LEAGUE
Publications Ltd

RUGBY LEAGUE
2012-2013
Keep on truckin'

League Publications Ltd

First published in Great Britain in 2012 by
League Publications Ltd
Wellington House
Briggate
Brighouse
West Yorkshire HD6 1DN

A CIP catalogue record for this book is available from the British Library
ISBN 978-1-901347-26-5

Designed and Typeset by League Publications Limited
Printed by Charlesworth Press, Wakefield

Contributing Editor
Tim Butcher

Statistics, production and design
Daniel Spencer

Contributors

Malcolm Andrews
Neil Barraclough
Peter Bird
Aaron Bower
Jeff Bowron
Martin Butcher
Phil Caplan
Ian Cheveau
Paul Clarke
Tom Coates
James Collins
Paul English
Simon Fitzjohn
Tim Groves
Malcolm Haigh
Roger Halstead
Phil Hodgson
Andrew Jackson
Chris Jackson
Conor Kelly
Steve Kilmartin
David Kuzio
Lorraine Marsden
Steve Mascord
Paddy McAteer
Keith McGhie

Joe Mills
David Parkinson
Arindam Rej
Ian Rigg
Mike Rylance
Martyn Sadler
David Saffer
James Stott
Gareth Walker
Jordan Walker
Chris Westwood
Ricky Wilby
Gavin Willacy
Ian Wilson

Pictures

Rugby League Photos
RLA Images
SWPix
Action Photographics,
Australia
CameraSport
Glenn Ashley
Richard Beattie
Bob Brough
Gordon Clayton
Paul Clayton
Paul English
Steve Gaunt
Peter Green
Magi Haroun
Dave Howarth
Wayne Keegan
Richard Land
Ian Lovell
Allan McKenzie
Mike McKenzie
Rob Terrace
Mal Walker
Bill Watkinson

CONTENTS

ACKNOWLEDGEMENTS

Gillette Rugby League 2012-2013 is the 17th of League Publications Ltd's annual series of Rugby League Yearbooks, the tenth year of its production with the backing of world-leading brand Gillette.

As always, in compiling this historical record of the Rugby League year, we rely on the hard work and dedication of all the contributors to *Rugby Leaguer & Rugby League Express* and *Rugby League World* magazine. Without their efforts this yearbook would not be possible.

We are able to include some wonderful action photography provided by, in particular RLphotos.com, Action Photographics in Sydney, Magi Haroun, Allan McKenzie, Dave Howarth and Peter Morley of RLAImages.

Thanks are due to the Rugby Football League for their help during the year, and to the historians and statisticians at clubs who help to keep us on our toes.

Acknowledgement also to the Rothmans Yearbook 1999, compiled by Ray Fletcher, the British Rugby Records Book from London Publications, and to the club officials, and some supporters, who helped us verify records.

The magnificent statistical review was put together meticulously, as always, by Daniel Spencer, who also designed the book.

Special mentions for Gareth Walker and Malcolm Andrews who wrote the Championship and NRL/State of Origin sections. Thanks also to Opta Sportdata, who compiled the Opta Index Analysis in our mind-boggling statistical section.

TIM BUTCHER
Contributing Editor
Gillette Rugby League 2012-2013

INTRODUCTION

The seventeenth season of Super League ended with Leeds pulling off another shock Grand Final win, although on the evidence of recent history it was far from a surprise, the Rhinos having all the know-how and experience to come from fifth in the table for the second year running, beating all challengers along the way. Truly a champion side again.

The Old Trafford win bookended Leeds' season, as they had produced an equally formidable display to beat 2011 NRL Premiers Manly Sea Eagles in the World Club Challenge in February.

It was a great year for Rhinos fans, despite them losing in the Challenge Cup Final at Wembley for the third year in a row.

Warrington were the victors this year in August, as fullback Brett Hodgson walked off with the Lance Todd Trophy after a convincing win. The Rhinos were able to gain full revenge six weeks later when the Grand Final was played on a bright autumn day, which wasn't the pattern for the year as a whole, as Britain suffered its wettest summer since records began.

Both showpiece finals were excellent and memorable events and Leeds and Warrington folk will remember them for years to come.

The financial crisis at Bradford was the major ongoing story of the year but out of that negative, which saw the Bulls' Super League status and very existence under serious threat, came plenty of good news stories, not least the rallying round of Rugby League fans, players and officials to raise hundreds of thousands of pounds, and the dignified way that head coach Mick Potter and his staff guided the side to ninth position, despite a six-point deduction for the club entering administration.

There was relief for Bradford supporters when the club was bought by local restaurateur Omar Khan, but even that didn't turn out too well in the very short term as Khan saw Hull FC beat the Bulls 70-6 at Odsal, in the first game of his ownership. The Bulls finished the year working hard to retain their players, but one of their first re-signings was Albert Goldthorpe Rookie of the Year, teenager John Bateman, who enjoyed a terrific campaign in the Bradford pack.

There were lots of other great stories coming out of 2012.

According to the Rugby Football League, a total of 1.88 million fans watched the 27 rounds of the regular season, a 6.7 per cent increase on 2011 and the highest aggregate attendance since Super League's inception in 1996.

We saw two new stadiums come into use, the Salford City Stadium and Langtree Park St Helens. The City Reds' bow at their new home in round one was dampened by heavy snow. The week after, it was still very cold in St Helens, but playable, as Saints played their first Super League game, coincidentally against the City Reds, at Langtree Park, after a season guesting in 2011 at Stobart Stadium Halton. A healthy crowd of over 15,500 Saints fans ignored the freezing weather as some of the club's former great players formed a guard of honour for Tom Van Vollenhoven to carry the matchball to the centre spot.

Salford went on to have their moments under coach Phil Veivers and his assistant Sean Long. When the Reds' backline clicked it was almost unstoppable. But financial troubles and the mid-season departure of scrum-half Matty Smith to Wigan saw their season fizzle out.

Promoted Widnes Vikings had the privilege of opening the show in round one with a Friday night TV game on the Stobart Stadium's new artificial-pitch. Sub-zero conditions meant several players suffered scratches and burns but complaints about the surface fell away as the season progressed.

The Vikings were beaten 32-14 by Wakefield Trinity Wildcats, who had been awarded a licence for Super League XVII because of the eleventh hour demise in 2011 of Crusaders. That meant their new coach, Richard Agar had to scrape a side together in the off-season to at least try and compete, but the Wildcats and Agar managed more than that and a seven-match winning run at the end of the regular season won them an unlikely play-off spot.

Widnes eventually finished bottom of the pile, but only on points difference and some major scalps along the way, most notably that of Wigan, saw them coming up to speed as the season progressed.

A record Super League comeback from 26-0 down secured Wigan's 42-36 win at Hull KR and the League Leaders Shield but when they were presented with it a week later after round 27, they weren't overjoyed, having just lost to St Helens at the DW Stadium. Wigan's regular season form had them favourites for the title but they were eliminated by Leeds, with the suspended Michael McIlorum and the injured Sam Tomkins in the stands looking on. It was still a great year for them, with winger Josh Charnley topping the try-scoring charts in an all-conquering regular season, the high point a 50-8 win at Leeds with a side racked by injury and suspension.

That game came a week after the Magic Weekend, held for the first time at Manchester's Etihad Stadium, and for a change the sun came out for the two-day extravaganza. A 26-man brawl and a 42-16 win by Wigan over Saints rounded off the weekend. Three players were sent off - Wigan's Lee Tuson and Gareth Hock and Saints' Shaun Magennis. They all got suspended, as did Lee Mossop, the Wigan prop.

The Saturday evening had finished in an equally explosive fashion with a cracking Hull derby as Hull KR came back from the dead and a magnificent last-second, long-range David Hodgson try secured a 32-30 win over Hull FC. All in all it was an enjoyable weekend.

There were three coaching casualties of the Super League season. Huddersfield's Nathan Brown went after a 33-6 defeat by Warrington in the semi-final of Challenge Cup, and admitting that he had been forced to change tactics by his players. The Giants had headed the table in late April and were an outside bet for the Grand Final but sunk almost without trace after that. The week before the Cup and coach exit, Nathan Brown already having signed to coach St Helens in 2013, the Giants had lost 52-6 at Castleford, who had a rough season all round with the tragic death of coach Ian Millward's teenage son, the resignation of their chief executive, player departures and the suspensions of Rangi Chase. One of those suspensions was for a dangerous tackle on Tangi Ropati in the Tigers' Challenge Cup exit at neighbours Featherstone, a rare and fully deserved giant killing. Featherstone pushed Wigan all the way too in the next round.

In March, a 12-8 defeat at Bradford meant a fifth game without a win for St Helens as they fell out of the top-eight and coach Royce Simmons was shown the door. And Rob Powell made way for Tony Rea at London Broncos in July in a season of struggle for the Broncos, despite some high-profile signings.

The other outpost club of Super League, Catalan Dragons, had a much better season, finishing fourth and building their home support impressively. They also produced the most exciting finish of the season when Daryl Millard's try after the final hooter, followed by Albert Goldthorpe Medal winner Scott Dureau's touchline conversion snatched a 34-32 win at St Helens in round four.

This year was the year the Joining Jack charity, set up to help former Wigan player Andy Johnson's young son, caught the public imagination. Many a try-scorer made the linked-finger gesture to the cameras to show their support. Tour de France winner and

Introduction

Wigan fan Bradley Wiggins joined in on the winner's podium and the Warriors wore a special kit in their last home game.

The international year was a bit of a damp squib. The England v Exiles two-match series got off to a bad start with the opening match played at St Helens in a deluge. It was even worse for Thomas Leuluai and Wigan as the Exiles captain broke his leg stopping Ryan Hall from scoring a try. England won that but with several players rested, lost the second leg at Huddersfield. The year ended with England testing out a high-altitude training camp in South Africa and a triangular tournament with Wales and France that turned into a training run for the World Cup to come in 2013, but was hailed as invaluable preparation for the 2013 World Cup, to be staged in the northern hemisphere.

April left Rugby League looking for a new chairman when Richard Lewis ended a ten-year tenure as he headed off for the manicured lawns of Wimbledon, where he was appointed chief executive of the All England Club. A cash-less, three-year title sponsorship for Super League with Stobart was ended after a year.

Jamie Peacock played his last game for England against the Exiles at St Helens before retiring from international Rugby League, got an MBE, had a public spat with former Great Britain great Garry Schofield who criticised him in his League Express column, and then played a giant part in Leeds' Championship win.

2012 was also the year of the Early Guilty Plea; the first Welsh professional derby in over 100 years; a school from the south of England, Howard of Effingham from Surrey, winning the Steven Mullaney year seven national title (and we had a Welsh-speaking school, Ystalyfera, in the year 10 final); Paul Wood giving more than could be reasonably expected in the Warrington cause at Old Trafford, with an accidental collision with Kallum Watkins' knee rupturing a testicle and the Wolves prop having to have it removed; and the first year when much of the amateur game played during the summer months.

In the Championships there were three excellent competitions. Sheffield Eagles beat League Leaders Featherstone 20-16 in a cracking Grand Final at Warrington to win the Co-operative Championship title while Halifax collected the Northern Rail Cup after a 21-12 win over Featherstone in Blackpool. Four weeks after being told they were champions by finishing top of the league, and then told they weren't, Doncaster finally won their first ever league title with a thrilling 16-13 win over Barrow Raiders in the Championship One decider.

Four clubs were promoted from Championship One to allow four clubs from outside the heartlands to enter the RFL. The first to be accepted, Northampton, changed their minds midway through the year, but Hemel, Oxford and University of Gloucester All Golds were ready to take their place in a nine-team competition.

That and more is detailed in the following three hundred and odd pages. We are sure you will enjoy reliving another eventful year.

The Gillette Yearbook contains the full story of the domestic year, details of the international season and the Australian NRL season, and match facts for every Super League, Challenge Cup games involving professional teams, Championship and Championship One and Northern Rail Cup game. Every player who has played Super League is also listed along with those players to have made their debuts this year. We have also selected five individuals who we judge to have made the biggest impact on Rugby League in 2012. We have published scoring and attendance records for every club and this year include a list of every club's longest serving player. League Publications publishes the weekly newspaper Rugby Leaguer & Rugby League Express, as well as the monthly glossy magazine Rugby League World and the website 'totalrl.com'. Many thanks once again to Gillette for their support for both this yearbook, and for the sport of Rugby League.

TIM BUTCHER
Contributing Editor
Gillette Rugby League 2012-2013

1
THE 2012 SEASON

DECEMBER 2011
Further horizons

In the wake of the Gillette Four Nations final, there was no hysterical reaction to another series loss to Australia and there was little time to draw breath before the announcement of the cities that would stage the round games of the 2013 World Cup. Thirty-four bids were submitted to the RFL by the July deadline, with Bristol, Limerick, Perpignan and Neath the only venues outside the north of England chosen to host games, although Bradford, Sheffield, Castleford and Wakefield all missed out. No games were allocated to Wembley and the venue for the final was not known. Former Wales international Gareth Thomas was to be an official ambassador for the tournament.

Bristol's amateur club, Bristol Sonics were one of the clubs in the running to enter Championship One in 2013. The Rugby Football League, under its Championship review undertaken in 2011, was to bring four new teams into the third tier from 2013, with Wakefield Trinity Wildcats set to form a twinning with the first new club to be announced, Northampton. Northampton Town FC Chairman David Cardoza was the man behind the successful bid.

Wigan had already announced a link with South Wales Scorpions and also with Wales Rugby League. One of the stipulations laid down in the agreement dictated that any player leaving Wales to play for Wigan must remain loyal at international level to his home nation.

On the international front, the French Rugby League Federation began the search for a successor to Bobbie Goulding as head coach of the France team. Goulding's three-year contract was not renewed when it ran out. Johnathan Thurston saw his name added to the illustrious roll call of Golden Boot winners when Rugby League World magazine confirmed him as the best player in the world in 2011. Thurston led the tributes to Arthur Beetson, the Australian Rugby League Immortal, who died of a heart attack on the Gold Coast.

On the domestic scene, a number of rule changes were to come into force from Boxing Day, the biggest changes being that the number of permitted interchanges during a match was to be reduced from 12 to 10 and that a player in possession of the ball coming into contact with the corner post would no longer be deemed in touch. Both these rules were already in operation in the NRL in Australia. Players would be permitted to drop kick for goal as well as place kick when adding a conversion after a try (it was already permitted to kick a two-point penalty with a drop kick). There would also be a greater leniency shown towards players who offloaded the ball after 'held' was called. If the referee believed that the player didn't hear the call then, instead of a penalty being awarded to the opposing team, play would be taken back to where the call was made and restarted.

The changes were approved by the RFL Council following proposals made by the RFL Laws Committee, made up of players, coaches and administrators past and present.

Two of the clubs struggling to build new stadia to satisfy Super League licensing criteria faced critical times towards the end of the year. A public inquiry called by the government into Wakefield Trinity Wildcats' new stadium at Newmarket began at Wakefield Town Hall, the result to be known in the spring of 2012, while Castleford Tigers' chief executive Richard Wright called for the continued backing of the club's supporters following news that their planned relocation to Glasshoughton might be delayed. The

Tigers had been hoping to be in their new home, for which they had already received planning permission, for the start of the 2013 season, but it emerged that a major supermarket operator involved in negotiations for the sale of their Wheldon Road home was reviewing its commitment.

Wigan and Hull KR both headed off for warm-weather training camps, the Robins to Tenerife and the Warriors to Florida. Former Sydney Roosters junior Anthony Gelling had been officially unveiled as a Wigan player and, within minutes, the 21-year-old was on board a flight destined for the USA. Gelling had been playing for Auckland Vulcans after being sacked by the Roosters for defecating in a hotel room.

Wakefield, with new coach Richard Agar assembling a virtually new team since the end of the 2011 season, signed PNG hooker Paul Aiton and Richard Mathers, on a season-long loan after he was told by new Castleford coach Ian Millward he was not in his plans.

Former Wakefield players Josh Veivers and Stuart Howarth were finding it hard to find a new club because of the Super League rules on club-trained players. Salford City Reds were interested in the pair, both aged 21, who had come through the Wigan Academy system before joining Wakefield in 2011, playing 31 games between them before being released by Agar. But the Reds had reached the limit of twelve Federation-trained players and were required to fill up their quota with eight club-trained players.

Huddersfield Giants appointed assistant coach Paul Anderson as their new head coach for three years from the start of the 2013 season. Anderson was to take over from current boss Nathan Brown who was to return to Australia at the end of 2012.

Warrington coach Tony Smith insisted halfback Richie Myler was not heading for the Halliwell Jones exit door after postings on the Internet suggested the former Widnes and Salford player was about to join Super League new boys Widnes Vikings. Myler played in the Boxing Day friendly but was thought likely to miss the start of the new season after dislocating an elbow in the 32-18 victory over the Vikings.

In the other Festive Friendlies, Castleford Tigers beat Bradford Bulls 28-18 at Probiz Coliseum. Bulls' new signing Manase Manuokafoa was set to be sidelined for at least the first two months of the season after picking up a knee injury in the club's final training session before the game. Leeds Rhinos beat Wakefield 26-10 at Headingley.

A crowd of around 1,200 hit the Hull Arena to watch the Super League Prizefighter tournament in aid of Lee Radford's Testimonial and the children's charity 'Life for a Kid'. Radford won the eight-player tournament on a points decision over Paul Sculthorpe in the final.

The biggest story of the month also emerged in Hull. Former Hull FC chief executive James Rule, who resigned from his post on 11 October 2011, and Hull's former strength and conditioning coach Ben Cooper both made history by becoming the first members of an athlete's entourage to be suspended after being convicted of anti-doping rule violations.

Rule and Cooper were charged by UK Anti-Doping (UKAD) with conspiring with former player Martin Gleeson to cover up the circumstances which led to Gleeson testing positive for a banned stimulant after the game against Salford on 13 May. Both Rule and Cooper were found to have deliberately misled UKAD when giving evidence in relation to the doping charges brought against Gleeson. They were both suspended for two years from any role that involved interaction with athletes.

The second year of Cooper's suspension would be lifted, however, if no further incriminating evidence came to light, while Rule would still be able to play a role in a professional sports club that did not involve having control over players. It meant he could still find a job that involved a financial, marketing, commercial or other related roles. The two suspensions were to run from 9 June 2011.

Gleeson was suspended for three years from the same date, although he would be able to return to action after 18 months provided no additional incriminating information came to light.

At the very end of the year star Sam Tomkins triumphed in the 2011 League Express Readers' Poll, winning the readers' vote as the Player of the Year.

JANUARY
On the road

Rugby League was recognised twice in the New Year's Honours List, with England captain Jamie Peacock receiving an MBE, and the former President of the Rugby Football League, and former Great Britain player, Bev Risman the OBE.

There was growing speculation as 2012 got underway that Super League would not have a main title sponsor after Engage had ended its sponsorship. But on 20 January it was revealed that logistics company Stobart would take up title sponsorship for the next three years, although the deal would not bring in any direct income to the Super League competition or its clubs. All the benefit accruing from the sponsorship would be benefits in kind, coming from a fleet of 100 Stobart lorries that was to carry Super League imagery. Each of the 14 Super League clubs was to have six lorries allocated to it, with images on their side of well-known players scoring tries.

Super League turned down £750,000 per annum from the gambling company Betfair. There had been a 9-5 vote in favour of the Stobart option at a clubs meeting at Red Hall. Nine clubs - Bradford, Huddersfield, Hull FC, Hull KR, Leeds Rhinos, London Broncos, Salford City Reds, Wakefield Trinity Wildcats and Widnes Vikings - were present at the meeting, while Castleford Tigers participated by means of video conferencing facilities. Catalan Dragons, St Helens, Warrington Wolves and Wigan Warriors were absent but had made their views known before the event. Hull FC, Hull Kingston Rovers, Leeds Rhinos, Salford City Reds and Castleford Tigers voted in favour of Betfair. Former RFL President Ronnie Teeman, who held the post in the 1994/5 season, issued a stinging criticism of the RFL for the deal in Rugby League Express.

St Helens played their first game at their new Langtree Park stadium, which had lost part of its roof during gales earlier in the month, beating Widnes 42-24 on a Friday night to retain the Karalius Cup. Salford's first game at their new stadium at Barton went less well as the Reds, without new captain Stephen Wild, suffered a 36-12 humbling at the hands of Championship side Leigh.

Pre-season friendlies were taking their toll on some clubs even before the start of the season.

Hard hit were Hull KR who, before a ball was kicked, lost Blake Green, who was ruled out for up to six months with a blood clot in his calf, and then saw newly appointed captain Ben Galea suffer a medial ligament knee injury early on in the 36-18 derby victory over Hull FC at the KC Stadium. Young forward Richard Beaumont also suffered a broken fibula. New signing Ryan O'Hara was out until late February, with the former Crusaders forward having returned from the Tenerife training camp with a shoulder injury that required surgery. Hull FC also lost Kiwi hooker Aaron Heremaia to a neck injury. New Hull FC captain Andy Lynch claimed that his club's recent pre-season training trip to Tenerife was a huge success, despite the derby defeat.

Catalan Dragons were also affected injury-wise. A week after looking impressive in a 46-10 win over Wakefield in Perpignan, they beat London 44-22 but lost their captain Gregory Mounis, who later required surgery on a knee problem; Cyril Stacul, underwent surgery on an ankle problem while Frederic Vaccari was expected to miss the entire 2012 season after learning that he needed a knee reconstruction. And to cap it off, Eloi Pelissier suffered a broken jaw in a reserve team game in the French Elite 1. Coach Trent Robinson agreed a two-month loan deal with Championship side Batley Bulldogs for former Hull KR hooker Ben Fisher.

Huddersfield Giants had a front-row crisis following the groin injury suffered by Keith Mason in a 30-18 win at Wigan in a testimonial game for Sean O'Loughlin. Larne Patrick (wrist) and Tony Tonks, signed from Featherstone Rovers and suspended from the previous season's Championship grand final, were also set to miss the opening game of the season, also away at Wigan. Other absentees were Luke O'Donnell (knee), David Fa'alogo (back), Kevin Brown (ankle) and David Faiumu (shoulder).

Leeds Rhinos' only pre-season run-out of January was a 66-0 romp over Championship champions Featherstone in the Rob Burrow testimonial game.

Warrington Wolves chose not to play any warm-up games in England, instead enjoying a three-week training camp in Sydney that culminated in a 34-28 friendly success over South Sydney Rabbitohs, only eight days before round one of Super League. Despite having to be without David Solomona for up to five months, after the ball-handling forward sustained a broken fibula and dislocated ankle injury early in the training camp, Richie Myler, injured on Boxing Day, made a surprise return in the win over Souths. The Wolves' 23-day tour was sponsored by Emirates Airlines.

Martin Aspinwall returned to pre-season training with Hull FC after his club suspension was lifted. The new signing from the Tigers had been suspended indefinitely pending an internal investigation by the club and the outcome of police charges following an incident the previous month. The subsequent investigation confirmed that Aspinwall was guilty of only a minor misdemeanour, and he was fined £200 by Hull Magistrates Court for being drunk and disorderly and swearing at police outside a nightclub.

Castleford Tigers fullback Richard Owen issued an apology to supporters after being sanctioned for a breach of club discipline. Owen was questioned by police after he was involved in a brawl in Pontefract with several men dressed as Santa Claus in the early hours of Christmas Day.

Karl Pryce returned to his first club Bradford Bulls on a one-year deal and his old mentor, former Great Britain coach Brian Noble, emerged as a leading contender to take over from Bobbie Goulding as the head of the France national team.

The Bulls were to have joint captains in the 2012 season in hookers Heath L'Estrange and Matt Diskin while Widnes Vikings appointed Jon Clarke as their captain for their return to Super League. Wakefield prop Oliver Wilkes was in a race to be fit for the start of the 2012 season after undergoing an emergency appendicitis operation.

The RFL strongly denied allegations in The Mail on Sunday that it was complicit in misleading UK Anti-Doping about the nature of Martin Gleeson's doping violation in 2011. In the article Gleeson alleged that when then Hull FC chief executive James Rule concocted a story about Hull coach Ben Cooper advising Gleeson to take the stimulant MHA, Rule sent three statements via email to RFL Operations Director Emma Rosewarne, who sent them on to UKAD. The newspaper article suggested that Rosewarne's actions demonstrated that she was a party to the fraud, but the RFL insisted that she was merely acting as a conduit for the email communications. The new owner of Hull FC, Adam Pearson, played down suggestions of a further inquiry.

FEBRUARY
Cold start

Round 1

Sub-zero temperatures greeted the launch of Super League XVII but all seven games in round one went ahead.

One game that was never in doubt was the Friday-night TV game between promoted Widnes Vikings and Wakefield Trinity Wildcats, the first Super League game to be played on an artificial playing surface. The Vikings, who had been awarded a licence the previous March, had the state-of-the-art i-pitch laid, and it had been passed for use by the Rugby Football League.

There was some doubt about whether the surface itself or the underlying frozen conditions were to blame, but several players suffered bad grazing to their knees and elbows. Wakefield fullback Richie Mathers posted a photograph on the social network Twitter of his badly cut knee, saying: "It's nothing aimed at Widnes, great club & happy they are bk in. It's just the surface, in my experience, isn't right for Super League." His Wakefield colleague Danny Kirmond tweeted, "pretty sore to be honest, but apparently it's softer when not frozen underneath, plenty of burns though."

Nevertheless the season opener, which drew impressive TV ratings, was a fast and ferocious affair thanks to the firm playing surface and Wakefield emerged 32-14 winners. The freezing-cold night couldn't deter over 8,000 fans gathering to witness the Vikings' first game back in Super League, and most of them were well content when the home side led 10-4 at half-time. But Wakefield levelled two minutes after the turnaround, and, though there was in no way a Widnes collapse, poor discipline saw them concede eight straight penalties, which their coach Denis Betts put down to fatigue, and Tim Smith orchestrated four more tries on the back of a mighty effort from his pack.

The Vikings were without captain Jon Clarke for the second half when a hamstring strain tightened during the break, and with Aussie halfback Anthony Watts missing the game with a hamstring injury of his own, Betts was shorn of halfback options. Fullback Shaun Briscoe was also sidelined with an injury suffered in the pre-season game at St Helens, although that gave 20-year-old Danny Craven the chance to show great promise on his Super League debut. Craven registered the Vikings' first try of their new Super League life when he grubbered into the in-goal and got a hand to the ball as Mathers waited for it to bounce dead.

Wakefield, under new coach Richard Agar, had recruited an almost completely new side after the surprise renewal of their Super League licence. Widnes had a few familiar faces from their Championship years. Thirty-two players out of 34 were making Super

League debuts for their new clubs, although some for the second time.

PNG captain Paul Aiton was excellent for the Wildcats in the first 53 minutes before Kyle Wood came on to inject pace from dummy-half. An even bigger standout was Kirmond, who came to Wakefield as part of a deal that took Aaron Murphy to Huddersfield.

Strangely, the RFL had scheduled another match on the season-launch night, champions Leeds Rhinos hosting Hull Kingston Rovers on an awful, sandy surface. Despite the game being in doubt until an hour before kick-off, more than 15,000 fans braved the elements and saw Rovers still in with a strong shout until seven minutes from time when Kallum Watkins finished off a game-turning hat-trick. Danny McGuire's last-minute try completed the 34-16 home win.

The Rhinos, in preparation for the World Club Challenge against Manly in a fortnight's time, were settled, their only debutant being Darrell Griffin. Rovers had six making their competitive bow, all in the starting 13, while new Aussie coach Craig Sandercock, in his first taste of Super League, also had to accommodate the loss of chief playmaker Blake Green, out for an indefinite period with a blood clot on his leg, and captain Ben Galea, who had damaged knee ligaments in the pre-season friendly win over Hull FC. Kevin Sinfield made his 400th appearance in blue and amber of Leeds.

If the playing surface wasn't ideal at Headingley the night after it was even worse as Salford opened the new Salford City Stadium with a 24-10 defeat by Castleford Tigers, who just about handled the freezing, snowy surface the better. If it hadn't been the Saturday night TV game the fixture might not have gone ahead and several players were left with raw knees that put them in doubt for the following week.

Salford lost hooker Wayne Godwin in the seventh minute with a rib injury and he was replaced by Stuart Howarth, released by Wakefield, who himself came off with concussion 15 minutes from time.

Seen as the club's first choice fullback after Richard Mathers' season-long loan departure to Wakefield, Richard Owen justified the belief new coach Ian Millward had placed in him with two fine tries in a hard-fought win. 2011 Albert Goldthorpe Medal winner Rangi Chase had a patchy game but still set up three of the Tigers' four tries.

Earlier that day, St Helens came back from a half-time deficit at the Twickenham Stoop to overpower a spirited, new-look London Broncos side in the latter stages by 34-24. The Broncos, reverting to their former name after six seasons as Harlequins, were almost unrecognisable from the team that finished the last season twelfth after a heavy final-day defeat to Saints. Craig Gower, returning to Rugby League after spending four years playing rugby union in France and for Italy, captained the home side, and was at the heart of most of their promising attacking play in the first half. Hemel product, young winger Kieran Dixon made an impressive debut for London. James Roby, who created the first try in each half with scything breaks, crashed over for the crucial score with just over five minutes left to finally shrug off the Broncos' challenge. Roby was acting captain in the absence of Paul Wellens, still recovering from minor surgery on his foot.

New Hull coach Peter Gentle declared himself happy with the 20-all draw against Warrington Wolves at the KC Stadium on the Sunday, despite being in the lead for much of the game and conceding a late try to Rhys Evans. Ben Westwood missed a tricky conversion attempt which would have snatched both points for the Wolves.

Hull came into the game without new signings, halfback Brett Seymour and prop forward Eamon O'Carroll. Seymour had injured his knee in a friendly against Bradford, and had an operation to clear the knee out, while signing from Wigan O'Carroll had suffered a back injury in training. Aaron Heremaia was also missing with a neck injury.

Warrington coach Tony Smith had left out Lee Briers for an unspecified breach of club discipline at the end of the training camp in Sydney but was able to play Richie Myler, who had made a remarkable recovery after dislocating an elbow in the Boxing Day friendly with Widnes. Hull's best was Danny Tickle.

February

Catalan Dragons made light of a spate of injuries - regular wingers Frederic Vaccari and Cyril Stacul and captain Gregory Mounis all out - increased by the omission of Leon Pryce, due to a hamstring problem, which put on hold the long-awaited first Super League appearance by an Englishman in a Dragons shirt - to hammer Bradford 34-12 at Odsal. The powerful French engine room - Remi Casty and Lopini Paea at the forefront - quickly battered the Bulls into submission and Ian Henderson and Scott Dureau made hay down the middle. Dureau's penalty just before half-time opened the gap to 20 points and it was 30-0 until just after the hour mark when Jamie Langley finally gave the beleaguered Bulls faithful something to cheer.

A heavy overnight snow flurry made little difference to the pitch, which was covered, but it necessitated a super-human effort by all of the Bulls' staff, including chief executive Ryan Duckett and coach Mick Potter to get the huge open Rooley Lane terrace fit for spectators.

Huddersfield coach Nathan Brown fielded a team containing a mixture of youth and experience and produced the shock of the round with a Sunday afternoon 20-16 victory at Wigan. Brown's injury-hit side had been rank outsiders going into the game, but showed tremendous commitment and, with Danny Brough pivotal, produced a superior kicking game to the Warriors. Brown was reluctant to put a timescale on the return of several injured first-teamers, including captain Kevin Brown, Keith Mason, Luke O'Donnell, David Fa'alogo and David Faiumu, and re-affirmed his confidence in the players he had available.

There were debuts for players on both sides, with Epalahame Lauaki and Ben Flower on the bench for Wigan, and Greg Eden, Luke George, Tommy Lee and Jason Chan starting the game for Huddersfield. Front-rower Larne Patrick was a major doubt before the game with a wrist injury, but climbed off the bench to score two crucial tries just after half-time. His second was a spectacular gamebreaker as he crashed through the first line of defence off Shaun Lunt's smart offload and showed remarkable pace and poise for a prop to ignore Scott Grix's support and dummy past Sam Tomkins to score.

Round 2

After a freezing opening to Super League in England the postponement of Hull FC's round-two fixture in the Mediterranean climes of Perpignan provided an unusual twist. Hull director of rugby Shaun McRae reacted angrily to the late decision to call off the Saturday evening match against the Dragons. Despite the low temperatures in the days leading up to the match, the game had been scheduled to go ahead as planned and the pitch was deemed playable on the Friday afternoon. But the following day referee Phil Bentham and match commissioner Gerry Kershaw acted on concerns raised by Catalan head coach Trent Robinson, and the match was postponed due to ice on the pitch at 2.00pm, four hours before the game was scheduled to begin. McRae said he had no problem with the decision to call off the game, and agreed that conditions were unsafe, but he was left fuming by the timing, which left thousands of travelling fans reflecting on a fruitless trip. McRae believed the decision to water the pitch the night before the game contributed to the match being postponed as it turned to ice.

It was still very cold in St Helens, but playable, as Saints played their first Super League game at their new home, Langtree Park, after a season guesting at Stobart Stadium Halton. A healthy crowd of over 15,500 Saints fans ignored the freezing weather as some of the club's former great players formed a guard of honour for Tom Van Vollenhoven to carry the matchball to the centre spot and James Roby had the privilege to lead out Saints at their new home for the first time.

It didn't all go to plan although St Helens' 38-10 win went down in the history books. The Reds fully deserved a 10-4 lead at half-time, with their halfback pairing of Matty Smith and Daniel Holdsworth - looking slightly more comfortable than on the snow and ice of the previous week - sharp and inventive, their pack doing a manful job in the tackle to prevent Saints getting on their trademark roll, and the outside backs, in particular right winger Danny Williams, snuffing out every threat when the ball was sent wide.

For St Helens it was an emotional night, with the former great players and the pre-match speech from the chairman setting the scene, and the players could have been forgiven for being caught up in the ceremony. The City Reds were already doing it tough injury-wise. Wayne Godwin was sidelined with a rib-cartilage injury picked up in the previous week's home defeat, with Stuart Howarth playing almost 70 minutes before being replaced by Gareth Owen, who was making his first senior appearance since 2010. Iafeta Palea'aesina and Vinnie Anderson were both named in the 19-man squad, but had to pull out with a hamstring injury sustained in training and illness respectively.

Signing from South Sydney, Shannan McPherson, made his Reds debut, with Jordan James dropping out. And Ashley Gibson, Chris Nero and Adam Sidlow were all called up for seasonal debuts, with Sean Gleeson dropped by coach Phil Veivers. On the night, Howarth broke his nose, McPherson had to have stitches inserted in his face and centre Joel Moon was taken to hospital a suspected broken wrist, his involvement in the game ending after 22 minutes.

Saints had injury problems too. Captain Paul Wellens was still recovering from foot surgery. Mark Flanagan suffered a chest injury in the win at London, and his place on the bench was taken by Nathan Ashe. Ade Gardner came in for his first game of the season after being unused off the bench in London, with Jamie Foster out with a quad injury. And Gary Wheeler continued to deputise for injured England centre Michael Shenton (dislocated elbow). Tony Puletua (shoulder and elbow surgery) returned. Unsung Andrew Dixon's pace and energy off the bench was a big factor in Saints' second-half blitz, the second-rower scoring two tries as Roby's all-action running from dummy-half left Salford helpless.

Bradford bounced back from their first-round mauling at the hands of Catalans with a 20-12 attritional win at Castleford, with the pitch having to be cleared of snow before kick-off. Luke Gale's penalty in the 67th minute, awarded when the Tigers' Jake Emmitt was caught offside, helped give Bradford an eight-point lead which, in the conditions, was enough.

Conditions were no better just down the road at Wakefield's Belle Vue where Hull KR registered their first win, by 22-10. Rovers weathered the loss of captain Michael Dobson after 32 minutes to a shoulder injury, were reduced to twelve men at one stage when prop Scott Taylor was sin-binned, and repelled a fierce second-half onslaught from the Wildcats. Trinity, including three former Robins players in Ben Cockayne, Peter Fox, and Frankie Mariano, elevated Oliver Wilkes from the bench to replace injured prop Kyle Amor (broken hand), but were otherwise unchanged from the side which came from behind to beat Widnes 32-14 in their season's opener. Tries to Josh Hodgson and Rhys Lovegrove in the last 20 minutes and a goal to Craig Hall were the only scores of a second half that Wakefield almost totally dominated.

Huddersfield went top of the table with their second win, as the Giants' exciting crop of British youngsters ripped Widnes Vikings apart at the Galpharm, with Leroy Cudjoe and Luke George sharing seven tries between them in a 66-6 win. Nathan Brown fielded a side with just one overseas player in the 17 – former Crusader Jason Chan – and watched on as they brushed the Vikings aside.

Cudjoe finished with four tries and George three, while the outstanding Joe Wardle and Greg Eden also crossed. 2011 Albert Goldthorpe Rookie of the Year Jermaine McGillvary was the only outside back not to touch down, but barely put a foot wrong, and with Danny Brough, Kevin Brown, Scott Grix and Luke Robinson pulling the strings, the home side had too much firepower for Widnes, for whom Paddy Flynn, Simon Finnigan and Ben Davies made a first appearances of the season. The Vikings barely touched the ball in the opening 15 minutes, and were trailing 18-0 and effectively already out of the contest.

Warrington welcomed back Lee Briers after a club disciplinary suspension and the Wolves' nine-try, 50-10 win at the Halliwell Jones Stadium was a fair reflection of their superiority over London Broncos, with Chris Bridge's mix of great handling, virtuoso offloading and impressive touchdowns the standout. The Wolves scored the try of the game on 58 minutes when fullback Stefan Ratchford's kick return broke the Broncos line. He slipped the ball out to Rhys Evans, who galloped downfield but was collared by Luke Dorn. The young winger managed an almost impossible offload in the collision to Ratchford who finished off the move he started by darting in from 20 metres out.

Josh Charnley grabbed his first senior hat-trick for Wigan in the 20-6 Saturday-night win over Leeds at the DW Stadium. Wigan looked to be back to their best as Sean O'Loughlin, Brett Finch, Sam Tomkins and Thomas Leuluai ran the show. Hooker Michael McIlorum also had a top game. New Wigan coach Shaun Wane made a handful of changes to the side defeated by the Giants a week earlier, however, including handing a debut to 20-year-old prop forward Tom Spencer, who came in to replace Liam Farrell, suspended for one match for making dangerous contact on Huddersfield's Leroy Cudjoe. Farrell had become the first player to make an 'early guilty plea' for the offence, thereby attracting a low-end suspension. Second-rower Jack Hughes came into the centre in place of George Carmont, who broke a thumb a week earlier.

Although they were clearly second best, Leeds coach Brian McDermott was refusing to panic and was confident of an improvement in the World Cub Challenge the following Friday.

Kallum Watkins, who scored a hat-trick in Leeds' opening day win against Hull Kingston Rovers, missed out on the trip to Wigan with a wrist injury but was thought likely to line up against the NRL Champions, although Lee Smith, who started on the wing, was forced out of the action in the first half with a rib injury.

World Club Challenge

Leeds Rhinos captain Kevin Sinfield praised the character of his team, and the backing of the Rhinos supporters in a sell-out crowd, after the club's 26-12 victory over NRL Premiers Manly at Headingley. Jamie Peacock, who won a record breaking fourth World Club Challenge-winning medal, was outstanding in the heat of battle. Ryan Hall, who trended worldwide on Twitter during the game, took the plaudits and enhanced his reputation as a world-class finisher, plaguing the Aussies with two quality tries

From the momentum-shifting 51st minute, when Manly's Daly Cherry-Evans scooted over and Jamie Lyon's conversion made it 16-12, Leeds were tested defensively to almost breaking point, at one stage surviving five consecutive sets in their own quarter. When Steve Matai touched down a Kieran Foran kick it could have been a different outcome but on replay video-referee Ian Smith saw that Glenn Stewart had pushed Kallum Watkins in the back to prevent him

Jamie Peacock looks for a way past Jamie Buhrer and Matt Ballin

leaping for the ball and the try was disallowed.

With the crowd's exhortations reaching boiling point, Leeds assumed control as they had in the later stages of the 2011 Grand Final. Peacock charged in, Paul McShane was hauled back from over the line by Glenn Stewart, before Rob Burrow found the chink, darting crossfield to draw in Matai and create an overlap. Watkins provided Ben Jones-Bishop with the scoring pass and enough space to sneak in at the corner. Sinfield's conversion hit the post, but with a two-score advantage, victory was assured, and even more so when the re-start failed to go ten metres. On the last tackle Sinfield's wickedly bouncing ball evaded Watkins, Michael Oldfield and Foran for Carl Ablett to pounce

The win - the first victory by a British club since the Rhinos defeated Melbourne Storm at Elland Road in 2008 - prompted RFL Chief Executive Nigel Wood to propose an expanded World Club Challenge tournament. Leeds chief executive Gary Hetherington had raised the issue with several NRL clubs on a recent visit to Australia, and claimed to have found significant levels of interest in the concept, with three teams from Australia coming to Europe to take on the three leading clubs in Super League on successive days on a weekend dedicated to the concept.

ARL Commission chief executive David Gallop said he would listen to any proposal tabled by British officials, although he was unsure about the logistics of expanding the World Club Challenge beyond an annual one-off clash between the winners of Super League and the NRL. The American National Rugby League (AMNRL) was hoping to interest the Hawaii Tourist Authority in a five-year plan to stage top-level matches in Honolulu, and AMNRL boss David Niu made it clear that hosting the World Club Challenge was among his aims.

HEINZ BIG SOUP WORLD CLUB CHALLENGE

Friday 17th February 2012

LEEDS RHINOS 26 MANLY SEA EAGLES 12

RHINOS: 1 Brent Webb; 2 Ben Jones-Bishop; 3 Kallum Watkins; 4 Zak Hardaker; 5 Ryan Hall; 13 Kevin Sinfield (C); 6 Danny McGuire; 8 Kylie Leuluai; 7 Rob Burrow; 10 Jamie Peacock; 11 Jamie Jones-Buchanan; 15 Brett Delaney; 12 Carl Ablett. Subs (all used): 16 Ryan Bailey; 20 Darrell Griffin; 9 Paul McShane; 18 Chris Clarkson.
Tries: Watkins (18), Hall (28, 37), Jones-Bishop (75), Ablett (78); **Goals:** Sinfield 3/5.
SEA EAGLES: 1 Brett Stewart; 2 David Williams; 3 Jamie Lyon (C); 4 Steve Matai; 5 Michael Oldfield; 6 Kieran Foran; 7 Daly Cherry-Evans; 8 Jason King (C); 9 Matt Ballin; 10 Brent Kite; 11 Anthony Watmough; 12 Tony Williams; 13 Glenn Stewart. Subs (all used): 14 Jamie Buhrer; 15 Vic Mauro; 16 Darcy Lussick; 17 George Rose.
Tries: B Stewart (33), Cherry-Evans (52); **Goals:** Lyon 2/2.
Rugby Leaguer & League Express Men of the Match:
Rhinos: Jamie Peacock; *Sea Eagles:* Tony Williams.
Penalty count: 13-12; **Half-time:** 16-6; **Referee:** Ashley Klein; **Attendance:** 21,062 *(at Headingley Carnegie).*

Round 3

Huddersfield Giants coach Nathan Brown admitted Warrington were still the team to beat after their 32-22 victory over the Giants at the Galpharm Stadium on the Saturday lifted them to the top of the table. Warrington were without flu victim Garreth Carvell and then saw both Simon Grix and Ben Harrison leave the field in the first half with knee injuries, but still had the resolve to come out on top in an expansive encounter, despite the cold, windy and wet conditions.

Chris Riley opened the scoring in the left corner before the Giants took ascendancy when Luke Robinson broke from deep and sent Danny Brough haring for the posts and then Eorl Crabtree celebrated his 300th career appearance with a try by the posts. The Wolves trailed by eight but found the points they needed before half-time to edge in front for a second time. Just before the half-hour, the ball was worked left to Ryan Atkins and the powerful centre broke before looking inside for Richie Myler, whose quick thinking put Riley in for his second. Then, after Jason Chan had coughed up possession for Huddersfield, Chris Bridge steamed over the line when the ball was flung to the right.

On the stroke of half-time Huddersfield's Tommy Lee was placed on report for a high shot on Lee Briers straight from a 20-metre restart. In the week, Lee took an early guilty plea and copped a two-match ban. The hooker should have been dismissed for the challenge, but he made the most of the let-off early in the second half, giving a dummy before finding Chan, who touched down despite the attention of four defenders.

Tempers flared when Bridge took exception to Huddersfield prop Jacob Fairbank's involvement in a tackle, and then on the next play the Wolves centre was penalised for a spear tackle. A melee ensued and several punches were thrown. The friction continued as the Giants looked to extend their lead, but this time Bridge was the victim of an elbow from Kevin Brown as he attempted to tackle the Huddersfield captain. Both Bridge and Brown were put on report but were found to have no charge to answer.

The latter penalty relieved the pressure on Warrington and, less than ten minutes later, Joel Monaghan plucked Ben Westwood's looping pass out of the air to score. Briers' grubber was pounced on by Matty Blythe shortly after, although Greg Eden's try just before the hour kept the Giants in touch. The decisive try came in the final ten minutes. Westwood drove the ball in to the heart of the defence and appeared to knock on. But Stefan Ratchford scooped up the loose ball before sending Myler over the line, and replays showed that the ball had been stripped by Joe Wardle.

In Perpignan, Castleford Tigers were in a strong position against the Dragons, leading 16-6 at the break before going down 28-20. Leon Pryce played in his first competitive game for the Dragons and just edged Rangi Chase in the battle of the England stand-offs. Pryce's run, dummy and break led to Daryl Millard's try in the 69th minute and saw the Dragons take the lead. Jason Baitieri went over under the posts seven minutes from time and Scott Dureau sealed the win with the simple conversion to give the Dragons an unassailable eight-point-lead.

Bradford coach Mick Potter dismissed accusations that his team was "soft" after the Sunday 54-16 mauling by Wigan Warriors. The Bulls fell to their second home defeat of the season in spectacular style, conceding ten tries against Shaun Wane's rampant side. Pat Richards guaranteed his place in Wigan's history books with a 16-point haul that saw him leapfrog Frano Botica into third place on the Warriors' all-time top points scorers list. Richards started the game four points short of Botica's final total of 1,931. Within 20 minutes, he had overtaken the Kiwi ace after first converting Josh Charnley's opening try and then scoring himself when Brett Finch regathered his own kick and sent the winger over. Bradford gave debuts to Keith Lulia and Phil Joseph, while Michael Platt also made his first appearance of the season after Adrian Purtell was sidelined with a torn pectoral muscle. The Bulls were hit with a hammer blow just 10 minutes into proceedings when playmaker Luke Gale was carried off with an ankle injury. Chris Tuson's try just before half-time that made it 22-10 punctured any momentum the Bulls were building.

Paul Wellens returned on the Sunday to face Hull Kingston Rovers at Craven Park, scoring a 50th minute try in a thrilling 36-all draw. Jamie Foster did not have his finest afternoon with the boot but, when it mattered, he delivered. His last kick at goal, the final action of a thrilling match in which momentum kept swinging, rescued a point for Saints after a gutsy display from a patched-up Hull KR side. Winger Foster, back in the side after injury, had already missed four out of seven attempts at goal and four minutes earlier had spurned a chance to snatch a draw - after Francis Meli's dramatic late try - as Foster's effort crashed against an upright. But, when he was handed a second chance, he held his nerve admirably. The penalty, for a high tackle by Mickey Paea on Gary Wheeler, was only the second conceded by the Robins in the whole match. Rovers' efforts were all the more impressive bearing in mind their poor start, as Saints breezed into a 14-0 lead with three quick tries. Craig Hall in particular rose to a play-making challenge while Constantine Mika scored twice. Saints had not won a Super League game on east Hull turf since June 2007.

After two excellent TV games from Leeds and Huddersfield, a Sunday night offering between Hull FC and London Broncos proved a poor spectacle, Hull eventually winning 22-14 after a Broncos fightback, helped by Sam Moa's 61st minute sending off for a mis-timed shoulder charge on Julien Rinaldi. It was a spectacular hit and led to much debate on whether the Tongan should have been sent off at all. Rinaldi was knocked out and on the following Tuesday Moa was banned for one game. Kirk Yeaman's try just after half-time after powerful work from Willie Manu made the score 22-4, giving London too much to do even with the help of the sending-off.

Salford City Reds coach Phil Veivers revealed that the RFL gave clearance to his players to wear protective tights for their trip to Widnes Vikings' i-pitch on the Sunday afternoon. Stephen Wild and Vinnie Anderson were among a handful of players to wear them following complaints of cuts and grazes from other players in recent weeks. The Reds were the side to get their first win of the season, threatening at one point to turn the match into a rout, the Widnes players booed off at half-time when trailing 32-6. Luke Patten, Daniel Holdsworth and Matty Smith were excellent for Salford, who were clearly benefitting from the expertise of assistant coach Sean Long.

Widnes could hardly have had a worse build-up to the game, with trio Scott Moore, Hep Cahill and Simon Finnigan suspended by the club for an off-field incident. Moore also broke his jaw. They were further disrupted by Ben Kavanagh snapping his Achilles in the first half and debutant Anthony Watts limping off after the break. They responded well, with two-try Patrick Ah Van, Kurt Haggerty and Anthony Mullally among their best, as they made the final scoreline a more respectable 38-18. Widnes coach Denis Betts admitted it was taking his side time to adjust to life in the top flight.

Round 4

Catalan Dragons produced one of the greatest comebacks in the history of Super League to grab a 34-32 win after the hooter in a thriller at Langtree Park in the Friday evening TV game.

Saints led 26-8 at one stage, with Jamie Foster, Gary Wheeler and Tommy Makinson all grabbing tries. But an amazing second-half fightback led by Scott Dureau, Ian Henderson and Leon Pryce sealed an unlikely victory. The clock was down to 30 seconds remaining with the Dragons, four points behind, needing to keep the ball alive, and they did that to some effect. After a penalty under the Saints posts, Dureau hoisted a kick to the right corner as the hooter sounded. Steve Menzies leapt highest and palmed the ball back to Damien Blanch on the bounce. The Saints cover smothered the winger, although he managed to fling the ball back on the ground.

February

Sebastien Raguin tried to dribble the ball into the corner, but missed it completely, allowing Leon Pryce to pick up and spread the ball back left. Jason Baitieri, Thomas Bosc, with an offload out of a tackle, Dureau with a flick on, and suddenly Setaimata Sa had an inch of space that he exploited brilliantly, giving Daryl Millard a one on one with the covering Jonny Lomax.

Millard stepped inside to score, but referee James Child had to go to the video referee, because, after a mesmerising 30 seconds of play, nobody was sure what had really happened. Steve Ganson rightly gave the nod, the scores were level, and Dureau capped it off with a stunning touchline conversion to leave the Saints faithful stunned.

The win left the Dragons as the only side with a 100 per cent record and they had a game in hand on top-of-the-table Warrington, who were undefeated still after a 42-10 home win over Hull KR. Ben Westwood produced another astonishing feat of endurance, despite suffering from flu and went clear at the top of the Albert Goldthorpe Medal table. Westwood had typically been among the Wolves best before somehow finding another gear in the closing stages, scoring twice and making another for Ryan Atkins to give the scoreline a lopsided look.

The Wolves never looked in danger of losing the game, with Atkins and winger Chris Riley also helping themselves to doubles to go alongside Chris Bridge's solitary effort. Brett Hodgson made his first appearance of the year after recovering from an off-season ankle operation.

Rovers were missing four players with injury from the side that drew against St Helens in Lincoln Withers, David Hodgson, Jordan Cox and Scott Murrell. But they welcomed back key halfback Michael Dobson - who had not been in the 19-man squad announced 48 hours earlier - with Sam Latus, Jason Netherton and Keal Carlile also coming into the 17.

Dobson could, however, do little to prevent the Robins wasting a host of good attacking opportunities in the first half, including twice getting the ball back from kick-offs. As a result they trailed 18-0 at the break, with the Wolves' vastly superior cutting edge the difference between the sides in a stop-start 40 minutes.

Danny Brough provided the magic as Huddersfield Giants ensured they stayed in touch with the Super League leaders with a hard-fought 30-16 win in London. Brough notched an interception try, created two other scores and provided the attacking impetus when needed to ensure the visitors emerged with the two points in a game that was touch and go for long periods. Had the Broncos taken their chances it could have been a very different story, with the point-less hosts having three tries chalked off. Kevin Brown's try right after the interval pushed the Giants into a match-winning 20-6 lead.

England captain Jamie Peacock was presented with his MBE by HM The Queen at Buckingham Palace and on the following Sunday was rested as the Rhinos enjoyed an eight-try 44-16 win at Widnes, who were still looking for their first league points.

The Rhinos, who were expected to be without Jamie Jones-Buchanan for up to

CARNEGIE CHALLENGE CUP - PRELIMINARY ROUND

Saturday 4th February 2012
Leeds Metropolitan University 15 Ovenden 14
Saturday 11th February 2012
Egremont Rangers 22 Bank Quay Bulls 16; Kells 20 Widnes West Bank 18 *(aet)*;
Seaton Rangers 8 Huddersfield Underbank Rangers 24
Sunday 12th February 2012
Blackbrook 18 Eccles 8; Millom 20 British Police 10;
Wigan St Cuthberts 24 Northumbria University 18
Wednesday 15th February 2012
Castleford Lock Lane 24 Elland 18 *(aet)*; Normanton Knights 32 Milford Marlins 30
Saturday 18th February 2012
Bradford Dudley Hill 38 Castleford Panthers 0; Eastmoor Dragons 22 Wigan St Judes 16;
Featherstone Lions 14 Askam 22; Loughborough University 22 Hunslet Warriors 50;
Nottingham Outlaws 0 Hunslet Old Boys 50; Oldham St Annes 40 Bentley Good
Companions 4; Rochdale Mayfield 14 University of Gloucestershire 33;
Stanley Rangers 60 Edinburgh Eagles 22; Warrington Wizards 18 East Leeds 28;
York Acorn 42 Norland Sharks 4
Sunday 19th February 2012
Hull University 10 Waterhead 68

Edge Hill University, drawn at Sharlston, withdrew;
Valley Cougars, drawn at Shaw Cross, withdrew

CARNEGIE CHALLENGE CUP - ROUND 1

Saturday 18th February 2012
Castleford Lock Lane 24 Sharlston Rovers 32;
Egremont Rangers 30 Leeds Metropolitan University 6
Saturday 25th February 2012
Blackbrook 24 East Leeds 20 *(aet)*; Bradford Dudley Hill 52 Askam 12;
Huddersfield Underbank Rangers 48 Stanley Rangers 10;
Hunslet Old Boys 26 Waterhead 14; Hunslet Warriors 32 Oldham St Annes 8;
Kells 34 Normanton Knights 12; Millom 36 University of Gloucestershire 8;
Shaw Cross Sharks 10 York Acorn 18; Wigan St Cuthberts 46 Eastmoor Dragons 22

CARNEGIE CHALLENGE CUP - ROUND 2

Saturday 10th March 2012
East Hull 32 RAF 14; Egremont Rangers 32 Ince Rose Bridge 22;
Hull Dockers 30 Kells 21; Hunslet Old Boys 16 Blackbrook 12;
Hunslet Warriors 30 Wigan St Patricks 0; Leigh East 6 Bradford Dudley Hill 16;
Oulton Raiders 19 British Army 5; Royal Navy 32 Leigh Miners Rangers 24;
Saddleworth Rangers 18 Myton Warriors 36; Sharlston Rovers 20 Wigan St Cuthberts 19;
Siddal 62 West Hull 12; Thatto Heath Crusaders 32 Millom 10;
York Acorn 26 Skirlaugh 10
Sunday 11th March 2012
Huddersfield Underbank Rangers 10 Wath Brow Hornets 24

three months after he underwent surgery to repair cartilage damaged in the World Club Challenge, turned the screw after the home side had made their best start yet to a Super League game. Widnes, whose marquee signing Anthony Watts was out with a long-term knee injury, gave Shaun Briscoe his Vikings debut and welcomed back Simon Finnigan and Hep Cahill who were missing previous week for internal disciplinary reasons.

The Rhinos had Richard Moore, the close-season signing from Crusaders, on the bench with Darrell Griffin making his first start for the club after his arrival from Huddersfield. Danny McGuire and Rob Burrow were at the centre of a creative Rhinos machine that opened up an 18-0 lead in the space of five minutes around the quarter-mark.

Winger Danny Williams and forward Vinnie Anderson missed a Friday night 24-22 victory over Hull FC at Salford City Stadium. A last-gasp penalty kick from Daniel Holdsworth for markers not square finally tipped the balance in Salford's favour.

The Saturday night TV game didn't match the game between Saints and Catalans for excitement but Bradford fans were highly satisfied to see their side come away from Wakefield with a 36-18 win. Ben Jeffries, who had had two spells with each club, created four of the Bulls' six tries, including three of the four in 14 minutes either side of the hour that swung a hitherto see-saw encounter decisively in the visitors favour. Jeffries had been forced to watch the Bulls erratic early season form and was only gifted his chance by the ankle ligament injury picked up by Luke Gale during the drubbing by Wigan the week before.

Mick Potter's side turned a 14-12 early second-half deficit into a winning advantage. Twice Jeffries' pin-point diagonal punts were capitalised upon by an alert Elliott Whitehead, while Keith Lulia and Brett Kearney also benefited from the stand-off's unerring accuracy.

After going down to an opening-day defeat against Huddersfield, Wigan had bounced back with a bang, with three successive wins culminating in a convincing 46-4 victory at Castleford Tigers on the Sunday.

The game was overshadowed by the sudden death seven days earlier of Robbie Millward, the 19-year-old son of Castleford Tigers and former Wigan coach Ian Millward, who was given compassionate leave, assistant Stuart Donlan left in charge. The match was preceded by a minute's applause in his memory and, once the action got under way, Sam Tomkins took control almost from the outset. Tomkins finished with a hat-trick and was just about untouchable.

Pat Richards was another huge figure for the visitors, with seven goals from eight attempts, including four from the touchline, plus two well-taken tries. Richards' second six minutes after half-time showed Tomkins at his mercurial best, running around in a circle on the Castleford '20' before somehow finding space on the left to send Richards into the left corner.

SUPER LEAGUE TABLE - *Sunday 26th February*

	P	W	D	L	F	A	D	PTS
Warrington Wolves	4	3	1	0	144	62	82	7
Wigan Warriors	4	3	0	1	136	46	90	6
Huddersfield Giants	4	3	0	1	138	70	68	6
Catalan Dragons	3	3	0	0	96	64	32	6
St Helens	4	2	1	1	140	104	36	5
Leeds Rhinos	3	2	0	1	84	52	32	4
Salford City Reds	4	2	0	2	82	102	-20	4
Bradford Bulls	4	2	0	2	84	118	-34	4
Hull FC	3	1	1	1	64	58	6	3
Hull Kingston Rovers	4	1	1	2	84	122	-38	3
Wakefield T Wildcats	3	1	0	2	60	72	-12	2
Castleford Tigers	4	1	0	3	60	104	-44	2
London Broncos	4	0	0	4	64	136	-72	0
Widnes Vikings	4	0	0	4	54	180	-126	0

MARCH
Bulls in bother

Round 5

Salford City Reds, unfancied at the start of the season, moved into the top-five with their third win out of five, a 44-12 home hammering of London, the Broncos' fifth successive defeat.

The Reds were 20-0 up at the break and with 20 minutes to go led by 44-0 before the Broncos scored two consolation tries. Iafeta Palea'aesina's effort from dummy half on the stroke of half-time ensured the win. Salford had chalked up a hat-trick of consecutive victories for the first time since April 2006.

Salford went above Catalans who lost 36-12 at Wigan on the Sunday. There were no last-minute miracles for the Dragons this week as Wigan extended their winning run to four matches in a brutal encounter that ended the French side's 100 per cent start to the season.

Wigan dominated the opening half but found themselves trailing at the break after a controversial try on the hooter when Gregory Mounis was adjudged to have grounded the ball. Two tries in six second-half minutes from Jack Hughes and Josh Charnley put the Warriors in full control and they managed a further two tries in the last ten minutes to take the points. Michael McIlorum and Gareth Hock were outstanding for Wigan with scrum-half Scott Dureau in top form in a losing side.

Leeds extended their winning sequence, including the World Club Challenge success over Manly Sea Eagles, to three games, with a 36-14 success at Castleford on the Friday night. At one stage Castleford looked as likely to prevail as the game went into the final quarter, having bounced back from an 18-point deficit to only four points down. But three converted tries in the last 15 minutes, including a hat-trick score by winger Ryan Hall and a touchdown on his debut by youngster Liam Hood, proved to be decisive.

Tigers assistant coach Stuart Donlan was still in charge after having earlier that day attended Robbie Millward's funeral in Leigh with other members of the Castleford staff.

The Tigers' focus began to drift 17 minutes from time, when a Ben Jones-Bishop break from deep in his own territory from a clearing kick by Castleford set up the position from which the ball was swept wide for stand-off Danny McGuire, fullback Brent Webb and centre Zak Hardaker to send Hall over in the corner for his hat-trick score.

In a game afflicted by the wet and windy weather at the KC Stadium, Richard Agar's former club Hull FC held off a stirring comeback from his Wakefield Wildcats side to win 14-10. The Black and Whites dominated field position for just over an hour - with Danny Houghton's swift dummy-half play pivotal - but Wakefield came back with tries to Ben Cockayne and Kyle Wood on 70 and 74 minutes and there were nervous closing minutes for the home fans.

On the same Sunday afternoon across town Hull KR were making short work of Widnes Vikings, winning 36-0. Widnes had boosted their squad following the arrivals of Cameron Phelps and Sione 'John' Kite. Phelps and front-rower Kite had both been in Australia waiting for visas and had arrived during midweek. But both men were left out of the 19-man squad for the Sunday game through their lack of match fitness. Vikings coach Denis Betts also confirmed 20-year-old scrum-half Gareth O'Brien was to join on loan from Warrington. Michael Dobson, aided by an admirably industrious display by the forwards, made Hull KR look a class above Widnes.

Some of Hull KR's players considered the weather to be the worst they had ever played in. Rovers' Constantine Mika could count himself lucky as he sat out the match after picking up a one-match ban for dangerous contact at Warrington the week before. Widnes were playing catch up after conceding two early tries to Lincoln Withers and Jake Webster and they looked a beaten side when Rovers added two more in a three-minute spell from Scott Murrell and Craig Hall.

Warrington had a tougher than expected 23-10 win at Bradford to maintain their unbeaten run. It was a third consecutive home defeat for the Bulls but they led for a huge proportion of the opening half after a trademark dive from dummy-half by Matt Diskin had given them a seventh-minute advantage, improved by Jarrod Sammut's conversion.

Even when the Wolves hit back midway through the half – a long Brett Hodgson pass sending Chris Riley over in the corner amid cries of "forward" - the hosts maintained their composure and might have extended their lead, had the video referee not twice ruled out home touchdowns in the space of four minutes.

First, when Stefan Ratchford's attempted clearance was charged down and Sammut gathered to cross, video scrutiny led to an offside decision. Then Michael Platt appeared to have scored after athletic work from Elliot Kear patted back a Ben Jeffries kick but again the Bulls missed out as replays proved a foot on the touchline fractionally before the ball was grounded.

Mickey Higham's try, a dummy through from two metres out just before the interval, created a mild injustice on the scoreboard. That reflection of play became even less balanced three minutes after the break when Ryan Atkins benefited from a favourable bounce after a Sammut last-tackle grubber kick rebounded straight into his hands. Bradford Academy product Atkins raced 80 metres up-field to score his 100th career try.

Another one-time Odsal favourite, Chris Bridge, incurred the wrath of his former fans by completing a tackle on Jeffries with an elbow into the chest, which resulted in only a penalty. Bridge took an early guilty plea in the week and settled for a one-match ban.

Trent Waterhouse reached out of a tackle to score and Bridge, backed by a predictable chorus of boos, slotted his third conversion to extend the lead to 16 points. Brett Kearney was helped off after accidentally cracking his head in a clash with Higham, before John Bateman put Jason Crookes over in the corner to reduce the margin to 12. But with eight minutes remaining Lee Briers, back on after having also left the field after colliding with the goal post while almost scoring a first-half try, added a field goal to finally put the game out of reach.

The Wolves missed Michael Monaghan, though his replacement Higham picked up three Goldthorpe points. Monaghan had undergone minor surgery on both knees and Ben Westwood was also absent with a hamstring injury. Tongan Manase Manuokafoa made a delayed Super League debut for the Bulls after recovering from a knee ligament problem.

Danny Brough played a key role in Huddersfield's dramatic 17-16 defeat of St Helens at the Galpharm Stadium on the Sunday, Saints ' second straight narrow loss.

Brough was at the centre of all the game's crucial moments, with the main three coming in the space of five second-half minutes.

First he collected a Lee Gaskell kick within ten metres of his own line, raced upfield on a dazzling run and created a genuine try of the season contender for Luke George, the winger's hat-trick score.

His conversion to that try then went over off both posts and the crossbar to give the Giants a four-point lead – one that he surprisingly extended by one with a field goal soon after. But that proved to be the all-important play, as when Ade Gardner dived over in the left corner with seven minutes remaining, Jonny Lomax's difficult conversion fell wide and Huddersfield hung on in a frantic finale.

Round 6

Vikings coach Denis Betts admitted he used Shaun Wane's decision to rest five senior players as motivation for his side ahead of the shock 37-36 Sunday afternoon win over Wigan at the Stobart Stadium, as Widnes registered their first points of the season. But he admitted he would have done the same thing as Wane if he'd been in the Warriors boss's shoes. Wane elected to rest Liam Farrell, Sam Tomkins, Thomas Leuluai, Sean O'Loughlin and Pat Richards, while giving debuts to Matthew Russell, Anthony Gelling, Joe Mellor and Logan Tomkins.

The Vikings came back from 18-6 and 36-18 down to level the scores at 36-36 through Frank Winterstein's try. Lloyd White then booted a field goal to edge Widnes ahead, but they were forced to withstand a nervous finish that included a failed 35-metre penalty attempt from Wigan winger Josh Charnley.

Referee Robert Hicks incensed the Widnes faithful with his decision to blow for a Willie Isa knock on, gifting Wigan one last chance with a minute to go. But Brett Finch was robbed from first receiver when White shot out of the line, made initial contact and then sprung the ball free. Betts' own selection included three debutants in Cameron Phelps, Sione Kite and Gareth O'Brien and there were six ex-Warriors in his starting line-up.

St Helens coach Royce Simmons reckoned his side "hit rock bottom" against Hull on the Friday night when they fell to a 22-10 defeat to the Black and Whites at Langtree Park. It was Saints' third defeat in a row and saw them slip out of the top eight.

Danny Tickle's boot, two tries from Wade McKinnon and a superb long-range effort from Jordan Turner combined to win the game for a Hull FC side under the radar. Hull overcame the first-half loss of Kirk Yeaman with a wrist injury to dominate the final half hour of the game against a Saints team lacking in confidence and direction without James Roby, who had suffered a knee injury in the defeat at Huddersfield. Tickle – who caught the eye offensively in a close first half – kicked five goals from as many attempts after the break, including three crucial penalties as the home side also lost its discipline.

Turner had helped his side level the scores with a stunning 90-metre try that sparked the Black and Whites' late charge, and McKinnon continued his impressive start to the season with two more tries and a hand in Turner's effort. Captain Andy Lynch set a terrific lead up front

Yeaman, who had been named that week in the England training squad, was set for a spell on the sidelines after sustaining a wrist injury while defending a St Helens attack. He used the expected time out to have surgery on a troublesome foot complaint.

London Broncos coach Rob Powell was visibly relieved after seeing his team record its first Super League win of the season against Castleford on the Saturday. They did it in style in the end with 20-unanswered second-half points completing a 42-16 victory. Former Crusaders halfback Michael Witt ran the game for the home side, making several crucial line breaks and kicking well. Jason Golden's sixth-minute try, set up by Craig Gower's scything break, broke the resistance of the Tigers, whose coach Ian Millward was still on compassionate leave, and who were missing Brett Ferres, banned for one game for dangerous contact in the defeat by Leeds.

Leeds were establishing themselves as the form side as they knocked Warrington off the top of the table with a 26-18 win at Headingley.

The Rhinos adapted better to the greasy conditions, Garreth Carvell knocking on within 26 seconds of the start, and by the 26th minute had scored two converted tries through the outstanding Danny McGuire and Zak Hardaker. But the Wolves were level at the break through converted tries to Matty Blythe and Chris Hill.

Three minutes after the turnaround, Rob Burrow broke clear in trademark fashion. Kevin Sinfield, McGuire and Brent Webb spread the ball at speed, Kallum Watkins providing a classic finish with a one-handed put down, Sinfield glossing the score with a touchline conversion. From the re-start, Ryan Bailey in his first game since the World Club Challenge, knocked on, Adrian Morley's charge gained a penalty, Chris Hill ramped up and Mickey Higham and Lee Briers shifted wide for Ben Westwood to just retain control of the ball as he trampled over Jay Pitts and Webb.

A Sinfield penalty edged Leeds two points ahead; Richie Myler had a try disallowed for offside and Ben Jones-Bishop likewise for an obstruction; and the crucial try came with 13 minutes remaining. Young hooker Liam Hood, who had scored on his debut at Castleford the week before, got to the ball first after Myler's fumble to acrobatically touch down.

Huddersfield moved to the top of the table with a not-always convincing 32-14 victory at neighbours Wakefield. The Giants, leading 18-4 at half-time, saw their advantage whittled away to just four points within 15 minutes of the restart but rallied to run in three further scores and cement top spot following Wigan's shock defeat by Widnes.

Trinity were in the game for long periods, forcing the Giants to drop-out on no fewer than four occasions – but even a well taken hat-trick from winger Ben Cockayne was ultimately not enough to prevent them slipping to a fourth straight defeat. Kevin Brown played a captain's knock to steady the Giants ship when it was wobbling midway through the second half, with a hand in all of their last three tries.

In Perpignan, Catalans, with eleven French players in the seventeen-man squad, ended Salford's three-match winning run in emphatic style on the Saturday afternoon, winning 40-18. Twenty points in 13 minutes after going behind turned the game and gave the hosts an unassailable lead by half-time. Setaimata Sa sat out the game after picking up a two-match suspension for dangerous contact in the defeat at Wigan.

The Saturday night TV game featured an astonishing comeback by Bradford at Hull KR. The Bulls went into the match without injured pack stars Craig Kopczak, Olivier Elima, Ian Sibbit and James Donaldson, but they overcame a 16-point deficit after 50 minutes to register a 36-24 victory. In the backs the Bulls were also missing Elliot Kear, Luke Gale and Adrian Purtell.

Bradford also had to contend with first-half injuries to Jamie Langley and Nick Scruton and trailed 24-8 with half an hour to go, but five second-half tries saw off a tiring Rovers, young winger Jason Crookes finishing with a try hat-trick.

Round 7

Leeds captain Kevin Sinfield became the greatest points scorer in the club's history on the Friday night, when he scored a try and kicked eight goals as the Rhinos demolished Salford City Reds 56-16. His tally now stood at 2,925 points, passing the record of 2,920 previously held by Lewis Jones. Oldham-born Sinfield made his debut for Leeds in a 22-24 home defeat to Sheffield Eagles on August 22, 1997, and had to wait over a year before scoring his first point. He crossed for a try in a 72-16 away win over Huddersfield on September 13, 1998, and his first goal came the season after, in a 62-18 away defeat to St Helens on May 4, 1999.

Zak Hardaker scored a hat-trick of touchdowns as Leeds made it four league wins in a row. The Rhinos were missing Ryan Bailey, who started the first of a three-match ban after pushing referee Richard Silverwood during the Warrington win the previous week.

Brent Webb escaped with a fine for a similar offence.

Pat Richards claimed 18 points as Wigan recovered from their shock defeat at Widnes with a seven-try 42-30 home win over determined London. Richards was now just one point short of becoming only the third Wigan player to register 2,000 points for the club.

The Broncos led 18-6 after half an hour, and briefly looked capable of threatening another shock when Chris Melling's try hauled them back to within six points, despite a Wigan rally either side of half-time. Brett Finch put in a second successive man-of-the-match display and his second try, on 56 minutes, put Wigan just out of reach as the Broncos threatened a second-half revival.

David Fa'alogo made an unexpected and successful comeback from injury during Huddersfield's impressive 42-4 defeat of Castleford on the Friday following major back surgery during the winter.

Ian Millward, back in charge of Castleford for the first time since the tragic death of his son Robbie, labelled Huddersfield genuine title contenders after the Giants, inspired by a Luke George hat-trick, consolidated top spot in the table with a sixth win of the season. George's impeccably executed treble was his third hat-trick, all on the same Galpharm Stadium stage, in his last five appearances following a winter move from Wakefield back to his home-town club. The 24-year-old one-time Giants Academy winger might have bagged four, but just failed to gather a slightly wayward long pass from Kevin Brown, before being taken off with an ankle sprain around the hour mark.

The Tigers, without leading scorer Josh Griffin (back) and playmaker Danny Orr (arm), had now suffered six straight defeats, their only win coming on the opening weekend of the season at Salford.

Leon Pryce made his 400th career appearance as the Dragons struggled past Hull KR in Perpignan, eventually winning 20-12. Rovers held the upper hand until just before the hour mark. On the 57th minute, Catalans had played their way down field, keeping the ball alive in style and only a last-gasp tackle by Graeme Horne prevented Jason Baitieri scoring. The next play saw Scott Dureau chip the ball wide to Damien Blanch who was challenged by Kris Welham. The ball came free and in an instant, the Dragons winger collected the ball and touched down, looking certain he had scored. The French touch-judge walked away from the incident, indicating he felt it was no try but after a discussion with him, referee Ben Thaler awarded the try. The ruling left Hull KR coach Craig Sandercock seething. Thomas Bosc's try five minutes from the end sealed the win.

Lee Briers' eight points for Warrington saw him pass the 2,500 milestone for his club as the Wolves struggled to beat Wakefield 32-30 at home. Isaac John's missed conversion with five minutes to go would have sealed a deserved point for Wakefield, but it dropped agonisingly short. It was his only miss of the day.

Warrington welcomed back hooker Michael Monaghan from double knee surgery and he replaced Mickey Higham who was serving the first of a two-match suspension for a high tackle against the Rhinos. Chris Riley started at fullback in place of the injured Stefan Ratchford, out for 12 weeks with a shoulder problem, while Rhys Williams took Riley's spot on the wing. Chris Hill replaced the injured Garreth Carvell in the front row, while there was a debut from the bench for youngster Brad Dwyer.

The Wildcats were by far the better team in the first half and the three tries to two scoreline was well deserved as the normally reliable Wolves defence struggled to cope with John, Tim Smith and Kyle Wood. Warrington improved after the break and led by the hard-working Ben Westwood they outscored their visitors four tries to two in the second period, although Simon Grix's try came on the seventh tackle.

Wakefield looked like they had grabbed a late draw when Vince Mellars went over in the last five minutes, but John's kick didn't have the legs.

Hull FC brought the Vikings back down to earth with a massive bump in a 58-10 rout at the KC Stadium, one week after the Vikings' shock home victory against Wigan. The Black and Whites embarrassed a woeful Vikings defence, with five tries providing 28 points in the first 27 minutes of the match. Danny Tickle was the star of the show for Hull, highlighting his multitude of skills with four tries, and nine goal kicks, in a 34-point haul that was two short of the club record set by Jim Kennedy in 1921.

Saints crashed to their fourth straight defeat at Bradford on the Saturday night, 12-8, and had now gone five games without a victory since winning their first two matches. Eighteen-year-old John Bateman stood out for the Bulls who were missing nine players through injury. For Saints, both James Roby and Jonny Lomax were a week away from returns. When Tony Puletua dropped Paul Wellens' pass with the line at his mercy in the 69th minute on their only meaningful attack of the second half, it was obviously not Saints' night.

The following day head coach Royce Simmons and his assistant Kieron Purtill were sacked.

Round 8

England captain Jamie Peacock, at the end of a week in which he signed a new two-year club contract until the end of the 2014 season, reacted angrily to his Leeds side being labelled unprofessional after their shock 46-6 defeat to a resurgent St Helens at Langtree Park in the Sunday evening TV game. The Rhinos' players had collectively dyed their hair red to raise money for Sport Relief, but they ran into a St Helens storm. "It's a fantastic effort by the lads to raise money for a superb cause," said Peacock. "All the lads find such comments completely disrespectful."

In many cases the red hair turned pink and, whatever the cause, St Helens, on the back of a win-less run of five matches and with caretaker coaches Mike Rush and Keiron Cunningham in charge, halted Leeds' early-season charge in spectacular fashion. St Helens ran in four unanswered tries in the opening 40 minutes - it was 18-0 after ten minutes, with Lance Hohaia pulling the strings alongside the returning James Roby and Jonny Lomax, who finished with 22 points. Four more tries in the second period saw Saints coast to a victory which was never in doubt from the first whistle as they kept Leeds to just one try. The Rhinos were without influential halfback Danny McGuire who had been ruled out for a fortnight after picking up a hamstring injury during training, and Brent Webb, who fell victim to illness before the game.

Widnes coach Denis Betts was delighted to record his second successive home win, with a dramatic 38-30 victory over London Broncos on the Sunday. For the first time the Vikings had pulled away from the bottom of the table, and now lay in twelfth place in Super League. Former Wigan boss Betts had to put a scratch side out due to injuries to influential captain and vice captain Jon Clarke and Shaun Briscoe, as well as leaving out prop Anthony Mullally and exciting youngster Danny Craven. In came Lloyd White at nine, Rhys Hanbury at stand-off, Ben Cross in the front row and Chris Dean on the edges. Welsh international White was the gamestar and collected two tries as Cameron's Phelps' 74th-minute try sealed it for Widnes after Tony Clubb's try converted by Michael Witt levelled the scores at 30-all with nine minutes to go. Gareth O'Brien's 77th minute penalty goal secured the points.

Huddersfield coach Nathan Brown denied that being linked to the St Helens job caused any distractions ahead of his team's surprise 40-22 defeat at Hull KR. The Giants' problems were compounded by an ankle injury to captain Kevin Brown and David Fa'alogo suffered a compound fracture to a finger.

Hull KR had been trailing 18-6 against the team who, at the start of the round, were top of Super League, just six minutes before the break, before a dramatic swing of momentum. Rovers piled on 34 further points, while conceding just a solitary unconverted try, on the way to a memorable victory. The fact that they were awarded just two penalties over the 80 minutes made their eventual tally all the more impressive.

Young prop Scott Taylor played a big part in the reversal of momentum and Michael Dobson was given licence by the Giants. Huddersfield's brief hopes of a recovery were dashed when Sam Latus managed to escape a swarm of defenders, showing relentless determination to find his way through, and establish a 12-point lead with eight minutes left on the clock.

Salford bounced back from two heavy defeats to stem Bradford's recent surge up the table with a 38-18 win at Odsal. The Reds arrived having conceded 18 tries and 96 points in successive defeats to Catalans and Leeds but showed few signs of lacking confidence as they capitalised on an error-strewn Bulls display to leapfrog above their opponents in the league table on points difference.

The Bulls, who went into the game on the back of three victories in four games, briefly held the lead, but five first-half tries, three in the last six minutes before the break, left them too big a mountain to climb. Bradford, without suspended Olivier Elima (dangerous contact on Lee Gaskell in the victory over Saints) but with Jamie Langley back, went into the break trailing 30-6 and although they tidied up their act and outscored the visitors in the second half, it proved too little too late.

Back-rower Elliott Whitehead that week signed a new deal that would keep him at Odsal until the end of 2016 and was hoping the Bulls would continue to plan for a promising future by signing up other younger players on long term deals.

Five-and-a-half years after leaving Sydney for Perpignan, Catalan Dragons' fullback Clint Greenshields announced he would leave the club at the end of the year to return home. Greenshields was back from injury on the Sunday as the Dragons surprisingly lost 32-22 at Wakefield. Buoyed by their excellent display in a two-point defeat at Warrington the previous weekend, Wakefield controlled the first half, with scrum-half Tim Smith guiding them to a 24-6 half-time lead. They then withstood a second-half comeback from the Dragons, who were plagued by handling errors throughout the game. Richard Agar had big efforts in the pack from Andy Raleigh and Paul Aiton among others, while Peter Fox scored two tries and barely put a foot wrong in general play. It proved too much for a Dragons team that couldn't discover their usual fluidity in attack, despite the best efforts of scrum-half Scott Dureau after the break.

Hull FC maintained their strong bid for a play-off spot with a 42-28 win, and Castleford regained much of their pride following a couple of indifferent displays, in a rousing display in the late-March heat of west Yorkshire. The result hinged on a number of factors, one of which was the superbly accurate kicking of Hull FC second row Danny Tickle, who landed seven goals from as many attempts, including four from the touchline. Tickle also grabbed a try in the second period, temporarily hurting his leg in the process, replacement kicker Richard Whiting's shot drifting narrowly wide from a testing angle. A try by Hull winger Tom Briscoe 10 minutes from time, moments after Castleford's Kirk Dixon appeared to be obstructed in pursuing a kick by Rangi Chase, transformed what could have been a two-point deficit facing the Tigers into an unbridgeable 14 points.

Shaun Wane warned Epalahame Lauaki he needed to be smarter, after the former Hull FC forward conceded the decisive penalty that cost the Warriors the points in their 22-20 home defeat by Warrington on the Friday.

Lauaki was twice placed on report by referee Richard Silverwood in a heated seven-minute spell late in the second half. First, as Wigan led 20-18 going into the final quarter, he led with the elbow while in possession in the 65th minute, then he produced a dangerous throw on Matty Blythe in the 72nd minute. Having levelled with another penalty, Wolves fullback Brett Hodgson then landed a 40-metre goal from the Blythe incident to secure a tense victory and take Warrington back to the top of the table.

Gareth Hock was back to form for Wigan and though it was rip-roaring game, neither side were at their best. Lauaki got a two-match ban for the tackle on Blythe.

Round 9

On the last Tuesday of March, four-times Super League champions Bradford Bulls announced they would go out of business unless supporters raised £1 million - at least half of it in the following ten days. The Bulls stated their problems had reached crisis point and the Good Friday visit of Leeds might be their last-ever game at Odsal.

Chairman Peter Hood said the recent sale of the lease on Odsal to the Rugby Football League had allowed the club to repay money owed to the game's governing body but the Royal Bank of Scotland had cut their overdraft facility, which meant they were unable to pay HMRC for tax due on historical image rights payments. The club needed to raise £500,000 by Friday, April 6, to stave off the threat of collapse and had written to every season-ticket holder, member and sponsor in a desperate plea for funds. The RFL's director of standards and licensing Blake Solly said they were aware of the crisis and were backing the club's survival bid.

Hood said the wages of players and staff had been paid for March but their ability to pay April wages would depend on the success of the plea for fresh cash. Several Bulls players manned the phones as supporters rang in to pledge money to the cause and several former players put up prized possessions for auction.

With that backdrop the Bulls put up a doughty display to go down 24-18 at Hull FC, who themselves went into second spot after their fifth win on a row. Amid all their financial problems the Bulls, missing Ben Jeffries through a hamstring injury, put in a determined performance as they came from behind to level on three separate occasions.

Hull, who drafted in youngsters Liam Kent and Chris Green for their competitive debuts, grabbed the lead for the last time in the 69th minute. An error from Bradford in their own half allowed a beautiful sweeping move right to left to be finished off classically by Tom Briscoe, after a perfectly weighted pass from Jordan Turner. The closing minutes saw great set control from the Airlie Birds, and a fine kicking game epitomised by Jamie Ellis's 40/20 with four minutes to go. After a penalty, Danny Tickle was allowed to extend Hull's lead to six, which ended up being too much for a tired but committed Bulls. Bradford's worries were compounded by a bad shoulder injury to young winger Jason Crookes, and a two-match ban for boom forward John Bateman for a dangerous tackle.

Castleford climbed off the foot of Super League with a last-gasp 34-30 home win over Hull Kingston Rovers, the day after one of the club's favourite sons, Malcolm Reilly, addressed the squad about their mental toughness, urging them to find the best in themselves.

A last-gasp try by Castleford winger Nick Youngquest, converted for good measure from the touchline by centre Kirk Dixon secured the sorely-needed victory. The touchdown, Youngquest's second of the contest, capped a rally from 10 points down midway through the second period. The decisive score, orchestrated by outstanding stand-off Rangi Chase, with enterprising fullback Richard Owen supplying the final pass, was questioned by Hull KR coach Craig Sandercock in the post-match press conference for an incident in the build-up that enabled the Tigers to gain possession.

Rovers, who had spent several minutes defending desperately and valiantly on their own line, appeared to be set for some respite when youngster Liam Salter collected the ball behind his own line.

From a distance, Salter then appeared to drop to the floor, risking being penalised for a `voluntary tackle'. Referee Robert Hicks' whistle, however, didn't blow – and three Tigers players picked the winger up and dropped him over the goal-line, forcing a drop-out that led to the decisive try. That episode, shortly after Robins fullback Shannon McDonnell had denied Owen with a superb tackle, gave Castleford the possession and territory from which Youngquest claimed his winner.

That Friday-night win put the Broncos bottom but they bounced straight back off the foot of the table on the Saturday afternoon with a resounding victory over Wakefield, outplaying the Wildcats in every facet of the game in a 36-0 win. Craig Gower's kicking game constantly flummoxed the hapless Wildcats and led to three of the Broncos' seven tries as the Broncos led 24-0 at half-time and Michael Robertson's second try just minutes into the second half killed off any slim hopes of a Wakefield comeback.

That result meant Widnes were back at the foot of the table on points difference after a 76-6 annihilation in Perpignan. Scott Dureau edged four-try debutant winger Damien Cardace to the gamestar award and took a commanding lead in the Albert Goldthorpe standings. The former Newcastle halfback dazzled with his skills and gave a place-kicking masterclass, kicking goals from both touchlines to post an impressive 11 goals from 11 attempts.

Widnes looked like rabbits in the headlights of a Catalan juggernaut that showed a ruthless edge to their play and showed no signs of letting up until the full-time whistle. Four tries in eight minutes before the break for the Dragons saw the home side race from a 12-6 lead to go 36-6 in front at the interval. It was also no co-incidence that the Dragons super show came as Ian Henderson returned from an ankle injury.

On the Friday night Warrington went into their 40th meeting with St Helens in Super League having won only three times and fell again to a 28-16 home defeat. The Saints raced into a 22-0 lead after 23 minutes, with skipper Paul Wellens grabbing a brace of tries as their recent run of four defeats started to become a distant memory. James Roby was back to his brilliant best, and he was backed up by the likes of Wellens, Jonny Lomax and Jon Wilkin, who was making his 300th career appearance, while Ade Gardner took the line on at every opportunity.

The Wolves missed the presence of Ben Westwood, who was out through suspension for a swinging arm on Epalahame Lauaki the week before, and made so many mistakes they were never in the game.

Wigan climbed quickly back onto the horse at Salford with a nine-try 40-20 win over an undisciplined Reds side which boasted six former Warriors players. Pat Richards was out with a thigh injury, which meant a starting berth for 18-year-old Matthew Russell on the wing. Skipper Sean O'Loughlin also sat the game out after picking a knee injury in training. Lee Mossop returned the squad and Gareth Hock was once again outstanding.

Huddersfield were back at the top of the table after a 22-12 win at Headingley on the Friday night in an error-strewn game. Two tries in as many minutes towards the start of the second half gave the defensively miserly Giants the foothold needed for a much merited win.

For the first, Lee Gilmour won the midfield, Danny Brough spread the ball to the right, Leroy Cudjoe freed Jermaine McGillvary, and the outstanding fullback Greg Eden raced onto his kick infield for his fifth try of the campaign. David Fa'alogo pressured Leeds from the re-start, and Eden linked gloriously up the middle with Scott Grix on a breakaway. Brough danced to the left again, and Cudjoe positioned McGillvary into the corner for a torpedo-like finish to a magnificent move.

SUPER LEAGUE TABLE - *Sunday 1st April*

	P	W	D	L	F	A	D	PTS
Huddersfield Giants	9	7	0	2	273	156	117	14
Hull FC	8	6	1	1	224	134	90	13
Warrington Wolves	9	6	1	2	255	176	79	13
Wigan Warriors	9	6	0	3	310	167	143	12
Catalan Dragons	8	6	0	2	266	168	98	12
Leeds Rhinos	8	5	0	3	220	168	52	10
St Helens	9	4	1	4	248	177	71	9
Salford City Reds	9	4	0	5	218	268	-50	8
Bradford Bulls	9	4	0	5	178	235	-57	8
Hull Kingston Rovers	9	3	1	5	226	234	-8	7
London Broncos	9	2	0	7	214	276	-62	4
Wakefield T Wildcats	8	2	0	6	146	208	-62	4
Castleford Tigers	9	2	0	7	156	296	-140	4
Widnes Vikings	9	2	0	7	145	416	-271	4

APRIL
The Giants stir

Round 10

Bradford Bulls reached their initial pledge target of £500,000, helped by a successful auction of Rugby League memorabilia on Maundy Thursday night, and the club now hoped to press on to try to reach its final target of £1 million. A bucket collection at Odsal on Good Friday night raised an extra £14,000. Almost 21,000 fans saw the Bulls defeat old rivals Leeds Rhinos 12-4. Leeds supporters turned out in force to cheer their team and in so doing lent their support to the Bulls' cause, helping to swell the holiday weekend's largest Super League crowd.

It was a typical, feisty battle played out in wet conditions. A Zak Hardaker try on 15 minutes gave Leeds a lead they hung onto for 50 minutes until Jamie Langley scored a scrambled try and Ben Jeffries sealed it five minutes later. The Rhinos, missing Danny McGuire and Rob Burrow, had now lost three games on the trot, against St Helens, Huddersfield and Bradford. Jamie Peacock was the victim of a spear tackle two minutes from time. Bryn Hargreaves was sent off but the following Wednesday, Bulls joint captain Heath L'Estrange, the real culprit, was banned for three games. Newly elected Bradford West MP George Galloway, who had won a surprise by-election victory standing for his Respect Party was there to witness the famous Bulls win.

The Bulls position was by no means secure and St Helens Chairman Eamonn McManus described the club's position as "a mere symptom" of "a systemic commercial weakness in the way Rugby League is structured and governed". McManus, writing in his programme notes for the St Helens v Wigan Good Friday fixture, called for an overhaul to ensure a future for the whole game. His comments came after Hull Kingston Rovers Chairman Neil Hudgell had circulated a letter to all the Super League clubs claiming that the game was "bankrupt".

The RFL denied a lack of transparency in the governance of the game. Leeds chief executive Gary Hetherington urged his fellow club officials to raise points of dispute in Super League meetings, which some never attended, rather than through the media.

Gareth Hock was in fine form on Good Friday as Wigan outplayed St Helens to claim a 28-10 victory in the first ever derby encounter at Langtree Park. Saints took the lead through a Francis Meli try from an error by Sam Tomkins, but Wigan hit back with tries from Darrell Goulding and George Carmont to lead 12-4 at the break. Saints scored first in the second half through Sia Soliola, but further tries from Tomkins, Hock and Jeff Lima sealed an eventually convincing win for the Warriors. Hock was also warned by the referee after he scored his try as he threw the ball into the Saints supporters, which left the majority of them baying for blood.

April

Saints went into the match having that week announced that Huddersfield coach Nathan Brown would take the head coach's job at Langtree Park at the end of the season on a three-year contract.

There were two games on the Thursday night. The Dragons blitzed London Broncos with four tries in the space of ten minutes at the start of the second half to record a 36-18 win in London. Damien Blanch's injury-affected start to 2012 continued as he broke a hand.

Thierry Alibert was once again at the centre of controversy after London Broncos coach Rob Powell accused him of awarding a try to the Dragons on the seventh tackle. The Frenchman had been dropped for round eight after miscounting and awarding a crucial try on the seventh tackle to Warrington in their match against Wakefield in round seven. He was suspended for one game again.

Warrington coach Tony Smith said he would face the music if the Rugby Football League decided to punish him for conducting a pitch-side team talk midway through the first half in Warrington's televised Thursday-night 46-12 derby victory over Widnes. Smith took the unusual step of leaving his seat to go to the touchline after the Vikings had taken a two-score lead, which had sent shock waves through the Halliwell Jones Stadium. After Chris Bridge had brought it back to 12-6 Smith decided to make his mark and he didn't know whether his move was in the rules or not. Young hooker Brad Dwyer scored the first try of his Super League career in the 73rd minute.

After Friday Huddersfield Giants remained top of the table after a 36-10 home win over Salford. Michael Lawrence made his 100th appearance for the Claret and Golds as Tommy Lee scored two tries

That week rugby union club Sale Sharks announced they would ground share with Salford City Reds at the Salford City Stadium in a move that had been anticipated for some time.

Castleford Tigers got one over near neighbours Wakefield with a Friday-night 34-16 win at Rapid Solicitors Stadium. It was the Tigers' best display of the season as they controlled the ball perfectly for Rangi Chase to orchestrate. Trinity's chances went when second row Ali Lauitiiti, who had been a constant threat in the first quarter, hobbled off on crutches at the interval with hamstring trouble.

It was a very Good Friday for the west side of Hull as Hull FC retained second place in the table with a comprehensive 36-6 derby win at the KC Stadium. In what was initially a close game, Brett Seymour's creation of FC's first two tries was key, and he scored a try of his own late in the game

The first play of the game was brutal, with Hull FC assistant coach Lee Radford knocking over his past apprentice, in ex-East Hull junior Josh Hodgson, with a bulldozing carry in his return from retirement to help out a front-row injury crisis. Radford was called up to bolster a Hull pack missing props Mark O'Meley, Eamon O'Carroll, Sam Moa and Chris Green, while new signing from Leeds Jay Pitts made his debut.

The bad luck for Hull KR had started before half-time in an incident in which Rhys Lovegrove and Kris Welham clashed heads, Lovegrove having to be helped off the field. Welham was also subdued for the rest of the game.

Round 11

RFL Chairman Richard Lewis announced he would leave the governing body at the end of April to become the new chief executive of The All England Lawn Tennis Club at Wimbledon. Non-executive director Maurice Watkins assumed interim chairmanship. Also making a departure was former England hooker Scott Moore who was sacked by the Vikings for a second unspecified disciplinary misdemeanour.

Seventeen-year-old Jack Owens made his debut for the Vikings in their 38-4 Easter Monday home defeat by Bradford, whose second win of the Easter weekend had them in seventh position. Wales prop Craig Kopczak returned to the Bulls line-up - having spent the previous five games on the sidelines with a broken finger - and was unstoppable when he made his appearance off the bench on 23 minutes, bagging himself a try on the stroke of half-time. With Jarrod Sammut's conversion, that gave the Bulls an 18-4 half-time lead, after Ben Jeffries and Michael Platt had already gone over in the opening 10 minutes, with Adrian Purtell playing a big part in both tries.

Rhys Hanbury got some points on the board for the Vikings on the half-hour with a fine try, but the Bulls ran riot in the second half. Platt got a second, while the club's three NRL signings for this season – Purtell, Manase Manuokafoa and Keith Lulia - got one each. By the time of Lulia's final try, Danny Addy had taken over the kicking duties following a knee injury to Sammut.

As well as cheering on a professional and efficient performance from their team, the Bulls fans were in fine voice, chanting Steve O'Connor's name to show their thanks for the Widnes boss's pledge towards their club's fight for survival. O'Connor had followed up his £10,000 pledge by donating 600 tickets for the Easter Monday game.

At Headingley, Leeds bagged 10 tries against the Broncos, who went down to their second Easter defeat by 52-10. Ryan Hall led the way with four. Zak Hardaker ended the afternoon with a wonderful brace, the first a long-distance individual effort, the second off a cheeky reverse pass from Brent Webb. Kevin Sinfield converted five second-half tries as Leeds remained sixth in the league.

After losing Jonny Lomax and Jon Wilkin during Good Friday's defeat to Wigan, injury once again hit St Helens as they claimed a hard-fought 18-12 away win against a Castleford side missing Rangi Chase, Danny Orr, Richard Owen and Daryl Clark, the main protagonists in their win at Wakefield three days earlier.

Try-scorer Ade Gardner (knee), Tony Puletua (shoulder) and Gary Wheeler (hamstring) all had to leave the field before the end of game at the Probiz Coliseum, but their teammates bounced back to claim Saints' third win in four matches under caretaker coaches Mike Rush and Keiron Cunningham.

It was mainly one-way traffic as Wigan beat Wakefield 36-6 at the DW Stadium. Thomas Leuluai, Sam Tomkins and Brett Finch excelled for the Warriors.

Prop Scott Taylor was the hero of the hour for Hull KR as the Robins fought back to take the spoils on their first trip to the Salford City Stadium. Two barnstorming tries in the last ten minutes from Taylor, both converted by Michael Dobson, quickly saw the Robins turn a 10-6 deficit into an 18-10 victory.

An eight-try 44-16 victory in the sun saw the Dragons leapfrog Warrington to move into third place in the table, and maintained the French side's perfect home record so far this season. Neither side played brilliantly but the capacity French crowd lapped it up as the Dragons ran in some spectacular scores. The Wolves also saw Richie Myler and Adrian Morley pick up injuries.

The clash of the top two went the way of the top side as the Giants won 22-4 at home to Hull FC, whose winning run was ended at six games. In the difficult, wet conditions there were no first-half tries, and it was 2-2 at the break as numerous spilled balls and knock-ons meant chances were at a premium. Danny Tickle and Danny Brough, who ran the show for the Giants, traded successful penalty kicks in the opening 16 minutes but despite enjoying most of the possession the Giants couldn't add to their score.

Tickle slotted over another penalty to give Hull the lead on 58 minutes after a Giants obstruction on a kick play. But the Giants finally opened up their opponents when Eorl Crabtree powered over from 10 metres out. The big prop and Jason Chan played big roles six minutes later in getting field position for Luke Robinson to burrow over from dummy-half. Brough converted both tries, and added a further penalty before making a long-range break from dummy-half and adding the conversion to Joe Wardle's touchdown in the left corner.

There was almost another Giants try in the final minute, but Tom Briscoe's pace denied Greg Eden. Tommy Lee was facing a possible four months on the sidelines after he damaged knee ligaments.

* On Easter Monday the first all-Wales clash at professional level in over 100 years took place at Wrexham when North Wales Crusaders, the club that had risen from the Ashes of the Crusaders Super League side, beat South Wales Scorpions by 34-22. The last derby had taken place on December 27th 1910, when Merthyr Tydfil beat Ebbw Vale 2-0.

Challenge Cup Round 4

Wigan were made favourites to win the 2012 Carnegie Challenge Cup by bookmaker William Hill, following their Sunday-afternoon 98-4 demolition of Championship One side North Wales Crusaders at the DW Stadium.

The Warriors were priced at 11/4, ahead of Warrington at 3/1 and St Helens and Leeds at 9/2. Super League leaders Huddersfield Giants, who came back from a half-time deficit to gain a convincing 42-16 victory at Hull FC on the Sunday, were the fifth favourites at 8/1, with the Catalan Dragons at 9/1.

Rob Burrow suffered a fractured cheekbone in Leeds' 38-18 win over Wakefield on the Friday evening as he clashed heads with Wakefield hooker Paul Aiton during the first half.

On the Saturday Widnes and St Helens produced a fantastic spectacle as a meagre crowd nearly witnessed the comeback of the season when the Vikings came from 40-16 down to almost take 12-time Cup winners Saints into golden point extra-time. Eventually, Patrick Ah Van's penultimate kick, in the 75th minute, which struck the upright, proved the difference in a 14-try thriller that ended 38-40.

Warrington progressed with a convincing 44-18 victory over a spirited Keighley side at Cougar Park. Jason Demetriou's Cougars, which included his former Wakefield teammates Sam Obst, Michael Korkidas and Semi Tadulala, went in just 16 points down at the interval, but Brad Dwyer's score early in the second half confirmed the result.

Eighteen-year-old John Bateman edged out hat-trick duo Elliott Whitehead and Shaun Ainscough for the gamestar honour in Bradford's 72-6 win over Championship One pacesetters Doncaster at Odsal; Castleford loanee Ryan Brierley plundered four tries in Leigh's 68-18 home win over Rochdale; Michael Witt scored two tries and booted seven goals as hosts London Broncos ran in 13 tries in a comprehensive 72-4 win over Dewsbury Rams.

After a heroic second-half fightback, from 20-0 down at the break, Hull KR made a Cup exit at Craven Park as Catalans emerged 20-18 victors. Leon Pryce's first-half double had helped ensure the Dragons possessed enough points to hold off the Robins surge though Rovers went on to out-score their opponents four tries to three. Ultimately, Michael Dobson's missed kicks proved crucial, although his chances were far more difficult than the ones Scott Dureau efficiently booted over. Dobson hit a post on two occasions so it was by a margin of inches that the Robins were edged out as stand-off Blake Green made his first appearance of the season after recovering from a blood clot in his leg.

The Challenge Cup threw up a rare and dramatic giant-killing as Championship champions Featherstone Rovers knocked neighbours and bitter rivals Castleford Tigers out with a 23-16 victory at Big Fellas Stadium (Post Office Road).

Live on Sky TV, a cricket score looked in prospect when Daryl Clark scored after four dominant minutes. But after only nine minutes a kick by Danny Orr ended up in the hands of Tangi Ropati, who thrilled the home fans by scorching in for a touchdown. Suddenly

Tom Saxton fends off the challenge of Danny Orr as Featherstone upset their local rivals Castleford

the pressure was on the Tigers, and Clark responded by holding down Jon Hepworth too long in the tackle and being sin-binned. Clark's absence was a great opportunity for Rovers, and they pounced twice, through Kyle Briggs and Ian Hardman, while the Tigers' hooker was off the field.

After 20 minutes Fev were leading 16-6, and we awaited the response from the Tigers when Clark returned. But after more great work from Hepworth, who had a stormer throughout, it was Featherstone who scored the next try through Greg Worthington. The Tigers nabbed one back through Josh Griffin before the break to cut the margin to ten points, and in a tense second half there would only be one try, from Nick Youngquest for the Tigers twelve minutes before the final hooter.

Liam Finn added a field goal to increase the margin to seven points, and the Tigers just couldn't get back into the tie. As the game had gone on, they had become more frustrated. 2011 Albert Goldthorpe Medal winner Rangi Chase put in a high challenge that left Ropati with two fractures in his jaw, and needing three plates and several pins inserted into his face. The foul wasn't penalised as it appeared to be a shoulder charge in real time, but on the following Tuesday the RFL Disciplinary Committee banned him for three games for a dangerous high tackle.

Round 12

Shaun Lunt made a dream start to his Leeds career in the Friday-night TV game by scoring a match-clinching try on the hour mark against the Catalan Dragons in the Rhinos' 34-18 win, after having joined the club on loan from Huddersfield for the rest of the season only a couple of days earlier.

Lunt's move came after Huddersfield coach Nathan Brown signed hooker Scott Moore to the club for a second spell. Moore spent the 2009 season on loan at the Giants under Brown, and sealed his return to the Galpharm Stadium less than a week after his contract with Widnes Vikings was cancelled. Lunt's arrival at Headingley saw rookie Liam Hood move to Dewsbury on a dual-registration deal.

April

Leeds produced their best 80-minute performance of the regular season as the Dragons, pre-match favourites, left Headingley Carnegie, where they had never won, for the eighth successive time without the spoils. Although particularly keen to highlight the finishing prowess of two-try Ben Jones-Bishop, coach Brian McDermott singled out his energised pack, with converted Aussie centre Brett Delaney to the fore, as being the key to a highly impressive victory.

Dragons fullback Clint Greenshields faced disciplinary action following comments made on Twitter about referee Ben Thaler during the clash. Greenshields, who missed the game with a hamstring injury, and was watching on TV from France, tweeted: 'Holy s*** thaler is retarded. F*** me!'.

He was suspended for the next weekend by the club and then fined £1000 by the RFL, half of it suspended.

St Helens interim coach Mike Rush paid tribute to rookie winger Adam Swift, after the youngster scored a hat-trick of tries against Widnes Vikings in Saints' 62-0 victory on the Friday night. Swift's grandfather Harold, the former Chairman of the famous Blackbrook amateur club, from which Adam joined St Helens, passed away before the winger made his first-team debut in the Cup the previous week. Denis Betts' team had pushed St Helens to the limit in their Challenge Cup tie seven days earlier, but failed to compete in front of a bumper Langtree Park crowd.

Two late Ashley Gibson tries set up a grandstand finish to a Saturday-night TV match between Salford and the Wildcats, that hosts Wakefield had looked like winning at a canter. Trinity led through two tries in the first six minutes and should have been out of sight by half-time. Dean Collis's opening score was added to by Danny Washbrook, Frankie Mariano and Peter Fox to forge a 22-6 lead at the break and, despite a Chris Nero reply early in the second half, two Paul Sykes penalties seemed have sealed both points for the Wildcats until Gibson's late brace. A frantic finale ensued in which Salford could easily have snatched it when Matty Ashurst seemed set to level things but, thanks to a desperate grasp by Danny Kirmond, just failed to hang on to a Joel Moon pass in the dying seconds with the line beckoning. It finished 26-22.

Apart from the clash between Bradford and Huddersfield on the Sunday all the games were one-sided - surprisingly so at Hull FC where Wigan took the home side to the cleaners with a 56-12 hammering. Injury-hit Hull, with an untested, young half-back pairing of Danny Nicklas and Jamie Ellis, plus an 18-year-old centre, Lee Crooks's son Ben Crooks making his first Super League start, were never in the contest. By the 52nd minute Wigan had stormed into a 40-0 lead. Shaun Wane's team were not in merciful mood on the way to 10 tries, with Pat Richards managing 26 points on his own by scoring a hat-trick and collecting seven goals from eight kicks. The only down side was that Richards - returning from a thigh injury - had to go off 10 minutes from the end with a knee injury that required surgery.

Hull fullback Wade McKinnon returned from a hamstring injury, following rumours he had requested to leave the club earlier in the week. The Australian had found it difficult to adapt to life in the UK, even though he had a deal running to the end of 2013.

Wigan stand-off Joe Mellor joined Widnes Vikings on a one-month loan deal. It was his second spell at the club as he spent time with them in the Championship in 2011. Utility back Amos Roberts announced his retirement after failing to fully recover from a knee injury suffered on Easter Monday in 2010. He had not played since the previous summer and had a third knee operation at the end of 2011.

Warrington finally clicked into gear in a one-sided encounter against an under-strength Castleford side, running in ten tries for a 54-6 win in what at times was an exhibition in the sunshine. The Wolves led 38-0 at the break and Brett Hodgson finished with 22 points from two tries and seven goals.

Hull KR bounced back from their exit in the Challenge Cup to Catalan Dragons with a thumping 44-16 victory against a London Broncos side lacking in experience. The

Robins were devastating down their left-hand side, with Michael Dobson, Kris Welham and David Hodgson all working together to great effect. Welham and Hodgson combined for five of their seven tries, but it was Dobson who stole the show, providing the type of performance that had him collecting the Albert Goldthorpe Medal in 2009. London lacked the creative flair of the injured Michael Witt, and with eight first-team players sidelined, the Broncos' inexperience was evident, particularly in defence.

Danny Brough produced another dominant display to maintain Huddersfield's grip on top spot in the Super League table, the Giants winning 20-6 at Odsal after a water-logged eighty minutes. Scrum-half Brough was superb, consistently kicking Bradford into difficulties as well as scoring a try, booting four goals and laying on another score for Jermaine McGillvary. Brough's third goal, a 57th minute penalty, put the Giants eight points clear - and out of the reach of the hosts.

SUPER LEAGUE TABLE - *Sunday 22nd April*

	P	W	D	L	F	A	D	PTS
Huddersfield Giants	12	10	0	2	351	176	175	20
Wigan Warriors	12	9	0	3	430	195	235	18
Warrington Wolves	12	8	1	3	371	238	133	17
Catalan Dragons	11	8	0	3	364	236	128	16
Hull FC	11	7	1	3	276	218	58	15
Leeds Rhinos	11	7	0	4	310	208	102	14
St Helens	12	6	1	5	338	217	121	13
Bradford Bulls	12	6	0	6	234	263	-29	12
Hull Kingston Rovers	12	5	1	6	294	296	-2	11
Salford City Reds	12	4	0	8	260	348	-88	8
Wakefield T Wildcats	11	3	0	8	194	300	-106	6
Castleford Tigers	12	3	0	9	208	384	-176	6
London Broncos	12	2	0	10	258	408	-150	4
Widnes Vikings	12	2	0	10	161	562	-401	4

Challenge Cup Round 5

The Featherstone Cup fairytale came to an end on the last Friday night of April when, again on live TV, they fell 32-16 to Wigan at Big Fellas Stadium. It was a far tighter contest than the scoreline suggested as again the Super League side went into the lead in the first five minutes, Sean O'Loughlin crossing from a Brett Finch pass. Rovers responded magnificently and it was a Wigan error that contributed to their first score. In the 19th minute Anthony Gelling lost the ball in contact coming out of his own '20'. Jonny Hepworth picked it up, before smart handling by Liam Finn and Greg Worthington allowed Tommy Saxton to win the race to the corner. Wigan were penalised for offside at the restart before an angled kick to the left by Liam Finn found Ian Hardman on the left, and the video ref said yes to onside and the grounding.

A Darrell Goulding try on the right on 24 minutes levelled. On the half-hour a Gelling touchdown was ruled out when the video ref spotted an obstruction by Gareth Hock in the build up. Four minutes later, after Harrison Hansen had left the field to have a cut face repaired when he clashed heads with Stuart Dickens, twice in the same tackle, Rovers took the lead when Michael Mcllorum was penalised for holding down in front of his own posts.

Finn kicked the goal before, on 37 minutes a key moment of the game occurred. Finn was penalised for holding Mcllorum down, and the ball was moved left to Hock, who shot like a bullet towards the posts, with Charnley converting

In the 53rd minute Thomas Leuluai gave the video-ref another job from first receiver on the right, after a big drive from Jeff Lima. Charnley's conversion was successful - it was a vital score for the Warriors. Rovers still believed, hanging on defensively inside their own '10' after Andy Kain lost the ball, only to retrieve it when Finn stole it from Brett Finch to race deep into Wigan territory on 58 minutes. The play-the-ball was quick, and the ball was moved wide to the right by Kyle Briggs, Hepworth and Sam Smeaton for Gareth Raynor to speed into the right corner, Finn missing the conversion.

With one score between the sides, and a quarter of the game left, nothing seemed impossible for Rovers. But on 63 minutes Mcllorum made a break towards Rovers' posts, and the ball was moved left on the next play to Gelling, who kicked for the line, but failed to touch down. Raynor was adjudged to have obstructed him. Within two minutes, Finch and Leuluai moved the ball quickly to the right, outflanking Rovers' cover. Charnley couldn't convert his own try, but on 78 minutes Hock grubbered on the last tackle and raced through almost unchallenged to touch down. Charnley's kick ended the scoring and Wigan went into the Tuesday-morning draw for the sixth round as the favourites.

Leigh went into the draw as the only Championship side remaining after a golden-point field goal from Martyn Ridyard seven minutes into extra time settled a pulsating tie at Leigh Sports Village with Halifax by 19-18.

On a cold and wet day, London just edged out Batley in a tie that almost had all the makings of a cup upset. Bulldogs coach John Kear had built up the game during the week perfectly by posing questions about whether London's Australian stars could hack it on the slope of Mount Pleasant. However, the Broncos key men Michael Witt and Craig Gower

Gareth Hock wraps up Stuart Dickens as Wigan end Featherstone's Challenge Cup fairytale

guided the visitors through to the quarter-finals by 22-16, amid a determined effort from the home side. The Broncos dominated possession with ball in hand and took a 16-0 lead early in the game. But they committed seven knock ons in the first half near the Bulldogs line, as Batley came back to close the gap to four points before the break.

The three other Championship sides didn't fare so well. Danny Brough grabbed 20 points from a try and eight goals at a wet and windy Galpharm as the Giants beat Swinton Lions 52-0; Scott Dureau ran riot behind a dominant pack in a 68-6 win over Sheffield Eagles in Perpignan; and Jonny Lomax's 28-point haul and Francis Meli's hat-trick were the features of St Helens' 76-0 win over Championship One Oldham, in a tie switched from Whitebank to Langtree Park.

Leeds Rhinos had a hard-fought 16-10 win at Salford but didn't get in front until the final eight minutes. The match-winning intervention came from Danny McGuire, who produced a determined, fleet-footed run and laid the ball off precisely for Shaun Lunt to force his way over for the match-winning try.

And in the Saturday TV game Warrington had a tough 32-16 home win over Bradford. The Bulls were buoyed by the return of scrum-half Luke Gale after a 10-game absence with an ankle injury. Adrian Purtell passed a fitness test on a hamstring to take his place on the wing and his 12th minute try gave the Bulls the lead. But by the time Joel Monaghan had scored the second try of his hat-trick four minutes after half-time the Wolves, guided by Brett Hodgson, with Michael Monaghan still absent with knee problems, had a stranglehold at 20-6. Hodgson was the victim of a crusher tackle by John Bateman which was put on report and earned the youngster a three-match suspension - his second ban within the space of a month.

MAY
Magic tricks

Round 13

Rugby League entered new territory on the first Sunday of May as London Broncos played their home match with Bradford at Leyton Orient's Brisbane Road ground in north-east London. A crowd of just under three thousand was the Broncos reward for testing the water, a larger attendance than some of their games at the Stoop that season. On the pitch, London, with Hull KR prop Scott Wheeldon making a loan debut, were unable to give their new or old fans much to cheer about after letting slip a 16-point lead before falling to a 29-22 defeat.

The Bulls had to cope without Adrian Purtell and Brett Kearney because of injury and were without John Bateman through suspension but Michael Platt scored four tries for a welcome win that kept them in eighth spot, level now with Leeds.

The Rhinos had gone down 34-20 to Hull FC at the KC Stadium on the Saturday night, Hull beating Leeds for the first time in twelve attempts. Hull coach Peter Gentle opted to play Richard Whiting at stand-off and the move proved pivotal, the former Featherstone junior picking up three Albert Goldthorpe points as the game's top performer.

The first half was an extremely tight affair with the lead switching hands four times, but FC just edged it, with good defence giving them a six-point advantage at the break. Hull came out the stronger in the second half as Danny Tickle added three penalty goals, but Ryan Hall pulled it back to eight points, before tries from Tom Briscoe, with his second, and Ben Crooks sealed it, and Danny McGuire added a late try for consolation. The Rhinos were hit by a crucial forward pass call that denied a try for Brent Webb when they trailed 20-10. Briscoe's second try was chosen as League Express Try of the Week as he burst through three tackles, and then beat three other defenders in a 70-metre dash to the line.

Meanwhile speculation was mounting that Jordan Turner would be following Willie Manu out of Hull to St Helens for 2013.

In a game in which the lead changed hands on five occasions, Huddersfield's winning run of four games came to an end with a 27-20 defeat at Catalan Dragons that saw them overtaken at the top of the table on points difference. The Giants dominated field position for much of the game and Joe Wardle's try seven minutes from time gave Danny Brough the chance to put them 22-20 ahead, but he couldn't land the touchline kick

Despite losing form halfback Scott Dureau six minutes into the second half with a leg injury, the Dragons had the resolve to go on and maintain their unbeaten home record in SLXVII. A penalty for offside allowed the Catalans to go down field and drives from Remi Casty and Jason Baitieri gave field position for Thomas Bosc to kick a field goal on the third tackle. With time running out, frustration got the better of Huddersfield, again pulled for offside. The Dragons made them pay with a superb try that saw Bosc and Leon Pryce heavily involved before Clint Greenshields put Vincent Duport over to secure the win. Bosc's conversion sent the crowd into raptures.

Wigan went top of the table after their 36-22 victory over Hull Kingston Rovers at the DW Stadium on the Friday night. The Warriors were at their scintillating best as they raced into a 26-0 lead inside the first 25 minutes. Michael McIlorum, Gareth Hock and Lee Mossop were all outstanding in driving the hosts forward during a match-winning opening quarter. Behind them, Brett Finch was scheming, Thomas Leuluai was solid and Sam Tomkins showed flashes of brilliance. On the flanks, Darrell Goulding and hat-trick hero Josh Charnley combined well, while George Carmont did enough to lay on the first of two tries for Anthony Gelling.

The abiding memory was the sight of referee Phil Bentham breaking his leg after 18 minutes in the build up to Mossop's try under the posts. In back play Bentham had accidentally stepped into Shannon McDonnell's path, and the 41-year-old official was eventually stretchered off after a seven-minute hold up, before being taken to Wigan Infirmary with a broken tibia. Touch judge Robert Hicks took over.

Despite resting several star names, Warrington ultimately proved too strong for Salford as they won at home by 24-20 with a solid if unspectacular performance which saw them almost snatch defeat from the jaws of victory. Wolves coach Tony Smith shuffled his pack ahead of the following week's Challenge Cup tie in Perpignan by recalling winger Rhys Williams, hooker Brad Dwyer and impressive 17-year old second-rower Ben Currie. Adrian Morley, Richie Myler, Stefan Ratchford and Michael Monaghan were all still missing through injury. Lee Briers was rested, as were Ben Westwood, Chris Bridge and Brett Hodgson.

Phil Veivers had plenty of first team players on the treatment table too. Shannan McPherson, Vinnie Anderson, Sean Gleeson, Chris Nero and Iafeta Palea'aesina were among the walking wounded, and Wayne Godwin broke his arm after only ten minutes.

At 24-10 down, Salford were tiring badly and with a man light on the bench it was proving difficult for them to get back into the game as the clock ticked down. However, when Chris Riley spilled a Daniel Holdsworth bomb on 74 minutes, Luke Adamson picked up the crumbs and a delightful one-handed offload found Holdsworth who coasted in under the posts to reduce the arrears to 24-16. Two minutes later, the Reds turned up the heat once more when a scuffed kick on the last play went into the Warrington in-goal and an alert Danny Williams pounced on the ball to stun the home crowd. Ultimately, Warrington held on for the win.

James Roby provided a dummy-half master class, and Chris Flannery a rare hat-trick, as St Helens eased past a Wakefield side that at least managed to break the home team's long-standing clean sheet. Saints hadn't conceded a try for 172 minutes when Francis Meli's error led to a Dean Collis try in the opening stages. But, for the most part, the home side was well in control, and the 38-12 margin could have been greater but for five missed conversions by Jonny Lomax and a late Peter Fox consolation.

On the Mayday Monday, boom hooker Daryl Clark came off the bench to light up a contest between two teams running low on confidence, Castleford winning at home over Widnes by 36-12. Winger Nick Youngquest scored a fine hat-trick as Widnes collapsed in the last 20 minutes, and to compound matters, back-rower Simon Finnigan was out for the rest of the season after suffering a fractured fibula.

They were probably also affected by the news that marquee signing Anthony Watts, who had played only a few minutes before suffering a season-ending injury had that weekend been arrested for being drunk and disorderly, days after signing a new one-year contract. On the Tuesday he said he was leaving the club to return to Australia because of "personal reasons." It emerged that he was also found to be possessing a small amount of cocaine on his arrest and had been sacked by the club.

Another making an exit was Bradford Bulls chairman Peter Hood, who resigned his post, former chairman Chris Caisley promising to head a strategic review into the Bulls' financial status.

* The RFL confirmed that Manchester would stage the final of the 2013 World Cup, while Wembley would stage both semi-finals as a double header.

Challenge Cup Quarter Finals

Alex Murphy, who as player-coach memorably led Leigh to lift the Challenge Cup with a shock 24-7 win over Leeds in the final, had called on Leigh Centurions to remember the class of 1971 when they played Leeds Rhinos on the Friday night, almost exactly 41 years since their famous Wembley win. Leeds won the game at canter by 60-12. Kevin Sinfield proved the star of the show with two tries and ten goals as the Rhinos blasted into the semi-finals, in which they were drawn with Wigan. Leigh were by no means easy beats but once Rob Burrow scored one of his specials from dummy-half nine minutes after half-time, and Sinfield goaled to bring up 30 points, Leeds were safely into the semis.

Huddersfield coach Nathan Brown described the prospect of a semi-final against their 2009 Challenge Cup Final conquerors Warrington as "quite exciting", after watching his high-flying Huddersfield side romp into the last four for the fourth time in eight years with a 50-14 demolition of London Broncos at the Galpharm Stadium on the Sunday. The 2004, 2006 and 2009 semi-finalists' free-scoring attack, allied to the best defence in the Super League, was always likely to be too good for struggling London, with just two wins against top-flight opposition all season.

In a dramatic opening, Broncos second-rower Matt Cook was helped off before a tackle had been completed after tangling with Jermaine McGillvary as both attempted to field the kick-off. Luke Robinson's two tries in as many minutes early in the second half put the game beyond London's reach, if Greg Eden's score just before the break hadn't already.

The Wolves ended the Catalan Dragons' unbeaten home record and gained revenge for their defeat on Easter Monday with a 32-22 win in Perpignan which was built in the first half when solid defence and ruthless attacking saw Warrington take a commanding 20-6 lead. Lee Briers kicked the home side into submission in the first half, into a testing breeze. He ran the game for the Wolves and laid Paul Wood's 52nd minute try on a plate to halt a mini Catalan revival. Chris Bridge's interception try six minutes from the end sealed the win for the Wolves.

Wigan coach Shaun Wane could not hide his delight as the Challenge Cup holders prevented fierce rivals St Helens from reaching their twelfth consecutive semi-final with an 18-4 win at the DW Stadium. Wane had promised to make life hell for St Helens in the previous week's League Express and Wigan were led around the park by Brett Finch and Thomas Leuluai, with the former controlling everything in attack, while Leuluai was awesome in defence.

Saints got off to a dream start with a Paul Wellens try but as the half rolled on the Cup holders grew in strength and could have been even further in front than the 12-4 half-time scoreline. Wigan extended their lead at the start of the second half, with Finch scoring a fine individual try, and from then on, with Saints dominating field position, they manned up in defence and ground out the victory.

There had been doubt after the draw as to whether the Warriors would be able to stage the game at their own stadium because the soccer club had a fixture the following day, the BBC insisting they wanted to televise the game on the Saturday afternoon, but the matter was eventually resolved.

Wane said he wanted to keep hold of his halfback Brett Finch. Finch's current contract ran until the end of the season, and after recent eye-catching performances there had been significant interest in his services both from the Super League and NRL.

Round 14

Wigan moved clear as the top-two sides clashed at the Galpharm Stadium in the Friday TV game, and they did it in some style with a 32-12 win over the Giants. Three tries in eight minutes midway through the second half gave Wigan the points, but the foundations had been laid before half-time. The Warriors led 12-6 at the break, but that could easily have been more had Josh Charnley managed to convert any of his side's three tries. Charnley's own try-double sandwiched a superb Sam Tomkins effort, all of which exposed Huddersfield's left-side defence.

Wigan's inability to make the most of their tries meant Greg Eden's score briefly levelled proceedings early in the second half. But the Giants fullback quickly fell from grace, spilling Brett Finch's kick to allow George Carmont to edge the Warriors back in front soon afterwards, and the floodgates were opened.

Thomas Leuluai's dummy sent Liam Farrell through quickly afterwards, before Carmont galloped on to Gareth Hock's pass to complete a match-winning burst. And with Wigan fans celebrating in the rain-sodden Galpharm Stadium, Jeff Lima added the finishing touches in the final seconds to complete an emphatic win.

Warrington moved into second place above Huddersfield, a point behind Wigan, after a 42-12 win at Wakefield on the Sunday, though an easy win was far from certain when Wakefield held them 12-12 at the break. Trinity, with the benefit of a fortnight's break due to the previous weekend's Carnegie Challenge Cup quarter-finals, welcomed back second-row duo Steve Southern and Ali Lauitiiti for the first time since they were injured during the Good Friday clash with Castleford. But coach Richard Agar was concerned at how Warrington chalked up four of their seven tries in the final quarter of the match.

Scott Dureau's late try eventually sealed a high-scoring, see-saw encounter in which hosts Widnes played their full part, despite considerable adversity. The Vikings looked as though they would be blown away when Catalans scored three tries inside the first 14 minutes, but hauled themselves back into the contest and led 22-20 early in the second half.

They then had to face more difficulties, as the visitors scored 12 points with Jon Clarke in the sin bin, and home playmakers Lloyd White and Joe Mellor were stretchered off in quick succession. But Denis Betts' charges dragged themselves off the canvas again, and well-worked tries to Kurt Haggerty and Patrick Ah Van put them back ahead with eight minutes on the clock. But crucially Catalans regained their next kick-off, and late tries to Thomas Bosc and the excellent Dureau eventually ensured the two points would head back to France after a 42-34 win.

Hull FC had a nailbiting 14-12 win against London Broncos at Gillingham on the Sunday, a game which drew a crowd of almost 4,000, as Rugby League returned to Kent for the first time since the demise of Kent Invicta in 1984. With Hull in a slender 12-6 lead, a 67th minute Danny Tickle penalty goal put two scores between the two sides, which proved enough as Michel Robertson's converted try two minutes later set up a tense final ten minutes.

Hull KR produced their best performance of the season to date with a powerful 12-try, 70-12 home win against a hapless Castleford Tigers on the Sunday. Three tries in the first nine minutes set Hull KR on their way, and gave the Tigers no chance. Eight of Rovers' twelve tries were created by pivots Michael Dobson, Blake Green and Shannon McDonnell. Castleford hooker Daryl Clark was set for a long spell on the sidelines after picking up a knee ligament injury.

On the Friday night Salford City Reds and the Bulls played out a tense 20-all draw, in a game which see-sawed both ways until Salford salvaged a point with a late try.

It was certainly a dramatic closing five minutes in the rain at Salford City Stadium as, with the Bulls clinging on to a 20-16 lead, Olivier Elima was wrongly sin-binned for holding back a Salford player on the Bradford line. From the penalty, the Reds moved the ball out wide, and Luke Patten chimed into the line to offload to Jodie Broughton, who crashed over in the corner. But Daniel Holdsworth couldn't pot the crucial touchline conversion. Karl Pryce scored a hat-trick.

In the first of Sky TV's 'Super League Mondays' St Helens got back to winning form at Headingley with a 31-18 win over the Rhinos. Saints were led superbly in the last half hour by halves Jonny Lomax and Lance Hohaia, with Jon Wilkin adding to their threat. Wilkin's try in the 65th minute opened up a ten-point gap and demonstrated the Leeds defence was running out of gas. Leeds coach Brian McDermott suggested he was panicking as Leeds fell into eighth spot at the end of a week in which it was announced fullback Brent Webb would leave the club at the end of the season.

Round 15 - Magic Weekend

The RFL was happy to celebrate a record-breaking attendance of 63,716 for two days of Super League at a sun-scorched Etihad Stadium in Manchester, on the re-positioned Magic Weekend, although this was only marginally better than the figure for the second Magic Weekend in 2008 in Cardiff, which featured only six games, not seven.

There were some cracking games, none better than the one that brought the curtain down on the Saturday, the Hull derby.

And no try was better than the final one of that game, which saw David Hodgson tearing down the left wing to score, and win the match in the most thrilling finish of all by 32-30. Rovers coach Craig Sandercock compared it with winning the NRL Grand Final with Manly in 2008.

The game was an extremely tight and intense affair but FC looked to have clinched it with Jordan Turner's try on 66 minutes leaving the score at 30-16. However, the Robins came back with three tries in the final 12 minutes to win the match, with a few slices of luck before Hodgson's winner.

First, in the build-up to Rovers' first comeback try, Tony Martin was down injured. Then the pass for Michael Dobson's score after that was forward.

David Hodgson finished with two tries on a weekend of scoring feats. Joel Monaghan scored five tries against Widnes Vikings on the Saturday in a 68-4 win after the Wolves led 40-0 at half-time. His centre Matty Blythe scored three in an impressive performance. Warrington ran in 12 tries altogether, and they came within the space of less than 50 minutes, due to an unusual half-an-hour scoreless patch either side of half-time. Widnes were never in the game from the moment Blythe sliced through after less than three minutes.

Danny McGuire scored five tries for Leeds Rhinos against Bradford Bulls on the Sunday in a game that wasn't so one-sided. The 37-22 win was far from a five-star showing from Leeds. Bradford, after a competitive effort for most of the match, could leave feeling hard done by at the final scoreline. McGuire's display included a first-half hat-trick, which helped Leeds come back from 18-6 down midway through that opening period and go into the break level at 18-18. In the opening part of that first half, Leeds' level of ill-discipline was surprising. But the champions did not concede again after that - until allowing the Bulls a late consolation try - and added 31 points to their own tally. A controversial moment did help them on the way to turning the momentum though as the second of McGuire's tries came from an apparent forward pass from Brent Webb.

Salford celebrate Adam Sidlow's late try that wins a Magic Weekend thriller against Huddersfield

After the game, Bulls' Adrian Purtell, after playing the full 80 minutes, was taken ill on the coach home from Manchester, and was quickly placed on a drip before being rushed to hospital. Purtell then underwent surgery to unblock an artery, and returned home on the following Wednesday afternoon.

Huddersfield captain Kevin Brown spoke to the media after captaining the Giants in a 38-34 Magic Weekend defeat to Salford City Reds on the Sunday. He explained why he had decided to sign a four-year contract from 2013 with Super League new boys Widnes Vikings, in the process giving up a contract with the Giants that was due to expire at the end of the 2015 season.

Prop Adam Sidlow was the unlikely late try-scoring hero, scoring his second try in the 76th minute, as Salford condemned Huddersfield to a shock third successive league defeat in another sun-drenched scoring-fest where the lead changed hands no fewer than six times. It was Salford's first league win for over two months - since they triumphed 38-18 at Bradford on March 25th. Luke Patten, who had announced he would be retiring at the end of the season, gave a superb display that the Giants struggled to handle.

In the opening Sunday game, the Catalans, having led 24-0 after a first half of total dominance, had to shake off a spirited comeback from the Broncos before securing a 42-18 win. Tries to Antonio Kaufusi, Ben Bolger and Chad Randall, all converted by Shane Rodney had London only six points behind at 24-18 before the hour mark and looking capable of going on and winning. But Remi Casty's try in the 62nd minute gained back the momentum for the Scott Dureau-inspired Dragons.

The weekend had got off to a blistering start amid the tropical conditions as great rivals Castleford and Wakefield served up an eleven-try thriller, with Trinity finishing 32-26 winners. Cas were buoyed by the return of Rangi Chase after his three-match suspension along with skipper Danny Orr who recovered from a back injury. Young centre Jordan Thompson opened the scoring after less than two minutes when Chase bamboozled Wakefield from dummy half. But Wakefield were thrown an unexpected route back into the game in the 13th minute as a cross-field move from the Tigers came to an abrupt end when a pass from Chase was intercepted by Kiwi centre Vince Mellars on his own 20-metre line and he raced 90 metres to score.

It was nip-and-tuck right until after the final whistle in one of the most exciting and bizarre finishes. First, a glorious no-look pass on the inside from Chase set up a Cas attack and, when Orr's over-the-shoulder pass bobbed into the hands of Nathan Massey, the Tigers prop wrestled his way over the line on 77 minutes. The Tigers' elation was short-lived however, when video referee James Child adjudged Orr's pass had gone forward and Massey had been offside.

Seizing on this reprieve, Wakefield sealed the game on 79 minutes when Tim Smith's lateral run and dummy opened up the gap for the Aussie maestro to dart through a tired defence from 30 metres.

Paul Sykes missed the kick and it wasn't all over. The Tigers got the kick-off back and launched one final attack, Chase's kick to the right finding Thompson, whose inside pass went to ground as the hooter sounded. Ben Cockayne hacked on, collected, raced away, performed a risky one-two with Ali Lauitiiti and scored in the left corner. The 'try' meant the video referee was called up and he ruled there had been a push on a Cas player after Thompson's pass hit the ground. Amazingly play was brought back for the penalty and Cas had one last attack. To the relief of the Trinity contingent, Frankie Mariano managed to stifle Chase as the ball was moved left.

The final game of the weekend was the most anticipated but Wigan's dominance of St Helens continued with a 42-16 win. A stunning opening saw Shaun Wane's side lead 26-0 after just 24 minutes, but much more was to unfold, with a second-half brawl at a scrum seeing three players shown the red card by referee Ben Thaler.

While that was undoubtedly a major talking point, it could not deflect any attention from a sparkling Wigan performance, with the likes of Brett Finch, Sam Tomkins and Darrell Goulding lighting up the sun-baked Etihad Stadium. Finch and halfback partner Thomas Leuluai tormented Saints throughout, Goulding had a hand in three Warriors tries, and Tomkins grabbed a brace, the second a marvellous individual effort. Gareth Hock was having a huge match before he was joined by Chris Tuson and Shaun Magennis in being dismissed in the 53rd minute, while Lee Mossop, Michael McIlorum and Sean O'Loughlin worked themselves to a standstill.

The following Tuesday Hock was banned for two matches and Tuson for one, while Shaun Magennis copped a three-match ban for an offside punch on Tuson.

SUPER LEAGUE TABLE - *Sunday 27th May*

	P	W	D	L	F	A	D	PTS
Wigan Warriors	15	12	0	3	540	245	295	24
Warrington Wolves	15	11	1	3	505	274	231	23
Catalan Dragons	14	11	0	3	475	308	167	22
Huddersfield Giants	15	10	0	5	417	273	144	20
Hull FC	14	9	1	4	354	282	72	19
St Helens	15	8	1	6	423	289	134	17
Leeds Rhinos	14	8	0	6	385	295	90	16
Hull Kingston Rovers	15	7	1	7	418	374	44	15
Bradford Bulls	15	7	1	7	305	342	-37	15
Salford City Reds	15	5	1	9	338	426	-88	11
Wakefield T Wildcats	14	4	0	10	250	406	-156	8
Castleford Tigers	15	4	0	11	282	498	-216	8
London Broncos	15	2	0	13	310	493	-183	4
Widnes Vikings	15	2	0	13	211	708	-497	4

JUNE
Warriors on the march

Round 16

Former Albert Goldthorpe Medal winners Michael Dobson and Sam Tomkins both earned three points for their performances in round 16.

At Headingley on the Friday night, Tomkins led a Wigan master class as the Warriors hammered World Club Champions Leeds 50-8. Coach Shaun Wane had been forced to throw in youngsters Logan Tomkins, Dominic Crosby and Rhodri Lloyd because of the suspensions the club suffered after the brawl in the Magic Weekend game against St Helens, but they slotted in seamlessly, with the relatively inexperienced Welshman Gil Dudson also starting at prop.

In the lead up, Wane had said: "I want a bad reception, I want people to hate us. I like that," though on the night it was hard to not to admire his side, who were looking invincible at this stage of the season. Wigan also had a stroke of luck, when Jeff Lima dropped the ball when scoring their opening try in the third minute, and referee James Child didn't go to the video referee. To his embarrassment the big screen clearly revealed his mistake within seconds of him awarding the try. It mattered not as Wigan went on to score another eight tries in front of a stunned home crowd.

On the Sunday, Hull Kingston Rovers defeated Warrington Wolves 23-22 in a thriller at Craven Park, with Michael Dobson landing a 77th-minute field goal to snatch the points after the Robins had been behind 18-0 after 15 minutes and 22-6 at half-time.

The rainiest and coldest June since records began was getting underway, as a plethora of handling errors by the Wolves at their own end gave Rovers opportunities. Lee Briers' wayward field-goal attempt in the 80th minute sealed the win for the Robins, as the veteran stand-off stood 20 metres out and in front of the post but missed the opportunity to level it, with the ball just swaying left of the uprights.

St Helens captain Paul Wellens predicted June would be a critical month for his side and urged his teammates to build on a much-improved defensive showing at Hull as Saints drew 18-18, after Hull recovered from being 12-0 down midway through the first half. A last-gasp Tom Makinson penalty snatched the point after Saints conceded eight goal-line drop-outs but their defence repeatedly proved a brick wall.

Wakefield Wildcats won their second game in a row for the first time in 2012 when they were 24-6 home winners over London Broncos on the Sunday.

Richard Agar's side did little wrong in difficult conditions, but neither did they have to stretch themselves after gaining an early lead. Agar had plenty of willing workers in his ranks, none more so than second-rower Danny Kirmond, whose sterling efforts were rewarded with a second-half try. Kyle Amor and Paul Aiton were others to provide plenty of industry, while on-loan Paul Sykes produced some key first-half contributions and Peter Fox excelled under the high ball on the right wing. It proved to be more than enough for a Broncos side that struggled to find any potency in attack. Ali Lauitiiti's first-half try provided an 18-point cushion that was always going to prove to be enough.

On the Friday night Salford produced a major shock when they beat Catalan Dragons at home 34-30. Matty Smith's exit from the club at the end of the season had grabbed the headlines in the week, but the City Reds somehow managed to remain focussed enough to build on their Magic Weekend heroics by coming back from 20-0 down on 25 minutes, despite then having both Daniel Holdsworth and Vinnie Anderson sin-binned just before half-time, to snatch a dramatic second win on the trot in an entertaining twelve-try thriller. Winger Jodie Broughton scored a brace of tries in a superb performance, and his 70th minute effort that made it 34-26 proved decisive.

The Giants continued their recent trend of signing British talent on long-term deals when Greg Eden committed his future to the club until the end of 2015. The 21-year-old fullback had recently described been by his coach Nathan Brown as the British equivalent of Australian superstar Billy Slater.

On the Sunday the Giants fell to their third consecutive defeat, by 26-22 at lowly Widnes, who moved off the bottom of the table thanks to an amazing last-minute try to Cameron Phelps. The Vikings had to work hard for their victory, despite racing into a 16-0 lead in the first 15 minutes. The Giants fought back and took the lead for the first time with five minutes remaining. But Widnes grabbed the win with the last play of the game, as fullback Phelps pounced on Rhys Hanbury's kick under the posts.

Coach Denis Betts handed hooker Paul McShane his Vikings debut following his loan move from champions Leeds Rhinos and he took the place of skipper Jon Clarke, who was serving a one-match suspension for a dangerous tackle in the 68-4 defeat by Warrington Wolves at the Magic Weekend. Betts was also pleased for front-rower Ben Cross, as the former Leeds Rhinos and Wigan Warriors prop scored his first try in his tenth season of first-grade Rugby League.

In the Monday night game Shaun Ainscough scored a hat-trick as Bradford beat Castleford 46-32 at Odsal. In a game that looked all over after 35 minutes, when the Bulls were 34-10 up, it was not until Ainscough's final try six minutes from time that Bradford finally had the game won.

* History was made on the first Saturday of June when four Englishmen played in an NRL match, with Canterbury's James Graham facing up to Souths' trio of Burgesses - Luke, Sam and debutant George.

Round 17

The run up to round 17 was dominated by England captain Jamie Peacock's Twitter outburst on the Friday afternoon, in which he called Garry Schofield, the 1990 Golden Boot winner as the world's-best player, a fat slob and a coward. The previous Monday in his weekly column in League Express, Schofield wrote: "Jamie Peacock thinks that 35 is the new 30, but he's playing like a 40-year-old at the moment." Peacock's day went from bad to worse just hours later, as his Leeds side quickly went 30-0 down at Warrington, before staging a mini-recovery to lose 37-18. Leeds remained in ninth place, a point behind Bradford Bulls in eighth, although they had a game in hand.

Warrington were still missing Michael Monaghan and Richie Myler through injury, and Leeds went into the game without Danny McGuire, who was out with a groin problem. But the Wolves' first half was blistering, Chris Riley's 28th-minute try leaving Leeds with far too big a mountain to climb in the wretched wet and windy conditions.

Wigan's match against the Catalan Dragons in Montpellier on the Saturday was the first Rugby League game televised live in France by the Al-Jazeera Sports channel under its new name of Beln Sport. Catalans lost their unbeaten league home record as Wigan ran out comfortable winners on the scoreboard by 36-14, but it was far from easy for the Warriors. Sam Tomkins' try seven minutes from the end finally extinguished any hopes of a Catalan comeback as Michael McIlorum continued his excellent form. That week, Brett Finch confirmed he was to leave the club at the end of the current season.

June

Steve Menzies surpassed Brad Davis' record as Super League's oldest ever player. Born on December 4, 1973, Menzies beat the record set by Davis in 2004, when he played for Castleford aged 38 years, six months and three days.

Castleford Tigers chief executive Richard Wright denied he was about to depart the club, after rumours circulated in Castleford on the Sunday, following their exciting 34-30 victory over Salford City Reds. A late try by Castleford prop Craig Huby, who rose in astonishing style above the Salford defence to collect a high kick by stand-off Rangi Chase, helped the Tigers to a stunning victory in an error-strewn but nevertheless thrilling game that ended a run of six successive league defeats for the home side. The man of the match was Castleford veteran Danny Orr, who came on as an early substitute for injured hooker Adam Milner and finished with a hat-trick, in addition to converting Huby's touchdown. Michael Shenton was to re-join the Tigers in 2013 after signing a four-year contract, even though he still had a year remaining at St Helens.

Jonny Lomax produced another sparkling home display and centre Josh Jones enhanced his growing reputation with a hat-trick as St Helens swept injury-hit Bradford aside 54-0. Mick Potter's side went into the game under the on-going cloud of uncertainty about their off-field situation, with 11 players missing through injury, and having played just four days earlier against Castleford. The Bulls back-row forward Ian Sibbit - playing only his second game since injuring his shoulder in the game at Castleford in round 2 - broke his arm

Paul Sykes, on loan from Bradford, scored a try and four goals, as the Wildcats edged Hull FC 32-30 at the Rapid Solicitors Stadium after launching a staggering second-half comeback to leave Hull shell-shocked for the third week in a row.

Wakefield trailed 14-0 and then 30-10 and, amid an error-strewn first 50 minutes, looked dead and buried. But three tries in eight minutes and a total of 22 points without reply during the last half hour turned the game on its head. It was the first time since early 2010 that the Wildcats had won three successive games, following successes over Castleford and London Broncos.

London left it late but finally snatched a 28-24 victory from the jaws of defeat with the last play of a see-saw battle with fellow strugglers Widnes at the Stoop. The Broncos were staring down the barrel as the clock ticked towards 80 minutes but summoned up the energy, spirit and resolve for one final successful attack that saw them move off the bottom of the table and above their opponents, courtesy of a far superior points difference. Antonio Kaufusi popped up to win the game with a try just as time expired.

In the Monday night TV game Hull KR coach Craig Sandercock hailed Michael Dobson the form halfback in the competition after he collected 24 points through two tries and eight goals in the Robins' 44-26 win at Huddersfield.

Craig Hall, at stand-off in place of hamstring injury-victim Blake Green, rounded off the evening by shooting through a gap created by a clever ruck move between Lincoln Withers and Constantine Mika before gracefully rounding Greg Eden for the Robins' seventh try.

There was no scheduled round for 15th to 17th June which was designated an international weekend.

* Matt King, the former London Broncos Academy player who had been paralysed in a game at Halifax, was awarded an OBE in the Queen's Birthday Honours List.

Round 3

Leeds beat Wakefield 44-40 after a 14-try spree at Headingley in the game postponed to accommodate the World Club Challenge. The match was ultimately determined by a disputed penalty in the 64th minute, Leeds given the put-in to a scrum on the Wakefield '30' after Shaun Lunt had raided down the blindside on the last, and his attempted pass deemed touched by a Wildcat.

The visitors objected rather too dogmatically for referee Richard Silverwood and Kevin

Sinfield landed the two points to re-establish a two-score lead his side had last held in the ninth minute of the game. That was part of an exemplary, accomplished evening of goal kicking on both sides, although the Wildcats elected not to attempt the extras after Peter Fox's late score out wide in an effort to have a complete, final set of six – on which they failed to capitalise.

Round 18

On another extremely wet night, Catalan Dragons edged out Hull KR 13-10 at Craven Park in a game full of spilled ball and penalties, but plenty of late drama, with Scott Dureau providing the game winner in the 77th minute with a long-range field goal.

Rovers' injury riddled season came back to bite them, with centre Kris Welham out for the season, and loose forward Rhys Lovegrove sidelined for a couple of months, with a fractured fibula and medial knee ligament injuries respectively. Welham's injury in the fifth minute of the game was the more innocuous, as he fell on the wet surface and rolled his ankle with the Robins close to the Dragons' line. Lovegrove picked up his injury whilst being tackled by former Rovers hooker Ben Fisher in the 48th minute.

Rain poured down heavily throughout the match and the quality of the game suffered as the Catalans' error count in their own half almost caused their downfall. But Rovers couldn't take advantage of their pressure and position, and were eventually made to pay, as Dureau and veteran Steve Menzies made major late contributions to help the Dragons win the game, after some controversial decisions had helped the French to level the match.

The major talking point was whether Clint Greenshields' 76th-minute try to make the score 10-10 was rightly or wrongly awarded by the video referee Ian Smith. Smith ruled that fullback-turned-winger-for-the-day had sufficient control and downward pressure.

Three converted late tries, all of them from kicks, gave St Helens a flattering 32-10 victory at Salford City Stadium over a Reds side that was fully in the game for the majority of the contest. As with the match at Langtree Park in February, the Reds established a 10-0 lead which they held until Josh Jones' try just before the break dragged Saints back into the contest. The visitors then slowly ground their opponents down in the second half, and Salford's inability to deal with their outstanding kicking game cost them dearly.

Jon Wilkin played his full part in that aspect of Saints' play, while Lance Hohaia had one of his best games for the club at stand-off and Michael Shenton provided some crucial touches in the right centre. Tom Makinson's 54th minute try, after Jodie Broughton had allowed Jon Wilkin's kick to bounce, gave Saints a lead they would never lose.

In wind and sun at Headingley on the Sunday, Leeds disposed of the Castleford Tigers by 40-22, to move up to sixth, in a clash they dominated for an hour before falling off the pace late on. The Tigers were facing a mini-crisis, with Rangi Chase having been left out of their side for internal disciplinary reasons, Daryl Clark having asked and been turned down for a transfer, and suggestions the club had had a major disagreement with its major sponsor Probiz.

With a crowd and atmosphere heightened by the after-match arrival of the Olympic torch, magnificent interplay between Ryan Hall and Carl Ablett fashioned a try right on half-time that took the score to 22-6 and gave confidence-shot Cas too much of a deficit to claw back. Brent Webb's injury absence looked to have left a void but Zak Hardaker was proving a revelation in the fullback's role.

Luke Robinson was facing a spell on the sidelines after suffering a hyper-extension to an elbow during the Giants' 46-10 home win over London on the Sunday, ending a run of five consecutive defeats. The Giants' previous win came against the same opponents, when they cruised to a 50-14 Challenge Cup home quarter-final win on May 13. Danny Brough was a menace and set up three tries, kicked seven goals and nailed a late 40/20.

Cash-strapped crisis club Bradford kept their play-off hopes alive with a hard-earned 34-26 home win over Wakefield. The Bulls raced into an 18-6 lead before Trinity hit back with three tries in 13 minutes to go in at the interval with a two-point lead. But the home side responded positively after the break and even weathered the late loss of Luke Gale to the sin bin to emerge with a victory that drew them back on the heels of eighth-placed Hull KR – level on match points but with an inferior points difference – in the race for a Super League play-off spot.

Wildcats coach Richard Agar questioned his players' commitment at the end of a week when the Wildcats were given the green light for a brand new stadium that could have ensured their Super League status.

Warrington produced a solid and at times spectacular seven-try 40-18 home win against an ill-disciplined Hull FC side who had threatened an upset. Ryan Atkins finished with a try hat-trick after a powerful display. Willie Manu's sin-binning on 57 minutes for interference at the play the ball scuppered Hull FC's chances as Warrington went over for two crucial tries, to Atkins and Garreth Carvell, while he was off the field.

Aaron Heremaia made his debut for Hull after recovering from a neck injury suffered in pre-season.

The Monday night game proved to be a mis-match as Wigan won their 13th straight game in all competitions, beating Widnes at home by 52-14. The Warriors tore into a 16-0 lead within the first 13 minutes and kept sporadic Widnes comebacks at bay thereafter.

Wigan coach Shaun Wane had expressed concern that the break in the season for the England-Exiles game might disrupt Wigan's formidable momentum. He spurned the option of recalling Joe Mellor from his loan spell at Widnes, after the loss of Thomas Leuluai, who broke a leg in the Exiles match against England, instead switching captain Sean O'Loughlin to stand-off. Josh Charnley scored a hat-trick of tries and also kicked seven goals for a 26-point haul.

Shaun Briscoe came off the bench late in the first half after three months out with a groin injury sustained in Widnes's March thrashing at Catalans and was now set for another spell on the sidelines after suffering a torn pectoral muscle in the second half.

* *The RFL ended a reported £5 million deal with Elonex, who provided the LED digital advertising boards for all televised games. All Super League clubs were asked by the RFL to remove all advertising from Elonex in their matchday programmes, and LED boards were switched off during the Hull KR v Catalan Dragons clash on Friday.*

Round 19

On the last Tuesday of June Bradford Bulls went into administration, with administrator Brendan Guilfoyle saying that a sale would have to be achieved within ten working days if the club was to survive.

The following Friday night the Bulls won an astonishing 30-22 victory at Wigan. The Bulls outscored the Warriors five tries to four, with a major talking point coming in the second half when Michael McIlorum was sent off for punching Olivier Elima. The following week McIlorum took an early guilty plea and no further action was taken.

The Warriors were without fullback Sam Tomkins after he picked up a dead leg in the win over Widnes, meaning 20-year-old Jack Murphy was thrown in at the deep end for his debut. Luke Gale pulled the strings for the Bulls, and his link-up play with Jarrod Sammut and Brett Kearney was top class, while he converted all five tries in terrible conditions. Karl

Pryce scored two tries against his old club.

The Bulls were due to face London Broncos at Odsal the following Sunday, and their coach Mick Potter was hoping to carry on as normal. The morning after, Potter, all his assistants and all the backroom staff at Odsal were sacked.

St Helens halfback Jonny Lomax pulled out of England's squad for the following Wednesday's second match against the Exiles at Huddersfield, after sustaining a rib injury late in St Helens' 34-28 win over Hull KR, also on the Friday night. Late tries from Anthony Laffranchi and Tony Puletua earned Saints the spoils in a see-saw game in which they were coasting to victory after the first 29 minutes, when they led 26-0, before Rovers came back to lead 28-26 after Josh Hodgson's try just after the hour mark.

Rovers arrived at the ground just after seven o'clock after their team bus broke down en route. Coach Craig Sandercock had apparently requested a short delay to prepare his team, but that was rejected.

Wolves coach Tony Smith rested several key players for the trip to Salford on the Friday and the result was a televised 48-24 thrashing. Those absent, either through injury or choice, included Lee Briers, Brett Hodgson, Simon Grix, Ryan Atkins, Joel and Michael Monaghan, Ben Westwood and Garreth Carvell. David Solomona made his return from pre-season injury but then picked up another leg knock in the 41st minute. At one stage Salford led 44-6 as halfbacks Matty Smith and Daniel Holdsworth combined superbly. Vinnie Anderson played great against his former club, scoring twice - a feat also achieved by England new boy Jodie Broughton, fellow winger Danny Williams and impressive Luke Patten.

Wakefield got away from the rain which had caused much flooding in many parts of England with a trip to Perpignan but an early kick-off time saw temperatures hitting over 30 degrees in the shade as the Wildcats lost 34-10. In total contrast to the previous Friday at Hull KR, the weather suited the home side and they made Wakefield pay, scoring two late tries to give a score that did not reflect the effort Wakefield put into the game.

On the same afternoon Danny McGuire scored four tries as Leeds inflicted a ten-try 58-12 rout on the Broncos at the Stoop. Broncos coach Rob Powell saw fit to apologise to fans in his post-match interview.

In the only Sunday game, Hull FC edged out Huddersfield at the KC Stadium by 28-24 as they got the better of a late flurry of four tries in the last 13 minutes, of which they grabbed three. Eorl Crabtree's 75th minute try for the Giants seemed to have won the game, but a short kick-off by Danny Tickle bemused Luke George and went out of play. Moments later Kirk Yeaman grabbed the game-winning try as Hull spread the ball wide left.

Liam Watts, Albert Goldthorpe Super League Rookie of the Year in 2010, made his debut off the bench after joining Hull FC on a three-and-a-half year deal from Hull Kingston Rovers.

In the Monday TV game, Widnes climbed back off the bottom of the table with a comprehensive win against the struggling Castleford Tigers. Eamon O'Carroll, on his debut after his midweek signing from Hull FC, scored a try as Widnes collected their fourth league win of the season.

Castleford were missing stand-off Rangi Chase, still absent for internal disciplinary reasons. And with skipper Danny Orr on the bench because of a knee problem sustained in the defeat at Leeds, Ryan McGoldrick and Brett Ferres filled the starting halfback roles. Richard Owen was also missing, serving a one-match ban for punching in the Leeds game.

At the end of June Jamie Peacock shocked the Rugby League world by announcing his international retirement.

SUPER LEAGUE TABLE - *Monday 2nd July*

	P	W	D	L	F	A	D	PTS
Wigan Warriors	19	15	0	4	702	309	393	30
Warrington Wolves	19	13	1	5	628	381	247	27
Catalan Dragons	18	13	0	5	566	398	168	26
St Helens	19	11	2	6	561	345	216	24
Huddersfield Giants	19	11	0	8	535	381	154	22
Leeds Rhinos	19	11	0	8	553	456	97	22
Hull FC	18	10	2	6	448	396	52	22
Bradford Bulls	19	10	1	8	415	476	-61	21
Hull Kingston Rovers	19	9	1	9	523	469	54	19
Salford City Reds	19	7	1	11	460	546	-86	15
Wakefield T Wildcats	19	6	0	13	382	554	-172	12
Castleford Tigers	19	5	0	14	380	654	-274	10
Widnes Vikings	19	4	0	15	313	822	-509	8
London Broncos	19	3	0	16	366	645	-279	6

JULY
Farewell to Stobart

Round 20

Mick Potter admitted he was close to tears after being given an emotional guard of honour following the Sunday 44-12 win over London Broncos at Odsal. After being made redundant the previous Monday, Potter was persuaded by Bradford's players two days later to return on a voluntary basis. The former St Helens and Catalans coach said: "It was touching. I'm not a guy that breaks out in tears very quickly, but I reckon I came close at one stage."

The threat of the Bulls' imminent liquidation hung heavy over Odsal. It was hoped the future ownership of the club would be determined that week, according to the club's administrator Brendan Guilfoyle, who was optimistic he would have the funds to pay the staff when their salaries were due on

the following Saturday. He also accepted criticism for pulling out of a meeting with the players the previous week, but said that he had other priorities. Joint captain Matt Diskin, sidelined with a shoulder injury, said that communication between the squad and the administrator had not improved since the controversial cancelled meeting between the two parties. Brett Kearney scored four tries in the win over London.

There was also change at Castleford where former Huddersfield coach and former Wakefield Trinity Wildcats and York City Knights chief executive Steve Ferres was appointed chief executive as the replacement for Richard Wright, who resigned the previous week after 15 years in the post. One of Ferres's first tasks was to deal with the disciplinary issue surrounding Rangi Chase and with requests by Daryl Clark and Ryan McGoldrick to leave the club.

On the Sunday the Tigers - lacking eight regulars - produced a stunning 52-6 home victory over Huddersfield. Former Leigh halfback Jamie Ellis, snapped up from Hull FC by coach Ian Millward, scored 24 points with a try and 10 goals from 11 attempts on debut. Ellis originally signed for two years from the start of the 2013 season, but then was released by Hull immediately. Fullback Richard Owen was the gamestar though, creating each of the Tigers' opening tries and claiming the third for himself. Former Leeds, Roosters and Hull utility player Jordan Tansey joined the Tigers from York City Knights for 2013.

Ryan McGoldrick had left the previous Thursday for Hull FC, who confirmed that Sam Moa and Danny Tickle were out for the rest of the season with bicep injuries that required urgent surgery. McGoldrick, 31, made his debut at fullback for Hull in the 21-6 televised defeat to Leeds at Headingley on a rainy Friday night. It was the Rhinos' fourth consecutive Super League win, a run which had coincided with the switch of Zak

Hardaker to fullback to cover the injury absence of Brent Webb, who was in his last season at Headingley. Leeds skipper Kevin Sinfield was the key to Leeds' ground-out win and his touchline conversion of Ryan Hall's try at the start of the second half, to make it 20-0, established a winning lead.

Wigan announced the previous Friday that they had signed scrum-half Matty Smith from Salford City Reds. Smith, 24, had expected to join Wigan for three seasons from 2013, but the Reds were happy to accept an undisclosed transfer fee for a player whose contract was due to expire at the end of the season. Smith had made his England debut the previous Wednesday against the Exiles, and made his Wigan debut, wearing squad number 38, off the bench in a 52-10 win at Wakefield on the Sunday.

The Wildcats debuted Lee Smith, who was on a month's loan from Leeds, with centre Vince Mellars needing an operation on a detached retina. Wigan also had Iain Thornley making his debut, picked on the wing in place of Josh Charnley, injured playing for England against the Exiles in midweek, with Logan Tomkins at hooker for Michael McIlorum, also injured. Brett Finch orchestrated the Wigan performance and time and again directed the Wigan attack at an overwhelmed, right-side Wakefield defence, with Sam Tomkins and George Carmont both collecting hat-tricks. A crowd of over nine thousand watched the game.

Marc Sneyd, 21, was the beneficiary of Matty Smith's earlier-than-anticipated move to Wigan and he stepped up to the mark for the Reds' clash with Hull Kingston Rovers at Craven Park on the Sunday, partnering Daniel Holdsworth at halfback, and helping his team to a shock 24-22 victory that put them only two points behind the Robins in tenth place.

With Bradford likely to suffer a points deduction, it meant the Reds were now effectively just outside the top eight. Rovers captain Ben Galea missed the game with a hamstring injury after the club confirmed he would leave Craven Park when his current contract expired at the end of the season, having failed to reach agreement on a new deal.

Widnes Vikings were left ruing a controversial disallowed conversion in their 24-23 home defeat to St Helens on the same day. Most people thought halfback Rhys Hanbury's 53rd minute kick went through the posts, but referee Robert Hicks was unable to give the goal because his touch-judges deemed it went wide, and, due to RFL directives, he was unable to overrule them. The decision proved decisive in the end, as Josh Jones' last-minute try and Lee Gaskell's touchline conversion condemned Denis Betts' improving side to a one-point defeat.

In the Monday-night TV game there was a cracking clash between second and fourth-placed Warrington and Catalans at Halliwell Jones Stadium, which the Wolves edged 15-6, with goal-line and scrambling defence the key to the Wolves win. Michael Monaghan had missed most of the season with knee problems but he came off the bench and his 67th minute field goal settled home nerves. Dragons prop David Ferriol received a two-match ban for a high tackle on Michael Monaghan, and his appeal was turned down.

Challenge Cup Semi-finals

Leeds Rhinos and Warrington Wolves won the right to face each other at Wembley in a repeat of the 2010 Challenge Cup Final.

On the Saturday Leeds caused a huge shock when they defeated Wigan 39-28 at the Galpharm Stadium, while Warrington beat Huddersfield Giants 33-6 at the Salford City Stadium on the Sunday.

Quoted as 3/1 outsiders by the bookmakers before the game and written off by most, including sections of their own support, the Rhinos again showed they were still a team for the big stage. Skipper Kevin Sinfield was imperious at stand-off, producing a masterful kicking game that was central to them establishing an unlikely but vital early 16-0 lead. Danny McGuire and Rob Burrow were outstanding, with Leeds coach Brian McDermott

Rob Burrow makes a break through the Wigan defence

praising McGuire's attacking contribution despite having to deal with a huge amount of traffic in defence as Wigan targeted the experienced halfback. Burrow was typically electric at hooker, providing a number of clean breaks and danger each time he took on the defensive line. Zak Hardaker took two tries well from fullback and produced one brilliant second-half cover tackle on Jack Hughes, while both wingers Ryan Hall and Ben Jones-Bishop finished with smart doubles.

Wigan never fully recovered from a shocking opening 11 minutes that left them 16-0 down after a series of uncharacteristic mistakes, most notably from Sam Tomkins, who Leeds admitted they had targeted to try and nullify his considerable attacking threat. Gareth Hock was their most effective forward with the ball and scored a tremendous first-half try, while subs Ben Flower, Liam Farrell and Hughes all ran strongly and Tomkins tried his best to atone for his early mistakes. But it was not enough, and dreams of back-to-back Wembley triumphs were over.

After the game Leeds' young star Stevie Ward pulled out of the England Academy tour to Australia, due to depart the next Thursday, in order to try to claim a place in the Rhinos' Challenge Cup Final squad.

Warrington coach Tony Smith paid tribute to his pack as his side booked a third trip to Wembley in four seasons with a tough win over Huddersfield. The Wolves ran in five tries as they finished 33-6 winners.

The Giants started the game well, with Danny Brough and Leroy Cudjoe controlling matters in attack and defence, and Scott Moore's converted try gave them an early lead.

Lee Briers tries to escape from Lee Gilmour as Dale Ferguson closes in

But a controversial decision allowed the Wolves back into the game and from that moment they never looked back. The decision to award Garreth Carvell the benefit-of-the-doubt try hurt the Giants and they seemed affected as Warrington ran in two more tries to lead 18-6 at the break. After the turnaround Huddersfield threw everything at Warrington but their defence didn't crack and a converted try from Brett Hodgson along with a field goal and penalty and a late Stefan Ratchford try made sure of the Wolves' Wembley return.

After the game Giants coach Nathan Brown, due to join St Helens from the end of the season, insisted he had no intention of stepping down before then. In the past couple of months the Giants had dropped from first on the Super League ladder to seventh, leaving many fans wondering if he would see the job through. Brown suggested there had been a clear-the-air meeting with the Huddersfield players and admitted he was forced into changing the way his side played the game. The following day he was sacked and assistant Paul Anderson, due to succeed him in November, took over as head coach.

Round 2

In a game postponed from an icy French February, the Dragons bounced back from their Monday-night defeat at Warrington with a 44-14 win over Hull FC. Scott Dureau registered 20 points with six goals and two tries, but was still overshadowed by the highly impressive Clint Greenshields. Although Hull were never close enough to challenge, it wasn't until Greenshields' try in the 68th minute that victory was assured.

Neither Hull FC nor Castleford Tigers were prepared to comment on reports that Hull were about to make a move to sign current Man of Steel and Albert Goldthorpe Medal holder Rangi Chase. Chase, who came back into the Castleford fold that week after being suspended on full pay on 25 June in relation to his alleged behaviour in the lead-up to the Tigers' game against Leeds, had a contract with three years unexpired. The Tigers were thought to have asked for a transfer fee of £350,000. Chase had issued a public apology for his behaviour.

Round 21

Another coach lost his job before round 21 when former coach Tony Rea took charge of bottom-of-the-table London Broncos on an interim basis after the dismissal of Rob Powell.

After seeing his new side thumped 44-6 by Wigan on the Saturday, Rea was quick to rule himself out of contention for a permanent role. Sam Tomkins delivered a virtuoso display, scoring four tries and 28 points on his own. The Broncos never looked likely to recover from conceding two tries in the opening six minutes but Sam Tomkins' try on the stroke of half-time and the one he laid on for Iain Thornley at the start of the second half made the result academic.

Warrington stayed within three points of leaders Wigan with a 40-26 win at Castleford in hot conditions after the Rangi Chase-inspired Tigers blasted back from 34-0 down early in the second period to within eight points. Stefan Ratchford's late try put paid to Castleford's revival.

The Tigers had confirmed the previous week that Brett Ferres was to join Huddersfield Giants with immediate effect.

Despite a change of coach things got no better for Huddersfield as they lost to Wakefield at home by 35-14. A sparkling second half from Wakefield ensured there would be no fairytale start to Paul Anderson's reign. Trinity ran in five tries and 29-unanswered points in even time to come from behind and emphatically end a run of four straight defeats. Quick-fire tries from Lee Smith - who had signed a permanent contract until the end of 2013 - and Richie Mathers, shortly after Keith Mason dropped the ball trying to touch down at the other end, seemed to prompt home heads to drop.

The beleaguered Giants had now suffered eight defeats in their last nine league matches and plummeted from the Super League summit to a position where their place in the top eight was now in jeopardy.

The Wildcats were missing hooker Paul Aiton who had been ruled out for six to eight weeks with a broken jaw sustained in a mugging while on holiday in Spain. The PNG captain was assaulted with a bat or an iron bar.

Rhys Hanbury produced 30 minutes of magic as Widnes chalked up their first Super League away win since June 2005 - by 46-8 at Salford on the Friday night. Hanbury was virtually untouchable for a half hour in which the Vikings scored 40 unanswered points and took the game completely away from the Reds. He scored two stunning solo tries, had a hand in two others, and eventually finished with a personal points haul of 22 points. Cameron Phelps and Patrick Ah Van also bagged try doubles

In a first, the Friday night TV game was broadcast from France as St Helens moved back into third after a 20-15 win in Perpignan.

Behind 15-10 at the break, Saints produced a backs-to-the-wall effort that saw their tryline remain intact for the second half, despite being hammered in the penalty count and having Tony Puletua sent off for a shoulder charge to Gregory Mounis's head. St Helens - for whom Lance Hohaia excelled - rode their luck too. They had to withstand the Dragons getting over their line three times in the last fifteen minutes only for the home side to drop the ball or the video referee to rule in the Saints' favour.

Most controversial was the incident five minutes from time as Scott Dureau's high kick to the left corner hung in the air. Tommy Makinson jumped for the ball early, Daryl Millard had the run on him and went to out-jump Makinson to claim the ball. As Millard went to raise his hands above his head, his left arm brushed against Makinson as the young Saints winger misjudged the flight. The ball bounced into the in-goal area and Damien Cardace touched the ball down. Referee Ben Thaler handed the decision on to video referee Ian Smith, who ruled that Millard had made enough contact with Makinson to put the Saints winger off and disallowed the try. The home crowd went berserk.

On the same Friday night the Bulls took thousands of supporters to Headingley to watch their 34-16 defeat, following the Rhinos' gesture of donating the money for tickets sold through the Odsal ticket office for the game. The offer was thought to have raised about $60,000 for the Bulls.

There was almost a packed house to see a rip-roaring game. Three of the Rhinos' six tries, including the momentum changer by Shaun Lunt early in the second half, came directly from the visitors spilling the ball, although they were hampered by the loss of in-form fullback Brett Kearney when he failed to reappear after the break having suffered concussion. At 18-6 going into the final quarter, Jamie Peacock held out Manase Manuokafoa and Leeds immediately went up the other end for Zak Hardaker to cross in a defining 12-point turnaround.

In the Monday-night game at Craven Park, Hull FC's second derby success of the season, and their second victory in eight games, lifted them above Huddersfield into sixth place. The 32-18 defeat also left the Robins struggling to make the top eight after a fourth consecutive defeat, at least before the Bulls' points deduction the following week left them two points clear in the last play-off spot.

Hull gave debuts to on-loan St Helens winger Jamie Foster and speedster Tom Lineham. Foster made a potentially disastrous start to his Hull career when he put the ball into touch on the full from the game's kick-off but he soon put that behind him by tackling Rovers winger David Hodgson into touch to save a try and went on to kick immaculately, finishing with six goals from six attempts. Danny Houghton returned from a four-match injury absence to torment the Robins from dummy-half.

Hull FC owner Adam Pearson had vowed his club would spend money to win success. He was thought to have agreed a transfer deal to take Rangi Chase from Castleford to the KC Stadium for 2013.

Round 22

Wigan made sure it was not a happy return for former coach Ian Millward who was facing up against his old team for the first time in a competitive match since his sacking in 2006 – but, despite a 40-16 home win, the league leaders did not have it all their own way against the Tigers. Wigan raced into a 16-0 lead inside the first 11 minutes, through two tries from Epalahame Lauaki and one from Iain Thornley, and it looked like they would hit 50 by half-time, but Castleford eventually got a foothold in the game and restricted them to only one more score before the break and crossed for a try of their own. Sam Tomkins was quiet for the majority of the game but when he got involved he was in superb form, scoring two tries and having a hand in a few others.

Warriors supporters had to do a name check on Josh Charnley when the winger ran onto the field shorn of all his hair. Charnley had an ambassadorial role for the charity Joining Jack, run by former Warrior Andy Johnson, who was searching for a cure for his son Jack's Duchenne Muscular Dystrophy. Charnley agreed to lose his curly locks, allowing Sam Tomkins to shave them off, if the charity could surpass 20,000 Twitter followers. He was forced to accept his fate when they did so after help from Tour de France winner and Warriors season ticket holder Bradley Wiggins.

On the Saturday, Catalan Dragons - without ten first-team players - overcame a stubborn and much-improved London Broncos outfit to maintain their top-four push with a 19-12 home win. The game was memorable for around 500 Catalan supporters getting up and leaving their seats in protest at the refereeing after a video decision went against the home side in the 19th minute when Remi Casty went over. Referee Tim Roby asked video referee Peter Brooke to check the grounding but he found an issue with an earlier obstruction.

Scott Dureau came up with a superb field goal from the narrowest of angles to seal the game that was in the balance until he put two scores between the sides on 71 minutes.

On the Sunday, the Wolves were in entertaining form as they accounted for Bradford 50-22 at home. Stefan Ratchford staked his claim for a Wembley shirt by ruthlessly grabbing four tries from fullback in Brett Hodgson's absence. Ratchford scored twice in each half during a nine-try romp, while Richie Myler also shone. Warrington's four-try, nine-minute burst inside the opening quarter left Bradford playing for pride, which they restored with four tries of their own, two from Danny Addy.

Hull KR put the previous Monday's derby disappointment behind them to get back to winning ways and hold off the resurgent Vikings at Stobart Stadium and gain a 32-26 win. Young fullback Louis Sheriff sealed the game for Rovers with a try with three minutes to go. Chris Heil and George Griffin made their Robins debuts.

Hull FC consolidated their sixth-placed position with a hard-fought, 34-26 home win against Salford as they held off a valiant second-half comeback and coped with the sin-binning of Mark O'Meley in the 66th minute. Much of Hull's good work was done in the first half as they ran in four of their five tries before the break to establish a 24-12 lead, with Tom Briscoe, starting at fullback, impressing as he laid on the opening score for the Tom Lineham, who grabbed two tries on his first Super League start. It was a two-point ball game until two minutes to go when Ryan McGoldrick showed great skill and deception to first dummy, and then swiftly pass the ball short to the on-running Jordan Turner for the game-winning try.

In a late Sunday-evening televised game James Roby and Lance Hohaia pulled the midfield strings as St Helens moved back into third place in Super League and continued Huddersfield's miserable recent run with a 46-12 home win. Saints established a 28-6 lead after less than half an hour though the Giants kept their line intact for 33 minutes in the middle of the game. Most of their best moments came courtesy of the boot of Danny Brough, who also produced one eye-catching second-half break.

In the Monday-night TV game, the Wildcats turned the tables on Leeds after two defeats at Headingley, a fine team performance producing a convincing 38-18 home win, despite a hat-trick from Ryan Hall in defeat. Tim Smith, who had signed a new one-year contract at Wakefield, and Paul Sykes had top games in the halves behind a ferocious pack performance. Leeds fullback Brent Webb, in his comeback game from injury, and Wakefield prop Oliver Wilkes were both banned for late high tackles, Webb getting two games and Wilkes one.

On the last day of July the Rugby Football League wrote to the consortium which had tabled an amended offer to purchase the club from the administrator of Bradford Bulls informing them that the conditional nature of their offer remained unacceptable.

SUPER LEAGUE TABLE - *Monday 30th July*

	P	W	D	L	F	A	D	PTS
Wigan Warriors	22	18	0	4	838	341	497	36
Warrington Wolves	22	16	1	5	733	435	298	33
St Helens	22	14	2	6	651	395	256	30
Catalan Dragons	22	15	0	7	650	459	191	30
Leeds Rhinos	22	13	0	9	626	516	110	26
Hull FC	22	12	2	8	534	505	29	26
Huddersfield Giants	22	11	0	11	567	514	53	22
Hull KR	22	10	1	11	595	551	44	21
Bradford Bulls *	22	11	1	10	497	572	-75	17
Salford City Reds	22	8	1	13	518	648	-130	17
Wakefield T Wildcats	22	8	0	14	465	638	-173	16
Castleford Tigers	22	6	0	16	474	740	-266	12
Widnes Vikings	22	5	0	17	408	886	-478	10
London Broncos	22	3	0	19	396	752	-356	6

* 6 points deducted for entering administration

* The Rugby Football League began the search for a new sponsor for Super League after calling time on the deal with the Stobart Group. The RFL had signed a three-year deal with Stobart in January, which involved no cash input although Super League clubs and players were advertised on 100 of Stobart's green trucks, but the clubs decided to exercise an opt-out clause after 12 months.

AUGUST
Wildcats wake up

Round 23

Bradford Bulls' future as a club became a little clearer after Super League (Europe) Limited, the company that ran the Super League competition, made a six-figure offer to Brendan Guilfoyle, the administrator who had been trying to sell the club since it went into administration on 27 June.

On the first Sunday of August, Mick Potter again deflected all credit towards his playing staff after the beleaguered Bulls moved back into the play-off reckoning with a 38-26 home win over Widnes. Bradford, despite recent back-to-back defeats against Leeds and Warrington and a potentially crippling six-point deduction, were again within striking distance of a top-eight place after a hard-fought victory in a rain-lashed encounter at Odsal.

The cash-strapped Bulls had to overcome the shock of conceding two tries in the opening ten minutes and found themselves 16-4 down midway through the first half before rallying bravely to claim the win which moved them to within two points of eighth-placed Hull KR. The Bulls, without England Academy tour captain John Bateman and with fullback Brett Kearney outstanding, weren't in the clear until winger Shaun Ainscough's second try four minutes from the end.

Hull KR fans were treated to another thriller at Craven Park on the same day, once again seeing their side edged in the closing stages as Leeds snatched a 25-24 victory with an impressive second-half performance encapsulated in a seven-minute spell, during which they turned the tide of the game with three tries to help them on their way to an important win for their top-four hopes.

Going in at half-time 18-6 down Leeds looked shaky, particularly in defence, as they allowed Michael Dobson to control the game. Dobson was less effective in the second half as the Rhinos gained the majority of possession and turned the screw with that special seven minutes of play, with the home side not even touching the ball. Rovers did manage to hit back and take the lead but it then became the Kevin Sinfield show as the Rhinos captain took the game by the scruff of the neck and his kicking game pushed Leeds over the line, with first a penalty goal to level, and then a late field goal to win the game.

That week Hull KR captain and veteran second-row forward Ben Galea announced he was probably set for retirement at the end of the season, having received no offers to continue playing since it was announced Hull KR would not renew his contract into 2013.

Wakefield Trinity Wildcats sat just three points adrift of eighth-placed Hull KR after a convincing Tim Smith-orchestrated 40-12 victory in the local derby at Castleford. Wakefield coach Richard Agar was delighted to see fullback Richard Mathers silence his Castleford critics and cross the line for two tries against his parent club at the Probiz Coliseum. Mathers made a significant contribution to what was a miserable afternoon for Tigers coach Ian Millward, the man who deemed him surplus to requirements ahead of the 2012 season.

Mathers was jeered by sections of the Tigers support every time he touched the ball in the first half, and in the second half a Castleford shirt was thrown in his direction when he played the ball near the main stand touchline. But the 29-year-old had the last laugh, and made no secret of his delight at completing a brace of tries in the dying minutes against the club that still held his registration.

Salford City Reds' play-off hopes were fading as they were leapfrogged by Wakefield after losing 40-28 at London on the Saturday. It was an amazing comeback by the Broncos as they overturned a 28-6 half-time deficit, scoring 34-unanswered points, with Craig Gower and Julien Rinaldi the architects in chief. Northampton-product Will Lovell's short-range try with five minutes left sealed the victory.

At the top of the table, Wigan looked unstoppable after their 48-10 home nine-try demolition of Hull FC on the Friday night. The game was billed as 'The Big One 4' by the Wigan club, and they were in the mood to inflict pain and misery on Hull. They led 24-4 at the break, thanks to a brace of tries each from Josh Charnley and Sam Tomkins, while Gareth Hock also crossed. The margin could have been greater if Charnley had brought his kicking boots, as the winger kicked only two from five conversions. Charnley completed his try hat-trick after the break, while there were further scores from Liam Farrell, Michael McIlorum and debutant Sam Powell. Matty Smith was in superb form for the Warriors with his accurate kicking game and organisational skills.

There was a shock on the Sunday at the newly named John Smith's Stadium as hosts Huddersfield Giants gave Paul Anderson his first win in three attempts as head coach, stunning Catalan Dragons 36-18. The Giants led the Super League table after round 10, but had collapsed over the last three months and had only one victory from their last 10 league games before the visit of the Dragons. But they were back to their gritty best against the Frenchmen, with impressive performances from Eorl Crabtree, Michael Lawrence and Jason Chan laying the foundations upon which Danny Brough, Scott Grix and Luke Robinson built the hosts' best attacking display since June. Michael Lawrence was an unsung hero for the Giants, producing an all-action and tireless display.

On the Monday night, Warrington just about made sure of a top-two finish with a 22-12 win at third-placed St Helens. Lee Briers ran the show for Warrington, and his kicks throughout the game gave the Wolves the edge.

* That week it was announced that as many as 43 people working in professional clubs and local authorities in the development of Rugby League in the community were likely to lose their jobs because of a cut in Sport England funding.

Round 24

Warrington Wolves moved to within one point of Wigan as they completely outplayed the Super League leaders in very warm conditions at the Halliwell Jones Stadium on the Saturday. Warrington came strongly at Wigan from the start of the game, and after seven minutes they had scored two converted tries from Ben Westwood and Ben Harrison, both of them converted by Brett Hodgson, and they went onto win 30-10.

Wigan looked to have stemmed the tide of Warrington attacks when Gareth Hock scored a relatively soft try when tapping a penalty and brushing off Westwood after 31 minutes, but a try from Joel Monaghan saw the Wolves take a 10-point lead into the interval. Wigan's opening 40 minutes were uncharacteristic, with plenty of unforced errors, and at times they struggled to get out of their own half. But Warrington looked hungrier and they took their chances well. Further tries in the second half from Stefan Ratchford and Richie Myler sealed a comprehensive victory. Trent Waterhouse ran his blood to water for the Warrington cause.

Third-placed St Helens fell back to the chasing pack after they were stunned at in-form Wakefield, Paul Sykes' dramatic late field goal sealing a thrilling 33-32 win. It was a fourth victory in a row for Richard Agar's side, and with Hull KR next up, a top-eight finish had suddenly becoming a serious prospect for the Wildcats. Sykes' one-point effort sealed an excellent performance from the former Bradford man, among many for the home side. His halfback partner Tim Smith was outstanding during a first half in which Trinity led 22-8 at one point, while skipper Danny Kirmond helped himself to two tries in a typically committed display.

St Helens had scored one of the quickest tries in Super League history. Just 27 seconds were on the clock when Tony Puletua touched down. And going into the later stages Saints levelled the scores when Francis Meli completed his hat-trick, brushing away from the otherwise excellent Kirmond for Makinson to convert. Sykes and Smith both missed field goal attempts, before a major turning point. Saints were trying to set up for their own field-goal attempt when Lee Gaskell offloaded in a tackle on halfway and debutant Danny Cowling – who produced three big tackles in the final quarter – swooped on the loose ball. Moments later Sykes was slotting his winning one-pointer to send the home support into raptures.

Bradford were one point ahead of the Wildcats, level on points with eighth-placed Hull KR after they beat the injury-hit Robins 32-26 in the televised Friday game. Jamie Langley claimed two vital tries as just reward for an outstanding 40-plus tackling effort which typified the Bulls' ever-eager defence. Elliott Whitehead's 71st minute try and Luke Gale's two late goals sealed it for the battling Bulls, with the club's future still not settled.

Bulls prop Tom Burgess that week announced he was to join brothers Sam, Luke and twin brother George at South Sydney Rabbitohs from next season.

Salford's top-eight chances were almost gone after they sank to a dour 30-20 home defeat by Huddersfield. Huddersfield's Scott Grix prompted and probed throughout the 80 minutes as Michael Lawrence's late try, and Grix's conversion, left Salford with an eight-point deficit with only two minutes remaining, and Grix kicked a penalty just before the hooter sounded.

London Broncos continued their revival under Tony Rea with a 42-20 win at Castleford. Luke Dorn raced over for four tries as the Broncos registered a first away victory in the league since March 2011. Dorn's fourth touchdown, seven minutes into the second period, restored a 20-point advantage after Castleford's Josh Griffin had notched his second try

Widnes Vikings went bottom of the table after a 68-24 Friday-night defeat at Headingley. Danny McGuire was poised to become the greatest tryscorer of the Super League era, needing one to overtake former team-mate Keith Senior. And, with a wonderful, weaving, long-distance run in the 12th minute it looked like he had got it, only for Rhys Hanbury to track back and ground him a few metres short. But, with barely 15 minutes remaining and the record still as elusive as his support play, McGuire was helped off the field with a knee injury that immediately cast doubt on his Wembley participation in a fortnight's time.

Widnes' free spirit at the start of the second half brought them back to 40-24 and forced a second drop-out in quick succession. Kevin Sinfield's precision and quick thinking saw him make touch from it, and the Vikings saw little ball after that.

Catalans' top-four push was faltering as they sank to a 30-10 defeat at Hull FC, the Airlie Birds simultaneously securing a play-off spot and keeping their top-four hopes alive. With Willie Manu outstanding, even though there was half hour left, Tom Briscoe's long-range score on 50 minutes gave the Black and Whites a 16-point lead that the Dragons never looked like bridging.

* Former St Helens star and current Rochdale Hornets coach John Stankevitch threatened to take his case to the European Court of Human Rights when he was banned from any involvement on Rugby League after refusing to pay a fine for abusing a match official following a Northern Rail Cup tie with Keighley Cougars earlier in the year. He had always disputed the allegation.

Round 25

Scott Dureau earned two Albert Goldthorpe points for his performance for the Catalan Dragons as they defeated Leeds Rhinos 38-34 in Perpignan, meaning he couldn't be caught in the race for the 2012 Medal. After 25 rounds he was eight points ahead of his nearest challenger, Hull KR's Michael Dobson, and ten ahead of Wigan's Brett Finch and Sam Tomkins.

In Perpignan on the Saturday the Dragons registered their first win in three games. On two occasions they allowed Leeds to come back into the game despite trailing by three and four-score margins. Remi Casty produced an all-action performance to outshine Dureau. Casty's two tries were the tip of the iceberg as the Catalan captain came up with some top defence and tough, hard running in attack. Daryl Millard's try and Dureau's goal five minutes from the end gave the hosts a ten-point lead and the Challenge Cup Finalists - missing Rob Burrow and Danny McGuire, with youngster Stevie Ward excelling - just too much to do.

The result meant the Dragons jumped above Leeds into the top four, level with St Helens.

St Helens put the disappointment of their last-minute reverse at Wakefield five days earlier firmly to bed, with a resounding eight-try 44-12 victory over a gutsy, but one-dimensional Castleford side, whose season was petering out. With a brace of tries, one an absolute stunner, Saints speedster Tommy Makinson was the standout performer alongside captain Paul Wellens. Chris Flannery's 38th-minute touchdown poured cold water on any Tigers fightback before a huge cloudburst hit the ground on 55 minutes, in what was the wettest summer on record.

Bulls star John Bateman left the field with an injured shoulder during the Bulls' 34-12 defeat of Huddersfield Giants at the John Smith's Stadium on the Sunday as Bradford made up their six-point deduction to climb back into the top eight. The Bulls responded to an early deficit to run in half-a-dozen tries en route to their sixth win in eight games as Luke Gale put in a display full of vision and precise kicking. Brett Kearney's try on the hour helped extend the Bulls lead to 18 points, less than two minutes after Jermaine McGillvary had one wiped out at the other end, and it was going to be the Bulls day.

Hull KR were the team to drop out of the eight when they fell to a 31-30 defeat to Wakefield - the fifth time Rovers had lost by three or fewer points at Craven Park in 2012, and they had drawn 30-all with St Helens in round 3.

Stand-off Paul Sykes was the match winner again for the Wildcats as he provided his second game-winning field goal in as many matches, to keep the Wildcats in the play-off mix and push the Robins down to tenth in the table. Trinity's fifth win in a row moved them up to ninth, a point off Bradford above them, after a win that was inspired by their half-back combination of Tim Smith and Sykes, who created five of six Wildcats' tries – four of them with the boot.

In the Saturday TV game, Widnes Vikings ran in eight tries, and there could of been many more, as they put Hull FC to the sword at the Stobart Stadium by 42-16. Peter Gentle's Hull side were lacklustre in every department, Widnes were better for most of the game, and totally deserved their victory, which was only their sixth of the season.

Willie Isa and Shaun Briscoe, on his return to the line-up after a long injury absence, were the heroes, popping up in the right places at the right time to claim two crucial tries each for the Vikings. Danny Craven's try on 43 minutes put Widnes 14 points ahead and allowed the Vikings to build on their late scores in the first half.

Luke Dorn grabbed four tries for the second time in less than a week as the Broncos thrashed Challenge Cup finalists Warrington by 62-18 at the Stoop on the Friday, becoming the first player to score four tries in successive Super League games. Dorn, who first joined the London club in 2005 before having spells at Salford and Castleford in 2007 and 2008, had also become the first player to score 100 tries for the London club since its birth as Fulham in 1980.

For the men from the capital it was a third straight win, easing them to 12th in Super League and continuing their revival under interim coach Tony Rea. A week before the Challenge Cup final Warrington coach Tony Smith elected to ring the changes ahead of the clash with as many as eight first-team regulars missing.

In a game switched to Monday night to accommodate the soccer club, Wigan Warriors moved three points clear of the Wolves with a convincing 38-6 home win over Salford. Pat Richards marked his return from injury with an 18-point haul as Wigan recovered from the defeat at Warrington and ran in seven tries, with Richards helping himself to two of them, as well as five goals.

The winger needed just 13 minutes to open his account on his first game back since suffering a serious knee injury in the win over Hull FC in round 12 on 22 April. He added a second eight minutes later, in between setting up Sam Tomkins, as the Warriors led 14-0 at the break in an otherwise uninspiring 40 minutes. Further tries from Darrell Goulding, Jack Hughes, Harrison Hansen and Sean O'Loughlin saw the Warriors cruise to victory.

Ben Davies and Cameron Phelps halt Tom Briscoe as Widnes record an impressive win against Hull FC

SUPER LEAGUE TABLE - *Monday 20th August*

	P	W	D	L	F	A	D	PTS
Wigan Warriors	25	20	0	5	934	387	547	40
Warrington Wolves	25	18	1	6	803	519	284	37
St Helens	25	15	2	8	739	462	277	32
Catalan Dragons	25	16	0	9	716	559	157	32
Leeds Rhinos	25	15	0	10	753	602	151	30
Hull FC	25	13	2	10	590	605	-15	28
Huddersfield Giants	25	13	0	12	645	586	59	26
Bradford Bulls *	25	14	1	10	601	636	-35	23
Wakefield T Wildcats	25	11	0	14	569	712	-143	22
Hull Kingston Rovers	25	10	1	14	675	639	36	21
Salford City Reds	25	8	1	16	572	756	-184	17
London Broncos	25	6	0	19	540	818	-278	12
Castleford Tigers	25	6	0	19	518	866	-348	12
Widnes Vikings	25	6	0	19	500	1008	-508	12

* 6 points deducted for entering administration

* *The RFL's plans to bring four new clubs into the Championship One in 2013 suffered a blow when the first club to have their application approved, Northampton Rebels, withdrew.*

* *A public work of art to be erected at Wembley Stadium was to incorporate all five players who featured in a final shortlist, Billy Boston, Eric Ashton, Martin Offiah, Gus Risman and Alex Murphy, decided by a public vote followed by a number of selection panels.*

CHALLENGE CUP FINAL
Three-timer for Wolves

The heavens opened in spectacular style 20 minutes into the game, but nothing could dampen the euphoria of Warrington's third Wembley win in four seasons as they beat Leeds Rhinos 35-18, Leeds' third consecutive Challenge Cup final defeat.

Wolves fullback Brett Hodgson was a convincing winner of the Lance Todd Trophy, gaining 27 of the 36 votes cast by members of the Rugby League Writers Association. Hodgson recovered from a huge tackle at the start of the second half by the Rhinos' Kylie Leuluai to play a key role, scoring the final Warrington try.

Warrington killed off the doughty Rhinos in a ten-minute spell before the hour mark, scoring three tries, two of them converted, before Lee Briers made it a four-score gap with a routine field goal. The ten minutes after half-time had also proved crucial, with

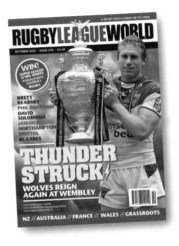

Leeds trailing only 12-10 and opening the half with a fierce barrage of defence. Hodgson had minutes before been clattered by Kevin Sinfield on a kick return when Kylie Leuluai, who had just come back on the field to replace Ian Kirke, hit Hodgson hard again, forcing the ball loose. Fellow tackler Brett Delaney picked it up and raced over in front of an ecstatic Leeds support.

A question mark hung over the legality of Leuluai's tackle. Was it a penalty? Video referee Phil Bentham took ages to rule it wasn't and spotted a fingertip touch of the ball by Leuluai, deeming that Hodgson had knocked on first, awarding Leeds the scrum.

Worse was to follow for Leeds fans. After Carl Ablett was tackled into touch by Stefan Ratchford when Ryan Hall caught Sinfield's bomb and passed to his centre, the Rhinos were penalised for not getting back ten and then Richie Myler tackled Zak Hardaker into in-goal. Briers dropped the restart and Leeds expected the scrum, but referee Richard Silverwood ruled the ball had gone back. Briers forced another GLDO when Hall had to scramble his kick dead and within a minute Chris Riley was over in the left corner to begin the ten-minute blitz.

Hodgson was instrumental, sending out a long pass, Trent Waterhouse the decoy, that sucked in Kallum Watkins and sent in Riley. Five minutes later Hodgson repeated the trick, this time missing out Riley to send in Ryan Atkins with a pin-point pass. The video referee gave the green light for the next try, this time on the other side of the field, when Ben Westwood managed to squeeze the ball out of a five-man tackle near the line after a thrilling attack from Ratchford and Joel Monaghan, Tyrone McCarthy the try scorer. Briers' field goal followed on the next Wolves attack.

McCarthy, who was a shock Wembley selection after only two first-grade games in 2009, repaid the faith of coach Smith after he chose to go without utility forward Simon

Adrian Morley and Lance Todd Trophy winner Brett Hodgson lift the Challenge Cup

Grix, who had also missed the Wolves' previous two cup finals. Mike Cooper also missed out, while Chris Bridge hadn't made the 19-man squad.

Leeds coach Brian McDermott named 22-year old rookie Jimmy Keinhorst on the bench after only three first-team starts. Chris Clarkson was omitted alongside prop Richard Moore. Rob Burrow was back and McDermott kept faith with 18-year-old Stevie Ward at halfback in place of Danny McGuire, out with a knee injury suffered against Widnes two weeks before.

Sinfield kicked off the game as the storm gathered, searching for his first Challenge Cup winners medal at the fifth attempt and the first thunder came from Jamie Jones-Buchanan and Leuluai's battering hit on Chris Hill, who lost control of the ball, though it shot out backwards.

Jamie Peacock, a huge presence for the Rhinos, showed his intent with a galloping 20-metre charge out of his own territory, while Westwood twice indicated where the Wolves thought a threat would come with no-questions-asked tackles on both Ward and Burrow, the latter on the last provoking a huge roar from the Warrington fans.

Brett Delaney celebrates with Kylie Leuluai, but the 'try' was subsequently ruled out by the video referee

The Wolves took the lead in the seventh minute with a try right out of the top drawer. Ben Harrison and Mickey Higham both offloaded around the Leeds '40', Higham's effort going to ground. Hill picked up and with a shimmy made a half break before feeding Myler on his side. There was no way through for the scrum-half but as he was closed down he looked up and saw Joel Monaghan unmarked on the right wing, produced a measured chip, and Monaghan junior collected on the full to maintain his record of scoring in every round.

Hodgson sent over the difficult conversion and within a minute the Wolves broke again, this time Hodgson cutting through from halfway off Briers' ball, but his pass to Westwood went behind the back-rower and a knock on was ruled.

Leeds responded with a break by Watkins and a scoot from Burrow but though Hall caught Sinfield's bomb on the last he was wrapped up as he fell by Joel Monaghan. After Hardaker had returned Higham's kick with interest and Westwood had dumped Ryan Bailey with a textbook tackle, Warrington invited the Rhinos back into the game with a series of handling errors. Carvell lost the ball on his own '40' as he regained his feet after Peacock's tackle; Atkins' inside pass to Riley missed its target, under pressure from Watkins, and rumbled into touch 40 metres out. The personal duel between Atkins and Watkins was one to savour.

Two penalties finally allowed Leeds enough pressure to level the scores. Carvell was caught within the ten metres and then deemed guilty of a ball steal on the ground on Bailey and two tackles later sub Ian Kirke, on the field all of four minutes, took Sinfield's inside ball and spun over to the left of the posts in the tackles of Hodgson and Higham. The conversion was easy for Sinfield.

Cue a huge deluge and things went pear-shaped for a few minutes, Hill knocking on a play-the-ball, Waterhouse spilling the ball on impact and Paul

Wood, just off the bench, swinging a punch at Ablett. Sinfield surprisingly, or not considering the conditions, took the two points from 38 metres out and Leeds led 8-6.

The rain eased and, with Adrian Morley - playing his 150th game for the Wolves - and Michael Monaghan off the bench, Warrington responded as Riley caught Briers' bomb to the left wing but couldn't keep hold as Ben Jones-Bishop grabbed him as he went for the corner.

A high tackle by sub Darrell Griffin on Michael Monaghan on the Leeds '40' gave the Wolves position to retake the lead. Two drives to the sticks and the ball was moved left for Myler to send Waterhouse charging through the tackles of Sinfield and Watkins, the former claiming the big back-rower had lost control. Mr Silverwood had no doubt and awarded the try for Hodgson to convert and it was now Leeds' turn to give Warrington a glut of possession.

Jones-Buchanan was penalised for interference in the tackle on Wood, Ablett was caught within the ten metres and a Briers grubber almost unlocked the Rhinos defence again, a knock on against the Wolves being ruled.

A great relieving kick from Sinfield, one of many, was spoilt by a high tackle by Bailey on Riley and Michael Monaghan ran at Peacock - brought back on to stem the tide - not square at marker on the last to try and win an easy penalty, but Mr Silverwood was having none of it.

Atkins fumbled a play the ball on halfway and Leeds, with three minutes of the half remaining, had a chance to make a significant mark before the break.

Up went the bomb to the left and so did Joel Monaghan who caught the ball cleanly and hared downfield, rounding Ward before being headed off by the covering Peacock and Kirke.

Back on the Wolves line, touch judge Tim Roby was waiting to advise Silverwood that Briers had illegally stood in the way of Hall as he went for the ball, Leeds got the penalty and Sinfield made it a two-point ball game with his third goal.

The rain stayed off after the turnaround as the action and the drama intensified.

After only three minutes, Rhinos fans were convinced they were back in front when Leuluai knocked out Hodgson and Delaney raced over and began to celebrate. Leuluai can only have got the slightest of touches on the ball as it emerged.

Within 20 minutes the Wolves were heading towards the far distance with the Rhinos chasing the game, finally getting a try back in the 70th minute when Hardaker broke his shackles at last and planted a fine grubber down the right wing for Watkins to collect on the bounce and cross. And with two minutes to go Watkins got on the outside of Atkins to get the ball down in the tackle for his second try.

But in between, just as the votes for the man of the match were being handed in, Hodgson was dummying his way through to the left of the posts for the Wolves' sixth try, before kicking his fifth conversion.

CARNEGIE CHALLENGE CUP FINAL

Saturday 25th August 2012

LEEDS RHINOS 18 WARRINGTON WOLVES 35

RHINOS: 4 Zak Hardaker; 2 Ben Jones-Bishop; 3 Kallum Watkins; 12 Carl Ablett; 5 Ryan Hall; 13 Kevin Sinfield (C); 25 Stevie Ward; 8 Kylie Leuluai; 7 Rob Burrow; 10 Jamie Peacock; 11 Jamie Jones-Buchanan; 15 Brett Delaney; 16 Ryan Bailey. Subs (all used): 20 Darrell Griffin; 31 Shaun Lunt; 17 Ian Kirke; 32 Jimmy Keinhorst.
Tries: Kirke (19), Watkins (70, 79); **Goals:** Sinfield 3/5.
WOLVES: 1 Brett Hodgson; 5 Joel Monaghan; 19 Stefan Ratchford; 4 Ryan Atkins; 2 Chris Riley; 6 Lee Briers; 7 Richard Myler; 10 Garreth Carvell; 14 Mick Higham; 20 Chris Hill; 11 Trent Waterhouse; 12 Ben Westwood; 13 Ben Harrison. Subs (all used): 8 Adrian Morley (C); 16 Paul Wood; 9 Michael Monaghan; 21 Tyrone McCarthy.
Tries: J Monaghan (7), Waterhouse (29), Riley (49), Atkins (54), McCarthy (59), Hodgson (74);
Goals: Hodgson 5/6; **Field goal:** Briers (63).
Rugby Leaguer & League Express Men of the Match:
Rhinos: Jamie Peacock; *Wolves:* Brett Hodgson.
Penalty count: 8-9; **Half-time:** 10-12;
Referee: Richard Silverwood;
Attendance: 79,180 *(at Wembley Stadium).*

---

* Howard of Effingham school from Leatherhead became the first school from the south of England to win a Champion Schools title when they beat Castleford Academy 24-22 in the Year 7 Steven Mullaney Memorial Trophy game, played as a curtain raiser at Wembley.

SEPTEMBER
Wigan take pole

Round 26

Wigan clinched the League Leaders' Shield on the first Sunday of September by staging the biggest comeback in the history of Super League to defeat Hull Kingston Rovers 42-36 at Craven Park. The Robins went ahead 26-0 in the 34th minute with a try by Jake Webster, goaled by Michael Dobson But two tries just before half-time for the Warriors ignited a tremendous comeback.

At a point in the second half it looked like the miracle wasn't on, as a series of errors from the Warriors gave the Robins the chance to push their lead out to 36-22, before an incredible four tries in 12 minutes sealed the win for the Warriors.

When George Carmont passed Pat Richards the ball near the half way line with three minutes on the clock and the Robins leading 36-32, the winger had plenty to do, expertly backing himself to beat Craig Hall down the sideline for pace to level the scores, and then the Australian calmly slotted the conversion which broke the home support's hearts. Josh Charnley's try at the death confirmed the pain.

Bradford Bulls were at last out of administration, although the RFL had not yet given their purchase the green light. The Bulls' administrator Brendan Guilfoyle announced on the Friday he had sold the club to local restaurateur Omar Khan, who had formed a new company, OK Bulls Ltd, with which to buy the club. Khan was to have a 100 per cent holding of shares in the new company with Gerry Sutcliffe MP becoming the club's new honorary chairman.

The administrator's report into the affairs of the Bulls revealed the insolvency practitioners had carried out 842 hours of work between 29 June and 24 August, and charged the club £172,551.90p. This was more than the £150,000 that Khan had paid for the club. Khan was in the crowd to witness the Saturday-night clash with Hull FC that was vital to the Bulls' top-eight chances. Bradford suffered a record home Super League defeat, by 70-6, as their backs-to-the-wall bubble burst spectacularly, Hull capitalising on the Bulls' numerous on-field deficiencies with some scintillating finishing to rack up 13 tries.

Tom Briscoe claimed a second-half hat-trick, Willie Manu and Aaron Heremaia grabbed braces, while Jamie Foster finished with a personal tally of 26 points through two tries and nine goals. A record all-time away score did wonders for the East Yorkshire side's confidence heading towards the play-offs, and that after the Bulls took an early lead when Keith Lulia, tackled on his back, brilliantly offloaded to find Jason Crookes in enough space to score in the corner. Luke Gale landed the touchline conversion, and then Karl Pryce and Gale combined down the other flank to almost increase the Bulls' advantage.

But a few minutes later the momentum swung dramatically after a controversial decision by referee Ben Thaler to award a penalty when Briscoe was bundled into touch after a threatening break down the wing. Heath L'Estrange did superbly to catch hold of Briscoe's shirt but never fully grasped the visitors' top try-scorer, who got up and appeared to attempt to play on before being pushed over the whitewash with the help of Ben Jeffries. Jeffries was sin-binned – a "ridiculous" decision in the eyes of coach Mick Potter. Almost immediately Ryan McGoldrick put Joe Westerman through a hole in the right channel to level the scores. and it was processional from then on.

The Bradford players received a standing ovation as they left the field for their efforts during the club's nightmare year.

Wakefield leap-frogged the Bulls into eighth spot after a scratchy 22-18 televised home win over Widnes on the Sunday night. Captain Danny Kirmond's try with five minutes to go, following a great break from Kyle Wood, was just enough for the Wildcats.

Brett Hodgson produced another man of the match performance as Warrington turned their attention to Super League success after the previous week's Wembley win with a 54-6 home win over Huddersfield.

Hodgson was outstanding for the Wolves, especially in the second half when the home side scored seven tries, to take the gamestar award from Stefan Ratchford who had been instrumental in getting the Wolves into a 16-6 interval lead.

St Helens, Catalans and Leeds were in a tussle for third and fourth places in the table, and all won their penultimate regular-season games.

Saints ended a three-game winning streak for the resurgent London Broncos with a 30-0 win at Langtree Park, Mark Flanagan and Paul Wellens getting two tries each and Louie McCarthy-Scarsbrook having a great game against his old club.

Leeds bounced back the week after their Wembley defeat with a 46-12 home win over Salford securing at least fifth spot, the position from which they launched their unprecedented 2011 title assault. Salford were denied a try, fumbling the ball in-goal, at the start of the second half and in the next set Stevie Ward set up Rob Burrow for his 150th try to make it 22-0 and the outcome was decided.

The Dragons served notice that they were ready and able to make an impact on the play-offs with a 46-26 win at Castleford, with Damien Blanch and Clint Greenshields both scoring hat-tricks.

It was an emotional day in which the Tigers said farewell to skipper Danny Orr, at least in a playing capacity as he was joining the club's coaching staff, another former captain in Ryan Hudson, Nick Youngquest, Stuart Jones and Steve Snitch.

The Dragons needed to beat the Bulls, who also had to win to have a chance of getting into the play-offs, the following Saturday and rely on St Helens to lose at Wigan, to make third place.

Round 27

The League Leaders' Shield was presented to Wigan at the DW Stadium on the Friday night but St Helens spoilt the celebrations with a 26-18 win to ensure they avoided playing the Warriors in the play-offs. The win secured third place and Saints would now go to second-placed Warrington the following weekend.

Wigan played most of the game with 12 men after referee James Child sent off Wigan hooker Michael McIlorum for a late, high hit on Anthony Laffranchi for which he was banned for three games. McIlorum, who was sent off earlier in the season for punching Bradford Bulls' Olivier Elima, became the fourth player to be red-carded in a Wigan-Saints fixture this season, following the brawl at the Magic Weekend in Manchester which saw Gareth Hock, Chris Tuson and Shaun Magennis all sent off. With the extra man, Saints led 12-6 at half-time, with James Roby and Tom Makinson crossing for tries to cancel out Thomas Leuluai's early score. Pat Richards' converted try early in the second half levelled but further tries from Andrew Dixon, Josh Jones and Jonny Lomax won the game before Sam Tomkins consolation in the last minute. Stuart Fielden started his first game for Wigan in over 18 months, following knee and pectoral injuries.

The game was dedicated to the Joining Jack charity with Wigan wearing a special kit for the night.

Warrington's 52-14 win at Widnes meant the Vikings finished bottom of the table on points difference below Castleford, also on 12 points. The Tigers' season ended with a seventh straight defeat, this time at Hull FC, who recorded a comfortable 36-10 win at the KC Stadium. The Black and Whites showed glimpses of the superb performance against the Bulls the week before in an eleven-minute period in the second half that saw three tries extend their lead from eight points to 24 to seal the game. Once again, Willie Manu, off to St Helens at the end of the season, was the gamestar.

London Broncos finished two points clear of the bottom two after emerging victorious by 48-42 over Hull KR in a 16-try thriller on a scorching afternoon to end the season at the Stoop. The sides scored eight tries apiece but London recorded their fourth win in just seven games under Tony Rea thanks to a flawless goal-kicking display from captain Craig Gower, who kicked eight goals from eight attempts and the extra points were the difference in the end.

Another scrum-half, Danny Brough, in his first game as captain, led the Giants to a 48-24 victory over Leeds Rhinos at the John Smith's Stadium. Despite suffering the loss of Luke O'Donnell to a red card, Brough created his side's first two tries, scored a solo effort and kicked eight goals from 10 attempts for a 20-point haul. His second conversion was his 1,000th goal as a senior player.

O'Donnell was sent off just 16 minutes into his comeback from a knee injury, after it appeared that the Giants prop had escaped initial punishment for a tackle on Leeds Rhinos prop Ian Kirke. O'Donnell collided with Kirke in a one-on-one tackle, dislodging the ball and knocking the Leeds man unconscious. Play continued, but was brought to a halt at the next tackle, allowing medical staff to treat Kirke, who had not moved.

A minor scuffle at the play-the-ball was defused, and the entire incident was placed on report, before coach Paul Anderson took the decision to substitute O'Donnell.

Kirke was treated on the field for nine minutes, before he was carried off on a stretcher. O'Donnell was called back onto the field by referee Thierry Alibert and then, following a conversation between the referee, a touch judge, Giants captain Brough and O'Donnell, the Australian was shown the red card. Kirke was taken straight to hospital, and, after being examined, was subsequently released with no significant ill effects on Sunday evening. O'Donnell was found not guilty by the RFL who ruled an accidental clash of heads.

Bradford Bulls needed to win in sun-baked Perpignan to have a chance of making eighth spot but they lost 50-26, with Clint Greenshields getting another hat-trick for the Dragons, who secured fourth place.

Catalans Trent Robinson had been appointed the new coach of Sydney Roosters on the previous Thursday after the sacking of Brian Smith.

Bulls prop forward Craig Kopczak didn't play after telling the Bulls that he was walking away from his contract with the club, citing the Transfer of Undertakings (Protection of Employment) regulations 2006, which gave an employee the power to pull out of an employment contract if a business was transferred to a new owner. It was also

Wigan captain Sean O'Loughlin lifts the League Leaders Shield

revealed that the Bulls had agreed to operate for the next two seasons with only a half of the TV money of other clubs, with the club awarded a probationary licence for the next 12 months.

Bulls coach Mick Potter decided the head back to Australia and his assistant Francis Cummins was announced as his successor.

Another club that had had its share of tough times in 2012 was Salford City Reds. Not only had the Reds had a moderate season, but they had been forced to share their stadium with the Sale Sharks rugby union club. The Reds were due to play Wakefield at home on Friday night in the last game of the season. Unfortunately for them, because Wakefield looked likely to qualify for the play-offs, Sky Sports want to screen the game on Saturday evening at 6.15pm. Sale were playing their first home game on the Saturday after switching from the Friday night to accommodate the Reds.

So the Reds had to move their game to the Leigh Sports Village meaning that a crowd of less than two and half thousand turned up - the vast majority from Wakefield - to see the Wildcats win 42-34. Fullback Luke Patten and centre Joel Moon both missed the game. Patten had now retired, while Moon appeared at a RFL tribunal on the Friday trying, unsuccessfully, to secure a release from his contract, which had another year to run.

It was a sad ending to Salford's season that had promised so much. Matty Smith had gone to Wigan in mid-season, Sean Gleeson was heading to Hull KR, Daniel Holdsworth to Hull and Luke Adamson, the club's longest serving player, was also leaving for rugby union.

On the positive side the Reds were expected to have new owners before the following season.

It was much easier than the scoreline suggested for the Tim Smith-inspired Wildcats, who having seen Bradford lose earlier in the day, didn't have to win to secure a trip to Leeds in an elimination play-off.

FINAL SUPER LEAGUE TABLE - *Sunday 9th September*

	P	W	D	L	F	A	D	PTS
Wigan Warriors	27	21	0	6	994	449	545	42
Warrington Wolves	27	20	1	6	909	539	370	41
St Helens	27	17	2	8	795	480	315	36
Catalan Dragons	27	18	0	9	812	611	201	36
Leeds Rhinos	27	16	0	11	823	662	161	32
Hull FC	27	15	2	10	696	621	75	32
Huddersfield Giants	27	14	0	13	699	664	35	28
Wakefield T Wildcats	27	13	0	14	633	764	-131	26
Bradford Bulls *	27	14	1	12	633	756	-123	23
Hull Kingston Rovers	27	10	1	16	753	729	24	21
Salford City Reds	27	8	1	18	618	844	-226	17
London Broncos	27	7	0	20	588	890	-302	14
Castleford Tigers	27	6	0	21	554	948	-394	12
Widnes Vikings	27	6	0	21	532	1082	-550	12

* 6 points deducted for entering administration

SUPER LEAGUE PLAY-OFFS
Rhinos' perfect charge

Week One

Qualifying Play-offs

WIGAN WARRIORS 46 CATALAN DRAGONS 6

Wigan annihilated fourth-placed Catalans with coach Shaun Wane revealing that Michael McIlorum's suspension was used as motivation. McIlorum's season was over after his appeal against a three-game ban for a late challenge on St Helens prop Anthony Laffranchi in round 27 failed.

Wigan started like a house on fire, with George Carmont crossing twice inside the first ten minutes before Thomas Leuluai's try saw them lead 16-0. The Dragons were by no means dead at this stage, and after plenty of pressure and a disallowed try they eventually got on the score sheet themselves through Louis Anderson, only for Wigan to hit them with a sucker punch just before the break with Darrell Goulding touching down.

A quick try just after the break from Liam Farrell killed the game off as a contest, as the Warriors crossed for eight tries in all to earn a week off and the club call for the Qualifying semi-finals.

WARRINGTON WOLVES 6 ST HELENS 28

St Helens moved one game away from a seventh straight Grand Final and raised more questions about Warrington's play-off temperament. Saints' dogged rearguard defence was breached just once, by Brett Hodgson's 22nd minute opening try, and provided the foundation for the early Saturday evening victory. It also laid the platform for another superb James Roby display, a terrific impact off the bench by Sia Soliola, and crucial contributions from both Jonny Lomax and Tom Makinson.

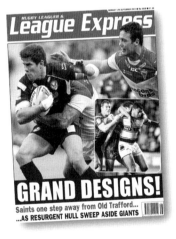

Roby had been handed the moniker "The Dynamo" in the RFL's new marketing campaign in midweek, and he could hardly have lived up to it more. His 64th minute try took the game firmly away from the misfiring Wolves who were missing Ben Westwood and Ben Harrison, with Garreth Carvell and Brett Hodgson both leaving the field with back injuries.

Form winger Makinson scored twice and kicked four goals, with the other tries coming from Soliola and Meli.

Elimination Play-offs

LEEDS RHINOS 42 WAKEFIELD TRINITY WILDCATS 20

Defending champions Leeds kept alive their hopes of another Grand Final appearance after bringing Wakefield's seven-match winning run to a halt in a Saturday night game at Headingley.

The Rhinos, boosted by the return of halfback Danny McGuire after a four-match absence with a knee injury, trailed three times before finally getting on top of eighth-placed Wakefield and finishing with a flourish with a Ben Jones-Bishop hat-trick to earn a trip to Catalan Dragons in the following Friday's preliminary semi-final.

Tim Smith's accurate cut-out passes enabled Ben Cockayne to open the scoring and for Lee Smith to take Cockayne's return pass to touch down. Kallum Watkins breaks put Rob Burrow in twice, the second try just after Leeds captain Kevin Sinfield crucially knocked down Cockayne's final pass with the tryline beckoning.

Wakefield led 16-12 early in the second half after Kyle Wood's inside pass sent Frankie Mariano racing from his own half and he sent in Richie Mathers. But Leeds took a lead they were never to lose when Ryan Hall broke clear on an interception. Super League's top tackler Danny Washbrook tracked back 70 metres to make an astonishing tackle before Kevin Sinfield responded to Jones-Bishop's call in open space with a wonderful chip into his hands for a stunning score.

HULL FC 46 HUDDERSFIELD GIANTS 10

Hull FC managed to keep the free-flowing Giants scoreless for 67 minutes before two late consolation tries in the Sunday night game. On-loan winger Jamie Foster claimed 22 points from two tries and seven goals, but it was Hull's defence that impressed. The Giants were top of the table after a third of the season, but just three wins from their last nine league games highlighted their problems for a third successive year.

Winger Tom Briscoe collected an early double to give Hull a lead they never surrendered. The Airlie Birds had reached a 22-0 lead early in the second half when Foster claimed his brace. Liam Watts, Aaron Heremaia, Andy Lynch and Richard Horne scored Hull's final tries, with Scott Grix and Eorl Crabtree touching down for the visitors.

Danny Houghton's 40/20 on 55 minutes effectively ended the game, as Watts scored soon after to post an unassailable lead.

The win meant Hull had to travel to Warrington on the Saturday, while Huddersfield's year finished and they duly parted company with forwards David Fa'alogo and Adam Walker and hookers Scott Moore and Tommy Lee.

Week Two

Preliminary Semi-finals

CATALAN DRAGONS 20 LEEDS RHINOS 27

Leeds Rhinos, missing Kylie Leuluai, suspended for one game for punching Wakefield winger Peter Fox the previous week, showed off their play-off pedigree in a tough battle in the south of France that was decided only in the dying minutes.

With 30 seconds remaining of the first half Leeds led 12-4 through Stevie Ward and Shaun Lunt tries, after Clint Greenshields had given the home side an early lead.

As they looked to put the game to bed, Danny McGuire's pass wide to Ryan Hall was intercepted by Damien Blanch and he raced 95 metres to score. Scott Dureau added the conversion to send the sides in at 10-12.

Eight minutes after the restart, McGuire was placed on report for a swinging arm on Louis Anderson. From the penalty Dureau put up a high kick to the right corner and Blanch rose above the Leeds defenders to claim the ball and touch down. Dureau hit the post with the conversion attempt.

Leeds again bounced back to retake the lead, as a low Sinfield kick trickled into the in-goal area before Carl Ablett pounced to score. Sinfield added the simple conversion to take the score to 18-14.

Again Leeds backed up with a second try, as Ryan Bailey charged downfield from the kick-off and handed off three would-be Catalan defenders before handing the ball onto the supporting McGuire who sprinted over to score. Sinfield again added the conversion to give the Rhinos a ten-point-lead.

Thomas Bosc went over under the posts and Dureau added the simple goal to narrow the lead to four points and set up a grandstand finish. With seven minutes remaining, Jamal Fakir conceded two penalties, the first while in possession for leading with the elbow, the second in front of his own posts for a high tackle on Burrow. Sinfield kicked the simple goal and extended the Leeds lead to six points.

It was left to Danny McGuire to drop a goal from twenty metres out after Sinfield had been closed down to seal the win with two minutes remaining.

WARRINGTON WOLVES 24 HULL FC 12

Halfbacks Richie Myler and Lee Briers played integral roles as Warrington moved a step closer to realising their dream of a first Grand Final.

Hull struggled to break down the well-organised Wolves defence, only crossing for their first try in the 66th minute with the contest effectively over at 24-0.

Coach Tony Smith praised the contribution of the increasingly influential Trent Waterhouse in the back row, as well as centre Stefan Ratchford, who scored the second-half try that took the game fully away from Hull with a moment of individual brilliance. Forwards Danny Houghton and Willie Manu – playing his last game for the club – never wavered in their efforts up front, but Hull looked a tired side.

The Wolves scored in the 14th minute when Briers' pin-point crossfield kick eluded both Hull's Jordan Turner and home centre Ryan Atkins, and Waterhouse reacted quickest to touch down. Six minutes before half-time Briers sent Myler over with a well-timed pass and Hodgson converted for a 12-0 lead at the break.

On 54 minutes Ratchford scored a great individual try, pushing off Aaron Heremaia and Manu and spotting a gap behind the defence, chipping through and collecting the ball off the post to make it 18-0.

The game was safe when Myler sliced through the Hull defence, after Atkins had popped an offload out the back, to put Hodgson under the posts for another converted try that made it 24-0.

Hull recorded two late tries to give their big away following something to cheer. Heremaia kicked for Tom Briscoe to touch down in the left corner. Soon after, Houghton, Brett Seymour and Richard Horne combined from a scrum to put Ben Crooks over on the opposite side.

Week Three

Qualifying Semi-finals

WIGAN WARRIORS 12 LEEDS RHINOS 13

Leeds kept their dream alive of winning the Super League title for a sixth time as they booked their place in the Grand Final with a last-gasp win at the Minor Premiers. It looked like the Warriors had pulled off an amazing comeback after trailing 11-0 at the break to lead 12-11 with minutes remaining, until Liam Farrell was caught offside as Rob Burrow darted for the posts, after stand-in fullback Jack Murphy had dropped a Kevin Sinfield bomb. The Rhinos skipper slotted over the winning penalty from almost in front of the posts.

Murphy started at fullback in place of the injured Sam Tomkins, who failed a late fitness test on a knee injury sustained in training, for only his second first-team appearance.

Leeds travelled without the suspended Danny McGuire, following his one-match ban for a swinging arm on Louis Anderson in the win over the Catalans in France but a virtuoso kicking display from Sinfield took them into their seventh Grand Final in nine years.

The Warriors were camped on the Rhinos' line after a bruising opening 13 minutes, but a panicked, wayward ball from Brett Finch was swooped upon by Kallum Watkins, and the centre raced 90 metres to score under the posts. Sinfield converted for a 6-0 lead. That was the end of Leeds' try scoring but by half-time it was 11-nil after two Sinfield penalties, a 40/20 and a field goal.

Wigan needed to score first in the second half to have any chance of getting back in the game and they did when Thomas Leuluai produced a great short ball for Harrison Hansen to charge over.

Rob Burrow scooted through a gap to go over, but video referee Ian Smith ruled the scrum-half had dropped the ball in George Carmont's desperate challenge. More Wigan pressure finally told as Finch ran across field and through Leeds' umbrella outside defence before sending Pat Richards in the corner. Richards kicked the conversion from the touchline, as Wigan led for the first time at 12-11 with 18 minutes to go.

After Sinfield's last penalty goal, Wigan had one last chance to win the game as Darrell Goulding broke down the right, but he could not get the ball away as Leeds scrambled back, and then Finch was off target with a field-goal attempt that would have sent the game into extra time.

ST HELENS 18 WARRINGTON WOLVES 36

Warrington finally made it to their first Grand Final and, in the process, denied Saints a seventh successive Old Trafford appearance. A Simon Grix try on the stroke of half-time tipped the balance in a contest that Saints were dominating at the time after scoring three tries to Warrington's one.

Saints took the initiative when a slick cross-field move to the right found Lance Hohaia and his fabulous cut-out pass found Flannery, who sucked in the Wolves fringe defence to slip the ball to Tom Makinson. The young winger's finish was one of the best of the season as he appeared to dive around Chris Riley and dextrously ground the ball

Trent Waterhouse holds off Andrew Dixon on the way to scoring Warrington's clinching try

with one hand when he hit the corner post. Saints held sway 4-0 after just 12 minutes.

The introduction of captain Adrian Morley for an under-firing Ben Westwood – back from a knee injury sustained at Wembley - seemed to give the Wolves a lift and when Jon Wilkin lost his footing, and the ball, inside his own half on 18 minutes, the Wolves sniffed their chance, as Brett Hodgson's pass sent Chris Riley in at the corner. Hodgson added a superb kick from the touchline to nudge the Wolves ahead at 6-4.

But tries to Francis Meli and Paul Wellens had Warrington staring down the barrel of a 14-6 scoreline until Richie Myler collected Jonny Lomax's grubber towards the Wolves line and raced 40 metres downfield. After a series of dazzling offloads Lee Briers' well-timed pass to the right found Simon Grix on a devastating angle to crash over for the try. Hodgson added the kick as the hooter sounded to reduce the deficit to 14-12 and Warrington knew that despite being out-enthused for the first 40 minutes they were still right in it.

On 49 minutes Briers to put up his first attacking kick into the corner. Joel Monaghan used his towering height to out-jump Meli and although the winger lost the ball, it went backwards and in the split-second of confusion, the prone Monaghan re-gathered the ball to score. Hodgson added the kick and the Wolves went in front at 18-14, a lead they were not to lose.

Ryan Atkins showed some sensational footwork to cut back on the inside to open up the Saints defence before delivering a superb offload to Trent Waterhouse, to make it 24-14.

Then Waterhouse, the big second-rower, somehow spun out of five tacklers to provide the killer try from ten metres out. Four minutes later Briers, Myler and Atkins dovetailed and Riley bagged his brace in the corner to make it 34-14.

Meli squeezed in at the corner for his second try but Hodgson rounded it off with a late penalty.

SUPER LEAGUE GRAND FINAL
Six of one...

Leeds captain Kevin Sinfield won the Harry Sunderland Trophy for the second time in three years and led his side to a sixth Super League title. The Rhinos had to recover twice, going behind after only four minutes to a Richie Myler try and then five minutes into the second half to a Ryan Atkins score, and more significantly Sinfield himself had to regain consciousness after a clash of heads with Michael Monaghan and, after a shaky few minutes, his composure to lead the Rhinos home.

For the second year running, Leeds had done it the hard way from fifth position, and this year after the regular season had ended with a hammering at Huddersfield. From that point the Rhinos once again embarked on an unbeaten march through the play-offs with a home win over Wakefield, and then victories on away soil in Perpignan and at league leaders Wigan. During that run, Sinfield's leadership had been outstanding and his kicking game crucial as he kicked 21 goals out of as many attempts.

On a sunlit Saturday evening, the swirling wind that had threatened to blow away the red carpet during the pre-match entertainment looked like being a factor with both Sinfield and Warrington's Lee Briers' kicking games expected to play a big part in the outcome.

After Leeds enjoyed the first two sets thanks to Zak Hardaker recovering his own kick that ricocheted of Ben Harrison, the Wolves were the first to exploit their kicking arsenal. Briers put up a bomb to the left that Ben Jones-Bishop couldn't take and his opposite, Chris Riley was held up over the line after forcing his way over. The ball was taken to the right and Myler scythed through, Jamie Peacock getting a despairing hand on his shoulder, to shoot over to the right of the posts. Wigan, the week before, had struggled to break down the Rhinos with their trademark wide plays, but it looked like the Wolves had almost instantly found a way to counter the Rhinos' smothering defence.

Brett Hodgson kicked the conversion and the Wolves looked energised, Chris Hill launching a midfield break with an offload to Mickey Higham. Briers' deep bomb was the first of several that were taken easily by Hardaker under no immediate pressure, although at this stage the Rhinos attack was looking anything but composed as Jamie Jones-

STOBART SUPER LEAGUE GRAND FINAL

Saturday 6th October 2012

LEEDS RHINOS 26 WARRINGTON WOLVES 18

RHINOS: 4 Zak Hardaker; 2 Ben Jones-Bishop; 3 Kallum Watkins; 12 Carl Ablett; 5 Ryan Hall; 13 Kevin Sinfield (C); 6 Danny McGuire; 8 Kylie Leuluai; 7 Rob Burrow; 10 Jamie Peacock; 11 Jamie Jones-Buchanan; 15 Brett Delaney; 16 Ryan Bailey. Subs (all used): 17 Ian Kirke; 20 Darrell Griffin; 25 Stevie Ward; 31 Shaun Lunt.
Tries: Sinfield (19), Jones-Bishop (28), Ablett (59), Hall (72);
Goals: Sinfield 5/5.
WOLVES: 1 Brett Hodgson; 5 Joel Monaghan; 19 Stefan Ratchford; 4 Ryan Atkins; 2 Chris Riley; 6 Lee Briers; 7 Richard Myler; 20 Chris Hill; 14 Mick Higham; 13 Ben Harrison; 12 Ben Westwood; 11 Trent Waterhouse; 15 Simon Grix. Subs (all used): 8 Adrian Morley (C); 9 Michael Monaghan; 16 Paul Wood; 17 Michael Cooper.
Tries: Myler (4), J Monaghan (38), Atkins (45);
Goals: Hodgson 3/4.
Rugby Leaguer & League Express Men of the Match:
Rhinos: Kevin Sinfield; *Wolves:* Richard Myler.
Penalty count: 6-5; **Half-time:** 14-14;
Referee: Richard Silverwood;
Attendance: 70,676 *(at Old Trafford, Manchester).*

Buchanan's rushed, last-tackle bomb rolled dead. JJB then got his head in the wrong place trying to tackle Harrison and took a while to come round before Briers caused Hardaker problems for the first, and as it turned out, only time when his kick bounced awkwardly.

When Trent Waterhouse knocked on on his own 30-metre line it signalled the end of the Wolves dominance for almost the rest of the first half.

Riley was trapped in-goal in the 11th minute by Delaney for the game's only goal-line drop-out. Within a minute Ryan Hall was in at the left corner but Sinfield's pass that missed out Carl Ablett was ruled forward. If it was it was marginal.

Rob Burrow was starting to buzz from dummy-half and Sinfield was getting his eye in, though Jones-Bishop couldn't take his attacking bomb to the right.

Briers meanwhile was getting a lot of attention from the robust Ablett. Not only was the second-rower-turned-centre running at him regularly with the ball, every time the stand-off shaped to kick Ablett was bearing down on him. The next time Briers smartly took the ball right instead of kicking and released Joel Monaghan down the right. The younger Monaghan chipped inside but it was Sinfield who gathered the bouncing ball in front of his own posts, getting hurt in a cruncher from Higham and Westwood. On the next attack Riley knocked on Briers' bomb to the left corner before Leeds profited from the same ploy at the other end of the field.

Joel Monaghan got to Sinfield's high kick before Ryan Hall but only managed to knock it back towards his own line and straight into the hands of Ablett. Ablett spotted Sinfield coming at pace behind him and his lobbed pass was good enough to send his skipper into the left corner, where he had to reach out one handed in Stefan Ratchford's desperate tackle.

Sinfield's towering kick from the touchline levelled the scores and within six minutes he was edging Leeds in front with a 35-metre penalty after Harrison was harshly adjudged to have kneed the ball from the grasp of Kallum Watkins as he tried to play the ball. Warrington had got themselves into that position because Michael Monaghan, just off the bench that second, couldn't take Atkins' unexpected and unwise offload on his own '40'.

The first penalty of the game had come after 25 minutes but the second soon followed as Mike Cooper was adjudged to have tackled Brett Delaney high as he ran the ball out of the Leeds '20', and again the Rhinos soon capitalised with a splendid try, this time from a perfectly executed set move. The old guard of Peacock, Sinfield and Danny McGuire, back from suspension and the only change to the line-ups from the previous week, combined, and McGuire's bullet pass to the right found Jones-Bishop at pace, stepping inside to shrug off Riley and then Hodgson to score a beauty.

Sinfield's third goal made it 14-6 and it could have been more if Atkins had not chased

back to bring down McGuire as he arced through on halfway. The lightning attack ended when Burrow, 20 metres out, couldn't take the last of a series of thrilling offloads.

Leeds' confidence was sky high and they attacked down the left at almost every opportunity, Hall unable to take Ablett's pass when he was clear at halfway.

The spirit of adventure gave the Wolves a way back into the game. Sinfield's quick pass to Ablett 35 metres out was spilled. The Wolves got their first penalty for offside at the scrum and then a repeat set when McGuire knocked down Briers' pass.

With two minutes left of the half, the ball was worked right, Briers' long looping pass found Joel Monaghan unmarked and he raced around towards the posts.

Ryan Hall shows his delight as he crosses to win the Super League Grand Final for Leeds

Hodgson cut the deficit to two points and after putting a monster hit on Adrian Morley straight from the restart, Jones-Buchanan was caught offside at marker and there was still time for one last Wolves attack. It reaped two points and levelled the scores as Hodgson converted a penalty when Leeds were caught within the ten metres on their own line after Cooper had charged through towards the posts.

Within two minutes of the second half it looked as though Leeds' fairytale was over when Michael Monaghan's head collided with Sinfield's jaw as he charged down the Leeds captain's kick. Sinfield eventually got back on his feet but Myler exploited his grogginess as he ran at him down the left and was away down the wing, Watkins' push just putting the scrum-half off his kick back infield.

Super League Grand Final

Myler was involved in the build-up to Warrington retaking the lead when he stripped the ball from Hardaker as he returned a kick, although replays showed he had caught the fullback in the face. The Wolves took full advantage and when Hodgson fed Atkins at short range from dummy-half, the centre had the strength to force his way over through Jones-Bishop and Watkins' tackles.

Jamie Peacock was brought back off the bench, the same had happened in the win over Wakefield when Leeds were under the cosh, although if Ratchford had been able to take Michael Monaghan's pass when he broke from the play-the-ball there could have been a different scenario.

From then on Warrington were their own worst enemies, giving Leeds possession and having to defend in their own half for almost all the next 20 minutes. Briers tried an audacious kick from his own '20' for Joel Monaghan to collect on the right wing. It was exciting stuff, but gave Leeds the ball 40 metres out. The Wolves managed to thwart several attacks, Joel Monaghan leaping brilliantly to take McGuire's chip; Morley and Hodgson forcing Sinfield to lose possession under the posts, and Jones-Buchanan being caught on the last in the left corner.

The defensive effort could not go on for ever.

In the 58th minute, Leeds' strategy of Ablett tiring out Briers paid off. Briers was penalised 40 metres out for a high slap on Ablett and then the Wolves were caught offside under their own posts. Ablett was almost over once, and then sub hooker Shaun Lunt created enough space to get him over with a clever dart left out of dummy-half. Briers couldn't stop him, Sinfield converted and Leeds were two points up.

The Wolves won repeat sets which gave them a rare foray into Leeds territory but Waterhouse lost control of the ball as he went for the line before Leeds produced a try worthy of winning a Grand Final.

Kylie Leuluai's monster hit on Higham on the 66th minute won Leeds possession and shook Old Trafford.

Sinfield's long kick from his own '20' pinned Warrington back. The Wolves countered but Harrison couldn't take Briers' inside pass and knocked on.

Leeds worked upfield, Burrow shot out off dummy-half and fed Delaney who passed on smartly to Watkins 20 metres out. The big centre was forced inside and found Hardaker who passed on to a stationary McGuire. The stand-off had time to think, and then boomed a pass to Ablett in the left centre and he sent Hall into the corner, directly in front of the joyous Leeds support.

Sinfield's conversion made it an eight-point ball game and although Warrington got the short kick-off back and produced a frenzied attack or two, Ratchford's attempt to flick on to Joel Monaghan ended in a knock on.

Burrow's 40/20 out of dummy-half ensured the win, and there was the unusual sight of Hodgson passing the ball out to no-one as the rest of the Wolves left-side attack was in back play trying to mediate in an altercation between Myler and Ryan Bailey.

Higham's knock on in midfield was the last act of the game and the Leeds players' celebrations began in earnest.

SUPER LEAGUE XVII AWARDS

MAN OF STEEL
Sam Tomkins
(Wigan Warriors)

*(chosen by
players poll)*

YOUNG PLAYER OF THE YEAR
Zak Hardaker (Leeds Rhinos)

COACH OF THE YEAR
Mick Potter (Bradford Bulls)

CLUB OF THE YEAR
Wigan Warriors

TOP TRY SCORER Josh Charnley (Wigan Warriors)
for scoring 31 regular season tries

TOP METRE MAKER James Roby (St Helens)
for making 3,971 regular season metres

TOP TACKLER Danny Washbrook
(Wakefield Trinity Wildcats)
for making 990 regular season tackles

MIKE GREGORY SPIRIT OF RUGBY LEAGUE AWARD
Jamie Peacock MBE (Leeds Rhinos)

SUPER LEAGUE DREAM TEAM
(previous appearances in italics)
1 Sam Tomkins (Wigan Warriors) *2009, 2010, 2011*
2 Josh Charnley (Wigan Warriors) *Debut*
3 George Carmont (Wigan Warriors) *2008, 2011*
4 Ryan Atkins (Warrington Wolves) *Debut*
5 Ryan Hall (Leeds Rhinos) *2009, 2010*
6 Brett Finch (Wigan Warriors) *Debut*
7 Scott Dureau (Catalan Dragons) *2011*
8 Chris Hill (Warrington Wolves) *Debut*
9 James Roby (St Helens) *2007, 2010, 2011*
10 Remi Casty (Catalan Dragons) *Debut*
11 Ben Westwood (Warrington Wolves)
2008, 2010, 2011
12 Gareth Hock (Wigan Warriors) *Debut*
13 Sean O'Loughlin (Wigan Warriors) *2010, 2011*

ALBERT GOLDTHORPE MEDAL
Scott Dureau (Catalan Dragons)

ROOKIE OF THE YEAR
John Bateman (Bradford Bulls)

CLUB OF THE YEAR
Wigan Warriors

LIFETIME ACHIEVEMENT AWARD
David Oxley MBE

CAREER ACHIEVEMENT AWARD
Paul Sculthorpe

2
CHAMPIONSHIPS 2012

CHAMPIONSHIP SEASON
Wild Rovers

FEATHERSTONE ROVERS achieved a league campaign of remarkable consistency for the third successive season, but narrow defeats in the two finals ensured it was ultimately a year of what might have been.

Just two league defeats meant that Daryl Powell's side lost just five matches in the Championship between 2010 and 2012.

But they fell short on the biggest stages in 2012, losing gripping Northern Rail Cup and Grand Finals to Halifax and Sheffield respectively. Rovers will feel they were capable of winning both, but had to settle for another League Leaders Shield on the silverware front.

Still, there was much to admire about the club and its squad yet again in 2012, not least a stirring Challenge Cup run that saw them beat Super League rivals Castleford Tigers on live television, before pushing Wigan all the way in the following round.

At the hub of everything good was again scrum-half Liam Finn, named Championship Player of the Year for the second time in three seasons, having also won the Championship One award in 2009. He was one of four Rovers in the All Stars team, with free-scoring halfback partner Andy Kain and models of consistency Sam Smeaton and Matty Dale joining him.

Elsewhere prop Anthony England emerged as a real force, a timely boost given Stuart Dickens' retirement at the end of the campaign, and Ian Hardman and Tom Saxton again terrorised opposition defences.

With extensive stadium developments taking place and the club continuing to produce promising youngsters at an impressive rate the future continued to look bright for Featherstone – though they were hoping for more success on the main stages in 2013.

LEIGH CENTURIONS' season of overachievement amid adversity saw Paul Rowley deservedly crowned Coach of the Year, before their tiny squad finally caught up with them in the play-offs.

Rowley took over in the New Year with the club's very existence under threat, and after the Centurions had publicly pursued a couple of overseas coaches. But Rowley's eventual appointment paid immediate dividends, as he pulled together a small squad at the last minute and started chalking up impressive results.

Rowley rarely had many more than 17 or 18 players available on a week-to-week basis, often including a handful of dual-registration signings. But they quickly started playing as a team, and their second placed league finish was fully deserved.

Hopes of an unlikely Grand Final appearance were dashed, however, by consecutive play-off defeats to Featherstone and then Sheffield, the second a genuine thriller as the patched up Centurions mounted a late comeback that fell just short.

Rowley had a host of outstanding contributors throughout the year, not least powerful centres Stuart Littler and Matt Gardner, the latter making the All Stars team. Gardner was joined by excellent young back-rowers Craig Briscoe and Sam Hopkins, while the experienced Bob Beswick was nominated for the Player of the Year award after another superb year.

Liam Finn was at the heart of the Featherstone Rovers side that won the League Leaders Shield

The back three of Gregg McNally, Jon Pownall and Steve Maden also earned constant praise from Rowley throughout the year. Martyn Ridyard was a key figure at stand-off and Ryan Brierley bagged 25 tries.

The Centurions finished the year on a much more stable footing, with Rowley's squad for 2013 in place months ahead of the turbulent previous close-season campaign.

A memorable Northern Rail Cup triumph in Blackpool was the obvious high for **HALIFAX** in a season of progress under new coach Karl Harrison. The former Great Britain prop returned to the club where he was a popular front-rower after a successful coaching spell with rivals Batley.

Harrison was left disappointed by the way his new side finished the 2012 campaign – a forgettable, thumping home defeat to Sheffield in the play-offs. But finishing third and lifting a first NRC can only be construed as an overall success, on which Harrison would look to build in coming seasons.

By the time Fax had edged past Keighley before being dumped by the Eagles in the play-offs, they looked a tired side, and for hooker Sean Penkywicz it was a frustrating end to an outstanding spell with the club. Penkywicz left for hometown club Leigh Centurions, but not before winning the man-of-the-match award in the NRC final, earning a nomination for Championship Player of the Year and earning a place in the competition's All Stars team.

Prop Sam Barlow also made the mythical 13, after a superb season in which he caused opposition defences all kinds of problems. Fellow front-rower Luke Ambler plus second rows Dane Manning and Adam Robinson were also among Fax's best as Harrison built a pack to match any team in the division.

Halfbacks Paul Handforth and Anthony Thackeray sparkled at times, with Thackeray finishing as the top try scorer with 19, edging out the likes of the improving Ryan Fieldhouse, Paul White and Rob Worrincy.

SHEFFIELD EAGLES produced a remarkable finish to the season to lift the Championship title after a thrilling Grand Final win over Featherstone.

The Eagles – who off the field continued their extensive youth development work - reached Warrington from fourth position for the second consecutive season. And after falling well short in the 2011 Grand Final, they stunned heavy pre-match favourites Featherstone at the second time of asking, giving coach Mark Aston another major high to go alongside his Lance Todd Trophy, Challenge Cup-winning success of 1998.

Aston and his squad had been left hugely disappointed by being largely overlooked at the Championship awards night just days before the Grand Final – with fullback Quentin Laulu-Togagae the only man recognised, through his selection in the All Stars team. But they more than made up for that the following Sunday in Warrington, with Laulu-Togagae scoring one of the tries of the season to extend his own new club record of 35 in a season.

Back-rower Michael Knowles capped a season of stunning consistency with the man-of-the-match award against Featherstone, and there were also big performances from the ever-reliable front row of Jack Howieson, Andrew Henderson and Mitchell Stringer.

Stand-off Simon Brown's kicking game came into its own during the play-off run, while winger Scott Turner emerged as a real talent on the left wing.

With Menzie Yere and Misi Taulapapa typically dangerous throughout the campaign, Sheffield always had the quality to succeed – and in 2012 timed their end-of-season run to perfection.

BATLEY BULLDOGS secured a major coup by landing former England coach John Kear for 2012, but a largely promising campaign stuttered to a halt in the closing stages.

Kear described the play-off defeat at Sheffield as his side's worst display of the season, which was a significant shame for a side that will have felt it could have emulated the Eagles' run to the Grand Final on their day. Kear did uncover the find of the season in the Championship, with front-rower Alex Walmsley making a massive impact after switching from Dewsbury Celtic. Walmsley was deservedly named the competition's Young Player of the Year, made the All Stars team and earned a four-year contract with Super League giants St Helens.

There were plenty of key contributors for the Bulldogs elsewhere. Winger Alex Brown was another to make the All Stars team and secure a top-flight contract when he switched to Hull KR in October, while Gareth Potts was also selected after an outstanding first season at the club in which he scored 19 tries.

In halfbacks Ben Black and Gareth Moore, Batley had one of the best combinations in the competition, while Paul Mennell proved a revelation after being switched permanently to hooker.

The likes of Byron Smith, Mark Applegarth and Ash Lindsay were models of consistency, giving the Bulldogs a strong platform up front. But they fell just short on several occasions against the best clubs in the competition, and Kear was keen to amend that in coming seasons.

KEIGHLEY COUGARS made the play-offs in their first season back in the Championship, a significant achievement for player-coach Jason Demetriou in his final year at the club.

Demetriou left to take up a coaching role with Northern Pride in North Queensland at the end of the campaign, and was replaced by Paul March.

But he did so having left a legacy at Cougar Park, guiding the club to promotion in his first year at the helm before establishing Keighley back at the higher level. They also pushed Halifax all the way in the play-offs before succumbing to a 28-24 defeat in a desperate finale.

Demetriou enlisted the help of his former Wakefield teammates Michael Korkidas, Semi Tadulala and Sam Obst, with all of them making an impact at different stages. Obst finished as the club's top try scorer with 15, striking up a good halfback partnership with Welsh international Danny Jones.

Centre James Haythornthwaite was developing into one of the competition's best centres before being forced to leave due to work commitments, while Richie Barnett enjoyed a successful first season at the club out wide.

Barnett, Danny Lawton and Craig Moss all made double figures in the try-scoring stakes, while Jy-Mel Coleman produced some genuine moments of brilliance off the bench. In the pack, Andy Shickell, Oliver Pursglove and James Feather all performed on a week-to-week basis, leaving March a solid platform on which to build.

After a promising start that saw them win four of their opening six league games, **DEWSBURY RAMS'** season faltered through the summer and they missed out on the play-offs.

Their results, which included five straight defeats in the middle of the campaign, ultimately cost long-serving coach Warren Jowitt his job. He was replaced by former Great Britain prop Paul Broadbent for the final three games of the season, but despite overseeing an upturn in performances, he missed out on the permanent job to Australian Glenn Morrison.

Jowitt's final season in charge had started with much promise, with the Rams second after beating York and Swinton early on. They pushed both Featherstone and Batley close before defeating Hunslet and Keighley, and were third in mid-May before their slump began. Their fading hopes of a play-off place were ended in Jowitt's final match in charge, a 34-6 loss at top six rivals the Cougars. The early-season retirement of Nick Fozzard – their major winter recruit – due to shoulder surgery certainly didn't help,

Top try scorer and the club's outstanding back was fullback James Craven, who continued his progression after stepping up from the amateur game. Steve Crossley was a huge presence up front, earning a move to Featherstone, while Brad Singleton was a welcome arrival from Leeds and Josh Tonks continued his progression in the back row.

Scott Spaven, Rob Spicer and Ben Jones were also mainstays of the side and all penned deals to remain under new coach Morrison.

SWINTON LIONS made solid progress on their return to the Championship, avoiding what would have been the relegation places – there were no sides relegated with four Championship One sides promoted - after winning five games and drawing one.

Northern Rail Cup defeats to York, Hunslet and Championship One side Barrow had hinted at a season of struggle, and they were then comfortably dispatched by Sheffield in the opening game of the league campaign. But a stirring home win over Batley Bulldogs on April Fools' Day kick-started their year, and they were generally much more competitive after that, late thrashings at Batley and Featherstone apart.

High points included back-to-back wins over York and Hunslet in May that briefly raised hopes of an unlikely play-off charge. That never materialised, but there was still much to be positive about during a season spent playing at Leigh Sports Village as the club continued to try and push through a move to a new stadium in Agecroft.

Top try scorer was stand-off or centre Martin Ainscough, while Tom Armstrong, Gavin Dodd and Adam Higson also reached double figures. Chaz I'Anson was an influential figure in any one of three positions; the Hawkyard brothers Richie and Darren mainstays of Steve McCormack's side, and Mike Morrison a big performer at prop.

The Lions finished the year by securing a new link-up with Super League Grand Finalists Warrington that they hoped would further aid their development in coming seasons.

Championship Season

HUNSLET HAWKS were most observers' favourites to finish bottom of the Championship, so a ninth-placed finish on the smallest budget in the competition was something of a success for coach Barry Eaton.

The former Keighley boss made no secret of the fact that he was operating on a fraction of the spending of his rivals, and that 2012 was a building year ahead of future seasons. Eaton managed to assemble a squad that made the quarter-finals of the Northern Rail Cup after three group wins out of four, and they also pushed Batley close in the fourth round of the Challenge Cup.

They were competitive most weeks in the league as well, although they will want to forget heavy whitewashes at Batley and Featherstone. The fact that Eaton had to contend with the competition's most crippling injury list – notably to their playmakers – hardly helped their cause.

The two wins over York proved their highlights, with Dennis Tuffour scoring twice in a 20-6 home win in April, and Liam Welham twice in a final day 26-28 win at the Knights.

Top try scorer was promising young centre Josh Nathaniel with seven, while the evergreen David March notched six in another year of endeavour at loose forward. Others to come out of the season with real credit included prop Andy Yates, hooker Luke Haigh and winger Lee Brickwood, and a new partnership with Leeds Rhinos saw the club finish the year with high hopes for the future.

YORK CITY KNIGHTS finished bottom of the Championship after chalking up just one win all season, a June home triumph over Swinton Lions.

It proved a difficult first season in charge for player-coach Chris Thorman, who left the club at the end of the year to take up an assistant's position at Huddersfield Giants. Thorman had to battle against injuries throughout the campaign, but was still left frustrated by his side's inability to turn winning positions into victories on a number of occasions.

The year had started promisingly with three straight Northern Rail Cup wins, but the fact they then blew a quarter-final place by losing heavily at Sheffield was probably a sign of things to come. The two defeats to Hunslet will have been particularly hard to take given that the Knights were favourites for those matches, but at least two Matt Garside tries helped them to that win over Swinton.

Garside's displays earned him a move to champions Sheffield Eagles, while assistant coach James Ford and his winger George Elliott both made double figures in the try stakes. Jack Lee rarely let his efforts waver up front, and the same could be said for Adam Sullivan, while Thorman himself consistently tried his all to turn matters around.

Thorman was replaced as coach by the experienced Gary Thornton once his move to Huddersfield was confirmed, and the Knights also announced a link-up with Hull FC in an attempt to progress up the Championship table.

CHAMPIONSHIP AWARDS

Liam Finn

PLAYER OF THE YEAR
Liam Finn
(Featherstone Rovers)

YOUNG PLAYER OF THE YEAR
Alex Walmsley
(Batley Bulldogs)

COACH OF THE YEAR
Paul Rowley
(Leigh Centurions)

CLUB OF THE YEAR
Featherstone Rovers

RUGBY LEAGUE WORLD TEAM OF THE YEAR
1 Quentin Laulu-Togagae (Sheffield Eagles)
2 Gareth Potts (Batley Bulldogs)
3 Stuart Littler (Leigh Centurions)
4 Sam Smeaton (Featherstone Rovers)
5 Tom Saxton (Featherstone Rovers)
6 Andy Kain (Featherstone Rovers)
7 Liam Finn (Featherstone Rovers)
8 Alex Walmsley (Batley Bulldogs)
9 Bob Beswick (Leigh Centurions)
10 Sam Barlow (Halifax)
11 Dane Manning (Halifax)
12 Michael Knowles (Sheffield Eagles)
13 Sam Hopkins (Leigh Centurions)

CHAMPIONSHIP ONE SEASON
Bonny Donny

DONCASTER recorded the most successful season in the club's history by finishing in pole position in Championship One and then winning the Grand Final against Barrow at Warrington.

The Dons had never topped a competition before, and although there was some unnecessary confusion over whether that constituted them being champions, they dispelled any doubt with an accomplished performance at the Halliwell Jones Stadium four weeks later.

The club cleaned up at the Championship awards dinner, with Tony Miller named Coach of the Year and marquee signing Paul Cooke the Player of the Year. Cooke also gained recognition for his work in the local community and the Dons were named Championship One Club of the Year.

Centre Lee Waterman, who finished the campaign at fullback after an injury to Mick Butterfield, broke the tries-in-a-season record with 36, earning him a place in the All Stars team alongside Cooke and winger Stewart Sanderson.

And there were plenty of heroes elsewhere for Miller, with prop Mark Castle outstanding up front alongside the likes of Craig Robinson and Mike Emmett. Kyle Kesik was a key figure whether at stand-off or hooker, Craig Fawcett finished with 18 tries and a man-of-the-match display in the Grand Final, and Tom Hodson was prolific out wide.

A link-up with Wakefield allowed youngsters Danny Cowling, Russ Spiers and Lucas Walshaw to play their part late in the season, ensuring 2012 was a year that Doncaster supporters will not forget.

Doncaster celebrate finishing top of Championship One after a big win at London Skolars

Championship One Season

BARROW RAIDERS had looked set to top Championship One for much of the second half of the season, until late defeats at Workington and Rochdale derailed their bid.

They then suffered further disappointment when they were edged out by Doncaster in a gripping Grand Final played in difficult conditions.

But despite that, the 2012 campaign was undoubtedly a resounding success for the Raiders and their rookie coach Darren Holt.

The club's very existence had come under serious threat at the end of 2011, and Holt effectively started his first coaching position with a clean slate and no players. But he built a squad almost completely of local players, and for much of the year the Raiders looked the strongest side in the competition, becoming the first club to earn promotion to the new-look Championship with a televised win over Whitehaven in July.

Stand-out throughout the year was captain Liam Harrison, who thrived in his new position of second row after being switched from the centres by Holt, earning a Player of the Year nomination and an All Stars place.

Dan Toal also clinched a place in that team after a terrific first year in the professional game at loose forward, along with Liam Campbell, who finished as top try scorer with 21. He formed an excellent halfback partnership with Scott Kaighan, ensuring that Holt's final season as a player saw him restricted to just ten appearances.

Fourth All Star Andy Ballard was a constant source of danger from fullback, Andy Bracek a big presence up front and James Dandy a willing worker at hooker. But arguably the most impressive aspect of their season was the way that amateurs Toal, Lee Haney and Andrew Dawson stepped up to the professional game.

WORKINGTON TOWN achieved their ultimate aim of promotion to the Championship, but a tough run of injuries late in the year scuppered their title hopes.

Joint coaches Martin Oglanby and Gary Charlton were again rightly praised for their continuing work at the West Cumbrian club, as they secured a handful of high-profile signings to work within the team they had been building for three years.

Peter Lupton, Mark Calderwood and especially Jamie Thackray all played their parts in the club's success, with the front-rower named in the All Stars team alongside hooker Graeme Mattinson and centre Jason Mossop.

Winger Elliott Miller won the Young Player of the Year prize after running in 26 tries – 15 more than his nearest Town rivals Thackray and ever-consistent Australian Jarrad Stack. Others worthy of mention for their efforts include fullback Brett Carter, utility Karl Olstrum and halfback Carl Forber.

Arguably the biggest success story of the season was back-rower Brett Phillips, who ended the year in the full Scotland squad after an outstanding first full campaign in the professional game.

After a 50-10 win over South Wales in July, Town were briefly top of the table entering the closing stages of the season. But with injuries taking their toll, three defeats in the space of four games, including a shock loss at previously winless Gateshead, saw them slip down to third, and their season finished with a 20-0 defeat at eventual champions Doncaster in the play-offs.

WHITEHAVEN became the fourth and final club to secure a promotion place, but Australian coach Don Gailer had still lost his job by the end of the year after an up-and-down season at the Recreation Ground.

Gailer had arrived to replace club legend David Seeds at the club and, after a stuttering start, began to get results from his side midway through the season. But the controversial policy of allowing half of the squad to train in Lancashire early in the week eventually caught up with Haven, with divisions in their ranks becoming a public issue around the time of Gailer's departure.

Still, there were highlights as well, although Whitehaven only beat a top-three side once, producing arguably their best performances of the season to see off Doncaster 25-18 in August.

Winger Craig Calvert continued his prolific career, scoring 27 tries to take his place in the All Stars team. The next closest was mid-year capture Jamie Rooney with ten, and he and Carl Rudd played key roles in getting Haven over the promotion finishing line late in the campaign. Front-rowers Paul Cullnean and Dave Houghton were Haven's best forwards, with Richard Varkulis and Lee Doran having their moments at different stages of the season as well.

Papua New Guinean centre Jessie Joe Parker also showed flashes of brilliance, but Haven ended the year hoping for more stability after appointing experienced coach Dave Woods as the man to replace Gailer for 2013.

A run of five league defeats in six games virtually ended **ROCHDALE HORNETS'** promotion hopes in coach John Stankevitch's final season in charge of the club.

Stankevitch moved to an off-field role at Spotland at the end of the campaign, having seen injuries ruin his hopes of leading the club into the Championship after two previous years of progression.

Halfbacks Paul Crook and Steve Roper were among those to spend extended spells on the sidelines, while Hornets were hardly helped by their best forward Gary Middlehurst picking up an early six-match ban after being sent off at North Wales Crusaders.

Though they briefly rallied with three straight wins in June and July, any chance of making the top four came to a halt when they lost 31-12 at home to nearest challengers Whitehaven. The same opponents comprehensively ended any play-off hopes they might have had as well, and at the end of the year Hornets announced an extensive link-up with St Helens that saw Ian Talbot take over as head coach.

Fullback turned winger Jonny Leather finished as top try scorer with 16, with Dale Bloomfield and popular local player Wayne English also making double figures.

Middlehurst was among the most destructive runners in the competition when he was on the field, and Stankevitch unveiled another real find from the amateur game in giant prop Phil Braddish.

The 2012 season also saw the introduction of a host of young players from a newly established under-23s squad but, overall, it was largely a campaign to forget for Rochdale supporters.

OLDHAM were another club to see their promotion hopes hit by injury, with coach Tony Benson battling against a weekly list that left the Roughyeds off the top-four pace almost from the off. Benson eventually paid for a run of nine games without a win with his job, and after his assistant Martin Roden took charge as a caretaker, the club began a new era with the appointment of former Salford and Bradford centre Scott Naylor at the end of the year.

Roden almost oversaw a stunning play-off win at Workington before then, only for a late Town surge to ensure a disappointing campaign ended on a losing note at Derwent Park.

There were undoubted bright spots though, particularly the performances of fullback Miles Greenwood, Oldham's stand-out player by some distance. The former Halifax player scored 20 tries in all competitions to earn his own move back into the Championship with Batley, and some felt he was unlucky to miss out on All Stars selection.

Forward Alex Thompson was another to impress, along with hooker John Clough, young scrum-half Jamie Dallimore and hooker Danny Whitmore. Dallimore and Whitmore were another two examples of the club's admirable development work on a shoestring budget.

With a host of 2012 players joining Benson at his new club in Oxford for 2013, Oldham underwent significant changes in personnel in Naylor's first weeks in charge.

LONDON SKOLARS came within a whisker of making the play-offs for the first time in another season of progress under coach Joe Mbu.

A stirring home win over Whitehaven in front of the television cameras on the club's now traditional Friday Night Lights game in August gave them a late chance of making the top six. But a final match win against champions Doncaster proved beyond them – though there was still much to admire in their 2013 campaign.

Forward Lamont Bryan made the Championship One All Stars team after a host of strong performances, whether playing in the front or back row. Australian Brad Hopkins finished as top try scorer after an excellent year, while winger Ade Adebisi and scrum-half Dylan Skee also reached double figures.

Skee broke the club's points-in-a-season record with 226 in total, and his combination with halfback partner Andy McLean was a major reason for the club winning four games from five late in the season. Only a sluggish start – one win from their opening eight games – prevented them from making a stronger play-off push.

Neil Thorman was something of a revelation after moving from the backs to hooker, while Dave Williams and Rob and Matt Thomas were also key figures.

With Mbu remaining in charge and the club strengthening its links with London Broncos, Skolars ended the year optimistic about future promotion chances.

NORTH WALES CRUSADERS were a welcome addition to Championship One after they rose from the ashes of the Crusaders club that lost its Super League place.

North Wales Crusaders' Jono Smith in action against South Wales Scorpions, during the first professional Welsh derby since 1910

Launched towards the very end of 2011, they were well behind the rest in terms of recruitment, but appointed the perfect coach in Clive Griffiths to ensure their competitiveness. The vastly experienced and popular Griffiths quickly set about signing a group of players that were a credit to the fledgling outfit throughout the year,

Among those was rookie winger Rob Massam, who ending his first season in the professional game with a full Welsh cap against France in Lens. Massam was excellent throughout and topped the try-scoring list with 11, just ahead of fellow rookie successes Leon Brennan and Andrew Moulsdale.

Danny Hulme caught the eye at fullback when injury didn't disrupt his season, while loose forward Jono Smith quickly became a cult hero with an impressive Crusaders support that roared their backing wherever the team played. Tommy Johnson, Jamie Durbin and Jonny Walker were among others that deserve mention for their efforts over a credible debut year.

Definite highlights included a league double over Oldham and an historic Easter Monday triumph over South Wales Scorpions in front of 1,204 fans.

With Griffiths remaining at the helm and with the benefit of a full close season, plus signings including former Great Britain winger Stuart Reardon, the club finished 2012 looking well placed to progress.

The appointment of Dave Clark as coach, a link with Wigan and high-profile signings including Jamie Rooney meant that **SOUTH WALES SCORPIONS** started the year with high hopes of a promotion push.

But that never came close to materialising, and with Rooney departing after just seven games for the Scorpions, and injuries disrupting their campaign, they finished a disappointing ninth having won just four league games. Two of those came back-to-back in May, against Rochdale and Oldham, during what was undoubtedly the side's best spell of the season.

But those wins apart, the Scorpions struggled badly for consistency, and weren't helped by a constant changing of the side that led to a larger playing roster than anyone else in the professional game – Clark used a staggering 69 players in the end.

There were some mainstays of the side among those, with Scorpions stalwarts Ashley Bateman, Steve Parry and Dalton Grant among them. New recruit Nathan Mossop and the returning David James also deserve mention for their efforts during what was generally a difficult campaign.

Amongst those 69 players used were a whole host of local players, who Clark hoped would grow in coming years after their 2012 experiences. With other South Wales youngsters joining the Wigan youth set-up as part of the partnership, the validity of having a professional club in the Valleys wasn't questioned, despite a first-team campaign that fell below expectations.

GATESHEAD THUNDER finished 2012 at the bottom of the pile again – but a major high late in their season ensured it wasn't all doom and gloom in the north-east.

That high came by ending a run of 64 games without a win against professional opposition when they stunned high-flying Workington Town on a midweek night in August. Skipper Jason Payne scored two tries in a memorable 24-22 triumph that also gave coach Kevin Neighbour his first win in Championship One in his second season in charge.

Neighbour ended the year hoping his side could build on that in a new-look Championship One that would see Thunder among the most experienced clubs in the league.

Payne was a constant credit to the club with his performances through the season, while Gateshead's top try scorer came in the unlikely form of prop Brett Waller. His displays earned a winter move to Championship side Doncaster, but Neighbour retained much of the rest of his squad and added some impressive new recruits at the end of the year.

Joe Brown, Paul Stamp and Ryan McBride were mainstays of the 2012 side, and though there was a handful of thrashings, there were also plenty of games in which Thunder competed fully.

CHAMPIONSHIP ONE AWARDS

Paul Cooke

PLAYER OF THE YEAR
Paul Cooke
(Doncaster)

YOUNG PLAYER OF THE YEAR
Elliott Miller
(Workington Town)

COACH OF THE YEAR
Tony Miller
(Doncaster)

CLUB OF THE YEAR
Doncaster

RUGBY LEAGUE WORLD TEAM OF THE YEAR
1 Andy Ballard (Barrow Raiders)
2 Elliott Miller (Workington Town)
3 Lee Waterman (Doncaster)
4 Jason Mossop (Workington Town)
5 Stewart Sanderson (Doncaster)
6 Paul Cooke (Doncaster)
7 Liam Campbell (Barrow Raiders)
8 Mark Castle (Doncaster)
9 Graeme Mattinson (Workington Town)
10 Jamie Thackray (Workington Town)
11 Liam Harrison (Barrow Raiders)
12 Brett Phillips (Workington Town)
13 Lamont Bryan (London Skolars)

CHAMPIONSHIPS - REFEREE OF THE YEAR
George Stokes

COMMUNITY PROGRAMME OF THE YEAR
Workington Town

NORTHERN RAIL
CUP FINAL
Fax of Life

Dane Manning
upends Andy Kain

RAIL STRIKE!
Halifax claim Northern Rail Cup
...as Powell slams Harrison

Steve Tyrer's late try settled a thrilling, bruising and controversial Northern Rail Cup final as Halifax edged out pre-match favourites Featherstone.

In a game likened to "State of Origin for the Championship" by the Premier Sports commentary team, Fax ripped into their opponents from the off, unsettling them from their usual game.

There had been plenty of pre-match controversy between coached Karl Harrison and Daryl Powell over allegations that Rovers over-used "wrestling" tactics, and the pair crossed swords verbally at the end as well. Powell claimed that Harrison's words had influenced the performance of the officials during the final, but what cannot be disputed is that Fax outplayed their opponents in an excellent advert for the competition.

NORTHERN RAIL CUP FINAL

Sunday 29th July 2012

FEATHERSTONE ROVERS 12 HALIFAX 21

ROVERS: 1 Ian Hardman; 2 Jack Briscoe; 3 Sam Smeaton; 4 Greg Worthington; 5 Tom Saxton; 6 Andy Kain; 7 Liam Finn; 8 Anthony England; 9 Ben Kaye; 10 Stuart Dickens; 11 Jon Grayshon; 12 Tim Spears; 13 Matty Dale. Subs (all used): 14 James Lockwood; 15 Dominic Maloney; 16 Michael Haley; 17 Andrew Bostock.
Tries: Finn (26), Smeaton (43); **Goals:** Finn 2/3.
HALIFAX: 1 Ryan Fieldhouse; 2 Rob Worrincy; 3 Lee Paterson; 4 Steve Tyrer; 5 Wayne Reittie; 6 Paul Handforth; 7 Anthony Thackeray; 8 Jim Gannon; 9 Craig Ashall; 10 Sean Hesketh; 11 Dane Manning; 12 Luke Ambler; 13 Adam Robinson. Subs (all used): 14 Anthony Bowman; 15 Makali Aizue; 16 Sam Barlow; 17 Sean Penkywicz.
Tries: Thackeray (4), S Barlow (36), Tyrer (78); **Goals:** Tyrer 4/5;
Field goal: Ashall (72).
Rugby Leaguer & League Express Men of the Match:
Rovers: Anthony England; *Halifax:* Sean Penkywicz.
Penalty count: 5-10; **Half-time:** 6-12; **Referee:** Jamie Leahy;
Attendance: 6,691 *(at Bloomfield Road, Blackpool).*

Halifax were ahead from the moment halfback Anthony Thackeray crossed in the fourth minute, and although Featherstone hit back through Liam Finn, Sam Barlow's strong effort made it 12-6 at the break.

Again Featherstone responded, with Sam Smeaton touching down to level the scores, before a Tyrer penalty and improvised Craig Ashall field goal edged Fax back in front.

They could then celebrate a first NRC title – and Harrison's third with three different clubs – when Tyrer was first to a Thackeray kick in the dying stages.

CHAMPIONSHIP PLAY-OFFS
Golden Eagles

Keighley Cougars came desperately close to stunning Halifax in the opening Championship play-off in Jason Demetriou's last game in charge.

In a see-saw game, James Feather's 76th-minute try put the Cougars level at 24-24 and set up a grandstand finale. But Fax, who had tries to forwards Makali Aizue, Jim Gannon and Sam Barlow, hit back with a last-gasp Lee Paterson score to win 28-24 and progress to the second weekend.

Sheffield Eagles started their march to the Grand Final with an accomplished 42-12 win over fancied Batley. Bulldogs coach John Kear would label his side's display as their worst of the season after they struggled to contain their opponents from the off. Winger Scott Turner helped himself to a hat-trick of tries and Misi Taulapapa and Joe Hirst bagged doubles, while Batley had two players sin-binned on an afternoon to forget for them.

That set up a televised trip to Halifax, and Sheffield's march gained further momentum with a stunning and unexpectedly one-sided 54-12 win at the Shay. Mark Aston's side dominated the game from the off and led 22-0 at the break,

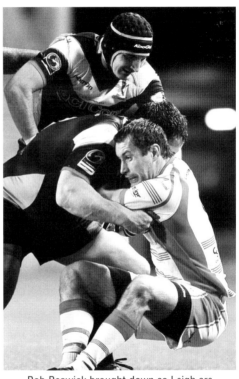

Bob Beswick brought down as Leigh are eliminated by Sheffield

with record try scorer Quentin Laulu-Togagae helping himself to another double. Winger Turner and centre Menzie Yere followed suite after the restart, as Fax looked a tired team despite consolation efforts from Paul Handforth, Rob Worrincy and Ryan Fieldhouse.

Elsewhere that weekend, Featherstone were booking a third straight Grand Final appearance by disposing of Leigh 32-14 in a match that was closer than the scoreline suggested. The Centurions led 14-6 at the interval, with Jon Pownall's brace and Craig Briscoe's early effort gaining control for them.

But with a significant swing in the penalty count taking place in the second half, Dominic Maloney's rare double and eight goals from the boot of Liam Finn saw Rovers home.

Championship Play-offs

That meant the Centurions had to face a home clash with Sheffield for the second consecutive year – and again they fell short, losing 22-32 in an outstanding spectacle. With Turner and Taulapapa among the tries again, the Eagles led for most of the game and were 20-4 up at the halfway point. But Leigh roared back with tries to Andy Thornley, Ryan Brierley and Dean McGilvray, and Sheffield needed a last-minute effort from Yere to assure their place in the Grand Final.

Championship Grand Final

Sheffield Eagles enjoyed their biggest success since the 1998 Challenge Cup final by lifting the Championship Grand Final in an upset win over Featherstone. Coach Mark Aston – the Lance Todd Trophy winner 14 years before – got one over on his old Eagles teammate Daryl Powell and avenged their heavy 2011 defeat in the same match.

Again Sheffield had to come from fourth place to reach the Grand Final, after wins against Batley, Halifax and Leigh. And this time Aston's side were much better prepared for the showcase clash, holding their own in a superb match despite the difficult conditions.

THE CO-OPERATIVE CHAMPIONSHIP GRAND FINAL

Sunday 30th September 2012

FEATHERSTONE ROVERS 16 SHEFFIELD EAGLES 20

ROVERS: 1 Ian Hardman; 2 Tangi Ropati; 3 Nathan Chappell; 4 Greg Worthington; 5 Tom Saxton; 6 Andy Kain; 7 Liam Finn; 8 Anthony England; 9 Ben Kaye; 10 James Lockwood; 11 Matty Dale; 12 Tim Spears; 13 Kyle Briggs. Subs (all used): 14 Dominic Maloney; 15 Stuart Dickens; 16 Andrew Bostock; 17 Jon Hepworth.
Tries: Hardman (17), Hepworth (51); **Goals:** Finn 4/4.
On report: Maloney (57) - alleged use of the elbow on Turner.
EAGLES: 1 Quentin Laulu-Togagae; 2 Misi Taulapapa; 3 Duane Straugheir; 4 Menzie Yere; 5 Scott Turner; 6 Simon Brown; 7 Dominic Brambani; 8 Jack Howieson; 9 Andrew Henderson; 10 Mitchell Stringer; 11 Michael Knowles; 12 Sam Scott; 13 Alex Szostak. Subs (all used): 14 James Davey; 15 Peter Green; 16 Dane McDonald; 17 Liam Higgins.
Tries: Turner (9), Laulu-Togagae (32), McDonald (46), Taulapapa (57); **Goals:** Brown 2/5.
Rugby Leaguer & League Express Men of the Match:
Rovers: Ian Hardman; *Eagles:* Michael Knowles.
Penalty count: 4-6; **Half-time:** 8-10; **Referee:** Tim Roby; **Attendance:** 6,409 *(at Halliwell Jones Stadium, Warrington).*

"We've come a very long way in a short space of time," Aston said. "I'm living the dream and we've worked very hard to get some recognition.

"The boys were outstanding, and they've set a new benchmark now for next year. I can't speak highly enough of the staff or directors – and the players today were immense."

Aston had a man-of-the-match performer in hard-working back-rower Michael Knowles, and a genuine try-of-the-season contender with Quentin Laulu-Togagae's stunning first-half team effort.

It meant a second defeat in finals for Featherstone after their Northern Rail Cup loss to Halifax.

"We're massively disappointed to have been in two finals this year and not played well enough," Powell said. "But the boys have worked so hard – we have a few guys leaving, and wanted to put on a big performance for them but it wasn't to be.

"We've lost a couple of real big games by nothing really. But we haven't played well enough, and couldn't play our natural game in the conditions. We should have been better than we were but there's no excuses from me."

Sheffield opened the scoring when left winger Scott Turner continued his excellent finish to the season with a try out wide, before Featherstone hit back through fullback Ian Hardman.

Then came the moment of magic from the Eagles, as a stunning move from off their own line ended with Laulu-Togagae finishing with panache for his 35th try of a record-breaking season.

That gave Sheffield a 10-8 interval lead, and they extended it when Dane McDonald touched down six minutes after the restart.

Back came Featherstone as the lead changed four hands in total, when Jon Hepworth stepped his way over from close range.

But the decisive try went the way of the Eagles and their Samoan centre Misi Taulapapa, as Aston's side held on in a desperate but try-less closing quarter to seal their return to the Rugby League spotlight.

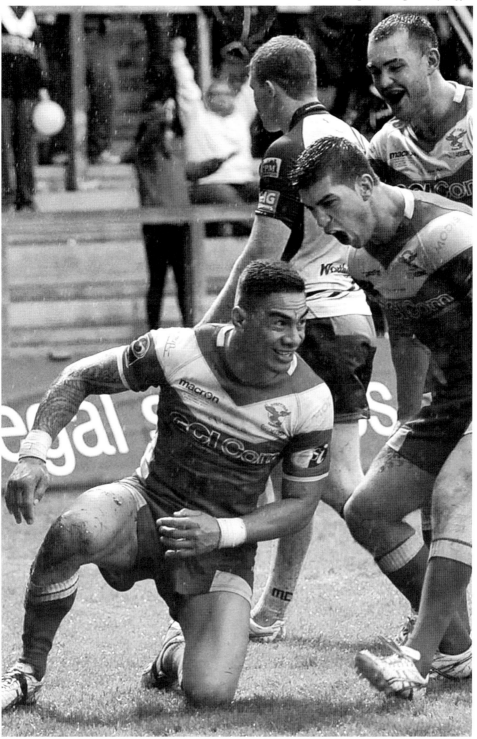

Duane Straugheir and Dane McDonald rush to congratulate Misi Taulapapa on scoring in the Championship Grand Final

CHAMPIONSHIP ONE PLAY-OFFS
South Yorkshire pride

West Cumbrian rivals Workington Town and Whitehaven saw off the respective challenges of Oldham and Rochdale Hornets on the opening weekend of the Championship One play-offs.

Town had to come from behind against the Roughyeds in a thrilling clash at Derwent Park. Oldham, with caretaker coach Martin Roden in charge, led for most of the game and Paul Smith's hat-trick try in the 70th minute looked certain to book their passage through. But Workington scored twice in the final six minutes to snatch victory and keep their Grand Final hopes alive.

There were no such problems up the road for Whitehaven, who swept past Rochdale 40-12 at the Recreation Ground. Two tries from Jessie Joe Parker and one each from Carl Rudd and ex-Hornet Lee Doran made it 20-0 at half-time. And further scores to Max Wiper, Lewis Palfrey, Paul Cullnean and Jamie Rooney ensured there would be no shock from a depleted Rochdale side.

Those wins set up a West Cumbrian derby on the second weekend, and Workington proved too strong in running out 26-2 winners. The first try didn't arrive until John Patrick's effort in the 33rd minute during a tight first half. But Town powered home after the restart, with Mark Calderwood and Marc Shackley scoring and Carl Forber kicking seven goals from as many attempts.

That meant Workington faced a final eliminator against Doncaster, after the league leaders were pipped 22-20 at home to Barrow Raiders in the Qualifying Semi-final. Kyle Kesik had given Tony Miller's side a dream start, but two tries in ten minutes from Aaron Low put Barrow in front. They looked in control when Chris Larkin and James Dandy crossed either side of the break, but Lucas Walshaw and Stewart Sanderson efforts set up a nervous finale for the Cumbrians.

Doncaster took the second chance they had earned by finishing top when a masterful defensive display saw them beat Workington 20-0 the following weekend. Chris Spurr, Stewart Sanderson, Craig Fawcett and Nathan Powley all crossed as the Dons won, despite the absence of injured talisman Paul Cooke. Town also had to deal with the 43rd minute dismissal of loose forward Chris Annakin as their season drew to a close.

Championship One Grand Final

Doncaster ended any ambiguity over who would be crowned Championship One champions by backing up their top-place finish with a gritty Grand Final triumph.

The Dons initially thought they had been crowned champions by topping the league, but after being told that was not the case, Tony Miller's side took matters into their own hands.

Lee Waterman dives over for a Doncaster try during the Championship One Grand Final

Despite missing Championship One Player of the Year Paul Cooke after he sustained a knee injury in the clash with Barrow two weeks earlier, Doncaster gained revenge for that loss and lifted the title on their own terms.

They had a man-of-the-match performance from scrum-half Craig Fawcett, who turned the game with three big plays in the second half. First he helped stop a certain James Nixon try with a last-gasp tackle, then he broke clear to send Lee Waterman over, before scoring himself in the 57th minute.

With Stewart Sanderson having crossed in the first half, the Dons looked in control in a match played in wet conditions. But Aaron Low's 77th-minute effort set up a nervous finale, in which the outstanding Doncaster defence held firm to secure the club's biggest day in the sun, metaphorically, as it was a wet afternoon in Warrington.

"It was very tough and we didn't make it easy for ourselves," Miller said. "I think it shows what we're all about, the way we defended when on our own goal-line. When it looked like Barrow were going to score we managed to somehow keep them out. That speaks volumes about us and how we have played all year."

Barrow – who had an outstanding display from skipper Liam Harrison - had three second-half tries correctly disallowed, but coach Darren Holt had no complaints. "When I look at the game, I think they maybe just deserved to win by the margin they did on the basis of their defence alone," Holt said. "The boys will learn from this.

"They will have their heads down for half an hour, but once that half-hour is over, they will get their heads back up, and hopefully they will then understand what they have achieved this year."

THE CO-OPERATIVE CHAMPIONSHIP ONE GRAND FINAL

Sunday 30th September 2012

BARROW RAIDERS 13 DONCASTER 16

RAIDERS: 1 Andy Ballard; 2 Lee Haney; 3 Chris Larkin; 4 Aaron Low; 5 James Nixon; 6 Scott Kaighan; 7 Liam Campbell; 8 Jamie Butler; 9 James Dandy; 10 Ryan Duffy; 11 Liam Harrison; 12 James Gordon; 13 Daniel Toal. Subs (all used): 14 Liam Finch; 15 Martin Ostler; 16 Ruairi McGoff; 17 Andrew Dawson.
Tries: Larkin (4), Low (77); **Goals:** Ballard 2/3; **Field goal:** Kaighan (39).
DONCASTER: 1 Lee Waterman; 2 Tom Hodson; 3 Chris Spurr; 4 Danny Cowling; 5 Stewart Sanderson; 6 Kyle Kesik; 7 Craig Fawcett; 8 Mark Castle; 9 Mike Emmett; 10 Russ Spiers; 11 Lucas Walshaw; 12 Michael Kelly; 13 Carl Hughes. Subs (all used): 14 Nathan Powley; 15 Craig Robinson; 16 Grant Edwards; 17 Liam Cunningham.
Tries: Sanderson (11), Waterman (46), Fawcett (57); **Goals:** Hodson 2/3.
Rugby Leaguer & League Express Men of the Match:
Raiders: Liam Harrison; *Doncaster:* Craig Fawcett.
Penalty count: 4-5; **Half-time:** 7-4; **Referee:** Jamie Leahy.
(at Halliwell Jones Stadium, Warrington).

3
INTERNATIONAL YEAR

AUTUMN INTERNATIONALS
A dry run

England duly won the end-of-season triangular series, designed by the Rugby Football League to assist England coach Steve McNamara in his preparations for the 2013 World Cup after both Australia and New Zealand turned down requests to play them, with a 48-4 win over France in the final at Salford

McNamara named a 24-man squad on Tuesday 2nd October for England's high-altitude training camp to South Africa and the games against France and Wales. Twenty-four year old Warrington prop Chris Hill, in his first season in Super League after joining the Wolves from Leigh, earned a call-up along with five clubmates, Ryan Atkins, Adrian Morley, Ben Harrison, Richard Myler and Ben Westwood. There were seven from Leeds Rhinos - Carl Ablett, Rob Burrow, Ryan Hall, Zak Hardaker, Jamie Jones-Buchanan, Kevin Sinfield and Kallum Watkins. Canterbury Bulldogs prop James Graham and South Sydney Rabbitohs' Sam Burgess were both named although Graham was in doubt having been put on report in the NRL Grand Final for allegedly biting Billy Slater's ear in a fight. He copped a 12-match suspension and was replaced by South Sydney Rabbitohs prop Luke Burgess.

Sam Burgess (knee) and the Warrington duo Ryan Atkins (shoulder) and Ben Westwood (knee and groin) withdrew with injury the day after the Super League Grand Final. The three were replaced by Wigan Warriors forward Liam Farrell and Warrington pair Ben Harrison and Stefan Ratchford, who didn't play because of illness.

Melbourne Storm halfback Gareth Widdop, who played a pivotal role in his club's

---

2012 AUTUMN INTERNATIONALS - SQUADS

ENGLAND: Carl Ablett (Leeds Rhinos), Tom Briscoe (Hull FC), Luke Burgess (South Sydney Rabbitohs), Rob Burrow (Leeds Rhinos), Josh Charnley (Wigan Warriors), Rangi Chase (Castleford Tigers), Leroy Cudjoe (Huddersfield Giants), Gareth Ellis (Wests Tigers), Liam Farrell (Wigan Warriors), Ryan Hall (Leeds Rhinos), Zak Hardaker (Leeds Rhinos), Ben Harrison (Warrington Wolves), Chris Hill (Warrington Wolves), Gareth Hock (Wigan Warriors), Jamie Jones-Buchanan (Leeds Rhinos), Michael McIlorum (Wigan Warriors), Adrian Morley (Warrington Wolves), Lee Mossop (Wigan Warriors), Richard Myler (Warrington Wolves), Sean O'Loughlin (Wigan Warriors), Stefan Ratchford (Warrington Wolves), Kevin Sinfield (Leeds Rhinos) (C), Sam Tomkins (Wigan Warriors), Kallum Watkins (Leeds Rhinos).

Coach Steve McNamara had named a revised Elite Training Squad (ETS) on September 2nd. Ryan Bailey (Leeds Rhinos), Chris Bridge (Warrington Wolves), Ian Henderson (Catalan Dragons) and East Yorkshire pair Kris Welham (Hull Kingston Rovers) and Kirk Yeaman (Hull FC) were all dropped from the squad he had named in March. Jamie Peacock (Leeds Rhinos) announced his international retirement in June.

From the September ETS, Danny Brough (Huddersfield Giants), Garreth Carvell (Warrington Wolves), Ben Jones-Bishop (Leeds Rhinos) and Jonny Lomax (St Helens) didn't make the final 24-man squad. Eorl Crabtree (Huddersfield Giants), Ben Westwood (Warrington Wolves) and Jon Wilkin (St Helens) were ruled out injured, with Danny McGuire (Leeds Rhinos) and James Roby (St Helens) rested.

FRANCE: Jason Baitieri (Catalan Dragons), William Barthau (Catalan Dragons), Romaric Bemba (Carcassonne), Andrew Bentley (Pia), Kane Bentley (Pia), Thomas Bosc (Catalan Dragons), Julian Bousquet (Catalan Dragons), Damien Cardace (Catalan Dragons), Remi Casty (Catalan Dragons), Vincent Duport (Catalan Dragons), Olivier Elima (Bradford Bulls) (C), Jamal Fakir (Catalan Dragons), David Ferriol (Catalan Dragons), Tony Gigot (Avignon), Mathieu Griffi (Lezignan), David Guasch (St Esteve), Kevin Larroyer (Catalan Dragons), Antoni Maria (Catalan Dragons), Samy Masselot (Toulouse Olympique), Gregory Mounis (Catalan Dragons), Mathias Pala (Catalan Dragons), Eloi Pelissier (Catalan Dragons), Sebastien Planas (Toulouse Olympique), Sebastien Raguin (Catalan Dragons), Stanislas Robin (St Esteve), Teddy Sadaoui (Carcassonne), Michael Simon (Catalan Dragons), Clement Soubeyras (Pia), Cyril Stacul (Catalan Dragons), Yoan Tisseyre (Lezignan).

WALES: Andy Bracek (Barrow Raiders), Owain Brown (North Wales Crusaders), Neil Budworth (Mackay Cutters), Joe Burke (South Wales Scorpions), Michael Channing (London Broncos), Courtney Davies (South Wales Scorpions), Ross Divorty (Halifax), Gil Dudson (Wigan Warriors), Jake Emmitt (Castleford Tigers), Ben Evans (Warrington Wolves), Daniel Fleming (Castleford Tigers), Ben Flower (Wigan Warriors), Andrew Gay (Mackay Cutters), David James (South Wales Scorpions), Jordan James (Salford City Reds), Alex Jones (South Wales Scorpions), Danny James (Keighley Cougars), Elliot Kear (Bradford Bulls), Craig Kopczak (unattached) (C), Rhodri Lloyd (Wigan Warriors), Rob Massam (North Wales Crusaders), Tom Morton (Newcastle Knights), Craig Moss (Keighley Cougars), Steve Parry (South Wales Scorpions), Osian Phillips (South Wales Scorpions), Jack Pring (Leeds Rhinos), Rhys Pugsley (Wigan Warriors), Christiaan Roets (North Wales Crusaders), Matt Seamark (Wynnum Manly), Ian Webster (Central Queensland Comets), Lee Williams (Mackay Cutters), Rhys Williams (Warrington Wolves).

Grand Final victory over Graham's Bulldogs, and Brisbane Broncos centre Jack Reed both missed out with shoulder injuries. Huddersfield Giants prop Eorl Crabtree (shoulder), St Helens forward Jon Wilkin (shoulder and elbow) and Hull FC's Danny Tickle (bicep) were also unavailable. St Helens hooker James Roby and Leeds halfback Danny McGuire were 'rested'. Wigan Warriors hooker Michael McIlrorum had one game still to serve of a three-match suspension picked up in round 27 of Super League, but was allowed to count England Knights' match in Ireland, so he was free to play.

ENGLAND ELITE TRAINING SQUAD *(March 2012)*
Carl Ablett (Leeds Rhinos), Ryan Bailey (Leeds Rhinos), Chris Bridge (Warrington Wolves), Tom Briscoe (Hull FC), Danny Brough (Huddersfield Giants), Rob Burrow (Leeds Rhinos), Garreth Carvell (Warrington Wolves), Josh Charnley (Wigan Warriors), Rangi Chase (Castleford Tigers), Eorl Crabtree (Huddersfield Giants), Leroy Cudjoe (Huddersfield Giants), Ryan Hall (Leeds Rhinos), Zak Hardaker (Leeds Rhinos), Ian Henderson (Catalan Dragons), Gareth Hock (Wigan Warriors), Ben Jones-Bishop (Leeds Rhinos), Jamie Jones-Buchanan (Leeds Rhinos), Jonny Lomax (St Helens), Danny McGuire (Leeds Rhinos), Michael McIlorum (Wigan Warriors), Adrian Morley (Warrington Wolves), Lee Mossop (Wigan Warriors), Sean O'Loughlin (Wigan Warriors), Jamie Peacock (Leeds Rhinos) (C), James Roby (St Helens), Kevin Sinfield (Leeds Rhinos), Sam Tomkins (Wigan Warriors), Kallum Watkins (Leeds Rhinos), Kris Welham (Hull Kingston Rovers), Ben Westwood (Warrington Wolves), Jon Wilkin (St Helens), Kirk Yeaman (Hull FC).

On 12th October, McNamara announced from South Africa that Kevin Sinfield was to succeed Jamie Peacock, who had retired from international rugby after the first Exiles game, as England captain.

Wales head coach Iestyn Harris named a 32-man squad for the series. Four of his senior players - Gil Dudson, Ben Flower, Craig Kopczak and Elliot Kear - all returned to the squad after missing the 28-16 defeat to France at Wrexham on June 16th through injury and Australia-based Andrew Gay, Matt Seamark, Ian Webster, Neil Budworth and Lee Williams were all available at the end of the season.

France had still not replaced Bobbie Goulding with a new national coach and Aurelien Cologni took interim charge for both the mid-season game in Wales and the Autumn International Series.

France had their revenge on the Welsh for the defeat two years before that put them out of the Four Nations, the win taking

AUTUMN INTERNATIONALS - GAME ONE

Saturday 20th October 2012

FRANCE 20 WALES 6

FRANCE: 1 Cyril Stacul (Catalan Dragons); 14 Mathias Pala (Catalan Dragons); 3 Vincent Duport (Catalan Dragons); 4 Kevin Larroyer (Catalan Dragons); 5 Clement Soubeyras (Pia); 6 Thomas Bosc (Catalan Dragons); 7 William Barthau (Catalan Dragons); 8 Olivier Elima (Bradford Bulls) (C); 9 Tony Gigot (Avignon); 10 Remi Casty (Catalan Dragons); 11 Antoni Maria (Catalan Dragons); 12 Sebastien Raguin (Catalan Dragons); 13 Gregory Mounis (Catalan Dragons). Subs (all used): 15 Mathieu Griffi (Lezignan); 16 Jason Baitieri (Catalan Dragons); 19 Eloi Pelissier (Catalan Dragons); 17 Romaric Bemba (Carcassonne). **Tries:** Bemba (32), Stacul (36), Bosc (38); **Goals:** Bosc 4/4. **Sin bin:** Mounis (49) - fighting.
WALES: 1 David James (South Wales Scorpions); 5 Elliot Kear (Bradford Bulls); 4 Michael Channing (London Broncos); 3 Christiaan Roets (North Wales Crusaders); 2 Rob Massam (North Wales Crusaders); 6 Danny Jones (Keighley Cougars); 7 Matt Seamark (Wynnum Manly); 8 Gil Dudson (Wigan Warriors); 9 Neil Budworth (Mackay Cutters); 10 Craig Kopczak (unattached) (C); 11 Rhodri Lloyd (Wigan Warriors); 12 Ben Evans (Warrington Wolves); 13 Ben Flower (Wigan Warriors). Subs (all used): 16 Rhys Pugsley (Wigan Warriors); 15 Jordan James (Salford City Reds); 14 Daniel Fleming (Castleford Tigers); 17 Craig Moss (Keighley Cougars).
Try: D James (2); **Goals:** Seamark 1/1.
Sin bin: Dudson (49) - late challenge on Barthau.
Rugby Leaguer & League Express Men of the Match:
France: Thomas Bosc; *Wales:* Craig Kopczak.
Penalty count: 8-4; **Half-time:** 18-6;
Referee: Richard Silverwood (England);
Attendance: 11,628 *(at Stade Felix Bollaert, Lens).*

place in the outpost northern town of Lens. An 11,628 crowd heartened the French Federation in their effort to expand the game. Just before half-time a brilliant spell from the French, which brought three tries in six minutes, turned the game after Wales had earlier caught France by surprise as they went 6-0 up in under two minutes, when Danny Jones and Matt Seamark combined in a well-worked move to put David James into a huge gap for the opening try, converted by Seamark. A stalemate of half an hour was broken emphatically by France's three tries, all involving Thomas Bosc.

Autumn Internationals

First, Bosc's grubber was touched down under the posts by Carcassonne substitute Romaric Bemba. Then the Catalan stand-off's 40/20 again put France into a strong attacking position, from which Cyril Stacul spun out of a Michael Channing tackle to go over from Bosc's pass. Then, following a dash from William Barthau, Jason Baitieri found the ubiquitous Bosc in support for the third. Bosc converted all three tries.

To their great credit, the Welsh refused to give in, in a battling second half. France came close. Bosc sliced through but was stopped in front of the line by a miraculous effort from Ben Flower. Larroyer had a try disallowed for a forward pass, and Soubeyras was held up over the line by Keighley fullback Craig Moss with three minutes to go. Remarkably the sole score of the second half came from a Bosc penalty in the 51st minute after Gil Dudson was yellow-carded for a late, high tackle on Barthau as he kicked downfield, which sparked the first of two minor brawls.

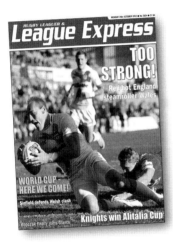

Fourteen tries was a fair reflection in the gulf between the cream of Super League and an essentially part-time Welsh team as a record score was conceded by Wales in Wrexham.

AUTUMN INTERNATIONALS - GAME TWO

Saturday 27th October 2012

WALES 12 ENGLAND 80

WALES: 1 Craig Moss (Keighley Cougars); 2 Elliot Kear (Bradford Bulls); 3 Michael Channing (London Broncos); 4 Christiaan Roets (North Wales Crusaders); 5 David James (South Wales Scorpions); 6 Danny Jones (Keighley Cougars); 7 Matt Seamark (Wynnum Manly); 8 Jordan James (Salford City Reds); 9 Neil Budworth (Mackay Cutters); 10 Craig Kopczak (unattached) (C); 11 Rhodri Lloyd (Wigan Warriors); 12 Ben Evans (Warrington Wolves); 13 Ben Flower (Wigan Warriors). Subs (all used): 14 Gil Dudson (Wigan Warriors); 16 Joe Burke (South Wales Scorpions); 15 Daniel Fleming (Castleford Tigers); 17 Steve Parry (South Wales Scorpions).
Tries: Roets (40), Fleming (47); **Goals:** Seamark 2/2.
ENGLAND: 1 Zak Hardaker (Leeds Rhinos); 2 Josh Charnley (Wigan Warriors); 3 Kallum Watkins (Leeds Rhinos); 4 Leroy Cudjoe (Huddersfield Giants); 5 Ryan Hall (Leeds Rhinos); 6 Kevin Sinfield (Leeds Rhinos) (C); 7 Richard Myler (Warrington Wolves); 8 Adrian Morley (Warrington Wolves); 9 Michael McIlorum (Wigan Warriors); 10 Chris Hill (Warrington Wolves); 11 Jamie Jones-Buchanan (Leeds Rhinos); 12 Gareth Ellis (Wests Tigers); 13 Sean O'Loughlin (Wigan Warriors). Subs (all used): 14 Rob Burrow (Leeds Rhinos); 15 Gareth Hock (Wigan Warriors); 16 Carl Ablett (Leeds Rhinos); 17 Lee Mossop (Wigan Warriors).
Tries: Hall (10, 42), Charnley (16, 58, 65, 71), Hardaker (19, 32), Watkins (26), Ellis (52), Burrow (60), Cudjoe (68, 77), Jones-Buchanan (75); **Goals:** Sinfield 12/14.
Rugby Leaguer & League Express Men of the Match:
Wales: Neil Budworth; *England:* Kevin Sinfield.
Penalty count: 7-8; **Half-time:** 6-26; **Referee:** Thierry Alibert (France); **Attendance:** 4,014
(at Glyndwr University Racecourse Stadium, Wrexham).

England had six players winning their first caps in Zak Hardaker, who was in at fullback for knee-injury victim Sam Tomkins, Josh Charnley, Kallum Watkins, Michael McIlorum, Chris Hill and Lee Mossop. Kevin Sinfield took the official man-of-the-match award and thrived on captaining England for the first time, describing the honour as "probably the proudest moment of my career."

Wales were overpowered from the word go. They did score tries either side of half-time through Christiaan Roets and Castleford junior Daniel Fleming to avoid a whitewash and South Wales hooker Steve Parry nearly sneaked a try at the end. But England finished with 14 tries, Sinfield kicking 12 straight conversions after missing the first two. Super League XVII's top try-scorer, Wigan winger Charnley got four of the tries and there were braces for the other winger, Ryan Hall, Hardaker and Leroy Cudjoe. Eleven of the 14 tries came from threequarters.

England proved far too strong for out-gunned France at Craven Park in Hull, who were badly handicapped by a string of injuries. Already without Sebastien Raguin and Jamal Fakir, they lost fullback Cyril Stacul to concussion in the 14th minute in a controversial Gareth Ellis tackle, prop Michael Simon to a chest injury and later back-rowers Kevin Larroyer (leg) and Gregory Mounis (sprung shoulder).

Saturday 3rd November 2012

ENGLAND 44 FRANCE 6

ENGLAND: 1 Sam Tomkins (Wigan Warriors); 2 Ryan Hall (Leeds Rhinos); 3 Kallum Watkins (Leeds Rhinos); 4 Leroy Cudjoe (Huddersfield Giants); 5 Tom Briscoe (Hull FC); 6 Kevin Sinfield (Leeds Rhinos) (C); 7 Richard Myler (Warrington Wolves); 8 Lee Mossop (Wigan Warriors); 9 Michael McIlorum (Wigan Warriors); 10 Chris Hill (Warrington Wolves); 11 Gareth Ellis (Wests Tigers); 12 Gareth Hock (Wigan Warriors); 13 Jamie Jones-Buchanan (Leeds Rhinos). Subs (all used): 14 Rob Burrow (Leeds Rhinos); 15 Adrian Morley (Warrington Wolves); 16 Carl Ablett (Leeds Rhinos); 17 Ben Harrison (Warrington Wolves).
Tries: Watkins (5, 23, 79), Briscoe (17, 48), Tomkins (29, 42), Sinfield (68); **Goals:** Sinfield 6/8.
On report: Ellis (14) - alleged high tackle on Stacul.
FRANCE: 1 Cyril Stacul (Catalan Dragons); 2 Damien Cardace (Catalan Dragons); 3 Mathias Pala (Catalan Dragons); 4 Vincent Duport (Catalan Dragons); 5 Clement Soubeyras (Pia); 6 Thomas Bosc (Catalan Dragons); 7 William Barthau (Catalan Dragons); 8 Olivier Elima (Bradford Bulls) (C); 9 Kane Bentley (Pia); 10 Remi Casty (Catalan Dragons); 11 Kevin Larroyer (Catalan Dragons); 12 Jason Baitieri (Catalan Dragons); 13 Gregory Mounis (Catalan Dragons). Subs (all used): 14 Eloi Pelissier (Catalan Dragons); 15 Mathieu Griffi (Lezignan); 16 Romaric Bemba (Carcassonne); 17 Michael Simon (Catalan Dragons).
Try: Bentley (72); **Goals:** Bosc 1/1.
Rugby Leaguer & League Express Men of the Match:
England: Kallum Watkins; *France:* Olivier Elima.
Penalty count: 7-13; **Half-time:** 20-0;
Referee: Shane Rehm (New Zealand);
Attendance: 7,173 *(at Craven Park, Hull).*

France had the benefit of a one-sided 11-2 second-half penalty count, but could still only manage a sole Kane Bentley try eight minutes from the end, despite the unwavering efforts of their captain Olivier Elima up front. Sam Tomkins' two tries, one either side of half-time, took him to 14 in as many games for his country, and past the 77-year-old record set by the St Helens winger Alf Ellaby, although Ellaby's tries were scored before England became Great Britain. As planned, Tomkins was withdrawn after an hour as a precaution following a recent knee injury, while centre Kallum Watkins stayed on to complete an impressive hat-trick. Fellow centre Leroy Cudjoe also caught the eye.

It was 32-0 with over half an hour remaining, and given the simplicity of Tom Briscoe's second try (the Hull FC winger in to replace Charnley), another huge England win looked on the cards. But with 12 minutes remaining, Sinfield stepped past two French defenders to reach out and score, before the visitors finally got themselves on the scoresheet when William Barthau's pass put Kane Bentley over by the posts. But England and Watkins deservedly had the final word, when he snared an interception try with the last play of the game.

England brought the curtain down on the autumn international series, with winger Ryan Hall scoring a record-equalling four tries in an accomplished win over France at Salford. In the first half the French restricted the home side to just three tries but Steve McNamara's side were much more clinical overall, and by the end had run in five more scores to complete their third one-sided win of the competition.

The value of the tournament was undisputed in the eyes of McNamara and his players, and there were undeniably a host of impressive performances. Hall produced another flawless wing performance as part of a threequarter line that looked sharp through the tournament. Sam Tomkins was typically dangerous each time he carried the ball, halfbacks Kevin Sinfield and Rangi Chase combined well throughout, and Chris Hill enhanced his growing reputation with another eye-

catching front-row performance. Sean O'Loughlin added an extra dimension to the side on his return at loose forward.

France were better than their performance at Craven Park eight days earlier, with Jason Baitieri and Remi Casty standing out in a hard-working pack, and scrum-half William Barthau lively throughout. McNamara was able to recall O'Loughlin at loose forward after he recovered from a hamstring injury sustained against Wales and Chase at scrum-half - who it had been thought had been ruled out of the tournament with a groin injury suffered during the South Africa training camp - and chose Wigan's Josh Charnley ahead of Tom Briscoe on the right wing. Richie Myler made way for Chase. France were able to welcome back key forwards Jamal Fakir and Sebastien Raguin, but were missing the influential Greg Mounis, Cyril Stacul and Eloi Pelissier.

While the French could stand toe-to-toe with their opponents up front, they lacked a cutting edge that was evident in each of England's three first-half tries.

After a strong run from the impressive O'Loughlin, Chase linked smoothly with Tomkins on the wraparound for Hall to grab his first – and 150th career – try of the evening. Sinfield began a perfect night with the boot with a touchline conversion. Tomkins scored a trademark try, stepping and dummying his way over from close range after Sinfield's pass, before the home attack again linked superbly three minutes later. Chase, Sinfield and O'Loughlin combined before the loose forward's looping pass put Hall in for his second. Sinfield's third from three made it 18-0 at the break, with the half finishing with one of several big hits, this time by Casty on lively substitute Rob Burrow.

The game was firmly taken away from the French in the opening 15 minutes of the second half, despite England losing Adrian Morley to a head injury after a collision with teammate Gareth Ellis. Sinfield and Ellis combined to put Charnley over in the corner, before an outstanding long pass from Chase allowed Hall to record his hat-trick try. Chase and Sinfield were involved in Tomkins' second as well, with the fullback again accelerating over

AUTUMN INTERNATIONALS - FINAL

Sunday 11th November 2012

ENGLAND 48 FRANCE 4

ENGLAND: 1 Sam Tomkins (Wigan Warriors); 2 Josh Charnley (Wigan Warriors); 3 Kallum Watkins (Leeds Rhinos); 4 Leroy Cudjoe (Huddersfield Giants); 5 Ryan Hall (Leeds Rhinos); 6 Kevin Sinfield (Leeds Rhinos) (C); 7 Rangi Chase (Castleford Tigers); 8 Lee Mossop (Wigan Warriors); 9 Michael McIlorum (Wigan Warriors); 10 Chris Hill (Warrington Wolves); 11 Jamie Jones-Buchanan (Leeds Rhinos); 12 Gareth Ellis (Wests Tigers); 13 Sean O'Loughlin (Wigan Warriors). Subs (all used): 14 Rob Burrow (Leeds Rhinos); 15 Carl Ablett (Leeds Rhinos); 16 Gareth Hock (Wigan Warriors); 17 Adrian Morley (Warrington Wolves).
Tries: Hall (9, 28, 47, 64), Tomkins (25, 56), Charnley (44), Burrow (71); **Goals:** Sinfield 8/8.
FRANCE: 1 Clement Soubeyras (Pia); 2 Teddy Sadaoui (Carcassonne); 3 Kevin Larroyer (Catalan Dragons); 4 Vincent Duport (Catalan Dragons); 5 Mathias Pala (Catalan Dragons); 6 Thomas Bosc (Catalan Dragons); 7 William Barthau (Catalan Dragons); 8 Jamal Fakir (Catalan Dragons); 9 Kane Bentley (Pia); 10 Remi Casty (Catalan Dragons); 11 Olivier Elima (Bradford Bulls) (C); 12 Sebastien Raguin (Catalan Dragons); 13 Jason Baitieri (Catalan Dragons). Subs (all used): 16 Romaric Bemba (Carcassonne); 19 Tony Gigot (Avignon); 15 Julian Bousquet (Catalan Dragons); 22 Mathieu Griffi (Lezignan).
Try: Pala (79); **Goals:** Bosc 0/1.
Rugby Leaguer & League Express Men of the Match:
England: Ryan Hall; *France:* Jason Baitieri.
Penalty count: 8-11; **Half-time:** 18-0;
Referee: Shane Rehm (New Zealand);
Attendance: 7,921 *(at City of Salford Community Stadium).*

and, with over a quarter of the game remaining, a huge scoreline looked on the cards. But France regrouped, restricted England to just two more scores and then recorded a try of their own in the closing stages.

England's best two tries of the game came within the space of seven minutes. The first was a breakaway effort, as Chase picked up a Thomas Bosc kick close to his own line, sprinted upfield and handed on to Tomkins. As the French cover came across he fed onto Hall, and when a gap opened up he grabbed the opportunity with both hands for his record-equalling fourth try. The second was a sharp team move, as Hill's excellent pass put Ellis through a hole, and Burrow supported to race away to the line. France eventually got over for a try that their efforts deserved with the clock ticking down. Bosc's low kick to the in-goal was fumbled by Charnley, and Mathias Pala pounced to put his side on the scoreboard.

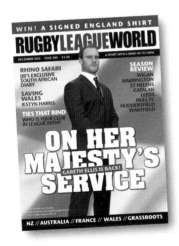

OTHER INTERNATIONALS
Wet and wild

International Origin

The two-match series between England and the Exiles ended all square, England winning the opening game in June by 18-10, but the Antipodeans recording a 32-20 victory at the Galpharm in early July. It meant the Exiles retained the trophy they had won last year with victory in a one-off game at Headingley. The mid-season clash - designed to give England a meaningful contest - was expanded to two games in 2012 at England coach Steve McNamara's request, the first leg being played on a Saturday, with no Super League games scheduled that weekend.

The event was ruined by torrential rain before and during the game at Langtree Park. England had to work very hard for their win, with all their tries coming via kicks, and clean breaks impossible to come by. Neither winger, Ryan Hall, nor Josh Charnley, got a running chance as the heavens re-opened just after kick-off to spoil any chance of an open contest. The Exiles tried to play more freely at times, but the strategy back-fired on them as the slippery ball regularly ended up on the ground. Late drop-outs from the squad didn't help. Michael Monaghan, Luke O'Donnell, Louis Anderson, George Carmont, Brett Finch and Lopini Paea were all ruled out with injury before the pre-match camp, which meant a call-up for Wigan prop Epalahame Lauaki, and then on the Friday captain Brett Hodgson (Warrington Wolves) and Setaimata Sa (Catalan Dragons) withdrew, with Hull KR's Shannon McDonnell drafted in.

Strangely, the Exiles played their best rugby after stand-in skipper Thomas Leuluai was carried off on a stretcher on the hour mark, after breaking a leg preventing Ryan Hall

INTERNATIONAL ORIGIN

GAME ONE

Saturday 16th June 2012

ENGLAND 18 EXILES 10

ENGLAND: 1 Sam Tomkins (Wigan Warriors); 2 Josh Charnley (Wigan Warriors); 3 Carl Ablett (Leeds Rhinos); 4 Ryan Atkins (Warrington Wolves); 5 Ryan Hall (Leeds Rhinos); 6 Kevin Sinfield (Leeds Rhinos); 7 Rangi Chase (Castleford Tigers); 8 Eorl Crabtree (Huddersfield Giants); 9 James Roby (St Helens); 10 Jamie Peacock (Leeds Rhinos) (C); 11 Gareth Hock (Wigan Warriors); 12 Danny Tickle (Hull FC); 13 Sean O'Loughlin (Wigan Warriors). Subs (all used): 14 Rob Burrow (Leeds Rhinos); 15 Garreth Carvell (Warrington Wolves); 16 Lee Mossop (Wigan Warriors); 17 Jamie Jones-Buchanan (Leeds Rhinos).
Tries: Hock (14), Tickle (28), Tomkins (45); **Goals:** Sinfield 3/3.
EXILES: 1 Shannon McDonnell (Hull Kingston Rovers); 2 Joel Monaghan (Warrington Wolves); 3 Iosia Soliola (St Helens); 4 Daryl Millard (Catalan Dragons); 5 Francis Meli (St Helens); 6 Thomas Leuluai (Wigan Warriors) (C); 7 Scott Dureau (Catalan Dragons); 8 Tony Puletua (St Helens); 9 Jeff Lima (Wigan Warriors); 10 Jeff Lima (Wigan Warriors); 11 Willie Manu (Hull FC); 12 Trent Waterhouse (Warrington Wolves); 13 David Fa'alogo (Huddersfield Giants). Subs (all used): 14 David Faiumu (Huddersfield Giants); 15 Anthony Laffranchi (St Helens); 16 Antonio Kaufusi (London Broncos); 17 Epalahame Lauaki (Wigan Warriors).
Tries: Meli (31), Millard (68); **Goals:** Dureau 1/2.
Rugby Leaguer & League Express Men of the Match:
England: James Roby; *Exiles:* Scott Dureau.
Penalty count: 4-3; **Half-time:** 12-4; **Referee:** Ben Thaler (England); **Attendance:** 11,083 *(at Langtree Park, St Helens).*

GAME TWO

Wednesday 4th July 2012

ENGLAND 20 EXILES 32

ENGLAND: 1 Stefan Ratchford (Warrington Wolves); 2 Josh Charnley (Wigan Warriors); 3 Leroy Cudjoe (Huddersfield Giants); 4 Ryan Atkins (Warrington Wolves); 5 Tom Briscoe (Hull FC); 6 Matty Smith (Salford City Reds); 7 Danny Brough (Huddersfield Giants); 8 Eorl Crabtree (Huddersfield Giants); 9 James Roby (St Helens); 10 Garreth Carvell (Warrington Wolves); 11 Carl Ablett (Leeds Rhinos); 12 Jon Wilkin (St Helens); 13 Jamie Jones-Buchanan (Leeds Rhinos). Subs (all used): 14 Rob Burrow (Leeds Rhinos); 15 Lee Mossop (Wigan Warriors); 16 Liam Farrell (Wigan Warriors); 17 Scott Taylor (Hull Kingston Rovers).
Tries: Atkins (23), Charnley (35), Briscoe (58), Cudjoe (78); **Goals:** Brough 2/4.
EXILES: 1 Brett Hodgson (Warrington Wolves) (C); 2 Joel Monaghan (Warrington Wolves); 4 Joel Moon (Salford City Reds); 3 Daryl Millard (Catalan Dragons); 5 Francis Meli (St Helens); 6 Daniel Holdsworth (Salford City Reds); 7 Scott Dureau (Catalan Dragons); 8 Anthony Laffranchi (St Helens); 9 Heath L'Estrange (Bradford Bulls); 10 Epalahame Lauaki (Wigan Warriors); 11 Willie Manu (Hull FC); 12 Steve Menzies (Catalan Dragons); 13 Iosia Soliola (St Helens). Subs (all used): 14 Lincoln Withers (Hull Kingston Rovers); 15 Kylie Leuluai (Leeds Rhinos); 16 Antonio Kaufusi (London Broncos); 17 Constantine Mika (Hull Kingston Rovers).
Tries: Hodgson (4, 55), Dureau (30), Monaghan (40), Meli (47, 61); **Goals:** Hodgson 4/6.
Rugby Leaguer & League Express Men of the Match:
England: Stefan Ratchford; *Exiles:* Brett Hodgson.
Penalty count: 1-1; **Half-time:** 10-16; **Referee:** Ben Thaler (England); **Attendance:** 7,865 *(at Galpharm Stadium, Huddersfield).*

Other Internationals

scoring in the left corner. Daryl Millard's try in the 68th minute had them within eight points and in control, though England held out.

In the Wednesday-night return leg, captain Brett Hodgson was back. The Warrington fullback scored two tries and kicked four goals to help Super League's overseas stars run out comfortable 32-20 winners. Francis Meli also touched down twice in the second half as the Exiles gained their revenge. Salford's Daniel Holdsworth got the official man-of-the-match award and there was an outstanding display from Steve Menzies.

England, without rested quartet Ryan Hall, Kevin Sinfield, Sean O'Loughlin and Sam Tomkins, as well as the now-retired Jamie Peacock, did manage four tries, though a young side led by Jon Wilkin were taught a harsh lesson by their more experienced opponents. McNamara's decision to throw in four new caps meant England struggled with the pace and intensity at times, although Stefan Ratchford, in at fullback for Sam Tomkins, made a fine debut.

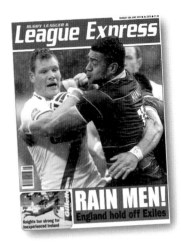

ANZAC TEST

Friday 20th April 2012

NEW ZEALAND 12 AUSTRALIA 20

NEW ZEALAND: 1 Josh Hoffman (Brisbane Broncos); 2 Jason Nightingale (St George Illawarra Dragons); 3 Shaun Kenny-Dowall (Sydney Roosters); 4 Simon Mannering (New Zealand Warriors); 5 Manu Vatuvei (New Zealand Warriors); 6 Benji Marshall (Wests Tigers) (C); 7 Shaun Johnson (New Zealand Warriors); 8 Sam McKendry (Penrith Panthers); 9 Issac Luke (South Sydney Rabbitohs); 10 Ben Matulino (New Zealand Warriors); 11 Frank Pritchard (Canterbury Bulldogs); 12 Adam Blair (Wests Tigers); 13 Jeremy Smith (Cronulla Sharks). Subs (all used): 14 Nathan Fien (St George Illawarra Dragons); 15 Jared Waerea-Hargreaves (Sydney Roosters); 16 Jesse Bromwich (Melbourne Storm); 17 Alex Glenn (Brisbane Broncos).
Tries: Luke (11), Johnson (46); **Goals:** Marshall 2/2.
AUSTRALIA: 1 Billy Slater (Melbourne Storm); 2 Darius Boyd (Newcastle Knights); 3 Greg Inglis (South Sydney Rabbitohs); 4 Justin Hodges (Brisbane Broncos); 5 Akuila Uate (Newcastle Knights); 6 Johnathan Thurston (North Queensland Cowboys); 7 Cooper Cronk (Melbourne Storm); 8 Paul Gallen (Cronulla Sharks); 9 Cameron Smith (Melbourne Storm) (C); 10 David Shillington (Canberra Raiders); 11 Dave Taylor (South Sydney Rabbitohs); 12 Sam Thaiday (Brisbane Broncos); 13 Luke Lewis (Penrith Panthers). Subs: 14 Daly Cherry-Evans (Manly Sea Eagles) (not used); 15 Ben Hannant (Brisbane Broncos); 16 James Tamou (North Queensland Cowboys); 17 Anthony Watmough (Manly Sea Eagles).
Tries: Thurston (20), Inglis (25), Smith (69); **Goals:** Thurston 4/4.
Sin bin: Slater (32) - professional foul.
Rugby Leaguer & League Express Men of the Match:
New Zealand: Josh Hoffman; *Australia:* Johnathan Thurston.
Penalty count: 7-7; **Half-time:** 6-14;
Referee: Richard Silverwood (England);
Attendance: 35,339 *(at Eden Park, Auckland).*

TEST MATCH

Saturday 13th October 2012

AUSTRALIA 18 NEW ZEALAND 10

AUSTRALIA: 1 Billy Slater (Melbourne Storm); 2 Darius Boyd (Newcastle Knights); 3 Greg Inglis (South Sydney Rabbitohs); 4 Josh Morris (Canterbury Bulldogs); 5 Brett Morris (St George Illawarra Dragons); 6 Johnathan Thurston (North Queensland Cowboys); 7 Cooper Cronk (Melbourne Storm); 8 Matt Scott (North Queensland Cowboys); 9 Cameron Smith (Melbourne Storm) (C); 10 James Tamou (North Queensland Cowboys); 11 Greg Bird (Gold Coast Titans); 12 Paul Gallen (Cronulla Sharks); 17 Tony Williams (Manly Sea Eagles). Subs (all used): 14 Robbie Farah (Wests Tigers); 15 Ryan Hoffman (Melbourne Storm); 16 David Shillington (Canberra Raiders); 13 Nate Myles (Gold Coast Titans).
Tries: Smith (23), Tamou (34), Boyd (71); **Goals:** Thurston 3/4.
NEW ZEALAND: 1 Josh Hoffman (Brisbane Broncos); 2 Sam Perrett (Canterbury Bulldogs); 3 Krisnan Inu (Canterbury Bulldogs); 4 Dean Whare (Manly Sea Eagles); 5 Gerard Beale (Brisbane Broncos); 6 Benji Marshall (Wests Tigers) (C); 7 Kieran Foran (Manly Sea Eagles); 8 Jesse Bromwich (Melbourne Storm); 9 Issac Luke (South Sydney Rabbitohs); 10 Sam Kasiano (Canterbury Bulldogs); 11 Frank Pritchard (Canterbury Bulldogs); 12 Kevin Proctor (Melbourne Storm); 13 Simon Mannering (New Zealand Warriors). Subs (all used): 14 Elijah Taylor (New Zealand Warriors); 15 Ben Matulino (New Zealand Warriors); 16 Greg Eastwood (Canterbury Bulldogs); 17 Adam Blair (Wests Tigers).
Tries: Luke (7), Beale (37); **Goals:** Inu 1/2.
Rugby Leaguer & League Express Men of the Match:
Australia: James Tamou; *New Zealand:* Issac Luke.
Penalty count: 4-4; **Half-time:** 10-10;
Referee: Ben Cummins (Australia);
Attendance: 26,479 *(at Dairy Farmers Stadium, Townsville).*

Australia-New Zealand Tests

Australia and New Zealand played each other twice in 2012, with the Kangaroos winning both the Anzac Day game at Eden Park in Auckland and the end-of-season match in Townsville.

The Kiwis suffered a 20-12 defeat in front of a big crowd on home soil on a Friday night in April. The New Zealanders had not won in the annual mid-season clash since 1998, and the final score of 20-12 in a dour encounter was not a true indication of the difference between the two nations. In their first encounter since the retirement of Darren Lockyer, the Australians showed there was life after the legend, with halves Johnathan

Thurston and Cooper Cronk showing real class as playmakers, and Cameron Smith turning in a true captain's role.

In October, it was an eight-point margin again, Australia winning 18-10 but the Kiwis pushed the Australians all the way in front of a sell-out 26,479 crowd at Townsville's Dairy Farmers Stadium. The half-time score was 10-10 and that's where it stayed until the 62nd minute, when Thurston landed his penalty goal before, nine minutes later, the Aussies sealed it with a superb try as Paul Gallen raced through the left channel and flicked the ball one-handed to Darius Boyd on a scissors run. Boyd tore to the posts to improve Thurston's position for the final conversion.

On the international weekend in June, a youthful Welsh side pushed their more experienced French counterparts all the way in an enthralling encounter at Glyndwr University Racecourse Stadium, Wrexham before falling to a 28-16 defeat. The Welsh had six youngsters making their debuts in the absence of five regulars through injury, in addition to their Australia-based players.

Rhys Williams became Wales' all-time leading try-scorer after touching down twice in Wales' first mid-season international for 11 years. David James also scored a try for the hosts but it was the visitors who ran out winners with five tries. Cyril Stacul and Mathieu Griffi both crossed twice to add to Gregory Mounis's try. Stacul's second try 13 minutes from time halted a Welsh revival.

England Knights

The England Knights programme ran for the second year in tandem with the Elite Training squad and played three games during 2012, all of them comfortable wins, including two to win the Alitalia European Cup in October.

Hull KR's Josh Hodgson was the standout in a 62-4 win over Ireland at St Helens' Langtree Park played as a curtain-raiser to the first England-Exiles game in June. Mark Aston's Irish trailed just 10-4 after competing fully in a rain-soaked opening half hour. But Hodgson made a terrific break with his first touch, and continued to have an influence as the Knights eventually ran in 11 tries against their inexperienced opponents. Centres Zak Hardaker and Ben Jones-Bishop, plus stand-off Stefan Ratchford, scored doubles.

The Knights cruised to a 56-4 victory over Ireland in Belfast before a 62-24 success over Scotland in Edinburgh to win the Alitalia European Cup.

In Belfast it was nip and tuck in the opening 20 minutes after Jodie Broughton opened the scoring after three minutes before a long pass from Ireland captain Liam Finn put Josh

INTERNATIONAL REPRESENTATIVE GAMES

Saturday 16th June 2012

WALES 16 FRANCE 28

WALES: 1 David James (South Wales Scorpions); 2 Jack Pring (Leeds Rhinos); 3 Michael Channing (London Broncos); 4 Christiaan Roets (North Wales Crusaders); 5 Rhys Williams (Warrington Wolves); 6 Danny Jones (Keighley Cougars); 7 Ollie Olds (Leeds Rhinos); 8 Jordan James (Salford City Reds) (C); 9 Steve Parry (South Wales Scorpions); 10 Jake Emmitt (Castleford Tigers); 11 Andy Bracek (Barrow Raiders); 12 Rhodri Lloyd (Wigan Warriors); 13 Ross Divorty (Halifax). Subs (all used): 14 Daniel Fleming (Castleford Tigers); 15 Iwan Brown (North Wales Crusaders); 16 Joe Burke (South Wales Scorpions); 17 Craig Moss (Keighley Cougars).
Tries: Williams (39, 60), D James (56); **Goals:** Jones 2/3.
FRANCE: 1 Cyril Stacul (Catalan Dragons); 2 Jeremy Guiraud (Carcassonne); 3 Jean-Philippe Baile (Catalan Dragons); 4 Mathias Pala (Catalan Dragons); 5 Clement Soubeyras (Pia); 18 Thomas Bosc (Catalan Dragons); 7 William Barthau (St Esteve); 20 Michael Simon (Catalan Dragons); 9 Kane Bentley (Lezignan); 8 Mathieu Griffi (Lezignan); 11 Olivier Elima (Bradford Bulls) (C); 12 Antoni Maria (St Esteve); 13 Gregory Mounis (Catalan Dragons). Subs (all used): 14 Eloi Pelissier (Catalan Dragons); 21 Romaric Bemba (Carcassonne); 16 Andrew Bentley (Lezignan); 17 Kevin Larroyer (Toulouse Olympique).
Tries: Stacul (15, 67), Mounis (32), Griffi (48, 52); **Goals:** Bosc 4/5.
Rugby Leaguer & League Express Men of the Match:
Wales: David James; *France:* Mathieu Griffi.
Penalty count: 8-5; **Half-time:** 4-12; **Referee:** James Child (England); **Attendance:** 1,464
(at The Glyndwr University Racecourse Stadium, Wrexham).

ENGLAND KNIGHTS 62 IRELAND 4

KNIGHTS: 1 Chris Riley (Warrington Wolves); 5 Jermaine McGillvary (Huddersfield Giants); 3 Zak Hardaker (Leeds Rhinos); 4 Ben Jones-Bishop (Leeds Rhinos); 2 Jodie Broughton (Salford City Reds); 6 Stefan Ratchford (Warrington Wolves); 7 Matty Smith (Salford City Reds) (C); 8 Michael Cooper (Warrington Wolves); 9 Shaun Lunt (Leeds Rhinos); 10 Scott Taylor (Hull Kingston Rovers); 11 Mark Flanagan (St Helens); 12 Liam Farrell (Wigan Warriors); 13 Dale Ferguson (Huddersfield Giants). Subs (all used): 14 Paul Clough (St Helens); 15 Josh Hodgson (Hull Kingston Rovers); 16 Chris Clarkson (Leeds Rhinos); 17 Gary Wheeler (St Helens).
Tries: Hardaker (5, 36), Jones-Bishop (19, 78), Ratchford (34, 66), Smith (49), Broughton (53), Flanagan (55), Hodgson (64), Lunt (76); **Goals:** Smith 5/7, Ratchford 4/4.
IRELAND: 1 Ian Cross (St Helens); 5 Joe Taylor (Dublin City Exiles); 3 Elliott Cosgrove (Dewsbury Rams); 4 John O'Donnell (Wigan Warriors); 2 Adam Hughes (Dublin City Exiles); 6 James Mendeika (Warrington Wolves); 7 Liam Finn (Featherstone Rovers); 8 Anthony Mullally (Widnes Vikings); 9 Pat Smith (Sheffield Eagles); 10 Michael Haley (Featherstone Rovers); 11 Dave Allen (Widnes Vikings); 12 Kurt Haggerty (Widnes Vikings); 13 Tyrone McCarthy (Warrington Wolves). Subs (all used): 14 Sean Casey (Leeds Rhinos); 18 Wayne Kerr (Country Cowboys); 16 Danny Bridge (Warrington Wolves); 17 Aaron McCloskey (St Helens).
Try: O'Donnell (28); **Goals:** Finn 0/1.
Rugby Leaguer & League Express Men of the Match:
Knights: Josh Hodgson; *Ireland:* Tyrone McCarthy.
Penalty count: 3-4; **Half-time:** 22-4; **Referee:** Steve Ganson (England).
(at Langtree Park, St Helens).

Toole in at the corner for his first international try. For ten minutes the sides battled it out without much joy until the 23rd minute when Michael Lawrence offloaded for Kieran Dixon to touch down. It was one-way traffic after that as Broughton and Tom Burgess finished with two tries each.

Ireland had opened the tournament with a 30-18 win over Scotland at Meggetland in Edinburgh. Warrington stand-off James Mendeika pulled the strings as Tim Bergin and Stuart Littler helped themselves to two tries each on the right.

In the final game in Edinburgh, Scotland took a shock lead after just four minutes when Mitchell Stringer barged over under the sticks from close range. The lead lasted three minutes before Mike Cooper sidestepped Brett Carter and fed Dan Sarginson to romp over for the first of two tries. Rhys Evans, Jodie Broughton and Scott Taylor also bagged braces, with one each for George Burgess, Keiran Dixon and Jordan Turner, who also booted nine goals for a personal haul of 22 points.

Stand-off Lee Paterson, and debutants Brett Phillips and Craig Borthwick crossed for Scotland, with David Scott kicking three conversions.

ENGLAND KNIGHTS - 2012 SQUADS

March: Joe Arundel (Castleford Tigers), Jodie Broughton (Salford City Reds), Chris Clarkson (Leeds Rhinos), Paul Clough (St Helens), Michael Cooper (Warrington Wolves), Rhys Evans (Warrington Wolves), Liam Farrell (Wigan Warriors), Dale Ferguson (Huddersfield Giants), Mark Flanagan (St Helens), Lee Gaskell (St Helens), Josh Hodgson (Hull Kingston Rovers), Danny Houghton (Hull FC), Shaun Lunt (Huddersfield Giants), Jermaine McGillvary (Huddersfield Giants), Richard Myler (Warrington Wolves), Larne Patrick (Huddersfield Giants), Stefan Ratchford (Warrington Wolves), Chris Riley (Warrington Wolves), Matty Smith (Salford City Reds), Scott Taylor (Hull Kingston Rovers), Joe Wardle (Huddersfield Giants), Liam Watts (Hull Kingston Rovers), Gary Wheeler (St Helens), Elliott Whitehead (Bradford Bulls).

Zak Hardaker (Leeds Rhinos) and Ben Jones-Bishop (Leeds Rhinos) were added to the squad for the Ireland game in June.

September: Jodie Broughton (Salford City Reds), Tom Burgess (Bradford Bulls), Daryl Clark (Castleford Tigers), Chris Clarkson (Leeds Rhinos), Paul Clough (St Helens), Michael Cooper (Warrington Wolves), Kieran Dixon (London Broncos), Greg Eden (Huddersfield Giants), Rhys Evans (Warrington Wolves), Liam Farrell (Wigan Warriors), Mark Flanagan (St Helens), Luke Gale (Bradford Bulls), Ben Harrison (Warrington Wolves), Chris Hill (Warrington Wolves), Josh Hodgson (Hull Kingston Rovers), Danny Houghton (Hull FC), Jack Hughes (Wigan Warriors), Michael Lawrence (Huddersfield Giants), Shaun Lunt (Leeds Rhinos), Jermaine McGillvary (Huddersfield Giants), Richard Myler (Warrington Wolves), Larne Patrick (Huddersfield Giants), Stefan Ratchford (Warrington Wolves), Chris Riley (Warrington Wolves), Matty Smith (Wigan Warriors), Scott Taylor (Hull Kingston Rovers), Jordan Turner (Hull FC), Joe Wardle (Huddersfield Giants), Joe Westerman (Hull FC).

October (*Alitalia European Cup***):** Jodie Broughton (Salford City Reds), George Burgess (South Sydney Rabbitohs), Tom Burgess (Bradford Bulls), Daryl Clark (Castleford Tigers), Chris Clarkson (Leeds Rhinos), Michael Cooper (Warrington Wolves), Kieran Dixon (London Broncos), Greg Eden (Huddersfield Giants), Rhys Evans (Warrington Wolves), Luke Gale (Bradford Bulls), Danny Houghton (Hull FC) (C), Jack Hughes (Wigan Warriors), Ben Jones-Bishop (Leeds Rhinos), Michael Lawrence (Huddersfield Giants), Shaun Lunt (Leeds Rhinos), Chris Riley (Warrington Wolves), Dan Sarginson (London Broncos), Scott Taylor (Hull Kingston Rovers), Jordan Turner (Hull FC).

ALITALIA EUROPEAN CUP

Sunday 14th October 2012

SCOTLAND 18 IRELAND 30

SCOTLAND: 1 Brett Carter (Workington Town); 2 Alex Hurst (Swinton Lions); 3 Shae Lyon-Fraser (Wigan Warriors); 4 Josh Barlow (Halifax); 5 David Scott (Hull Kingston Rovers); 6 Lee Paterson (Mackay Cutters); 7 Liam Hood (Leeds Rhinos); 8 Paul Jackson (Castleford Tigers); 9 Andrew Henderson (Sheffield Eagles) (C); 10 Mitchell Stringer (Sheffield Eagles); 11 Sam Barlow (Halifax); 12 Dale Ferguson (Huddersfield Giants); 13 Alex Szostak (Sheffield Eagles). Subs (all used): 14 Ben Fisher (Catalan Dragons); 15 Adam Walker (Huddersfield Giants); 16 Jonathan Walker (Castleford Tigers); 17 Callum Cockburn (Edinburgh Eagles).
Tries: Fisher (58), Stringer (61), Cockburn (74); **Goals:** Scott 3/3.
IRELAND: 1 Gregg McNally (Leigh Centurions); 2 Tim Bergin (Sheffield Eagles); 3 Stuart Littler (Leigh Centurions); 4 Joshua Toole (Mounties); 5 John O'Donnell (Wigan Warriors); 6 James Mendeika (Warrington Wolves); 7 Liam Finn (Featherstone Rovers) (C); 8 Sean Hesketh (Halifax); 9 Carl Sice (Whitehaven); 10 Luke Ambler (Halifax); 11 Elliott Cosgrove (Dewsbury Rams); 12 Callum Casey (Halifax); 13 Tyrone McCarthy (Warrington Wolves). Subs (all used): 14 Colton Roche (Leeds Rhinos); 15 Sam Wellings (Ireland Students); 16 Matty Hadden (Antrim Eels); 17 Tom McKeown (Dublin City Exiles).
Tries: Bergin (14, 33), Littler (22, 37), Cosgrove (43); **Goals:** Finn 5/6.
Rugby Leaguer & League Express Men of the Match:
Scotland: Mitchell Stringer; *Ireland:* James Mendeika.
Penalty count: 4-6; **Half-time:** 0-22; **Referee:** Ben Thaler (England); **Attendance:** 726 *(at Meggetland, Edinburgh).*

Saturday 20th October 2012

IRELAND 4 ENGLAND KNIGHTS 56

IRELAND: 1 Gregg McNally (Leigh Centurions); 2 Tim Bergin (Sheffield Eagles); 3 Stuart Littler (Leigh Centurions); 4 Joshua Toole (Mounties); 5 John O'Donnell (Wigan Warriors); 6 James Mendeika (Warrington Wolves); 7 Liam Finn (Featherstone Rovers) (C); 10 Luke Ambler (Halifax); 9 Carl Sice (Whitehaven); 8 Sean Hesketh (Halifax); 11 Callum Casey (Halifax); 12 Elliott Cosgrove (Dewsbury Rams); 13 Tyrone McCarthy (Warrington Wolves). Subs (all used): 14 Colton Roche (Leeds Rhinos); 15 Wayne Kerr (Country Cowboys); 16 Matty Hadden (Antrim Eels); 17 Sam Wellings (Ireland Students).
Try: Toole (4). **Goals:** Finn 0/1.
ENGLAND KNIGHTS: 1 Chris Riley (Warrington Wolves); 2 Kieran Dixon (London Broncos); 3 Jordan Turner (Hull FC); 4 Rhys Evans (Warrington Wolves); 5 Jodie Broughton (Salford City Reds); 6 Dan Sarginson (London Broncos); 7 Luke Gale (Bradford Bulls); 8 Scott Taylor (Hull Kingston Rovers); 9 Danny Houghton (Hull FC) (C); 10 George Burgess (South Sydney Rabbitohs); 11 Jack Hughes (Wigan Warriors); 12 Michael Lawrence (Huddersfield Giants); 13 Michael Cooper (Warrington Wolves). Subs (all used): 14 Tom Burgess (Bradford Bulls); 15 Shaun Lunt (Leeds Rhinos); 16 Chris Clarkson (Leeds Rhinos); 17 Ben Jones-Bishop (Leeds Rhinos).
Tries: Broughton (3, 53), Dixon (24), Turner (27), T Burgess (32, 79), Houghton (38), Gale (57), Lawrence (64), G Burgess (75);
Goals: Gale 8/10.
Rugby Leaguer & League Express Men of the Match:
Ireland: Luke Ambler; *England Knights:* Luke Gale.
Penalty count: 7-7; **Half-time:** 4-26; **Referee:** Ben Thaler (England); **Attendance:** 774 *(at Deramore Park, Belfast).*

Sunday 28th October 2012

SCOTLAND 24 ENGLAND KNIGHTS 62

SCOTLAND: 1 Brett Carter (Workington Town); 2 Alex Hurst (Swinton Lions); 3 Josh Barlow (Halifax); 4 Ben Hellewell (Warrington Wolves); 5 David Scott (Hull Kingston Rovers); 6 Lee Paterson (Mackay Cutters); 7 Andrew Henderson (Sheffield Eagles) (C); 8 Jack Howieson (Sheffield Eagles); 9 Ben Fisher (Catalan Dragons); 10 Mitchell Stringer (Sheffield Eagles); 11 Brett Phillips (Workington Town); 12 Alex Szostak (Sheffield Eagles); 13 Sam Barlow (Halifax). Subs (all used): 14 Callum Cockburn (Edinburgh Eagles); 15 Jonathan Walker (Castleford Tigers); 16 Adam Walker (Huddersfield Giants); 17 Craig Borthwick (Edinburgh Eagles).
Tries: Stringer (4), Paterson (31), Phillips (53), Borthwick (74);
Goals: Scott 4/4.
ENGLAND KNIGHTS: 1 Ben Jones-Bishop (Leeds Rhinos); 2 Kieran Dixon (London Broncos); 3 Jordan Turner (Hull FC); 4 Rhys Evans (Warrington Wolves); 5 Jodie Broughton (Salford City Reds); 6 Greg Eden (Huddersfield Giants); 7 Dan Sarginson (London Broncos); 8 George Burgess (South Sydney Rabbitohs); 9 Danny Houghton (Hull FC) (C); 10 Tom Burgess (Bradford Bulls); 11 Jack Hughes (Wigan Warriors); 12 Chris Clarkson (Leeds Rhinos); 13 Michael Cooper (Warrington Wolves). Subs (all used): 14 Scott Taylor (Hull Kingston Rovers); 15 Chris Riley (Warrington Wolves); 16 Ben Currie (Warrington Wolves); 17 Daryl Clark (Castleford Tigers).
Tries: Sarginson (8, 27), G Burgess (11), Broughton (13, 48), Turner (37), Evans (42, 55), Taylor (64, 66), Dixon (69); **Goals:** Turner 9/11.
On report: G Burgess (74) - alleged use of the elbow.
Rugby Leaguer & League Express Men of the Match:
Scotland: Ben Hellewell; *England Knights:* Jordan Turner.
Penalty count: 6-3; **Half-time:** 12-28; **Referee:** Shane Rehm (New Zealand); **Attendance:** 742 *(at Meggetland, Edinburgh).*

Academy Tour

England's under-18s side fell to a 2-0 series defeat to the Australian Schoolboys on their four-match tour of Australia. Two impressive wins in their warm-up games, by 42-18 over Parramatta and 28-18 over New South Wales, raised hopes of a first ever series win on Australian soil. But the Aussies proved far too strong in both Tests.

England were outscored by seven tries to two in a 41-10 defeat in the opening Test, played at Bruce Stadium, Canberra. England were in control of a very physical game until the 17th-minute mark when Australian winger Jack Goodsell crossed under the posts. The home side quickly opened up a 24-0 margin within a whirlwind ten-minute spell though when England got their hands on the ball Leeds centre Luke Briscoe managed to get the Academy on the scoreboard. Warrington's James Saltonstall scored the try of the game with ten minutes left on the clock with an 80-metre effort, after clubmate Ben Currie had burst through a gap from his own '20'.

A week later England lost 40-14 at Wynnum-Manly. It took just five minutes for animosity between the sides to surface when a 26-man brawl broke out in centre field and after winger Saltonstall got on the end of a deft chip from skipper John Bateman to open the scoring, the Schoolboys by half-time had a 24-6 advantage. Centre Briscoe got two late tries for England.

ENGLAND ACADEMY SQUAD - TOUR TO AUSTRALIA

Peter Aspinall (Huddersfield Giants), Jordan Baldwinson (Leeds Rhinos), John Bateman (Bradford Bulls) (C), Gavin Bennion (Warrington Wolves), Luke Briscoe (Leeds Rhinos), Joe Burgess (Wigan Warriors), James Cunningham (Hull FC), Ben Currie (Warrington Wolves), James Duckworth (Leeds Rhinos), Connor Farrell (Wigan Warriors), Jon Ford (Salford City Reds), Ryan Hampshire (Wigan Warriors), Josh Johnson (Huddersfield Giants), Liam McAvoy (Bradford Bulls), Mark Percival (St Helens), James Saltonstall (Warrington Wolves), Dominic Speakman (St Helens), Liam Sutcliffe (Leeds Rhinos), Ryan Sutton (Wigan Warriors), Luke Thompson (St Helens), Lewis Tierney (Wigan Warriors), Greg Wilde (St Helens), George Williams (Wigan Warriors).

Stevie Ward (Leeds Rhinos) and Oliver Roberts (Bradford Bulls) withdrew from the original 24-man squad. Roberts was replaced by Greg Wilde.

Sunday 5th August 2012

AUSTRALIAN SCHOOLBOYS 41 ENGLAND ACADEMY 10

AUSTRALIAN SCHOOLBOYS: 1 Alex Johnston (South Sydney Rabbitohs); 2 Jack Goodsell (Keebra Park State High School); 3 Clint Gutherson (Manly Sea Eagles); 4 Paul Simona (Wests Tigers); 5 Willis Meehan (Sydney Roosters); 6 Mitchell Moses (Wests Tigers); 7 Luke Brooks (Wests Tigers); 8 Matthew Lodge (Penrith Panthers); 9 Brad Deitz (Wests Tigers); 10 Jeremy Cropper (Canberra Raiders); 11 Kelepi Tanginoa (Parramatta Eels); 12 Adam Elliot (Canterbury Bulldogs) (C); 13 Chad McGill (Parramatta Eels). Subs (all used): 14 Dylan Walker (South Sydney Rabbitohs); 15 Chris Smith (Penrith Panthers); 16 Jai Arrow (Keebra Park State High School); 17 Pauli Pauli (Parramatta Eels).
Tries: Goodsell (17), Deitz (20), Simona (24), Moses (30, 55, 61), Meehan (74); **Goals:** Gutherson 6/7; **Field goal:** Moses (80).
ENGLAND ACADEMY: 1 Lewis Tierney (Wigan Warriors); 2 James Saltonstall (Warrington Wolves); 3 Luke Briscoe (Leeds Rhinos); 4 Jon Ford (Salford City Reds); 5 Joe Burgess (Wigan Warriors); 6 Ryan Hampshire (Wigan Warriors); 7 George Williams (Wigan Warriors); 8 Liam McAvoy (Bradford Bulls); 9 Dominic Speakman (St Helens); 10 Gavin Bennion (Warrington Wolves); 11 John Bateman (Bradford Bulls) (C); 12 Connor Farrell (Wigan Warriors); 13 Ben Currie (Warrington Wolves). Subs (all used): 14 Luke Thompson (St Helens); 15 Ryan Sutton (Wigan Warriors); 16 Jordan Baldwinson (Leeds Rhinos); 17 Josh Johnson (Huddersfield Giants).
Tries: Briscoe (35), Saltonstall (70); **Goals:** Hampshire 1/2.
(at Bruce Stadium, Canberra).

Sunday 12th August 2012

AUSTRALIAN SCHOOLBOYS 40 ENGLAND ACADEMY 14

AUSTRALIAN SCHOOLBOYS: 1 Alex Johnston (South Sydney Rabbitohs); 2 Jack Goodsell (Keebra Park State High School); 3 Clint Gutherson (Manly Sea Eagles); 4 Paul Simona (Wests Tigers); 5 Willis Meehan (Sydney Roosters); 6 Mitchell Moses (Wests Tigers); 7 Luke Brooks (Wests Tigers); 8 Matthew Lodge (Penrith Panthers); 9 Brad Deitz (Wests Tigers); 10 Jeremy Cropper (Canberra Raiders); 11 Kelepi Tanginoa (Parramatta Eels); 12 Adam Elliot (Canterbury Bulldogs) (C); 13 Chad McGill (Parramatta Eels). Subs (all used): 14 Dylan Walker (Manly Sea Eagles); 15 Chris Smith (Penrith Panthers); 16 Jai Arrow (Keebra Park State High School); 17 Pauli Pauli (Parramatta Eels).
Tries: Pauli (15), Gutherson (20), Goodsell (28, 50), McGill (39), Walker (57), Johnston (74); **Goals:** Gutherson 6/7.
ENGLAND ACADEMY: 1 Greg Wilde (St Helens); 2 James Saltonstall (Warrington Wolves); 3 Luke Briscoe (Leeds Rhinos); 4 Mark Percival (St Helens); 5 James Duckworth (Leeds Rhinos); 6 Liam Sutcliffe (Leeds Rhinos); 7 George Williams (Wigan Warriors); 8 Gavin Bennion (Warrington Wolves); 9 James Cunningham (Hull FC); 10 John Bateman (Bradford Bulls) (C); 11 Jordan Baldwinson (Leeds Rhinos); 12 Connor Farrell (Wigan Warriors); 13 Ben Currie (Warrington Wolves). Subs (all used): 14 Dominic Speakman (St Helens); 15 Luke Thompson (St Helens); 16 Josh Johnson (Huddersfield Giants); 17 Liam McAvoy (Bradford Bulls).
Tries: Saltonstall (10), Briscoe (68, 78); **Goals:** Percival 1/3.
(at Kougari Oval, Manly).

Friday 15th June 2012

ENGLAND ACADEMY 38 FRANCE UNDER-18s 18

ENGLAND ACADEMY: 1 Lewis Tierney (Wigan Warriors); 2 James Saltonstall (Warrington Wolves); 3 Jordan Harper (Leeds Rhinos); 4 Jon Ford (Salford City Reds); 5 Joe Burgess (Wigan Warriors); 6 Ryan Hampshire (Wigan Warriors); 7 George Williams (Wigan Warriors); 8 Rob Mulhern (Leeds Rhinos); 9 Dominic Speakman (St Helens); 10 Ryan Sutton (Wigan Warriors); 11 John Bateman (Bradford Bulls) (C). Subs (all used): 14 Tom Gilmore (Widnes Vikings); 15 Luke Thompson (St Helens); 16 Josh Johnson (Huddersfield Giants); 17 Luke Briscoe (Leeds Rhinos).
Tries: Tierney (14), Saltonstall (17), Burgess (35), Hampshire (44), Speakman (54), Baldwinson (71), Briscoe (75); **Goals:** Hampshire 5/7.
FRANCE UNDER-18s: 1 Valentin Ferret (Lezignan); 2 Alexis Escamilla (Carcassonne); 3 Charles Bouzinac (Lezignan); 4 Hakim Miloudi (St Esteve); 5 Ségoire Ghanem (Entraigues); 6 Joris Bissiere (Avignon); 7 Theo Fages (Salford City Reds); 8 Gadwin Springer (Toulouse Olympique); 9 Joan Guasch (St Esteve) (C); 10 Mickael Rouch (Limoux); 11 Benjamin Garcia (Wynnum Manly); 12 Yohan Didone (Toulouse Olympique); 13 Martial Romano (Carpentras). Subs (all used): 14 Alexandre Labarchede (Tonneins); 15 Karim Madani (Toulouse Olympique); 16 Ugo Perez (St Esteve); 17 Alexis Meresta-Doucet (St Esteve).
Tries: Rouch (8), Ferret (48), Miloudi (64); **Goals:** Guasch 3/3.
(at Odsal Stadium, Bradford).

WOMEN'S INTERNATIONAL

Friday 15th June 2012

ENGLAND WOMEN 48 FRANCE WOMEN 0

ENGLAND WOMEN: Tara Stanley (Widnes Vikings); Lauren Stallwood (Bradford Thunderbirds); Amy Hardcastle (Bradford Thunderbirds); Jodie Cunningham (Warrington); Hannah Bairstow (Featherstone Rovers); Gemma Walsh (Warrington); Kirsty Moroney (Bradford Thunderbirds); Emma Slowe (Featherstone Rovers); Lois Forsell (Hunslet Hawks); Andrea Dobson (Featherstone Rovers); Holly Freestone (Warrington); Emily Rudge (Warrington); Kim Field (Featherstone Rovers). Subs: Danielle Bound (Warrington); Rebecca Williams (Nottingham Outlaws); Clare Robinson (Warrington); Rachel Twibill (Bradford Thunderbirds).
FRANCE WOMEN: Sonia Benchoug; Angelique Degas; Lauraine Guigue; Hayate Choukri; Gaelle Delas; Elisa Ciria; Sonia Zaghdoudi; Maud Signoret; Elise Labrunie; Audrey Pene; Estelle Fauvelle; Delphine Lacoste; Virgine Calvo. Subs: Anais Mikalef; Coralie Mauroudar; Mira M'Raidi; Houita Benchoug.
(at Odsal Stadium, Bradford).

| EUROPEAN SHIELD | NORDIC CUP | Vanuatu 14 Greece 24 *(20th October 2012)* |

EUROPEAN SHIELD
(biennial home and away championship involving Italy, Serbia, Russia and Germany in 2012 and 2013)
Russia 21 Serbia 20; Russia 32 Italy 18;
Italy 72 Germany 10; Serbia 24 Italy 18;
Germany 26 Russia 32; Germany 25 Serbia 24

EUROPEAN BOWL
Czech Republic 42 Hungary 16

AMATEUR FOUR NATIONS
Scotland 36 Wales 16; Ireland 0 England 34;
Wales 28 Ireland 26; Scotland 14 England 48;
England 56 Wales 8
Ireland v Scotland didn't take place - waterlogged pitch

NORDIC CUP
Sweden 10 Norway 36; Norway 36 Denmark 6

OTHER INTERNATIONALS
Denmark 122 Sweden 8 *(28th April 2012)*
Malta 24 Denmark 12 *(9th June 2012)*
Jamaica 10 BARLA GB 23s 54 *(11th June 2012)*
Jamaica 28 BARLA GB 23s 56 *(16th June 2012)*
Canada 18 Jamaica 12 *(21st July 2012)*
Canada 36 Lebanon 18 *(11th August 2012)*
Canada 24 USA 28 *(8th September 2012)*
USA 36 Canada 14 *(23rd September 2012)*
Denmark 12 Malta 74 *(29th September 2012)*
Canada 4 English Lions 68 *(6th October 2012)*
Lebanon 24 Cook Islands 28 *(7th October 2012)*

Vanuatu 14 Greece 24 *(20th October 2012)*
Thailand 0 Philippines 84 *(21st October 2012)*

Belgrade under-18s festival *(17th-19th August 2012)*
English Lions 46 Lebanon 4; Serbia 46 Lebanon 4;
Serbia 0 English Lions 30

English Lions under-18s tour
Lebanon 0 English Lions 40; Lebanon 0 English Lions 56

Other youth internationals
Czech Youth 0 BARLA GB Lions under-17s 68
Italy under-18s 32 Germany 16
Germany under-16s 10 Serbia 4
Germany under-16s 14 Serbia 8

SEASON DOWN UNDER
Melbourne back on top

When the Melbourne Storm won two Premierships within the space of three seasons they were hailed as the finest Australian side of the 21st century. Then two years ago they were exposed as cheats, blatantly breaking the NRL salary cap rules. They were stripped of their 2007 and 2009 crowns and told they would lose all competition points for 2010. To get under their cap the Storm had to let most of their stars go, including Greg Inglis to South Sydney and three others to Wigan Warriors.

In 2012 they earned redemption. 'We were all down about what happened,' said captain Cameron Smith. 'It was a tough period. But we didn't look back. We were one match short of a grand final last year. But we didn't let that close call affect us, either. And it's all paid off.'

In one of the finest grand finals in decades the Storm overcame the Canterbury Bulldogs 14-4, and in doing so, proved themselves to be the legitimate champions of Rugby League in Australia. The Storm rebuilt their club around the big three of Cameron Smith, Cooper Cronk and Billy Slater and a host of players unwanted by other clubs. And they reaped the reward. Certainly the trio played a major role in orchestrating the success – with Cronk winning the Clive Churchill Medal as man of the match – but it was the other lesser known players who provided the rock-like defence that kept the Bulldogs at bay in a stirring second half.

Even the Canterbury fans in the capacity attendance of 82,976 would not have been disappointed with the spectacle that unfolded before them. Englishman James Graham was hit by a double whammy. Not only did he miss out in another grand final after a succession of five losses with St Helens, but he was charged with biting an ear of Australia's Test fullback Billy Slater in a melee, and later copped a 12-match ban.

What a game it was! Five minutes into the action, Canterbury's will-o'-the-wisp fullback Ben Barba raced 90 metres to touch down behind the Melbourne line. But referee Tony Archer had already ruled the Bulldogs' winger Johnathan Wright had spilled a bomb forward. It was a costly mistake. From the ensuing scrum Ryan Hoffman ran diagonally across the pitch to score. Smith missed with his conversion attempt. 'The Hoff' had had a sensational year since returning from Wigan. And the try ensured he was given a place in the Australian side for the Trans-Tasman encounter two weeks later.

The Bulldogs were next to score with Kiwi international Sam Perrett touching down in the right-hand corner. The try precipitated an all-in brawl with most of the players involved. It was then that Graham was caught on video apparently biting Slater.

Two of Melbourne's 'Three Musketeers' combined to regain the lead. Cronk fooled the defence with a dummy and sent Slater on his way to score his 16th try of the season. A minute before the interval, Cronk was pivotal again. He sent a low bomb across the field to an unmarked Justin O'Neill who obliged with a vital try to send the Storm off for the break with a 10-point lead.

The second half was all that one would expect from a gripping grand final. No more points were scored. And there were incredible defensive efforts from both sides, neither of which was willing to concede anything. Who said you have to score heaps of tries to have an exciting game? Melbourne Storm – worthy Premiers.

Here's how the sides fared in 2012.

MELBOURNE STORM (Premiers)

A bitterness had festered inside the hearts of Melbourne fans since the Storm were stripped of the 2007 and 2009 Premierships for cheating on the salary cap. The fans saw it as a Sydney conspiracy. The stirring victory over Canterbury in the grand final did much to cauterise the wound. Indeed, it probably proved the Storm might well have won both the disputed titles even without cheating.

However as captain Cameron Smith explained: 'It was extremely tough to get through that period. But we didn't look back, we looked forward.'

Melbourne started the season like a house on fire. Indeed some critics were even suggesting the unthinkable, going the through the season unbeaten. No side had done that since the great St George combination, in 1959. But today such a record truly is unthinkable. A mid-season slump around Origin time saw the Storm lose seven out of ten, including five straight losses.

Nevertheless there was a lot of self-belief. 'I've said it before and I'll say it again – these guys [the players] are the ones who have got us to where we are,' said Bellamy. 'They are the ones who have believed in the club and they are the ones who have worked so hard. It's been one hell of an effort.'

Although Bellamy will never admit the fact, the Storm success was built around the 'Three Musketeers', Slater, Cronk and Smith. They lost Slater injured for a few matches and the lack of his influence showed. But it was truly a combined effort. Ryan Hoffman had the best season of his career and was justly rewarded with a spot in the Australian Test side. Will Chambers relished the extra room to move after languishing in the boredom of rugby union. The other centre Dane Nielsen showed the class that had won him Origin selection for Queensland. And there were several players, unwanted by other clubs who under Bellamy's tutelage blossomed.

The most telling factor was Melbourne's ability to not only attack in a devastating fashion but defend stoically. They scored more tries than any of the other NRL clubs (119) – and they conceded the fewest (72).

CANTERBURY BULLDOGS (2nd & Minor Premiers)

The Bulldogs may have lost the grand final, a disappointment that resulted in some of their more unruly fans on going on a rampage. However the Canterbury supporters should have been over the moon as new coach Des Hasler performed a minor miracle. He took a side that could not even make the top eight for the play-offs the previous season to the Minor Premiership and, with a couple of solid finals victories including a comprehensive thrashing of South Sydney, through to the season decider.

In doing so, Hasler became the first coach in history to reach consecutive grand finals with different clubs. But, once there, he couldn't repeat his success of the previous season with Manly. Captain Michael Ennis summed up Hasler's effort: 'Part of me says how proud I am for where we came from. The other part is just devastated. But taking the emotion out of it, I am so proud of the boys. We've all learned off Des. He is the first to deflect away from himself. He is a very caring man and a very humble man. And he has each of our best interests at heart.'

His attitude paid dividends when he signed up mid-season two players who were out of favour at other clubs – Krisnan Inu (Warriors) and Sam Perrett (Roosters). Both thrived under his guidance. So, too, did some of the younger players. Five-eighth Josh Reynolds relished the chance offered to him by Hasler. Prop Sam Kasiano became one of the most feared props in the game and won a spot in the Kiwis squad for the October Trans-Tasman Test (after a tug-o'-war with Queensland who wanted him to relinquish his New Zealand affiliation and play Origin for the Maroons). Rookie forwards Josh Jackson and Dale Finucane also emerged.

But undoubtedly the star of the season was wil-o'-the-wisp fullback Ben Barba who came of age in 2012 to win the Dally M Medal as the best player in the NRL. What an attacking machine! He topped the tryscoring lists with 22 in 27 appearances. But that's not all. He made 23 try assists and 27 line breaks.

Four-Nations centre Josh Morris had a great season. His 17 tries had him up among the NRL leaders and earned him selection in the Australian squad for the Trans-Tasman Test. England Test prop James Graham was one of the best forwards in the Premiership. Sadly, he badly blotted his copybook with the 'brain explosion' in the grand final in which he was found guilty of biting Billy Slater's ear.

SOUTH SYDNEY RABBITOHS (3rd)

South Sydney had for far too many seasons promised so much, but delivered so little. But the arrival of coach Michael Maguire from Melbourne via Wigan seemed to change the whole culture of the Rabbitohs. At last they looked as if they could live up to their nickname of years gone by, 'The Pride of the League'.

From 10th spot on the ladder in 2011 they forced their way into the top four and reached the penultimate weekend of the play-offs, only to be hammered 32-8 by Canterbury. And there was a reason that the score in the preliminary final was so lopsided. There was little between the two sides in the first 26 minutes. Then Souths playmaker Adam Reynolds, the Dally M Rookie of the Year, tore a hamstring and was lost to the game. We'll never know had he stayed on the field whether the Rabbitohs could have lifted to beat the Bulldogs.

Michael Crocker, who had emerged as regular skipper after Souths started the season with a five-man captain's squad, summed it up: 'We've come a long way in 12 months. We're all about building our own history and culture. We are all really proud of what we have achieved this year. We'll work hard in the off-season and make sure we're better next year.' Souths also suffered a significant loss in the first week of the finals, but fought back to overwhelm the Canberra Raiders 38-16. To be beaten by both grand finalists in the play-offs was nothing of which to be ashamed.

Maguire's biggest gamble proved one of the NRL's most successful moves. At the start of the year he switched Australian Test centre Greg Inglis to fullback. It caught everyone by surprise. Well, not everyone. 'It wasn't a surprise to me,' Inglis said. 'I just had to work harder on my game. I had to keep developing.' And develop he did ... becoming one of the world's finest in the No 1 shirt.

Nathan Merritt's 14 tries took his career tally with Souths to 129 – and he had a real chance of becoming the greatest try-scorer in the history of the Rabbitohs the next season. Only Benny Wearing with 144 stood above him. Andrew Everingham's 17 tries was the greatest tally by a South Sydney player in his rookie season in almost six decades.

MANLY SEA EAGLES (4th)

No one expected Manly Sea Eagles to be a real threat this year, especially after losing their exciting youngster Will Hopoate to two years of Mormon missionary work. Even though they were reigning Premiers they had lost the brains behind their 2011 success – coach Des Hasler – and there was plenty of infighting among board members.

As it turned out they had a ready-made replacement in Hasler's assistant and one of Manly's favourite sons, Geoff Toovey. He rose to the occasion. Toovey rushed around and found the right support staff to replace those who had defected to Canterbury with Hasler. Toovey was buoyed by the fact that the nucleus of experienced performers had remained loyal. And, despite a loss to Leeds Rhinos in the World Club Challenge to kick off the Sea Eagles season, it proved to be a relatively good year. Good because Manly finished in the top four and then won though to the preliminary final. However that is the weekend all the players and fans would like to forget. The Sea Eagles saved their worst for last.

Melbourne Storm hammered Manly 40-12 after a diabolically bad display at AAMI Park. The Sea Eagles suffered their biggest loss of the season, had the worst completion rate of their sets of six tackles, made fewer metres than in any other game and the least number of line-breaks. 'It really was disappointing,' said Toovey. 'We dropped the ball from the kick-off and it never got any better. I don't mind us losing if we play well. But to lose like that with so many errors really gutted us. We we were way off the mark.' They weren't helped by co-captain Jamie Lyon taking a calf injury into the match. He tried to inspire his teammates but it was a lost cause.

Lyon had arguably the best season of his career – including that in which he was named Super League's Man of Steel. How sad that his retirement from representative League means we could no longer can enjoy his efforts in the Test and Origin arenas. His 190 points was his highest for a club season in the NRL.

The experienced forwards Anthony Watmough, Glenn Stewart and Brent Kite and backs Brett Stewart, Steve Matai and Daly Cherry Evans all had great seasons, while rookie winger Jorge Taufua was one of the discoveries of the year. The Sea Eagles lost Tony 'T-Rex' Williams for 2013. He was set to link with Hasler at the Bulldogs. And young fullback/winger Dean Whare, named in the Kiwis Trans-Tasman Test squad, was headed for Penrith.

NORTH QUEENSLAND COWBOYS (5th)
Critics had been predicting all year that mistakes by match officials could very well decide the results of matches in the finals series. And it came to pass in the second week of the play-offs when controversial decisions by the video referees, Steve Clark and Paul Simpkins, handed two tries to Manly and ended the season for the North Queensland Cowboys.

One ruling was a 50/50 call but the other was clear-cut – and the two officials were sacked for their mistake. Cowboys coach Neil Henry was livid: 'We've been dudded. It leaves a bitter taste in our mouths. I am not saying they (the match officials) are biased. I'd say they are incompetent.'

The Cowboys were entertaining, scoring more points than any other (597). Helping them were co-captain Johnathan Thurston (with 192 points), winger Ash Graham (21 tries, the second best in the NRL) and fullback Matt Bowen (13 tries). Bowen may have been 30 years old but he was still good enough to finish as runner-up in the voting for the Dally M Medal.

Then there were the bookends – props Matt Scott and James Tamou - who averaged 145 and 155 metres repectively in bullocking runs. Tamou created a furore when he turned his back on his native New Zealand to play Tests for Australia – just because he wanted to be involved in State of Origin.

CANBERRA RAIDERS (6th)
In June, after a 40-nil hammering by Wests Tigers, Canberra Raiders sat in second-last place on the NRL Ladder. They had won just four of their 12 games and there were widespread calls for their coach David Furner to be sacked. But the club hierarchy stood firm behind the beleaguered Furner. And they reaped their reward when, after winning the last five games of the regular season, they sneaked into the play-offs before beating Cronulla in the first weekend of the finals, scoring seven tries to one. Sadly for their fans they were no match for South Sydney the following week.

But the Raiders finished with their heads held high. 'I told the boys I was proud of where they finished,' said Furner. 'I am very happy with what we achieved.'

Loose forward Shaun Fensom was arguably their best player all season, averaging 44 tackles per game and running 105 metres. Jarrod Croker topped the NRL pointscoring with 226 after missing the last couple of games through injury. Prop David Shillington was a must choice for Australia's Test side. Stand-off Josh McCrone stepped up a notch after yet another injury to Raiders' strike weapon Terry Campese. And forward Josh Papalii and winger Edrick Lee showed immense promise.

CRONULLA SHARKS (7th)

Cronulla's first match of the season set the trend for the rest of the year, beaten by one point after a dodgy refereeing decision cost them victory. The Sharks did recover to sit in sixth place at the halfway mark but some more unfortunate rulings by referees, injuries to inspirational captain Paul Gallen and enigmatic playmaker Todd Carney all cost them dearly.

Then they saved two of their worst displays for their final two games of the season. 'We had some distractions and some hurdles to get over, but there are no excuses,' said coach Shane Flanagan. And Gallen added: 'We can learn from it all and come back a better side next season.'

Flanagan has such faith in his side that he knocked back an offer to take over the reins of the New Zealand Warriors in Auckland at a salary that would have doubled that he had been getting at Cronulla, and with a host of fringe benefits. The reason for his confidence was obvious. Not only were all his stars staying at Cronulla but his recruits included veteran utility Test man Luke Lewis and goal-kicking winger Michael Gordon from Penrith, improving winger Jonathan Wright (Canterbury) and the Wests Tigers' duo of joking winger Beau Ryan and England Four Nations loose forward Chris Heighington.

BRISBANE BRONCOS (8th)

Brisbane had a season that promised so much and returned so little. It was their first year of the post Darren Lockyer era. But they still hoped to send the old warhorse Petero Civoniceva into retirement as a winner. For a while they were on track, poised in third place on the NRL Ladder after 16 rounds. But seven losses in the final nine rounds of the home-and-away action saw them plummet out of finals contention.

With the drop in form came some interesting statistics. They averaged only 20 points per game – the fewest for the Broncos in 23 seasons. For only the second time in history no Broncos topped the century of points. They won only three games against teams that ultimately finished in the play-offs.

Injuries took their toll, with the most vital loss being that of exciting young Four Nations winger Jharal Yow Yeh, who suffered an horrific season-ending injury after just four outings. Some of the injuries forced captain Sam Thaiday to soldier on despite being hampered with his own problems.

Without Darren Lockyer inside him, centre Justin Hodges did not get enough clean passes. Yet he still helped lift the enthusiasm of his teammates with some wonderful displays. Hooker Andrew McCullough played in every game and averaged 42 tackles per appearance. A consistent season saw back-rower Ben Te'o chosen as 18th man for Australia in the October Test against the Kiwis, but Te'o was off to South Sydney the next season.

ST GEORGE ILLAWARRA DRAGONS (9th)

It was perhaps predictable that the Dragons were going to struggle in 2012 after supercoach Wayne Bennett left to accept a Kings Ransom from mining magnate Nathan Tinkler to take over the Newcastle Knights. And taking Test back Darius Boyd with him didn't help St George Illawarra's chances either.

And so it transpired. The Dragons struggled all season to stay in touch with the NRL front-runners. Indeed, such was their lack of attacking ability that they finished with the lowest scoring rate in the merged club's history – just under 17 points per game. And you don't win Premierships with those sort of figures.

Rookie coach Steve Price survived the setbacks but needed to pull a rabbit out of the hat if he was to continue on after 2013. The Dragons would be without the two retired veterans, captain Ben Hornby and utility Dean Young. And international Beau Scott joined Bennett at Newcastle, too. With the trio's departure Price had a war chest on which to draw if he needed to recruit. However, there were not too many established stars on the market.

WESTS TIGERS (10th)

What a wretched season it was for the Wests Tigers. Before a ball was kicked the bookmakers had them as favourites to win the Premiership. And with good reason! They had an impressive line-up with eight internationals (including England's Gareth Ellis and Chris Heighington and the Kiwis captain Benji Marshall). And they were schooled by Australia's Test coach Tim Sheens. But, with injuries to figures who were expected to play major roles in the surge towards a title – not the least Ellis and captain Robbie Farah – it didn't take long for everything to go pear-shaped. Even a mid-season run of seven straight wins hardly instilled confidence in the Wests' fans.

The awful season came to a dramatic end after the final two matches saw them miss out on the play-offs. There was in-fighting between members of the board from the two former clubs which had merged, Wests Magpies and Balmain Tigers. The popular pair of Heighington and Beau Ryan, the club's best player in 2012, were given a nudge and signed with Cronulla. Another talented young player Blake Ayshford was told to look elsewhere. This precipitated a player revolt with the result that Sheens was relieved of his coaching role, and the board and he struggled to find a solution to what he would do in the future.

New coach Mick Potter would have to deal with the fractured board but had the nucleus of a strong team, not the least promising prop Aaron Woods and lightning-fast Fijian winger Marika Koroibete, a member of the Tigers grand final-winning under-20s side. Koroibete scored 34 tries in as many Toyota Cup appearances in that youth competition over the past two years to add to his seven in six NRL games after he made his debut for the top side late in 2012.

As well, Wests had two other fine young players – fullback James Tedesco and stand-off Curtis Sironen. Both were cut down by injury shortly after they made it into the NRL ranks.

GOLD COAST TITANS (11th)

The Gold Coast Titans made a dramatic improvement in 2012. The previous year they were handed the wooden spoon (on points-difference from Canberra Raiders) and after nine rounds this time around they were in 14th place and looking at again finishing at the foot of the table. The club was also facing a financial crisis.

Then the Titans sparked to win seven of their next 10 games and were a chance of making the play-offs. They didn't, but gave coach John Carwright a glimpse of form that indicated more improvement was possible.

The most impressive debutant was 21-year-old stand-off Aiden Sezer. Fullback William Zillman had arguably the best season of his career. And then there was the evergreen forward Nate Myles. He was a revelation. He won the Wally Lewis Medal as Man of the Origin Series in Queensland's seventh victory over the Blues and was recalled to Australia's Test side for the October Trans-Tasman encounter. 'Nate went above and beyond for us,' Cartwright explained. 'He kept backing up, busted and wounded, but was still leading the way. Inspirational!'

Big signing Jamal Idris was a disappointment – but his lack of impact could be attributed to a series of niggling injuries. Internationals Greg Bird and Ashley Harrison also had to overcome injuries at vital stages of the season.

NEWCASTLE KNIGHTS (12th)

Newcastle fans were expecting new coach Wayne Bennett to perform miracles when he took over the reins at the start of the season. After all he was the most successful coach in Premiership history and had steered the Dragons out of the doldrums and to a title in his second year at the helm.

But Bennett warned everyone about expecting too much. He was proved right. And he missed the play-offs for the first time in 21 years. His task wasn't helped when captain

Kurt Gidley missed most of the season through injuries. Luckily there was another Test veteran, Danny Buderus, back from Leeds Rhinos, there to help out. And while critics scoffed when Bennett signed Willie Mason, back from French rugby union, the big fella surprised everyone with stout-hearted displays all season.

Four Nations flyer Akuila Uate had a quiet start to the season but then hit his straps to finish with 18 tries, the third best tally in the NRL. Fellow international Darius Boyd had a modest season after following Bennett to Newcastle from the Dragons, but kept his Test and Origin spots. And they were to be joined by yet another two internationals in 2013. Kiwi back-rower Jeremy Smith would be with his fourth NRL club after the Storm, Dragons and Sharks, while Four Nations utility Beau Scott had also spent time with Cronulla and St George Illawarra.

SYDNEY ROOSTERS (13th)

When the Roosters made the grand final in 2010 it seemed only a matter of time before there would be another title and coach Brian Smith looked ready to get the monkey off his back. After almost three decades as a senior coach, including stints with Hull FC and Bradford Bulls, his first Premiership was beckoning.

But it was back-to-back seasons of failure as the Roosters fell completely off their perch and had to fight to avoid the wooden spoon. And in the end, with the Roosters dropping from 11th to 13th on the NRL Ladder Smith was shown the door. It was predicted be the end to a career to one of the finest technical coaches of the modern era.

It was also a sad end to his time at Bondi for captain Braith Anasta who was off to finish his career with Wests Tigers.

But there was light at the end of the tunnel. New coach Trent Robinson, former assistant to Smith, was hailed as one of the mentors of the future after his stint with Catalan Dragons. The Roosters players were gutted when he left to join the French outfit and those under his tutelage at Perpignan had shouted his praises. He was seen as one the few individuals tough enough to stand-up to the demands of Sonny Bill Williams, returning from rugby union for the big bucks offered by Roosters boss Nick Politis.

Goal-kicking stand-off James Maloney is returning from Auckland to Australia as Anasta's replacement. He will link with NSW Origin scrum-half Mitchell Pearce. Fullback Anthony Minichiello, the former Golden Boot winner, is still in great form despite his veteran status. And in Roger Tuivasa-Sheck, the club has one of the most exciting youngsters in the game. The 19-year-old Samoan winger, a former New Zealand rugby union schoolboys representative, is ready to take over the No 1 shirt once Minichiello calls it a day.

A bonus was that the Roosters reached the finals' series of the Toyota Cup (Under-20s) with a number of those players ready to graduate to the big league.

NEW ZEALAND WARRIORS (14th)

What a dramatic nose-dive it was for the beaten side in the previous year's grand final. The Warriors allowed their coach Ivan Cleary to leave while he still had a year remaining on his contract and replaced him with Brian 'Bluey' McClennan, who had such success with New Zealand in the 2005 Tri-Nations Tournament and with Leeds Rhinos when they won the Super League in 2008 and 2009. But he could not replicate that success in the NRL. After winning just eight times in the first 22 encounters (with two losses after the Warriors had led 18-nil), McClennan was shown the door, even though the club did not have anyone in mind as his replacement.

The main problems for the Warriors were their lack of fitness, poor defence, lack of experience in the backs and poor interchange tactics (often with blockbusting forwards Russell Packer and Ben Matulino cooling their heels on the bench at the same time). And they sorely missed the veteran loose forward Micheal Luck through injury for much of the season. Yet, surprisingly, they still had a chance of making the play-offs with a few weeks remaining. However this coincided with a five-week spell on the sideline for captain Simon Mannering, so often a steadying influence for the Warriors. When he returned it was too late.

The 23-year-old Matulino truly came of age, carrying more than his share of the load. The Warriors would need a repeat from him in 2013 as it was going to be another tough year. They lost two of their better players – utility Lewis Brown who joined his former coach Cleary at Penrith and goal-kicking stand-off James Maloney who was to replace Braith Anasta at the Roosters.

PENRITH PANTHERS (15th)

Much was expected of Penrith in 2012 after the appointment of former Origin coach Phil Gould to direct the front office and the appointment as coach of Ivan Cleary who had steered the New Zealand Warriors to the previous year's grand final. But it all came to nothing and the Panthers were still fighting to avoid the wooden spoon with a couple of weeks left in the home-and-away clashes.

Such was the inner turmoil that international centre Michael Jennings was dropped to Penrith's feeder club (from where he was recruited by coach Ricky Stuart for the NSW Origin line-up) and the Panthers' favourite son (and captain) Luke Lewis decided to quit and join Cronulla in 2013. The latter was a real blow to the fans as they knew Lewis had hoped to finish his career as a one-club player. And a thyroid cancer scare robbed him of one last appearance in Penrith strip after 208 appearances.

The Panthers also lost goal-kicking winger Michael Gordon for 2013. After 102 club appearances he, too, was off to the Sharks.

PARRAMATTA EELS (16th)

What a disappointing season for the Eels, who picked up their first wooden spoon in 40 years – an embarrassment that led to the sacking of coach Stephen Kearney before the season was over. Worse was the fact that it was the final season for one of the Parramatta greats, captain Nathan Hindmarsh. He deserved better from his teammates after 22 Tests for Australia, 17 Origin games for New South Wales, and a record 340 appearances for the Eels since his debut in 1998.

There was no significance about the result of the final match of the 2012 season proper against the Dragons, but such was Hindmarsh's standing in the sport that 45,863 fans turned up at Homebush to say goodbye. The attendance figure broke the previous record for an NRL match outside the play-offs that turned up to farewell Hazem El Masri in 2009. Hindmarsh may not have been on the winning side, but a penalty in the closing minute of the encounter gave him the chance to kick the first goal of his career. He didn't need a tee, like the modern goalkickers – just a mound of sand, as he booted the goal from 22 metres out.

Also saying farewell that night was Eels goalkicking wiz Luke Burt, whose record boasted one appearance for the Prime Minister's XIII versus Papua New Guinea and 264 matches for Parramatta, with a club record of 124 tries and the second most points in Eels history.

Big-name signing Chris Sandow didn't fire and media darling Jarryd Hayne missed half the season though injury. That didn't help. New coach Ricky Stuart, the NSW Origin coach and former Test mentor, faced an uphill battle in his first season at the helm.

SEASON DOWN UNDER - ROUND-UP

NRL PREMIERSHIP FINALS SERIES

QUALIFYING FINALS

Friday 7th September 2012
Canterbury Bulldogs 16 ....Manly Sea Eagles 10
Saturday 8th September 2012
Melbourne Storm 24..South Sydney Rabbitohs 6

ELIMINATION FINALS

Saturday 8th September 2012
North Queensland Cowboys 33 ....Brisbane Broncos 16
Sunday 9th September 2012
Canberra Raiders 34 ....Cronulla Sharks 16

SEMI-FINALS

Friday 14th September 2012
Manly Sea Eagles 22 ....North Queensland Cowboys 12
Saturday 15th September 2012
South Sydney Rabbitohs 38 ....Canberra Raiders 16

PRELIMINARY FINALS

Friday 21st September 2012
Melbourne Storm 40 ....Manly Sea Eagles 12
Saturday 22nd September 2012
Canterbury Bulldogs 32 ....South Sydney Rabbitohs 8

GRAND FINAL

Sunday 30th September 2012

CANTERBURY BULLDOGS 4 MELBOURNE STORM 14

BULLDOGS: 1 Ben Barba; 2 Sam Perrett; 3 Josh Morris; 4 Krisnan Inu; 5 Jonathan Wright; 6 Josh Reynolds; 7 Kris Keating; 8 Aiden Tolman; 9 Michael Ennis (C); 10 Sam Kasiano; 11 Frank Pritchard; 12 Josh Jackson; 13 Greg Eastwood. Subs (all used): 14 James Graham; 15 Dale Finucane; 16 Corey Payne; 17 David Stagg.
Try: Perrett (25); **Goals:** Inu 0/1.
On report: Graham (25) - alleged bite on Slater.
STORM: 1 Billy Slater; 2 Sisa Waqa; 3 Dane Nielsen; 4 Will Chambers; 5 Justin O'Neill; 6 Gareth Widdop; 7 Cooper Cronk; 8 Jesse Bromwich; 9 Cameron Smith (C); 10 Bryan Norrie; 11 Sika Manu; 12 Ryan Hoffman; 13 Todd Lowrie. Subs (all used): 14 Ryan Hinchcliffe; 15 Kevin Proctor; 16 Jaiman Lowe; 17 Richard Fa'aoso.
Tries: Hoffman (6), Slater (31), O'Neill (39); **Goals:** Smith 1/5.
Rugby Leaguer & League Express Men of the Match:
Bulldogs: Ben Barba; *Storm:* Cooper Cronk.
Clive Churchill Medal (Man of the Match):
Cooper Cronk (Melbourne Storm).
Half-time: 4-14; **Referees:** Tony Archer & Ben Cummins;
Attendance: 82,976 *(at ANZ Stadium, Sydney).*

FINAL NRL PREMIERSHIP TABLE

	P	W	D	L	B	F	A	D	Pts
Canterbury Bulldogs	24	18	0	6	2	568	369	199	40
Melbourne Storm	24	17	0	7	2	579	361	218	38
South Sydney Rabbitohs	24	16	0	8	2	559	438	121	36
Manly Sea Eagles	24	16	0	8	2	497	403	94	36
North Queensland Cowboys	24	15	0	9	2	597	445	152	34
Canberra Raiders	24	13	0	11	2	545	536	9	30
Cronulla Sharks	24	12	1	11	2	455	441	14	29
Brisbane Broncos	24	12	0	12	2	481	447	34	28
St George Illawarra Dragons	24	11	0	13	2	405	438	-33	26
Wests Tigers	24	11	0	13	2	506	551	-45	26
Gold Coast Titans	24	10	0	14	2	449	477	-28	24
Newcastle Knights	24	10	0	14	2	448	488	-40	24
Sydney Roosters	24	8	1	15	2	462	626	-164	21
New Zealand Warriors	24	8	0	16	2	497	609	-112	20
Penrith Panthers	24	8	0	16	2	409	575	-166	20
Parramatta Eels	24	6	0	18	2	431	674	-243	16

TOP POINTSCORERS

		T	G	FG	Pts
Jarrod Croker	Canberra Raiders	16	81	0	226
Adam Reynolds	South Sydney Rabbitohs	3	97	2	208
Johnathan Thurston	North Queensland Cowboys	3	90	0	192
Jamie Lyon	Manly Sea Eagles	11	73	0	190
Benji Marshall	Wests Tigers	5	72	3	167

TOP TRYSCORERS

Ben Barba	Canterbury Bulldogs	22
Ashley Graham	North Queensland Cowboys	21
Akuila Uate	Newcastle Knights	18
Andrew Everingham	South Sydney Rabbitohs	17
Josh Morris	Canterbury Bulldogs	17

TOYOTA CUP GRAND FINAL *(Under-20s)*
Sunday 30th September 2012
Canberra Raiders 6 ....Wests Tigers 46
(at ANZ Stadium, Sydney)

NEW SOUTH WALES CUP GRAND FINAL
Sunday 30th September 2012
Balmain Ryde Tigers 18...Newtown Jets 22
(at ANZ Stadium, Sydney)

QUEENSLAND CUP GRAND FINAL
Sunday 23rd September 2012
Redcliffe Dolphins 10 ....Wynnum Manly Seagulls 20
(at Suncorp Stadium, Brisbane)

DALLY M AWARDS
Dally M Medal (Player of the Year): Ben Barba (Canterbury Bulldogs)
Provan Summons Medal (People's Choice):
Ben Barba (Canterbury Bulldogs)
Coach of the Year: Des Hasler (Canterbury Bulldogs)
Captains of the Year: Jamie Lyon & Jason King (Manly Sea Eagles)
Representative Player of the Year: Nate Myles (Gold Coast Titans)
Rookie of the Year: Adam Reynolds (South Sydney Rabbitohs)
Toyota Cup Player of the Year (Under-20s):
David Klemmer (Canterbury Bulldogs)

ALL STARS GAME

Saturday 4th February 2012

NRL INDIGENOUS ALL STARS 28 NRL ALL STARS 36

NRL INDIGENOUS ALL STARS: 1 Ben Barba (Canterbury Bulldogs); 2 Jharal Yow Yeh (Brisbane Broncos); 3 Greg Inglis (South Sydney Rabbitohs); 4 Justin Hodges (Brisbane Broncos); 5 Nathan Merritt (South Sydney Rabbitohs); 6 Johnathan Thurston (North Queensland Cowboys) (C); 7 Chris Sandow (Parramatta Eels); 8 Tom Learoyd-Lahrs (Canberra Raiders); 9 Travis Waddell (Canberra Raiders); 10 George Rose (Manly Sea Eagles); 11 Sam Thaiday (Brisbane Broncos); 12 Jamal Idris (Gold Coast Titans); 13 Greg Bird (Gold Coast Titans. Subs (all used): 14 Andrew Fifita (Cronulla Sharks); 15 Cory Paterson (North Queensland Cowboys); 16 Matt Bowen (North Queensland Cowboys); 17 Scott Prince (Gold Coast Titans); 18 Anthony Mitchell (Sydney Roosters); 19 Joel Thompson (Canberra Raiders); 20 Nathan Peats (South Sydney Rabbitohs).
Tries: Yow Yeh (5), Merritt (18, 38), Bowen (29), Inglis (67);
Goals: Thurston 3/4, Sandow 1/1.
NRL ALL STARS: 1 Josh Dugan (Canberra Raiders); 2 Jason Nightingale (St George Illawarra Dragons); 3 Jack Reed (Brisbane Broncos); 4 Michael Jennings (Penrith Panthers); 5 Manu Vatuvei (New Zealand Warriors); 6 Benji Marshall (Wests Tigers) (C); 7 Cooper Cronk (Melbourne Storm); 8 Kade Snowden (Newcastle Knights); 9 Aaron Payne (North Queensland Cowboys); 10 Luke Bailey (Gold Coast Titans); 11 Nathan Hindmarsh (Parramatta Eels); 12 Dave Taylor (South Sydney Rabbitohs); 13 Paul Gallen (Cronulla Sharks). Subs (all used): 14 Adam Blair (Wests Tigers); 15 Frank Pritchard (Canterbury Bulldogs); 16 Jared Waerea-Hargreaves (Sydney Roosters); 17 Anthony Watmough (Manly Sea Eagles); 18 Brent Tate (North Queensland Cowboys); 19 Luke Lewis (Penrith Panthers); 20 Nathan Fien (St George Illawarra Dragons).
Tries: Pritchard (26), Lewis (35), Bailey (44), Dugan (50), Reed (63), Vatuvei (72);
Goals: Marshall 6/6.
Rugby Leaguer & League Express Men of the Match:
NRL Indigenous All Stars: Nathan Merritt; *NRL All Stars:* Benji Marshall.
Preston Campbell Medal (Man of the Match, voted by fans):
Nathan Merritt (NRL Indigenous All Stars).
Half-time: 22-12; **Referees:** Ashley Klein, Jason Robinson,
Shayne Hayne & Gerard Sutton; **Attendance:** 25,700 *(at Skilled Park, Robina).*

REPRESENTATIVE GAME

Sunday 23rd September 2012

PAPUA NEW GUINEA 18 AUSTRALIAN PRIME MINISTER'S XIII 24

PAPUA NEW GUINEA: 1 Josiah Abavu (Port Moresby Vipers); 2 Matthew Puke (Mendi Muruks); 3 Richard Kambo (Port Moresby Vipers); 4 Jason Tali (Mount Hagen Eagles); 5 Albert Patak (Rabaul Gurias); 6 Dion Aiye (Rabaul Gurias); 7 Israel Eliab (Port Moresby Vipers); 8 Rodney Pora (Rabaul Gurias); 9 Charlie Wabo (Mendi Muruks); 10 Gonzella Urakusie (Goroka Lahanis); 11 David Loko (Mendi Mioks); 12 Mark Mexico (Kundiawa Tigers); 13 Glen Nami (Goroka Lahanis) (C). Subs (all used): 14 Wesley Mohokule (Goroka Lahanis); 15 Larson Marabe (Rabaul Gurias); 16 Enoch Maki (Mendi Muruks); 17 Wartovo Puara Jr (Rabaul Gurias); 18 Essau Siune (Kundiawa Lions).
Tries: Puke (14), Patak (47), Loko (65), Kambo (73); **Goals:** Eliab 1/4.
AUSTRALIAN PRIME MINISTER'S XIII: 1 Darius Boyd (Newcastle Knights); 2 Akuila Uate (Newcastle Knights); 3 Michael Jennings (Penrith Panthers); 4 Chris Lawrence (Wests Tigers); 5 Beau Ryan (Wests Tigers); 6 Lachlan Coote (Penrith Panthers); 7 Scott Prince (Gold Coast Titans) (C); 8 Aaron Woods (Wests Tigers); 9 Kevin Kingston (Penrith Panthers); 10 Tim Mannah (Parramatta Eels); 11 Ben Te'o (Brisbane Broncos); 12 Feleti Mateo (New Zealand Warriors); 13 Wade Graham (Penrith Panthers). Subs (all used): 14 Dan Hunt (St George Illawarra Dragons); 15 Martin Kennedy (Sydney Roosters); 16 Josh McGuire (Brisbane Broncos); 17 Matt Ryan (Parramatta Eels); 18 Nathan Stapleton (Cronulla Sharks).
Tries: Ryan (9), Jennings (12), Ryan (38), Uate (80); **Goals:** Prince 4/4.
Half-time: 4-18; **Attendance:** 14,500 *(at Lloyd Robson Oval, Port Moresby).*

State of Origin

There had been plenty of dramatic moments in the 31-year history of State of Origin and the game that sealed Queensland's seventh successive State of Origin series win ranked amongst them as Cooper Cronk's 40-metre field goal less than five minutes from time won a wonderful decider by 21-20.

'It was the best game I've been involved in, both teams ripped in,' NSW's losing captain Paul Gallen said. 'We'll come back next year and we'll be ready again.'

The third match of the series produced record TV ratings - setting a new record as the highest rating game in OzTam history and pulled its biggest ever audience in AFL-dominated Melbourne.

Even the absence of retired Darren Lockyer for the first time in 14 years couldn't stop the Queenslanders. Winning skipper Cameron Smith was a strong contender along with fellow Maroon Greg Inglis for the Wally Lewis Medal as man of the series which eventually went to Gold Coast forward Nate Myles, as veteran prop Petero Civoniceva - at the age of 36 and playing his farewell 33rd State of Origin game in the third leg at Suncorp – went out a winner.

Ricky Stuart stepped down as New South Wales head coach after the series in August, shortly after signing a contract to coach the Parramatta Eels from 2013 onwards.

Queensland were already well on track to extend their record-breaking run to seven consecutive series wins after their controversial 18-10 victory over New South Wales at the Etihad Stadium in Melbourne.

There were several disputed refereeing decisions. The biggest controversy concerned a try awarded to Maroons centre Greg Inglis with eight minutes left on the clock. At the time the result was hanging in the balance, with Queensland clinging to a 12-10 lead when Inglis swooped on a ball that had gone loose after a Blues bomb. As he went to plant the ball down for a four-pointer, NSW hooker Robbie Farah knocked it out of Inglis's hands. Video referee Sean Hampstead ruled that Farah had deliberately kicked it and so it was not a knock-on.

NSW coach Ricky Stuart later admitted he thought it was a try. But Blues captain Paul Gallen was furious. 'How is that a try?' he demanded of referees Matt Cecchin and Ben Cummins as Queensland goal-kicker Johnathan Thurston lined up the conversion to seal the eight-point victory. 'This is out of control. This is ridiculous.'

In the eyes of many critics Cecchin and Cummins seemed to be out of their depth and had confirmed pre-game doubts over why the two most experienced referees, Tony Archer and Shayne Hayne, were only spectators and not controlling the showcase feature.

The first confrontation of the night typified the Origin slogan – 'state against state, mate against mate'. It involved the two Newcastle teammates Darius Boyd (Queensland) and Akuila Uate (NSW).

The two wingers went for a bomb from Farah out wide. And video referee

STATE OF ORIGIN - GAME I

Wednesday 23rd May 2012

NEW SOUTH WALES 10 QUEENSLAND 18

NEW SOUTH WALES: 1 Brett Stewart (Manly Sea Eagles); 5 Akuila Uate (Newcastle Knights); 4 Josh Morris (Canterbury Bulldogs); 3 Michael Jennings (Penrith Panthers); 2 Jarryd Hayne (Parramatta Eels); 6 Todd Carney (Cronulla Sharks); 7 Mitchell Pearce (Sydney Roosters); 8 Paul Gallen (Cronulla Sharks) (C); 9 Robbie Farah (Wests Tigers); 10 James Tamou (North Queensland Cowboys); 11 Glenn Stewart (Manly Sea Eagles); 12 Luke Lewis (Penrith Panthers); 13 Greg Bird (Gold Coast Titans). Subs (all used): 14 Trent Merrin (St George Illawarra Dragons); 15 Jamie Buhrer (Manly Sea Eagles); 16 Ben Creagh (St George Illawarra Dragons); 17 Tony Williams (Manly Sea Eagles).
Tries: Uate (6), Jennings (42); **Goals:** Carney 1/2.
Sin bin: Jennings (21) - fighting.
QUEENSLAND: 1 Billy Slater (Melbourne Storm); 5 Brent Tate (North Queensland Cowboys); 4 Justin Hodges (Brisbane Broncos); 3 Greg Inglis (South Sydney Rabbitohs); 2 Darius Boyd (Newcastle Knights); 6 Johnathan Thurston (North Queensland Cowboys); 7 Cooper Cronk (Melbourne Storm); 8 Matt Scott (North Queensland Cowboys); 9 Cameron Smith (Melbourne Storm) (C); 10 Petero Civoniceva (Brisbane Broncos); 11 Nate Myles (Gold Coast Titans); 12 Sam Thaiday (Brisbane Broncos); 13 Ashley Harrison (Gold Coast Titans). Subs (all used): 14 Matt Gillett (Brisbane Broncos); 15 Dave Taylor (South Sydney Rabbitohs); 16 Ben Hannant (Brisbane Broncos); 17 David Shillington (Canberra Raiders).
Tries: Boyd (26, 39), Inglis (72); **Goals:** Thurston 3/3.
Rugby Leaguer & League Express Men of the Match:
New South Wales: Paul Gallen; *Queensland:* Nate Myles.
Half-time: 4-12; **Referees:** Matt Cecchin & Ben Cummins;
Attendance: 56,021 *(at Etihad Stadium, Melbourne).*

Hampstead, in a difficult decision, ruled Uate had not knocked on before he touched down for the first try.

With a wealth of possession for New South Wales, Farah was having a great game – showing the determination that followed his Origin snubs in recent years. He went close to scoring between the posts in the 17th minute but was held up after a wonderful tackle by prop Matt Scott and fullback Billy Slater.

The game exploded midway through the half with almost very player involved in an all-in brawl. But only NSW centre Michael Jennings was despatched to the sin bin – for running more than 20 metres to join the mayhem.

How sad for Jennings. He had already been told by Penrith coach Ivan Cleary he would be back with the Panthers' feeder club Wentworthville Wolves again on the weekend. But after being charged with contrary conduct he was suspended for one game.

With an extra man, the Maroons machine started to click. Moments later Queensland looked certain to score as Brent Tate stormed for the right corner, but he was bundled into touch just centimetres out from the line. Within two minutes Slater sliced into the backline, caught the ball and sent it on in one motion for Boyd to score wide out. Thurston converted from the sideline to put the Maroons in the front. As the siren was about to sound for half-time, Thurston drew Uate back into him in defence to give Boyd a clear run to the corner for his second try. And JT converted again from the sideline to give the Queenslanders a 12-4 lead.

The Blues were right back in contention after the break, when Jennings scored. It, too, was contentious with Jarryd Hayne looking to have knocked it forward to the Panthers centre.

As the half continued the Blues were definitely on top. Cooper Cronk made a try-saving tackle on Brett Stewart before Sam Thaiday beat the NSW fullback in a race to get to a Jennings kick behind the tryline.

The excitement continued to build - until that Inglis try.

So often the accolades in Origin games go to the flashy backs such as Slater, Inglis and Thurston. With his controversial try, Inglis set a new Origin record of 13 (in 16 appearances). Brent Tate, in his return to the Origin arena after four years, was also outstanding. But none was better than Nate Myles.

Back in the Origin mix after three years, Robbie Farah was close to being New South Wales' best in the first encounter. But he was truly inspirational as the Blues squared the series at Homebush, sending it to a decider in Brisbane. Farah played the full 80 minutes, during which time he set a new Origin record of 63 for the number of tackles made, beating the previous mark of 60 set in 2007 by Queensland's Dallas Johnson. Farah did not miss a single tackle all night.

'I didn't want to let anyone down,' Farah explained. Not his teammates. Not the NSW fans. But, most of all, not his mum, Sonia. She had been battling pancreatic cancer since November, when he rushed home from the Gillette Four Nations to be at her side. Sonia had hoped to watch from a private box provided by the stadium chiefs. In the end, she wasn't well enough and watched on television in her room in a nearby hospital. And the following day she told her exhausted son how proud she had been of his efforts. Five days later she died.

It was the usual spine-tingling Origin clash, right from the kick-off as the old confronted the new. Queensland prop Petero Civoniceva hit debutant Tim Grant in the first tackle of the match. It was meant to intimidate the rookie. Instead the veteran went reeling backwards as the Penrith youngster showed he had no intention of being threatened by the 36-year-old hard man.

The rain that had swept through Sydney for several days made handling difficult. The torrid nature of the game took its toll and, when the final tally was made, it was the Queenslanders who suffered most. Billy Slater was no real threat after he strained a cruciate ligament in his left knee midway through the half. The medicos allowed him to stay out on the field, because he could do little extra damage to the knee. Nevertheless his characteristic attacking flair was missing and he was out for the decider. NSW captain Paul Gallen went into the game with a serious injury to his right knee, but refused to succumb. Brent Tate and Justin Hodges struggled at times for Queensland. And then, soon after half-time, Queensland's Corey Parker ended his evening when he suffered a massive gash to his left shin.

In the 25th minute, the ball spread across the NSW backline. Brett Stewart sliced in as an extra man and plunged for the tryline. Thurston and Slater couldn't hold him up. Then, a struggling Slater took the ball over the sideline half-a-metre out from the left-hand corner with six minutes

STATE OF ORIGIN - GAME II

Wednesday 13th June 2012

NEW SOUTH WALES 16 QUEENSLAND 12

NEW SOUTH WALES: 1 Brett Stewart (Manly Sea Eagles); 5 Akuila Uate (Newcastle Knights); 4 Josh Morris (Canterbury Bulldogs); 3 Michael Jennings (Penrith Panthers); 2 Jarryd Hayne (Parramatta Eels); 6 Todd Carney (Cronulla Sharks); 7 Mitchell Pearce (Sydney Roosters); 8 Tim Grant (Penrith Panthers); 9 Robbie Farah (Wests Tigers); 10 James Tamou (North Queensland Cowboys); 11 Greg Bird (Gold Coast Titans); 12 Glenn Stewart (Manly Sea Eagles); 13 Paul Gallen (Cronulla Sharks) (C). Subs (all used): 14 Trent Merrin (St George Illawarra Dragons); 15 Luke Lewis (Penrith Panthers); 16 Ben Creagh (St George Illawarra Dragons); 17 Anthony Watmough (Manly Sea Eagles).
Tries: B Stewart (25, 43), Morris (47); **Goals:** Carney 2/4.
QUEENSLAND: 1 Billy Slater (Melbourne Storm); 5 Brent Tate (North Queensland Cowboys); 4 Justin Hodges (Brisbane Broncos); 3 Greg Inglis (South Sydney Rabbitohs); 2 Darius Boyd (Newcastle Knights); 6 Johnathan Thurston (North Queensland Cowboys); 7 Cooper Cronk (Melbourne Storm); 8 Matt Scott (North Queensland Cowboys); 9 Cameron Smith (Melbourne Storm) (C); 10 Petero Civoniceva (Brisbane Broncos); 11 Nate Myles (Gold Coast Titans); 12 Dave Taylor (South Sydney Rabbitohs); 13 Ashley Harrison (Gold Coast Titans). Subs (all used): 14 Matt Gillett (Brisbane Broncos); 15 Corey Parker (Brisbane Broncos); 16 Ben Hannant (Brisbane Broncos); 17 David Shillington (Canberra Raiders).
Tries: Hannant (39), Inglis (61); **Goals:** Thurston 2/2.
Sin bin: Cronk (42) - professional foul.
Rugby Leaguer & League Express Men of the Match:
New South Wales: Robbie Farah; *Queensland:* Matt Scott.
Half-time: 4-6; **Referees:** Tony Archer & Ben Cummins; **Attendance:** 83,110 *(at ANZ Stadium, Sydney).*

remaining. But the Queenslanders held on, with Cameron Smith taking a dangerous kick from Farah. Up the other end of the field, Cronk put up a bomb from 40 metres out. The Blues threequarters watched the ball instead of trying of take it on the full and Ashley Harrison scooped it up and flung it to Ben Hannant, who was across the stripe to even up the scores. And Thurston's conversion put the Queenslanders in front.

Moments after Parker's departure early in the second half the Blues almost scored, but Todd Carney was held back by Cronk as he and Slater went for the ball. It was not a penalty try. But the New South Welshmen were handed a penalty goal and Cronk was dispatched to the sin bin. The Queenslanders were made to pay dearly. From the restart Carney sent Brett Stewart on a long run to score between the posts and the Blues were in front 12-6. Then, less than four minutes later, Thurston pulled the ball out of Jarryd Hayne's hands. Everyone stopped except Josh Morris, who raced 60 metres to score and stretch the lead to 10 points.

Akuila Uate got caught again when he didn't go for a bomb. Darius Boyd leaped high and punched it to his left into the waiting arms of Greg Inglis, who extended his Origin tryscoring record to 14 in 17 matches. And when Thurston booted the conversion from the left sideline the Maroons were back within one try.

Cooper Cronk's 40-metre field goal less than five minutes from time won a game that ebbed and flowed in breathtaking, and at times brutal, fashion from beginning to end. There was one minute and 25 seconds on the clock when Paul Gallen was penalised for throwing a punch at Brent Tate after the winger's play the ball, with a melee ensuing and Tate getting in a sly punch on Greg Bird as he was being held on the ground.

The Maroons had the better of the opening, with veteran prop Petero Civoniceva leading the charge. A Johnathan Thurston kick trapped Jarryd Hayne in-goal and a Cooper Cronk bomb was knocked on by Inglis. But a sensational burst from his own territory by left wing Brett Morris took him through Sam Thaiday's tackle and around Inglis, though Cronk and Thurston combined to drag him down short. On the next play Queensland were penalised for offside and Todd Carney kicked the goal for a 2-0 NSW lead. It got even better for the Blues when Brett Morris managed to squeeze over from dummy-half, the video referee ruling that Thaiday had not managed to stop the Dragons winger grounding the ball. Carney converted and NSW looked set fair at 8-0.

But adversity only inspired the Maroons, with Thurston increasingly influential even though Origin II's man of the match, NSW hooker Robbie Farah was knocked senseless in a three-man tackle but carried on, making 54 tackles in the match and producing some influential kicks.

The pressure told when, after Civoniceva and Dane Nielson both went close, Corey Parker produced the first of a series of skilful offloads for Cameron Smith and Thurston to get the ball out wide for Darius Boyd to race into the left corner through Hayne's tackle. Thurston missed the conversion but the momentum was back with the Maroons. Anthony Watmough intercepted a Justin Hodges pass after a thrilling raid down the right and sub Ben Creagh was the next player knocked out and was led off the field to have a huge head gash repaired.

Queensland took the lead in thrilling style just after the half-hour mark. Thurston slipped Mitchell Pearce on the Maroons' 20-metre line and raced away, linked with Tate and then Cronk, who was tracked down by Carney. From the play the ball Queensland looked to have blown it but Parker got another offload away and Thurston was diving over to the left of the posts. His conversion was easy.

NSW kicked out on the full and within two minutes Hodges was over for a crucial score, running across field before straightening up for the converted score. The video referee was called in for what looked an obvious shepherd but ruled a fair dinkum try.

It was all Queensland straight after the break before a penalty against Thaiday for interference at a play the ball released the pressure. The Blues worked upfield and Farah's kick into the in-goal was grounded by the on-rushing Brett Stewart, the video referee ruling, before the ball reached dead. Carney kicked the goal and we had a two-point ball game.

Straight from the kick-off Tony Williams' attempted pass out of the tackle was spilled by Michael Jennings and James Tamou was penalised in front of the posts for Thurston to stretch the lead to four points. Just after the hour mark another Thurston penalty goal made it six points when Williams temporarily knocked out Cronk with a swinging arm.

NSW weren't done and with nine minutes left on the clock Farah was kicking again, this time a high ball to the right corner. Josh Morris acrobatically rose above Boyd to catch the ball and ground as he fell to the ground. Carney converted from the touchline to stun the partisan home crowd.

It was over to Cronk to provide a one-point lead that proved to be enough, Pearce putting a field-goal attempt wide with 30 seconds left on the clock.

'You don't really think too much, the clock's winding down,' Cronk said of his match-winner. 'It's why you do the practise I think.'

STATE OF ORIGIN - GAME III

Wednesday 4th July 2012

QUEENSLAND 21 NEW SOUTH WALES 20

QUEENSLAND: 1 Greg Inglis (South Sydney Rabbitohs); 5 Brent Tate (North Queensland Cowboys); 4 Justin Hodges (Brisbane Broncos); 3 Dane Nielsen (Melbourne Storm); 2 Darius Boyd (Newcastle Knights); 6 Johnathan Thurston (North Queensland Cowboys); 7 Cooper Cronk (Melbourne Storm); 8 Matt Scott (North Queensland Cowboys); 9 Cameron Smith (Melbourne Storm) (C); 10 Petero Civoniceva (Brisbane Broncos); 11 Nate Myles (Gold Coast Titans); 12 Sam Thaiday (Brisbane Broncos); 13 Corey Parker (Brisbane Broncos). Subs (all used): 14 Matt Gillett (Brisbane Broncos); 15 Ben Te'o (Brisbane Broncos); 16 Ben Hannant (Brisbane Broncos); 17 David Shillington (Canberra Raiders).
Tries: Boyd (19), Thurston (32), Hodges (35); **Goals:** Thurston 4/5; **Field goal:** Cronk (75).
On report: Shillington (75) - alleged high tackle.
NEW SOUTH WALES: 1 Brett Stewart (Manly Sea Eagles); 2 Jarryd Hayne (Parramatta Eels); 4 Josh Morris (Canterbury Bulldogs); 3 Michael Jennings (Penrith Panthers); 5 Brett Morris (St George Illawarra Dragons); 6 Todd Carney (Cronulla Sharks); 7 Mitchell Pearce (Sydney Roosters); 8 Tim Grant (Penrith Panthers); 9 Robbie Farah (Wests Tigers); 10 James Tamou (North Queensland Cowboys); 11 Beau Scott (St George Illawarra Dragons); 12 Greg Bird (Gold Coast Titans); 13 Paul Gallen (Cronulla Sharks) (C). Subs (all used): 14 Tony Williams (Manly Sea Eagles); 15 Luke Lewis (Penrith Panthers); 16 Ben Creagh (St George Illawarra Dragons); 17 Anthony Watmough (Manly Sea Eagles).
Tries: B Morris (13), B Stewart (47), J Morris (70); **Goals:** Carney 4/4.
Rugby Leaguer & League Express Men of the Match:
Queensland: Johnathan Thurston; *New South Wales:* Robbie Farah.
Half-time: 16-8; **Referees:** Tony Archer & Ben Cummins; **Attendance:** 52,437 *(at Suncorp Stadium, Brisbane).*

Wally Lewis Medal (Man of the Series): Nate Myles (Queensland).

2012 SEASON
MONTH BY MONTH

FEBRUARY

Round 1

ABOVE: Adam Milner touches down in the snow as Castleford defeat Salford in the Reds' first game at their new stadium

LEFT: Thomas Leuluai tackled by Carl Ablett as Wigan defeat Leeds

Round 2

Round 2

ABOVE: Scott Dureau is mobbed after kicking Catalan Dragons a memorable win at St Helens

LEFT: Mickey Paea collared by James Roby as Hull KR and St Helens fight out a draw

RIGHT: Featherstone's Ian Hardman crashes over to score during victory against Halifax

Round 3

Round 3

NORTHERN RAIL CUP

WORLD CLUB CHALLENGE

LEEDS RHINOS 26
MANLY SEA EAGLES 12

RIGHT: Rob Burrow takes on Tony Williams and George Rose

BELOW: Daly Cherry-Evans feels the force of Jamie Jones-Buchanan

BELOW: Fireworks as Kevin Sinfield holds aloft the World Club Challenge trophy

MARCH

Round 6

LEFT: Cameron Phelps and Jon Clarke celebrate a thrilling Widnes win over Wigan

BELOW: Sam Moa and Willie Manu get to grips with Louie McCarthy-Scarsbrook as Hull FC shock St Helens

RIGHT: Luke George on the charge during Huddersfield's victory against St Helens

BELOW: Leon Brennan makes a break as North Wales Crusaders are edged out by Barrow in their first game

Round 5

RIGHT: Kevin Sinfield becomes Leeds' all-time leading pointscorer during the Rhinos' win at Salford

FAR RIGHT: Bryn Hargreaves takes on the St Helens defence as Bradford emerge victorious

Round 1

Round

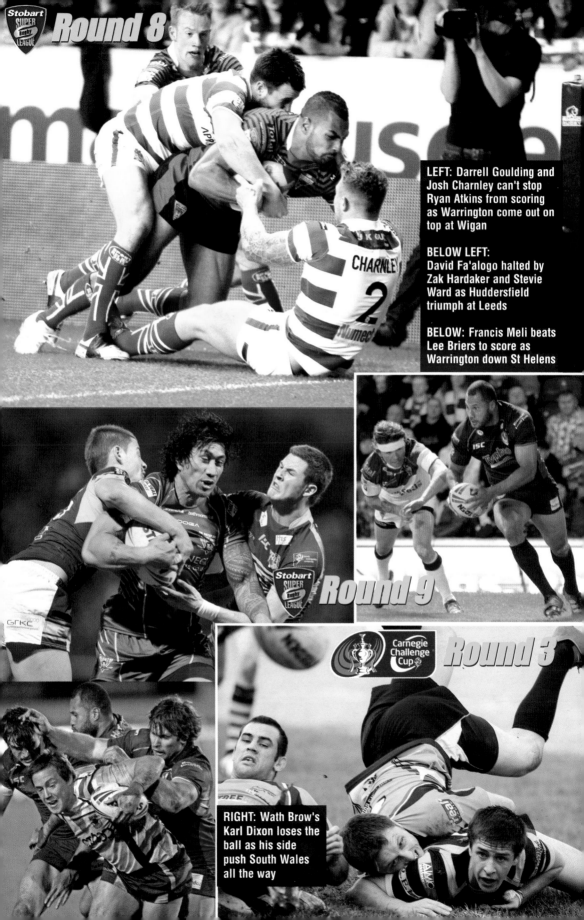

Round 8

LEFT: Darrell Goulding and Josh Charnley can't stop Ryan Atkins from scoring as Warrington come out on top at Wigan

BELOW LEFT: David Fa'alogo halted by Zak Hardaker and Stevie Ward as Huddersfield triumph at Leeds

BELOW: Francis Meli beats Lee Briers to score as Warrington down St Helens

Round 9

Carnegie Challenge Cup

Round 3

RIGHT: Wath Brow's Karl Dixon loses the ball as his side push South Wales all the way

APRIL

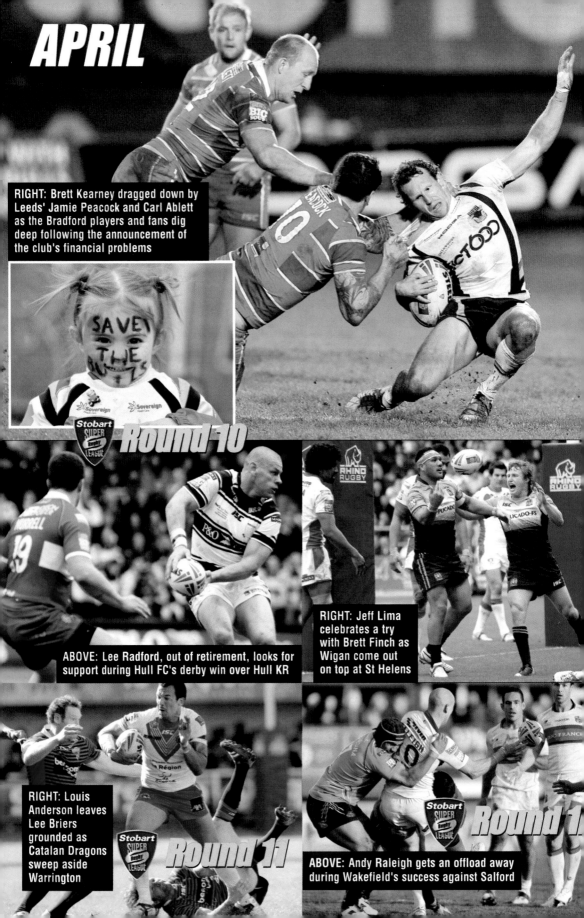

RIGHT: Brett Kearney dragged down by Leeds' Jamie Peacock and Carl Ablett as the Bradford players and fans dig deep following the announcement of the club's financial problems

Round 10

ABOVE: Lee Radford, out of retirement, looks for support during Hull FC's derby win over Hull KR

RIGHT: Jeff Lima celebrates a try with Brett Finch as Wigan come out on top at St Helens

RIGHT: Louis Anderson leaves Lee Briers grounded as Catalan Dragons sweep aside Warrington

Round 11

ABOVE: Andy Raleigh gets an offload away during Wakefield's success against Salford

Round 11

Round 4

ABOVE: Stuart Dickens leads the celebrations as Featherstone knock out fierce rivals Castleford

OW:
n Demetriou
ed by Andrew
erson as
hley edge out
field

The co-operative
CHAMPIONSHIP
Round 5

RIGHT: Craig Gower makes his way through the Mount Pleasant mud as London Broncos battle past Batley

Carnegie Challenge Cup
Round 5

LEFT: Jubilation for Leigh following golden-point victory against Halifax

ANZAC Test

ABOVE: Frank Pritchard gets the ball away during New Zealand's defeat to Australia

MAY

LEFT: Sheffield's Mitchell Stringer brought down by Bob Beswick and Tommy Goulden as Leigh edge a thriller

The co-operative **CHAMPIONSHIP**
Round 6

Stobart SUPER RUGBY LEAGUE
Round 13

ABOVE: Debutant Matthew Russell goes past Ryan Hall during a comprehensive Hull FC win over Leeds

BELOW: Tom Makinson scores a spectacular try in the corner as St Helens defeat Leeds in the first of nine televised Monday night fixtures

Carnegie Challenge Cup
Quarter Final

ABOVE: Ian Henderson wrapped up by Lee Briers and Chris Bridge as Warrington progress at the expense of Catalan Dragons

Stobart SUPER RUGBY LEAGUE
Round 14

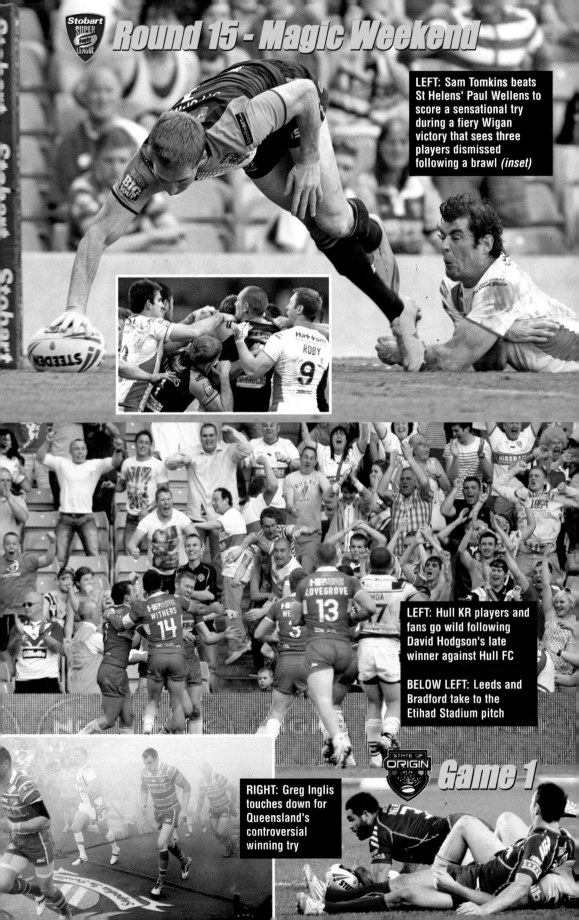

Round 15 - Magic Weekend

LEFT: Sam Tomkins beats St Helens' Paul Wellens to score a sensational try during a fiery Wigan victory that sees three players dismissed following a brawl *(inset)*

LEFT: Hull KR players and fans go wild following David Hodgson's late winner against Hull FC

BELOW LEFT: Leeds and Bradford take to the Etihad Stadium pitch

RIGHT: Greg Inglis touches down for Queensland's controversial winning try

Game 1

JUNE

Round 16

ABOVE: Thomas Leuluai crashes past Brent Webb to score as red-hot Wigan demolish Leeds

BELOW: Josh Hodgson wrapped up as Catalan Dragons edge out Hull KR

LEFT: Antonio Kaufusi shows his delight at grabbing London Broncos' late winning try against Widnes

Round 17

Round 18

RIGHT: Matty Dale on the charge during Featherstone's Anglo French Challenge success against Pia

Round 19

Anglo French Challenge

ABOVE: Brett Kearney brought to ground by Logan Tomkins as Bradford defy the odds to defeat Wigan

ORIGIN MATCH

Game 1

LEFT: Danny Tickle meets Hull FC teammate Willie Manu head on during England's victory against The Exiles

BELOW: Lee Paterson leaves Barrow's Ryan Shaw grasping at air as Halifax advance

BELOW: Michael Cooper tackled during England Knights' win against Ireland

NORTHERN RAIL CUP

Quarter Final

Internationals

The co-operative **CHAMPIONSHIP 1**

Round 11

STATE OF ORIGIN

Game 2

RIGHT: Antoni Maria takes on Jake Emmitt as France down Wales

LEFT: Michael Jennings congratulates Brett Stewart on scoring as New South Wales square the series

ABOVE: Jamie Thackray halted by Whitehaven's Carl Rudd as Workington take the Cumbrian derby

JULY

SALTER 29

Round 20

Game 2

ABOVE: Luke Patten looks for a gap during Salford's narrow win at Hull KR

ABOVE: Epalahame Lauaki collars Eorl Crabtree as The Exiles gain revenge over England

RIGHT: Sheffield's Michael Knowles upends Wayne Reittie as Halifax mount a famous fightback

Semi-finals

Semi-final

ABOVE: Joy for Warrington and despair for Huddersfield as the Wolves reach their third Challenge Cup Final in four seasons

BELOW: Ryan Bailey holds off Wigan trio Harrison Hansen, Michael McIlorum and Sam Tomkins to score as Leeds upset the formbook to march to Wembley

ABOVE: Tom Briscoe dragged down at Hull KR as Hull FC triumph in the Monday night derby

RIGHT: Rhys Hanbury bursts clear as Widnes record a big win at Salford

Round 21

Round 22

RIGHT: Paul Sykes celebrates scoring during Wakefield's impressive home victory against Leeds

RIGHT: Jon Grayshon halts Byron Smith during Featherstone's success against Batley

The co-operative CHAMPIONSHIP

Round 14

BELOW: Cooper Cronk lands a late field goal to win a seventh consecutive State of Origin series for Queensland

STATE OF ORIGIN

Game 3

FEATHERSTONE ROVERS 12
HALIFAX 21

ABOVE: Halifax celebrate as Anthony Thackeray scores the first try

NORTHERN RAIL CUP
N northern

FINAL

ABOVE: Tom Saxton gets a pass away under pressure from Lee Paterson, Adam Robinson and Luke Ambler

RIGHT: Sean Penkywicz lifts the Northern Rail Cup

LEFT: Stuart Dickens tackled by Dane Manning and Anthony Thackeray

AUGUST

RIGHT: Tony Clubb gets an offload away as London Broncos mount an incredible comeback to defeat Salford

Round 23

The co-operative CHAMPIONSHIP
Round 16

ABOVE: Joel Monaghan takes the ball away from Francis Meli as Warrington power past St Helens

BELOW: Ryan Atkins jumps for joy following a Warrington try in their win against Wigan

ABOVE: Alex Brown takes on the Dewsbury defence as Batley take the derby spoils

Round 24

The co-operative **CHAMPIONSHIP**

Round 17

ABOVE: Ryan Brierley beats Paul Handforth for a try during Leigh's victory against Halifax

BELOW: Daniel Barker, Tom Hodgson and James Pocklington show their delight as Gateshead record a r win, against Workington

The co-operative **CHAMPIONSHIP 1**

Round 15

Stobart SUPER LEAGUE

Round 24

Stobart SUPER LEAGUE

Round 25

An amazing few days for Wakefield's Paul Sykes who lands last-minute game-winning field goals in consecutive matches - against St Helens *(above)* and Hull KR *(below)*

LEFT: Adrian Morley, flanked by Lee Briers and Ryan Atkins, lifts the Challenge Cup

FINAL

RIGHT: Darrell Griffin halted by Paul Wood and Adrian Morley

BELOW: The rain pours out of the Wembley sky as Lee Briers takes the ball forward

SEPTEMBER

Round 26

ABOVE: James Roby touches down during St Helens' triumph at Warrington

RIGHT: Andy Lynch tackled by Brett Kearney and Manase Manuokafoa as Hull FC demolish Bradford

Qualifying Play-offs

Round 27

ABOVE: Wigan's Josh Charnley, Sam Tomkins and coach Shaun Wane show off the League Leaders Shield, picked up despite the Warriors going down at home to St Helens

ABOVE: Harrison Hansen meets Ian Henderson head on during Wigan's comfortable win over Catalan Dragons

The co-operative CHAMPIONSHIP

Elimination Play-off

ABOVE: Sam Barlow crashes over to score during Halifax's thrilling victory against Keighley

BELOW: Tom Briscoe beats Eorl Crabtree to score a spectacular try as Hull FC end Huddersfield's season

ABOVE: Jamie Peacock wrapped up by Danny Washbrook and Oliver Wilkes as Leeds end Wakefield's winning run

Elimination Play-offs

RIGHT: Trent Waterhouse halted by Joe Westerman and Brett Seymour as Warrington eliminate Hull FC

Preliminary Semi-finals

ABOVE: Simon Grix and Lance Hohaia chase a loose ball as Warrington reach their first Grand Final at the expense of St Helens

RIGHT: Danny McGuire takes a pass from Ryan Bailey on the way to scoring as Leeds edge past Catalan Dragons

Qualifying Semi-finals

RIGHT: Kallum Watkins races away to score an interception try during Leeds' win at Wigan

RIGHT: Blake Ferguson holds off Colin Best to score as Canberra end Cronulla's campaign

NRL Elimination Final

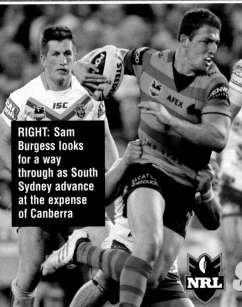

RIGHT: Sam Burgess looks for a way through as South Sydney advance at the expense of Canberra

BELOW: A rampaging Tony Williams charges through the North Queensland defence as Manly progress

NRL Semi-finals

LEFT: Manly's Jorge Taufua and Melbourne's Justin O'Neill contest a high ball as the Storm triumph

ABOVE: James Graham looks to escape from South Sydney's Luke Burgess as Canterbury charge to the Grand F

NRL Preliminary Finals

ABOVE: Billy Slater and Cameron Smith celebrate with Melbourne's fans

ABOVE RIGHT: Dally M Medal winner Ben Barba takes on Justin O'Neill

RIGHT: Tempers flare while the teams clash, as James Graham allegedly bites Billy Slater *(far right)*

The co-operative CHAMPIONSHIP GRAND FINAL

The co-operative Championship Grand Final Winners

FEATHERSTONE ROVERS 16
SHEFFIELD EAGLES 20

ABOVE: Sheffield Eagles celebrate their Grand Final win

ABOVE: Misi Taulapapa wrapped up by Anthony England, Andrew Bostock and Kyle Briggs

RIGHT: Quentin Laulu-Togagae evades Nathan Chappell on the way to a spectacular try

BARROW RAIDERS 13
DONCASTER 16

BELOW: Liam Harrison driven back by the Doncaster defence

BELOW: The champagne flows following Doncaster's Grand Final success

The co-operative CHAMPIONSHIP 1 GRAND FINAL

GRAND FINAL

LEEDS RHINOS 26
WARRINGTON WOLVES 18

CLOCKWISE, FROM TOP LEFT:

Kylie Leuluai tackled by Simon Grix
and Mick Higham

Kevin Sinfield and Brian McDermott
show off the Super League Trophy

Ryan Atkins crashes past Kallum
Watkins to score in the corner

No way through for Jamie Peacock

LEFT: Olympic gold medal-winning cyclist Bradley Wiggins presents Sam Tomkins with the 2012 Man of Steel Award

ABOVE: England Knights celebrate winning the Alitalia European Cup

Test Match

ABOVE: 2012 Super League Young Player of the Year - Zak Hardaker

ABOVE: Cameron Smith crashes over for a try during Australia's victory over New Zealand

BELOW: Kallum Watkins, Sam Tomkins and Luke Burgess relax on a break from England's training trip to South Africa

ABOVE: Action from the first ever international in Asia, as Philippines take on Thailand

ABOVE: Tom Burgess reaches out to score an England Knights try against Ireland

Alitalia Official Sponsor

European Cup

LEFT: England Knights' Scott Taylor takes on the Scotland defence

RIGHT: Ireland's Gregg McNally tries to escape from Scotland's David Scott

Autumn Internationals

ABOVE: Jordan James looks for a way through as Wales go down in France

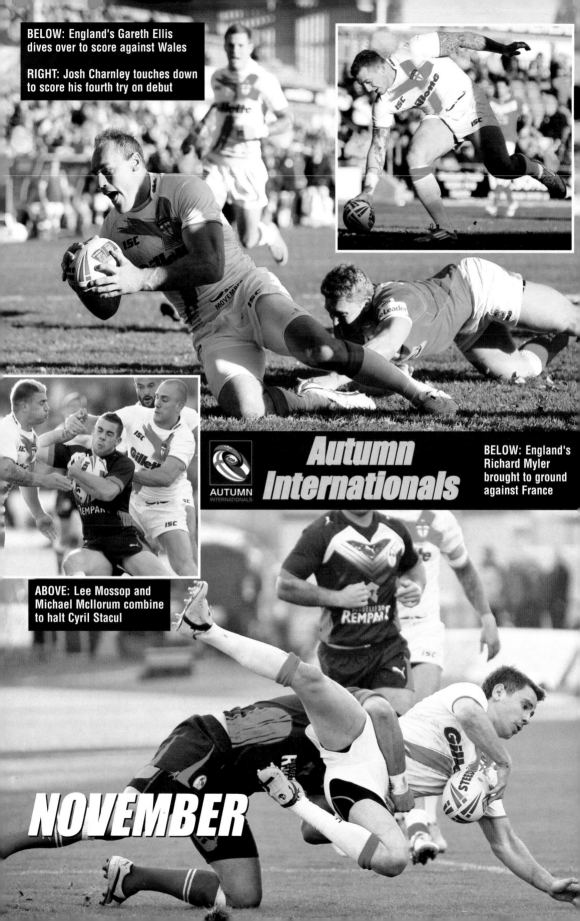

BELOW: England's Gareth Ellis dives over to score against Wales

RIGHT: Josh Charnley touches down to score his fourth try on debut

Autumn Internationals

AUTUMN INTERNATIONALS

BELOW: England's Richard Myler brought to ground against France

ABOVE: Lee Mossop and Michael McIlorum combine to halt Cyril Stacul

NOVEMBER

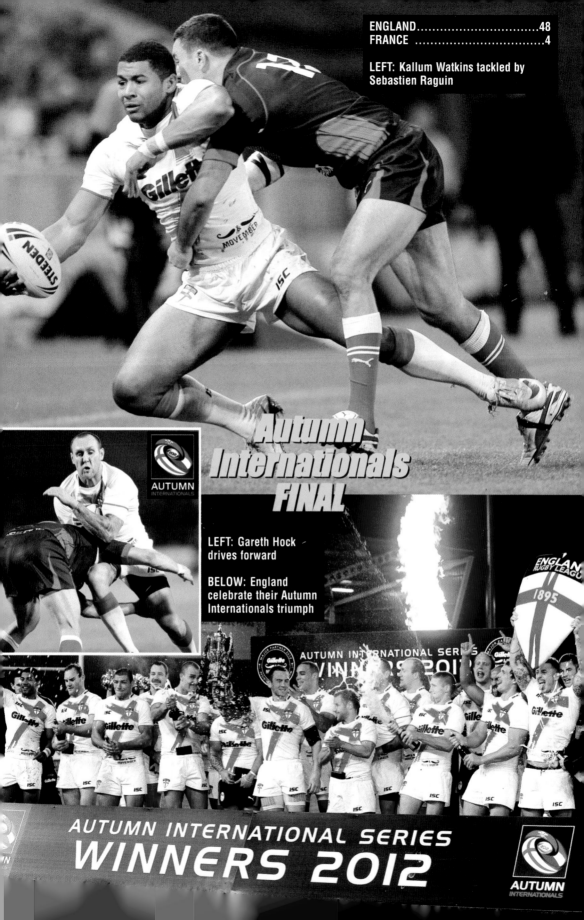

ENGLAND................................48
FRANCE 4

LEFT: Kallum Watkins tackled by
Sebastien Raguin

Autumn Internationals FINAL

LEFT: Gareth Hock
drives forward

BELOW: England
celebrate their Autumn
Internationals triumph

AUTUMN INTERNATIONAL SERIES
WINNERS 2012

THE TETLEY'S STAND

Mick Potter

Coach,
Bradford Bulls

No coach in Rugby League had the year that Mick Potter experienced in 2012.

Bradford Bulls was the nagging story of the year after the club announced it needed a million pounds to survive after its bank withdrew its overdraft facility. What followed was an, at times, agonising drama that saw a power battle between the current chairman and former chief Chris Caisley, a lengthy period of financial administration and uncertainty as to whether the Bulls would keep their Super League place at the end of the year.

In the middle of it all was former Catalans and St Helens coach Potter, whose own three months of uncertainty seemed to have ended at the start of July, when he and 15 other members of staff were sacked, three days after an astounding 30-22 win at top-of-the-table Wigan. Potter and his staff were persuaded to voluntarily go back and guide the team and if it hadn't been for a six-point penalty for going into administration, the Bulls would have made the play-offs for the first time since 2008.

But it was no wonder he headed home at the end of the year, and he certainly got his rewards when he landed the Wests Tigers head-coaching job.

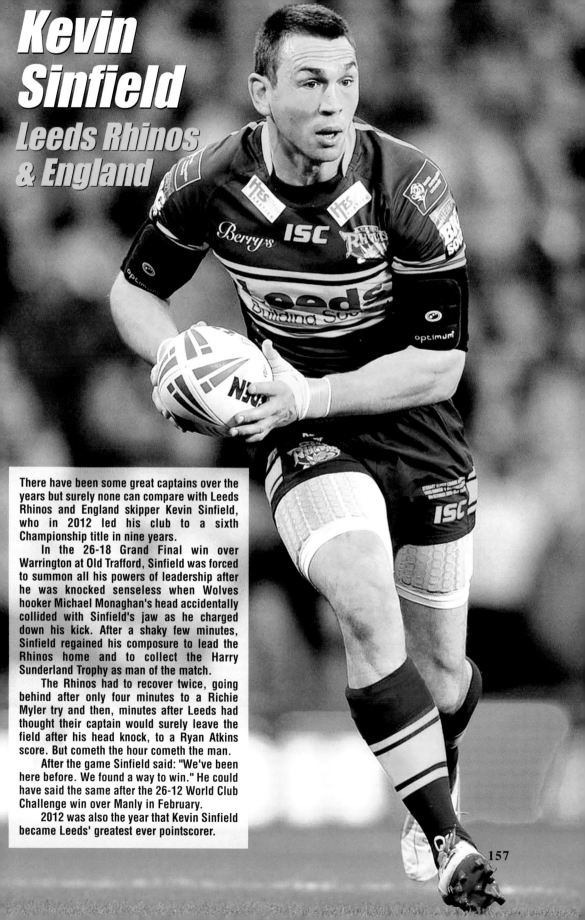

Kevin Sinfield

Leeds Rhinos & England

There have been some great captains over the years but surely none can compare with Leeds Rhinos and England skipper Kevin Sinfield, who in 2012 led his club to a sixth Championship title in nine years.

In the 26-18 Grand Final win over Warrington at Old Trafford, Sinfield was forced to summon all his powers of leadership after he was knocked senseless when Wolves hooker Michael Monaghan's head accidentally collided with Sinfield's jaw as he charged down his kick. After a shaky few minutes, Sinfield regained his composure to lead the Rhinos home and to collect the Harry Sunderland Trophy as man of the match.

The Rhinos had to recover twice, going behind after only four minutes to a Richie Myler try and then, minutes after Leeds had thought their captain would surely leave the field after his head knock, to a Ryan Atkins score. But cometh the hour cometh the man.

After the game Sinfield said: "We've been here before. We found a way to win." He could have said the same after the 26-12 World Club Challenge win over Manly in February.

2012 was also the year that Kevin Sinfield became Leeds' greatest ever pointscorer.

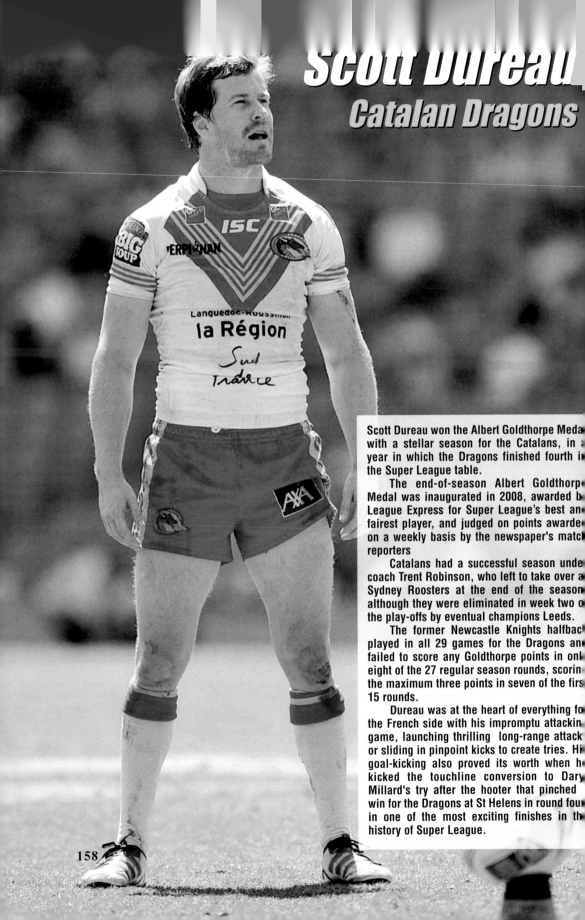

Scott Dureau
Catalan Dragons

Scott Dureau won the Albert Goldthorpe Medal with a stellar season for the Catalans, in a year in which the Dragons finished fourth in the Super League table.

The end-of-season Albert Goldthorpe Medal was inaugurated in 2008, awarded by League Express for Super League's best and fairest player, and judged on points awarded on a weekly basis by the newspaper's match reporters

Catalans had a successful season under coach Trent Robinson, who left to take over at Sydney Roosters at the end of the season, although they were eliminated in week two of the play-offs by eventual champions Leeds.

The former Newcastle Knights halfback played in all 29 games for the Dragons and failed to score any Goldthorpe points in only eight of the 27 regular season rounds, scoring the maximum three points in seven of the first 15 rounds.

Dureau was at the heart of everything for the French side with his impromptu attacking game, launching thrilling long-range attacks or sliding in pinpoint kicks to create tries. His goal-kicking also proved its worth when he kicked the touchline conversion to Daryl Millard's try after the hooter that pinched a win for the Dragons at St Helens in round four in one of the most exciting finishes in the history of Super League.

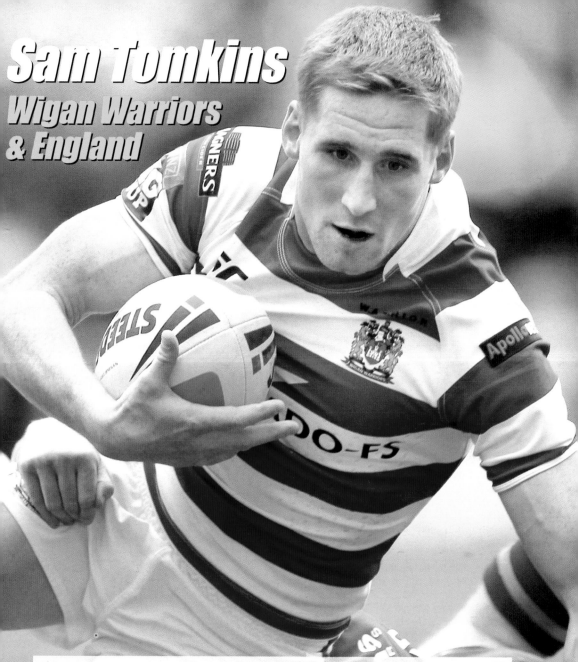

Sam Tomkins
Wigan Warriors & England

Sam Tomkins, one of our five personalities of 2011, cemented his reputation in 2012, voted by his peers as the Man of Steel after another season of box-office performances for Wigan Warriors.

The 23-year-old had lit up Super League since he made his Warriors debut in February of 2009 against Harlequins and went on to be named Super League Young Player of the Year. He had already made his Wigan debut in a Challenge Cup tie with Whitehaven, scoring five tries in a 106-8 win, in May of 2008.

Tomkins, a stand-off turned into a fullback by former Wigan coach Michael Maguire, was a player like no other, with his unique running style and speed off the mark, and Wigan fans were in for a treat every time he got his hands on the ball. He was Wigan's top-rated player by miles in the Opta ratings, making more metres, tackle busts, clean breaks and try assists than any of his teammates. He also finished the season with 36 tries to his name. When Tomkins got the ball, whatever the situation, anything could happen.

Chris Hill's rise within the space of 12 months from Championship player to full England international was one of the great stories of the Rugby League year.

Hill was 23-years old and in his fifth full season with Leigh Centurions when Warrington coach Tony Smith offered him the opportunity to step up to Super League at the end of 2011.

He took his chance, sweeping the board at Warrington's end-of-season awards night, just reward for being the Wolves' hardest-working forward in Super League XVII. On the day he turned 25, he won his second full England cap, against France at Hull after only 34 Super League games.

Hill didn't emerge from nowhere. In 2006 he had played for England Academy against an undefeated Australian Schoolboys side that included the likes of Chris Lawrence, Mitchell Pearce, Chris Sandow, Aiden Tolman and Israel Folau. And he had already made one Super League appearance, for Leigh in 2005, when he played as a substitute in a 78-4 hammering by St Helens at Hilton Park. Not getting picked up by a Super League club would have spelt the end of many young players' ambitions. Thankfully for Warrington and England, Hill never gave up the dream.

5
STATISTICAL REVIEW

SUPER LEAGUE PLAYERS
1996-2012

Super League Players 1996-2012

PLAYER	CLUB	YEAR	APP	TRIES	GOALS	FG	PTS
Carl Ablett	Leeds	2004, 2006-12	113(32)	32	0	0	128
	London	2005	3(2)	0	0	0	0
Darren Abram	Oldham	1996-97	25(2)	11	0	0	44
Darren Adams	Paris	1996	9(1)	1	0	0	4
Guy Adams	Huddersfield	1998	1(2)	0	0	0	0
Luke Adamson	Salford	2006-07, 2009-12	73(39)	11	1	0	46
Matt Adamson	Leeds	2002-04	54(8)	9	0	0	36
Phil Adamson	St Helens	1999	(1)	0	0	0	0
Toby Adamson	Salford	2010	(1)	0	0	0	0
Danny Addy	Bradford	2010-12	12(26)	3	7	0	26
Ade Adebisi	London	2004	(1)	0	0	0	0
Patrick Ah Van	Widnes	2012	19	14	29	0	114
	Bradford	2011	26	9	87	0	210
Jamie Ainscough	Wigan	2002-03	30(2)	18	0	0	72
Shaun Ainscough	Bradford	2011-12	27	15	0	0	60
	Wigan	2009-10	12	13	0	0	52
	Castleford	2010	7	4	0	0	16
Glen Air	London	1998-2001	57(13)	27	0	1	109
Paul Aiton	Wakefield	2012	18(2)	1	0	0	4
Makali Aizue	Hull KR	2007-09	18(32)	4	0	0	16
Darren Albert	St Helens	2002-05	105	77	0	0	308
Paul Alcock	Widnes	2003, 2005	1(7)	1	0	0	4
Neil Alexander	Salford	1998	(1)	0	0	0	0
Malcolm Alker	Salford	1997-2002, 2004-07, 2009-10	271(2)	40	0	1	161
Danny Allan	Leeds	2008-09	2(5)	0	0	0	0
Chris Allen	Castleford	1996	(1)	0	0	0	0
Dave Allen	Widnes	2012	23(3)	1	0	0	4
	Wigan	2003, 2005	6(15)	2	0	0	8
Gavin Allen	London	1996	10	0	0	0	0
John Allen	Workington	1996	20(1)	6	0	0	24
Ray Allen	London	1996	5(3)	3	0	0	12
Richard Allwood	Gateshead	1999	(4)	0	0	0	0
Sean Allwood	Gateshead	1999	3(17)	1	0	0	4
David Alstead	Warrington	2000-02	23(10)	3	0	0	12
Luke Ambler	Harlequins	2011	5(17)	1	0	0	4
	Leeds	2010	1(8)	1	0	0	4
Asa Amone	Halifax	1996-97	32(7)	10	0	0	40
Kyle Amor	Wakefield	2011-12	40(9)	8	0	0	32
	Leeds	2010	(3)	0	0	0	0
Thibaut Ancely	Catalans	2011	(2)	0	0	0	0
Grant Anderson	Castleford	1996-97	15(6)	3	0	0	12
Louis Anderson	Catalans	2012	15(2)	9	0	0	36
	Warrington	2008-11	92	18	0	0	72
Paul Anderson	St Helens	2005-06	48(5)	7	1	0	30
	Bradford	1997-2004	74(104)	30	0	0	120
	Halifax	1996	5(1)	1	0	0	4
Paul Anderson	Sheffield	1999	3(7)	1	0	0	4
	St Helens	1996-98	2(28)	4	1	0	18
Vinnie Anderson	Salford	2011-12	33(3)	14	0	0	56
	Warrington	2007-10	57(19)	22	0	0	88
	St Helens	2005-06	28(14)	17	0	0	68
Phil Anderton	St Helens	2004	1	0	0	0	0
Eric Anselme	Leeds	2008	2(2)	2	0	0	8
	Halifax	1997	(2)	0	0	0	0
Mark Applegarth	Wakefield	2004-07	20(5)	3	0	0	12
Graham Appo	Warrington	2002-05	60(13)	35	80	0	300
	Huddersfield	2001	7	4	0	0	16
Anthony Armour	London	2005	11(7)	1	0	0	4
Colin Armstrong	Workington	1996	11(2)	1	0	0	4
Tom Armstrong	St Helens	2009-11	10(5)	9	0	0	36
Richard Armswood	Workington	1996	5(1)	1	0	0	4
Danny Arnold	Salford	2001-02	26(13)	13	0	0	52
	Huddersfield	1998-2000	55(7)	26	0	0	104
	Castleford	2000	(4)	0	0	0	0
	St Helens	1996-97	40(1)	33	0	0	132
Joe Arundel	Castleford	2008, 2010-12	35(4)	14	2	0	60
Craig Ashall	St Helens	2006	1	1	0	0	4
Nathan Ashe	St Helens	2011-12	1(4)	0	0	0	0
Chris Ashton	Wigan	2005-07	44(2)	25	2	0	104
Matty Ashurst	Salford	2012	26	5	0	0	20
	St Helens	2009-11	12(39)	8	0	0	32
Martin Aspinwall	Hull	2012	12(15)	0	0	0	0
	Castleford	2011	12(6)	2	0	0	8
	Huddersfield	2006-10	72(8)	22	0	0	88
	Wigan	2001-05	85(13)	27	0	0	108
Mark Aston	Sheffield	1996-99	67(6)	6	243	6	516
Paul Atcheson	Widnes	2002-04	16(35)	4	0	0	16
	St Helens	1998-2000	58(4)	18	0	0	72
	Oldham	1996-97	40	21	0	0	84
David Atkins	Huddersfield	2001	26(1)	4	0	0	16
Ryan Atkins	Warrington	2010-12	82	57	0	0	228
	Wakefield	2006-09	86(2)	45	0	0	180
Josh Atkinson	Castleford	2012	2	0	0	0	0
Brad Attwood	Halifax	2003	(3)	0	0	0	0
Warren Ayres	Salford	1999	2(9)	1	2	0	8
Jerome Azema	Paris	1997	(1)	0	0	0	0
Marcus Bai	Bradford	2006	24	9	0	0	36
	Leeds	2004-05	57	42	0	0	168
David Baildon	Hull	1998-99	26(2)	4	0	0	16
Jean-Philippe Baile	Catalans	2008-12	59(8)	21	0	0	84
Andy Bailey	Hull	2004-05	2(8)	1	0	0	4
Chris Bailey	London	2012	24	6	0	0	24
	Harlequins	2011	24	3	0	0	12
Julian Bailey	Huddersfield	2003-04	47	13	0	0	52
Phil Bailey	Wigan	2007-10	84(4)	13	0	0	52
Ryan Bailey	Leeds	2002-12	152(89)	12	0	0	48
Jason Baitieri	Catalans	2011-12	35(20)	9	0	0	36
Simon Baldwin	Salford	2004-06	20(29)	3	0	0	12
	Sheffield	1999	7(15)	2	0	0	8
	Halifax	1996-98	41(15)	16	0	1	65
Rob Ball	Wigan	1998-2000	3(4)	0	0	0	0
Paul Ballard	Celtic	2009	2	0	0	0	0
	Widnes	2005	3(1)	2	0	0	8
Darren Bamford	Salford	2005	2(1)	0	0	0	0
Michael Banks	Bradford	1998	(1)	0	0	0	0
Steve Bannister	Harlequins	2007	(6)	0	0	0	0
	St Helens	2006-07	(3)	0	0	0	0
Frederic Banquet	Paris	1996	16(2)	7	4	0	36
Lee Bardauskas	Castleford	1996-97	(2)	0	0	0	0
Craig Barker	Workington	1996	(2)	0	0	0	0
Dwayne Barker	Harlequins	2008	5(5)	1	0	0	4
	London	2004	3	1	0	0	4
	Hull	2003	(1)	0	0	0	0
Mark Barlow	Wakefield	2002	(1)	0	0	0	0
Danny Barnes	Halifax	1999	2	0	0	0	0
Richie Barnett	Salford	2007	7	4	0	0	16
	Warrington	2006-07	26(10)	15	0	0	60
	Hull	2004-05	21(5)	21	0	0	84
	Widnes	2005	4	2	0	0	8
Richie Barnett	Hull	2003-04	31(1)	17	0	0	68
	London	2001-02	31(4)	13	0	0	52
David Barnhill	Leeds	2000	20(8)	5	0	0	20
Trent Barrett	Wigan	2007-08	53(1)	22	4	4	92
Paul Barrow	Warrington	1996-97	1(10)	1	0	0	4
Scott Barrow	St Helens	1997-2000	9(13)	1	0	0	4
Steve Barrow	London	2000	2	0	0	0	0
	Hull	1998-99	4(17)	1	0	0	4
	Wigan	1996	(8)	3	0	0	12
William Barthau	Catalans	2010, 2012	6(2)	0	3	0	6
Ben Barton	Huddersfield	1998	1(6)	1	0	0	4
Danny Barton	Salford	2001	1	0	0	0	0
Wayne Bartrim	Castleford	2002-03	41(2)	9	157	0	350
Greg Barwick	London	1996-97	30(4)	21	110	2	306
David Bastian	Halifax	1996	(2)	0	0	0	0
Ashley Bateman	Celtic	2009	1	0	0	0	0
John Bateman	Bradford	2011-12	15(3)	3	0	0	12
David Bates	Castleford	2001-02	(4)	0	0	0	0
	Warrington	2001	1(2)	0	0	0	0
Nathan Batty	Wakefield	2001	1(1)	0	0	0	0
Andreas Bauer	Hull KR	2007	10(2)	5	0	0	20
Russell Bawden	London	1996-97, 2002-04	50(49)	15	0	0	60
Neil Baxter	Salford	2001	1	0	0	0	0
Neil Baynes	Salford	1999-2002, 2004	84(19)	10	0	0	40
	Wigan	1996-98	1(0)	1	0	0	4
Chris Beasley	Celtic	2009	15(5)	2	0	0	8
Chris Beattie	Catalans	2006	22(5)	3	0	0	12
Richard Beaumont	Hull KR	2011-12	(3)	1	0	0	4
Robbie Beazley	London	1997-99	48(15)	13	0	0	52
Robbie Beckett	Halifax	2002	27	15	0	0	60
Dean Bell	Leeds	1996	1	1	0	0	4
Ian Bell	Hull	2003	(1)	0	0	0	0
Mark Bell	Wigan	1998	22	12	0	0	48
Paul Bell	Leeds	2000	1	0	0	0	0
Steven Bell	Catalans	2009-10	43	14	0	0	56
Troy Bellamy	Paris	1997	5(10)	0	0	0	0
Adrian Belle	Huddersfield	1998	10(2)	0	0	0	0
	Oldham	1996	19	8	0	0	32
Jamie Benn	Castleford	1998, 2000	3(8)	1	15	0	34
Andy Bennett	Warrington	1996	6(5)	1	0	0	4
Mike Bennett	St Helens	2000-08	74(70)	15	0	0	60
Andrew Bentley	Catalans	2007-10	9(15)	1	0	0	4
John Bentley	Huddersfield	1999	13(4)	3	0	0	12
	Halifax	1996, 1998	22(3)	24	0	0	96
Kane Bentley	Catalans	2007-10	11(19)	5	0	0	20
Phil Bergman	Paris	1997	20(1)	14	0	0	56
Shaun Berrigan	Hull	2008-10	60(8)	12	0	0	48
Joe Berry	Huddersfield	1998-99	25(14)	3	0	0	12
David Berthezene	Salford	2007	9(1)	0	0	0	0
	Catalans	2006-07	5(14)	0	0	0	0
Colin Best	Hull	2003-04	57	34	0	0	136
Roger Best	London	1997-98	1(5)	1	0	0	4
Bob Beswick	Wigan	2004-05	5(14)	2	0	0	8
Monty Betham	Wakefield	2006	26	2	0	0	8
Mike Bethwaite	Workington	1996	17(3)	1	0	0	4
Denis Betts	Wigan	1998-2001	82(24)	33	0	0	132
Cliff Beverley	Salford	2004-05	47(1)	14	0	0	56
Kyle Bibb	Wakefield	2008-10	1(24)	0	0	0	0
	Harlequins	2010	(2)	0	0	0	0
	Hull KR	2009	(2)	0	0	0	0

PLAYER	CLUB	YEAR	APP	TRIES	GOALS	FG	PTS
Adam Bibey	Widnes	2004	(1)	0	0	0	0
Ricky Bibey	Wakefield	2007-09	32(25)	1	0	0	4
	St Helens	2004	4(14)	0	0	0	0
	Wigan	2001-03	5(29)	0	0	0	0
Chris Birchall	Halifax	2002-03	24(22)	4	0	0	16
	Bradford	2000	(1)	0	0	0	0
Deon Bird	Castleford	2006	17(6)	5	0	0	20
	Widnes	2003-04	39(6)	9	0	0	36
	Wakefield	2002	10(1)	1	0	0	4
	Hull	2000-02	37(22)	20	0	0	80
	Gateshead	1999	19(3)	13	0	0	52
	Paris	1996-97	30	12	2	0	52
Greg Bird	Catalans	2009	20(2)	5	3	0	26
Nathan Blacklock	Hull	2005-06	44(3)	33	0	0	132
Ben Blackmore	Castleford	2012	1	0	0	0	0
Richie Blackmore	Leeds	1997-2000	63	25	0	0	100
Anthony Blackwood	Crusaders	2010	1	0	0	0	0
	Celtic	2009	25	5	0	0	20
Luke Blake	Wakefield	2009	(2)	0	0	0	0
Matthew Blake	Wakefield	2003-04	1(5)	0	0	0	0
Steve Blakeley	Salford	1997-2002	103(5)	26	241	2	588
	Warrington	2000	4(3)	1	9	0	22
Richard Blakeway	Castleford	2002-04	1(14)	0	0	0	0
Damien Blanch	Catalans	2011-12	49	35	0	0	140
	Wakefield	2008-10	44(3)	31	0	0	124
	Castleford	2006	3(2)	0	0	0	0
Matt Blaymire	Wakefield	2007-11	96(3)	26	0	1	105
Ian Blease	Salford	1997	(1)	0	0	0	0
Jamie Bloem	Huddersfield	2003	18(4)	3	11	0	34
	Halifax	1998-2002	82(25)	25	100	2	302
Vea Bloomfield	Paris	1996	4(14)	3	0	0	12
Matty Blythe	Warrington	2007-12	28(27)	12	0	0	48
Ben Bolger	London	2012	2(7)	1	0	0	4
	Harlequins	2010-11	4(15)	0	0	0	0
Pascal Bomati	Paris	1996	17(1)	10	0	0	40
Simon Booth	Hull	1998-99	15(9)	2	0	0	8
	St Helens	1996-97	10(4)	1	0	0	4
Steve Booth	Huddersfield	1998-99	16(4)	2	3	0	14
Alan Boothroyd	Halifax	1997	2(3)	0	0	0	0
Thomas Bosc	Catalans	2006-12	124(3)	38	294	4	744
John Boslem	Paris	1996	(5)	0	0	0	0
Liam Bostock	St Helens	2004	1	0	0	0	0
Liam Botham	Wigan	2005	5	0	0	0	0
	Leeds	2003-05	2(11)	4	0	0	16
	London	2004	6(2)	3	6	0	24
Frano Botica	Castleford	1996	21	5	84	2	190
Matthew Bottom	Leigh	2005	(1)	0	0	0	0
Hadj Boudebza	Paris	1996	(2)	0	0	0	0
David Boughton	Huddersfield	1999	26(1)	4	0	0	16
Julian Bousquet	Catalans	2012	(2)	0	0	0	0
David Bouveng	Halifax	1997-99	66(2)	19	0	0	76
Josh Bowden	Hull	2012	(7)	0	0	0	0
Tony Bowes	Huddersfield	1998	3(2)	0	0	0	0
Radney Bowker	London	2004	3	1	0	0	4
	St Helens	2001	(1)	0	0	0	0
David Boyle	Bradford	1999-2000	36(13)	15	0	1	61
Ryan Boyle	Salford	2010-12	56(7)	3	0	0	12
	Castleford	2006, 2008-09	(29)	2	0	0	8
Andy Bracek	Crusaders	2011	(2)	0	0	0	0
	Warrington	2005-08	7(49)	7	0	0	28
	St Helens	2004	(1)	0	0	0	0
David Bradbury	Hudds-Sheff	2000	21(2)	1	0	0	4
	Salford	1997-99	23(10)	6	0	0	24
	Oldham	1996-97	19(6)	9	0	0	36
John Braddish	St Helens	2001-02	1(1)	0	3	0	6
Graeme Bradley	Bradford	1996-98	62(1)	29	0	0	116
Nick Bradley-Qalilawa	Harlequins	2006	27	6	0	0	24
	London	2005	28	19	0	0	76
Darren Bradstreet	London	1999-2000	1(3)	0	0	0	0
Dominic Brambani	Castleford	2004	2(2)	0	0	0	0
Liam Bretherton	Wigan	1999	(5)	0	0	0	0
	Warrington	1997	(2)	0	0	0	0
Johnny Brewer	Halifax	1996	4(2)	2	0	0	8
Chris Bridge	Warrington	2005-12	132(14)	71	178	1	641
	Bradford	2003-04	2(14)	4	6	0	28
Lee Briers	Warrington	1997-2012	349(12)	126	831	67	2233
	St Helens	1997	3	0	11	0	22
Carl Briggs	Salford	1999	8(5)	3	0	1	13
	Halifax	1996	5(3)	1	0	0	4
Kyle Briggs	Bradford	2011	6	4	0	0	16
	Harlequins	2011	3	0	0	0	0
Mike Briggs	Widnes	2002	1(2)	1	0	0	4
Shaun Briscoe	Widnes	2012	7(1)	4	0	0	16
	Hull KR	2008-11	92	27	0	0	108
	Hull	2004-07	83(9)	50	0	0	200
	Wigan	2002-03	23(5)	11	0	0	44
Tom Briscoe	Hull	2008-12	105(3)	67	0	0	268
Darren Britt	St Helens	2002-03	41	3	0	0	12
Gary Broadbent	Salford	1997-2002	117(2)	22	0	0	88
Paul Broadbent	Wakefield	2002	16(5)	0	0	0	0
	Hull	2000-01	40(9)	3	0	0	12
	Halifax	1999	26(1)	2	0	0	8
	Sheffield	1996-98	63(1)	6	0	0	24
Andrew Brocklehurst	Salford	2004-07	34(23)	5	0	0	20
	London	2004	12(6)	2	0	0	8
	Halifax	2001-03	37(8)	2	0	0	8
Justin Brooker	Wakefield	2001	25	9	0	0	36
	Bradford	2000	17(4)	11	0	0	44
Danny Brough	Huddersfield	2010-12	68(3)	19	205	4	490
	Wakefield	2008-10	50(1)	14	174	4	408
	Castleford	2006	10	1	31	2	68
	Hull	2005-06	25(12)	3	85	1	183
Jodie Broughton	Salford	2010-12	71	41	0	0	164
	Hull	2008-09	9(3)	6	0	0	24
Alex Brown	Huddersfield	2009	1	0	0	0	0
Darren Brown	Salford	1999-2001	47(9)	11	6	0	56
Gavin Brown	Leeds	1996-97	5(2)	1	2	0	8
Kevin Brown	Huddersfield	2006-12	156	43	0	1	173
	Wigan	2003-06	46(18)	27	0	0	108
Lee Brown	Hull	1999	(1)	0	0	0	0
Michael Brown	Huddersfield	2008	(1)	0	0	0	0
Michael Brown	London	1996	(2)	0	0	0	0
Todd Brown	Paris	1996	8(1)	2	0	0	8
Adrian Brunker	Wakefield	1999	17	6	0	0	24
Lamont Bryan	Harlequins	2008-11	9(22)	2	0	0	8
Justin Bryant	Paris	1996	4(1)	0	0	0	0
	London	1996	7(8)	1	0	0	4
Mark Bryant	London	2012	8(19)	1	0	0	4
	Crusaders	2010-11	42(8)	1	0	0	4
	Celtic	2009	23(3)	0	0	0	0
Austin Buchanan	Wakefield	2005-06	6	2	0	0	8
	London	2003	3(1)	2	0	0	8
Danny Buderus	Leeds	2009-11	57(14)	14	0	0	56
Neil Budworth	Celtic	2009	8(19)	0	0	0	0
	Harlequins	2006	2(19)	0	0	0	0
	London	2002-05	59(11)	4	1	0	18
James Bunyan	Huddersfield	1998-99	8(7)	2	0	0	8
Andy Burgess	Salford	1997	3(12)	0	0	0	0
Luke Burgess	Leeds	2008-11	10(63)	6	0	0	24
	Harlequins	2007	(3)	0	0	0	0
Sam Burgess	Bradford	2006-09	46(34)	14	5	0	66
Tom Burgess	Bradford	2011-12	1(41)	3	0	0	12
Joe Burke	Crusaders	2011	(1)	0	0	0	0
Mike Burnett	Harlequins	2011	16(4)	1	0	0	4
	Hull	2008-10	13(21)	3	0	0	12
Darren Burns	Warrington	2002-04	66(6)	19	0	0	76
Gary Burns	Oldham	1996	6	1	0	0	4
Paul Burns	Workington	1996	5(2)	1	0	0	4
Rob Burrow	Leeds	2001-12	233(82)	134	123	5	787
Dean Busby	Warrington	1999-2002	34(34)	7	0	0	28
	Hull	1998	8(6)	0	0	0	0
	St Helens	1996-98	1(7)	0	0	0	0
Tom Bush	Leeds	2010	3(1)	1	0	0	4
Ikram Butt	London	1996	5(1)	0	0	0	0
Shane Byrne	Huddersfield	1998-99	1(5)	0	0	0	0
Todd Byrne	Hull	2008-09	20	4	0	0	16
Didier Cabestany	Paris	1996-97	20(6)	2	0	0	8
Hep Cahill	Widnes	2012	24	1	0	0	4
	Crusaders	2011	16	2	0	0	8
Joel Caine	Salford	2004	24	8	13	0	58
	London	2003	6	4	1	0	18
Mark Calderwood	Harlequins	2011	13	2	0	0	8
	Hull	2009-10	23	6	0	0	24
	Wigan	2006-08	64	23	0	0	92
	Leeds	2001-05	117(9)	88	0	0	352
Mike Callan	Warrington	2002	(4)	0	0	0	0
Matt Calland	Huddersfield	2003	2	0	0	0	0
	Hull	1999	1	0	0	0	0
	Bradford	1996-98	44(5)	24	0	0	96
Dean Callaway	London	1999-2000	26(24)	12	0	0	48
Laurent Cambres	Paris	1996	(1)	0	0	0	0
Chris Campbell	Warrington	2000	7(1)	2	0	0	8
Liam Campbell	Wakefield	2005	(1)	0	0	0	0
Logan Campbell	Hull	1998-99, 2001	70(13)	14	0	0	56
	Castleford	2000	14(2)	3	0	0	12
	Workington	1996	7(1)	1	0	0	4
Blake Cannova	Widnes	2002	(1)	0	0	0	0
Phil Cantillon	Widnes	2002-03	27(21)	18	0	0	72
	Leeds	1997	(1)	0	0	0	0
Damien Cardace	Catalans	2012	9	5	0	0	20
Daryl Cardiss	Warrington	2003-04	23(2)	3	4	0	20
	Halifax	1999-2003	91(8)	39	4	0	164
	Wigan	1996-98	12(6)	4	0	0	16
Dale Cardoza	Warrington	2002	5	1	0	0	4
	Halifax	2001	3	1	0	0	4
	Huddersfield	2000-01	20(9)	11	0	0	44
	Sheffield	1998-99	11(7)	3	0	0	12
Paul Carige	Salford	1999	24(1)	7	0	0	28
Dane Carlaw	Catalans	2008-10	58(15)	9	0	0	36
Keal Carlile	Hull KR	2012	(3)	0	0	0	0
	Huddersfield	2009, 2011	2(1)	1	0	0	4
	Bradford	2008	(1)	0	0	0	0

Super League Players 1996-2012

PLAYER	CLUB	YEAR	APP	TRIES	GOALS	FG	PTS
Jim Carlton	Huddersfield	1999	3(11)	2	0	0	8
George Carmont	Wigan	2008-12	136	71	0	0	284
Brian Carney	Warrington	2009	4	2	0	0	8
	Wigan	2001-05	91(10)	42	1	0	170
	Hull	2000	13(3)	7	0	0	28
	Gateshead	1999	3(2)	2	0	0	8
Martin Carney	Warrington	1997	(1)	0	0	0	0
Omari Caro	London	2012	11	4	0	0	16
Paul Carr	Sheffield	1996-98	45(5)	15	0	0	60
Bernard Carroll	London	1996	2(1)	1	0	0	4
Mark Carroll	London	1998	15(3)	1	0	0	4
Tonie Carroll	Leeds	2001-02	42(2)	30	0	0	120
Darren Carter	Workington	1996	10(3)	0	1	0	2
Steve Carter	Widnes	2002	14(7)	4	0	0	16
John Cartwright	Salford	1997	9	0	0	0	0
Garreth Carvell	Warrington	2009-12	73(17)	10	0	0	40
	Hull	2001-08	69(83)	22	0	0	88
	Leeds	1997-2000	(4)	0	0	0	0
	Gateshead	1999	4(4)	1	0	0	4
Garen Casey	Salford	1999	13(5)	3	23	0	58
Ray Cashmere	Salford	2009-11	63(3)	5	0	0	20
Mick Cassidy	Widnes	2005	24	0	0	0	0
	Wigan	1996-2004	184(36)	30	0	0	120
Remi Casty	Catalans	2006-12	62(83)	16	0	0	64
Ned Catic	Castleford	2008	7(7)	3	0	0	12
	Wakefield	2006-07	17(29)	4	0	0	16
Chris Causey	Warrington	1997-99	(18)	1	0	0	4
Jason Cayless	St Helens	2006-09	62(9)	7	0	0	28
Arnaud Cervello	Paris	1996	4	4	0	0	16
Marshall Chalk	Celtic	2009	13	4	0	0	16
Gary Chambers	Warrington	1996-2000	65(28)	2	0	0	8
Pierre Chamorin	Paris	1996-97	27(3)	8	3	0	38
Alex Chan	Catalans	2008	59(19)	11	0	0	44
Jason Chan	Huddersfield	2012	20(8)	4	0	0	16
	Crusaders	2010-11	48(1)	10	0	0	40
	Celtic	2009	17(6)	3	0	0	12
Joe Chandler	Leeds	2008	(1)	0	0	0	0
Michael Channing							
	London	2012	3(3)	1	0	0	4
Chris Chapman	Leeds	1999	(1)	0	0	0	0
Damien Chapman	London	1998	6(2)	3	4	1	21
David Chapman	Castleford	1996-98	24(6)	8	0	0	32
Jaymes Chapman	Halifax	2002-03	5(8)	1	0	0	4
Richard Chapman							
	Sheffield	1996	1	2	0	0	8
Chris Charles	Salford	2004-06	59(16)	6	140	0	304
	Castleford	2001	1(4)	1	0	0	4
Olivier Charles	Catalans	2007	2	2	0	0	8
Josh Charnley	Wigan	2010-12	55(2)	56	61	0	346
	Hull KR	2010	5	5	0	0	20
Rangi Chase	Castleford	2009-12	89(5)	31	0	3	127
Andy Cheetham	Huddersfield	1998-99	30	11	0	0	44
Kris Chesney	London	1998	1(2)	0	0	0	0
Chris Chester	Hull KR	2007-08	28(6)	4	0	0	16
	Hull	2002-06	67(25)	13	0	0	52
	Wigan	1999-2001	21(22)	5	0	0	20
	Halifax	1996-99	47(14)	16	15	1	95
Lee Chilton	Workington	1996	10(3)	6	0	0	24
Gary Christie	Bradford	1996-97	4(7)	1	0	0	4
James Clare	Castleford	2012	3	1	0	0	4
Daryl Clark	Castleford	2011-12	5(27)	10	0	0	40
Dean Clark	Leeds	1996	11(2)	3	0	0	12
Des Clark	St Helens	1999	4	0	0	0	0
	Halifax	1998-99	35(13)	6	0	0	24
Greg Clarke	Halifax	1997	1(1)	0	0	0	0
John Clarke	Oldham	1996-97	27(4)	5	0	0	20
Jon Clarke	Widnes	2012	17(1)	0	0	0	0
	Warrington	2001-11	217(25)	56	2	0	228
	London	2000-01	19(11)	2	0	0	8
	Wigan	1997-99	13(10)	3	0	0	12
Chris Clarkson	Leeds	2010-12	40(22)	7	0	0	28
Adam Clay	Salford	2011	2	3	0	0	12
Ryan Clayton	Castleford	2004,					
		2008-10	36(24)	5	0	0	20
	Salford	2006	3(8)	2	0	0	8
	Huddersfield	2005	4(6)	0	0	0	0
	Halifax	2000,					
		2002-03	28(12)	6	0	0	24
Gavin Clinch	Salford	2004	21(1)	1	0	1	5
	Halifax	1998-99,					
		2001-02	88(2)	26	45	5	199
	Hudds-Sheff	2000	18(2)	5	0	1	21
	Wigan	1999	10(2)	4	12	0	40
Joel Clinton	Hull KR	2010-12	42(14)	2	0	0	8
John Clough	Salford	2004-06	1(16)	0	0	0	0
Paul Clough	St Helens	2005-12	50(99)	15	0	0	60
Tony Clubb	London	2012	22(2)	6	0	0	24
	Harlequins	2006-11	100(11)	29	0	0	116
Bradley Clyde	Leeds	2001	7(5)	1	0	0	4
Michael Coady	Leeds	2010	1	0	0	0	0
Evan Cochrane	London	1996	5(1)	1	0	0	4
Ben Cockayne	Wakefield	2012	27	16	0	0	64
	Hull KR	2007-11	76(26)	27	0	0	108
Liam Colbon	London	2012	8	2	0	0	8
	Hull KR	2009-11	51	20	0	0	80
	Wigan	2004-05,					
		2007-08	37(14)	15	0	0	60
Anthony Colella	Huddersfield	2003	5(1)	2	0	0	8
Liam Coleman	Leigh	2005	1(4)	0	0	0	0
Andy Coley	Wigan	2008-11	100(10)	8	0	0	32
	Salford	2001-02,					
		2004-07	112(34)	34	0	0	136
Richard Colley	Bradford	2004	1	0	0	0	0
Steve Collins	Hull	2000	28	17	0	0	68
	Gateshead	1999	20(4)	13	0	0	52
Wayne Collins	Leeds	1997	21	3	0	0	12
Dean Collis	Wakefield	2012	21	10	0	0	40
Aurelien Cologni	Catalans	2006	4(1)	3	0	0	12
Gary Connolly	Widnes	2005	20	4	1	0	18
	Wigan	1996-2002,					
		2004	168(10)	70	5	0	290
	Leeds	2003-04	27	6	0	0	24
Matt Cook	London	2012	7(3)	2	0	0	8
	Hull KR	2010-11	9(16)	7	0	0	28
	Bradford	2005-09	11(52)	4	0	0	16
	Castleford	2008	2(1)	1	0	0	4
Mick Cook	Sheffield	1996	9(10)	2	0	0	8
Paul Cook	Huddersfield	1998-99	11(6)	2	13	0	34
	Bradford	1996-97	14(8)	7	38	1	105
Peter Cook	St Helens	2004	(1)	0	0	0	0
Paul Cooke	Wakefield	2010	16(1)	3	36	1	85
	Hull KR	2007-10	54(5)	8	76	2	186
	Hull	1999-2007	177(27)	32	333	4	798
Ben Cooper	Leigh	2005	25(1)	5	0	0	20
	Huddersfield	2000-01,					
		2003-04	28(12)	3	0	0	12
Michael Cooper	Warrington	2006-12	15(77)	5	0	0	20
	Castleford	2010	1(5)	2	0	0	8
Ged Corcoran	Halifax	2003	1(11)	0	0	0	0
Wayne Corcoran	Halifax	2003	4(2)	0	0	0	0
Jamie Cording	Huddersfield	2011-12	2(6)	1	0	0	4
Josh Cordoba	Hull	2009	8	1	0	0	4
Mark Corvo	Salford	2002	7(5)	0	0	0	0
Brandon Costin	Huddersfield	2001,					
		2003-04	69	42	93	3	357
	Bradford	2002	20(1)	8	0	0	32
Wes Cotton	London	1997-98	12	3	0	0	12
Phil Coussons	Salford	1997	7(2)	3	0	0	12
Alex Couttet	Paris	1997	1	0	0	0	0
Nick Couttet	Paris	1997	1	0	0	0	0
Jamie Coventry	Castleford	1996	1	0	0	0	0
Jimmy Cowan	Oldham	1996-97	2(8)	0	0	0	0
Will Cowell	Warrington	1998-2000	6(8)	1	0	0	4
Neil Cowie	Wigan	1996-2001	116(27)	10	0	1	41
Danny Cowling	Wakefield	2012	1	0	0	0	0
Jordan Cox	Hull KR	2011-12	1(15)	0	0	0	0
Mark Cox	London	2003	(3)	0	0	0	0
James Coyle	Wigan	2005	2(3)	1	0	0	4
Thomas Coyle	Wigan	2008	2(1)	0	0	0	0
Eorl Crabtree	Huddersfield	2001,					
		2003-12	116(130)	36	0	0	144
Andy Craig	Halifax	1999	13(7)	1	3	0	10
	Wigan	1996	5(5)	2	0	0	8
Owen Craigie	Widnes	2005	15	7	0	2	30
Scott Cram	London	1999-2002	65(7)	4	0	0	16
Danny Craven	Widnes	2012	12(5)	5	2	0	24
Steve Craven	Hull	1998-2003	53(42)	4	0	0	16
Nicky Crellin	Workington	1996	(2)	0	0	0	0
Jason Critchley	Wakefield	2000	7(1)	4	0	0	16
	Castleford	1997-98	27(3)	11	0	0	44
Jason Croker	Catalans	2007-09	56(2)	11	0	1	45
Martin Crompton	Salford	1998-2000	30(6)	11	6	2	58
	Oldham	1996-97	36(1)	16	0	3	67
Paul Crook	Wigan	2005	2(2)	0	5	1	11
Paul Crook	Oldham	1996	4(9)	0	3	0	6
Jason Crookes	Bradford	2009-12	25(1)	7	0	0	28
Ben Crooks	Hull	2012	13(2)	7	0	0	28
Lee Crooks	Castleford	1996-97	27(2)	2	14	0	36
Dominic Crosby	Wigan	2012	(7)	1	0	0	4
Alan Cross	St Helens	1997	(2)	0	0	0	0
Ben Cross	Widnes	2012	19(1)	2	0	0	8
	Wigan	2011	(4)	0	0	0	0
	Leeds	2011	(9)	0	0	0	0
Steve Crossley	Bradford	2010-11	(9)	1	0	0	4
Garret Crossman	Hull KR	2008	8(18)	0	0	0	0
Steve Crouch	Castleford	2004	4(1)	2	0	0	8
Kevin Crouthers	Warrington	2001-03	12(1)	4	0	0	16
	London	2000	6(4)	1	0	0	4
	Wakefield	1999	4(4)	1	0	0	4
	Bradford	1997-98	3(9)	2	0	0	8
Matt Crowther	Hull	2001-03	48	20	166	0	412
	Hudds-Sheff	2000	10(4)	5	22	0	64
	Sheffield	1996-99	43(4)	22	10	0	108
Heath Cruckshank							
	Halifax	2003	19(1)	0	0	0	0
	St Helens	2001	1(12)	0	0	0	0
Leroy Cudjoe	Huddersfield	2008-12	120(1)	61	45	0	334

Super League Players 1996-2012

PLAYER	CLUB	YEAR	APP	TRIES	GOALS	FG	PTS
Paul Cullen	Warrington	1996	19	3	0	0	12
Francis Cummins	Leeds	1996-2005	217(13)	120	26	2	534
James Cunningham							
	Hull	2012	(1)	0	0	0	0
Keiron Cunningham							
	St Helens	1996-2010	357(24)	138	0	0	552
Liam Cunningham							
	Hull	2010	(1)	0	0	0	0
Ben Currie	Warrington	2012	2(3)	2	0	0	8
Andy Currier	Warrington	1996-97	(2)	1	0	0	4
Peter Cusack	Hull	2008-10	34(22)	3	0	0	12
Joe Dakuitoga	Sheffield	1996	6(3)	0	0	0	0
Matty Dale	Hull	2006, 2008	(7)	1	0	0	4
	Wakefield	2008	1(1)	0	0	0	0
Brett Dallas	Wigan	2000-06	156	89	0	0	356
Mark Dalle Cort	Celtic	2009	23	4	0	0	16
Paul Darbyshire	Warrington	1997	(6)	0	0	0	0
James Davey	Wakefield	2009-11	3(14)	1	0	0	4
Maea David	Hull	1998	1	0	0	0	0
Alex Davidson	Salford	2011	(1)	0	0	0	0
Paul Davidson	Halifax	2001-03	22(30)	10	0	0	40
	London	2000	6(10)	4	0	0	16
	St Helens	1998-99	27(16)	7	0	0	28
	Oldham	1996-97	17(18)	14	0	1	57
Ben Davies	Widnes	2012	10(14)	3	0	0	12
	Castleford	2011	3(2)	2	0	0	8
	Wigan	2010	(5)	0	0	0	0
Gareth Davies	Warrington	1996-97	1(6)	0	0	0	0
Geraint Davies	Celtic	2009	(7)	0	0	0	0
John Davies	Castleford	2010-12	1(6)	1	0	0	4
Wes Davies	Wigan	1998-2001	22(22)	11	0	0	44
Brad Davis	Castleford	1997-2000,					
		2004, 2006	102(3)	31	43	10	220
	Wakefield	2001-03	51(12)	15	22	5	109
Matty Dawson	Huddersfield	2012	1	0	0	0	0
Matt Daylight	Hull	2000	17(1)	7	0	0	28
	Gateshead	1999	30	25	0	0	100
Michael De Vere	Huddersfield	2005-06	36	6	74	0	172
Paul Deacon	Wigan	2010-11	32(11)	4	14	0	44
	Bradford	1998-2009	258(43)	72	1029	23	2369
	Oldham	1997	(2)	0	0	0	0
Chris Dean	Widnes	2012	19	4	0	0	16
	Wakefield	2011	20	8	0	0	32
	St Helens	2007-10	18(3)	9	0	0	36
Craig Dean	Halifax	1996-97	25(11)	12	1	1	51
Gareth Dean	London	2002	(4)	0	0	0	0
Yacine Dekkiche	Hudds-Sheff	2000	11(3)	3	0	0	12
Brett Delaney	Leeds	2010-12	75	16	0	0	64
Jason Demetriou	Wakefield	2004-10	174(3)	50	2	0	204
	Widnes	2002-03	47(1)	15	1	0	62
Martin Dermott	Warrington	1997	1	0	0	0	0
David Despin	Paris	1996	(1)	0	0	0	0
Fabien Devecchi	Paris	1996-97	17(10)	2	0	0	8
Paul Devlin	Widnes	2002-04	32	16	0	0	64
Stuart Dickens	Salford	2005	4(5)	0	4	0	8
Matt Diskin	Bradford	2011-12	32(10)	7	0	0	28
	Leeds	2001-10	195(37)	40	0	0	160
Andrew Dixon	St Helens	2009-12	19(41)	12	0	0	48
Kieran Dixon	London	2012	23(1)	12	1	0	50
Kirk Dixon	Castleford	2008-12	102(1)	40	220	0	600
	Hull	2004-06	13(4)	7	4	0	36
Paul Dixon	Sheffield	1996-97	5(9)	1	0	0	4
Gareth Dobson	Castleford	1998-2000	(10)	0	0	0	0
Michael Dobson	Hull KR	2008-12	117	45	416	10	1022
	Wigan	2006	14	5	61	0	142
	Catalans	2006	10	4	31	1	79
Michael Docherty	Hull	2000-01	(6)	0	0	0	0
Sid Domic	Hull	2006-07	39(4)	15	0	0	60
	Wakefield	2004-05	48	30	0	0	120
	Warrington	2002-03	41(4)	17	0	0	68
Scott Donald	Leeds	2006-10	131	77	0	0	308
James Donaldson							
	Bradford	2009-12	7(25)	2	0	0	8
Glen Donkin	Hull	2002-03	(10)	1	0	0	4
Stuart Donlan	Castleford	2008	20	8	0	0	32
	Huddersfield	2004-06	59(3)	15	0	0	60
	Halifax	2001-03	65(2)	22	0	0	88
Jason Donohue	Bradford	1996	(4)	0	0	0	0
Jeremy Donougher							
	Bradford	1996-99	40(21)	13	0	0	52
Justin Dooley	London	2000-01	37(18)	2	0	0	8
Dane Dorahy	Halifax	2003	20	7	45	0	118
	Wakefield	2000-01	16(2)	4	19	1	55
Luke Dorn	London	2005, 2012	44(6)	38	0	0	152
	Harlequins	2006,					
		2009-11	83(1)	57	0	0	228
	Castleford	2008	25(1)	19	0	0	76
	Salford	2007	19(8)	11	0	0	44
Ewan Dowes	Hull	2003-11	169(51)	10	0	0	40
	Leeds	2001-03	1(9)	0	0	0	0
Adam Doyle	Warrington	1998	9(3)	4	0	0	16
Rod Doyle	Sheffield	1997-99	52(10)	10	0	0	40
Brad Drew	Huddersfield	2005-07,					
		2010	78(13)	18	13	1	99
	Wakefield	2008-09	27(9)	7	14	1	57
Damien Driscoll	Salford	2001	23(1)	1	0	0	4
Gil Dudson	Wigan	2012	5(4)	0	0	0	0
	Crusaders	2011	3(7)	0	0	0	0
	Celtic	2009	(1)	0	0	0	0
Jason Duffy	Leigh	2005	3(1)	0	0	0	0
John Duffy	Leigh	2005	21	6	0	0	24
	Salford	2000	3(11)	0	1	1	3
	Warrington	1997-99	12(12)	0	0	0	0
Tony Duggan	Celtic	2009	4	3	0	0	12
Andrew Duncan	London	1997	2(4)	2	0	0	8
	Warrington	1997	(1)	0	0	0	0
Andrew Dunemann							
	Salford	2006	25	1	0	2	6
	Leeds	2003-05	76(4)	11	0	2	46
	Halifax	1999-2002	68	19	0	1	77
Matt Dunford	London	1997-98	18(20)	3	0	1	13
Vincent Duport	Catalans	2007-09,					
		2011-12	59(14)	30	0	0	120
Jamie Durbin	Widnes	2005	1	0	0	0	0
	Warrington	2003	(1)	0	0	0	0
Scott Dureau	Catalans	2011-12	54	23	209	8	518
James Durkin	Paris	1997	(5)	0	0	0	0
Bernard Dwyer	Bradford	1996-2000	65(10)	14	0	0	56
Brad Dwyer	Warrington	2012	1(6)	2	0	0	8
Luke Dyer	Crusaders	2010	23(1)	5	0	0	20
	Celtic	2009	21	6	0	0	24
	Hull KR	2007	26	13	0	0	52
	Castleford	2006	17(2)	5	0	0	20
Adam Dykes	Hull	2008	12	1	0	2	6
Jim Dymock	London	2001-04	94(1)	15	0	1	61
Leo Dynevor	London	1996	8(11)	5	7	0	34
Jason Eade	Paris	1997	9	4	0	0	16
Michael Eagar	Hull	2004-05	12	4	0	0	16
	Castleford	1999-2003	130(2)	60	0	0	240
	Warrington	1998	21	6	0	0	24
Kyle Eastmond	St Helens	2007-11	46(20)	35	117	3	377
Greg Eastwood	Leeds	2010	5(12)	1	0	0	4
Barry Eaton	Widnes	2002	25	2	49	4	110
	Castleford	2000	1(4)	0	3	0	6
Greg Ebrill	Salford	2002	15(6)	1	0	0	4
Cliff Eccles	Salford	1997-98	30(5)	1	0	0	4
Chris Eckersley	Warrington	1996	1	0	0	0	0
Greg Eden	Huddersfield	2012	24	8	0	0	32
	Castleford	2011	2	1	0	0	4
Steve Edmed	Sheffield	1997	15(1)	0	0	0	0
Mark Edmondson	Salford	2007	10(2)	0	0	0	0
	St Helens	1999-2005	27(75)	10	0	0	40
Diccon Edwards	Castleford	1996-97	10(5)	1	0	0	4
Grant Edwards	Castleford	2006	(2)	0	0	0	0
Max Edwards	Harlequins	2010	1	0	0	0	0
Peter Edwards	Salford	1997-98	35(2)	4	0	0	16
Shaun Edwards	London	1997-2000	32(8)	16	1	0	66
	Bradford	1998	8(2)	4	0	0	16
	Wigan	1996	17(3)	12	1	0	50
Danny Ekis	Halifax	2001	(1)	0	0	0	0
Abi Ekoku	Bradford	1997-98	21(4)	6	0	0	24
	Halifax	1996	15(1)	5	0	0	20
Shane Elford	Huddersfield	2007-08	26(1)	7	0	0	28
Olivier Elima	Bradford	2011-12	37(3)	12	0	0	48
	Catalans	2008-10	56(10)	30	0	0	120
	Wakefield	2003-07	40(47)	13	0	0	52
	Castleford	2002	(1)	1	0	0	4
Abderazak Elkhalouki							
	Paris	1997	(1)	0	0	0	0
George Elliott	Leeds	2011	1	0	0	0	0
Andy Ellis	Wakefield	2012	10	0	0	0	0
	Harlequins	2010-11	26(11)	8	0	0	32
Gareth Ellis	Leeds	2005-08	109	24	1	0	98
	Wakefield	1999-2004	86(17)	21	2	0	88
Jamie Ellis	Castleford	2012	4(1)	1	13	0	30
	Hull	2012	4(5)	1	0	0	4
	St Helens	2009	1(2)	0	1	0	2
Danny Ellison	Castleford	1998-99	7(16)	6	0	0	24
	Wigan	1996-97	15(1)	13	0	0	52
Andrew Emelio	Widnes	2005	22(2)	8	0	0	32
Jake Emmitt	Castleford	2011-12	30(14)	0	0	0	0
	St Helens	2008-10	1(16)	1	0	0	4
Patrick Entat	Paris	1996	22	2	0	0	8
Jason Erba	Sheffield	1997	1(4)	0	0	0	0
Ryan Esders	Harlequins	2009-10	9(11)	3	0	0	12
	Hull KR	2009	(1)	0	0	0	0
James Evans	Castleford	2009-10	26(1)	13	0	0	52
	Bradford	2007-08	43(5)	20	0	0	80
	Wakefield	2006	6	3	0	0	12
	Huddersfield	2004-06	51	22	0	0	88
Paul Evans	Paris	1997	18	8	0	0	32
Rhys Evans	Warrington	2010-12	11(3)	3	0	0	12
Wayne Evans	London	2002	11(6)	2	0	0	8
Richie Eyres	Warrington	1997	2(5)	0	0	0	0
	Sheffield	1997	2(3)	0	0	0	0
Henry Fa'afili	Warrington	2004-07	90(1)	70	0	0	280
David Fa'alogo	Huddersfield	2010-12	38(16)	13	0	0	52
Sala Fa'alogo	Widnes	2004-05	8(15)	2	0	0	8
Richard Fa'aoso	Castleford	2006	10(15)	5	0	0	20

Super League Players 1996-2012

PLAYER	CLUB	YEAR	APP	TRIES	GOALS	FG	PTS
Maurie Fa'asavalu							
	St Helens	2004-10	5(137)	29	0	0	116
Bolouagi Fagborun							
	Huddersfield	2004-06	4(2)	1	0	0	4
Esene Faimalo	Salford	1997-99	23(25)	2	0	0	8
	Leeds	1996	3(3)	0	0	0	0
Joe Faimalo	Salford	1998-2000	23(47)	7	0	0	28
	Oldham	1996-97	37(5)	7	0	0	28
Jacob Fairbank	Huddersfield	2011-12	6(1)	0	0	0	0
Karl Fairbank	Bradford	1996	17(2)	4	0	0	16
David Fairleigh	St Helens	2001	26(1)	8	0	0	32
David Faiumu	Huddersfield	2008-12	33(69)	10	0	0	40
Jamal Fakir	Catalans	2006-12	52(77)	11	0	0	44
Jim Fallon	Leeds	1996	10	5	0	0	20
Ben Farrar	Catalans	2011	13	3	0	0	12
Danny Farrar	Warrington	1998-2000	76	13	0	0	52
Andy Farrell	Wigan	1996-2004	230	77	1026	16	2376
Anthony Farrell	Widnes	2002-03	24(22)	4	1	0	18
	Leeds	1997-2001	99(23)	18	0	0	72
	Sheffield	1996	14(5)	5	0	0	20
Craig Farrell	Hull	2000-01	1(3)	0	0	0	0
Liam Farrell	Wigan	2010-12	23(45)	26	0	0	104
Abraham Fatnowna							
	London	1997-98	7(2)	2	0	0	8
	Workington	1996	5	2	0	0	8
Sione Faumuina	Castleford	2009	18	1	0	0	4
	Hull	2005	3	1	0	0	4
Vince Fawcett	Wakefield	1999	13(1)	2	0	0	8
	Warrington	1998	4(7)	1	0	0	4
	Oldham	1997	5	3	0	0	12
Danny Fearon	Huddersfield	2001	(1)	0	0	0	0
	Halifax	1999-2000	5(6)	0	0	0	0
Chris Feather	Castleford	2009	1(23)	0	0	0	0
	Bradford	2007-08	7(20)	1	0	0	4
	Leeds	2003-04, 2006	16(35)	6	0	0	24
	Wakefield	2001-02, 2004-05	29(32)	9	0	0	36
Dom Feaunati	Leigh	2005	4	1	0	0	4
	St Helens	2004	10(7)	7	0	0	28
Adel Fellous	Hull	2008	1(2)	0	0	0	0
	Catalans	2006-07	16(22)	4	0	0	16
Luke Felsch	Hull	2000-01	46(6)	7	0	0	28
	Gateshead	1999	28(1)	2	0	0	8
Leon Felton	Warrington	2002	4(2)	0	0	0	0
	St Helens	2001	1(1)	0	0	0	0
Dale Ferguson	Huddersfield	2011-12	16(14)	8	0	0	32
	Wakefield	2007-11	40(14)	12	0	0	48
Brett Ferres	Huddersfield	2012	7	0	0	0	0
	Castleford	2009-12	78(5)	26	0	0	104
	Wakefield	2007-08	36(2)	6	5	0	34
	Bradford	2005-06	18(17)	11	2	0	48
David Ferriol	Catalans	2007-12	72(55)	8	0	0	32
Jason Ferris	Leigh	2005	4	1	0	0	4
Jamie Field	Wakefield	1999-2006	133(59)	19	0	0	76
	Huddersfield	1998	15(5)	0	0	0	0
	Leeds	1996-97	3(11)	0	0	0	0
Mark Field	Wakefield	2003-07	28(7)	3	0	0	12
Jamie Fielden	London	2003	(1)	0	0	0	0
	Huddersfield	1998-2000	4(8)	0	0	0	0
Stuart Fielden	Wigan	2006-12	105(24)	2	0	0	8
	Bradford	1998-2006	142(78)	41	0	0	164
Lafaele Filipo	Workington	1996	15(4)	3	0	0	12
Salesi Finau	Warrington	1996-97	16(15)	8	0	0	32
Brett Finch	Wigan	2011-12	49(3)	16	0	0	64
Vinny Finigan	Bradford	2010	4(1)	4	0	0	16
Liam Finn	Wakefield	2004	1(1)	0	1	0	2
	Halifax	2002-03	16(5)	2	30	1	69
Lee Finnerty	Halifax	2003	18(2)	5	2	0	24
Phil Finney	Warrington	1998	1	0	0	0	0
Simon Finnigan	Widnes	2003-05, 2012	56(24)	21	0	0	84
	Huddersfield	2009-10	22(5)	6	0	0	24
	Bradford	2008	14(13)	8	0	0	32
	Salford	2006-07	50	17	0	0	68
Matt Firth	Halifax	2000-01	12(2)	0	0	0	0
Andy Fisher	Wakefield	1999-2000	31(8)	4	0	0	16
Ben Fisher	Catalans	2012	9(5)	1	0	0	4
	Hull KR	2007-11	78(46)	18	0	0	72
Craig Fitzgibbon	Hull	2010-11	42(1)	9	8	0	52
Daniel Fitzhenry	Hull KR	2008-09	36(11)	14	0	0	56
Karl Fitzpatrick	Salford	2004-07, 2009-10	89(11)	33	2	0	136
Mark Flanagan	St Helens	2012	6(17)	3	0	0	12
	Wigan	2009	3(7)	1	0	0	4
Chris Flannery	St Helens	2007-12	108(11)	32	0	0	128
Darren Fleary	Leigh	2005	24	1	0	0	4
	Huddersfield	2003-04	43(8)	4	0	0	16
	Leeds	1997-2002	98(9)	3	0	0	12
Greg Fleming	London	1999-2001	64(1)	40	2	0	164
Adam Fletcher	Castleford	2006, 2008	16(7)	11	0	0	44
Bryan Fletcher	Wigan	2006-07	47(2)	14	0	0	56
Richard Fletcher	Castleford	2006	13(5)	3	4	0	20
	Hull	1999-2004	11(56)	5	0	0	20
Greg Florimo	Halifax	2000	26	6	4	0	32
	Wigan	1999	18(2)	7	1	0	30
Ben Flower	Wigan	2012	6(11)	1	0	0	4
	Crusaders	2010-11	10(23)	2	0	0	8
	Celtic	2009	2(15)	0	0	0	0
Jason Flowers	Salford	2004	6(1)	0	0	0	0
	Halifax	2002	24(4)	4	0	0	16
	Castleford	1996-2001	119(19)	33	0	1	133
Stuart Flowers	Castleford	1996	(3)	0	0	0	0
Adrian Flynn	Castleford	1996-97	19(2)	10	0	0	40
Paddy Flynn	Widnes	2012	20	9	0	0	36
Wayne Flynn	Sheffield	1997	3(5)	0	0	0	0
Adam Fogerty	Warrington	1998	4	0	0	0	0
	St Helens	1996	13	1	0	0	4
Carl Forber	Leigh	2005	4	1	0	0	4
	St Helens	2004	1(1)	0	6	0	12
Paul Forber	Salford	1997-98	19(12)	4	0	0	16
Byron Ford	Hull KR	2007	13	6	0	0	24
James Ford	Castleford	2009	3(5)	1	0	0	4
Mike Ford	Castleford	1997-98	25(12)	5	0	3	23
	Warrington	1996	3	0	0	0	0
Jim Forshaw	Salford	1999	(1)	0	0	0	0
Mike Forshaw	Warrington	2004	20(1)	5	0	0	20
	Bradford	1997-2003	162(7)	32	0	0	128
	Leeds	1996	11(3)	5	0	0	20
Carl Forster	St Helens	2011-12	(3)	0	0	0	0
Mark Forster	Warrington	1996-2000	102(1)	40	0	0	160
David Foster	Halifax	2000-01	4(9)	0	0	0	0
Jamie Foster	Hull	2012	9	5	45	0	110
	St Helens	2010-12	44(3)	30	201	0	522
Peter Fox	Wakefield	2007, 2012	51	25	0	0	100
	Hull KR	2008-11	95	52	0	0	208
Nick Fozzard	Castleford	2011	7(10)	0	0	0	0
	St Helens	2004-08, 2010	100(25)	7	0	0	28
	Hull KR	2009	18(4)	1	0	0	4
	Warrington	2002-03	43(11)	2	0	0	8
	Huddersfield	1998-2000	24(8)	2	0	0	8
	Leeds	1996-97	6(16)	3	0	0	12
David Fraisse	Workington	1996	8	0	0	0	0
Daniel Frame	Widnes	2002-05	100(6)	24	0	0	96
Paul Franze	Castleford	2006	2(1)	0	0	0	0
Laurent Frayssinous							
	Catalans	2006	14(2)	3	32	0	76
Andrew Frew	Halifax	2003	17	5	0	0	20
	Wakefield	2002	21	8	0	0	32
	Huddersfield	2001	26	15	0	0	60
Dale Fritz	Castleford	1999-2003	120(4)	9	0	0	36
Gareth Frodsham	St Helens	2008-09	1(9)	0	0	0	0
Liam Fulton	Huddersfield	2009	12(3)	4	0	0	16
David Furner	Leeds	2003-04	45	8	23	0	78
	Wigan	2001-02	51(2)	21	13	0	110
David Furness	Castleford	1996	(1)	0	0	0	0
Matt Gafa	Harlequins	2006-09	81	26	16	0	136
Luke Gale	Bradford	2012	18	2	65	1	139
	Harlequins	2009-11	56(12)	18	86	3	247
Ben Galea	Hull KR	2008-12	115(2)	33	0	0	132
Tommy Gallagher	Hull KR	2007	1(7)	0	0	0	0
	Widnes	2004	(6)	0	0	0	0
	London	2003	1(9)	1	0	0	4
Mark Gamson	Sheffield	1996	3	0	0	0	0
Jim Gannon	Hull KR	2007	7(16)	1	0	0	4
	Huddersfield	2003-06	79(14)	11	0	0	44
	Halifax	1999-2002	83(4)	14	0	0	56
Steve Garcia	Salford	2001	(1)	0	0	0	0
Jean-Marc Garcia	Sheffield	1996-97	35(3)	22	0	0	88
Ade Gardner	St Helens	2002-12	227(12)	142	0	0	568
Matt Gardner	Harlequins	2009	6(3)	2	0	0	8
	Huddersfield	2006-07	22(3)	7	0	0	28
	Castleford	2004	1	1	0	0	4
Steve Gartland	Oldham	1996	1(1)	0	1	0	2
Daniel Gartner	Bradford	2001-03	74(1)	26	0	0	104
Dean Gaskell	Warrington	2002-05	58(1)	10	0	0	40
Lee Gaskell	St Helens	2010-12	30(9)	13	7	1	67
George Gatis	Huddersfield	2008	5(5)	1	0	0	4
Richard Gay	Castleford	1996-2002	94(16)	39	0	0	156
Andrew Gee	Warrington	2000-01	33(1)	4	0	0	16
Anthony Gelling	Wigan	2012	10	7	0	0	28
Stanley Gene	Hull KR	2007-09	37(17)	9	0	0	36
	Bradford	2006	5(16)	8	0	0	32
	Huddersfield	2001, 2003-05	70(6)	27	0	0	108
	Hull	2000-01	5(23)	6	0	0	24
Steve Georgallis	Warrington	2001	5(1)	2	0	0	8
Luke George	Huddersfield	2012	23	15	0	0	60
	Wakefield	2007-11	38(3)	24	0	0	96
Shaun Geritas	Warrington	1997	(5)	1	0	0	4
Alex Gerrard	Widnes	2012	(8)	0	0	0	0
Anthony Gibbons	Leeds	1996	9(4)	2	0	1	9
David Gibbons	Leeds	1996	3(4)	2	0	0	8
Scott Gibbs	St Helens	1996	9	3	0	0	12
Ashley Gibson	Salford	2010-12	57(2)	34	0	0	136
	Leeds	2005-09	25(7)	13	9	0	70

PLAYER	CLUB	YEAR	APP	TRIES	GOALS	FG	PTS
Damian Gibson	Castleford	2003-04	40(3)	5	0	0	20
	Salford	2002	28	3	0	0	12
	Halifax	1998-2001	104(1)	39	0	0	156
	Leeds	1997	18	3	0	0	12
Matt Gidley	St Helens	2007-10	105	40	6	0	172
Tony Gigot	Catalans	2010-11	9(13)	0	3	0	6
Ian Gildart	Oldham	1996-97	31(7)	0	0	0	0
Chris Giles	Widnes	2003-04	35	12	0	0	48
	St Helens	2002	(1)	0	0	0	0
Peter Gill	London	1996-99	75(6)	20	0	0	80
Carl Gillespie	Halifax	1996-99	47(36)	13	0	0	52
Michael Gillett	London	2001-02	23(21)	12	2	0	52
Simon Gillies	Warrington	1999	28	6	0	0	24
Tom Gilmore	Widnes	2012	(1)	0	0	0	0
Lee Gilmour	Huddersfield	2010-12	71(1)	17	0	0	68
	St Helens	2004-09	149(3)	41	0	0	164
	Bradford	2001-03	44(31)	20	0	0	80
	Wigan	1997-2000	44(39)	22	0	0	88
Marc Glanville	Leeds	1998-99	43(3)	5	0	0	20
Eddie Glaze	Castleford	1996	1	0	0	0	0
Paul Gleadhill	Leeds	1996	4	0	0	0	0
Ben Gledhill	Salford	2012	3(7)	1	0	0	4
	Wakefield	2010-11	(16)	0	0	0	0
Mark Gleeson	Warrington	2000-08	38(102)	12	0	0	48
Martin Gleeson	Hull	2011	6	4	0	0	16
	Wigan	2009-11	46(1)	19	0	0	76
	Warrington	2005-09	110(1)	44	0	0	176
	St Helens	2002-04	56(1)	25	0	0	100
	Huddersfield	1999-2001	47(9)	18	0	0	72
Sean Gleeson	Salford	2011-12	35	14	0	0	56
	Wakefield	2007-10	67(6)	20	0	0	80
	Wigan	2005-06	3(3)	0	0	0	0
Jon Goddard	Hull KR	2007	20	2	0	0	8
	Castleford	2000-01	(2)	0	0	0	0
Richard Goddard	Castleford	1996-97	11(3)	2	10	0	28
Brad Godden	Leeds	1998-99	47	15	0	0	60
Wayne Godwin	Salford	2011-12	22(5)	2	0	0	8
	Bradford	2008-10	16(44)	9	0	0	36
	Hull	2007	3(13)	1	0	0	4
	Wigan	2005-06	9(38)	6	0	0	24
	Castleford	2001-04	30(33)	18	56	0	184
Jason Golden	London	2012	7(2)	1	0	0	4
	Harlequins	2009-11	34(12)	3	0	0	12
	Wakefield	2007-08	26(5)	1	0	0	4
Marvin Golden	Widnes	2003	4	1	0	0	4
	London	2001	17(2)	1	0	0	4
	Halifax	2000	20(2)	5	0	0	20
	Leeds	1996-99	43(11)	19	0	0	76
Brett Goldspink	Halifax	2000-02	64(5)	2	0	0	8
	Wigan	1999	6(16)	1	0	0	4
	St Helens	1998	19(4)	2	0	0	8
	Oldham	1997	13(2)	0	0	0	0
Lee Gomersall	Hull KR	2008	1	0	0	0	0
Luke Goodwin	London	1998	9(2)	3	1	1	15
	Oldham	1997	16(4)	10	17	2	76
Grant Gore	Widnes	2012	(1)	0	0	0	0
Aaron Gorrell	Catalans	2007-08	23	6	14	0	52
Andy Gorski	Salford	2001-02	(2)	0	0	0	0
Cyrille Gossard	Catalans	2006-12	54(30)	5	0	0	20
Bobbie Goulding	Salford	2001-02	31(1)	2	56	4	124
	Wakefield	2000	12	3	25	3	65
	Huddersfield	1998-99	27(1)	3	65	4	146
	St Helens	1996-98	42(2)	9	210	4	460
Darrell Goulding	Wigan	2005-12	95(22)	62	0	0	248
	Salford	2009	9	5	0	0	20
Mick Govin	Leigh	2005	5(6)	4	0	0	16
Craig Gower	London	2012	26	4	24	0	64
David Gower	Salford	2006-07	(16)	0	0	0	0
James Graham	St Helens	2003-11	132(63)	47	0	0	188
Nathan Graham	Bradford	1996-98	17(28)	4	0	1	17
Nick Graham	Wigan	2003	13(1)	2	0	0	8
Dalton Grant	Crusaders	2011	(1)	0	0	0	0
Jon Grayshon	Harlequins	2007-09	10(32)	4	0	0	16
	Huddersfield	2003-06	7(43)	5	0	0	20
Blake Green	Hull KR	2011-12	35	14	0	0	56
Brett Green	Gateshead	1999	10(2)	0	0	0	0
Chris Green	Hull	2012	(10)	2	0	0	8
James Green	Hull KR	2012	(1)	0	0	0	0
Toby Green	Huddersfield	2001	3(1)	1	0	0	4
Craig Greenhill	Castleford	2004	21(4)	1	0	0	4
	Hull	2002-03	56	3	2	0	16
Clint Greenshields	Catalans	2007-12	137	81	0	0	324
Brandon Greenwood	Halifax	1996	1	0	0	0	0
Gareth Greenwood	Huddersfield	2003	(1)	0	0	0	0
	Halifax	2002	1	0	0	0	0
Joe Greenwood	St Helens	2012	(2)	0	0	0	0
Lee Greenwood	Huddersfield	2005	7	3	0	0	12
	London	2004-05	30(2)	19	0	0	76
	Halifax	2000-03	38(2)	17	0	0	68
	Sheffield	1999	1(1)	0	0	0	0
James Grehan	Castleford	2012	2(2)	0	0	0	0
Maxime Greseque	Wakefield	2007	2(1)	0	0	0	0
Mathieu Griffi	Catalans	2006-08	1(25)	0	0	0	0
Darrell Griffin	Leeds	2012	8(19)	2	0	0	8
	Huddersfield	2007-11	65(60)	13	0	0	52
	Wakefield	2003-06	55(37)	9	3	0	42
George Griffin	Hull KR	2012	2(2)	0	0	0	0
Josh Griffin	Castleford	2012	20	13	1	0	54
	Wakefield	2011	17	5	21	0	62
	Huddersfield	2009	2	0	0	0	0
Jonathan Griffiths	Paris	1996	(4)	1	0	0	4
Andrew Grima	Workington	1996	2(9)	2	0	0	8
Tony Grimaldi	Hull	2000-01	56(1)	14	0	0	56
	Gateshead	1999	27(2)	10	0	0	40
Danny Grimley	Sheffield	1996	4(1)	1	0	0	4
Scott Grix	Huddersfield	2010-12	58(11)	28	25	0	162
	Wakefield	2008-09	39(3)	18	0	0	72
Simon Grix	Warrington	2006-12	93(24)	30	0	0	120
	Halifax	2003	2(4)	0	0	0	0
Brett Grogan	Gateshead	1999	14(7)	3	0	0	12
Brent Grose	Warrington	2003-07	134(1)	55	0	0	220
David Guasch	Catalans	2010	1	0	0	0	0
Renaud Guigue	Catalans	2006	14(4)	3	0	0	12
Jerome Guisset	Catalans	2006-10	102(23)	9	0	0	36
	Wigan	2005	20(2)	3	0	0	12
	Warrington	2000-04	59(65)	21	0	0	84
Awen Guttenbeil	Castleford	2008	19	0	0	0	0
Reece Guy	Oldham	1996	3(4)	0	0	0	0
Tom Haberecht	Castleford	2008	2(2)	1	0	0	4
Gareth Haggerty	Harlequins	2008-09	8(28)	6	0	0	24
	Salford	2004-07	1(93)	15	0	0	60
	Widnes	2002	1(2)	1	0	0	4
Kurt Haggerty	Widnes	2012	6(8)	3	0	0	12
Andy Haigh	St Helens	1996-98	20(16)	11	0	0	44
Scott Hale	St Helens	2011	(3)	1	0	0	4
Michael Haley	Leeds	2008	(1)	0	0	0	0
Carl Hall	Leeds	1996	7(2)	3	0	0	12
Craig Hall	Hull KR	2011-12	35	19	25	0	126
	Hull	2007-10	59(9)	39	11	0	178
Glenn Hall	Bradford	2010	7(18)	2	0	0	8
Martin Hall	Halifax	1998	2(10)	1	0	0	4
	Hull	1999	7	0	0	0	0
	Castleford	1998	4	0	0	0	0
	Wigan	1996-97	31(5)	7	6	0	40
Ryan Hall	Leeds	2007-12	137(2)	122	0	0	488
Steve Hall	Widnes	2004	1	0	0	0	0
	London	2002-03	35(3)	10	0	0	40
	St Helens	1999-2001	36(22)	19	0	0	76
Graeme Hallas	Huddersfield	2001	1	0	0	0	0
	Hull	1998-99	30(10)	6	39	1	103
	Halifax	1996	11(4)	5	0	0	20
Dave Halley	Bradford	2007-10	63(12)	20	0	0	80
	Wakefield	2009	5	4	0	0	16
Danny Halliwell	Salford	2007	2(3)	0	0	0	0
	Leigh	2005	5	3	0	0	12
	Halifax	2000-03	17(8)	4	0	0	16
	Warrington	2002	9(1)	8	0	0	32
	Salford	2002	3	0	0	0	0
Colum Halpenny	Wakefield	2003-06	103(1)	36	0	0	144
	Halifax	2002	22	12	0	0	48
Jon Hamer	Bradford	1996	(1)	0	0	0	0
Andrew Hamilton	London	1997, 2003	1(20)	3	0	0	12
John Hamilton	St Helens	1998	3	0	0	0	0
Karle Hammond	Halifax	2002	10(2)	2	14	0	36
	Salford	2001	2(3)	1	0	0	4
	London	1999-2000	47	23	2	3	99
	St Helens	1996-98	58(8)	28	0	4	116
Rhys Hanbury	Widnes	2012	24	13	25	1	103
	Crusaders	2010-11	26(1)	14	0	0	56
Anthony Hancock	Paris	1997	8(6)	1	0	0	4
Michael Hancock	Salford	2001-02	12(24)	7	0	0	28
Gareth Handford	Castleford	2001	7(2)	0	0	0	0
	Bradford	2000	1(1)	0	0	0	0
Paul Handforth	Castleford	2006	2(15)	2	1	0	10
	Wakefield	2000-04	17(44)	10	13	0	66
Paddy Handley	Leeds	1996	1(1)	2	0	0	8
Dean Hanger	Warrington	1999	7(11)	3	0	0	12
	Huddersfield	1998	20(1)	5	0	0	20
Josh Hannay	Celtic	2009	17	2	24	0	56
Harrison Hansen	Wigan	2004-12	139(61)	38	0	0	152
Lee Hansen	Wigan	1997	10(5)	0	0	0	0
Shontayne Hape	Bradford	2003-08	123(2)	79	0	0	316
Lionel Harbin	Wakefield	2001	(1)	0	0	0	0
Zak Hardaker	Leeds	2011-12	45	28	1	0	114
Ian Hardman	Hull KR	2007	18	4	0	0	16
	St Helens	2003-07	32(11)	9	5	0	46
Jeff Hardy	Hudds-Sheff	2000	20(5)	6	0	1	25
	Sheffield	1999	22(4)	7	0	0	28
Spencer Hargrave	Castleford	1996-99	(6)	0	0	0	0
Bryn Hargreaves	Bradford	2011-12	45(5)	1	0	0	4
	St Helens	2007-10	53(44)	7	0	0	28
	Wigan	2004-06	16(12)	1	0	0	4

169

Super League Players 1996-2012

PLAYER	CLUB	YEAR	APP	TRIES	GOALS	FG	PTS
Lee Harland	Castleford	1996-2004	148(35)	20	0	0	80
Neil Harmon	Halifax	2003	13(3)	0	0	0	0
	Salford	2001	6(5)	0	0	0	0
	Bradford	1998-2000	15(13)	2	0	0	8
	Huddersfield	1998	12	1	0	0	4
	Leeds	1996	10	1	0	0	4
Ben Harris	Bradford	2005-07	70(4)	24	0	0	96
Iestyn Harris	Bradford	2004-08	109(11)	35	87	2	316
	Leeds	1997-2001	111(7)	57	490	6	1214
	Warrington	1996	16	4	63	2	144
Ben Harrison	Warrington	2007-12	80(44)	7	0	0	28
Karl Harrison	Hull	1999	26	2	0	0	8
	Halifax	1996-98	60(2)	2	0	0	8
Andrew Hart	London	2004	12(1)	2	0	0	8
Tim Hartley	Harlequins	2006	2	1	0	0	4
	Salford	2004-05	6(7)	5	0	0	20
Carlos Hassan	Bradford	1996	6(4)	2	0	0	8
Phil Hassan	Wakefield	2002	9(1)	0	0	0	0
	Halifax	2000-01	25(4)	3	0	0	12
	Salford	1998	15	2	0	0	8
	Leeds	1996-97	38(4)	12	0	0	48
Tom Haughey	Castleford	2006	1(3)	1	0	0	4
	London	2003-04	10(8)	1	0	0	4
	Wakefield	2001-02	5(12)	0	0	0	0
Simon Haughton	Wigan	1996-2002	63(46)	32	0	0	128
Solomon Haumono							
	Harlequins	2006	10(9)	6	0	0	24
	London	2005	24(5)	8	0	0	32
Weller Hauraki	Leeds	2011-12	18(17)	6	0	0	24
	Crusaders	2010	26(1)	11	0	0	44
Richie Hawkyard	Bradford	2007	1(2)	1	0	0	4
Andy Hay	Widnes	2003-04	50(2)	7	0	0	28
	Leeds	1997-2002	112(27)	43	0	0	172
	Sheffield	1996-97	17(3)	5	0	0	20
Adam Hayes	Hudds-Sheff	2000	2(1)	0	0	0	0
Joey Hayes	Salford	1999	9	2	0	0	8
	St Helens	1996-98	11(6)	7	0	0	28
James Haynes	Hull KR	2009	1	0	0	0	0
Mathew Head	Hull	2007	9(1)	1	0	1	5
Mitch Healey	Castleford	2001-03	68(1)	10	16	0	72
Daniel Heckenberg							
	Harlequins	2006-09	31(39)	4	0	0	16
Chris Heil	Hull KR	2012	2	1	0	0	4
Ricky Helliwell	Salford	1997-99	(2)	0	0	0	0
Tom Hemingway	Huddersfield	2005-09	7(7)	1	17	0	38
Bryan Henare	St Helens	2000-01	4(12)	1	0	0	4
Richard Henare	Warrington	1996-97	28(2)	24	0	0	96
Andrew Henderson							
	Castleford	2006, 2008	44(11)	4	0	0	16
Ian Henderson	Catalans	2011-12	47(6)	4	0	0	16
	Bradford	2005-07	33(37)	13	0	0	52
Kevin Henderson	Wakefield	2005-11	52(68)	9	0	0	36
	Leigh	2005	(1)	0	0	0	0
Mark Henry	Salford	2009-11	67	22	0	0	88
Brad Hepi	Castleford	1999, 2001	9(21)	3	0	0	12
	Salford	2000	3(5)	0	0	0	0
	Hull	1998	15(1)	3	0	0	12
Jon Hepworth	Castleford	2003-04	19(23)	7	8	0	44
	Leeds	2003	(1)	0	0	0	0
	London	2002	(2)	0	0	0	0
Marc Herbert	Bradford	2011	20	4	2	0	20
Aaron Heremaia	Hull	2012	10(3)	5	0	0	20
Ian Herron	Hull	2000	9	1	17	0	38
	Gateshead	1999	25	4	105	0	226
Jason Hetherington							
	London	2001-02	37	9	0	0	36
Gareth Hewitt	Salford	1999	2(1)	0	0	0	0
Andrew Hick	Hull	2000	9(9)	1	0	0	4
	Gateshead	1999	12(5)	2	0	0	8
Jarrad Hickey	Wakefield	2011	(8)	2	0	0	8
Chris Hicks	Warrington	2008-10	72	56	119	0	462
Paul Hicks	Wakefield	1999	(1)	0	0	0	0
Darren Higgins	London	1998	5(6)	2	0	0	8
Iain Higgins	London	1997-98	1(7)	2	0	0	8
Liam Higgins	Wakefield	2011	4(12)	0	0	0	0
	Castleford	2008-10	42(32)	2	0	0	8
	Hull	2003-06	1(34)	0	0	0	0
Mick Higham	Warrington	2009-12	31(51)	20	0	0	80
	Wigan	2006-08	61(28)	13	0	0	52
	St Helens	2001-05	43(56)	32	0	0	128
Chris Highton	Warrington	1997	1(1)	0	0	0	0
David Highton	London	2004-05	21(24)	2	0	0	8
	Salford	2002	4(5)	2	0	0	8
	Warrington	1998-2001	18(14)	2	0	0	8
Paul Highton	Salford	1998-2002, 2004-07	114(80)	14	0	0	56
	Halifax	1996-98	12(18)	2	0	0	8
Andy Hill	Huddersfield	1999	(4)	0	0	0	0
	Castleford	1999	4(4)	0	0	0	0
Chris Hill	Warrington	2012	19(9)	4	0	0	16
	Leigh	2005	(1)	0	0	0	0
Danny Hill	Wigan	2006-07	1(10)	0	0	0	0
	Hull KR	2007	2	0	0	0	0
	Hull	2004-06	4(6)	0	0	0	0
Howard Hill	Oldham	1996-97	22(12)	4	0	0	16
John Hill	St Helens	2003	(1)	0	0	0	0
	Halifax	2003	1(2)	0	0	0	0
	Warrington	2001-02	(4)	0	0	0	0
Scott Hill	Harlequins	2007-08	41(2)	13	0	0	52
Mark Hilton	Warrington	1996-2000, 2002-06	141(40)	7	0	0	28
Ian Hindmarsh	Catalans	2006	25	3	0	0	12
Brendan Hlad	Castleford	2008	(3)	0	0	0	0
Andy Hobson	Widnes	2004	5(13)	0	0	0	0
	Halifax	1998-2003	51(85)	8	0	0	32
Gareth Hock	Wigan	2003-09, 2011-12	126(43)	38	0	0	152
Tommy Hodgkinson							
	St Helens	2006	(1)	0	0	0	0
Andy Hodgson	Wakefield	1999	14(2)	2	1	0	10
	Bradford	1997-98	8(2)	4	0	0	16
Brett Hodgson	Warrington	2011-12	45	26	203	0	510
	Huddersfield	2009-10	45	13	166	0	384
David Hodgson	Hull KR	2012	18	16	0	0	64
	Huddersfield	2008-11	84	59	0	0	236
	Salford	2005-07	81	30	47	0	214
	Wigan	2000-04	90(19)	43	0	0	172
	Halifax	1999	10(3)	5	0	0	20
Elliot Hodgson	Huddersfield	2009	1	0	0	0	0
Josh Hodgson	Hull KR	2010-12	46(28)	16	0	0	64
	Hull	2009	(2)	0	0	0	0
Ryan Hoffman	Wigan	2011	28(1)	11	0	0	44
Darren Hogg	London	1996	(1)	0	0	0	0
Michael Hogue	Paris	1997	5(7)	0	0	0	0
Lance Hohaia	St Helens	2012	26(2)	6	0	0	24
Chris Holden	Warrington	1996-97	2(1)	0	0	0	0
Daniel Holdsworth							
	Salford	2010-12	71	18	183	1	439
Stephen Holgate	Halifax	2000	1(10)	0	0	0	0
	Hull	1999	1	0	0	0	0
	Wigan	1997-98	11(26)	2	0	0	8
	Workington	1996	19	3	0	0	12
Martyn Holland	Wakefield	2000-03	52(3)	6	0	0	24
Oliver Holmes	Castleford	2010-12	31(12)	5	0	0	20
Tim Holmes	Widnes	2004-05	15(4)	0	0	0	0
Graham Holroyd	Huddersfield	2003					
	Salford	2000-02	40(11)	8	75	5	187
	Halifax	1999	24(2)	3	74	5	165
	Leeds	1996-98	40(26)	22	101	8	298
Dallas Hood	Wakefield	2003-04	18(9)	1	0	0	4
Liam Hood	Leeds	2012	1(4)	3	0	0	12
Jason Hooper	St Helens	2003-07	89(6)	35	30	0	200
Lee Hopkins	Harlequins	2006-07	44(3)	11	0	0	44
	London	2005	29	6	0	0	24
Sean Hoppe	St Helens	1999-2002	69(16)	32	0	0	128
Graeme Horne	Hull KR	2012	23(2)	6	0	0	24
	Huddersfield	2010-11	23(17)	11	0	0	44
	Hull	2003-09	49(74)	24	0	0	96
Richard Horne	Hull	1999-2012	306(13)	108	12	6	462
John Hough	Warrington	1996-97	9	2	0	0	8
Danny Houghton	Hull	2007-12	86(45)	14	0	0	56
Sylvain Houles	Wakefield	2003, 2005	8(1)	1	0	0	4
	London	2001-02	17(10)	11	0	0	44
	Hudds-Sheff	2000	5(2)	1	0	0	4
Harvey Howard	Wigan	2001-02	25(27)	1	0	0	4
	Bradford	1998	4(2)	1	0	0	4
	Leeds	1996	8	0	0	0	0
Kim Howard	London	1997	4(5)	1	0	0	4
Stuart Howarth	Salford	2012	23(4)	1	0	0	4
	Wakefield	2011	17(2)	1	0	0	4
Stuart Howarth	Workington	1996	(2)	0	0	0	0
David Howell	London	2012	19	3	0	0	12
	Harlequins	2008-11	76	26	0	0	104
Phil Howlett	Bradford	1999	5(1)	2	0	0	8
Craig Huby	Castleford	2003-04, 2006, 2008-12	88(47)	21	41	0	166
Ryan Hudson	Castleford	2002-04, 2009-12	138(12)	31	0	0	124
	Huddersfield	1998-99, 2007-08	51(22)	10	0	0	40
	Wakefield	2000-01	42(9)	11	0	1	45
Adam Hughes	Widnes	2002-05	89(2)	45	51	0	282
	Halifax	2001	8(8)	8	0	0	32
	Wakefield	1999-2000	43(3)	21	34	0	152
	Leeds	1996-97	4(5)	4	0	0	16
Ian Hughes	Sheffield	1996	9(8)	4	0	0	16
Jack Hughes	Wigan	2011-12	9(10)	3	0	0	12
Mark Hughes	Catalans	2006	23	9	0	0	36
Steffan Hughes	London	1999-2001	1(13)	1	0	0	4
David Hulme	Salford	1997-99	53(1)	5	0	0	20
	Leeds	1996	8(1)	2	0	0	8
Paul Hulme	Warrington	1996-97	23(1)	2	0	0	8
Gary Hulse	Widnes	2005	12(5)	2	0	0	8
	Warrington	2001-04	20(28)	8	0	1	33
Alan Hunte	Salford	2002	19(2)	9	0	0	36
	Warrington	1999-2001	83	49	0	0	196
	Hull	1998	21	7	0	0	28
	St Helens	1996-97	30(2)	28	0	0	112

Super League Players 1996-2012

PLAYER	CLUB	YEAR	APP	TRIES	GOALS	FG	PTS
Kieran Hyde	Wakefield	2010-11	11	4	4	0	24
Nick Hyde	Paris	1997	5(5)	1	0	0	4
Chaz I'Anson	Hull KR	2007-10	17(13)	3	0	0	12
Andy Ireland	Hull	1998-99	22(15)	0	0	0	0
	Bradford	1996	1	0	0	0	0
Kevin Iro	St Helens	1999-2001	76	39	0	0	156
	Leeds	1996	16	9	0	0	36
Willie Isa	Widnes	2012	24(2)	2	0	0	8
	Castleford	2011	7(2)	6	0	0	24
Andrew Isherwood							
	Wigan	1998-99	(5)	0	0	0	0
Olu Iwenofu	London	2000-01	2(1)	0	0	0	0
Chico Jackson	Hull	1999	(4)	0	0	0	0
Lee Jackson	Hull	2001-02	37(9)	12	1	0	50
	Leeds	1999-2000	28(24)	7	0	0	28
Michael Jackson	Sheffield	1998-99	17(17)	2	0	0	8
	Halifax	1996-97	27(6)	11	0	0	44
Paul Jackson	Castleford	2003-04, 2010-12	44(30)	5	0	0	20
	Huddersfield	1998, 2005-09	50(73)	4	0	0	16
	Wakefield	1999-2002	57(41)	2	0	0	8
Rob Jackson	Leigh	2005	20(3)	5	0	0	20
	London	2002-04	26(14)	9	0	0	36
Wayne Jackson	Halifax	1996-97	17(5)	2	0	0	8
Aled James	Crusaders	2011	1	0	0	0	0
	Celtic	2009	3(3)	1	0	0	4
	Widnes	2003	3	0	0	0	0
Andy James	Halifax	1996	(4)	0	0	0	0
Jordan James	Salford	2012	1(18)	2	0	0	8
	Crusaders	2010-11	5(24)	3	0	0	12
	Celtic	2009	17(4)	1	0	0	4
	Wigan	2006	2(4)	3	0	0	12
Matt James	Wakefield	2012	(4)	0	0	0	0
	Harlequins	2010	(2)	0	0	0	0
	Bradford	2006-09	1(23)	0	0	0	0
Pascal Jampy	Catalans	2006	4(7)	0	0	0	0
	Paris	1996-97	3(2)	0	0	0	0
Adam Janowski	Harlequins	2008	(1)	0	0	0	0
Ben Jeffries	Bradford	2008-09, 2011-12	76(3)	20	0	0	80
	Wakefield	2003-07, 2010-11	151(10)	70	20	6	326
Mick Jenkins	Hull	2000	24	2	0	0	8
	Gateshead	1999	16	3	0	0	12
Ed Jennings	London	1998-99	1(2)	0	0	0	0
Rod Jensen	Huddersfield	2007-08	26(3)	13	0	0	52
Anthony Jerram	Warrington	2007	(2)	0	0	0	0
Lee Jewitt	Salford	2007, 2009-12	23(59)	2	0	0	8
	Wigan	2005	(2)	0	0	0	0
Isaac John	Wakefield	2012	13	1	19	0	42
Andrew Johns	Warrington	2005	3	1	12	1	29
Matthew Johns	Wigan	2001	24	3	0	1	13
Andy Johnson	Salford	2004-05	8(26)	7	0	0	28
	Castleford	2002-03	32(16)	11	0	0	44
	London	2000-01	24(21)	12	0	0	48
	Huddersfield	1999	5	1	0	0	4
	Wigan	1996-99	24(20)	19	0	0	76
Bruce Johnson	Widnes	2004-05	(4)	0	0	0	0
Dallas Johnson	Catalans	2010	26	1	0	0	4
Greg Johnson	Wakefield	2011	12	2	0	0	8
Jason Johnson	St Helens	1997-99	2	0	0	0	0
Mark Johnson	Salford	1999-2000	22(9)	16	0	0	64
	Hull	1998	10(1)	4	0	0	16
	Workington	1996	12	4	0	0	16
Nick Johnson	Hull KR	2012	1	0	0	0	0
Nick Johnson	London	2003	(1)	0	0	0	0
Paul Johnson	Crusaders	2011	6(4)	0	0	0	0
	Wakefield	2010	12(3)	4	0	0	16
	Warrington	2007-09	37(9)	17	0	0	68
	Bradford	2004-06	46(8)	19	0	0	76
	Wigan	1996-2003	74(46)	54	0	0	216
Paul Johnson	Wakefield	2011-12	25(21)	6	0	0	24
	St Helens	2010	(2)	0	0	0	0
Richard Johnson	Bradford	2008	(2)	0	0	0	0
Ben Johnston	Castleford	2012	2	0	0	0	0
Ben Jones	Harlequins	2010	(2)	0	0	0	0
Chris Jones	Leigh	2005	1(1)	0	0	0	0
Danny Jones	Halifax	2003	1	0	0	0	0
David Jones	Oldham	1997	14(1)	5	0	0	20
Josh Jones	St Helens	2012	18	8	0	0	32
Mark Jones	Warrington	1996	8(11)	2	0	0	8
Phil Jones	Leigh	2005	16	8	31	0	94
	Wigan	1999-2001	14(7)	6	25	0	74
Stacey Jones	Catalans	2006-07	39	11	43	3	133
Stephen Jones	Huddersfield	2005	(1)	0	0	0	0
Stuart Jones	Castleford	2009-12	69(27)	14	0	0	56
	Huddersfield	2004-08	96(22)	17	0	0	68
	St Helens	2003	(18)	2	0	0	8
	Wigan	2002	5(3)	1	0	0	4
Ben Jones-Bishop							
	Leeds	2008-09, 2011-12	44(2)	27	0	0	108
	Harlequins	2010	17	10	0	0	40
Jamie Jones-Buchanan							
	Leeds	1999-2012	196(58)	56	0	0	224
Tim Jonkers	Wigan	2006	3(1)	0	0	0	0
	Salford	2004-06	5(11)	0	0	0	0
	St Helens	1999-2004	41(64)	12	0	0	48
Darren Jordan	Wakefield	2003	(1)	0	0	0	0
Phil Joseph	Bradford	2012	(6)	0	0	0	0
	Huddersfield	2004	7(6)	0	0	0	0
Warren Jowitt	Hull	2003	(2)	0	0	0	0
	Salford	2001-02	17(4)	2	0	0	8
	Wakefield	2000	19(3)	8	0	0	32
	Bradford	1996-99	13(25)	5	0	0	20
Chris Joynt	St Helens	1996-2004	201(14)	68	0	0	272
Gregory Kacala	Paris	1996	7	1	0	0	4
Andy Kain	Castleford	2004, 2006	9(7)	3	10	0	32
Antonio Kaufusi	London	2012	24(2)	5	0	0	20
Mal Kaufusi	London	2004	1(3)	0	0	0	0
Ben Kavanagh	Widnes	2012	1(5)	0	0	0	0
Liam Kay	Wakefield	2012	1	0	0	0	0
Ben Kaye	Harlequins	2009-10	2(13)	0	0	0	0
	Leeds	2008	2(2)	1	0	0	4
Elliot Kear	Bradford	2012	9	2	0	0	8
	Crusaders	2010-11	16(1)	4	0	0	16
	Celtic	2009	3	0	0	0	0
Brett Kearney	Bradford	2010-12	66	33	0	0	132
Stephen Kearney	Hull	2005	22(2)	5	0	0	20
Damon Keating	Wakefield	2002	7(17)	1	0	0	4
Shaun Keating	London	1996	1(3)	0	0	0	0
Mark Keenan	Workington	1996	3(4)	1	0	0	4
Jimmy Keinhorst	Leeds	2012	2(3)	3	0	0	12
Tony Kemp	Wakefield	1999-2000	15(5)	2	0	1	9
	Leeds	1996-98	23(2)	5	0	2	22
Damien Kennedy	London	2003	5(11)	1	0	0	4
Ian Kenny	St Helens	2004	(1)	0	0	0	0
Jason Kent	Leigh	2005	23	1	0	0	4
Liam Kent	Hull	2012	(5)	0	0	0	0
Shane Kenward	Wakefield	1999	28	6	0	0	24
	Salford	1998	1	0	0	0	0
Jason Keough	Paris	1997	2	1	0	0	4
Keiran Kerr	Widnes	2005	6	2	0	0	8
Martin Ketteridge	Halifax	1996	7(5)	0	0	0	0
Ronnie Kettlewell	Warrington	1996	(1)	0	0	0	0
Younes Khattabi	Catalans	2006-08	24(4)	10	0	0	40
David Kidwell	Warrington	2001-02	14(12)	9	0	0	36
Andrew King	London	2003	23(1)	15	0	0	60
Dave King	Huddersfield	1998-99	11(17)	2	0	0	8
James King	Leigh	2005	5(7)	0	0	0	0
Kevin King	Wakefield	2005	8(1)	2	0	0	8
	Castleford	2004	(1)	0	0	0	0
Matt King	Warrington	2008-11	91	58	0	0	232
Paul King	Wakefield	2010-11	10(19)	0	0	1	1
	Hull	1999-2009	136(93)	20	0	1	81
Andy Kirk	Wakefield	2005	6(3)	1	0	0	4
	Salford	2004	20	5	0	0	20
	Leeds	2001-02	4(4)	0	0	0	0
Ian Kirke	Leeds	2006-12	47(95)	8	0	0	32
John Kirkpatrick	London	2004-05	18(1)	5	0	0	20
	St Helens	2001-03	10(11)	10	0	0	40
	Halifax	2003	1	1	0	0	4
Danny Kirmond	Wakefield	2010, 2012	35(4)	10	0	0	40
	Huddersfield	2008-11	18(31)	9	0	0	36
Wayne Kitchin	Workington	1996	11(6)	3	17	1	47
Sione Kite	Widnes	2012	6(8)	1	0	0	4
Ian Knott	Leigh	2005	8(1)	2	0	0	8
	Wakefield	2002-03	34(5)	7	79	0	186
	Warrington	1996-2001	68(41)	24	18	0	132
Matt Knowles	Wigan	1996	(3)	0	0	0	0
Michael Knowles	Castleford	2006	(1)	0	0	0	0
Phil Knowles	Salford	1997	1	0	0	0	0
Simon Knox	Halifax	1999	(6)	0	0	0	0
	Salford	1998	1(1)	0	0	0	0
	Bradford	1996-98	9(19)	7	0	0	28
Toa Kohe-Love	Warrington	1996-2001, 2005-06	166(3)	90	0	0	360
	Bradford	2004	1(1)	0	0	0	0
	Hull	2002-03	42	19	0	0	76
Paul Koloi	Wigan	1997	1(2)	1	0	0	4
Craig Kopczak	Bradford	2006-12	32(83)	10	0	0	40
Michael Korkidas	Wakefield	2003-06, 2009-11	133(36)	15	0	0	60
	Huddersfield	2009	4(1)	1	0	0	4
	Castleford	2008	15(6)	1	0	0	4
	Salford	2007	26(1)	1	0	0	4
Nick Kouparitsas	Harlequins	2011	2(13)	1	0	0	4
Olsi Krasniqi	London	2012	(16)	2	0	0	8
	Harlequins	2010-11	3(20)	1	0	0	4
David Krause	London	1996-97	22(1)	7	0	0	28
Ben Kusto	Huddersfield	2001	21(4)	9	0	1	37
Anthony Laffranchi							
	St Helens	2012	8	7	0	0	32
James Laithwaite	Hull KR	2012	1(2)	1	0	0	4
Adrian Lam	Wigan	2001-04	105(2)	40	1	9	171
Mark Lane	Paris	1996	(2)	0	0	0	0
Allan Langer	Warrington	2000-01	47	13	4	0	60

171

Super League Players 1996-2012

PLAYER	CLUB	YEAR	APP	TRIES	GOALS	FG	PTS
Kevin Langer	London	1996	12(4)	2	0	0	8
Junior Langi	Salford	2005-06	27(7)	7	0	0	28
Chris Langley	Huddersfield	2000-01	18(1)	3	0	0	12
Gareth Langley	St Helens	2006	1	1	3	0	10
Jamie Langley	Bradford	2002-12	172(48)	35	0	0	140
Kevin Larroyer	Catalans	2012	(2)	0	0	0	0
Andy Last	Hull	1999-2005	16(10)	4	0	0	16
Sam Latus	Hull KR	2010-12	33(3)	13	0	0	52
Epalahame Lauaki							
	Wigan	2012	13(11)	2	0	0	8
	Hull	2009-11	3(50)	4	0	0	16
Dale Laughton	Warrington	2002	15(1)	0	0	0	0
	Huddersfield	2000-01	36(2)	4	0	0	16
	Sheffield	1996-99	48(22)	5	0	0	20
Ali Lauitiiti	Wakefield	2012	22(1)	8	0	0	32
	Leeds	2004-11	64(117)	58	0	0	232
Jason Laurence	Salford	1997	1	0	0	0	0
Graham Law	Wakefield	1999-2002	34(30)	6	40	0	104
Neil Law	Wakefield	1999-2002	83	39	0	0	156
	Sheffield	1998	1(1)	1	0	0	4
Dean Lawford	Widnes	2003-04	17(1)	5	2	4	28
	Halifax	2001	1(1)	0	0	0	0
	Leeds	1997-2000	15(8)	2	3	0	14
	Huddersfield	1999	6(1)	0	6	1	13
	Sheffield	1996	9(5)	2	1	1	11
Johnny Lawless	Halifax	2001-03	73(1)	10	0	0	40
	Hudds-Sheff	2000	19(6)	3	0	0	12
	Sheffield	1996-99	76(4)	11	0	0	44
Michael Lawrence							
	Huddersfield	2007-12	105(5)	32	0	0	128
Charlie Leaeno	Wakefield	2010	7(3)	2	0	0	8
Mark Leafa	Castleford	2008	5(9)	1	0	0	4
	Leigh	2005	28	2	0	0	8
Leroy Leapai	London	1996	2	0	0	0	0
Jim Leatham	Hull	1998-99	20(18)	4	0	0	16
	Leeds	1997	(1)	0	0	0	0
Andy Leathem	Warrington	1999	2(8)	0	0	0	0
	St Helens	1996-98	20(1)	1	0	0	4
Danny Lee	Gateshead	1999	16(2)	0	0	0	0
Jason Lee	Halifax	2001	10(1)	2	0	0	8
Mark Lee	Salford	1997-2000	25(11)	1	0	4	8
Robert Lee	Hull	1999	4(3)	0	0	0	0
Tommy Lee	Huddersfield	2012	11(7)	3	0	0	12
	Wakefield	2011	25	6	0	0	24
	Crusaders	2010	3(9)	0	0	0	0
	Hull	2005-09	44(27)	6	0	0	24
Matthew Leigh	Salford	2000	(6)	0	0	0	0
Chris Leikvoll	Warrington	2004-07	72(18)	4	0	0	16
Jim Lenihan	Huddersfield	1999	19(1)	10	0	0	40
Mark Lennon	Celtic	2009	10(3)	1	8	0	20
	Hull KR	2007	11(4)	5	7	0	34
	Castleford	2001-03	30(21)	10	21	0	82
Tevita Leo-Latu	Wakefield	2006-10	28(49)	10	0	0	40
Gary Lester	Hull	1998-99	46	17	0	0	68
Stuart Lester	Wigan	1997	1(3)	0	0	0	0
Heath L'Estrange	Bradford	2010-12	45(22)	7	0	0	28
Afi Leuila	Oldham	1996-97	17(3)	2	0	0	8
Kylie Leuluai	Leeds	2007-12	136(27)	16	0	0	64
Macgraff Leuluai	Widnes	2012	1(9)	0	0	0	0
Phil Leuluai	Salford	2007, 2009-10	7(47)	3	0	0	12
Thomas Leuluai	Wigan	2007-12	167(1)	51	0	0	204
	Harlequins	2006	15(2)	6	0	0	24
	London	2005	20	13	0	0	52
Simon Lewis	Castleford	2001	4	3	0	0	12
Paul Leyland	St Helens	2006	1	0	0	0	0
Jon Liddell	Leeds	2001	1	0	0	0	0
Jason Lidden	Castleford	1997	15(1)	7	0	0	28
Danny Lima	Wakefield	2007	(3)	0	0	0	0
	Salford	2006	7(2)	0	0	0	0
	Warrington	2004-06	15(47)	9	0	0	36
Jeff Lima	Wigan	2011-12	24(29)	4	0	0	16
Tom Lineham	Hull	2012	4(1)	4	0	0	16
Craig Littler	St Helens	2006	1	1	0	0	4
Stuart Littler	Salford	1998-2002, 2004-07, 2009-10	217(30)	65	0	0	260
Peter Livett	Workington	1996	3(1)	0	0	0	0
Rhodri Lloyd	Wigan	2012	1(2)	0	0	0	0
Scott Logan	Wigan	2006	10(11)	0	0	0	0
	Hull	2001-03	27(20)	5	0	0	20
Jamahl Lolesi	Huddersfield	2007-10	75(9)	27	0	0	108
Filimone Lolohea	Harlequins	2006	3(6)	0	0	0	0
	London	2005	8(15)	0	0	0	0
David Lomax	Huddersfield	2000-01	45(9)	4	0	0	16
	Paris	1997	19(2)	1	0	0	4
Jonny Lomax	St Helens	2009-12	73(2)	31	57	2	240
Dave Long	London	1999	(1)	0	0	0	0
Karl Long	London	2003	(1)	0	0	0	0
	Widnes	2002	4	1	0	0	4
Sean Long	Hull	2010-11	22	6	0	0	24
	St Helens	1997-2009	263(8)	126	826	20	2176
	Wigan	1996-97	1(5)	0	0	0	0
Davide Longo	Bradford	1996	1(3)	0	0	0	0

PLAYER	CLUB	YEAR	APP	TRIES	GOALS	FG	PTS
Gary Lord	Oldham	1996-97	28(12)	3	0	0	12
Paul Loughlin	Huddersfield	1998-99	34(2)	4	4	0	24
	Bradford	1996-97	36(4)	15	8	0	76
Rhys Lovegrove	Hull KR	2007-12	52(57)	12	0	0	48
Karl Lovell	Hudds-Sheff	2000	14	5	0	0	20
	Sheffield	1999	22(4)	8	0	0	32
Will Lovell	London	2012	7(3)	3	0	0	12
James Lowes	Bradford	1996-2003	205	84	2	2	342
Laurent Lucchese	Paris	1996	13(5)	2	0	0	8
Zebastian Luisi	Harlequins	2006-07	23(2)	4	0	0	16
	London	2004-05	21(1)	7	0	0	28
Keith Lulia	Bradford	2012	25	8	0	0	32
Shaun Lunt	Leeds	2012	10(9)	7	0	0	28
	Huddersfield	2009-12	30(35)	32	0	0	128
Peter Lupton	Crusaders	2010-11	37(9)	10	0	0	40
	Celtic	2009	16(4)	4	0	0	16
	Castleford	2006, 2008	40	11	0	0	44
	Hull	2003-06	19(26)	10	3	0	46
	London	2000-02	10(15)	2	2	0	12
Andy Lynch	Hull	2012	27(2)	3	0	0	12
	Bradford	2005-11	159(29)	46	0	0	184
	Castleford	1999-2004	78(48)	15	0	0	60
Reece Lyne	Hull	2010-11	11(1)	2	0	0	8
Jamie Lyon	St Helens	2005-06	54(1)	39	172	0	500
Duncan MacGillivray							
	Wakefield	2004-08	75(18)	6	0	0	24
Brad Mackay	Bradford	2000	24(2)	8	0	0	32
Graham Mackay	Hull	2002	27	18	24	0	120
	Bradford	2001	16(3)	12	1	0	50
	Leeds	2000	12(8)	10	2	0	44
Keiron Maddocks	Leigh	2005	1(3)	0	0	0	0
Steve Maden	Leigh	2005	23	9	0	0	36
	Warrington	2002	3	0	0	0	0
Mateaki Mafi	Warrington	1996-97	7(8)	7	0	0	28
Shaun Magennis	St Helens	2010-12	7(19)	3	0	0	12
Brendan Magnus	London	2000	3	1	0	0	4
Mark Maguire	London	1996-97	11(4)	7	13	0	54
Adam Maher	Hull	2000-03	88(4)	24	0	0	96
	Gateshead	1999	21(5)	3	0	0	12
Lee Maher	Leeds	1996	4(1)	0	0	0	0
Shaun Mahony	Paris	1997	5	0	0	0	0
Hutch Maiava	Hull	2007	(19)	1	0	0	4
David Maiden	Hull	2000-01	32(10)	11	0	0	44
	Gateshead	1999	5(16)	8	0	0	32
Craig Makin	Salford	1999-2001	24(20)	2	0	0	8
Tom Makinson	St Helens	2011-12	36(5)	20	54	0	188
Brady Malam	Wigan	2000	5(20)	1	0	0	4
Dominic Maloney	Wigan	2009	(7)	0	0	0	0
Francis Maloney	Castleford	1998-99, 2003-04	71(7)	24	33	3	165
	Salford	2001-02	45(1)	26	5	0	114
	Wakefield	2000	1(1)	1	1	0	6
	Oldham	1996-97	39(2)	12	91	2	232
George Mann	Warrington	1997	14(5)	1	0	0	4
	Leeds	1996	11(4)	2	0	0	8
Dane Manning	Leeds	2009	(1)	0	0	0	0
Misili Manu	Widnes	2005	1	0	0	0	0
Willie Manu	Hull	2007-12	133(18)	33	0	0	132
	Castleford	2006	19(4)	9	0	0	36
Manase Manuokafoa							
	Bradford	2012	13(10)	2	0	0	8
Darren Mapp	Celtic	2009	9(2)	1	0	0	4
David March	Wakefield	1999-2007	164(23)	34	126	0	388
Paul March	Wakefield	1999-2001, 2007	42(31)	17	23	0	114
	Huddersfield	2003-06	71(19)	17	36	1	141
Nick Mardon	London	1997-98	14	2	0	0	8
Remy Marginet	Catalans	2011	2	0	9	0	18
Antoni Maria	Catalans	2012	(1)	0	0	0	0
Frankie Mariano	Wakefield	2011-12	29(9)	11	0	0	44
	Hull KR	2010	(3)	0	0	0	0
Oliver Marns	Halifax	1996-2002	54(19)	23	0	0	92
Paul Marquet	Warrington	2002	23(2)	0	0	0	0
Callum Marriott	Salford	2011	1	0	0	0	0
Iain Marsh	Salford	1998-2001	1(4)	0	0	0	0
Lee Marsh	Salford	2001-02	3(4)	0	0	0	0
Stefan Marsh	Widnes	2012	20	7	0	0	28
	Wigan	2010-11	12	3	0	0	12
Richard Marshall	Leigh	2005	4(16)	1	0	0	4
	London	2002-03	33(11)	1	0	0	4
	Huddersfield	2000-01	35(14)	1	0	0	4
	Halifax	1996-99	38(34)	2	0	0	8
Jason Martin	Paris	1997	15(2)	3	0	0	12
Scott Martin	Salford	1997-99	32(18)	8	0	0	32
Tony Martin	Hull	2012	1	0	0	0	0
	Crusaders	2010-11	40(1)	14	1	0	58
	Wakefield	2008-09	33	10	33	0	106
	London	1996-97, 2001-03	97(1)	36	170	1	485
Mick Martindale	Halifax	1996	(4)	0	0	0	0
Sebastien Martins							
	Catalans	2006, 2009-11	(21)	2	0	0	8
Tommy Martyn	St Helens	1996-2003	125(20)	87	63	12	486

PLAYER	CLUB	YEAR	APP	TRIES	GOALS	FG	PTS
Dean Marwood	Workington	1996	9(6)	0	22	0	44
Martin Masella	Warrington	2001	10(14)	5	0	0	20
	Wakefield	2000	14(8)	4	0	0	16
	Leeds	1997-1999	59(5)	1	0	0	4
Colin Maskill	Castleford	1996	8	1	1	0	6
Keith Mason	Huddersfield	2006-12	118(14)	4	0	0	16
	Castleford	2006	(2)	0	0	0	0
	St Helens	2003-05	33(23)	4	0	0	16
	Wakefield	2000-01	5(17)	1	0	0	4
Willie Mason	Hull KR	2011	6	1	0	0	4
Sammy Masselot	Wakefield	2011	(1)	0	0	0	0
Nathan Massey	Castleford	2008-12	16(29)	1	0	0	4
Vila Matautia	St Helens	1996-2001	31(68)	9	0	0	36
Feleti Mateo	London	2005	4(10)	1	0	0	4
Barrie-Jon Mather							
	Castleford	1998, 2000-02	50(12)	21	0	0	84
Richard Mathers	Wakefield	2012	27	9	0	0	36
	Castleford	2011	21(1)	7	0	0	28
	Warrington	2002, 2009-10	42(3)	11	0	0	44
	Wigan	2008-09	23(1)	2	0	0	8
	Leeds	2002-06	85(2)	26	0	0	104
Jamie Mathiou	Leeds	1997-2001	31(82)	3	0	0	12
Terry Matterson	London	1996-98	46	15	90	6	246
Luke May	Harlequins	2009-10	(3)	0	0	0	0
Casey Mayberry	Halifax	2000	1(1)	0	0	0	0
Chris Maye	Halifax	2003	3(4)	0	0	0	0
Joe Mbu	Harlequins	2006-09	33(20)	3	0	0	12
	London	2003-05	29(19)	4	0	0	16
Danny McAllister	Gateshead	1999	3(3)	1	0	0	4
	Sheffield	1996-97	33(7)	10	0	0	40
John McAtee	St Helens	1996	2(1)	0	0	0	0
Nathan McAvoy	Bradford	1998-2002, 2007	83(31)	46	0	0	184
	Wigan	2006	15(2)	5	0	0	20
	Salford	1997-98, 2004-05	57(4)	18	0	0	72
Tyrone McCarthy	Warrington	2009-12	10(17)	2	0	0	8
	Wakefield	2011	2(5)	1	0	0	4
Louie McCarthy-Scarsbrook							
	St Helens	2011-12	23(31)	11	0	0	44
	Harlequins	2006-10	41(50)	17	0	0	68
Dave McConnell	London	2003	(4)	0	0	0	0
	St Helens	2001-02	3(2)	4	0	0	16
Robbie McCormack							
	Wigan	1998	24	2	0	0	8
Steve McCurrie	Leigh	2005	7(3)	1	0	0	4
	Widnes	2002-04	55(22)	10	0	0	40
	Warrington	1998-2001	69(26)	31	0	0	124
Barrie McDermott							
	Leeds	1996-2005	163(69)	28	0	0	112
Brian McDermott	Bradford	1996-2002	138(32)	33	0	0	132
Ryan McDonald	Widnes	2002-03	6(4)	0	0	0	0
Wayne McDonald	Huddersfield	2005-06	11(23)	1	0	0	4
	Wigan	2005	(4)	0	0	0	0
	Leeds	2002-05	34(47)	14	0	0	56
	St Helens	2001	7(11)	4	0	0	16
	Hull	2000	5(8)	4	0	0	16
	Wakefield	1999	9(17)	8	0	0	32
Shannon McDonnell							
	Hull KR	2012	21	6	0	0	24
Craig McDowell	Huddersfield	2003	(1)	0	0	0	0
	Warrington	2002	(1)	0	0	0	0
	Bradford	2000	(1)	0	0	0	0
Wes McGibbon	Halifax	1999	1	0	0	0	0
Jermaine McGillvary							
	Huddersfield	2010-12	54	32	0	0	128
Dean McGilvray	Salford	2009-10	14	4	0	0	16
	St Helens	2006-08	5(1)	1	0	0	4
Billy McGinty	Workington	1996	1	0	0	0	0
Ryan McGoldrick	Hull	2012	8	1	0	0	4
	Castleford	2006, 2008-12	129(5)	24	11	0	118
Kevin McGuinness							
	Salford	2004-07	63(3)	11	0	0	44
Casey McGuire	Catalans	2007-10	87(4)	27	0	0	108
Danny McGuire	Leeds	2001-12	222(37)	201	0	3	807
Gary McGuirk	Workington	1996	(4)	0	0	0	0
Michael McIlorum							
	Wigan	2007-12	63(51)	12	0	0	48
Richard McKell	Castleford	1997-98	22(7)	2	0	0	8
Chris McKenna	Bradford	2006-07	40(7)	7	0	0	28
	Leeds	2003-05	65(4)	18	0	0	72
Phil McKenzie	Workington	1996	4	0	0	0	0
Chris McKinney	Oldham	1996-97	4(9)	2	0	0	8
Wade McKinnon	Hull	2012	10	4	0	0	16
Mark McLinden	Harlequins	2006-08	46(1)	20	0	1	81
	London	2005	22(3)	8	0	0	32
Mike McMeeken	London	2012	(3)	0	0	0	0
Shayne McMenemy							
	Hull	2003-07	80(8)	12	0	0	48
	Halifax	2001-03	63	11	0	0	44
Andy McNally	London	2004	5(3)	0	0	0	0
	Castleford	2001, 2003	2(5)	1	0	0	4
Gregg McNally	Huddersfield	2011	1	0	6	0	12
Steve McNamara	Huddersfield	2001, 2003	41(9)	3	134	1	281
	Wakefield	2000	15(2)	2	32	0	72
	Bradford	1996-99	90(3)	14	348	7	759
Paul McNicholas	Hull	2004-05	28(12)	4	0	0	16
Neil McPherson	Salford	1997	(1)	0	0	0	0
Shannan McPherson							
	Salford	2012	11(2)	0	0	0	0
Duncan McRae	London	1996	11(2)	3	0	1	13
Paul McShane	Widnes	2012	6(5)	3	4	0	20
	Leeds	2009-12	9(25)	5	0	0	20
	Hull	2010	(4)	0	0	0	0
Derek McVey	St Helens	1996-97	28(4)	6	1	0	26
Dallas Mead	Warrington	1997	2	0	0	0	0
Robbie Mears	Leigh	2005	8(6)	0	0	0	0
	Leeds	2001	23	6	0	0	24
Paul Medley	Bradford	1996-98	6(35)	9	0	0	36
Francis Meli	St Helens	2006-12	170(1)	106	0	0	424
Vince Mellars	Wakefield	2012	16(2)	3	0	0	12
	Crusaders	2010-11	46	17	0	0	68
Chris Melling	London	2012	10(9)	3	2	0	16
	Harlequins	2007-11	100(11)	33	6	0	144
	Wigan	2004-05	8(2)	1	3	0	10
Joe Mellor	Widnes	2012	11	4	0	0	16
	Wigan	2012	1(1)	1	0	0	4
	Harlequins	2011	(2)	0	0	0	0
Paul Mellor	Castleford	2003-04	36(3)	18	0	0	72
Craig Menkins	Paris	1997	4(5)	0	0	0	0
Luke Menzies	Hull KR	2008	(1)	0	0	0	0
Steve Menzies	Catalans	2011-12	36(6)	22	0	0	88
	Bradford	2009-10	52(1)	24	1	0	98
Gary Mercer	Castleford	2002	(1)	0	0	0	0
	Leeds	1996-97, 2001	40(2)	9	0	0	36
	Warrington	2001	18	2	0	0	8
	Halifax	1998-2001	73(2)	16	0	0	64
Tony Mestrov	London	1996-97, 2001	59(8)	4	0	0	16
	Wigan	1998-2000	39(39)	3	0	0	12
Keiran Meyer	London	1996	4	1	0	0	4
Brad Meyers	Bradford	2005-06	40(11)	13	0	0	52
Gary Middlehurst	Widnes	2004	(2)	0	0	0	0
Simon Middleton	Castleford	1996-97	19(3)	8	0	0	32
Constantine Mika	Hull KR	2012	21(1)	6	0	0	24
Daryl Millard	Catalans	2011-12	49	22	1	0	90
	Wakefield	2010-11	21(1)	11	0	0	44
Shane Millard	Wigan	2007	19(6)	3	0	0	12
	Leeds	2006	6(21)	3	0	0	12
	Widnes	2003-05	69	23	0	0	92
	London	1998-2001	72(14)	11	1	0	46
Grant Millington	Castleford	2012	16(6)	4	0	0	16
David Mills	Harlequins	2006-07, 2010	25(32)	2	0	0	8
	Hull KR	2008-09	20(11)	1	0	0	4
	Widnes	2002-05	17(77)	8	0	0	32
Lewis Mills	Celtic	2009	(4)	0	0	0	0
Adam Milner	Castleford	2010-12	33(11)	8	0	0	32
Lee Milner	Halifax	1999	(1)	0	0	0	0
John Minto	London	1996	13	4	0	0	16
Lee Mitchell	Castleford	2012	13(10)	2	0	0	8
	Warrington	2007-11	8(27)	4	0	0	16
	Harlequins	2011	11(1)	1	0	0	4
Sam Moa	Hull	2009-12	29(44)	6	0	0	24
Martin Moana	Salford	2004	6(3)	1	0	0	4
	Halifax	1996-2001, 2003	126(22)	62	0	1	249
	Wakefield	2002	19(2)	10	0	0	40
	Huddersfield	2001	3(3)	2	0	0	8
Adam Mogg	Catalans	2007-10	74	19	0	1	77
Jon Molloy	Huddersfield	2011-12	2(1)	0	0	0	0
Steve Molloy	Huddersfield	2000-01	26(20)	3	0	0	12
	Sheffield	1998-99	32(17)	3	0	0	12
Chris Molyneux	Huddersfield	2000-01	1(18)	0	0	0	0
	Sheffield	1999	1(2)	0	0	0	0
Joel Monaghan	Warrington	2011-12	50	48	0	0	192
Michael Monaghan							
	Warrington	2008-12	114(10)	22	0	4	92
Joel Moon	Salford	2012	17	9	0	0	36
Adrian Moore	Huddersfield	1998-99	1(4)	0	0	0	0
Danny Moore	London	2000	7	0	0	0	0
	Wigan	1998-99	49(3)	18	0	0	72
Gareth Moore	Wakefield	2011	5	1	14	1	33
Jason Moore	Workington	1996	(5)	0	0	0	0
Richard Moore	Leeds	2012	(14)	1	0	0	4
	Crusaders	2011	11(10)	1	0	0	4
	Wakefield	2007-10	50(44)	8	0	0	32
	Leigh	2005	2(5)	0	0	0	0
	Bradford	2002-04	1(26)	0	0	0	0
	London	2002, 2004	5(9)	2	0	0	8
Scott Moore	Huddersfield	2009, 2012	29(7)	9	0	0	36
	Widnes	2012	3(3)	0	0	0	0
	St Helens	2004-07, 2010-11	29(37)	9	0	0	36
	Castleford	2008	11(5)	1	0	0	4

173

PLAYER	CLUB	YEAR	APP	TRIES	GOALS	FG	PTS
Dennis Moran	Wigan	2005-06	39	17	1	1	71
	London	2001-04	107(2)	74	2	5	305
Willie Morganson	Sheffield	1997-98	18(12)	5	3	0	26
Paul Moriarty	Halifax	1996	3(2)	0	0	0	0
Adrian Morley	Warrington	2007-12	132(9)	7	0	0	28
	Bradford	2005	2(4)	0	0	0	0
	Leeds	1996-2000	95(14)	25	0	0	100
Chris Morley	Salford	1999	3(5)	0	0	0	0
	Warrington	1998	2(8)	0	0	0	0
	St Helens	1996-97	21(16)	4	0	0	16
Glenn Morrison	Wakefield	2010-11	43(1)	9	0	0	36
	Bradford	2007-09	48(2)	19	0	0	76
Iain Morrison	Hull KR	2007	5(6)	1	0	0	4
	Huddersfield	2003-05	11(23)	0	0	0	0
	London	2001	(1)	0	0	0	0
Dale Morton	Wakefield	2009-11	22(3)	8	5	0	42
Gareth Morton	Hull KR	2007	7(4)	3	23	0	58
	Leeds	2001-02	1(1)	0	0	0	0
Lee Mossop	Wigan	2008-12	35(40)	5	0	0	20
	Huddersfield	2009	1(4)	1	0	0	4
Aaron Moule	Salford	2006-07	45	17	0	0	68
	Widnes	2004-05	29	12	0	0	48
Wilfried Moulinec	Paris	1996	1	0	0	0	0
Gregory Mounis	Catalans	2006-12	115(59)	22	17	0	122
Mark Moxon	Huddersfield	1998-2001	20(5)	1	0	1	5
Anthony Mullally	Widnes	2012	(9)	0	0	0	0
Brett Mullins	Leeds	2001	5(3)	1	0	0	4
Damian Munro	Widnes	2002	8(2)	1	0	0	4
	Halifax	1996-97	9(6)	8	0	0	32
Matt Munro	Oldham	1996-97	26(5)	8	0	0	32
Craig Murdock	Salford	2000	(2)	0	0	0	0
	Hull	1998-99	21(6)	8	0	2	34
	Wigan	1996-98	18(17)	14	0	0	56
Aaron Murphy	Huddersfield	2012	12	5	0	0	20
	Wakefield	2008-11	57(2)	12	0	0	48
Jack Murphy	Wigan	2012	2	1	0	0	4
Jamie Murphy	Crusaders	2011	(2)	0	0	0	0
Justin Murphy	Catalans	2006-08	59	49	0	0	196
	Widnes	2004	5	1	0	0	4
Doc Murray	Warrington	1997	(2)	0	0	0	0
	Wigan	1997	6(2)	0	0	0	0
Scott Murrell	Hull KR	2007-12	114(24)	24	26	1	149
	Leeds	2005	(1)	0	0	0	0
	London	2004	3(3)	2	0	0	8
David Mycoe	Sheffield	1996-97	12(13)	1	0	0	4
Richard Myler	Warrington	2010-12	69(1)	41	1	0	166
	Salford	2009	18	11	0	0	44
Rob Myler	Oldham	1996-97	19(2)	6	0	0	24
Stephen Myler	Salford	2006	4(8)	1	15	0	34
	Widnes	2003-05	35(14)	8	74	0	180
Vinny Myler	Salford	2004	(4)	0	0	0	0
	Bradford	2003	(1)	0	0	0	0
Matt Nable	London	1997	2(2)	1	0	0	4
Brad Nairn	Workington	1996	14	4	0	0	16
Frank Napoli	London	2000	14(6)	2	0	0	8
Carlo Napolitano	Salford	2000	(3)	1	0	0	4
Stephen Nash	Castleford	2012	3(4)	0	0	0	0
	Salford	2007, 2009	2(18)	1	0	0	4
	Widnes	2005	4(1)	0	0	0	0
Jim Naylor	Halifax	2000	7(6)	2	0	0	8
Scott Naylor	Salford	1997-98, 2004	30(1)	9	0	0	36
	Bradford	1999-2003	127(1)	51	0	0	204
Adam Neal	Salford	2010-12	9(25)	0	0	0	0
Mike Neal	Salford	1998	(1)	0	0	0	0
	Oldham	1996-97	6(4)	3	0	0	12
Jonathan Neill	Huddersfield	1998-99	20(11)	0	0	0	0
	St Helens	1996	1	0	0	0	0
Chris Nero	Salford	2011-12	30(11)	6	0	0	24
	Bradford	2008-10	65(5)	24	0	0	96
	Huddersfield	2004-07	97(8)	38	0	0	152
Jason Netherton	Hull KR	2007-12	48(62)	4	0	0	16
	London	2003-04	6	0	0	0	0
	Halifax	2002	2(3)	0	0	0	0
	Leeds	2001	(3)	0	0	0	0
Kirk Netherton	Castleford	2009-10	5(23)	3	0	0	12
	Hull KR	2007-08	9(15)	2	0	0	8
Paul Newlove	Castleford	2004	5	1	0	0	4
	St Helens	1996-2003	162	106	0	0	424
Richard Newlove	Wakefield	2003	17(5)	8	0	0	32
Clint Newton	Hull KR	2008-11	90(3)	37	0	0	148
Terry Newton	Wakefield	2010	(2)	0	0	0	0
	Bradford	2006-09	83(6)	26	0	0	104
	Wigan	2000-05	157(9)	62	0	0	248
	Leeds	1996-1999	55(14)	4	0	0	16
Gene Ngamu	Huddersfield	1999-2000	29(2)	9	67	0	170
Danny Nicklas	Hull	2010, 2012	2(8)	0	0	0	0
Sonny Nickle	St Helens	1999-2002	86(18)	14	0	0	56
	Bradford	1996-98	25(16)	9	0	0	36
Jason Nicol	Salford	2000-02	52(7)	11	0	0	44
Tawera Nikau	Warrington	2000-01	51	7	0	0	28
Rob Nolan	Hull	1998-99	20(11)	6	0	0	24
Paul Noone	Harlequins	2006	5(2)	0	0	0	0
	Warrington	2000-06	60(59)	12	20	0	88
Chris Norman	Halifax	2003	13(3)	2	0	0	8
Paul Norman	Oldham	1996	(1)	0	0	0	0
Andy Northey	St Helens	1996-97	8(17)	2	0	0	8
Danny Nutley	Castleford	2006	28	3	0	0	12
	Warrington	1998-2001	94(1)	3	0	0	12
Tony Nuttall	Oldham	1996-97	1(7)	0	0	0	0
Adam O'Brien	Bradford	2011-12	(8)	0	0	0	0
Clinton O'Brien	Wakefield	2003	(2)	0	0	0	0
Gareth O'Brien	Warrington	2011-12	11(1)	4	28	0	72
	Widnes	2012	4	0	15	0	30
Sam Obst	Hull	2011	17(6)	6	0	0	24
	Wakefield	2005-11	100(28)	40	7	0	174
Jamie O'Callaghan	London	2012	24	2	0	0	8
	Harlequins	2008-11	54(3)	12	0	0	48
Eamon O'Carroll	Widnes	2012	(3)	1	0	0	4
	Hull	2012	1(9)	0	0	0	0
	Wigan	2006-11	2(59)	3	0	0	12
Matt O'Connor	Paris	1997	11(4)	1	26	2	58
Terry O'Connor	Widnes	2005	25	2	0	0	8
	Wigan	1996-2004	177(45)	9	0	0	36
Jarrod O'Doherty	Huddersfield	2003	26	3	0	0	12
David O'Donnell	Paris	1997	21	3	0	0	12
Luke O'Donnell	Huddersfield	2011-12	21(2)	2	0	0	8
Martin Offiah	Salford	2000-01	41	20	0	2	82
	London	1996-99	29(3)	21	0	0	84
	Wigan	1996	8	7	0	0	28
Mark O'Halloran	London	2004-05	34(3)	10	0	0	40
Ryan O'Hara	Hull KR	2012	8(7)	1	0	0	4
	Crusaders	2010-11	41(8)	3	0	0	12
	Celtic	2009	27	3	0	0	12
Hefin O'Hare	Huddersfield	2001, 2003-05	72(10)	27	0	0	108
	Hull	1998	21(1)	0	0	0	0
Hitro Okesene	Hull	1998	21(1)	0	0	0	0
Anderson Okiwe	Sheffield	1997	1	0	0	0	0
Tom Olbison	Bradford	2009-12	16(19)	2	0	0	8
Jamie Olejnik	Paris	1997	11	8	0	0	32
Kevin O'Loughlin	Halifax	1997-98	2(4)	0	0	0	0
	St Helens	1997	(3)	0	0	0	0
Sean O'Loughlin	Wigan	2002-12	245(21)	55	3	2	228
Mark O'Meley	Hull	2010-12	52(8)	10	0	0	40
Jules O'Neill	Widnes	2003-05	57(3)	14	158	7	379
	Wakefield	2005	10(2)	2	4	0	16
	Wigan	2002-03	29(1)	12	72	0	192
Julian O'Neill	Widnes	2002-05	57(39)	3	0	0	12
	Wakefield	2001	24(1)	2	0	0	8
	St Helens	1997-2000	95(8)	5	0	0	20
Mark O'Neill	Hull KR	2007	17	5	0	0	20
	Leeds	2006	1(8)	0	0	0	0
Steve O'Neill	Gateshead	1999	1(1)	0	0	0	0
Tom O'Reilly	Warrington	2001-02	8(6)	1	0	0	4
Matt Orford	Bradford	2010	12	3	31	2	76
Chris Orr	Huddersfield	1998	19(3)	2	0	0	8
Danny Orr	Castleford	1997-2003, 2011-12	197(23)	75	308	3	919
	Harlequins	2007-10	90(4)	13	96	0	244
	Wigan	2004-06	66(2)	18	12	0	96
Gareth Owen	Salford	2010, 2012	(21)	4	0	0	16
Nick Owen	Leigh	2005	8(1)	1	11	0	26
Richard Owen	Castleford	2008-12	90(3)	44	0	0	176
Jack Owens	Widnes	2012	3	0	0	0	0
Lopini Paea	Catalans	2011-12	36(8)	8	0	0	32
Mickey Paea	Hull KR	2012	17(10)	5	0	0	20
Mathias Pala	Catalans	2011-12	7(1)	0	0	0	0
Iafeta Palea'aesina	Salford	2011-12	4(37)	3	0	0	12
	Wigan	2006-10	55(77)	16	0	0	64
Jason Palmada	Workington	1996	12	2	0	0	8
Junior Paramore	Castleford	1996	5(5)	3	0	0	12
Paul Parker	Hull	1999-2002	23(18)	9	0	0	36
Rob Parker	Castleford	2011	4(2)	2	0	0	8
	Salford	2009-11	23(14)	4	0	0	16
	Warrington	2006-08	10(56)	6	0	0	24
	Bradford	2000, 2002-05	19(76)	14	0	0	56
	London	2001	9	1	0	0	4
Wayne Parker	Halifax	1996-97	12(1)	0	0	0	0
Ian Parry	Warrington	2001	(1)	0	0	0	0
Jules Parry	Paris	1996	10(2)	0	0	0	0
Regis Pastre-Courtine	Paris	1996	4(3)	4	0	0	16
Andrew Patmore	Oldham	1996	8(5)	3	0	0	12
Larne Patrick	Huddersfield	2009-12	8(71)	17	0	0	68
Luke Patten	Salford	2011-12	53	16	0	0	64
Henry Paul	Harlequins	2006-08	60(1)	8	94	2	222
	Bradford	1999-2001	81(5)	29	350	6	822
	Wigan	1996-98	60	37	23	0	194
Junior Paul	London	1996	3	1	0	0	4
Robbie Paul	Salford	2009	2(24)	2	0	0	8
	Huddersfield	2006-07	44(8)	7	0	0	28
	Bradford	1996-2005	198(31)	121	3	0	490
Jason Payne	Castleford	2006	1(1)	0	0	0	0
Danny Peacock	Bradford	1997-99	32(2)	15	0	0	60

PLAYER	CLUB	YEAR	APP	TRIES	GOALS	FG	PTS
Jamie Peacock	Leeds	2006-12	162(10)	18	0	0	72
	Bradford	1999-2005	163(25)	38	0	0	152
Martin Pearson	Wakefield	2001	21(1)	3	60	3	135
	Halifax	1997-98, 2000	55(6)	24	181	0	458
	Sheffield	1999	17(6)	9	36	2	110
Jacques Pech	Paris	1996	16	0	0	0	0
Mike Pechey	Warrington	1998	6(3)	2	0	0	8
Bill Peden	London	2003	21(3)	7	0	0	28
Adam Peek	Crusaders	2010-11	5(22)	1	0	0	4
	Celtic	2009	5(12)	3	0	0	12
Eloi Pelissier	Catalans	2011-12	1(37)	2	0	0	8
Dimitri Pelo	Catalans	2007-10	79	37	0	0	148
Sean Penkywicz	Huddersfield	2004-05	21(11)	7	0	0	28
	Halifax	2000-03	29(27)	8	0	0	32
Julian Penni	Salford	1998-99	4	0	0	0	0
Kevin Penny	Wakefield	2011	5	1	0	0	4
	Harlequins	2010	5	3	0	0	12
	Warrington	2006-09	39(1)	26	0	0	104
Lee Penny	Warrington	1996-2003	140(5)	54	0	0	216
Paul Penrice	Workington	1996	11(2)	2	0	0	8
Chris Percival	Widnes	2002-03	26	6	0	0	24
Apollo Perelini	St Helens	1996-2000	103(16)	27	0	0	108
Mark Perrett	Halifax	1996-97	15(4)	4	0	0	16
Josh Perry	St Helens	2011-12	26(9)	0	0	0	0
Shane Perry	Catalans	2009	8(8)	1	0	0	4
Adam Peters	Paris	1997	16(3)	0	0	0	0
Dominic Peters	London	1998-2003	58(11)	12	0	0	48
Mike Peters	Warrington	2000	2(12)	1	0	0	4
	Halifax	2000	1	0	0	0	0
Willie Peters	Widnes	2004	9	3	0	2	14
	Wigan	2000	29	15	5	6	76
	Gateshead	1999	27	11	1	6	52
Dave Petersen	Hull KR	2012	2(2)	1	0	0	4
Matt Petersen	Wakefield	2008-09	14	3	0	0	12
Adrian Petrie	Workington	1996	(1)	0	0	0	0
Cameron Phelps	Widnes	2012	20	8	0	0	32
	Hull	2011	19	2	0	0	8
	Wigan	2008-10	43(1)	14	4	0	64
Rowland Phillips	Workington	1996	22	1	0	0	4
Nathan Picchi	Leeds	1996	(1)	0	0	0	0
Ian Pickavance	Hull	1999	4(2)	2	0	0	8
	Huddersfield	1999	3(14)	0	0	0	0
	St Helens	1996-98	12(44)	6	0	0	24
James Pickering	Castleford	1999	1(19)	0	0	0	0
Steve Pickersgill	Widnes	2012	15(7)	0	0	0	0
	Warrington	2005-09	1(36)	0	0	0	0
Nick Pinkney	Salford	2000-02	64	29	0	0	116
	Halifax	1999	26(2)	13	0	0	52
	Sheffield	1997-98	33	10	0	0	40
Mikhail Piskunov	Paris	1996	1(1)	1	0	0	4
Darryl Pitt	London	1996	2(16)	4	0	1	17
Jay Pitts	Hull	2012	8(13)	0	0	0	0
	Leeds	2009-12	10(15)	2	0	0	8
	Wakefield	2008-09	9(8)	2	0	0	8
Andy Platt	Salford	1997-98	20(3)	1	0	0	4
Michael Platt	Bradford	2007-12	110(5)	40	0	0	160
	Castleford	2006	26	7	0	0	28
	Salford	2001-02	3	1	0	0	4
Willie Poching	Leeds	2002-06	58(73)	44	0	0	176
	Wakefield	1999-2001	65(4)	20	0	0	80
Quentin Pongia	Wigan	2003-04	15(10)	0	0	0	0
Dan Potter	Widnes	2002-03	34(2)	6	0	0	24
	London	2001	1(3)	1	0	0	4
Craig Poucher	Hull	1999-2002	31(5)	5	0	0	20
Bryn Powell	Salford	2004	1(1)	0	0	0	0
Daio Powell	Sheffield	1999	13(1)	2	0	0	8
	Halifax	1997-98	30(3)	17	0	0	68
Daryl Powell	Leeds	1998-2000	49(30)	12	0	2	50
Sam Powell	Wigan	2012	1	1	0	0	4
Karl Pratt	Bradford	2003-05	35(19)	18	0	0	72
	Leeds	1999-2002	62(12)	33	0	0	132
Paul Prescott	Wigan	2004-12	48(75)	4	0	0	16
Steve Prescott	Hull	1▲3-99, 2001-03	99	46	191	3	569
	Wakefield	2000	22(1)	3	13	0	38
	St Helens	1996-97	32	15	17	0	94
Lee Prest	Workington	1996	(1)	0	0	0	0
Gareth Price	Salford	2002	(2)	0	0	0	0
	London	2002	2(2)	3	0	0	12
	St Helens	1999	(11)	2	0	0	8
Gary Price	Wakefield	1999-2001	55(13)	11	0	0	44
Richard Price	Sheffield	1996	1(2)	0	0	0	0
Tony Priddle	Paris	1997	11(7)	3	0	0	12
Karl Pryce	Bradford	2003-06, 2012	47(19)	46	1	0	186
	Harlequins	2011	11(7)	12	0	0	48
	Wigan	2009-10	11(2)	12	0	0	48
Leon Pryce	Catalans	2012	23(2)	8	0	0	32
	St Helens	2006-11	133(3)	64	0	0	256
	Bradford	1998-2005	159(29)	86	0	0	344
Waine Pryce	Wakefield	2007	10(2)	4	0	0	16
	Castleford	2000-06	97(12)	49	0	0	196
Tony Puletua	St Helens	2009-12	88(14)	37	0	0	148
Andrew Purcell	Castleford	2000	15(5)	3	0	0	12
	Hull	1999	27	4	0	0	16
Rob Purdham	Harlequins	2006-11	112(3)	18	131	1	335
	London	2002-05	53(15)	16	2	1	69
Adrian Purtell	Bradford	2012	8	1	0	0	4
Luke Quigley	Catalans	2007	16(1)	1	0	0	4
Damien Quinn	Celtic	2009	20(1)	4	12	0	40
Scott Quinnell	Wigan	1996	6(3)	1	0	0	4
Florian Quintilla	Catalans	2008-09	1(4)	0	0	0	0
Lee Radford	Hull	1998, 2006-12	138(30)	23	1	0	94
	Bradford	1999-2005	79(65)	18	12	0	96
Kris Radlinski	Wigan	1996-2006	236(1)	134	1	0	538
Sebastien Raguin	Catalans	2007-12	103(22)	28	0	0	112
Adrian Rainey	Castleford	2002	4(7)	1	0	0	4
Andy Raleigh	Wakefield	2012	23(4)	6	0	0	24
	Huddersfield	2006-11	74(46)	13	0	0	52
Jean-Luc Ramondou	Paris	1996	1(1)	1	0	0	4
Chad Randall	London	2012	22(5)	2	0	0	8
	Harlequins	2006-11	141(2)	37	0	1	149
Craig Randall	Halifax	1999	8(11)	4	0	0	16
	Salford	1997-98	12(18)	4	0	0	16
Scott Ranson	Oldham	1996-97	19(2)	7	0	0	28
Aaron Raper	Castleford	1999-2001	48(4)	4	2	1	21
Stefan Ratchford	Warrington	2012	20(4)	15	3	0	66
	Salford	2007, 2009-11	65(5)	23	20	0	132
Mike Ratu	Hull KR	2010	5	1	0	0	4
	Leeds	2007, 2009	1(5)	1	0	0	4
Paul Rauhihi	Warrington	2006-09	67(20)	10	0	0	40
Ben Rauter	Wakefield	2001	15(6)	4	0	0	16
Gareth Raynor	Bradford	2011	18	4	0	0	16
	Crusaders	2010	7	4	0	0	16
	Hull	2001-09	186	102	0	0	408
	Leeds	2000	(3)	0	0	0	0
Tony Rea	London	1996	22	4	0	0	16
Stuart Reardon	Crusaders	2011	25	11	0	0	44
	Bradford	2003-05, 2010	78(11)	37	0	0	148
	Warrington	2006-08	48	12	0	0	48
	Salford	2002	7(1)	3	0	0	12
Mark Reber	Wigan	1999-2000	9(9)	5	0	0	20
Alan Reddicliffe	Warrington	2001	1	0	0	0	0
Tahi Reihana	Bradford	1997-98	17(21)	0	0	0	0
Paul Reilly	Wakefield	2008	5(2)	1	0	0	4
	Huddersfield	1999-2001, 2003-07	150(8)	35	1	0	142
Robert Relf	Widnes	2002-04	68(2)	5	0	0	20
Steve Renouf	Wigan	2000-01	55	40	0	0	160
Steele Retchless	London	1998-2004	177(6)	13	0	0	52
Scott Rhodes	Hull	2000	2	0	0	0	0
Phillipe Ricard	Paris	1996-97	2	0	0	0	0
Andy Rice	Huddersfield	2000-01	2(13)	1	0	0	4
Basil Richards	Huddersfield	1998-99	28(17)	1	0	0	4
Craig Richards	Oldham	1996	1	0	0	0	0
Pat Richards	London	2006-12	174	131	658	3	1843
Andy Richardson	Hudds-Sheff	2000	(2)	0	0	0	0
Sean Richardson	Widnes	2002	2(18)	1	0	0	4
	Wakefield	1999	5(1)	0	0	0	0
	Castleford	1996-97	3(8)	1	0	0	4
Mark Riddell	Wigan	2009-10	45(11)	5	2	0	24
Neil Rigby	St Helens	2006	(1)	0	0	0	0
Shane Rigon	Bradford	2001	14(11)	12	0	0	48
Craig Rika	Halifax	1996	2	0	0	0	0
Chris Riley	Warrington	2005-12	116(11)	86	0	0	344
	Harlequins	2011	3	2	0	0	8
Peter Riley	Workington	1996	7(5)	0	0	0	0
Julien Rinaldi	London	2012	4(16)	1	0	0	4
	Wakefield	2002, 2010-11	27(9)	6	0	0	24
	Bradford	2009	(7)	1	0	0	4
	Harlequins	2007-08	4(43)	9	0	0	36
	Catalans	2006	16(6)	3	1	0	14
Dean Ripley	Castleford	2004	3(4)	1	0	0	4
Leroy Rivett	Warrington	2002	9	1	0	0	4
	Hudds-Sheff	2000	5(1)	1	0	0	4
	Leeds	1996-2000	39(15)	21	0	0	84
Jason Roach	Warrington	1998-99	29(7)	15	0	0	60
	Castleford	1997	7	4	0	0	16
Ben Roarty	Castleford	2000	11(6)	2	0	0	8
	Huddersfield	2003-05	52	5	0	0	20
Amos Roberts	Wigan	2009-11	47(2)	27	5	0	118
Mark Roberts	Wigan	2003	(3)	0	0	0	0
Robert Roberts	Huddersfield	2001	(1)	0	0	0	0
	Halifax	2000	(3)	0	0	0	0
	Hull	1999	24(2)	4	13	4	46
Michael Robertson	London	2012	24	15	0	0	60
Chad Robinson	Harlequins	2009	13(1)	2	0	0	8
Craig Robinson	Wakefield	2005	(1)	0	0	0	0
Jason Robinson	Wigan	1996-2000	126(1)	87	0	1	349
Jeremy Robinson	Paris	1997	10(3)	1	21	0	46
John Robinson	Widnes	2003-04	7	1	0	0	4

Super League Players 1996-2012

PLAYER	CLUB	YEAR	APP	TRIES	GOALS	FG	PTS
Luke Robinson	Huddersfield	2008-12	114(14)	31	4	0	132
	Salford	2005-07	79	28	10	2	134
	Wigan	2002-04	17(25)	9	6	1	49
	Castleford	2004	9	4	3	0	22
Will Robinson	Hull	2000	22	4	0	0	16
	Gateshead	1999	28	9	0	0	36
James Roby	St Helens	2004-12	121(114)	64	1	0	258
Mike Roby	St Helens	2004	(1)	0	0	0	0
Carl Roden	Warrington	1997	1	0	0	0	0
Shane Rodney	London	2012	12	2	12	0	32
Matt Rodwell	Warrington	2002	10	3	0	0	12
Darren Rogers	Castleford	1999-2004	162(1)	81	0	0	324
	Salford	1997-98	42	16	0	0	64
Jamie Rooney	Wakefield	2003-09	113(7)	60	321	21	903
	Castleford	2001	2(1)	0	6	0	12
Jonathan Roper	Castleford	2001	13	7	12	0	52
	Salford	2000	1(4)	1	3	0	10
	London	2000	4	0	0	0	0
	Warrington	1996-2000	75(8)	33	71	0	274
Scott Roskell	London	1996-97	30(2)	16	0	0	64
Steve Rosolen	London	1996-98	25(9)	10	0	0	40
Adam Ross	London	1996	(1)	0	0	0	0
Paul Round	Castleford	1996	(3)	0	0	0	0
Steve Rowlands	Widnes	2004-05	18(3)	2	15	0	38
	St Helens	2003	(1)	0	0	0	0
Paul Rowley	Leigh	2005	15(7)	3	0	0	12
	Huddersfield	2001	24	3	0	0	12
	Halifax	1996-2000	107(3)	27	1	3	113
Nigel Roy	London	2001-04	100	39	0	0	156
Nicky Royle	Widnes	2004	13	7	0	0	28
Shad Royston	Bradford	2011	17(1)	10	0	0	40
Chris Rudd	Warrington	1996-98	31(17)	10	16	0	72
Sean Rudder	Catalans	2006	22(1)	6	0	0	24
	Castleford	2004	9(3)	2	0	0	8
James Rushforth	Halifax	1997	(4)	0	0	0	0
Danny Russell	Huddersfield	1998-2000	50(13)	8	0	0	32
Ian Russell	Oldham	1997	1(3)	1	0	0	4
	Paris	1996	3	0	0	0	0
Matthew Russell	Hull	2012	6	0	0	0	0
	Wigan	2012	2	3	0	0	12
Richard Russell	Castleford	1996-98	37(4)	2	0	0	8
Robert Russell	Salford	1998-99	2(1)	0	1	0	2
Sean Rutgerson	Salford	2004-06	60(9)	4	0	0	16
Chris Ryan	London	1998-99	44(3)	17	10	0	88
Sean Ryan	Castleford	2004	11(5)	2	0	0	8
	Hull	2002-03	53	8	0	0	32
Justin Ryder	Wakefield	2004	19(3)	11	0	0	44
Jason Ryles	Catalans	2009	19(2)	2	0	0	8
Setaimata Sa	Catalans	2010-12	58(5)	21	0	0	84
Teddy Sadaoui	Catalans	2006	7	0	0	0	0
Liam Salter	Hull KR	2012	11	3	0	0	12
Matt Salter	London	1997-99	14(34)	0	0	0	0
Ben Sammut	Hull	2000	20	4	67	0	150
	Gateshead	1999	26(2)	6	17	0	58
Jarrod Sammut	Bradford	2012	14(1)	6	25	0	74
	Crusaders	2010-11	17(16)	17	0	0	68
Dean Sampson	Castleford	1996-2003	124(28)	24	0	0	96
Paul Sampson	London	2004	1(2)	1	0	0	4
	Wakefield	2000	17	8	0	0	32
Lee Sanderson	London	2004	1(5)	1	7	0	18
Jason Sands	Paris	1996-97	28	0	0	0	0
Mitchell Sargent	Castleford	2008-10	37(21)	6	0	0	24
Dan Sarginson	London	2012	16(1)	4	0	0	16
	Harlequins	2011	8	5	0	0	20
Lokeni Savelio	Halifax	2000	2(11)	0	0	0	0
	Salford	1997-98	18(20)	0	0	0	0
Tom Saxton	Salford	2007	5	0	0	0	0
	Wakefield	2006	9(6)	2	0	0	8
	Hull	2005	19(8)	3	0	0	12
	Castleford	2002-04	37(12)	11	0	0	44
Jonathan Scales	Halifax	2000	1	0	0	0	0
	Bradford	1996-98	46(4)	24	0	0	96
Andrew Schick	Castleford	1996-98	45(13)	10	0	0	40
Clinton Schifcofske							
	Crusaders	2010-11	44	5	115	0	250
Garry Schofield	Huddersfield	1998	(2)	0	0	0	0
Gary Schubert	Workington	1996	(1)	0	0	0	0
Matt Schultz	Hull	1998-99	23(9)	2	0	0	8
	Leeds	1996	2(4)	0	0	0	0
John Schuster	Halifax	1996-97	31	9	127	3	293
Nick Scruton	Bradford	2009-12	43(26)	4	0	0	16
	Leeds	2002, 2004-08	11(53)	3	0	0	12
	Hull	2004	2(16)	3	0	0	12
Danny Sculthorpe							
	Huddersfield	2009	5(8)	0	0	0	0
	Wakefield	2007-09	14(28)	1	0	0	4
	Castleford	2006	18(1)	4	0	1	17
	Wigan	2002-05	13(49)	7	0	0	28
Paul Sculthorpe	St Helens	1998-2008	223(4)	94	356	7	1095
	Warrington	1996-97	40	6	0	0	24
Mick Seaby	London	1997	3(2)	1	0	0	4
Danny Seal	Halifax	1996-99	8(17)	3	0	0	12
Matt Seers	Wakefield	2003	11(1)	2	0	0	8
Anthony Seibold	London	1999-2000	33(19)	5	0	0	20
Keith Senior	Leeds	1999-2011	319(2)	159	0	0	636
	Sheffield	1996-99	90(2)	40	0	0	160
Fili Seru	Hull	1998-99	37(1)	13	0	0	52
Anthony Seuseu	Halifax	2003	1(11)	1	0	0	4
Jerry Seuseu	Wigan	2005-06	29(9)	1	0	0	4
Brett Seymour	Hull	2012	24(1)	7	0	0	28
Will Sharp	Hull	2011-12	27(8)	10	0	0	40
	Harlequins	2008-10	65(1)	19	0	0	76
Darren Shaw	Salford	2002	5(9)	1	0	0	4
	London	1996, 2002	22(8)	3	0	0	12
	Castleford	2000-01	50(6)	1	0	0	4
	Sheffield	1998-99	51(1)	3	0	1	13
Mick Shaw	Halifax	1999	5	1	0	0	4
	Leeds	1996	12(2)	7	0	0	28
Phil Shead	Paris	1996	3(2)	0	0	0	0
Richard Sheil	St Helens	1997	(1)	0	0	0	0
Kelly Shelford	Warrington	1996-97	25(3)	4	0	2	18
Michael Shenton	St Helens	2011-12	51	15	0	0	60
	Castleford	2004, 2006, 2008-10	97(2)	46	0	0	184
Ryan Sheridan	Castleford	2004	2	0	0	0	0
	Widnes	2003	14(3)	2	0	0	8
	Leeds	1997-2002	123(7)	46	0	1	185
	Sheffield	1996	9(3)	5	0	1	21
Louis Sheriff	Hull KR	2011-12	8	3	0	0	12
Rikki Sheriffe	Bradford	2009-10	51	14	0	0	56
	Harlequins	2006-08	35(1)	16	0	0	64
	Halifax	2003	6(1)	3	0	0	12
Ian Sherratt	Oldham	1996	5(3)	1	0	0	4
Brent Sherwin	Catalans	2010	12	1	0	1	5
	Castleford	2008-10	48(1)	4	0	3	19
Peter Shiels	St Helens	2001-02	44(3)	11	0	0	44
Gary Shillabeer	Huddersfield	1999	(2)	0	0	0	0
Mark Shipway	Salford	2004-05	30(12)	3	0	0	12
Ian Sibbit	Bradford	2011-12	11(7)	0	0	0	0
	Salford	2005-07, 2009-10	64(17)	11	0	0	44
	Warrington	1999-2001, 2003-04	63(18)	24	0	0	96
Mark Sibson	Huddersfield	1999	2	2	0	0	8
Adam Sidlow	Salford	2009-12	34(44)	14	0	0	56
Jon Simms	St Helens	2002	(1)	0	0	0	0
Craig Simon	Hull	2000	23(2)	8	0	0	32
	Gateshead	1999	25(4)	6	0	0	24
Michael Simon	Catalans	2010-12	2(34)	1	0	0	4
Darren Simpson	Huddersfield	1998-99	17(1)	5	0	0	20
Jamie Simpson	Huddersfield	2011	8(1)	0	0	0	0
Robbie Simpson	London	1999	6(7)	0	0	0	0
Kevin Sinfield	Leeds	1997-2012	356(25)	58	1278	25	2813
Matt Sing	Hull	2007-08	41	14	0	0	56
Wayne Sing	Paris	1997	18(1)	2	0	0	8
Brad Singleton	Leeds	2011-12	(2)	0	0	0	0
Fata Sini	Salford	1997	22	7	0	0	28
John Skandalis	Huddersfield	2007-08	37(5)	4	0	0	16
Dylan Skee	Harlequins	2008-09	(3)	0	0	0	0
Ben Skerrett	Castleford	2003	(1)	0	0	0	0
Kelvin Skerrett	Halifax	1997-99	31(6)	2	0	0	8
	Wigan	1996	1(8)	0	0	0	0
Troy Slattery	Wakefield	2002-03	33(5)	4	0	0	16
	Huddersfield	1999	3	1	0	0	4
Mick Slicker	Huddersfield	2001, 2003-05	17(48)	2	0	0	8
	Sheffield	1999	(3)	1	0	0	4
	Halifax	1997	2(5)	0	0	0	0
Ian Smales	Castleford	1996-97	10(8)	5	0	0	20
Aaron Smith	Castleford	2006	(2)	0	0	0	0
	Bradford	2003-04	12(1)	3	0	0	12
Andy Smith	Harlequins	2007	6(3)	3	0	0	12
	Bradford	2004-06	9(9)	4	0	0	16
	Salford	2005	4	1	0	0	4
Byron Smith	Castleford	2004	(9)	0	0	0	0
	Halifax	2003	6(1)	0	0	0	0
Chris Smith	Hull	2001-02	12	3	0	0	12
	St Helens	1998-2000	62(9)	26	0	0	104
	Castleford	1996-97	36(1)	12	0	0	48
Craig Smith	Wigan	2002-04	77(3)	10	0	0	40
Damien Smith	St Helens	1998	21(1)	8	0	0	32
Danny Smith	Paris	1996	10(2)	1	15	0	34
	London	1996	2(1)	1	0	0	4
Darren Smith	St Helens	2003	25(1)	14	0	0	56
Gary Smith	Castleford	2001	(1)	0	0	0	0
Hudson Smith	Bradford	2000	8(22)	2	0	0	8
	Salford	1999	23(2)	5	0	0	20
James Smith	Salford	2000	23(3)	6	0	0	24
Jamie Smith	Hull	1998-99	24(6)	6	12	0	48
	Workington	1996	5(3)	0	1	0	2
Jason Smith	Hull	2001-04	61(3)	17	0	1	69
Jeremy Smith	Wakefield	2011	9(1)	1	0	0	4
	Salford	2009-10	27(17)	2	0	0	8
Kris Smith	London	2001	(1)	0	0	0	0
	Halifax	2001	(1)	0	0	0	0
Lee Smith	Wakefield	2012	9	6	0	0	24
	Leeds	2005-12	125(10)	60	34	1	309

PLAYER	CLUB	YEAR	APP	TRIES	GOALS	FG	PTS
Leigh Smith	Workington	1996	9	4	0	0	16
Mark Smith	Widnes	2005	12(15)	4	0	0	16
	Wigan	1999-2004	35(77)	8	0	0	32
Martyn Smith	Harlequins	2010	(2)	0	0	0	0
Matty Smith	Wigan	2012	6(3)	1	0	0	4
	Salford	2010-12	67(4)	13	6	1	65
	St Helens	2006-08, 2010	17(2)	3	10	1	33
	Celtic	2009	15(1)	3	2	1	17
Michael Smith	Hull KR	2007	(3)	1	0	0	4
	Castleford	1998, 2001-04	86(33)	32	0	0	128
	Hull	1999	12(6)	3	0	0	12
Paul Smith	Huddersfield	2004-06	52(17)	13	0	0	52
Paul Smith	Warrington	2001	(1)	0	0	0	0
	Castleford	1997-2000	6(37)	3	0	0	12
Paul Smith	London	1997	7(1)	2	0	0	8
Peter Smith	Oldham	1996	2	0	0	0	0
Richard Smith	Wakefield	2001	8(1)	1	0	0	4
	Salford	1997	(1)	1	0	0	4
Tim Smith	Wakefield	2012	27	6	0	0	24
	Wigan	2008-09	13(8)	2	0	0	8
Tony Smith	Hull	2001-03	43(5)	26	0	0	104
	Wigan	1997-2000	66(5)	46	0	0	184
	Castleford	1996-97	18(2)	10	0	0	40
Tony Smith	Workington	1996	9	1	0	0	4
Tyrone Smith	Harlequins	2006-07	49(3)	13	0	0	52
	London	2005	20(4)	11	0	0	44
Rob Smyth	Leigh	2005	15(1)	4	0	0	16
	Warrington	2000-03	65	35	20	0	180
	London	1998-2000	32(2)	9	15	0	66
	Wigan	1996	11(5)	16	0	0	64
Marc Sneyd	Salford	2010-12	9(12)	1	6	0	16
Steve Snitch	Castleford	2010-12	38(18)	10	0	0	40
	Wakefield	2002-05, 2009	33(55)	9	0	0	36
	Huddersfield	2006-08	24(35)	12	0	0	48
Bright Sodje	Wakefield	2000	15	4	0	0	16
	Sheffield	1996-99	54	34	0	0	136
Iosia Soliola	St Helens	2010-12	49(6)	12	0	0	48
David Solomona	Warrington	2010-12	8(49)	16	1	0	66
	Bradford	2007-09	44(9)	19	0	0	76
	Wakefield	2004-06	73(3)	26	0	0	104
Alfred Songoro	Wakefield	1999	8(5)	4	0	0	16
Romain Sort	Paris	1997	(1)	0	0	0	0
Paul Southern	Salford	1997-2002	79(33)	6	13	0	50
	St Helens	2002	1(1)	0	0	0	0
Steve Southern	Wakefield	2012	7(8)	3	0	0	12
Cain Southernwood	Bradford	2010	2	0	0	0	0
Roy Southernwood	Wakefield	1999	1	0	0	0	0
	Halifax	1996	2	0	0	0	0
Jason Southwell	Huddersfield	2004	(1)	0	0	0	0
Waisale Sovatabua	Wakefield	2001-03	44(3)	19	0	0	76
	Hudds-Sheff	2000	23(1)	8	0	0	32
	Sheffield	1996-99	56(17)	19	0	1	77
Yusef Sozi	London	2000-01	(5)	0	0	0	0
Scott Spaven	Hull KR	2010	(2)	0	0	0	0
Andy Speak	Castleford	2001	4(4)	0	0	0	0
	Wakefield	2000	6(5)	2	0	0	8
	Leeds	1999	4	1	0	0	4
Tim Spears	Castleford	2003	(3)	0	0	0	0
Ady Spencer	London	1996-99	8(36)	5	0	0	20
Jack Spencer	Salford	2009-11	(7)	0	0	0	0
Tom Spencer	Wigan	2012	(4)	0	0	0	0
Rob Spicer	Wakefield	2002-05	28(18)	4	0	0	16
Russ Spiers	Wakefield	2011	(2)	0	0	0	0
Stuart Spruce	Widnes	2002-03	45(4)	19	0	0	76
	Bradford	1996-2001	107(2)	57	0	0	228
Lee St Hilaire	Castleford	1997	4(2)	0	0	0	0
Marcus St Hilaire	Bradford	2006-07	34(1)	12	0	0	48
	Huddersfield	2003-05	72(2)	30	0	0	120
	Leeds	1996-2002	59(33)	31	0	0	124
Cyril Stacul	Catalans	2007-12	61(1)	18	0	0	72
Dylan Stainton	Workington	1996	2(3)	0	0	0	0
Mark Stamper	Workington	1996	(1)	0	0	0	0
John Stankevitch	Widnes	2005	17(5)	0	0	0	0
	St Helens	2000-04	74(40)	25	0	0	100
Gareth Stanley	Bradford	2000	1	1	0	0	4
Craig Stapleton	Salford	2009	24	2	0	0	8
	Leigh	2005	27(1)	4	0	0	16
Graham Steadman	Castleford	1996-97	11(17)	5	0	0	20
Jon Steel	Hull KR	2007-08	18	6	0	0	24
Jamie Stenhouse	Warrington	2000-01	9(3)	3	0	0	12
Gareth Stephens	Sheffield	1997-99	23(6)	2	0	0	8
David Stephenson	Hull	1998	11(7)	3	0	0	12
	Oldham	1997	10(8)	2	0	0	8
Francis Stephenson	London	2002-05	42(34)	5	0	0	20
	Wigan	2001	2(9)	0	0	0	0
	Wakefield	1999-2000	50(1)	6	0	0	24
Paul Sterling	Leeds	1997-2000	79(12)	50	0	0	200
Paul Stevens	Oldham	1996	2(1)	0	0	0	0
	London	1996	(1)	0	0	0	0
Warren Stevens	Leigh	2005	4(14)	1	0	0	4
	Warrington	1996-99, 2002-05	17(66)	1	0	0	4
	Salford	2001	(8)	0	0	0	0
Anthony Stewart	Harlequins	2006	4	0	0	0	0
	Salford	2004-06	51(2)	15	0	0	60
	St Helens	1997-2003	93(23)	44	0	0	176
Troy Stone	Widnes	2002	18(6)	1	0	0	4
	Huddersfield	2001	12(1)	1	0	0	4
James Stosic	Wakefield	2009	8(10)	1	0	0	4
Lynton Stott	Wakefield	1999	21	4	6	1	29
	Sheffield	1996-98	40(4)	15	0	0	60
Mitchell Stringer	Salford	2005-06	12(4)	0	0	0	0
	London	2004-05	10(19)	0	0	0	0
Graham Strutton	London	1996	9(1)	2	0	0	8
Matt Sturm	Leigh	2005	8(19)	3	0	0	12
	Warrington	2002-04	1(18)	0	0	0	0
	Huddersfield	1998-99	46	8	0	0	32
Anthony Sullivan	St Helens	1996-2001	137(2)	105	0	0	420
Michael Sullivan	Warrington	2006-07	21(16)	8	1	0	34
Phil Sumner	Warrington	1996	(5)	0	0	0	0
Simon Svabic	Salford	1998-2000	13(5)	3	19	0	50
Luke Swain	Salford	2009-10	54	3	0	0	12
Richard Swain	Hull	2004-07	89	5	0	0	20
Anthony Swann	Warrington	2001	3	1	0	0	4
Logan Swann	Warrington	2005-06	49(1)	17	0	0	68
	Bradford	2004	25	6	0	0	24
Willie Swann	Warrington	1996-97	25(2)	6	0	0	24
Adam Swift	St Helens	2012	3	5	0	0	20
Nathan Sykes	Castleford	1996-2004	158(52)	3	0	0	12
Paul Sykes	Wakefield	2012	21	3	70	3	155
	Bradford	1999-2002, 2008-12	99(4)	35	64	2	270
	Harlequins	2006-07	31(2)	15	47	1	155
	London	2001-05	95(1)	26	220	3	547
Wayne Sykes	London	1999	(2)	0	0	0	0
Semi Tadulala	Wakefield	2004-07, 2011	92	37	0	0	148
	Bradford	2008-09	49	30	0	0	120
Whetu Taewa	Sheffield	1997-98	33(7)	8	0	0	32
Alan Tait	Leeds	1996	3(3)	1	0	0	4
Willie Talau	Salford	2009-10	22	4	0	0	16
	St Helens	2003-08	130(1)	50	0	0	200
Ian Talbot	Wakefield	1999	9(5)	2	31	0	70
	Wigan	1997	3	1	0	0	4
Albert Talipeau	Wakefield	2004	2(3)	0	0	0	0
Gael Tallec	Halifax	2000	5(19)	3	0	0	12
	Castleford	1998-99	19(21)	3	0	0	12
	Wigan	1996-97	8(12)	3	0	0	12
Joe Tamani	Bradford	1996	11(3)	4	0	0	16
Ryan Tandy	Hull KR	2007	8(4)	2	0	0	8
Andrew Tangata-Toa	Huddersfield	1999	15	2	0	0	8
David Tangata-Toa	Celtic	2009	1(18)	4	0	0	16
	Hull KR	2007	(17)	3	0	0	12
Jordan Tansey	Crusaders	2011	14(4)	5	0	0	20
	Hull	2009-10	30	9	0	0	36
	Leeds	2006-08	18(32)	19	3	0	82
Kris Tassell	Wakefield	2002	24	10	0	0	40
	Salford	2000-01	35(10)	12	0	0	48
Shem Tatupu	Wigan	1996	(3)	0	0	0	0
Tony Tatupu	Wakefield	2000-01	20	2	0	0	8
	Warrington	1997	21(1)	6	0	0	24
James Taylor	Leigh	2005	(4)	0	0	0	0
Joe Taylor	Paris	1997	9(5)	2	0	0	8
Lawrence Taylor	Sheffield	1996	(1)	0	0	0	0
Scott Taylor	Hull KR	2009-12	21(29)	8	0	0	32
Frederic Teixido	Sheffield	1999	(4)	0	0	0	0
	Paris	1996-97	2(3)	1	0	0	4
Lionel Teixido	Catalans	2006-07	11(13)	3	0	0	12
Karl Temata	London	2005, 2012	1(8)	1	0	0	4
	Harlequins	2006-11	94(12)	7	0	0	28
Jason Temu	Hull	1998	13(2)	1	0	0	4
	Oldham	1996-97	25(3)	1	0	0	4
Paul Terry	London	1997	(1)	0	0	0	0
Anthony Thackeray	Castleford	2008	3(6)	0	0	0	0
	Hull	2007	2	0	0	0	0
Jamie Thackray	Crusaders	2010	1(16)	2	0	0	8
	Hull	2005-06, 2008-09	37(45)	6	0	0	24
	Leeds	2006-07	5(27)	7	0	0	28
	Castleford	2003-04	7(11)	3	0	0	12
	Halifax	2000-02	10(38)	3	0	0	12
Adam Thaler	Castleford	2002	(1)	0	0	0	0
Gareth Thomas	Crusaders	2010-11	27(1)	6	0	0	24
Giles Thomas	London	1997-99	1(2)	0	0	0	0
Rob Thomas	Harlequins	2011	(2)	0	0	0	0
Steve Thomas	London	2004	4(2)	0	0	0	0
	Warrington	2001	2	0	0	0	0

177

Super League Players 1996-2012

PLAYER	CLUB	YEAR	APP	TRIES	GOALS	FG	PTS
Alex Thompson	Warrington	2009	(1)	1	0	0	4
Alex Thompson	Sheffield	1997	4(11)	0	0	0	0
Bobby Thompson	Salford	1999	28	5	2	0	24
Jordan Thompson							
	Castleford	2009-12	35(12)	17	0	0	68
Sam Thompson	Harlequins	2009	(2)	0	0	0	0
	St Helens	2008	(5)	0	0	0	0
Chris Thorman	Hull	2009	19(2)	1	0	0	4
	Huddersfield	2000-01,					
		2005-08	126(20)	51	320	3	847
	London	2003	26(1)	7	81	1	191
	Sheffield	1999	5(13)	2	8	1	25
Tony Thorniley	Warrington	1997	(5)	0	0	0	0
Andy Thornley	Salford	2009	(1)	1	0	0	4
Iain Thornley	Wigan	2012	5	5	0	0	20
Danny Tickle	Hull	2007-12	146(1)	42	478	1	1125
	Wigan	2002-06	94(36)	34	200	2	538
	Halifax	2000-02	25(17)	10	91	2	224
Kris Tickle	Warrington	2001	(1)	0	0	0	0
John Timu	London	1998-2000	57(3)	11	0	0	44
Kerrod Toby	London	1997	2(2)	0	0	0	0
Tulsen Tollett	London	1996-2001	105(5)	38	49	1	251
Joel Tomkins	Wigan	2005-11	95(39)	46	0	0	184
Logan Tomkins	Wigan	2012	2(6)	0	0	0	0
Sam Tomkins	Wigan	2009-12	103(5)	84	28	1	393
Glen Tomlinson	Wakefield	1999-2000	41(5)	8	0	0	32
	Hull	1998	5	1	0	0	4
	Bradford	1996-97	27(13)	12	0	0	48
Ryan Tongia	Wakefield	2011	4	2	0	0	8
Ian Tonks	Castleford	1996-2001	32(50)	11	13	0	70
Tony Tonks	Huddersfield	2012	(1)	0	0	0	0
Motu Tony	Wakefield	2011-12	7(3)	1	0	0	4
	Hull	2005-09	76(20)	25	0	0	100
	Castleford	2004	8(1)	1	0	0	4
Mark Tookey	Harlequins	2006	12(14)	1	0	0	4
	London	2005	13(14)	5	0	0	20
	Castleford	2004	2(8)	1	0	0	4
Clinton Toopi	Leeds	2006-08	40(3)	9	0	0	36
David Tootill	Harlequins	2008	(4)	0	0	0	0
Paul Topping	Oldham	1996-97	23(10)	1	19	0	42
Patrick Torreilles	Paris	1996	9(1)	1	25	0	54
Albert Torrens	Huddersfield	2006	7	5	0	0	20
Mat Toshack	London	1998-2004	120(21)	24	0	0	96
Julien Touxagas	Catalans	2006-11	14(45)	4	0	0	16
Darren Treacy	Salford	2002	24(1)	6	1	0	26
Dean Treister	Hull	2003	16(1)	3	0	0	12
Rocky Trimarchi	Crusaders	2010	16(8)	0	0	0	0
Steve Trindall	London	2003-05	40(20)	3	0	0	12
Shane Tronc	Wakefield	2010	8(3)	2	0	0	8
Kyle Trout	Wakefield	2012	(11)	2	0	0	8
George Truelove	Wakefield	2002	2	1	0	0	4
	London	2000	5	1	0	0	4
Va'aiga Tuigamala							
	Wigan	1996	21	10	3	0	46
Fereti Tuilagi	St Helens	1999-2000	43(15)	21	0	0	84
	Halifax	1996-98	55(3)	27	0	0	108
Sateki Tuipulotu	Leeds	1996	6(3)	1	2	0	8
Tame Tupou	Bradford	2007-08	10(7)	8	0	0	32
Neil Turley	Leigh	2005	6(3)	2	20	1	49
Darren Turner	Huddersfield	2000-01,					
		2003-04	42(13)	13	0	0	52
	Sheffield	1996-99	41(29)	15	0	0	60
Ian Turner	Paris	1996	1(1)	1	0	0	4
Jordan Turner	Hull	2010-12	62(5)	28	0	0	112
	Salford	2006-07,					
		2009	22(10)	4	1	0	18
Chris Tuson	Wigan	2008,					
		2010-12	10(42)	5	0	0	20
	Castleford	2010	3(5)	0	0	0	0
Gregory Tutard	Paris	1996	1(1)	0	0	0	0
Brendon Tuuta	Warrington	1998	18(2)	4	0	0	16
	Castleford	1996-97	41(1)	3	0	0	12
Steve Tyrer	Salford	2010	20	6	9	0	42
	Celtic	2009	8	2	5	0	18
	St Helens	2006-08	17(3)	12	42	0	132
Mike Umaga	Halifax	1996-97	38(1)	16	5	0	74
Kava Utoikamanu	Paris	1996	6(3)	0	0	0	0
Frederic Vaccari	Catalans	2010-11	31	17	0	0	68
David Vaealiki	Wigan	2005-07	67(1)	17	0	0	68
Joe Vagana	Bradford	2001-08	176(44)	17	0	0	68
Nigel Vagana	Warrington	1997	20	17	0	0	68
Tevita Vaikona	Bradford	1998-2004	145(2)	89	0	0	356
Lesley Vainikolo	Bradford	2002-07	132(4)	136	1	0	546
Eric Van Brussell	Paris	1996	2	0	0	0	0
Jace Van Dijk	Celtic	2009	19	1	1	0	6
Richard Varkulis	Warrington	2004	4(1)	3	0	0	12
Marcus Vassilakopoulos							
	Sheffield	1997-99	15(11)	3	10	2	34
	Leeds	1996-97	1(3)	0	0	0	0
Josh Veivers	Salford	2012	5	2	0	0	8
	Wakefield	2011	10(2)	2	22	0	52
Phil Veivers	Huddersfield	1998	7(6)	1	0	0	4
	St Helens	1996	(1)	1	0	0	4
Michael Vella	Hull KR	2007-11	111(5)	13	0	0	52

PLAYER	CLUB	YEAR	APP	TRIES	GOALS	FG	PTS
Bruno Verges	Catalans	2006	25	6	0	0	24
Eric Vergniol	Paris	1996	14(1)	6	0	0	24
Gray Viane	Salford	2007	9	2	0	0	8
	Castleford	2006	20(7)	14	0	0	56
	Widnes	2005	20	13	0	0	52
	St Helens	2004	4	1	0	0	4
Adrian Vowles	Castleford	1997-2001,					
		2003	125(1)	29	1	1	119
	Wakefield	2002-03	24(3)	6	1	0	26
	Leeds	2002	14(3)	2	0	0	8
Michael Wainwright							
	Castleford	2008-10	70	22	0	0	88
	Wakefield	2004-05	21(10)	8	0	0	32
Mike Wainwright	Salford	2000-02,					
		2007	75(3)	9	0	0	36
	Warrington	1996-99,					
		2003-07	168(14)	23	0	0	92
Adam Walker	Huddersfield	2010-12	1(5)	0	0	0	0
Ben Walker	Leeds	2002	23(1)	8	100	0	232
Chev Walker	Bradford	2011-12	15(12)	1	0	0	4
	Hull KR	2008-09	24(7)	5	0	0	20
	Leeds	1999-2006	142(19)	77	0	0	308
Chris Walker	Catalans	2010	11	6	2	0	28
Jonathan Walker	Castleford	2010-12	10(19)	1	0	0	4
Jonny Walker	Wigan	2010	(1)	0	0	0	0
Matt Walker	Huddersfield	2001	3(6)	0	0	0	0
Anthony Wall	Paris	1997	9	3	3	0	18
Mark Wallace	Workington	1996	14(1)	3	0	0	12
Adam Walne	Salford	2012	(2)	0	0	0	0
Joe Walsh	Huddersfield	2009	1(1)	1	0	0	4
	Harlequins	2007-08	1(4)	0	0	0	0
Lucas Walshaw	Wakefield	2011-12	4(4)	0	0	0	0
Kerrod Walters	Gateshead	1999	10(12)	2	1	0	10
Kevin Walters	Warrington	2001	1	0	0	0	0
Jason Walton	Salford	2009	(5)	0	0	0	0
Barry Ward	St Helens	2002-03	20(30)	4	0	0	16
Danny Ward	Harlequins	2008-11	89(7)	4	0	0	16
	Hull KR	2007	11(9)	0	0	0	0
	Castleford	2006	18(7)	2	0	0	8
	Leeds	1999-2005	70(48)	9	0	1	37
Stevie Ward	Leeds	2012	10(9)	2	0	0	8
Joe Wardle	Huddersfield	2011-12	31	12	0	0	48
	Bradford	2010	1(1)	0	0	0	0
Phil Waring	Salford	1997-99	6(8)	2	0	0	8
Brett Warton	London	1999-2001	49(7)	14	133	0	322
Kyle Warren	Castleford	2002	13(14)	3	0	0	12
Danny Washbrook							
	Wakefield	2012	28	5	0	0	20
	Hull	2005-11	92(30)	11	0	0	44
Adam Watene	Wakefield	2006-08	45(8)	5	0	0	20
	Bradford	2006	(4)	0	0	0	0
Frank Watene	Wakefield	1999-2001	24(37)	6	0	0	24
Trent Waterhouse	Warrington	2012	26	8	0	0	32
Kallum Watkins	Leeds	2008-12	53(7)	34	0	0	136
Dave Watson	Sheffield	1998-99	41(4)	4	0	0	16
Ian Watson	Salford	1997, 2002	24(17)	8	3	5	43
	Workington	1996	4(1)	1	15	0	34
Kris Watson	Warrington	1996	11(2)	2	0	0	8
Anthony Watts	Widnes	2012	(1)	0	0	0	0
Brad Watts	Widnes	2005	6	3	0	0	12
Liam Watts	Hull	2012	10(2)	1	0	0	4
	Hull KR	2008,					
		2010-12	31(26)	6	0	0	24
Michael Watts	Warrington	2002	3	0	0	0	0
Brent Webb	Leeds	2007-12	137(1)	73	0	0	292
Jason Webber	Salford	2000	25(1)	10	0	0	40
Ian Webster	St Helens	2006	1	0	0	0	0
Jake Webster	Hull KR	2008-12	95(1)	34	7	0	150
James Webster	Hull	2008	1	0	0	0	0
	Hull KR	2007-08	36	2	0	2	10
Pat Weisner	Hull KR	2007	(2)	0	0	0	0
	Harlequins	2006	10(6)	3	0	0	12
Taylor Welch	Warrington	2008	1	0	0	0	0
Kris Welham	Hull KR	2007-12	108(2)	70	1	0	282
Paul Wellens	St Helens	1998-2012	359(23)	182	34	1	797
Jon Wells	Harlequins	2006-09	66	10	0	0	40
	London	2004-05	42(2)	19	0	0	76
	Wakefield	2003	22(1)	1	0	0	4
	Castleford	1996-2002	114(14)	49	0	0	196
Dwayne West	St Helens	2000-02	8(16)	6	0	0	24
	Wigan	1999	1(1)	0	0	0	0
Joe Westerman	Hull	2011-12	34(10)	13	22	0	96
	Castleford	2008-10	68(7)	29	151	0	418
Craig Weston	Widnes	2002, 2004	23(9)	2	1	2	12
	Huddersfield	1998-99	46(1)	15	15	0	90
Ben Westwood	Warrington	2002-12	242(8)	86	62	0	468
	Wakefield	1999-2002	31(7)	8	1	0	34
Andrew Whalley	Workington	1996	(2)	0	0	0	0
Paul Whatuira	Huddersfield	2008-10	59	23	0	0	92
Scott Wheeldon	London	2012	14(1)	2	0	0	8
	Hull KR	2009-12	30(42)	4	0	0	16
	Hull	2006-08	2(60)	4	0	0	16
Gary Wheeler	St Helens	2008-12	34(10)	14	9	0	74

178

PLAYER	CLUB	YEAR	APP	TRIES	GOALS	FG	PTS
Matt Whitaker	Castleford	2006	8(2)	0	0	0	0
	Widnes	2004-05	10(20)	9	0	0	36
	Huddersfield	2003-04	3(14)	0	0	0	0
David White	Wakefield	2000	(1)	0	0	0	0
Josh White	Salford	1998	18(3)	5	5	1	31
	London	1997	14(2)	8	0	1	33
Lloyd White	Widnes	2012	6(8)	3	0	1	13
	Crusaders	2010-11	13(11)	8	0	0	32
	Celtic	2009	6	1	0	0	4
Paul White	Salford	2009	1	1	0	0	4
	Wakefield	2006-07	24(12)	12	0	0	48
	Huddersfield	2003-05	11(32)	17	16	0	100
Elliott Whitehead	Bradford	2009-12	73(10)	27	0	0	108
Richard Whiting	Hull	2004-12	135(43)	52	8	2	226
Danny Whittle	Warrington	1998	(2)	0	0	0	0
David Whittle	St Helens	2002	1(2)	0	0	0	0
	Warrington	2001	1(2)	0	0	0	0
Jon Whittle	Wakefield	2006	8(2)	3	0	0	12
	Widnes	2005	13	2	0	0	8
	Wigan	2003	1	0	0	0	0
Dean Widders	Castleford	2009-11	25(32)	23	0	0	92
Stephen Wild	Salford	2011-12	48	2	0	0	8
	Huddersfield	2006-10	116(2)	33	0	0	132
	Wigan	2001-05	67(20)	24	0	0	96
Matthew Wildie	Wakefield	2010-12	6(14)	2	0	0	8
Oliver Wilkes	Wakefield	2008-09, 2012	46(32)	7	0	0	28
	Harlequins	2010-11	39(13)	4	0	0	16
	Wigan	2006	1(5)	0	0	0	0
	Leigh	2005	13(1)	1	0	0	4
	Huddersfield	2000-01	1(6)	0	0	0	0
	Sheffield	1998	(1)	0	0	0	0
Jon Wilkin	St Helens	2003-12	196(27)	62	0	1	249
Alex Wilkinson	Hull	2003-04	11(4)	1	0	0	4
	Huddersfield	2003	8	4	0	0	16
	London	2002	5(1)	0	0	0	0
	Bradford	2000-01	3(3)	1	0	0	4
Bart Williams	London	1998	5(3)	1	0	0	4
Daley Williams	Salford	2006-07	9(2)	4	0	0	16
Danny Williams	Harlequins	2006	9(13)	4	0	0	16
	London	2005	1(16)	0	0	0	0
Danny Williams	Salford	2011-12	28	20	0	0	80
	Leeds	2006, 2008	13(2)	7	0	0	28
	Hull	2008	3	0	0	0	0
Dave Williams	Harlequins	2008-11	1(17)	0	0	0	0
Desi Williams	Wigan	2004	2	0	0	0	0
Jonny Williams	London	2004	(4)	0	0	0	0
Lee Williams	Crusaders	2011	1(7)	0	0	0	0
Rhys Williams	Warrington	2010-12	18(1)	13	0	0	52
	Castleford	2012	8	4	0	0	16
	Crusaders	2011	6	3	0	0	12
Luke Williamson	Harlequins	2009-10	39	6	0	0	24
John Wilshere	Salford	2006-07, 2009	72(2)	32	142	0	412
	Leigh	2005	26	8	6	0	44
	Warrington	2004	5	2	0	0	8
Craig Wilson	Hull	2000	2(16)	1	0	1	5
	Gateshead	1999	17(11)	5	0	1	21
George Wilson	Paris	1996	7(2)	3	0	0	12
John Wilson	Catalans	2006-08	69	23	0	0	92
Richard Wilson	Hull	1998-99	(13)	0	0	0	0
Scott Wilson	Warrington	1998-99	23(2)	6	0	0	24
Johan Windley	Hull	1999	2(2)	1	0	0	4
Paul Wingfield	Warrington	1997	5(3)	6	1	0	26
Frank Winterstein	Widnes	2012	26	7	0	0	28
	Crusaders	2010-11	26(19)	4	0	0	16
	Wakefield	2009	(5)	0	0	0	0
Lincoln Withers	Hull KR	2012	14(12)	7	0	0	28
	Crusaders	2010-11	47	4	0	0	16
	Celtic	2009	21	6	0	0	24
Michael Withers	Wigan	2007	6(1)	1	0	0	4
	Bradford	1999-2006	156(6)	94	15	4	410
Michael Witt	London	2012	19	6	45	0	114
	Crusaders	2010-11	39	13	47	4	150
Jeff Wittenberg	Huddersfield	1998	18(1)	1	0	0	4
	Bradford	1997	8(9)	4	0	0	16
Kyle Wood	Wakefield	2012	1(27)	6	0	0	24
	Huddersfield	2011	1(5)	0	0	0	0
	Castleford	2010	1(4)	0	0	0	0
Martin Wood	Sheffield	1997-98	24(11)	4	18	2	54
Nathan Wood	Warrington	2002-05	90	38	0	3	155
	Wakefield	2002	11	2	0	0	8
Paul Wood	Warrington	2000-12	115(158)	39	0	0	156
Phil Wood	Widnes	2004	2(1)	0	0	0	0
Darren Woods	Widnes	2005	(1)	0	0	0	0
David Woods	Halifax	2002	18(2)	8	0	0	32
Simon Worrall	Leeds	2008-09	5(16)	1	0	0	4
Michael Worrincy	Bradford	2009-10	12(34)	12	0	0	48
	Harlequins	2006-08	20(12)	10	0	0	40
Rob Worrincy	Castleford	2004	1	0	0	0	0
Troy Wozniak	Widnes	2004	13(7)	1	0	0	4
Matthew Wray	Wakefield	2002-03	13(3)	2	0	0	8
David Wrench	Wakefield	2002-06	28(52)	6	0	0	24
	Leeds	1999-2001	7(17)	0	0	0	0
Craig Wright	Castleford	2000	1(9)	0	0	0	0
Nigel Wright	Huddersfield	1999	4(6)	1	0	0	4
	Wigan	1996-97	5(5)	2	0	1	9
Ricky Wright	Sheffield	1997-99	2(13)	0	0	0	0
Vincent Wulf	Paris	1996	13(4)	4	0	0	16
Andrew Wynyard	London	1999-2000	34(6)	4	0	0	16
Bagdad Yaha	Paris	1996	4(4)	2	4	0	16
Malakai Yasa	Sheffield	1996	1(3)	0	0	0	0
Kirk Yeaman	Hull	2001-12	235(17)	135	0	0	540
Grant Young	London	1998-99	22(2)	2	0	0	8
Nick Youngquest	Castleford	2011-12	37	28	0	0	112
	Crusaders	2010	26(1)	9	0	0	36
Ronel Zenon	Paris	1996	(4)	0	0	0	0
Nick Zisti	Bradford	1999	6(1)	0	0	0	0
Freddie Zitter	Catalans	2006	1	0	0	0	0

NEW FACES - Players making their Super League debuts in 2012

PLAYER	CLUB	DEBUT vs	ROUND	DATE
Paul Aiton	Wakefield	Widnes (a)	1	3/2/12
Josh Atkinson	Castleford	St Helens (h)	11	9/4/12
Ben Blackmore	Castleford	Hull (a)	27	8/9/12
Julian Bousquet	Catalans	Hull (h)	2	14/7/12
Josh Bowden	Hull	Salford (a)	4	24/2/12
Damien Cardace	Catalans	Widnes (h)	9	31/3/12
Omari Caro	London	Salford (a)	5	2/3/12
Michael Channing	London	Hull KR (a)	12	22/4/12
James Clare	Castleford	Huddersfield (a)	7	16/3/12
Dean Collis	Wakefield	Widnes (a)	1	3/2/12
Danny Cowling	Wakefield	St Helens (h)	24	12/8/12
Danny Craven	Widnes	Wakefield (h)	1	3/2/12
	(club debut: Whitehaven (a), ChR16, 1/7/10)			
Ben Crooks	Hull	Wigan (h)	12	22/4/12
	(club debut: Huddersfield (h), CCR4, 15/4/12)			
Dominic Crosby	Wigan	Huddersfield (a)	14	18/5/12
	(club debut: North Wales (h), CCR4, 15/4/12)			
James Cunningham	Hull	Catalans (a)	2	14/7/12
Ben Currie	Warrington	Widnes (h)	10	5/4/12
Matty Dawson	Huddersfield	Warrington (a)	26	2/9/12
Kieran Dixon	London	St Helens (h)	1	4/2/12
Brad Dwyer	Warrington	Wakefield (h)	7	18/3/12
Paddy Flynn	Widnes	Huddersfield (a)	2	12/2/12
	(club debut: Barrow (a), NRCR6, 16/3/08)			
Anthony Gelling	Wigan	Widnes (a)	6	11/3/12
Alex Gerrard	Widnes	Warrington (a)	10	5/4/12
	(club debut: Wigan (h), CCR5, 8/5/10)			
Tom Gilmore	Widnes	London (a)	17	9/6/12
Grant Gore	Widnes	Leeds (a)	24	10/8/12
	(club debut: London Skolars (a), NRCR1, 6/2/11)			
Craig Gower	London	St Helens (h)	1	4/2/12
Chris Green	Hull	Bradford (h)	9	30/3/12
James Green	Hull KR	Bradford (a)	24	10/8/12
Joe Greenwood	St Helens	Wakefield (h)	13	4/5/12
	(club debut: Oldham (a), CCR5, 27/4/12)			
James Grehan	Castleford	Wigan (h)	4	26/2/12
George Griffin	Hull KR	Widnes (a)	22	29/7/12
Kurt Haggerty	Widnes	Wakefield (h)	1	3/2/12
	(club debut: Featherstone (a), ChR15, 27/6/10)			
Chris Heil	Hull KR	Widnes (a)	22	29/7/12
Aaron Heremaia	Hull	Warrington (a)	18	24/6/12
Lance Hohaia	St Helens	London (a)	1	4/2/12
Liam Hood	Leeds	Castleford (a)	5	2/3/12
Isaac John	Wakefield	Widnes (a)	1	3/2/12
Nick Johnson	Hull KR	London (a)	27	8/9/12
Ben Johnston	Castleford	London (h)	24	12/8/12
Josh Jones	St Helens	Warrington (a)	9	30/3/12
Antonio Kaufusi	London	St Helens (h)	1	4/2/12
Ben Kavanagh	Widnes	Wakefield (h)	1	3/2/12
	(club debut: Blackpool (a), NRCR1, 3/2/08)			
Liam Kay	Wakefield	Wigan (a)	11	9/4/12
Jimmy Keinhorst	Leeds	Wakefield (a)	22	30/7/12
Liam Kent	Hull	Bradford (h)	9	30/3/12
	(club debut: Oldham (h), CCR4, 7/5/11)			
Sione Kite	Widnes	Wigan (h)	6	11/3/12
Anthony Laffranchi	St Helens	London (a)	1	4/2/12
James Laithwaite	Hull KR	Salford (h)	20	8/7/12
Kevin Larroyer	Catalans	Huddersfield (a)	23	5/8/12
Macgraff Leuluai	Widnes	Salford (h)	3	19/2/12
	(club debut: London Skolars (a), NRCR1, 6/2/11)			
Tom Lineham	Hull	Hull KR (a)	21	23/7/12
Rhodri Lloyd	Wigan	Leeds (a)	16	1/6/12
Will Lovell	London	Catalans (MW)	15	27/5/12
Keith Lulia	Bradford	Wigan (h)	3	19/2/12
Manase Manuokafoa	Bradford	Warrington (h)	5	3/3/12
Antoni Maria	Catalans	Castleford (a)	26	2/9/12
Shannon McDonnell	Hull KR	Leeds (a)	1	3/2/12
Wade McKinnon	Hull	Warrington (h)	1	5/2/12
Mike McMeeken	London	Warrington (h)	25	17/8/12
Shannan McPherson	Salford	St Helens (a)	2	10/2/12
Constantine Mika	Hull KR	Leeds (a)	1	3/2/12
Grant Millington	Castleford	Leeds (h)	5	2/3/12
Joel Moon	Salford	Castleford (h)	1	4/2/12
Anthony Mullally	Widnes	Wakefield (h)	1	3/2/12
	(club debut: Saddleworth (h), CCR3, 7/3/09)			
Jack Murphy	Wigan	Bradford (h)	19	29/6/12
Jack Owens	Widnes	Bradford (h)	11	9/4/12
	(club debut: Siddal (a), CCR3, 6/3/11)			
Mickey Paea	Hull KR	Leeds (a)	1	3/2/12
Dave Petersen	Hull KR	Salford (a)	11	9/4/12
Sam Powell	Wigan	Hull (h)	23	3/8/12
Adrian Purtell	Bradford	Catalans (h)	1	5/2/12
Michael Robertson	London	St Helens (h)	1	4/2/12
Shane Rodney	London	St Helens (h)	1	4/2/12
Matthew Russell	Wigan	Widnes (a)	6	11/3/12
Liam Salter	Hull KR	Catalans (a)	7	17/3/12
Brett Seymour	Hull	London (h)	3	19/2/12
Steve Southern	Wakefield	Widnes (a)	1	3/2/12
Tom Spencer	Wigan	Leeds (h)	2	11/2/12
Adam Swift	St Helens	Widnes (h)	12	20/4/12
	(club debut: Widnes (a), CCR4, 14/4/12)			
Iain Thornley	Wigan	Wakefield (a)	20	8/7/12
Logan Tomkins	Wigan	Widnes (a)	6	11/3/12
Tony Tonks	Huddersfield	Hull KR (a)	8	25/3/12
Kyle Trout	Wakefield	Bradford (h)	4	25/2/12
Adam Walne	Salford	Wigan (a)	25	20/8/12
Stevie Ward	Leeds	St Helens (a)	8	25/3/12
Trent Waterhouse	Warrington	Hull (a)	1	5/2/12
Anthony Watts	Widnes	Salford (h)	3	19/2/12

OLD FACES - Players making their Super League debuts for new clubs in 2012

PLAYER	CLUB	DEBUT vs	ROUND	DATE
Patrick Ah Van	Widnes	Wakefield (h)	1	3/2/12
Dave Allen	Widnes	Wakefield (h)	1	3/2/12
(club debut: Swinton (h), NRCR1, 12/2/06)				
Louis Anderson	Catalans	Bradford (a)	1	5/2/12
Matty Ashurst	Salford	Castleford (h)	1	4/2/12
Martin Aspinwall	Hull	Warrington (h)	1	5/2/12
Shaun Briscoe	Widnes	Leeds (h)	4	26/2/12
Mark Bryant	London	St Helens (h)	1	4/2/12
Hep Cahill	Widnes	Wakefield (h)	1	3/2/12
Keal Carlile	Hull KR	Warrington (a)	4	26/2/12
Jason Chan	Huddersfield	Wigan (a)	1	5/2/12
Jon Clarke	Widnes	Wakefield (h)	1	3/2/12
Ben Cockayne	Wakefield	Widnes (a)	1	3/2/12
Liam Colbon	London	St Helens (h)	1	4/2/12
Matt Cook	London	Warrington (a)	2	12/2/12
Ben Cross	Widnes	Wakefield (h)	1	3/2/12
Ben Davies	Widnes	Huddersfield (a) (D2)	2	12/2/12
Chris Dean	Widnes	Wakefield (h) (D3)	1	3/2/12
Gil Dudson	Wigan	St Helens (a)	10	6/4/12
Greg Eden	Huddersfield	Wigan (a)	1	5/2/12
Andy Ellis	Wakefield	Wigan (a)	11	9/4/12
Jamie Ellis	Castleford	Huddersfield (h)	20	8/7/12
	Hull	Wakefield (h)	5	4/3/12
Brett Ferres	Huddersfield	St Helens (a)	22	29/7/12
Simon Finnigan	Widnes	Huddersfield (a) (D2-SL)	2	12/2/12
(club debut: London Skolars (a) (D2), NRCR1, 6/2/11)				
Ben Fisher	Catalans	Bradford (a)	1	5/2/12
Mark Flanagan	St Helens	London (a)	1	4/2/12
Ben Flower	Wigan	Huddersfield (h)	1	5/2/12
Jamie Foster	Hull	Hull KR (a)	21	23/7/12
Peter Fox	Wakefield	Widnes (a) (D2)	1	3/2/12
Luke Gale	Bradford	Catalans (h)	1	5/2/12
Luke George	Huddersfield	Wigan (a)	1	5/2/12
Ben Gledhill	Salford	Castleford (h)	1	4/2/12
Darrell Griffin	Leeds	Hull KR (h)	1	3/2/12
Josh Griffin	Castleford	Salford (a)	1	4/2/12
Rhys Hanbury	Widnes	Wakefield (h)	1	3/2/12
Chris Hill	Warrington	Huddersfield (h)	3	18/2/12
David Hodgson	Hull KR	Leeds (a)	1	3/2/12
Graeme Horne	Hull KR	Leeds (a)	1	3/2/12
Stuart Howarth	Salford	Castleford (h)	1	4/2/12
Willie Isa	Widnes	Wakefield (h)	1	3/2/12
Jordan James	Salford	Castleford (h)	1	4/2/12
Matt James	Wakefield	Salford (h)	12	21/4/12
(club debut: Leeds (a), CCR4, 13/4/12)				
Phil Joseph	Bradford	Wigan (h)	3	19/2/12
Elliot Kear	Bradford	Catalans (h)	1	5/2/12
Danny Kirmond	Wakefield	Widnes (a) (D2)	1	3/2/12
Epalahame Lauaki	Wigan	Huddersfield (h)	1	5/2/12
Ali Lauitiiti	Wakefield	Widnes (a)	1	3/2/12
Tommy Lee	Huddersfield	Wigan (a)	1	5/2/12
Shaun Lunt	Leeds	Catalans (h)	12	20/4/12
Andy Lynch	Hull	Warrington (h)	1	5/2/12
Stefan Marsh	Widnes	Wakefield (h) (D2)	1	3/2/12
Tony Martin	Hull	Warrington (h)	1	5/2/12
Richard Mathers	Wakefield	Widnes (a)	1	3/2/12
Ryan McGoldrick	Hull	Leeds (a)	20	6/7/12
Paul McShane	Widnes	Huddersfield (h)	16	3/6/12
Vince Mellars	Wakefield	Widnes (a)	1	3/2/12
Joe Mellor	Widnes	St Helens (a) (D2)	12	20/4/12
	Wigan	Widnes (a)	6	11/3/12
Lee Mitchell	Castleford	Salford (a)	1	4/2/12
Richard Moore	Leeds	Widnes (a)	4	26/2/12
Scott Moore	Huddersfield	Wigan (h)	14	18/5/12
(club debut: Swinton (h) (D2), CCR5, 29/4/12)				
	Widnes	Wakefield (h)	1	3/2/12
Aaron Murphy	Huddersfield	London (a)	4	26/2/12
Stephen Nash	Castleford	Salford (a)	1	4/2/12
Gareth O'Brien	Widnes	Wigan (h)	6	11/3/12
Eamon O'Carroll	Widnes	Castleford (h)	19	2/7/12
	Hull	Wakefield (h)	5	4/3/12
Ryan O'Hara	Hull KR	Wigan (a)	13	4/5/12
Cameron Phelps	Widnes	Wigan (h)	6	11/3/12
Steve Pickersgill	Widnes	Wakefield (h)	1	3/2/12
(club debut: Gateshead (h), ChR11, 23/5/09)				
Jay Pitts	Hull	Hull KR (h)	10	6/4/12
Karl Pryce	Bradford	Hull KR (a) (D2)	6	10/3/12
Leon Pryce	Catalans	Castleford (h)	3	18/2/12
Andy Raleigh	Wakefield	Widnes (a)	1	3/2/12
Stefan Ratchford	Warrington	Hull (a)	1	5/2/12
Julien Rinaldi	London	St Helens (h) (D2)	1	4/2/12
Matthew Russell	Hull	Leeds (h)	13	5/5/12
Jarrod Sammut	Bradford	Catalans (h)	1	5/2/12
Lee Smith	Wakefield	Wigan (h)	20	8/7/12
Matty Smith	Wigan	Wakefield (a)	20	8/7/12
Tim Smith	Wakefield	Widnes (a)	1	3/2/12
Paul Sykes	Wakefield	London (a)	9	31/3/12
Josh Veivers	Salford	Catalans (a)	6	10/3/12
Danny Washbrook	Wakefield	Widnes (a)	1	3/2/12
Liam Watts	Hull	Huddersfield (h)	19	1/7/12
Scott Wheeldon	London	Bradford (h)	13	6/5/12
Lloyd White	Widnes	Wakefield (h)	1	3/2/12
Oliver Wilkes	Wakefield	Widnes (a) (D2)	1	3/2/12
Rhys Williams	Castleford	Wakefield (MW)	15	26/5/12
Frank Winterstein	Widnes	Wakefield (h)	1	3/2/12
Lincoln Withers	Hull KR	Leeds (a)	1	3/2/12
Michael Witt	London	St Helens (h)	1	4/2/12
Kyle Wood	Wakefield	Widnes (a)	1	3/2/12

SUPER LEAGUE XVII
Club by Club

27 October 2011 - prop forward Steve Crossley released and joins Dewsbury; Cain Southernwood goes to same club on season-long loan.

26 December 2011 - Manase Manuokafoa suffers serious knee injury in training ahead of 28-18 Boxing Day friendly defeat at Castleford.

12 January 2012 - Karl Pryce re-signs on one-year contract.

26 January 2012 - Heath L'Estrange and Matt Diskin appointed joint captains for 2012.

2 February 2012 - Swinton prop Phil Joseph signs 12-month contract after successful trials.

5 February 2012 - 34-12 home defeat by Catalans in round one.

5 February 2012 - Kyle Briggs rejoins Featherstone on season-long loan.

12 February 2012 - James Donaldson ruptures anterior cruciate ligament and Adrian Purtell tears pectoral in 20-12 win at Castleford in round 2.

19 February 2012 - Keith Lulia makes debut and Luke Gale injures ankle in 54-16 home defeat by Wigan.

25 February 2012 - Elliott Whitehead scores hat-trick in 36-18 win at Wakefield.

3 March 2012 - Manase Manuokafoa makes debut in 23-10 home defeat to Warrington. Craig Kopczak suffers badly-broken finger and Elliot Kear broken wrist.

10 March 2012 - Jason Crookes scores hat-trick in come back from 24-8 to win 36-24 at Hull KR. Jarrod Sammut banned for one game for use of forearm. Nick Scruton needs shoulder re-construction.

17 March 2012 - 12-8 success over St Helens is first home win of season. Olivier Elima makes seasonal debut and gets one-match ban for dangerous contact after early guilty plea.

20 March 2012 - Elliott Whitehead signs new five-year deal to end of 2016.

25 March 2012 - 38-18 home defeat to Salford in round 8.

27 March 2012 - Bulls warn they will go out of business unless supporters raise £1 million – at least half in the next 10 days.

30 March 2012 - John Bateman gets two matches for dangerous contact in 24-18 defeat at Hull.

6 April 2012 - 12-4 Good Friday home win over Leeds in front of over 20,000 people. Heath L'Estrange gets three-game ban for spear tackle on Jamie Peacock.

10 April 2012 - initial target of £500,000 reached to avoid immediate threat of administration.

11 April 2012 - Jarrod Sammut ruptures cruciate knee ligament in Easter Monday 38-4 win at Widnes.

22 April 2012 - chairman Peter Hood reveals he will be forced out at upcoming EGM.

28 April 2012 - 32-16 Challenge Cup exit at Warrington.

1 May 2012 - John Bateman banned for three games for crusher tackle on Brett Hodgson in Warrington defeat.

9 May 2012 - chairman Peter Hood stands down.

27 May 2012 - Adrian Purtell hospitalised with heart scare after 37-22 Magic Weekend defeat by Leeds.

KEY DATES - BRADFORD BULLS

14 June 2012 - HMRC gives notice of a winding-up petition.

26 June 2012 - club enters administration, administrator Brendan Guilfoyle claims he has 10 days to find a buyer to save the club from liquidation.

29 June 2012 - Bulls pull off remarkable 22-30 win at Wigan.

2 July 2012 - coach Mick Potter and chief executive Ryan Duckett among 16 members of staff made redundant by administrator.

3 July 2012 - players turn up for a pre-arranged meeting with administrator, only to find it cancelled. Brian Noble admits he was approached by administrator to take charge of next game, but was shocked by negative reaction.

4 July 2012 - Gary Tasker returns as interim chief executive. Mick Potter, Francis Cummins and Lee St Hilaire all return without pay.

8 July 2012 - Bradford beat London 44-12 at Odsal.

11 July 2012 - RFL agree to advance Bradford's monthly share of TV money to allow them to cover players' wages. Fans set up hardship fund to help coaching and backroom staff.

19 July 2012 - The ABC Consortium formally submit a bid for the club, conditional on them buying back Odsal from the RFL and the club retaining its Super League status.

24 July 2012 - RFL confirm a formal written offer has been made by the ABC Consortium for the club.

25 July 2012 - Bulls deduction of six points by RFL for entering administration leaves them four points adrift of play-offs after 50-22 defeat at Warrington.

26 July 2012 - RFL rejects conditional bid from consortium who want to buy back Odsal.

2 August 2012 - Super League (Europe) Ltd tables offer to purchase club from the administrator on behalf of the Super League clubs.

5 August 2012 - 38-26 home win over Widnes moves Bulls within two points of eighth-placed Hull KR.

6 August 2012 - Tom Burgess to join brothers at Souths at end of season.

10 August 2012 - 32-26 home win over Hull KR brings them level on points.

19 August 2012 - 34-12 win at Huddersfield moves Bulls into eighth.

22 August 2012 - Super League clubs confirm commitment to 14-team competition in 2013, raising hopes that the Bulls will survive as a Super League club.

31 August 2012 - club bought by Omar Khan, with local MP and former Sports Minister Gerry Sutcliffe as Honorary Chairman.

1 September 2012 - 70-6 defeat by Hull FC at Odsal sees Bulls drop out of play-off spots.

5 September 2012 - Ben Jeffries to retire and return to Australia at end of season.

6 September 2012 - Olivier Elima to rejoin Catalan Dragons at end of season.

8 September 2012 - Craig Kopczak terminates his own contract before 50-26 defeat at Catalans ends play-off hopes.

11 September 2012 - Bulls granted membership of RFL under new owners.

11 September 2012 - John Bateman named Albert Goldthorpe Rookie of the Year.

14 September 2012 - Mick Potter announces he is to return to Australia.

14 September 2012 - Bulls awarded one-year probationary licence for 2013.

17 September 2012 - assistant Francis Cummins appointed new head coach.

19 September 2012 - Jason Crookes joins Hull FC.

20 September 2012 - 26-year-old Bryn Hargreaves retires.

26 September 2012 - Chev Walker signs new 12-month deal.

5 October 2012 - Albert Goldthorpe Rookie of the Year John Bateman signs new improved three-year contract to end of 2015 season.

9 October 20121 - Karl Pryce and Phil Joseph released.

10 October 2012 - Matty Blythe signs on one-year's loan from Warrington.

13 October 2012 - Luke Gale signs new contract to end of 2015.

16 October 2012 - Manase Manuokafoa signs new two-year deal.

19 October 2012 - Jarrod Sammut signs new two-year contract to end of 2015 season.

24 October 2012 - Mick Potter appointed head coach at Wests Tigers.

24 October 2012 - Danny Addy signs new one-year contract.

29 October 2012 - Shaun Ainscough rejects reduced terms and leaves club.

CLUB RECORDS

Highest score:
98-6 v Toulouse, 19/4/2008
Highest score against:
18-75 v Leeds, 14/9/31
Record attendance:
69,429 v Huddersfield, 14/3/53

MATCH RECORDS

Tries:
6 Eric Batten v Leeds, 15/9/45
Trevor Foster v Wakefield, 10/4/48
Steve McGowan v Barrow, 8/11/92
Lesley Vainikolo v Hull, 2/9/2005
Goals:
15 Iestyn Harris v Toulouse, 15/4/2008
Points:
36 John Woods v Swinton, 13/10/85

SEASON RECORDS

Tries: 63 Jack McLean 1951-52
Goals: 213 *(inc 5fg)* Henry Paul 2001
Points: 457 Henry Paul 2001

CAREER RECORDS

Tries: 261 Jack McLean 1950-56
Goals:
1,165 *(inc 25fg)* Paul Deacon 1998-2009
Points: 2,605 Paul Deacon 1998-2009
Appearances:
588 Keith Mumby 1973-90; 1992-93

BRADFORD BULLS

DATE	FIXTURE	RESULT	SCORERS	LGE	ATT
5/2/12	Catalan Dragons (h)	L12-34	t:Langley,Kear g:Gale(2)	14th	10,610
12/2/12	Castleford (a)	W12-20	t:Sammut,Burgess,Kearney g:Gale(4)	10th	8,050
19/2/12	Wigan (h)	L16-54	t:Crookes,Sammut,Kearney g:Sammut(2)	12th	12,909
25/2/12	Wakefield (a)	W18-36	t:Lulia,Whitehead(3),Kearney(2) g:Sammut(6)	8th	6,934
3/3/12	Warrington (h)	L10-23	t:Diskin,Crookes g:Sammut	10th	11,318
10/3/12	Hull KR (a)	W24-36	t:Crookes(3),Pryce,Diskin,Kearney,Lulia g:Sammut(4)	8th	7,486
17/3/12	St Helens (h)	W12-8	t:Whitehead,Pryce g:Sykes(2)	7th	11,360
25/3/12	Salford (h)	L18-38	t:Kearney,Whitehead,Hargreaves g:Sammut(3)	8th	11,219
30/3/12	Hull FC (a)	L24-18	t:Lulia,Pryce,Bateman g:Sammut(3)	9th	11,673
6/4/12	Leeds (h)	W12-4	t:Langley,Jeffries g:Sammut(2)	7th	20,851
9/4/12	Widnes (a)	W4-38	t:Jeffries,Platt(2),Kopczak,Purtell,Manuokafoa,Lulia g:Sammut(4),Addy	7th	5,687
15/4/12	Doncaster (h) (CCR4)	W72-6	t:Whitehead(3),Jeffries,Diskin(2),Ainscough(3),Bateman,Kopczak,Lulia(2) g:Addy(10)	N/A	3,210
22/4/12	Huddersfield (h)	L6-20	t:Platt g:Addy	8th	11,182
28/4/12	Warrington (a) (CCR5)	L32-16	t:Purtell,Lulia,Elima g:Gale(2)	N/A	5,505
6/5/12	London Broncos (a) ●	W22-29	t:Pryce,Platt(4) g:Gale(4) fg:Gale	8th	2,844
18/5/12	Salford (a)	D20-20	t:Pryce(3),Burgess g:Gale(2)	7th	6,121
27/5/12	Leeds (MW) ●●	L22-37	t:Whitehead,Jeffries,Diskin,Kear g:Gale(3)	9th	N/A
4/6/12	Castleford (h)	W46-32	t:Lulia,Kearney(2),Bateman,Elima,Ainscough(3) g:Gale(7)	8th	10,906
8/6/12	St Helens (a)	L54-0		8th	13,025
24/6/12	Wakefield (h)	W34-26	t:Whitehead,Lulia(2),Ainscough,Elima g:Gale(7)	9th	11,236
29/6/12	Wigan (a)	W22-30	t:Pryce(2),Kearney,Lulia,Whitehead g:Gale(5)	8th	19,628
8/7/12	London Broncos (h)	W44-12	t:Manuokafoa,Kearney(4),Gale,Whitehead,Platt g:Gale(6)	6th	10,132
20/7/12	Leeds (a)	L34-16	t:Whitehead,Elima,Pryce g:Gale(2)	7th	18,520
29/7/12	Warrington (a)	L50-22	t:Addy(2),Whitehead,Pryce g:Gale(3)	9th	10,750
5/8/12	Widnes (h)	W38-26	t:Platt(2),Kearney,Ainscough(2),Jeffries,L'Estrange g:Gale(5)	9th	10,261
10/8/12	Hull KR (a)	W32-26	t:Langley(2),Ainscough,Crookes,Whitehead g:Gale(6)	9th	10,217
19/8/12	Huddersfield (a)	W12-34	t:Ainscough,Diskin,Gale,Kearney,Pryce(2) g:Gale(5)	8th	7,477
1/9/12	Hull FC (h)	L6-70	t:Crookes g:Gale	9th	10,616
8/9/12	Catalan Dragons (a)	L50-26	t:Platt,Sammut(4) g:Gale(3)	9th	9,284

● Played at Brisbane Road, Leyton
●● Played at Etihad Stadium, Manchester

	APP		TRIES		GOALS		FG		PTS	
	D.O.B.	ALL	SL	ALL	SL	ALL	SL	ALL	SL	ALL	SL
Danny Addy	15/1/91	4(11)	3(10)	2	2	12	2	0	0	32	12
Shaun Ainscough	27/11/89	18	16	11	8	0	0	0	0	44	32
John Bateman	30/9/93	14(3)	13(2)	3	2	0	0	0	0	12	8
Tom Burgess	21/4/92	(26)	(24)	2	2	0	0	0	0	8	8
Jason Crookes	21/4/90	13	13	7	7	0	0	0	0	28	28
Matt Diskin	27/1/82	17(4)	15(4)	6	4	0	0	0	0	24	16
James Donaldson	14/9/91	(2)	(2)	0	0	0	0	0	0	0	0
Olivier Elima	19/5/83	14(3)	12(3)	4	3	0	0	0	0	16	12
Luke Gale	22/6/88	19	18	2	2	67	65	1	1	143	139
Bryn Hargreaves	14/11/85	28	26	1	1	0	0	0	0	4	4
Ben Jeffries	4/9/80	21	19	5	4	0	0	0	0	20	16
Phil Joseph	10/1/85	(6)	(6)	0	0	0	0	0	0	0	0
Elliot Kear	29/11/88	9	9	2	2	0	0	0	0	8	8
Brett Kearney	29/9/83	22	22	15	15	0	0	0	0	60	60
Craig Kopczak	20/12/86	13(4)	12(3)	2	1	0	0	0	0	8	4
Jamie Langley	21/12/83	25	23	4	4	0	0	0	0	16	16
Heath L'Estrange	21/5/85	12(15)	12(14)	1	1	0	0	0	0	4	4
Keith Lulia	17/6/87	27	25	11	8	0	0	0	0	44	32
Manase Manuokafoa	24/3/85	14(11)	13(10)	2	2	0	0	0	0	8	8
Adam O'Brien	11/7/93	(3)	(3)	0	0	0	0	0	0	0	0
Tom Olbison	20/3/91	8(6)	7(6)	0	0	0	0	0	0	0	0
Michael Platt	23/3/84	18	17	11	11	0	0	0	0	44	44
Karl Pryce	27/7/86	20	19	13	13	0	0	0	0	52	52
Adrian Purtell	31/1/85	10	8	2	1	0	0	0	0	8	4
Jarrod Sammut	15/2/87	14(1)	14(1)	6	6	25	25	0	0	74	74
Nick Scruton	24/12/84	(7)	(7)	0	0	0	0	0	0	0	0
Ian Sibbit	15/10/80	2(2)	2(2)	0	0	0	0	0	0	0	0
Paul Sykes	11/8/81	2	2	0	0	2	2	0	0	4	4
Chev Walker	9/10/82	6(10)	6(10)	0	0	0	0	0	0	0	0
Elliott Whitehead	4/9/89	27(1)	25(1)	15	12	0	0	0	0	60	48
Callum Windley	26/1/91	(1)	0	0	0	0	0	0	0	0	0

Elliott Whitehead

LEAGUE RECORD
P27-W14-D1-L12
(9th, SL)
F633, A756, Diff-123
23 points. *(6 points deducted for entering administration)*

CHALLENGE CUP
Round Five

ATTENDANCES
Best - v Leeds (SL - 20,851)
Worst - v Doncaster (CC - 3,210)
Total (SL only) - 152,817
Average (SL only) - 11,755
(Down by 2,212 on 2011)

185

10 November 2011 - Canterbury Bulldogs prop Grant Millington signs two-year contract; Warrington back-rower Lee Mitchell joins on 12-month loan.

15 December 2011 - Richie Mathers joins Wakefield on season-long loan.

26 December 2011 - 28-18 victory over Bradford in home Boxing Day friendly.

3 January 2012 - Ryan Shaw joins on one-month's loan from Warrington.

4 January 2012 - Richard Owen 'sanctioned' for undisclosed breach of club discipline.

5 January 2012 - Ryan Brierley joins Leigh Centurions on dual-contract.

13 January 2012 - 32-22 home friendly win over Huddersfield.

23 January 2012 - Australian centre or back row forward James Grehan signs one-year contract from French club Limoux.

4 February 2012 - Richard Owen scores two tries in 24-10, round-one win at snowbound Salford.

12 February 2012 - 20-12 round-two defeat at home to Bradford in wintry conditions.

18 February 2012 - Josh Griffin scores hat-trick in 28-20 defeat to Catalans in Perpignan.

20 February 2012 - Ian Millward on compassionate leave following the sudden death of teenage son. Assistant Stuart Donlan takes temporary charge.

26 February 2012 - 46-4 home defeat by Wigan.

2 March 2012 - Grant Millington makes debut in 36-14 home defeat to Leeds. Brett Ferres gets one-match ban for dangerous contact.

12 March 2012 - coach Ian Millward returns to work.

16 March 2012 - 42-4 televised defeat at Huddersfield.

19 March 2012 - 42-16 round-six defeat at London Broncos.

25 March 2012 - 42-28 round-8, home defeat by Hull FC is seventh on a row.

30 March 2012 - Jonathan Walker signs new two-year contract extension to end of 2014.

30 March 2012 - last-minute Nick Youngquest try secures 34-30 home win over Hull KR.

6 April 2012 - 34-16 Good Friday win at Wakefield.

9 April 2012 - injury-hit side falls 18-12 at home to St Helens.

12 April 2012 - Jake Emmitt signs new two-year contract to end of 2014.

KEY DATES - CASTLEFORD TIGERS

14 April 2012 - Craig Huby returns and Rangi Chase gets three-match ban for breaking Tangi Ropati's jaw in shock 23-16 Cup defeat at Featherstone.

22 April 2012 - 54-6 round-11 defeat at Warrington.

25 April 2012 - James Grehan goes on loan to Batley.

7 May 2012 - 36-12 win over Widnes, Ryan McGoldrick gets two-match ban for leading with forearm.

22 May 2012 - Tigers players apologise after 70-12 defeat at Hull KR.

23 May 2012 - Warrington winger Rhys Williams joins on month's loan.

26 May 2012 - 32-26 Magic Weekend defeat by Wakefield.

29 May 2012 - Joe Arundel to leave for Hull FC at end of season.

6 June 2012 - Michael Shenton to rejoin club on four-year contract from 2013.

10 June 2012 - last-minute Craig Huby try claims 34-30 home win over Salford.

23 June 2012 - transfer request by Daryl Clark rejected.

24 June 2012 - Rangi Chase suspended on full pay while club investigates disciplinary matter and absent for 40-22 defeat at Leeds.

25 June 2012 - young front-rower Daniel Fleming joins Batley on dual contract.

26 June 2012 - Hull KR centre Jake Webster, three years, and Hull FC halfback Jamie Ellis, two, sign for 2013. Nick Youngquest to retire at end of season.

28 June 2012 - Huddersfield's Lee Gilmour signs two-year deal from 2013.

2 July 2012 - 40-10 televised defeat at Widnes.

3 July 2012 - Ryan McGoldrick granted request to leave with immediate effect.

4 July 2012 - Jamie Ellis joins from Hull FC.

5 July 2012 - Jordan Tansey signs one-year deal for 2013.

7 July 2012 - chief executive Richard Wright leaves with immediate effect.

8 July 2012 - Steve Ferres appointed chief executive.

8 July 2012 - Jamie Ellis kicks 10 goals and scores a try on debut in 52-6 home win over Huddersfield.

11 July 2012 - Rangi Chase suspension lifted and he apologises.

18 July 2012 - Ryan Hudson to retire at end of season.

19 July 2012 - Hull FC make unsuccessful bid to sign Rangi Chase.

20 July 2012 - Brett Ferres joins Huddersfield with immediate effect.

26 July 2012 - Danny Orr to retire at end of season.

2 August 2012 - Stuart Jones to step down from full-time rugby at end of season.

5 August 2012 - 40-12 home defeat to Wakefield is fifth defeat in six games.

9 August 2012 - Sydney Roosters winger Justin Carney signs two-year deal from 2013.

12 August 2012 - Ben Johnston makes debut in 42-20 home defeat by London. Jamie Ellis suspended for one game for dangerous throw. Tigers fall to 13th spot.

29 August 2012 - Josh Griffin leaves to play rugby union at Leeds.

31 August 2012 - Steve Snitch released and joins Australian club Northern Pride.

8 September 2012 - 36-10 defeat at Hull means 13th-placed finish.

13 September 2012 - Weller Hauraki signs from Leeds on two-year contract.

11 October 2012 - Ben Johnston signs new two-year contract.

24 October 2012 - Rangi Chase to stay in 2013 after move to St George Illawarra breaks down.

CLUB RECORDS

Highest score:
106-0 v Rochdale, 9/9/2007
Highest score against:
12-76 v Leeds, 14/8/2009
Record attendance:
25,449 v Hunslet, 9/3/35

MATCH RECORDS

Tries:
5 Derek Foster v Hunslet, 10/11/72
John Joyner v Millom, 16/9/73
Steve Fenton v Dewsbury, 27/1/78
Ian French v Hunslet, 9/2/86
St John Ellis v Whitehaven, 10/12/89
Goals: 17 Sammy Lloyd v Millom, 16/9/73
Points: 43 Sammy Lloyd v Millom, 16/9/73

SEASON RECORDS

Tries: 40 St John Ellis 1993-94
Goals: 158 Sammy Lloyd 1976-77
Points: 334 Bob Beardmore 1983-84

CAREER RECORDS

Tries: 206 Alan Hardisty 1958-71
Goals: 875 Albert Lunn 1951-63
Points: 1,870 Albert Lunn 1951-63
Appearances: 613 John Joyner 1973-92

CASTLEFORD TIGERS

DATE	FIXTURE	RESULT	SCORERS	LGE	ATT
4/2/12	Salford (a)	W10-24	t:Owen(2),Griffin,Milner g:Dixon(4)	4th	5,242
12/2/12	Bradford (h)	L12-20	t:Griffin,Owen g:Dixon(2)	7th	8,050
18/2/12	Catalan Dragons (a)	L28-20	t:Griffin(3),Arundel g:Dixon(2)	10th	7,488
26/2/12	Wigan (h)	L4-46	t:Griffin	12th	8,156
2/3/12	Leeds (h)	L14-36	t:Clark,Dixon,Griffin g:Dixon	12th	9,237
10/3/12	London Broncos (a)	L42-16	t:Youngquest,Dixon,McGoldrick g:Dixon(2)	13th	2,381
16/3/12	Huddersfield (a)	L42-4	t:Youngquest	13th	6,928
25/3/12	Hull FC (h)	L28-42	t:Youngquest,Walker,Millington,Griffin,Ferres g:Dixon(4)	14th	9,050
30/3/12	Hull KR (h)	W34-30	t:Griffin,Youngquest(2),Owen,Dixon,Snitch g:Dixon(5)	13th	6,396
6/4/12	Wakefield (a)	W16-34	t:Owen(2),Millington,Snitch,Ferres,Holmes g:Dixon(5)	11th	9,786
9/4/12	St Helens (h)	L12-18	t:Ferres(2) g:Dixon(2)	11th	6,492
14/4/12	Featherstone (a) (CCR4)	L23-16	t:Clark,Griffin,Youngquest g:Dixon,Orr	N/A	4,165
22/4/12	Warrington (a)	L54-6	t:Mitchell g:Orr	12th	10,519
7/5/12	Widnes (h)	W36-12	t:Ferres,Clark(2),Thompson,Youngquest(3) g:Orr(2),Huby,Griffin	11th	5,580
20/5/12	Hull KR (a)	L70-12	t:Thompson,Griffin g:Dixon(2)	11th	7,312
26/5/12	Wakefield (MW) ●	L26-32	t:Thompson,Jones,Youngquest,Holmes,Orr g:Dixon(2),Orr	12th	N/A
4/6/12	Bradford (a)	L46-32	t:Thompson,Chase(2),Massey,Williams(2) g:Dixon(4)	12th	10,906
10/6/12	Salford (h)	W34-30	t:Youngquest,Orr(3),Thompson,Huby g:Dixon(3),Huby,Orr	12th	5,877
24/6/12	Leeds (a)	L40-22	t:Jackson,Huby,Ferres(2) g:Orr,Huby,McGoldrick	12th	16,153
2/7/12	Widnes (a)	L40-10	t:Youngquest,Jones g:Huby	12th	4,501
8/7/12	Huddersfield (h)	W52-6	t:Clare,Thompson,Youngquest,Owen(2),Griffin,Milner,Ellis g:Ellis(10)	12th	5,012
22/7/12	Warrington (h)	L26-40	t:Youngquest(2),Williams,Owen,Mitchell g:Ellis,Orr(2)	12th	6,167
27/7/12	Wigan (a)	L40-16	t:Williams,Holmes,Jones g:Youngquest(2)	12th	13,975
5/8/12	Wakefield (h)	L12-40	t:Jackson,Youngquest g:Orr(2)	12th	7,050
12/8/12	London Broncos (h)	L20-42	t:Milner,Orr,Griffin(2) g:Ellis(2)	12th	5,149
17/8/12	St Helens (a)	L44-12	t:Jackson,Millington g:Orr(2)	13th	12,224
2/9/12	Catalan Dragons (h)	L26-46	t:Hudson,Jones,Youngquest,Millington,Owen g:Orr(3)	13th	5,005
8/9/12	Hull FC (a)	L36-10	t:Thompson,Holmes g:Orr	13th	11,607

● Played at Etihad Stadium, Manchester

		APP		TRIES		GOALS		FG		PTS	
	D.O.B.	ALL	SL	ALL	SL	ALL	SL	ALL	SL	ALL	SL
Joe Arundel	22/8/91	4	4	1	1	0	0	0	0	4	4
Josh Atkinson	4/10/91	2	2	0	0	0	0	0	0	0	0
Ben Blackmore	19/2/93	1	1	0	0	0	0	0	0	0	0
Rangi Chase	11/4/86	17	16	2	2	0	0	0	0	8	8
James Clare	13/4/91	3	3	1	1	0	0	0	0	4	4
Daryl Clark	10/2/93	5(10)	4(10)	4	3	0	0	0	0	16	12
John Davies	8/1/91	1	1	0	0	0	0	0	0	0	0
Kirk Dixon	19/7/84	17	16	3	3	39	38	0	0	90	88
Jamie Ellis	4/10/89	4(1)	4(1)	1	1	13	13	0	0	30	30
Jake Emmitt	4/10/88	16(9)	15(9)	0	0	0	0	0	0	0	0
Brett Ferres	17/4/86	16(2)	15(2)	7	7	0	0	0	0	28	28
James Grehan	17/3/87	2(2)	2(2)	0	0	0	0	0	0	0	0
Josh Griffin	9/5/90	21	20	14	13	1	1	0	0	58	54
Oliver Holmes	7/8/92	18(5)	17(5)	4	4	0	0	0	0	16	16
Craig Huby	21/5/86	15(2)	15(1)	2	2	4	4	0	0	16	16
Ryan Hudson	20/11/79	9(3)	9(3)	1	1	0	0	0	0	4	4
Paul Jackson	29/9/78	6(2)	6(2)	3	3	0	0	0	0	12	12
Ben Johnston	8/3/92	2	2	0	0	0	0	0	0	0	0
Stuart Jones	7/12/81	15(11)	15(10)	4	4	0	0	0	0	16	16
Nathan Massey	11/7/89	11(16)	10(16)	1	1	0	0	0	0	4	4
Ryan McGoldrick	12/1/81	13(5)	13(4)	1	1	1	1	0	0	6	6
Grant Millington	1/11/86	16(7)	16(6)	4	4	0	0	0	0	16	16
Adam Milner	19/12/91	17(4)	17(4)	3	3	0	0	0	0	12	12
Lee Mitchell	8/9/88	13(10)	13(10)	2	2	0	0	0	0	8	8
Stephen Nash	14/1/86	3(4)	3(4)	0	0	0	0	0	0	0	0
Danny Orr	17/5/78	22(3)	21(3)	5	5	17	16	0	0	54	52
Richard Owen	25/4/90	24	23	10	10	0	0	0	0	40	40
Steve Snitch	22/2/83	12(8)	11(8)	2	2	0	0	0	0	8	8
Jordan Thompson	4/9/91	16(1)	16(1)	7	7	0	0	0	0	28	28
Jonathan Walker	20/2/91	11(7)	10(7)	1	1	0	0	0	0	4	4
Rhys Williams	8/12/89	8	8	4	4	0	0	0	0	16	16
Nick Youngquest	28/7/83	24	23	17	16	2	2	0	0	72	68

Nick Youngquest

LEAGUE RECORD
P27-W6-D0-L21
(13th, SL)
F554, A948, Diff-394
12 points.

CHALLENGE CUP
Round Four

ATTENDANCES
Best - v Leeds (SL - 9,237)
Worst - v Catalan Dragons
(SL - 5,005)
Total (SL only) - 87,221
Average (SL only) - 6,709
(Down by 447 on 2011)

14 January 2012 - Leon Pryce stars in 46-10 home friendly victory over Wakefield.

21 January 2012 - Clint Greenshields scores hat-trick in 44-22 friendly win over London Broncos in Perpignan. Cyril Stacul breaks ankle; Frederic Vaccari suffers knee ligament damage.

21 January 2012 - Eloi Pelissier breaks jaw in reserve team game.

27 January 2012 - Ben Fisher signed on two-month deal to cover for Greg Mounis, who suffered knee injury in London win.

5 February 2012 - 34-12 win at Bradford in round one.

11 February 2012 - Leon Pryce's debut delayed when home game with Hull FC is called off at last minute because of frozen pitch.

18 February 2012 - Leon Pryce makes debut in 28-20 home win over Castleford.

24 February 2012 - Daryl Millard try and Scott Dureau touchline conversion after the hooter snatches 34-32 win at St Helens.

4 March 2012 - 36-12 defeat at Wigan ends winning start. Setaimata Sa banned for two matches for dangerous contact. Ian Henderson injures ankle and Louis Anderson picks up hamstring problem.

10 March 2012 - 17-man squad featuring 11 French players records 40-18 home win over Salford.

17 March 2012 - second-half comeback secures 20-12 home win over Hull KR.

22 March 2012 - Clint Greenshields announces he will return to Australia at end of season.

25 March 2012 - 32-22 defeat at Wakefield in round 8.

5 April 2012 - 36-18 win at London in round 10.

9 April 2012 - 44-16 home win over Warrington on Easter Monday.

15 April 2012 - 20-18 round four Challenge Cup win at Hull KR.

20 April 2012 - 34-18 defeat at Leeds ends four-match winning run.

27 April 2012 - Clint Greenshields fined and suspended for three days by club for describing referee Ben Thaler as 'a retard' on Twitter.

28 April 2012 - 68-6 home win over Sheffield Eagles in Challenge Cup round five.

2 May 2012 - Clint Greenshields fined £1,000 by RFL for Twitter comments, half suspended.

KEY DATES - CATALAN DRAGONS

2 May 2012 - Setaimata Sa to leave for rugby union at end of season.

3 May 2012 - Scott Dureau signs three-year contract extension to end of 2015.

16 May 2012 - Newcastle back-rower/centre Zeb Taia signs three-year deal from 2013.

24 May 2012 - Jason Baitieri signs new three-year contract to end of 2015.

22 June 2012 - William Barthau signs new one-year contract to end of 2013 season.

28 June 2012 - Daryl Millard signs new two-year contract to end of 2014 season.

5 July 2012 - Mathias Pala signs new one-year deal.

6 July 2012 - Lopini Paea signs new two-year contract to end of 2014.

21 July 2012 - 20-15 home defeat by St Helens.

28 July 2012 - Jean-Philippe Baile out for season after suffering ruptured bicep in 19-12 home win over London Broncos.

8 August 2012 - Sebastien Raguin to take up two-year contract as football manager at end of season.

12 August 2012 - 30-10 defeat at Hull FC sees Dragons drop out of top four.

17 August 2012 - Trent Robinson fined £500 for comments made to match official Thierry Alibert at half-time of 36-18 round 23 defeat at Huddersfield.

18 August 2012 - Leon Pryce suffers knee injury as 38-34 home defeat of Leeds sees Dragons leapfrog the Rhinos into fourth.

2 September 2012 - 46-26 round 26 win at Castleford.

4 September 2012 - Leeds Rhinos fullback Brent Webb signs for 2013 on two-year deal.

6 September 2012 - France captain Olivier Elima re-joins from Bradford on two-year deal.

7 September 2012 - Trent Robinson to take over as Sydney Roosters head coach at end of season.

10 September 2012 - David Ferriol to retire at end of season.

11 September 2012 - Scott Dureau collects Albert Goldthorpe Medal at glittering ceremony at Langtree Park.

12 September 2012 - Damien Blanch signs new two-year contract to end of 2014.

14 September 2012 - 46-6 qualifying play-off defeat at Wigan.

18 September 2012 - Steve Menzies signs new one-year contract for 2013.

21 September 2012 - 27-20 Preliminary semi-final home defeat to Leeds means play-off exit.

3 October 2012 - assistant Laurent Frayssinous appointed new head coach.

13 October 2012 - Eloi Pelissier signs new two-year contract.

19 October 2012 - Vincent Duport signs new four-year contract to end of 2016 season.

7 November 2012 - Former GB boss David Waite appointed assistant coach.

CLUB RECORDS

Highest score: 76-6 v Widnes, 31/3/2012
Highest score against:
12-60 v Leeds, 15/9/2006
Record attendance: 18,150 v Warrington, 20/6/2009 *(Barcelona)*
11,500 v Warrington, 9/4/2012
(Stade Gilbert Brutus)

MATCH RECORDS

Tries:
4 Justin Murphy v Warrington, 13/9/2008
Damien Cardace v Widnes, 31/3/2012
Goals:
11 Thomas Bosc v Featherstone, 31/3/2007
Thomas Bosc v Batley, 29/5/2010
Scott Dureau v Widnes, 31/3/2012
Points:
26 Thomas Bosc v Featherstone, 31/3/2007

SEASON RECORDS

Tries: 27 Justin Murphy 2006
Goals: 134 Scott Dureau 2012
Points: 319 Scott Dureau 2012

CAREER RECORDS

Tries: 86 Clint Greenshields 2007-2012
Goals:
355 *(inc 6fg)* Thomas Bosc 2006-2012
Points: 882 Thomas Bosc 2006-2012
Appearances:
186 Gregory Mounis 2006-2012

CATALAN DRAGONS

DATE	FIXTURE	RESULT	SCORERS	LGE	ATT
5/2/12	Bradford (a)	W12-34	t:Baitieri,Greenshields,Bosc,Sa,Millard,Raguin g:Dureau(5)	1st	10,610
18/2/12	Castleford (h)	W28-20	t:Bosc,Duport,Millard(2),Baitieri g:Dureau(4)	5th	7,488
24/2/12	St Helens (a)	W32-34	t:Casty,Blanch,Duport,Dureau,Sa,Millard g:Dureau(5)	4th	13,108
4/3/12	Wigan (a)	L36-12	t:Dureau,Mounis g:Dureau(2)	6th	14,464
10/3/12	Salford (h)	W40-18	t:Blanch(2),Dureau,Bosc,Pryce,Duport(2),Millard g:Dureau(4)	5th	8,158
17/3/12	Hull KR (h)	W20-12	t:Paea,Blanch,Bosc g:Dureau(4)	5th	7,133
25/3/12	Wakefield (a)	L32-22	t:Mounis,Dureau,Duport,Greenshields g:Dureau(3)	6th	7,254
31/3/12	Widnes (h)	W76-6	t:Greenshields(3),Casty,Sa,Cardace(4),Anderson,Blanch,Millard, Duport g:Dureau(11),Millard	5th	9,156
5/4/12	London Broncos (a)	W18-36	t:Anderson(2),Duport(2),Menzies,Dureau,Pryce g:Dureau(4)	5th	1,829
9/4/12	Warrington (h)	W44-16	t:Paea,Bosc,Menzies(2),Anderson,Sa(2),Millard g:Dureau(5),Bosc	3rd	11,500
15/4/12	Hull KR (a) (CCR4)	W18-20	t:Pryce(2),Henderson g:Dureau(4)	N/A	4,425
20/4/12	Leeds (a)	L34-18	t:Anderson,Menzies,Pryce g:Dureau(3)	4th	13,282
28/4/12	Sheffield (h) (CCR5)	W68-6	t:Cardace(3),Duport,Pryce(2),Bosc(2),Menzies,Pellissier(2),Stacul g:Dureau(10)	N/A	3,102
5/5/12	Huddersfield (h)	W27-20	t:Cardace,Greenshields,Pryce,Casty,Duport g:Dureau,Bosc(2) fg:Bosc	4th	10,624
13/5/12	Warrington (h) (CCQF)	L22-32	t:Paea,Simon,Fisher,Duport g:Dureau(3)	N/A	7,476
20/5/12	Widnes (a)	W34-42	t:Greenshields,Pryce,Duport,Anderson(2),Paea,Bosc,Dureau g:Dureau(5)	4th	4,684
27/5/12	London Broncos (MW) ●	W42-18	t:Paea,Pryce(2),Casty(2),Menzies,Fakir g:Dureau(7)	3rd	N/A
1/6/12	Salford (a)	L34-30	t:Millard,Dureau,Stacul,Paea,Casty,Duport g:Dureau(3)	3rd	4,220
9/6/12	Wigan (h) ●●	L14-36	t:Greenshields,Dureau g:Dureau(3)	3rd	13,858
22/6/12	Hull KR (a)	W10-13	t:Sa,Greenshields g:Dureau(2) fg:Dureau	3rd	7,142
30/6/12	Wakefield (h)	W34-10	t:Blanch(3),Menzies(2),Greenshields g:Dureau(5)	3rd	8,842
9/7/12	Warrington (a)	L15-6	t:Baitieri g:Dureau	4th	10,570
14/7/12	Hull FC (h)	W44-14	t:Pryce,Dureau(2),Millard(2),Blanch,Greenshields(2) g:Dureau(6)	3rd	7,388
20/7/12	St Helens (h)	L15-20	t:Duport,Raguin g:Dureau(3) fg:Dureau	4th	10,387
28/7/12	London Broncos (h)	W19-12	t:Baitieri,Fisher,Millard g:Dureau(3) fg:Dureau	4th	7,673
5/8/12	Huddersfield (a)	L36-18	t:Casty,Millard,Blanch g:Dureau(3)	4th	5,822
12/8/12	Hull FC (a)	L30-10	t:Duport(2) g:Dureau	5th	10,769
18/8/12	Leeds (h)	W38-34	t:Sa,Dureau,Casty(2),Duport,Millard g:Dureau(7)	4th	10,269
2/9/12	Castleford (a)	W26-46	t:Duport,Blanch(3),Sa,Greenshields(3) g:Dureau(7)	4th	5,005
8/9/12	Bradford (h)	W50-26	t:Greenshields(3),Duport,Sa,Anderson,Menzies,Millard,Dureau g:Dureau(7)	4th	9,284
14/9/12	Wigan (a) (QPO)	L46-6	t:Anderson g:Dureau	N/A	7,232
21/9/12	Leeds (h) (PSF)	L20-27	t:Greenshields,Blanch(2),Bosc g:Dureau(2)	N/A	8,156

● Played at Etihad Stadium, Manchester   ●● Played at Stade de la Mosson, Montpellier

		APP		TRIES		GOALS		FG		PTS	
	D.O.B.	ALL	SL	ALL	SL	ALL	SL	ALL	SL	ALL	SL
Louis Anderson	27/6/85	17(2)	15(2)	9	9	0	0	0	0	36	36
Jean-Philippe Baile	7/6/87	5(1)	5(1)	0	0	0	0	0	0	0	0
Jason Baitieri	2/7/89	30(1)	27(1)	4	4	0	0	0	0	16	16
William Barthau	30/1/90	(1)	(1)	0	0	0	0	0	0	0	0
Damien Blanch	24/5/83	21	21	15	15	0	0	0	0	60	60
Thomas Bosc	5/8/83	20	18	9	7	3	3	1	1	43	35
Julian Bousquet	18/7/91	(2)	(2)	0	0	0	0	0	0	0	0
Damien Cardace	16/10/92	12	9	8	5	0	0	0	0	32	20
Remi Casty	5/2/85	31(1)	29	9	9	0	0	0	0	36	36
Vincent Duport	15/12/87	32	29	19	17	0	0	0	0	76	68
Scott Dureau	29/7/86	32	29	12	12	134	117	3	3	319	285
Jamal Fakir	30/8/82	(28)	(25)	1	1	0	0	0	0	4	4
David Ferriol	24/4/79	13(9)	12(8)	0	0	0	0	0	0	0	0
Ben Fisher	4/2/81	9(6)	9(5)	2	1	0	0	0	0	8	4
Cyrille Gossard	7/2/82	1(3)	1(3)	0	0	0	0	0	0	0	0
Clint Greenshields	11/1/82	23	22	19	19	0	0	0	0	76	76
Ian Henderson	23/4/83	23(4)	20(4)	1	0	0	0	0	0	4	0
Kevin Larroyer	19/6/89	(2)	(2)	0	0	0	0	0	0	0	0
Antoni Maria	21/3/87	(1)	(1)	0	0	0	0	0	0	0	0
Steve Menzies	4/12/73	17(5)	15(4)	9	8	0	0	0	0	36	32
Daryl Millard	20/2/85	30	27	14	14	1	1	0	0	58	58
Gregory Mounis	18/1/85	2(20)	2(20)	2	2	0	0	0	0	8	8
Lopini Paea	19/4/84	24(2)	22(2)	6	5	0	0	0	0	24	20
Mathias Pala	14/6/89	5(1)	5(1)	0	0	0	0	0	0	0	0
Eloi Pelissier	18/6/91	(17)	(15)	2	0	0	0	0	0	8	0
Leon Pryce	9/10/81	26(2)	23(2)	12	8	0	0	0	0	48	32
Sebastien Raguin	14/2/79	13(11)	13(9)	2	2	0	0	0	0	8	8
Setaimata Sa	14/9/87	19(1)	17(1)	9	9	0	0	0	0	36	36
Michael Simon	2/4/87	3(8)	1(7)	1	0	0	0	0	0	4	0
Cyril Stacul	12/10/84	8	6	2	1	0	0	0	0	8	4

Clint Greenshields

LEAGUE RECORD
P27-W18-D0-L9
(4th, SL/Preliminary Semi-Final)
F812, A611, Diff+201
36 points.

CHALLENGE CUP
Quarter Finalists

ATTENDANCES
Best - v Wigan (SL - 13,858)
Worst - v Sheffield (CC - 3,102)
Total (SL, inc play-offs) - 129,916
Average (SL, inc play-offs) - 9,280
(Up by 893 on 2011)

12 November 2011 - Jamahl Lolesi confirms retirement and will remain on coaching staff.

21 November 2011 - Elliot Hodgson released from final year of contract by mutual consent.

16 December 2011 - Jamie Simpson released.

17 December 2011 - Paul Anderson announced as successor to Nathan Brown at end of 2012 season.

13 January 2012 - 32-22 friendly defeat at Castleford.

19 January 2012 - 30-18 friendly win at Wigan.

5 February 2012 - Larne Patrick stars in 20-16 round one win at Wigan.

12 February 2012 - Leroy Cudjoe scores four tries and Luke George a hat-trick in 66-6 home win over Widnes.

18 February 2012 - Eorl Crabtree makes 300th career appearance in end-to-end 32-22 home defeat by Warrington. Tommy Lee put on report and banned for two games for high tackle on Lee Briers.

26 February 2012 - Danny Brough stars and Leroy Cudjoe scores two tries in 30-16 win at London.

4 March 2012 - Danny Brough field goal is the difference in 17-16 home win over St Helens as Luke George scores second hat-trick.

11 March 2012 - 32-14 win at Wakefield moves Giants to top of Super League.

16 March 2012 - Luke George scores third home hat-trick in 42-4 win over Castleford.

19 March 2012 - club rules out Nathan Brown succeeding sacked St Helens coach Royce Simmons.

25 March 2012 - 40-22 defeat at Hull KR.

30 March 2012 - Luke O'Donnell plays first game of season in 22-12, round 9 win at Leeds.

3 April 2012 - St Helens appoint Nathan Brown as new head coach.

5 April 2012 - Larne Patrick signs new contract to end of 2016.

9 April 2012 - 22-4 Easter Monday home win over second-placed Hull FC maintains top spot.

15 April 2012 - 42-16 win at Hull FC secures passage into Challenge Cup fifth round.

17 April 2012 - Scott Moore signs to end of season less than a week after being sacked by Widnes.

18 April 2012 - Shaun Lunt joins Leeds Rhinos on loan for rest of the season.

18 April 2012 - Jacob Fairbank signs three-year contract extension to end of 2015 season.

22 April 2012 - round 12, 20-6 win at Bradford.

29 April 2012 - 52-0 home win over Swinton in Challenge Cup round five.

13 May 2012 - 50-14 home Challenge Cup quarter-final win over London.

KEY DATES - HUDDERSFIELD GIANTS

18 May 2012 - 32-12 home defeat by Wigan.

26 May 2012 - Kevin Brown to leave for Widnes at end of season.

29 May 2012 - Greg Eden signs new contract to end of 2015 season.

29 May 2012 - Kevin Brown gets one-match ban after early guilty plea for high tackle in 38-34 Magic Weekend defeat to Salford.

3 June 2012 - 26-22 defeat at Widnes.

11 June 2012 - 44-26 televised Monday night home defeat by Hull KR.

24 June 2012 - 46-10 home win over London ends five-match losing run.

25 June 2012 - former assistant coach Kieron Purtill to rejoin club in November.

28 June 2012 - Lee Gilmour to leave for Castleford at end of season.

1 July 2012 - last-minute 28-24 defeat at Hull FC.

8 July 2012 - 52-6 defeat at Castleford sinks Giants into seventh spot.

10 July 2012 - Tony Tonks released.

12 July 2012 - Luke O'Donnell suffers training injury.

15 July 2012 - 33-6 defeat by Warrington in semi-final of Challenge Cup.

16 July 2012 - Nathan Brown sacked, Paul Anderson steps up to head coach with immediate effect.

20 July 2012 - Brett Ferres joins immediately from Castleford on three-and-a-half-year deal.

22 July 2012 - 35-14 home defeat by Wakefield in Paul Anderson's first game in charge.

25 July 2012 - Kieron Purtill joins as assistant coach with immediate effect.

27 July 2012 - Kevin Brown ruled out for season with ankle injury.

29 July 2012 - Brett Ferres makes debut in 46-12 defeat at St Helens.

31 July 2012 - assistant coach Jamahl Lolesi leaves the club.

2 August 2012 - 21-year-old prop Anthony Mullally joins from Widnes on three-year deal.

5 August 2012 - 36-18 win over high-flying Catalans.

10 August 2012 - 30-20 win at Salford.

17 August 2012 - 34-12 home defeat by Bradford.

2 September 2012 - Matt Dawson makes debut in 54-6 hammering at Warrington.

9 September 2012 - Luke O'Donnell returns from injury and is sent off after 12 minutes for a tackle on Ian Kirke. Giants go on to win 48-24. O'Donnell is cleared of wrongdoing by RFL.

11 September 2012 - 25-year-old Tongan International forward Ukuma Ta'ai signs from NZ Warriors on three-year contract.

16 September 2012 - 46-10 elimination play-off defeat at Hull FC.

19 September 2012 - David Fa'alogo, Adam Walker, Scott Moore and Tommy Lee released.

21 September 2012 - Tommy Lee joins London Broncos.

12 October 2012 - Stuart Fielden, released by Wigan, joins on two-year contract.

16 October 2012 - Shaun Lunt returns from loan after starring in Leeds' Grand Final win.

25 October 2012 - Wales captain Craig Kopczak signs three-year deal.

CLUB RECORDS

Highest score:
142-4 v Blackpool G, 26/11/94
Highest score against:
12-94 v Castleford, 18/9/88
Record attendance:
32,912 v Wigan, 4/3/50 *(Fartown)*
15,629 v Leeds, 10/2/2008
(McAlpine/Galpharm/John Smiths Stadium)

MATCH RECORDS

Tries:
10 Lionel Cooper v Keighley, 17/11/51
Goals:
18 Major Holland v Swinton Park, 28/2/14
Points:
39 Major Holland v Swinton Park, 28/2/14

SEASON RECORDS

Tries: 80 Albert Rosenfeld 1913-14
Goals: 147 Ben Gronow 1919-20
Points: 332 Pat Devery 1952-53

CAREER RECORDS

Tries: 420 Lionel Cooper 1947-55
Goals: 958 Frank Dyson 1949-63
Points: 2,072 Frank Dyson 1949-63
Appearances: 485 Douglas Clark 1909-29

HUDDERSFIELD GIANTS

DATE	FIXTURE	RESULT	SCORERS	LGE	ATT
5/2/12	Wigan (a)	W16-20	t:Gilmour,Patrick(2) g:Brough(4)	6th	16,771
12/2/12	Widnes (h)	W66-6	t:Robinson,Cudjoe(4),Grix,George(3),Chan,Wardle,Eden g:Brough(9)	1st	8,869
18/2/12	Warrington (h)	L22-32	t:Brough,Crabtree,Chan,Eden g:Brough(3)	3rd	8,184
26/2/12	London Broncos (a)	W16-30	t:Brough,Cudjoe(2),Brown,Wardle g:Brough(5)	3rd	1,970
4/3/12	St Helens (h)	W17-16	t:George(3) g:Brough(2) fg:Brough	3rd	9,194
11/3/12	Wakefield (a)	W14-32	t:McGillvary(2),Patrick,Wardle(2),Brown g:Brough(4)	1st	8,794
16/3/12	Castleford (h)	W42-4	t:George(3),Eden,Wardle,Patrick,Brown,Lawrence g:Brough(5)	1st	6,928
25/3/12	Hull KR (a)	L40-22	t:George,Grix,Eden,Lunt g:Brough(3)	2nd	7,616
30/3/12	Leeds (a)	W12-22	t:Crabtree,Chan,Eden,McGillvary g:Brough(3)	1st	15,408
6/4/12	Salford (h)	W36-10	t:McGillvary,Lawrence,Lee(2),Lunt,Eden g:Brough(6)	1st	6,988
9/4/12	Hull FC (h)	W22-4	t:Crabtree,Robinson,Wardle g:Brough(5)	1st	9,950
15/4/12	Hull FC (a) (CCR4)	W16-42	t:George(2),Eden,Cudjoe(2),Wardle,Robinson,Chan g:Brough(5)	N/A	8,327
22/4/12	Bradford (a)	W6-20	t:McGillvary,George,Brough g:Brough(4)	1st	11,182
29/4/12	Swinton (h) (CCR5)	W52-0	t:Brough,Faiumu,Gilmour,Eden(2),Chan,Grix,Cording(2) g:Brough(8)	N/A	2,617
5/5/12	Catalan Dragons (a)	L27-20	t:Robinson,Ferguson,Grix,Wardle g:Brough(2)	2nd	10,624
13/5/12	London Broncos (h) (CCQF)	W50-14	t:Murphy(2),Eden(2),Patrick,Robinson(2),McGillvary,Ferguson g:Brough(5),Grix(2)	N/A	2,574
18/5/12	Wigan (h)	L12-32	t:McGillvary,Eden g:Brough(2)	3rd	10,123
27/5/12	Salford (MW) ●	L34-38	t:Brown,Brough(2),Lawrence,Crabtree(2) g:Brough(5)	4th	N/A
3/6/12	Widnes (a)	L26-22	t:Ferguson,Fa'alogo,Grix g:Brough(5)	4th	4,644
11/6/12	Hull KR (h)	L26-44	t:Cudjoe,Crabtree,Murphy(2),Patrick g:Brough(3)	5th	4,962
24/6/12	London Broncos (h)	W46-10	t:George,Brown,Murphy,Lawrence,Grix,Crabtree(2),Patrick g:Brough(7)	5th	6,019
1/7/12	Hull FC (a)	L28-24	t:Cudjoe,Faiumu,Murphy,Crabtree g:Brough(4)	5th	11,142
8/7/12	Castleford (a)	L52-6	t:Cudjoe g:Brough	7th	5,012
15/7/12	Warrington (CCSF) ●●	L6-33	t:Moore g:Brough	N/A	9,473
22/7/12	Wakefield (h)	L14-35	t:George(2),Crabtree g:Brough	8th	6,579
29/7/12	St Helens (a)	L46-12	t:Mason,Grix g:Brough(2)	7th	14,070
5/8/12	Catalan Dragons (h)	W36-18	t:McGillvary(2),Grix,Murphy,Fa'alogo,Gilmour g:Brough(6)	7th	5,822
10/8/12	Salford (a)	W20-30	t:McGillvary,Lee,Eden,Chan,Lawrence g:Grix(5)	7th	3,615
19/8/12	Bradford (h)	L12-34	t:Wardle,Cudjoe g:Brough(2)	7th	7,477
2/9/12	Warrington (a)	L54-6	t:Grix g:Grix	7th	10,515
9/9/12	Leeds (h)	W48-24	t:Cudjoe(2),George,Lawrence,Brough,Robinson(2),Grix g:Brough(8)	7th	9,128
16/9/12	Hull FC (a) (EPO)	L46-10	t:Crabtree,Grix g:Grix	N/A	8,662

● Played at Etihad Stadium, Manchester
●● Played at City of Salford Community Stadium

		APP		TRIES		GOALS		FG		PTS	
	D.O.B.	ALL	SL	ALL	SL	ALL	SL	ALL	SL	ALL	SL
Danny Brough	15/1/83	30	26	7	6	120	101	1	1	269	227
Kevin Brown	2/10/84	20	17	5	5	0	0	0	0	20	20
Jason Chan	26/1/84	23(8)	20(8)	6	4	0	0	0	0	24	16
Jamie Cording	30/12/89	(5)	(4)	2	0	0	0	0	0	8	0
Eorl Crabtree	2/10/82	27(3)	24(3)	11	11	0	0	0	0	44	44
Leroy Cudjoe	7/4/88	32	28	14	12	0	0	0	0	56	48
Matty Dawson	2/10/90	1	1	0	0	0	0	0	0	0	0
Greg Eden	14/11/90	27	24	13	8	0	0	0	0	52	32
David Fa'alogo	4/9/80	10(10)	9(9)	2	2	0	0	0	0	8	8
Jacob Fairbank	4/3/90	5(2)	5(1)	0	0	0	0	0	0	0	0
David Faiumu	30/4/88	4(21)	2(19)	2	1	0	0	0	0	8	4
Dale Ferguson	13/4/88	7(9)	5(8)	3	2	0	0	0	0	12	8
Brett Ferres	17/4/86	7	7	0	0	0	0	0	0	0	0
Luke George	30/10/87	25	23	17	15	0	0	0	0	68	60
Lee Gilmour	12/3/78	21(1)	17(1)	3	2	0	0	0	0	12	8
Scott Grix	1/5/84	29	25	11	10	9	7	0	0	62	54
Michael Lawrence	12/4/90	24(4)	21(4)	6	6	0	0	0	0	24	24
Tommy Lee	1/2/88	11(7)	11(7)	3	3	0	0	0	0	12	12
Shaun Lunt	15/4/86	(6)	(6)	2	2	0	0	0	0	8	8
Keith Mason	20/1/82	15(5)	14(3)	1	1	0	0	0	0	4	4
Jermaine McGillvary	16/5/88	24	21	10	9	0	0	0	0	40	36
Jon Molloy	23/3/91	1(1)	1	0	0	0	0	0	0	0	0
Scott Moore	23/1/88	7(6)	6(5)	1	0	0	0	0	0	4	0
Aaron Murphy	26/11/88	15	12	7	5	0	0	0	0	28	20
Luke O'Donnell	22/10/80	7(3)	6(2)	0	0	0	0	0	0	0	0
Larne Patrick	3/11/88	3(23)	3(20)	7	6	0	0	0	0	28	24
Luke Robinson	25/7/84	19(10)	17(8)	8	5	0	0	0	0	32	20
Tony Tonks	27/4/85	(1)	(1)	0	0	0	0	0	0	0	0
Adam Walker	20/2/91	1(3)	1(3)	0	0	0	0	0	0	0	0
Joe Wardle	22/9/91	21	18	9	8	0	0	0	0	36	32

Leroy Cudjoe

LEAGUE RECORD
P27-W14-D0-L13
(7th, SL/Elimination Play-Off)
F699, A664, Diff+35
28 points.

CHALLENGE CUP
Semi-Finalists

ATTENDANCES
Best - v Wigan (SL - 10,123)
Worst - v London Broncos
(CC - 2,574)
Total (SL only) - 100,223
Average (SL only) - 7,709
(Up by 562 on 2011)

2 November 2011 - Epalahame Lauaki signs for Wigan.

10 November 2011, who spent the 2011 season with Castleford Tigers signs one-year deal.

1 December 2011 - Sam Obst released from last year of contract and joins Keighley.

19 December 2011 - Martin Aspinwall suspended pending internal investigation.

29 December 2011 - Martin Gleeson, three years half-suspended; former chief executive James Rule and former conditioner Ben Cooper, two years half suspended, banned from game for misleading UK Anti-Doping Panel.

31 December 2011 - Martin Aspinwall suspension lifted after being fined by court for being drunk and aggressive.

9 January 2012 - Tony Martin misses pre-season training camp in Tenerife because of flu.

19 January 2012 - Andy Lynch, signed from Bradford the previous September on two-year deal, named captain.

22 January 2012 - 36-18 friendly defeat to Hull KR at KC Stadium. Aaron Heremaia damages disc in spine.

29 January 2012 - 46-6 home friendly win over Bradford in Lee Radford testimonial.

5 February 2012 - Last-second try snatches 20-20 draw for Warrington at KC Stadium.

11 February 2012 - round-two game at Catalans called off because of frozen pitch.

19 February 2012 - Sam Moa sent off and banned for one game for mis-timed shoulder charge on Julien Rinaldi in 22-14 home win over London. Joe Westerman dislocates shoulder.

25 February 2012 - late penalty snatches Salford a 24-22 win over Hull FC in round four.

4 March 2012 - Eamon O'Carroll makes debut in 14-10 home win over Wakefield.

9 March 2012 - Wade McKinnon scores two tries in 22-10 win at St Helens. Mark O'Meley accepts one-match ban for dangerous play.

12 March 2012 - Kirk Yeaman undergoes surgery on injured foot after picking up arm injury in win at St Helens.

15 March 2012 - SLXVII derbies reversed because of impending building work at Craven Park.

18 March 2012 - Danny Tickle scores four tries and kicks nine goals in 58-10 home win over Widnes.

21 March 2012 - England forward Gareth Ellis signs three-year contract from 2013.

23 March 2012 - Josh Bowden signs new two-year contract.

25 March 2012 - 42-28 win at Castleford moves Hull into third spot.

29 March 2012 - Aaron Heremaia told he needs neck operation.

29 March 2012 - Jay Pitts signs immediately on two-and-a-half-year deal on free transfer from Leeds Rhinos.

6 April 2012 - Jay Pitts makes debut in 36-6 home win over Hull KR as Hull move into second spot.

9 April 2012 - 22-4 defeat at leaders Huddersfield.

15 April 2012 - Challenge Cup exit after 42-16 home defeat to Huddersfield.

21 April 2012 - 56-12 hammering at home to Wigan in round 12.

30 April 2012 - Willie Manu turns down contract offer.

1 May 2012 - fullback Wade McKinnon leaves for personal reasons, six months into three-year contract. Matthew Russell joins on month's loan from Wigan.

KEY DATES - HULL F.C.

2 May 2012 - Andy Lynch signs new contract to end of 2014.

10 May 2012 - Liam Kent signs new two-year contract.

10 May 2012 - Jack Briscoe joins Featherstone on dual-registration.

22 May 2012 - Richard Whiting banned for one game for dangerous contact in 14-12 win over London in Gillingham.

26 May 2012 - last-second try ensures 32-30 derby defeat at Magic Weekend. Tony Martin out for season with ruptured Achilles heel.

29 May 2012 - Castleford centre Joe Arundel signs four-year deal from 2013. Matthew Russell extends loan for another month.

1 June 2012 - Richard Whiting signs new two-year contract.

3 June 2012 - late penalty gains St Helens 18-all draw at KC Stadium.

10 June 2012 - 32-30 defeat at Wakefield.

11 June 2012 - Willie Manu to join St Helens at end of season.

22 June 2012 - Liam Watts signs from Hull KR with immediate effect on three-and-a-half-year contract.

24 June 2012 - Aaron Heremaia makes debut in 40-18 defeat at Warrington.

25 June 2012 - Eamon O'Carroll and Jamie Ellis given permission to speak to other clubs. Matthew Russell extends loan for another month.

26 June 2012 - Jamie Ellis to leave at end of season to join Castleford.

27 June 2012 - Eamon O'Carroll leaves by mutual consent.

3 July 2012 - Jordan Turner to leave at end of season to join St Helens. Jamie Ellis goes to Castleford with immediate effect.

5 July 2012 - Sam Moa and Danny Tickle out for rest of season with arm injuries sustained in 28-24 home win over Huddersfield on 1 July.

6 July 2012 - Ryan McGoldrick signs from Castleford until end of season.

10 July 2012 - Ryan McGoldrick suspended for one game for touching official in 21-6 defeat at Leeds, but wins appeal.

14 July 2012 - 44-14 defeat at Catalans in re-scheduled round 2 game.

18 July 2012 - Matthew Russell returns to parent club Wigan.

18 July 2012 - St Helens winger Jamie Foster joins on loan for at least a month.

20 July 2012 - attempt to sign Rangi Chase with immediate effect founders.

23 July 2012 - Hull FC move into sixth place as Jamie Foster kicks six from six in 32-18 win over Hull KR at Craven Park.

29 July 2012 - Tom Lineham, on his home debut, scores two tries in dramatic 34-26 home victory over Salford.

3 August 2012 - Joe Westerman banned for a game for striking in 48-10 defeat at Wigan.

8 August 2012 - Tony Martin retires.

10 August 2012 - Ben Crooks signs contract to end of 2015.

12 August 2012 - move back up into sixth place after impressive 30-10 home victory over Catalans. Richard Whiting breaks foot.

15 August 2012 - young forward Chris Green signs new two-year contract.

18 August 2012 - Tom Lineham breaks ankle in shock 42-16 televised defeat at bottom-of-the-table Widnes.

21 August 2012 - Jamie Foster to remain on loan on week-by-week basis.

23 August 2012 - Sam Moa to return to Australia at end of season to join Sydney Roosters.

24 August 2012 - Danny Nicklas signs contract extension to end of 2013 season.

1 September 2012 - 70-6 victory at Bradford is record club away win. Ryan McGoldrick dislocates shoulder.

9 September 2012 - Peter Gentle signs one-year contract extension to end of 2015.

10 September 2012 - Salford's Australian stand-off Daniel Holdsworth joins for 2013 on two-year contract.

11 September 2012 - Ben Galea, released by Hull KR, signs on 12-month contract after reversing decision to retire.

14 September 2012 - Danny Houghton signs new contract to end of 2017.

15 September 2012 - Mark O'Meley signs new one-year contract.

16 September 2012 - 46-10 home elimination play-off win over Huddersfield.

19 September 2012 - Bradford winger Jason Crookes joins on three-year contract.

22 September 2012 - 24-12 Preliminary semi-final defeat at Warrington means play-off exit.

24 September 2012 - Wakefield prop Paul Johnson signs on two-year deal.

24 September 2012 - Martin Aspinwall leaves and joins Leigh.

19 October 2012 - young hooker James Cunningham extends contract to end of 2015.

CLUB RECORDS

Highest score: 88-0 v Sheffield, 2/3/2003
Highest score against:
16-74 v St Helens, 18/7/99
Record attendance:
28,798 v Leeds, 7/3/36 *(The Boulevard)*
23,004 v Hull KR, 2/9/2007 *(KC Stadium)*

MATCH RECORDS

Tries: 7 Clive Sullivan v Doncaster, 15/4/68
Goals: 14 Jim Kennedy v Rochdale, 7/4/21
Sammy Lloyd v Oldham, 10/9/78
Matt Crowther v Sheffield, 2/3/2003
Points: 36 Jim Kennedy v Keighley, 29/1/21

SEASON RECORDS

Tries: 52 Jack Harrison 1914-15
Goals: 170 Sammy Lloyd 1978-79
Points: 369 Sammy Lloyd 1978-79

CAREER RECORDS

Tries: 250 Clive Sullivan 1961-74; 1981-85
Goals: 687 Joe Oliver 1928-37; 1943-45
Points: 1,842 Joe Oliver 1928-37; 1943-45
Appearances: 500 Edward Rogers 1906-25

HULL F.C.

HULL F.C.

DATE	FIXTURE	RESULT	SCORERS	LGE	ATT
5/2/12	Warrington (h)	D20-20	t:Yeaman,Tickle(2),Briscoe g:Tickle(2)	7th	12,710
19/2/12	London Broncos (h)	W22-14	t:Briscoe,Westerman,McKinnon,Yeaman g:Tickle(3)	6th	10,096
24/2/12	Salford (a)	L24-22	t:Seymour(2),McKinnon,Briscoe g:Tickle(3)	9th	5,186
4/3/12	Wakefield (h)	W14-10	t:Yeaman,Sharp g:Tickle(3)	8th	11,105
9/3/12	St Helens (a)	W10-22	t:McKinnon(2),Turner g:Tickle(5)	6th	14,875
18/3/12	Widnes (h)	W58-10	t:Tickle(4),Manu(2),Lynch,Whiting,Moa,Briscoe g:Tickle(9)	6th	10,705
25/3/12	Castleford (a)	W28-42	t:Moa,Manu(2),Turner,Tickle,Seymour,Briscoe g:Tickle(7)	3rd	9,050
30/3/12	Bradford (h)	W24-18	t:Horne(2),Manu,Briscoe g:Tickle(4)	2nd	11,673
6/4/12	Hull KR (h)	W36-6	t:Radford,Turner(3),Yeaman,Seymour g:Tickle(6)	2nd	18,979
9/4/12	Huddersfield (a)	L22-4	g:Tickle(2)	4th	9,950
15/4/12	Huddersfield (h) (CCR4)	L16-42	t:Briscoe(2) g:Tickle(4)	N/A	8,327
22/4/12	Wigan (h)	L12-56	t:Ellis,Sharp g:Tickle(2)	5th	11,549
5/5/12	Leeds (h)	W34-20	t:Tickle,Sharp,Briscoe(2),Crooks g:Tickle(7)	5th	11,667
20/5/12	London Broncos (a) ●	W12-14	t:Crooks,Whiting g:Tickle(3)	5th	3,930
26/5/12	Hull KR (MW) ●●	L30-32	t:Seymour,Horne,Manu,Martin,Turner g:Tickle(5)	5th	N/A
3/6/12	St Helens (h)	D18-18	t:Whiting,Horne,Tickle g:Tickle(3)	5th	11,727
10/6/12	Wakefield (a)	L32-30	t:Manu,Seymour,Crooks,Yeaman(2) g:Tickle(5)	6th	8,986
24/6/12	Warrington (a)	L40-18	t:Yeaman,Manu,Westerman g:Tickle(3)	7th	10,582
1/7/12	Huddersfield (h)	W28-24	t:Crooks,Briscoe,Heremaia,Yeaman(2) g:Tickle(4)	7th	11,142
6/7/12	Leeds (a)	L21-6	t:Horne g:Westerman	8th	13,250
14/7/12	Catalan Dragons (a)	L44-14	t:Crooks,Briscoe(2) g:Westerman	8th	7,388
23/7/12	Hull KR (a)	W18-32	t:McGoldrick,Turner,Yeaman,Whiting,Briscoe g:Foster(6)	6th	9,086
29/7/12	Salford (a)	W34-26	t:Lineham(2),Yeaman,Westerman,Turner g:Foster(7)	6th	10,766
3/8/12	Wigan (a)	L48-10	t:Lineham,Seymour g:Foster	6th	17,736
12/8/12	Catalan Dragons (h)	W30-10	t:Manu,Lineham,Green,Briscoe,Foster g:Foster(5)	6th	10,769
18/8/12	Widnes (h)	L42-16	t:Turner,Westerman,Heremaia g:Foster(2)	6th	5,008
1/9/12	Bradford (a)	W6-70	t:Westerman,Foster(2),Manu(2),Houghton,Heremaia(2),Briscoe(3), Crooks,Lynch g:Foster(9)	6th	10,616
8/9/12	Castleford (h)	W36-10	t:Manu,Briscoe,Horne,Houghton,O'Meley,Green g:Foster(6)	6th	11,607
16/9/12	Huddersfield (h) (EPO)	W46-10	t:Briscoe(2),Foster(2),Watts,Heremaia,Lynch,Horne g:Foster(7)	N/A	8,662
22/9/12	Warrington (a) (PSF)	L24-12	t:Briscoe,Crooks g:Foster(2)	N/A	7,323

● Played at Priestfield Stadium, Gillingham ●● Played at Etihad Stadium, Manchester

		APP		TRIES		GOALS		FG		PTS	
	D.O.B.	ALL	SL	ALL	SL	ALL	SL	ALL	SL	ALL	SL
Martin Aspinwall	21/10/81	12(15)	12(15)	0	0	0	0	0	0	0	0
Josh Bowden	14/1/92	(7)	(7)	0	0	0	0	0	0	0	0
Tom Briscoe	19/3/90	30	29	22	20	0	0	0	0	88	80
Ben Crooks	15/6/93	13(3)	13(2)	7	7	0	0	0	0	28	28
James Cunningham	3/4/94	(1)	(1)	0	0	0	0	0	0	0	0
Jamie Ellis	4/10/89	5(5)	4(5)	1	1	0	0	0	0	4	4
Jamie Foster	27/7/90	9	9	5	5	45	45	0	0	110	110
Chris Green	3/1/90	(11)	(10)	2	2	0	0	0	0	8	8
Aaron Heremaia	19/9/82	10(3)	10(3)	5	5	0	0	0	0	20	20
Richard Horne	16/7/82	20(2)	20(2)	7	7	0	0	0	0	28	28
Danny Houghton	25/9/88	25	24	2	2	0	0	0	0	8	8
Liam Kent	9/4/91	(6)	(5)	0	0	0	0	0	0	0	0
Tom Lineham	21/9/91	4(1)	4(1)	4	4	0	0	0	0	16	16
Andy Lynch	20/10/79	28(2)	27(2)	3	3	0	0	0	0	12	12
Reece Lyne	2/12/92	1	0	0	0	0	0	0	0	0	0
Willie Manu	20/3/80	29(1)	28(1)	12	12	0	0	0	0	48	48
Tony Martin	7/10/78	11	10	1	1	0	0	0	0	4	4
Ryan McGoldrick	12/1/81	8	8	1	1	0	0	0	0	4	4
Wade McKinnon	12/2/81	10	10	4	4	0	0	0	0	16	16
Sam Moa	14/6/86	12(3)	11(3)	2	2	0	0	0	0	8	8
Danny Nicklas	29/6/91	2(5)	2(5)	0	0	0	0	0	0	0	0
Eamon O'Carroll	13/6/87	1(9)	1(9)	0	0	0	0	0	0	0	0
Mark O'Meley	22/5/81	6(8)	6(8)	1	1	0	0	0	0	4	4
Jay Pitts	9/12/89	9(13)	8(13)	0	0	0	0	0	0	0	0
Lee Radford	26/3/79	2(2)	2(2)	1	1	0	0	0	0	4	4
Matthew Russell	6/6/93	6	6	0	0	0	0	0	0	0	0
Brett Seymour	27/9/84	25(1)	24(1)	7	7	0	0	0	0	28	28
Will Sharp	12/5/86	16	15	3	3	0	0	0	0	12	12
Danny Tickle	10/3/83	19(1)	18(1)	9	9	80	76	0	0	196	188
Jordan Turner	9/1/89	22(3)	21(3)	9	9	0	0	0	0	36	36
Liam Watts	8/7/90	10(2)	10(2)	1	1	0	0	0	0	4	4
Joe Westerman	15/11/89	15(3)	15(3)	5	5	2	2	0	0	24	24
Richard Whiting	20/12/84	12(11)	12(10)	4	4	0	0	0	0	16	16
Kirk Yeaman	15/9/83	18	18	11	11	0	0	0	0	44	44

Tom Briscoe

LEAGUE RECORD
P27-W15-D2-L10
(6th, SL/Preliminary Semi-Final)
F696, A621, Diff+75
32 points.

CHALLENGE CUP
Round Four

ATTENDANCES
Best - v Hull KR (SL - 18,979)
Worst - v Huddersfield (CC - 8,327)
Total (SL, inc play-offs) - 163,157
Average (SL, inc play-offs) - 11,654
(Down by 777 on 2011)

193

25 November 2011 - Misi Taulapapa released from 12-month contract and re-joins Sheffield.

21 December 2011 - Ben Galea named team captain.

18 January 2012 - Blake Green ruled out indefinitely after discovery of blood clot in leg.

22 January 2012 - Ben Galea suffers medial knee ligament injury in 36-18 friendly win over Hull FC at KC Stadium; youngster Richard Beaumont breaks fibula.

2 February 2012 - Kris Welham signs three-year contract extension to end of 2015.

3 February 2012 - 34-16 round-one defeat at Leeds.

12 February 2012 - Michael Dobson injures shoulder in 22-10 round-two win at Wakefield.

19 February 2012 - Jamie Foster penalty after final hooter rescues St Helens a 36-all draw at Craven Park.

26 February 2012 - Constantine Mika accepts Early Guilty Plea for dangerous contact in 42-10 defeat at Warrington and is banned for one match.

4 March 2012 - Michael Dobson stars in 36-0 home win over Widnes.

10 March 2012 - Jake Webster suffers hip injury as 24-8 lead ends in 36-24 home defeat to Bradford.

15 March 2012 - SLXVII derbies reversed because of impending building work at Craven Park.

17 March 2012 - 20-12 defeat to Catalans in Perpignan despite 12-8 half-time lead.

25 March 2012 - 40-22 home win at Craven Park knocks Huddersfield off top of table.

30 March 2012 - last-minute 34-30 defeat at Castleford.

6 April 2012 - Ben Galea makes first appearance of season in 36-6 Good Friday defeat at Hull.

9 April 2012 - 18-10 Easter Monday win at Salford.

15 April 2012 - round-four Challenge Cup exit after 20-18 home defeat to Catalans.

21 April 2012 - 44-16 round-12 win over London at Craven Park.

25 April 2012 - Liam Salter and James Green both sign two-year contract extensions to end of 2014.

1 May 2012 - prop Scott Wheeldon released and signs for London for rest of season.

4 May 2012 - Jordan Cox ruptures spleen in under-20s match.

4 May 2012 - Ryan O'Hara makes debut in 36-22 defeat at Wigan.

KEY DATES - HULL KINGSTON ROVERS

9 May 2012 - Shannon McDonnell turns down new contract offer.

26 May 2012 - last-second David Hodgson try secures 32-30 win over Hull FC at Magic Weekend.

3 June 2012 - Michael Dobson field goal two minutes from time secures 23-22 home win over Warrington.

11 June 2012 - Liam Watts requests release from contract which runs to end of 2013.

11 June 2012 - 44-26 Monday night win at Huddersfield.

22 June 2012 - Kris Welham breaks leg as late field goal secures Catalans' 13-10 win at Craven Park. Liam Watts joins Hull FC.

26 June 2012 - Jake Webster to join Castleford at end of season.

27 June 2012 - North Queensland Cowboys back-rower Cory Paterson signs on two-year deal from 2013.

4 July 2012 - Warrington back-rower James Laithwaite arrives on loan.

5 July 2012 - Rhys Lovegrove signs new three-year deal to end of 2015 season.

6 July 2012 - Ben Galea to leave at end of season.

8 July 2012 - shock 24-22 home defeat by Salford.

10 July 2012 - Salford City Reds centre Sean Gleeson signs three-year deal from 2013.

17 July 2012 - Craig Hall signs new two-year deal.

23 July 2012 - Shannon McDonnell suffers season-ending knee injury in 32-18 home defeat to Hull FC.

26 July 2012 - Newcastle Knights prop Evarn Tuimavave signs two-year contract from 2013.

5 August 2012 - late Kevin Sinfield field goal secures 25-24 win for Leeds at Craven Park.

10 August 2012 - 32-26 defeat at Bradford.

14 August 2012 - Scott Murrell to leave at end of season.

19 August 2012 - late Paul Sykes field goal earns Wakefield 31-30 win at Craven Park, as Rovers drop from eighth to tenth.

2 September 2012 - 42-36 home defeat to Wigan, after leading 26-0 means no play-off spot in 2012.

5 September 2012 - Penrith halfback Travis Burns signs three-year contract from 2013.

13 September 2012 - Blake Green, two years into a four-year contract, joins Wigan for "a substantial settlement fee".

1 October 2012 - Omari Caro signs from London on two-year contract.

9 October 2012 - Batley winger Alex Brown joins on one-year contract with a further year's option.

9 October 2012 - Louis Sheriff joins Queensland Cup club Redcliffe Dolphins.

16 October 2012 - Scott Taylor, with two years left on Rovers contract, signs for Wigan with a transfer fee payable.

19 October 2012 - Josh Hodgson signs new four-year contract.

7 November 2012 - Adam Walker, released by Huddersfield, joins on three-year deal.

CLUB RECORDS

Highest score:
100-6 v Nottingham City, 19/8/90
Highest score against:
8-76 v Halifax, 20/10/91
Record attendance:
27,670 v Hull FC, 3/4/53 *(Boothferry Park)*
10,250 v Hull FC, 5/6/2011 *(Craven Park)*

MATCH RECORDS

Tries: 11 George West
v Brooklands Rovers, 4/3/1905
Goals:
14 Alf Carmichael v Merthyr, 8/10/1910
Mike Fletcher v Whitehaven, 18/3/90
Colin Armstrong v Nottingham City, 19/8/90
Damien Couturier v Halifax, 23/4/2006
Points: 53 George West
v Brooklands Rovers, 4/3/1905

SEASON RECORDS

Tries: 45 Gary Prohm 1984-85
Goals: 199 Mike Fletcher 1989-90
Points: 450 Mike Fletcher 1989-90

CAREER RECORDS

Tries: 207 Roger Millward 1966-80
Goals: 1,268 Mike Fletcher 1987-98
Points: 2,760 Mike Fletcher 1987-98
Appearances: 489 Mike Smith 1975-91

HULL KINGSTON ROVERS

DATE	FIXTURE	RESULT	SCORERS	LGE	ATT
3/2/12	Leeds (a)	L34-16	t:Horne(2),Welham,D Hodgson	12th	15,343
12/2/12	Wakefield (a)	W10-22	t:Paea,Mika,J Hodgson,Lovegrove g:Dobson(2),Hall	9th	8,612
19/2/12	St Helens (h)	D36-36	t:D Hodgson,Mika,McDonnell,J Hodgson(2),Welham g:Hall(6)	7th	7,610
26/2/12	Warrington (a)	L42-10	t:Lovegrove,Hall g:Dobson	10th	11,916
4/3/12	Widnes (h)	W36-0	t:Withers,Webster,Murrell,Hall(2),J Hodgson g:Dobson(6)	9th	7,423
10/3/12	Bradford (h)	L24-36	t:Welham,Paea,J Hodgson,Hall g:Dobson(4)	10th	7,486
17/3/12	Catalan Dragons (a)	L20-12	t:Dobson,Welham g:Dobson(2)	10th	7,133
25/3/12	Huddersfield (h)	W40-22	t:Watts,D Hodgson,Welham,J Hodgson,Taylor,Latus,Paea g:Dobson(6)	10th	7,616
30/3/12	Castleford (a)	L34-30	t:Welham(3),J Hodgson,Withers g:Dobson(5)	10th	6,396
6/4/12	Hull FC (a)	L36-6	t:Hall g:Dobson	10th	18,979
9/4/12	Salford (a)	W10-18	t:Withers,Taylor(2) g:Dobson(3)	9th	5,000
15/4/12	Catalan Dragons (h) (CCR4)	L18-20	t:Taylor,B Green,J Hodgson,Latus g:Dobson	N/A	4,425
22/4/12	London Broncos (h)	W44-16	t:D Hodgson(3),Welham(2),Horne,B Green g:Dobson(8)	9th	6,713
4/5/12	Wigan (a)	L36-22	t:Galea,McDonnell,J Hodgson,Welham g:Dobson(3)	9th	14,457
20/5/12	Castleford (h)	W70-12	t:McDonnell(3),D Hodgson(4),Latus,Welham,Withers,Mika,Hall g:Dobson(11)	9th	7,312
26/5/12	Hull FC (MW) ●	W30-32	t:Hall,McDonnell,D Hodgson(2),Latus,Dobson g:Hall,Dobson(3)	8th	N/A
3/6/12	Warrington (h)	W23-22	t:J Hodgson,Dobson,Latus,Hall g:Dobson(3) fg:Dobson	7th	7,661
11/6/12	Huddersfield (a)	W26-44	t:D Hodgson(2),Dobson(2),Welham,Galea,Hall g:Dobson(8)	7th	4,962
22/6/12	Catalan Dragons (h)	L10-13	t:Webster,Murrell g:Dobson	8th	7,142
29/6/12	St Helens (a)	L34-28	t:Taylor(2),Latus(2),J Hodgson g:Dobson(4)	9th	12,435
8/7/12	Salford (h)	L22-24	t:Mika,B Green,Hall,Dobson g:Dobson(3)	9th	7,213
23/7/12	Hull FC (h)	L18-32	t:Laithwaite,Paea,J Hodgson g:Dobson(3)	9th	9,086
29/7/12	Widnes (a)	W26-32	t:Dobson,O'Hara,J Hodgson,Galea,Horne,Sheriff g:Dobson(4)	8th	5,325
5/8/12	Leeds (h)	L24-25	t:Horne,J Hodgson,Dobson,Sheriff g:Dobson(4)	8th	8,379
10/8/12	Bradford (a)	L32-26	t:Taylor,D Hodgson,Salter,Hall g:Dobson(5)	8th	10,217
19/8/12	Wakefield (h)	L30-31	t:Salter(2),Horne,Withers,Galea,J Hodgson g:Dobson(3)	10th	8,726
2/9/12	Wigan (h)	L36-42	t:Hall,Withers(2),Galea,Webster,D Hodgson g:Dobson(6)	10th	8,845
8/9/12	London Broncos (a)	L48-42	t:Paea,Beaumont,Petersen,Heil,Mika(2),Galea,Dobson g:Dobson(4),Hall	10th	2,525

● Played at Etihad Stadium, Manchester

		APP		TRIES		GOALS		FG		PTS	
	D.O.B.	ALL	SL	ALL	SL	ALL	SL	ALL	SL	ALL	SL
Richard Beaumont	2/2/88	(1)	(1)	1	1	0	0	0	0	4	4
Keal Carlile	20/3/90	(3)	(3)	0	0	0	0	0	0	0	0
Joel Clinton	8/12/81	12(7)	12(7)	0	0	0	0	0	0	0	0
Jordan Cox	27/5/92	1(9)	1(9)	0	0	0	0	0	0	0	0
Michael Dobson	29/5/86	27	26	9	9	104	103	1	1	245	243
Ben Galea	16/8/78	17(1)	16(1)	6	6	0	0	0	0	24	24
Blake Green	19/9/86	10	9	3	2	0	0	0	0	12	8
James Green	29/11/90	(1)	(1)	0	0	0	0	0	0	0	0
George Griffin	26/6/92	2(2)	2(2)	0	0	0	0	0	0	0	0
Craig Hall	21/2/88	22	21	12	12	9	9	0	0	66	66
Chris Heil	18/8/92	2	2	1	1	0	0	0	0	4	4
David Hodgson	8/8/81	18	18	16	16	0	0	0	0	64	64
Josh Hodgson	31/10/89	20(7)	20(6)	15	14	0	0	0	0	60	56
Graeme Horne	22/3/85	24(2)	23(2)	6	6	0	0	0	0	24	24
Nick Johnson	18/12/90	1	1	0	0	0	0	0	0	0	0
James Laithwaite	23/9/91	1(2)	1(2)	1	1	0	0	0	0	4	4
Sam Latus	21/10/89	16	15	7	6	0	0	0	0	28	24
Rhys Lovegrove	11/3/87	16(6)	16(5)	2	2	0	0	0	0	8	8
Shannon McDonnell	5/8/87	22	21	6	6	0	0	0	0	24	24
Constantine Mika	14/9/89	22(1)	21(1)	6	6	0	0	0	0	24	24
Scott Murrell	5/9/85	12(10)	12(9)	2	2	0	0	0	0	8	8
Jason Netherton	5/10/82	2(9)	2(9)	0	0	0	0	0	0	0	0
Ryan O'Hara	18/8/80	8(7)	8(7)	1	1	0	0	0	0	4	4
Mickey Paea	25/3/86	18(10)	17(10)	5	5	0	0	0	0	20	20
Dave Petersen	6/3/92	2(2)	2(2)	1	1	0	0	0	0	4	4
Liam Salter	14/6/93	12	11	3	3	0	0	0	0	12	12
Louis Sheriff	6/9/92	6	6	2	2	0	0	0	0	8	8
Scott Taylor	27/2/91	14(12)	14(11)	7	6	0	0	0	0	28	24
Liam Watts	8/7/90	8(2)	7(2)	1	1	0	0	0	0	4	4
Jake Webster	29/10/83	13	13	3	3	0	0	0	0	12	12
Kris Welham	12/5/87	19	18	13	13	0	0	0	0	52	52
Scott Wheeldon	23/2/86	2(6)	2(6)	0	0	0	0	0	0	0	0
Lincoln Withers	7/5/81	15(12)	14(12)	7	7	0	0	0	0	28	28

Mickey Paea

LEAGUE RECORD
P27-W10-D1-L16
(10th, SL)
F753, A729, Diff+24
21 points.

CHALLENGE CUP
Round Four

ATTENDANCES
Best - v Hull FC (SL - 9,086)
Worst - v Catalan Dragons
(CC - 4,425)
Total (SL only) - 101,212
Average (SL only) - 7,786
(Down by 534 on 2011)

18 October 2011 - teenagers Stevie Ward, Liam Hood and Brad Singleton promoted to 25-man squad.

9 December 2011 - Jamie Jones-Buchanan signs new three-year deal.

23 December 2011 - Chris Clarkson agrees new five-year contract.

26 December 2011 - 26-10 Boxing Day friendly win over Wakefield at Headingley.

1 January 2012 - Jamie Peacock awarded MBE.

26 January 2012 - Kallum Watkins signs new five-year contract to end of 2016.

26 January 2012 - 66-0 home win over Featherstone in Rob Burrow Testimonial game.

3 February 2012 - Kallum Watkins scores hat-trick in muddy round one 34-16 home win over Hull KR.

8 February 2012 - Brett Delaney signs three-year contract extension to end of 2015 season.

11 February 2012 - 20-6 defeat at Wigan.

17 February 2012 - 26-12 World Club Challenge win over Manly at Headingley.

20 February 2012 - Jamie Jones-Buchanan out for up to three months with a knee injury aggravated in WCC.

1 March 2012 - Kevin Sinfield gives talk to Eton Sports Society.

2 March 2012 - Liam Hood scores try on debut in 36-14 win at Castleford.

9 March 2012 - 26-18 home win over Warrington. Ryan Bailey suspended for three matches for pushing referee.

16 March 2012 - Kevin Sinfield scores a try and kicks eight goals in 56-16 win at Salford to become club's all-time leading scorer.

23 March 2012 - Jamie Peacock MBE signs new two-year deal running to end of 2014.

25 March 2012 - Danny McGuire misses 46-6 defeat at St Helens, with Rhinos sporting red hair in support of charity.

29 March 2012 - Jay Pitts joins Hull FC with immediate effect.

6 April 2012 - 12-4 Good Friday defeat at Bradford.

13 April 2012 - Rob Burrow fractures cheekbone in 38-18 Challenge Cup round four win over Wakefield at Headingley.

18 April 2012 - Huddersfield hooker Shaun Lunt joins on loan for rest of season. Liam Hood joins Dewsbury on dual-registration.

20 April 2012 - Shaun Lunt scores decisive try in 34-18 home win over Catalans.

29 April 2012 - late 16-10 win at Salford in Challenge Cup fifth round.

2 May 2012 - Brad Singleton joins Dewsbury on dual-registration.

5 May 2012 - 34-20 round-13 defeat at Hull FC.

KEY DATES - LEEDS RHINOS

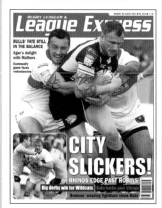

9 May 2012 - Zak Hardaker signs new five-year deal to end of 2016.

18 May 2012 - Brent Webb turns down contract offer.

21 May 2012 - 31-18 Monday-night home defeat by St Helens.

27 May 2012 - Danny McGuire scores five tries in 37-22 Magic Weekend win over Bradford.

31 May 2012 - Carl Ablett signs new five-year contract to end of 2016 season. Paul McShane joins Widnes on season-long loan.

1 June 2012 - 50-8 home defeat by Wigan.

9 June 2012 - 37-18 defeat at Warrington.

18 June 2012 - 44-40 home win over Wakefield in re-arranged round 3 game.

26 June 2012 - Jamie Peacock announces retirement from international Rugby League.

5 July 2012 - Lee Smith joins Wakefield on month's loan.

9 July 2012 - Luke Ambler given permission to speak to other clubs .

12 July 2012 - young Welsh halfback Ollie Olds joins York on dual registration.

14 July 2012 - Kevin Sinfield inspires 39-28 Challenge Cup semi-final win over Wigan.

17 July 2012 - Stevie Ward signs five-year contract to end of 2017 Super League season.

20 July 2012 - Lee Smith signs permanent deal with Wakefield.

30 July 2012 - Jimmy Keinhorst makes debut in 38-18 Monday-night TV defeat at Wakefield.

1 August 2012 - Brent Webb gets two-match ban for high tackle.

5 August 2012 - late Kevin Sinfield field goal secures 25-24 win at Hull KR.

8 August 2012 - Penrith Panthers forward Mitch Achurch signs four-year contract from the 2013 season.

10 August 2012 - Danny McGuire suffers knee injury in 68-24 win over Widnes and is ruled out of Challenge Cup Final.

18 August 2012 - Rob Burrow misses 38-34 defeat to Catalans in Perpignan.

20 August 2012 - official partnership with Hunslet Hawks announced.

25 August 2012 - 35-18 defeat to Warrington at Wembley.

29 August 2012 - Brent Webb ruled out for rest of season with knee injury and will join Catalans for 2013.

7 September 2012 - Jimmy Keinhorst signs new three-year contract to end of 2015.

13 September 2012 - Weller Hauraki joins Castleford.

15 September 2012 - Danny McGuire become's Super League's all-time leading tryscorer with 200th try in Rhinos' 42-20 elimination play-off win over Wakefield.

21 September 2012 - 27-20 Preliminary semi-final win at Catalans. Danny McGuire suspended for one game for high tackle.

23 September 2012 - Wigan elect to play Leeds in Qualifying semi-final.

28 September 2012 - late Kevin Sinfield penalty secures 13-12 play-off win at Wigan.

6 October 2012 - Kevin Sinfield wins second Harry Sunderland Trophy in 26-18 Grand Final win over Warrington.

16 October 2012 - Shaun Lunt returns to Huddersfield after starring in Grand Final win.

CLUB RECORDS

Highest score:
106-10 v Swinton, 11/2/2001
Highest score against:
6-74 v Wigan, 20/5/92
Record attendance:
40,175 v Bradford, 21/5/47

MATCH RECORDS

Tries:
8 Fred Webster v Coventry, 12/4/13
Eric Harris v Bradford, 14/9/31
Goals:
17 Iestyn Harris v Swinton, 11/2/2001
Points:
42 Iestyn Harris v Huddersfield, 16/7/99

SEASON RECORDS

Tries: 63 Eric Harris 1935-36
Goals: 173 *(inc 5fg)* Kevin Sinfield 2012
Points: 431 Lewis Jones 1956-57

CAREER RECORDS

Tries: 391 Eric Harris 1930-39
Goals:
1,479 *(inc 32fg)* Kevin Sinfield 1997-2012
Points: 3,222 Kevin Sinfield 1997-2012
Appearances: 625 John Holmes 1968-89

LEEDS RHINOS

DATE	FIXTURE	RESULT	SCORERS	LGE	ATT
3/2/12	Hull KR (h)	W34-16	t:Delaney,Webb,Watkins(3),McGuire g:Sinfield(5)	3rd	15,343
11/2/12	Wigan (a)	L20-6	t:Griffin g:Sinfield	8th	15,370
17/2/12	Manly (WCC) ●	W26-12	t:Watkins,Hall(2),Jones-Bishop,Ablett g:Sinfield(3)	N/A	21,062
26/2/12	Widnes (a)	W16-44	t:Jones-Bishop(2),Burrow(2),Hall(2),Hardaker,Watkins g:Sinfield(6)	6th	6,046
2/3/12	Castleford (a)	W14-36	t:Hall(3),Watkins,McGuire,Hood g:Sinfield(6)	4th	9,237
9/3/12	Warrington (h)	W26-18	t:McGuire,Hardaker,Watkins,Hood g:Sinfield(5)	4th	17,120
16/3/12	Salford (a)	W16-56	t:Hardaker(3),Delaney,Watkins,Sinfield,Hood,McGuire,Burrow,Ablett g:Sinfield(8)	4th	6,891
25/3/12	St Helens (a)	L46-6	t:Hardaker g:Sinfield	5th	15,195
30/3/12	Huddersfield (h)	L12-22	t:Hardaker,Leuluai g:Sinfield(2)	6th	15,408
6/4/12	Bradford (a)	L12-4	t:Hardaker	6th	20,851
9/4/12	London Broncos (h)	W52-10	t:Ablett,Jones-Bishop(2),Hall(4),Webb,Hardaker(2) g:Sinfield(6)	6th	13,109
13/4/12	Wakefield (h) (CCR4)	W38-18	t:Bailey,McGuire,Hardaker(2),Ablett,McShane,Jones-Bishop g:Sinfield(5)	N/A	7,140
20/4/12	Catalan Dragons (h)	W34-18	t:Jones-Bishop(2),Hall,Hardaker,Lunt,Bailey g:Sinfield(5)	6th	13,282
29/4/12	Salford (a) (CCR5)	W10-16	t:Webb,Jones-Bishop,Lunt g:Sinfield(2)	N/A	4,500
5/5/12	Hull FC (a)	L34-20	t:Jones-Bishop,Ablett,Hall,McGuire g:Sinfield(2)	7th	11,667
11/5/12	Leigh (a) (CCQF)	W12-60	t:McGuire,Webb,Jones-Bishop,Hall(2),Burrow,Lunt,Sinfield(2),Smith g:Sinfield(10)	N/A	5,290
21/5/12	St Helens (h)	L18-31	t:McGuire,Delaney,Jones-Buchanan g:Sinfield(3)	8th	15,343
27/5/12	Bradford (MW) ●●	W22-37	t:McGuire(5),Ablett g:Sinfield(6) fg:Sinfield	7th	N/A
1/6/12	Wigan (h)	L8-50	t:Hall(2)	9th	16,113
8/6/12	Warrington (a)	L37-18	t:Sinfield,Burrow(2) g:Sinfield(3)	9th	10,835
18/6/12	Wakefield (h)	W44-40	t:Hardaker,Jones-Bishop(3),Jones-Buchanan,Hauraki,Ablett g:Sinfield(8)	8th	12,272
24/6/12	Castleford (h)	W40-22	t:Jones-Bishop(2),Burrow(2),Hall(2),Watkins g:Sinfield(6)	6th	16,153
30/6/12	London Broncos (a)	W12-58	t:Lunt(2),McGuire(4),Ablett,Hardaker,Burrow,Leuluai g:Sinfield(9)	6th	3,628
6/7/12	Hull FC (h)	W21-6	t:Ablett,Delaney,Hall g:Sinfield(4) fg:Sinfield	5th	13,250
14/7/12	Wigan (CCSF) ●●●	W39-28	t:Hall(2),Jones-Bishop(2),Hardaker(2),Bailey g:Sinfield(5) fg:Sinfield	N/A	12,860
20/7/12	Bradford (h)	W34-16	t:Watkins(2),Lunt,Hardaker,McGuire,Sinfield g:Sinfield(4),Hardaker	5th	18,520
30/7/12	Wakefield (a)	L38-18	t:Watkins,Hall(3) g:Sinfield	5th	9,547
5/8/12	Hull KR (a)	W24-25	t:McGuire(2),Hall,Ablett g:Sinfield(4) fg:Sinfield	5th	8,379
10/8/12	Widnes (h)	W68-24	t:Bailey,Hall(2),Lunt,Hardaker(2),Moore,Delaney,Griffin,Leuluai,Ward,Keinhorst g:Sinfield(10)	4th	13,326
18/8/12	Catalan Dragons (a)	L38-34	t:Lunt,Watkins(2),Hall(2),Keinhorst g:Sinfield(5)	5th	10,269
25/8/12	Warrington (CCF) ●●●●	L18-35	t:Kirke,Watkins(2) g:Sinfield(3)	N/A	79,180
31/8/12	Salford (a)	W46-12	t:Jones-Bishop,Hall,Sinfield,Burrow,Watkins(2),Hauraki,Jones-Buchanan g:Sinfield(7)	5th	15,081
9/9/12	Huddersfield (a)	L48-24	t:Keinhorst,Hall,Watkins,Ablett,Peacock g:Sinfield(2)	5th	9,128
15/9/12	Wakefield (h) (EPO)	W42-20	t:Burrow(2),Jones-Bishop(3),McGuire,Hardaker g:Sinfield(7)	N/A	9,044
21/9/12	Catalan Dragons (a) (PSF)	W20-27	t:Ward,Lunt,Ablett,McGuire g:Sinfield(5) fg:McGuire	N/A	8,156
28/9/12	Wigan (a) (QSF)	W12-13	t:Watkins g:Sinfield(4) fg:Sinfield	N/A	12,334
6/10/12	Warrington (GF) ●●●●●	W26-18	t:Sinfield,Jones-Bishop,Ablett,Hall g:Sinfield(5)	N/A	70,676

● Played at Headingley Carnegie   ●● Played at Etihad Stadium, Manchester   ●●● Played at Galpharm Stadium, Huddersfield
●●●● Played at Wembley Stadium   ●●●●● Played at Old Trafford, Manchester

APP TRIES GOALS FG PTS

	D.O.B.	ALL	SL	ALL	SL	ALL	SL	ALL	SL	ALL	SL
Carl Ablett	19/12/85	34	29	13	11	0	0	0	0	52	44
Ryan Bailey	11/11/83	18(10)	14(8)	4	2	0	0	0	0	16	8
Rob Burrow	26/9/82	27(3)	22(3)	12	11	0	0	0	0	48	44
Chris Clarkson	7/4/90	12(15)	9(14)	0	0	0	0	0	0	0	0
Brett Delaney	26/10/85	34	29	5	5	0	0	0	0	20	20
Darrell Griffin	19/6/81	8(24)	8(19)	2	2	0	0	0	0	8	8
Ryan Hall	27/11/87	37	31	33	27	0	0	0	0	132	108
Zak Hardaker	17/10/91	37	31	21	17	1	1	0	0	86	70
Weller Hauraki	18/2/85	5(7)	4(7)	2	2	0	0	0	0	8	8
Liam Hood	6/1/92	1(4)	1(4)	3	3	0	0	0	0	12	12
Ben Jones-Bishop	24/8/88	32	26	23	17	0	0	0	0	92	68
Jamie Jones-Buchanan	1/8/81	24	20	3	3	0	0	0	0	12	12
Jimmy Keinhorst	14/7/90	2(4)	2(3)	3	3	0	0	0	0	12	12
Ian Kirke	26/12/80	3(22)	2(19)	1	0	0	0	0	0	4	0
Kylie Leuluai	29/3/78	31(4)	25(4)	3	3	0	0	0	0	12	12
Shaun Lunt	15/4/86	11(12)	10(9)	9	7	0	0	0	0	36	28
Danny McGuire	6/12/82	26	21	22	20	0	0	1	1	89	81
Paul McShane	19/11/89	3(6)	3(3)	1	0	0	0	0	0	4	0
Richard Moore	2/2/81	(16)	(14)	1	1	0	0	0	0	4	4
Jamie Peacock	14/12/77	31(1)	26(1)	1	1	0	0	0	0	4	4
Jay Pitts	9/12/89	2(1)	2(1)	0	0	0	0	0	0	0	0
Kevin Sinfield	12/9/80	37	31	7	5	168	140	5	4	369	304
Brad Singleton	29/10/92	(1)	(1)	0	0	0	0	0	0	0	0
Lee Smith	8/8/86	9(5)	8(3)	1	0	0	0	0	0	4	0
Stevie Ward	17/11/93	11(10)	10(9)	2	2	0	0	0	0	8	8
Kallum Watkins	12/3/91	27	24	20	17	0	0	0	0	80	68
Brent Webb	8/11/80	19	15	4	2	0	0	0	0	16	8

Zak Hardaker

LEAGUE RECORD
P27-W16-D0-L11
(5th, SL/Grand Final Winners,
Champions)
F823, A662, Diff+161
32 points.

CHALLENGE CUP
Runners-Up

ATTENDANCES
Best - v Manly (WCC - 21,062)
Worst - v Wakefield (CC - 7,140)
Total (SL, inc play-offs) - 203,364
Average (SL, inc play-offs) - 14,526
(Down by 143 on 2011)

23 November 2011 - Olsi Krasniqi signs new three-year contract to end of 2014.

21 January 2012 - Karl Temata suffers knee ligament injury in 44-22 friendly defeat in Perpignan.

27 January 2012 - 42-14 win over London Skolars at HAC.

4 February 2012 - Kieran Dixon makes debut in 34-24 home defeat to St Helens in round one.

12 February 2012 - David Howell returns from 2011 suspension in 50-10 defeat at Warrington.

19 February 2012 - Shane Rodney suffers knee injury in 22-14 defeat at Hull FC.

26 February 2012 - Tony Clubb dislocates jaw in 30-16 home defeat by Huddersfield..

2 March 2012 - Omari Caro makes debut in 44-12 reverse at Salford, making it five defeats from first five games.

10 March 2012 - 42-16 home win over Castleford in round 6.

18 March 2012 - Michael Witt scores 18 points in 42-30 defeat at Wigan.

25 March 2012 - 38-30 defeat at Widnes.

31 March 2012 - 36-0 home win over Wakefield takes Broncos off bottom of table.

5 April 2012 - 36-18 defeat at home to Catalans in round 10.

9 April 2012 - 52-10 Easter Monday defeat at Leeds.

15 April 2012 - 72-4 home win over Dewsbury secures Challenge Cup place in fifth round.

22 April 2012 - 44-16 round 12 defeat at Hull KR.

29 April 2012 - 22-16 round-five Challenge Cup win at Championship Batley.

1 May 2012 - prop Scott Wheeldon signs for rest of season after being released by Hull KR.

3 May 2012 - Jarrad Hickey released six months after it was realised he would not fit within quota.

6 May 2012 - 29-22 defeat to Bradford at Leyton.

13 May 2012 - 50-14 Challenge Cup quarter-final exit at Huddersfield.

20 May 2012 - 14-12 defeat to Hull FC at Gillingham.

27 May 2012 - 42-18 Magic Weekend defeat to Catalans.

KEY DATES - LONDON BRONCOS

9 June 2012 - 28-24 home win over Widnes Vikings.

25 June 2012 - Michael Robertson and Scott Wheeldon both sign new two year-contracts to end of 2014.

27 June 2012 - Omari Caro wins League's fastest man race at Headingley.

7 July 2012 - 44-12 defeat at Bradford

13 July 2012 - former Widnes utility back Shane Grady joins on two-year contract from Australian side Thirroul Butchers.

17 July 2012 - Rob Powell steps down with immediate effect. Tony Rea takes over as interim head coach for the last seven games.

21 July 2012 - 44-6 home defeat to Wigan in Tony Rea's first game in charge.

29 July 2012 - 19-12 round-22 away defeat to Catalan.

4 August 2012 - 40-28 home comeback win over Salford ends losing run at five games.

12 August 2012 - Luke Dorn scores four tries in 42-20 win at Castleford.

17 August 2012 - Luke Dorn scores another four tries in 62-18 home win over Warrington to become first London player to score 100 tries.

20 August 2012 - Tony Rea signs two-year head coaching contract.

31 August 2012 - 30-0 defeat at St Helens.

7 September 2012 - Julien Rinaldi announces he is to retire at end of season; Karl Temata to join Limoux.

8 September 2012 - 48-42 home round-27 win over Hull KR means 12th place finish.

19 September 2012 - Broncos to remain at Twickenham Stoop in 2013.

21 September 2012 - Tommy Lee signs on two-year contract.

CLUB RECORDS

Highest score: 82-0 v Highfield, 12/11/95
82-2 v Barrow, 20/5/2006
Highest score against:
6-82 v Warrington, 20/3/2011
Record attendance:
15,013 v Wakefield, 15/2/81

MATCH RECORDS

Tries:
5 Martin Offiah v Whitehaven, 14/3/99
Goals:
13 Rob Purdham v Barrow, 20/5/2006
Points:
34 Rob Purdham v Barrow, 20/5/2006

SEASON RECORDS

Tries: 43 Mark Johnson 1993-94
Goals: 159 John Gallagher 1993-94
Points: 384 John Gallagher 1993-94

CAREER RECORDS

Tries:
103 Luke Dorn 2005-2006; 2009-2012
Goals: 309 Steve Diamond 1981-84
Points: 772 Paul Sykes 2001-2007
Appearances:
202 Steele Retchless 1998-2004

LONDON BRONCOS

DATE	FIXTURE	RESULT	SCORERS	LGE	ATT
4/2/12	St Helens (h)	L24-34	t:Robertson,Krasniqi,Bailey,Witt g:Witt(4)	10th	4,924
12/2/12	Warrington (a)	L50-10	t:Witt,Robertson g:Witt	13th	10,834
19/2/12	Hull FC (a)	L22-14	t:Robertson,Dorn,Melling g:Witt	13th	10,096
26/2/12	Huddersfield (h)	L16-30	t:Kaufusi(2),O'Callaghan g:Witt(2)	13th	1,970
2/3/12	Salford (a)	L44-12	t:Howell,Kaufusi g:Witt(2)	13th	5,250
10/3/12	Castleford (h)	W42-16	t:Howell(2),Bailey,Gower,Cook,Sarginson,Golden,Melling g:Witt(5)	12th	2,381
18/3/12	Wigan (a)	L42-30	t:Witt(2),Robertson,Sarginson,Melling g:Witt(5)	12th	12,608
25/3/12	Widnes (a)	L38-30	t:Dorn,Bryant,Witt,Colbon,Clubb g:Witt(5)	13th	6,535
31/3/12	Wakefield (h)	W36-0	t:Clubb,Sarginson,Dixon,Robertson(2),Colbon,Dorn g:Witt(4)	11th	2,268
5/4/12	Catalan Dragons (h)	L18-36	t:Rodney,Dorn,Robertson g:Witt,Rodney(2)	12th	1,829
9/4/12	Leeds (a)	L52-10	t:Dixon,Dorn g:Witt	13th	13,109
15/4/12	Dewsbury (h) (CCR4)	W72-4	t:Kaufusi(2),Dixon(2),Randall,Sarginson,Dorn,O'Callaghan(2),Witt(2), Bailey,Cook g:Witt(7),Gower(3)	N/A	652
22/4/12	Hull KR (a)	L44-16	t:Rodney,Randall,Dixon g:Rodney(2)	13th	6,713
29/4/12	Batley (a) (CCR5)	W16-22	t:O'Callaghan,Cook,Kaufusi,Randall g:Rodney(3)	N/A	1,025
6/5/12	Bradford (h) ●	L22-29	t:Robertson,Cook,Channing,Witt g:Witt(3)	13th	2,844
13/5/12	Huddersfield (a) (CCQF)	L50-14	t:Dixon(2),Wheeldon g:Witt	N/A	2,574
20/5/12	Hull FC (h) ●●	L12-14	t:Dixon,Robertson g:Witt,Rodney	13th	3,930
27/5/12	Catalan Dragons (MW) ●●●	L42-18	t:Kaufusi,B Bolger,Randall g:Rodney(3)	13th	N/A
3/6/12	Wakefield (a)	L24-6	t:Wheeldon g:Rodney	14th	5,876
9/6/12	Widnes (h)	W28-24	t:Gower,Caro,Clubb,Sarginson,Kaufusi g:Rodney(3),Dixon	13th	2,117
24/6/12	Huddersfield (a)	L46-10	t:Robertson,Gower g:Gower	13th	6,019
30/6/12	Leeds (h)	L12-58	t:Bailey,Dixon g:Witt(2)	14th	3,628
8/7/12	Bradford (a)	L44-12	t:Dixon(2),Lovell	14th	10,132
21/7/12	Wigan (h)	L6-44	t:Robertson g:Witt	14th	4,309
28/7/12	Catalan Dragons (a)	L19-12	t:Clubb,Wheeldon g:Gower(2)	14th	7,673
4/8/12	Salford (h)	W40-28	t:Caro,Gower,Clubb,Dixon,Bailey,O'Callaghan,Lovell,Dorn g:Gower(4)	14th	1,517
12/8/12	Castleford (a)	W20-42	t:Bailey,Dorn(4),Dixon,Clubb g:Witt(7)	13th	5,149
17/8/12	Warrington (h)	W62-18	t:Dixon,Lovell,Dorn(4),Caro,Robertson(2),Rinaldi g:Gower(9),Melling(2)	12th	2,261
31/8/12	St Helens (a)	L30-0		12th	13,262
8/9/12	Hull KR (h)	W48-42	t:Robertson(2),Caro,Dixon(2),Bailey,Krasniqi,Dorn g:Gower(8)	12th	2,525

● Played at Brisbane Road, Leyton
●● Played at Priestfield Stadium, Gillingham
●●● Played at Etihad Stadium, Manchester

		APP		TRIES		GOALS		FG		PTS	
	D.O.B.	ALL	SL	ALL	SL	ALL	SL	ALL	SL	ALL	SL
Chris Bailey	5/7/82	27	24	7	6	0	0	0	0	28	24
Ben Bolger	13/9/89	2(7)	2(7)	1	1	0	0	0	0	4	4
Sam Bolger	1/11/91	(1)	0	0	0	0	0	0	0	0	0
Mark Bryant	10/4/81	10(20)	8(19)	1	1	0	0	0	0	4	4
Omari Caro	7/3/91	12	11	4	4	0	0	0	0	16	16
Michael Channing	30/6/92	5(3)	3(3)	1	1	0	0	0	0	4	4
Tony Clubb	12/6/87	23(3)	22(2)	6	6	0	0	0	0	24	24
Liam Colbon	30/9/84	8	8	2	2	0	0	0	0	8	8
Matt Cook	14/11/86	10(3)	7(3)	4	2	0	0	0	0	16	8
Kieran Dixon	22/8/92	26(1)	23(1)	16	12	1	1	0	0	66	50
Luke Dorn	2/7/82	17(7)	16(6)	15	15	0	0	0	0	64	60
Jason Golden	6/11/85	7(2)	7(2)	1	1	0	0	0	0	4	4
Craig Gower	29/4/78	29	26	4	4	27	24	0	0	70	64
David Howell	18/11/83	20	19	3	3	0	0	0	0	12	12
Antonio Kaufusi	27/11/84	27(2)	24(2)	8	5	0	0	0	0	32	20
Olsi Krasniqi	26/6/92	(17)	(16)	2	2	0	0	0	0	8	8
Will Lovell	10/5/93	7(3)	7(3)	3	3	0	0	0	0	12	12
Mike McMeeken	10/5/94	(3)	(3)	0	0	0	0	0	0	0	0
Chris Melling	21/9/84	10(12)	10(9)	3	3	2	2	0	0	16	16
Jamie O'Callaghan	21/9/90	27	24	5	2	0	0	0	0	20	8
Chad Randall	30/12/80	25(5)	22(5)	4	2	0	0	0	0	16	8
Julien Rinaldi	27/4/79	4(16)	4(16)	1	1	0	0	0	0	4	4
Michael Robertson	14/4/83	26	24	15	15	0	0	0	0	60	60
Shane Rodney	15/8/83	15	12	2	2	15	12	0	0	38	32
Dan Sarginson	26/5/93	18(1)	16(1)	5	4	0	0	0	0	20	16
Karl Temata	12/7/78	(9)	(6)	0	0	0	0	0	0	0	0
Scott Wheeldon	23/2/86	14(2)	14(1)	3	2	0	0	0	0	12	8
Michael Witt	1/1/84	22	19	8	6	53	45	0	0	138	114

Kieran Dixon

LEAGUE RECORD
P27-W7-D0-L20
(12th, SL)
F588, A890, Diff-302
14 points.

CHALLENGE CUP
Quarter Finalists

ATTENDANCES
Best - v St Helens (SL - 4,924)
Worst - v Dewsbury (CC - 652)
Total (SL only) - 36,503
Average (SL only) - 2,808
(Down by 324 on 2011, Harlequins)

23 November 2011 - Phil Veivers appointed new head coach.

30 November 2011 - Rob Parker joins Leigh Centurions.

3 December 2011 - young winger Adam Clay joins Leigh Centurions.

6 January 2012 - Stephen Wild named captain for 2012.

7 January 2012 - first game at City of Salford Stadium ends in 36-12 defeat to Leigh in pre-season friendly.

4 February 2012 - 24-10 defeat to Castleford in snow-bound first league game at new stadium. Wayne Godwin out for up to two months with rib cartilage damage.

10 February 2012 - 38-10 defeat in St Helens' first game at Langtree Park after leading 10-4 at half-time. Joel Moon breaks hand.

19 February 2012 - Daniel Holdsworth and Luke Patten get try braces in first win of the season by 38-18 at Widnes.

24 February 2012 - Daniel Holdsworth kicks late penalty goal to secure 24-22 home win over Hull FC.

2 March 2012 - Joel Moon makes a quicker than expected return as 44-12 home win over London makes it three in a row and moves Reds in to top-five.

10 March 2012 - Joel Moon suffers recurrence of hand injury in 40-18 defeat at Catalan Dragons.

16 March 2012 - COS Stadium witnesses Kevin Sinfield become Leeds' all-time record scorer as Rhinos win 56-16 at Salford.

24 March 2012 - Joel Moon returns and gets two tries in 38-18 win at Bradford.

30 March 2012 - 40-20 home defeat to Wigan Warriors.

4 April 2012 - Sale Sharks rugby union to share City of Salford Stadium from start of their season.

6 April 2012 - 36-10 Good Friday defeat at Huddersfield.

9 April 2012 - two late Hull KR tries mean 18-10 home, Easter Monday defeat; Vinnie Anderson suffers elbow injury.

15 April 2012 - 58-18 round four Challenge Cup win at Whitehaven.

17 April 2012 - Luke Patten announces he will retire at end of season and return Down Under.

21 April 2012 - 26-22 defeat at Wakefield in televised Saturday night game.

29 April 2012 - 16-10 home defeat to Leeds leads to Cup exit.

KEY DATES - SALFORD CITY REDS

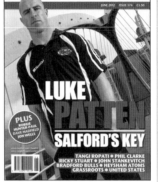

4 May 2012 - halfback Théo Fages signs new five-year deal.

6 May 2012 - Wayne Godwin unlikely to play again this season after suffering double fracture of arm in 24-20 defeat at Warrington.

10 May 2012 - Australian fullback Luke Towers signs from French club Limoux.

18 May 2012 - late Jodie Broughton try earns 20-20 home draw with Bradford.

27 May 2012 - 38-34 win over Huddersfield at Magic Weekend.

1 June 2012 - 34-30 home win over Catalan Dragons.

10 June 2012 - 34-30 defeat at Castleford.

11 June 2012 - chief executive David Tarry leaves club due to redundancy.

21 June 2012 - Danny Williams signs new two-year contract.

22 June 2012 - Shannan McPherson tears MCL in 32-10 home defeat to St Helens and is out for season.

29 June 2012 - 48-24 home thrashing of Warrington.

6 July 2012 - halfback Matty Smith joins Wigan with immediate effect after substantial offer.

8 July 2012 - 24-22 Super League win at Hull KR two days after Matty Smith's departure to Wigan.

11 July 2012 - Sean Gleeson to join Hull KR at end of season.

13 July 2012 - Ashley Gibson signs new one-year deal.

14 July 2012 - England Academy International back Jonathan Ford signs three-year contract.

20 July 2012 - 46-8 home hammering by Widnes Vikings

29 July 2012 - 34-26 defeat at Hull FC.

4 August 2012 - second-half collapse at Twickenham ends in 40-28 defeat to Broncos as play-off hopes end.

10 August 2012 - 30-20 home defeat by Huddersfield.

20 August 2012 - Adam Walne makes debut in 38-6 defeat at Wigan in Monday-night re-arranged game.

31 August 2012 - 46-12 defeat at Leeds in round 26.

7 September 2012 - Joel Moon fails in attempt at RFL tribunal to be released half way into two-year contract.

8 September 2012 - 42-34 defeat to Wakefield in game switched to Leigh means 11th placed finish.

10 September 2012 - Daniel Holdsworth joins Hull FC.

SALFORD CITY REDS

DATE	FIXTURE	RESULT	SCORERS	LGE	ATT
4/2/12	Castleford (h)	L10-24	t:Smith,Ashurst g:Holdsworth	11th	5,242
10/2/12	St Helens (a)	L38-10	t:Broughton,Gibson g:Holdsworth	12th	15,547
19/2/12	Widnes (a)	W18-38	t:Holdsworth(2),Patten(2),Broughton,Owen,Palea'aesina g:Holdsworth(5)	11th	5,053
24/2/12	Hull FC (h)	W24-22	t:Gibson(2),Ashurst,Gleeson g:Holdsworth(4)	7th	5,186
2/3/12	London Broncos (h)	W44-12	t:Nero(2),Adamson,Smith,Palea'aesina,Gleeson(2),Moon g:Holdsworth(6)	5th	5,250
10/3/12	Catalan Dragons (a)	L40-18	t:Howarth,Veivers,Owen g:Holdsworth(3)	7th	8,158
16/3/12	Leeds (h)	L16-56	t:Anderson,Owen,Patten g:Holdsworth(2)	8th	6,891
25/3/12	Bradford (a)	W18-38	t:Veivers,Moon(2),Patten,Gibson,Ashurst,Owen g:Holdsworth(5)	7th	11,219
30/3/12	Wigan (h)	L20-40	t:Holdsworth,Williams,Patten,James g:Holdsworth(2)	8th	6,774
6/4/12	Huddersfield (a)	L36-10	t:Broughton,Moon g:Holdsworth	9th	6,988
9/4/12	Hull KR (h)	L10-18	t:Patten,Gibson g:Holdsworth	10th	5,000
15/4/12	Whitehaven (a) (CCR4)	W18-58	t:Nero,Sneyd(2),Moon(2),Adamson,Gleeson,Veivers,Smith,Ashurst g:Sneyd(9)	N/A	751
21/4/12	Wakefield (a)	L26-22	t:Holdsworth,Nero,Gibson(2) g:Holdsworth(3)	10th	6,748
29/4/12	Leeds (h) (CCR5)	L10-16	t:Jewitt,Broughton g:Holdsworth	N/A	4,500
6/5/12	Warrington (a)	L24-20	t:Gibson(2),Holdsworth,Williams g:Holdsworth(2)	10th	10,437
18/5/12	Bradford (h)	D20-20	t:Sidlow,Williams(2),Broughton g:Holdsworth(2)	10th	6,121
27/5/12	Huddersfield (MW) ●	W34-38	t:Moon(2),Gleeson,Broughton(2),Sidlow(2) g:Holdsworth(5)	10th	N/A
1/6/12	Catalan Dragons (h)	W34-30	t:Moon,Holdsworth,Gleeson,Broughton(2),Patten g:Holdsworth(3),Smith(2)	10th	4,220
10/6/12	Castleford (a)	L34-30	t:Anderson,Broughton,Moon,Wild,Gleeson g:Sneyd(5)	10th	5,877
22/6/12	St Helens (h)	L10-32	t:Anderson,Williams g:Holdsworth	10th	5,447
29/6/12	Warrington (h)	W48-24	t:Williams(2),Broughton(2),Anderson(2),Patten(2),Smith g:Holdsworth(6)	10th	6,179
8/7/12	Hull KR (a)	W22-24	t:Broughton,Williams(2),Gledhill,Moon g:Holdsworth(2)	10th	7,213
20/7/12	Widnes (h)	L8-46	t:Gibson,Williams	10th	5,196
29/7/12	Hull FC (a)	L34-26	t:Gibson(2),Broughton,Gleeson(2) g:Holdsworth(3)	10th	10,766
4/8/12	London Broncos (a)	L40-28	t:Gleeson,Anderson,Gibson(2),Ashurst,Broughton g:Holdsworth(2)	11th	1,517
10/8/12	Huddersfield (h)	L20-30	t:Anderson,Broughton,Williams,Gleeson g:Holdsworth(2)	11th	3,615
20/8/12	Wigan (a)	L38-6	t:James g:Holdsworth	11th	13,703
31/8/12	Leeds (a)	L46-12	t:Patten(2) g:Holdsworth(2)	11th	15,081
8/9/12	Wakefield (h) ●●	L34-42	t:Williams,Gleeson,Anderson,Gibson(2),Ashurst g:Holdsworth(4),Adamson	11th	2,380

● Played at Etihad Stadium, Manchester
●● Played at Leigh Sports Village

	APP		TRIES		GOALS		FG		PTS	
	D.O.B.	ALL	SL	ALL	SL	ALL	SL	ALL SL	ALL	SL
Luke Adamson	17/11/87	14(7)	12(7)	2	1	1	1	0 0	10	6
Vinnie Anderson	14/2/79	17(2)	17(2)	8	8	0	0	0 0	32	32
Matty Ashurst	1/11/89	27(1)	26	6	5	0	0	0 0	24	20
Ryan Boyle	17/10/87	14(3)	14(3)	0	0	0	0	0 0	0	0
Jodie Broughton	9/1/88	22	21	16	15	0	0	0 0	64	60
Ashley Gibson	25/9/86	18	16	16	16	0	0	0 0	64	64
Ben Gledhill	18/9/89	3(7)	3(7)	1	1	0	0	0 0	4	4
Sean Gleeson	29/11/87	25	23	12	11	0	0	0 0	48	44
Wayne Godwin	13/3/82	6	4	0	0	0	0	0 0	0	0
Daniel Holdsworth	27/4/84	27	26	6	6	70	69	0 0	164	162
Stuart Howarth	25/1/90	23(6)	23(4)	1	1	0	0	0 0	4	4
Jordan James	24/5/80	1(20)	1(18)	2	2	0	0	0 0	8	8
Lee Jewitt	14/2/87	13(8)	12(7)	1	0	0	0	0 0	4	0
Shannan McPherson	12/12/85	11(2)	11(2)	0	0	0	0	0 0	0	0
Joel Moon	20/5/88	19	17	11	9	0	0	0 0	44	36
Adam Neal	21/5/90	2(4)	1(4)	0	0	0	0	0 0	0	0
Chris Nero	14/2/81	9(12)	8(11)	4	3	0	0	0 0	16	12
Gareth Owen	3/7/92	(18)	(18)	4	4	0	0	0 0	16	16
Iafeta Palea'aesina	10/2/82	3(18)	2(17)	2	2	0	0	0 0	8	8
Luke Patten	9/1/80	27	26	11	11	0	0	0 0	44	44
Adam Sidlow	25/10/87	13(6)	11(6)	3	3	0	0	0 0	12	12
Matty Smith	23/7/87	21	19	4	3	2	2	0 0	20	16
Marc Sneyd	9/2/91	5	4	2	0	14	5	0 0	36	10
Josh Veivers	9/12/89	6	5	3	2	0	0	0 0	12	8
Adam Walne	3/10/90	(2)	(2)	0	0	0	0	0 0	0	0
Stephen Wild	26/4/81	28	27	1	1	0	0	0 0	4	4
Danny Williams	26/9/86	23	22	12	12	0	0	0 0	48	48

Stuart Howarth

LEAGUE RECORD
P27-W8-D1-L18
(11th, SL)
F618, A844, Diff-226
17 points.

CHALLENGE CUP
Round Five

ATTENDANCES
Best - v Leeds (SL - 6,891)
Worst - v Wakefield (SL - 2,380)
Total (SL only) - 67,501
Average (SL only) - 5,192
(Up by 438 on 2011, The Willows)

29 November 2011 - Jonny Lomax signs new four-year contract to end of 2015.

6 December 2011 - Jon Wilkin signs new four-year deal until end of 2015.

12 January 2012 - Jamie Foster signs new two-year contract.

4 February 2012 - Paul Wellens and Tony Puletua miss 34-24 round-one win at London.

10 February 2012 - 38-unanswered points secure 38-10 win over Salford in first game at Langtree Park.

19 February 2012 - last-minute Jamie Foster penalty ensures 36-all draw at Hull KR, after leading 14-0.

22 February 2012 - Chris Flannery announces he is to retire at end of season.

24 February 2012 - sensational Catalan try after the hooter and touchline conversion means 34-32 round four home defeat.

2 March 2012 - Gary Wheeler signs two-year contract extension to end of 2014.

4 March 2102 - James Roby suffers leg injury in 17-16 defeat at Huddersfield.

9 March 2012 - 22-10 home defeat to Hull FC.

11 March 2012 - three men arrested after Sia Soliola beaten and injured outside city-centre bar.

17 March 2012 - 12-8 defeat at Bradford is fifth game without a win as Saints fall out of top-eight.

18 March 2012 - coach Royce Simmons and assistant Kieron Purtill sacked.

19 March 2012 - Head of Performance Mike Rush appointed acting head coach with Keiron Cunningham as assistant.

25 March 2012 - 46-6 televised Sunday night home win over Leeds.

30 March 2012 - 28-16 win at Warrington after leading 22-0 until one minute from half-time.

3 April 2012 - Nathan Brown appointed new head coach on three-year deal from end of 2012.

3 April 2012 - Paul Wellens and Anthony Laffranchi to miss Good Friday derby with Wigan after both getting one-match bans for dangerous tackles.

6 April 2012 - 28-10 home, Good Friday defeat to Wigan.

9 April 2012 - 18-12 win at Castleford on Easter Monday.

14 April 2012 - Adam Swift makes debut as Saints hang on for 40-38 Challenge Cup round four win at Widnes.

KEY DATES - ST HELENS

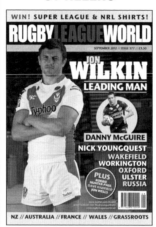

20 April 2012 - Adam Swift scores hat-trick in 62-0 round-12, home defeat of Widnes.

27 April 2012 - Francis Meli gets hat-trick, Jonny Lomax 28 points in 72-0 Cup win over Oldham in switched tie at Langtree Park.

1 May 2012 - Saints draw Wigan away in Challenge Cup quarter-finals.

12 May 2012 - 18-4 defeat at Wigan means Saints miss Challenge Cup semis for first time in 12 years.

21 May 2012 - 31-18 round 14 win at Leeds.

27 May 2012 - Shaun Magennis one of three players sent off after brawl in 46-12 hammering by Wigan in Magic Weekend derby.

29 May 2012 - Shaun Magennis banned for three matches for part in Magic fight.

3 June 2012 - last-minute Tommy Makinson penalty earns 18-all draw at Hull FC.

7 June 2012 - Josh Jones signs new three-year contract; prop Carl Forster pens two-year deal.

7 June 2012 - Michael Shenton to re-join Castleford at end of season.

8 June 2012 - 54-0 home win over Bradford moves Saints back into top four.

11 June 2012 - Willie Manu signs from Hull FC on two-year contract from 2013.

29 June 2012 - after leading 26-0 Saints hold on to win 34-26 at home to Hull KR to go third.

3 July 2012 - Jordan Turner signs from Hull FC on two-year contract from 2013.

18 July 2012 - Jamie Foster goes to Hull FC on month's loan.

20 July 2012 - Tony Puletua sent off and banned for one match after mis-timed shoulder charge in 20-15 win at Catalans.

17 August 2012 - Mike Rush handed £500 suspended fine for comments made about the match referee following 33-32 defeat at Wakefield Trinity Wildcats on August 12.

7 September 2012 - 26-18 win at Wigan in round 27 ensures third-placed finish.

11 September 2012 - Paul Wellens and Francis Meli sign one-year extensions; Paul Clough nets three-year deal.

13 September 2012 - Alex Walmsley signs from Batley on three-year contract.

15 September 2012 - 28-6 qualifying play-off win at Warrington.

29 September 2012 - 36-18 Qualifying semi-final defeat at home to Warrington.

CLUB RECORDS

Highest score:
112-0 v Carlisle, 14/9/86
Highest score against:
6-78 v Warrington, 12/4/1909
Record attendance:
35,695 v Wigan, 26/12/49 *(Knowsley Road)*
17,980 v Wigan, 6/4/2012 *(Langtree Park)*

MATCH RECORDS

Tries: 6 Alf Ellaby v Barrow, 5/3/32
Steve Llewellyn v Castleford, 3/3/56
Steve Llewellyn v Liverpool, 20/8/56
Tom van Vollenhoven v Wakefield, 21/12/57
Tom van Vollenhoven v Blackpool, 23/4/62
Frank Myler v Maryport, 1/9/69
Shane Cooper v Hull, 17/2/88
Goals: 16 Paul Loughlin v Carlisle, 14/9/86
Points:
40 Paul Loughlin v Carlisle, 14/9/86

SEASON RECORDS

Tries 62 Tom van Vollenhoven 1958-59
Goals: 214 Kel Coslett 1971-72
Points: 452 Kel Coslett 1971-72

CAREER RECORDS

Tries: 392 Tom van Vollenhoven 1957-68
Goals: 1,639 Kel Coslett 1962-76
Points: 3,413 Kel Coslett 1962-76
Appearances: 531 Kel Coslett 1962-76

ST HELENS

DATE	FIXTURE	RESULT	SCORERS	LGE	ATT
4/2/12	London Broncos (a)	W24-34	t:Lomax,Dixon,Foster,Meli,Roby g:Foster(7)	5th	4,924
10/2/12	Salford (h)	W38-10	t:Soliola,Roby,Meli,Dixon(2),Wilkin,Laffranchi g:Makinson(5)	2nd	15,547
19/2/12	Hull KR (a)	D36-36	t:Soliola,Shenton,Roby,Flannery,Meli(2),Wellens g:Foster(4)	2nd	7,610
24/2/12	Catalan Dragons (h)	L32-34	t:Foster,Laffranchi,Wheeler(2),Makinson g:Foster(6)	5th	13,108
4/3/12	Huddersfield (a)	L17-16	t:Gaskell,Lomax,Gardner g:Lomax(2)	7th	9,194
9/3/12	Hull FC (a)	L10-22	t:Gardner,Puletua g:Foster	9th	14,875
17/3/12	Bradford (a)	L12-8	t:Dixon,Meli	9th	11,360
25/3/12	Leeds (h)	W46-6	t:Gardner(2),Lomax(2),Wheeler(2),Wellens,Hohaia g:Lomax(7)	9th	15,195
30/3/12	Warrington (a)	W16-28	t:Gardner,Wellens(2),Meli,Soliola g:Lomax(4)	7th	15,000
6/4/12	Wigan (h)	L10-28	t:Meli,Soliola g:Makinson	8th	17,980
9/4/12	Castleford (a)	W12-18	t:Gardner,Soliola,Shenton,Meli g:Roby	8th	6,492
14/4/12	Widnes (a) (CCR4)	W38-40	t:Jones(2),Wellens(2),Flannery,Hohaia,McCarthy-Scarsbrook g:Lomax(6)	N/A	3,069
20/4/12	Widnes (h)	W62-0	t:Soliola,Wellens,Laffranchi(2),Swift(3),McCarthy-Scarsbrook,Dixon, Shenton,Flanagan g:Lomax(9)	7th	14,243
27/4/12	Oldham (a) (CCR5) ●	W0-76	t:Lomax(2),Clough,McCarthy-Scarsbrook,Jones(2),Soliola,Makinson, Wellens,Meli(3),Shenton,Magennis g:Lomax(10)	N/A	5,746
4/5/12	Wakefield (h)	W38-12	t:Flannery(3),Soliola(2),Lomax,Makinson,Roby g:Lomax(3)	6th	13,177
12/5/12	Wigan (a) (CCQF)	L18-4	t:Wellens	N/A	12,864
21/5/12	Leeds (a)	W18-31	t:Lomax(2),Wellens,Makinson,Wilkin g:Makinson(3),Lomax(2) fg:Lomax	6th	15,343
27/5/12	Wigan (MW) ●●	L16-42	t:Clough,McCarthy-Scarsbrook,Wellens g:Lomax(2)	6th	N/A
3/6/12	Hull FC (h)	D18-18	t:Swift,Hohaia,Wilkin g:Makinson(3)	6th	11,727
8/6/12	Bradford (h)	W54-0	t:Wellens(2),Jones(3),Lomax(2),Meli,Makinson,Hohaia g:Makinson(7)	4th	13,025
22/6/12	Salford (a)	W10-32	t:Jones,Hohaia,Makinson,Lomax,Shenton,Wellens g:Makinson,Gaskell(3)	4th	5,447
29/6/12	Hull KR (h)	W34-28	t:Lomax,Wellens(2),Jones(2),Laffranchi,Puletua g:Makinson(3)	4th	12,435
8/7/12	Widnes (a)	W23-24	t:Soliola,Wilkin,Shenton,Jones g:Gaskell(4)	3rd	7,023
20/7/12	Catalan Dragons (a)	W15-20	t:Hohaia,Meli,Flannery,Makinson g:Makinson(2)	3rd	10,387
29/7/12	Huddersfield (h)	W46-12	t:Makinson,Lomax,Meli,Hohaia,McCarthy-Scarsbrook,Laffranchi,Roby, Wellens g:Makinson(7)	3rd	14,070
6/8/12	Warrington (h)	L12-22	t:Shenton,Wellens g:Makinson(2)	3rd	15,728
12/8/12	Wakefield (a)	L33-32	t:Puletua,Meli(3),Wellens(2) g:Makinson(4)	3rd	7,876
17/8/12	Castleford (h)	W44-12	t:Laffranchi,Wellens,Makinson(2),Flannery,Wheeler,Swift,Lomax g:Makinson(2),Wheeler(4)	3rd	12,224
31/8/12	London Broncos (h)	W30-0	t:Puletua,Flanagan(2),Wellens(2),Laffranchi g:Lomax,Wheeler(2)	3rd	13,262
7/9/12	Wigan (a)	W18-26	t:Roby,Makinson,Dixon,Jones,Lomax g:Makinson(3)	3rd	21,522
15/9/12	Warrington (a) (QPO)	W6-28	t:Soliola,Makinson(2),Roby,Meli g:Makinson(4)	N/A	10,190
29/9/12	Warrington (h) (QSF)	L18-36	t:Makinson,Meli(2),Wellens g:Makinson	N/A	12,715

● Played at Langtree Park
●● Played at Etihad Stadium, Manchester

		APP		TRIES		GOALS		FG		PTS	
	D.O.B.	ALL	SL	ALL	SL	ALL	SL	ALL	SL	ALL	SL
Nathan Ashe	15/10/91	(2)	(2)	0	0	0	0	0	0	0	0
Paul Clough	27/9/87	4(27)	3(25)	2	1	0	0	0	0	8	4
Andrew Dixon	28/2/90	3(17)	2(16)	6	6	0	0	0	0	24	24
Mark Flanagan	4/12/87	8(18)	6(17)	3	3	0	0	0	0	12	12
Chris Flannery	5/6/80	21(5)	19(4)	7	6	0	0	0	0	28	24
Carl Forster	4/6/92	(3)	(2)	0	0	0	0	0	0	0	0
Jamie Foster	27/7/90	5	5	2	2	18	18	0	0	44	44
Ade Gardner	24/6/83	9	9	6	6	0	0	0	0	24	24
Lee Gaskell	28/10/90	8(3)	8(3)	1	1	7	7	0	0	18	18
Joe Greenwood	2/4/93	(3)	(2)	0	0	0	0	0	0	0	0
Lance Hohaia	1/4/83	29(2)	26(2)	7	6	0	0	0	0	28	24
Josh Jones	12/5/93	20	18	12	8	0	0	0	0	48	32
Anthony Laffranchi	16/11/80	29	27	8	8	0	0	0	0	32	32
Jonny Lomax	4/9/90	29	26	16	14	46	30	1	1	157	117
Shaun Magennis	2/12/89	2(7)	2(4)	1	0	0	0	0	0	4	0
Tom Makinson	10/10/91	24	22	14	13	48	48	0	0	152	148
Louie McCarthy-Scarsbrook	14/1/86	4(26)	3(24)	5	3	0	0	0	0	20	12
Francis Meli	20/8/80	30	27	20	17	0	0	0	0	80	68
Josh Perry	4/2/81	21(5)	19(5)	0	0	0	0	0	0	0	0
Tony Puletua	25/6/79	22(2)	22(2)	4	4	0	0	0	0	16	16
James Roby	22/11/85	30	27	7	7	1	1	0	0	30	30
Michael Shenton	22/7/86	26	23	7	6	0	0	0	0	28	24
Iosia Soliola	4/8/86	22(5)	19(5)	11	10	0	0	0	0	44	40
Adam Swift	20/2/93	4	3	5	5	0	0	0	0	20	20
Paul Wellens	27/2/80	29	26	24	20	0	0	0	0	96	80
Gary Wheeler	30/9/89	12(2)	11(2)	5	5	6	6	0	0	32	32
Jon Wilkin	1/11/83	25	24	4	4	0	0	0	0	16	16

James Roby

LEAGUE RECORD
P27-W17-D2-L8
(3rd, SL/Qualifying Semi-Final)
F795, A480, Diff+315
36 points.

CHALLENGE CUP
Quarter Finalists

ATTENDANCES
Best - v Wigan (SL - 17,980)
Worst - v Oldham (CC - 5,746)
Total (SL, inc play-offs) - 197,584
Average (SL, inc play-offs) - 14,113
(Up by 6,138 on 2011,
Stobart Stadium)

28 November 2011 - Matt James joins on two-year deal from Barrow.

15 December 2011 - Richard Mathers joins on one-year loan from Castleford.

16 December 2011 - PNG captain Paul Aiton signs two-year contract.

24 December 2011 - Steve Southern announced as 2012 captain.

26 December 2011 - 26-10 Boxing Day friendly defeat at Headingley.

14 January 2012 - 46-10 friendly defeat to Catalans at end of training camp in France.

20 January 2012 - Gareth Moore released and joins Batley.

22 January 2012 - 40-20 home friendly win over Castleford.

27 January 2012 - Matt James joins Halifax on month's loan.

31 January 2012 - Kyle Trout signs new contract to end of 2015.

3 February 2012 - 32-14 round-one win at Widnes Vikings. Kyle Amor breaks hand.

12 February 2012 - 22-10 home defeat by Hull KR.

25 February 2012 - Ben Jeffries kicks Bradford to televised 36-18 win at Rapid Solicitors Stadium.

3 March 2012 - Kieran Hyde joins Doncaster on dual-registration.

4 March 2012 - 14-10 defeat at Hull FC despite late fightback.

11 March 2012 - Ben Cockayne scores hat-trick in 32-14 home defeat by Huddersfield.

18 March 2012 - late Isaac John conversion drops just short to mean 32-30 defeat at Warrington.

25 March 2012 - Peter Fox scores two tries in 32-22 home win over high-flying Catalans.

29 March 2012 - Paul Sykes joins on loan from Bradford for rest of season.

31 March 2012 - Paul Sykes makes debut in 36-0 televised defeat at London.

2 April 2012 - Ben Cockayne signs new two-year contract to end of 2014.

6 April 2012 - 34-16 home, Good Friday defeat to Castleford.

9 April 2012 - 36-6 Easter Monday defeat at Wigan.

13 April 2012 - 38-18 Challenge Cup round-four exit at Leeds.

21 April 2012 - Oliver Wilkes snaps thumb ligaments in 26-22 home, televised win over Salford.

4 May 2012 - Matt James banned for one game for use of elbow in 38-12 defeat at St Helens.

KEY DATES - WAKEFIELD T WILDCATS

11 May 2012 - Andy Ellis joins Featherstone on one-month loan.

20 May 2012 - round 14, 42-12 home defeat by Warrington.

26 May 2012 - late Tim Smith try claims 32-26 win over Castleford at Magic Weekend.

3 June 2012 - rain-soaked 24-6 home win over London Broncos.

9 June 2012 - Danny Kirmond takes over captaincy from Steve Southern.

10 June 2012 - late Ali Lauitiiti try secures 32-30 home win over Hull FC.

18 June 2012 - controversial Monday night 44-40 defeat at Leeds in re-arranged round 3 game.

24 June 2012 - 34-26 defeat at Bradford.

30 June 2012 - 34-10 defeat at Catalans.

5 July 2012 - Lee Smith joins on one-month loan from Leeds.

8 July 2012 - 52-10 home defeat to Wigan.

19 July 2012 - Paul Aiton out for up to eight weeks with broken jaw after mugging in Spain.

20 July 2012 - Lee Smith signs contract until end of 2013.

21 July 2012 - new stadium at Newmarket gets green light from government.

22 July 2012 - Ali Lauitiiti banned for one game for use of knees in tackle after 35-18 win at Huddersfield.

26 July 2012 - Tim Smith signs new 12-month contract for 2013.

30 July 2012 - Oliver Wilkes banned for one game for high tackle in 38-18 Monday-night home win over Leeds.

5 August 2012 - 40-12 derby win at Castleford. Dean Collis cops one-game ban for dangerous throw.

12 August 2012 - last-minute Paul Sykes field goal secures 33-32 home win over St Helens. Danny Cowling makes debut.

13 August 2012 - Paul Aiton signs two-year contract extension to end of 2015.

19 August 2012 - last-minute Paul Sykes field goal secures 31-30 win at Hull KR.

24 August 2012 - Ali Lauitiiti signs one-year contract extension to end of 2014.

2 September 2012 - 22-18 home win over Widnes moves Wakefield into top-eight

6 September 2012 - Frankie Mariano signs 12-month contract extension to end of 2013 season.

8 September 2012 - 42-34 round-27 win over Salford at Leigh is seventh win in row and secures eighth spot.

15 September 2012 - 42-20 elimination play-off defeat at Leeds.

21 September 2102 - Kyle Amor signs contract until end of 2014.

24 September 2012 - Paul Johnson leaves to join Hull FC.

1 October 2012 - Reece Lyne signs from Hull FC on three-year contract.

2 October 2012 - Paul Sykes signs permanent contract for 2013.

19 October 2012 - forward Justin Poore joins from Parramatta on two-year deal.

23 October 2012 - Richard Mathers signs permanent two-year deal.

2 November 2012 - Tim Smith extends contract to end of 2014.

CLUB RECORDS

Highest score:
90-12 v Highfield, 27/10/92
Highest score against:
0-86 v Castleford, 17/4/95
Record attendance:
30,676 v Huddersfield, 26/2/21

MATCH RECORDS

Tries:
7 Fred Smith v Keighley, 25/4/59
Keith Slater v Hunslet, 6/2/71
Goals:
13 Mark Conway v Highfield, 27/10/92
Points:
36 Jamie Rooney v Chorley, 27/2/2004

SEASON RECORDS

Tries: 38 Fred Smith 1959-60
David Smith 1973-74
Goals: 163 Neil Fox 1961-62
Points: 407 Neil Fox 1961-62

CAREER RECORDS

Tries: 272 by Neil Fox 1956-69; 1970-74
Goals: 1,836 by Neil Fox 1956-69; 1970-74
Points: 4,488 by Neil Fox 1956-69; 1970-74
Appearances:
605 Harry Wilkinson 1930-49

WAKEFIELD T WILDCATS

DATE	FIXTURE	RESULT	SCORERS	LGE	ATT
3/2/12	Widnes (a)	W14-32	t:Lauitiiti,Raleigh,Mathers,T Smith,Fox(2) g:John(4)	2nd	8,120
12/2/12	Hull KR (h)	L10-22	t:Cockayne,Raleigh g:John	6th	8,612
25/2/12	Bradford (h)	L18-36	t:Cockayne,Southern,Kirmond,Mathers g:John	11th	6,934
4/3/12	Hull FC (a)	L14-10	t:Cockayne,Wood g:John	11th	11,105
11/3/12	Huddersfield (h)	L14-32	t:Cockayne(3) g:John	11th	8,794
18/3/12	Warrington (a)	L32-30	t:Washbrook,John,Mathers,Lauitiiti,Mellars g:John(5)	11th	10,686
25/3/12	Catalan Dragons (h)	W32-22	t:Cockayne,Fox(2),Raleigh,Kirmond g:John(6)	11th	7,254
31/3/12	London Broncos (a)	L36-0		12th	2,268
6/4/12	Castleford (h)	L16-34	t:Fox,Sykes,Wood g:Sykes(2)	13th	9,786
9/4/12	Wigan (a)	L36-6	t:Wood g:Sykes	12th	13,609
13/4/12	Leeds (a) (CCR4)	L38-18	t:Amor,Kirmond,John g:Sykes(3)	N/A	7,140
21/4/12	Salford (h)	W26-22	t:Collis,Washbrook,Mariano,Fox g:Sykes(5)	11th	6,748
4/5/12	St Helens (a)	L38-12	t:Collis,Fox g:Sykes(2)	12th	13,177
20/5/12	Warrington (h)	L12-42	t:Mariano,Southern g:Sykes(2)	12th	8,483
26/5/12	Castleford (MW) ●	W26-32	t:Mellars,Mathers,Southern,Washbrook,Fox,T Smith g:Sykes(4)	11th	N/A
3/6/12	London Broncos (h)	W24-6	t:Mellars,Collis,Lauitiiti,Kirmond g:Sykes(4)	11th	5,876
10/6/12	Hull FC (h)	W32-30	t:Collis,Fox,Sykes,Washbrook,Amor,Lauitiiti g:Sykes(4)	11th	8,986
18/6/12	Leeds (a)	L44-40	t:Cockayne,T Smith,Collis,Lauitiiti,Trout,Wilkes,Fox g:Sykes(6)	11th	12,272
24/6/12	Bradford (a)	L34-26	t:Aiton,Cockayne,T Smith,Mariano,Amor g:Sykes(3)	11th	11,236
30/6/12	Catalan Dragons (a)	L34-10	t:Lauitiiti,Trout g:Sykes	11th	8,842
8/7/12	Wigan (h)	L10-52	t:Fox,Cockayne g:Sykes	11th	9,107
22/7/12	Huddersfield (a)	W14-35	t:Cockayne,Collis,L Smith,Mathers,T Smith,Kirmond g:Sykes(5) fg:Sykes	11th	6,579
30/7/12	Leeds (h)	W38-18	t:Raleigh,Sykes,Kirmond,Washbrook,Wood,Collis,Fox g:Sykes(5)	11th	9,547
5/8/12	Castleford (a)	W12-40	t:Cockayne,Mathers(2),T Smith,Collis,Kirmond,L Smith g:Sykes(6)	10th	7,050
12/8/12	St Helens (h)	W33-32	t:L Smith(2),Raleigh,Kirmond(2),Wood g:Sykes(4) fg:Sykes	10th	7,876
19/8/12	Hull KR (a)	W30-31	t:Cockayne(2),Fox,Mariano,Collis,Wood g:Sykes(3) fg:Sykes	9th	8,726
2/9/12	Widnes (h)	W22-18	t:Amor,Mathers,Lauitiiti,Kirmond g:Sykes(3)	8th	8,234
8/9/12	Salford (a) ●●	W34-42	t:Mariano,Raleigh,Collis,Johnson,Cockayne,Fox,L Smith g:Sykes(7)	8th	2,380
15/9/12	Leeds (a) (EPO)	L42-20	t:Cockayne,L Smith,Mathers,Lauitiiti g:Sykes(2)	N/A	9,044

● Played at Etihad Stadium, Manchester
●● Played at Leigh Sports Village

	D.O.B.	APP		TRIES		GOALS		FG		PTS	
		ALL	SL	ALL	SL	ALL	SL	ALL	SL	ALL	SL
Paul Aiton	29/5/85	19(2)	18(2)	1	1	0	0	0	0	4	4
Kyle Amor	26/5/87	23(2)	22(2)	4	3	0	0	0	0	16	12
Ben Cockayne	20/7/83	28	27	16	16	0	0	0	0	64	64
Dean Collis	21/10/85	22	21	10	10	0	0	0	0	40	40
Danny Cowling	20/12/92	1	1	0	0	0	0	0	0	0	0
Andy Ellis	15/12/84	10	10	0	0	0	0	0	0	0	0
Peter Fox	5/11/83	29	28	14	14	0	0	0	0	56	56
Matt James	26/3/87	(5)	(4)	0	0	0	0	0	0	0	0
Isaac John	12/12/88	13(1)	13	2	1	19	19	0	0	46	42
Paul Johnson	13/3/88	1(20)	1(20)	1	1	0	0	0	0	4	4
Liam Kay	17/12/91	1	1	0	0	0	0	0	0	0	0
Danny Kirmond	11/11/85	24	23	10	9	0	0	0	0	40	36
Ali Lauitiiti	13/7/79	22(1)	22(1)	8	8	0	0	0	0	32	32
Frankie Mariano	10/5/87	7(8)	7(8)	5	5	0	0	0	0	20	20
Richard Mathers	24/10/83	28	27	9	9	0	0	0	0	36	36
Vince Mellars	27/1/84	16(3)	16(2)	3	3	0	0	0	0	12	12
Andy Raleigh	17/3/81	24(4)	23(4)	6	6	0	0	0	0	24	24
Lee Smith	8/8/86	9	9	6	6	0	0	0	0	24	24
Tim Smith	13/1/85	28	27	6	6	0	0	0	0	24	24
Steve Southern	29/4/82	7(8)	7(8)	3	3	0	0	0	0	12	12
Paul Sykes	11/8/81	22	21	3	3	73	70	3	3	161	155
Motu Tony	29/5/81	1	1	0	0	0	0	0	0	0	0
Kyle Trout	1/3/91	(11)	(11)	2	2	0	0	0	0	8	8
Lucas Walshaw	4/8/92	5(3)	4(3)	0	0	0	0	0	0	0	0
Danny Washbrook	18/9/85	29	28	5	5	0	0	0	0	20	20
Matthew Wildie	25/10/90	1(1)	1(1)	0	0	0	0	0	0	0	0
Oliver Wilkes	2/5/80	5(20)	5(19)	1	1	0	0	0	0	4	4
Kyle Wood	18/6/89	2(27)	1(27)	6	6	0	0	0	0	24	24

Ben Cockayne

LEAGUE RECORD
P27-W13-D0-L14
(8th, SL/Elimination Play-Off)
F633, A764, Diff-131
26 points.

CHALLENGE CUP
Round Four

ATTENDANCES
Best - v Castleford (SL - 9,786)
Worst - v London Broncos
(SL - 5,876)
Total (SL only) - 106,237
Average (SL only) - 8,172
(Up by 1,620 on 2011)

10 November 2011 - Lee Mitchell signs one-year extension for 2012 with additional one-year option and joins Castleford on loan for SLXVII.

15 November 2011 - Tyrone McCarthy signs new two-year contract to end of 2013.

17 November 2011 - assistant coaches Willie Poching and Richard Marshall sign contracts for 2012.

8 December 2011 - prop Adrian Morley granted three-month Testimonial for services to the game.

26 December 2011 - Stefan Ratchford and Chris Hill both make debuts in 32-18 home Boxing Day win over Widnes.

3 January 2012 - Lee Briers, Ryan Atkins and Ben Westwood named in League Express Team of the Year.

3 January 2012 - centre Ryan Shaw joins Castleford Tigers on month's loan.

9 January 2012 - Ben Hellewell and Brooke Broughton join York on dual registration.

9 January 2012 - squad arrives in Australia for three-week training camp.

15 January 2012 - David Solomona breaks leg in training and undergoes surgery in Sydney.

28 January 2012 - 34-28 win over South Sydney with Matt King in opposition.

5 February 2012 - Lee Briers dropped as disciplinary measure as late Rhys Evans try secures 20-20 draw at Hull FC in Super League opener.

12 February 2012 - Lee Briers returns as nine-try Wolves beat London Broncos 50-10 in round 2.

18 February 2012 - Ben Harrison suffers knee injury in 32-22 win at Huddersfield.

1 March 2012 - Ryan Shaw joins Leigh Centurions on dual registration.

3 March 2012 - Ryan Atkins crosses for 100th career try as 23-10 win at Bradford keeps Wolves top.

5 March 2012 - Gareth O'Brien joins Widnes on month's loan.

9 March 2012 - unbeaten start to the season ends with 26-18 defeat at Leeds. Mickey Higham banned for two games for high tackle.

13 March 2012 - Stefan Ratchford undergoes surgery on shoulder injury sustained at Leeds.

14 March 2012 - Brett Hodgson named captain of Exiles team.

18 March 2012 - Brad Dwyer makes debut as Wolves hold on for 32-30 home win over Wakefield.

23 March 2012 - two late Brett Hodgson penalty goals secure 22-20 round-eight win at Wigan. Ben Westwood suspended for one match for striking with the arm.

28 March 2012 - James Laithwaite joins Leigh on dual registration.

30 March 2012 - 28-16 home defeat to St Helens after trailing 22-0 until 39th minute.

KEY DATES - WARRINGTON WOLVES

3 April 2012 - Gareth O'Brien in squad to face Widnes on Easter Thursday after returning from loan spell with the Vikings.

5 April 2012 - Ben Currie makes debut in 46-12 home win over Widnes. Garreth Carvell banned for two games the following Wednesday for kicking out in tackle.

9 April 2012 - Richie Myler suffers groin injury and Adrian Morley neck problem in 44-16 defeat at Catalans on Easter Monday.

15 April 2012 - Jordan Burke makes debut in 44-18 round-four Challenge Cup win at Keighley.

19 April 2012 - young prop Glenn Riley joins Swinton on loan until end of season.

22 April 2012 - 54-6 home, round 12 win over Castleford after leading 38-0 at half-time.

28 April 2012 - 32-16 home win over Bradford secures Cup quarter-final berth.

1 May 2012 - draw Catalans away in last-eight.

13 May 2012 - 32-22 win in Perpignan secures semi-final berth.

20 May 2012 - 42-12 win at Wakefield moves Wolves into second place.

23 May 2012 - Rhys Williams joins Castleford on one-month loan.

26 May 2012 - Joel Monaghan scores five tries in 68-4 Magic Weekend win over Widnes.

3 June 2012 - cold, wet 23-22 defeat at Hull KR after leading 22-6.

9 June 2012 - Chris Riley and Gareth O'Brien score try-braces in 37-18 home win over Leeds.

24 June 2012 - Ryan Atkins hat-trick in 40-18 home win over Hull FC.

29 June 2012 - 48-24 hammering at Salford.

2 July 2012 - James Laithwaite goes on month's loan to Hull KR.

9 July 2012 - 15-6 home win over Catalan Dragons.

15 July 2012 - 33-6 win over Huddersfield in Challenge Cup semi-final at Salford.

6 August 2012 - 22-12 win at St Helens all but secures second spot in table.

9 August 2012 - 10 players sign contract extensions. Adrian Morley, Lee Briers, Mickey Higham and James Laithwaite to end of 2013 season; Brett Hodgson, Brad Dwyer and Mike Cooper 2014; Ben Westwood and Gareth O'Brien to 2015; Chris Hill until the end of 2016.

11 August 2012 - 30-10 home win over Wigan moves Wolves one point behind table-toppers. Lee Briers makes 400th appearance.

17 August 2012 - 62-18 defeat at London Broncos the week before Wembley.

25 August 2012 - 35-18 win over Leeds is third Wembley success in four seasons. Brett Hodgson wins Lance Todd Trophy.

2 September 2012 - 54-6 round-26 home win over Huddersfield.

9 September 2012 - 52-14 win at Widnes in last round.

15 September 2012 - 28-6 home qualifying play-off defeat to St Helens.

22 September 2012 - 32-22 Preliminary semi-final home defeat by Hull FC.

29 September 2012 - 36-18 Qualifying semi-final win at St Helens.

6 October 2012 - Paul Wood has ruptured testicle removed after 26-18 Grand Final defeat to Leeds.

10 October 2012 - Matty Blythe joins Bradford on one-year's loan.

19 October 2012 - coach Tony Smith signs contract extension to November 2015.

CLUB RECORDS
Highest score:
112-0 v Swinton, 20/5/2011
Highest score against:
12-84 v Bradford, 9/9/2001
Record attendance:
34,404 v Wigan, 22/1/49 *(Wilderspool)*
15,000 v St Helens, 30/3/2012
(Halliwell Jones Stadium)

MATCH RECORDS
Tries:
7 Brian Bevan v Leigh, 29/3/48
Brian Bevan v Bramley, 22/4/53
Goals:
16 Lee Briers v Swinton, 20/5/2011
Points:
44 Lee Briers v Swinton, 20/5/2011

SEASON RECORDS
Tries: 66 Brian Bevan 1952-53
Goals: 170 Steve Hesford 1978-79
Points: 363 Harry Bath 1952-53

CAREER RECORDS
Tries: 740 Brian Bevan 1945-62
Goals: 1,159 Steve Hesford 1975-85
Points: 2,543 Lee Briers 1997-2012
Appearances: 620 Brian Bevan 1945-62

WARRINGTON WOLVES

DATE	FIXTURE	RESULT	SCORERS	LGE	ATT
5/2/12	Hull FC (a)	D20-20	t:Waterhouse,Williams,Grix,Evans g:Westwood(2)	7th	12,710
12/2/12	London Broncos (h)	W50-10	t:Bridge(2),J Monaghan(2),Atkins(2),Ratchford,Briers(2) g:Westwood(5),Briers(2)	3rd	10,834
18/2/12	Huddersfield (a)	W22-32	t:Riley(2),Bridge,J Monaghan,Blythe,Myler g:Briers(4)	1st	8,184
26/2/12	Hull KR (h)	W42-10	t:Riley(2),Bridge,Atkins(2),Westwood(2) g:Hodgson(7)	1st	11,916
3/3/12	Bradford (a)	W10-23	t:Riley,Higham,Atkins,Waterhouse g:Bridge(3) fg:Briers	1st	11,318
9/3/12	Leeds (a)	L26-18	t:Blythe,Hill,Westwood g:Briers(3)	2nd	17,120
18/3/12	Wakefield (h)	W32-30	t:Atkins,Myler(2),Westwood,Grix,J Monaghan g:Briers(4)	2nd	10,686
23/3/12	Wigan (a)	W20-22	t:Atkins,J Monaghan,Briers g:Hodgson(5)	1st	21,267
30/3/12	St Helens (h)	L16-28	t:Hodgson,J Monaghan,Atkins g:Hodgson(2)	3rd	15,000
5/4/12	Widnes (h)	W46-12	t:Bridge(2),Riley(3),Hodgson,Atkins,Dwyer g:Hodgson(7)	3rd	12,042
9/4/12	Catalan Dragons (a)	L44-16	t:Higham,Riley,Dwyer g:Hodgson(2)	5th	11,500
15/4/12	Keighley (a) (CCR4)	W18-44	t:J Monaghan,Westwood,Hill,Williams,Dwyer,Riley,Harrison,Wood g:Briers(6)	N/A	2,196
22/4/12	Castleford (h)	W54-6	t:Bridge,Waterhouse,J Monaghan(2),Hodgson(2),Atkins(2),Riley,Grix g:Hodgson(7)	3rd	10,519
28/4/12	Bradford (h) (CCR5)	W32-16	t:J Monaghan(3),Hodgson,Riley,Atkins g:Hodgson(4)	N/A	5,505
6/5/12	Salford (h)	W24-20	t:Williams(2),Currie,Carvell g:O'Brien(4)	3rd	10,437
13/5/12	Catalan Dragons (a) (CCQF)	W22-32	t:J Monaghan,Hodgson,Riley,Wood,Bridge g:Hodgson(6)	N/A	7,476
20/5/12	Wakefield (a)	W12-42	t:Atkins(3),Riley(2),Ratchford(2) g:Hodgson(7)	2nd	8,483
26/5/12	Widnes (MW) ●	W68-4	t:Blythe(3),Carvell,J Monaghan(5),Atkins,Ratchford,Currie g:O'Brien(10)	2nd	N/A
3/6/12	Hull KR (a)	L23-22	t:O'Brien,Westwood,Riley(2) g:Hodgson(3)	2nd	7,661
8/6/12	Leeds (h)	W37-18	t:Waterhouse,Riley(2),O'Brien(2),Atkins g:Hodgson(5),O'Brien fg:Briers	2nd	10,835
24/6/12	Hull FC (h)	W40-18	t:Atkins(3),Riley,Briers,Carvell,J Monaghan g:O'Brien(6)	2nd	10,582
29/6/12	Salford (a)	L48-24	t:Ratchford,Myler,Riley,Blythe g:O'Brien(4)	2nd	6,179
9/7/12	Catalan Dragons (h)	W15-6	t:Westwood,Atkins g:Hodgson(2),O'Brien fg:M Monaghan	2nd	10,570
15/7/12	Huddersfield (CCSF) ●●	W6-33	t:Carvell,Atkins,J Monaghan,Hodgson,Ratchford g:Hodgson(6) fg:Hodgson	N/A	9,473
22/7/12	Castleford (a)	W26-40	t:Westwood(2),J Monaghan,Atkins,Riley,Solomona,Ratchford g:Hodgson(6)	2nd	6,167
29/7/12	Bradford (h)	W50-22	t:J Monaghan,Myler,Riley,Ratchford(4),Grix,Solomona g:Briers(5),O'Brien(2)	2nd	10,750
6/8/12	St Helens (a)	W12-22	t:Hodgson,Hill,Waterhouse,Riley g:Hodgson(3)	2nd	15,728
11/8/12	Wigan (h)	W30-10	t:Westwood,Harrison,J Monaghan,Ratchford,Myler g:Hodgson(5)	2nd	13,859
17/8/12	London Broncos (a)	L62-18	t:Ratchford,Myler,Williams g:Ratchford(3)	2nd	2,261
25/8/12	Leeds (CCF) ●●●	W18-35	t:J Monaghan,Waterhouse,Riley,Atkins,McCarthy,Hodgson g:Hodgson(5) fg:Briers	N/A	79,180
2/9/12	Huddersfield (h)	W54-6	t:J Monaghan(3),Bridge,Ratchford,Myler,Hodgson,Williams,Atkins,Hill g:Hodgson(7)	2nd	10,515
9/9/12	Widnes (a)	W14-52	t:Higham(2),Williams,Riley(2),Ratchford,Solomona,Hill,Atkins,Wood g:Briers(5),Solomona	2nd	8,617
15/9/12	St Helens (h) (QPO)	L6-28	t:Hodgson g:Hodgson	N/A	10,190
22/9/12	Hull FC (h) (PSF)	W24-12	t:Waterhouse,Myler,Ratchford,Hodgson g:Hodgson(4)	N/A	7,323
29/9/12	St Helens (a) (QSF)	W18-36	t:Riley(2),Grix,J Monaghan,Waterhouse(2) g:Hodgson(6)	N/A	12,715
6/10/12	Leeds (GF) ●●●●	L26-18	t:Myler,J Monaghan,Atkins g:Hodgson(3)	N/A	70,676

● Played at Etihad Stadium, Manchester ●● Played at City of Salford Community Stadium
●●● Played at Wembley Stadium ●●●● Played at Old Trafford, Manchester

		APP		TRIES		GOALS		FG		PTS	
	D.O.B.	ALL	SL	ALL	SL	ALL	SL	ALL	SL	ALL	SL
Ryan Atkins	7/10/85	32	28	27	24	0	0	0	0	108	96
Matty Blythe	20/11/88	11(7)	10(7)	6	6	0	0	0	0	24	24
Chris Bridge	5/7/84	20(2)	17(2)	9	8	3	3	0	0	42	38
Lee Briers	14/6/78	27	22	4	4	29	23	3	2	77	64
Jordan Burke	16/11/91	1	0	0	0	0	0	0	0	0	0
Garreth Carvell	21/4/80	14(10)	11(9)	4	3	0	0	0	0	16	12
Michael Cooper	15/9/88	8(23)	8(20)	0	0	0	0	0	0	0	0
Ben Currie	15/7/94	2(4)	2(3)	2	2	0	0	0	0	8	8
Brad Dwyer	28/4/93	1(7)	1(6)	3	2	0	0	0	0	12	8
Rhys Evans	30/10/92	5	5	1	1	0	0	0	0	4	4
Simon Grix	28/9/85	18(8)	18(6)	5	5	0	0	0	0	20	20
Ben Harrison	24/2/88	18(6)	15(4)	2	1	0	0	0	0	8	4
Mick Higham	18/9/80	23(5)	18(5)	4	4	0	0	0	0	16	16
Chris Hill	3/11/87	24(9)	19(9)	5	4	0	0	0	0	20	16
Brett Hodgson	12/2/78	23	19	12	8	103	82	1	0	255	196
Tyrone McCarthy	21/4/88	11(11)	9(8)	1	0	0	0	0	0	4	0
Joel Monaghan	22/4/82	31	26	29	22	0	0	0	0	116	88
Michael Monaghan	13/5/80	10(11)	10(9)	0	0	0	0	1	1	1	1
Adrian Morley	10/5/77	19(9)	19(7)	0	0	0	0	0	0	0	0
Richard Myler	21/5/90	24	23	10	10	0	0	0	0	40	40
Gareth O'Brien	31/10/91	13(1)	10(1)	3	3	28	28	0	0	68	68
Stefan Ratchford	19/7/88	22(4)	20(4)	16	15	3	3	0	0	70	66
Chris Riley	22/2/88	34(1)	29(1)	29	25	0	0	0	0	116	100
David Solomona	26/1/78	(5)	(5)	3	3	1	1	0	0	14	14
Trent Waterhouse	8/1/81	31	26	9	8	0	0	0	0	36	32
Ben Westwood	25/7/81	25	20	10	9	7	7	0	0	54	50
Rhys Williams	8/12/89	9	8	7	6	0	0	0	0	28	24
Paul Wood	10/10/81	12(20)	10(17)	3	1	0	0	0	0	12	4

Chris Riley

LEAGUE RECORD
P27-W20-D1-L6
(2nd, SL/Grand Final Runners-Up)
F909, A539, Diff+370
41 points.

CHALLENGE CUP
Winners

ATTENDANCES
Best - v St Helens (SL - 15,000)
Worst - v Bradford (CC - 5,505)
Total (SL, inc play-offs) - 166,058
Average (SL, inc play-offs) - 11,070
(Down by 79 on 2011)

31 March 2011 - Widnes awarded Grade C Super League licence.

10 May 2011 - Denis Betts announced as new head coach on two-year contract.

11 May 2011 - Chris Gerrard released and leaves with immediate effect.

12 July 2011 - Crusaders' Hep Cahill signs three-year deal; Ben Cross, released by Leeds, signs one-year contract. Paddy Flynn, Steve Pickersgill and Ben Kavanagh all retained.

15 July 2011 - Shaun Briscoe signs from Hull KR on a two-year deal from 2012. Current player Macgraff Leuluai earns two-year Super League contract.

27 July 2011 - current players Dave Allen and Thomas Coyle sign new two-year deals; Kurt Haggerty one year with one-year option.

31 July 2011 - local products Danny Craven, Jack Owens and Tom Gilmore sign three-year Super League contracts.

1 August 2011 - Patrick Ah Van signs from Bradford on two-year deal.

7 August 2011 - Crusaders' Lloyd White signs three-year contract. Ben Davies, Chris Dean and Frank Winterstein join on two-year contracts.

26 August 2011 - Dean Gaskell, Richard Varkulis, Gareth Haggerty, Danny Hulme, Shane Grady, Chris Lunt, Chaz I'Anson, Matt Gardner, Greg Scott, Daniel Heckenberg, Danny Sculthorpe, Tangi Ropati and Dave Houghton all released.

2 September 2011 - Willie Isa joins from Castleford on two-year deal.

6 September 2011 - Warrington hooker Jon Clarke signs two-year deal.

7 September 2011 - former Crusader Rhys Hanbury joins on two-year contract.

18 September 2011 - Anthony Thackeray, Steve Tyrer and James Coyle all released.

5 October 2011 - Australian stand-off Anthony Watts, out of the game in 2011, joins on one-year deal.

11 October 2011 - St Helens hooker Scott Moore joins on three-year deal.

29 November 2011 - Wigan centre Stefan Marsh joins on season-long loan.

7 December 2011 - Academy forward Anthony Mullally handed 12-month contract on return from Brisbane.

26 December 2011 - Anthony Watts limps off with hamstring problem after five minutes of 32-18 Boxing Day defeat to Warrington.

3 January 2012 - Jon Clarke and Shaun Briscoe named captain and vice captain.

8 January 2012 - 28-6 pre-season win over Swinton.

20 January 2012 - former Wigan and Hull FC fullback Cameron Phelps signs two-year contract.

20 January 2012 - Paddy Flynn scores hat-trick in 42-24 friendly defeat at St Helens. Anthony Watts leaves field early with hamstring problem.

25 January 2012 - Melbourne Storm prop Sione 'John' Kite signs one-year deal.

3 February 2012 - 32-14 round-one defeat by Wakefield on icy Stobart Stadium i-pitch.

4 February 2012 - Thomas Coyle suffers compound fracture of left tibia and fibula in under-20s game.

KEY DATES - WIDNES VIKINGS

12 February 2012 - Jon Clarke misses 66-6 round-two defeat at Huddersfield with hamstring injury.

17 February 2012 - Scott Moore, Hep Cahill and Simon Finnigan suspended for breach of club discipline. Moore suffers broken jaw in training.

19 February 2012 - Anthony Watts, on debut, ruled out for season with knee injury and Ben Kavanagh snaps Achilles tendon in 38-18 home loss to Salford.

24 February 2012 - suspended Hep Cahill and Simon Finnigan return to squad to face Leeds.

26 February 2012 - Shaun Briscoe debuts in home 44-16 round-4 defeat to Leeds. Simon Finnigan picks up Widnes's first Albert Goldthorpe medal point.

29 February 2012 - Cameron Phelps gets visa and makes arrival.

1 March 2012 - Sione Kite links up with the club after obtaining visa.

4 March 2012 - Ben Cross picks up calf injury in second minute of 36-0 defeat at Hull KR.

5 March 2012 - Warrington reserve scrum-half Gareth O'Brien arrives on month's loan.

11 March 2012 - Lloyd White kicks 71st minute field goal to seal shock 37-36 win over Wigan. Cameron Phelps, Gareth O'Brien and Sione Kite all debut.

18 March 2012 - Paddy Flynn bags two tries and Shaun Briscoe leaves field with concussion in 58-10 defeat at Hull FC.

25 March 2012 - Widnes off bottom of the table for the first time after 38-30 home win over London. Hep Cahill banned for one game for striking with forearm.

28 March 2012 - Kurt Haggerty signs for North Wales Crusaders on dual registration.

2 April 2012 - Paddy Flynn signs two-year contract extension to end of 2014.

12 April 2012 - Scott Moore leaves by mutual consent and signs for Huddersfield.

14 April 2012 - 40-38 Challenge Cup round-four exit at home to St Helens.

17 April 2012 - Wigan halfback Joe Mellor re-joins on a month's loan.

20 April 2012 - 62-0 round-12 defeat at St Helens.

1 May 2012 - Anthony Mullally rejects improved contract offer.

1 May 2012 - Anthony Watts, out for season, signs new deal for 2013.

7 May 2012 - Anthony Watts released due to personal reasons.

18 May 2012 - deal to sign former Wakefield forward Jarrad Hickey, released by London, falls through.

26 May 2012 - Vikings pay transfer fee to Huddersfield to sign Kevin Brown on four-year deal from 2013.

26 May 2012 - 68-4 hammering by Warrington at Magic Weekend. Jon Clarke gets one match for dangerous throw.

30 May 2012 - Leeds hooker Paul McShane joins on loan for rest of season.

3 June 2012 - last-minute Cameron Phelps try seals 26-22 home win over Huddersfield. Joe Mellor banned for one game for dangerous throw.

8 June 2012 - Anthony Mullally joins Whitehaven on loan for rest of season.

9 June 2012 - last-second defeat at London by 28-24.

29 June 2012 - Eamon O'Carroll signs from Hull FC with immediate effect until end of 2014.

2 July 2012 - 40-10 televised Monday-night home win over Castleford.

6 July 2012 - Steve Pickersgill signs new 12-month contract until end of 2013.

8 July 2012 - last-second touchline conversion gains St Helens 24-23 win at Stobart Stadium.

19 July 2012 - MacGraff Leuluai goes to Leigh on initial one-month loan.

20 July 2012 - 46-8 win at Salford.

18 August 2012 - 42-16 home TV win over Hull FC.

23 August 2012 - Simon Finnigan to join Leigh.

2 September 2012 - late try means 22-18 defeat at Wakefield.

5 September 2012 - Sione Kite and Kurt Haggerty released.

9 September 2012 - 52-14 home defeat by Warrington means last-place finish on points difference.

10 September 2012 - former Hull FC chief executive James Rule takes over as CEO.

10 October 2012 - Stefan Marsh and Joe Mellor sign permanent two-year contracts. Ben Davies and Alex Gerrard sign for one year.

16 October 2012 - Thomas Coyle released.

CLUB RECORDS

Highest score:
90-4 v Doncaster, 10/6/2007
Highest score against:
6-76 v Catalan Dragons, 31/3/2012
Record attendance:
24,205 v St Helens, 16/2/61

MATCH RECORDS

Tries: 7 Phil Cantillon v York, 18/2/2001
Goals: 14 Mark Hewitt v Oldham, 25/7/99
Tim Hartley v Saddleworth, 7/3/2009
Points:
38 Gavin Dodd v Doncaster, 10/6/2007

SEASON RECORDS

Tries: 58 Martin Offiah 1988-89
Goals: 161 Mick Nanyan 2007
Points: 434 Mick Nanyan 2007

CAREER RECORDS

Tries: 234 Mal Aspey 1964-80
Goals: 1,083 Ray Dutton 1966-78
Points: 2,195 Ray Dutton 1966-78
Appearances: 591 Keith Elwell 1970-86

WIDNES VIKINGS

DATE	FIXTURE	RESULT	SCORERS	LGE	ATT
3/2/12	Wakefield (h)	L14-32	t:Craven,Ah Van,Cahill g:Ah Van	13th	8,120
12/2/12	Huddersfield (a)	L66-6	t:Flynn g:Ah Van	14th	8,869
19/2/12	Salford (h)	L18-38	t:Ah Van(2),Flynn g:Ah Van(2),Hanbury	14th	5,053
26/2/12	Leeds (h)	L16-44	t:Ah Van,Hanbury,Flynn g:Ah Van(2)	14th	6,046
4/3/12	Hull KR (a)	L36-0		14th	7,423
11/3/12	Wigan (h)	W37-36	t:Flynn,Marsh,Briscoe(2),White,Winterstein g:O'Brien(6) fg:White	14th	7,357
18/3/12	Hull FC (a)	L58-10	t:Flynn(2) g:O'Brien	14th	10,705
25/3/12	London Broncos (h)	W38-30	t:White(2),Dean,Hanbury,Davies,Phelps g:O'Brien(7)	12th	6,535
31/3/12	Catalan Dragons (a)	L76-6	t:Kite g:O'Brien	14th	9,156
5/4/12	Warrington (a)	L46-12	t:Dean,Allen g:Ah Van(2)	14th	12,042
9/4/12	Bradford (h)	L4-38	t:Hanbury	14th	5,687
14/4/12	St Helens (h) (CCR4)	L38-40	t:Ah Van(2),Hanbury,White(2),Haggerty,Cahill g:Ah Van(5)	N/A	3,069
20/4/12	St Helens (a)	L62-0		14th	14,243
7/5/12	Castleford (a)	L36-12	t:Flynn,Marsh g:Hanbury(2)	14th	5,580
20/5/12	Catalan Dragons (h)	L34-42	t:Marsh,Mellor,Hanbury,Dean,Haggerty,Ah Van g:Hanbury(5)	14th	4,684
26/5/12	Warrington (MW) ●	L68-4	t:Haggerty	14th	N/A
3/6/12	Huddersfield (h)	W26-22	t:Ah Van,Hanbury,Cross,Phelps g:Ah Van(5)	13th	4,644
9/6/12	London Broncos (a)	L28-24	t:Phelps(2),Winterstein(2) g:Ah Van(4)	14th	2,117
25/6/12	Wigan (a)	L54-12	t:Cross,Mellor g:Ah Van(2)	14th	13,445
2/7/12	Castleford (h)	W40-10	t:Marsh,Winterstein,Davies,McShane,Mellor,O'Carroll,Ah Van g:Ah Van(5),Hanbury	13th	4,501
8/7/12	St Helens (h)	L23-24	t:Ah Van(3),Dean,Phelps g:Hanbury fg:Hanbury	13th	7,023
20/7/12	Salford (a)	W8-46	t:Phelps(2),Ah Van(2),Hanbury(2),McShane,Craven g:Hanbury(7)	13th	5,196
29/7/12	Hull KR (h)	L26-32	t:Mellor,Marsh,Haggerty,Craven,Hanbury g:Hanbury(3)	13th	5,325
5/8/12	Bradford (a)	L38-26	t:Ah Van(2),Davies,Craven,Hanbury g:Hanbury(2),Ah Van	13th	10,261
10/8/12	Leeds (a)	L68-24	t:Marsh(2),Winterstein,Phelps g:Ah Van(4)	14th	13,326
18/8/12	Hull FC (h)	W42-16	t:Isa(2),Flynn,Briscoe(2),Winterstein,Craven,Hanbury g:Craven(2),McShane(3)	14th	5,008
2/9/12	Wakefield (a)	L22-18	t:Hanbury(2),Flynn g:Hanbury(2),McShane	14th	8,234
9/9/12	Warrington (h)	L14-52	t:Winterstein,McShane,Hanbury g:Hanbury	14th	8,617

● Played at Etihad Stadium, Manchester

		APP		TRIES		GOALS		FG		PTS	
	D.O.B.	ALL	SL	ALL	SL	ALL	SL	ALL	SL	ALL	SL
Patrick Ah Van	17/3/88	20	19	16	14	34	29	0	0	132	114
Dave Allen	15/9/85	23(3)	23(3)	1	1	0	0	0	0	4	4
Shaun Briscoe	23/2/83	7(1)	7(1)	4	4	0	0	0	0	16	16
Hep Cahill	15/10/86	25	24	2	1	0	0	0	0	8	4
Jon Clarke	4/4/79	18(1)	17(1)	0	0	0	0	0	0	0	0
Danny Craven	21/11/91	13(5)	12(5)	5	5	2	2	0	0	24	24
Ben Cross	6/12/78	20(1)	19(1)	2	2	0	0	0	0	8	8
Ben Davies	2/11/89	10(14)	10(14)	3	3	0	0	0	0	12	12
Chris Dean	17/1/88	20	19	4	4	0	0	0	0	16	16
Simon Finnigan	8/12/81	5(5)	5(5)	0	0	0	0	0	0	0	0
Paddy Flynn	11/12/87	21	20	9	9	0	0	0	0	36	36
Alex Gerrard	5/11/91	(8)	(8)	0	0	0	0	0	0	0	0
Tom Gilmore	2/2/94	(1)	(1)	0	0	0	0	0	0	0	0
Grant Gore	21/11/91	(1)	(1)	0	0	0	0	0	0	0	0
Kurt Haggerty	8/1/89	7(8)	6(8)	4	3	0	0	0	0	16	12
Rhys Hanbury	27/8/85	25	24	14	13	25	25	1	1	107	103
Willie Isa	1/1/89	25(2)	24(2)	2	2	0	0	0	0	8	8
Ben Kavanagh	4/3/88	1(5)	1(5)	0	0	0	0	0	0	0	0
Sione Kite	14/1/88	6(9)	6(8)	1	1	0	0	0	0	4	4
Macgraff Leuluai	9/2/90	1(10)	1(9)	0	0	0	0	0	0	0	0
Stefan Marsh	3/9/90	20	20	7	7	0	0	0	0	28	28
Paul McShane	19/11/89	6(5)	6(5)	3	3	4	4	0	0	20	20
Joe Mellor	28/11/90	11	11	4	4	0	0	0	0	16	16
Scott Moore	23/1/88	3(3)	3(3)	0	0	0	0	0	0	0	0
Anthony Mullally	28/6/91	(10)	(9)	0	0	0	0	0	0	0	0
Gareth O'Brien	31/10/91	4	4	0	0	15	15	0	0	30	30
Eamon O'Carroll	13/6/87	(3)	(3)	1	1	0	0	0	0	4	4
Jack Owens	3/6/94	4	3	0	0	0	0	0	0	0	0
Cameron Phelps	11/2/85	20	20	8	8	0	0	0	0	32	32
Steve Pickersgill	28/11/85	16(7)	15(7)	0	0	0	0	0	0	0	0
Anthony Watts	12/9/86	(1)	(1)	0	0	0	0	0	0	0	0
Lloyd White	9/10/88	6(9)	6(8)	5	3	0	0	1	1	21	13
Frank Winterstein	17/12/86	27	26	7	7	0	0	0	0	28	28

Rhys Hanbury

LEAGUE RECORD
P27-W6-D0-L21
(14th, SL)
F532, A1082, Diff-550
12 points.

CHALLENGE CUP
Round Four

ATTENDANCES
Best - v Warrington (SL - 8,617)
Worst - v St Helens (CC - 3,069)
Total (SL only) - 78,600
Average (SL only) - 6,046
(Up by 2,302 on 2011,
Championship)

17 November 2011 - former Crusaders Gil Dudson and Ben Flower sign two-year contracts as Warriors announce tie-up with Wales Rugby League.

19 November 2011 - Thomas Leuluai announces he will join NZ Warriors at end of 2012.

21 November 2011 - Sam Tomkins selected to play for Barbarians rugby union team and scores only try in 60-11 defeat.

29 November 2011 - centre Stefan Marsh joins Widnes on one-year loan deal.

12 December 2011 - centre-second row Anthony Gelling joins from Auckland Vulcans.

3 January 2012 - Sam Tomkins voted Player of 2011 by readers of League Express newspaper.

15 January 2012 - Pat Richards scores two tries and three goals in 22-6 pre-season win at Hull KR.

19 January 2012 - 30-18 home defeat by Huddersfield in Sean O'Loughlin Testimonial match.

24 January 2012 - hard-fought 16-10 friendly win over Reds at Salford's new stadium.

5 February 2012 - George Carmont breaks thumb in 20-16 home, opening-round defeat to Huddersfield.

7 February 2012 - Liam Farrell suspended for one match for dangerous contact against Huddersfield in first early guilty plea in English game.

11 February 2012 - Josh Charnley scores hat trick in 20-6 home win over Leeds.

15 February 2012 - Tom Spencer joins Leigh on dual registration.

19 February 2012 - Pat Richards becomes club's third all-time leading scorer with a try and six goals in 54-16 win at Bradford.

26 February 2012 - Sam Tomkins marks 100th Wigan appearance with hat-trick in 46-4 win at Castleford.

2 March 2012 - Paul Prescott joins South Wales Scorpions on short-term loan. Gil Dudson and Greg Burke also join the Welsh side on dual registration.

4 March 2012 - Josh Charnley bags another two tries in 36-12 home win over Catalans.

6 March 2012 - Jack Hughes signs to end of 2014, with extra two-year option for club.

11 March 2012 - Matt Russell, Joe Mellor, Anthony Gelling and Logan Tomkins make debuts in 37-36 defeat at win-less Widnes.

18 March 2012 - Brett Finch crosses twice in 42-30 home win over London.

23 March 2012 - Pat Richards' eight points in 22-20 home defeat to Warrington takes him past the 2,000 mark for Wigan. Epalahame Lauaki gets two-match ban for dangerous tackle.

30 March 2012 - Lee Mossop, ankle, and Ben Flower, hamstring out for up to six weeks after 40-20 win at Salford.

6 April 2012 - Gil Dudson makes debut in 28-10 Good Friday win at St Helens.

9 April 2012 - 36-6 home, Easter Monday win over Wakefield.

15 April 2012 - Sam Tomkins scores six tries in 98-4 home hammering of North Wales Crusaders in Challenge Cup.

KEY DATES - WIGAN WARRIORS

17 April 2012 - halfback Joe Mellor re-joins Widnes on month's loan.

22 April 2012 - Pat Richards scores hat-trick and 26 points and damages knee in 56-12 win at Hull FC.

27 April 2012 - battling 32-16 win at Featherstone in fifth round of Cup.

1 May 2012 - St Helens drawn at home in quarter-final. Matthew Russell joins Hull FC on month's loan.

9 May 2012 - Iain Thornley returns from Sale Sharks on three-and-a-half year contract.

11 May 2012 - Amos Roberts gives up injury battles and retires from playing.

12 May 2012 - 18-4 home win over St Helens ensures Challenge Cup semi-finals.

18 May 2012 - 32-12 win at Huddersfield moves Warriors a point clear at top.

25 May 2012 - Jeff Lima to join South Sydney at end of season.

27 May 2012 - Harrison Hansen breaks jaw, Gareth Hock and Chris Tuson sent off in 42-16 Magic Weekend win over St Helens.

29 May 2012 - Hock two, Tuson and Lee Mossop one each, banned for their parts in Magic brawl.

1 June 2012 - 50-8 win at Leeds.

9 June 2012 - 36-14 win over Catalans in Montpellier makes it 12 games unbeaten.

16 June 2012 - Thomas Leuluai breaks leg in Exiles game against England.

29 June 2012 - 30-22 home defeat to Bradford ends 13-match unbeaten run. Michael McIlorum sent off for punching Olivier Elima and takes one-match early guilty plea.

6 July 2012 - Matty Smith signs from Salford with immediate effect on three-year deal.

8 July 2012 - Sam Tomkins and George Carmont score hat-tricks in 52-10 win at Wakefield.

14 July 2012 - 39-28 Challenge Cup semi-final defeat to Leeds.

21 July 2012 - 44-6 victory at London Broncos.

4 August 2012 - Sam Powell makes debut in 48-10 home win over Hull FC.

11 August 2012 - 30-10 defeat at Warrington.

20 August 2012 - Pat Richards returns from 17-week injury lay-off with two tries and five goals in 38-6 home win over Salford.

2 September 2012 - record SL comeback from 26-0 secures 42-36 win at Hull KR and League Leaders Shield.

7 September 2012 - Stuart Fielden returns and Michael McIlorum sent off for late tackle on Anthony Laffranchi in 26-18 home defeat by St Helens.

11 September 2012 - Michael McIlorum suspended for three matches for reckless high tackle.

11 September 2012 - Wigan named Albert Goldthorpe Team of the Year.

13 September 2012 - Hull KR stand-off Blake Green signs on two-year contract.

14 September 2012 - George Carmont scores hat-trick in 46-6 home qualifying play-off win over fourth-placed Catalans.

23 September 2012 - Wigan elect to play Leeds in Qualifying semi-final.

28 September 2012 - Stuart Fielden released.

28 September 2012 - late Kevin Sinfield penalty means 13-12 Qualifying semi-final exit to Leeds.

2 October 2012 - Sam Tomkins awarded Man of Steel.

5 October 2012 - Stefan Marsh, Joe Mellor and Ryan King released.

16 October 2012 - Scott Taylor signs for two years with another year option, with a transfer fee payable to Hull KR.

CLUB RECORDS

Highest score:
116-0 v Flimby & Fothergill, 14/2/25
Highest score against:
0-75 v St Helens, 26/6/2005
Record attendance:
47,747 v St Helens, 27/3/59 *(Central Park)*
25,004 v St Helens, 25/3/2005
(JJB/DW Stadium)

MATCH RECORDS

Tries: 10 Martin Offiah v Leeds, 10/5/92
Shaun Edwards v Swinton, 29/9/92
Goals: 22 Jim Sullivan
v Flimby & Fothergill, 14/2/25
Points: 44 Jim Sullivan
v Flimby & Fothergill, 14/2/25

SEASON RECORDS

Tries: 62 Johnny Ring 1925-26
Goals: 186 Frano Botica 1994-95
Points: 462 Pat Richards 2010

CAREER RECORDS

Tries: 478 Billy Boston 1953-68
Goals: 2,317 Jim Sullivan 1921-46
Points: 4,883 Jim Sullivan 1921-46
Appearances: 774 Jim Sullivan 1921-46

WIGAN WARRIORS

DATE	FIXTURE	RESULT	SCORERS	LGE	ATT
5/2/12	Huddersfield (h)	L16-20	t:S Tomkins,Farrell,O'Loughlin g:Richards(2)	9th	16,771
11/2/12	Leeds (h)	W20-6	t:Charnley(3) g:Richards(4)	5th	15,370
19/2/12	Bradford (a)	W16-54	t:Charnley(2),Richards,Hock,Tuson(2),Goulding(2),Farrell(2) g:Richards(6),S Tomkins	4th	12,909
26/2/12	Castleford (a)	W4-46	t:O'Loughlin,S Tomkins(3),Richards(2),Charnley(2) g:Richards(7)	2nd	8,156
4/3/12	Catalan Dragons (h)	W36-12	t:Leuluai,Richards,Hughes,Charnley(2),O'Loughlin g:Richards(6)	2nd	14,464
11/3/12	Widnes (a)	L37-36	t:Hock,Hansen,Russell(2),Finch,Mellor g:Charnley(6)	3rd	7,357
18/3/12	London Broncos (h)	W42-30	t:Finch(2),Hock,Goulding,Carmont,Richards,S Tomkins g:Richards(7)	3rd	12,608
23/3/12	Warrington (h)	L20-22	t:Hock,McIlorum,Richards g:Richards(2),Charnley(2)	4th	21,267
30/3/12	Salford (a)	W20-40	t:Goulding(2),Charnley,S Tomkins(2),Carmont,Farrell,Russell g:Charnley(4)	4th	6,774
6/4/12	St Helens (a)	W10-28	t:Goulding,Carmont,S Tomkins,Hock,Lima g:Charnley(4)	4th	17,980
9/4/12	Wakefield (h)	W36-6	t:Leuluai,Gelling,Goulding(2),Carmont(2),Charnley g:Charnley(4)	2nd	13,609
15/4/12	North Wales (h) (CCR4)	W98-4	t:King(2),S Tomkins(6),Charnley(2),Farrell(3),Mellor,Tuson,Prescott, L Tomkins,Crosby g:Charnley(13)	N/A	4,198
22/4/12	Hull FC (a)	W12-56	t:Richards(3),Hock,S Tomkins,Charnley(2),McIlorum,Leuluai,Finch g:Richards(7),Charnley	2nd	11,549
27/4/12	Featherstone (a) (CCR5)	W16-32	t:O'Loughlin,Goulding,Hock(2),Leuluai,Charnley g:Charnley(3),S Tomkins	N/A	4,082
4/5/12	Hull KR (h)	W36-22	t:Charnley(3),S Tomkins,Mossop,Gelling(2) g:Charnley(4)	1st	14,457
12/5/12	St Helens (h) (CCQF)	W18-4	t:S Tomkins,O'Loughlin,Finch g:Charnley(3)	N/A	12,864
18/5/12	Huddersfield (a)	W12-32	t:Charnley(2),S Tomkins,Carmont(2),Farrell,Lima g:S Tomkins(2)	1st	10,123
27/5/12	St Helens (MW) ●	W16-42	t:S Tomkins(2),Hock,Charnley(2),O'Loughlin,Carmont,Farrell g:Charnley(5)	1st	N/A
1/6/12	Leeds (a)	W8-50	t:Lima,Farrell,O'Loughlin,Carmont,Leuluai(2),Charnley,Gelling,Finch g:Charnley(7)	1st	16,113
9/6/12	Catalan Dragons (a) ●●	W14-36	t:Tuson,Gelling,Charnley,Carmont(2),S Tomkins,Hughes g:Charnley(2),S Tomkins(2)	1st	13,858
25/6/12	Widnes (h)	W54-12	t:Charnley(3),McIlorum,Carmont,Prescott,Gelling,Finch(2),S Tomkins g:Charnley(7)	1st	13,445
29/6/12	Bradford (h)	L22-30	t:Gelling,Murphy,Flower,Crosby g:Charnley(3)	1st	19,628
8/7/12	Wakefield (a)	W10-52	t:S Tomkins(3),Hock,Carmont(3),Hansen,Thornley(2) g:S Tomkins(6)	1st	9,107
14/7/12	Leeds (CCSF) ●●●	L39-28	t:Carmont,Hock,Flower,O'Loughlin,Charnley g:S Tomkins(4)	N/A	12,860
21/7/12	London Broncos (a)	W6-44	t:S Tomkins(4),Charnley,Thornley,Smith,Finch g:S Tomkins(6)	1st	4,309
27/7/12	Castleford (h)	W40-16	t:Lauaki(2),Thornley,Farrell,Carmont,S Tomkins(2),Charnley g:S Tomkins(4)	1st	13,975
3/8/12	Hull FC (h)	W48-10	t:S Tomkins(2),Hock,Charnley(3),Farrell,McIlorum,Powell g:Charnley(6)	1st	17,736
11/8/12	Warrington (a)	L30-10	t:Hock,Thornley g:Charnley	1st	13,859
20/8/12	Salford (h)	W38-6	t:Richards(2),S Tomkins,Goulding,Hughes,Hansen,O'Loughlin g:Richards(5)	1st	13,703
2/9/12	Hull KR (a)	W36-42	t:Finch,Goulding,Hock,Richards(2),Carmont,Farrell,Charnley g:Richards(5)	1st	8,845
7/9/12	St Helens (h)	L18-26	t:Leuluai,Richards,S Tomkins g:Richards(3)	1st	21,522
14/9/12	Catalan Dragons (h) (QPO)	W46-6	t:Carmont(3),Leuluai,Goulding,Farrell,S Tomkins,Charnley g:Richards(7)	N/A	7,232
28/9/12	Leeds (h) (QSF)	L12-13	t:Hansen,Richards g:Richards(2)	N/A	12,334

● Played at Etihad Stadium, Manchester ●● Played at Stade de la Mosson, Montpellier ●●● Played at Galpharm Stadium, Huddersfield

		APP		TRIES		GOALS		FG		PTS	
	D.O.B.	ALL	SL	ALL	SL	ALL	SL	ALL	SL	ALL	SL
George Carmont	30/6/78	27	24	21	20	0	0	0	0	84	80
Josh Charnley	26/6/91	32	28	36	32	75	56	0	0	294	240
Dominic Crosby	11/12/90	(8)	(7)	2	1	0	0	0	0	8	4
Gil Dudson	16/6/90	5(5)	5(4)	0	0	0	0	0	0	0	0
Liam Farrell	2/7/90	8(21)	7(18)	14	11	0	0	0	0	56	44
Stuart Fielden	14/9/79	1	1	0	0	0	0	0	0	0	0
Brett Finch	20/8/81	31	28	10	9	0	0	0	0	40	36
Ben Flower	19/10/87	6(12)	6(11)	2	1	0	0	0	0	8	4
Anthony Gelling	18/10/90	13	10	7	7	0	0	0	0	28	28
Darrell Goulding	3/3/88	31	28	12	11	0	0	0	0	48	44
Harrison Hansen	26/10/85	28	25	4	4	0	0	0	0	16	16
Gareth Hock	5/9/83	30	26	14	11	0	0	0	0	56	44
Jack Hughes	4/1/92	12(10)	9(9)	3	3	0	0	0	0	12	12
Ryan King	23/1/92	1	0	2	0	0	0	0	0	8	0
Epalahame Lauaki	27/1/84	14(14)	13(11)	2	2	0	0	0	0	8	8
Thomas Leuluai	22/6/85	22(1)	19(1)	8	7	0	0	0	0	32	28
Jeff Lima	4/7/82	10(19)	8(18)	3	3	0	0	0	0	12	12
Rhodri Lloyd	22/7/93	1(2)	1(2)	0	0	0	0	0	0	0	0
Michael McIlorum	10/1/88	28(2)	25(1)	4	4	0	0	0	0	16	16
Joe Mellor	28/11/90	2(1)	1(1)	2	1	0	0	0	0	8	4
Lee Mossop	17/1/89	22(4)	20(3)	1	1	0	0	0	0	4	4
Jack Murphy	18/3/92	2	2	1	1	0	0	0	0	4	4
Sean O'Loughlin	24/11/82	27	24	9	6	0	0	0	0	36	24
Sam Powell	3/7/92	1	1	1	1	0	0	0	0	4	4
Paul Prescott	1/1/86	9(2)	6(2)	2	1	0	0	0	0	8	4
Pat Richards	27/2/82	14	14	15	15	63	63	0	0	186	186
Matthew Russell	6/6/93	2	2	3	3	0	0	0	0	12	12
Matty Smith	23/7/87	6(3)	6(3)	1	1	0	0	0	0	4	4
Tom Spencer	2/1/91	(4)	(4)	0	0	0	0	0	0	0	0
Iain Thornley	11/9/91	5	5	5	5	0	0	0	0	20	20
Logan Tomkins	1/8/91	3(6)	2(6)	1	0	0	0	0	0	4	0
Sam Tomkins	23/3/89	30	26	36	29	26	21	0	0	196	158
Chris Tuson	25/2/90	6(18)	5(15)	4	3	0	0	0	0	16	12

Josh Charnley

LEAGUE RECORD
P27-W21-D0-L6
(1st, SL/Qualifying Semi-Final)
F994, A449, Diff+545
42 points.

CHALLENGE CUP
Semi-Finalists

ATTENDANCES
Best - v St Helens (SL - 21,522)
Worst - v North Wales (CC - 4,198)
Total (SL, inc play-offs) - 228,121
Average (SL, inc play-offs) - 15,208
(Down by 79 on 2011)

SUPER LEAGUE XVII
Round by Round

ROUND 1

Friday 3rd February 2012

LEEDS RHINOS 34 HULL KINGSTON ROVERS 16

RHINOS: 1 Brent Webb; 14 Lee Smith; 3 Kallum Watkins; 4 Zak Hardaker; 5 Ryan Hall; 13 Kevin Sinfield (C); 6 Danny McGuire; 16 Ryan Bailey; 7 Rob Burrow; 10 Jamie Peacock; 11 Jamie Jones-Buchanan; 15 Brett Delaney; 12 Carl Ablett. Subs (all used): 8 Kylie Leuluai; 19 Weller Hauraki; 20 Darrell Griffin (D); 9 Paul McShane.
Tries: Delaney (5), Webb (25), Watkins (59, 63, 73), McGuire (78); **Goals:** Sinfield 5/6.
ROVERS: 1 Shannon McDonnell (D); 2 Craig Hall; 3 Kris Welham; 4 Jake Webster; 5 David Hodgson (D); 19 Scott Murrell; 7 Michael Dobson (C); 8 Joel Clinton; 14 Lincoln Withers (D); 23 Mickey Paea (D); 18 Graeme Horne (D); 11 Constantine Mika (D); 13 Rhys Lovegrove. Subs (all used): 10 Scott Taylor; 22 Scott Wheeldon; 9 Josh Hodgson; 20 Jordan Cox.
Tries: Horne (8, 38), Welham (48), D Hodgson (69); **Goals:** Dobson 0/4.
Rugby Leaguer & League Express Men of the Match: *Rhinos:* Brett Delaney; *Rovers:* Mickey Paea.
Penalty count: 12-5; **Half-time:** 10-8;
Referee: Phil Bentham; **Attendance:** 15,343.

WIDNES VIKINGS 14 WAKEFIELD TRINITY WILDCATS 32

VIKINGS: 25 Danny Craven; 3 Chris Dean (D3); 20 Stefan Marsh (D2); 4 Willie Isa (D); 5 Patrick Ah Van (D); 13 Jon Clarke (C) (D); 7 Rhys Hanbury (D); 8 Ben Cross (D); 9 Scott Moore (D); 16 Ben Kavanagh; 11 Frank Winterstein (D); 21 Dave Allen; 12 Hep Cahill (D). Subs (all used): 6 Lloyd White (D); 17 Steve Pickersgill; 24 Kurt Haggerty; 26 Anthony Mullally.
Tries: Craven (8), Ah Van (39), Cahill (56); **Goals:** Ah Van 1/3.
Sin bin: Cross (71) - dissent.
WILDCATS: 1 Richard Mathers (D); 2 Peter Fox (D2); 3 Dean Collis (D); 4 Vince Mellars (D); 5 Ben Cockayne (D); 6 Isaac John (D); 20 Tim Smith (D); 15 Kyle Amor; 14 Paul Aiton (D); 12 Steve Southern (C) (D); 11 Ali Lauitiiti (D); 17 Danny Kirmond (D2); 13 Danny Washbrook (D). Subs (all used): 7 Kyle Wood (D); 8 Oliver Wilkes (D2); 10 Andy Raleigh (D); 16 Paul Johnson.
Tries: Lauitiiti (21), Raleigh (42), Mathers (60), T Smith (65), Fox (72, 74); **Goals:** John 4/6.
Rugby Leaguer & League Express Men of the Match: *Vikings:* Frank Winterstein; *Wildcats:* Danny Kirmond.
Penalty count: 6-13; **Half-time:** 10-4;
Referee: Ben Thaler; **Attendance:** 8,120.

Saturday 4th February 2012

LONDON BRONCOS 24 ST HELENS 34

BRONCOS: 1 Luke Dorn; 5 Michael Robertson (D); 2 Liam Colbon (D); 3 Jamie O'Callaghan; 21 Kieran Dixon (D); 6 Michael Witt (D); 7 Craig Gower (C) (D); 8 Antonio Kaufusi (D); 9 Chad Randall; 13 Tony Clubb; 12 Chris Bailey; 11 Shane Rodney (D); 17 Jason Golden. Subs (all used): 16 Chris Melling; 18 Olsi Krasniqi; 14 Julien Rinaldi (D2); 10 Mark Bryant (D).
Tries: Robertson (9), Krasniqi (32), Bailey (37), Witt (65); **Goals:** Witt 4/4.
SAINTS: 6 Lance Hohaia (D); 21 Tom Makinson; 17 Gary Wheeler; 5 Francis Meli; 22 Jamie Foster; 20 Lee Gaskell; 7 Jonny Lomax; 14 Anthony Laffranchi (D); 9 James Roby (C); 10 Louie McCarthy-Scarsbrook; 19 Andrew Dixon; 4 Iosia Soliola; 12 Jon Wilkin. Subs: 8 Josh Perry; 16 Paul Clough; 15 Mark Flanagan (D); 2 Ade Gardner (not used).
Tries: Lomax (4), Dixon (19), Foster (48), Meli (60), Roby (74); **Goals:** Foster 7/7.
Rugby Leaguer & League Express Men of the Match: *Broncos:* Craig Gower; *Saints:* James Roby.
Penalty count: 6-6; **Half-time:** 18-16;
Referee: Robert Hicks; **Attendance:** 4,924.

SALFORD CITY REDS 10 CASTLEFORD TIGERS 24

CITY REDS: 1 Luke Patten; 2 Jodie Broughton; 3 Sean Gleeson; 4 Joel Moon (D); 5 Danny Williams; 6 Daniel Holdsworth; 7 Matty Smith; 21 Jordan James (D); 9 Wayne Godwin; 8 Lee Jewitt; 11 Matty Ashurst (D); 27 Vinnie Anderson; 13 Stephen Wild (C). Subs (all used): 24 Stuart Howarth (D); 17 Iafeta Palea'aesina; 16 Luke Adamson; 20 Ben Gledhill (D).
Tries: Smith (17), Ashurst (75); **Goals:** Holdsworth 1/2.
TIGERS: 1 Richard Owen; 4 Kirk Dixon; 3 Joe Arundel; 23 Ryan McGoldrick; 5 Josh Griffin (D); 6 Rangi Chase; 7 Danny Orr (C); 8 Jake Emmitt; 15 Adam Milner; 12 Jonathan Walker; 17 Lee Mitchell (D); 21 Oliver Holmes; 14 Stuart Jones. Subs (all used): 9 Daryl Clark; 11 Brett Ferres; 22 Nathan Massey; 24 Stephen Nash (D).
Tries: Owen (35, 78), Griffin (47), Milner (68); **Goals:** Dixon 4/4.
Rugby Leaguer & League Express Men of the Match: *City Reds:* Matty Smith; *Tigers:* Richard Owen.
Penalty count: 6-4; **Half-time:** 4-6;
Referee: Thierry Alibert; **Attendance:** 5,242.

Sunday 5th February 2012

BRADFORD BULLS 12 CATALAN DRAGONS 34

BULLS: 1 Brett Kearney; 24 Jason Crookes; 2 Adrian Purtell (D); 4 Chev Walker; 5 Elliot Kear (D); 22 Jarrod Sammut (D); 7 Luke Gale (D); 10 Craig Kopczak; 14 Matt Diskin (C); 15 Bryn Hargreaves; 26 John Bateman; 17 Ian Sibbit; 13 Jamie Langley. Subs (all used): 9 Heath L'Estrange (C); 8 Nick Scruton; 20 James Donaldson; 21 Tom Burgess.
Tries: Langley (63), Kear (80); **Goals:** Gale 2/2.
DRAGONS: 1 Clint Greenshields; 6 Thomas Bosc; 25 Vincent Duport; 14 Sebastien Raguin; 18 Daryl Millard; 4 Setaimata Sa; 7 Scott Dureau; 23 Lopini Paea; 9 Ian Henderson; 10 Remi Casty (C); 17 Cyrille Gossard; 12 Louis Anderson (D); 24 Jason Baitieri. Subs (all used): 11 Steve Menzies; 8 David Ferriol; 22 Jamal Fakir; 26 Ben Fisher (D).
Tries: Baitieri (7), Greenshields (21), Bosc (31), Sa (42), Millard (55), Raguin (76); **Goals:** Dureau 5/7.
Rugby Leaguer & League Express Men of the Match: *Bulls:* Elliot Kear; *Dragons:* Scott Dureau.
Penalty count: 12-9; **Half-time:** 0-20;
Referee: James Child; **Attendance:** 10,610.

HULL FC 20 WARRINGTON WOLVES 20

HULL: 1 Wade McKinnon (D); 2 Will Sharp; 3 Tony Martin (D); 4 Kirk Yeaman; 5 Tom Briscoe; 6 Richard Horne; 28 Danny Nicklas; 8 Mark O'Meley; 9 Danny Houghton; 10 Andy Lynch (C) (D); 11 Willie Manu; 12 Danny Tickle; 13 Joe Westerman. Subs (all used): 17 Sam Moa; 19 Jordan Turner; 15 Richard Whiting; 22 Martin Aspinwall (D).
Tries: Yeaman (2), Tickle (33, 54), Briscoe (42); **Goals:** Tickle 2/4.
WOLVES: 2 Chris Riley; 23 Rhys Evans; 3 Chris Bridge; 4 Ryan Atkins; 22 Rhys Williams; 19 Stefan Ratchford (D); 7 Richard Myler; 8 Adrian Morley (C); 9 Michael Monaghan; 10 Garreth Carvell; 11 Trent Waterhouse (D); 12 Ben Westwood; 15 Simon Grix. Subs (all used): 13 Ben Harrison; 17 Michael Cooper; 14 Mick Higham; 16 Paul Wood.
Tries: Waterhouse (11), Williams (13), Grix (37), Evans (79); **Goals:** Westwood 2/4.
Rugby Leaguer & League Express Men of the Match: *Hull:* Danny Tickle; *Wolves:* Simon Grix.
Penalty count: 3-6; **Half-time:** 10-16;
Referee: Steve Ganson; **Attendance:** 12,710.

WIGAN WARRIORS 16 HUDDERSFIELD GIANTS 20

WARRIORS: 1 Sam Tomkins; 2 Josh Charnley; 3 Darrell Goulding; 4 George Carmont; 5 Pat Richards; 6 Brett Finch; 7 Thomas Leuluai; 10 Lee Mossop; 9 Michael McIlorum; 14 Jeff Lima; 11 Harrison Hansen; 12 Gareth Hock; 13 Sean O'Loughlin (C). Subs (all used): 16 Liam Farrell; 17 Chris Tuson; 21 Epalahame Lauaki (D); 23 Ben Flower (D).
Tries: S Tomkins (33), Farrell (54), O'Loughlin (75); **Goals:** Richards 2/3.
GIANTS: 29 Greg Eden (D); 5 Jermaine McGillvary; 3 Leroy Cudjoe; 17 Joe Wardle; 20 Luke George (D); 1 Scott Grix (C); 7 Danny Brough; 8 Eorl Crabtree; 9 Luke Robinson; 23 Jacob Fairbank; 18 Jason Chan (D); 4 Lee Gilmour; 19 Tommy Lee (D). Subs (all used): 14 Shaun Lunt; 15 Larne Patrick; 2 Michael Lawrence; 24 Adam Walker.
Tries: Gilmour (21), Patrick (49, 57); **Goals:** Brough 4/4.
Rugby Leaguer & League Express Men of the Match: *Warriors:* Liam Farrell; *Giants:* Larne Patrick.
Penalty count: 5-5; **Half-time:** 6-8;
Referee: Richard Silverwood; **Attendance:** 16,771.

ROUND 2

Friday 10th February 2012

ST HELENS 38 SALFORD CITY REDS 10

SAINTS: 6 Lance Hohaia; 21 Tom Makinson; 17 Gary Wheeler; 5 Francis Meli; 2 Ade Gardner; 20 Lee Gaskell; 7 Jonny Lomax; 11 Tony Puletua; 9 James Roby (C); 14 Anthony Laffranchi; 13 Chris Flannery; 4 Iosia Soliola; 12 Jon Wilkin. Subs (all used): 19 Andrew Dixon; 8 Josh Perry; 16 Paul Clough; 24 Nathan Ashe.
Tries: Soliola (28), Roby (49), Meli (54), Dixon (57, 72), Wilkin (67), Laffranchi (80); **Goals:** Makinson 5/7.
CITY REDS: 1 Luke Patten; 2 Jodie Broughton; 18 Ashley Gibson; 4 Joel Moon; 5 Danny Williams; 6 Daniel Holdsworth; 7 Matty Smith; 12 Shannan McPherson (D); 24 Stuart Howarth; 20 Ben Gledhill; 11 Matty Ashurst; 16 Luke Adamson; 13 Stephen Wild (C). Subs (all used): 8 Lee Jewitt; 14 Chris Nero; 15 Adam Sidlow; 23 Gareth Owen.
Tries: Broughton (8), Gibson (24); **Goals:** Holdsworth 1/2.
Rugby Leaguer & League Express Men of the Match: *Saints:* Andrew Dixon; *City Reds:* Danny Williams.
Penalty count: 6-5; **Half-time:** 4-10;
Referee: Richard Silverwood; **Attendance:** 15,547.

Saturday 11th February 2012

WIGAN WARRIORS 20 LEEDS RHINOS 6

WARRIORS: 1 Sam Tomkins; 2 Josh Charnley; 3 Darrell Goulding; 26 Jack Hughes; 5 Pat Richards; 6 Brett Finch; 7 Thomas Leuluai; 10 Lee Mossop; 9 Michael McIlorum; 23 Ben Flower; 11 Harrison Hansen; 12 Gareth Hock; 13 Sean O'Loughlin (C). Subs (all used): 14 Jeff Lima; 17 Chris Tuson; 21 Epalahame Lauaki; 32 Tom Spencer (D).
Tries: Charnley (16, 30, 57); **Goals:** Richards 4/4.
RHINOS: 1 Brent Webb; 14 Lee Smith; 12 Carl Ablett; 4 Zak Hardaker; 5 Ryan Hall; 13 Kevin Sinfield (C); 6 Danny McGuire; 16 Ryan Bailey; 7 Rob Burrow; 10 Jamie Peacock; 11 Jamie Jones-Buchanan; 15 Brett Delaney; 19 Weller Hauraki. Subs: 8 Kylie Leuluai; 18 Chris Clarkson; 20 Darrell Griffin; 9 Paul McShane (not used).
Try: Griffin (54); **Goals:** Sinfield 1/1.
Rugby Leaguer & League Express Men of the Match: *Warriors:* Josh Charnley; *Rhinos:* Rob Burrow.
Penalty count: 9-6; **Half-time:** 12-0;
Referee: Thierry Alibert; **Attendance:** 15,370.

Sunday 12th February 2012

HUDDERSFIELD GIANTS 66 WIDNES VIKINGS 6

GIANTS: 29 Greg Eden; 5 Jermaine McGillvary; 3 Leroy Cudjoe; 17 Joe Wardle; 20 Luke George; 1 Scott Grix; 7 Danny Brough; 8 Eorl Crabtree; 9 Luke Robinson; 4 Lee Gilmour; 23 Jacob Fairbank; 18 Jason Chan; 6 Kevin Brown (C). Subs (all used): 16 Dale Ferguson; 19 Tommy Lee; 2 Michael Lawrence; 24 Adam Walker.
Tries: Robinson (3), Cudjoe (12, 23, 25, 58), Grix (15), George (37, 48, 65), Chan (61), Wardle (72), Eden (78); **Goals:** Brough 9/12.
VIKINGS: 25 Danny Craven; 2 Paddy Flynn; 3 Chris Dean; 4 Willie Isa; 5 Patrick Ah Van; 6 Lloyd White; 7 Rhys Hanbury; 8 Ben Cross (C); 9 Scott Moore; 10 Ben Davies (D2); 11 Frank Winterstein; 21 David Allen; 12 Hep Cahill. Subs (all used): 15 Simon Finnigan; 16 Ben Kavanagh; 24 Kurt Haggerty; 26 Anthony Mullally.
Try: Flynn (52); **Goals:** Ah Van 1/1.
Rugby Leaguer & League Express Men of the Match: *Giants:* Joe Wardle; *Vikings:* Anthony Mullally.
Penalty count: 6-8; **Half-time:** 34-0;
Referee: Steve Ganson; **Attendance:** 8,869.

WARRINGTON WOLVES 50 LONDON BRONCOS 10

WOLVES: 19 Stefan Ratchford; 5 Joel Monaghan; 3 Chris Bridge; 4 Ryan Atkins; 23 Rhys Evans; 6 Lee Briers; 7 Richard Myler; 10 Garreth Carvell; 9 Michael Monaghan; 8 Adrian Morley (C); 11 Trent Waterhouse; 12 Ben Westwood; 15 Simon Grix. Subs (all used): 2 Chris Riley; 13 Ben Harrison; 16 Paul Wood; 17 Michael Cooper.
Tries: Bridge (14, 31), J Monaghan (23, 44), Atkins (36, 48), Ratchford (58), Briers (71, 78); **Goals:** Westwood 5/7, Briers 2/2.
BRONCOS: 1 Luke Dorn; 5 Michael Robertson; 4 David Howell; 3 Jamie O'Callaghan; 21 Kieran Dixon; 6 Michael Witt; 7 Craig Gower (C); 8 Antonio Kaufusi; 9 Chad Randall; 10 Mark Bryant; 12 Chris Bailey; 11 Shane Rodney; 13 Tony Clubb. Subs (all used): 14 Julien Rinaldi; 16 Chris Melling; 18 Olsi Krasniqi; 20 Matt Cook (D).
Tries: Witt (8), Robertson (39); **Goals:** Witt 1/2.
Rugby Leaguer & League Express Men of the Match: *Wolves:* Chris Bridge; *Broncos:* Olsi Krasniqi.
Penalty count: 10-7; **Half-time:** 22-10;
Referee: James Child; **Attendance:** 10,834.

CASTLEFORD TIGERS 12 BRADFORD BULLS 20

TIGERS: 1 Richard Owen; 5 Josh Griffin; 23 Ryan McGoldrick; 3 Joe Arundel; 4 Kirk Dixon; 6 Rangi Chase; 7 Danny Orr (C); 8 Jake Emmitt; 15 Adam Milner; 12 Jonathan Walker; 21 Oliver Holmes; 17 Lee Mitchell; 14 Stuart Jones. Subs (all used): 22 Nathan Massey; 24 Stephen Nash; 9 Daryl Clark; 11 Brett Ferres.
Tries: Griffin (49), Owen (78); **Goals:** Dixon 2/2.
Sin bin: Emmitt (67) - deliberate offside.
BULLS: 1 Brett Kearney; 24 Jason Crookes; 2 Adrian Purtell; 4 Chev Walker; 5 Elliot Kear; 22 Jarrod Sammut; 7 Luke Gale; 10 Craig Kopczak; 14 Matt Diskin (C); 15 Bryn Hargreaves; 17 Ian Sibbit; 12 Elliott Whitehead; 13 Jamie Langley. Subs (all used): 20 James Donaldson; 8 Nick Scruton; 21 Tom Burgess; 9 Heath L'Estrange (C).
Tries: Sammut (9), Burgess (38), Kearney (76); **Goals:** Gale 4/4.
Sin bin: L'Estrange (56) - holding down.
Rugby Leaguer & League Express Men of the Match: *Tigers:* Danny Orr; *Bulls:* Jamie Langley.
Penalty count: 11-5; **Half-time:** 0-12;
Referee: Ben Thaler; **Attendance:** 8,050.

WAKEFIELD TRINITY WILDCATS 10 HULL KINGSTON ROVERS 22

WILDCATS: 1 Richard Mathers; 2 Peter Fox; 3 Dean Collis; 4 Vince Mellars; 5 Ben Cockayne; 6 Isaac John; 20 Tim Smith; 8 Oliver Wilkes; 14 Paul Aiton; 12 Steve Southern (C); 17 Danny Kirmond; 11 Ali Lauitiiti; 13 Danny Washbrook. Subs (all used): 7 Kyle Wood; 10 Andy Raleigh; 16 Paul Johnson; 19 Frankie Mariano.
Tries: Cockayne (17), Raleigh (31); **Goals:** John 1/2.
ROVERS: 1 Shannon McDonnell; 2 Craig Hall; 3 Kris Welham; 4 Jake Webster; 5 David Hodgson; 19 Scott Murrell; 7 Michael Dobson (C); 8 Joel Clinton; 14 Lincoln Withers; 23 Mickey Paea; 18 Graeme Horne; 11 Constantine Mika; 13 Rhys Lovegrove. Subs (all used): 9 Josh Hodgson; 20 Jordan Cox; 10 Scott Taylor; 22 Scott Wheeldon.
Tries: Paea (7), Mika (22), J Hodgson (59), Lovegrove (69); **Goals:** Dobson 2/2, Hall 1/2.
Sin bin: Taylor (48) - professional foul.
Rugby Leaguer & League Express Men of the Match: *Wildcats:* Paul Johnson; *Rovers:* Constantine Mika.
Penalty count: 12-9; **Half-time:** 10-12;
Referee: Robert Hicks; **Attendance:** 8,612.

ROUND 3

Saturday 18th February 2012

HUDDERSFIELD GIANTS 22 WARRINGTON WOLVES 32

GIANTS: 29 Greg Eden; 5 Jermaine McGillvary; 3 Leroy Cudjoe; 17 Joe Wardle; 20 Luke George; 7 Danny Brough; 1 Scott Grix; 8 Eorl Crabtree; 9 Luke Robinson; 16 Dale Ferguson; 4 Lee Gilmour; 18 Jason Chan; 6 Kevin Brown (C). Subs (all used): 19 Tommy Lee; 23 Jacob Fairbank; 13 David Faiumu; 24 Adam Walker.
Tries: Brough (16), Crabtree (22), Chan (44), Eden (59); **Goals:** Brough 3/4.
On report: Lee (40) - alleged high tackle on Briers; Brown (47) - alleged use of the elbow on Bridge.

WOLVES: 19 Stefan Ratchford; 2 Chris Riley; 3 Chris Bridge; 4 Ryan Atkins; 5 Joel Monaghan; 6 Lee Briers; 7 Richard Myler; 8 Adrian Morley (C); 9 Michael Monaghan; 16 Paul Wood; 11 Trent Waterhouse; 12 Ben Westwood; 15 Simon Grix. Subs (all used): 13 Ben Harrison; 17 Michael Cooper; 18 Matty Blythe; 20 Chris Hill (D).
Tries: Riley (1, 27), Bridge (32), J Monaghan (54), Blythe (57), Myler (72); **Goals:** Westwood 0/2, Briers 4/4.
On report: Bridge (46) - alleged dangerous tackle.
Rugby Leaguer & League Express Men of the Match: *Giants:* Danny Brough; *Wolves:* Lee Briers.
Penalty count: 9-10; **Half-time:** 12-14;
Referee: Phil Bentham; **Attendance:** 8,184.

CATALAN DRAGONS 28 CASTLEFORD TIGERS 20

DRAGONS: 1 Clint Greenshields; 2 Damien Blanch; 25 Vincent Duport; 18 Daryl Millard; 6 Thomas Bosc; 3 Leon Pryce (D); 7 Scott Dureau; 23 Lopini Paea; 9 Ian Henderson; 10 Remi Casty (C); 4 Setaimata Sa; 14 Sebastien Raguin; 24 Jason Baitieri. Subs (all used): 8 David Ferriol; 11 Steve Menzies; 22 Jamal Fakir; 26 Ben Fisher.
Tries: Bosc (12), Duport (45), Millard (55, 69), Baitieri (73); **Goals:** Dureau 4/5.
Sin bin: Baitieri (15) - retaliation.
TIGERS: 1 Richard Owen; 5 Josh Griffin; 23 Ryan McGoldrick; 3 Joe Arundel; 4 Kirk Dixon; 6 Rangi Chase; 7 Danny Orr (C); 24 Stephen Nash; 9 Daryl Clark; 22 Nathan Massey; 21 Oliver Holmes; 11 Brett Ferres; 14 Stuart Jones. Subs (all used): 8 Jake Emmitt; 13 Steve Snitch; 15 Adam Milner; 17 Lee Mitchell.
Tries: Griffin (1, 20, 50), Arundel (24); **Goals:** Dixon 2/4.
Sin bin: Nash (15) - high tackle on Baitieri.
Rugby Leaguer & League Express Men of the Match: *Dragons:* Leon Pryce; *Tigers:* Rangi Chase.
Penalty count: 10-4; **Half-time:** 6-16;
Referee: Tim Roby; **Attendance:** 7,488.

Sunday 19th February 2012

BRADFORD BULLS 16 WIGAN WARRIORS 54

BULLS: 1 Brett Kearney; 24 Jason Crookes; 3 Keith Lulia (D); 29 Michael Platt; 5 Elliot Kear; 22 Jarrod Sammut; 7 Luke Gale; 10 Craig Kopczak; 14 Matt Diskin (C); 15 Bryn Hargreaves; 12 Elliott Whitehead; 4 Chev Walker; 13 Jamie Langley. Subs (all used): 9 Heath L'Estrange (C); 8 Nick Scruton; 34 Phil Joseph (D); 21 Tom Burgess.
Tries: Crookes (29), Sammut (34), Kearney (68);
Goals: Sammut 2/3.
WARRIORS: 1 Sam Tomkins; 2 Josh Charnley; 3 Darrell Goulding; 26 Jack Hughes; 5 Pat Richards; 6 Brett Finch; 7 Thomas Leuluai; 10 Lee Mossop; 9 Michael McIlorum; 23 Ben Flower; 11 Harrison Hansen; 12 Gareth Hock; 13 Sean O'Loughlin (C). Subs (all used): 14 Jeff Lima; 17 Chris Tuson; 21 Epalahame Lauaki; 16 Liam Farrell.
Tries: Charnley (16, 58), Richards (20), Hock (23), Tuson (37, 45), Goulding (42, 54), Farrell (47, 76);
Goals: Richards 6/9, S Tomkins 1/1.
Rugby Leaguer & League Express Men of the Match: *Bulls:* Craig Kopczak; *Warriors:* Brett Finch.
Penalty count: 7-7; **Half-time:** 10-22;
Referee: Steve Ganson; **Attendance:** 12,909.

HULL KINGSTON ROVERS 36 ST HELENS 36

ROVERS: 1 Shannon McDonnell; 2 Craig Hall; 3 Kris Welham; 4 Jake Webster; 5 David Hodgson; 13 Rhys Lovegrove; 19 Scott Murrell (C); 8 Joel Clinton; 14 Lincoln Withers; 23 Mickey Paea; 11 Constantine Mika; 18 Graeme Horne; 15 Liam Watts. Subs (all used): 22 Scott Wheeldon; 10 Scott Taylor; 9 Josh Hodgson; 20 Jordan Cox.
Tries: D Hodgson (17), Mika (21), McDonnell (24), J Hodgson (35, 54), Welham (63); **Goals:** Hall 6/6.
SAINTS: 1 Paul Wellens (C); 2 Ade Gardner; 3 Michael Shenton; 5 Francis Meli; 22 Jamie Foster; 6 Lance Hohaia; 7 Jonny Lomax; 14 Anthony Laffranchi; 9 James Roby; 11 Tony Puletua; 13 Chris Flannery; 4 Iosia Soliola; 12 Jon Wilkin. Subs (all used): 8 Josh Perry; 10 Louie McCarthy-Scarsbrook; 19 Andrew Dixon; 17 Gary Wheeler.
Tries: Soliola (7), Shenton (11), Roby (14), Flannery (32), Meli (46, 76), Wellens (51); **Goals:** Foster 4/8.
Rugby Leaguer & League Express Men of the Match: *Rovers:* Craig Hall; *Saints:* Jonny Lomax.
Penalty count: 6-2; **Half-time:** 24-20;
Referee: Ben Thaler; **Attendance:** 7,610.

WIDNES VIKINGS 18 SALFORD CITY REDS 38

VIKINGS: 25 Danny Craven; 2 Paddy Flynn; 20 Stefan Marsh; 4 Willie Isa; 5 Patrick Ah Van; 6 Lloyd White; 7 Rhys Hanbury; 8 Ben Cross (C); 13 Jon Clarke; 10 Ben Davies; 11 Frank Winterstein; 21 Dave Allen; 24 Kurt Haggerty. Subs (all used): 14 Anthony Watts (D); 16 Ben Kavanagh; 22 Macgraff Leuluai; 26 Anthony Mullally.
Tries: Ah Van (24, 59), Flynn (76);
Goals: Ah Van 2/2, Hanbury 1/1.
Sin bin: Watts (39) - dissent.
CITY REDS: 1 Luke Patten; 2 Jodie Broughton; 14 Chris Nero; 18 Ashley Gibson; 5 Danny Williams; 6 Daniel Holdsworth; 7 Matty Smith; 12 Shannan McPherson; 24 Stuart Howarth; 20 Ben Gledhill; 16 Luke Adamson; 27 Vinnie Anderson; 13 Stephen Wild (C). Subs (all used): 23 Gareth Owen; 15 Adam Sidlow; 8 Lee Jewitt; 17 Iafeta Palea'aesina.
Tries: Holdsworth (2, 28), Patten (13, 17), Broughton (33), Owen (40), Palea'aesina (45);
Goals: Holdsworth 5/7.
Rugby Leaguer & League Express Men of the Match: *Vikings:* Patrick Ah Van; *City Reds:* Luke Patten.
Penalty count: 6-11; **Half-time:** 6-32;
Referee: James Child; **Attendance:** 5,053.

HULL FC 22 LONDON BRONCOS 14

HULL: 1 Wade McKinnon; 2 Will Sharp; 3 Tony Martin; 4 Kirk Yeaman; 5 Tom Briscoe; 6 Richard Horne; 7 Brett Seymour (D); 17 Sam Moa; 9 Danny Houghton; 10 Andy Lynch (C); 11 Willie Manu; 12 Danny Tickle; 22 Martin Aspinwall. Subs (all used): 28 Danny Nicklas; 8 Mark O'Meley; 15 Richard Whiting; 13 Joe Westerman.
Tries: Briscoe (16), Westerman (28), McKinnon (32), Yeaman (47); **Goals:** Tickle 3/4.
Dismissal: Moa (61) - high tackle on Rinaldi.
BRONCOS: 1 Luke Dorn; 5 Michael Robertson; 4 David Howell; 3 Jamie O'Callaghan; 21 Kieran Dixon; 6 Michael Witt; 7 Craig Gower (C); 8 Antonio Kaufusi; 9 Chad Randall; 10 Mark Bryant; 11 Shane Rodney; 12 Chris Bailey; 13 Tony Clubb. Subs (all used): 14 Julien Rinaldi; 16 Chris Melling; 17 Jason Golden; 18 Olsi Krasniqi.
Tries: Robertson (24), Dorn (68), Melling (70);
Goals: Witt 1/3.
Rugby Leaguer & League Express Men of the Match: *Hull:* Willie Manu; *Broncos:* Craig Gower.
Penalty count: 12-13; **Half-time:** 16-4;
Referee: Richard Silverwood; **Attendance:** 10,096.

ROUND 4

Friday 24th February 2012

SALFORD CITY REDS 24 HULL FC 22

CITY REDS: 1 Luke Patten; 2 Jodie Broughton; 14 Chris Nero; 3 Sean Gleeson; 18 Ashley Gibson; 6 Daniel Holdsworth; 7 Matty Smith; 12 Shannan McPherson; 24 Stuart Howarth; 10 Ryan Boyle; 11 Matty Ashurst; 16 Luke Adamson; 13 Stephen Wild (C). Subs (all used): 8 Lee Jewitt; 15 Adam Sidlow; 17 Iafeta Palea'aesina; 23 Gareth Owen.
Tries: Gibson (10, 23), Ashurst (49), Gleeson (68);
Goals: Holdsworth 4/5.
HULL: 1 Wade McKinnon; 2 Will Sharp; 3 Tony Martin; 4 Kirk Yeaman; 5 Tom Briscoe; 6 Richard Horne; 7 Brett Seymour; 8 Mark O'Meley; 9 Danny Houghton; 10 Andy Lynch (C); 11 Willie Manu; 12 Danny Tickle; 22 Martin Aspinwall. Subs: 15 Richard Whiting; 19 Jordan Turner; 28 Danny Nicklas (not used); 30 Josh Bowden (D).
Tries: Seymour (25, 36), McKinnon (31), Briscoe (64);
Goals: Tickle 3/4.
Rugby Leaguer & League Express Men of the Match: *City Reds:* Luke Patten; *Hull:* Brett Seymour.
Penalty count: 9-5; **Half-time:** 10-16;
Referee: Phil Bentham; **Attendance:** 5,186.

ST HELENS 32 CATALAN DRAGONS 34

SAINTS: 1 Paul Wellens (C); 21 Tom Makinson; 3 Michael Shenton; 17 Gary Wheeler; 22 Jamie Foster; 20 Lee Gaskell; 7 Jonny Lomax; 14 Anthony Laffranchi; 9 James Roby; 10 Louie McCarthy-Scarsbrook; 4 Iosia Soliola; 12 Jon Wilkin; 11 Tony Puletua. Subs (all used): 6 Lance Hohaia; 13 Chris Flannery; 15 Mark Flanagan; 16 Paul Clough.
Tries: Foster (4), Laffranchi (16), Wheeler (34, 69), Makinson (45); **Goals:** Foster 6/6.
DRAGONS: 1 Clint Greenshields; 2 Damien Blanch; 25 Vincent Duport; 18 Daryl Millard; 6 Thomas Bosc; 3 Leon Pryce; 7 Scott Dureau; 23 Lopini Paea; 9 Ian Henderson; 10 Remi Casty (C); 4 Setaimata Sa; 11 Steve Menzies; 24 Jason Baitieri. Subs (all used): 8 David Ferriol; 13 Gregory Mounis; 14 Sebastien Raguin; 22 Jamal Fakir.
Tries: Casty (8), Blanch (58), Duport (64), Dureau (66), Sa (71), Millard (80); **Goals:** Dureau 5/7.
Rugby Leaguer & League Express Men of the Match: *Saints:* Jonny Lomax; *Dragons:* Scott Dureau.
Penalty count: 8-8; **Half-time:** 20-8;
Referee: James Child; **Attendance:** 13,108.

Saturday 25th February 2012

WAKEFIELD TRINITY WILDCATS 18
BRADFORD BULLS 36

WILDCATS: 1 Richard Mathers; 2 Peter Fox; 3 Dean Collis; 4 Vince Mellars; 5 Ben Cockayne; 6 Isaac John; 20 Tim Smith; 8 Oliver Wilkes; 14 Paul Aiton; 12 Steve Southern (C); 17 Danny Kirmond; 11 Ali Lauitiiti; 13 Danny Washbrook. Subs (all used): 7 Kyle Wood; 10 Andy Raleigh; 16 Paul Johnson; 22 Kyle Trout (D).
Tries: Cockayne (1), Southern (13), Kirmond (44), Mathers (70); **Goals:** John 1/3, Cockayne 0/1.
BULLS: 1 Brett Kearney; 5 Elliot Kear; 29 Michael Platt; 3 Keith Lulia; 24 Jason Crookes; 22 Jarrod Sammut; 6 Ben Jeffries; 10 Craig Kopczak; 14 Matt Diskin (C); 15 Bryn Hargreaves; 26 John Bateman; 12 Elliott Whitehead; 13 Jamie Langley. Subs (all used): 9 Heath L'Estrange (C); 8 Nick Scruton; 34 Phil Joseph; 21 Tom Burgess.
Tries: Lulia (8), Whitehead (35, 55, 61), Kearney (51, 64); **Goals:** Sammut 6/6.
Rugby Leaguer & League Express Men of the Match: *Wildcats:* Paul Aiton; *Bulls:* Ben Jeffries.
Penalty count: 10-8; **Half-time:** 10-12;
Referee: Ben Thaler; **Attendance:** 6,934.

Sunday 26th February 2012

LONDON BRONCOS 16 HUDDERSFIELD GIANTS 30

BRONCOS: 5 Michael Robertson; 21 Kieran Dixon; 3 Jamie O'Callaghan; 4 David Howell; 2 Liam Colbon; 6 Michael Witt; 7 Craig Gower (C); 8 Antonio Kaufusi; 9 Chad Randall; 10 Mark Bryant; 17 Jason Golden; 12 Chris Bailey; 13 Tony Clubb. Subs (all used): 16 Chris Melling; 1 Luke Dorn; 22 Ben Bolger; 18 Olsi Krasniqi.
Tries: Kaufusi (12, 52), O'Callaghan (75); **Goals:** Witt 2/3.
GIANTS: 21 Aaron Murphy (D); 5 Jermaine McGillvary; 3 Leroy Cudjoe; 17 Joe Wardle; 20 Luke George; 7 Danny Brough; 1 Scott Grix; 8 Eorl Crabtree; 9 Luke Robinson; 23 Jacob Fairbank; 4 Lee Gilmour; 18 Jason Chan; 6 Kevin Brown (C). Subs (all used): 10 Keith Mason; 13 David Faiumu; 15 Larne Patrick; 14 Shaun Lunt.
Tries: Brough (20), Cudjoe (24, 78), Brown (41), Wardle (56); **Goals:** Brough 5/6.
Rugby Leaguer & League Express Men of the Match: *Broncos:* Kieran Dixon; *Giants:* Danny Brough.
Penalty count: 10-10; **Half-time:** 6-14;
Referee: Tim Roby; **Attendance:** 1,970.

WIDNES VIKINGS 16 LEEDS RHINOS 44

VIKINGS: 1 Shaun Briscoe (D); 2 Paddy Flynn; 20 Stefan Marsh; 4 Willie Isa; 5 Patrick Ah Van; 6 Lloyd White; 7 Rhys Hanbury; 8 Ben Cross; 13 Jon Clarke (C); 10 Ben Davies; 11 Frank Winterstein; 21 Dave Allen; 12 Hep Cahill. Subs (all used): 15 Simon Finnigan; 17 Steve Pickersgill; 25 Danny Craven; 26 Anthony Mullally.
Tries: Ah Van (24), Hanbury (27), Flynn (70);
Goals: Ah Van 2/3.
RHINOS: 1 Brent Webb; 2 Ben Jones-Bishop; 3 Kallum Watkins; 4 Zak Hardaker; 5 Ryan Hall; 13 Kevin Sinfield (C); 6 Danny McGuire; 20 Darrell Griffin; 7 Rob Burrow; 8 Kylie Leuluai; 15 Brett Delaney; 19 Weller Hauraki; 12 Carl Ablett. Subs (all used): 9 Paul McShane; 17 Ian Kirke; 21 Richard Moore (D); 22 Jay Pitts.
Tries: Jones-Bishop (16, 29), Burrow (18, 21), Hall (50, 75), Hardaker (60), Watkins (73);
Goals: Sinfield 6/8.
Rugby Leaguer & League Express Men of the Match: *Vikings:* Simon Finnigan; *Rhinos:* Danny McGuire.
Penalty count: 11-5; **Half-time:** 10-22;
Referee: Steve Ganson; **Attendance:** 6,046.

WARRINGTON WOLVES 42
HULL KINGSTON ROVERS 10

WOLVES: 1 Brett Hodgson; 2 Chris Riley; 3 Chris Bridge; 4 Ryan Atkins; 5 Joel Monaghan; 6 Lee Briers; 7 Richard Myler; 8 Adrian Morley (C); 9 Michael Monaghan; 16 Paul Wood; 11 Trent Waterhouse; 12 Ben Westwood; 17 Michael Cooper. Subs (all used): 19 Stefan Ratchford; 10 Garreth Carvell; 20 Chris Hill; 18 Matty Blythe.
Tries: Riley (14, 63), Bridge (23), Atkins (34, 79), Westwood (74, 76); **Goals:** Hodgson 7/7.
ROVERS: 1 Shannon McDonnell; 13 Rhys Lovegrove; 3 Kris Welham; 4 Jake Webster; 21 Sam Latus; 2 Craig Hall; 7 Michael Dobson (C); 8 Joel Clinton; 9 Josh Hodgson; 23 Mickey Paea; 11 Constantine Mika; 18 Graeme Horne; 15 Liam Watts. Subs (all used): 25 Keal Carlile (D); 10 Scott Taylor; 22 Scott Wheeldon; 16 Jason Netherton.
Tries: Lovegrove (44), Hall (57); **Goals:** Dobson 1/2.
Rugby Leaguer & League Express Men of the Match: *Wolves:* Ben Westwood; *Rovers:* Josh Hodgson.
Penalty count: 7-10; **Half-time:** 18-0;
Referee: Richard Silverwood; **Attendance:** 11,916.

CASTLEFORD TIGERS 4 WIGAN WARRIORS 46

TIGERS: 1 Richard Owen; 2 Nick Youngquest; 4 Kirk Dixon; 23 Ryan McGoldrick; 5 Josh Griffin; 6 Rangi Chase; 7 Danny Orr (C); 8 Jake Emmitt; 15 Adam Milner; 24 Stephen Nash; 21 Oliver Holmes; 17 Lee Mitchell; 14 Stuart Jones. Subs (all used): 9 Daryl Clark; 13 Steve Snitch; 22 Nathan Massey; 28 James Grehan (D).
Try: Griffin (14); **Goals:** Dixon 0/1.
WARRIORS: 1 Sam Tomkins; 2 Josh Charnley; 3 Darrell Goulding; 26 Jack Hughes; 5 Pat Richards; 6 Brett Finch; 7 Thomas Leuluai; 21 Epalahame Lauaki; 9 Michael McIlorum; 10 Lee Mossop; 11 Harrison Hansen; 12 Gareth Hock; 13 Sean O'Loughlin (C). Subs (all used): 14 Jeff Lima; 16 Liam Farrell; 17 Chris Tuson; 32 Tom Spencer.
Tries: O'Loughlin (3), S Tomkins (8, 38, 43), Richards (16, 46), Charnley (50, 78); **Goals:** Richards 7/8.
Rugby Leaguer & League Express Men of the Match: *Tigers:* Rangi Chase; *Warriors:* Sam Tomkins.
Penalty count: 8-5; **Half-time:** 4-24;
Referee: Thierry Alibert; **Attendance:** 8,156.

ROUND 5

Friday 2nd March 2012

CASTLEFORD TIGERS 14 LEEDS RHINOS 36

TIGERS: 1 Richard Owen; 2 Nick Youngquest; 4 Kirk Dixon; 23 Ryan McGoldrick; 5 Josh Griffin; 6 Rangi Chase; 7 Danny Orr (C); 8 Jake Emmitt; 15 Adam Milner; 20 Grant Millington (D); 11 Brett Ferres; 21 Oliver Holmes; 14 Stuart Jones. Subs (all used): 9 Daryl Clark; 13 Steve Snitch; 17 Lee Mitchell; 22 Nathan Massey.
Tries: Clark (34), Dixon (37), Griffin (45);
Goals: Dixon 1/3.
RHINOS: 1 Brent Webb; 2 Ben Jones-Bishop; 3 Kallum Watkins; 4 Zak Hardaker; 5 Ryan Hall; 13 Kevin Sinfield (C); 6 Danny McGuire; 8 Kylie Leuluai; 7 Rob Burrow; 10 Jamie Peacock; 22 Jay Pitts; 15 Brett Delaney; 12 Carl Ablett. Subs (all used): 17 Ian Kirke; 18 Chris Clarkson; 20 Darrell Griffin; 24 Liam Hood (D).
Tries: Hall (11, 24, 63), Watkins (27), McGuire (75), Hood (77); **Goals:** Sinfield 6/6.
Rugby Leaguer & League Express Men of the Match: *Tigers:* Danny Orr; *Rhinos:* Ryan Hall.
Penalty count: 5-6; **Half-time:** 10-18;
Referee: James Child; **Attendance:** 9,237.

SALFORD CITY REDS 44 LONDON BRONCOS 12

CITY REDS: 1 Luke Patten; 14 Chris Nero; 4 Joel Moon; 3 Sean Gleeson; 18 Ashley Gibson; 6 Daniel Holdsworth; 7 Matty Smith; 12 Shannan McPherson; 24 Stuart Howarth; 10 Ryan Boyle; 11 Matty Ashurst; 16 Luke Adamson; 13 Stephen Wild (C). Subs (all used): 8 Lee Jewitt; 17 Iafeta Palea'aesina; 21 Jordan James; 23 Gareth Owen.
Tries: Nero (13, 57), Adamson (20), Smith (33), Palea'aesina (38), Gleeson (46, 59), Moon (48);
Goals: Holdsworth 6/8.
BRONCOS: 5 Michael Robertson; 23 Omari Caro (D); 3 Jamie O'Callaghan; 4 David Howell; 2 Liam Colbon; 6 Michael Witt; 7 Craig Gower (C); 8 Antonio Kaufusi; 9 Chad Randall; 10 Mark Bryant; 12 Chris Bailey; 17 Jason Golden; 16 Chris Melling. Subs (all used): 1 Luke Dorn; 14 Julien Rinaldi; 18 Olsi Krasniqi; 20 Matt Cook.
Tries: Howell (65), Kaufusi (70); **Goals:** Witt 2/2.
Rugby Leaguer & League Express Men of the Match: *City Reds:* Iafeta Palea'aesina; *Broncos:* Craig Gower.
Penalty count: 5-6; **Half-time:** 20-0;
Referee: Ben Thaler; **Attendance:** 5,250.

Saturday 3rd March 2012

BRADFORD BULLS 10 WARRINGTON WOLVES 23

BULLS: 1 Brett Kearney; 24 Jason Crookes; 3 Keith Lulia; 29 Michael Platt; 5 Elliot Kear; 22 Jarrod Sammut; 6 Ben Jeffries; 10 Craig Kopczak; 14 Matt Diskin (C); 15 Bryn Hargreaves; 12 Elliott Whitehead; 26 John Bateman; 13 Jamie Langley. Subs (all used): 9 Heath L'Estrange (C); 21 Tom Burgess; 34 Phil Joseph; 16 Manase Manuokafoa (D).
Tries: Diskin (7), Crookes (67); **Goals:** Sammut 1/2.
WOLVES: 1 Brett Hodgson; 2 Chris Riley; 3 Chris Bridge; 4 Ryan Atkins; 5 Joel Monaghan; 6 Lee Briers; 7 Richard Myler; 8 Adrian Morley (C); 14 Mick Higham; 16 Paul Wood; 11 Trent Waterhouse; 18 Matty Blythe; 17 Michael Cooper. Subs (all used): 19 Stefan Ratchford; 10 Garreth Carvell; 20 Chris Hill; 21 Tyrone McCarthy.
Tries: Riley (19), Higham (38), Atkins (43), Waterhouse (61); **Goals:** Hodgson 0/1, Bridge 3/3;
Field goal: Briers (72).
Rugby Leaguer & League Express Men of the Match: *Bulls:* Matt Diskin; *Wolves:* Mick Higham.
Penalty count: 11-8; **Half-time:** 6-10;
Referee: Thierry Alibert; **Attendance:** 11,318.

Sunday 4th March 2012

HUDDERSFIELD GIANTS 17 ST HELENS 16

GIANTS: 29 Greg Eden; 5 Jermaine McGillvary; 3 Leroy Cudjoe; 17 Joe Wardle; 20 Luke George; 1 Scott Grix; 7 Danny Brough; 8 Eorl Crabtree; 9 Luke Robinson; 24 Adam Walker; 18 Jason Chan; 2 Michael Lawrence; 6 Kevin Brown (C). Subs (all used): 13 David Faiumu; 14 Shaun Lunt; 15 Larne Patrick; 4 Lee Gilmour.
Tries: George (18, 46, 65); **Goals:** Brough 2/4;
Field goal: Brough (69).
SAINTS: 1 Paul Wellens (C); 21 Tom Makinson; 3 Michael Shenton; 5 Francis Meli; 2 Ade Gardner; 20 Lee Gaskell; 7 Jonny Lomax; 14 Anthony Laffranchi; 9 James Roby; 10 Louie McCarthy-Scarsbrook; 12 Jon Wilkin; 4 Iosia Soliola; 11 Tony Puletua. Subs (all used): 16 Paul Clough; 19 Andrew Dixon; 15 Mark Flanagan; 6 Lance Hohaia.
Tries: Gaskell (29), Lomax (32), Gardner (73);
Goals: Lomax 2/3.
Rugby Leaguer & League Express Men of the Match: *Giants:* Danny Brough; *Saints:* Iosia Soliola.
Penalty count: 9-3; **Half-time:** 4-12;
Referee: Phil Bentham; **Attendance:** 9,194.

HULL FC 14 WAKEFIELD TRINITY WILDCATS 10

HULL: 1 Wade McKinnon; 2 Will Sharp; 3 Tony Martin; 4 Kirk Yeaman; 5 Tom Briscoe; 6 Richard Horne; 7 Brett Seymour; 8 Mark O'Meley; 9 Danny Houghton; 10 Andy Lynch (C); 11 Willie Manu; 12 Danny Tickle; 22 Martin Aspinwall. Subs (all used): 20 Jamie Ellis (D); 15 Richard Whiting; 16 Eamon O'Carroll (D); 17 Sam Moa.
Tries: Yeaman (18), Sharp (62); **Goals:** Tickle 3/3.
On report: Moa (67) - alleged high tackle on Southern.
WILDCATS: 1 Richard Mathers; 2 Peter Fox; 3 Dean Collis; 4 Vince Mellars; 5 Ben Cockayne; 6 Isaac John; 20 Tim Smith; 8 Oliver Wilkes; 14 Paul Aiton; 12 Steve Southern (C); 17 Danny Kirmond; 11 Ali Lauitiiti; 13 Danny Washbrook. Subs (all used): 7 Kyle Wood; 10 Andy Raleigh; 16 Paul Johnson; 33 Lucas Walshaw.
Tries: Cockayne (70), Wood (74); **Goals:** John 1/2.
Rugby Leaguer & League Express Men of the Match: *Hull:* Danny Houghton; *Wildcats:* Kyle Wood.
Penalty count: 9-9; **Half-time:** 8-0;
Referee: Steve Ganson; **Attendance:** 11,105.

HULL KINGSTON ROVERS 36 WIDNES VIKINGS 0

ROVERS: 1 Shannon McDonnell; 2 Craig Hall; 3 Kris Welham; 4 Jake Webster; 21 Sam Latus; 13 Rhys Lovegrove; 7 Michael Dobson (C); 8 Joel Clinton; 14 Lincoln Withers; 10 Scott Taylor; 9 Josh Hodgson; 18 Graeme Horne; 15 Liam Watts. Subs (all used): 19 Scott Murrell; 16 Jason Netherton; 23 Mickey Paea; 20 Jordan Cox.
Tries: Withers (2), Webster (11), Murrell (26), Hall (29, 50), J Hodgson (72); **Goals:** Dobson 6/6.
VIKINGS: 1 Shaun Briscoe; 2 Paddy Flynn; 20 Stefan Marsh; 4 Willie Isa; 5 Patrick Ah Van; 6 Lloyd White; 7 Rhys Hanbury; 8 Ben Cross; 13 Jon Clarke (C); 10 Ben Davies; 11 Frank Winterstein; 21 Dave Allen; 12 Hep Cahill. Subs (all used): 15 Simon Finnigan; 17 Steve Pickersgill; 25 Danny Craven; 26 Anthony Mullally.
Rugby Leaguer & League Express Men of the Match: *Rovers:* Michael Dobson; *Vikings:* Jon Clarke.
Penalty count: 10-8; **Half-time:** 24-0;
Referee: Tim Roby; **Attendance:** 7,423.

WIGAN WARRIORS 36 CATALAN DRAGONS 12

WARRIORS: 1 Sam Tomkins; 2 Josh Charnley; 3 Darrell Goulding; 26 Jack Hughes; 5 Pat Richards; 6 Brett Finch; 7 Thomas Leuluai; 21 Epalahame Lauaki; 9 Michael McIlorum; 10 Lee Mossop; 11 Harrison Hansen; 12 Gareth Hock; 13 Sean O'Loughlin (C). Subs (all used): 14 Jeff Lima; 16 Liam Farrell; 17 Chris Tuson; 23 Ben Flower.
Tries: Leuluai (17), Richards (34), Hughes (50), Charnley (56, 79), O'Loughlin (75); **Goals:** Richards 6/7.
DRAGONS: 1 Clint Greenshields; 2 Damien Blanch; 15 Jean-Philippe Baile; 25 Vincent Duport; 18 Daryl Millard; 6 Thomas Bosc; 7 Scott Dureau; 23 Lopini Paea; 9 Ian Henderson; 10 Remi Casty (C); 4 Setaimata Sa; 12 Louis Anderson; 24 Jason Baitieri. Subs (all used): 8 David Ferriol; 13 Gregory Mounis; 3 Leon Pryce; 22 Jamal Fakir.
Tries: Dureau (21), Mounis (39);
Goals: Dureau 2/2, Bosc 0/1.
Rugby Leaguer & League Express Men of the Match: *Warriors:* Michael McIlorum; *Dragons:* Scott Dureau.
Penalty count: 12-10; **Half-time:** 10-12;
Referee: Richard Silverwood; **Attendance:** 14,464.

ROUND 6

Friday 9th March 2012

LEEDS RHINOS 26 WARRINGTON WOLVES 18

RHINOS: 1 Brent Webb; 2 Ben Jones-Bishop; 3 Kallum Watkins; 4 Zak Hardaker; 5 Ryan Hall; 13 Kevin Sinfield (C); 6 Danny McGuire; 8 Kylie Leuluai; 7 Rob Burrow; 10 Jamie Peacock; 22 Jay Pitts; 15 Brett Delaney; 12 Carl Ablett. Subs (all used): 16 Ryan Bailey; 18 Chris Clarkson; 20 Darrell Griffin; 24 Liam Hood.
Tries: McGuire (21), Hardaker (26), Watkins (43), Hood (67); **Goals:** Sinfield 5/5.
WOLVES: 19 Stefan Ratchford; 2 Chris Riley; 18 Matty Blythe; 4 Ryan Atkins; 5 Joel Monaghan; 6 Lee Briers; 7 Richard Myler; 8 Adrian Morley (C); 14 Mick Higham; 10 Garreth Carvell; 11 Trent Waterhouse; 12 Ben Westwood; 16 Paul Wood. Subs (all used): 20 Chris Hill; 15 Simon Grix; 17 Michael Cooper; 21 Tyrone McCarthy.
Tries: Blythe (31), Hill (36), Westwood (49);
Goals: Briers 3/3.
Rugby Leaguer & League Express Men of the Match: *Rhinos:* Danny McGuire; *Wolves:* Lee Briers.
Penalty count: 8-9; **Half-time:** 12-12;
Referee: Richard Silverwood; **Attendance:** 17,120.

ST HELENS 10 HULL FC 22

SAINTS: 1 Paul Wellens (C); 2 Ade Gardner; 3 Michael Shenton; 5 Francis Meli; 22 Jamie Foster; 20 Lee Gaskell; 7 Jonny Lomax; 14 Anthony Laffranchi; 6 Lance Hohaia; 11 Tony Puletua; 12 Jon Wilkin; 4 Iosia Soliola; 16 Paul Clough. Subs (all used): 8 Josh Perry; 10 Louie McCarthy-Scarsbrook; 17 Gary Wheeler; 19 Andrew Dixon.
Tries: Gardner (20), Puletua (45); **Goals:** Foster 1/2.
HULL: 1 Wade McKinnon; 2 Will Sharp; 3 Tony Martin; 4 Kirk Yeaman; 5 Tom Briscoe; 6 Richard Horne; 7 Brett Seymour; 8 Mark O'Meley; 9 Danny Houghton; 10 Andy Lynch (C); 11 Willie Manu; 12 Danny Tickle; 15 Richard Whiting. Subs (all used): 16 Eamon O'Carroll; 17 Sam Moa; 19 Jordan Turner; 20 Jamie Ellis.
Tries: McKinnon (29, 79), Turner (52); **Goals:** Tickle 5/6.
Rugby Leaguer & League Express Men of the Match: *Saints:* Tony Puletua; *Hull:* Danny Tickle.
Penalty count: 9-10; **Half-time:** 4-4;
Referee: Ben Thaler; **Attendance:** 14,875.

Saturday 10th March 2012

LONDON BRONCOS 42 CASTLEFORD TIGERS 16

BRONCOS: 1 Luke Dorn; 5 Michael Robertson; 4 David Howell; 19 Dan Sarginson; 2 Liam Colbon; 6 Michael Witt; 7 Craig Gower (C); 8 Antonio Kaufusi; 9 Chad Randall; 13 Tony Clubb; 20 Matt Cook; 17 Jason Golden; 12 Chris Bailey. Subs (all used): 10 Mark Bryant; 14 Julien Rinaldi; 15 Karl Temata; 16 Chris Melling.
Tries: Howell (6, 76), Bailey (9), Gower (30), Cook (37), Sarginson (59), Golden (67), Melling (76);
Goals: Witt 5/8.
TIGERS: 1 Richard Owen; 2 Nick Youngquest; 4 Kirk Dixon; 23 Ryan McGoldrick; 5 Josh Griffin; 6 Rangi Chase; 7 Danny Orr (C); 8 Jake Emmitt; 15 Adam Milner; 20 Grant Millington; 17 Lee Mitchell; 21 Oliver Holmes; 14 Stuart Jones. Subs (all used): 9 Daryl Clark; 12 Jonathan Walker; 13 Steve Snitch; 22 Nathan Massey.
Tries: Youngquest (12), Dixon (22), McGoldrick (45);
Goals: Dixon 2/3.
Rugby Leaguer & League Express Men of the Match: *Broncos:* Michael Witt; *Tigers:* Rangi Chase.
Penalty count: 5-9; **Half-time:** 22-12;
Referee: Phil Bentham; **Attendance:** 2,381.

CATALAN DRAGONS 40 SALFORD CITY REDS 18

DRAGONS: 6 Thomas Bosc; 2 Damien Blanch; 25 Vincent Duport; 15 Jean-Philippe Baile; 18 Daryl Millard; 3 Leon Pryce; 7 Scott Dureau; 8 David Ferriol; 26 Ben Fisher; 10 Remi Casty (C); 23 Lopini Paea; 14 Sebastien Raguin; 24 Jason Baitieri. Subs (all used): 13 Gregory Mounis; 17 Cyrille Gossard; 20 Michael Simon; 22 Jamal Fakir.
Tries: Blanch (14, 23), Dureau (17), Bosc (27), Pryce (39), Duport (54, 73), Millard (76);
Goals: Dureau 4/7, Bosc 0/1.
CITY REDS: 1 Luke Patten; 25 Josh Veivers (D); 3 Sean Gleeson; 4 Joel Moon; 14 Chris Nero; 6 Daniel Holdsworth; 7 Matty Smith; 12 Shannan McPherson; 24 Stuart Howarth; 10 Ryan Boyle; 11 Matty Ashurst; 16 Luke Adamson; 13 Stephen Wild (C). Subs (all used): 8 Lee Jewitt; 17 Iafeta Palea'aesina; 21 Jordan James; 23 Gareth Owen.
Tries: Howarth (12), Veivers (64), Owen (66);
Goals: Holdsworth 3/3.
Rugby Leaguer & League Express Men of the Match: *Dragons:* Scott Dureau; *City Reds:* Gareth Owen.
Penalty count: 9-8; **Half-time:** 26-6;
Referee: Thierry Alibert; **Attendance:** 8,158.

HULL KINGSTON ROVERS 24 BRADFORD BULLS 36

ROVERS: 1 Shannon McDonnell; 13 Rhys Lovegrove; 4 Jake Webster; 3 Kris Welham; 21 Sam Latus; 2 Craig Hall; 7 Michael Dobson (C); 10 Scott Taylor; 14 Lincoln Withers; 23 Mickey Paea; 11 Constantine Mika; 18 Graeme Horne; 9 Josh Hodgson. Subs (all used): 19 Scott Murrell; 16 Jason Netherton; 15 Liam Watts; 8 Joel Clinton.
Tries: Welham (3), Paea (7), J Hodgson (39), Hall (43);
Goals: Dobson 4/4.
BULLS: 1 Brett Kearney; 33 Karl Pryce (D2); 4 Chev Walker; 3 Keith Lulia; 24 Jason Crookes; 22 Jarrod Sammut; 6 Ben Jeffries; 15 Bryn Hargreaves; 14 Matt Diskin (C); 16 Manase Manuokafoa; 12 Elliott Whitehead; 26 John Bateman; 13 Jamie Langley. Subs (all used): 9 Heath L'Estrange (C); 8 Nick Scruton; 23 Danny Addy; 21 Tom Burgess.
Tries: Crookes (21, 53, 77), Pryce (31), Diskin (64), Kearney (67), Lulia (80); **Goals:** Sammut 4/7.
Rugby Leaguer & League Express Men of the Match: *Rovers:* Mickey Paea; *Bulls:* Jason Crookes.
Penalty count: 6-4; **Half-time:** 18-8;
Referee: Steve Ganson; **Attendance:** 7,486.

Sunday 11th March 2012

WIDNES VIKINGS 37 WIGAN WARRIORS 36

VIKINGS: 1 Shaun Briscoe; 2 Paddy Flynn; 20 Stefan Marsh; 19 Cameron Phelps (D); 4 Willie Isa; 32 Gareth O'Brien (D); 25 Danny Craven; 17 Steve Pickersgill; 13 Jon Clarke (C); 10 Ben Davies; 11 Frank Winterstein; 21 Dave Allen; 12 Hep Cahill. Subs (all used): 6 Lloyd White; 15 Simon Finnigan; 18 Sione Kite (D); 26 Anthony Mullally.
Tries: Flynn (20), Marsh (34), Briscoe (36, 61), White (54), Winterstein (64); **Goals:** O'Brien 6/6;
Field goal: White (71).
WARRIORS: 27 Matthew Russell (D); 24 Anthony Gelling (D); 3 Darrell Goulding; 26 Jack Hughes; 2 Josh Charnley; 6 Brett Finch (C); 25 Joe Mellor (D); 14 Jeff Lima; 9 Michael McIlorum; 10 Lee Mossop; 11 Harrison Hansen; 12 Gareth Hock; 17 Chris Tuson. Subs (all used): 21 Epalahame Lauaki; 23 Ben Flower; 28 Logan Tomkins (D); 32 Tom Spencer.
Tries: Hock (4), Hansen (7), Russell (30, 50), Finch (44), Mellor (46); **Goals:** Charnley 6/7.
Rugby Leaguer & League Express Men of the Match: *Vikings:* Shaun Briscoe; *Warriors:* Brett Finch.
Penalty count: 9-7; **Half-time:** 18-18;
Referee: Robert Hicks; **Attendance:** 7,357.

WAKEFIELD TRINITY WILDCATS 14 HUDDERSFIELD GIANTS 32

WILDCATS: 1 Richard Mathers; 2 Peter Fox; 3 Dean Collis; 4 Vince Mellars; 5 Ben Cockayne; 6 Isaac John; 20 Tim Smith; 10 Andy Raleigh; 14 Paul Aiton; 12 Steve Southern (C); 17 Danny Kirmond; 11 Ali Lauitiiti; 13 Danny Washbrook. Subs (all used): 7 Kyle Wood; 33 Lucas Walshaw; 16 Paul Johnson; 8 Oliver Wilkes.
Tries: Cockayne (31, 44, 55);
Goals: Cockayne 0/1, Smith 0/1, John 1/1.
GIANTS: 29 Greg Eden; 5 Jermaine McGillvary; 3 Leroy Cudjoe; 17 Joe Wardle; 21 Aaron Murphy; 1 Scott Grix; 7 Danny Brough; 8 Eorl Crabtree; 19 Tommy Lee; 4 Lee Gilmour; 18 Jason Chan; 23 Jacob Fairbank; 6 Kevin Brown (C). Subs (all used): 13 David Faiumu; 14 Shaun Lunt; 15 Larne Patrick; 2 Michael Lawrence.
Tries: McGillvary (6, 20), Patrick (36), Wardle (62, 72), Brown (69); **Goals:** Brough 4/7.
Rugby Leaguer & League Express Men of the Match: *Wildcats:* Ben Cockayne; *Giants:* Kevin Brown.
Penalty count: 10-11; **Half-time:** 4-18;
Referee: James Child; **Attendance:** 8,794.

ROUND 7

Friday 16th March 2012

HUDDERSFIELD GIANTS 42 CASTLEFORD TIGERS 4

GIANTS: 29 Greg Eden; 5 Jermaine McGillvary; 3 Leroy Cudjoe; 17 Joe Wardle; 20 Luke George; 7 Danny Brough; 1 Scott Grix; 8 Eorl Crabtree; 9 Luke Robinson; 4 Lee Gilmour; 18 Jason Chan; 2 Michael Lawrence; 6 Kevin Brown (C). Subs (all used): 12 David Fa'alogo; 13 David Faiumu; 15 Larne Patrick; 19 Tommy Lee.
Tries: George (11, 38, 41), Eden (15), Wardle (24), Patrick (36), Brown (43), Lawrence (64);
Goals: Brough 5/8.
Sin bin:
Chan (32) - alleged dangerous tackle on Youngquest.
On report:
Chan (32) - alleged dangerous tackle on Youngquest.

TIGERS: 1 Richard Owen; 26 James Clare (D); 3 Joe Arundel; 4 Kirk Dixon; 2 Nick Youngquest; 23 Ryan McGoldrick; 6 Rangi Chase (C); 12 Jonathan Walker; 16 Ryan Hudson; 20 Grant Millington; 11 Brett Ferres; 28 James Grehan; 13 Steve Snitch. Subs (all used): 9 Daryl Clark; 17 Lee Mitchell; 8 Jake Emmitt; 22 Nathan Massey.
Try: Youngquest (30); **Goals:** Dixon 0/1.
Rugby Leaguer & League Express Men of the Match: *Giants:* Luke George; *Tigers:* Rangi Chase.
Penalty count: 7-6; **Half-time:** 26-4;
Referee: Steve Ganson; **Attendance:** 6,928.

SALFORD CITY REDS 16 LEEDS RHINOS 56

CITY REDS: 1 Luke Patten; 18 Ashley Gibson; 14 Chris Nero; 3 Sean Gleeson; 5 Danny Williams; 6 Daniel Holdsworth; 7 Matty Smith; 12 Shannan McPherson; 24 Stuart Howarth; 8 Lee Jewitt; 11 Matty Ashurst; 27 Vinnie Anderson; 13 Stephen Wild (C). Subs (all used): 16 Luke Adamson; 17 Iafeta Palea'aesina; 21 Jordan James; 23 Gareth Owen.
Tries: Anderson (10), Owen (76), Patten (80);
Goals: Holdsworth 2/3.
RHINOS: 1 Brent Webb; 2 Ben Jones-Bishop; 3 Kallum Watkins; 4 Zak Hardaker; 5 Ryan Hall; 13 Kevin Sinfield (C); 6 Danny McGuire; 8 Kylie Leuluai; 7 Rob Burrow; 10 Jamie Peacock; 18 Chris Clarkson; 15 Brett Delaney; 12 Carl Ablett. Subs (all used): 17 Ian Kirke; 20 Darrell Griffin; 21 Richard Moore; 24 Liam Hood.
Tries: Hardaker (14, 48, 61), Delaney (21), Watkins (25), Sinfield (27), Hood (32), McGuire (36), Burrow (65), Ablett (71); **Goals:** Sinfield 8/10.
Rugby Leaguer & League Express Men of the Match: *City Reds:* Lee Jewitt; *Rhinos:* Kevin Sinfield.
Penalty count: 7-4; **Half-time:** 4-32;
Referee: Robert Hicks; **Attendance:** 6,891.

Saturday 17th March 2012

BRADFORD BULLS 12 ST HELENS 8

BULLS: 1 Brett Kearney; 33 Karl Pryce; 2 Adrian Purtell; 3 Keith Lulia; 24 Jason Crookes; 28 Paul Sykes; 6 Ben Jeffries; 16 Manase Manuokafoa; 14 Matt Diskin (C); 15 Bryn Hargreaves; 12 Elliott Whitehead; 4 Chev Walker; 26 John Bateman. Subs (all used): 9 Heath L'Estrange (C); 21 Tom Burgess; 11 Olivier Elima; 23 Danny Addy.
Tries: Whitehead (33), Pryce (42); **Goals:** Sykes 2/3.
SAINTS: 1 Paul Wellens (C); 21 Tom Makinson; 3 Michael Shenton; 5 Francis Meli; 22 Jamie Foster; 20 Lee Gaskell; 17 Gary Wheeler; 14 Anthony Laffranchi; 6 Lance Hohaia; 11 Tony Puletua; 12 Jon Wilkin; 19 Andrew Dixon; 16 Paul Clough. Subs (all used): 8 Josh Perry; 15 Mark Flanagan; 24 Nathan Ashe; 13 Chris Flannery.
Tries: Dixon (22), Meli (80); **Goals:** Foster 0/2.
Sin bin: Foster (61) - professional foul.
Rugby Leaguer & League Express Men of the Match: *Bulls:* John Bateman; *Saints:* Paul Wellens.
Penalty count: 11-8; **Half-time:** 8-4;
Referee: Richard Silverwood; **Attendance:** 11,360.

CATALAN DRAGONS 20 HULL KINGSTON ROVERS 12

DRAGONS: 6 Thomas Bosc; 2 Damien Blanch; 25 Vincent Duport; 15 Jean-Philippe Baile; 18 Daryl Millard; 3 Leon Pryce; 7 Scott Dureau; 8 David Ferriol; 26 Ben Fisher; 10 Remi Casty (C); 23 Lopini Paea; 14 Sebastien Raguin; 24 Jason Baitieri. Subs (all used): 13 Gregory Mounis; 16 Eloi Pelissier; 17 Cyrille Gossard; 20 Michael Simon.
Tries: Paea (25), Blanch (57), Bosc (75);
Goals: Dureau 4/5.
ROVERS: 1 Shannon McDonnell; 29 Liam Salter (D); 18 Graeme Horne; 3 Kris Welham; 21 Sam Latus; 19 Scott Murrell; 7 Michael Dobson (C); 8 Joel Clinton; 14 Lincoln Withers; 23 Mickey Paea; 11 Constantine Mika; 9 Josh Hodgson; 16 Jason Netherton. Subs (all used): 13 Rhys Lovegrove; 20 Jordan Cox; 22 Scott Wheeldon; 25 Keal Carlile.
Tries: Dobson (33), Welham (40); **Goals:** Dobson 2/2.
Rugby Leaguer & League Express Men of the Match: *Dragons:* Remi Casty; *Rovers:* Michael Dobson.
Penalty count: 7-4; **Half-time:** 6-12;
Referee: Ben Thaler; **Attendance:** 7,133.

Sunday 18th March 2012

HULL FC 58 WIDNES VIKINGS 10

HULL: 1 Wade McKinnon; 2 Will Sharp; 3 Tony Martin; 19 Jordan Turner; 5 Tom Briscoe; 6 Richard Horne; 7 Brett Seymour; 17 Sam Moa; 9 Danny Houghton; 10 Andy Lynch (C); 11 Willie Manu; 12 Danny Tickle; 22 Martin Aspinwall. Subs (all used): 20 Jamie Ellis; 30 Josh Bowden; 15 Richard Whiting; 16 Eamon O'Carroll.
Tries: Tickle (5, 20, 27, 55), Manu (11, 43), Lynch (14), Whiting (49), Moa (53), Briscoe (60); **Goals:** Tickle 9/10.
VIKINGS: 1 Shaun Briscoe; 2 Paddy Flynn; 20 Stefan Marsh; 19 Cameron Phelps; 4 Willie Isa; 25 Danny Craven; 32 Gareth O'Brien; 17 Steve Pickersgill; 13 Jon Clarke (C); 10 Ben Davies; 11 Frank Winterstein; 21 Dave Allen; 12 Hep Cahill. Subs (all used): 6 Lloyd White; 15 Simon Finnigan; 18 Sione Kite; 26 Anthony Mullally.
Tries: Flynn (70, 78); **Goals:** O'Brien 1/2.
Rugby Leaguer & League Express Men of the Match: *Hull:* Danny Tickle; *Vikings:* Paddy Flynn.
Penalty count: 9-1; **Half-time:** 28-0;
Referee: Phil Bentham; **Attendance:** 10,705.

WARRINGTON WOLVES 32
WAKEFIELD TRINITY WILDCATS 30

WOLVES: 2 Chris Riley; 5 Joel Monaghan; 3 Chris Bridge; 4 Ryan Atkins; 22 Rhys Williams; 6 Lee Briers; 7 Richard Myler; 8 Adrian Morley (C); 9 Michael Monaghan; 20 Chris Hill; 11 Trent Waterhouse; 12 Ben Westwood; 15 Simon Grix. Subs (all used): 16 Paul Wood; 17 Michael Cooper; 18 Matty Blythe; 33 Brad Dwyer (D).
Tries: Atkins (13), Myler (33, 42), Westwood (48), Grix (61), J Monaghan (67); **Goals:** Briers 4/6.
Sin bin: Wood (38) - persistent offending.
WILDCATS: 1 Richard Mathers; 2 Peter Fox; 17 Danny Kirmond; 4 Vince Mellars; 5 Ben Cockayne; 6 Isaac John; 20 Tim Smith; 10 Andy Raleigh; 14 Paul Aiton; 15 Kyle Amor; 12 Steve Southern (C); 11 Ali Lauitiiti; 13 Danny Washbrook. Subs (all used): 7 Kyle Wood; 33 Lucas Walshaw; 16 Paul Johnson; 8 Oliver Wilkes.
Tries: Washbrook (5), John (25), Mathers (31), Lauitiiti (46), Mellars (75); **Goals:** John 5/6.
Rugby Leaguer & League Express Men of the Match: *Wolves:* Ben Westwood; *Wildcats:* Tim Smith.
Penalty count: 11-11; **Half-time:** 12-20;
Referee: Thierry Alibert; **Attendance:** 10,686.

WIGAN WARRIORS 42 LONDON BRONCOS 30

WARRIORS: 1 Sam Tomkins; 2 Josh Charnley; 3 Darrell Goulding; 4 George Carmont; 5 Pat Richards; 6 Brett Finch; 7 Thomas Leuluai; 8 Paul Prescott; 9 Michael McIlorum; 21 Epalahame Lauaki; 11 Harrison Hansen; 12 Gareth Hock; 13 Sean O'Loughlin (C). Subs (all used): 17 Chris Tuson; 16 Liam Farrell; 14 Jeff Lima; 23 Ben Flower.
Tries: Finch (10, 56), Hock (31), Goulding (35), Carmont (38), Richards (42), S Tomkins (65);
Goals: Richards 7/7.
BRONCOS: 1 Luke Dorn; 5 Michael Robertson; 4 David Howell; 19 Dan Sarginson; 3 Jamie O'Callaghan; 6 Michael Witt; 7 Craig Gower (C); 8 Antonio Kaufusi; 9 Chad Randall; 13 Tony Clubb; 20 Matt Cook; 17 Jason Golden; 12 Chris Bailey. Subs (all used): 10 Mark Bryant; 14 Julien Rinaldi; 15 Karl Temata; 16 Chris Melling.
Tries: Witt (5, 71), Robertson (17), Sarginson (28), Melling (46); **Goals:** Witt 5/5.
Rugby Leaguer & League Express Men of the Match: *Warriors:* Brett Finch; *Broncos:* Michael Witt.
Penalty count: 8-8; **Half-time:** 24-18;
Referee: James Child; **Attendance:** 12,608.

ROUND 8

Friday 23rd March 2012

WIGAN WARRIORS 20 WARRINGTON WOLVES 22

WARRIORS: 1 Sam Tomkins; 2 Josh Charnley; 3 Darrell Goulding; 4 George Carmont; 5 Pat Richards; 6 Brett Finch; 7 Thomas Leuluai; 8 Paul Prescott; 9 Michael McIlorum; 21 Epalahame Lauaki; 11 Harrison Hansen; 12 Gareth Hock; 13 Sean O'Loughlin (C). Subs (all used): 17 Chris Tuson; 16 Liam Farrell; 14 Jeff Lima; 23 Ben Flower.
Tries: Hock (19), McIlorum (27), Richards (41);
Goals: Richards 2/2, Charnley 2/4.
On report: Lauaki (65) - alleged use of the forearm, (72) - alleged dangerous tackle on Blythe.
WOLVES: 1 Brett Hodgson; 2 Chris Riley; 3 Chris Bridge; 4 Ryan Atkins; 5 Joel Monaghan; 6 Lee Briers; 7 Richard Myler; 8 Adrian Morley (C); 9 Michael Monaghan; 17 Michael Cooper; 11 Trent Waterhouse; 12 Ben Westwood; 15 Simon Grix. Subs: 16 Paul Wood; 33 Brad Dwyer (not used); 18 Matty Blythe; 20 Chris Hill.
Tries: Atkins (7), J Monaghan (35), Briers (49);
Goals: Hodgson 5/6.
On report: Westwood (65) - alleged high tackle.
Rugby Leaguer & League Express Men of the Match: *Warriors:* Gareth Hock; *Wolves:* Brett Hodgson.
Penalty count: 8-12; **Half-time:** 12-12;
Referee: Richard Silverwood; **Attendance:** 21,267.

Sunday 25th March 2012

BRADFORD BULLS 18 SALFORD CITY REDS 38

BULLS: 1 Brett Kearney; 33 Karl Pryce; 28 Paul Sykes; 3 Keith Lulia; 24 Jason Crookes; 22 Jarrod Sammut; 6 Ben Jeffries; 16 Manase Manuokafoa; 14 Matt Diskin (C); 15 Bryn Hargreaves; 12 Elliott Whitehead; 4 Chev Walker; 13 Jamie Langley. Subs (all used): 9 Heath L'Estrange (C); 21 Tom Burgess; 26 John Bateman; 23 Danny Addy.
Tries: Kearney (15), Whitehead (46), Hargreaves (60);
Goals: Sammut 3/3.
CITY REDS: 1 Luke Patten; 18 Ashley Gibson; 3 Sean Gleeson; 4 Joel Moon; 25 Josh Veivers; 6 Daniel Holdsworth; 7 Matty Smith; 8 Lee Jewitt; 24 Stuart Howarth; 10 Ryan Boyle; 11 Matty Ashurst; 27 Vinnie Anderson; 13 Stephen Wild (C). Subs (all used): 16 Luke Adamson; 17 Iafeta Palea'aesina; 21 Jordan James; 23 Gareth Owen.
Tries: Veivers (9), Moon (22, 34), Patten (24), Gibson (37), Ashurst (40), Owen (50); **Goals:** Holdsworth 5/9.
Rugby Leaguer & League Express Men of the Match: *Bulls:* Brett Kearney; *City Reds:* Luke Patten.
Penalty count: 9-11; **Half-time:** 6-30;
Referee: Ben Thaler; **Attendance:** 11,219.

HULL KINGSTON ROVERS 40
HUDDERSFIELD GIANTS 22

ROVERS: 1 Shannon McDonnell; 21 Sam Latus; 3 Kris Welham; 18 Graeme Horne; 5 David Hodgson; 19 Scott Murrell; 7 Michael Dobson (C); 8 Joel Clinton; 14 Lincoln Withers; 22 Scott Wheeldon; 11 Constantine Mika; 9 Josh Hodgson; 15 Liam Watts. Subs (all used): 23 Mickey Paea; 10 Scott Taylor; 13 Rhys Lovegrove; 20 Jordan Cox.
Tries: Watts (10), D Hodgson (35), Welham (39), J Hodgson (44), Taylor (57), Latus (72), Paea (78);
Goals: Dobson 6/7.
GIANTS: 29 Greg Eden; 5 Jermaine McGillvary; 3 Leroy Cudjoe; 17 Joe Wardle; 20 Luke George; 7 Danny Brough; 1 Scott Grix; 8 Eorl Crabtree; 19 Tommy Lee; 15 Larne Patrick; 18 Jason Chan; 2 Michael Lawrence; 6 Kevin Brown (C). Subs (all used): 12 David Fa'alogo; 13 David Faiumu; 14 Shaun Lunt; 22 Tony Tonks (D).
Tries: George (4), Grix (11), Eden (18), Lunt (63);
Goals: Brough 3/4.
Rugby Leaguer & League Express Men of the Match: *Rovers:* Scott Taylor; *Giants:* Kevin Brown.
Penalty count: 2-8; **Half-time:** 18-18;
Referee: Steve Ganson; **Attendance:** 7,616.

WIDNES VIKINGS 38 LONDON BRONCOS 30

VIKINGS: 19 Cameron Phelps; 2 Paddy Flynn; 20 Stefan Marsh; 3 Chris Dean; 4 Willie Isa; 32 Gareth O'Brien; 7 Rhys Hanbury; 8 Ben Cross (C); 6 Lloyd White; 18 Sione Kite; 11 Frank Winterstein; 15 Simon Finnigan; 12 Hep Cahill. Subs (all used): 9 Scott Moore; 10 Ben Davies; 21 Dave Allen; 17 Steve Pickersgill.
Tries: White (2, 67), Dean (6), Hanbury (29), Davies (42), Phelps (74); **Goals:** O'Brien 7/8.
Sin bin: Cross (53) - late challenge on Gower.
BRONCOS: 1 Luke Dorn; 3 Jamie O'Callaghan; 4 David Howell; 19 Dan Sarginson; 2 Liam Colbon; 6 Michael Witt; 7 Craig Gower (C); 8 Antonio Kaufusi; 9 Chad Randall; 13 Tony Clubb; 16 Chris Melling; 20 Matt Cook; 12 Chris Bailey. Subs (all used): 10 Mark Bryant; 15 Karl Temata; 14 Julien Rinaldi; 21 Kieran Dixon.
Tries: Dorn (12), Bryant (46), Witt (55), Colbon (63), Clubb (71); **Goals:** Witt 5/5.
Sin bin: Clubb (77) - late challenge on O'Brien.
Rugby Leaguer & League Express Men of the Match: *Vikings:* Lloyd White; *Broncos:* Craig Gower.
Penalty count: 7-12; **Half-time:** 18-6;
Referee: Richard Silverwood; **Attendance:** 6,535.

CASTLEFORD TIGERS 28 HULL FC 42

TIGERS: 1 Richard Owen; 2 Nick Youngquest; 28 James Grehan; 4 Kirk Dixon; 5 Josh Griffin; 6 Rangi Chase; 7 Danny Orr (C); 22 Nathan Massey; 16 Ryan Hudson; 12 Jonathan Walker; 11 Brett Ferres; 21 Oliver Holmes; 8 Jake Emmitt. Subs (all used): 13 Steve Snitch; 14 Stuart Jones; 20 Grant Millington; 23 Ryan McGoldrick.
Tries: Youngquest (16), Walker (19), Millington (29), Griffin (58), Ferres (78); **Goals:** Dixon 4/5.
HULL: 1 Wade McKinnon; 2 Will Sharp; 3 Tony Martin; 19 Jordan Turner; 5 Tom Briscoe; 6 Richard Horne; 7 Brett Seymour; 17 Sam Moa; 9 Danny Houghton; 10 Andy Lynch (C); 11 Willie Manu; 12 Danny Tickle; 22 Martin Aspinwall. Subs (all used): 30 Josh Bowden; 20 Jamie Ellis; 15 Richard Whiting; 16 Eamon O'Carroll.
Tries: Moa (9), Manu (23, 76), Turner (37), Tickle (46), Seymour (52), Briscoe (70);
Goals: Tickle 7/7, Whiting 0/1.
Rugby Leaguer & League Express Men of the Match: *Tigers:* Danny Orr; *Hull:* Danny Tickle.
Penalty count: 6-10; **Half-time:** 16-20;
Referee: Matthew Thomason; **Attendance:** 9,050.

WAKEFIELD TRINITY WILDCATS 32
CATALAN DRAGONS 22

WILDCATS: 1 Richard Mathers; 2 Peter Fox; 3 Dean Collis; 4 Vince Mellars; 5 Ben Cockayne; 6 Isaac John; 20 Tim Smith; 15 Kyle Amor; 14 Paul Aiton; 10 Andy Raleigh; 11 Ali Lauitiiti; 17 Danny Kirmond; 13 Danny Washbrook. Subs (all used): 7 Kyle Wood; 12 Steve Southern (C); 16 Paul Johnson; 8 Oliver Wilkes.
Tries: Cockayne (12), Fox (18, 40), Raleigh (25), Kirmond (52); **Goals:** John 6/6, Cockayne 0/1.
DRAGONS: 6 Thomas Bosc; 1 Clint Greenshields; 15 Jean-Philippe Baile; 25 Vincent Duport; 18 Daryl Millard; 3 Leon Pryce; 7 Scott Dureau; 23 Lopini Paea; 26 Ben Fisher; 10 Remi Casty (C); 4 Setaimata Sa; 14 Sebastien Raguin; 24 Jason Baitieri. Subs (all used): 8 David Ferriol; 13 Gregory Mounis; 16 Eloi Pelissier; 22 Jamal Fakir.
Tries: Mounis (34), Dureau (54), Duport (65), Greenshields (74); **Goals:** Dureau 3/4.
On report: Mounis (44) - alleged dangerous tackle on Fox.
Rugby Leaguer & League Express Men of the Match: *Wildcats:* Tim Smith; *Dragons:* Scott Dureau.
Penalty count: 9-5; **Half-time:** 24-6;
Referee: Robert Hicks; **Attendance:** 7,254.

ST HELENS 46 LEEDS RHINOS 6

SAINTS: 1 Paul Wellens (C); 2 Ade Gardner; 3 Michael Shenton; 5 Francis Meli; 17 Gary Wheeler; 6 Lance Hohaia; 7 Jonny Lomax; 14 Anthony Laffranchi; 9 James Roby; 8 Josh Perry; 13 Chris Flannery; 12 Jon Wilkin; 11 Tony Puletua. Subs (all used): 10 Louie McCarthy-Scarsbrook; 15 Mark Flanagan; 16 Paul Clough; 18 Shaun Magennis.
Tries: Gardner (3, 67), Lomax (6, 20), Wheeler (10, 78), Wellens (43), Hohaia (65); **Goals:** Lomax 7/8.
RHINOS: 14 Lee Smith; 2 Ben Jones-Bishop; 3 Kallum Watkins; 4 Zak Hardaker; 5 Ryan Hall; 13 Kevin Sinfield (C); 7 Rob Burrow; 8 Kylie Leuluai; 9 Paul McShane; 10 Jamie Peacock; 18 Chris Clarkson; 15 Brett Delaney; 12 Carl Ablett. Subs (all used): 17 Ian Kirke; 20 Darrell Griffin; 21 Richard Moore; 25 Stevie Ward (D).
Try: Hardaker (52); **Goals:** Sinfield 1/1.
Rugby Leaguer & League Express Men of the Match: *Saints:* Lance Hohaia; *Rhinos:* Rob Burrow.
Penalty count: 4-1; **Half-time:** 24-0;
Referee: Phil Bentham; **Attendance:** 15,195.

ROUND 9

Friday 30th March 2012

CASTLEFORD TIGERS 34 HULL KINGSTON ROVERS 30

TIGERS: 1 Richard Owen; 2 Nick Youngquest; 17 Lee Mitchell; 4 Kirk Dixon; 5 Josh Griffin; 6 Rangi Chase; 7 Danny Orr (C); 12 Jonathan Walker; 9 Daryl Clark; 22

Nathan Massey; 11 Brett Ferres; 21 Oliver Holmes; 8 Jake Emmitt. Subs (all used): 13 Steve Snitch; 14 Stuart Jones; 20 Grant Millington; 23 Ryan McGoldrick.
Tries: Griffin (7), Youngquest (33, 80), Owen (38), Dixon (54), Snitch (62); **Goals:** Dixon 5/6.
ROVERS: 1 Shannon McDonnell; 29 Liam Salter; 18 Graeme Horne; 3 Kris Welham; 5 David Hodgson; 19 Scott Murrell; 7 Michael Dobson (C); 8 Joel Clinton; 14 Lincoln Withers; 22 Scott Wheeldon; 11 Constantine Mika; 9 Josh Hodgson; 15 Liam Watts. Subs (all used): 23 Mickey Paea; 10 Scott Taylor; 13 Rhys Lovegrove; 20 Jordan Cox.
Tries: Welham (2, 19, 44), J Hodgson (40), Withers (50); **Goals:** Dobson 5/6.
Rugby Leaguer & League Express Men of the Match: *Tigers:* Rangi Chase; *Rovers:* Shannon McDonnell.
Penalty count: 6-5; **Half-time:** 18-16;
Referee: Robert Hicks; **Attendance:** 6,396.

HULL FC 24 BRADFORD BULLS 18

HULL: 6 Richard Horne; 2 Will Sharp; 3 Tony Martin; 19 Jordan Turner; 5 Tom Briscoe; 20 Jamie Ellis; 7 Brett Seymour; 16 Eamon O'Carroll; 9 Danny Houghton; 10 Andy Lynch (C); 11 Willie Manu; 12 Danny Tickle; 22 Martin Aspinwall. Subs (all used): 15 Richard Whiting; 30 Josh Bowden; 24 Liam Kent; 27 Chris Green (D).
Tries: Horne (8, 58), Manu (20), Briscoe (69);
Goals: Tickle 4/5.
BULLS: 1 Brett Kearney; 33 Karl Pryce; 2 Adrian Purtell; 3 Keith Lulia; 24 Jason Crookes; 23 Danny Addy; 22 Jarrod Sammut; 15 Bryn Hargreaves; 14 Matt Diskin (C); 16 Manase Manuokafoa; 12 Elliott Whitehead; 26 John Bateman; 13 Jamie Langley. Subs (all used): 9 Heath L'Estrange (C); 34 Phil Joseph; 11 Olivier Elima; 21 Tom Burgess.
Tries: Lulia (15), Pryce (45), Bateman (67);
Goals: Sammut 3/3.
Rugby Leaguer & League Express Men of the Match: *Hull:* Will Sharp; *Bulls:* John Bateman.
Penalty count: 7-7; **Half-time:** 12-6;
Referee: Thierry Alibert; **Attendance:** 11,673.

LEEDS RHINOS 12 HUDDERSFIELD GIANTS 22

RHINOS: 2 Ben Jones-Bishop; 14 Lee Smith; 3 Kallum Watkins; 4 Zak Hardaker; 5 Ryan Hall; 13 Kevin Sinfield (C); 25 Stevie Ward; 8 Kylie Leuluai; 9 Paul McShane; 10 Jamie Peacock; 18 Chris Clarkson; 15 Brett Delaney; 12 Carl Ablett. Subs (all used): 20 Darrell Griffin; 17 Ian Kirke; 21 Richard Moore; 24 Liam Hood.
Tries: Hardaker (25), Leuluai (67); **Goals:** Sinfield 2/2.
GIANTS: 29 Greg Eden; 5 Jermaine McGillvary; 3 Leroy Cudjoe; 17 Joe Wardle; 20 Luke George; 7 Danny Brough; 1 Scott Grix (C); 8 Eorl Crabtree; 9 Luke Robinson; 12 David Fa'alogo; 4 Lee Gilmour; 18 Jason Chan; 19 Tommy Lee. Subs (all used): 11 Luke O'Donnell; 13 David Faiumu; 15 Larne Patrick; 2 Michael Lawrence.
Tries: Crabtree (31), Chan (36), Eden (52), McGillvary (54); **Goals:** Brough 3/4.
Rugby Leaguer & League Express Men of the Match: *Rhinos:* Stevie Ward; *Giants:* Greg Eden.
Penalty count: 7-6; **Half-time:** 6-12;
Referee: Richard Silverwood; **Attendance:** 15,408.

SALFORD CITY REDS 20 WIGAN WARRIORS 40

CITY REDS: 1 Luke Patten; 25 Josh Veivers; 4 Joel Moon; 3 Sean Gleeson; 5 Danny Williams; 6 Daniel Holdsworth; 7 Matty Smith; 10 Ryan Boyle; 24 Stuart Howarth; 8 Lee Jewitt; 11 Matty Ashurst; 27 Vinnie Anderson; 13 Stephen Wild (C). Subs (all used): 16 Luke Adamson; 17 Iafeta Palea'aesina; 21 Jordan James; 23 Gareth Owen.
Tries: Holdsworth (7), Williams (12), Patten (56), James (79); **Goals:** Holdsworth 2/4.
WARRIORS: 1 Sam Tomkins; 2 Josh Charnley; 3 Darrell Goulding; 4 George Carmont; 27 Matthew Russell; 6 Brett Finch (C); 7 Thomas Leuluai; 10 Lee Mossop; 9 Michael McIlorum; 8 Paul Prescott; 12 Gareth Hock; 11 Harrison Hansen; 16 Liam Farrell. Subs (all used): 14 Jeff Lima; 17 Chris Tuson; 23 Ben Flower; 25 Joe Mellor.
Tries: Goulding (2, 16), Charnley (21), S Tomkins (23, 45), Carmont (30), Farrell (37), Russell (60); **Goals:** Charnley 4/8.
Rugby Leaguer & League Express Men of the Match: *City Reds:* Danny Williams; *Warriors:* Michael McIlorum.
Penalty count: 5-13; **Half-time:** 8-30;
Referee: James Child; **Attendance:** 6,774.

WARRINGTON WOLVES 16 ST HELENS 28

WOLVES: 1 Brett Hodgson; 2 Chris Riley; 18 Matty Blythe; 4 Ryan Atkins; 5 Joel Monaghan; 6 Lee Briers; 7 Richard Myler; 8 Adrian Morley (C); 9 Michael Monaghan; 16 Paul Wood; 11 Trent Waterhouse; 15 Simon Grix; 17 Michael Cooper. Subs (all used): 10 Garreth Carvell; 14 Mick Higham; 3 Chris Bridge; 20 Chris Hill.
Tries: Hodgson (39), J Monaghan (47), Atkins (80);
Goals: Hodgson 2/3.
SAINTS: 1 Paul Wellens (C); 2 Ade Gardner; 3 Michael Shenton; 26 Josh Jones (D); 5 Francis Meli; 6 Lance Hohaia; 7 Jonny Lomax; 14 Anthony Laffranchi; 9 James Roby; 8 Josh Perry; 13 Chris Flannery; 4 Iosia Soliola; 12 Jon Wilkin. Subs (all used): 10 Louie McCarthy-Scarsbrook; 15 Mark Flanagan; 16 Paul Clough; 18 Shaun Magennis.
Tries: Gardner (3), Wellens (11, 15), Meli (23), Soliola (68); **Goals:** Lomax 4/5.
Rugby Leaguer & League Express Men of the Match: *Wolves:* Chris Hill; *Saints:* Jon Wilkin.
Penalty count: 9-5; **Half-time:** 6-22;
Referee: Ben Thaler; **Attendance:** 15,000.

Saturday 31st March 2012

CATALAN DRAGONS 76 WIDNES VIKINGS 6

DRAGONS: 1 Clint Greenshields; 2 Damien Blanch; 25 Vincent Duport; 18 Daryl Millard; 28 Damien Cardace (D); 3 Leon Pryce; 7 Scott Dureau; 20 Michael Simon; 9 Ian Henderson; 10 Remi Casty (C); 23 Lopini Paea; 4 Setaimata Sa; 24 Jason Baitieri. Subs (all used): 8 David Ferriol; 12 Louis Anderson; 16 Eloi Pelissier; 22 Jamal Fakir.
Tries: Greenshields (1, 32, 79), Casty (7), Sa (35), Cardace (37, 39, 64, 68), Anderson (45), Blanch (51), Millard (54), Duport (59);
Goals: Dureau 11/11, Millard 1/2.
VIKINGS: 1 Shaun Briscoe; 2 Paddy Flynn; 19 Cameron Phelps; 3 Chris Dean; 4 Willie Isa; 32 Gareth O'Brien; 7 Rhys Hanbury; 8 Ben Cross (C); 6 Lloyd White; 18 Sione Kite; 11 Frank Winterstein; 21 Dave Allen; 15 Simon Finnigan. Subs (all used): 9 Scott Moore; 10 Ben Davies; 17 Steve Pickersgill; 22 Macgraff Leuluai.
Try: Kite (9); **Goals:** O'Brien 1/1.
Rugby Leaguer & League Express Men of the Match: *Dragons:* Scott Dureau; *Vikings:* Gareth O'Brien.
Penalty count: 11-3; **Half-time:** 36-6;
Referee: Phil Bentham; **Attendance:** 9,156.

LONDON BRONCOS 36 WAKEFIELD TRINITY WILDCATS 0

BRONCOS: 5 Michael Robertson; 2 Liam Colbon; 19 Dan Sarginson; 3 Jamie O'Callaghan; 21 Kieran Dixon; 6 Michael Witt; 7 Craig Gower (C); 8 Antonio Kaufusi; 9 Chad Randall; 13 Tony Clubb; 12 Chris Bailey; 11 Shane Rodney; 20 Matt Cook. Subs (all used): 10 Mark Bryant; 15 Karl Temata; 14 Julien Rinaldi; 1 Luke Dorn.
Tries: Clubb (4), Sarginson (16), Dixon (31), Robertson (35, 44), Colbon (57), Dorn (75);
Goals: Witt 4/6, Rodney 0/1, Gower 0/1.
WILDCATS: 1 Richard Mathers; 2 Peter Fox; 34 Paul Sykes (D); 4 Vince Mellars; 5 Ben Cockayne; 6 Isaac John; 20 Tim Smith; 10 Andy Raleigh; 14 Paul Aiton; 15 Kyle Amor; 17 Danny Kirmond; 11 Ali Lauitiiti; 13 Danny Washbrook. Subs (all used): 7 Kyle Wood; 16 Paul Johnson; 8 Oliver Wilkes; 12 Steve Southern (C).
Rugby Leaguer & League Express Men of the Match: *Broncos:* Craig Gower; *Wildcats:* Isaac John.
Penalty count: 5-4; **Half-time:** 24-0;
Referee: Steve Ganson; **Attendance:** 2,268.

ROUND 10

Thursday 5th April 2012

LONDON BRONCOS 18 CATALAN DRAGONS 36

BRONCOS: 5 Michael Robertson; 2 Liam Colbon; 19 Dan Sarginson; 3 Jamie O'Callaghan; 21 Kieran Dixon; 6 Michael Witt; 7 Craig Gower (C); 8 Antonio Kaufusi; 9 Chad Randall; 13 Tony Clubb; 20 Matt Cook; 11 Shane Rodney; 12 Chris Bailey. Subs (all used): 10 Mark Bryant; 15 Karl Temata; 14 Julien Rinaldi; 1 Luke Dorn.
Tries: Rodney (36), Dorn (63), Robertson (68);
Goals: Witt 1/1, Rodney 2/2.
DRAGONS: 1 Clint Greenshields; 2 Damien Blanch; 18 Daryl Millard; 25 Vincent Duport; 6 Thomas Bosc; 3 Leon Pryce; 7 Scott Dureau; 23 Lopini Paea; 26 Ben Fisher; 10 Remi Casty (C); 4 Setaimata Sa; 12 Louis Anderson; 13 Gregory Mounis. Subs (all used): 9 Ian Henderson; 11 Steve Menzies; 20 Michael Simon; 22 Jamal Fakir.
Tries: Anderson (8, 48), Duport (14, 45), Menzies (50), Dureau (54), Pryce (76); **Goals:** Dureau 4/7.
Sin bin: Henderson (72) - late challenge on Gower.
Rugby Leaguer & League Express Men of the Match: *Broncos:* Shane Rodney; *Dragons:* Scott Dureau.
Penalty count: 7-4; **Half-time:** 6-10;
Referee: Thierry Alibert; **Attendance:** 1,829.

WARRINGTON WOLVES 46 WIDNES VIKINGS 12

WOLVES: 1 Brett Hodgson (C); 2 Chris Riley; 5 Joel Monaghan; 4 Ryan Atkins; 22 Rhys Williams; 24 Gareth O'Brien; 7 Richard Myler; 20 Chris Hill; 14 Mick Higham; 10 Garreth Carvell; 32 Ben Currie (D); 12 Ben Westwood; 3 Chris Bridge. Subs (all used): 17 Michael Cooper; 33 Brad Dwyer; 16 Paul Wood; 21 Tyrone McCarthy.
Tries: Bridge (21, 24), Riley (29, 77, 80), Hodgson (53), Atkins (57), Dwyer (73); **Goals:** Hodgson 7/8.
VIKINGS: 19 Cameron Phelps; 2 Paddy Flynn; 3 Chris Dean; 4 Willie Isa; 5 Patrick Ah Van; 25 Danny Craven; 7 Rhys Hanbury; 18 Sione Kite; 9 Scott Moore; 12 Hep Cahill; 21 Dave Allen; 15 Simon Finnigan; 22 Macgraff Leuluai. Subs (all used): 6 Lloyd White; 8 Ben Cross (C); 24 Kurt Haggerty; 28 Alex Gerrard.
Tries: Dean (3), Allen (9); **Goals:** Ah Van 2/2.
Rugby Leaguer & League Express Men of the Match: *Wolves:* Brett Hodgson; *Vikings:* Cameron Phelps.
Penalty count: 11-8; **Half-time:** 18-12;
Referee: James Child; **Attendance:** 12,042.

Friday 6th April 2012

HULL FC 36 HULL KINGSTON ROVERS 6

HULL: 1 Wade McKinnon; 2 Will Sharp; 19 Jordan Turner; 4 Kirk Yeaman; 5 Tom Briscoe; 6 Richard Horne; 7 Brett Seymour; 35 Lee Radford; 9 Danny Houghton; 10 Andy Lynch (C); 11 Willie Manu; 12 Danny Tickle; 15 Richard Whiting. Subs (all used): 20 Jamie Ellis; 22 Martin Aspinwall; 30 Josh Bowden; 34 Jay Pitts (D).
Tries: Radford (36), Turner (42, 64, 80), Yeaman (68), Seymour (71); **Goals:** Tickle 6/7.
ROVERS: 1 Shannon McDonnell; 2 Craig Hall; 18 Graeme Horne; 3 Kris Welham; 5 David Hodgson; 19 Scott Murrell; 7 Michael Dobson; 8 Joel Clinton; 14 Lincoln Withers; 10 Scott Taylor; 11 Constantine Mika; 9 Josh Hodgson; 15 Liam Watts. Subs (all used): 22 Scott Wheeldon; 23 Mickey Paea; 13 Rhys Lovegrove; 12 Ben Galea (C).
Try: Hall (33); **Goals:** Dobson 1/1.
Rugby Leaguer & League Express Men of the Match: *Hull:* Brett Seymour; *Rovers:* Lincoln Withers.
Penalty count: 9-9; **Half-time:** 6-6;
Referee: Richard Silverwood; **Attendance:** 18,979.

ST HELENS 10 WIGAN WARRIORS 28

SAINTS: 21 Tom Makinson; 2 Ade Gardner; 3 Michael Shenton; 26 Josh Jones; 5 Francis Meli; 6 Lance Hohaia; 7 Jonny Lomax; 8 Josh Perry; 9 James Roby (C); 18 Shaun Magennis; 13 Chris Flannery; 11 Tony Puletua; 12 Jon Wilkin. Subs (all used): 4 Iosia Soliola; 10 Louie McCarthy-Scarsbrook; 15 Mark Flanagan; 16 Paul Clough.
Tries: Meli (11), Soliola (51);
Goals: Lomax 0/1, Makinson 1/1.
Sin bin: Shenton (71) - obstruction.
WARRIORS: 1 Sam Tomkins; 2 Josh Charnley; 3 Darrell Goulding; 4 George Carmont; 5 Pat Richards; 6 Brett Finch (C); 7 Thomas Leuluai; 8 Paul Prescott; 9 Michael McIlorum; 14 Jeff Lima; 12 Gareth Hock; 11 Harrison Hansen; 17 Chris Tuson. Subs (all used): 22 Gil Dudson (D); 26 Jack Hughes; 28 Logan Tomkins; 32 Tom Spencer.
Tries: Goulding (16), Carmont (26), S Tomkins (61), Hock (72), Lima (77); **Goals:** Charnley 4/5.
Rugby Leaguer & League Express Men of the Match: *Saints:* James Roby; *Warriors:* Gareth Hock.
Penalty count: 8-10; **Half-time:** 4-12;
Referee: Phil Bentham; **Attendance:** 17,980.

HUDDERSFIELD GIANTS 36 SALFORD CITY REDS 10

GIANTS: 29 Greg Eden; 5 Jermaine McGillvary; 3 Leroy Cudjoe; 2 Michael Lawrence; 20 Luke George; 7 Danny Brough; 9 Luke Robinson; 8 Eorl Crabtree; 19 Tommy Lee; 11 Luke O'Donnell; 4 Lee Gilmour; 18 Jason Chan; 6 Kevin Brown (C). Subs (all used): 13 David Faiumu; 14 Shaun Lunt; 15 Larne Patrick; 16 Dale Ferguson.
Tries: McGillvary (9), Lawrence (15), Lee (31, 52), Lunt (48), Eden (76); **Goals:** Brough 6/6.
CITY REDS: 1 Luke Patten; 2 Jodie Broughton; 3 Sean Gleeson; 4 Joel Moon; 5 Danny Williams; 6 Daniel Holdsworth; 7 Matty Smith; 8 Lee Jewitt; 24 Stuart Howarth; 12 Shannan McPherson; 11 Matty Ashurst; 27 Vinnie Anderson; 13 Stephen Wild (C). Subs (all used): 10 Ryan Boyle; 16 Luke Adamson; 23 Gareth Owen; 17 Iafeta Palea'aesina.
Tries: Broughton (4), Moon (25); **Goals:** Holdsworth 1/2.
Rugby Leaguer & League Express Men of the Match: *Giants:* Tommy Lee; *City Reds:* Joel Moon.
Penalty count: 7-11; **Half-time:** 18-10;
Referee: Robert Hicks; **Attendance:** 6,988.

WAKEFIELD TRINITY WILDCATS 16 CASTLEFORD TIGERS 34

WILDCATS: 1 Richard Mathers; 2 Peter Fox; 4 Vince Mellars; 34 Paul Sykes; 5 Ben Cockayne; 6 Isaac John; 20 Tim Smith; 15 Kyle Amor; 14 Paul Aiton; 10 Andy Raleigh; 11 Ali Lauitiiti; 12 Steve Southern (C); 13 Danny Washbrook. Subs (all used): 7 Kyle Wood; 22 Kyle Trout; 16 Paul Johnson; 8 Oliver Wilkes.
Tries: Fox (25), Sykes (39), Wood (78); **Goals:** Sykes 2/3.
TIGERS: 1 Richard Owen; 2 Nick Youngquest; 11 Brett Ferres; 4 Kirk Dixon; 5 Josh Griffin; 6 Rangi Chase; 7 Danny Orr (C); 12 Jonathan Walker; 9 Daryl Clark; 22 Nathan Massey; 21 Oliver Holmes; 13 Steve Snitch; 8 Jake Emmitt. Subs (all used): 14 Stuart Jones; 17 Lee Mitchell; 20 Grant Millington; 23 Ryan McGoldrick.
Tries: Owen (11, 32), Millington (35), Snitch (47), Ferres (64), Holmes (69); **Goals:** Dixon 5/6.
Rugby Leaguer & League Express Men of the Match: *Wildcats:* Isaac John; *Tigers:* Rangi Chase.
Penalty count: 3-2; **Half-time:** 10-18;
Referee: Steve Ganson; **Attendance:** 9,786.

BRADFORD BULLS 12 LEEDS RHINOS 4

BULLS: 1 Brett Kearney; 33 Karl Pryce; 2 Adrian Purtell; 3 Keith Lulia; 18 Shaun Ainscough; 22 Jarrod Sammut; 6 Ben Jeffries; 16 Manase Manuokafoa; 14 Matt Diskin (C); 15 Bryn Hargreaves; 11 Olivier Elima; 12 Elliott Whitehead; 13 Jamie Langley. Subs (all used): 9 Heath L'Estrange (C); 21 Tom Burgess; 34 Phil Joseph; 23 Danny Addy.
Tries: Langley (65), Jeffries (73); **Goals:** Sammut 2/2.
Dismissal: Hargreaves (78) - spear tackle on Peacock.
Sin bin: Elima (61) - dissent.
RHINOS: 1 Brent Webb; 2 Ben Jones-Bishop; 3 Kallum Watkins; 4 Zak Hardaker; 5 Ryan Hall; 13 Kevin Sinfield (C); 25 Stevie Ward; 20 Darrell Griffin; 9 Paul McShane; 10 Jamie Peacock; 18 Chris Clarkson; 15 Brett Delaney; 12 Carl Ablett. Subs (all used): 16 Ryan Bailey; 17 Ian Kirke; 8 Kylie Leuluai; 14 Lee Smith.
Try: Hardaker (15); **Goals:** Sinfield 0/1.
On report: Griffin (62) - alleged punching.
Rugby Leaguer & League Express Men of the Match: *Bulls:* Jamie Langley; *Rhinos:* Paul McShane.
Penalty count: 6-3; **Half-time:** 0-4;
Referee: Ben Thaler; **Attendance:** 20,851.

ROUND 11

Monday 9th April 2012

CATALAN DRAGONS 44 WARRINGTON WOLVES 16

DRAGONS: 1 Clint Greenshields; 25 Vincent Duport; 4 Setaimata Sa; 18 Daryl Millard; 6 Thomas Bosc; 3 Leon Pryce; 7 Scott Dureau; 23 Lopini Paea; 9 Ian Henderson; 10 Remi Casty (C); 11 Steve Menzies; 12 Louis Anderson; 24 Jason Baitieri. Subs (all used): 8 David Ferriol; 13 Gregory Mounis; 16 Eloi Pelissier; 22 Jamal Fakir.
Tries: Paea (4), Bosc (6), Menzies (26, 73), Anderson (37), Sa (50, 71), Millard (68);
Goals: Dureau 5/6, Bosc 1/2.
WOLVES: 1 Brett Hodgson; 2 Chris Riley; 3 Chris Bridge; 18 Matty Blythe; 5 Joel Monaghan; 6 Lee Briers; 7 Richard Myler; 8 Adrian Morley (C); 14 Mick Higham; 20 Chris Hill; 11 Trent Waterhouse; 12 Ben Westwood; 15 Simon Grix. Subs (all used): 10 Garreth Carvell; 16 Paul Wood; 17 Michael Cooper; 33 Brad Dwyer.
Tries: Higham (14), Riley (30), Dwyer (78);
Goals: Hodgson 2/3.
Rugby Leaguer & League Express Men of the Match:
Dragons: Gregory Mounis; *Wolves:* Mick Higham.
Penalty count: 14-7; **Half-time:** 22-12;
Referee: Steve Ganson; **Attendance:** 11,500.

HUDDERSFIELD GIANTS 22 HULL FC 4

GIANTS: 29 Greg Eden; 21 Aaron Murphy; 3 Leroy Cudjoe; 17 Joe Wardle; 5 Jermaine McGillvary; 7 Danny Brough; 1 Scott Grix; 10 Keith Mason; 19 Tommy Lee; 12 David Fa'alogo; 2 Michael Lawrence; 25 Jon Molloy; 6 Kevin Brown (C). Subs (all used): 15 Larne Patrick; 18 Jason Chan; 8 Eorl Crabtree; 9 Luke Robinson.
Tries: Crabtree (62), Robinson (68), Wardle (73);
Goals: Brough 5/5.
HULL: 1 Wade McKinnon; 2 Will Sharp; 19 Jordan Turner; 4 Kirk Yeaman; 5 Tom Briscoe; 20 Jamie Ellis; 7 Brett Seymour; 35 Lee Radford; 9 Danny Houghton; 10 Andy Lynch (C); 11 Willie Manu; 12 Danny Tickle; 15 Richard Whiting. Subs (all used): 30 Josh Bowden; 22 Martin Aspinwall; 34 Jay Pitts; 24 Liam Kent.
Goals: Tickle 2/2.
Rugby Leaguer & League Express Men of the Match:
Giants: Danny Brough; *Hull:* Danny Houghton.
Penalty count: 8-4; **Half-time:** 2-2;
Referee: James Child; **Attendance:** 9,950.

LEEDS RHINOS 52 LONDON BRONCOS 10

RHINOS: 1 Brent Webb; 2 Ben Jones-Bishop; 12 Carl Ablett; 4 Zak Hardaker; 5 Ryan Hall; 13 Kevin Sinfield (C); 14 Lee Smith; 20 Darrell Griffin; 7 Rob Burrow; 10 Jamie Peacock; 18 Chris Clarkson; 15 Brett Delaney; 16 Ryan Bailey. Subs (all used): 8 Kylie Leuluai; 17 Ian Kirke; 9 Paul McShane; 23 Brad Singleton.
Tries: Ablett (24), Jones-Bishop (31, 38), Hall (34, 51, 62, 68), Webb (71), Hardaker (73, 77);
Goals: Sinfield 6/10.
BRONCOS: 5 Michael Robertson; 21 Kieran Dixon; 3 Jamie O'Callaghan; 19 Dan Sarginson; 2 Liam Colbon; 6 Michael Witt; 7 Craig Gower (C); 8 Antonio Kaufusi; 9 Chad Randall; 13 Tony Clubb; 20 Matt Cook; 11 Shane Rodney; 12 Chris Bailey. Subs (all used): 15 Karl Temata; 10 Mark Bryant; 1 Luke Dorn; 18 Olsi Krasniqi.
Tries: Dixon (43), Dorn (46); **Goals:** Witt 1/2.
Rugby Leaguer & League Express Men of the Match:
Rhinos: Carl Ablett; *Broncos:* Michael Witt.
Penalty count: 6-7; **Half-time:** 18-0;
Referee: Robert Hicks; **Attendance:** 13,109.

SALFORD CITY REDS 10 HULL KINGSTON ROVERS 18

CITY REDS: 1 Luke Patten; 5 Danny Williams; 3 Sean Gleeson; 4 Joel Moon; 18 Ashley Gibson; 6 Daniel Holdsworth; 7 Matty Smith; 12 Shannan McPherson; 9 Wayne Godwin; 17 Iafeta Palea'aesina; 11 Matty Ashurst; 19 Adam Neal; 13 Stephen Wild (C). Subs (all used): 24 Stuart Howarth; 27 Vinnie Anderson; 21 Jordan James; 8 Lee Jewitt.
Tries: Patten (13), Gibson (68); **Goals:** Holdsworth 1/2.
ROVERS: 1 Shannon McDonnell; 2 Craig Hall; 18 Graeme Horne; 3 Kris Welham; 21 Sam Latus; 19 Scott Murrell; 7 Michael Dobson; 23 Mickey Paea; 14 Lincoln Withers; 10 Scott Taylor; 11 Constantine Mika; 20 Jordan Cox; 12 Ben Galea (C). Subs (all used): 8 Joel Clinton; 15 Liam Watts; 25 Keal Carlile; 28 Dave Petersen (D).
Tries: Withers (37), Taylor (71, 78); **Goals:** Dobson 3/3.
Rugby Leaguer & League Express Men of the Match:
City Reds: Luke Patten; *Rovers:* Scott Taylor.
Penalty count: 8-10; **Half-time:** 4-6;
Referee: Tim Roby; **Attendance:** 5,000.

WIDNES VIKINGS 4 BRADFORD BULLS 38

VIKINGS: 29 Jack Owens; 2 Paddy Flynn; 3 Chris Dean; 4 Willie Isa; 5 Patrick Ah Van; 25 Danny Craven; 7 Rhys Hanbury; 8 Ben Cross; 13 Jon Clarke (C); 18 Sione Kite; 11 Frank Winterstein; 15 Simon Finnigan; 12 Hep Cahill. Subs (all used): 6 Lloyd White; 9 Scott Moore; 10 Ben Davies; 21 Dave Allen.
Try: Hanbury (29); **Goals:** Ah Van 0/1.
BULLS: 1 Brett Kearney; 29 Michael Platt; 2 Adrian Purtell; 3 Keith Lulia; 18 Shaun Ainscough; 6 Ben Jeffries; 22 Jarrod Sammut; 15 Bryn Hargreaves; 14 Matt Diskin (C); 16 Manase Manuokafoa; 11 Olivier Elima; 12 Elliott Whitehead; 13 Jamie Langley. Subs (all used): 9 Heath L'Estrange (C); 10 Craig Kopczak; 23 Danny Addy; 19 Tom Olbison.
Tries: Jeffries (6), Platt (9, 50), Kopczak (38), Purtell (42), Manuokafoa (65), Lulia (77);
Goals: Sammut 4/6, Addy 1/1.
Rugby Leaguer & League Express Men of the Match:
Vikings: Rhys Hanbury; *Bulls:* Craig Kopczak.
Penalty count: 9-9; **Half-time:** 4-18;
Referee: Phil Bentham; **Attendance:** 5,687.

WIGAN WARRIORS 36 WAKEFIELD TRINITY WILDCATS 6

WARRIORS: 1 Sam Tomkins; 2 Josh Charnley; 3 Darrell Goulding; 4 George Carmont; 24 Anthony Gelling; 6 Brett Finch (C); 7 Thomas Leuluai; 8 Paul Prescott; 28 Logan Tomkins; 21 Epalahame Lauaki; 11 Harrison Hansen; 12 Gareth Hock; 17 Chris Tuson. Subs (all used): 14 Jeff Lima; 22 Gil Dudson; 26 Jack Hughes; 9 Michael McIlorum.
Tries: Leuluai (15), Gelling (28), Goulding (33, 60), Carmont (47, 71), Charnley (52); **Goals:** Charnley 4/8.
WILDCATS: 18 Motu Tony; 2 Peter Fox; 34 Paul Sykes; 4 Vince Mellars; 31 Liam Kay (D); 6 Isaac John; 7 Kyle Wood; 8 Oliver Wilkes; 9 Andy Ellis (D); 15 Kyle Amor; 33 Lucas Walshaw; 19 Frankie Mariano; 13 Danny Washbrook (C). Subs (all used): 14 Paul Aiton; 16 Paul Johnson; 21 Matthew Wildie; 22 Kyle Trout.
Try: Wood (67); **Goals:** Sykes 1/1.
Rugby Leaguer & League Express Men of the Match:
Warriors: Thomas Leuluai; *Wildcats:* Kyle Amor.
Penalty count: 8-6; **Half-time:** 16-0;
Referee: Ben Thaler; **Attendance:** 13,609.

CASTLEFORD TIGERS 12 ST HELENS 18

TIGERS: 4 Kirk Dixon; 29 Josh Atkinson (D); 11 Brett Ferres; 25 Jordan Thompson; 5 Josh Griffin; 23 Ryan McGoldrick (C); 15 Adam Milner; 12 Jonathan Walker; 16 Ryan Hudson (C); 24 Stephen Nash; 17 Lee Mitchell; 21 Oliver Holmes; 27 John Davies. Subs (all used): 8 Jake Emmitt; 13 Steve Snitch; 14 Stuart Jones; 28 James Grehan.
Tries: Ferres (26, 67); **Goals:** Dixon 2/2.
SAINTS: 1 Paul Wellens (C); 2 Ade Gardner; 3 Michael Shenton; 26 Josh Jones; 5 Francis Meli; 17 Gary Wheeler; 6 Lance Hohaia; 8 Josh Perry; 9 James Roby; 14 Anthony Laffranchi; 11 Tony Puletua; 4 Iosia Soliola; 13 Chris Flannery. Subs (all used): 10 Louie McCarthy-Scarsbrook; 15 Mark Flanagan; 16 Paul Clough; 18 Shaun Magennis.
Tries: Gardner (19), Soliola (30), Shenton (48), Meli (61); **Goals:** Wheeler 0/3, Roby 1/1.
Rugby Leaguer & League Express Men of the Match:
Tigers: Adam Milner; *Saints:* James Roby.
Penalty count: 11-7; **Half-time:** 6-8;
Referee: Richard Silverwood; **Attendance:** 6,492.

ROUND 12

Friday 20th April 2012

LEEDS RHINOS 34 CATALAN DRAGONS 18

RHINOS: 1 Brent Webb; 2 Ben Jones-Bishop; 12 Carl Ablett; 4 Zak Hardaker; 5 Ryan Hall; 13 Kevin Sinfield (C); 6 Danny McGuire; 8 Kylie Leuluai; 31 Shaun Lunt (D); 10 Jamie Peacock; 18 Chris Clarkson; 15 Brett Delaney; 16 Ryan Bailey. Subs (all used): 20 Darrell Griffin; 21 Richard Moore; 17 Ian Kirke; 14 Lee Smith.
Tries: Jones-Bishop (4, 26), Hall (11), Hardaker (47), Lunt (60), Bailey (63); **Goals:** Sinfield 5/6.
DRAGONS: 18 Daryl Millard; 28 Damien Cardace; 14 Sebastien Raguin; 25 Vincent Duport; 5 Cyril Stacul; 3 Leon Pryce; 7 Scott Dureau; 23 Lopini Paea; 9 Ian Henderson; 10 Remi Casty (C); 11 Steve Menzies; 12 Louis Anderson; 4 Setaimata Sa. Subs (all used): 22 Jamal Fakir; 20 Michael Simon; 24 Jason Baitieri; 26 Ben Fisher.
Tries: Anderson (23), Menzies (51), Pryce (77);
Goals: Dureau 3/3.
Rugby Leaguer & League Express Men of the Match:
Rhinos: Brett Delaney; *Dragons:* Steve Menzies.
Penalty count: 9-10; **Half-time:** 16-6;
Referee: Ben Thaler; **Attendance:** 13,282.

ST HELENS 62 WIDNES VIKINGS 0

SAINTS: 1 Paul Wellens (C); 34 Adam Swift; 3 Michael Shenton; 26 Josh Jones; 5 Francis Meli; 6 Lance Hohaia; 7 Jonny Lomax; 14 Anthony Laffranchi; 9 James Roby; 18 Shaun Magennis; 13 Chris Flannery; 4 Iosia Soliola; 15 Mark Flanagan. Subs (all used): 10 Louie McCarthy-Scarsbrook; 16 Paul Clough; 19 Andrew Dixon; 25 Carl Forster.
Tries: Soliola (11), Wellens (14), Laffranchi (21, 25), Swift (37, 65, 74), McCarthy-Scarsbrook (43), Dixon (51), Shenton (54), Flanagan (57); **Goals:** Lomax 9/11.
VIKINGS: 19 Cameron Phelps; 2 Paddy Flynn; 20 Stefan Marsh; 4 Willie Isa; 5 Patrick Ah Van; 25 Danny Craven; 34 Joe Mellor (D2); 8 Ben Cross; 13 Jon Clarke (C); 17 Steve Pickersgill; 24 Kurt Haggerty; 11 Frank Winterstein; 12 Hep Cahill. Subs (all used): 6 Lloyd White; 21 Dave Allen; 22 Macgraff Leuluai; 26 Anthony Mullally.
Rugby Leaguer & League Express Men of the Match:
Saints: Adam Swift; *Vikings:* Paddy Flynn.
Penalty count: 10-4; **Half-time:** 26-0;
Referee: Tim Roby; **Attendance:** 14,243.

Saturday 21st April 2012

WAKEFIELD TRINITY WILDCATS 26 SALFORD CITY REDS 22

WILDCATS: 1 Richard Mathers; 2 Peter Fox; 3 Dean Collis; 34 Paul Sykes; 5 Ben Cockayne; 6 Isaac John; 20 Tim Smith; 10 Andy Raleigh; 14 Paul Aiton; 8 Oliver Wilkes; 17 Danny Kirmond (C); 19 Frankie Mariano; 13 Danny Washbrook. Subs (all used): 7 Kyle Wood; 15 Kyle Amor; 4 Vince Mellars; 25 Matt James.
Tries: Collis (3), Washbrook (6), Mariano (30), Fox (36);
Goals: Sykes 5/6.
CITY REDS: 1 Luke Patten; 18 Ashley Gibson; 3 Sean Gleeson; 4 Joel Moon; 2 Jodie Broughton; 6 Daniel Holdsworth; 7 Matty Smith; 12 Shannan McPherson; 9 Wayne Godwin; 17 Iafeta Palea'aesina; 11 Matty Ashurst; 16 Luke Adamson; 13 Stephen Wild (C). Subs (all used): 24 Stuart Howarth; 14 Chris Nero; 8 Lee Jewitt; 21 Jordan James.
Tries: Holdsworth (24), Nero (48), Gibson (75, 77);
Goals: Holdsworth 3/4.
Rugby Leaguer & League Express Men of the Match:
Wildcats: Danny Kirmond; *City Reds:* Chris Nero.
Penalty count: 9-5; **Half-time:** 22-6;
Referee: Phil Bentham; **Attendance:** 6,748.

Sunday 22nd April 2012

BRADFORD BULLS 6 HUDDERSFIELD GIANTS 20

BULLS: 33 Karl Pryce; 2 Adrian Purtell; 29 Michael Platt; 3 Keith Lulia; 18 Shaun Ainscough; 23 Danny Addy; 6 Ben Jeffries; 16 Manase Manuokafoa; 14 Matt Diskin (C); 15 Bryn Hargreaves; 11 Olivier Elima; 12 Elliott Whitehead; 13 Jamie Langley. Subs (all used): 26 John Bateman; 21 Tom Burgess; 19 Tom Olbison; 10 Craig Kopczak.
Try: Platt (34); **Goals:** Addy 1/1, Jeffries 0/1.
GIANTS: 21 Aaron Murphy; 5 Jermaine McGillvary; 3 Leroy Cudjoe; 17 Joe Wardle; 20 Luke George; 7 Danny Brough; 1 Scott Grix; 8 Eorl Crabtree; 9 Luke Robinson; 10 Keith Mason; 2 Michael Lawrence; 11 Luke O'Donnell; 6 Kevin Brown (C). Subs (all used): 13 David Faiumu; 16 Dale Ferguson; 15 Larne Patrick; 18 Jason Chan.
Tries: McGillvary (15), George (39), Brough (76);
Goals: Brough 4/5.
Sin bin: O'Donnell (64) - punching.
Rugby Leaguer & League Express Men of the Match:
Bulls: Matt Diskin; *Giants:* Danny Brough.
Penalty count: 7-5; **Half-time:** 6-10;
Referee: Thierry Alibert; **Attendance:** 11,182.

HULL FC 12 WIGAN WARRIORS 56

HULL: 1 Wade McKinnon; 2 Will Sharp; 3 Tony Martin; 23 Ben Crooks; 5 Tom Briscoe; 28 Danny Nicklas; 20 Jamie Ellis; 17 Sam Moa; 9 Danny Houghton; 10 Andy Lynch (C); 11 Willie Manu; 12 Danny Tickle; 34 Jay Pitts. Subs (all used): 15 Richard Whiting; 35 Lee Radford; 24 Liam Kent; 30 Josh Bowden.
Tries: Ellis (54), Sharp (58); **Goals:** Tickle 2/2.
WARRIORS: 1 Sam Tomkins; 2 Josh Charnley; 3 Darrell Goulding; 4 George Carmont; 5 Pat Richards; 6 Brett Finch; 7 Thomas Leuluai; 8 Paul Prescott; 9 Michael McIlorum; 22 Gil Dudson; 12 Gareth Hock; 11 Harrison Hansen; 13 Sean O'Loughlin (C). Subs (all used): 16 Liam Farrell; 17 Chris Tuson; 21 Epalahame Lauaki; 14 Jeff Lima.
Tries: Richards (2, 7, 42), Hock (17), S Tomkins (36), Charnley (39, 65), McIlorum (52), Leuluai (70), Finch (79); **Goals:** Richards 7/8, Charnley 1/2.
Rugby Leaguer & League Express Men of the Match:
Hull: Will Sharp; *Warriors:* Pat Richards.
Penalty count: 6-5; **Half-time:** 0-28;
Referee: Steve Ganson; **Attendance:** 11,549.

HULL KINGSTON ROVERS 44 LONDON BRONCOS 16

ROVERS: 1 Shannon McDonnell; 2 Craig Hall; 29 Liam Salter; 3 Kris Welham; 5 David Hodgson; 6 Blake Green; 7 Michael Dobson; 13 Rhys Lovegrove; 9 Josh Hodgson; 23 Mickey Paea; 11 Constantine Mika; 12 Ben Galea (C); 19 Scott Murrell. Subs (all used): 14 Lincoln Withers; 10 Scott Taylor; 16 Jason Netherton; 18 Graeme Horne.
Tries: D Hodgson (5, 11, 33), Welham (7, 59), Horne (62), B Green (64); **Goals:** Dobson 8/8.
BRONCOS: 1 Luke Dorn; 23 Omari Caro; 3 Jamie O'Callaghan; 19 Dan Sarginson; 21 Kieran Dixon; 12 Chris Bailey; 7 Craig Gower (C); 8 Antonio Kaufusi; 9 Chad Randall; 10 Mark Bryant; 11 Shane Rodney; 16 Chris Melling; 13 Tony Clubb. Subs (all used): 20 Matt Cook; 22 Ben Bolger; 18 Olsi Krasniqi; 28 Michael Channing (D).
Tries: Rodney (18), Randall (24), Dixon (55);
Goals: Rodney 2/3.
Rugby Leaguer & League Express Men of the Match:
Rovers: Michael Dobson; *Broncos:* Luke Dorn.
Penalty count: 8-9; **Half-time:** 26-12;
Referee: James Child; **Attendance:** 6,713.

WARRINGTON WOLVES 54 CASTLEFORD TIGERS 6

WOLVES: 1 Brett Hodgson (C); 2 Chris Riley; 4 Ryan Atkins; 3 Chris Bridge; 5 Joel Monaghan; 6 Lee Briers; 24 Gareth O'Brien; 20 Chris Hill; 14 Mick Higham; 16 Paul Wood; 11 Trent Waterhouse; 12 Ben Westwood; 21 Tyrone McCarthy. Subs (all used): 13 Ben Harrison; 15 Simon Grix; 17 Michael Cooper; 33 Brad Dwyer.
Tries: Bridge (5), Waterhouse (14), J Monaghan (20, 23), Hodgson (35, 37), Atkins (40, 56), Riley (74), Grix (78); **Goals:** Hodgson 7/10.
TIGERS: 2 Nick Youngquest; 29 Josh Atkinson; 25 Jordan Thompson; 11 Brett Ferres; 5 Josh Griffin; 23 Ryan McGoldrick; 7 Danny Orr (C); 22 Nathan Massey; 15 Adam Milner; 12 Jonathan Walker; 17 Lee Mitchell; 21 Oliver Holmes; 8 Jake Emmitt. Subs (all used): 9 Daryl Clark; 10 Craig Huby; 14 Stuart Jones; 20 Grant Millington.
Try: Mitchell (62); **Goals:** Orr 1/1.
Rugby Leaguer & League Express Men of the Match:
Wolves: Brett Hodgson; *Tigers:* Danny Orr.
Penalty count: 8-11; **Half-time:** 38-0;
Referee: Robert Hicks; **Attendance:** 10,519.

Castleford's Jordan Thompson bursts past Widnes duo Jon Clarke and Lloyd White

ROUND 13

Friday 4th May 2012

ST HELENS 38 WAKEFIELD TRINITY WILDCATS 12

SAINTS: 1 Paul Wellens (C); 21 Tom Makinson; 3 Michael Shenton; 26 Josh Jones; 5 Francis Meli; 6 Lance Hohaia; 7 Jonny Lomax; 14 Anthony Laffranchi; 9 James Roby; 16 Paul Clough; 13 Chris Flannery; 4 Iosia Soliola; 15 Mark Flanagan. Subs (all used): 10 Louie McCarthy-Scarsbrook; 19 Andrew Dixon; 25 Carl Forster; 28 Joe Greenwood.
Tries: Flannery (6, 44, 48), Soliola (22, 28), Lomax (38), Makinson (65), Roby (68); **Goals:** Lomax 3/8.
WILDCATS: 1 Richard Mathers; 2 Peter Fox; 3 Dean Collis; 34 Paul Sykes; 5 Ben Cockayne; 21 Matthew Wildie; 20 Tim Smith; 10 Andy Raleigh; 9 Andy Ellis; 15 Kyle Amor; 19 Frankie Mariano; 17 Danny Kirmond (C); 13 Danny Washbrook. Subs (all used): 4 Vince Mellars; 7 Kyle Wood; 14 Paul Aiton; 25 Matt James.
Tries: Collis (10), Fox (71); **Goals:** Sykes 2/2.
Rugby Leaguer & League Express Men of the Match:
Saints: James Roby; *Wildcats:* Richard Mathers.
Penalty count: 8-13; **Half-time:** 22-6;
Referee: Thierry Alibert; **Attendance:** 13,177.

WIGAN WARRIORS 36 HULL KINGSTON ROVERS 22

WARRIORS: 1 Sam Tomkins; 2 Josh Charnley; 3 Darrell Goulding; 4 George Carmont; 24 Anthony Gelling; 6 Brett Finch; 7 Thomas Leuluai; 21 Epalahame Lauaki; 9 Michael McIlorum; 10 Lee Mossop; 11 Harrison Hansen; 12 Gareth Hock; 13 Sean O'Loughlin (C). Subs (all used): 14 Jeff Lima; 16 Liam Farrell; 17 Chris Tuson; 26 Jack Hughes.
Tries: Charnley (5, 25, 42), S Tomkins (14), Mossop (18), Gelling (22, 59); **Goals:** Charnley 4/7.
ROVERS: 1 Shannon McDonnell; 2 Craig Hall; 3 Kris Welham; 29 Liam Salter; 5 David Hodgson; 6 Blake Green; 7 Michael Dobson; 23 Mickey Paea; 14 Lincoln Withers; 10 Scott Taylor; 11 Constantine Mika; 12 Ben Galea (C); 15 Liam Watts. Subs (all used): 17 Ryan O'Hara (D); 8 Joel Clinton; 13 Rhys Lovegrove; 9 Josh Hodgson.
Tries: Galea (36), McDonnell (53), J Hodgson (72), Welham (74); **Goals:** Dobson 3/4.
Rugby Leaguer & League Express Men of the Match:
Warriors: Anthony Gelling; *Rovers:* Shannon McDonnell.
Penalty count: 7-5; **Half-time:** 26-6;
Referee: Phil Bentham *(replaced by Robert Hicks, 18)*; **Attendance:** 14,457.

Saturday 5th May 2012

CATALAN DRAGONS 27 HUDDERSFIELD GIANTS 20

DRAGONS: 1 Clint Greenshields; 6 Thomas Bosc; 25 Vincent Duport; 18 Daryl Millard; 28 Damien Cardace; 3 Leon Pryce; 7 Scott Dureau; 23 Lopini Paea; 9 Ian Henderson; 10 Remi Casty; 11 Steve Menzies; 4

Setaimata Sa; 24 Jason Baitieri. Subs (all used): 12 Louis Anderson; 16 Eloi Pelissier; 20 Michael Simon; 22 Jamal Fakir.
Tries: Cardace (16), Greenshields (27), Pryce (35), Casty (54), Duport (78);
Goals: Dureau 1/3, Bosc 2/2; **Field goal:** Bosc (76).
GIANTS: 29 Greg Eden; 5 Jermaine McGillvary; 3 Leroy Cudjoe; 17 Joe Wardle; 20 Luke George; 7 Danny Brough; 1 Scott Grix; 8 Eorl Crabtree; 9 Luke Robinson; 11 Luke O'Donnell; 18 Jason Chan; 2 Michael Lawrence; 6 Kevin Brown (C). Subs (all used): 10 Keith Mason; 13 David Faiumu; 15 Larne Patrick; 16 Dale Ferguson.
Tries: Robinson (23), Ferguson (30), Grix (48), Wardle (73); **Goals:** Brough 2/4.
Rugby Leaguer & League Express Men of the Match:
Dragons: Remi Casty; *Giants:* Michael Lawrence.
Penalty count: 12-8; **Half-time:** 14-12;
Referee: Richard Silverwood; **Attendance:** 10,624.

HULL FC 34 LEEDS RHINOS 20

HULL: 36 Matthew Russell (D); 2 Will Sharp; 19 Jordan Turner; 23 Ben Crooks; 5 Tom Briscoe; 15 Richard Whiting; 7 Brett Seymour; 17 Sam Moa; 9 Danny Houghton; 10 Andy Lynch (C); 11 Willie Manu; 12 Danny Tickle; 34 Jay Pitts. Subs: 20 Jamie Ellis (not used); 8 Mark O'Meley; 16 Eamon O'Carroll; 22 Martin Aspinwall.
Tries: Tickle (14), Sharp (26), Briscoe (28, 74), Crooks (77); **Goals:** Tickle 7/8.
RHINOS: 1 Brent Webb; 2 Ben Jones-Bishop; 12 Carl Ablett; 4 Zak Hardaker; 5 Ryan Hall; 13 Kevin Sinfield (C); 6 Danny McGuire; 8 Kylie Leuluai; 31 Shaun Lunt; 10 Jamie Peacock; 18 Chris Clarkson; 15 Brett Delaney; 11 Jamie Jones-Buchanan. Subs (all used): 14 Lee Smith; 20 Darrell Griffin; 17 Ian Kirke; 21 Richard Moore.
Tries: Jones-Bishop (10), Ablett (23), Hall (66), McGuire (80); **Goals:** Sinfield 2/4.
Rugby Leaguer & League Express Men of the Match:
Hull: Richard Whiting; *Rhinos:* Brent Webb.
Penalty count: 12-10; **Half-time:** 16-10;
Referee: James Child; **Attendance:** 11,667.

Sunday 6th May 2012

LONDON BRONCOS 22 BRADFORD BULLS 29

BRONCOS: 5 Michael Robertson; 21 Kieran Dixon; 28 Michael Channing; 19 Dan Sarginson; 3 Jamie O'Callaghan; 6 Michael Witt; 7 Craig Gower (C); 8 Antonio Kaufusi; 9 Chad Randall; 10 Mark Bryant; 11 Shane Rodney; 20 Matt Cook; 12 Chris Bailey. Subs: 22 Ben Bolger (not used); 16 Chris Melling; 30 Scott Wheeldon (D); 1 Luke Dorn.
Tries: Robertson (2), Cook (7), Channing (10), Witt (37); **Goals:** Witt 3/4.
BULLS: 5 Elliot Kear; 18 Shaun Ainscough; 29 Michael Platt; 3 Keith Lulia; 33 Karl Pryce; 6 Ben Jeffries; 7 Luke Gale; 15 Bryn Hargreaves; 14 Matt Diskin (C); 10 Craig Kopczak; 13 Jamie Langley; 12 Elliott Whitehead; 11 Olivier Elima. Subs (all used): 9 Heath L'Estrange (C); 23 Danny Addy; 16 Manase Manuokafoa; 21 Tom Burgess.

Tries: Pryce (17), Platt (27, 39, 42, 65); **Goals:** Gale 4/6; **Field goal:** Gale (76).
Rugby Leaguer & League Express Men of the Match:
Broncos: Michael Robertson; *Bulls:* Michael Platt.
Penalty count: 5-10; **Half-time:** 22-16; **Referee:** Robert Hicks; **Attendance:** 2,844 *(at Brisbane Road, Leyton)*.

WARRINGTON WOLVES 24 SALFORD CITY REDS 20

WOLVES: 2 Chris Riley; 22 Rhys Williams; 18 Matty Blythe; 4 Ryan Atkins; 5 Joel Monaghan; 15 Simon Grix; 24 Gareth O'Brien; 17 Michael Cooper; 33 Brad Dwyer; 10 Garreth Carvell; 11 Trent Waterhouse (C); 32 Ben Currie; 13 Ben Harrison. Subs (all used): 14 Mick Higham; 16 Paul Wood; 20 Chris Hill; 21 Tyrone McCarthy.
Tries: Williams (3, 38), Currie (57), Carvell (62);
Goals: O'Brien 4/4.
CITY REDS: 1 Luke Patten; 2 Jodie Broughton; 4 Joel Moon; 18 Ashley Gibson; 5 Danny Williams; 6 Daniel Holdsworth; 7 Matty Smith; 8 Lee Jewitt; 9 Wayne Godwin; 15 Adam Sidlow; 11 Matty Ashurst; 16 Luke Adamson; 13 Stephen Wild (C). Subs (all used): 10 Ryan Boyle; 19 Adam Neal; 21 Jordan James; 24 Stuart Howarth.
Tries: Gibson (12, 25), Holdsworth (74), Williams (76); **Goals:** Holdsworth 2/4.
Sin bin: Patten (62) - dissent.
Rugby Leaguer & League Express Men of the Match:
Wolves: Trent Waterhouse; *City Reds:* Ashley Gibson.
Penalty count: 8-3; **Half-time:** 12-10;
Referee: Ben Thaler; **Attendance:** 10,437.

Monday 7th May 2012

CASTLEFORD TIGERS 36 WIDNES VIKINGS 12

TIGERS: 1 Richard Owen; 5 Josh Griffin; 4 Kirk Dixon; 11 Brett Ferres; 2 Nick Youngquest; 23 Ryan McGoldrick; 7 Danny Orr (C); 22 Nathan Massey; 16 Ryan Hudson; 10 Craig Huby; 17 Lee Mitchell; 20 Grant Millington; 14 Stuart Jones. Subs (all used): 9 Daryl Clark; 8 Jake Emmitt; 12 Jonathan Walker; 25 Jordan Thompson.
Tries: Ferres (12), Clark (33, 78), Thompson (53), Youngquest (59, 69, 73);
Goals: Orr 2/3, Huby 1/1, Dixon 0/2, Griffin 1/1.
On report:
McGoldrick (42) - alleged use of the elbow on Pickersgill.
VIKINGS: 19 Cameron Phelps; 2 Paddy Flynn; 20 Stefan Marsh; 3 Chris Dean; 4 Willie Isa; 7 Rhys Hanbury; 34 Joe Mellor; 8 Ben Cross; 13 Jon Clarke (C); 12 Hep Cahill; 11 Frank Winterstein; 21 Dave Allen; 15 Simon Finnigan. Subs (all used): 10 Ben Davies; 17 Steve Pickersgill; 22 Macgraff Leuluai.
Tries: Flynn (18), Marsh (80); **Goals:** Hanbury 2/3.
On report:
Cahill (77) - alleged dangerous tackle on Youngquest.
Rugby Leaguer & League Express Men of the Match:
Tigers: Daryl Clark; *Vikings:* Paddy Flynn.
Penalty count: 11-11; **Half-time:** 10-8;
Referee: Steve Ganson; **Attendance:** 5,580.

ROUND 14

Friday 18th May 2012

HUDDERSFIELD GIANTS 12 WIGAN WARRIORS 32

GIANTS: 29 Greg Eden; 5 Jermaine McGillvary; 3 Leroy Cudjoe; 18 Jason Chan; 20 Luke George; 7 Danny Brough; 1 Scott Grix; 8 Eorl Crabtree; 9 Luke Robinson; 12 David Fa'alogo; 2 Michael Lawrence; 4 Lee Gilmour; 6 Kevin Brown (C). Subs (all used): 13 David Faiumu; 15 Larne Patrick; 16 Dale Ferguson; 35 Scott Moore.
Tries: McGillvary (16), Eden (48); **Goals:** Brough 2/3.
WARRIORS: 1 Sam Tomkins; 2 Josh Charnley; 3 Darrell Goulding; 4 George Carmont; 24 Anthony Gelling; 6 Brett Finch; 7 Thomas Leuluai; 22 Gil Dudson; 9 Michael McIlorum; 10 Lee Mossop; 11 Harrison Hansen; 12 Gareth Hock; 13 Sean O'Loughlin (C). Subs (all used): 14 Jeff Lima; 16 Liam Farrell; 17 Chris Tuson; 33 Dominic Crosby.
Tries: Charnley (18, 38), S Tomkins (29), Carmont (50, 58), Farrell (54), Lima (80);
Goals: Charnley 0/4, S Tomkins 2/3.
Rugby League & League Express Men of the Match:
Giants: Greg Eden; *Warriors:* Michael McIlorum.
Penalty count: 3-8; **Half-time:** 6-12;
Referee: Ben Thaler; **Attendance:** 10,123.

SALFORD CITY REDS 20 BRADFORD BULLS 20

CITY REDS: 1 Luke Patten; 2 Jodie Broughton; 4 Joel Moon; 3 Sean Gleeson; 5 Danny Williams; 6 Daniel Holdsworth; 7 Matty Smith; 8 Lee Jewitt; 24 Stuart Howarth; 15 Adam Sidlow; 11 Matty Ashurst; 16 Luke Adamson; 13 Stephen Wild (C). Subs (all used): 10 Ryan Boyle; 14 Chris Nero; 17 Iafeta Palea'aesina; 23 Gareth Owen.
Tries: Sidlow (5), Williams (47, 55), Broughton (77);
Goals: Holdsworth 2/4.
BULLS: 5 Elliot Kear; 33 Karl Pryce; 29 Michael Platt; 3 Keith Lulia; 18 Shaun Ainscough; 6 Ben Jeffries; 7 Luke Gale; 10 Craig Kopczak; 14 Matt Diskin (C); 15 Bryn Hargreaves; 11 Olivier Elima; 12 Elliott Whitehead; 13 Jamie Langley. Subs (all used): 9 Heath L'Estrange (C); 16 Manase Manuokafoa; 21 Tom Burgess; 23 Danny Addy.
Tries: Pryce (31, 36, 49), Burgess (72); **Goals:** Gale 2/4.
Sin bin: Elima (76) - obstruction.
Rugby League & League Express Men of the Match:
City Reds: Luke Patten; *Bulls:* Karl Pryce.
Penalty count: 11-10; **Half-time:** 6-10;
Referee: Richard Silverwood; **Attendance:** 6,121.

Sunday 20th May 2012

LONDON BRONCOS 12 HULL FC 14

BRONCOS: 5 Michael Robertson; 21 Kieran Dixon; 28 Michael Channing; 3 Jamie O'Callaghan; 23 Omari Caro; 19 Dan Sarginson; 7 Craig Gower (C); 30 Scott Wheeldon; 6 Michael Witt; 13 Tony Clubb; 16 Chris Melling; 11 Shane Rodney; 12 Chris Bailey. Subs (all used): 8 Antonio Kaufusi; 10 Mark Bryant; 9 Chad Randall; 22 Ben Bolger.
Tries: Dixon (9), Robertson (69);
Goals: Witt 1/1, Rodney 1/1.
HULL: 36 Matthew Russell; 2 Will Sharp; 19 Jordan Turner; 23 Ben Crooks; 5 Tom Briscoe; 15 Richard Whiting; 7 Brett Seymour; 17 Sam Moa; 9 Danny Houghton; 10 Andy Lynch (C); 11 Willie Manu; 12 Danny Tickle; 34 Jay Pitts. Subs (all used): 16 Eamon O'Carroll; 22 Martin Aspinwall; 13 Joe Westerman; 6 Richard Horne.
Tries: Crooks (24), Whiting (50); **Goals:** Tickle 3/3.
Rugby League & League Express Men of the Match:
Broncos: Kieran Dixon; *Hull:* Willie Manu.
Penalty count: 9-10; **Half-time:** 6-6;
Referee: Thierry Alibert; **Attendance:** 3,930
(at Priestfield Stadium, Gillingham).

HULL KINGSTON ROVERS 70 CASTLEFORD TIGERS 12

ROVERS: 1 Shannon McDonnell; 21 Sam Latus; 2 Craig Hall; 3 Kris Welham; 5 David Hodgson; 6 Blake Green; 7 Michael Dobson; 23 Mickey Paea; 9 Josh Hodgson; 10 Scott Taylor; 11 Constantine Mika; 12 Ben Galea (C); 13 Rhys Lovegrove. Subs (all used): 14 Lincoln Withers; 19 Scott Murrell; 17 Ryan O'Hara; 8 Joel Clinton.
Tries: McDonnell (3, 15, 55), D Hodgson (5, 22, 43, 76), Latus (9), Welham (33), Withers (57), Mika (65), Hall (72); **Goals:** Dobson 11/12.
TIGERS: 1 Richard Owen; 2 Nick Youngquest; 25 Jordan Thompson; 4 Kirk Dixon; 5 Josh Griffin; 11 Brett Ferres; 15 Adam Milner; 22 Nathan Massey; 16 Ryan Hudson (C); 10 Craig Huby; 17 Lee Mitchell; 20 Grant Millington; 14 Stuart Jones. Subs (all used): 9 Daryl Clark; 8 Jake Emmitt; 12 Jonathan Walker; 21 Oliver Holmes.
Tries: Thompson (36), Griffin (70); **Goals:** Dixon 2/2.
Rugby League & League Express Men of the Match:
Rovers: Shannon McDonnell; *Tigers:* Daryl Clark.
Penalty count: 9-5; **Half-time:** 36-6;
Referee: James Child; **Attendance:** 7,312.

WIDNES VIKINGS 34 CATALAN DRAGONS 42

VIKINGS: 19 Cameron Phelps; 2 Paddy Flynn; 20 Stefan Marsh; 3 Chris Dean; 5 Patrick Ah Van; 34 Joe Mellor; 7 Rhys Hanbury; 8 Ben Cross; 13 Jon Clarke (C); 17 Steve Pickersgill; 11 Frank Winterstein; 21 Dave Allen; 12 Hep Cahill. Subs (all used): 6 Lloyd White; 10 Ben Davies; 24 Kurt Haggerty; 26 Anthony Mullally.
Tries: Marsh (21), Mellor (27), Hanbury (40), Dean (42), Haggerty (64), Ah Van (72); **Goals:** Hanbury 5/6.
Sin bin: Clarke (51) - late challenge on Dureau.
DRAGONS: 1 Clint Greenshields; 6 Thomas Bosc; 11 Steve Menzies; 25 Vincent Duport; 28 Damien Cardace; 3 Leon Pryce; 7 Scott Dureau; 23 Lopini Paea; 9 Ian Henderson; 10 Remi Casty (C); 14 Sebastien Raguin; 12 Louis Anderson; 24 Jason Baitieri. Subs (all used): 20 Michael Simon; 22 Jamal Fakir; 27 William Barthau; 29 Mathias Pala.
Tries: Greenshields (2), Pryce (11), Duport (14), Anderson (32, 57), Paea (60), Bosc (73), Dureau (80);
Goals: Dureau 5/8.
Rugby League & League Express Men of the Match:
Vikings: Rhys Hanbury; *Dragons:* Scott Dureau.
Penalty count: 7-10; **Half-time:** 18-20;
Referee: Robert Hicks; **Attendance:** 4,684.

WAKEFIELD TRINITY WILDCATS 12 WARRINGTON WOLVES 42

WILDCATS: 1 Richard Mathers (C); 2 Peter Fox; 3 Dean Collis; 34 Paul Sykes; 5 Ben Cockayne; 6 Isaac John; 20 Tim Smith; 16 Paul Johnson; 14 Paul Aiton; 10 Andy Raleigh; 11 Ali Lauitiiti; 19 Frankie Mariano; 13 Danny Washbrook. Subs (all used): 7 Kyle Wood; 15 Kyle Amor; 12 Steve Southern; 22 Kyle Trout.
Tries: Mariano (5), Southern (34); **Goals:** Sykes 2/2.
WOLVES: 1 Brett Hodgson (C); 22 Rhys Williams; 18 Matty Blythe; 4 Ryan Atkins; 2 Chris Riley; 19 Stefan Ratchford; 24 Gareth O'Brien; 20 Chris Hill; 14 Mick Higham; 16 Paul Wood; 21 Tyrone McCarthy; 12 Ben Westwood; 13 Ben Harrison. Subs (all used): 10 Garreth Carvell; 17 Michael Cooper; 15 Simon Grix; 32 Ben Currie.
Tries: Atkins (8, 65, 72), Riley (22, 76), Ratchford (49, 62); **Goals:** Hodgson 7/7.
Rugby League & League Express Men of the Match:
Wildcats: Paul Aiton; *Wolves:* Ryan Atkins.
Penalty count: 11-6; **Half-time:** 12-12;
Referee: Tim Roby; **Attendance:** 8,483.

Monday 21st May 2012

LEEDS RHINOS 18 ST HELENS 31

RHINOS: 1 Brent Webb; 14 Lee Smith; 3 Kallum Watkins; 4 Zak Hardaker; 5 Ryan Hall; 13 Kevin Sinfield (C); 6 Danny McGuire; 8 Kylie Leuluai; 7 Rob Burrow; 10 Jamie Peacock; 11 Jamie Jones-Buchanan; 15 Brett Delaney; 12 Carl Ablett. Subs: 16 Ryan Bailey; 18 Chris Clarkson; 20 Darrell Griffin; 31 Shaun Lunt (not used).
Tries: McGuire (11), Delaney (38), Jones-Buchanan (48);
Goals: Sinfield 3/3.
On report: Sinfield (63) - alleged high tackle on Makinson.
SAINTS: 1 Paul Wellens (C); 21 Tom Makinson; 3 Michael Shenton; 17 Gary Wheeler; 5 Francis Meli; 6 Lance Hohaia; 7 Jonny Lomax; 14 Anthony Laffranchi; 9 James Roby; 8 Josh Perry; 13 Chris Flannery; 4 Iosia Soliola; 12 Jon Wilkin. Subs (all used): 10 Louie McCarthy-Scarsbrook; 11 Tony Puletua; 15 Mark Flanagan; 16 Paul Clough.
Tries: Lomax (21, 58), Wellens (31), Makinson (51), Wilkin (65); **Goals:** Makinson 3/4, Lomax 2/2;
Field goal: Lomax (76).
Rugby League & League Express Men of the Match:
Rhinos: Jamie Peacock; *Saints:* Jon Wilkin.
Penalty count: 5-6; **Half-time:** 12-12;
Referee: Steve Ganson; **Attendance:** 15,343.

ROUND 15 - MAGIC WEEKEND

Saturday 26th May 2012

CASTLEFORD TIGERS 26 WAKEFIELD TRINITY WILDCATS 32

TIGERS: 1 Richard Owen; 32 Rhys Williams (D); 4 Kirk Dixon; 25 Jordan Thompson; 2 Nick Youngquest; 6 Rangi Chase; 7 Danny Orr (C); 19 Paul Jackson; 14 Stuart Jones; 10 Craig Huby; 11 Brett Ferres; 21 Oliver Holmes; 17 Lee Mitchell. Subs (all used): 12 Jonathan Walker; 15 Adam Milner; 20 Grant Millington; 22 Nathan Massey.
Tries: Thompson (2), Jones (22), Youngquest (34), Holmes (39), Orr (70); **Goals:** Dixon 2/4, Orr 1/1.
WILDCATS: 1 Richard Mathers (C); 2 Peter Fox; 3 Dean Collis; 4 Vince Mellars; 5 Ben Cockayne; 34 Paul Sykes; 20 Tim Smith; 15 Kyle Amor; 14 Paul Aiton; 10 Andy Raleigh; 19 Frankie Mariano; 17 Danny Kirmond; 13 Danny Washbrook. Subs (all used): 7 Kyle Wood; 11 Ali Lauitiiti; 12 Steve Southern; 25 Matt James.
Tries: Mellars (13), Mathers (16), Southern (29), Washbrook (37), Fox (53), T Smith (79);
Goals: Sykes 4/6.
Rugby League & League Express Men of the Match:
Tigers: Danny Orr; *Wildcats:* Ben Cockayne.
Penalty count: 6-5; **Half-time:** 20-24;
Referee: Robert Hicks.

WARRINGTON WOLVES 68 WIDNES VIKINGS 4

WOLVES: 19 Stefan Ratchford; 5 Joel Monaghan; 18 Matty Blythe; 4 Ryan Atkins; 2 Chris Riley; 6 Lee Briers; 24 Gareth O'Brien; 20 Chris Hill; 15 Simon Grix; 10 Garreth Carvell; 11 Trent Waterhouse; 21 Tyrone McCarthy; 13 Ben Harrison. Subs (all used): 8 Adrian Morley (C); 17 Michael Cooper; 32 Ben Currie; 33 Brad Dwyer.
Tries: Blythe (3, 29, 63), Carvell (6), J Monaghan (12, 22, 24, 60, 80), Atkins (19), Ratchford (66), Currie (68); **Goals:** O'Brien 10/12.
VIKINGS: 19 Cameron Phelps; 2 Paddy Flynn; 20 Stefan Marsh; 3 Chris Dean; 5 Patrick Ah Van; 34 Joe Mellor; 7 Rhys Hanbury; 8 Ben Cross; 13 Jon Clarke (C); 17 Steve Pickersgill; 11 Frank Winterstein; 24 Kurt Haggerty; 12 Hep Cahill. Subs (all used): 4 Willie Isa; 10 Ben Davies; 22 Macgraff Leuluai; 28 Alex Gerrard.
Try: Haggerty (47); **Goals:** Hanbury 0/1.
Rugby League & League Express Men of the Match:
Wolves: Joel Monaghan; *Vikings:* Ben Cross.
Penalty count: 9-3; **Half-time:** 40-0;
Referee: George Stokes.

HULL FC 30 HULL KINGSTON ROVERS 32

HULL: 36 Matthew Russell; 2 Will Sharp; 19 Jordan Turner; 3 Tony Martin; 5 Tom Briscoe; 6 Richard Horne; 7 Brett Seymour; 17 Sam Moa; 9 Danny Houghton; 10 Andy Lynch (C); 12 Danny Tickle; 11 Willie Manu; 34 Jay Pitts. Subs (all used): 16 Eamon O'Carroll; 22 Martin Aspinwall; 13 Joe Westerman; 24 Liam Kent.
Tries: Seymour (11), Horne (26), Manu (32), Martin (60), Turner (66); **Goals:** Tickle 5/5.
ROVERS: 1 Shannon McDonnell; 21 Sam Latus; 2 Craig Hall; 3 Kris Welham; 5 David Hodgson; 6 Blake Green; 7 Michael Dobson; 23 Mickey Paea; 9 Josh Hodgson; 10 Scott Taylor; 18 Graeme Horne; 12 Ben Galea (C); 13 Rhys Lovegrove. Subs (all used): 14 Lincoln Withers; 17 Ryan O'Hara; 8 Joel Clinton; 19 Scott Murrell.
Tries: Hall (18), McDonnell (22), D Hodgson (51, 79), Latus (68), Dobson (72); **Goals:** Hall 1/1, Dobson 3/5.
Sin bin: Dobson (10) - holding down.
Rugby League & League Express Men of the Match:
Hull: Willie Manu; *Rovers:* David Hodgson.
Penalty count: 4-11; **Half-time:** 18-12;
Referee: Steve Ganson.

Attendance: 30,763 *(at Etihad Stadium, Manchester).*

Sunday 27th May 2012

CATALAN DRAGONS 42 LONDON BRONCOS 18

DRAGONS: 1 Clint Greenshields; 6 Thomas Bosc; 25 Vincent Duport; 29 Mathias Pala; 5 Cyril Stacul; 3 Leon Pryce; 7 Scott Dureau; 23 Lopini Paea; 26 Ben Fisher; 10 Remi Casty (C); 11 Steve Menzies; 12 Louis Anderson; 24 Jason Baitieri. Subs (all used): 9 Ian Henderson; 14 Sebastien Raguin; 20 Michael Simon; 22 Jamal Fakir.
Tries: Paea (11), Pryce (14, 36), Casty (20, 62), Menzies (69), Fakir (74); **Goals:** Dureau 7/7.
Sin bin: Baitieri (55) - late challenge on Gower.
BRONCOS: 5 Michael Robertson; 21 Kieran Dixon; 23 Omari Caro; 3 Jamie O'Callaghan; 28 Michael Channing; 19 Dan Sarginson; 7 Craig Gower (C); 8 Antonio Kaufusi; 6 Michael Witt; 30 Scott Wheeldon; 11 Shane Rodney; 16 Chris Melling; 13 Tony Clubb. Subs (all used): 9 Chad Randall; 10 Mark Bryant; 22 Ben Bolger; 31 Will Lovell (D).
Tries: Kaufusi (42), B Bolger (48), Randall (56);
Goals: Rodney 3/3.
Rugby League & League Express Men of the Match:
Dragons: Scott Dureau; *Broncos:* Chad Randall.
Penalty count: 10-9; **Half-time:** 24-0;
Referee: James Child.

HUDDERSFIELD GIANTS 34 SALFORD CITY REDS 38

GIANTS: 29 Greg Eden; 5 Jermaine McGillvary; 3 Leroy Cudjoe; 17 Joe Wardle; 20 Luke George; 1 Scott Grix; 7 Danny Brough; 10 Keith Mason; 35 Scott Moore; 16 Dale Ferguson; 2 Michael Lawrence; 18 Jason Chan; 6 Kevin Brown (C). Subs (all used): 8 Eorl Crabtree; 9 Luke Robinson; 12 David Fa'alogo; 13 David Faiumu.
Tries: Brown (6), Brough (13, 73), Lawrence (40), Crabtree (48, 51); **Goals:** Brough 5/6.
CITY REDS: 1 Luke Patten; 2 Jodie Broughton; 4 Joel Moon; 3 Sean Gleeson; 5 Danny Williams; 6 Daniel Holdsworth; 7 Matty Smith; 8 Lee Jewitt; 24 Stuart Howarth; 15 Adam Sidlow; 11 Matty Ashurst; 14 Chris Nero; 13 Stephen Wild (C). Subs (all used): 23 Gareth Owen; 27 Vinnie Anderson; 17 Iafeta Palea'aesina; 12 Shannan McPherson.
Tries: Moon (3, 19), Gleeson (27), Broughton (36, 60), Sidlow (66, 76); **Goals:** Holdsworth 5/7.
Rugby League & League Express Men of the Match:
Giants: Scott Grix; *City Reds:* Luke Patten.
Penalty count: 8-7; **Half-time:** 16-22; **Referee:** Tim Roby.

BRADFORD BULLS 22 LEEDS RHINOS 37

BULLS: 1 Brett Kearney; 5 Elliot Kear; 2 Adrian Purtell; 3 Keith Lulia; 33 Karl Pryce; 6 Ben Jeffries; 7 Luke Gale; 10 Craig Kopczak; 14 Matt Diskin (C); 15 Bryn Hargreaves; 26 John Bateman; 12 Elliott Whitehead; 11 Olivier Elima. Subs (all used): 9 Heath L'Estrange (C); 16 Manase Manuokafoa; 21 Tom Burgess; 4 Chev Walker.
Tries: Whitehead (9), Jeffries (14), Diskin (20), Kear (78); **Goals:** Gale 3/4.
RHINOS: 1 Brent Webb; 14 Lee Smith; 3 Kallum Watkins; 4 Zak Hardaker; 5 Ryan Hall; 13 Kevin Sinfield (C); 6 Danny McGuire; 10 Jamie Peacock; 31 Shaun Lunt; 8 Kylie Leuluai; 11 Jamie Jones-Buchanan; 12 Carl Ablett; 15 Brett Delaney. Subs (all used): 7 Rob Burrow; 21 Richard Moore; 16 Ryan Bailey; 19 Weller Hauraki.
Tries: McGuire (2, 26, 33, 48, 76), Ablett (70);
Goals: Sinfield 6/6; **Field goal:** Sinfield (72).
Rugby League & League Express Men of the Match:
Bulls: Luke Gale; *Rhinos:* Danny McGuire.
Penalty count: 9-4; **Half-time:** 18-18;
Referee: Thierry Alibert.

ST HELENS 16 WIGAN WARRIORS 42

SAINTS: 1 Paul Wellens (C); 2 Ade Gardner; 3 Michael Shenton; 17 Gary Wheeler; 5 Francis Meli; 6 Lance Hohaia; 7 Jonny Lomax; 8 Josh Perry; 9 James Roby; 14 Anthony Laffranchi; 4 Iosia Soliola; 13 Chris Flannery; 12 Jon Wilkin. Subs (all used): 16 Paul Clough; 10 Louie McCarthy-Scarsbrook; 11 Tony Puletua; 18 Shaun Magennis.
Tries: Clough (36), McCarthy-Scarsbrook (56), Wellens (74); **Goals:** Lomax 2/3.
Dismissal: Magennis (53) - fighting.
WARRIORS: 1 Sam Tomkins; 2 Josh Charnley; 3 Darrell Goulding; 4 George Carmont; 24 Anthony Gelling; 6 Brett Finch; 7 Thomas Leuluai; 22 Gil Dudson; 9 Michael

McIlorum; 10 Lee Mossop; 11 Harrison Hansen; 12 Gareth Hock; 13 Sean O'Loughlin (C). Subs (all used): 14 Jeff Lima; 16 Liam Farrell; 17 Chris Tuson; 21 Epalahame Lauaki.
Tries: S Tomkins (5, 22), Hock (11), Charnley (15, 40), O'Loughlin (24), Carmont (43), Farrell (65);
Goals: Charnley 5/10.
Dismissals: Hock (53) - fighting; Tuson (53) - fighting.
Rugby Leaguer & League Express Men of the Match: *Saints:* Louie McCarthy-Scarsbrook; *Warriors:* Brett Finch.
Penalty count: 10-10; **Half-time:** 6-30;
Referee: Ben Thaler.

Attendance: 32,953 *(at Etihad Stadium, Manchester).*

ROUND 16

Friday 1st June 2012

LEEDS RHINOS 8 WIGAN WARRIORS 50

RHINOS: 1 Brent Webb; 14 Lee Smith; 12 Carl Ablett; 4 Zak Hardaker; 5 Ryan Hall; 13 Kevin Sinfield (C); 6 Danny McGuire; 8 Kylie Leuluai; 31 Shaun Lunt; 10 Jamie Peacock; 11 Jamie Jones-Buchanan; 15 Brett Delaney; 18 Chris Clarkson. Subs (all used): 7 Rob Burrow; 16 Ryan Bailey; 19 Weller Hauraki; 21 Richard Moore.
Tries: Hall (14, 65); **Goals:** Sinfield 0/2.
WARRIORS: 1 Sam Tomkins; 2 Josh Charnley; 3 Darrell Goulding; 4 George Carmont; 24 Anthony Gelling; 6 Brett Finch; 7 Thomas Leuluai; 22 Gil Dudson; 9 Michael McIlorum; 14 Jeff Lima; 16 Liam Farrell; 26 Jack Hughes; 13 Sean O'Loughlin (C). Subs (all used): 21 Epalahame Lauaki; 33 Dominic Crosby; 36 Rhodri Lloyd (D); 28 Logan Tomkins.
Tries: Lima (3), Farrell (6), O'Loughlin (27), Carmont (29), Leuluai (39, 72), Charnley (48), Gelling (60), Finch (76); **Goals:** Charnley 7/9.
Rugby Leaguer & League Express Men of the Match: *Rhinos:* Jamie Jones-Buchanan; *Warriors:* Sam Tomkins.
Penalty count: 7-15; **Half-time:** 4-26;
Referee: James Child; **Attendance:** 16,113.

SALFORD CITY REDS 34 CATALAN DRAGONS 30

CITY REDS: 1 Luke Patten; 5 Danny Williams; 3 Sean Gleeson; 4 Joel Moon; 2 Jodie Broughton; 6 Daniel Holdsworth; 7 Matty Smith; 8 Lee Jewitt; 24 Stuart Howarth; 15 Adam Sidlow; 11 Matty Ashurst; 27 Vinnie Anderson; 13 Stephen Wild (C). Subs (all used): 12 Shannan McPherson; 14 Chris Nero; 17 Iafeta Palea'aesina; 23 Gareth Owen.
Tries: Moon (28), Holdsworth (31), Gleeson (42), Broughton (44, 70), Patten (55);
Goals: Holdsworth 3/4, Smith 2/2.
DRAGONS: 6 Thomas Bosc; 18 Daryl Millard; 15 Jean-Philippe Baile; 25 Vincent Duport; 5 Cyril Stacul; 3 Leon Pryce; 7 Scott Dureau; 10 Remi Casty (C); 26 Ben Fisher; 23 Lopini Paea; 11 Steve Menzies; 12 Louis Anderson; 24 Jason Baitieri. Subs (all used): 8 David Ferriol; 9 Ian Henderson; 13 Gregory Mounis; 14 Sebastien Raguin.
Tries: Millard (6), Dureau (8), Stacul (15), Paea (24), Casty (59), Duport (76); **Goals:** Dureau 3/6.
Rugby Leaguer & League Express Men of the Match: *City Reds:* Jodie Broughton; *Dragons:* Jason Baitieri.
Penalty count: 9-7; **Half-time:** 12-20;
Referee: Steve Ganson; **Attendance:** 4,220.

Sunday 3rd June 2012

HULL FC 18 ST HELENS 18

HULL: 36 Matthew Russell; 2 Will Sharp; 19 Jordan Turner; 23 Ben Crooks; 5 Tom Briscoe; 6 Richard Horne; 7 Brett Seymour; 17 Sam Moa; 9 Danny Houghton; 10 Andy Lynch (C); 11 Willie Manu; 12 Danny Tickle; 13 Joe Westerman. Subs (all used): 22 Martin Aspinwall; 15 Richard Whiting; 34 Jay Pitts; 16 Eamon O'Carroll.
Tries: Whiting (26), Horne (52), Tickle (63);
Goals: Tickle 3/4.
SAINTS: 1 Paul Wellens (C); 21 Tom Makinson; 3 Michael Shenton; 26 Josh Jones; 34 Adam Swift; 6 Lance Hohaia; 7 Jonny Lomax; 8 Josh Perry; 9 James Roby; 11 Tony Puletua; 4 Iosia Soliola; 13 Chris Flannery; 12 Jon Wilkin. Subs (used): 10 Louie McCarthy-Scarsbrook; 16 Paul Clough; 20 Lee Gaskell; 15 Mark Flanagan.
Tries: Swift (18), Hohaia (21), Wilkin (57);
Goals: Makinson 3/4.
Rugby Leaguer & League Express Men of the Match: *Hull:* Danny Tickle; *Saints:* Tom Makinson.
Penalty count: 9-6; **Half-time:** 6-12;
Referee: Thierry Alibert; **Attendance:** 11,727.

HULL KINGSTON ROVERS 23 WARRINGTON WOLVES 22

ROVERS: 1 Shannon McDonnell; 21 Sam Latus; 18 Graeme Horne; 3 Kris Welham; 5 David Hodgson; 2 Craig Hall; 7 Michael Dobson; 23 Mickey Paea; 9 Josh Hodgson; 10 Scott Taylor; 11 Constantine Mika; 12 Ben Galea (C); 13 Rhys Lovegrove. Subs (all used): 14 Lincoln Withers; 17 Ryan O'Hara; 8 Joel Clinton; 19 Scott Murrell.
Tries: J Hodgson (28), Dobson (49), Latus (51), Hall (68); **Goals:** Dobson 3/4; **Field goal:** Dobson (77).
WOLVES: 1 Brett Hodgson; 5 Joel Monaghan; 18 Matty Blythe; 4 Ryan Atkins; 2 Chris Riley; 6 Lee Briers; 24 Gareth O'Brien; 8 Adrian Morley (C); 15 Simon Grix; 10 Garreth Carvell; 11 Trent Waterhouse; 12 Ben Westwood; 13 Ben Harrison. Subs (all used): 14 Mick Higham; 20 Chris Hill; 19 Stefan Ratchford; 3 Chris Bridge.
Tries: O'Brien (3), Westwood (10), Riley (15, 37);
Goals: Hodgson 3/4.
Rugby Leaguer & League Express Men of the Match: *Rovers:* Michael Dobson; *Wolves:* Chris Riley.
Penalty count: 12-8; **Half-time:** 6-22;
Referee: Robert Hicks; **Attendance:** 7,661.

WIDNES VIKINGS 26 HUDDERSFIELD GIANTS 22

VIKINGS: 19 Cameron Phelps; 2 Paddy Flynn; 20 Stefan Marsh; 3 Chris Dean; 5 Patrick Ah Van; 34 Joe Mellor; 7 Rhys Hanbury (C); 8 Ben Cross; 35 Paul McShane (D); 12 Hep Cahill; 11 Frank Winterstein; 24 Kurt Haggerty; 21 Dave Allen. Subs (all used): 4 Willie Isa; 10 Ben Davies; 22 Macgraff Leuluai; 17 Steve Pickersgill.
Tries: Ah Van (3), Hanbury (8), Cross (11), Phelps (80);
Goals: Ah Van 5/6.
Sin bin: Pickersgill (35) - holding down.
On report: Haggerty (30) - alleged dangerous tackle.
GIANTS: 21 Aaron Murphy; 5 Jermaine McGillvary; 20 Luke George; 2 Michael Lawrence; 29 Greg Eden; 1 Scott Grix; 7 Danny Brough; 8 Eorl Crabtree; 9 Luke Robinson (C); 4 Lee Gilmour; 16 Dale Ferguson; 18 Jason Chan; 3 Leroy Cudjoe. Subs (all used): 10 Keith Mason; 12 David Fa'alogo; 15 Larne Patrick; 35 Scott Moore.
Tries: Ferguson (30), Fa'alogo (35), Grix (67);
Goals: Brough 5/5.
On report:
Lawrence (42) - alleged high tackle on Hanbury.
Rugby Leaguer & League Express Men of the Match: *Vikings:* Rhys Hanbury; *Giants:* David Fa'alogo.
Penalty count: 8-16; **Half-time:** 16-12;
Referee: George Stokes; **Attendance:** 4,644.

WAKEFIELD TRINITY WILDCATS 24 LONDON BRONCOS 6

WILDCATS: 1 Richard Mathers; 2 Peter Fox; 3 Dean Collis; 4 Vince Mellars; 5 Ben Cockayne; 34 Paul Sykes; 20 Tim Smith; 15 Kyle Amor; 14 Paul Aiton; 10 Andy Raleigh; 11 Ali Lauitiiti; 17 Danny Kirmond (C); 13 Danny Washbrook. Subs (all used): 7 Kyle Wood; 19 Frankie Mariano; 12 Steve Southern; 8 Oliver Wilkes.
Tries: Mellars (6), Collis (20), Lauitiiti (28), Kirmond (53); **Goals:** Sykes 4/6.
BRONCOS: 1 Luke Dorn; 21 Kieran Dixon; 4 David Howell; 3 Jamie O'Callaghan; 5 Michael Robertson; 6 Michael Witt; 7 Craig Gower (C); 8 Antonio Kaufusi; 9 Chad Randall; 30 Scott Wheeldon; 11 Shane Rodney; 16 Chris Melling; 12 Chris Bailey. Subs: 13 Tony Clubb; 10 Mark Bryant; 19 Dan Sarginson; 23 Omari Caro (not used).
Try: Wheeldon (63); **Goals:** Rodney 1/1.
Rugby Leaguer & League Express Men of the Match: *Wildcats:* Danny Kirmond; *Broncos:* Kieran Dixon.
Penalty count: 11-10; **Half-time:** 18-0;
Referee: Tim Roby; **Attendance:** 5,876.

Monday 4th June 2012

BRADFORD BULLS 46 CASTLEFORD TIGERS 32

BULLS: 1 Brett Kearney; 18 Shaun Ainscough; 29 Michael Platt; 3 Keith Lulia; 33 Karl Pryce; 6 Ben Jeffries; 7 Luke Gale; 16 Manase Manuokafoa; 9 Heath L'Estrange (C); 15 Bryn Hargreaves; 26 John Bateman; 19 Tom Olbison; 11 Olivier Elima. Subs (all used): 21 Tom Burgess; 12 Elliott Whitehead; 17 Ian Sibbit; 23 Danny Addy.
Tries: Lulia (6), Kearney (9, 60), Bateman (18), Elima (22), Ainscough (29, 32, 74); **Goals:** Gale 7/8.
TIGERS: 2 Nick Youngquest; 32 Rhys Williams; 4 Kirk Dixon; 25 Jordan Thompson; 5 Josh Griffin; 6 Rangi Chase; 7 Danny Orr (C); 19 Paul Jackson; 14 Stuart Jones; 10 Craig Huby; 11 Brett Ferres; 21 Oliver Holmes; 17 Lee Mitchell. Subs (all used): 12 Jonathan Walker; 23 Ryan McGoldrick; 20 Grant Millington; 22 Nathan Massey.
Tries: Thompson (12), Chase (26, 62), Massey (36), Williams (51, 53); **Goals:** Dixon 4/6.
Rugby Leaguer & League Express Men of the Match: *Bulls:* Brett Kearney; *Tigers:* Rangi Chase.
Penalty count: 9-5; **Half-time:** 34-16;
Referee: Ben Thaler; **Attendance:** 10,906.

ROUND 17

Friday 8th June 2012

ST HELENS 54 BRADFORD BULLS 0

SAINTS: 1 Paul Wellens (C); 21 Tom Makinson; 3 Michael Shenton; 26 Josh Jones; 5 Francis Meli; 6 Lance Hohaia; 7 Jonny Lomax; 8 Josh Perry; 9 James Roby; 14 Anthony Laffranchi; 11 Tony Puletua; 4 Iosia Soliola; 12 Jon Wilkin. Subs (all used): 10 Louie McCarthy-Scarsbrook; 13 Chris Flannery; 15 Mark Flanagan; 16 Paul Clough.
Tries: Wellens (6, 50), Jones (20, 31, 79), Lomax (24, 62), Meli (40), Makinson (54), Hohaia (57);
Goals: Makinson 7/10.
BULLS: 29 Michael Platt; 18 Shaun Ainscough; 12 Elliott Whitehead; 3 Keith Lulia; 33 Karl Pryce; 6 Ben Jeffries; 7 Luke Gale; 13 Jamie Langley; 9 Heath L'Estrange (C); 15 Bryn Hargreaves; 19 Tom Olbison; 26 John Bateman; 11 Olivier Elima. Subs (all used): 16 Manase Manuokafoa; 17 Ian Sibbit; 21 Tom Burgess; 23 Danny Addy.
Rugby Leaguer & League Express Men of the Match: *Saints:* Jonny Lomax; *Bulls:* Elliott Whitehead.
Penalty count: 10-8; **Half-time:** 28-0;
Referee: Tim Roby; **Attendance:** 13,025.

WARRINGTON WOLVES 37 LEEDS RHINOS 18

WOLVES: 1 Brett Hodgson; 5 Joel Monaghan; 3 Chris Bridge; 4 Ryan Atkins; 2 Chris Riley; 6 Lee Briers; 24 Gareth O'Brien; 20 Chris Hill; 14 Mick Higham; 10 Garreth Carvell; 11 Trent Waterhouse; 12 Ben Westwood; 13 Ben Harrison. Subs (all used): 8 Adrian Morley (C); 15 Simon Grix; 17 Michael Cooper; 19 Stefan Ratchford.
Tries: Waterhouse (2), Riley (4, 28), O'Brien (11, 18), Atkins (71); **Goals:** Hodgson 5/5, O'Brien 1/2;
Field goal: Briers (65).
RHINOS: 1 Brent Webb; 2 Ben Jones-Bishop; 12 Carl Ablett; 4 Zak Hardaker; 5 Ryan Hall; 13 Kevin Sinfield (C); 7 Rob Burrow; 8 Kylie Leuluai; 31 Shaun Lunt; 10 Jamie Peacock; 11 Jamie Jones-Buchanan; 15 Brett Delaney; 16 Ryan Bailey. Subs (all used): 17 Ian Kirke; 18 Chris Clarkson; 20 Darrell Griffin; 25 Stevie Ward.
Tries: Sinfield (34), Burrow (46, 68); **Goals:** Sinfield 3/3.
Rugby Leaguer & League Express Men of the Match: *Wolves:* Gareth O'Brien; *Rhinos:* Rob Burrow.
Penalty count: 6-5; **Half-time:** 30-6;
Referee: Ben Thaler; **Attendance:** 10,835.

Saturday 9th June 2012

CATALAN DRAGONS 14 WIGAN WARRIORS 36

DRAGONS: 1 Clint Greenshields; 2 Damien Blanch; 4 Setaimata Sa; 25 Vincent Duport; 18 Daryl Millard; 3 Leon Pryce; 7 Scott Dureau; 8 David Ferriol; 9 Ian Henderson; 10 Remi Casty (C); 11 Steve Menzies; 12 Louis Anderson; 24 Jason Baitieri. Subs (all used): 13 Gregory Mounis; 14 Sebastien Raguin; 23 Lopini Paea; 26 Ben Fisher.
Tries: Greenshields (18, pen), Dureau (70);
Goals: Dureau 3/3.
WARRIORS: 1 Sam Tomkins; 2 Josh Charnley; 3 Darrell Goulding; 4 George Carmont; 24 Anthony Gelling; 6 Brett Finch; 7 Thomas Leuluai; 22 Gil Dudson; 9 Michael McIlorum; 10 Lee Mossop; 16 Liam Farrell; 17 Chris Tuson; 13 Sean O'Loughlin (C). Subs (all used): 14 Jeff Lima; 21 Epalahame Lauaki; 26 Jack Hughes; 28 Logan Tomkins.
Tries: Tuson (12), Gelling (15), Charnley (38), Carmont (50, 60), S Tomkins (73), Hughes (79);
Goals: Charnley 2/6, S Tomkins 2/2.
Sin bin: Dudson (10) - late challenge on Dureau.
Rugby Leaguer & League Express Men of the Match: *Dragons:* Scott Dureau; *Warriors:* Michael McIlorum.
Penalty count: 9-13; **Half-time:** 8-14;
Referee: James Child; **Attendance:** 13,858
(at Stade de la Mosson, Montpellier).

LONDON BRONCOS 28 WIDNES VIKINGS 24

BRONCOS: 5 Michael Robertson; 21 Kieran Dixon; 4 David Howell; 3 Jamie O'Callaghan; 23 Omari Caro; 19 Dan Sarginson; 7 Craig Gower (C); 30 Scott Wheeldon; 9 Chad Randall; 8 Antonio Kaufusi; 17 Jason Golden; 11 Shane Rodney; 12 Chris Bailey. Subs (all used): 10 Mark Bryant; 31 Will Lovell; 14 Julien Rinaldi; 13 Tony Clubb.
Tries: Gower (13), Caro (33), Clubb (49), Sarginson (73), Kaufusi (80); **Goals:** Rodney 3/4, Dixon 1/1.
VIKINGS: 19 Cameron Phelps; 2 Paddy Flynn; 4 Willie Isa; 3 Chris Dean; 5 Patrick Ah Van; 13 Jon Clarke (C); 7 Rhys Hanbury; 8 Ben Cross; 35 Paul McShane; 17 Steve Pickersgill; 11 Frank Winterstein; 21 Dave Allen; 12 Hep Cahill. Subs (all used): 10 Ben Davies; 22 Macgraff Leuluai; 24 Kurt Haggerty; 30 Tom Gilmore (D).
Tries: Phelps (3, 43), Winterstein (39, 60);
Goals: Ah Van 4/5.
Rugby Leaguer & League Express Men of the Match: *Broncos:* Julien Rinaldi; *Vikings:* Frank Winterstein.
Penalty count: 8-6; **Half-time:** 12-12;
Referee: Robert Hicks; **Attendance:** 2,117.

Sunday 10th June 2012

CASTLEFORD TIGERS 34 SALFORD CITY REDS 30

TIGERS: 1 Richard Owen; 2 Nick Youngquest; 4 Kirk Dixon; 25 Jordan Thompson; 32 Rhys Williams; 6 Rangi Chase; 23 Ryan McGoldrick; 12 Jonathan Walker; 15 Adam Milner; 10 Craig Huby; 11 Brett Ferres; 20 Grant Millington; 14 Stuart Jones. Subs (all used): 7 Danny Orr (C); 8 Jake Emmitt; 21 Oliver Holmes; 22 Nathan Massey.
Tries: Youngquest (14), Orr (38, 48, 77), Thompson (40), Huby (79); **Goals:** Dixon 3/4, Huby 1/1, Orr 1/1.
Sin bin: Ferres (17) - delaying restart.
CITY REDS: 1 Luke Patten; 2 Jodie Broughton; 3 Sean Gleeson; 4 Joel Moon; 5 Danny Williams; 22 Marc Sneyd; 7 Matty Smith; 12 Shannan McPherson; 24 Stuart Howarth; 15 Adam Sidlow; 11 Matty Ashurst; 27 Vinnie Anderson; 13 Stephen Wild (C). Subs (all used): 14 Chris Nero; 17 Iafeta Palea'aesina; 20 Ben Gledhill; 23 Gareth Owen.
Tries: Anderson (20), Broughton (24), Moon (55), Wild (58), Gleeson (73); **Goals:** Sneyd 5/5.
Rugby Leaguer & League Express Men of the Match: *Tigers:* Danny Orr; *City Reds:* Luke Patten.
Penalty count: 4-5; **Half-time:** 16-12;
Referee: George Stokes; **Attendance:** 5,877.

WAKEFIELD TRINITY WILDCATS 32 HULL FC 30

WILDCATS: 1 Richard Mathers (C); 2 Peter Fox; 3 Dean Collis; 4 Vince Mellars; 5 Ben Cockayne; 34 Paul Sykes; 20 Tim Smith; 15 Kyle Amor; 14 Paul Aiton; 10 Andy Raleigh; 11 Ali Lauitiiti; 33 Lucas Walshaw; 13 Danny Washbrook. Subs (all used): 7 Kyle Wood; 8 Oliver Wilkes; 12 Steve Southern; 22 Kyle Trout.
Tries: Collis (25), Fox (38), Sykes (51), Washbrook (55), Amor (59), Lauitiiti (72); **Goals:** Sykes 4/6.
HULL: 36 Matthew Russell; 23 Ben Crooks; 19 Jordan Turner; 4 Kirk Yeaman; 5 Tom Briscoe; 20 Jamie Ellis; 7 Brett Seymour; 10 Andy Lynch (C); 9 Danny Houghton; 17 Sam Moa; 11 Willie Manu; 12 Danny Tickle; 13 Joe Westerman. Subs (all used): 15 Richard Whiting; 22 Martin Aspinwall; 34 Jay Pitts; 16 Eamon O'Carroll.
Tries: Manu (10), Seymour (22), Crooks (35), Yeaman (43, 47); **Goals:** Tickle 5/6.
On report: Westerman (24) - alleged dangerous tackle.

Rugby Leaguer & League Express Men of the Match: *Wildcats:* Paul Sykes; *Hull:* Willie Manu.
Penalty count: 7-5; **Half-time:** 10-18;
Referee: Steve Ganson; **Attendance:** 8,986.

Monday 11th June 2012

HUDDERSFIELD GIANTS 26
HULL KINGSTON ROVERS 44

GIANTS: 29 Greg Eden; 20 Luke George; 3 Leroy Cudjoe; 2 Michael Lawrence; 21 Aaron Murphy; 19 Tommy Lee; 7 Danny Brough; 8 Eorl Crabtree; 35 Scott Moore; 12 David Fa'alogo; 4 Lee Gilmour; 16 Dale Ferguson; 6 Kevin Brown (C). Subs (all used): 18 Jason Chan; 15 Larne Patrick; 13 David Faiumu; 9 Luke Robinson.
Tries: Cudjoe (7), Crabtree (24), Murphy (62, 73), Patrick (76); **Goals:** Brough 3/5.
ROVERS: 1 Shannon McDonnell; 4 Jake Webster; 18 Graeme Horne; 3 Kris Welham; 5 David Hodgson; 2 Craig Hall; 7 Michael Dobson; 17 Ryan O'Hara; 9 Josh Hodgson; 10 Scott Taylor; 11 Constantine Mika; 12 Ben Galea (C); 13 Rhys Lovegrove. Subs (all used): 23 Mickey Paea; 14 Lincoln Withers; 16 Jason Netherton; 19 Scott Murrell.
Tries: D Hodgson (3, 58), Dobson (27, 65), Welham (35), Galea (43), Hall (79); **Goals:** Dobson 8/9.
Rugby Leaguer & League Express Men of the Match: *Giants:* Eorl Crabtree; *Rovers:* Michael Dobson.
Penalty count: 7-7; **Half-time:** 12-18;
Referee: Thierry Alibert; **Attendance:** 4,962.

ROUND 3

Monday 18th June 2012

LEEDS RHINOS 44 WAKEFIELD TRINITY WILDCATS 40

RHINOS: 4 Zak Hardaker; 2 Ben Jones-Bishop; 12 Carl Ablett; 15 Brett Delaney; 5 Ryan Hall; 13 Kevin Sinfield (C); 6 Danny McGuire; 8 Kylie Leuluai; 7 Rob Burrow; 20 Darrell Griffin; 11 Jamie Jones-Buchanan; 18 Chris Clarkson; 16 Ryan Bailey. Subs (all used): 10 Jamie Peacock; 19 Weller Hauraki; 25 Stevie Ward; 31 Shaun Lunt.
Tries: Hardaker (7), Jones-Bishop (11, 36, 60), Jones-Buchanan (26), Hauraki (51), Ablett (75);
Goals: Sinfield 8/8.
WILDCATS: 1 Richard Mathers (C); 2 Peter Fox; 3 Dean Collis; 4 Vince Mellars; 5 Ben Cockayne; 34 Paul Sykes; 20 Tim Smith; 15 Kyle Amor; 14 Paul Aiton; 10 Andy Raleigh; 11 Ali Lauitiiti; 33 Lucas Walshaw; 13 Danny Washbrook. Subs (all used): 8 Oliver Wilkes; 12 Steve Southern; 22 Kyle Trout; 7 Kyle Wood.
Tries: Cockayne (16), T Smith (19), Collis (23), Lauitiiti (32), Trout (47), Wilkes (72), Fox (78);
Goals: Sykes 6/6 *(last conversion attempt declined).*
Rugby Leaguer & League Express Men of the Match: *Rhinos:* Jamie Jones-Buchanan; *Wildcats:* Paul Aiton.
Penalty count: 5-8; **Half-time:** 24-24;
Referee: Richard Silverwood; **Attendance:** 12,272.

ROUND 18

Friday 22nd June 2012

HULL KINGSTON ROVERS 10 CATALAN DRAGONS 13

ROVERS: 1 Shannon McDonnell; 4 Jake Webster; 18 Graeme Horne; 3 Kris Welham; 2 Craig Hall; 6 Blake Green; 7 Michael Dobson; 10 Scott Taylor; 9 Josh Hodgson; 17 Ryan O'Hara; 11 Constantine Mika; 12 Ben Galea (C); 13 Rhys Lovegrove. Subs (all used): 14 Lincoln Withers; 23 Mickey Paea; 19 Scott Murrell; 16 Jason Netherton.
Tries: Webster (20), Murrell (61); **Goals:** Dobson 1/2.
DRAGONS: 3 Leon Pryce; 2 Damien Blanch; 25 Vincent Duport; 18 Daryl Millard; 1 Clint Greenshields; 6 Thomas Bosc; 7 Scott Dureau; 8 David Ferriol; 9 Ian Henderson; 10 Remi Casty (C); 11 Steve Menzies; 4 Setaimata Sa; 24 Jason Baitieri. Subs (all used): 26 Ben Fisher; 22 Jamal Fakir; 14 Sebastien Raguin; 13 Gregory Mounis.
Tries: Sa (14), Greenshields (75); **Goals:** Dureau 2/4;
Field goal: Dureau (77).
Rugby Leaguer & League Express Men of the Match: *Rovers:* Scott Taylor; *Dragons:* Steve Menzies.
Penalty count: 12-12; **Half-time:** 6-4;
Referee: Richard Silverwood; **Attendance:** 7,142.

SALFORD CITY REDS 10 ST HELENS 32

CITY REDS: 1 Luke Patten; 2 Jodie Broughton; 4 Joel Moon; 3 Sean Gleeson; 5 Danny Williams; 6 Daniel Holdsworth; 7 Matty Smith; 12 Shannan McPherson; 24 Stuart Howarth; 15 Adam Sidlow; 11 Matty Ashurst; 27 Vinnie Anderson; 13 Stephen Wild (C). Subs (all used): 20 Ben Gledhill; 17 Iafeta Palea'aesina; 21 Jordan James; 14 Chris Nero.
Tries: Anderson (21), Williams (30);
Goals: Holdsworth 1/2.
SAINTS: 1 Paul Wellens (C); 21 Tom Makinson; 3 Michael Shenton; 26 Josh Jones; 5 Francis Meli; 6 Lance Hohaia; 7 Jonny Lomax; 11 Tony Puletua; 9 James Roby; 14 Anthony Laffranchi; 13 Chris Flannery; 4 Iosia Soliola; 12 Jon Wilkin. Subs (all used): 10 Louie McCarthy-Scarsbrook; 16 Paul Clough; 20 Lee Gaskell; 15 Mark Flanagan.
Tries: Jones (37), Hohaia (43), Makinson (54), Lomax (71), Shenton (74), Wellens (77);
Goals: Makinson 1/3, Gaskell 3/3.
Rugby Leaguer & League Express Men of the Match: *City Reds:* Joel Moon; *Saints:* Jon Wilkin.
Penalty count: 9-6; **Half-time:** 10-6;
Referee: James Child; **Attendance:** 5,447.

Sunday 24th June 2012

BRADFORD BULLS 34
WAKEFIELD TRINITY WILDCATS 26

BULLS: 1 Brett Kearney; 18 Shaun Ainscough; 29 Michael Platt; 3 Keith Lulia; 33 Karl Pryce; 6 Ben Jeffries; 7 Luke Gale; 11 Olivier Elima; 9 Heath L'Estrange (C); 15 Bryn Hargreaves; 26 John Bateman; 12 Elliott Whitehead; 13 Jamie Langley. Subs (all used): 21 Tom Burgess; 16 Manase Manuokafoa; 22 Jarrod Sammut; 19 Tom Olbison.
Tries: Whitehead (2), Lulia (8, 47), Ainscough (20), Elima (67); **Goals:** Gale 7/7.
Sin bin: Gale (74) - holding down.
WILDCATS: 1 Richard Mathers; 2 Peter Fox; 3 Dean Collis; 4 Vince Mellars; 5 Ben Cockayne; 34 Paul Sykes; 20 Tim Smith; 15 Kyle Amor; 14 Paul Aiton; 10 Andy Raleigh; 11 Ali Lauitiiti; 17 Danny Kirmond (C); 13 Danny Washbrook. Subs (all used): 7 Kyle Wood; 8 Oliver Wilkes; 12 Steve Southern; 19 Frankie Mariano.
Tries: Aiton (15), Cockayne (24), T Smith (30), Mariano (37), Amor (64); **Goals:** Sykes 3/5.
Rugby Leaguer & League Express Men of the Match: *Bulls:* Luke Gale; *Wildcats:* Ali Lauitiiti.
Penalty count: 7-9; **Half-time:** 18-20;
Referee: Robert Hicks; **Attendance:** 11,236.

HUDDERSFIELD GIANTS 46 LONDON BRONCOS 10

GIANTS: 29 Greg Eden; 21 Aaron Murphy; 3 Leroy Cudjoe; 4 Lee Gilmour; 20 Luke George; 7 Danny Brough; 1 Scott Grix; 8 Eorl Crabtree; 35 Scott Moore; 10 Keith Mason; 12 David Fa'alogo; 2 Michael Lawrence; 6 Kevin Brown (C). Subs (all used): 9 Luke Robinson; 15 Larne Patrick; 16 Dale Ferguson; 18 Jason Chan.
Tries: George (13), Brown (16), Murphy (40), Lawrence (55), Grix (58), Crabtree (65, 79), Patrick (73);
Goals: Brough 7/8.
BRONCOS: 1 Luke Dorn; 5 Michael Robertson; 31 Will Lovell; 4 David Howell; 21 Kieran Dixon; 19 Dan Sarginson; 7 Craig Gower (C); 8 Antonio Kaufusi; 14 Julien Rinaldi; 30 Scott Wheeldon; 17 Jason Golden; 12 Chris Bailey; 13 Tony Clubb. Subs (all used): 9 Chad Randall; 10 Mark Bryant; 22 Ben Bolger; 28 Michael Channing.
Tries: Robertson (5), Gower (48); **Goals:** Gower 1/2.
Rugby Leaguer & League Express Men of the Match: *Giants:* Danny Brough; *Broncos:* Michael Robertson.
Penalty count: 9-5; **Half-time:** 16-4;
Referee: Steve Ganson; **Attendance:** 6,019.

LEEDS RHINOS 40 CASTLEFORD TIGERS 22

RHINOS: 4 Zak Hardaker; 2 Ben Jones-Bishop; 3 Kallum Watkins; 12 Carl Ablett; 5 Ryan Hall; 13 Kevin Sinfield (C); 6 Danny McGuire; 8 Kylie Leuluai; 7 Rob Burrow; 20 Darrell Griffin; 11 Jamie Jones-Buchanan; 15 Brett Delaney; 25 Stevie Ward. Subs (all used): 16 Ryan Bailey; 21 Richard Moore; 31 Shaun Lunt; 19 Weller Hauraki.
Tries: Jones-Bishop (11, 54), Burrow (15, 24), Hall (39, 57), Watkins (46); **Goals:** Sinfield 6/7.
TIGERS: 2 Nick Youngquest; 1 Richard Owen; 25 Jordan Thompson; 11 Brett Ferres; 32 Rhys Williams; 23 Ryan McGoldrick; 7 Danny Orr (C); 22 Nathan Massey; 15 Adam Milner; 10 Craig Huby; 20 Grant Millington; 21 Oliver Holmes; 8 Jake Emmitt. Subs (all used): 19 Paul Jackson; 12 Jonathan Walker; 13 Steve Snitch; 14 Stuart Jones.
Tries: Jackson (31), Huby (61), Ferres (66, 76);
Goals: Orr 1/1, Huby 1/2, McGoldrick 1/1.
Sin bin: Owen (60) - retaliation.
Rugby Leaguer & League Express Men of the Match: *Rhinos:* Zak Hardaker; *Tigers:* Ryan McGoldrick.
Penalty count: 9-11; **Half-time:** 22-6;
Referee: Tim Roby; **Attendance:** 16,153.

WARRINGTON WOLVES 40 HULL FC 18

WOLVES: 19 Stefan Ratchford; 2 Chris Riley; 3 Chris Bridge; 4 Ryan Atkins; 5 Joel Monaghan; 6 Lee Briers (C); 24 Gareth O'Brien; 20 Chris Hill; 14 Mick Higham; 10 Garreth Carvell; 11 Trent Waterhouse; 17 Michael Cooper; 13 Ben Harrison. Subs (all used): 9 Michael Monaghan; 16 Paul Wood; 21 Tyrone McCarthy; 32 Ben Currie.
Tries: Atkins (11, 32, 61), Riley (29), Briers (51), Carvell (66), J Monaghan (72); **Goals:** O'Brien 6/7.
HULL: 36 Matthew Russell; 23 Ben Crooks; 19 Jordan Turner; 4 Kirk Yeaman; 5 Tom Briscoe; 6 Richard Horne; 7 Brett Seymour; 17 Sam Moa; 15 Richard Whiting; 10 Andy Lynch (C); 11 Willie Manu; 12 Danny Tickle; 13 Joe Westerman. Subs (all used): 14 Aaron Heremaia (D); 22 Martin Aspinwall; 24 Liam Kent; 34 Jay Pitts.
Tries: Yeaman (5), Manu (9), Westerman (18);
Goals: Tickle 3/4.
Sin bin: Manu (57) - interference.
Rugby Leaguer & League Express Men of the Match: *Wolves:* Ryan Atkins; *Hull:* Brett Seymour.
Penalty count: 15-8; **Half-time:** 18-18;
Referee: Ben Thaler; **Attendance:** 10,582.

Monday 25th June 2012

WIGAN WARRIORS 54 WIDNES VIKINGS 12

WARRIORS: 1 Sam Tomkins; 2 Josh Charnley; 3 Darrell Goulding; 4 George Carmont; 24 Anthony Gelling; 13 Sean O'Loughlin (C); 6 Brett Finch; 21 Epalahame Lauaki; 9 Michael McIlorum; 10 Lee Mossop; 26 Jack Hughes; 12 Gareth Hock; 16 Liam Farrell. Subs (all used): 8 Paul Prescott; 28 Logan Tomkins; 33 Dominic Crosby; 36 Rhodri Lloyd.
Tries: Charnley (2, 56, 68), McIlorum (10), Carmont (13), Prescott (35), Gelling (38), Finch (43, 72), S Tomkins (79); **Goals:** Charnley 7/10.
VIKINGS: 19 Cameron Phelps; 2 Paddy Flynn; 3 Chris Dean; 4 Willie Isa; 5 Patrick Ah Van; 7 Rhys Hanbury; 34 Joe Mellor; 8 Ben Cross (C); 35 Paul McShane; 17 Steve Pickersgill; 11 Frank Winterstein; 21 Dave Allen; 12 Hep Cahill. Subs (all used): 1 Shaun Briscoe; 10 Ben Davies; 25 Danny Craven; 28 Alex Gerrard.
Tries: Cross (18), Mellor (40); **Goals:** Ah Van 2/2.
Rugby Leaguer & League Express Men of the Match: *Warriors:* Brett Finch; *Vikings:* Joe Mellor.
Penalty count: 9-4; **Half-time:** 28-12;
Referee: Thierry Alibert; **Attendance:** 13,445.

ROUND 19

Friday 29th June 2012

SALFORD CITY REDS 48 WARRINGTON WOLVES 24

CITY REDS: 1 Luke Patten; 5 Danny Williams; 3 Sean Gleeson; 4 Joel Moon; 2 Jodie Broughton; 6 Daniel Holdsworth; 7 Matty Smith; 20 Ben Gledhill; 24 Stuart Howarth; 10 Ryan Boyle; 11 Matty Ashurst; 27 Vinnie Anderson; 13 Stephen Wild (C). Subs (all used): 21 Jordan James; 17 Iafeta Palea'aesina; 16 Luke Adamson; 14 Chris Nero.
Tries: Williams (5, 56), Broughton (24, 43), Anderson (26, 52), Patten (30, 80), Smith (49);
Goals: Holdsworth 6/9.
WOLVES: 19 Stefan Ratchford; 2 Chris Riley; 18 Matty Blythe; 3 Chris Bridge; 23 Rhys Evans; 24 Gareth O'Brien; 7 Richard Myler; 16 Paul Wood; 14 Mick Higham; 20 Chris Hill; 11 Trent Waterhouse; 17 Michael Cooper; 13 Ben Harrison. Subs (used): 8 Adrian Morley (C); 33 Brad Dwyer; 21 Tyrone McCarthy; 26 David Solomona.
Tries: Ratchford (37), Myler (68), Riley (71), Blythe (77); **Goals:** O'Brien 4/4.
Rugby Leaguer & League Express Men of the Match: *City Reds:* Matty Smith; *Wolves:* David Solomona.
Penalty count: 9-6; **Half-time:** 24-6;
Referee: Richard Silverwood; **Attendance:** 6,179.

ST HELENS 34 HULL KINGSTON ROVERS 28

SAINTS: 1 Paul Wellens (C); 21 Tom Makinson; 3 Michael Shenton; 26 Josh Jones; 5 Francis Meli; 20 Lee Gaskell; 7 Jonny Lomax; 8 Josh Perry; 9 James Roby; 14 Anthony Laffranchi; 11 Tony Puletua; 4 Iosia Soliola; 12 Jon Wilkin. Subs (all used): 10 Louie McCarthy-Scarsbrook; 13 Chris Flannery; 15 Mark Flanagan; 16 Paul Clough.
Tries: Lomax (5), Wellens (9, 16), Jones (21, 25), Laffranchi (72), Puletua (80); **Goals:** Makinson 3/7.
ROVERS: 1 Shannon McDonnell; 2 Craig Hall; 4 Jake Webster; 18 Graeme Horne; 21 Sam Latus; 6 Blake Green; 7 Michael Dobson; 8 Joel Clinton; 9 Josh Hodgson; 17 Ryan O'Hara; 11 Constantine Mika; 12 Ben Galea (C); 16 Jason Netherton. Subs (all used): 10 Scott Taylor; 14 Lincoln Withers; 19 Scott Murrell; 23 Mickey Paea.
Tries: Taylor (30, 50), Latus (38, 39), J Hodgson (61);
Goals: Dobson 4/5.
Rugby Leaguer & League Express Men of the Match: *Saints:* Tony Puletua; *Rovers:* Lincoln Withers.
Penalty count: 6-7; **Half-time:** 26-16;
Referee: Thierry Alibert; **Attendance:** 12,435.

WIGAN WARRIORS 22 BRADFORD BULLS 30

WARRIORS: 35 Jack Murphy (D); 2 Josh Charnley; 3 Darrell Goulding; 4 George Carmont; 24 Anthony Gelling; 13 Sean O'Loughlin (C); 6 Brett Finch; 21 Epalahame Lauaki; 9 Michael McIlorum; 10 Lee Mossop; 36 Rhodri Lloyd; 12 Gareth Hock; 16 Liam Farrell. Subs (all used): 28 Logan Tomkins; 26 Jack Hughes; 33 Dominic Crosby; 23 Ben Flower.
Tries: Gelling (3), Murphy (16), Flower (37), Crosby (51); **Goals:** Charnley 3/4.
Dismissal: McIlorum (55) - punching Elima.
BULLS: 1 Brett Kearney; 18 Shaun Ainscough; 29 Michael Platt; 3 Keith Lulia; 33 Karl Pryce; 22 Jarrod Sammut; 7 Luke Gale; 11 Olivier Elima; 9 Heath L'Estrange (C); 16 Manase Manuokafoa; 26 John Bateman; 12 Elliott Whitehead; 13 Jamie Langley. Subs (all used): 21 Tom Burgess; 4 Chev Walker; 25 Adam O'Brien; 19 Tom Olbison.
Tries: Pryce (23, 73), Kearney (31), Lulia (40), Whitehead (61); **Goals:** Gale 5/5.
Sin bin: Pryce (9) - holding down.
Rugby Leaguer & League Express Men of the Match: *Warriors:* Liam Farrell; *Bulls:* Luke Gale.
Penalty count: 13-7; **Half-time:** 16-18;
Referee: Tim Roby; **Attendance:** 19,628.

Saturday 30th June 2012

CATALAN DRAGONS 34
WAKEFIELD TRINITY WILDCATS 10

DRAGONS: 1 Clint Greenshields; 2 Damien Blanch; 25 Vincent Duport; 29 Mathias Pala; 18 Daryl Millard; 3 Leon Pryce; 7 Scott Dureau; 8 David Ferriol; 9 Ian Henderson; 10 Remi Casty (C); 11 Steve Menzies; 23 Lopini Paea; 24 Jason Baitieri. Subs (all used): 13 Gregory Mounis; 14 Sebastien Raguin; 16 Eloi Pelissier; 22 Jamal Fakir.
Tries: Blanch (4, 65, 74), Menzies (18, 30), Greenshields (41); **Goals:** Dureau 5/6.

WILDCATS: 1 Richard Mathers; 2 Peter Fox; 34 Paul Sykes; 4 Vince Mellars; 5 Ben Cockayne; 6 Isaac John; 20 Tim Smith; 10 Andy Raleigh; 14 Paul Aiton; 15 Kyle Amor; 17 Danny Kirmond (C); 11 Ali Lauitiiti; 13 Danny Washbrook. Subs (all used): 7 Kyle Wood; 8 Oliver Wilkes; 16 Paul Johnson; 22 Kyle Trout.
Tries: Lauitiiti (24), Trout (45); **Goals:** Sykes 1/2.
Rugby Leaguer & League Express Men of the Match: *Dragons:* Clint Greenshields; *Wildcats:* Danny Kirmond.
Penalty count: 11-5; **Half-time:** 18-6;
Referee: Ben Thaler; **Attendance:** 8,842.

LONDON BRONCOS 12 LEEDS RHINOS 58

BRONCOS: 19 Dan Sarginson; 5 Michael Robertson; 31 Will Lovell; 3 Jamie O'Callaghan; 21 Kieran Dixon; 6 Michael Witt; 7 Craig Gower (C); 8 Antonio Kaufusi; 14 Julien Rinaldi; 30 Scott Wheeldon; 12 Chris Bailey; 4 David Howell; 13 Tony Clubb. Subs (all used): 10 Mark Bryant; 9 Chad Randall; 28 Michael Channing; 18 Olsi Krasniqi.
Tries: Bailey (23), Dixon (45); **Goals:** Witt 2/2.
RHINOS: 4 Zak Hardaker; 2 Ben Jones-Bishop; 3 Kallum Watkins; 12 Carl Ablett; 5 Ryan Hall; 13 Kevin Sinfield (C); 6 Danny McGuire; 8 Kylie Leuluai; 7 Rob Burrow; 20 Darrell Griffin; 11 Jamie Jones-Buchanan; 19 Weller Hauraki; 25 Stevie Ward. Subs (all used): 31 Shaun Lunt; 17 Ian Kirke; 16 Ryan Bailey; 18 Chris Clarkson.
Tries: Lunt (26, 31), McGuire (36, 39, 62, 69), Ablett (65), Hardaker (72), Burrow (74), Leuluai (78);
Goals: Sinfield 9/10.
Rugby Leaguer & League Express Men of the Match: *Broncos:* Craig Gower; *Rhinos:* Danny McGuire.
Penalty count: 4-7; **Half-time:** 6-24;
Referee: Robert Hicks; **Attendance:** 3,628.

Sunday 1st July 2012

HULL FC 28 HUDDERSFIELD GIANTS 24

HULL: 6 Richard Horne; 23 Ben Crooks; 19 Jordan Turner; 4 Kirk Yeaman; 5 Tom Briscoe; 15 Richard Whiting; 7 Brett Seymour; 17 Sam Moa; 14 Aaron Heremaia; 10 Andy Lynch (C); 11 Willie Manu; 12 Danny Tickle; 13 Joe Westerman. Subs (all used): 28 Danny Nicklas; 34 Jay Pitts; 37 Liam Watts (D); 22 Martin Aspinwall.
Tries: Crooks (3), Briscoe (33), Heremaia (67), Yeaman (71, 77); **Goals:** Tickle 4/5.
GIANTS: 29 Greg Eden; 21 Aaron Murphy; 3 Leroy Cudjoe; 4 Lee Gilmour; 20 Luke George; 7 Danny Brough; 1 Scott Grix; 8 Eorl Crabtree; 35 Scott Moore; 10 Keith Mason; 15 Larne Patrick; 2 Michael Lawrence; 6 Kevin Brown (C). Subs (all used): 19 Tommy Lee; 18 Jason Chan; 11 Luke O'Donnell; 13 David Faiumu.
Tries: Cudjoe (21), Faiumu (40), Murphy (55), Crabtree (75); **Goals:** Brough 4/4.
Rugby Leaguer & League Express Men of the Match: *Hull:* Richard Horne; *Giants:* Greg Eden.
Penalty count: 8-6; **Half-time:** 10-12;
Referee: James Child; **Attendance:** 11,142.

Monday 2nd July 2012

WIDNES VIKINGS 40 CASTLEFORD TIGERS 10

VIKINGS: 19 Cameron Phelps; 4 Willie Isa; 20 Stefan Marsh; 3 Chris Dean; 5 Patrick Ah Van; 34 Joe Mellor; 8 Ben Cross; 13 Jon Clarke (C); 17 Steve Pickersgill; 11 Frank Winterstein; 21 Dave Allen; 12 Hep Cahill. Subs (all used): 36 Eamon O'Carroll (D); 35 Paul McShane; 10 Ben Davies; 18 Sione Kite.
Tries: Marsh (2), Winterstein (23), Davies (39), McShane (45), Mellor (50), O'Carroll (66), Ah Van (72); **Goals:** Ah Van 5/6, Hanbury 1/1.
TIGERS: 2 Nick Youngquest; 32 Rhys Williams; 5 Josh Griffin; 25 Jordan Thompson; 26 James Clare; 11 Brett Ferres; 23 Ryan McGoldrick; 12 Jonathan Walker; 15 Adam Milner; 10 Craig Huby; 20 Grant Millington; 21 Oliver Holmes; 13 Steve Snitch. Subs (all used): 7 Danny Orr (C); 8 Jake Emmitt; 14 Stuart Jones; 22 Nathan Massey.
Tries: Youngquest (14), Jones (56); **Goals:** Huby 1/2.
Rugby Leaguer & League Express Men of the Match: *Vikings:* Paul McShane; *Tigers:* Adam Milner.
Penalty count: 8-6; **Half-time:** 18-4;
Referee: Steve Ganson; **Attendance:** 4,501.

ROUND 20

Friday 6th July 2012

LEEDS RHINOS 21 HULL FC 6

RHINOS: 4 Zak Hardaker; 2 Ben Jones-Bishop; 3 Kallum Watkins; 12 Carl Ablett; 5 Ryan Hall; 13 Kevin Sinfield (C); 6 Danny McGuire; 10 Jamie Peacock; 31 Shaun Lunt; 20 Darrell Griffin; 25 Stevie Ward; 15 Brett Delaney; 16 Ryan Bailey. Subs (all used): 17 Ian Kirke; 18 Chris Clarkson; 21 Richard Moore; 7 Rob Burrow.
Tries: Ablett (12), Delaney (20), Hall (44);
Goals: Sinfield 4/4; **Field goal:** Sinfield (76).
HULL: 38 Ryan McGoldrick (D); 23 Ben Crooks; 19 Jordan Turner; 4 Kirk Yeaman; 5 Tom Briscoe; 6 Richard Horne; 7 Brett Seymour; 10 Andy Lynch (C); 14 Aaron Heremaia; 37 Liam Watts; 13 Joe Westerman; 15 Richard Whiting; 34 Jay Pitts. Subs (all used): 22 Martin Aspinwall; 11 Willie Manu; 28 Danny Nicklas; 35 Lee Radford.
Try: Horne (52); **Goals:** Westerman 1/1.
Rugby Leaguer & League Express Men of the Match: *Rhinos:* Kevin Sinfield; *Hull:* Richard Whiting.
Penalty count: 13-5; **Half-time:** 14-0;
Referee: Tim Roby; **Attendance:** 13,250.

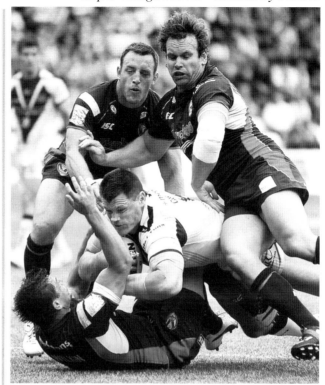

Widnes' Ben Cross brought to ground by St Helens' James Roby, Josh Perry and Jon Wilkin

Sunday 8th July 2012

BRADFORD BULLS 44 LONDON BRONCOS 12

BULLS: 1 Brett Kearney; 18 Shaun Ainscough; 29 Michael Platt; 3 Keith Lulia; 33 Karl Pryce; 6 Ben Jeffries; 7 Luke Gale; 16 Manase Manuokafoa; 9 Heath L'Estrange (C); 15 Bryn Hargreaves; 26 John Bateman; 12 Elliott Whitehead; 13 Jamie Langley. Subs (all used): 21 Tom Burgess; 25 Adam O'Brien; 4 Chev Walker; 19 Tom Olbison.
Tries: Manuokafoa (13), Kearney (16, 42, 58, 76), Gale (19), Whitehead (27), Platt (32); **Goals:** Gale 6/8.
BRONCOS: 19 Dan Sarginson; 5 Michael Robertson; 31 Will Lovell; 3 Jamie O'Callaghan; 21 Kieran Dixon; 6 Michael Witt; 1 Luke Dorn; 10 Mark Bryant; 14 Julien Rinaldi; 30 Scott Wheeldon; 12 Chris Bailey; 4 David Howell; 13 Tony Clubb. Subs (all used): 9 Chad Randall (C); 16 Chris Melling; 18 Olsi Krasniqi; 22 Ben Bolger.
Tries: Dixon (21, 50), Lovell (79); **Goals:** Witt 0/3.
Rugby Leaguer & League Express Men of the Match: *Bulls:* Brett Kearney; *Broncos:* Mark Bryant.
Penalty count: 8-5; **Half-time:** 26-4;
Referee: Richard Silverwood; **Attendance:** 10,132.

HULL KINGSTON ROVERS 22 SALFORD CITY REDS 24

ROVERS: 1 Shannon McDonnell; 2 Craig Hall; 29 Liam Salter; 4 Jake Webster; 21 Sam Latus; 6 Blake Green; 7 Michael Dobson (C); 23 Mickey Paea; 9 Josh Hodgson; 17 Ryan O'Hara; 11 Constantine Mika; 18 Graeme Horne; 10 Scott Murrell. Subs (all used): 14 Lincoln Withers; 10 Scott Taylor; 16 Jason Netherton; 35 James Laithwaite (D).
Tries: Mika (24), B Green (26), Hall (42), Dobson (67); **Goals:** Dobson 3/4.
CITY REDS: 1 Luke Patten; 2 Jodie Broughton; 18 Ashley Gibson; 4 Joel Moon; 5 Danny Williams; 6 Daniel Holdsworth; 22 Marc Sneyd; 8 Lee Jewitt; 24 Stuart Howarth; 10 Ryan Boyle; 11 Matty Ashurst; 27 Vinnie Anderson; 13 Stephen Wild (C). Subs (all used): 14 Chris Nero; 15 Adam Sidlow; 21 Jordan James; 20 Ben Gledhill.
Tries: Broughton (2), Williams (14, 49), Gledhill (30), Moon (53); **Goals:** Holdsworth 2/5.
Rugby Leaguer & League Express Men of the Match: *Rovers:* Michael Dobson; *City Reds:* Daniel Holdsworth.
Penalty count: 7-9; **Half-time:** 12-16;
Referee: Steve Ganson; **Attendance:** 7,213.

WIDNES VIKINGS 23 ST HELENS 24

VIKINGS: 19 Cameron Phelps; 4 Willie Isa; 20 Stefan Marsh; 3 Chris Dean; 5 Patrick Ah Van; 34 Joe Mellor; 7 Rhys Hanbury; 8 Ben Cross; 13 Jon Clarke (C); 17 Steve Pickersgill; 11 Frank Winterstein; 21 Dave Allen; 12 Hep Cahill. Subs (all used): 10 Ben Davies; 18 Sione Kite; 35 Paul McShane; 36 Eamon O'Carroll.
Tries: Ah Van (35, 55, 64), Dean (52), Phelps (77);
Goals: Hanbury 1/4, Marsh 0/1; **Field goal:** Hanbury (73).
SAINTS: 1 Paul Wellens (C); 21 Tom Makinson; 3 Michael Shenton; 26 Josh Jones; 5 Francis Meli; 20 Lee Gaskell; 6 Lance Hohaia; 8 Josh Perry; 9 James Roby; 14 Anthony Laffranchi; 13 Chris Flannery; 11 Tony Puletua; 12 Jon Wilkin. Subs (all used): 4 Iosia Soliola; 10 Louie McCarthy-Scarsbrook; 16 Paul Clough; 19 Andrew Dixon.
Tries: Soliola (32), Wilkin (44), Shenton (60), Jones (79); **Goals:** Gaskell 4/4.
Rugby Leaguer & League Express Men of the Match: *Vikings:* Patrick Ah Van; *Saints:* Jon Wilkin.
Penalty count: 10-8; **Half-time:** 6-6;
Referee: Robert Hicks; **Attendance:** 7,023.

CASTLEFORD TIGERS 52 HUDDERSFIELD GIANTS 6

TIGERS: 1 Richard Owen; 2 Nick Youngquest; 25 Jordan Thompson; 5 Josh Griffin; 26 James Clare; 7 Danny Orr (C); 33 Jamie Ellis (D); 19 Paul Jackson; 15 Adam Milner; 10 Craig Huby; 20 Grant Millington; 13 Steve Snitch; 8 Jake Emmitt. Subs (all used): 14 Stuart Jones; 16 Ryan Hudson; 17 Lee Mitchell; 22 Nathan Massey.
Tries: Clare (4), Thompson (19), Youngquest (27), Owen (32, 67), Griffin (62), Milner (72), Ellis (76);
Goals: Ellis 10/11.
GIANTS: 29 Greg Eden; 21 Aaron Murphy; 3 Leroy Cudjoe; 2 Michael Lawrence; 20 Luke George; 7 Danny Brough; 9 Luke Robinson; 10 Keith Mason; 35 Scott Moore; 4 Lee Gilmour; 11 Luke O'Donnell; 15 Larne Patrick; 6 Kevin Brown (C). Subs (all used): 12 David Fa'alogo; 19 Tommy Lee; 13 David Faiumu; 18 Jason Chan.
Try: Cudjoe (11); **Goals:** Brough 1/1.
Rugby Leaguer & League Express Men of the Match: *Tigers:* Richard Owen; *Giants:* Luke O'Donnell.
Penalty count: 13-6; **Half-time:** 22-6;
Referee: Ben Thaler; **Attendance:** 5,012.

WAKEFIELD TRINITY WILDCATS 10 WIGAN WARRIORS 52

WILDCATS: 1 Richard Mathers; 2 Peter Fox; 17 Danny Kirmond (C); 35 Lee Smith (D); 5 Ben Cockayne; 34 Paul Sykes; 20 Tim Smith; 15 Kyle Amor; 14 Paul Aiton; 10 Andy Raleigh; 11 Ali Lauitiiti; 33 Lucas Walshaw; 13 Danny Washbrook. Subs (all used): 7 Kyle Wood; 8 Oliver Wilkes; 16 Paul Johnson; 22 Kyle Trout.
Tries: Fox (4), Cockayne (72); **Goals:** Sykes 1/2.

WARRIORS: 1 Sam Tomkins; 37 Iain Thornley (D); 3 Darrell Goulding; 4 George Carmont; 24 Anthony Gelling; 13 Sean O'Loughlin (C); 6 Brett Finch; 23 Ben Flower; 28 Logan Tomkins; 10 Lee Mossop; 11 Harrison Hansen; 12 Gareth Hock; 17 Chris Tuson. Subs (all used): 16 Liam Farrell; 21 Epalahame Lauaki; 33 Dominic Crosby; 38 Matty Smith (D).
Tries: S Tomkins (17, 34, 69), Hock (28), Carmont (37, 60, 76), Hansen (47), Thornley (52, 58);
Goals: S Tomkins 6/10.
Rugby Leaguer & League Express Men of the Match:
Wildcats: Kyle Amor; *Warriors:* Brett Finch.
Penalty count: 10-6; **Half-time:** 4-22;
Referee: Thierry Alibert; **Attendance:** 9,107.

Monday 9th July 2012

WARRINGTON WOLVES 15 CATALAN DRAGONS 6

WOLVES: 1 Brett Hodgson; 5 Joel Monaghan; 3 Chris Bridge; 4 Ryan Atkins; 2 Chris Riley; 19 Stefan Ratchford; 24 Gareth O'Brien; 10 Garreth Carvell; 14 Mick Higham; 20 Chris Hill; 11 Trent Waterhouse; 12 Ben Westwood; 13 Ben Harrison. Subs (all used): 8 Adrian Morley (C); 9 Michael Monaghan; 17 Michael Cooper; 21 Tyrone McCarthy.
Tries: Westwood (14), Atkins (51); **Goals:** Hodgson 2/3, O'Brien 1/1; **Field goal:** M Monaghan (67).
DRAGONS: 1 Clint Greenshields; 2 Damien Blanch; 25 Vincent Duport; 18 Daryl Millard; 28 Damien Cardace; 3 Leon Pryce; 7 Scott Dureau; 8 David Ferriol; 9 Ian Henderson; 10 Remi Casty (C); 11 Steve Menzies; 23 Lopini Paea; 24 Jason Baitieri. Subs (all used): 13 Gregory Mounis; 14 Sebastien Raguin; 16 Eloi Pelissier; 22 Jamal Fakir.
Try: Baitieri (58); **Goals:** Dureau 1/1.
On report:
Ferriol (63) - alleged high tackle on M Monaghan.
Rugby Leaguer & League Express Men of the Match:
Wolves: Chris Hill; *Dragons:* Leon Pryce.
Penalty count: 7-6; **Half-time:** 6-0;
Referee: James Child; **Attendance:** 10,570.

ROUND 2

Saturday 14th July 2012

CATALAN DRAGONS 44 HULL FC 14

DRAGONS: 1 Clint Greenshields; 2 Damien Blanch; 25 Vincent Duport; 29 Mathias Pala; 18 Daryl Millard; 3 Leon Pryce; 7 Scott Dureau; 23 Lopini Paea; 26 Ben Fisher; 10 Remi Casty (C); 11 Steve Menzies; 14 Sebastien Raguin; 24 Jason Baitieri. Subs (all used): 13 Gregory Mounis; 16 Eloi Pelissier; 21 Julian Bousquet (D); 22 Jamal Fakir.
Tries: Pryce (13), Dureau (22, 39), Millard (31, 42), Blanch (48), Greenshields (68, 74); **Goals:** Dureau 6/8.
HULL: 38 Ryan McGoldrick; 23 Ben Crooks; 19 Jordan Turner; 4 Kirk Yeaman; 5 Tom Briscoe; 6 Richard Horne; 7 Brett Seymour; 22 Martin Aspinwall; 14 Aaron Heremaia; 10 Andy Lynch (C); 11 Willie Manu; 13 Joe Westerman; 15 Richard Whiting. Subs (all used): 27 Chris Green; 31 James Cunningham (D); 34 Jay Pitts; 37 Liam Watts.
Tries: Crooks (8), Briscoe (35, 63);
Goals: Westerman 1/3.
Rugby Leaguer & League Express Men of the Match:
Dragons: Clint Greenshields; *Hull:* Kirk Yeaman.
Penalty count: 10-6; **Half-time:** 22-8;
Referee: Thierry Alibert; **Attendance:** 7,388.

ROUND 21

Friday 20th July 2012

CATALAN DRAGONS 15 ST HELENS 20

DRAGONS: 5 Cyril Stacul; 2 Damien Blanch; 25 Vincent Duport; 18 Daryl Millard; 28 Damien Cardace; 3 Leon Pryce; 7 Scott Dureau; 23 Lopini Paea; 9 Ian Henderson; 10 Remi Casty (C); 11 Steve Menzies; 14 Sebastien Raguin; 24 Jason Baitieri. Subs (all used): 13 Gregory Mounis; 16 Eloi Pelissier; 21 Julian Bousquet; 22 Jamal Fakir.
Tries: Duport (5), Raguin (38); **Goals:** Dureau 3/3;
Field goal: Dureau (40).
SAINTS: 1 Paul Wellens (C); 21 Tom Makinson; 3 Michael Shenton; 26 Josh Jones; 5 Francis Meli; 6 Lance Hohaia; 7 Jonny Lomax; 8 Josh Perry; 9 James Roby; 14 Anthony Laffranchi; 11 Tony Puletua; 13 Chris Flannery; 12 Jon Wilkin. Subs (all used): 4 Iosia Soliola; 10 Louie McCarthy-Scarsbrook; 16 Paul Clough; 19 Andrew Dixon.
Tries: Hohaia (14), Meli (30), Flannery (48), Makinson (54); **Goals:** Makinson 2/4.
Dismissal: Puletua (74) - high tackle on Mounis.
Rugby Leaguer & League Express Men of the Match:
Dragons: Remi Casty; *Saints:* Lance Hohaia.
Penalty count: 10-5; **Half-time:** 15-10;
Referee: Ben Thaler; **Attendance:** 10,387.

LEEDS RHINOS 34 BRADFORD BULLS 16

RHINOS: 4 Zak Hardaker; 2 Ben Jones-Bishop; 3 Kallum Watkins; 15 Brett Delaney; 5 Ryan Hall; 13 Kevin Sinfield (C); 6 Danny McGuire; 8 Kylie Leuluai; 7 Rob Burrow; 10 Jamie Peacock; 11 Jamie Jones-Buchanan; 25 Stevie Ward; 16 Ryan Bailey. Subs (all used): 20 Darrell Griffin; 31 Shaun Lunt; 17 Ian Kirke; 21 Richard Moore.
Tries: Watkins (21, 46), Lunt (48), Hardaker (64), McGuire (71), Sinfield (79);
Goals: Sinfield 4/5, Hardaker 1/1.
Sin bin: Sinfield (57) - professional foul.

BULLS: 1 Brett Kearney; 18 Shaun Ainscough; 29 Michael Platt; 3 Keith Lulia; 33 Karl Pryce; 22 Jarrod Sammut; 7 Luke Gale; 16 Manase Manuokafoa; 9 Heath L'Estrange (C); 15 Bryn Hargreaves; 11 Olivier Elima; 12 Elliott Whitehead; 13 Jamie Langley. Subs (all used): 4 Chev Walker; 19 Tom Olbison; 21 Tom Burgess; 25 Adam O'Brien.
Tries: Whitehead (4), Elima (69), Pryce (76);
Goals: Gale 2/3.
Rugby Leaguer & League Express Men of the Match:
Rhinos: Ben Jones-Bishop; *Bulls:* Bryn Hargreaves.
Penalty count: 4-9; **Half-time:** 6-6;
Referee: Steve Ganson; **Attendance:** 18,520.

SALFORD CITY REDS 8 WIDNES VIKINGS 46

CITY REDS: 1 Luke Patten; 2 Jodie Broughton; 18 Ashley Gibson; 3 Sean Gleeson; 5 Danny Williams; 6 Daniel Holdsworth; 22 Marc Sneyd; 8 Lee Jewitt; 24 Stuart Howarth; 10 Ryan Boyle; 11 Matty Ashurst; 27 Vinnie Anderson; 13 Stephen Wild (C). Subs (all used): 21 Jordan James; 17 Iafeta Palea'aesina; 15 Adam Sidlow; 14 Chris Nero.
Tries: Gibson (58), Williams (65); **Goals:** Holdsworth 0/2.
VIKINGS: 19 Cameron Phelps; 4 Willie Isa; 3 Chris Dean; 20 Stefan Marsh; 5 Patrick Ah Van; 34 Joe Mellor; 7 Rhys Hanbury; 8 Ben Cross (C); 35 Paul McShane; 17 Steve Pickersgill; 11 Frank Winterstein; 21 Dave Allen; 12 Hep Cahill. Subs (all used): 10 Ben Davies; 18 Sione Kite; 25 Danny Craven; 36 Eamon O'Carroll.
Tries: Phelps (24, 51), Ah Van (28, 36), Hanbury (40, 54), McShane (48), Craven (73); **Goals:** Hanbury 7/8.
Rugby Leaguer & League Express Men of the Match:
City Reds: Luke Patten; *Vikings:* Rhys Hanbury.
Penalty count: 8-11; **Half-time:** 0-24;
Referee: James Child; **Attendance:** 5,196.

Saturday 21st July 2012

LONDON BRONCOS 6 WIGAN WARRIORS 44

BRONCOS: 19 Dan Sarginson; 21 Kieran Dixon; 3 Jamie O'Callaghan; 4 David Howell; 5 Michael Robertson; 6 Michael Witt; 7 Craig Gower (C); 10 Mark Bryant; 9 Chad Randall; 30 Scott Wheeldon; 12 Chris Bailey; 16 Chris Melling; 13 Tony Clubb. Subs (all used): 31 Will Lovell; 14 Julien Rinaldi; 8 Antonio Kaufusi; 18 Olsi Krasniqi.
Try: Robertson (66); **Goals:** Witt 1/1.
WARRIORS: 1 Sam Tomkins; 2 Josh Charnley; 3 Darrell Goulding; 4 George Carmont; 37 Iain Thornley; 6 Brett Finch; 38 Matty Smith; 23 Ben Flower; 9 Michael McIlorum; 21 Epalahame Lauaki; 11 Harrison Hansen; 12 Gareth Hock; 13 Sean O'Loughlin (C). Subs (all used): 14 Jeff Lima; 10 Lee Mossop; 16 Liam Farrell; 17 Chris Tuson.
Tries: S Tomkins (2, 39, 55, 71), Charnley (6), Thornley (43), Smith (50), Finch (61); **Goals:** S Tomkins 6/8.
Rugby Leaguer & League Express Men of the Match:
Broncos: Michael Robertson; *Warriors:* Sam Tomkins.
Penalty count: 5-7; **Half-time:** 0-16;
Referee: Thierry Alibert; **Attendance:** 4,309.

Sunday 22nd July 2012

HUDDERSFIELD GIANTS 14
WAKEFIELD TRINITY WILDCATS 35

GIANTS: 1 Scott Grix; 20 Luke George; 3 Leroy Cudjoe; 4 Lee Gilmour; 29 Greg Eden; 7 Danny Brough; 9 Luke Robinson (C); 8 Eorl Crabtree; 35 Scott Moore; 10 Keith Mason; 16 Dale Ferguson; 18 Jason Chan; 23 Jacob Fairbank. Subs (all used): 12 David Fa'alogo; 15 Larne Patrick; 19 Tommy Lee; 26 Jamie Cording.
Tries: George (17, 39), Crabtree (46); **Goals:** Brough 1/3.
WILDCATS: 1 Richard Mathers; 2 Peter Fox; 3 Dean Collis; 35 Lee Smith; 5 Ben Cockayne; 34 Paul Sykes; 20 Tim Smith; 15 Kyle Amor; 9 Andy Ellis; 10 Andy Raleigh; 11 Ali Lauitiiti; 17 Danny Kirmond (C); 13 Danny Washbrook. Subs (all used): 7 Kyle Wood; 8 Oliver Wilkes; 16 Paul Johnson; 22 Kyle Trout.
Tries: Cockayne (25), Collis (52), L Smith (62), Mathers (67), T Smith (71), Kirmond (78);
Goals: Sykes 5/6; **Field goal:** Sykes (74).
Rugby Leaguer & League Express Men of the Match:
Giants: Luke George; *Wildcats:* Tim Smith.
Penalty count: 7-5; **Half-time:** 8-6;
Referee: Tim Roby; **Attendance:** 6,579.

CASTLEFORD TIGERS 26 WARRINGTON WOLVES 40

TIGERS: 1 Richard Owen; 32 Rhys Williams; 25 Jordan Thompson; 5 Josh Griffin; 2 Nick Youngquest; 6 Rangi Chase; 33 Jamie Ellis; 19 Paul Jackson; 15 Adam Milner; 10 Craig Huby; 13 Steve Snitch; 20 Grant Millington; 8 Jake Emmitt. Subs (all used): 7 Danny Orr (C); 14 Stuart Jones; 17 Lee Mitchell; 22 Nathan Massey.
Tries: Youngquest (50, 61), Williams (57), Owen (64), Mitchell (69); **Goals:** Ellis 1/2, Orr 2/3.
WOLVES: 1 Brett Hodgson; 5 Joel Monaghan; 18 Matty Blythe; 4 Ryan Atkins; 2 Chris Riley; 19 Stefan Ratchford; 7 Richard Myler; 20 Chris Hill; 14 Mick Higham; 8 Adrian Morley (C); 21 Tyrone McCarthy; 12 Ben Westwood; 17 Michael Cooper. Subs (all used): 16 Paul Wood; 26 David Solomona; 10 Garreth Carvell; 9 Michael Monaghan.
Tries: Westwood (3, 35), J Monaghan (9), Atkins (27), Riley (39), Solomona (50), Ratchford (78);
Goals: Hodgson 6/7.
Rugby Leaguer & League Express Men of the Match:
Tigers: Rangi Chase; *Wolves:* Richard Myler.
Penalty count: 5-3; **Half-time:** 0-30;
Referee: Robert Hicks; **Attendance:** 6,167.

Monday 23rd July 2012

HULL KINGSTON ROVERS 18 HULL FC 32

ROVERS: 1 Shannon McDonnell; 21 Sam Latus; 4 Jake Webster; 18 Graeme Horne; 5 David Hodgson; 6 Blake Green; 7 Michael Dobson; 23 Mickey Paea; 14 Lincoln Withers; 10 Scott Taylor; 11 Constantine Mika; 12 Ben Galea (C); 9 Josh Hodgson. Subs (all used): 17 Ryan O'Hara; 19 Scott Murrell; 8 Joel Clinton; 35 James Laithwaite.
Tries: Laithwaite (48), Paea (57), J Hodgson (61);
Goals: Dobson 3/4.
On report: Mika (24) - alleged high tackle on Turner.
HULL: 6 Richard Horne; 40 Jamie Foster (D); 19 Jordan Turner; 4 Kirk Yeaman; 5 Tom Briscoe; 38 Ryan McGoldrick; 14 Aaron Heremaia; 37 Liam Watts; 9 Danny Houghton; 10 Andy Lynch (C); 11 Willie Manu; 13 Joe Westerman; 15 Richard Whiting. Subs (all used): 27 Chris Green; 34 Jay Pitts; 22 Martin Aspinwall; 39 Tom Lineham (D).
Tries: McGoldrick (7), Turner (16), Yeaman (52), Whiting (66), Briscoe (75); **Goals:** Foster 6/6.
Rugby Leaguer & League Express Men of the Match:
Rovers: Michael Dobson; *Hull:* Danny Houghton.
Penalty count: 7-5; **Half-time:** 2-14;
Referee: Richard Silverwood; **Attendance:** 9,086.

ROUND 22

Friday 27th July 2012

WIGAN WARRIORS 40 CASTLEFORD TIGERS 16

WARRIORS: 1 Sam Tomkins; 2 Josh Charnley; 3 Darrell Goulding; 4 George Carmont; 37 Iain Thornley; 6 Brett Finch (C); 38 Matty Smith; 21 Epalahame Lauaki; 9 Michael McIlorum; 10 Lee Mossop; 11 Harrison Hansen; 12 Gareth Hock; 23 Ben Flower. Subs (all used): 14 Jeff Lima; 16 Liam Farrell; 17 Chris Tuson; 33 Dominic Crosby.
Tries: Lauaki (3, 8), Thornley (11), Farrell (40), Carmont (52), S Tomkins (65, 80), Charnley (74);
Goals: S Tomkins 4/8.
TIGERS: 1 Richard Owen; 32 Rhys Williams; 25 Jordan Thompson; 14 Stuart Jones; 2 Nick Youngquest; 21 Oliver Holmes; 7 Danny Orr (C); 19 Paul Jackson; 15 Adam Milner; 10 Craig Huby; 13 Steve Snitch; 20 Grant Millington; 8 Jake Emmitt. Subs (all used): 16 Ryan Hudson; 24 Stephen Nash; 17 Lee Mitchell; 22 Nathan Massey.
Tries: Williams (37), Holmes (47), Jones (77);
Goals: Youngquest 2/2, Huby 0/1.
Rugby Leaguer & League Express Men of the Match:
Warriors: Sam Tomkins; *Tigers:* Rhys Williams.
Penalty count: 4-4; **Half-time:** 20-6;
Referee: George Stokes; **Attendance:** 13,975.

Saturday 28th July 2012

CATALAN DRAGONS 19 LONDON BRONCOS 12

DRAGONS: 5 Cyril Stacul; 2 Damien Blanch; 25 Vincent Duport; 18 Daryl Millard; 28 Damien Cardace; 3 Leon Pryce; 7 Scott Dureau; 8 David Ferriol; 26 Ben Fisher; 23 Lopini Paea; 10 Remi Casty (C); 14 Sebastien Raguin; 24 Jason Baitieri. Subs (all used): 13 Gregory Mounis; 15 Jean-Philippe Baile; 16 Eloi Pelissier; 17 Cyrille Gossard.
Tries: Baitieri (8), Fisher (31), Millard (59);
Goals: Dureau 3/3; **Field goal:** Dureau (71).
BRONCOS: 5 Michael Robertson; 23 Omari Caro; 4 David Howell; 3 Jamie O'Callaghan; 21 Kieran Dixon; 1 Luke Dorn; 7 Craig Gower (C); 8 Antonio Kaufusi; 9 Chad Randall; 30 Scott Wheeldon; 16 Chris Melling; 12 Chris Bailey; 13 Tony Clubb. Subs (all used): 10 Mark Bryant; 14 Julien Rinaldi; 17 Jason Golden; 18 Olsi Krasniqi.
Tries: Clubb (1), Wheeldon (15); **Goals:** Gower 2/2.
Rugby Leaguer & League Express Men of the Match:
Dragons: Lopini Paea; *Broncos:* Craig Gower.
Penalty count: 11-5; **Half-time:** 12-12;
Referee: Tim Roby; **Attendance:** 7,673.

Sunday 29th July 2012

HULL FC 34 SALFORD CITY REDS 26

HULL: 5 Tom Briscoe; 40 Jamie Foster; 19 Jordan Turner; 4 Kirk Yeaman; 39 Tom Lineham; 38 Ryan McGoldrick; 14 Aaron Heremaia; 37 Liam Watts; 9 Danny Houghton; 8 Mark O'Meley; 11 Willie Manu; 13 Joe Westerman; 22 Martin Aspinwall. Subs (all used): 10 Andy Lynch (C); 34 Jay Pitts; 27 Chris Green; 28 Danny Nicklas.
Tries: Lineham (5, 40), Yeaman (8), Westerman (27), Turner (78); **Goals:** Foster 7/7.
Sin bin: O'Meley (66) - punching.
CITY REDS: 1 Luke Patten; 5 Danny Williams; 3 Sean Gleeson; 18 Ashley Gibson; 2 Jodie Broughton; 6 Daniel Holdsworth; 22 Marc Sneyd; 8 Lee Jewitt; 24 Stuart Howarth; 10 Ryan Boyle; 11 Matty Ashurst; 16 Luke Adamson; 13 Stephen Wild (C). Subs (all used): 14 Chris Nero; 15 Adam Sidlow; 20 Ben Gledhill; 21 Jordan James.
Tries: Gibson (19, 61), Broughton (22), Gleeson (55, 70); **Goals:** Holdsworth 3/5.
Rugby Leaguer & League Express Men of the Match:
Hull: Tom Briscoe; *City Reds:* Sean Gleeson.
Penalty count: 12-7; **Half-time:** 24-12;
Referee: Robert Hicks; **Attendance:** 10,766.

WARRINGTON WOLVES 50 BRADFORD BULLS 22

WOLVES: 19 Stefan Ratchford; 2 Chris Riley; 23 Rhys Evans; 15 Simon Grix; 5 Joel Monaghan; 6 Lee Briers; 7 Richard Myler; 10 Garreth Carvell; 9 Michael Monaghan;

8 Adrian Morley (C); 12 Ben Westwood; 21 Tyrone McCarthy; 13 Ben Harrison. Subs (all used): 17 Michael Cooper; 16 Paul Wood; 26 David Solomona; 24 Gareth O'Brien.
Tries: J Monaghan (1), Myler (12), Riley (15), Ratchford (17, 34, 63, 68), Grix (21), Solomona (53);
Goals: Briers 5/7, O'Brien 2/2.
BULLS: 22 Jarrod Sammut; 18 Shaun Ainscough; 3 Keith Lulia; 29 Michael Platt; 33 Karl Pryce; 23 Danny Addy; 7 Luke Gale; 16 Manase Manuokafoa; 9 Heath L'Estrange (C); 15 Bryn Hargreaves; 19 Tom Olbison; 12 Elliott Whitehead; 13 Jamie Langley. Subs (all used): 21 Tom Burgess; 4 Chev Walker; 10 Craig Kopczak; 8 Nick Scruton.
Tries: Addy (38, 46), Whitehead (49), Pryce (73);
Goals: Gale 3/4.
Rugby Leaguer & League Express Men of the Match:
Wolves: Stefan Ratchford; *Bulls:* Danny Addy.
Penalty count: 8-6; **Half-time:** 32-6;
Referee: Ben Thaler; **Attendance:** 10,750.

WIDNES VIKINGS 26 HULL KINGSTON ROVERS 32

VIKINGS: 29 Jack Owens; 4 Willie Isa; 20 Stefan Marsh; 3 Chris Dean; 5 Patrick Ah Van; 34 Joe Mellor; 7 Rhys Hanbury; 8 Ben Cross (C); 35 Paul McShane; 17 Steve Pickersgill; 11 Frank Winterstein; 21 Dave Allen; 12 Hep Cahill. Subs (all used): 10 Ben Davies; 18 Sione Kite; 24 Kurt Haggerty; 25 Danny Craven.
Tries: Mellor (1), Marsh (39), Haggerty (46), Craven (58), Hanbury (73); **Goals:** Hanbury 3/5.
ROVERS: 27 Louis Sheriff; 29 Liam Salter; 4 Jake Webster; 32 Chris Heil (D); 5 David Hodgson; 6 Blake Green; 7 Michael Dobson; 8 Joel Clinton; 9 Josh Hodgson; 17 Ryan O'Hara; 35 James Laithwaite; 12 Ben Galea (C); 28 Dave Petersen. Subs (all used): 23 Mickey Paea; 14 Lincoln Withers; 18 Graeme Horne; 26 George Griffin (D).
Tries: Dobson (7), O'Hara (17), J Hodgson (27), Galea (50), Horne (63), Sheriff (77); **Goals:** Dobson 4/6.
Rugby Leaguer & League Express Men of the Match:
Vikings: Stefan Marsh; *Rovers:* Ben Galea.
Penalty count: 6-8; **Half-time:** 8-18;
Referee: Thierry Alibert; **Attendance:** 5,325.

ST HELENS 46 HUDDERSFIELD GIANTS 12

SAINTS: 1 Paul Wellens (C); 21 Tom Makinson; 3 Michael Shenton; 26 Josh Jones; 5 Francis Meli; 6 Lance Hohaia; 7 Jonny Lomax; 8 Josh Perry; 9 James Roby; 14 Anthony Laffranchi; 4 Iosia Soliola; 13 Chris Flannery; 12 Jon Wilkin. Subs (all used): 16 Paul Clough; 15 Mark Flanagan; 19 Andrew Dixon; 10 Louie McCarthy-Scarsbrook.
Tries: Makinson (5), Lomax (14), Meli (17), Hohaia (22), McCarthy-Scarsbrook (27), Laffranchi (60), Roby (66), Wellens (73); **Goals:** Makinson 7/8.
GIANTS: 29 Greg Eden; 3 Leroy Cudjoe; 2 Michael Lawrence; 4 Lee Gilmour; 20 Luke George; 1 Scott Grix; 7 Danny Brough; 8 Eorl Crabtree; 9 Luke Robinson (C); 10 Keith Mason; 18 Jason Chan; 12 David Fa'alogo; 36 Brett Ferres (D). Subs (all used): 35 Scott Moore; 13 David Faiumu; 15 Larne Patrick; 19 Tommy Lee.
Tries: Mason (19), Grix (30); **Goals:** Brough 2/2.
Rugby Leaguer & League Express Men of the Match:
Saints: James Roby; *Giants:* Danny Brough.
Penalty count: 8-2; **Half-time:** 28-12;
Referee: James Child; **Attendance:** 14,070.

Monday 30th July 2012

WAKEFIELD TRINITY WILDCATS 38 LEEDS RHINOS 18

WILDCATS: 1 Richard Mathers; 2 Peter Fox; 3 Dean Collis; 35 Lee Smith; 5 Ben Cockayne; 34 Paul Sykes; 20 Tim Smith; 15 Kyle Amor; 9 Andy Ellis; 10 Andy Raleigh; 19 Frankie Mariano; 17 Danny Kirmond (C); 13 Danny Washbrook. Subs (all used): 7 Kyle Wood; 8 Oliver Wilkes; 16 Paul Johnson; 22 Kyle Trout.
Tries: Raleigh (8), Sykes (28), Kirmond (30), Washbrook (56), Wood (60), Collis (75), Fox (79); **Goals:** Sykes 5/7.
On report: Wilkes (43) - alleged late challenge on Burrow.
RHINOS: 1 Brent Webb; 2 Ben Jones-Bishop; 3 Kallum Watkins; 4 Zak Hardaker; 5 Ryan Hall; 25 Stevie Ward; 13 Kevin Sinfield (C); 8 Kylie Leuluai; 7 Rob Burrow; 10 Jamie Peacock; 11 Jamie Jones-Buchanan; 19 Weller Hauraki; 17 Ian Kirke. Subs (all used): 20 Darrell Griffin; 31 Shaun Lunt; 32 Jimmy Keinhorst (D); 21 Richard Moore.
Tries: Watkins (13), Hall (45, 47, 70); **Goals:** Sinfield 1/4.
On report: Webb (3) - alleged late challenge on Kirmond.
Rugby Leaguer & League Express Men of the Match:
Wildcats: Ben Cockayne; *Rhinos:* Jamie Peacock.
Penalty count: 8-9; **Half-time:** 18-4;
Referee: Richard Silverwood; **Attendance:** 9,547.

ROUND 23

Friday 3rd August 2012

WIGAN WARRIORS 48 HULL FC 10

WARRIORS: 1 Sam Tomkins; 2 Josh Charnley; 26 Jack Hughes; 4 George Carmont; 37 Iain Thornley; 38 Matty Smith; 29 Sam Powell (D); 21 Epalahame Lauaki; 9 Michael McIlorum; 10 Lee Mossop; 11 Harrison Hansen; 12 Gareth Hock; 13 Sean O'Loughlin (C). Subs (all used): 14 Jeff Lima; 16 Liam Farrell; 17 Chris Tuson; 33 Dominic Crosby.
Tries: S Tomkins (2, 40), Hock (7), Charnley (16, 27, 52), Farrell (65), McIlorum (68), Powell (75); **Goals:** Charnley 6/9.
HULL: 5 Tom Briscoe; 40 Jamie Foster; 15 Richard Whiting; 4 Kirk Yeaman; 39 Tom Lineham; 38 Ryan McGoldrick; 7 Brett Seymour; 37 Liam Watts; 14 Aaron Heremaia; 10 Andy Lynch (C); 11 Willie Manu; 13 Joe Westerman; 22 Martin Aspinwall. Subs (all used): 8 Mark O'Meley; 34 Jay Pitts; 27 Chris Green; 28 Danny Nicklas.
Tries: Lineham (34), Seymour (72); **Goals:** Foster 1/2.
On report: Westerman (66) - alleged high tackle on Lauaki.
Rugby Leaguer & League Express Men of the Match:
Warriors: Matty Smith; *Hull:* Richard Whiting.
Penalty count: 6-5; **Half-time:** 22-4;
Referee: James Child; **Attendance:** 17,736.

Saturday 4th August 2012

LONDON BRONCOS 40 SALFORD CITY REDS 28

BRONCOS: 5 Michael Robertson; 21 Kieran Dixon; 3 Jamie O'Callaghan; 4 David Howell; 23 Omari Caro; 1 Luke Dorn; 7 Craig Gower (C); 8 Antonio Kaufusi; 9 Chad Randall; 30 Scott Wheeldon; 31 Will Lovell; 12 Chris Bailey; 13 Tony Clubb. Subs (all used): 14 Julien Rinaldi; 10 Mark Bryant; 18 Olsi Krasniqi; 16 Chris Melling.
Tries: Caro (5), Gower (47), Clubb (52), Dixon (67), Bailey (69), O'Callaghan (71), Lovell (76), Dorn (79);
Goals: Gower 4/8.
CITY REDS: 1 Luke Patten; 2 Jodie Broughton; 3 Sean Gleeson; 18 Ashley Gibson; 5 Danny Williams; 6 Daniel Holdsworth; 24 Stuart Howarth; 15 Adam Sidlow; 27 Vinnie Anderson; 10 Ryan Boyle; 16 Luke Adamson; 11 Matty Ashurst; 13 Stephen Wild (C). Subs (all used): 20 Ben Gledhill; 21 Jordan James; 14 Chris Nero; 23 Gareth Owen.
Tries: Gleeson (8), Anderson (13), Gibson (16, 21), Ashurst (31), Broughton (33); **Goals:** Holdsworth 2/6.
Rugby Leaguer & League Express Men of the Match:
Broncos: Craig Gower; *City Reds:* Ashley Gibson.
Penalty count: 10-4; **Half-time:** 6-28;
Referee: George Stokes; **Attendance:** 1,517.

Sunday 5th August 2012

BRADFORD BULLS 38 WIDNES VIKINGS 26

BULLS: 1 Brett Kearney; 18 Shaun Ainscough; 3 Keith Lulia; 29 Michael Platt; 33 Karl Pryce; 6 Ben Jeffries; 7 Luke Gale; 10 Craig Kopczak; 9 Heath L'Estrange (C); 15 Bryn Hargreaves; 19 Tom Olbison; 12 Elliott Whitehead; 13 Jamie Langley. Subs (all used): 21 Tom Burgess; 16 Manase Manuokafoa; 4 Chev Walker; 23 Danny Addy.
Tries: Platt (13, 62), Kearney (24), Ainscough (31, 76), Jeffries (36), L'Estrange (58); **Goals:** Gale 5/7.
VIKINGS: 19 Cameron Phelps; 4 Willie Isa; 20 Stefan Marsh; 3 Chris Dean; 5 Patrick Ah Van; 25 Danny Craven; 7 Rhys Hanbury; 10 Ben Davies; 35 Paul McShane; 17 Steve Pickersgill; 11 Frank Winterstein; 21 Dave Allen; 12 Hep Cahill. Subs (all used): 13 Jon Clarke (C); 18 Sione Kite; 24 Kurt Haggerty; 28 Alex Gerrard.
Tries: Ah Van (6, 65), Davies (10), Craven (21), Hanbury (40); **Goals:** Hanbury 2/4, Ah Van 1/1.
Rugby Leaguer & League Express Men of the Match:
Bulls: Brett Kearney; *Vikings:* Danny Craven.
Penalty count: 9-8; **Half-time:** 22-20;
Referee: Steve Ganson; **Attendance:** 10,261.

HUDDERSFIELD GIANTS 36 CATALAN DRAGONS 18

GIANTS: 29 Greg Eden; 5 Jermaine McGillvary; 3 Leroy Cudjoe; 4 Lee Gilmour; 21 Aaron Murphy; 1 Scott Grix; 7 Danny Brough; 8 Eorl Crabtree; 19 Tommy Lee; 10 Keith Mason; 36 Brett Ferres; 18 Jason Chan; 2 Michael Lawrence. Subs (all used): 13 David Faiumu; 12 David Fa'alogo; 9 Luke Robinson (C); 26 Jamie Cording.
Tries: McGillvary (13, 26), Grix (34), Murphy (40), Fa'alogo (52), Gilmour (56); **Goals:** Brough 6/6.
DRAGONS: 5 Cyril Stacul; 2 Damien Blanch; 18 Daryl Millard; 25 Vincent Duport; 28 Damien Cardace; 3 Leon Pryce; 7 Scott Dureau; 8 David Ferriol; 26 Ben Fisher; 23 Lopini Paea; 10 Remi Casty (C); 14 Sebastien Raguin; 24 Jason Baitieri. Subs (all used): 9 Ian Henderson; 13 Gregory Mounis; 22 Jamal Fakir; 32 Kevin Larroyer (D).
Tries: Casty (18), Millard (60), Blanch (68);
Goals: Dureau 3/3.
Rugby Leaguer & League Express Men of the Match:
Giants: Michael Lawrence; *Dragons:* Scott Dureau.
Penalty count: 7-11; **Half-time:** 24-6;
Referee: Thierry Alibert; **Attendance:** 5,822.

HULL KINGSTON ROVERS 24 LEEDS RHINOS 25

ROVERS: 27 Louis Sheriff; 21 Sam Latus; 29 Liam Salter; 18 Graeme Horne; 5 David Hodgson; 19 Scott Murrell; 7 Michael Dobson; 8 Joel Clinton; 9 Josh Hodgson; 17 Ryan O'Hara; 13 Rhys Lovegrove; 12 Ben Galea (C); 28 Dave Petersen. Subs (all used): 14 Lincoln Withers; 10 Scott Taylor; 23 Mickey Paea; 26 George Griffin.
Tries: Horne (4), J Hodgson (15), Dobson (32), Sheriff (61); **Goals:** Dobson 4/4.
RHINOS: 4 Zak Hardaker; 2 Ben Jones-Bishop; 3 Kallum Watkins; 12 Carl Ablett; 5 Ryan Hall; 13 Kevin Sinfield (C); 6 Danny McGuire; 8 Kylie Leuluai; 7 Rob Burrow; 10 Jamie Peacock; 11 Jamie Jones-Buchanan; 25 Stevie Ward; 15 Brett Delaney. Subs (all used): 16 Ryan Bailey; 18 Chris Clarkson; 20 Darrell Griffin; 31 Shaun Lunt.
Tries: McGuire (10, 46), Hall (44), Ablett (51);
Goals: Sinfield 4/5; **Field goal:** Sinfield (72).
Rugby Leaguer & League Express Men of the Match:
Rovers: Michael Dobson; *Rhinos:* Kevin Sinfield.
Penalty count: 7-5; **Half-time:** 18-6;
Referee: Tim Roby; **Attendance:** 8,379.

CASTLEFORD TIGERS 12
WAKEFIELD TRINITY WILDCATS 40

TIGERS: 1 Richard Owen; 2 Nick Youngquest; 5 Josh Griffin; 25 Jordan Thompson; 32 Rhys Williams; 7 Danny Orr (C); 15 Adam Milner; 19 Paul Jackson; 16 Ryan Hudson; 10 Craig Huby; 20 Grant Millington; 13 Steve Snitch; 8 Jake Emmitt. Subs (all used): 14 Stuart Jones; 17 Lee Mitchell; 22 Nathan Massey; 33 Jamie Ellis.
Tries: Jackson (61), Youngquest (74); **Goals:** Orr 2/2.
WILDCATS: 1 Richard Mathers; 2 Peter Fox; 3 Dean Collis; 35 Lee Smith; 5 Ben Cockayne; 34 Paul Sykes; 20 Tim Smith; 15 Kyle Amor; 9 Andy Ellis; 10 Andy Raleigh; 11 Ali Lauitiiti; 17 Danny Kirmond (C); 13 Danny Washbrook. Subs (all used): 7 Kyle Wood; 19 Frankie Mariano; 16 Paul Johnson; 25 Matt James.
Tries: Cockayne (11), Mathers (15, 78), T Smith (33), Collis (44), Kirmond (52), L Smith (57); **Goals:** Sykes 6/7.
Rugby Leaguer & League Express Men of the Match:
Tigers: Danny Orr; *Wildcats:* Tim Smith.
Penalty count: 6-6; **Half-time:** 0-16;
Referee: Ben Thaler; **Attendance:** 7,050.

Monday 6th August 2012

ST HELENS 12 WARRINGTON WOLVES 22

SAINTS: 1 Paul Wellens (C); 21 Tom Makinson; 3 Michael Shenton; 26 Josh Jones; 5 Francis Meli; 6 Lance Hohaia; 7 Jonny Lomax; 8 Josh Perry; 9 James Roby; 14 Anthony Laffranchi; 11 Tony Puletua; 13 Chris Flannery; 12 Jon Wilkin. Subs (all used): 10 Louie McCarthy-Scarsbrook; 15 Mark Flanagan; 16 Paul Clough; 19 Andrew Dixon.
Tries: Shenton (19), Wellens (74); **Goals:** Makinson 2/2.
WOLVES: 1 Brett Hodgson; 2 Chris Riley; 19 Stefan Ratchford; 4 Ryan Atkins; 5 Joel Monaghan; 6 Lee Briers; 7 Richard Myler; 8 Adrian Morley (C); 14 Mick Higham; 20 Chris Hill; 11 Trent Waterhouse; 12 Ben Westwood; 21 Tyrone McCarthy. Subs (all used): 9 Michael Monaghan; 15 Simon Grix; 16 Paul Wood; 17 Michael Cooper.
Tries: Hodgson (2), Hill (7), Waterhouse (42), Riley (62);
Goals: Hodgson 3/4.
Rugby Leaguer & League Express Men of the Match:
Saints: James Roby; *Wolves:* Brett Hodgson.
Penalty count: 8-5; **Half-time:** 6-10;
Referee: Richard Silverwood; **Attendance:** 15,728.

ROUND 24

Friday 10th August 2012

BRADFORD BULLS 32 HULL KINGSTON ROVERS 26

BULLS: 1 Brett Kearney; 18 Shaun Ainscough; 29 Michael Platt; 3 Keith Lulia; 24 Jason Crookes; 6 Ben Jeffries; 7 Luke Gale; 10 Craig Kopczak; 9 Heath L'Estrange (C); 15 Bryn Hargreaves; 19 Tom Olbison; 12 Elliott Whitehead; 13 Jamie Langley. Subs (all used): 21 Tom Burgess; 16 Manase Manuokafoa; 14 Matt Diskin (C); 4 Chev Walker.
Tries: Langley (17, 59), Ainscough (25), Crookes (54), Whitehead (71); **Goals:** Gale 6/6.
ROVERS: 27 Louis Sheriff; 21 Sam Latus; 2 Craig Hall; 29 Liam Salter; 5 David Hodgson; 19 Scott Murrell; 7 Michael Dobson; 23 Mickey Paea; 9 Josh Hodgson; 17 Ryan O'Hara; 12 Ben Galea (C); 18 Graeme Horne; 26 George Griffin. Subs (all used): 14 Lincoln Withers; 10 Scott Taylor; 33 James Green (D); 20 Jordan Cox.
Tries: Taylor (20), D Hodgson (32), Salter (64), Hall (80); **Goals:** Dobson 5/5.
On report:
J Green (42) - alleged use of the knees on Olbison.
Rugby Leaguer & League Express Men of the Match:
Bulls: Jamie Langley; *Rovers:* Michael Dobson.
Penalty count: 7-11; **Half-time:** 12-14;
Referee: James Child; **Attendance:** 10,217.

LEEDS RHINOS 68 WIDNES VIKINGS 24

RHINOS: 4 Zak Hardaker; 2 Ben Jones-Bishop; 3 Kallum Watkins; 12 Carl Ablett; 5 Ryan Hall; 13 Kevin Sinfield (C); 6 Danny McGuire; 8 Kylie Leuluai; 31 Shaun Lunt; 20 Darrell Griffin; 15 Brett Delaney; 25 Stevie Ward; 16 Ryan Bailey. Subs (all used): 17 Ian Kirke; 21 Richard Moore; 18 Chris Clarkson; 32 Jimmy Keinhorst.
Tries: Bailey (6), Hall (9, 29), Lunt (12), Hardaker (21, 76), Moore (25), Delaney (38), Griffin (61), Leuluai (68), Ward (71), Keinhorst (78); **Goals:** Sinfield 10/12.
VIKINGS: 19 Cameron Phelps; 4 Willie Isa; 20 Stefan Marsh; 3 Chris Dean; 5 Patrick Ah Van; 25 Danny Craven; 7 Rhys Hanbury (C); 17 Steve Pickersgill; 24 Kurt Haggerty; 10 Ben Davies; 11 Frank Winterstein; 21 Dave Allen; 12 Hep Cahill. Subs (all used): 28 Alex Gerrard; 22 Macgraff Leuluai; 27 Grant Gore; 18 Sione Kite.
Tries: Marsh (18, 53), Winterstein (33), Phelps (51);
Goals: Ah Van 4/4.
Sin bin: Haggerty (61) - late challenge on McGuire.
Rugby Leaguer & League Express Men of the Match:
Rhinos: Brett Delaney; *Vikings:* Dave Allen.
Penalty count: 10-5; **Half-time:** 40-12;
Referee: George Stokes; **Attendance:** 13,326.

SALFORD CITY REDS 20 HUDDERSFIELD GIANTS 30

CITY REDS: 1 Luke Patten; 5 Danny Williams; 3 Sean Gleeson; 18 Ashley Gibson; 2 Jodie Broughton; 6 Daniel Holdsworth; 24 Stuart Howarth; 15 Adam Sidlow; 27 Vinnie Anderson; 10 Ryan Boyle; 16 Luke Adamson; 11 Matty Ashurst; 13 Stephen Wild (C). Subs (all used): 17 Iafeta Palea'aesina; 20 Ben Gledhill; 21 Jordan James; 23 Gareth Owen.

Tries: Anderson (29), Broughton (37), Williams (61), Gleeson (63); **Goals:** Holdsworth 2/4.
GIANTS: 29 Greg Eden; 5 Jermaine McGillvary; 3 Leroy Cudjoe; 17 Joe Wardle; 21 Aaron Murphy; 1 Scott Grix; 19 Tommy Lee; 8 Eorl Crabtree; 9 Luke Robinson (C); 10 Keith Mason; 18 Jason Chan; 36 Brett Ferres; 2 Michael Lawrence. Subs (all used): 12 David Fa'alogo; 13 David Faiumu; 26 Jamie Cording; 35 Scott Moore.
Tries: McGillvary (9), Lee (23), Eden (42), Chan (47), Lawrence (78); **Goals:** Grix 5/7.
Sin bin: Cudjoe (20) - interference.
Rugby Leaguer & League Express Men of the Match: *City Reds:* Vinnie Anderson; *Giants:* Scott Grix.
Penalty count: 8-9; **Half-time:** 12-10;
Referee: Ben Thaler; **Attendance:** 3,615.

Saturday 11th August 2012

WARRINGTON WOLVES 30 WIGAN WARRIORS 10

WOLVES: 1 Brett Hodgson; 2 Chris Riley; 19 Stefan Ratchford; 4 Ryan Atkins; 5 Joel Monaghan; 6 Lee Briers; 7 Richard Myler; 8 Adrian Morley (C); 14 Mick Higham; 20 Chris Hill; 11 Trent Waterhouse; 12 Ben Westwood; 13 Ben Harrison. Subs (all used): 16 Paul Wood; 9 Michael Monaghan; 10 Garreth Carvell; 15 Simon Grix.
Tries: Westwood (2), Harrison (7), J Monaghan (35), Ratchford (55), Myler (68); **Goals:** Hodgson 5/6.
WARRIORS: 1 Sam Tomkins; 2 Josh Charnley; 3 Darrell Goulding; 4 George Carmont; 37 Iain Thornley; 6 Brett Finch; 38 Matty Smith; 21 Epalahame Lauaki; 9 Michael McIlorum; 10 Lee Mossop; 11 Harrison Hansen; 12 Gareth Hock; 13 Sean O'Loughlin (C). Subs (all used): 8 Paul Prescott; 14 Jeff Lima; 16 Liam Farrell; 26 Jack Hughes.
Tries: Hock (32), Thornley (58); **Goals:** Charnley 1/2.
Rugby Leaguer & League Express Men of the Match: *Wolves:* Trent Waterhouse; *Warriors:* George Carmont.
Penalty count: 8-7; **Half-time:** 16-6;
Referee: Steve Ganson; **Attendance:** 13,859.

Sunday 12th August 2012

HULL FC 30 CATALAN DRAGONS 10

HULL: 5 Tom Briscoe; 39 Tom Lineham; 19 Jordan Turner; 23 Ben Crooks; 40 Jamie Foster; 38 Ryan McGoldrick; 7 Brett Seymour; 37 Liam Watts; 9 Danny Houghton; 8 Mark O'Meley; 11 Willie Manu; 15 Richard Whiting; 22 Martin Aspinwall. Subs (all used): 14 Aaron Heremaia; 10 Andy Lynch (C); 34 Jay Pitts; 27 Chris Green.
Tries: Manu (4), Lineham (31), Green (47), Briscoe (50), Foster (74); **Goals:** Foster 5/6.
DRAGONS: 1 Clint Greenshields; 2 Damien Blanch; 25 Vincent Duport; 18 Daryl Millard; 28 Damien Cardace; 3 Leon Pryce; 7 Scott Dureau; 8 David Ferriol; 9 Ian Henderson; 10 Remi Casty (C); 12 Louis Anderson; 14 Sebastien Raguin; 24 Jason Baitieri. Subs (all used): 16 Eloi Pelissier; 13 Gregory Mounis; 22 Jamal Fakir; 4 Setaimata Sa.
Tries: Duport (16, 61); **Goals:** Dureau 1/2.
On report: Ferriol (55) - alleged punching.
Rugby Leaguer & League Express Men of the Match: *Hull:* Willie Manu; *Dragons:* Vincent Duport.
Penalty count: 9-7; **Half-time:** 12-6;
Referee: Robert Hicks; **Attendance:** 10,769.

CASTLEFORD TIGERS 20 LONDON BRONCOS 42

TIGERS: 1 Richard Owen; 2 Nick Youngquest; 5 Josh Griffin; 13 Steve Snitch; 25 Jordan Thompson; 30 Ben Johnston (D); 33 Jamie Ellis; 20 Grant Millington; 7 Danny Orr (C); 10 Craig Huby; 17 Lee Mitchell; 14 Stuart Jones; 15 Adam Milner. Subs (all used): 8 Jake Emmitt; 16 Ryan Hudson; 21 Oliver Holmes; 22 Nathan Massey.
Tries: Milner (3), Orr (33), Griffin (41, 67);
Goals: Ellis 2/4.
BRONCOS: 1 Luke Dorn; 21 Kieran Dixon; 3 Jamie O'Callaghan; 4 David Howell; 23 Omari Caro; 6 Michael Witt; 7 Craig Gower (C); 8 Antonio Kaufusi; 9 Chad Randall; 30 Scott Wheeldon; 16 Chris Melling; 12 Chris Bailey; 13 Tony Clubb. Subs (all used): 10 Mark Bryant; 14 Julien Rinaldi; 18 Olsi Krasniqi; 22 Ben Bolger.
Tries: Bailey (11), Dorn (16, 27, 35, 47), Dixon (29), Clubb (71); **Goals:** Witt 7/7.
Rugby Leaguer & League Express Men of the Match: *Tigers:* Danny Orr; *Broncos:* Craig Gower.
Penalty count: 2-3; **Half-time:** 10-30;
Referee: Richard Silverwood; **Attendance:** 5,149.

WAKEFIELD TRINITY WILDCATS 33 ST HELENS 32

WILDCATS: 1 Richard Mathers; 2 Peter Fox; 27 Danny Cowling (D); 35 Lee Smith; 5 Ben Cockayne; 34 Paul Sykes; 20 Tim Smith; 15 Kyle Amor; 9 Andy Ellis; 10 Andy Raleigh; 11 Ali Lauitiiti; 17 Danny Kirmond (C); 13 Danny Washbrook. Subs (all used): 7 Kyle Wood; 8 Oliver Wilkes; 19 Frankie Mariano; 16 Paul Johnson.
Tries: L Smith (8, 61), Raleigh (14), Kirmond (27, 30), Wood (68); **Goals:** Sykes 4/6; **Field goal:** Sykes (80).
SAINTS: 1 Paul Wellens (C); 21 Tom Makinson; 3 Michael Shenton; 26 Josh Jones; 5 Francis Meli; 6 Lance Hohaia; 7 Jonny Lomax; 8 Josh Perry; 9 James Roby; 14 Anthony Laffranchi; 11 Tony Puletua; 13 Chris Flannery; 15 Mark Flanagan. Subs (all used): 10 Louie McCarthy-Scarsbrook; 16 Paul Clough; 19 Andrew Dixon; 20 Lee Gaskell.
Tries: Puletua (1), Meli (17, 50, 72), Wellens (35, 58);
Goals: Makinson 4/6.
Rugby Leaguer & League Express Men of the Match: *Wildcats:* Paul Sykes; *Saints:* Francis Meli.
Penalty count: 8-5; **Half-time:** 22-14;
Referee: Thierry Alibert; **Attendance:** 7,876.

ROUND 25

Friday 17th August 2012

LONDON BRONCOS 62 WARRINGTON WOLVES 18

BRONCOS: 5 Michael Robertson; 21 Kieran Dixon; 4 David Howell; 3 Jamie O'Callaghan; 23 Omari Caro; 1 Luke Dorn; 7 Craig Gower (C); 8 Antonio Kaufusi; 9 Chad Randall; 30 Scott Wheeldon; 16 Chris Melling; 31 Will Lovell; 22 Ben Bolger. Subs (all used): 10 Mark Bryant; 18 Olsi Krasniqi; 32 Mike McMeeken (D); 14 Julien Rinaldi.
Tries: Dixon (2), Lovell (6), Dorn (20, 45, 71, 78), Caro (28), Robertson (59, 75), Rinaldi (66);
Goals: Gower 9/9, Melling 2/2.
WOLVES: 2 Chris Riley; 23 Rhys Evans; 3 Chris Bridge; 4 Ryan Atkins; 22 Rhys Williams; 19 Stefan Ratchford; 7 Richard Myler; 8 Adrian Morley (C); 9 Michael Monaghan; 16 Paul Wood; 21 Tyrone McCarthy; 11 Trent Waterhouse; 15 Simon Grix. Subs (all used): 17 Michael Cooper; 18 Matty Blythe; 20 Chris Hill; 26 David Solomona.
Tries: Ratchford (14), Myler (23), Williams (32);
Goals: Ratchford 3/3.
Sin bin: Hill (62) - late challenge on Gower.
Rugby Leaguer & League Express Men of the Match: *Broncos:* Luke Dorn; *Wolves:* Stefan Ratchford.
Penalty count: 7-5; **Half-time:** 24-18;
Referee: Ben Thaler; **Attendance:** 2,261.

ST HELENS 44 CASTLEFORD TIGERS 12

SAINTS: 1 Paul Wellens (C); 21 Tom Makinson; 34 Adam Swift; 17 Gary Wheeler; 5 Francis Meli; 6 Lance Hohaia; 7 Jonny Lomax; 8 Josh Perry; 9 James Roby; 14 Anthony Laffranchi; 4 Iosia Soliola; 13 Chris Flannery; 11 Tony Puletua. Subs (all used): 10 Louie McCarthy-Scarsbrook; 15 Mark Flanagan; 16 Paul Clough; 19 Andrew Dixon.
Tries: Laffranchi (7), Wellens (20), Makinson (32, 51), Flannery (38), Wheeler (59), Swift (61), Lomax (68);
Goals: Makinson 2/4, Wheeler 4/4.
TIGERS: 1 Richard Owen; 2 Nick Youngquest; 13 Steve Snitch; 25 Jordan Thompson; 5 Josh Griffin; 7 Danny Orr (C); 30 Ben Johnston; 8 Jake Emmitt; 16 Ryan Hudson; 10 Craig Huby; 20 Grant Millington; 14 Stuart Jones; 17 Lee Mitchell. Subs (all used): 15 Adam Milner; 19 Paul Jackson; 21 Oliver Holmes; 22 Nathan Massey.
Tries: Jackson (25), Millington (72); **Goals:** Orr 2/2.
Rugby Leaguer & League Express Men of the Match: *Saints:* Tom Makinson; *Tigers:* Danny Orr.
Penalty count: 9-7; **Half-time:** 20-6;
Referee: George Stokes; **Attendance:** 12,224.

Saturday 18th August 2012

CATALAN DRAGONS 38 LEEDS RHINOS 34

DRAGONS: 1 Clint Greenshields; 2 Damien Blanch; 25 Vincent Duport; 18 Daryl Millard; 29 Mathias Pala; 3 Leon Pryce; 7 Scott Dureau; 8 David Ferriol; 9 Ian Henderson; 10 Remi Casty (C); 4 Setaimata Sa; 12 Louis Anderson; 24 Jason Baitieri. Subs (all used): 13 Gregory Mounis; 14 Sebastien Raguin; 16 Eloi Pelissier; 22 Jamal Fakir.
Tries: Sa (6), Dureau (14), Casty (21, 59), Duport (45), Millard (75); **Goals:** Dureau 7/7.
RHINOS: 4 Zak Hardaker; 2 Ben Jones-Bishop; 3 Kallum Watkins; 12 Carl Ablett; 5 Ryan Hall; 25 Stevie Ward; 13 Kevin Sinfield (C); 8 Kylie Leuluai; 31 Shaun Lunt; 10 Jamie Peacock; 11 Jamie Jones-Buchanan; 15 Brett Delaney; 16 Ryan Bailey. Subs (all used): 17 Ian Kirke; 18 Chris Clarkson; 21 Richard Moore; 32 Jimmy Keinhorst.
Tries: Lunt (28), Watkins (40, 78), Hall (65, 73), Keinhorst (68); **Goals:** Sinfield 5/6.
On report: Bailey (41) - alleged dangerous contact.
Rugby Leaguer & League Express Men of the Match: *Dragons:* Remi Casty; *Rhinos:* Stevie Ward.
Penalty count: 7-7; **Half-time:** 20-12;
Referee: James Child; **Attendance:** 10,269.

WIDNES VIKINGS 42 HULL FC 16

VIKINGS: 1 Shaun Briscoe; 2 Paddy Flynn; 20 Stefan Marsh; 19 Cameron Phelps; 4 Willie Isa; 25 Danny Craven; 7 Rhys Hanbury; 10 Ben Davies; 13 Jon Clarke (C); 18 Sione Kite; 11 Frank Winterstein; 21 Dave Allen; 12 Hep Cahill. Subs (all used): 16 Ben Kavanagh; 24 Kurt Haggerty; 28 Alex Gerrard; 35 Paul McShane.
Tries: Isa (14, 48), Flynn (16), Briscoe (38, 70), Winterstein (40), Craven (43), Hanbury (74);
Goals: Hanbury 0/2, Craven 2/3, McShane 3/3.
On report: Phelps (49) - challenge on Lineham.
HULL: 5 Tom Briscoe; 39 Tom Lineham; 23 Ben Crooks; 19 Jordan Turner; 40 Jamie Foster; 38 Ryan McGoldrick; 7 Brett Seymour; 37 Liam Watts; 9 Danny Houghton; 10 Andy Lynch (C); 11 Willie Manu; 13 Joe Westerman; 34 Jay Pitts. Subs (all used): 6 Richard Horne; 14 Aaron Heremaia; 22 Martin Aspinwall; 8 Mark O'Meley.
Tries: Turner (8), Westerman (20), Heremaia (56);
Goals: Foster 2/3.
On report:
McGoldrick (59) - alleged high tackle on Hanbury.
Rugby Leaguer & League Express Men of the Match: *Vikings:* Shaun Briscoe; *Hull:* Danny Houghton.
Penalty count: 9-5; **Half-time:** 20-10;
Referee: Steve Ganson; **Attendance:** 5,008.

Sunday 19th August 2012

HUDDERSFIELD GIANTS 12 BRADFORD BULLS 34

GIANTS: 29 Greg Eden; 5 Jermaine McGillvary; 3 Leroy Cudjoe; 17 Joe Wardle; 20 Luke George; 1 Scott Grix; 7 Danny Brough; 8 Eorl Crabtree; 19 Tommy Lee; 10 Keith Mason; 36 Brett Ferres; 18 Jason Chan; 2 Michael Lawrence. Subs (all used): 9 Luke Robinson (C); 12 David Fa'alogo; 13 David Faiumu; 15 Larne Patrick.
Tries: Wardle (5), Cudjoe (75); **Goals:** Brough 2/2.
BULLS: 1 Brett Kearney; 18 Shaun Ainscough; 33 Karl Pryce; 3 Keith Lulia; 24 Jason Crookes; 6 Ben Jeffries; 7 Luke Gale; 15 Bryn Hargreaves; 9 Heath L'Estrange (C); 10 Craig Kopczak; 26 John Bateman; 12 Elliott Whitehead; 13 Jamie Langley. Subs (all used): 16 Manase Manuokafoa; 21 Tom Burgess; 14 Matt Diskin (C); 4 Chev Walker.
Tries: Ainscough (17), Diskin (29), Gale (38), Kearney (59), Pryce (66, 79); **Goals:** Gale 5/6.
Rugby Leaguer & League Express Men of the Match: *Giants:* Eorl Crabtree; *Bulls:* Luke Gale.
Penalty count: 7-13; **Half-time:** 6-18;
Referee: Thierry Alibert; **Attendance:** 7,477.

HULL KINGSTON ROVERS 30 WAKEFIELD TRINITY WILDCATS 31

ROVERS: 27 Louis Sheriff; 21 Sam Latus; 29 Liam Salter; 18 Graeme Horne; 5 David Hodgson; 2 Craig Hall; 7 Michael Dobson; 17 Ryan O'Hara; 9 Josh Hodgson; 10 Scott Taylor; 13 Rhys Lovegrove; 12 Ben Galea (C); 26 George Griffin. Subs (all used): 14 Lincoln Withers; 16 Jason Netherton; 11 Constantine Mika; 23 Mickey Paea.
Tries: Salter (21, 37), Horne (25), Withers (62), Galea (65), J Hodgson (72); **Goals:** Dobson 3/6.
WILDCATS: 1 Richard Mathers; 2 Peter Fox; 3 Dean Collis; 35 Lee Smith; 5 Ben Cockayne; 34 Paul Sykes; 20 Tim Smith; 15 Kyle Amor; 9 Andy Ellis; 10 Andy Raleigh; 11 Ali Lauitiiti; 17 Danny Kirmond (C); 13 Danny Washbrook. Subs (all used): 7 Kyle Wood; 19 Frankie Mariano; 16 Paul Johnson; 8 Oliver Wilkes.
Tries: Cockayne (7, 50), Fox (40), Mariano (41), Collis (53), Wood (75); **Goals:** Sykes 3/6;
Field goal: Sykes (80).
On report: Mathers (25) - challenge on Horne.
Rugby Leaguer & League Express Men of the Match: *Rovers:* Mickey Paea; *Wildcats:* Paul Sykes.
Penalty count: 9-8; **Half-time:** 14-8;
Referee: Richard Silverwood; **Attendance:** 8,726.

Monday 20th August 2012

WIGAN WARRIORS 38 SALFORD CITY REDS 6

WARRIORS: 1 Sam Tomkins; 2 Josh Charnley; 3 Darrell Goulding; 4 George Carmont; 5 Pat Richards; 6 Brett Finch; 38 Matty Smith; 14 Jeff Lima; 9 Michael McIlorum; 10 Lee Mossop; 11 Harrison Hansen; 12 Gareth Hock; 13 Sean O'Loughlin (C). Subs (all used): 23 Ben Flower; 21 Epalahame Lauaki; 16 Liam Farrell; 26 Jack Hughes.
Tries: Richards (13, 21), S Tomkins (15), Goulding (46), Hughes (52), Hansen (64), O'Loughlin (70);
Goals: Richards 5/7.
CITY REDS: 1 Luke Patten; 2 Jodie Broughton; 3 Sean Gleeson; 25 Josh Veivers; 5 Danny Williams; 6 Daniel Holdsworth; 24 Stuart Howarth; 15 Adam Sidlow; 27 Vinnie Anderson; 10 Ryan Boyle; 16 Luke Adamson; 11 Matty Ashurst; 13 Stephen Wild (C). Subs (all used): 19 Adam Neal; 28 Adam Walne (D); 21 Jordan James; 23 Gareth Owen.
Try: James (79); **Goals:** Holdsworth 1/1.
Rugby Leaguer & League Express Men of the Match: *Warriors:* Pat Richards; *City Reds:* Luke Patten.
Penalty count: 8-7; **Half-time:** 14-0;
Referee: Tim Roby; **Attendance:** 13,703.

ROUND 26

Friday 31st August 2012

LEEDS RHINOS 46 SALFORD CITY REDS 12

RHINOS: 4 Zak Hardaker; 2 Ben Jones-Bishop; 3 Kallum Watkins; 32 Jimmy Keinhorst; 5 Ryan Hall; 13 Kevin Sinfield (C); 7 Rob Burrow; 8 Kylie Leuluai; 31 Shaun Lunt; 10 Jamie Peacock; 15 Brett Delaney; 11 Jamie Jones-Buchanan; 12 Carl Ablett. Subs (all used): 17 Ian Kirke; 25 Stevie Ward; 19 Weller Hauraki; 18 Chris Clarkson.
Tries: Jones-Bishop (11), Hall (16), Sinfield (22), Burrow (42), Watkins (46, 55), Hauraki (47), Jones-Buchanan (61); **Goals:** Sinfield 7/8.
CITY REDS: 1 Luke Patten; 2 Jodie Broughton; 3 Sean Gleeson; 18 Ashley Gibson; 5 Danny Williams; 6 Daniel Holdsworth; 24 Stuart Howarth; 10 Ryan Boyle; 27 Vinnie Anderson; 15 Adam Sidlow; 14 Chris Nero; 11 Matty Ashurst; 13 Stephen Wild (C). Subs (all used): 21 Jordan James; 28 Adam Walne; 23 Gareth Owen; 19 Adam Neal.
Tries: Patten (64, 78); **Goals:** Holdsworth 2/2.
Rugby Leaguer & League Express Men of the Match: *Rhinos:* Jamie Peacock; *City Reds:* Vinnie Anderson.
Penalty count: 8-7; **Half-time:** 16-0;
Referee: Robert Hicks; **Attendance:** 15,081.

ST HELENS 30 LONDON BRONCOS 0

SAINTS: 1 Paul Wellens (C); 21 Tom Makinson; 17 Gary Wheeler; 26 Josh Jones; 5 Francis Meli; 6 Lance Hohaia; 7 Jonny Lomax; 8 Josh Perry; 9 James Roby; 14 Anthony Laffranchi; 4 Iosia Soliola; 11 Tony Puletua; 12 Jon Wilkin. Subs (all used): 10 Louie McCarthy-Scarsbrook; 15 Mark Flanagan; 16 Paul Clough; 19 Andrew Dixon.
Tries: Puletua (3), Flanagan (35, 47), Wellens (50, 59), Laffranchi (80); **Goals:** Lomax 1/4, Wheeler 2/4.
BRONCOS: 5 Michael Robertson; 21 Kieran Dixon; 3 Jamie O'Callaghan; 4 David Howell; 23 Omari Caro; 1 Luke Dorn; 7 Craig Gower (C); 8 Antonio Kaufusi; 9 Chad Randall; 30 Scott Wheeldon; 31 Will Lovell; 13 Tony Clubb; 22 Ben Bolger. Subs (all used): 10 Mark Bryant; 14 Julien Rinaldi; 18 Olsi Krasniqi; 32 Mike McMeeken.

Rugby Leaguer & League Express Men of the Match:
Saints: Louie McCarthy-Scarsbrook;
Broncos: Kieran Dixon.
Penalty count: 12-9; **Half-time:** 10-0;
Referee: Richard Silverwood; **Attendance:** 13,262.

Saturday 1st September 2012

BRADFORD BULLS 6 HULL FC 70

BULLS: 1 Brett Kearney; 18 Shaun Ainscough; 33 Karl Pryce; 3 Keith Lulia; 24 Jason Crookes; 6 Ben Jeffries; 7 Luke Gale; 10 Craig Kopczak; 9 Heath L'Estrange (C); 15 Bryn Hargreaves; 19 Tom Olbison; 12 Elliott Whitehead; 13 Jamie Langley. Subs (all used): 11 Olivier Elima; 16 Manase Manuokafoa; 14 Matt Diskin (C); 4 Chev Walker.
Try: Crookes (3); **Goals:** Gale 1/1.
Sin bin: Jeffries (8) - professional foul.
HULL: 6 Richard Horne; 40 Jamie Foster; 19 Jordan Turner; 23 Ben Crooks; 5 Tom Briscoe; 38 Ryan McGoldrick; 14 Aaron Heremaia; 37 Liam Watts; 9 Danny Houghton; 10 Andy Lynch (C); 11 Willie Manu; 13 Joe Westerman; 34 Jay Pitts. Subs (all used): 7 Brett Seymour; 8 Mark O'Meley; 22 Martin Aspinwall; 27 Chris Green.
Tries: Westerman (9), Foster (11, 73), Manu (18, 32), Houghton (28), Heremaia (45, 68), Briscoe (47, 59, 80), Crooks (62), Lynch (66); **Goals:** Foster 9/13.
Rugby Leaguer & League Express Men of the Match:
Bulls: Brett Kearney; *Hull:* Willie Manu.
Penalty count: 8-13; **Half-time:** 6-28;
Referee: Ben Thaler; **Attendance:** 10,616.

Sunday 2nd September 2012

CASTLEFORD TIGERS 26 CATALAN DRAGONS 46

TIGERS: 1 Richard Owen; 2 Nick Youngquest; 13 Steve Snitch; 14 Stuart Jones; 25 Jordan Thompson; 6 Rangi Chase; 33 Jamie Ellis; 22 Nathan Massey; 7 Danny Orr (C); 10 Craig Huby; 20 Grant Millington; 16 Ryan Hudson; 15 Adam Milner. Subs (all used): 9 Daryl Clark; 17 Lee Mitchell; 21 Oliver Holmes; 24 Stephen Nash.
Tries: Hudson (18), Jones (28), Youngquest (61), Millington (64), Owen (77); **Goals:** Orr 3/5.
DRAGONS: 1 Clint Greenshields; 2 Damien Blanch; 18 Daryl Millard; 25 Vincent Duport; 29 Mathias Pala; 6 Thomas Bosc; 7 Scott Dureau; 13 Gregory Mounis; 9 Ian Henderson; 10 Remi Casty (C); 4 Setaimata Sa; 12 Louis Anderson; 24 Jason Baitieri. Subs (all used): 16 Eloi Pelissier; 22 Jamal Fakir; 31 Antoni Maria (D); 32 Kevin Larroyer.
Tries: Duport (6), Blanch (12, 40, 79), Sa (25), Greenshields (37, 49, 55); **Goals:** Dureau 7/8.
Rugby Leaguer & League Express Men of the Match:
Tigers: Danny Orr; *Dragons:* Scott Dureau.
Penalty count: 7-5; **Half-time:** 12-30;
Referee: Tim Roby; **Attendance:** 5,005.

HULL KINGSTON ROVERS 36 WIGAN WARRIORS 42

ROVERS: 27 Louis Sheriff; 4 Jake Webster; 18 Graeme Horne; 29 Liam Salter; 5 David Hodgson; 2 Craig Hall; 7 Michael Dobson; 10 Scott Taylor; 14 Lincoln Withers; 23 Mickey Paea; 11 Constantine Mika; 12 Ben Galea (C); 13 Rhys Lovegrove. Subs (all used): 9 Josh Hodgson; 16 Jason Netherton; 20 Jordan Cox; 17 Ryan O'Hara.
Tries: Hall (3), Withers (13, 43), Galea (23), Webster (34), D Hodgson (64); **Goals:** Dobson 6/8.
WARRIORS: 1 Sam Tomkins; 2 Josh Charnley; 3 Darrell Goulding; 4 George Carmont; 5 Pat Richards; 6 Brett Finch; 38 Matty Smith; 14 Jeff Lima; 9 Michael McIlorum; 23 Ben Flower; 11 Harrison Hansen; 12 Gareth Hock; 13 Sean O'Loughlin (C). Subs (all used): 7 Thomas Leuluai; 10 Lee Mossop; 16 Liam Farrell; 26 Jack Hughes.
Tries: Finch (37), Goulding (40), Hock (55), Richards (57, 77), Carmont (68), Farrell (72), Charnley (80); **Goals:** Richards 5/8.
Rugby Leaguer & League Express Men of the Match:
Rovers: Mickey Paea; *Warriors:* Pat Richards.
Penalty count: 7-7; **Half-time:** 26-12;
Referee: Thierry Alibert; **Attendance:** 8,845.

WARRINGTON WOLVES 54 HUDDERSFIELD GIANTS 6

WOLVES: 1 Brett Hodgson; 5 Joel Monaghan; 3 Chris Bridge; 4 Ryan Atkins; 22 Rhys Williams; 19 Stefan Ratchford; 7 Richard Myler; 8 Adrian Morley (C); 9 Michael Monaghan; 20 Chris Hill; 15 Simon Grix; 11 Trent Waterhouse; 13 Ben Harrison. Subs (all used): 10 Garreth Carvell; 14 Mick Higham; 16 Paul Wood; 18 Matty Blythe.
Tries: J Monaghan (18, 73, 76), Bridge (34), Ratchford (37), Myler (52), Hodgson (58), Williams (68), Atkins (70), Hill (80); **Goals:** Hodgson 7/10.
GIANTS: 29 Greg Eden; 21 Aaron Murphy; 3 Leroy Cudjoe; 17 Joe Wardle; 28 Matty Dawson (D); 1 Scott Grix; 19 Tommy Lee; 10 Keith Mason; 9 Luke Robinson (C); 12 David Fa'alogo; 36 Brett Ferres; 18 Jason Chan; 2 Michael Lawrence. Subs (all used): 8 Eorl Crabtree; 15 Larne Patrick; 26 Jamie Cording; 35 Scott Moore.
Try: Grix (32); **Goals:** Grix 1/1.
Rugby Leaguer & League Express Men of the Match:
Wolves: Brett Hodgson; *Giants:* Scott Grix.
Penalty count: 7-7; **Half-time:** 16-6;
Referee: George Stokes; **Attendance:** 10,515.

WAKEFIELD TRINITY WILDCATS 22
WIDNES VIKINGS 18

WILDCATS: 1 Richard Mathers; 2 Peter Fox; 3 Dean Collis; 35 Lee Smith; 5 Ben Cockayne; 34 Paul Sykes; 20 Tim Smith; 15 Kyle Amor; 9 Andy Ellis; 10 Andy Raleigh; 11 Ali Lauitiiti; 17 Danny Kirmond (C); 13 Danny Washbrook. Subs (all used): 7 Kyle Wood; 19 Frankie Mariano; 16 Paul Johnson; 8 Oliver Wilkes.
Tries: Amor (12), Mathers (51), Lauitiiti (62), Kirmond (75); **Goals:** Sykes 3/5.
VIKINGS: 1 Shaun Briscoe; 2 Paddy Flynn; 20 Stefan Marsh; 19 Cameron Phelps; 4 Willie Isa; 25 Danny Craven; 7 Rhys Hanbury; 17 Steve Pickersgill; 13 Jon Clarke (C); 18 Sione Kite; 11 Frank Winterstein; 21 Dave Allen; 12 Hep Cahill. Subs (all used): 16 Ben Kavanagh; 10 Ben Davies; 28 Alex Gerrard; 35 Paul McShane.
Tries: Hanbury (6, 40), Flynn (57);
Goals: Hanbury 2/2, McShane 1/2.
Sin bin: Flynn (67) - high tackle on Wood.
Rugby Leaguer & League Express Men of the Match:
Wildcats: Kyle Wood; *Vikings:* Rhys Hanbury.
Penalty count: 10-5; **Half-time:** 6-10;
Referee: James Child; **Attendance:** 8,234.

ROUND 27

Friday 7th September 2012

WIGAN WARRIORS 18 ST HELENS 26

WARRIORS: 1 Sam Tomkins; 2 Josh Charnley; 3 Darrell Goulding; 4 George Carmont; 5 Pat Richards; 6 Brett Finch; 7 Thomas Leuluai; 15 Stuart Fielden; 9 Michael McIlorum; 14 Jeff Lima; 11 Harrison Hansen; 12 Gareth Hock; 13 Sean O'Loughlin (C). Subs (all used): 10 Lee Mossop; 16 Liam Farrell; 22 Gil Dudson; 23 Ben Flower.
Tries: Leuluai (11), Richards (44), S Tomkins (80);
Goals: Richards 3/3.
Dismissal: McIlorum (15) - late, high tackle on Laffranchi.
SAINTS: 1 Paul Wellens (C); 21 Tom Makinson; 3 Michael Shenton; 26 Josh Jones; 5 Francis Meli; 6 Lance Hohaia; 7 Jonny Lomax; 8 Josh Perry; 9 James Roby; 14 Anthony Laffranchi; 15 Mark Flanagan; 11 Tony Puletua; 12 Jon Wilkin. Subs (all used): 10 Louie McCarthy-Scarsbrook; 28 Joe Greenwood; 16 Paul Clough; 19 Andrew Dixon.
Tries: Roby (23), Makinson (28), Dixon (57), Jones (70), Lomax (72); **Goals:** Makinson 3/5.
Rugby Leaguer & League Express Men of the Match:
Warriors: Sean O'Loughlin; *Saints:* Tony Puletua.
Penalty count: 11-7; **Half-time:** 6-12;
Referee: James Child; **Attendance:** 21,522.

Saturday 8th September 2012

LONDON BRONCOS 48 HULL KINGSTON ROVERS 42

BRONCOS: 5 Michael Robertson; 21 Kieran Dixon; 4 David Howell; 19 Dan Sarginson; 23 Omari Caro; 1 Luke Dorn; 7 Craig Gower (C); 8 Antonio Kaufusi; 9 Chad Randall; 30 Scott Wheeldon; 12 Chris Bailey; 31 Will Lovell; 13 Tony Clubb. Subs (all used): 10 Mark Bryant; 18 Olsi Krasniqi; 32 Mike McMeeken; 14 Julien Rinaldi.
Tries: Robertson (2, 55), Caro (11), Dixon (25, 45), Bailey (29), Krasniqi (68), Dorn (75); **Goals:** Gower 8/8.
ROVERS: 27 Louis Sheriff; 29 Liam Salter; 32 Chris Heil; 18 Graeme Horne; 31 Nick Johnson (D); 2 Craig Hall; 7 Michael Dobson; 23 Mickey Paea; 14 Lincoln Withers; 10 Scott Taylor; 12 Ben Galea (C); 11 Constantine Mika; 13 Rhys Lovegrove. Subs (all used): 17 Ryan O'Hara; 24 Richard Beaumont; 9 Josh Hodgson; 28 Dave Petersen.
Tries: Paea (33), Beaumont (36), Petersen (51), Heil (58), Mika (63, 77), Galea (72), Dobson (74);
Goals: Dobson 4/6, Hall 1/2.
Sin bin: Dobson (55) - dissent.
Rugby Leaguer & League Express Men of the Match:
Broncos: Craig Gower; *Rovers:* Mickey Paea.
Penalty count: 5-7; **Half-time:** 24-12;
Referee: Tim Roby; **Attendance:** 2,525.

CATALAN DRAGONS 50 BRADFORD BULLS 26

DRAGONS: 1 Clint Greenshields; 2 Damien Blanch; 25 Vincent Duport; 4 Setaimata Sa; 18 Daryl Millard; 6 Thomas Bosc; 7 Scott Dureau; 8 David Ferriol; 9 Ian Henderson; 10 Remi Casty (C); 14 Sebastien Raguin; 12 Louis Anderson; 24 Jason Baitieri. Subs (all used): 11 Steve Menzies; 13 Gregory Mounis; 16 Eloi Pelissier; 22 Jamal Fakir.
Tries: Greenshields (7, 61, 80), Duport (13), Sa (16), Anderson (24), Menzies (48), Millard (55), Dureau (65);
Goals: Dureau 7/9.
BULLS: 1 Brett Kearney; 5 Elliot Kear; 29 Michael Platt; 3 Keith Lulia; 24 Jason Crookes; 22 Jarrod Sammut; 7 Luke Gale; 15 Bryn Hargreaves; 9 Heath L'Estrange (C); 16 Manase Manuokafoa; 19 Tom Olbison; 12 Elliott Whitehead; 11 Olivier Elima. Subs (all used): 4 Chev Walker; 8 Nick Scruton; 14 Matt Diskin (C); 34 Phil Joseph.
Tries: Platt (2), Sammut (5, 33, 40, 73); **Goals:** Gale 3/5.
Rugby Leaguer & League Express Men of the Match:
Dragons: Clint Greenshields; *Bulls:* Jarrod Sammut.
Penalty count: 6-5; **Half-time:** 22-20;
Referee: Richard Silverwood; **Attendance:** 9,284.

HULL FC 36 CASTLEFORD TIGERS 10

HULL: 6 Richard Horne; 40 Jamie Foster; 23 Ben Crooks; 4 Kirk Yeaman; 5 Tom Briscoe; 7 Brett Seymour; 14 Aaron Heremaia; 37 Liam Watts; 9 Danny Houghton; 10 Andy Lynch (C); 11 Willie Manu; 13 Joe Westerman; 34 Jay Pitts. Subs (all used): 8 Mark O'Meley; 22 Martin Aspinwall; 12 Danny Tickle; 27 Chris Green.
Tries: Manu (6), Briscoe (35), Horne (45), Houghton (50), O'Meley (56), Green (76); **Goals:** Foster 6/7.
TIGERS: 1 Richard Owen; 34 Ben Blackmore (D); 13 Steve Snitch; 25 Jordan Thompson; 2 Nick Youngquest; 6 Rangi Chase; 7 Danny Orr (C); 10 Craig Huby; 9 Daryl Clark; 22 Nathan Massey; 20 Grant Millington; 21 Oliver Holmes; 16 Ryan Hudson. Subs (all used): 15 Adam Milner; 8 Jake Emmitt; 12 Jonathan Walker; 17 Lee Mitchell.
Tries: Thompson (11), Holmes (66);
Goals: Orr 1/1, Youngquest 0/1.
Rugby Leaguer & League Express Men of the Match:
Hull: Willie Manu; *Tigers:* Jordan Thompson.
Penalty count: 11-7; **Half-time:** 14-6;
Referee: Robert Hicks; **Attendance:** 11,607.

SALFORD CITY REDS 34
WAKEFIELD TRINITY WILDCATS 42

CITY REDS: 25 Josh Veivers; 5 Danny Williams; 3 Sean Gleeson; 18 Ashley Gibson; 2 Jodie Broughton; 6 Daniel Holdsworth; 24 Stuart Howarth; 10 Ryan Boyle; 27 Vinnie Anderson; 15 Adam Sidlow; 14 Chris Nero; 11 Matty Ashurst; 13 Stephen Wild (C). Subs (all used): 16 Luke Adamson; 19 Adam Neal; 21 Jordan James; 23 Gareth Owen.
Tries: Williams (31), Gleeson (36), Anderson (49), Gibson (73, 80), Ashurst (78);
Goals: Holdsworth 4/5, Adamson 1/1.
WILDCATS: 1 Richard Mathers; 2 Peter Fox; 3 Dean Collis; 35 Lee Smith; 5 Ben Cockayne; 34 Paul Sykes; 20 Tim Smith; 15 Kyle Amor; 9 Andy Ellis; 10 Andy Raleigh; 19 Frankie Mariano; 17 Danny Kirmond (C); 13 Danny Washbrook. Subs (all used): 7 Kyle Wood; 8 Oliver Wilkes; 16 Paul Johnson; 22 Kyle Trout.
Tries: Mariano (18), Raleigh (21), Collis (25), Johnson (40), Cockayne (45), Fox (60), L Smith (67);
Goals: Sykes 7/7.
Rugby Leaguer & League Express Men of the Match:
City Reds: Vinnie Anderson; *Wildcats:* Tim Smith.
Penalty count: 7-7; **Half-time:** 12-24;
Referee: Ben Thaler; **Attendance:** 2,380
(at Leigh Sports Village).

Sunday 9th September 2012

HUDDERSFIELD GIANTS 48 LEEDS RHINOS 24

GIANTS: 3 Leroy Cudjoe; 5 Jermaine McGillvary; 2 Michael Lawrence; 17 Joe Wardle; 20 Luke George; 1 Scott Grix; 7 Danny Brough (C); 8 Eorl Crabtree; 13 David Faiumu; 10 Keith Mason; 12 David Fa'alogo; 36 Brett Ferres; 11 Luke O'Donnell. Subs (all used): 9 Luke Robinson; 15 Larne Patrick; 16 Dale Ferguson; 18 Jason Chan.
Tries: Cudjoe (4, 73), George (8), Lawrence (28), Brough (40), Robinson (57, 70), Grix (68);
Goals: Brough 8/10.
Dismissal: O'Donnell (12) - challenge on Kirke.
RHINOS: 4 Zak Hardaker; 2 Ben Jones-Bishop; 32 Jimmy Keinhorst; 3 Kallum Watkins; 5 Ryan Hall; 13 Kevin Sinfield (C); 7 Rob Burrow; 8 Kylie Leuluai; 24 Liam Hood; 10 Jamie Peacock; 11 Jamie Jones-Buchanan; 15 Brett Delaney; 12 Carl Ablett. Subs (all used): 17 Ian Kirke; 19 Weller Hauraki; 20 Darrell Griffin; 25 Stevie Ward.
Tries: Keinhorst (34), Hall (62), Watkins (75), Ablett (78), Peacock (80); **Goals:** Sinfield 2/5.
Rugby Leaguer & League Express Men of the Match:
Giants: Danny Brough; *Rhinos:* Jamie Peacock.
Penalty count: 8-9; **Half-time:** 22-4;
Referee: Thierry Alibert; **Attendance:** 9,128.

WIDNES VIKINGS 14 WARRINGTON WOLVES 52

VIKINGS: 29 Jack Owens; 2 Paddy Flynn; 3 Chris Dean; 19 Cameron Phelps; 4 Willie Isa; 34 Joe Mellor; 7 Rhys Hanbury; 10 Ben Davies; 13 Jon Clarke (C); 17 Steve Pickersgill; 11 Frank Winterstein; 21 Dave Allen; 24 Kurt Haggerty. Subs (all used): 16 Ben Kavanagh; 22 Macgraff Leuluai; 28 Alex Gerrard; 35 Paul McShane.
Tries: Winterstein (5), McShane (45), Hanbury (71);
Goals: Hanbury 1/2, Haggerty 0/1.
WOLVES: 19 Stefan Ratchford; 2 Chris Riley; 3 Chris Bridge; 4 Ryan Atkins; 22 Rhys Williams; 6 Lee Briers; 7 Richard Myler; 16 Paul Wood; 14 Mick Higham; 20 Chris Hill; 21 Tyrone McCarthy; 15 Simon Grix; 13 Ben Harrison. Subs (all used): 8 Adrian Morley (C); 17 Michael Cooper; 18 Matty Blythe; 26 David Solomona.
Tries: Higham (10, 66), Williams (18), Riley (28, 41), Ratchford (33), Solomona (37), Hill (56), Atkins (76), Wood (79);
Goals: Briers 5/8, Ratchford 0/1, Solomona 1/1.
Rugby Leaguer & League Express Men of the Match:
Vikings: Jon Clarke; *Wolves:* Richard Myler.
Penalty count: 4-5; **Half-time:** 6-22;
Referee: Steve Ganson; **Attendance:** 8,617.

PLAY-OFFS

QUALIFYING PLAY-OFFS

Friday 14th September 2012

WIGAN WARRIORS 46 CATALAN DRAGONS 6

WARRIORS: 1 Sam Tomkins; 2 Josh Charnley; 3 Darrell Goulding; 4 George Carmont; 5 Pat Richards; 6 Brett Finch; 7 Thomas Leuluai; 21 Epalahame Lauaki; 13 Sean O'Loughlin (C); 10 Lee Mossop; 11 Harrison Hansen; 26 Jack Hughes; 16 Liam Farrell. Subs (all used): 14 Jeff Lima; 38 Matty Smith; 22 Gil Dudson; 23 Ben Flower.
Tries: Carmont (5, 10, 68), Leuluai (24), Goulding (39), Farrell (43), S Tomkins (53), Charnley (74);
Goals: Richards 7/8.
DRAGONS: 1 Clint Greenshields; 2 Damien Blanch; 4 Setaimata Sa; 25 Vincent Duport; 18 Daryl Millard; 6 Thomas Bosc; 7 Scott Dureau; 23 Lopini Paea; 9 Ian Henderson; 10 Remi Casty (C); 11 Steve Menzies; 12 Louis Anderson; 24 Jason Baitieri. Subs (all used): 13 Gregory Mounis; 16 Eloi Pelissier; 22 Jamal Fakir; 14 Sebastien Raguin.
Try: Anderson (35); **Goals:** Dureau 1/1.
Rugby Leaguer & League Express Men of the Match:
Warriors: George Carmont; *Dragons:* Louis Anderson.
Penalty count: 9-8; **Half-time:** 22-6;
Referee: Richard Silverwood; **Attendance:** 7,232.

Saturday 15th September 2012

WARRINGTON WOLVES 6 ST HELENS 28

WOLVES: 1 Brett Hodgson; 5 Joel Monaghan; 19 Stefan Ratchford; 4 Ryan Atkins; 2 Chris Riley; 6 Lee Briers; 7 Richard Myler; 8 Adrian Morley (C); 14 Mick Higham; 20 Chris Hill; 11 Trent Waterhouse; 15 Simon Grix; 21 Tyrone McCarthy. Subs (all used): 9 Michael Monaghan; 10 Garreth Carvell; 16 Paul Wood; 17 Michael Cooper.
Try: Hodgson (22); **Goals:** Hodgson 1/1.
SAINTS: 1 Paul Wellens (C); 21 Tom Makinson; 17 Gary Wheeler; 26 Josh Jones; 5 Francis Meli; 6 Lance Hohaia; 7 Jonny Lomax; 8 Josh Perry; 9 James Roby; 14 Anthony Laffranchi; 11 Tony Puletua; 15 Mark Flanagan; 12 Jon Wilkin. Subs (all used): 4 Iosia Soliola; 10 Louie McCarthy-Scarsbrook; 16 Paul Clough; 19 Andrew Dixon.
Tries: Soliola (33), Makinson (36, 51), Roby (64), Meli (67); **Goals:** Makinson 4/6.
Rugby Leaguer & League Express Men of the Match:
Wolves: Chris Hill; *Saints:* James Roby.
Penalty count: 7-8; **Half-time:** 6-12;
Referee: Ben Thaler; **Attendance:** 10,190.

ELIMINATION PLAY-OFFS

Saturday 15th September 2012

LEEDS RHINOS 42 WAKEFIELD TRINITY WILDCATS 20

RHINOS: 4 Zak Hardaker; 2 Ben Jones-Bishop; 3 Kallum Watkins; 12 Carl Ablett; 5 Ryan Hall; 13 Kevin Sinfield (C); 6 Danny McGuire; 8 Kylie Leuluai; 7 Rob Burrow; 10 Jamie Peacock; 11 Jamie Jones-Buchanan; 15 Brett Delaney; 16 Ryan Bailey. Subs (all used): 25 Stevie Ward; 20 Darrell Griffin; 31 Shaun Lunt; 18 Chris Clarkson.
Tries: Burrow (21, 39), Jones-Bishop (49, 72, 74), McGuire (61), Hardaker (64); **Goals:** Sinfield 7/7.
WILDCATS: 1 Richard Mathers; 2 Peter Fox; 3 Dean Collis; 35 Lee Smith; 5 Ben Cockayne; 34 Paul Sykes; 20 Tim Smith; 15 Kyle Amor; 9 Andy Ellis; 10 Andy Raleigh; 11 Ali Lauititi; 17 Danny Kirmond (C); 13 Danny Washbrook. Subs (all used): 8 Oliver Wilkes; 19 Frankie Mariano; 7 Kyle Wood; 16 Paul Johnson.
Tries: Cockayne (15), L Smith (32), Mathers (41), Lauititi (68); **Goals:** Sykes 2/4.
Rugby Leaguer & League Express Men of the Match:
Rhinos: Rob Burrow; *Wildcats:* Tim Smith.
Penalty count: 6-7; **Half-time:** 12-10;
Referee: Steve Ganson; **Attendance:** 9,044.

Sunday 16th September 2012

HULL FC 46 HUDDERSFIELD GIANTS 10

HULL: 6 Richard Horne; 40 Jamie Foster; 19 Jordan Turner; 4 Kirk Yeaman; 5 Tom Briscoe; 7 Brett Seymour; 14 Aaron Heremaia; 37 Liam Watts; 9 Danny Houghton; 10 Andy Lynch (C); 11 Willie Manu; 13 Joe Westerman; 22 Martin Aspinwall. Subs (all used): 8 Mark O'Meley; 34 Jay Pitts; 23 Ben Crooks; 27 Chris Green.
Tries: Briscoe (8, 13), Foster (41, 50), Watts (57), Heremaia (62), Lynch (71), Horne (74); **Goals:** Foster 7/9.
GIANTS: 3 Leroy Cudjoe; 5 Jermaine McGillvary; 2 Michael Lawrence; 17 Joe Wardle; 20 Luke George; 1 Scott Grix; 7 Danny Brough (C); 8 Eorl Crabtree; 13 David Faiumu; 10 Keith Mason; 36 Brett Ferres; 12 David Fa'alogo; 11 Luke O'Donnell. Subs (all used): 9 Luke Robinson; 18 Jason Chan; 15 Larne Patrick; 16 Dale Ferguson.
Tries: Crabtree (67), Grix (69); **Goals:** Grix 1/2.
Rugby Leaguer & League Express Men of the Match:
Hull: Danny Houghton; *Giants:* Eorl Crabtree.
Penalty count: 8-5; **Half-time:** 12-0;
Referee: James Child; **Attendance:** 8,662.

Catalan Dragons' Vincent Duport looks to escape from Wigan's George Carmont and Brett Finch

PRELIMINARY SEMI-FINALS

Friday 21st September 2012

CATALAN DRAGONS 20 LEEDS RHINOS 27

DRAGONS: 1 Clint Greenshields; 2 Damien Blanch; 25 Vincent Duport; 4 Setaimata Sa; 18 Daryl Millard; 6 Thomas Bosc; 7 Scott Dureau; 8 David Ferriol; 9 Ian Henderson; 10 Remi Casty (C); 11 Steve Menzies; 12 Louis Anderson; 24 Jason Baitieri. Subs (all used): 3 Leon Pryce; 13 Gregory Mounis; 22 Jamal Fakir; 23 Lopini Paea.
Tries: Greenshields (7), Blanch (40, 48), Bosc (68);
Goals: Dureau 2/4.
On report: Fakir (72) - alleged high tackle on Burrow.
RHINOS: 4 Zak Hardaker; 2 Ben Jones-Bishop; 3 Kallum Watkins; 12 Carl Ablett; 5 Ryan Hall; 13 Kevin Sinfield (C); 6 Danny McGuire; 17 Ian Kirke; 7 Rob Burrow; 10 Jamie Peacock; 11 Jamie Jones-Buchanan; 15 Brett Delaney; 16 Ryan Bailey. Subs (all used): 18 Chris Clarkson; 20 Darrell Griffin; 25 Stevie Ward; 31 Shaun Lunt.
Tries: Ward (34), Lunt (36), Ablett (63), McGuire (65);
Goals: Sinfield 5/5; **Field goal:** McGuire (77).
On report: McGuire (47) - alleged high tackle on Anderson.
Rugby Leaguer & League Express Men of the Match:
Dragons: Louis Anderson; *Rhinos:* Danny McGuire.
Penalty count: 15-7; **Half-time:** 10-12;
Referee: Ben Thaler; **Attendance:** 8,156.

Saturday 22nd September 2012

WARRINGTON WOLVES 24 HULL FC 12

WOLVES: 1 Brett Hodgson; 5 Joel Monaghan; 19 Stefan Ratchford; 4 Ryan Atkins; 2 Chris Riley; 6 Lee Briers; 7 Richard Myler; 8 Adrian Morley (C); 14 Mick Higham; 20 Chris Hill; 11 Trent Waterhouse; 15 Simon Grix; 13 Ben Harrison. Subs (all used): 9 Michael Monaghan; 21 Tyrone McCarthy; 17 Michael Cooper; 16 Paul Wood.
Tries: Waterhouse (14), Myler (34), Ratchford (54), Hodgson (62); **Goals:** Hodgson 4/4.
HULL: 6 Richard Horne; 40 Jamie Foster; 19 Jordan Turner; 4 Kirk Yeaman; 5 Tom Briscoe; 7 Brett Seymour; 14 Aaron Heremaia; 37 Liam Watts; 9 Danny Houghton; 10 Andy Lynch (C); 11 Willie Manu; 13 Joe Westerman; 22 Martin Aspinwall. Subs (all used): 23 Ben Crooks; 8 Mark O'Meley; 27 Chris Green; 34 Jay Pitts.
Tries: Briscoe (66), Crooks (71); **Goals:** Foster 2/2.
On report:
Westerman (23) - alleged high tackle on M Monaghan.
Rugby Leaguer & League Express Men of the Match:
Wolves: Richard Myler; *Hull:* Danny Houghton.
Penalty count: 6-6; **Half-time:** 12-0;
Referee: Richard Silverwood; **Attendance:** 7,323.

QUALIFYING SEMI-FINALS

Friday 28th September 2012

WIGAN WARRIORS 12 LEEDS RHINOS 13

WARRIORS: 35 Jack Murphy; 2 Josh Charnley; 3 Darrell Goulding; 4 George Carmont; 5 Pat Richards; 6 Brett Finch; 7 Thomas Leuluai; 14 Jeff Lima; 13 Sean O'Loughlin (C); 10 Lee Mossop; 11 Harrison Hansen; 12 Gareth Hock; 16 Liam Farrell. Subs (all used): 21 Epalahame Lauaki; 38 Matty Smith; 26 Jack Hughes; 23 Ben Flower.

Tries: Hansen (42), Richards (61); **Goals:** Richards 2/2.
RHINOS: 4 Zak Hardaker; 2 Ben Jones-Bishop; 3 Kallum Watkins; 12 Carl Ablett; 5 Ryan Hall; 13 Kevin Sinfield (C); 7 Rob Burrow; 8 Kylie Leuluai; 31 Shaun Lunt; 10 Jamie Peacock; 11 Jamie Jones-Buchanan; 15 Brett Delaney; 16 Ryan Bailey. Subs (all used): 17 Ian Kirke; 18 Chris Clarkson; 20 Darrell Griffin; 25 Stevie Ward.
Try: Watkins (13); **Goals:** Sinfield 4/4;
Field goal: Sinfield (30).
Rugby Leaguer & League Express Men of the Match:
Warriors: Thomas Leuluai; *Rhinos:* Kevin Sinfield.
Penalty count: 7-5; **Half-time:** 0-11;
Referee: Richard Silverwood; **Attendance:** 12,334.

Saturday 29th September 2012

ST HELENS 18 WARRINGTON WOLVES 36

SAINTS: 1 Paul Wellens (C); 21 Tom Makinson; 13 Chris Flannery; 26 Josh Jones; 5 Francis Meli; 6 Lance Hohaia; 7 Jonny Lomax; 8 Josh Perry; 9 James Roby; 14 Anthony Laffranchi; 11 Tony Puletua; 15 Mark Flanagan; 12 Jon Wilkin. Subs (all used): 4 Iosia Soliola; 10 Louie McCarthy-Scarsbrook; 16 Paul Clough; 19 Andrew Dixon.
Tries: Makinson (12), Meli (27, 71), Wellens (34);
Goals: Makinson 1/4.
WOLVES: 1 Brett Hodgson; 5 Joel Monaghan; 19 Stefan Ratchford; 4 Ryan Atkins; 2 Chris Riley; 6 Lee Briers; 7 Richard Myler; 20 Chris Hill; 14 Mick Higham; 13 Ben Harrison; 12 Ben Westwood; 11 Trent Waterhouse; 15 Simon Grix. Subs (all used): 8 Adrian Morley (C); 9 Michael Monaghan; 16 Paul Wood; 17 Michael Cooper.
Tries: Riley (18, 66), Grix (38), J Monaghan (49), Waterhouse (59, 62); **Goals:** Hodgson 6/7.
Rugby Leaguer & League Express Men of the Match:
Saints: Iosia Soliola; *Wolves:* Trent Waterhouse.
Penalty count: 5-6; **Half-time:** 14-12;
Referee: Ben Thaler; **Attendance:** 12,715.

GRAND FINAL

Saturday 6th October 2012

LEEDS RHINOS 26 WARRINGTON WOLVES 18

RHINOS: 4 Zak Hardaker; 2 Ben Jones-Bishop; 3 Kallum Watkins; 12 Carl Ablett; 5 Ryan Hall; 13 Kevin Sinfield (C); 6 Danny McGuire; 8 Kylie Leuluai; 7 Rob Burrow; 10 Jamie Peacock; 11 Jamie Jones-Buchanan; 15 Brett Delaney; 16 Ryan Bailey. Subs (all used): 17 Ian Kirke; 20 Darrell Griffin; 25 Stevie Ward; 31 Shaun Lunt.
Tries: Sinfield (19), Jones-Bishop (28), Ablett (59), Hall (72); **Goals:** Sinfield 5/5.
WOLVES: 1 Brett Hodgson; 5 Joel Monaghan; 19 Stefan Ratchford; 4 Ryan Atkins; 2 Chris Riley; 6 Lee Briers; 7 Richard Myler; 20 Chris Hill; 14 Mick Higham; 13 Ben Harrison; 12 Ben Westwood; 11 Trent Waterhouse; 15 Simon Grix. Subs (all used): 8 Adrian Morley (C); 9 Michael Monaghan; 16 Paul Wood; 17 Michael Cooper.
Tries: Myler (4), J Monaghan (38), Atkins (45);
Goals: Hodgson 3/4.
Rugby Leaguer & League Express Men of the Match:
Rhinos: Kevin Sinfield; *Wolves:* Richard Myler.
Penalty count: 6-5; **Half-time:** 14-14;
Referee: Richard Silverwood;
Attendance: 70,676 *(at Old Trafford, Manchester).*

Leeds' Jamie Peacock and Kallum Watkins tackle Warrington's Chris Riley during the
Super League Grand Final

SUPER LEAGUE XVII
Opta Analysis

SUPER LEAGUE XVII
TOP PERFORMERS

TACKLES
Danny Washbrook	Wakefield	990
James Roby	St Helens	966
Danny Houghton	Hull FC	841
Jason Baitieri	Catalan Dragons	830
Michael Lawrence	Huddersfield	792
Jon Wilkin	St Helens	787
Chad Randall	London Broncos	782
Ian Henderson	Catalan Dragons	781
Paul Aiton	Wakefield	780
Hep Cahill	Widnes	779

TACKLES MADE *(% success)*
Jacob Fairbank	Huddersfield	99.56
Stephen Nash	Castleford	99.29
Ben Currie	Warrington	99.07
Paul Jackson	Castleford	98.97
Eorl Crabtree	Huddersfield	98.61
Gil Dudson	Wigan	98.60
Liam Farrell	Wigan	98.29
James Roby	St Helens	98.07
Paul Prescott	Wigan	97.89
Lopini Paea	Catalan Dragons	97.80

OFFLOADS
Gareth Hock	Wigan	72
Jamie Peacock	Leeds	55
Ryan Atkins	Warrington	51
Ali Lauitiiti	Wakefield	51
Willie Manu	Hull FC	51
Joel Moon	Salford	50
Luke Patten	Salford	48
Andy Lynch	Hull FC	47
Leon Pryce	Catalan Dragons	47
Rangi Chase	Castleford	44

CLEAN BREAKS
Sam Tomkins	Wigan	39
Ryan Hall	Leeds	31
Josh Charnley	Wigan	30
Ryan Atkins	Warrington	26
George Carmont	Wigan	26
Chris Riley	Warrington	25
Jodie Broughton	Salford	24
Scott Dureau	Catalan Dragons	24
Clint Greenshields	Catalan Dragons	24
Ben Jones-Bishop	Leeds	23

TRY ASSISTS
Michael Dobson	Hull KR	35
Tim Smith	Wakefield	34
Sam Tomkins	Wigan	33
Rangi Chase	Castleford	29
Scott Dureau	Catalan Dragons	28
Brett Finch	Wigan	28
Daniel Holdsworth	Salford	23
Craig Gower	London Broncos	21
Jonny Lomax	St Helens	21
James Roby	St Helens	20

MOST OFFLOADS -
Gareth Hock

MARKER TACKLES
Jon Wilkin	St Helens	159
Danny Houghton	Hull FC	148
Danny Washbrook	Wakefield	145
Lincoln Withers	Hull KR	144
Anthony Laffranchi	St Helens	141
Jamie Langley	Bradford	140
Brett Delaney	Leeds	135
Rhys Lovegrove	Hull KR	135
Paul Aiton	Wakefield	131
Chad Randall	London Broncos	131

METRES
James Roby	St Helens	3971
Sam Tomkins	Wigan	3438
Andy Lynch	Hull FC	3386
Ben Cockayne	Wakefield	3292
Mickey Paea	Hull KR	3054
Peter Fox	Wakefield	3047
Tom Briscoe	Hull FC	2924
Nick Youngquest	Castleford	2911
Jeff Lima	Wigan	2910
Louie McCarthy-Scarsbrook	St Helens	2859

CARRIES
James Roby	St Helens	845
Craig Gower	London Broncos	579
Andy Lynch	Hull FC	515
Kevin Sinfield	Leeds	514
Danny Houghton	Hull FC	511
Michael McIlorum	Wigan	483
Sam Tomkins	Wigan	465
Tim Smith	Wakefield	455
Chris Bailey	London Broncos	450
Richard Mathers	Wakefield	442

AVERAGE GAIN PER CARRY *(Metres)*
Luke George	Huddersfield	9.69
Rhys Williams	Warrington/Castleford	9.68
Francis Meli	St Helens	9.28
Patrick Ah Van	Widnes	9.21
Jermaine McGillvary	Huddersfield	9.05
Josh Griffin	Castleford	8.87
Kieran Dixon	London Broncos	8.81
Tom Briscoe	Hull FC	8.78
Joe Wardle	Huddersfield	8.63
David Hodgson	Hull KR	8.62

TACKLE BUSTS
Sam Tomkins	Wigan	156
Willie Manu	Hull FC	105
Zak Hardaker	Leeds	98
Luke Patten	Salford	85
Vincent Duport	Catalan Dragons	78
Rangi Chase	Castleford	76
Danny Brough	Huddersfield	72
Gareth Hock	Wigan	72
Peter Fox	Wakefield	70
Paul Wellens	St Helens	69

40/20s
Danny Brough	Huddersfield	5
Scott Dureau	Catalan Dragons	5
Paul Sykes	Wakefield	3
Michael Dobson	Hull KR	2
Luke Gale	Bradford	2
Craig Gower	London Broncos	2
Blake Green	Hull KR	2
Daniel Holdsworth	Salford	2
Kevin Sinfield	Leeds	2

PENALTIES CONCEDED
Chris Bailey	London Broncos	28
Michael McIlorum	Wigan	28
Steve Pickersgill	Widnes	28
Keith Mason	Huddersfield	25
Ben Cross	Widnes	24
Gareth Hock	Wigan	24
Jason Chan	Huddersfield	23
Kevin Sinfield	Leeds	23
Stephen Wild	Salford	23
Jon Wilkin	St Helens	23

opta

All statistics in Opta Analysis include
Super League regular season games only

Richard Myler and Chris Riley celebrate as Ryan Atkins scores against Hull KR. Warrington scored the most tries from their own half in Super League XVII

SUPER LEAGUE XVII AVERAGES PER MATCH

TACKLES		OFFLOADS		METRES		ERRORS	
Warrington Wolves	313.0	Warrington Wolves	14.7	St Helens	1473.0	Warrington Wolves	14.8
St Helens	306.0	Hull FC	14.2	Wigan Warriors	1411.8	Catalan Dragons	14.7
Huddersfield Giants	305.1	Salford City Reds	14.0	Warrington Wolves	1381.1	Huddersfield Giants	13.0
Castleford Tigers	304.4	Catalan Dragons	13.5	Leeds Rhinos	1363.3	Leeds Rhinos	12.9
Salford City Reds	303.4	Leeds Rhinos	12.8	Catalan Dragons	1324.8	Widnes Vikings	12.9
Leeds Rhinos	303.0	Castleford Tigers	11.0	Hull FC	1324.6	Bradford Bulls	12.6
Wakefield T Wildcats	301.4	Widnes Vikings	11.0	Hull Kingston Rovers	1276.9	Hull FC	12.6
Bradford Bulls	298.9	Bradford Bulls	10.7	Wakefield T Wildcats	1263.6	Castleford Tigers	12.4
London Broncos	293.6	St Helens	10.6	Huddersfield Giants	1259.5	London Broncos	12.1
Widnes Vikings	289.5	Wakefield T Wildcats	9.9	Bradford Bulls	1250.9	Salford City Reds	12.0
Hull Kingston Rovers	288.4	Huddersfield Giants	9.5	Castleford Tigers	1249.9	Wigan Warriors	11.6
Catalan Dragons	284.7	Wigan Warriors	9.5	London Broncos	1246.3	Hull Kingston Rovers	11.1
Hull FC	284.1	Hull Kingston Rovers	7.5	Salford City Reds	1179.6	Wakefield T Wildcats	10.5
Wigan Warriors	280.3	London Broncos	7.3	Widnes Vikings	1129.9	St Helens	10.2

MISSED TACKLES		CLEAN BREAKS		CARRIES		KICKS IN GENERAL PLAY	
Widnes Vikings	30.7	Wigan Warriors	9.7	St Helens	227.4	St Helens	21.4
London Broncos	28.3	Catalan Dragons	7.6	Wigan Warriors	218.6	Hull Kingston Rovers	18.3
Hull Kingston Rovers	26.8	Huddersfield Giants	7.6	Hull FC	215.0	London Broncos	18.2
Salford City Reds	26.6	Warrington Wolves	7.6	Leeds Rhinos	205.5	Wakefield T Wildcats	18.1
Bradford Bulls	23.8	Leeds Rhinos	7.5	Wakefield T Wildcats	203.8	Castleford Tigers	17.9
Castleford Tigers	22.6	Hull FC	7.1	Warrington Wolves	201.3	Huddersfield Giants	17.9
Hull FC	22.3	St Helens	6.7	Catalan Dragons	201.1	Bradford Bulls	17.7
Wakefield T Wildcats	21.7	Salford City Reds	6.2	Bradford Bulls	200.9	Hull FC	17.3
Catalan Dragons	21.1	Hull Kingston Rovers	6.0	Castleford Tigers	200.7	Leeds Rhinos	17.3
Leeds Rhinos	20.7	Wakefield T Wildcats	5.9	London Broncos	200.7	Wigan Warriors	16.9
Warrington Wolves	20.3	Bradford Bulls	5.6	Hull Kingston Rovers	193.7	Salford City Reds	16.8
Huddersfield Giants	19.5	Castleford Tigers	5.5	Salford City Reds	192.6	Warrington Wolves	16.5
St Helens	17.2	Widnes Vikings	5.0	Huddersfield Giants	185.4	Widnes Vikings	16.2
Wigan Warriors	16.1	London Broncos	4.7	Widnes Vikings	176.8	Catalan Dragons	15.2

SUPER LEAGUE XVII TRIES SCORED/CONCEDED

TOTAL TRIES SCORED		TOTAL TRIES CONCEDED		SCORED FROM KICKS		CONCEDED FROM KICKS	
Wigan Warriors	183	Widnes Vikings	194	St Helens	23	Wakefield T Wildcats	32
Warrington Wolves	160	Castleford Tigers	168	Wakefield T Wildcats	22	Castleford Tigers	25
St Helens	146	London Broncos	157	Bradford Bulls	21	Hull Kingston Rovers	22
Leeds Rhinos	145	Salford City Reds	150	Hull Kingston Rovers	21	Huddersfield Giants	20
Catalan Dragons	143	Wakefield T Wildcats	146	Warrington Wolves	21	Leeds Rhinos	19
Hull Kingston Rovers	132	Bradford Bulls	138	Catalan Dragons	20	Hull FC	18
Huddersfield Giants	121	Hull Kingston Rovers	131	Leeds Rhinos	17	St Helens	18
Hull FC	117	Leeds Rhinos	128	London Broncos	17	Catalan Dragons	16
Salford City Reds	116	Huddersfield Giants	127	Wigan Warriors	16	Widnes Vikings	15
Wakefield T Wildcats	114	Catalan Dragons	120	Widnes Vikings	15	Bradford Bulls	14
Bradford Bulls	111	Hull FC	118	Huddersfield Giants	13	Salford City Reds	14
London Broncos	105	Warrington Wolves	111	Hull FC	13	London Broncos	11
Castleford Tigers	101	St Helens	91	Castleford Tigers	12	Warrington Wolves	10
Widnes Vikings	95	Wigan Warriors	80	Salford City Reds	12	Wigan Warriors	9

SUPER LEAGUE XVII TRIES SCORED/CONCEDED

TRIES SCORED FROM OWN HALF

Warrington Wolves	29
Catalan Dragons	25
Leeds Rhinos	23
Wigan Warriors	21
Salford City Reds	20
Huddersfield Giants	19
Hull Kingston Rovers	16
Hull FC	15
St Helens	15
Widnes Vikings	15
Bradford Bulls	10
London Broncos	9
Castleford Tigers	8
Wakefield T Wildcats	7

TRIES CONCEDED FROM OVER 50M

Castleford Tigers	29
London Broncos	24
Wakefield T Wildcats	23
Widnes Vikings	22
Bradford Bulls	21
Hull Kingston Rovers	21
Catalan Dragons	18
Leeds Rhinos	18
Salford City Reds	18
Warrington Wolves	16
Hull FC	13
Wigan Warriors	10
St Helens	8
Huddersfield Giants	6

TRIES SCORED FROM UNDER 10M

Wigan Warriors	81
Warrington Wolves	70
St Helens	69
London Broncos	64
Bradford Bulls	62
Wakefield T Wildcats	61
Hull FC	60
Hull Kingston Rovers	60
Huddersfield Giants	58
Castleford Tigers	56
Catalan Dragons	54
Leeds Rhinos	52
Salford City Reds	49
Widnes Vikings	42

TRIES CONCEDED FROM UNDER 10M

Widnes Vikings	90
Salford City Reds	70
Huddersfield Giants	66
Castleford Tigers	65
Leeds Rhinos	65
Catalan Dragons	63
Hull Kingston Rovers	63
London Broncos	63
Wakefield T Wildcats	62
Bradford Bulls	61
Warrington Wolves	58
Hull FC	54
St Helens	48
Wigan Warriors	36

SUPER LEAGUE XVII PENALTIES

TOTAL PENALTIES AWARDED

Catalan Dragons	277
Wigan Warriors	251
Warrington Wolves	244
Wakefield T Wildcats	243
Bradford Bulls	235
Hull FC	229
Hull Kingston Rovers	219
Leeds Rhinos	213
St Helens	211
London Broncos	208
Salford City Reds	206
Huddersfield Giants	204
Widnes Vikings	195
Castleford Tigers	189

TOTAL PENALTIES CONCEDED

Widnes Vikings	255
Leeds Rhinos	245
Hull FC	244
Warrington Wolves	235
St Helens	234
Catalan Dragons	230
London Broncos	221
Bradford Bulls	219
Huddersfield Giants	218
Salford City Reds	218
Wigan Warriors	208
Wakefield T Wildcats	203
Hull Kingston Rovers	202
Castleford Tigers	192

FOUL PLAY - AWARDED

Catalan Dragons	71
Warrington Wolves	62
Bradford Bulls	60
Wakefield T Wildcats	58
St Helens	57
Hull Kingston Rovers	54
Huddersfield Giants	52
Hull FC	52
Wigan Warriors	52
London Broncos	46
Leeds Rhinos	45
Salford City Reds	43
Widnes Vikings	43
Castleford Tigers	38

FOUL PLAY - CONCEDED

Warrington Wolves	72
Widnes Vikings	67
Wigan Warriors	60
Huddersfield Giants	58
St Helens	58
Leeds Rhinos	54
Wakefield T Wildcats	53
London Broncos	52
Catalan Dragons	48
Castleford Tigers	47
Salford City Reds	43
Hull FC	42
Bradford Bulls	40
Hull Kingston Rovers	39

OFFSIDE - AWARDED

Leeds Rhinos	33
Warrington Wolves	33
Huddersfield Giants	32
Bradford Bulls	26
Castleford Tigers	26
London Broncos	26
St Helens	26
Widnes Vikings	26
Catalan Dragons	25
Hull Kingston Rovers	23
Wigan Warriors	18
Hull FC	18
Salford City Reds	18
Wakefield T Wildcats	15

OFFSIDE - CONCEDED

Hull Kingston Rovers	37
Wigan Warriors	35
Hull FC	34
Salford City Reds	31
Castleford Tigers	29
Catalan Dragons	26
Leeds Rhinos	25
Warrington Wolves	25
St Helens	23
Widnes Vikings	23
London Broncos	21
Huddersfield Giants	20
Bradford Bulls	12
Wakefield T Wildcats	9

INTERFERENCE - AWARDED

Wakefield T Wildcats	92
Wigan Warriors	83
Hull FC	77
Leeds Rhinos	75
Salford City Reds	75
Warrington Wolves	75
Bradford Bulls	74
Catalan Dragons	73
London Broncos	67
Castleford Tigers	64
Huddersfield Giants	64
Hull Kingston Rovers	63
St Helens	58
Widnes Vikings	50

INTERFERENCE - CONCEDED

Widnes Vikings	85
Hull FC	81
Bradford Bulls	79
Leeds Rhinos	77
London Broncos	75
St Helens	75
Huddersfield Giants	73
Castleford Tigers	68
Warrington Wolves	67
Salford City Reds	65
Wakefield T Wildcats	65
Hull Kingston Rovers	64
Catalan Dragons	61
Wigan Warriors	55

OBSTRUCTION - AWARDED

Catalan Dragons	20
Hull FC	18
Wakefield T Wildcats	16
London Broncos	15
Bradford Bulls	14
St Helens	14
Wigan Warriors	14
Widnes Vikings	13
Castleford Tigers	11
Leeds Rhinos	11
Hull Kingston Rovers	10
Huddersfield Giants	9
Salford City Reds	8
Warrington Wolves	8

OBSTRUCTION - CONCEDED

Catalan Dragons	20
Leeds Rhinos	18
Salford City Reds	16
London Broncos	15
Widnes Vikings	15
Warrington Wolves	14
Hull FC	13
St Helens	13
Wakefield T Wildcats	13
Huddersfield Giants	12
Bradford Bulls	10
Hull Kingston Rovers	10
Wigan Warriors	8
Castleford Tigers	4

BALL STEALING - AWARDED

Hull Kingston Rovers	32
Wigan Warriors	30
Catalan Dragons	24
Widnes Vikings	23
Bradford Bulls	20
London Broncos	19
Warrington Wolves	18
St Helens	17
Hull FC	16
Salford City Reds	15
Wakefield T Wildcats	14
Leeds Rhinos	11
Castleford Tigers	10
Huddersfield Giants	8

BALL STEALING - CONCEDED

Leeds Rhinos	28
Hull FC	26
Warrington Wolves	26
Bradford Bulls	22
Salford City Reds	21
Wakefield T Wildcats	21
Catalan Dragons	20
London Broncos	16
Huddersfield Giants	15
Hull Kingston Rovers	14
Wigan Warriors	14
St Helens	13
Widnes Vikings	11
Castleford Tigers	10

OFFSIDE MARKERS - AWARDED

Wigan Warriors	31
Catalan Dragons	30
Bradford Bulls	20
Castleford Tigers	18
Hull FC	18
Salford City Reds	17
Warrington Wolves	16
Wakefield T Wildcats	14
Widnes Vikings	14
London Broncos	13
St Helens	11
Huddersfield Giants	10
Leeds Rhinos	8
Hull Kingston Rovers	7

OFFSIDE MARKERS - CONCEDED

St Helens	24
Leeds Rhinos	20
Hull FC	19
Catalan Dragons	18
Salford City Reds	18
Warrington Wolves	18
Widnes Vikings	18
Bradford Bulls	17
Wakefield T Wildcats	17
Huddersfield Giants	14
London Broncos	13
Hull Kingston Rovers	11
Wigan Warriors	11
Castleford Tigers	9

NOT PLAYING BALL CORRECTLY - AWARDED

Leeds Rhinos	4
Widnes Vikings	2
Bradford Bulls	1
Castleford Tigers	1
Hull Kingston Rovers	1
Salford City Reds	1
Wakefield T Wildcats	1
Catalan Dragons	0
Huddersfield Giants	0
Hull FC	0
London Broncos	0
St Helens	0
Warrington Wolves	0
Wigan Warriors	0

NOT PLAYING BALL CORRECTLY - CONCEDED

Hull Kingston Rovers	3
Bradford Bulls	2
Hull FC	2
Widnes Vikings	2
Salford City Reds	1
Wakefield T Wildcats	1
Castleford Tigers	0
Catalan Dragons	0
Huddersfield Giants	0
Leeds Rhinos	0
London Broncos	0
St Helens	0
Warrington Wolves	0
Wigan Warriors	0

DISSENT - AWARDED
(including advances)

Hull FC	9
Salford City Reds	7
Catalan Dragons	6
Hull Kingston Rovers	6
Wakefield T Wildcats	6
Huddersfield Giants	5
Leeds Rhinos	5
Widnes Vikings	5
Castleford Tigers	4
St Helens	4
Warrington Wolves	4
Bradford Bulls	3
London Broncos	2
Wigan Warriors	2

DISSENT - CONCEDED
(including advances)

Catalan Dragons	13
Wigan Warriors	7
Bradford Bulls	6
Salford City Reds	6
St Helens	6
Widnes Vikings	6
Castleford Tigers	5
Huddersfield Giants	4
Hull FC	4
Wakefield T Wildcats	4
Hull Kingston Rovers	3
London Broncos	2
Leeds Rhinos	1
Warrington Wolves	1

BRADFORD BULLS

**Elliott
Whitehead**

MARKER TACKLES

Jamie Langley	140
Elliott Whitehead	124
Heath L'Estrange	99
Bryn Hargreaves	91
Olivier Elima	70

METRES

Brett Kearney	2446
Bryn Hargreaves	2312
Heath L'Estrange	2136
Elliott Whitehead	2117
Manase Manuokafoa	2057

CARRIES

Heath L'Estrange	433
Bryn Hargreaves	389
Brett Kearney	361
Jamie Langley	319
Elliott Whitehead	317

TACKLES

Elliott Whitehead	744
Jamie Langley	740
Bryn Hargreaves	690
Heath L'Estrange	657
Manase Manuokafoa	488

CLEAN BREAKS

Brett Kearney	17
Jarrod Sammut	16
Elliott Whitehead	15
Shaun Ainscough	13
Karl Pryce	13

TACKLE BUSTS

Brett Kearney	51
Shaun Ainscough	44
Jarrod Sammut	37
Keith Lulia	36
Elliott Whitehead	35

OFFLOADS

Elliott Whitehead	28
Olivier Elima	26
Keith Lulia	21
Michael Platt	21
Manase Manuokafoa	18

TRY ASSISTS

Ben Jeffries	13
Luke Gale	12
Brett Kearney	8
Keith Lulia	8
Elliott Whitehead	7

TOTAL OPTA INDEX

Elliott Whitehead	11716
Jamie Langley	10958
Bryn Hargreaves	10309
Heath L'Estrange	10047
Brett Kearney	9840

**Jamie
Langley**

CASTLEFORD TIGERS

**Richard
Owen**

MARKER TACKLES

Nathan Massey	112
Jake Emmitt	99
Lee Mitchell	95
Oliver Holmes	93
Steve Snitch	74

METRES

Nick Youngquest	2911
Richard Owen	2733
Jake Emmitt	2550
Josh Griffin	2067
Rangi Chase	1995

CARRIES

Rangi Chase	436
Richard Owen	405
Nick Youngquest	391
Jake Emmitt	390
Danny Orr	379

TACKLES

Jake Emmitt	681
Oliver Holmes	635
Nathan Massey	618
Stuart Jones	592
Lee Mitchell	571

CLEAN BREAKS

Rangi Chase	12
Richard Owen	12
Nick Youngquest	12
Brett Ferres	11
Rhys Williams	11

TACKLE BUSTS

Rangi Chase	76
Richard Owen	61
Daryl Clark	44
Danny Orr	36
Brett Ferres	33

OFFLOADS

Rangi Chase	44
Craig Huby	32
Grant Millington	32
Richard Owen	31
Danny Orr	18

TRY ASSISTS

Rangi Chase	29
Ryan McGoldrick	9
Richard Owen	8
Danny Orr	5
Ryan Hudson	4

TOTAL OPTA INDEX

Richard Owen	9958
Rangi Chase	9897
Jake Emmitt	9739
Danny Orr	9121
Nathan Massey	8692

**Rangi
Chase**

233

CATALAN DRAGONS

Scott
Dureau

Jason
Baitieri

TACKLES
Jason Baitieri.................830
Ian Henderson 781
Remi Casty 615
Lopini Paea 489
Gregory Mounis............422

OFFLOADS
Leon Pryce 47
Steve Menzies 32
Jason Baitieri.................28
Gregory Mounis.............24
Ian Henderson 20

CLEAN BREAKS
Scott Dureau 24
Clint Greenshields 24
Vincent Duport 22
Daryl Millard 19
Damien Blanch 18

TRY ASSISTS
Scott Dureau 28
Leon Pryce 18
Vincent Duport 10
Ian Henderson 10
Setaimata Sa 9

MARKER TACKLES
Ian Henderson 125
Jason Baitieri................117
Remi Casty 88
Lopini Paea 57
Gregory Mounis.............55

METRES
Jason Baitieri..............2483
Clint Greenshields 2472
Vincent Duport 2400
Scott Dureau 2304
Daryl Millard 2182

CARRIES
Jason Baitieri................414
Scott Dureau 414
Ian Henderson 369
Vincent Duport 356
Clint Greenshields 327

TACKLE BUSTS
Vincent Duport 78
Clint Greenshields 59
Scott Dureau 53
Remi Casty 49
Jamal Fakir 48

TOTAL OPTA INDEX
Jason Baitieri............13284
Scott Dureau 12468
Vincent Duport 11494
Remi Casty 11341
Ian Henderson 11047

HUDDERSFIELD GIANTS

Eorl
Crabtree

Danny
Brough

TACKLES
Michael Lawrence 792
Jason Chan 713
Eorl Crabtree 708
Luke Robinson 658
Leroy Cudjoe 541

OFFLOADS
Leroy Cudjoe 29
David Faiumu..................27
Jason Chan 23
Eorl Crabtree 22
Greg Eden 17

CLEAN BREAKS
Danny Brough 22
Greg Eden 22
Luke George 19
Joe Wardle.....................17
Jermaine McGillvary 16

TRY ASSISTS
Danny Brough 18
Scott Grix 14
Kevin Brown 9
Leroy Cudjoe 9
Tommy Lee 5

MARKER TACKLES
Michael Lawrence 130
Eorl Crabtree 118
Luke Robinson 109
Jason Chan 90
Leroy Cudjoe 66

METRES
Eorl Crabtree 2841
Greg Eden 2808
Luke George 2627
Jermaine McGillvary 2345
Jason Chan 2153

CARRIES
Eorl Crabtree 394
Luke Robinson 360
Greg Eden 359
Danny Brough 319
Jason Chan 310

TACKLE BUSTS
Danny Brough 72
Greg Eden 67
Leroy Cudjoe 56
Scott Grix 53
Eorl Crabtree 52

TOTAL OPTA INDEX
Danny Brough 14716
Eorl Crabtree 13781
Jason Chan 11519
Michael Lawrence 11412
Leroy Cudjoe 11144

HULL F.C.

HULL F.C.

Danny Houghton

Andy Lynch

MARKER TACKLES
Danny Houghton	148
Andy Lynch	122
Danny Tickle	83
Richard Whiting	76
Martin Aspinwall	66

METRES
Andy Lynch	3386
Tom Briscoe	2924
Willie Manu	2674
Danny Houghton	2161
Jordan Turner	2119

CARRIES
Andy Lynch	515
Danny Houghton	511
Willie Manu	392
Brett Seymour	372
Tom Briscoe	333

TACKLES
Danny Houghton	841
Andy Lynch	774
Willie Manu	572
Danny Tickle	544
Richard Whiting	459

CLEAN BREAKS
Tom Briscoe	22
Jordan Turner	19
Ben Crooks	16
Willie Manu	16
Richard Horne	13

TACKLE BUSTS
Willie Manu	105
Tom Briscoe	59
Jordan Turner	46
Matthew Russell	42
Will Sharp	39

OFFLOADS
Willie Manu	51
Andy Lynch	47
Tom Briscoe	37
Brett Seymour	30
Richard Whiting	25

TRY ASSISTS
Richard Horne	14
Willie Manu	12
Brett Seymour	12
Danny Houghton	9
Tom Briscoe	7

TOTAL OPTA INDEX
Danny Houghton	14258
Andy Lynch	13468
Willie Manu	13451
Brett Seymour	10322
Tom Briscoe	10044

HULL KINGSTON ROVERS

Michael Dobson

Lincoln Withers

MARKER TACKLES
Lincoln Withers	144
Rhys Lovegrove	135
Josh Hodgson	99
Graeme Horne	84
Mickey Paea	65

METRES
Mickey Paea	3054
Josh Hodgson	2297
Scott Taylor	2160
Craig Hall	2106
Shannon McDonnell	1880

CARRIES
Michael Dobson	402
Mickey Paea	368
Lincoln Withers	367
Josh Hodgson	347
Scott Taylor	309

TACKLES
Lincoln Withers	770
Josh Hodgson	639
Rhys Lovegrove	615
Graeme Horne	511
Mickey Paea	483

CLEAN BREAKS
Craig Hall	20
Michael Dobson	17
David Hodgson	15
Kris Welham	15
Ben Galea	12

TACKLE BUSTS
Shannon McDonnell	59
Craig Hall	55
Michael Dobson	48
Constantine Mika	41
Josh Hodgson	38

OFFLOADS
Constantine Mika	24
Craig Hall	22
Mickey Paea	21
Josh Hodgson	15
Scott Taylor	13

TRY ASSISTS
Michael Dobson	35
Craig Hall	12
Shannon McDonnell	11
Lincoln Withers	11
Kris Welham	5

TOTAL OPTA INDEX
Michael Dobson	13291
Lincoln Withers	11349
Josh Hodgson	10946
Mickey Paea	9541
Scott Taylor	8820

LEEDS RHINOS

Kevin Sinfield

Zak Hardaker

TACKLES
Brett Delaney 769
Jamie Peacock...............698
Carl Ablett 619
Jamie Jones-Buchanan ..531
Kevin Sinfield.................522

OFFLOADS
Jamie Peacock..................55
Kevin Sinfield...................43
Carl Ablett 29
Ryan Hall 28
Jamie Jones-Buchanan 25

CLEAN BREAKS
Ryan Hall 31
Ben Jones-Bishop 23
Zak Hardaker 22
Kallum Watkins 21
Danny McGuire 19

TRY ASSISTS
Kevin Sinfield...................18
Brent Webb 14
Rob Burrow 11
Danny McGuire 11
Carl Ablett 9

METRES
Ryan Hall 2819
Jamie Peacock.............2810
Zak Hardaker 2751
Rob Burrow 2442
Brett Delaney 2201

TACKLE BUSTS
Zak Hardaker 98
Rob Burrow 57
Kallum Watkins 56
Carl Ablett 48
Danny McGuire 48

MARKER TACKLES
Brett Delaney 135
Jamie Peacock.................94
Chris Clarkson 92
Kevin Sinfield...................86
Jamie Jones-Buchanan 77

CARRIES
Kevin Sinfield.................514
Jamie Peacock...............438
Rob Burrow 384
Ryan Hall 367
Zak Hardaker 351

TOTAL OPTA INDEX
Zak Hardaker 13503
Kevin Sinfield..............13494
Jamie Peacock...........11555
Ryan Hall 11494
Brett Delaney 11464

LONDON BRONCOS

Chris Bailey

Craig Gower

TACKLES
Chad Randall 782
Chris Bailey 710
Mark Bryant....................590
Tony Clubb......................567
Antonio Kaufusi 520

OFFLOADS
Mark Bryant.....................32
Chris Bailey 30
Michael Witt 18
Craig Gower.....................15
Luke Dorn 11

CLEAN BREAKS
Kieran Dixon 12
Luke Dorn 12
Chris Bailey 10
Omari Caro 10
Michael Robertson 10

TRY ASSISTS
Craig Gower.....................21
Luke Dorn 11
Chad Randall 9
Michael Witt 9
Julien Rinaldi.....................7

METRES
Chris Bailey 2743
Craig Gower.................2606
Kieran Dixon 2556
Mark Bryant.................2493
Michael Robertson 2059

TACKLE BUSTS
Kieran Dixon 51
Craig Gower.....................37
Dan Sarginson.................35
Michael Robertson 33
Chris Bailey 32

MARKER TACKLES
Chad Randall 131
Julien Rinaldi...................93
Chris Bailey 84
Mark Bryant.....................80
Tony Clubb.......................68

CARRIES
Craig Gower...................579
Chris Bailey 450
Mark Bryant...................369
Michael Robertson 321
Chad Randall 294

TOTAL OPTA INDEX
Craig Gower...............11835
Chris Bailey 11281
Chad Randall 10077
Mark Bryant.................9190
Michael Robertson 8880

SALFORD CITY REDS

Luke Patten

MARKER TACKLES
Matty Ashurst 115
Lee Jewitt 95
Stuart Howarth 90
Stephen Wild 88
Daniel Holdsworth 86

METRES
Jodie Broughton 2736
Luke Patten 2623
Danny Williams 2110
Lee Jewitt 1729
Matty Ashurst 1682

CARRIES
Luke Patten 430
Daniel Holdsworth 377
Jodie Broughton 344
Matty Ashurst 299
Danny Williams 299

Daniel Holdsworth

TACKLES
Stephen Wild 776
Matty Ashurst 708
Stuart Howarth 646
Daniel Holdsworth 575
Lee Jewitt 552

CLEAN BREAKS
Jodie Broughton 24
Danny Williams 21
Luke Patten 20
Sean Gleeson 15
Ashley Gibson 14

TACKLE BUSTS
Luke Patten 85
Jodie Broughton 55
Danny Williams 50
Sean Gleeson 47
Joel Moon 36

OFFLOADS
Joel Moon 50
Luke Patten 48
Sean Gleeson 39
Vinnie Anderson 34
Stephen Wild 31

TRY ASSISTS
Daniel Holdsworth 23
Luke Patten 18
Sean Gleeson 10
Joel Moon 8
Matty Smith 6

TOTAL OPTA INDEX
Luke Patten 11541
Daniel Holdsworth 10900
Matty Ashurst 9599
Jodie Broughton 8989
Stephen Wild 8745

ST HELENS

James Roby

MARKER TACKLES
Jon Wilkin 159
Anthony Laffranchi 141
James Roby 131
Chris Flannery 78
Josh Perry 75

METRES
James Roby 3971
Louie McCarthy-Scarsbrook..2859
Paul Clough 2629
Francis Meli 2580
Paul Wellens 2544

CARRIES
James Roby 845
Paul Wellens 417
Jon Wilkin 389
Jonny Lomax 386
Lance Hohaia 384

Jon Wilkin

TACKLES
James Roby 966
Jon Wilkin 787
Anthony Laffranchi 601
Louie McCarthy-Scarsbrook..540
Iosia Soliola 524

CLEAN BREAKS
Paul Wellens 18
Jonny Lomax 16
Francis Meli 16
James Roby 14
Lance Hohaia 12

TACKLE BUSTS
Paul Wellens 69
Lance Hohaia 55
Francis Meli 52
Jonny Lomax 48
James Roby 47

OFFLOADS
James Roby 29
Anthony Laffranchi 25
Louie McCarthy-Scarsbrook ..23
Tony Puletua 21
Jonny Lomax 17

TRY ASSISTS
Jonny Lomax 21
James Roby 20
Lance Hohaia 12
Paul Wellens 12
Michael Shenton 10

TOTAL OPTA INDEX
James Roby 20312
Jon Wilkin 13133
Paul Wellens 12826
Lance Hohaia 11874
Jonny Lomax 10808

WAKEFIELD T WILDCATS

Tim Smith

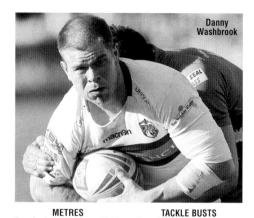

Danny Washbrook

TACKLES
Danny Washbrook	990
Paul Aiton	780
Andy Raleigh	729
Danny Kirmond	572
Oliver Wilkes	462

OFFLOADS
Ali Lauitiiti	51
Ben Cockayne	25
Danny Washbrook	23
Richard Mathers	19
Andy Raleigh	19

CLEAN BREAKS
Ben Cockayne	22
Peter Fox	19
Danny Kirmond	13
Richard Mathers	12
Paul Sykes	12

TRY ASSISTS
Tim Smith	34
Richard Mathers	9
Paul Sykes	9
Danny Washbrook	7
Ali Lauitiiti	6

METRES
Ben Cockayne	3292
Peter Fox	3047
Richard Mathers	2589
Andy Raleigh	2430
Kyle Amor	2345

TACKLE BUSTS
Peter Fox	70
Ben Cockayne	64
Richard Mathers	49
Danny Kirmond	38
Paul Sykes	38

MARKER TACKLES
Danny Washbrook	145
Paul Aiton	131
Andy Raleigh	114
Danny Kirmond	88
Kyle Wood	81

CARRIES
Tim Smith	455
Richard Mathers	442
Ben Cockayne	426
Peter Fox	386
Andy Raleigh	368

TOTAL OPTA INDEX
Danny Washbrook	13082
Tim Smith	12405
Andy Raleigh	11325
Paul Aiton	11025
Ben Cockayne	10419

WARRINGTON WOLVES

Chris Riley

Ryan Atkins

TACKLES
Trent Waterhouse	630
Chris Hill	562
Adrian Morley	544
Michael Cooper	520
Paul Wood	517

OFFLOADS
Ryan Atkins	51
Trent Waterhouse	43
Paul Wood	34
Ben Westwood	27
Chris Bridge	26

CLEAN BREAKS
Ryan Atkins	26
Chris Riley	25
Stefan Ratchford	22
Chris Bridge	17
Joel Monaghan	17

TRY ASSISTS
Richard Myler	19
Lee Briers	18
Ryan Atkins	14
Brett Hodgson	14
Chris Bridge	12

METRES
Chris Riley	2492
Ryan Atkins	2462
Chris Hill	2414
Adrian Morley	2019
Paul Wood	2011

TACKLE BUSTS
Ryan Atkins	66
Chris Riley	66
Stefan Ratchford	51
Ben Westwood	36
Richard Myler	34

MARKER TACKLES
Trent Waterhouse	102
Ben Westwood	102
Mick Higham	87
Chris Hill	83
Paul Wood	83

CARRIES
Chris Hill	319
Chris Riley	305
Ryan Atkins	286
Paul Wood	275
Ben Westwood	273

TOTAL OPTA INDEX
Ryan Atkins	12040
Chris Riley	9910
Trent Waterhouse	9905
Chris Hill	9701
Stefan Ratchford	9697

WIDNES VIKINGS

Hep Cahill

MARKER TACKLES
Hep Cahill	125
Dave Allen	104
Jon Clarke	67
Ben Davies	64
Ben Cross	61

METRES
Hep Cahill	2626
Frank Winterstein	2226
Ben Davies	2123
Willie Isa	2058
Rhys Hanbury	1987

CARRIES
Hep Cahill	385
Rhys Hanbury	330
Frank Winterstein	330
Ben Davies	290
Willie Isa	287

Frank Winterstein

TACKLES
Hep Cahill	779
Dave Allen	760
Frank Winterstein	526
Ben Davies	513
Steve Pickersgill	457

CLEAN BREAKS
Patrick Ah Van	22
Rhys Hanbury	20
Paddy Flynn	14
Stefan Marsh	10
Joe Mellor	10

TACKLE BUSTS
Rhys Hanbury	65
Paddy Flynn	52
Stefan Marsh	39
Patrick Ah Van	32
Willie Isa	22

OFFLOADS
Frank Winterstein	42
Rhys Hanbury	28
Dave Allen	24
Hep Cahill	21
Stefan Marsh	20

TRY ASSISTS
Rhys Hanbury	18
Willie Isa	6
Paul McShane	5
Jon Clarke	4
Cameron Phelps	3

TOTAL OPTA INDEX
Hep Cahill	10764
Frank Winterstein	9273
Dave Allen	8748
Rhys Hanbury	8691
Ben Davies	8087

WIGAN WARRIORS

Sam Tomkins

MARKER TACKLES
Harrison Hansen	126
Michael McIlorum	119
Liam Farrell	102
Lee Mossop	86
Jeff Lima	85

METRES
Sam Tomkins	3438
Jeff Lima	2910
Josh Charnley	2826
Gareth Hock	2238
Michael McIlorum	2210

CARRIES
Michael McIlorum	483
Sam Tomkins	465
Brett Finch	439
Jeff Lima	378
Sean O'Loughlin	364

Brett Finch

TACKLES
Michael McIlorum	746
Harrison Hansen	584
Sean O'Loughlin	581
Liam Farrell	516
Jeff Lima	501

CLEAN BREAKS
Sam Tomkins	39
Josh Charnley	30
George Carmont	26
Darrell Goulding	21
Brett Finch	19

TACKLE BUSTS
Sam Tomkins	156
Gareth Hock	72
George Carmont	59
Josh Charnley	57
Liam Farrell	47

OFFLOADS
Gareth Hock	72
Brett Finch	24
George Carmont	22
Sam Tomkins	21
Michael McIlorum	18

TRY ASSISTS
Sam Tomkins	33
Brett Finch	28
Darrell Goulding	15
George Carmont	11
Thomas Leuluai	11

TOTAL OPTA INDEX
Sam Tomkins	18629
Brett Finch	12166
Michael McIlorum	11159
Josh Charnley	10484
Liam Farrell	10339

CHAMPIONSHIP 2012
Club by Club

BATLEY BULLDOGS

DATE	FIXTURE	RESULT	SCORERS	LGE	ATT
12/2/12	Keighley (a) (NRC)	W16-22	t:Mennell,Walker,Maun,Applegarth,Potts g:Moore	N/A	1,095
19/2/12	London Skolars (h) (NRC)	W50-16	t:Potts,Mennell,Maun(2),Preece,Lythe,Black,Moore,Mills g:Moore(6),Mennell	3rd(P1)	601
25/2/12	Toulouse (h) (NRC)	W34-12	t:Moore,Lythe,Walton,A Walmsley,Preece,Campbell g:Moore(5)	2nd(P1)	620
4/3/12	Featherstone (a) (NRC)	W22-34	t:Potter,Frodsham,Campbell,Daley Williams,Buttery(2) g:Palfrey(5)	1st(P1)	1,652
8/3/12	Leigh (a)	W18-24	t:Bretherton,Preece(2),Potts g:Moore(4)	5th	1,663
18/3/12	Keighley (h)	L8-10	t:Moore g:Moore(2)	5th	848
25/3/12	Workington (a) (CCR3)	W6-22	t:Lindsay,Bretherton,Brown,Black g:Palfrey(3)	N/A	601
1/4/12	Swinton (a)	L26-18	t:Daley Williams(2),Palfrey g:Moore(3)	6th	707
6/4/12	Dewsbury (h)	W18-16	t:Moore(2),Walton g:Moore(3)	6th	1,353
15/4/12	Hunslet (a) (CCR4)	W18-21	t:Preece,Moore,A Walmsley,Potts g:Moore(2) fg:Moore	N/A	664
22/4/12	York (a)	W16-30	t:Bretherton(2),Daley Williams,Potts,Moore g:Moore(5)	5th	691
29/4/12	London Broncos (h) (CCR5)	L16-22	t:Maun,Applegarth,Preece g:Moore(2)	N/A	1,025
6/5/12	Hunslet (a)	W0-48	t:Maun,Preece,Potts(4),Brown(2),Grehan g:Moore(6)	2nd	506
13/5/12	Featherstone (h)	L24-31	t:Walton,Potts(2),Hirst g:Moore(3),Mennell	2nd	1,317
20/5/12	Halifax (h)	W23-16	t:Bretherton,A Walmsley,Black g:Moore(5) fg:Moore	2nd	1,553
24/5/12	Sheffield (a) ●	L26-16	t:Black,Bretherton,Potts g:Moore(2)	5th	1,117
10/6/12	Hunslet (h)	W56-10	t:Black(3),Moore(2),Walton(3),Brown,Bretherton g:Moore(8)	4th	705
17/6/12	Leigh (a) (NRCQF)	L32-12	t:Potts,Wildie g:Moore(2)	N/A	2,002
24/6/12	Keighley (a)	W30-34	t:Maun,Brown,Bretherton,Potts,Campbell,Applegarth g:Moore(5)	3rd	878
1/7/12	Leigh (h)	W42-20	t:Mennell,Scott,Potts(2),Moore,Applegarth,Campbell g:Moore(7)	3rd	1,003
12/7/12	Sheffield (h)	L24-32	t:Applegarth,Potts,Brown,Lythe g:Moore(4)	3rd	874
22/7/12	Featherstone (a)	L31-28	t:Black(2),Maun,Preece,Brown g:Moore(4)	4th	2,304
2/8/12	Swinton (h)	W62-6	t:Applegarth(2),Potts,A Walmsley,Wildie,Moore(2),L Walmsley,Brown,Smith,Campbell g:Moore(9)	3rd	720
12/8/12	Dewsbury (a)	W12-26	t:Campbell,Brown,Wildie,A Walmsley g:Moore(5)	3rd	1,705
19/8/12	York (h)	W50-0	t:Campbell,Black,Maun,Potts,Wildie,Brown(2),Lindsay,Walton g:Moore(7)	3rd	741
2/9/12	Halifax (a)	L26-20	t:A Walmsley(2),Black g:Moore(4)	5th	2,344
9/9/12	Sheffield (a) (EPO) ●●	L42-12	t:Campbell,A Walmsley g:Moore(2)	N/A	722

● Played at Bramall Lane
●● Played at Don Valley Stadium

	D.O.B.	APP		TRIES		GOALS		FG		PTS	
		ALL	Ch	ALL	Ch	ALL	Ch	ALL	Ch	ALL	Ch
Mark Applegarth	10/12/84	20(7)	16(3)	7	5	0	0	0	0	28	20
Ben Black	29/4/81	25	18	11	9	0	0	0	0	44	36
Alex Bretherton	5/12/82	23(1)	17	8	7	0	0	0	0	32	28
Alex Brown	28/8/87	22(1)	18	11	10	0	0	0	0	44	40
Chris Buttery	23/12/85	1(1)	0	2	0	0	0	0	0	8	0
Johnny Campbell	17/7/87	15(1)	11(1)	8	6	0	0	0	0	32	24
Gareth Frodsham	18/12/89	(2)	(1)	1	0	0	0	0	0	4	0
James Green	29/11/90	6(3)	6(3)	0	0	0	0	0	0	0	0
James Grehan	17/3/87	4(1)	4	1	1	0	0	0	0	4	4
Tom Henderson	4/3/91	4	1	0	0	0	0	0	0	0	0
Keegan Hirst	13/12/88	3(18)	2(14)	1	1	0	0	0	0	4	4
Ashley Lindsay	31/7/83	11(10)	10(6)	2	1	0	0	0	0	8	4
Kris Lythe	29/3/83	12(6)	6(5)	3	1	0	0	0	0	12	4
Danny Maun	5/1/81	21	16	8	4	0	0	0	0	32	16
Paul Mennell	26/10/86	21(4)	15(2)	3	1	2	1	0	0	16	6
Luke Menzies	29/6/88	4(1)	1(1)	0	0	0	0	0	0	0	0
Danny Mills	10/8/82	4	0	1	0	0	0	0	0	4	0
Gareth Moore	3/6/89	24(1)	19	12	9	106	88	2	1	262	213
Lewis Palfrey	25/2/90	3(9)	1(6)	1	1	8	0	0	0	20	4
Craig Potter	17/12/80	13(1)	7(1)	1	0	0	0	0	0	4	0
Gareth Potts	25/7/90	24	19	19	15	0	0	0	0	76	60
Ian Preece	13/6/85	15(2)	9(2)	8	4	0	0	0	0	32	16
Adam Scott	1/1/85	5(2)	3(2)	1	1	0	0	0	0	4	4
Byron Smith	5/3/84	24(6)	18(1)	1	1	0	0	0	0	4	4
Mark Toohey	16/6/82	2(1)	1(1)	0	0	0	0	0	0	0	0
Jonny Walker	26/3/88	12	7	1	0	0	0	0	0	4	0
Alex Walmsley	10/4/90	1(18)	1(13)	8	6	0	0	0	0	32	24
Liam Walmsley	27/3/89	(5)	(5)	1	1	0	0	0	0	4	4
Jason Walton	13/6/90	24	17	7	6	0	0	0	0	28	24
Matthew Wildie	25/10/90	1(10)	1(9)	4	3	0	0	0	0	16	12
Daley Williams	15/5/86	6	3	4	3	0	0	0	0	16	12
Darren Williams	28/6/89	1	0	0	0	0	0	0	0	0	0

Gareth Moore

LEAGUE RECORD
P18-W11-D0-L7-BP7
(5th, Championship/
Elimination Play-Off)
F551, A326, Diff+225
40 points.

CHALLENGE CUP
Round Five

NORTHERN RAIL CUP
Quarter Finalists/1st, Pool 1

ATTENDANCES
Best - v Halifax (Ch - 1,553)
Worst - v London Skolars (NRC - 601)
Total (excluding Challenge Cup) - 10,335
Average (excluding Challenge Cup) - 939
(Down by 126 on 2011)

CLUB RECORDS **MATCH RECORDS**	Highest score: 100-4 v Gateshead, 17/3/2010 Highest score against: 9-78 v Wakefield, 26/8/67 Record attendance: 23,989 v Leeds, 14/3/25 Tries: 5 Joe Oakland v Bramley, 19/12/1908; Tommy Brannan v Swinton, 17/1/20; Jim Wale v Bramley, 4/12/26; Jim Wale v Cottingham, 12/2/27; Tommy Oldroyd v Highfield, 6/3/94; Ben Feehan v Halifax, 10/8/2008; Jermaine McGillvary v Whitehaven, 24/5/2009 Goals: 16 Gareth Moore v Gateshead, 17/3/2010 Points: 40 Gareth Moore v Gateshead, 17/3/2010
SEASON RECORDS **CAREER RECORDS**	Tries: 30 Johnny Campbell 2010 Goals: 144 Barry Eaton 2004 Points: 308 Richard Price 1997 Tries: 142 Craig Lingard 1998-2008 Goals: 463 Wharton 'Wattie' Davies 1897-1912 Points: 1,297 Wharton 'Wattie' Davies 1897-1912 Appearances: 421 Wharton 'Wattie' Davies 1897-1912

DEWSBURY RAMS

DATE	FIXTURE	RESULT	SCORERS	LGE	ATT
12/2/12	Halifax (h) (NRC)	L6-36	t:Crossley g:Walker	N/A	1,347
19/2/12	Featherstone (a) (NRC)	L38-6	t:Esders g:Spaven	10th(P1)	1,943
26/2/12	Oldham (a) (NRC)	W28-30	t:Faal,Jones,Barber,Barker,Olpherts,Nicholson g:Spaven(3)	7th(P1)	573
4/3/12	Rochdale (h) (NRC)	W32-10	t:Faal,Crossley,Esders,Akaidere(2),Craven g:Walker(4)	5th(P1)	701
11/3/12	York (h)	W30-10	t:Buchanan,Faal(2),Barker,Tonks g:Walker(5)	3rd	1,059
18/3/12	Swinton (a)	W16-34	t:Crossley,Cook,Faal,Flanagan,Nicholson g:Walker(7)	2nd	654
25/3/12	Thatto Heath (h) (CCR3)	W84-12	t:Barber,Buchanan(5),Flanagan(2),Spicer,Craven(3),Esders,Harris,Wainwright g:Walker(12)	N/A	606
1/4/12	Featherstone (h)	L12-24	t:Esders,Buchanan g:Walker(2)	4th	1,597
6/4/12	Batley (a)	L18-16	t:Craven,Flanagan,Southernwood g:Walker(2)	5th	1,353
15/4/12	London Broncos (a) (CCR4)	L72-4	t:Akaidere	N/A	652
22/4/12	Hunslet (h)	W16-8	t:Craven(2),Buchanan g:Walker(2)	4th	850
6/5/12	Keighley (h)	W29-22	t:Wainwright,Spicer,Buchanan,Smith,Spaven g:Walker(4) fg:Walker	3rd	992
13/5/12	Halifax (a)	L50-22	t:Esders,Hood,Singleton,Faal g:Walker(3)	5th	2,377
18/5/12	Sheffield (a) ●	L42-10	t:Faal,Craven g:Walker	7th	1,154
27/5/12	Leigh (h)	L18-34	t:Walker,Craven,Flanagan g:Walker(3)	7th	922
10/6/12	Featherstone (a)	L60-18	t:Spaven,Craven,Barber g:Walker(3)	7th	2,241
21/6/12	Halifax (h)	L24-34	t:Crossley,Craven,Cosgrove,Buchanan g:Walker(4)	8th	1,092
29/6/12	York (a)	W24-32	t:Esders(2),Craven(2),Spaven,Faal g:Walker(4)	7th	906
13/7/12	Leigh (a)	L50-6	t:Craven g:Walker	7th	1,536
22/7/12	Swinton (h)	W32-24	t:Buchanan,Flanagan(3),Scott g:Walker(6)	7th	835
5/8/12	Keighley (a)	L34-6	t:Craven g:Walker	7th	814
12/8/12	Batley (h)	L12-26	t:Samuel,Wainwright g:Walker(2)	7th	1,705
19/8/12	Hunslet (a)	W22-34	t:Walker,Esders,Spaven,Cosgrove,Hood,Scott g:Walker(5)	7th	463
2/9/12	Sheffield (h)	L20-30	t:Tebb,Akaidere,Scott,Esders g:Walker(2)	7th	1,156

● Played at Bramall Lane

		APP		TRIES		GOALS		FG		PTS	
	D.O.B.	ALL	Ch	ALL	Ch	ALL	Ch	ALL	Ch	ALL	Ch
Jermaine Akaidere	19/5/91	8	6	4	1	0	0	0	0	16	4
Ed Barber	26/4/90	7(1)	2(1)	3	1	0	0	0	0	12	4
Dwayne Barker	21/9/83	14	9	2	1	0	0	0	0	8	4
Mark Barlow	16/2/84	2(3)	2(1)	0	0	0	0	0	0	0	0
Luke Blake	10/8/89	10(4)	8(3)	0	0	0	0	0	0	0	0
Ben Bolger	13/9/89	1(1)	1(1)	0	0	0	0	0	0	0	0
Austin Buchanan	22/5/84	21	16	11	6	0	0	0	0	44	24
Joe Chandler	2/11/88	2(3)	2(3)	0	0	0	0	0	0	0	0
Craig Cook	26/5/83	8	3	1	1	0	0	0	0	4	4
Elliott Cosgrove	31/3/91	2(6)	2(6)	2	2	0	0	0	0	8	8
James Craven	14/10/88	20	17	15	11	0	0	0	0	60	44
Steve Crossley	28/11/89	19(1)	13(1)	4	2	0	0	0	0	16	8
John Davies	8/1/91	1(1)	0	0	0	0	0	0	0	0	0
Ryan Esders	20/10/86	22(1)	17(1)	9	6	0	0	0	0	36	24
Ayden Faal	12/12/86	16	13	8	6	0	0	0	0	32	24
George Flanagan	8/10/86	2(14)	2(12)	8	6	0	0	0	0	32	24
Nick Fozzard	22/7/77	1(1)	0	0	0	0	0	0	0	0	0
Billy Harris	6/1/92	1(8)	(5)	1	0	0	0	0	0	4	0
Liam Hood	6/1/92	9(3)	9(3)	2	2	0	0	0	0	8	8
Ben Jones	8/10/88	18(1)	14	1	0	0	0	0	0	4	0
Matt Nicholson	11/9/91	3(14)	2(10)	2	1	0	0	0	0	8	4
Derrell Olpherts	7/1/92	3(1)	0	1	0	0	0	0	0	4	0
Danny Samuel	8/8/85	(4)	(1)	1	1	0	0	0	0	4	4
Jonathan Schofield	17/4/90	(2)	(1)	0	0	0	0	0	0	0	0
Greg Scott	21/6/91	10(3)	9(2)	3	3	0	0	0	0	12	12
Brad Singleton	29/10/92	9(3)	9(3)	1	1	0	0	0	0	4	4
Andy Smith	6/7/84	5(6)	3(5)	1	1	0	0	0	0	4	4
Cain Southernwood	4/5/92	2(3)	1(3)	1	1	0	0	0	0	4	4
Scott Spaven	6/3/90	21	17	4	4	4	0	0	0	24	16
Rob Spicer	22/9/84	19	15	2	1	0	0	0	0	8	4
Matthew Tebb	4/9/90	(5)	(3)	1	1	0	0	0	0	4	4
Josh Tonks	14/8/91	22(2)	16(2)	1	1	0	0	0	0	4	4
Michael Wainwright	4/11/80	9(3)	4(3)	3	2	0	0	0	0	12	8
Pat Walker	24/3/86	21	18	2	2	74	57	1	1	157	123
Daley Williams	15/5/86	4(1)	4(1)	0	0	0	0	0	0	0	0

James Craven

LEAGUE RECORD
P18-W7-D0-L11-BP4
(7th, Championship)
F371, A528, Diff-157
25 points.

CHALLENGE CUP
Round Four

NORTHERN RAIL CUP
6th, Pool 1

ATTENDANCES
Best - v Batley (Ch - 1,705)
Worst - v Thatto Heath (CC - 606)
Total (excluding Challenge Cup) - 12,256
Average (excluding Challenge Cup) - 1,114
(Up by 66 on 2011)

CLUB RECORDS	**Highest score:** 90-5 v Blackpool, 4/4/93 **Highest score against:** 0-82 v Widnes, 30/11/86
MATCH RECORDS	**Record attendance:** 26,584 v Halifax, 30/10/20 *(Crown Flatt)*; 3,995 v Batley, 26/12/94; v Bradford, 18/4/2010 *(new ground)*
	Tries: 8 Dai Thomas v Liverpool, 13/4/1907
SEASON RECORDS	**Goals:** 13 Greg Pearce v Blackpool Borough, 4/4/93; Francis Maloney v Hunslet, 25/3/2007 **Points:** 32 Les Holliday v Barrow, 11/9/94
CAREER RECORDS	**Tries:** 40 Dai Thomas 1906-07 **Goals:** 169 Barry Eaton 2000 **Points:** 394 Barry Eaton 2000
	Tries: 144 Joe Lyman 1913-31 **Goals:** 863 Nigel Stephenson 1967-78; 1984-86 **Points:** 2,082 Nigel Stephenson 1967-78; 1984-86
	Appearances: 454 Joe Lyman 1913-31

FEATHERSTONE ROVERS

DATE	FIXTURE	RESULT	SCORERS	LGE	ATT
15/2/12	Oldham (a) (NRC)	W0-68	t:Ropati,Finn(3),Grayshon(2),Kain(3),Hardman(2),Worthington g:Finn(10)	N/A	672
19/2/12	Dewsbury (h) (NRC)	W38-6	t:Smeaton,Kain,Briggs(2),Ropati,Kaye,Hardman g:Finn(5)	1st(P1)	1,943
26/2/12	Halifax (a) (NRC)	W32-34	t:Hardman(3),Ropati,Bostock,Worthington g:Finn(5)	1st(P1)	2,530
4/3/12	Batley (h) (NRC)	L22-34	t:Worthington,Spears,Dickens,Dale,Ropati g:Finn	2nd(P1)	1,652
11/3/12	Keighley (a)	W12-22	t:Hardman,England,Smeaton(2) g:Finn(3)	4th	1,621
15/3/12	Leigh (h)	W36-16	t:Worthington,Hardman,Bostock,Kain(2),Ropati g:Finn(6)	4th	2,382
25/3/12	Hunslet Old Boys (a) (CCR3) ●	W12-86	t:Dickens(2),Briggs(3),Hardman(4),Mvududu(2),Finn(2),Saxton,Hepworth g:Finn(13)	N/A	785
1/4/12	Dewsbury (a)	W12-24	t:Hardman,Kain(2),Dale g:Finn(4)	2nd	1,597
7/4/12	Sheffield (h)	L40-60	t:Worthington,Dale,Ropati,Saxton,Kain(2),Haley g:Finn(6)	3rd	2,293
14/4/12	Castleford (h) (CCR4)	W23-16	t:Ropati,Briggs,Hardman,Worthington g:Finn(3) fg:Finn	N/A	4,165
22/4/12	Swinton (a)	W24-26	t:Smeaton,Finn(2),Raynor(2) g:Finn(3)	2nd	866
27/4/12	Wigan (h) (CCR5)	L16-32	t:Saxton,Hardman,Raynor g:Finn(2)	N/A	4,082
6/5/12	Halifax (h)	L12-60	t:Haley,Dale g:Finn(2)	6th	2,806
13/5/12	Batley (a)	W24-31	t:Dale,Chappell(2),Bostock,Worthington,England g:Finn(3) fg:Kain	3rd	1,317
19/5/12	York (h)	W34-14	t:Bostock(2),Kain,Chappell(3) g:Finn(5)	3rd	1,620
27/5/12	Hunslet (a)	W10-54	t:Kaye,Dickens,Bostock,Finn,Chappell(2),Hepworth(2),Saxton g:Finn(9)	2nd	724
3/6/12	Pia (h) (AFC)	W48-22	t:Kain(2),Spears,Grayshon,Briscoe(2),Worthington,Hepworth g:Finn(8)	N/A	1,150
10/6/12	Dewsbury (h)	W60-18	t:Kain(4),Smeaton(2),Worthington,Finn(2),Saxton g:Finn(10)	2nd	2,241
14/6/12	Keighley (a) (NRCQF)	W12-60	t:England,Briscoe,Finn,Spears,Bostock,Kain(2),Hardman,Lockwood,Saxton g:Finn(10)	N/A	828
22/6/12	Leigh (a)	W16-22	t:Kain,Chappell(2),Ellis g:Finn(3)	2nd	1,837
28/6/12	Halifax (a)	W4-24	t:Finn,Dale,Ellis,Worthington g:Finn(4)	1st	2,792
5/7/12	Leigh (h) (NRCSF)	W54-16	t:Briscoe(2),Smeaton(4),Saxton(2),Dickens,Finn g:Finn(7)	N/A	1,721
15/7/12	Hunslet (h)	W68-0	t:England,Smeaton,Kain(2),Grayshon,Finn,Dickens,Lockwood,Saxton,Bussey,Worthington,Dale g:Finn(10)	1st	2,021
22/7/12	Batley (h)	W31-28	t:Grayshon,Kain(3),Finn g:Finn(5) fg:Finn	1st	2,304
29/7/12	Halifax (NRCF) ●●	L12-21	t:Finn,Smeaton g:Finn(2)	N/A	6,691
3/8/12	York (a)	W12-40	t:Ropati(2),Smeaton,Maloney,Chappell(2),Briggs g:Finn(6)	1st	1,015
12/8/12	Swinton (h)	W86-12	t:Worthington(3),Ropati(5),Kain,Smeaton,Finn(2),Hardman,Grayshon,Dale g:Finn(13)	1st	2,068
16/8/12	Sheffield (a) ●●●	D28-28	t:Ropati,Kain(3),Hardman g:Finn(4)	1st	1,449
2/9/12	Keighley (h)	W46-4	t:Worthington,Hardman,Chappell,Grayshon,Dickens,Smeaton,Kain,Ropati g:Finn(7)	1st	2,816
13/9/12	Leigh (h) (QSF)	W32-14	t:Maloney(2),Dickens,Hardman g:Finn(8)	N/A	1,828
30/9/12	Sheffield (GF) ●●●●	L16-20	t:Hardman,Hepworth g:Finn(4)	N/A	6,409

● Played at Big Fellas Stadium　●● Played at Bloomfield Road, Blackpool
●●● Played at Don Valley Stadium　●●●● Played at Halliwell Jones Stadium, Warrington

		APP		TRIES		GOALS		FG		PTS	
	D.O.B.	ALL	Ch	ALL	Ch	ALL	Ch	ALL	Ch	ALL	Ch
Andrew Bostock	25/2/85	4(16)	3(10)	7	5	0	0	0	0	28	20
Kyle Briggs	7/12/87	13(5)	8(3)	7	1	0	0	0	0	28	4
Jack Briscoe	25/10/91	9	5	5	0	0	0	0	0	20	0
Jack Bussey	17/8/92	1(5)	1(3)	1	1	0	0	0	0	4	4
Tom Carr	16/7/91	2	1	0	0	0	0	0	0	0	0
Nathan Chappell	4/12/89	7(3)	7(3)	12	12	0	0	0	0	48	48
Matty Dale	10/10/86	28	19	8	7	0	0	0	0	32	28
Stuart Dickens	23/3/80	23(4)	13(4)	8	4	0	0	0	0	32	16
Andy Ellis	15/12/84	1(6)	1(5)	2	2	0	0	0	0	8	8
Anthony England	19/10/86	21(6)	15(3)	4	3	0	0	0	0	16	12
Liam Finn	2/11/83	31	20	18	10	181	115	2	1	436	271
Nathan Freer	21/5/89	(2)	0	0	0	0	0	0	0	0	0
Jon Grayshon	10/5/83	13(9)	8(7)	7	4	0	0	0	0	28	16
Michael Haley	19/9/87	7(14)	6(6)	2	2	0	0	0	0	8	8
Ian Hardman	8/12/84	30	20	21	8	0	0	0	0	84	32
Jon Hepworth	25/12/82	12(6)	6(6)	5	3	0	0	0	0	20	12
Lewis Jones	3/11/91	(1)	0	0	0	0	0	0	0	0	0
Andy Kain	1/9/85	23(6)	17(2)	30	22	0	0	1	1	121	89
Ben Kaye	19/12/88	29(1)	18(1)	2	1	0	0	0	0	8	4
James Lockwood	21/3/86	17(12)	9(10)	2	1	0	0	0	0	8	4
Liam Mackay	26/10/90	(2)	(1)	0	0	0	0	0	0	0	0
Dominic Maloney	12/3/87	1(23)	1(16)	3	3	0	0	0	0	12	12
Mufaro Mvududu	29/8/91	1(2)	0	2	0	0	0	0	0	8	0
Dave Nurse	11/10/89	(1)	0	0	0	0	0	0	0	0	0
Gareth Raynor	24/2/78	4	2	3	2	0	0	0	0	12	8
Tangi Ropati	15/11/84	16	10	16	11	0	0	0	0	64	44
Tom Saxton	3/10/83	26	16	9	4	0	0	0	0	36	16
Sam Smeaton	26/10/88	28	18	15	9	0	0	0	0	60	36
Tim Spears	27/7/84	27	17	3	0	0	0	0	0	12	0
Greg Worthington	17/7/90	29	19	15	10	0	0	0	0	60	40

Andy Kain

LEAGUE RECORD
P18-W15-D1-L2-BP0
(1st, Championship/
Grand Final Runners-Up)
F684, A354, Diff+330
47 points.

CHALLENGE CUP
Round Five

NORTHERN RAIL CUP
Runners-Up/2nd, Pool 1

ATTENDANCES
Best - v Castleford (CC - 4,165)
Worst - v Hunslet Old Boys (CC - 785)
Total (excluding Challenge Cup) - 28,845
Average (excluding
Challenge Cup) - 2,060
(Up by 385 on 2011)

CLUB RECORDS **MATCH RECORDS**	**Highest score:** 96-0 v Castleford Lock Lane, 8/2/2004　**Highest score against:** 14-80 v Bradford, 3/4/2005　**Record attendance:** 17,531 v St Helens, 21/3/59 **Tries:** 6 Mike Smith v Doncaster, 13/4/68; Chris Bibb v Keighley, 17/9/89 **Goals:** 13 Mark Knapper v Keighley, 17/9/89; Liam Finn v Hunslet Old Boys, 25/3/2012; Liam Finn v Swinton, 12/8/2012 **Points:** 40 Martin Pearson v Whitehaven, 26/11/95
SEASON RECORDS **CAREER RECORDS**	**Tries:** 48 Paul Newlove 1992-93　**Goals:** 183 *(inc 2fg)* Liam Finn 2012　**Points:** 436 Liam Finn 2012 **Tries:** 162 Don Fox 1953-66　**Goals:** 1,210 Steve Quinn 1975-88　**Points:** 2,654 Steve Quinn 1975-88　**Appearances:** 440 Jim Denton 1921-34

HALIFAX

DATE	FIXTURE	RESULT	SCORERS	LGE	ATT
12/2/12	Dewsbury (a) (NRC)	W6-36	t:Ashall,Reittie,Penkywicz,Bowman,Robinson,Thackeray,Handforth g:Tyrer(4)	N/A	1,347
19/2/12	Rochdale (h) (NRC)	W38-6	t:Fieldhouse,Thackeray,Gannon,Worrincy,White,Ashall,Tyrer g:Tyrer(5)	2nd(P1)	1,881
26/2/12	Featherstone (h) (NRC)	L32-34	t:Tyrer,Heaton(2),Ashall,Hesketh,White g:Tyrer(4)	3rd(P1)	2,530
4/3/12	London Skolars (a) (NRC)	W12-16	t:Fieldhouse,Tyrer,Reittie g:Tyrer(2)	3rd(P1)	613
11/3/12	Hunslet (h)	W44-18	t:Penkywicz,Casey(2),Thackeray,Heaton,Chandler,Fieldhouse(2) g:Tyrer(4),Handforth(2)	2nd	2,052
18/3/12	York (a)	W18-24	t:Heaton(2),Manning,Penkywicz g:Paterson(4)	3rd	967
25/3/12	Myton (a) (CCR3) ●	W4-94	t:White(2),Manning,S Barlow(2),Worrincy,Bowman,Chandler,Thackeray,Tyrer,Ashall,Casey,Paterson,Reittie(2),J Barlow g:Paterson(13)	N/A	1,011
29/3/12	Sheffield (a) ●●	W18-50	t:Ashall(2),Penkywicz(2),Manning,Ambler,Divorty,Paterson,Heaton g:Paterson(7)	1st	1,412
6/4/12	Keighley (h)	W13-12	t:Thackeray,Tyrer g:Paterson(2) fg:Handforth	1st	2,378
14/4/12	South Wales (a) (CCR4) ●	W28-84	t:Casey,Ashall,Bowman(2),Paterson,White(2),Chandler,Handforth,Tyrer(2),Hesketh,Manning,Aizue,Penkywicz g:Paterson(12)	N/A	879
19/4/12	Leigh (h)	L18-32	t:Ashall,Reittie,Heaton g:Tyrer(3)	1st	2,062
29/4/12	Leigh (a) (CCR5)	L19-18		N/A	2,182
		(aet)	t:Thackeray,Worrincy,Paterson g:Paterson(2),Handforth		
6/5/12	Featherstone (a)	W12-60	t:Robinson(2),Ashall,Divorty(3),Handforth,Thackeray,Worrincy,Reittie g:Paterson(10)	1st	2,806
13/5/12	Dewsbury (h)	W50-22	t:Tyrer,Worrincy(2),Penkywicz,S Barlow(2),Ashall,Thackeray,Hesketh g:Paterson(7)	1st	2,377
20/5/12	Batley (a)	L23-16	t:Penkywicz,Paterson,Manning g:Paterson(2)	1st	1,553
25/5/12	Swinton (a)	W18-24	t:Ambler(2),Thackeray,Bowman g:Paterson(4)	1st	822
2/6/12	Toulouse (a) (AFC)	W26-54	t:Paterson,S Barlow,Chandler,Thackeray,White(2),Handforth,Bowman,Divorty g:Paterson(9)	N/A	300
10/6/12	Keighley (a)	W16-30	t:S Barlow,Penkywicz,Fieldhouse(2),Paterson g:Paterson(5)	1st	1,723
17/6/12	Barrow (h) (NRCQF)	W54-24	t:S Barlow,Thackeray(2),Paterson,Robinson(2),Penkywicz,Fieldhouse,Bowman,Worrincy g:Paterson(7)	N/A	1,448
21/6/12	Dewsbury (a)	W24-34	t:S Barlow,Hesketh,Gannon,Robinson,Bowman,Penkywicz g:Paterson(5)	1st	1,092
28/6/12	Featherstone (h)	L4-24	t:Reittie	2nd	2,792
6/7/12	Sheffield (a) (NRCSF) ●●●	W22-24	t:Fieldhouse,Worrincy,Thackeray,Reittie g:Tyrer(4)	N/A	671
15/7/12	Swinton (a)	W50-28	t:Tyrer,Fieldhouse(4),Paterson(2),Bowman,S Barlow g:Tyrer(7)	2nd	2,089
22/7/12	Hunslet (a)	W22-52	t:White(3),Tonks,Penkywicz,Thackeray(3),S Barlow g:Tyrer(5),Paterson(3)	2nd	664
29/7/12	Featherstone (NRCF) ●●●●	W12-21	t:Thackeray,S Barlow,Tyrer g:Tyrer(4) fg:Ashall	N/A	6,691
5/8/12	Sheffield (h)	W30-26	t:Worrincy,Thackeray(2),White,Ambler,Handforth,Tyrer(4)	2nd	1,912
12/8/12	York (h)	W44-12	t:Heaton,S Barlow,Handforth,White(2),Worrincy(2),Bowman g:Handforth(6)	2nd	1,989
17/8/12	Leigh (a)	L32-28	t:S Barlow,Fieldhouse,Worrincy(2),White g:Tyrer(4)	2nd	2,122
2/9/12	Batley (h)	W26-20	t:Ambler(2),Aizue,Fieldhouse g:Tyrer(5)	3rd	2,344
6/9/12	Keighley (h) (EPO)	W28-24	t:Gannon,Aizue,Tyrer,S Barlow,Paterson g:Tyrer(4)	N/A	1,203
16/9/12	Sheffield (h) (ESF)	L12-54	t:Handforth,Worrincy,Fieldhouse	N/A	1,513

● Played at The Shay   ●● Played at Bramall Lane
●●● Played at Don Valley Stadium   ●●●● Played at Bloomfield Road, Blackpool

		APP		TRIES		GOALS		FG		PTS	
	D.O.B.	ALL	Ch	ALL	Ch	ALL	Ch	ALL	Ch	ALL	Ch
Makali Aizue	30/12/77	5(14)	4(11)	3	2	0	0	0	0	12	8
Luke Ambler	18/12/89	21(4)	16(2)	6	6	0	0	0	0	24	24
Craig Ashall	26/9/85	25(4)	15(4)	11	5	0	0	1	0	45	20
Josh Barlow	15/5/91	(8)	(1)	1	0	0	0	0	0	4	0
Sam Barlow	7/3/88	7(16)	4(12)	14	9	0	0	0	0	56	36
Anthony Bowman	18/3/92	5(14)	1(8)	10	4	0	0	0	0	40	16
Callum Casey	6/6/90	5(14)	3(11)	4	2	0	0	0	0	16	8
Joe Chandler	2/11/88	1(7)	1(2)	4	1	0	0	0	0	16	4
Iain Davies	11/9/90	(1)	0	0	0	0	0	0	0	0	0
Ross Divorty	27/11/88	10(4)	6(4)	5	4	0	0	0	0	20	16
Ryan Fieldhouse	10/4/88	27	18	15	11	0	0	0	0	60	44
Jim Gannon	16/6/77	13(13)	9(9)	3	2	0	0	0	0	12	8
Mark Goodman	3/10/90	(1)	0	0	0	0	0	0	0	0	0
James Haley	2/7/85	7	5	0	0	0	0	0	0	0	0
Paul Handforth	6/10/81	29(1)	19(1)	6	3	10	9	1	1	45	31
Ben Heaton	12/3/90	16	10	8	6	0	0	0	0	32	24
Sean Hesketh	17/8/86	17(4)	9(3)	4	2	0	0	0	0	16	8
Matt James	26/3/87	(1)	0	0	0	0	0	0	0	0	0
Dane Manning	15/4/89	24(2)	13(2)	5	3	0	0	0	0	20	12
Iain Morrison	6/5/83	2(2)	(1)	0	0	0	0	0	0	0	0
Lee Paterson	20/7/82	24(3)	17(2)	11	6	92	49	0	0	228	122
Sean Penkywicz	18/5/82	24(5)	17(2)	12	9	0	0	0	0	48	36
Wayne Reittie	21/1/88	18	11	8	3	0	0	0	0	32	12
Adam Robinson	8/4/87	24(1)	16(1)	6	3	0	0	0	0	24	12
Anthony Thackeray	19/2/86	29(1)	20	19	10	0	0	0	0	76	40
Tony Tonks	27/4/85	4(3)	4(3)	1	1	0	0	0	0	4	4
Steve Tyrer	16/3/89	23	15	11	4	59	36	0	0	162	88
Paul White	7/12/82	19(1)	12(1)	15	7	0	0	0	0	60	28
Rob Worrincy	9/7/85	24	15	14	9	0	0	0	0	56	36

Anthony Thackeray

LEAGUE RECORD
P18-W14-D0-L4-BP2
(3rd, Championship/
Elimination Semi-Final)
F597, A377, Diff+220
44 points.

CHALLENGE CUP
Round Five

NORTHERN RAIL CUP
Winners/3rd, Pool 1

ATTENDANCES
Best - v Featherstone (Ch - 2,792)
Worst - v South Wales (CC - 879)
Total (excluding Challenge Cup) - 28,570
Average (excluding
Challenge Cup) - 2,041
(Down by 20 on 2011)

CLUB RECORDS Highest score: 94-4 v Myton, 25/3/2012 Highest score against: 6-88 v Hull KR, 23/4/2006
Record attendance: 29,153 v Wigan, 21/3/59 *(Thrum Hall)*; 9,827 v Bradford, 12/3/2000 *(The Shay)*
MATCH RECORDS Tries: 8 Keith Williams v Dewsbury, 9/11/57 Goals: 14 Bruce Burton v Hunslet, 27/8/72 Points: 32 John Schuster v Doncaster, 9/10/94
SEASON RECORDS Tries: 48 Johnny Freeman 1956-57 Goals: 156 Graham Holroyd 2008 Points: 362 John Schuster 1994-95
CAREER RECORDS Tries: 290 Johnny Freeman 1954-67 Goals: 1,028 Ronnie James 1961-71 Points: 2,191 Ronnie James 1961-71 Appearances: 482 Stan Kielty 1946-58

HUNSLET HAWKS

DATE	FIXTURE	RESULT	SCORERS	LGE	ATT
15/2/12	Whitehaven (h) (NRC)	W34-18	t:Nathaniel,March,Ratcliffe(2),Lewis,Oakes g:Ratcliffe(5)	N/A	305
19/2/12	Swinton (a) (NRC)	W18-24	t:Brickwood,Clayton(2),Nathaniel,Helliwell g:Ratcliffe,Allan	1st(P2)	475
26/2/12	Leigh (a) (NRC)	L30-12	t:Ratcliffe(2) g:Ratcliffe(2)	4th(P2)	1,374
4/3/12	Doncaster (h) (NRC)	W20-10	t:Lewis,Haigh,Oakes,Brickwood g:Ratcliffe(2)	3rd(P2)	310
11/3/12	Halifax (a)	L44-18	t:Lowe,Watson,Benjafield g:Ratcliffe(3)	9th	2,052
18/3/12	Sheffield (h)	L22-40	t:Davies(2),Nathaniel,Allan g:Ratcliffe(3)	9th	419
25/3/12	Royal Navy (h) (CCR3)	W34-14	t:Clayton,Watson,March,Ratcliffe,Tuffour,Nathaniel,Benjafield g:Ratcliffe(2),Allan	N/A	302
1/4/12	Keighley (a)	L48-6	t:Nathaniel g:Ratcliffe	10th	1,069
8/4/12	York (h)	W20-6	t:Tuffour(2),Brickwood,Helliwell g:Helliwell(2)	8th	505
15/4/12	Batley (h) (CCR4)	L18-21	t:Yates(2),March(2) g:Helliwell	N/A	664
22/4/12	Dewsbury (a)	L16-8	t:Oakes g:McLocklan(2)	9th	850
6/5/12	Batley (h)	L0-48		9th	506
13/5/12	Swinton (h)	L12-38	t:Oakes,McLocklan g:Helliwell(2)	9th	426
20/5/12	Leigh (a)	L30-10	t:Hodgson,Brickwood g:Helliwell	9th	1,716
27/5/12	Featherstone (h)	L10-54	t:Kain(2) g:T Henderson	9th	724
10/6/12	Batley (a)	L56-10	t:Yates,Haughey g:Helliwell	10th	705
15/6/12	Sheffield (a) (NRCQF) ●	L48-0		N/A	286
24/6/12	Swinton (a)	L36-22	t:Yates,Kain,Welham,Nathaniel g:Dobek(3)	10th	567
1/7/12	Keighley (h)	L12-22	t:A Henderson,Kain g:T Henderson(2)	10th	505
15/7/12	Featherstone (a)	L68-0		10th	2,021
22/7/12	Halifax (h)	L22-52	t:Benjafield,Karalius,March,Haigh g:March(3)	10th	664
5/8/12	Leigh (h)	L6-36	t:Nathaniel g:Helliwell	10th	608
10/8/12	Sheffield (a) ●	L30-20	t:Welham(2),Haigh,Brickwood g:Helliwell(2)	10th	777
19/8/12	Dewsbury (h)	L22-34	t:Haigh,Kain,Welham,March g:Helliwell(3)	9th	463
2/9/12	York (a)	W26-28	t:Kain,Lewis,Welham(2),Tuffour g:Helliwell(4)	9th	913

● Played at Don Valley Stadium

	D.O.B.	APP		TRIES		GOALS		FG		PTS	
		ALL	Ch	ALL	Ch	ALL	Ch	ALL	Ch	ALL	Ch
Danny Allan	9/4/89	6	2	1	1	2	0	0	0	8	4
Ryan Benjafield	3/8/82	11(13)	10(7)	3	2	0	0	0	0	12	8
Richard Blakeway	22/7/83	6(6)	2(6)	0	0	0	0	0	0	0	0
Jack Bradbury	4/11/90	(2)	(1)	0	0	0	0	0	0	0	0
Lee Brickwood	20/7/91	25	18	5	3	0	0	0	0	20	12
David Clayton	23/9/88	17(2)	12(2)	3	0	0	0	0	0	12	0
Gareth Davies	26/9/84	7(1)	6	2	2	0	0	0	0	8	8
Aaron Dobek	10/9/87	3	2	0	0	3	3	0	0	6	6
Steve Dooler	31/12/77	2(4)	1(1)	0	0	0	0	0	0	0	0
Danny Grimshaw	25/2/86	1	0	0	0	0	0	0	0	0	0
Luke Haigh	24/7/87	25	18	4	3	0	0	0	0	16	12
Tom Haughey	30/1/82	7(1)	6(1)	1	1	0	0	0	0	4	4
Luke Helliwell	1/3/88	17(1)	10(1)	2	1	17	16	0	0	42	36
Anthony Henderson	9/12/82	4(7)	3(6)	1	1	0	0	0	0	4	4
Tom Henderson	4/3/91	4(1)	4	0	0	3	3	0	0	6	6
Elliot Hodgson	2/11/90	11(1)	9(1)	1	1	0	0	0	0	4	4
Stuart Kain	18/9/85	18	13	6	6	0	0	0	0	24	24
Ben Karalius	6/12/91	6	6	1	1	0	0	0	0	4	4
Steve Lewis	22/10/86	12(5)	8(3)	3	1	0	0	0	0	12	4
Neil Lowe	20/12/78	3(5)	2(5)	1	1	0	0	0	0	4	4
Lee Mapals	17/7/85	6	6	0	0	0	0	0	0	0	0
David March	25/7/79	24	17	6	2	3	3	0	0	30	14
Joe McLocklan	2/10/86	5(19)	5(13)	1	1	2	2	0	0	8	8
Luke Menzies	29/6/88	4(4)	4(4)	0	0	0	0	0	0	0	0
Josh Nathaniel	24/5/91	17(3)	12(2)	7	4	0	0	0	0	28	16
John Oakes	12/2/88	24	18	4	2	0	0	0	0	16	8
Joe Parkinson	1/7/91	(1)	(1)	0	0	0	0	0	0	0	0
Joe Pickets	27/11/90	(1)	0	0	0	0	0	0	0	0	0
Danny Ratcliffe	14/3/87	8	3	5	0	19	7	0	0	58	14
Ryan Smith	25/10/88	5	4	0	0	0	0	0	0	0	0
David Tootill	22/5/86	1(14)	(9)	0	0	0	0	0	0	0	0
Dennis Tuffour	17/2/89	13(1)	9(1)	4	3	0	0	0	0	16	12
Scott Watson	16/3/88	4(4)	2(4)	2	1	0	0	0	0	8	4
Liam Welham	11/11/88	8	8	6	6	0	0	0	0	24	24
Andrew Yates	23/2/90	21(4)	14(4)	4	2	0	0	0	0	16	8

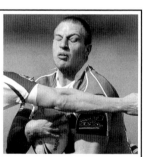

Andrew Yates

LEAGUE RECORD
P18-W2-D0-L16-BP4
(9th, Championship)
F248, A684, Diff-436
10 points.

CHALLENGE CUP
Round Four

NORTHERN RAIL CUP
Quarter Finalists/3rd, Pool 2

ATTENDANCES
Best - v Featherstone (Ch - 724)
Worst - v Royal Navy (CC - 302)
Total (excluding Challenge Cup) - 5,435
Average (excluding Challenge Cup) - 494
(Down by 255 on 2011)

CLUB RECORDS	
	Highest score: 82-0 v Highfield, 21/1/96 **Highest score against:** 0-82 v Bradford, 2/3/2003
	Record attendance: 24,700 v Wigan, 15/3/24 *(Parkside)*; 2,454 v Wakefield, 13/4/98 *(South Leeds Stadium)*
MATCH RECORDS	**Tries:** 7 George Dennis v Bradford, 20/1/34 **Goals:** 12 Billy Langton v Keighley, 18/8/59 **Points:** 30 Simon Wilson v Highfield, 21/1/96
SEASON RECORDS	**Tries:** 34 Alan Snowden 1956-57 **Goals:** 181 Billy Langton 1958-59 **Points:** 380 Billy Langton 1958-59
CAREER RECORDS	**Tries:** 154 Fred Williamson 1943-55 **Goals:** 1,044 Billy Langton 1955-66 **Points:** 2,202 Billy Langton 1955-66 **Appearances:** 579 Geoff Gunney 1951-73

KEIGHLEY COUGARS

DATE	FIXTURE	RESULT	SCORERS	LGE	ATT
12/2/12	Batley (h) (NRC)	L16-22	t:Demetriou,Barnett,Feather g:D Jones(2)	N/A	1,095
18/2/12	Toulouse (a) (NRC)	D24-24	t:Feather,Demetriou,March,Lawton g:Lawton(4)	4th(P1)	650
26/2/12	Rochdale (a) (NRC)	W16-40	t:Parata(4),Feather,Obst,Coleman,Lawton g:D Jones(4)	4th(P1)	604
4/3/12	Oldham (h) (NRC)	W26-12	t:Obst(2),R Jones,Barnett,Duffy g:D Jones(3)	4th(P1)	827
11/3/12	Featherstone (h)	L12-22	t:Lawton,Tadulala g:D Jones(2)	7th	1,621
18/3/12	Batley (a)	W8-10	t:Coleman,Haythornthwaite g:D Jones	6th	848
25/3/12	Bradford Dudley Hill (a) (CCR3) ●	W6-58	t:Duffy,Jesse Sheriffe,Lawton(4),Shepherd,R Jones(2),Shickell,D Jones g:D Jones(7)	N/A	814
1/4/12	Hunslet (h)	W48-6	t:Pursglove,Moss,Shickell,Jode Sheriffe,Tadulala,Obst,Haythornthwaite,Feather g:D Jones(8)	3rd	1,069
6/4/12	Halifax (a)	L13-12	t:R Jones,D Jones g:D Jones(2)	4th	2,378
15/4/12	Warrington (h) (CCR4)	L18-44	t:Barnett,Obst(2) g:D Jones(3)	N/A	2,196
22/4/12	Sheffield (h)	W23-16	t:Moss,Obst,Coleman,Lawton g:Lawton(3) fg:Obst	3rd	948
6/5/12	Dewsbury (a)	L29-22	t:Pursglove,Haythornthwaite,Moss(2) g:D Jones(3)	5th	992
17/5/12	Swinton (h)	W36-4	t:Haythornthwaite(3),Tadulala,Feather,Coleman,Barnett g:D Jones(4)	6th	716
27/5/12	York (a)	W18-42	t:Haythornthwaite,Tadulala(2),Obst,Moss,Lawton,Coleman g:Lawton(7)	6th	918
10/6/12	Halifax (a)	L16-30	t:Haythornthwaite,Demetriou,Barnett(2)	6th	1,723
14/6/12	Featherstone (h) (NRCQF)	L12-60	t:Coleman,Obst g:Lawton(2)	N/A	828
24/6/12	Batley (h)	L30-34	t:Jesse Sheriffe,Obst(2),Coleman,Barnett g:Lawton(5)	6th	878
1/7/12	Hunslet (a)	W12-22	t:Lawton,Obst,Duffy,Moss g:Lawton(3)	6th	505
15/7/12	York (h)	W46-24	t:Lawton,Moss(2),Barnett(3),Tadulala,Duffy(2) g:Lawton(5)	6th	972
20/7/12	Sheffield (a) ●●	L16-6	t:Wray g:Lawton	6th	854
5/8/12	Dewsbury (h)	W34-6	t:Moss,Rawlins,Barnett,Lawton(2),Demetriou g:Lawton(5)	6th	814
9/8/12	Leigh (h)	L0-26		6th	831
19/8/12	Swinton (a)	D18-18	t:Feather,Obst(2) g:Lawton(3)	6th	515
23/8/12	Leigh (a)	L40-14	t:Obst,Demetriou,Tadulala g:Lawton	6th	1,597
2/9/12	Featherstone (a)	L46-4	t:Duffy	6th	2,816
6/9/12	Halifax (a) (EPO)	L28-24	t:Moss,March,D Jones,Feather g:Lawton(4)	N/A	1,203

● Played at Cougar Park
●● Played at Don Valley Stadium

		APP		TRIES		GOALS		FG		PTS	
	D.O.B.	ALL	Ch	ALL	Ch	ALL	Ch	ALL	Ch	ALL	Ch
Richie Barnett	26/4/81	23	18	11	8	0	0	0	0	44	32
Neil Cherryholme	20/12/86	19(4)	16(1)	0	0	0	0	0	0	0	0
Chris Clough	20/1/87	1(3)	(1)	0	0	0	0	0	0	0	0
Jy-Mel Coleman	13/10/88	10(8)	8(5)	7	5	0	0	0	0	28	20
James Davey	21/8/89	(5)	(4)	0	0	0	0	0	0	0	0
Jason Demetriou	13/1/76	10(10)	7(9)	5	3	0	0	0	0	20	12
Gavin Duffy	9/4/87	13	10	6	4	0	0	0	0	24	16
James Feather	15/4/84	22(1)	16(1)	7	4	0	0	0	0	28	16
James Haythornthwaite	19/10/90	20	14	8	8	0	0	0	0	32	32
Danny Jones	6/3/86	18(1)	13(1)	3	2	39	20	0	0	90	48
Richard Jones	7/7/89	12	7	4	1	0	0	0	0	16	4
Michael Korkidas	12/1/81	10(16)	6(13)	0	0	0	0	0	0	0	0
Danny Lawton	10/3/90	22	17	13	7	43	37	0	0	138	102
Paul March	25/7/79	14(5)	10(4)	2	1	0	0	0	0	8	4
Craig Moss	4/8/84	22	17	10	10	0	0	0	0	40	40
Jake Normington	11/10/91	2	0	0	0	0	0	0	0	0	0
Sam Obst	26/11/80	24	18	15	9	0	0	1	1	61	37
Matt Parata	15/1/88	5	1	4	0	0	0	0	0	16	0
Oliver Pursglove	18/1/86	24(1)	18(1)	2	2	0	0	0	0	8	8
Brendan Rawlins	28/1/86	6(10)	5(7)	1	1	0	0	0	0	4	4
Lewis Reed	24/3/91	2(1)	2(1)	0	0	0	0	0	0	0	0
Ben Sagar	19/12/89	4	4	0	0	0	0	0	0	0	0
Jamie Shepherd	14/8/90	12(1)	8	1	0	0	0	0	0	4	0
Jesse Sheriffe	12/1/90	6	4	2	1	0	0	0	0	8	4
Jode Sheriffe	4/7/86	6(13)	4(10)	1	1	0	0	0	0	4	4
Andy Shickell	9/5/81	14(10)	10(7)	2	1	0	0	0	0	8	4
Ryan Smith	25/10/88	2(2)	2(1)	0	0	0	0	0	0	0	0
Semi Tadulala	3/3/78	15	12	7	7	0	0	0	0	28	28
Jamaine Wray	15/3/84	(13)	(10)	1	1	0	0	0	0	4	4

Danny Lawton

LEAGUE RECORD
P18-W8-D1-L9-BP5
(6th, Championship/
Elimination Play-Off)
F395, A368, Diff+27
31 points.

CHALLENGE CUP
Round Four

NORTHERN RAIL CUP
Quarter Finalists/4th, Pool 1

ATTENDANCES
Best - v Warrington (CC - 2,196)
Worst - v Swinton (Ch - 716)
Total (excluding Challenge Cup) - 12,322
Average (excluding
Challenge Cup) - 1,027
(Up by 197 on 2011, Championship One)

CLUB RECORDS
MATCH RECORDS Highest score: 104-4 v Highfield, 23/4/95 Highest score against: 2-92 v Leigh, 30/4/86 Record attendance: 14,500 v Halifax, 3/3/51
Tries: 6 Jason Critchley v Widnes, 18/8/96
Goals: 15 John Wasyliw v Nottingham City, 1/11/92; Martyn Wood v Lancashire Lynx, 1/5/2000 Points: 36 John Wasyliw v Nottingham City, 1/11/92
SEASON RECORDS Tries: 45 Nick Pinkney 1994-95 Goals: 187 John Wasyliw 1992-93 Points: 490 John Wasyliw 1992-93
CAREER RECORDS Tries: 155 Sam Stacey 1904-20 Goals: 967 Brian Jefferson 1965-77 Points: 2,116 Brian Jefferson 1965-77
Appearances: 372 Hartley Tempest 1902-15; David McGoun 1925-38

LEIGH CENTURIONS

DATE	FIXTURE	RESULT	SCORERS	LGE	ATT
12/2/12	Barrow (h) (NRC)	W48-16	t:Goulden,Littler(2),Worrincy,McGilvray,Brierley(2),Parker g:Ridyard(5),Brierley(3)	N/A	1,860
19/2/12	Sheffield (a) (NRC) ●	L23-22	t:Hopkins(2),McNally,Brierley g:Ridyard(3)	3rd(P2)	1,045
26/2/12	Hunslet (h) (NRC)	W30-12	t:Taylor,Hopkins,Littler,Nicholson,McNally,Worrincy g:Ridyard(3)	3rd(P2)	1,374
4/3/12	Gateshead (a) (NRC) ●●	W0-42	t:Russell(2),Shaw,Gallagher,Taylor,Gardner,Spencer,Clay g:Ridyard(5)	2nd(P2)	276
8/3/12	Batley (h)	L18-24	t:Parker,Shaw(2),Clay g:Ridyard	6th	1,663
15/3/12	Featherstone (a)	L36-16	t:Gardner,Spencer,Russell g:Shaw,Ridyard	7th	2,382
24/3/12	London Skolars (a) (CCR3)	W26-43	t:Pownall,Littler(3),Maden,Gardner,Worrincy,McNally g:Ridyard(5) fg:Beswick	N/A	376
30/3/12	York (h)	W36-6	t:Duffy,McNally,Pownall(3),Ridyard,Gardner g:Ridyard(4)	7th	1,700
6/4/12	Swinton (h)	W38-4	t:Taylor(2),Briscoe,Maden(2),Gardner,Brierley g:Ridyard(5)	7th	2,135
15/4/12	Rochdale (h) (CCR4)	W68-18	t:Briscoe,Ridyard,Brierley(4),Littler(2),Maden,Hopkins(2),Gardner g:Ridyard(10)	N/A	1,229
19/4/12	Halifax (a)	W18-32	t:McNally(2),Duffy,Brierley(2),Gardner g:Ridyard(4)	6th	2,062
29/4/12	Halifax (h) (CCR5)	W19-18			
		(aet)	t:Duffy,Goulden,Laithwaite g:Ridyard(3) fg:Ridyard	N/A	2,182
6/5/12	Sheffield (a) ●	W32-34	t:Taylor,Pownall,Brierley,Laithwaite,Hopkins g:Ridyard(7)	4th	1,237
11/5/12	Leeds (h) (CCQF)	L12-60	t:Goulden,McNally g:Ridyard(2)	N/A	5,290
20/5/12	Hunslet (h)	W30-10	t:Nicholson,Laithwaite,Gallagher,Brierley,Parker g:Ridyard(5)	5th	1,716
27/5/12	Dewsbury (a)	W18-34	t:Duffy,Goulden,Littler,Spencer,Briscoe,Hopkins g:Ridyard(5)	4th	922
2/6/12	Avignon (h) (AFC)	W44-10	t:Brierley(3),Gallagher,Ridyard(3),McGilvray g:Brierley(2),Ridyard(4)	N/A	773
7/6/12	Sheffield (h)	W40-12	t:McNally,Littler,Pownall,Brierley(2),Ridyard(2) g:Ridyard(6)	3rd	1,645
17/6/12	Batley (h) (NRCQF)	W32-12	t:Gardner,Maden(2),Littler,McNally,Beswick g:Ridyard(4)	N/A	2,002
22/6/12	Featherstone (h)	L16-22	t:Goulden,Brierley,Maden g:Ridyard(2)	4th	1,837
1/7/12	Batley (a)	L42-20	t:Clay,Brierley,Thornley,McGilvray g:Ridyard(2)	5th	1,003
5/7/12	Featherstone (a) (NRCSF)	L54-16	t:Henderson,Hopkins,Littler g:Ridyard(2)	N/A	1,721
13/7/12	Dewsbury (a)	W50-6	t:Hopkins(2),Maden,Briscoe,Gardner(2),McNally,Goulden,Mendeika g:Ridyard(7)	5th	1,536
22/7/12	York (a)	W20-66	t:Gardner,Ridyard(2),McNally(2),Goulden,Briscoe,Hopkins,Thornley,Nicholson,		
			Brierley,Littler g:Ridyard(9)	5th	806
5/8/12	Hunslet (a)	W6-36	t:Goulden,Gardner(2),Hopkins,Parker,McNally,Littler g:Ridyard(4)	5th	608
9/8/12	Keighley (a)	W0-26	t:McNally(2),Ridyard,Pownall(2) g:Ridyard(3)	5th	831
17/8/12	Halifax (h)	W32-28	t:Beswick,McNally,Ridyard(2),Littler,Brierley g:Ridyard(4)	4th	2,122
23/8/12	Keighley (h)	W40-14	t:Henderson,Ridyard,McGilvray(2),Brierley(3) g:Ridyard(6)	2nd	1,597
2/9/12	Swinton (a)	W12-48	t:Pownall,Beswick,Ridyard,Gallagher(2),Gardner,McNally,Nicholson		
			g:Ridyard(7),McNally	2nd	1,796
13/9/12	Featherstone (a) (QSF)	L32-14	t:Briscoe,Pownall(2) g:Ridyard	N/A	1,828
20/9/12	Sheffield (h) (FE)	L22-32	t:Pownall,Thornley,Brierley,McGilvray g:Ridyard(3)	N/A	1,725

● Played at Don Valley Stadium   ●● Played at Kingston Park, Newcastle

	D.O.B.	APP		TRIES		GOALS		FG		PTS	
		ALL	Ch	ALL	Ch	ALL	Ch	ALL	Ch	ALL	Ch
Bob Beswick	8/12/84	23(3)	17(1)	3	2	0	0	1	0	13	8
Ricky Bibey	22/9/81	6(1)	3	0	0	0	0	0	0	0	0
Ryan Brierley	13/2/92	7(20)	3(15)	25	15	5	0	0	0	110	60
Craig Briscoe	8/12/92	20(10)	13(6)	6	5	0	0	0	0	24	20
Greg Burke	12/2/93	(1)	0	0	0	0	0	0	0	0	0
Adam Clay	7/10/90	5	2	3	2	0	0	0	0	12	8
John Duffy	2/7/80	18(1)	12	4	3	0	0	0	0	16	12
Tommy Gallagher	10/9/83	1(20)	(11)	5	3	0	0	0	0	20	12
Matt Gardner	24/8/84	30	20	14	10	0	0	0	0	56	40
Lee Gittins	6/12/87	1	0	0	0	0	0	0	0	0	0
Tommy Goulden	30/6/81	23	16	8	5	0	0	0	0	32	20
Kevin Henderson	1/10/81	5(9)	4(7)	2	1	0	0	0	0	8	4
Sam Hopkins	17/2/90	15(10)	10(6)	12	6	0	0	0	0	48	24
James Laithwaite	23/9/91	12	8	3	2	0	0	0	0	12	8
Macgraff Leuluai	9/2/90	2	2	0	0	0	0	0	0	0	0
Stuart Littler	19/2/79	29	19	15	5	0	0	0	0	60	20
Steve Maden	13/9/82	27(1)	18	8	4	0	0	0	0	32	16
Dean McGilvray	24/4/88	8(1)	4(1)	6	4	0	0	0	0	24	16
Gregg McNally	2/1/91	28	19	17	12	1	1	0	0	70	50
James Mendeika	16/12/91	1(1)	1(1)	1	1	0	0	0	0	4	4
Stephen Nash	14/1/86	3(4)	1(3)	0	0	0	0	0	0	0	0
Anthony Nicholson	28/11/90	14(10)	8(7)	4	3	0	0	0	0	16	12
Michael Ostick	23/1/88	18(5)	14(1)	0	0	0	0	0	0	0	0
Rob Parker	5/9/81	21(2)	13(1)	4	3	0	0	0	0	16	12
Jonathan Pownall	22/8/91	19	14	12	11	0	0	0	0	48	44
Martyn Ridyard	25/7/86	29(2)	19(1)	14	10	132	86	1	0	321	212
Alex Robson	29/9/90	(2)	(1)	0	0	0	0	0	0	0	0
Chris Rowe	8/2/94	1	0	0	0	0	0	0	0	0	0
Matthew Russell	6/6/93	2	1	3	1	0	0	0	0	12	4
Ryan Shaw	27/2/92	3	2	3	2	1	1	0	0	14	10
Sam Singleton	16/2/93	1	0	0	0	0	0	0	0	0	0
Tom Spencer	2/1/91	11(7)	7(6)	3	2	0	0	0	0	12	8
James Taylor	11/9/84	9(7)	5(6)	5	3	0	0	0	0	20	12
Andy Thornley	1/3/89	5(5)	4(5)	3	3	0	0	0	0	12	12
Josh Ward	16/6/95	1	0	0	0	0	0	0	0	0	0
Michael Worrincy	16/2/86	5(2)	1(1)	3	0	0	0	0	0	12	0

Martyn Ridyard

LEAGUE RECORD
P18-W14-D0-L4-BP2
(2nd, Championship/Final Eliminator)
F612, A310, Diff+302
44 points.

CHALLENGE CUP
Quarter Finalists

NORTHERN RAIL CUP
Semi-Finalists/2nd, Pool 2

ATTENDANCES
Best - v Leeds (CC - 5,290)
Worst - v Avignon (AFC - 773)
Total (excluding Challenge Cup) - 23,685
Average (excluding
Challenge Cup) - 1,692
(Down by 556 on 2011)

CLUB RECORDS
Highest score: 92-2 v Keighley, 30/4/86 **Highest score against:** 4-94 v Workington, 26/2/95
Record attendance: 31,326 v St Helens, 14/3/53 *(Hilton Park)*; 5,290 v Leeds, 11/5/2012 *(Leigh Sports Village)*

MATCH RECORDS
Tries: 6 Jack Wood v York, 4/10/47; Neil Turley v Workington, 31/1/2001
Goals: 15 Mick Stacey v Doncaster, 28/3/76 **Points:** 42 Neil Turley v Chorley, 4/4/2004

SEASON RECORDS
Tries: 55 Neil Turley 2001 **Goals:** 187 Neil Turley 2004 **Points:** 468 Neil Turley 2004

CAREER RECORDS
Tries: 189 Mick Martyn 1954-67 **Goals:** 1,043 Jimmy Ledgard 1948-58 **Points:** 2,492 John Woods 1976-85; 1990-92
Appearances: 503 Albert Worrall 1920-38

SHEFFIELD EAGLES

DATE	FIXTURE	RESULT	SCORERS	LGE	ATT
12/2/12	Workington (a) (NRC)	W14-28	t:Scott,Taulapapa,Henderson,Morrison,Szostak g:Brown(2),Brambani(2)	N/A	532
19/2/12	Leigh (h) (NRC) ●	W23-22	t:Szostak,Hirst,Scott,Finigan g:Brown(3) fg:Brambani	2nd(P2)	1,045
26/2/12	Doncaster (a) (NRC)	W12-56	t:Morrison,Hirst(2),Szostak,Taulapapa,Laulu-Togagae(2),Stringer,Brambani(2) g:Brown(8)	1st(P2)	731
2/3/12	York (h) (NRC) ●	W36-4	t:Morrison,Brambani(2),Yere,Straugheir,Taulapapa g:Brown(6)	1st(P2)	725
11/3/12	Swinton (h) ●	W56-22	t:Szostak,Yere,Brambani,Hepworth,Finigan,Morrison,Straugheir,Hirst(2),Laulu-Togagae g:Brown(8)	1st	1,815
18/3/12	Hunslet (a)	W22-40	t:Morrison(2),Laulu-Togagae,Higgins,Yere,Henderson(2) g:Brown(6)	1st	419
24/3/12	Oulton (a) (CCR3)	W6-58	t:Laulu-Togagae(4),McDonald(2),Morrison,Hepworth,Scott,P Smith,Straugheir g:Brown(3),Knowles(4)	N/A	360
29/3/12	Halifax (h) ●●	L18-50	t:Brambani,Higgins,McDonald g:Brown(3)	5th	1,412
7/4/12	Featherstone (a)	W40-60	t:Taulapapa(3),Turner,Morrison,Yere,Szostak,Laulu-Togagae(2),Hirst,McDonald g:Brambani(5),Brown(3)	2nd	2,293
15/4/12	York (a) (CCR4)	W12-50	t:Brambani,Morrison(2),Henderson,Yere,Turner,Szostak,Laulu-Togagae(2) g:Brambani(7)	N/A	551
22/4/12	Keighley (a)	L23-16	t:Taulapapa(2),Morrison g:Brown(2)	7th	948
28/4/12	Catalan Dragons (a) (CCR5)	L68-6	t:Finigan g:Brown	N/A	3,102
6/5/12	Leigh (h) ●	L32-34	t:Knowles(2),Morrison,Finigan,Taulapapa,Laulu-Togagae g:Brown(4)	7th	1,237
10/5/12	York (a)	W18-25	t:Laulu-Togagae(2),Finigan,Brambani g:Brown(4) fg:Brown	4th	462
18/5/12	Dewsbury (h) ●●	W42-10	t:Yere(2),Hirst,Morrison,Taulapapa,Brown,Henderson g:Brown(7)	4th	1,154
24/5/12	Batley (h) ●●	W26-16	t:Yere(2),Laulu-Togagae(2),Straugheir g:Brown(3)	3rd	1,117
2/6/12	Carcassonne (a) (AFC)	W12-40	t:Szostak,Turner,Laulu-Togagae(2),Yere(2),Brambani g:Brown(4),Brambani(2)	N/A	3,250
7/6/12	Leigh (a)	L40-12	t:Knowles,Laulu-Togagae g:Brown(2)	5th	1,645
15/6/12	Hunslet (h) (NRCQF) ●	W48-0	t:Laulu-Togagae(4),McDonald,Morrison,Yere,Henderson,Szostak g:Brown(3),Brambani(3)	N/A	286
22/6/12	York (h) ●	W44-10	t:Brambani,Yere(3),Knowles(2),Laulu-Togagae(2) g:Brambani(6)	5th	784
1/7/12	Swinton (a)	W24-32	t:Knowles(2),Hirst,Yere,Straugheir,Taulapapa g:Brambani(3),Brown	4th	506
6/7/12	Halifax (h) (NRCSF) ●	L22-24	t:Knowles(2),Henderson,Turner g:Brown(3)	N/A	671
12/7/12	Batley (a)	W24-32	t:Finigan(2),Morrison,Laulu-Togagae,Turner,Stringer g:Brown(4)	4th	874
20/7/12	Keighley (h) ●	W16-6	t:Laulu-Togagae(2),Turner g:Brown(2)	3rd	854
5/8/12	Halifax (a)	L30-26	t:Finigan,Turner,Knowles(2),Laulu-Togagae g:Brown(3)	4th	1,912
10/8/12	Hunslet (h) ●	W30-20	t:Morrison,Davey,Straugheir,Hirst(2) g:Brown(5)	4th	777
16/8/12	Featherstone (h) ●	D28-28	t:Knowles,Turner,Davey,Laulu-Togagae(2) g:Brambani(4)	5th	1,449
2/9/12	Dewsbury (a)	W20-30	t:McDonald,Morrison,Taulapapa,Yere,Davey,Brambani g:Brambani(3)	4th	1,156
9/9/12	Batley (h) (EPO) ●	W42-12	t:Turner(3),Taulapapa(2),Hirst(2) g:Brown(7)	N/A	722
16/9/12	Halifax (a) (ESF)	W12-54	t:Straugheir,Laulu-Togagae(2),Turner(2),Knowles,Yere(2),Stringer,Brambani g:Brown(7)	N/A	1,513
20/9/12	Leigh (a) (FE)	W22-32	t:Knowles,Straugheir,Taulapapa,Turner,Yere g:Brown(6)	N/A	1,725
30/9/12	Featherstone (GF) ●●●	W16-20	t:Turner,Laulu-Togagae,McDonald,Taulapapa g:Brown(2)	N/A	6,409

● Played at Don Valley Stadium ●● Played at Bramall Lane ●●● Played at Halliwell Jones Stadium, Warrington

APP   TRIES   GOALS   FG   PTS

	D.O.B.	ALL	Ch	ALL	Ch	ALL	Ch	ALL	Ch	ALL	Ch
Tim Bergin	29/7/85	1	0	0	0	0	0	0	0	0	0
Dominic Brambani	10/5/85	32	22	12	6	35	21	1	0	119	66
Simon Brown	23/6/89	26(2)	17(2)	1	1	112	79	1	1	229	163
James Davey	21/8/89	1(10)	1(10)	3	3	0	0	0	0	12	12
Vinny Finigan	4/8/89	19	11	9	7	0	0	0	0	36	28
Peter Green	2/12/81	12(15)	8(11)	0	0	0	0	0	0	0	0
Andrew Henderson	17/6/79	29(1)	21(1)	7	3	0	0	0	0	28	12
Ryan Hepworth	16/1/81	3(13)	(10)	2	1	0	0	0	0	8	4
Liam Higgins	19/7/83	7(22)	3(18)	2	2	0	0	0	0	8	8
Joe Hirst	21/4/87	21(4)	14(3)	12	9	0	0	0	0	48	36
Jack Howieson	28/7/81	30	22	0	0	0	0	0	0	0	0
Michael Knowles	2/5/87	23(4)	17(3)	14	12	4	0	0	0	64	48
Jack Latus	14/9/88	(1)	0	0	0	0	0	0	0	0	0
Quentin Laulu-Togagae	1/12/84	30(1)	22	35	21	0	0	0	0	140	84
Dane McDonald	14/7/87	10(5)	8(4)	7	4	0	0	0	0	28	16
Nev Morrison	27/5/90	27	17	17	10	0	0	0	0	68	40
Alex Rowe	11/3/85	(7)	(2)	0	0	0	0	0	0	0	0
Leigh Sanders	12/11/91	(1)	0	0	0	0	0	0	0	0	0
Sam Scott	5/6/90	14(9)	10(5)	3	0	0	0	0	0	12	0
Aaron Smith	10/9/82	(1)	0	0	0	0	0	0	0	0	0
Pat Smith	4/3/90	4(4)	2(1)	1	0	0	0	0	0	4	0
Duane Straugheir	29/9/89	6(12)	5(8)	8	6	0	0	0	0	32	24
Mitchell Stringer	1/11/83	24(5)	19(2)	3	2	0	0	0	0	12	8
Alex Szostak	4/3/86	18(8)	12(6)	8	2	0	0	0	0	32	8
Misi Taulapapa	25/1/82	29	20	16	13	0	0	0	0	64	52
Scott Turner	15/4/88	20(2)	15(2)	14	11	0	0	0	0	56	44
Nathan Walmsley	29/9/89	(1)	0	0	0	0	0	0	0	0	0
Menzie Yere	24/10/83	30	20	20	15	0	0	0	0	80	60

Quentin Laulu-Togagae

LEAGUE RECORD
P18-W12-D1-L5-BP3
(4th, Championship/
Grand Final Winners, Champions)
F565, A437, Diff+128
41 points.

CHALLENGE CUP
Round Five

NORTHERN RAIL CUP
Semi-Finalists/1st, Pool 2

ATTENDANCES
Best - v Swinton (Ch - 1,815)
Worst - v Hunslet (NRCQF - 286)
Total (excluding Challenge Cup) - 14,048
Average (excluding
Challenge Cup) - 1,003
(Down by 115 on 2011)

CLUB RECORDS	**Highest score:** 98-4 v London Skolars, 3/8/2003 **Highest score against:** 0-88 v Hull, 2/3/2003 **Record attendance:** 10,603 v Bradford, 16/8/97
MATCH RECORDS	**Tries:** 5 Daryl Powell v Mansfield, 2/1/89 **Goals:** 13 Gavin Brown v London Skolars, 3/8/2003 **Points:** 32 Roy Rafferty v Fulham, 21/9/86
SEASON RECORDS	**Tries:** 35 Quentin Laulu-Togagae 2012 **Goals:** 148 Mark Aston 1988-89 **Points:** 307 Mark Aston 1988-89
CAREER RECORDS	**Tries:** 114 Daryl Powell 1984-95 **Goals:** 986 Mark Aston 1986-2004 **Points:** 2,142 Mark Aston 1986-2004 **Appearances:** 389 Mark Aston 1986-2004

SWINTON LIONS

DATE	FIXTURE	RESULT	SCORERS	LGE	ATT
19/2/12	Hunslet (h) (NRC)	L18-24	t:Armstrong,Ainscough,Dodd g:Mort(3)	8th(P2)	475
23/2/12	York (a) (NRC)	L30-22	t:R Hawkyard,Mort,Morrison,Cunniffe g:Mort(3)	8th(P2)	504
26/2/12	Barrow (a) (NRC)	L32-16	t:Dodd,Watson,I'Anson g:Dodd(2)	9th(P2)	1,083
4/3/12	Workington (h) (NRC)	W30-12	t:Armstrong(2),Ainscough,D Hawkyard(2),Dodd g:Dodd(2),Ashall	6th(P2)	503
11/3/12	Sheffield (a) ●	L56-22	t:Foxen,Higson(2),D Hawkyard g:Dodd(3)	10th	1,815
18/3/12	Dewsbury (h)	L16-34	t:Higson,Ainscough,Hurst g:Mort(2)	10th	654
25/3/12	Siddal (h) (CCR3)	W66-0	t:Higson(2),I'Anson,Ashall(2),Holland,Ainscough(2),Mort(2),Armstrong, D Hawkyard g:Mort(9)	N/A	404
1/4/12	Batley (h)	W26-18	t:Dodd,I'Anson,Cunniffe,Armstrong,Hale g:Mort(3)	8th	707
6/4/12	Leigh (a)	L38-4	t:Cunniffe	9th	2,135
14/4/12	Gateshead (h) (CCR4)	W70-10	t:Mills,Meekin,Watson,Penny(2),Higson,Cunniffe,Ainscough(2),D Hawkyard, Gorski,I'Anson g:Mort(11)	N/A	415
22/4/12	Featherstone (h)	L24-26	t:Cunniffe,Ainscough,Higson,Penny g:Mort(4)	8th	866
29/4/12	Huddersfield (a) (CCR5)	L52-0		N/A	2,617
6/5/12	York (h)	W32-12	t:Higson(2),Penny,Armstrong(2),Ainscough g:Dodd(4)	8th	410
13/5/12	Hunslet (a)	W12-38	t:Ainscough(2),Dodd(3),Penny,Cunniffe g:Dodd(5)	8th	426
17/5/12	Keighley (a)	L36-4	t:Dodd	8th	716
25/5/12	Halifax (h)	L18-24	t:R Hawkyard,Dodd,Ainscough g:Dodd(3)	8th	822
10/6/12	York (a)	L26-22	t:Penny,R Hawkyard,Armstrong,Higson,Dodd g:Dodd	8th	631
24/6/12	Hunslet (h)	W36-22	t:Walker(2),Dodd(2),Ainscough,I'Anson g:Mort(6)	7th	567
1/7/12	Sheffield (h)	L24-32	t:I'Anson,Ainscough,Penny,Armstrong g:Mort(4)	8th	506
15/7/12	Halifax (a)	L50-28	t:Mills,Mort,Ashall,Armstrong,Holland g:Mort(4)	8th	2,089
22/7/12	Dewsbury (a)	L32-24	t:Cunniffe,Armstrong(2),Penny g:Mort(4)	8th	835
2/8/12	Batley (a)	L62-6	t:Penny g:Mort	8th	720
12/8/12	Featherstone (a)	L86-12	t:Hurst(2),D Hawkyard	8th	2,068
19/8/12	Keighley (h)	D18-18	t:Ainscough,Armstrong,Cunniffe g:Dodd(3)	8th	515
2/9/12	Leigh (h)	L12-48	t:Reay,Ainscough g:Mort(2)	8th	1,796

● Played at Don Valley Stadium

	APP		TRIES		GOALS		FG		PTS	
	D.O.B.	ALL	Ch	ALL	Ch	ALL	Ch	ALL	Ch	ALL	Ch

	D.O.B.	ALL	Ch	ALL	Ch	ALL	Ch	ALL	Ch	ALL	Ch
Martin Ainscough	23/10/85	25	18	16	10	0	0	0	0	64	40
Tom Armstrong	12/9/89	24(1)	17(1)	13	9	0	0	0	0	52	36
Karl Ashall	3/11/89	4(16)	3(12)	3	1	1	0	0	0	14	4
Chris Clarke	9/4/87	5(1)	5	0	0	0	0	0	0	0	0
Dale Cunniffe	25/3/87	23(1)	17	8	6	0	0	0	0	32	24
Gavin Dodd	28/2/81	17	14	12	9	23	19	0	0	94	74
Carl Forster	4/6/92	11(1)	11(1)	0	0	0	0	0	0	0	0
Rob Foxen	12/12/87	4(3)	3	1	1	0	0	0	0	4	4
Andy Gorski	31/3/81	2(4)	(2)	1	0	0	0	0	0	4	0
Scott Hale	14/12/91	1(4)	1(4)	1	1	0	0	0	0	4	4
Darren Hawkyard	14/10/84	19(1)	13(1)	6	2	0	0	0	0	24	8
Richie Hawkyard	21/1/86	19(3)	13(3)	3	2	0	0	0	0	12	8
Adam Higson	19/5/87	15	11	10	7	0	0	0	0	40	28
Neil Holland	24/2/89	5(11)	2(9)	2	1	0	0	0	0	8	4
Alex Hurst	17/3/90	7(1)	4(1)	3	3	0	0	0	0	12	12
Chaz I'Anson	30/11/86	21(3)	15(2)	6	3	0	0	0	0	24	12
Dave McConnell	25/3/81	(2)		0	0	0	0	0	0	0	0
Danny Meekin	16/3/89	6(9)	3(6)	1	0	0	0	0	0	4	0
David Mills	1/6/81	14(8)	10(5)	2	1	0	0	0	0	8	4
Mike Morrison	9/9/87	12(10)	9(8)	1	0	0	0	0	0	4	0
Ian Mort	21/6/88	15	10	4	1	56	30	0	0	128	64
Kevin Penny	3/10/87	15	11	9	7	0	0	0	0	36	28
Sam Reay	23/5/84	6(3)	4(2)	1	1	0	0	0	0	4	4
Glenn Riley	21/9/92	2(10)	2(9)	0	0	0	0	0	0	0	0
Mark Smith	18/8/81	21(3)	15(3)	0	0	0	0	0	0	0	0
Adam Walker	20/2/91	5(2)	5(2)	2	2	0	0	0	0	8	8
Ian Watson	27/10/76	24	17	2	2	0	0	0	0	8	8
Lee Wingfield	9/6/81	3(2)	1	0	0	0	0	0	0	0	0

Martin Ainscough

LEAGUE RECORD
P18-W4-D1-L13-BP5
(8th, Championship)
F366, A632, Diff-266
19 points.

CHALLENGE CUP
Round Five

NORTHERN RAIL CUP
6th, Pool 2

ATTENDANCES
Best - v Leigh (Ch - 1,796)
Worst - v Siddal (CC - 404)
Total (excluding Challenge Cup) - 7,821
Average (excluding Challenge Cup) - 711
(Up by 2 on 2011, Championship One,
The Willows)

CLUB RECORDS	Highest score: 94-0 v Gateshead, 22/8/2010 Highest score against: 0-112 v Warrington, 20/5/2011
	Record attendance: 26,891 v Wigan, 12/2/64 *(Station Road)*
MATCH RECORDS	Tries: 6 Mark Riley v Prescot, 11/8/96 Goals: 12 Ken Gowers v Liverpool City, 3/10/59
	Points: 30 Greg Pearce v Prescot, 11/8/96; Mick Nanyn v York, 25/3/2001; Gavin Dodd v Gateshead, 22/8/2010; Ian Mort v South Wales, 17/4/2011
SEASON RECORDS	Tries: 42 John Stopford 1963-64 Goals: 128 Albert Blan 1960-61 Points: 338 Ian Mort 2011
CAREER RECORDS	Tries: 197 Frank Evans 1921-31 Goals: 970 Ken Gowers 1954-73 Points: 2,105 Ken Gowers 1954-73 Appearances: 601 Ken Gowers 1954-73

YORK CITY KNIGHTS

DATE	FIXTURE	RESULT	SCORERS	LGE	ATT
19/2/12	Doncaster (a) (NRC)	W18-29	t:Ford(2),Lee,Clarke,Pryce g:Thorman(4) fg:Thorman	5th(P2)	702
23/2/12	Swinton (h) (NRC)	W30-22	t:Pryce,Elliott,Bush,Lee(2) g:Thorman(5)	2nd(P2)	504
26/2/12	Gateshead (h) (NRC)	W26-22	t:Turner,Hemmings(2),Green(2) g:Bush(3)	2nd(P2)	635
2/3/12	Sheffield (a) (NRC) ●	L36-4	t:Clarke	5th(P2)	725
11/3/12	Dewsbury (a)	L30-10	t:Bush,Sutton g:Thorman	8th	1,059
18/3/12	Halifax (h)	L18-24	t:Green,Lee,Benson g:Thorman(3)	8th	967
25/3/12	Hull Dockers (h) (CCR3)	W40-14	t:Lee,Haughey,Elliott,Garside,Ford(3),Turner g:Bush(2),Turner(2)	N/A	346
30/3/12	Leigh (a)	L36-6	t:Turner g:Thorman	9th	1,700
8/4/12	Hunslet (a)	L20-6	t:Hellewell g:Thorman	10th	505
15/4/12	Sheffield (h) (CCR4)	L12-50	t:Elliott,Sutton g:Thorman(2)	N/A	551
22/4/12	Batley (h)	L16-30	t:Houston,Davies,King g:Thorman(2)	10th	691
6/5/12	Swinton (a)	L32-12	t:Ford,Elliott(2)	10th	410
10/5/12	Sheffield (h)	L18-25	t:Johnston,Ford,Elliott g:Thorman(3)	10th	462
19/5/12	Featherstone (a)	L34-14	t:Ford(2),Tansey g:Thorman	10th	1,620
27/5/12	Keighley (h)	L18-42	t:Lee,Bush(2) g:Thorman(3)	10th	918
10/6/12	Swinton (h)	W26-22	t:Elliott,Garside(2),Davies,Ford g:Thorman(3)	9th	631
22/6/12	Sheffield (a) ●	L44-10	t:Ford,Turner g:Thorman	9th	784
29/6/12	Dewsbury (h)	L24-32	t:Bush,Davies(2),Thorman g:Thorman(4)	9th	906
15/7/12	Keighley (a)	L46-24	t:Garside,Brining,Esposito,Elliott g:Thorman(4)	9th	972
22/7/12	Leigh (h)	L20-66	t:Lee,Sullivan,Brining,Esposito g:Thorman(2)	9th	806
3/8/12	Featherstone (h)	L12-40	t:Bush,Clarke g:Thorman(2)	9th	1,015
12/8/12	Halifax (a)	L44-12	t:Elliott,Bush g:Thorman(2)	9th	1,989
19/8/12	Batley (a)	L50-0		10th	741
2/9/12	Hunslet (h)	L26-28	t:Elliott,Pryce,Poutney(2),Lee g:Thorman(3)	10th	913

● Played at Don Valley Stadium

APP TRIES GOALS FG PTS

	D.O.B.	ALL	Ch	ALL	Ch	ALL	Ch	ALL	Ch	ALL	Ch
Jack Aldous	3/4/91	20(3)	16(2)	0	0	0	0	0	0	0	0
Alex Benson	22/5/85	2(6)	1(2)	1	1	0	0	0	0	4	4
Kris Brining	16/11/93	3(7)	1(6)	2	2	0	0	0	0	8	8
Brooke Broughton	30/10/90	2(5)	1(3)	0	0	0	0	0	0	0	0
Davey Burns	22/6/86	(1)	0	0	0	0	0	0	0	0	0
Tom Bush	25/1/90	20(3)	15(2)	7	6	5	0	0	0	38	24
Harry Carter	10/2/94	(1)	(1)	0	0	0	0	0	0	0	0
Rhys Clarke	12/3/91	11(6)	7(5)	3	1	0	0	0	0	12	4
Tyler Craig	4/7/93	2(1)	2(1)	0	0	0	0	0	0	0	0
John Davies	8/1/91	13	13	4	4	0	0	0	0	16	16
Ben Dent	27/9/91	5	3	0	0	0	0	0	0	0	0
George Elliott	21/9/91	19(3)	15(2)	10	7	0	0	0	0	40	28
Liam Ellis	24/7/95	(3)	(3)	0	0	0	0	0	0	0	0
Dario Esposito	25/9/88	2(5)	2(5)	2	2	0	0	0	0	8	8
James Ford	29/9/82	18	13	11	6	0	0	0	0	44	24
Nathan Freer	21/5/89	7(7)	6(7)	0	0	0	0	0	0	0	0
Matt Garside	1/10/90	23	18	4	3	0	0	0	0	16	12
John Gay	8/7/91	(1)	0	0	0	0	0	0	0	0	0
Chris Green	3/1/90	2(5)	2(3)	3	1	0	0	0	0	12	4
Tom Haughey	30/1/82	7(2)	4	1	0	0	0	0	0	4	0
Ben Hellewell	30/1/92	7	4	1	1	0	0	0	0	4	4
Joe Hemmings	10/1/89	2(4)	(3)	2	0	0	0	0	0	8	0
James Houston	28/12/82	9(3)	5(2)	1	1	0	0	0	0	4	4
Adam Howard	22/7/87	(4)	(2)	0	0	0	0	0	0	0	0
Ben Johnston	8/3/92	3	3	1	1	0	0	0	0	4	4
Paul King	28/6/79	11(1)	9(1)	1	1	0	0	0	0	4	4
Jack Lee	1/11/88	21(2)	17	8	4	0	0	0	0	32	16
Danny Nicklas	29/6/91	2	2	0	0	0	0	0	0	0	0
Ollie Olds	14/8/93	2	2	0	0	0	0	0	0	0	0
Gareth Poutney	5/10/91	2(2)	2(2)	2	2	0	0	0	0	8	8
Waine Pryce	3/10/81	11	9	3	1	0	0	0	0	12	4
Ed Smith	12/11/92	11(1)	7(1)	0	0	0	0	0	0	0	0
Jack Stearman	30/1/88	(1)	(1)	0	0	0	0	0	0	0	0
Tim Stubbs	6/5/95	(2)	(2)	0	0	0	0	0	0	0	0
Adam Sullivan	14/11/82	23	18	1	1	0	0	0	0	4	4
Dave Sutton	21/9/89	7(9)	4(8)	2	1	0	0	0	0	8	4
Jordan Tansey	9/9/86	17	11	1	1	0	0	0	0	4	4
Chris Thorman	26/9/80	21	18	1	1	47	36	1	0	99	76
Brett Turner	1/12/87	7(7)	4(7)	4	2	2	0	0	0	20	8

Chris Thorman

LEAGUE RECORD
P18-W1-D0-L17-BP4
(10th, Championship)
F272, A645, Diff-373
7 points.

CHALLENGE CUP
Round Four

NORTHERN RAIL CUP
5th, Pool 2

ATTENDANCES
Best - v Featherstone (Ch - 1,015)
Worst - v Hull Dockers (CC - 346)
Total (excluding Challenge Cup) - 8,448
Average (excluding Challenge Cup) - 768
(Down by 381 on 2011)

CLUB RECORDS
MATCH RECORDS
Highest score: 132-0 v Northumbria University, 6/3/2011 **Highest score against:** 0-98 v Rochdale, 8/4/2001
Record attendance: 14,689 v Swinton, 10/2/34 *(Clarence Street)*; 4,977 v Halifax, 5/1/90 *(Ryedale/Huntington Stadium)*
Tries: 7 Brad Davis v Highfield, 17/9/95 **Goals:** 20 Chris Thorman v Northumbria University, 6/3/2011
Points: 56 Chris Thorman v Northumbria University, 6/3/2011

SEASON RECORDS
CAREER RECORDS
Tries: 35 John Crossley 1980-81 **Goals:** 178 *(inc 4fg)* Danny Brough 2004 **Points:** 412 Danny Brough 2004
Tries: 167 Peter Foster 1955-67 **Goals:** 1,060 Vic Yorke 1954-67 **Points:** 2,159 Vic Yorke 1954-67 **Appearances:** 449 Willie Hargreaves 1952-65

CHAMPIONSHIP 2012
Round by Round

ROUND 1

Thursday 8th March 2012

LEIGH CENTURIONS 18 BATLEY BULLDOGS 24

CENTURIONS: 1 Gregg McNally; 2 Steve Maden; 3 Ryan Shaw; 4 Matt Gardner; 5 Adam Clay; 6 Martyn Ridyard; 7 John Duffy; 8 Rob Parker; 9 Bob Beswick; 10 Ricky Bibey; 11 Craig Briscoe; 12 Tommy Goulden; 13 Sam Hopkins. Subs (all used): 14 Ryan Brierley; 15 Michael Worrincy; 16 James Taylor; 17 Michael Ostick.
Tries: Parker (3), Shaw (6, 57), Clay (72);
Goals: Ridyard 1/2, Brierley 0/2.
BULLDOGS: 1 Ian Preece; 2 Gareth Potts; 3 Jason Walton; 4 Danny Maun; 5 Alex Brown; 6 Ben Black; 7 Gareth Moore; 8 Byron Smith; 9 Paul Mennell; 10 Craig Potter; 11 Alex Bretherton; 12 Jonny Walker; 13 Kris Lythe. Subs (all used): 14 Ashley Lindsay; 15 Alex Walmsley; 16 Mark Applegarth; 17 Lewis Palfrey.
Tries: Bretherton (13), Preece (15, 43), Potts (48);
Goals: Moore 4/5.
Rugby Leaguer & League Express Men of the Match:
Centurions: John Duffy; *Bulldogs:* Jonny Walker.
Penalty count: 15-13; **Half-time:** 10-10;
Referee: Matthew Thomason; **Attendance:** 1,663.

Sunday 11th March 2012

KEIGHLEY COUGARS 12 FEATHERSTONE ROVERS 22

COUGARS: 1 Craig Moss; 2 James Haythornthwaite; 3 Matt Parata; 4 Danny Lawton; 5 Semi Tadulala; 6 Danny Jones; 7 Sam Obst; 8 Andy Shickell; 9 James Feather; 10 Neil Cherryholme; 11 Oliver Pursglove; 12 Richard Jones; 13 Jason Demetriou. Subs (all used): 14 Jy-Mel Coleman; 15 Jamaine Wray; 16 Brendan Rawlins; 17 Michael Korkidas.
Tries: Lawton (25), Tadulala (78); **Goals:** D Jones 2/3.
ROVERS: 1 Ian Hardman; 2 Tom Saxton; 3 Sam Smeaton; 4 Greg Worthington; 5 Tangi Ropati; 6 Andy Kain; 7 Liam Finn; 8 Anthony England; 9 Ben Kaye; 10 Michael Haley; 11 Jon Grayshon; 12 Tim Spears; 13 Matty Dale. Subs (all used): 14 Jon Hepworth; 15 Jack Bussey; 16 James Lockwood; 17 Dominic Maloney.
Tries: Hardman (9), England (54), Smeaton (59, 63);
Goals: Finn 3/4.
Rugby Leaguer & League Express Men of the Match:
Cougars: Craig Moss; *Rovers:* Liam Finn.
Penalty count: 11-5; **Half-time:** 8-6;
Referee: Gareth Hewer; **Attendance:** 1,621.

DEWSBURY RAMS 30 YORK CITY KNIGHTS 10

RAMS: 1 James Craven; 2 Jermaine Akaidere; 3 Ryan Esders; 4 Ayden Faal; 5 Austin Buchanan; 6 Pat Walker; 7 Scott Spaven; 8 Ben Jones; 9 Craig Cook; 10 Steve Crossley; 11 Josh Tonks; 12 Dwayne Barker; 13 Luke Blake. Subs (all used): 14 George Flanagan; 15 Matt Nicholson; 16 Andy Smith; 17 Billy Harris.
Tries: Buchanan (2), Faal (12, 66), Barker (56), Tonks (75); **Goals:** Walker 5/6.
CITY KNIGHTS: 1 Ben Hellewell; 2 Tom Bush; 3 James Ford; 4 Matt Garside; 5 Dave Sutton; 6 Chris Thorman; 7 Jordan Tansey; 8 Adam Sullivan; 9 Jack Lee; 10 James Houston; 11 Rhys Clarke; 12 Tom Haughey; 13 Jack Aldous. Subs (all used): 14 George Elliott; 15 Chris Green; 16 Alex Benson; 17 Brooke Broughton.
Tries: Bush (49), Sutton (68); **Goals:** Thorman 1/2.
Rugby Leaguer & League Express Men of the Match:
Rams: Dwayne Barker; *City Knights:* Ben Hellewell.
Penalty count: 7-6; **Half-time:** 12-0;
Referee: Ronnie Laughton; **Attendance:** 1,059.

HALIFAX 44 HUNSLET HAWKS 18

HALIFAX: 1 Ryan Fieldhouse; 2 Rob Worrincy; 3 Ben Heaton; 4 Steve Tyrer; 5 Paul White; 6 Paul Handforth; 7 Anthony Thackeray; 8 Jim Gannon; 9 Sean Penkywicz; 10 Sean Hesketh; 11 Joe Chandler; 12 Adam Robinson; 13 Callum Casey. Subs (all used): 14 Anthony Bowman; 15 Josh Barlow; 16 Luke Ambler; 17 Lee Paterson.
Tries: Penkywicz (9), Casey (16, 27), Thackeray (36), Heaton (40), Chandler (46), Fieldhouse (70, 76);
Goals: Tyrer 4/6, Handforth 2/2.
HAWKS: 1 Danny Ratcliffe; 2 Lee Brickwood; 3 David Clayton; 4 Gareth Davies; 5 Dennis Tuffour; 6 Danny Allan; 7 David March; 8 Andrew Yates; 9 Luke Haigh; 10 Steve Lewis; 11 Richard Blakeway; 12 John Oakes; 13 Ryan Benjafield. Subs (all used): 14 Joe McLocklan; 15 Scott Watson; 16 David Tootill; 17 Neil Lowe.
Tries: Lowe (32), Watson (51), Benjafield (66);
Goals: Ratcliffe 3/3.
Rugby Leaguer & League Express Men of the Match:
Halifax: Paul Handforth; *Hawks:* Joe McLocklan.
Penalty count: 7-7; **Half-time:** 28-6;
Referee: Tim Roby; **Attendance:** 2,052.

SHEFFIELD EAGLES 56 SWINTON LIONS 22

EAGLES: 1 Quentin Laulu-Togagae; 2 Vinny Finigan; 3 Menzie Yere; 4 Misi Taulapapa; 5 Nev Morrison; 6 Simon Brown; 7 Dominic Brambani; 8 Jack Howieson; 9 Andrew Henderson; 10 Mitchell Stringer; 11 Alex Szostak; 12 Peter Green; 13 Joe Hirst. Subs (all used): 14 Pat Smith; 15 Sam Scott; 16 Duane Straugheir; 17 Ryan Hepworth.
Tries: Szostak (2), Yere (7), Brambani (20), Hepworth (32), Finigan (50), Morrison (54), Straugheir (57), Hirst (65, 70), Laulu-Togagae (72); **Goals:** Brown 8/10.
LIONS: 1 Richie Hawkyard; 2 Gavin Dodd; 3 Adam Higson; 4 Tom Armstrong; 5 Rob Foxen; 6 Martin Ainscough; 7 Ian Watson; 8 Neil Holland; 9 Mark Smith; 10 David Mills; 11 Dale Cunniffe; 12 Darren Hawkyard; 13 Chaz I'Anson. Subs (all used): 14 Mike Morrison; 15 Carl Forster; 16 Karl Ashall; 17 Scott Hale.
Tries: Foxen (23), Higson (42, 46), D Hawkyard (77);
Goals: Dodd 3/4.
Rugby Leaguer & League Express Men of the Match:
Eagles: Quentin Laulu-Togagae; *Lions:* Mark Smith.
Penalty count: 4-3; **Half-time:** 24-6; **Referee:** Jamie Leahy; **Attendance:** 1,815 *(at Don Valley Stadium)*.

ROUND 2

Thursday 15th March 2012

FEATHERSTONE ROVERS 36 LEIGH CENTURIONS 16

ROVERS: 1 Ian Hardman; 2 Tom Saxton; 3 Sam Smeaton; 4 Greg Worthington; 5 Tangi Ropati; 6 Andy Kain; 7 Liam Finn; 8 Anthony England; 9 Ben Kaye; 10 Michael Haley; 11 Jon Grayshon; 12 James Lockwood; 13 Matty Dale. Subs (all used): 14 Jon Hepworth; 15 Kyle Briggs; 16 Dominic Maloney; 17 Andrew Bostock.
Tries: Worthington (15), Hardman (21), Bostock (28), Kain (34, 43), Ropati (55); **Goals:** Finn 6/6.
CENTURIONS: 1 Matthew Russell; 2 Steve Maden; 3 Stuart Littler; 4 Matt Gardner; 5 Ryan Shaw; 6 Ryan Brierley; 7 John Duffy; 8 Ricky Bibey; 9 Bob Beswick; 10 Tom Spencer; 11 Michael Worrincy; 12 James Taylor; 13 Sam Hopkins. Subs (all used): 14 Martyn Ridyard; 15 Craig Briscoe; 16 Anthony Nicholson; 17 Rob Parker.
Tries: Gardner (39), Spencer (47), Russell (79);
Goals: Shaw 1/1, Ridyard 1/3.
Rugby Leaguer & League Express Men of the Match:
Rovers: Andy Kain; *Centurions:* John Duffy.
Penalty count: 7-11; **Half-time:** 24-8;
Referee: Ronnie Laughton; **Attendance:** 2,382.

Sunday 18th March 2012

BATLEY BULLDOGS 8 KEIGHLEY COUGARS 10

BULLDOGS: 1 Ian Preece; 2 Gareth Potts; 3 Jason Walton; 4 Danny Maun; 5 Alex Brown; 6 Ben Black; 7 Gareth Moore; 8 Byron Smith; 9 Paul Mennell; 10 Craig Potter; 11 Jonny Walker; 12 Adam Scott; 13 Kris Lythe. Subs (all used): 14 Ashley Lindsay; 15 Gareth Frodsham; 16 Mark Applegarth; 17 Mark Toohey.
Try: Moore (2); **Goals:** Moore 2/2.
COUGARS: 1 Craig Moss; 2 Richie Barnett; 3 James Haythornthwaite; 4 Danny Lawton; 5 Semi Tadulala; 6 Danny Jones; 7 Sam Obst; 8 Michael Korkidas; 9 James Feather; 10 Neil Cherryholme; 11 Oliver Pursglove; 12 Richard Jones; 13 Jy-Mel Coleman. Subs (all used): 14 Paul March; 15 Jason Demetriou; 16 Jode Sheriffe; 17 Andy Shickell.
Tries: Coleman (39), Haythornthwaite (69);
Goals: D Jones 1/2.
Rugby Leaguer & League Express Men of the Match:
Bulldogs: Ian Preece; *Cougars:* Danny Jones.
Penalty count: 7-6; **Half-time:** 6-6;
Referee: Clint Sharrad; **Attendance:** 848.

SWINTON LIONS 16 DEWSBURY RAMS 34

LIONS: 1 Richie Hawkyard; 2 Alex Hurst; 3 Adam Higson; 4 Tom Armstrong; 5 Ian Mort; 6 Martin Ainscough; 7 Ian Watson; 8 Carl Forster; 9 Mark Smith; 10 Lee Wingfield; 11 Scott Hale; 12 Darren Hawkyard; 13 Chaz I'Anson. Subs (all used): 14 Mike Morrison; 15 Danny Meekin; 16 Karl Ashall; 17 David Mills.
Tries: Higson (19), Ainscough (31), Hurst (67);
Goals: Mort 2/3.
RAMS: 1 James Craven; 2 Jermaine Akaidere; 3 Ryan Esders; 4 Ayden Faal; 5 Austin Buchanan; 6 Pat Walker; 7 Scott Spaven; 8 Ben Jones; 9 Craig Cook; 10 Steve Crossley; 11 Josh Tonks; 12 Dwayne Barker; 13 Luke Blake. Subs (all used): 14 George Flanagan; 15 Matt Nicholson; 16 Andy Smith; 17 Billy Harris.
Tries: Crossley (7), Cook (10), Faal (35), Flanagan (39), Nicholson (76); **Goals:** Walker 7/7.
Rugby Leaguer & League Express Men of the Match:
Lions: Richie Hawkyard; *Rams:* Pat Walker.
Penalty count: 4-7; **Half-time:** 10-26;
Referee: Tim Roby; **Attendance:** 654.

HUNSLET HAWKS 22 SHEFFIELD EAGLES 40

HAWKS: 1 David Clayton; 2 Lee Brickwood; 3 Josh Nathaniel; 4 Gareth Davies; 5 Dennis Tuffour; 6 Danny Ratcliffe; 7 Danny Allan; 8 Andrew Yates; 9 Luke Haigh; 10 Neil Lowe; 11 Steve Lewis; 12 John Oakes; 13 David March. Subs (all used): 14 Joe McLocklan; 15 Scott Watson; 16 David Tootill; 17 Ryan Benjafield.
Tries: Davies (38, 66), Nathaniel (42), Allan (61);
Goals: Ratcliffe 3/4.
Sin bin: Ratcliffe (23) - dissent.
EAGLES: 1 Quentin Laulu-Togagae; 2 Vinny Finigan; 3 Menzie Yere; 4 Misi Taulapapa; 5 Nev Morrison; 6 Simon Brown; 7 Dominic Brambani; 8 Jack Howieson; 9 Andrew Henderson; 10 Liam Higgins; 11 Alex Szostak; 12 Peter Green; 13 Joe Hirst. Subs (all used): 14 Sam Scott; 15 Mitchell Stringer; 16 Duane Straugheir; 17 Ryan Hepworth.
Tries: Morrison (3, 13), Laulu-Togagae (16), Higgins (19), Yere (23), Henderson (30, 76); **Goals:** Brown 6/7.
Sin bin: Higgins (60) - holding down.
Rugby Leaguer & League Express Men of the Match:
Hawks: Danny Allan; *Eagles:* Simon Brown.
Penalty count: 8-8; **Half-time:** 4-36;
Referee: Matthew Thomason; **Attendance:** 419.

YORK CITY KNIGHTS 18 HALIFAX 24

CITY KNIGHTS: 1 Ben Hellewell; 2 Tom Bush; 3 James Ford; 4 Matt Garside; 5 Dave Sutton; 6 Chris Thorman; 7 Jordan Tansey; 8 Adam Sullivan; 9 Jack Lee; 10 Chris Green; 11 Tom Haughey; 12 Ed Smith; 13 Jack Aldous. Subs (all used): 14 Brett Turner; 15 Alex Benson; 16 James Houston; 17 Brooke Broughton.
Tries: Green (29), Lee (38), Benson (73);
Goals: Thorman 3/3.
HALIFAX: 1 Ryan Fieldhouse; 2 Paul White; 3 Lee Paterson; 4 Ben Heaton; 5 Wayne Reittie; 6 Paul Handforth; 7 Anthony Thackeray; 8 Jim Gannon; 9 Sean Penkywicz; 10 Sean Hesketh; 11 Dane Manning; 12 Adam Robinson; 13 Craig Ashall. Subs (all used): 14 Anthony Bowman; 15 Joe Chandler; 16 Sam Barlow; 17 Luke Ambler.
Tries: Heaton (11, 15), Manning (40), Penkywicz (80);
Goals: Paterson 4/4.
Rugby Leaguer & League Express Men of the Match:
City Knights: Chris Thorman; *Halifax:* Adam Robinson.
Penalty count: 4-3; **Half-time:** 12-18;
Referee: Gareth Hewer; **Attendance:** 967.

ROUND 3

Thursday 29th March 2012

SHEFFIELD EAGLES 18 HALIFAX 50

EAGLES: 1 Quentin Laulu-Togagae; 2 Scott Turner; 3 Menzie Yere; 4 Misi Taulapapa; 5 Nev Morrison; 6 Simon Brown; 7 Dominic Brambani; 8 Jack Howieson; 9 Andrew Henderson; 10 Mitchell Stringer; 11 Alex Szostak; 12 Peter Green; 13 Joe Hirst. Subs (all used): 14 Dane McDonald; 15 Liam Higgins; 16 Michael Knowles; 17 Alex Rowe.
Tries: Brambani (37), Higgins (43), McDonald (63);
Goals: Brown 3/3.
HALIFAX: 1 Ryan Fieldhouse; 2 Wayne Reittie; 3 Steve Tyrer; 4 Ben Heaton; 5 Lee Paterson; 6 Paul Handforth; 7 Anthony Thackeray; 8 Luke Ambler; 9 Sean Penkywicz; 10 Jim Gannon; 11 Dane Manning; 12 Adam Robinson; 13 Craig Ashall. Subs (all used): 14 Callum Casey; 15 Ross Divorty; 16 Sean Hesketh; 17 Makali Aizue.
Tries: Ashall (14, 28), Penkywicz (17, 67), Manning (20), Ambler (50), Divorty (69), Paterson (71), Heaton (76); **Goals:** Paterson 7/9.
Rugby Leaguer & League Express Men of the Match:
Eagles: Andrew Henderson; *Halifax:* Dane Manning.
Penalty count: 11-5; **Half-time:** 6-20;
Referee: Gareth Hewer; **Attendance:** 1,412 *(at Bramall Lane)*.

Friday 30th March 2012

LEIGH CENTURIONS 36 YORK CITY KNIGHTS 6

CENTURIONS: 1 Gregg McNally; 2 Steve Maden; 3 Stuart Littler; 4 Matt Gardner; 5 Jonathan Pownall; 6 Martyn Ridyard; 7 John Duffy; 8 Ricky Bibey; 9 Bob Beswick; 10 Rob Parker; 11 Craig Briscoe; 12 James Laithwaite; 13 James Taylor. Subs (all used): 14 Ryan Brierley; 15 Sam Hopkins; 16 Anthony Nicholson; 17 Tommy Gallagher.
Tries: Duffy (6), McNally (14), Pownall (19, 33, 78), Ridyard (26), Gardner (66); **Goals:** Ridyard 4/7.
CITY KNIGHTS: 1 Jordan Tansey; 2 Tom Bush; 3 George Elliott; 4 Matt Garside; 5 Ben Hellewell; 6 James Ford; 7 Chris Thorman; 8 Adam Sullivan; 9 Jack Lee; 10 Alex Benson; 11 James Houston; 12 Tom Haughey; 13 Jack Aldous. Subs (all used): 14 Brett Turner; 15 Dave Sutton; 16 Nathan Freer; 17 Brooke Broughton.
Try: Turner (42); **Goals:** Thorman 1/1.
Rugby Leaguer & League Express Men of the Match:
Centurions: Craig Briscoe;
City Knights: Brooke Broughton.
Penalty count: 6-7; **Half-time:** 26-0;
Referee: Jamie Leahy; **Attendance:** 1,700.

Sunday 1st April 2012

KEIGHLEY COUGARS 48 HUNSLET HAWKS 6

COUGARS: 1 Craig Moss; 2 Richie Barnett; 3 James Haythornthwaite; 4 Danny Lawton; 5 Semi Tadulala; 6 Danny Jones; 7 Sam Obst; 8 Andy Shickell; 9 James Feather; 10 Neil Cherryholme; 11 Oliver Pursglove; 12 Richard Jones; 13 Paul March. Subs (all used): 14 James Davey; 15 Jason Demetriou; 16 Michael Korkidas; 17 Jode Sheriffe.
Tries: Pursglove (32), Moss (34), Shickell (52), Jode Sheriffe (54), Tadulala (63), Obst (66), Haythornthwaite (75), Feather (78); **Goals:** D Jones 8/8.
HAWKS: 1 David Clayton; 2 Lee Brickwood; 3 Gareth Davies; 4 Josh Nathaniel; 5 Dennis Tuffour; 6 Danny Ratcliffe; 7 Luke Helliwell; 8 Andrew Yates; 9 Luke Haigh; 10 Neil Lowe; 11 Scott Watson; 12 John Oakes; 13 David March. Subs (all used): 14 Joe McLocklan; 15 Richard Blakeway; 16 Anthony Henderson; 17 Ryan Benjafield.
Try: Nathaniel (42); **Goals:** Ratcliffe 1/1.
Rugby Leaguer & League Express Men of the Match:
Cougars: Sam Obst; *Hawks:* Luke Helliwell.
Penalty count: 4-6; **Half-time:** 12-0;
Referee: Ronnie Laughton; **Attendance:** 1,069.

SWINTON LIONS 26 BATLEY BULLDOGS 18

LIONS: 1 Richie Hawkyard; 2 Ian Mort; 3 Adam Higson; 4 Tom Armstrong; 5 Gavin Dodd; 6 Martin Ainscough; 7 Ian Watson; 8 Mike Morrison; 9 Karl Ashall; 10 Carl Forster; 11 Dale Cunniffe; 12 Darren Hawkyard; 13 Chaz I'Anson. Subs (all used): 14 Neil Holland; 15 Scott Hale; 16 Andy Gorski; 17 Mark Smith.
Tries: Dodd (13), I'Anson (17), Cunniffe (54), Armstrong (61), Hale (78); **Goals:** Mort 3/5.
On report:
Cunniffe (31) - alleged late challenge on Moore.

Hunslet's John Oakes on the charge through the York defence

BULLDOGS: 1 Johnny Campbell; 2 Gareth Potts; 3 Mark Toohey; 4 Daley Williams; 5 Alex Brown; 6 Gareth Moore; 7 Lewis Palfrey; 8 Luke Menzies; 9 Tom Henderson; 10 Keegan Hirst; 11 Alex Bretherton; 12 Mark Applegarth; 13 Ashley Lindsay. Subs (all used): 14 Paul Mennell; 15 Alex Walmsley; 16 Ian Preece; 17 Byron Smith.
Tries: Daley Williams (10, 37), Palfrey (33);
Goals: Moore 3/3.
Rugby Leaguer & League Express Men of the Match:
Lions: Ian Watson; *Bulldogs:* Ashley Lindsay.
Penalty count: 7-11; **Half-time:** 10-18;
Referee: Matthew Thomason; **Attendance:** 707.

DEWSBURY RAMS 12 FEATHERSTONE ROVERS 24

RAMS: 1 James Craven; 2 Greg Scott; 3 Ryan Esders; 4 Ayden Faal; 5 Austin Buchanan; 6 Pat Walker; 7 Scott Spaven; 8 Ben Jones; 9 Luke Blake; 10 Steve Crossley; 11 Rob Spicer; 12 Dwayne Barker; 13 Josh Tonks. Subs (all used): 14 George Flanagan; 15 Matt Nicholson; 16 Ben Bolger; 17 Cain Southernwood.
Tries: Esders (35), Buchanan (63); **Goals:** Walker 2/4.
ROVERS: 1 Ian Hardman; 2 Tom Saxton; 3 Sam Smeaton; 4 Greg Worthington; 5 Tangi Ropati; 6 Andy Kain; 7 Liam Finn; 8 Anthony England; 9 Ben Kaye; 10 Stuart Dickens; 11 James Lockwood; 12 Tim Spears; 13 Matty Dale. Subs (all used): 14 Jon Hepworth; 15 Dominic Maloney; 16 Michael Haley; 17 Jon Grayson.
Tries: Hardman (32), Kain (43, 67), Dale (48);
Goals: Finn 4/5.
Rugby Leaguer & League Express Men of the Match:
Rams: Steve Crossley; *Rovers:* Andy Kain.
Penalty count: 10-7; **Half-time:** 6-4;
Referee: George Stokes; **Attendance:** 1,597.

ROUND 4

Friday 6th April 2012

LEIGH CENTURIONS 38 SWINTON LIONS 4

CENTURIONS: 1 Gregg McNally; 2 Steve Maden; 3 Stuart Littler; 4 Matt Gardner; 5 Jonathan Pownall; 6 Martyn Ridyard; 7 Bob Beswick; 8 Michael Ostick; 9 Anthony Nicholson; 10 Rob Parker; 11 James Laithwaite; 12 Tommy Goulden; 13 James Taylor. Subs (all used): 14 Ryan Brierley; 15 Sam Hopkins; 16 Craig Briscoe; 17 Tommy Gallagher.
Tries: Taylor (9, 53), Briscoe (27), Maden (39, 79), Gardner (64), Brierley (73); **Goals:** Ridyard 5/7.
On report: Brawl (31).
LIONS: 1 Richie Hawkyard; 2 Ian Mort; 3 Adam Higson; 4 Tom Armstrong; 5 Gavin Dodd; 6 Martin Ainscough; 7 Ian Watson; 8 Mike Morrison; 9 Karl Ashall; 10 Carl Forster; 11 Dale Cunniffe; 12 Darren Hawkyard; 13 Chaz l'Anson. Subs (all used): 14 Neil Holland; 15 Scott Hale; 16 Andy Gorski; 17 Mark Smith.
Try: Cunniffe (19); **Goals:** Mort 0/1.

On report: Brawl (31).
Rugby Leaguer & League Express Men of the Match:
Centurions: Bob Beswick; *Lions:* Richie Hawkyard.
Penalty count: 6-6; **Half-time:** 18-4;
Referee: Ronnie Laughton; **Attendance:** 2,135.

BATLEY BULLDOGS 18 DEWSBURY RAMS 16

BULLDOGS: 1 Ian Preece; 2 Gareth Potts; 3 Jason Walton; 4 Daley Williams; 5 Alex Brown; 6 Ben Black; 7 Gareth Moore; 8 Byron Smith; 9 Paul Mennell; 10 Craig Potter; 11 Alex Bretherton; 12 Jonny Walker; 13 Kris Lythe. Subs (all used): 14 Ashley Lindsay; 15 Alex Walmsley; 16 Mark Applegarth; 17 Adam Scott.
Tries: Moore (21, 49), Walton (29); **Goals:** Moore 3/4.
RAMS: 1 James Craven; 2 Greg Scott; 3 Ryan Esders; 4 Ayden Faal; 5 Austin Buchanan; 6 Pat Walker; 7 Scott Spaven; 8 Ben Jones; 9 Craig Cook; 10 Steve Crossley; 11 Rob Spicer; 12 Ben Bolger; 13 Josh Tonks. Subs (all used): 14 George Flanagan; 15 Andy Smith; 16 Matt Nicholson; 17 Cain Southernwood.
Tries: Craven (41), Flanagan (70), Southernwood (75);
Goals: Walker 2/3.
Rugby Leaguer & League Express Men of the Match:
Bulldogs: Gareth Moore; *Rams:* Ryan Esders.
Penalty count: 4-7; **Half-time:** 10-0;
Referee: Clint Sharrad; **Attendance:** 1,353.

HALIFAX 13 KEIGHLEY COUGARS 12

HALIFAX: 1 Ryan Fieldhouse; 2 Wayne Reittie; 3 Steve Tyrer; 4 Ben Heaton; 5 Lee Paterson; 6 Paul Handforth; 7 Anthony Thackeray; 8 Luke Ambler; 9 Sean Penkywicz; 10 Jim Gannon; 11 Dane Manning; 12 Adam Robinson; 13 Craig Ashall. Subs (all used): 14 Callum Casey; 15 Ross Divorty; 16 Joe Chandler; 17 Makali Aizue.
Tries: Thackeray (11), Tyrer (18); **Goals:** Paterson 2/2;
Field goal: Handforth (68).
COUGARS: 1 Craig Moss; 2 Richie Barnett; 3 James Haythornthwaite; 4 Danny Lawton; 5 Semi Tadulala; 6 Danny Jones; 7 Sam Obst; 8 Michael Korkidas; 9 James Feather; 10 Neil Cherryholme; 11 Oliver Pursglove; 12 Richard Jones; 13 Paul March. Subs (all used): 14 James Davey; 15 Jason Demetriou; 16 Andy Shickell; 17 Jode Sheriffe.
Tries: R Jones (15), D Jones (29); **Goals:** D Jones 2/2.
Rugby Leaguer & League Express Men of the Match:
Halifax: Anthony Thackeray; *Cougars:* Paul March.
Penalty count: 4-2; **Half-time:** 12-12;
Referee: Jamie Leahy; **Attendance:** 2,378.

Saturday 7th April 2012

FEATHERSTONE ROVERS 40 SHEFFIELD EAGLES 60

ROVERS: 1 Ian Hardman; 2 Tom Saxton; 3 Sam Smeaton; 4 Greg Worthington; 5 Tangi Ropati; 6 Kyle Briggs; 7 Liam Finn; 8 Dominic Maloney; 9 Andy Kain; 10 Michael Haley; 11 Jon Grayson; 12 Tim Spears; 13

Matty Dale. Subs (all used): 14 Jon Hepworth; 15 James Lockwood; 16 Stuart Dickens; 17 Anthony England.
Tries: Worthington (19), Dale (23), Ropati (33), Saxton (54), Kain (56, 60), Haley (63); **Goals:** Finn 6/7.
EAGLES: 1 Quentin Laulu-Togagae; 2 Scott Turner; 3 Menzie Yere; 4 Misi Taulapapa; 5 Nev Morrison; 6 Simon Brown; 7 Dominic Brambani; 8 Jack Howieson; 9 Andrew Henderson; 10 Liam Higgins; 11 Alex Szostak; 12 Peter Green; 13 Joe Hirst. Subs (all used): 14 Dane McDonald; 15 Ryan Hepworth; 16 Michael Knowles; 17 Alex Rowe.
Tries: Taulapapa (3, 15, 47), Turner (11), Morrison (30), Yere (36), Szostak (41), Laulu-Togagae (49, 77), Hirst (65), McDonald (79); **Goals:** Brambani 5/7, Brown 3/4.
Rugby Leaguer & League Express Men of the Match:
Rovers: Kyle Briggs; *Eagles:* Dominic Brambani.
Penalty count: 5-8; **Half-time:** 16-26;
Referee: Tim Roby; **Attendance:** 2,293.

Sunday 8th April 2012

HUNSLET HAWKS 20 YORK CITY KNIGHTS 6

HAWKS: 1 Elliot Hodgson; 2 Lee Brickwood; 3 Gareth Davies; 4 David Clayton; 5 Dennis Tuffour; 6 Luke Helliwell; 7 Ryan Smith; 8 Andrew Yates; 9 Luke Haigh; 10 Anthony Henderson; 11 Scott Watson; 12 John Oakes; 13 David March. Subs (all used): 14 Joe McLocklan; 15 Richard Blakeway; 16 David Tootill; 17 Ryan Mansfield.
Tries: Tuffour (13, 40), Brickwood (54), Helliwell (80);
Goals: Helliwell 2/4.
CITY KNIGHTS: 1 Jordan Tansey; 2 Tom Bush; 3 James Ford; 4 Matt Garside; 5 Ben Hellewell; 6 Chris Thorman; 7 Brett Turner; 8 Adam Sullivan; 9 Jack Lee; 10 James Houston; 11 Nathan Freer; 12 Brooke Broughton; 13 Tom Haughey. Subs (all used): 14 George Elliott; 15 Jack Aldous; 16 Rhys Clarke; 17 Paul King.
Try: Hellewell (67); **Goals:** Thorman 1/1.
Sin bin: Tansey (52) - dissent.
Rugby Leaguer & League Express Men of the Match:
Hawks: Gareth Davies; *City Knights:* Tom Haughey.
Penalty count: 5-6; **Half-time:** 10-0;
Referee: Warren Turley; **Attendance:** 505.

ROUND 5

Thursday 19th April 2012

HALIFAX 18 LEIGH CENTURIONS 32

HALIFAX: 1 Ryan Fieldhouse; 2 Wayne Reittie; 3 Steve Tyrer; 4 Ben Heaton; 5 Paul White; 6 Paul Handforth; 7 Anthony Thackeray; 8 Jim Gannon; 9 Sean Penkywicz; 10 Luke Ambler; 11 Dane Manning; 12 Adam Robinson; 13 Craig Ashall. Subs (all used): 14 Callum Casey; 15 Ross Divorty; 16 Sean Hesketh; 17 Makali Aizue.
Tries: Ashall (6), Reittie (75), Heaton (78);
Goals: Tyrer 3/3.

Dewsbury's Scott Spaven gets a pass away as Keighley's Jy-Mel Coleman closes in

CENTURIONS: 1 Gregg McNally; 2 Steve Maden; 3 Stuart Littler; 4 Matt Gardner; 5 Jonathan Pownall; 6 Martyn Ridyard; 7 John Duffy; 8 Michael Ostick; 9 Bob Beswick; 10 Rob Parker; 11 James Laithwaite; 12 Tommy Goulden; 13 Craig Briscoe. Subs (all used): 14 Ryan Brierley; 15 Tom Spencer; 16 Sam Hopkins; 17 Tommy Gallagher.
Tries: McNally (31, 52), Duffy (35), Brierley (42, 72), Gardner (65); **Goals:** Ridyard 4/6.
Rugby Leaguer & League Express Men of the Match:
Halifax: Adam Robinson; *Centurions:* Bob Beswick.
Penalty count: 9-4; **Half-time:** 6-10;
Referee: George Stokes; **Attendance:** 2,062.

Sunday 22nd April 2012

KEIGHLEY COUGARS 23 SHEFFIELD EAGLES 16

COUGARS: 1 Craig Moss; 2 Richie Barnett; 3 James Haythornthwaite; 4 Danny Lawton; 5 Gavin Duffy; 6 Jy-Mel Coleman; 7 Sam Obst; 8 Andy Shickell; 9 James Feather; 10 Michael Korkidas; 11 Oliver Pursglove; 12 Jamie Shepherd; 13 Paul March. Subs (all used): 14 James Davey; 15 Jason Demetriou; 16 Jode Sheriffe; 17 Neil Cherryholme.
Tries: Moss (5), Obst (18), Coleman (48), Lawton (51); **Goals:** Lawton 3/5; **Field goal:** Obst (78).
EAGLES: 1 Quentin Laulu-Togagae; 2 Scott Turner; 3 Menzie Yere; 4 Misi Taulapapa; 5 Nev Morrison; 6 Dane McDonald; 7 Dominic Brambani; 8 Jack Howieson; 9 Andrew Henderson; 10 Liam Higgins; 11 Alex Szostak; 12 Peter Green; 13 Joe Hirst. Subs (all used): 14 Simon Brown; 15 Ryan Hepworth; 16 Michael Knowles; 17 Mitchell Stringer.
Tries: Taulapapa (26, 67), Morrison (38);
Goals: Brambani 0/1, Brown 2/2.
Rugby Leaguer & League Express Men of the Match:
Cougars: Andy Shickell; *Eagles:* Simon Brown.
Penalty count: 9-14; **Half-time:** 10-10;
Referee: Matthew Thomason; **Attendance:** 948.

SWINTON LIONS 24 FEATHERSTONE ROVERS 26

LIONS: 1 Richie Hawkyard; 2 Ian Mort; 3 Adam Higson; 4 Tom Armstrong; 5 Kevin Penny; 6 Martin Ainscough; 7 Ian Watson; 8 David Mills; 9 Mark Smith; 10 Danny Meekin; 11 Dale Cunniffe; 12 Darren Hawkyard; 13 Chaz I'Anson. Subs (all used): 14 Mike Morrison; 15 Glenn Riley; 16 Scott Hale; 17 Karl Ashall.
Tries: Cunniffe (29), Ainscough (29), Higson (31), Penny (70); **Goals:** Mort 4/4.
ROVERS: 1 Ian Hardman; 2 Gareth Raynor; 3 Sam Smeaton; 4 Greg Worthington; 5 Tom Saxton; 6 Kyle Briggs; 7 Liam Finn; 8 Michael Haley; 9 Ben Kaye; 10 James Lockwood; 11 Jon Grayshon; 12 Tim Spears; 13 Jon Hepworth. Subs (all used): 14 Andy Kain; 15 Dominic Maloney; 16 Anthony England; 17 Andrew Bostock.
Tries: Smeaton (12), Finn (25, 46), Raynor (55, 76);
Goals: Finn 3/5.

Rugby Leaguer & League Express Men of the Match:
Lions: Chaz I'Anson; *Rovers:* Liam Finn.
Penalty count: 5-4; **Half-time:** 18-10;
Referee: Clint Sharrad; **Attendance:** 866.

DEWSBURY RAMS 16 HUNSLET HAWKS 8

RAMS: 1 James Craven; 2 Greg Scott; 3 Ryan Esders; 4 Ayden Faal; 5 Austin Buchanan; 6 Pat Walker; 7 Scott Spaven; 8 Ben Jones; 9 George Flanagan; 10 Steve Crossley; 11 Rob Spicer; 12 Dwayne Barker; 13 Josh Tonks. Subs (all used): 14 Liam Hood; 15 Matt Nicholson; 16 Michael Wainwright; 17 Cain Southernwood.
Tries: Craven (31, 59), Buchanan (64); **Goals:** Walker 2/3.
HAWKS: 1 Elliot Hodgson; 2 Lee Brickwood; 3 Gareth Davies; 4 David Clayton; 5 Stuart Kain; 6 Joe McClocklan; 7 Ryan Smith; 8 Andrew Yates; 9 Luke Haigh; 10 Anthony Henderson; 11 Richard Blakeway; 12 John Oakes; 13 David March. Subs (all used): 14 Jack Bradbury; 15 Steve Lewis; 16 Neil Lowe; 17 David Tootill.
Try: Oakes (35); **Goals:** McLocklan 2/2.
Rugby Leaguer & League Express Men of the Match:
Rams: James Craven; *Hawks:* Joe McLocklan.
Penalty count: 3-6; **Half-time:** 6-8;
Referee: Gareth Hewer; **Attendance:** 850.

YORK CITY KNIGHTS 16 BATLEY BULLDOGS 30

CITY KNIGHTS: 1 Jordan Tansey; 2 Tom Bush; 3 James Ford; 4 Matt Garside; 5 George Elliott; 6 Chris Thorman; 7 Brett Turner; 8 Adam Sullivan; 9 Jack Lee; 10 Nathan Freer; 11 John Davies; 12 Ed Smith; 13 Paul King. Subs (all used): 14 Jack Aldous; 15 Rhys Clarke; 16 Joe Hemmings; 17 James Houston.
Tries: Houston (29), Davies (59), King (79);
Goals: Thorman 2/3.
Sin bin: Garside (48) - fighting.
BULLDOGS: 1 Johnny Campbell; 2 Gareth Potts; 3 Jason Walton; 4 Daley Williams; 5 Alex Brown; 6 Ben Black; 7 Gareth Moore; 8 Byron Smith; 9 Paul Mennell; 10 Alex Walmsley; 11 Alex Bretherton; 12 Jonny Walker; 13 Mark Applegarth. Subs (all used): 14 Lewis Palfrey; 15 Keegan Hirst; 16 Luke Menzies; 17 Kris Lythe.
Tries: Bretherton (8, 76), Daley Williams (21), Potts (39), Moore (68); **Goals:** Moore 5/5.
Sin bin: Moore (48) - fighting; Bretherton (58) - dissent.
Rugby Leaguer & League Express Men of the Match:
City Knights: John Davies; *Bulldogs:* Mark Applegarth.
Penalty count: 8-7; **Half-time:** 6-18;
Referee: Jamie Leahy; **Attendance:** 691.

ROUND 6

Sunday 6th May 2012

SWINTON LIONS 32 YORK CITY KNIGHTS 12

LIONS: 1 Richie Hawkyard; 2 Gavin Dodd; 3 Adam

Higson; 4 Tom Armstrong; 5 Kevin Penny; 6 Martin Ainscough; 7 Ian Watson; 8 David Mills; 9 Mark Smith; 10 Danny Meekin; 11 Dale Cunniffe; 12 Darren Hawkyard; 13 Chaz I'Anson. Subs (all used): 14 Mike Morrison; 15 Adam Walker; 16 Glenn Riley; 17 Karl Ashall.
Tries: Higson (8, 44), Penny (13), Armstrong (25, 30), Ainscough (80); **Goals:** Dodd 4/7.
CITY KNIGHTS: 1 Jordan Tansey; 2 Tom Bush; 3 James Ford; 4 Matt Garside; 5 George Elliott; 6 Chris Thorman; 7 Ben Johnston; 8 Adam Sullivan; 9 Jack Lee; 10 Jack Aldous; 11 John Davies; 12 James Houston; 13 Paul King. Subs (all used): 14 Brett Turner; 15 Rhys Clarke; 16 Dave Sutton; 17 Joe Hemmings.
Tries: Ford (16), Elliott (39, 62); **Goals:** Thorman 0/3.
Rugby Leaguer & League Express Men of the Match:
Lions: Adam Higson; *City Knights:* Ben Johnston.
Penalty count: 8-7; **Half-time:** 18-8;
Referee: George Stokes; **Attendance:** 410.

DEWSBURY RAMS 29 KEIGHLEY COUGARS 22

RAMS: 1 James Craven; 2 Michael Wainwright; 3 Ryan Esders; 4 Ayden Faal; 5 Austin Buchanan; 6 Pat Walker; 7 Scott Spaven; 8 Ben Jones; 9 Liam Hood; 10 Steve Crossley; 11 Rob Spicer; 12 Dwayne Barker; 13 Josh Tonks. Subs (all used): 14 Brad Singleton; 15 Matt Nicholson; 16 Andy Smith; 17 Luke Blake.
Tries: Wainwright (10), Spicer (26), Buchanan (33), Smith (62), Spaven (77); **Goals:** Walker 4/5;
Field goal: Walker (72).
COUGARS: 1 Craig Moss; 2 Richie Barnett; 3 James Haythornthwaite; 4 Semi Tadulala; 5 Gavin Duffy; 6 Danny Jones; 7 Sam Obst; 8 Richard Jones; 9 James Feather; 10 Neil Cherryholme; 11 Oliver Pursglove; 12 Lewis Reed; 13 Jy-Mel Coleman. Subs (all used): 14 James Davey; 15 Jason Demetriou; 16 Jode Sheriffe; 17 Michael Korkidas.
Tries: Pursglove, Haythornthwaite (38), Moss (44, 55); **Goals:** D Jones 3/4.
Rugby Leaguer & League Express Men of the Match:
Rams: Steve Crossley; *Cougars:* Jy-Mel Coleman.
Penalty count: 3-5; **Half-time:** 18-12;
Referee: Ronnie Laughton; **Attendance:** 992.

FEATHERSTONE ROVERS 12 HALIFAX 60

ROVERS: 1 Ian Hardman; 2 Gareth Raynor; 3 Sam Smeaton; 4 Jon Hepworth; 5 Andrew Bostock; 6 Kyle Briggs; 7 Liam Finn; 8 Michael Haley; 9 Ben Kaye; 10 Stuart Dickens; 11 James Lockwood; 12 Tim Spears; 13 Matty Dale. Subs (all used): 14 Andy Kain; 15 Dominic Maloney; 16 Jon Grayshon; 17 Anthony England.
Tries: Haley (1), Dale (23); **Goals:** Finn 2/2.
HALIFAX: 1 Ryan Fieldhouse; 2 Rob Worrincy; 3 Steve Tyrer; 4 Lee Paterson; 5 Wayne Reittie; 6 Paul Handforth; 7 Anthony Thackeray; 8 Adam Robinson; 9 Sean Penkywicz; 10 Luke Ambler; 11 Dane Manning; 12 Ross Divorty; 13 Craig Ashall. Subs (all used): 14 Callum Casey; 15 Jim Gannon; 16 Sam Barlow; 17 Iain Morrison.

Tries: Robinson (9, 70), Ashall (13), Divorty (19, 29, 33), Handforth (39), Thackeray (48), Worrincy (50), Reittie (79); **Goals:** Paterson 10/10.
Rugby Leaguer & League Express Men of the Match: *Rovers:* Andy Kain; *Halifax:* Ross Divorty.
Penalty count: 3-10; **Half-time:** 12-36; **Referee:** Tim Roby; **Attendance:** 2,806.

HUNSLET HAWKS 0 BATLEY BULLDOGS 48

HAWKS: 1 Elliot Hodgson; 2 Lee Brickwood; 3 Josh Nathaniel; 4 David Clayton; 5 Gareth Davies; 6 Joe McLocklan; 7 Ryan Smith; 8 Andrew Yates; 9 Luke Haigh; 10 Anthony Henderson; 11 Tom Haughey; 12 John Oakes; 13 David March. Subs (all used): 14 Steve Dooler; 15 Richard Blakeway; 16 Ryan Benjafield; 17 Neil Lowe.
BULLDOGS: 1 Ian Preece; 2 Gareth Potts; 3 Jason Walton; 4 Danny Maun; 5 Alex Brown; 6 Ben Black; 7 Gareth Moore; 8 Byron Smith; 9 Paul Mennell; 10 Craig Potter; 11 Alex Bretherton; 12 James Grehan; 13 Mark Applegarth. Subs (all used): 14 Alex Walmsley; 15 Lewis Palfrey; 16 Keegan Hirst; 17 Kris Lythe.
Tries: Maun (19), Preece (22), Potts (24, 58, 75, 78), Brown (30, 46), Grehan (52); **Goals:** Moore 6/9.
Rugby Leaguer & League Express Men of the Match: *Hawks:* Josh Nathaniel; *Bulldogs:* Gareth Potts.
Penalty count: 4-6; **Half-time:** 0-20; **Referee:** Dave Merrick; **Attendance:** 506.

SHEFFIELD EAGLES 32 LEIGH CENTURIONS 34

EAGLES: 1 Quentin Laulu-Togagae; 2 Vinny Finigan; 3 Menzie Yere; 4 Misi Taulapapa; 5 Nev Morrison; 6 Simon Brown; 7 Dominic Brambani; 8 Jack Howieson; 9 Andrew Henderson; 10 Mitchell Stringer; 11 Michael Knowles; 12 Peter Green; 13 Joe Hirst. Subs (all used): 14 Sam Scott; 15 Liam Higgins; 16 Duane Straugheir; 17 Ryan Hepworth.
Tries: Knowles (15, 24), Morrison (22), Finigan (42), Taulapapa (53), Laulu-Togagae (63); **Goals:** Brown 4/6.
CENTURIONS: 1 Gregg McNally; 2 Steve Maden; 3 Stuart Littler; 4 Matt Gardner; 5 Jonathan Pownall; 6 Martyn Ridyard; 7 Ryan Brierley; 8 Stephen Nash; 9 Bob Beswick; 10 Rob Parker; 11 James Laithwaite; 12 Tommy Goulden; 13 James Taylor. Subs (all used): 14 Anthony Nicholson; 15 Craig Briscoe; 16 Sam Hopkins; 17 Tom Spencer.
Tries: Taylor (5), Pownall (10), Brierley (29), Laithwaite (37), Hopkins (58); **Goals:** Ridyard 7/7.
Rugby Leaguer & League Express Men of the Match: *Eagles:* Michael Knowles; *Centurions:* Ryan Brierley.
Penalty count: 4-5; **Half-time:** 14-24; **Referee:** Jamie Leahy; **Attendance:** 1,237 *(at Don Valley Stadium).*

ROUND 7

Thursday 10th May 2012

YORK CITY KNIGHTS 18 SHEFFIELD EAGLES 25

CITY KNIGHTS: 1 Jordan Tansey; 2 Tom Bush; 3 James Ford; 4 Matt Garside; 5 George Elliott; 6 Chris Thorman; 7 Ben Johnston; 8 Adam Sullivan; 9 Jack Lee; 10 Jack Aldous; 11 John Davies; 12 James Houston; 13 Paul King. Subs (all used): 14 Brett Turner; 15 Dave Sutton; 16 Rhys Clarke; 17 Joe Hemmings.
Tries: Johnston (26), Ford (51), Elliott (54); **Goals:** Thorman 3/3.
Sin bin: Lee (79) - fighting.
EAGLES: 1 Quentin Laulu-Togagae; 2 Vinny Finigan; 3 Menzie Yere; 4 Misi Taulapapa; 5 Nev Morrison; 6 Simon Brown; 7 Dominic Brambani; 8 Jack Howieson; 9 Andrew Henderson; 10 Mitchell Stringer; 11 Michael Knowles; 12 Peter Green; 13 Joe Hirst. Subs (all used): 14 Sam Scott; 15 Liam Higgins; 16 Duane Straugheir; 17 Ryan Hepworth.
Tries: Laulu-Togagae (20, 34), Finigan (48), Brambani (67); **Goals:** Brown 4/4; **Field goal:** Brown (76).
Sin bin: Taulapapa (79) - fighting.
Rugby Leaguer & League Express Men of the Match: *City Knights:* John Davies; *Eagles:* Quentin Laulu-Togagae.
Penalty count: 5-4; **Half-time:** 6-12; **Referee:** Gareth Hewer; **Attendance:** 462.

Sunday 13th May 2012

BATLEY BULLDOGS 24 FEATHERSTONE ROVERS 31

BULLDOGS: 1 Ian Preece; 2 Gareth Potts; 3 Jason Walton; 4 Danny Maun; 5 Alex Brown; 6 Ben Black; 7 Gareth Moore; 8 Byron Smith; 9 Paul Mennell; 10 Craig Potter; 11 Mark Applegarth; 12 James Grehan; 13 Kris Lythe. Subs (all used): 14 Johnny Campbell; 15 Keegan Hirst; 16 James Green; 17 Ashley Lindsay.
Tries: Walton (8), Potts (43, 54), Hirst (50); **Goals:** Moore 3/3, Mennell 1/1.
ROVERS: 1 Ian Hardman; 2 Nathan Chappell; 3 Sam Smeaton; 4 Jon Hepworth; 5 Greg Worthington; 6 Andy Kain; 7 Liam Finn; 8 Anthony England; 9 Ben Kaye; 10 Stuart Dickens; 11 Matty Dale; 12 Tim Spears; 13 Kyle Briggs. Subs (all used): 14 James Lockwood; 15 Andrew Bostock; 16 Jon Grayshon; 17 Michael Haley.
Tries: Dale (4), Chappell (13, 40), Bostock (38), Worthington (69), England (77); **Goals:** Finn 3/6; **Field goal:** Kain (73).
Rugby Leaguer & League Express Men of the Match: *Bulldogs:* Keegan Hirst; *Rovers:* Andy Kain.
Penalty count: 13-10; **Half-time:** 6-20; **Referee:** Matthew Thomason; **Attendance:** 1,317.

Batley's Alex Brown makes a break against Halifax

HALIFAX 50 DEWSBURY RAMS 22

HALIFAX: 1 Ryan Fieldhouse; 2 Rob Worrincy; 3 Steve Tyrer; 4 Lee Paterson; 5 Paul White; 6 Paul Handforth; 7 Anthony Thackeray; 8 Sean Hesketh; 9 Sean Penkywicz; 10 Luke Ambler; 11 Ross Divorty; 12 Adam Robinson; 13 Craig Ashall. Subs (all used): 14 Callum Casey; 15 Jim Gannon; 16 Sam Barlow; 17 Makali Aizue.
Tries: Tyrer (5), Worrincy (8, 22), Penkywicz (33), S Barlow (39, 48), Ashall (59), Thackeray (61), Hesketh (64); **Goals:** Paterson 7/9.
RAMS: 1 James Craven; 2 Jermaine Akaidere; 3 Ryan Esders; 4 Ayden Faal; 5 Austin Buchanan; 6 Pat Walker; 7 Scott Spaven; 8 Ben Jones; 9 Liam Hood; 10 Steve Crossley; 11 Rob Spicer; 12 Dwayne Barker; 13 Josh Tonks. Subs (all used): 14 George Flanagan; 15 Matt Nicholson; 16 Brad Singleton; 17 Andy Smith.
Tries: Esders (17), Hood (55), Singleton (76), Faal (79); **Goals:** Walker 3/4.
Rugby Leaguer & League Express Men of the Match: *Halifax:* Sean Penkywicz; *Rams:* Ayden Faal.
Penalty count: 7-4; **Half-time:** 26-4; **Referee:** Jamie Leahy; **Attendance:** 2,377.

HUNSLET HAWKS 12 SWINTON LIONS 38

HAWKS: 1 Elliot Hodgson; 2 Stuart Kain; 3 Lee Brickwood; 4 Steve Lewis; 5 Dennis Tuffour; 6 Luke Helliwell; 7 Ryan Smith; 8 Andrew Yates; 9 Luke Haigh; 10 Ryan Benjafield; 11 Tom Haughey; 12 John Oakes; 13 David March. Subs (all used): 14 Joe McLocklan; 15 Luke Menzies; 16 Josh Nathaniel; 17 Neil Lowe.
Tries: Oakes (28), McLocklan (78); **Goals:** Helliwell 2/2.
LIONS: 1 Richie Hawkyard; 2 Gavin Dodd; 3 Adam Higson; 4 Tom Armstrong; 5 Kevin Penny; 6 Martin Ainscough; 7 Ian Watson; 8 David Mills; 9 Mark Smith; 10 Carl Forster; 11 Dale Cunniffe; 12 Darren Hawkyard; 13 Chaz I'Anson. Subs (all used): 14 Mike Morrison; 15 Adam Walker; 16 Karl Ashall; 17 Glenn Riley.
Tries: Ainscough (9, 57), Dodd (35, 72, 80), Penny (37), Cunniffe (64); **Goals:** Dodd 5/7.
Rugby Leaguer & League Express Men of the Match: *Hawks:* Elliot Hodgson; *Lions:* Ian Watson.
Penalty count: 9-5; **Half-time:** 6-16; **Referee:** Ronnie Laughton; **Attendance:** 426.

ROUND 8

Thursday 17th May 2012

KEIGHLEY COUGARS 36 SWINTON LIONS 4

COUGARS: 1 Craig Moss; 2 Richie Barnett; 3 James Haythornthwaite; 4 Danny Lawton; 5 Semi Tadulala; 6 Danny Jones; 7 Sam Obst; 8 Andy Shickell; 9 James Feather; 10 Neil Cherryholme; 11 Oliver Pursglove; 12 Richard Jones; 13 Paul March. Subs (all used): 14 Jy-Mel Coleman; 15 Jason Demetriou; 16 Brendan Rawlins; 17 Michael Korkidas.
Tries: Haythornthwaite (33, 65, 74), Tadulala (43), Feather (51), Coleman (70), Barnett (72); **Goals:** D Jones 4/7.
LIONS: 1 Richie Hawkyard; 2 Gavin Dodd; 3 Adam Higson; 4 Tom Armstrong; 5 Kevin Penny; 6 Martin Ainscough; 7 Ian Watson; 8 David Mills; 9 Mark Smith; 10 Adam Walker; 11 Dale Cunniffe; 12 Darren Hawkyard; 13 Chaz I'Anson. Subs (all used): 14 Neil Holland; 15 Mike Morrison; 16 Karl Ashall; 17 Glenn Riley.
Try: Dodd (21); **Goals:** Dodd 0/1.
Rugby Leaguer & League Express Men of the Match: *Cougars:* James Haythornthwaite; *Lions:* Ian Watson.
Penalty count: 8-4; **Half-time:** 4-4; **Referee:** Jamie Leahy; **Attendance:** 716.

Friday 18th May 2012

SHEFFIELD EAGLES 42 DEWSBURY RAMS 10

EAGLES: 1 Quentin Laulu-Togagae; 2 Vinny Finigan; 3 Menzie Yere; 4 Misi Taulapapa; 5 Nev Morrison; 6 Simon Brown; 7 Dominic Brambani; 8 Jack Howieson; 9 Andrew Henderson; 10 Mitchell Stringer; 11 Michael Knowles; 12 Joe Hirst; 13 Dane McDonald. Subs (all used): 14 Peter Green; 15 Duane Straugheir; 16 Alex Szostak; 17 Liam Higgins.
Tries: Yere (3, 14), Hirst (27), Morrison (33), Taulapapa (38), Brown (54), Henderson (62); **Goals:** Brown 7/7.
RAMS: 1 James Craven; 2 Andy Smith; 3 Ryan Esders; 4 Ayden Faal; 5 Austin Buchanan; 6 Pat Walker; 7 Cain Southernwood; 8 Brad Singleton; 9 Luke Blake; 10 Steve Crossley; 11 Rob Spicer; 12 Dwayne Barker; 13 Josh Tonks. Subs (all used): 14 Billy Harris; 15 Ed Barber; 16 Michael Wainwright; 17 Liam Hood.
Tries: Faal (59), Craven (79); **Goals:** Walker 1/2.
Rugby Leaguer & League Express Men of the Match: *Eagles:* Michael Knowles; *Rams:* Liam Hood.
Penalty count: 6-9; **Half-time:** 30-0; **Referee:** Clint Sharrad; **Attendance:** 1,154 *(at Bramall Lane).*

Saturday 19th May 2012

FEATHERSTONE ROVERS 34 YORK CITY KNIGHTS 14

ROVERS: 1 Ian Hardman; 2 Jack Briscoe; 3 Sam Smeaton; 4 Greg Worthington; 5 Nathan Chappell; 6 Andy Kain; 7 Liam Finn; 8 Anthony England; 9 Ben Kaye; 10 Stuart Dickens; 11 Matty Dale; 12 Tim Spears; 13 Jon Hepworth. Subs (all used): 14 Andy Ellis; 15 Andrew Bostock; 16 Michael Haley; 17 Dominic Maloney.
Tries: Bostock (44, 56), Kain (68), Chappell (73, 75, 78); **Goals:** Finn 5/6.
Sin bin: Worthington (36) - fighting.
CITY KNIGHTS: 1 Jordan Tansey; 2 Tom Bush; 3 James Ford; 4 Matt Garside; 5 George Elliott; 6 Chris Thorman; 7 Ben Johnston; 8 Adam Sullivan; 9 Jack Lee; 10 Jack Aldous; 11 Rhys Clarke; 12 John Davies; 13 Paul King. Subs (all used): 14 Brett Turner; 15 Dave Sutton; 16 Ed Smith; 17 Adam Howard.
Tries: Ford (24, 37), Tansey (39); **Goals:** Thorman 1/3.
Sin bin: Bush (36) - fighting.
Rugby Leaguer & League Express Men of the Match: *Rovers:* Dominic Maloney; *City Knights:* Chris Thorman.
Penalty count: 4-4; **Half-time:** 0-14; **Referee:** Ronnie Laughton; **Attendance:** 1,620.

Sunday 20th May 2012

BATLEY BULLDOGS 23 HALIFAX 16

BULLDOGS: 1 Ian Preece; 2 Gareth Potts; 3 Jason Walton; 4 Danny Maun; 5 Alex Brown; 6 Ben Black; 7 Gareth Moore; 8 Byron Smith; 9 Kris Lythe; 10 James Green; 11 Alex Bretherton; 12 James Grehan; 13 Mark Applegarth. Subs (all used): 14 Lewis Palfrey; 15 Keegan Hirst; 16 Alex Walmsley; 17 Ashley Lindsay.

256

Leigh's Rob Parker loses the ball as he makes a break against Dewsbury

Tries: Bretherton (24), A Walmsley (34), Black (78); **Goals:** Moore 5/5; **Field goal:** Moore (75). **Sin bin:** Maun (76) - fighting.
HALIFAX: 1 Ryan Fieldhouse; 2 Wayne Reittie; 3 Steve Tyrer; 4 Lee Paterson; 5 Rob Worrincy; 6 Paul Handforth; 7 Anthony Thackeray; 8 Jim Gannon; 9 Sean Penkywicz; 10 Luke Ambler; 11 Ross Divorty; 12 Adam Robinson; 13 Craig Ashall. Subs (all used): 14 Callum Casey; 15 Dane Manning; 16 Sam Barlow; 17 Makali Aizue.
Tries: Penkywicz (17), Paterson (45), Manning (56); **Goals:** Paterson 2/4.
Dismissal: Reittie (61) - headbutt on Moore.
Sin bin: S Barlow (76) - fighting.
Rugby Leaguer & League Express Men of the Match: *Bulldogs:* Ben Black; *Halifax:* Lee Paterson.
Penalty count: 8-8; **Half-time:** 12-6;
Referee: George Stokes; **Attendance:** 1,553.

LEIGH CENTURIONS 30 HUNSLET HAWKS 10

CENTURIONS: 1 Gregg McNally; 2 Steve Maden; 3 Stuart Littler; 4 Matt Gardner; 5 Jonathan Pownall; 6 Martyn Ridyard; 7 Bob Beswick; 8 Michael Ostick; 9 Anthony Nicholson; 10 Rob Parker; 11 James Laithwaite; 12 Tommy Goulden; 13 Craig Briscoe. Subs (all used): 14 Ryan Brierley; 15 Stephen Nash; 16 Sam Hopkins; 17 Tommy Gallagher.
Tries: Nicholson (20), Laithwaite (32), Gallagher (40), Brierley (42), Parker (55); **Goals:** Ridyard 5/5.
HAWKS: 1 Elliot Hodgson; 2 Stuart Kain; 3 David Clayton; 4 Josh Nathaniel; 5 Lee Brickwood; 6 Luke Helliwell; 7 Tom Henderson; 8 Andrew Yates; 9 Luke Haigh; 10 Ryan Benjafield; 11 Tom Haughey; 12 John Oakes; 13 David March. Subs (all used): 14 Joe McLocklan; 15 Luke Menzies; 16 Richard Blakeway; 17 Neil Lowe.
Tries: Hodgson (13), Brickwood (71); **Goals:** Helliwell 1/2.
Rugby Leaguer & League Express Men of the Match: *Centurions:* James Laithwaite; *Hawks:* Luke Haigh.
Penalty count: 6-6; **Half-time:** 18-6;
Referee: Dave Merrick; **Attendance:** 1,716.

ROUND 9

Thursday 24th May 2012

SHEFFIELD EAGLES 26 BATLEY BULLDOGS 16

EAGLES: 1 Quentin Laulu-Togagae; 2 Vinny Finigan; 3 Menzie Yere; 4 Duane Straugheir; 5 Nev Morrison; 6 Simon Brown; 7 Dominic Brambani; 8 Jack Howieson; 9 Andrew Henderson; 10 Mitchell Stringer; 11 Michael Knowles; 12 Dane McDonald; 13 Joe Hirst. Subs (all used): 14 Scott Turner; 15 Peter Green; 16 Alex Szostak; 17 Liam Higgins.

Tries: Yere (9, 64), Laulu-Togagae (33, 46), Straugheir (36); **Goals:** Brown 3/5.
BULLDOGS: 1 Ian Preece; 2 Gareth Potts; 3 Jason Walton; 4 Danny Maun; 5 Alex Brown; 6 Ben Black; 7 Gareth Moore; 8 Byron Smith; 9 Kris Lythe; 10 James Green; 11 Alex Bretherton; 12 James Grehan; 13 Mark Applegarth. Subs (all used): 14 Lewis Palfrey; 15 Keegan Hirst; 16 Alex Walmsley; 17 Ashley Lindsay.
Tries: Black (17), Bretherton (24), Potts (67); **Goals:** Moore 2/3.
Rugby Leaguer & League Express Men of the Match: *Eagles:* Quentin Laulu-Togagae; *Bulldogs:* James Green.
Penalty count: 10-5; **Half-time:** 16-10;
Referee: Ronnie Laughton; **Attendance:** 1,117
(at Bramall Lane).

Friday 25th May 2012

SWINTON LIONS 18 HALIFAX 24

LIONS: 1 Richie Hawkyard; 2 Gavin Dodd; 3 Adam Higson; 4 Tom Armstrong; 5 Kevin Penny; 6 Martin Ainscough; 7 Ian Watson; 8 Adam Walker; 9 Mark Smith; 10 Carl Forster; 11 Dale Cunniffe; 12 Darren Hawkyard; 13 Chaz I'Anson. Subs (all used): 14 Mike Morrison; 15 David Mills; 16 Glenn Riley; 17 Karl Ashall.
Tries: R Hawkyard (6), Dodd (16), Ainscough (50); **Goals:** Dodd 3/3.
HALIFAX: 1 Ryan Fieldhouse; 2 Rob Worrincy; 3 Lee Paterson; 4 James Haley; 5 Paul White; 6 Paul Handforth; 7 Anthony Thackeray; 8 Makali Aizue; 9 Sean Penkywicz; 10 Luke Ambler; 11 Dane Manning; 12 Adam Robinson; 13 Craig Ashall. Subs (all used): 14 Anthony Bowman; 15 Ross Divorty; 16 Sam Barlow; 17 Jim Gannon.
Tries: Ambler (22, 79), Thackeray (47), Bowman (58); **Goals:** Paterson 4/5.
Rugby Leaguer & League Express Men of the Match: *Lions:* Richie Hawkyard; *Halifax:* Luke Ambler.
Penalty count: 6-11; **Half-time:** 12-6;
Referee: Jamie Leahy; **Attendance:** 822.

Sunday 27th May 2012

DEWSBURY RAMS 18 LEIGH CENTURIONS 34

RAMS: 1 James Craven; 2 Andy Smith; 3 Ryan Esders; 4 Ayden Faal; 5 Austin Buchanan; 6 Pat Walker; 7 Scott Spaven; 8 Ben Jones; 9 Liam Hood; 10 Steve Crossley; 11 Rob Spicer; 12 Dwayne Barker; 13 Ed Barber. Subs (all used): 14 Brad Singleton; 15 Elliott Cosgrove; 16 Josh Tonks; 17 George Flanagan.
Tries: Walker (25), Craven (32), Flanagan (52); **Goals:** Walker 3/3.
CENTURIONS: 1 Gregg McNally; 2 Steve Maden; 3 Stuart Littler; 4 Matt Gardner; 5 Jonathan Pownall; 6 Martyn Ridyard; 7 John Duffy; 8 Michael Ostick; 9 Bob Beswick; 10 Rob Parker; 11 James Laithwaite; 12

Tommy Goulden; 13 Sam Hopkins. Subs (all used): 14 Anthony Nicholson; 15 Craig Briscoe; 16 Stephen Nash; 17 Tom Spencer.
Tries: Duffy (20), Goulden (44), Littler (48), Spencer (65), Briscoe (75), Hopkins (79); **Goals:** Ridyard 5/6.
Rugby Leaguer & League Express Men of the Match: *Rams:* James Craven; *Centurions:* Martyn Ridyard.
Penalty count: 7-6; **Half-time:** 12-6;
Referee: Gareth Hewer; **Attendance:** 922.

HUNSLET HAWKS 10 FEATHERSTONE ROVERS 54

HAWKS: 1 Elliot Hodgson; 2 Stuart Kain; 3 Lee Brickwood; 4 Josh Nathaniel; 5 Dennis Tuffour; 6 Joe McLocklan; 7 Tom Henderson; 8 Andrew Yates; 9 Luke Haigh; 10 Ryan Benjafield; 11 Tom Haughey; 12 John Oakes; 13 David March. Subs (all used): 14 Steve Lewis; 15 Luke Menzies; 16 Richard Blakeway; 17 Anthony Henderson.
Tries: Kain (15, 53); **Goals:** T Henderson 1/2.
ROVERS: 1 Ian Hardman; 2 Jack Briscoe; 3 Andrew Bostock; 4 Greg Worthington; 5 Tom Saxton; 6 Andy Kain; 7 Liam Finn; 8 Anthony England; 9 Ben Kaye; 10 Stuart Dickens; 11 Matty Dale; 12 Jon Grayshon; 13 Jon Hepworth. Subs (all used): 14 Nathan Chappell; 15 James Lockwood; 16 Dominic Maloney; 17 Andy Ellis.
Tries: Kaye (3), Dickens (6), Bostock (21), Finn (32), Chappell (40, 43), Hepworth (60, 67), Saxton (77); **Goals:** Finn 9/9.
Dismissal: England (80) - punching.
Rugby Leaguer & League Express Men of the Match: *Hawks:* John Oakes; *Rovers:* Liam Finn.
Penalty count: 9-4; **Half-time:** 4-30;
Referee: Matthew Kidd; **Attendance:** 724.

YORK CITY KNIGHTS 18 KEIGHLEY COUGARS 42

CITY KNIGHTS: 1 Jordan Tansey; 2 Tom Bush; 3 James Ford; 4 Matt Garside; 5 George Elliott; 6 Chris Thorman; 7 Brett Turner; 8 Adam Sullivan; 9 Jack Lee; 10 Jack Aldous; 11 Rhys Clarke; 12 Ed Smith; 13 Paul King. Subs (all used): 14 Kris Brining; 15 Dave Sutton; 16 Nathan Freer; 17 Adam Howard.
Tries: Lee (6), Bush (9, 24); **Goals:** Thorman 3/3.
COUGARS: 1 Craig Moss; 2 Richie Barnett; 3 James Haythornthwaite; 4 Danny Lawton; 5 Semi Tadulala; 6 Jy-Mel Coleman; 7 Sam Obst; 8 Andy Shickell; 9 James Feather; 10 Neil Cherryholme; 11 Oliver Pursglove; 12 Richard Jones; 13 Paul March. Subs (all used): 14 Jason Demetriou; 15 Danny Jones; 16 Michael Korkidas; 17 Brendan Rawlins.
Tries: Haythornthwaite (29), Tadulala (31, 43), Obst (40), Moss (60), Lawton (70), Coleman (80); **Goals:** Lawton 7/9.
Rugby Leaguer & League Express Men of the Match: *City Knights:* Chris Thorman; *Cougars:* Brendan Rawlins.
Penalty count: 4-10; **Half-time:** 18-18;
Referee: Dave Merrick; **Attendance:** 918.

ANGLO FRENCH CHALLENGE

Saturday 2nd June 2012

LEIGH CENTURIONS 44 AVIGNON 10

CENTURIONS: 1 Ryan Brierley; 2 Adam Clay; 3 Lee Gittins; 4 Kevin Henderson; 5 Dean McGilvray; 6 Josh Ward; 7 John Duffy; 8 Tom Spencer; 9 Sam Singleton; 10 Tommy Gallagher; 11 James Laithwaite; 12 Chris Rowe; 13 Craig Briscoe. Subs (all used): 14 Martyn Ridyard; 15 Greg Burke; 16 Anthony Nicholson; 17 Alex Robson.
Tries: Brierley (4, 36, 43), Gallagher (13), Ridyard (49, 51, 74), McGilvray (59);
Goals: Brierley 2/2, Ridyard 4/6.
AVIGNON: 1 Olivier Arnaud; 2 Kevin Liguoro; 3 Brett Kelly; 4 Yannick Ruh; 5 Jeremy Fuste; 6 Younes Khattabi; 7 Florian Bissiere; 8 Said Tamghart; 9 Gregory Marsal; 10 Joris Cagnac; 11 Teli Pelo; 12 Aaron Wood; 13 Joris Clement. Subs (all used): 14 Alexis Rodriguez; 15 Benjamin Genin; 16 Thomas Viloni; 17 Alexis Corona.
Tries: Rodriguez (65), Cagnac (68);
Goals: Arnaud 1/2.
Rugby Leaguer & League Express Men of the Match: *Centurions:* Ryan Brierley; *Avignon:* Joris Cagnac.
Penalty count: 4-9; **Half-time:** 18-0;
Referee: Jamie Leahy; **Attendance:** 773.

TOULOUSE OLYMPIQUE 26 HALIFAX 54

OLYMPIQUE: 1 Adam Innes; 2 Erwan Maze; 3 Bruno Ormeno; 4 Damien Couturier; 5 Antoine Reveillon; 6 Sebastien Planas; 7 Yoanne Didone; 8 David Delpoux; 9 Mourad Kriouache; 10 Jerome Gout; 11 Cyril Moliner; 12 Olivier Saintignan; 13 Sylvain Houles. Subs (all used): 14 Yohan Barthau; 15 Theo Gonzalez-Trique; 16 Joris Canton; 17 Tony Maurel.
Tries: Maze (35), Canton (67), Kriouache (70), Saintignan (77), Barthau (80); **Goals:** Couturier 3/5.
HALIFAX: 1 Ryan Fieldhouse; 2 Rob Worrincy; 3 James Haley; 4 Lee Paterson; 5 Paul White; 6 Anthony Bowman; 7 Anthony Thackeray; 8 Luke Ambler; 9 Paul Handforth; 10 Sean Hesketh; 11 Dane Manning; 12 Ross Divorty; 13 Sam Barlow. Subs (all used): 14 Sean Penkywicz; 15 Joe Chandler; 16 Josh Barlow; 17 Iain Davies.
Tries: Paterson (6), S Barlow (13), Chandler (29), Thackeray (35), White (41, 51), Handforth (44), Bowman (59), Divorty (73); **Goals:** Paterson 9/9.
Rugby Leaguer & League Express Men of the Match: *Olympique:* Mourad Kriouache; *Halifax:* Sam Barlow.
Penalty count: 7-8; **Half-time:** 6-24;
Referee: Mohammed Drizza; **Attendance:** 300.

CARCASSONNE 12 SHEFFIELD EAGLES 40

CARCASSONNE: 1 Jeremy Guiraud; 2 Alexis Escamilla; 3 Stuart Reardon; 4 Thomas Barrau; 5 Greg Mazard; 6 Russell Aitken; 7 Mathieu Alberola; 8 Romaric Bemba; 9 Jonathan Soum; 10 Osea Sadrau; 11 Tyrone Pau; 12 Anthony Rastouil; 13 Amar Sabri. Subs (all used): 14 Baptiste Delpech; 15 Quentin Nicol; 16 Sebastien Canet; 17 Maxime Peault.
Tries: Sadrau (22), Sabri (78); **Goals:** Alberola 2/2.
EAGLES: 1 Quentin Laulu-Togagae; 2 Vinny Finigan; 3 Menzie Yere; 4 Scott Turner; 5 Nev Morrison; 6 Simon Brown; 7 Dominic Brambani; 8 Ryan Hepworth; 9 Pat Smith; 10 Mitchell Stringer; 11 Alex Szostak; 12 Sam Scott; 13 Misi Taulapapa. Subs (all used): 14 Nathan Walmsley; 15 Leigh Sanders; 16 Jack Latus; 17 Alex Rowe.
Tries: Szostak (8), Turner (13), Laulu-Togagae (24, 70), Yere (27, 41), Brambani (60); **Goals:** Brown 4/5, Brambani 2/2.
Sin bin: Sanders (72) - interference.
Rugby Leaguer & League Express Men of the Match: *Carcassonne:* Osea Sadrau; *Eagles:* Menzie Yere.
Penalty count: 11-10; **Half-time:** 6-22;
Referee: Stephan Vincent; **Attendance:** 3,250.

Sunday 3rd June 2012

FEATHERSTONE ROVERS 48 PIA 22

ROVERS: 1 Ian Hardman; 2 Jack Briscoe; 3 Jon Grayshon; 4 Greg Worthington; 5 Tom Saxton; 6 Andy Kain; 7 Liam Finn; 8 Anthony England; 9 Ben Kaye; 10 James Lockwood; 11 Matty Dale; 12 Tim Spears; 13 Jon Hepworth. Subs (all used): 14 Jack Bussey; 15 Mufaro Mvududu; 16 Dominic Maloney; 17 Michael Haley.
Tries: Kain (7, 11), Spears (19), Grayshon (22), Briscoe (26, 80), Worthington (30), Hepworth (34);
Goals: Finn 8/8.
PIA: 1 Clement Soubeyras; 2 Wendy Buche; 3 Mathieu Mayans; 4 Steve Naughton; 5 Thomas Ambert; 6 Maxime Greseque; 7 Anthony Carrere; 8 Arty Shead; 9 Christophe Moly; 10 Ben Vaeau; 11 Mark Cantoni; 12 Dustin Cooper; 13 Boderick Wright. Subs (all used): 14 Unaloto Lamelangi; 15 Anthony Leger; 16 John Boudebza; 17 Vincent Comtat.
Tries: Mayans (38), Greseque (48), Buche (55, 68);
Goals: Greseque 3/4.
Rugby Leaguer & League Express Men of the Match: *Rovers:* Liam Finn; *Pia:* Maxime Greseque.
Penalty count: 5-2; **Half-time:** 42-6;
Referee: Gareth Hewer; **Attendance:** 1,150.

ROUND 10

Thursday 7th June 2012

LEIGH CENTURIONS 40 SHEFFIELD EAGLES 12

CENTURIONS: 1 Gregg McNally; 2 Steve Maden; 3 Stuart Littler; 4 Matt Gardner; 5 Jonathan Pownall; 6 Martyn Ridyard; 7 Craig Briscoe; 8 Michael Ostick; 9 Bob Beswick; 10 Rob Parker; 11 James Laithwaite; 12 Tommy Goulden; 13 Sam Hopkins. Subs (all used): 14 Ryan Brierley; 15 Kevin Henderson; 16 Tom Spencer; 17 Tommy Gallagher.
Tries: McNally (2), Littler (8), Pownall (52), Brierley (58, 76), Ridyard (61, 68); **Goals:** Ridyard 6/7.
EAGLES: 1 Quentin Laulu-Togagae; 2 Vinny Finigan; 3 Menzie Yere; 4 Misi Taulapapa; 5 Nev Morrison; 6 Simon Brown; 7 Dominic Brambani; 8 Jack Howieson; 9 Andrew Henderson; 10 Mitchell Stringer; 11 Michael Knowles; 12 Joe Hirst; 13 Dane McDonald. Subs (all used): 14 Scott Turner; 15 Alex Szostak; 16 Peter Green; 17 Liam Higgins.
Tries: Knowles (18), Laulu-Togagae (26);
Goals: Brown 2/2.
Rugby Leaguer & League Express Men of the Match: *Centurions:* Martyn Ridyard; *Eagles:* Andrew Henderson.
Penalty count: 7-6; **Half-time:** 12-12;
Referee: George Stokes; **Attendance:** 1,645.

Sunday 10th June 2012

BATLEY BULLDOGS 56 HUNSLET HAWKS 10

BULLDOGS: 1 Johnny Campbell; 2 Gareth Potts; 3 Jason Walton; 4 Danny Maun; 5 Alex Brown; 6 Ben Black; 7 Gareth Moore; 8 Byron Smith; 9 Paul Mennell; 10 Craig Potter; 11 Alex Bretherton; 12 Jonny Walker; 13 Mark Applegarth. Subs (all used): 14 Matthew Wildie; 15 Keegan Hirst; 16 Kris Lythe; 17 Ian Preece.
Tries: Black (4, 11, 58), Moore (27, 77), Walton (40, 60, 62), Brown (50), Bretherton (80); **Goals:** Moore 8/10.
HAWKS: 1 Elliot Hodgson; 2 Stuart Kain; 3 Lee Brickwood; 4 Steve Lewis; 5 Dennis Tuffour; 6 Joe McLocklan; 7 Aaron Dobek; 8 Luke Menzies; 9 Luke Haigh; 10 Ryan Benjafield; 11 Tom Haughey; 12 John Oakes; 13 David March. Subs (all used): 14 Luke Helliwell; 15 Richard Blakeway; 16 Anthony Henderson; 17 Andrew Yates.
Tries: Yates (68), Haughey (71); **Goals:** Helliwell 1/2.
Rugby Leaguer & League Express Men of the Match: *Bulldogs:* Ben Black; *Hawks:* Ryan Benjafield.
Penalty count: 8-7; **Half-time:** 22-0;
Referee: Jamie Leahy; **Attendance:** 705.

KEIGHLEY COUGARS 16 HALIFAX 30

COUGARS: 1 Craig Moss; 2 Richie Barnett; 3 James Haythornthwaite; 4 Danny Lawton; 5 Jesse Sheriffe; 6 Danny Jones; 7 Sam Obst; 8 Jode Sheriffe; 9 James Feather; 10 Michael Korkidas; 11 Oliver Pursglove; 12 Jamie Shepherd; 13 Paul March. Subs (all used): 14 Jy-Mel Coleman; 15 Jason Demetriou; 16 Brendan Rawlins; 17 Andy Shickell.
Tries: Haythornthwaite (28), Demetriou (63), Barnett (75, 79); **Goals:** D Jones 0/4.
HALIFAX: 1 Ryan Fieldhouse; 2 Rob Worrincy; 3 Lee Paterson; 4 James Haley; 5 Paul White; 6 Paul Handforth; 7 Anthony Thackeray; 8 Luke Ambler; 9 Sean Penkywicz; 10 Sean Hesketh; 11 Dane Manning; 12 Ross Divorty; 13 Sam Barlow. Subs (all used): 14 Craig Ashall; 15 Jim Gannon; 16 Adam Robinson; 17 Makali Aizue.
Tries: S Barlow (9), Penkywicz (44), Fieldhouse (55, 58), Paterson (65); **Goals:** Paterson 5/5.
Rugby Leaguer & League Express Men of the Match: *Cougars:* Jy-Mel Coleman; *Halifax:* Craig Ashall.
Penalty count: 3-7; **Half-time:** 4-6;
Referee: Clint Sharrad; **Attendance:** 1,723.

FEATHERSTONE ROVERS 60 DEWSBURY RAMS 18

ROVERS: 1 Ian Hardman; 2 Jack Briscoe; 3 Sam Smeaton; 4 Greg Worthington; 5 Tom Saxton; 6 Andy Kain; 7 Liam Finn; 8 James Lockwood; 9 Ben Kaye; 10 Stuart Dickens; 11 Matty Dale; 12 Tim Spears; 13 Jon Hepworth. Subs (all used): 14 Andy Ellis; 15 Dominic Maloney; 16 Michael Haley; 17 Andrew Bostock.
Tries: Kain (3, 47, 50, 69), Smeaton (6, 44), Worthington (26), Finn (30, 63), Saxton (65);
Goals: Finn 10/10.
RAMS: 1 James Craven; 2 Andy Smith; 3 Ryan Esders; 4 Greg Scott; 5 Austin Buchanan; 6 Pat Walker; 7 Scott Spaven; 8 Ben Jones; 9 Luke Blake; 10 Brad Singleton; 11 Rob Spicer; 12 Dwayne Barker; 13 Ed Barber. Subs (all used): 14 Josh Tonks; 15 Matt Nicholson; 16 Steve Crossley; 17 Liam Hood.
Tries: Spaven (19), Craven (55), Barber (74);
Goals: Walker 3/3.
Rugby Leaguer & League Express Men of the Match: *Rovers:* Andy Kain; *Rams:* Austin Buchanan.
Penalty count: 1-3; **Half-time:** 24-6;
Referee: Ronnie Laughton; **Attendance:** 2,241.

YORK CITY KNIGHTS 26 SWINTON LIONS 22

CITY KNIGHTS: 1 Jordan Tansey; 2 Waine Pryce; 3 James Ford; 4 Matt Garside; 5 George Elliott; 6 Chris Thorman; 7 Danny Nicklas; 8 Adam Sullivan; 9 Jack Lee; 10 Jack Aldous; 11 Rhys Clarke; 12 John Davies; 13 Paul King. Subs (all used): 14 Brett Turner; 15 Tom Bush; 16 Nathan Freer; 17 Chris Green.
Tries: Elliott (2), Garside (14, 74), Davies (18), Ford (63); **Goals:** Thorman 3/5.
LIONS: 1 Richie Hawkyard; 2 Gavin Dodd; 3 Adam Higson; 4 Tom Armstrong; 5 Kevin Penny; 6 Martin Ainscough; 7 Ian Watson; 8 Adam Walker; 9 Mark Smith; 10 Carl Forster; 11 Dale Cunniffe; 12 Chris Clarke; 13 Chaz I'Anson. Subs (all used): 14 Mike Morrison; 15 Glenn Riley; 16 Neil Holland; 17 Karl Ashall.
Tries: Penny (8), R Hawkyard (11), Armstrong (33), Higson (42), Dodd (58); **Goals:** Dodd 1/5.
Rugby Leaguer & League Express Men of the Match: *City Knights:* Matt Garside; *Lions:* Mark Smith.
Penalty count: 5-5; **Half-time:** 16-14;
Referee: Gareth Hewer; **Attendance:** 631.

ROUND 11

Thursday 21st June 2012

DEWSBURY RAMS 24 HALIFAX 34

RAMS: 1 James Craven; 2 Daley Williams; 3 Ryan Esders; 4 Ayden Faal; 5 Austin Buchanan; 6 Pat Walker; 7 Scott Spaven; 8 Ben Jones; 9 Liam Hood; 10 Steve Crossley; 11 Rob Spicer; 12 Josh Tonks; 13 Brad Singleton. Subs (all used): 14 Greg Scott; 15 Elliott Cosgrove; 16 Billy Harris; 17 George Flanagan.
Tries: Crossley (19), Craven (26), Cosgrove (60), Buchanan (62); **Goals:** Walker 4/5.
HALIFAX: 1 Ryan Fieldhouse; 2 Rob Worrincy; 3 Lee Paterson; 4 James Haley; 5 Paul White; 6 Paul Handforth; 7 Anthony Thackeray; 8 Sam Barlow; 9 Sean Penkywicz; 10 Luke Ambler; 11 Ross Divorty; 12 Adam Robinson; 13 Craig Ashall. Subs (all used): 14 Anthony Bowman; 15 Dane Manning; 16 Sean Hesketh; 17 Jim Gannon.
Tries: S Barlow (9), Hesketh (28), Gannon (47), Robinson (69), Bowman (74), Penkywicz (79);
Goals: Paterson 5/6.
Rugby Leaguer & League Express Men of the Match: *Rams:* Steve Crossley; *Halifax:* Sean Penkywicz.
Penalty count: 5-3; **Half-time:** 14-12;
Referee: Clint Sharrad; **Attendance:** 1,092.

Friday 22nd June 2012

LEIGH CENTURIONS 16 FEATHERSTONE ROVERS 22

CENTURIONS: 1 Gregg McNally; 2 Steve Maden; 3 Stuart Littler; 4 Matt Gardner; 5 Jonathan Pownall; 6 Martyn Ridyard; 7 Craig Briscoe; 8 Michael Ostick; 9 Bob Beswick; 10 Rob Parker; 11 James Laithwaite; 12 Tommy Goulden; 13 Sam Hopkins. Subs (all used): 14 Ryan Brierley; 15 Kevin Henderson; 16 Tom Spencer; 17 Stephen Nash.
Tries: Goulden (13), Brierley (70), Maden (77);
Goals: Ridyard 2/3.
ROVERS: 1 Ian Hardman; 2 Nathan Chappell; 3 Sam Smeaton; 4 Greg Worthington; 5 Tom Saxton; 6 Andy Kain; 7 Liam Finn; 8 Anthony England; 9 Ben Kaye; 10 Stuart Dickens; 11 James Lockwood; 12 Tim Spears; 13 Matty Dale. Subs (all used): 14 Andy Ellis; 15 Dominic Maloney; 16 Jon Grayshon; 17 Andrew Bostock.
Tries: Kain (20), Chappell (40, 74), Ellis (52);
Goals: Finn 3/4.
Rugby Leaguer & League Express Men of the Match: *Centurions:* Tommy Goulden; *Rovers:* Matty Dale.
Penalty count: 13-5; **Half-time:** 6-10;
Referee: Gareth Hewer; **Attendance:** 1,837.

SHEFFIELD EAGLES 44 YORK CITY KNIGHTS 10

EAGLES: 1 Quentin Laulu-Togagae; 2 Scott Turner; 3 Menzie Yere; 4 Misi Taulapapa; 5 Nev Morrison; 6 Pat Smith; 7 Dominic Brambani; 8 Jack Howieson; 9 Andrew Henderson; 10 Mitchell Stringer; 11 Michael Knowles; 12 Peter Green; 13 Joe Hirst. Subs (all used): 14 James Davey; 15 Sam Scott; 16 Alex Szostak; 17 Liam Higgins.
Tries: Brambani (2), Yere (16, 41, 79), Knowles (53, 55), Laulu-Togagae (59, 66); **Goals:** Brambani 6/8.
Dismissal: Stringer (64) - head-butt.
CITY KNIGHTS: 1 Jordan Tansey; 2 Waine Pryce; 3 James Ford; 4 Matt Garside; 5 George Elliott; 6 Chris Thorman; 7 Danny Nicklas; 8 Adam Sullivan; 9 Jack Lee; 10 Jack Aldous; 11 Rhys Clarke; 12 John Davies; 13 Paul King. Subs (all used): 14 Brett Turner; 15 Tom Bush; 16 Nathan Freer; 17 Chris Green.
Tries: Ford (12), Turner (39); **Goals:** Thorman 1/2.
Rugby Leaguer & League Express Men of the Match: *Eagles:* Jack Howieson; *City Knights:* John Davies.
Penalty count: 7-7; **Half-time:** 12-10; **Referee:** Jamie Leahy; **Attendance:** 784 *(at Don Valley Stadium).*

Sunday 24th June 2012

SWINTON LIONS 36 HUNSLET HAWKS 22

LIONS: 1 Ian Mort; 2 Gavin Dodd; 3 Adam Higson; 4 Tom Armstrong; 5 Kevin Penny; 6 Martin Ainscough; 7 Ian Watson; 8 Adam Walker; 9 Mark Smith; 10 Mike Morrison; 11 Dale Cunniffe; 12 Chris Clarke; 13 Carl Forster. Subs (all used): 14 David Mills; 15 Glenn Riley; 16 Richie Hawkyard; 17 Chaz I'Anson.
Tries: Walker (4, 22), Dodd (45, 70), Ainscough (64), I'Anson (75); **Goals:** Mort 6/6.
HAWKS: 1 Elliot Hodgson; 2 Stuart Kain; 3 Lee Brickwood; 4 Liam Welham; 5 Dennis Tuffour; 6 Luke Helliwell; 7 Aaron Dobek; 8 Andrew Yates; 9 Luke Haigh; 10 Ryan Benjafield; 11 Steve Lewis; 12 John Oakes; 13 David March. Subs (all used): 14 Joe McLocklan; 15 Josh Nathaniel; 16 David Tootill; 17 Anthony Henderson.
Tries: Yates (8), Kain (14), Welham (35), Nathaniel (51);
Goals: Dobek 3/6.
Rugby Leaguer & League Express Men of the Match: *Lions:* Ian Mort; *Hawks:* Luke Helliwell.
Penalty count: 3-5; **Half-time:** 12-16;
Referee: Chris Leatherbarrow; **Attendance:** 567.

Featherstone's Tim Spears and Sam Smeaton bring down Halifax's Dane Manning

KEIGHLEY COUGARS 30 BATLEY BULLDOGS 34

COUGARS: 1 Craig Moss; 2 Gavin Duffy; 3 Richie Barnett; 4 Danny Lawton; 5 Jesse Sheriffe; 6 Jy-Mel Coleman; 7 Paul March; 8 Michael Korkidas; 9 Sam Obst; 10 Neil Cherryholme; 11 Oliver Pursglove; 12 Brendan Rawlins; 13 Jamie Shepherd. Subs (all used): 14 Ryan Smith; 15 Jason Demetriou; 16 Andy Shickell; 17 Jode Sheriffe. **Tries:** Jesse Sheriffe (32), Obst (37, 77), Coleman (45), Barnett (80); **Goals:** Lawton 5/5.
BULLDOGS: 1 Johnny Campbell; 2 Gareth Potts; 3 Jason Walton; 4 Danny Maun; 5 Alex Brown; 6 Ben Black; 7 Gareth Moore; 8 Byron Smith; 9 Paul Mennell; 10 Mark Applegarth; 11 Alex Bretherton; 12 Jonny Walker; 13 Ashley Lindsay. Subs (all used): 14 Matthew Wildie; 15 Keegan Hirst; 16 Lewis Palfrey; 17 James Green. **Tries:** Maun (2), Brown (12), Bretherton (18), Potts (22), Campbell (27), Applegarth (56); **Goals:** Moore 5/6.
Sin bin: Hirst (39) - interference.
Rugby Leaguer & League Express Men of the Match: *Cougars:* Sam Obst; *Bulldogs:* Johnny Campbell.
Penalty count: 8-5; **Half-time:** 12-30;
Referee: Ronnie Laughton; **Attendance:** 878.

ROUND 12

Thursday 28th June 2012

HALIFAX 4 FEATHERSTONE ROVERS 24

HALIFAX: 1 Ryan Fieldhouse; 2 Rob Worrincy; 3 Steve Tyrer; 4 Lee Paterson; 5 Wayne Reittie; 6 Paul Handforth; 7 Anthony Thackeray; 8 Sean Hesketh; 9 Sean Penkywicz; 10 Luke Ambler; 11 Dane Manning; 12 Adam Robinson; 13 Sam Barlow. Subs (all used): 14 Anthony Bowman; 15 Makali Aizue; 16 Craig Ashall; 17 Jim Gannon.
Try: Reittie (37); **Goals:** Paterson 0/1.
ROVERS: 1 Ian Hardman; 2 Jack Briscoe; 3 Sam Smeaton; 4 Greg Worthington; 5 Tom Saxton; 6 Andy Kain; 7 Liam Finn; 8 James Lockwood; 9 Ben Kaye; 10 Stuart Dickens; 11 Jon Grayshon; 12 Tim Spears; 13 Matty Dale. Subs (all used): 14 Andy Ellis; 15 Andrew Bostock; 16 Michael Haley; 17 Dominic Maloney. **Tries:** Finn (3), Dale (26), Ellis (49), Worthington (73); **Goals:** Finn 4/4.
Rugby Leaguer & League Express Men of the Match: *Halifax:* Adam Robinson; *Rovers:* Andy Ellis.
Penalty count: 15-10; **Half-time:** 4-12;
Referee: Matthew Thomason; **Attendance:** 2,792.

Friday 29th June 2012

YORK CITY KNIGHTS 24 DEWSBURY RAMS 32

CITY KNIGHTS: 1 Tom Bush; 2 Waine Pryce; 3 James Ford; 4 Matt Garside; 5 George Elliott; 6 Chris Thorman; 7 Brett Turner; 8 Adam Sullivan; 9 Jack Lee; 10 Jack Aldous; 11 John Davies; 12 Chris Green; 13 Paul King. Subs: 14 Kris Brining (not used); 15 Rhys Clarke; 16 Nathan Freer; 17 Dario Esposito.
Tries: Bush (43), Davies (45, 77), Thorman (49); **Goals:** Thorman 4/4.
RAMS: 1 James Craven; 2 Daley Williams; 3 Ryan Esders; 4 Ayden Faal; 5 Austin Buchanan; 6 Pat Walker; 7 Scott Spaven; 8 Ben Jones; 9 Liam Hood; 10 Steve Crossley; 11 Rob Spicer; 12 Josh Tonks; 13 Brad Singleton. Subs: 14 Greg Scott (not used); 15 Elliott Cosgrove; 16 Billy Harris; 17 George Flanagan. **Tries:** Esders (19, 80), Craven (22, 60), Spaven (55), Faal (77); **Goals:** Walker 4/6.
Rugby Leaguer & League Express Men of the Match: *City Knights:* John Davies; *Rams:* James Craven.
Penalty count: 10-6; **Half-time:** 0-10;
Referee: Chris Leatherbarrow; **Attendance:** 906.

Sunday 1st July 2012

BATLEY BULLDOGS 42 LEIGH CENTURIONS 20

BULLDOGS: 1 Johnny Campbell; 2 Gareth Potts; 3 Jason Walton; 4 Danny Maun; 5 Alex Brown; 6 Ben Black; 7 Gareth Moore; 8 Byron Smith; 9 Paul Mennell; 10 James Green; 11 Mark Applegarth; 12 Alex Bretherton; 13 Ashley Lindsay. Subs (all used): 14 Matthew Wildie; 15 Keegan Hirst; 16 Alex Walmsley; 17 Adam Scott.
Tries: Mennell (24), Scott (28), Potts (37, 39), Moore (60), Applegarth (76), Campbell (78); **Goals:** Moore 7/8.
CENTURIONS: 1 Gregg McNally; 2 Adam Clay; 3 Stuart Littler; 4 Matt Gardner; 5 Dean McGilvray; 6 Martyn Ridyard; 7 Ryan Brierley; 8 Michael Ostick; 9 Bob Beswick; 10 Rob Parker; 11 Andy Thornley; 12 Kevin Henderson; 13 Craig Briscoe. Subs (all used): 14 Alex Robson; 15 Sam Hopkins; 16 Anthony Nicholson; 17 Tommy Gallagher.
Tries: Clay (10), Brierley (16), Thornley (53), McGilvray (55); **Goals:** Ridyard 2/4.
Sin bin: Littler (79) - interference.
Rugby Leaguer & League Express Men of the Match: *Bulldogs:* Gareth Moore; *Centurions:* Anthony Nicholson.
Penalty count: 12-10; **Half-time:** 24-8;
Referee: George Stokes; **Attendance:** 1,003.

SWINTON LIONS 24 SHEFFIELD EAGLES 32

LIONS: 1 Ian Mort; 2 Gavin Dodd; 3 Martin Ainscough; 4 Tom Armstrong; 5 Kevin Penny; 6 Chaz I'Anson; 7 Ian Watson; 8 Glenn Riley; 9 Mark Smith; 10 Mike Morrison; 11 Dale Cunniffe; 12 Chris Clarke; 13 Adam Walker. Subs: 14 David Mills; 15 Danny Meekin; 16 Richie Hawkyard; 17 Sam Reay (not used).
Tries: I'Anson (8), Ainscough (39), Penny (59), Armstrong (71); **Goals:** Mort 4/4.
EAGLES: 1 Quentin Laulu-Togagae; 2 Scott Turner; 3 Menzie Yere; 4 Misi Taulapapa; 5 Nev Morrison; 6 Pat Smith; 7 Dominic Brambani; 8 Jack Howieson; 9 Andrew Henderson; 10 Mitchell Stringer; 11 Michael Knowles; 12 Sam Scott; 13 Joe Hirst. Subs (all used): 14 Simon Brown; 15 Peter Green; 16 Duane Straugheir; 17 Liam Higgins.
Tries: Knowles (20, 32), Hirst (23), Yere (45), Straugheir (63), Taulapapa (74); **Goals:** Brambani 3/4, Brown 1/2.
Rugby Leaguer & League Express Men of the Match: *Lions:* Kevin Penny; *Eagles:* Dominic Brambani.
Penalty count: 3-4; **Half-time:** 12-18;
Referee: Gareth Hewer; **Attendance:** 506.

HUNSLET HAWKS 12 KEIGHLEY COUGARS 22

HAWKS: 1 Stuart Kain; 2 Lee Mapals; 3 Josh Nathaniel; 4 Liam Welham; 5 Lee Brickwood; 6 Tom Henderson; 7 Ben Karalius; 8 Andrew Yates; 9 Luke Haigh; 10 Ryan Benjafield; 11 Steve Dooler; 12 John Oakes; 13 David March. Subs (all used): 14 Joe McLocklan; 15 David Clayton; 16 David Tootill; 17 Anthony Henderson.
Tries: A Henderson (51), Kain (70).
Goals: T Henderson 2/2.
COUGARS: 1 Craig Moss; 2 Richie Barnett; 3 James Haythornthwaite; 4 Danny Lawton; 5 Gavin Duffy; 6 Jason Demetriou; 7 Sam Obst; 8 Andy Shickell; 9 James Feather; 10 Neil Cherryholme; 11 Oliver Pursglove; 12 Brendan Rawlins; 13 Jamie Shepherd. Subs (all used): 14 Jamaine Wray; 15 Chris Clough; 16 Jode Sheriffe; 17 Michael Korkidas.
Tries: Lawton (18), Obst (60), Duffy (65), Moss (73); **Goals:** Lawton 3/4.
Rugby Leaguer & League Express Men of the Match: *Hawks:* Stuart Kain; *Cougars:* Craig Moss.
Penalty count: 11-7; **Half-time:** 0-6;
Referee: Jamie Leahy; **Attendance:** 505.

ROUND 13

Thursday 12th July 2012

BATLEY BULLDOGS 24 SHEFFIELD EAGLES 32

BULLDOGS: 1 Gareth Potts; 2 Johnny Campbell; 3 Jonny Walker; 4 Danny Maun; 5 Alex Brown; 6 Ben Black; 7 Gareth Moore; 8 Byron Smith; 9 Paul Mennell; 10 Mark Applegarth; 11 Alex Bretherton; 12 Adam Scott; 13 Ashley Lindsay. Subs (all used): 14 Matthew Wildie; 15 Keegan Hirst; 16 Kris Lythe; 17 James Green.
Tries: Applegarth (14), Potts (24), Brown (31), Lythe (35); **Goals:** Moore 4/4.
EAGLES: 1 Quentin Laulu-Togagae; 2 Nev Morrison; 3 Misi Taulapapa; 4 Scott Turner; 5 Vinny Finigan; 6 Simon Brown; 7 Dominic Brambani; 8 Jack Howieson; 9 Andrew Henderson; 10 Mitchell Stringer; 11 Michael Knowles; 12 Sam Scott; 13 Joe Hirst. Subs (all used): 14 James Davey; 15 Ryan Hepworth; 16 Alex Szostak; 17 Liam Higgins.
Tries: Finigan (22, 57), Morrison (64), Laulu-Togagae (68), Turner (72), Stringer (79); **Goals:** Brown 4/6.
Rugby Leaguer & League Express Men of the Match: *Bulldogs:* Keegan Hirst; *Eagles:* Quentin Laulu-Togagae.
Penalty count: 4-6; **Half-time:** 24-6;
Referee: George Stokes; **Attendance:** 874.

Swinton's Kevin Penny looks for a way past Dewsbury's Pat Walker and Joe Chandler

Friday 13th July 2012

LEIGH CENTURIONS 50 DEWSBURY RAMS 6

CENTURIONS: 1 Gregg McNally; 2 Steve Maden; 3 James Mendeika; 4 Matt Gardner; 5 Dean McGilvray; 6 Martyn Ridyard; 7 John Duffy; 8 Andy Thornley; 9 Anthony Nicholson; 10 Rob Parker; 11 Stuart Littler; 12 Tommy Goulden; 13 Sam Hopkins. Subs (all used): 14 Ryan Brierley; 15 Kevin Henderson; 16 Craig Briscoe; 17 Tommy Gallagher.
Tries: Hopkins (7, 76), Maden (11), Briscoe (36), Gardner (42, 57), McNally (51), Goulden (67), Mendeika (80); **Goals:** Ridyard 7/9.
RAMS: 1 James Craven; 2 Greg Scott; 3 Ryan Esders; 4 Daley Williams; 5 Austin Buchanan; 6 Pat Walker; 7 Scott Spaven; 8 Ben Jones; 9 Liam Hood; 10 Steve Crossley; 11 Josh Tonks; 12 Rob Spicer; 13 Brad Singleton. Subs (all used): 14 Luke Blake; 15 Elliott Cosgrove; 16 Joe Chandler; 17 George Flanagan.
Try: Craven (5); **Goals:** Walker 1/1.
Sin bin: Flanagan (63) - interference.
Rugby Leaguer & League Express Men of the Match:
Centurions: Sam Hopkins; *Rams:* Steve Crossley.
Penalty count: 10-6; **Half-time:** 16-6;
Referee: Matthew Thomason; **Attendance:** 1,536.

Sunday 15th July 2012

KEIGHLEY COUGARS 46 YORK CITY KNIGHTS 24

COUGARS: 1 Craig Moss; 2 Gavin Duffy; 3 Richie Barnett; 4 Danny Lawton; 5 Semi Tadulala; 6 Danny Jones; 7 Sam Obst; 8 Brendan Rawlins; 9 James Feather; 10 Neil Cherryholme; 11 Oliver Pursglove; 12 Jamie Shepherd; 13 Jy-Mel Coleman. Subs (all used): 14 Jamaine Wray; 15 Paul March; 16 Andy Shickell; 17 Michael Korkidas.
Tries: Lawton (16), Moss (20, 51), Barnett (27, 55, 68), Tadulala (34), Duffy (39, 72); **Goals:** Lawton 5/9.
CITY KNIGHTS: 1 Tom Bush; 2 Waine Pryce; 3 James Ford; 4 Matt Garside; 5 George Elliott; 6 Chris Thorman; 7 Ollie Olds; 8 Adam Sullivan; 9 Jack Lee; 10 Jack Aldous; 11 John Davies; 12 Ed Smith; 13 Paul King. Subs (all used): 14 Kris Brining; 15 Tyler Craig; 16 Nathan Freer; 17 Dario Esposito.
Tries: Garside (8), Brining (49), Esposito (60), Elliott (34), Duffy 4/4.
Rugby Leaguer & League Express Men of the Match:
Cougars: Richie Barnett; *City Knights:* Dario Esposito.
Penalty count: 4-6; **Half-time:** 24-6;
Referee: Ronnie Laughton; **Attendance:** 972.

FEATHERSTONE ROVERS 68 HUNSLET HAWKS 0

ROVERS: 1 Ian Hardman; 2 Tom Carr; 3 Sam Smeaton; 4 Greg Worthington; 5 Tom Saxton; 6 Andy Kain; 7 Liam Finn; 8 Anthony England; 9 Andy Ellis; 10 Michael Haley; 11 Jon Grayshon; 12 Matty Dale; 13 Jack Bussey. Subs

(all used): 14 Ben Kaye; 15 James Lockwood; 16 Liam Mackay; 17 Stuart Dickens.
Tries: England (3), Smeaton (9), Kain (17, 67), Grayshon (20), Finn (23), Dickens (36), Lockwood (39), Saxton (41), Bussey (46), Worthington (56), Dale (74); **Goals:** Finn 10/12.
HAWKS: 1 Stuart Kain; 2 Lee Mapals; 3 Josh Nathaniel; 4 Liam Welham; 5 Lee Brickwood; 6 Tom Henderson; 7 Ben Karalius; 8 Andrew Yates; 9 Luke Haigh; 10 Ryan Benjafield; 11 Tom Haughey; 12 John Oakes; 13 David March. Subs (all used): 14 Joe McLocklan; 15 David Clayton; 16 David Tootill; 17 Anthony Henderson.
Rugby Leaguer & League Express Men of the Match:
Rovers: Andy Kain; *Hawks:* Anthony Henderson.
Penalty count: 4-9; **Half-time:** 40-0;
Referee: Clint Sharrad; **Attendance:** 2,021.

HALIFAX 50 SWINTON LIONS 28

HALIFAX: 1 Ryan Fieldhouse; 2 Rob Worrincy; 3 Steve Tyrer; 4 Lee Paterson; 5 Wayne Reittie; 6 Paul Handforth; 7 Anthony Thackeray; 8 Sam Barlow; 9 Sean Penkywicz; 10 Sean Hesketh; 11 Dane Manning; 12 Adam Robinson; 13 Craig Ashall. Subs (all used): 14 Anthony Bowman; 15 Callum Casey; 16 Tony Tonks; 17 Jim Gannon.
Tries: Tyrer (4), Fieldhouse (6, 55, 72, 77), Paterson (33, 38), Bowman (50), S Barlow (69); **Goals:** Tyrer 7/9.
LIONS: 1 Ian Mort; 2 Gavin Dodd; 3 Sam Reay; 4 Tom Armstrong; 5 Kevin Penny; 6 Martin Ainscough; 7 Chaz I'Anson; 8 David Mills; 9 Karl Ashall; 10 Mike Morrison; 11 Dale Cunniffe; 12 Chris Clarke; 13 Carl Forster. Subs (all used): 14 Neil Holland; 15 Danny Meekin; 16 Alex Hurst; 17 Mark Smith.
Tries: Mills (14), Mort (19), Ashall (22), Armstrong (59), Holland (80); **Goals:** Mort 4/5.
Rugby Leaguer & League Express Men of the Match:
Halifax: Ryan Fieldhouse; *Lions:* Ian Mort.
Penalty count: 5-6; **Half-time:** 24-16;
Referee: Gareth Hewer; **Attendance:** 2,089.

ROUND 14

Friday 20th July 2012

SHEFFIELD EAGLES 16 KEIGHLEY COUGARS 6

EAGLES: 1 Quentin Laulu-Togagae; 2 Vinny Finigan; 3 Scott Turner; 4 Misi Taulapapa; 5 Nev Morrison; 6 Simon Brown; 7 Dominic Brambani; 8 Jack Howieson; 9 Andrew Henderson; 10 Mitchell Stringer; 11 Michael Knowles; 12 Sam Scott; 13 Alex Szostak. Subs (all used): 14 James Davey; 15 Peter Green; 16 Ryan Hepworth; 17 Liam Higgins.
Tries: Laulu-Togagae (4, 23), Finigan (15);
Goals: Brown 2/3.
COUGARS: 1 Craig Moss; 2 Gavin Duffy; 3 Richie Barnett; 4 Danny Lawton; 5 Semi Tadulala; 6 Danny Jones; 7 Sam Obst; 8 Jode Sheriffe; 9 Paul March; 10

Neil Cherryholme; 11 Jason Demetriou; 12 Jamie Shepherd; 13 James Haythornthwaite. Subs (all used): 14 Jamaine Wray; 15 Oliver Pursglove; 16 Michael Korkidas; 17 Andy Shickell.
Try: Wray (72); **Goals:** Lawton 1/1.
Sin bin: March (62) - high tackle.
Rugby Leaguer & League Express Men of the Match:
Eagles: Alex Szostak; *Cougars:* Jamaine Wray.
Penalty count: 11-11; **Half-time:** 16-0;
Referee: Matthew Thomason;
Attendance: 854 *(at Don Valley Stadium).*

Sunday 22nd July 2012

DEWSBURY RAMS 32 SWINTON LIONS 24

RAMS: 1 Greg Scott; 2 Daley Williams; 3 Ryan Esders; 4 Ayden Faal; 5 Austin Buchanan; 6 Pat Walker; 7 Scott Spaven; 8 Ben Jones; 9 Luke Blake; 10 Steve Crossley; 11 Brad Singleton; 12 Rob Spicer; 13 Josh Tonks. Subs (all used): 14 Matt Nicholson; 15 Elliott Cosgrove; 16 Joe Chandler; 17 George Flanagan.
Tries: Buchanan (25), Flanagan (39, 46, 79), Scott (53);
Goals: Walker 6/7.
LIONS: 1 Richie Hawkyard; 2 Ian Mort; 3 Sam Reay; 4 Tom Armstrong; 5 Kevin Penny; 6 Martin Ainscough; 7 Ian Watson; 8 David Mills; 9 Mark Smith; 10 Mike Morrison; 11 Dale Cunniffe; 12 Darren Hawkyard; 13 Carl Forster. Subs (all used): 14 Neil Holland; 15 Glenn Riley; 16 Karl Ashall; 17 Danny Meekin.
Tries: Cunniffe (55), Armstrong (60, 64), Penny (70);
Goals: Mort 4/4.
Rugby Leaguer & League Express Men of the Match:
Rams: George Flanagan; *Lions:* Ian Watson.
Penalty count: 10-8; **Half-time:** 16-0;
Referee: Warren Turley; **Attendance:** 835.

FEATHERSTONE ROVERS 31 BATLEY BULLDOGS 28

ROVERS: 1 Ian Hardman; 2 Jack Briscoe; 3 Sam Smeaton; 4 Greg Worthington; 5 Tom Saxton; 6 Andy Kain; 7 Liam Finn; 8 Anthony England; 9 Ben Kaye; 10 Stuart Dickens; 11 Jon Grayshon; 12 Tim Spears; 13 Matty Dale. Subs (all used): 14 Dominic Maloney; 15 Michael Haley; 16 James Lockwood; 17 Jack Bussey.
Tries: Grayshon (9), Kain (19, 24, 33), Finn (61);
Goals: Finn 5/5; **Field goal:** Finn (74).
BULLDOGS: 1 Ian Preece; 2 Gareth Potts; 3 Jason Walton; 4 Danny Maun; 5 Alex Brown; 6 Ben Black; 7 Gareth Moore; 8 Byron Smith; 9 Matthew Wildie; 10 Keegan Hirst; 11 Alex Bretherton; 12 Mark Applegarth; 13 Ashley Lindsay. Subs (all used): 14 Paul Mennell; 15 Craig Potter; 16 Alex Walmsley; 17 Kris Lythe.
Tries: Black (5, 43), Maun (28), Preece (55), Brown (80); **Goals:** Moore 4/5.
Rugby Leaguer & League Express Men of the Match:
Rovers: Andy Kain; *Bulldogs:* Alex Walmsley.
Penalty count: 4-9; **Half-time:** 24-12;
Referee: Ronnie Laughton; **Attendance:** 2,304.

Featherstone's Stuart Dickens takes on York duo Jack Aldous and Jack Lee

HUNSLET HAWKS 22 HALIFAX 52

HAWKS: 1 Stuart Kain; 2 Lee Mapals; 3 Josh Nathaniel; 4 Liam Welham; 5 Lee Brickwood; 6 Luke Helliwell; 7 Ben Karalius; 8 Andrew Yates; 9 Luke Haigh; 10 Ryan Benjafield; 11 David Clayton; 12 John Oakes; 13 David March. Subs (all used): 14 Joe McLocklan; 15 Elliot Hodgson; 16 David Tootill; 17 Luke Menzies.
Tries: Benjafield (2), Karalius (51), March (76), Haigh (79); **Goals:** March 3/4.
HALIFAX: 1 Paul White; 2 Lee Paterson; 3 Steve Tyrer; 4 James Haley; 5 Wayne Reittie; 6 Paul Handforth; 7 Anthony Thackeray; 8 Tony Tonks; 9 Sean Penkywicz; 10 Sean Hesketh; 11 Dane Manning; 12 Adam Robinson; 13 Craig Ashall. Subs (all used): 14 Anthony Bowman; 15 Callum Casey; 16 Sam Barlow; 17 Makali Aizue.
Tries: White (7, 37, 73), Tonks (14), Penkywicz (27), Thackeray (30, 43, 55), S Barlow (34);
Goals: Tyrer 5/6, Paterson 3/3.
Rugby Leaguer & League Express Men of the Match: *Hawks:* Ben Karalius; *Halifax:* Anthony Thackeray.
Penalty count: 8-5; **Half-time:** 6-34;
Referee: Dave Merrick; **Attendance:** 664.

YORK CITY KNIGHTS 20 LEIGH CENTURIONS 66

CITY KNIGHTS: 1 Tom Bush; 2 Waine Pryce; 3 Dave Sutton; 4 Matt Garside; 5 George Elliott; 6 Chris Thorman; 7 Ollie Olds; 8 Adam Sullivan; 9 Jack Lee; 10 Jack Aldous; 11 John Davies; 12 Ed Smith; 13 Rhys Clarke. Subs (all used): 14 Kris Brining; 15 Nathan Freer; 16 Jack Stearman; 17 Dario Esposito.
Tries: Lee (2), Sullivan (15), Brining (72), Esposito (79);
Goals: Thorman 2/4.
Sin bin: Bush (52) - dissent.
CENTURIONS: 1 Gregg McNally; 2 Steve Maden; 3 Stuart Littler; 4 Kevin Henderson; 5 Matt Gardner; 6 Martyn Ridyard; 7 John Duffy; 8 Michael Ostick; 9 Anthony Nicholson; 10 Rob Parker; 11 Macgraff Leuluai; 12 Tommy Goulden; 13 Sam Hopkins. Subs (all used): 14 Ryan Brierley; 15 Andy Thornley; 16 Craig Briscoe; 17 Tom Spencer.
Tries: Gardner (6), Ridyard (12, 35), McNally (24, 46), Goulden (38), Briscoe (40), Hopkins (52), Thornley (59), Nicholson (63), Brierley (67), Littler (80);
Goals: Ridyard 9/12.
Rugby Leaguer & League Express Men of the Match: *City Knights:* Ollie Olds; *Centurions:* Martyn Ridyard.
Penalty count: 4-9; **Half-time:** 10-32;
Referee: George Stokes; **Attendance:** 806.

ROUND 15

Thursday 2nd August 2012

BATLEY BULLDOGS 62 SWINTON LIONS 6

BULLDOGS: 1 Johnny Campbell; 2 Gareth Potts; 3 Jason Walton; 4 Danny Maun; 5 Alex Brown; 6 Ben Black; 7 Gareth Moore; 8 Byron Smith; 9 Paul Mennell; 10 James Green; 11 Alex Bretherton; 12 Mark Applegarth; 13 Ashley Lindsay. Subs (all used): 14 Matthew Wildie; 15 Keegan Hirst; 16 Alex Walmsley; 17 Liam Walmsley.
Tries: Applegarth (9, 73), Potts (23), A Walmsley (31), Wildie (39), Moore (40, 48), L Walmsley (59), Brown (61), Smith (75), Campbell (79); **Goals:** Moore 9/11.
LIONS: 1 Richie Hawkyard; 2 Ian Mort; 3 Sam Reay; 4 Tom Armstrong; 5 Kevin Penny; 6 Martin Ainscough; 7 Ian Watson; 8 David Mills; 9 Mark Smith; 10 Mike Morrison; 11 Dale Cunniffe; 12 Darren Hawkyard; 13 Carl Forster. Subs (all used): 14 Karl Ashall; 15 Glenn Riley; 16 Neil Holland; 17 Chaz l'Anson.
Try: Penny (14); **Goals:** Mort 1/1.
Rugby Leaguer & League Express Men of the Match: *Bulldogs:* Ben Black; *Lions:* David Mills.
Penalty count: 9-5; **Half-time:** 28-6;
Referee: Dave Merrick; **Attendance:** 720.

Friday 3rd August 2012

YORK CITY KNIGHTS 12 FEATHERSTONE ROVERS 40

CITY KNIGHTS: 1 Tom Bush; 2 Waine Pryce; 3 George Elliott; 4 Matt Garside; 5 Ben Dent; 6 Rhys Clarke; 7 Chris Thorman; 8 Adam Sullivan; 9 Jack Lee; 10 Jack Aldous; 11 John Davies; 12 Dario Esposito; 13 Nathan Freer. Subs (all used): 14 Kris Brining; 15 Dave Sutton; 16 Gareth Poutney; 17 Tim Stubbs.
Tries: Bush (15), Clarke (64); **Goals:** Thorman 2/2.
ROVERS: 1 Ian Hardman; 2 Tom Saxton; 3 Sam Smeaton; 4 Greg Worthington; 5 Tangi Ropati; 6 Kyle Briggs; 7 Liam Finn; 8 Anthony England; 9 Ben Kaye; 10 Stuart Dickens; 11 Andrew Bostock; 12 Tim Spears; 13 Matty Dale. Subs (all used): 14 Jack Bussey; 15 James Lockwood; 16 Nathan Chappell; 17 Dominic Maloney.
Tries: Ropati (3, 43), Smeaton (10), Maloney (28), Chappell (30, 51), Briggs (76); **Goals:** Finn 6/7.
Rugby Leaguer & League Express Men of the Match: *City Knights:* Rhys Clarke; *Rovers:* Nathan Chappell.
Penalty count: 4-6; **Half-time:** 6-24;
Referee: Gareth Hewer; **Attendance:** 1,015.

Sunday 5th August 2012

KEIGHLEY COUGARS 34 DEWSBURY RAMS 6

COUGARS: 1 Craig Moss; 2 Richie Barnett; 3 James Haythornthwaite; 4 Danny Lawton; 5 Semi Tadulala; 6 Danny Jones; 7 Sam Obst; 8 Andy Shickell; 9 James Feather; 10 Jode Sheriffe; 11 Lewis Reed; 12 Oliver Pursglove; 13 Jason Demetriou. Subs (all used): 14 Jamaine Wray; 15 Jy-Mel Coleman; 16 Brendan Rawlins; 17 Michael Korkidas.
Tries: Moss (11), Rawlins (19), Barnett (32), Lawton (44, 72), Demetriou (55); **Goals:** Lawton 5/7.
RAMS: 1 James Craven; 2 Jermaine Akaidere; 3 Ryan Esders; 4 Ayden Faal; 5 Austin Buchanan; 6 Pat Walker; 7 Scott Spaven; 8 Ben Jones; 9 Liam Hood; 10 Brad Singleton; 11 Josh Tonks; 12 Rob Spicer; 13 Luke Blake. Subs (all used): 14 Michael Wainwright; 15 Greg Scott; 16 George Flanagan; 17 Matt Nicholson.
Try: Craven (4); **Goals:** Walker 1/1.
Rugby Leaguer & League Express Men of the Match: *Cougars:* Jy-Mel Coleman; *Rams:* James Craven.
Penalty count: 7-4; **Half-time:** 14-6;
Referee: Jamie Leahy; **Attendance:** 814.

HALIFAX 30 SHEFFIELD EAGLES 26

HALIFAX: 1 Ryan Fieldhouse; 2 Rob Worrincy; 3 Lee Paterson; 4 Steve Tyrer; 5 Paul White; 6 Paul Handforth; 7 Anthony Thackeray; 8 Tony Tonks; 9 Sean Penkywicz; 10 Luke Ambler; 11 Dane Manning; 12 Adam Robinson; 13 Jim Gannon. Subs (all used): 14 Anthony Bowman; 15 Craig Ashall; 16 Sam Barlow; 17 Makali Aizue.
Tries: Worrincy (21), Thackeray (27, 77), White (46), Ambler (75); **Goals:** Handforth 1/1, Tyrer 4/4.
Sin bin: Gannon (68) - fighting.
EAGLES: 1 Quentin Laulu-Togagae; 2 Vinny Finigan; 3 Menzie Yere; 4 Misi Taulapapa; 5 Scott Turner; 6 Simon Brown; 7 Dominic Brambani; 8 Jack Howieson; 9 Andrew Henderson; 10 Mitchell Stringer; 11 Michael Knowles; 12 Sam Scott; 13 Alex Szostak. Subs (all used): 14 James Davey; 15 Dane McDonald; 16 Duane Straugheir; 17 Liam Higgins.
Tries: Finigan (5), Turner (11), Knowles (15, 30), Laulu-Togagae (56); **Goals:** Brown 3/6.
Sin bin: Straugheir (68) - fighting.
Rugby Leaguer & League Express Men of the Match: *Halifax:* Dane Manning; *Eagles:* Michael Knowles.
Penalty count: 8-9; **Half-time:** 12-22;
Referee: Chris Leatherbarrow; **Attendance:** 1,912.

HUNSLET HAWKS 6 LEIGH CENTURIONS 36

HAWKS: 1 Stuart Kain; 2 Lee Mapals; 3 Josh Nathaniel; 4 Liam Welham; 5 Lee Brickwood; 6 Luke Helliwell; 7 Ben Karalius; 8 Andrew Yates; 9 Luke Haigh; 10 Ryan Benjafield; 11 David Clayton; 12 John Oakes; 13 Elliot Hodgson. Subs (all used): 14 Joe McLocklan; 15 Scott Watson; 16 Steve Lewis; 17 David Tootill.
Try: Nathaniel (75); **Goals:** Helliwell 1/1.
CENTURIONS: 1 Gregg McNally; 2 Steve Maden; 3 Stuart Littler; 4 Matt Gardner; 5 Jonathan Pownall; 6 Martyn Ridyard; 7 John Duffy; 8 Michael Ostick; 9 Anthony Nicholson; 10 Rob Parker; 11 Macgraff Leuluai; 12 Tommy Goulden; 13 Sam Hopkins. Subs (all used): 14 Bob Beswick; 15 Kevin Henderson; 16 Andy Thornley; 17 James Taylor.
Tries: Goulden (5), Gardner (7, 39), Hopkins (11), Parker (18), McNally (28), Littler (46); **Goals:** Ridyard 4/7.
Rugby Leaguer & League Express Men of the Match: *Hawks:* Andrew Yates; *Centurions:* John Duffy.
Penalty count: 9-10; **Half-time:** 0-32;
Referee: Matthew Thomason; **Attendance:** 608.

ROUND 16

Thursday 9th August 2012

KEIGHLEY COUGARS 0 LEIGH CENTURIONS 26

COUGARS: 1 Craig Moss; 2 Gavin Duffy; 3 James Haythornthwaite; 4 Richie Barnett; 5 Semi Tadulala; 6 Danny Jones; 7 Sam Obst; 8 Andy Shickell; 9 James Feather; 10 Neil Cherryholme; 11 Jamie Shepherd; 12 Oliver Pursglove; 13 Jason Demetriou. Subs (all used): 14 Jamaine Wray; 15 Jy-Mel Coleman; 16 Brendan Rawlins; 17 Michael Korkidas.
CENTURIONS: 1 Gregg McNally; 2 Steve Maden; 3 Stuart Littler; 4 Matt Gardner; 5 Jonathan Pownall; 6 Martyn Ridyard; 7 John Duffy; 8 Michael Ostick; 9 Bob Beswick; 10 Tom Spencer; 11 Craig Briscoe; 12 Tommy Goulden; 13 Sam Hopkins. Subs (all used): 14 Ryan Brierley; 15 Anthony Nicholson; 16 Kevin Henderson; 17 Andy Thornley.
Tries: McNally (29, 31), Ridyard (38), Pownall (71, 77); **Goals:** Ridyard 3/5.
Sin bin: Hopkins (65) - interference.
Rugby Leaguer & League Express Men of the Match: *Cougars:* Andy Shickell; *Centurions:* Martyn Ridyard.
Penalty count: 15-8; **Half-time:** 0-14;
Referee: Jamie Leahy; **Attendance:** 831.

Friday 10th August 2012

SHEFFIELD EAGLES 30 HUNSLET HAWKS 20

EAGLES: 1 Quentin Laulu-Togagae; 2 Vinny Finigan; 3 Menzie Yere; 4 Scott Turner; 5 Nev Morrison; 6 Simon Brown; 7 Dominic Brambani; 8 Jack Howieson; 9 James Davey; 10 Mitchell Stringer; 11 Michael Knowles; 12 Joe Hirst; 13 Dane McDonald. Subs (all used): 14 Andrew Henderson; 15 Alex Szostak; 16 Duane Straugheir; 17 Liam Higgins.
Tries: Morrison (5), Davey (13), Straugheir (50), Hirst (65, 68); **Goals:** Brown 5/5.
HAWKS: 1 Stuart Kain; 2 Dennis Tuffour; 3 Josh Nathaniel; 4 Liam Welham; 5 Lee Brickwood; 6 Luke Helliwell; 7 Joe McLocklan; 8 Callum Menzies; 9 Luke Haigh; 10 Steve Lewis; 11 David Clayton; 12 John Oakes; 13 David March. Subs (all used): 14 Joe Parkinson; 15 Scott Watson; 16 Ryan Benjafield; 17 Andrew Yates.
Tries: Welham (17, 38), Haigh (21), Brickwood (24); **Goals:** Helliwell 2/4.
Rugby Leaguer & League Express Men of the Match: *Eagles:* Michael Knowles; *Hawks:* David March.
Penalty count: 10-8; **Half-time:** 12-20;
Referee: Matthew Thomason; **Attendance:** 777 *(at Don Valley Stadium).*

Sunday 12th August 2012

DEWSBURY RAMS 12 BATLEY BULLDOGS 26

RAMS: 1 James Craven; 2 Michael Wainwright; 3 Ryan Esders; 4 Greg Scott; 5 Austin Buchanan; 6 Pat Walker; 7 Scott Spaven; 8 Joe Chandler; 9 George Flanagan; 10 Matt Nicholson; 11 Elliott Cosgrove; 12 Josh Tonks; 13 Mark Barlow. Subs (all used): 14 Daley Williams; 15 Matthew Tebb; 16 Danny Samuel; 17 Jonathan Schofield.
Tries: Samuel (38), Wainwright (75); **Goals:** Walker 2/2.
Sin bin: Spaven (50) - fighting.
On report: Esders (15) - alleged dangerous contact; Brawl (50).
BULLDOGS: 1 Johnny Campbell; 2 Gareth Potts; 3 Jason Walton; 4 Danny Maun; 5 Alex Brown; 6 Ben Black; 7 Gareth Moore; 8 Byron Smith; 9 Paul Mennell; 10 Craig Potter; 11 Alex Bretherton; 12 Mark Applegarth; 13 Ashley Lindsay. Subs (all used): 14 Matthew Wildie; 15 Keegan Hirst; 16 Alex Walmsley; 17 Liam Walmsley.
Tries: Campbell (23), Brown (53), Wildie (69), A Walmsley (78); **Goals:** Moore 5/5.
Sin bin: Wildie (50) - fighting.
On report: Brawl (50).
Rugby Leaguer & League Express Men of the Match: *Rams:* Matt Nicholson; *Bulldogs:* Ben Black.
Penalty count: 9-13; **Half-time:** 6-8;
Referee: Ronnie Laughton; **Attendance:** 1,705.

FEATHERSTONE ROVERS 86 SWINTON LIONS 12

ROVERS: 1 Ian Hardman; 2 Tangi Ropati; 3 Sam Smeaton; 4 Greg Worthington; 5 Tom Saxton; 6 Andy Kain; 7 Liam Finn; 8 Anthony England; 9 Ben Kaye; 10 Stuart Dickens; 11 Nathan Chappell; 12 Tim Spears; 13 Matty Dale. Subs (all used): 14 Kyle Briggs; 15 Jon Lockwood; 16 Jon Grayshon; 17 Dominic Maloney.
Tries: Hardman (6, 60, 79), Ropati (10, 18, 30, 45, 53), Kain (13), Smeaton (21), Finn (25, 48), Hardman (33), Grayshon (42), Dale (75); **Goals:** Finn 13/15.
LIONS: 1 Richie Hawkyard; 2 Gavin Dodd; 3 Sam Reay; 4 Martin Ainscough; 5 Alex Hurst; 6 Chaz I'Anson; 7 Ian Watson; 8 Glenn Riley; 9 Mark Smith; 10 David Mills; 11 Dale Cunniffe; 12 Danny Meekin; 13 Chris Clarke. Subs (all used): 14 Neil Holland; 15 Darren Hawkyard; 16 Tom Armstrong; 17 Karl Ashall.
Tries: Hurst (2, 76), D Hawkyard (51); **Goals:** Dodd 0/3.
Rugby Leaguer & League Express Men of the Match: *Rovers:* Tangi Ropati; *Lions:* Chaz I'Anson.
Penalty count: 7-1; **Half-time:** 46-4;
Referee: Warren Turley; **Attendance:** 2,068.

HALIFAX 44 YORK CITY KNIGHTS 12

HALIFAX: 1 Paul White; 2 Rob Worrincy; 3 Anthony Bowman; 4 James Haley; 5 Ben Heaton; 6 Paul Handforth; 7 Anthony Thackeray; 8 Tony Tonks; 9 Craig Ashall; 10 Sean Hesketh; 11 Dane Manning; 12 Callum Casey; 13 Luke Ambler. Subs (all used): 14 Lee Paterson; 15 Jim Gannon; 16 Sam Barlow; 17 Makali Aizue.
Tries: Heaton (6), S Barlow (23), Handforth (33), White (39, 44), Worrincy (63, 72), Bowman (69); **Goals:** Handforth 6/8.
CITY KNIGHTS: 1 Tom Bush; 2 Waine Pryce; 3 George Elliott; 4 Matt Garside; 5 Ben Dent; 6 Chris Thorman; 7 Tyler Craig; 8 Adam Sullivan; 9 Jack Lee; 10 Jack Aldous; 11 Dario Esposito; 12 John Davies; 13 Nathan Freer. Subs (all used): 14 Kris Brining; 15 Dave Sutton; 16 Gareth Poutney; 17 Liam Ellis.
Tries: Elliott (10), Bush (17); **Goals:** Thorman 2/2.
Rugby Leaguer & League Express Men of the Match: *Halifax:* Paul Handforth; *City Knights:* John Davies.
Penalty count: 5-3; **Half-time:** 22-12;
Referee: Clint Sharrad; **Attendance:** 1,989.

Keighley's Jode Sheriffe wrapped up by the Swinton defence

ROUND 17

Thursday 16th August 2012

SHEFFIELD EAGLES 28 FEATHERSTONE ROVERS 28

EAGLES: 1 Quentin Laulu-Togagae; 2 Nev Morrison; 3 Menzie Yere; 4 Misi Taulapapa; 5 Scott Turner; 6 Dane McDonald; 7 Dominic Brambani; 8 Jack Howieson; 9 Andrew Henderson; 10 Mitchell Stringer; 11 Michael Knowles; 12 Sam Scott; 13 Alex Szostak. Subs (all used): 14 James Davey; 15 Peter Green; 16 Ryan Hepworth; 17 Liam Higgins.
Tries: Knowles (39), Turner (44), Davey (47), Laulu-Togagae (69, 73); **Goals:** Brambani 4/5.
ROVERS: 1 Ian Hardman; 2 Tangi Ropati; 3 Sam Smeaton; 4 Greg Worthington; 5 Tom Saxton; 6 Andy Kain; 7 Liam Finn; 8 Anthony England; 9 Ben Kaye; 10 Stuart Dickens; 11 Nathan Chappell; 12 Tim Spears; 13 Matty Dale. Subs (all used): 14 Kyle Briggs; 15 James Lockwood; 16 Jon Grayshon; 17 Dominic Maloney.
Tries: Ropati (9), Kain (16, 31, 63), Hardman (54); **Goals:** Finn 4/5.
Rugby Leaguer & League Express Men of the Match: *Eagles:* Michael Knowles; *Rovers:* Liam Finn.
Penalty count: 8-3; **Half-time:** 6-16; **Referee:** Gareth Hewer; **Attendance:** 1,449 *(at Don Valley Stadium).*

Friday 17th August 2012

LEIGH CENTURIONS 32 HALIFAX 28

CENTURIONS: 1 Gregg McNally; 2 Steve Maden; 3 Stuart Littler; 4 Matt Gardner; 5 Jonathan Pownall; 6 Martyn Ridyard; 7 Bob Beswick; 8 Michael Ostick; 9 Anthony Nicholson; 10 Tom Spencer; 11 Craig Briscoe; 12 Tommy Goulden; 13 Sam Hopkins. Subs (all used): 14 Ryan Brierley; 15 Kevin Henderson; 16 Andy Thornley; 17 James Taylor.
Tries: Beswick (2), McNally (10), Ridyard (23, 64), Littler (35), Brierley (76); **Goals:** Ridyard 4/6.
HALIFAX: 1 Ryan Fieldhouse; 2 Rob Worrincy; 3 Anthony Thackeray; 8 Tony Tonks; 9 Sean Penkywicz; 10 Sean Hesketh; 11 Dane Manning; 12 Ben Heaton; 13 Luke Ambler. Subs (all used): 14 Callum Casey; 15 Craig Ashall; 16 Sam Barlow; 17 Makali Aizue.
Tries: S Barlow (17), Fieldhouse (19), Worrincy (47, 80), White (73); **Goals:** Tyrer 4/5.
Tyrer; 4 Lee Paterson; 5 Paul White; 6 Paul Handforth; 7

Rugby Leaguer & League Express Men of the Match: *Centurions:* Martyn Ridyard; *Halifax:* Sean Penkywicz.
Penalty count: 12-8; **Half-time:** 20-12;
Referee: Tim Roby; **Attendance:** 2,122.

Sunday 19th August 2012

BATLEY BULLDOGS 50 YORK CITY KNIGHTS 0

BULLDOGS: 1 Johnny Campbell; 2 Gareth Potts; 3 Jason Walton; 4 Danny Maun; 5 Alex Brown; 6 Ben Black; 7 Gareth Moore; 8 Byron Smith; 9 Paul Mennell; 10 Adam Scott; 11 Alex Bretherton; 12 Mark Applegarth; 13 Ashley Lindsay. Subs (all used): 14 Matthew Wildie; 15 Keegan Hirst; 16 Alex Walmsley; 17 Liam Walmsley.
Tries: Campbell (5), Black (12), Maun (22), Potts (31), Wildie (40), Brown (42, 48), Lindsay (44), Walton (65); **Goals:** Moore 7/9.
CITY KNIGHTS: 1 Ben Dent; 2 Waine Pryce; 3 Gareth Poutney; 4 Matt Garside; 5 George Elliott; 6 Chris Thorman; 7 Tyler Craig; 8 Adam Sullivan; 9 Kris Brining; 10 Jack Aldous; 11 Ed Smith; 12 John Davies; 13 Nathan Freer. Subs (all used): 14 Harry Carter; 15 Dave Sutton; 16 Liam Ellis; 17 Dario Esposito.
Rugby Leaguer & League Express Men of the Match: *Bulldogs:* Alex Brown; *City Knights:* Harry Carter.
Penalty count: 5-5; **Half-time:** 28-0;
Referee: Matthew Thomason; **Attendance:** 741.

SWINTON LIONS 18 KEIGHLEY COUGARS 18

LIONS: 1 Gavin Dodd; 2 Rob Foxen; 3 Martin Ainscough; 4 Tom Armstrong; 5 Alex Hurst; 6 Chaz I'Anson; 7 Ian Watson; 8 Neil Holland; 9 Mark Smith; 10 Mike Morrison; 11 Dale Cunniffe; 12 Darren Hawkyard; 13 Carl Forster. Subs (all used): 14 David Mills; 15 Danny Meekin; 16 Sam Reay; 17 Richie Hawkyard.
Tries: Ainscough (9), Armstrong (30), Cunniffe (37); **Goals:** Dodd 3/4.
COUGARS: 1 Craig Moss; 2 Gavin Duffy; 3 James Haythornthwaite; 4 Danny Lawton; 5 Richie Barnett; 6 Jy-Mel Coleman; 7 Sam Obst; 8 Michael Korkidas; 9 James Feather; 10 Neil Cherryholme; 11 Oliver Pursglove; 12 Sam Obst; Subs (all used): 14 Jamaine Wray; 15 Brendan Rawlins; 16 Jode Sheriffe; 17 Andy Shickell.
Tries: Feather (3), Obst (17, 26); **Goals:** Lawton 3/3.
Rugby Leaguer & League Express Men of the Match: *Lions:* Chaz I'Anson; *Cougars:* Sam Obst.
Penalty count: 3-8; **Half-time:** 18-18;
Referee: Ronnie Laughton; **Attendance:** 515.

HUNSLET HAWKS 22 DEWSBURY RAMS 34

HAWKS: 1 Stuart Kain; 2 Lee Mapals; 3 Josh Nathaniel; 4 Liam Welham; 5 Lee Brickwood; 6 Luke Helliwell; 7 Ben Karalius; 8 Steve Lewis; 9 Luke Haigh; 10 Luke Menzies; 11 David Clayton; 12 John Oakes; 13 David March. Subs (all used): 14 Joe McLocklan; 15 Tom Haughey; 16 Ryan Benjafield; 17 Andrew Yates.
Tries: Haigh (24), Kain (32), Welham (44), March (63); **Goals:** Helliwell 3/4.
RAMS: 1 James Craven; 2 Michael Wainwright; 3 Ryan Esders; 4 Greg Scott; 5 Jermaine Akaidere; 6 Pat Walker; 7 Scott Spaven; 8 Matt Nicholson; 9 Liam Hood; 10 Brad Singleton; 11 Rob Spicer; 12 Josh Tonks; 13 Mark Barlow. Subs (all used): 14 Joe Chandler; 15 Elliott Cosgrove; 16 Luke Blake; 17 Matthew Tebb.

Sheffield's Quentin Laulu-Togagae looks to break free against Dewsbury

Tries: Walker (12), Esders (35), Spaven (49), Cosgrove (52), Hood (67), Scott (73); **Goals:** Walker 5/6.
Rugby Leaguer & League Express Men of the Match: *Hawks:* David March; *Rams:* Liam Hood.
Penalty count: 10-6; **Half-time:** 10-12;
Referee: Jamie Leahy; **Attendance:** 463.

ROUND 7

Thursday 23rd August 2012

LEIGH CENTURIONS 40 KEIGHLEY COUGARS 14

CENTURIONS: 1 Gregg McNally; 2 Steve Maden; 3 Stuart Littler; 4 Matt Gardner; 5 Dean McGilvray; 6 Martyn Ridyard; 7 Bob Beswick; 8 Michael Ostick; 9 Anthony Nicholson; 10 Tom Spencer; 11 Craig Briscoe; 12 Tommy Goulden; 13 Kevin Henderson. Subs (all used): 14 Ryan Brierley; 15 James Mendeika; 16 James Taylor; 17 Tommy Gallagher.
Tries: Henderson (14), Ridyard (43), McGilvray (54, 61), Brierley (58, 72, 76); **Goals:** Ridyard 6/7.
COUGARS: 1 Craig Moss; 2 Gavin Duffy; 3 Danny Lawton; 4 Richie Barnett; 5 Semi Tadulala; 6 Jason Demetriou; 7 Sam Obst; 8 Andy Shickell; 9 James Feather; 10 Neil Cherryholme; 11 Oliver Pursglove; 12 Brendan Rawlins; 13 Ben Sagar. Subs (all used): 14 Jamaine Wray; 15 Paul March; 16 Jode Sheriff; 17 Michael Korkidas.
Tries: Obst (4), Demetriou (45), Tadulala (66);
Goals: Lawton 1/3.
Sin bin: Tadulala (50) - delaying restart.
Rugby Leaguer & League Express Men of the Match: *Centurions:* Martyn Ridyard; *Cougars:* Andy Shickell.
Penalty count: 13-3; **Half-time:** 6-4;
Referee: Gareth Hewer; **Attendance:** 1,597.

ROUND 18

Sunday 2nd September 2012

SWINTON LIONS 12 LEIGH CENTURIONS 48

LIONS: 1 Ian Mort; 2 Rob Foxen; 3 Gavin Dodd; 4 Tom Armstrong; 5 Alex Hurst; 6 Martin Ainscough; 7 Ian Watson; 8 David Mills; 9 Mark Smith; 10 Mike Morrison; 11 Dale Cunniffe; 12 Darren Hawkyard; 13 Chaz I'Anson. Subs (all used): 14 Danny Meekin; 15 Neil Holland; 16 Sam Reay; 17 Karl Ashall.
Tries: Reay (33), Ainscough (46); **Goals:** Mort 2/2.

CENTURIONS: 1 Gregg McNally; 2 Dean McGilvray; 3 Stuart Littler; 4 Matt Gardner; 5 Jonathan Pownall; 6 Martyn Ridyard; 7 John Duffy; 8 James Taylor; 9 Bob Beswick; 10 Tom Spencer; 11 Craig Briscoe; 12 Tommy Goulden; 13 Kevin Henderson. Subs (all used): 14 Ryan Brierley; 15 Anthony Nicholson; 16 Andy Thornley; 17 Tommy Gallagher.
Tries: Pownall (14), Beswick (21), Ridyard (24), Gallagher (30, 43), Gardner (37), McNally (52), Nicholson (80); **Goals:** Ridyard 7/7, McNally 1/1.
Rugby Leaguer & League Express Men of the Match: *Lions:* Darren Hawkyard; *Centurions:* Martyn Ridyard.
Penalty count: 3-10; **Half-time:** 6-30;
Referee: Jamie Leahy; **Attendance:** 1,796.

DEWSBURY RAMS 20 SHEFFIELD EAGLES 30

RAMS: 1 James Craven; 2 Jermaine Akaidere; 3 Greg Scott; 4 Elliott Cosgrove; 5 Michael Wainwright; 6 Pat Walker; 7 Scott Spaven; 8 Brad Singleton; 9 Liam Hood; 10 Joe Chandler; 11 Rob Spicer; 12 Josh Tonks; 13 Luke Blake. Subs (all used): 14 Matthew Tebb; 15 Ryan Esders; 16 Mark Barlow; 17 George Flanagan.
Tries: Tebb (38), Akaidere (47), Scott (73), Esders (76);
Goals: Walker 2/4.
EAGLES: 1 Quentin Laulu-Togagae; 2 Nev Morrison; 3 Menzie Yere; 4 Misi Taulapapa; 5 Scott Turner; 6 Dane McDonald; 7 Dominic Brambani; 8 Jack Howieson; 9 Andrew Henderson; 10 Mitchell Stringer; 11 Michael Knowles; 12 Sam Scott; 13 Alex Szostak. Subs (all used): 14 James Davey; 15 Peter Green; 16 Ryan Hepworth; 17 Liam Higgins.
Tries: McDonald (6), Morrison (9), Taulapapa (25), Yere (43), Davey (51), Brambani (79); **Goals:** Brambani 3/6.
Rugby Leaguer & League Express Men of the Match: *Rams:* Matthew Tebb; *Eagles:* Dominic Brambani.
Penalty count: 9-6; **Half-time:** 6-12;
Referee: Warren Turley; **Attendance:** 1,156.

FEATHERSTONE ROVERS 46 KEIGHLEY COUGARS 4

ROVERS: 1 Ian Hardman; 2 Nathan Chappell; 3 Sam Smeaton; 4 Greg Worthington; 5 Tangi Ropati; 6 Andy Kain; 7 Liam Finn; 8 Anthony England; 9 Ben Kaye; 10 Stuart Dickens; 11 Matty Dale; 12 Tim Spears; 13 Kyle Briggs. Subs (all used): 14 Jon Hepworth; 15 James Lockwood; 16 Jon Grayshon; 17 Andrew Bostock.
Tries: Worthington (5), Hardman (11), Chappell (20), Grayshon (45), Dickens (57), Smeaton (60), Kain (64), Ropati (69); **Goals:** Finn 7/8.
COUGARS: 1 Ryan Smith; 2 Jesse Sheriffe; 3 Danny Lawton; 4 Ben Sagar; 5 Gavin Duffy; 6 Jy-Mel Coleman; 7 Danny Jones; 8 Jode Sheriffe; 9 Paul March; 10 Neil

Cherryholme; 11 Jamie Shepherd; 12 Oliver Pursglove; 13 Richie Barnett. Subs (all used): 14 Jamaine Wray; 15 James Feather; 16 Lewis Reed; 17 Michael Korkidas.
Try: Duffy (34); **Goals:** Lawton 0/1.
Rugby Leaguer & League Express Men of the Match: *Rovers:* Andy Kain; *Cougars:* Michael Korkidas.
Penalty count: 12-6; **Half-time:** 18-4;
Referee: Dave Merrick; **Attendance:** 2,816.

HALIFAX 26 BATLEY BULLDOGS 20

HALIFAX: 1 Ryan Fieldhouse; 2 Rob Worrincy; 3 Lee Paterson; 4 Steve Tyrer; 5 Paul White; 6 Sean Penkywicz; 7 Anthony Thackeray; 8 Luke Ambler; 9 Craig Ashall; 10 Makali Aizue; 11 Ben Heaton; 12 Adam Robinson; 13 Jim Gannon. Subs (all used): 14 Callum Casey; 15 Tony Tonks; 16 Sam Barlow; 17 Paul Handforth.
Tries: Ambler (15, 77), Aizue (50), Fieldhouse (63);
Goals: Tyrer 5/5.
BULLDOGS: 1 Johnny Campbell; 2 Gareth Potts; 3 Jason Walton; 4 Danny Maun; 5 Alex Brown; 6 Ben Black; 7 Gareth Moore; 8 Byron Smith; 9 Paul Mennell; 10 James Green; 11 Alex Bretherton; 12 Mark Applegarth; 13 Ashley Lindsay. Subs (all used): 14 Matthew Wildie; 15 Keegan Hirst; 16 Alex Walmsley; 17 Liam Walmsley.
Tries: A Walmsley (24, 43), Black (28); **Goals:** Moore 4/4.
Rugby Leaguer & League Express Men of the Match: *Halifax:* Ryan Fieldhouse; *Bulldogs:* Alex Walmsley.
Penalty count: 10-5; **Half-time:** 6-14;
Referee: Matthew Thomason; **Attendance:** 2,344.

YORK CITY KNIGHTS 26 HUNSLET HAWKS 28

CITY KNIGHTS: 1 Tom Bush; 2 Waine Pryce; 3 Dave Sutton; 4 Matt Garside; 5 Gareth Poutney; 6 Chris Thorman; 7 George Elliott; 8 Adam Sullivan; 9 Jack Lee; 10 Jack Aldous; 11 John Davies; 12 Ed Smith; 13 Nathan Freer. Subs (all used): 14 Kris Brining; 15 Liam Ellis; 16 Tim Stubbs; 17 Dario Esposito.
Tries: Elliott (24), Pryce (50), Poutney (60, 76), Lee (67); **Goals:** Thorman 3/5.
HAWKS: 1 Stuart Kain; 2 Lee Mapals; 3 Josh Nathaniel; 4 Liam Welham; 5 Lee Brickwood; 6 Luke Helliwell; 7 Ben Karalius; 8 Luke Menzies; 9 Luke Haigh; 10 Steve Lewis; 11 David Clayton; 12 John Oakes; 13 David March. Subs (all used): 14 Joe McLocklan; 15 Dennis Tuffour; 16 Andrew Yates; 17 Ryan Benjafield.
Tries: Kain (4), Lewis (16), Welham (32, 41), Tuffour (56); **Goals:** Helliwell 4/6.
Rugby Leaguer & League Express Men of the Match: *City Knights:* Adam Sullivan; *Hawks:* David March.
Penalty count: 8-4; **Half-time:** 4-16;
Referee: Gareth Hewer; **Attendance:** 913.

Leigh's Gregg McNally tries in vain to stop Featherstone's Dominic Maloney from scoring

PLAY-OFFS

ELIMINATION PLAY-OFFS

Thursday 6th September 2012

HALIFAX 28 KEIGHLEY COUGARS 24

HALIFAX: 1 Ryan Fieldhouse; 2 Rob Worrincy; 3 Lee Paterson; 4 Steve Tyrer; 5 Wayne Reittie; 6 Paul Handforth; 7 Anthony Thackeray; 8 Luke Ambler; 9 Craig Ashall; 10 Makali Aizue; 11 Callum Casey; 12 Ben Heaton; 13 Jim Gannon. Subs (all used): 14 Paul White; 15 Sean Penkywicz; 16 Sam Barlow; 17 Tony Tonks. **Tries:** Gannon (13), Aizue (20), Tyrer (28), S Barlow (66), Paterson (80); **Goals:** Tyrer 4/6.
COUGARS: 1 Craig Moss; 2 Richie Barnett; 3 Ben Sagar; 4 Danny Lawton; 5 Gavin Duffy; 6 Danny Jones; 7 Sam Obst; 8 Andy Shickell; 9 James Feather; 10 Neil Cherryholme; 11 Oliver Pursglove; 12 Brendan Rawlins; 13 Jason Demetriou. Subs (all used): 14 Jamaine Wray; 15 Paul March; 16 Jode Sheriffe; 17 Michael Korkidas. **Tries:** Moss (8), March (38), D Jones (44), Feather (76); **Goals:** Lawton 4/4.
Rugby Leaguer & League Express Men of the Match: *Halifax:* Paul Handforth; *Cougars:* Jason Demetriou.
Penalty count: 10-7; **Half-time:** 16-12;
Referee: Jamie Leahy; **Attendance:** 1,203.

Sunday 9th September 2012

SHEFFIELD EAGLES 42 BATLEY BULLDOGS 12

EAGLES: 1 Quentin Laulu-Togagae; 2 Misi Taulapapa; 3 Duane Straugheir; 4 Menzie Yere; 5 Scott Turner; 6 Simon Brown; 7 Dominic Brambani; 8 Jack Howieson; 9 Andrew Henderson; 10 Mitchell Stringer; 11 Michael Knowles; 12 Sam Scott; 13 Dane McDonald. Subs (all used): 14 James Davey; 15 Peter Green; 16 Joe Hirst; 17 Liam Higgins. **Tries:** Turner (22, 34, 74), Taulapapa (28, 57), Hirst (32, 64); **Goals:** Brown 7/8.
BULLDOGS: 1 Johnny Campbell; 2 Ian Preece; 3 Jason Walton; 4 Danny Maun; 5 Gareth Potts; 6 Ben Black; 7 Gareth Moore; 8 Byron Smith; 9 Paul Mennell; 10 James Green; 11 Alex Bretherton; 12 Mark Applegarth; 13 Ashley Lindsay. Subs (all used): 14 Matthew Wildie; 15 Keegan Hirst; 16 Alex Walmsley; 17 Liam Walmsley. **Tries:** Campbell (68), A Walmsley (77); **Goals:** Moore 2/3.
Sin bin: Mennell (62) - punching;
Applegarth (66) - interference.
Rugby Leaguer & League Express Men of the Match: *Eagles:* Simon Brown; *Bulldogs:* Alex Walmsley.
Penalty count: 13-8; **Half-time:** 24-2;
Referee: George Stokes; **Attendance:** 722
(at Don Valley Stadium).

QUALIFYING SEMI-FINAL

Thursday 13th September 2012

FEATHERSTONE ROVERS 32 LEIGH CENTURIONS 14

ROVERS: 1 Ian Hardman; 2 Tangi Ropati; 3 Sam Smeaton; 4 Greg Worthington; 5 Tom Saxton; 6 Andy Kain; 7 Liam Finn; 8 Anthony England; 9 Ben Kaye; 10 James Lockwood; 11 Matty Dale; 12 Tim Spears; 13 Kyle Briggs. Subs (all used): 14 Nathan Chappell; 15 Andrew Bostock; 16 Dominic Maloney; 17 Stuart Dickens. **Tries:** Maloney (22, 59), Dickens (49), Hardman (66); **Goals:** Finn 8/8.
CENTURIONS: 1 Gregg McNally; 2 Steve Maden; 3 Stuart Littler; 4 Matt Gardner; 5 Jonathan Pownall; 6 Martyn Ridyard; 7 John Duffy; 8 Michael Ostick; 9 Bob Beswick; 10 Tom Spencer; 11 Craig Briscoe; 12 Tommy Goulden; 13 Andy Thornley. Subs (all used): 14 Ryan Brierley; 15 James Taylor; 16 Kevin Henderson; 17 Tommy Gallagher.
Tries: Briscoe (2), Pownall (10, 40); **Goals:** Ridyard 1/3.
Dismissal: Henderson (76) - high tackle on Briggs.
Rugby Leaguer & League Express Men of the Match: *Rovers:* Dominic Maloney; *Centurions:* Martyn Ridyard.
Penalty count: 16-8; **Half-time:** 6-14;
Referee: George Stokes; **Attendance:** 1,828.

ELIMINATION SEMI-FINAL

Sunday 16th September 2012

HALIFAX 12 SHEFFIELD EAGLES 54

HALIFAX: 1 Ryan Fieldhouse; 2 Rob Worrincy; 3 Lee Paterson; 4 Steve Tyrer; 5 Wayne Reittie; 6 Paul Handforth; 7 Anthony Thackeray; 8 Luke Ambler; 9 Craig Ashall; 10 Makali Aizue; 11 Ben Heaton; 12 Ross Divorty; 13 Adam Robinson. Subs (all used): 14 Callum Casey; 15 Sean Penkywicz; 16 Sam Barlow; 17 Jim Gannon. **Tries:** Handforth (50), Worrincy (67), Fieldhouse (76); **Goals:** Tyrer 0/2, Gannon 0/1.
EAGLES: 1 Quentin Laulu-Togagae; 2 Misi Taulapapa; 3 Duane Straugheir; 4 Menzie Yere; 5 Scott Turner; 6 Simon Brown; 7 Dominic Brambani; 8 Jack Howieson; 9 Andrew Henderson; 10 Mitchell Stringer; 11 Michael Knowles; 12 Sam Scott; 13 Alex Szostak. Subs (all used): 14 James Davey; 15 Peter Green; 16 Joe Hirst; 17 Liam Higgins. **Tries:** Straugheir (7), Laulu-Togagae (9, 14), Turner (36, 47), Knowles (57), Yere (59, 73), Stringer (63), Brambani (69); **Goals:** Brown 7/11.
Rugby Leaguer & League Express Men of the Match: *Halifax:* Sam Barlow; *Eagles:* Simon Brown.
Penalty count: 5-11; **Half-time:** 0-22;
Referee: Tim Roby; **Attendance:** 1,513.

FINAL ELIMINATOR

Thursday 20th September 2012

LEIGH CENTURIONS 22 SHEFFIELD EAGLES 32

CENTURIONS: 1 Gregg McNally; 2 Steve Maden; 3 Stuart Littler; 4 Matt Gardner; 5 Jonathan Pownall; 6 Martyn Ridyard; 7 John Duffy; 8 Michael Ostick; 9 Bob Beswick; 10 Tom Spencer; 11 Craig Briscoe; 12 Andy Thornley; 13 Anthony Nicholson. Subs (all used): 14 Ryan Brierley; 15 Dean McGilvray; 16 James Taylor; 17 Tommy Gallagher.
Tries: Pownall (36), Thornley (50), Brierley (72), McGilvray (75); **Goals:** Ridyard 3/4.
EAGLES: 1 Quentin Laulu-Togagae; 2 Scott Turner; 3 Menzie Yere; 4 Duane Straugheir; 5 Misi Taulapapa; 6 Simon Brown; 7 Dominic Brambani; 8 Jack Howieson; 9 Andrew Henderson; 10 Mitchell Stringer; 11 Michael Knowles; 12 Sam Scott; 13 Alex Szostak. Subs (all used): 14 James Davey; 15 Peter Green; 16 Joe Hirst; 17 Liam Higgins.
Tries: Knowles (1), Straugheir (24), Taulapapa (29), Turner (47), Yere (79); **Goals:** Brown 6/8.
On report: Laulu-Togagae (55) - late challenge on McNally.
Rugby Leaguer & League Express Men of the Match: *Centurions:* Tom Spencer; *Eagles:* Michael Knowles.
Penalty count: 7-8; **Half-time:** 4-20;
Referee: Tim Roby; **Attendance:** 1,725.

GRAND FINAL

Sunday 30th September 2012

FEATHERSTONE ROVERS 16 SHEFFIELD EAGLES 20

ROVERS: 1 Ian Hardman; 2 Tangi Ropati; 3 Nathan Chappell; 4 Greg Worthington; 5 Tom Saxton; 6 Andy Kain; 7 Liam Finn; 8 Anthony England; 9 Ben Kaye; 10 James Lockwood; 11 Matty Dale; 12 Tim Spears; 13 Kyle Briggs. Subs (all used): 14 Dominic Maloney; 15 Stuart Dickens; 16 Andrew Bostock; 17 Jon Hepworth. **Tries:** Hardman (17), Hepworth (51); **Goals:** Finn 4/4.
On report:
Maloney (57) - alleged use of the elbow on Turner.
EAGLES: 1 Quentin Laulu-Togagae; 2 Misi Taulapapa; 3 Duane Straugheir; 4 Menzie Yere; 5 Scott Turner; 6 Simon Brown; 7 Dominic Brambani; 8 Jack Howieson; 9 Andrew Henderson; 10 Mitchell Stringer; 11 Michael Knowles; 12 Sam Scott; 13 Alex Szostak. Subs (all used): 14 James Davey; 15 Peter Green; 16 Dane McDonald; 17 Liam Higgins.
Tries: Turner (9), Laulu-Togagae (32), McDonald (46), Taulapapa (57); **Goals:** Brown 2/5.
Rugby Leaguer & League Express Men of the Match: *Rovers:* Ian Hardman; *Eagles:* Michael Knowles.
Penalty count: 4-6; **Half-time:** 8-10;
Referee: Tim Roby; **Attendance:** 6,409
(at Halliwell Jones Stadium, Warrington).

Sheffield's Sam Scott charges past Featherstone's Kyle Briggs during the Championship Grand Final

CHAMPIONSHIP ONE 2012
Club by Club

BARROW RAIDERS

DATE	FIXTURE	RESULT	SCORERS	LGE	ATT
12/2/12	Leigh (a) (NRC)	L48-16	t:Toal,Nixon,Campbell g:Holt(2)	N/A	1,860
19/2/12	Workington (h) (NRC)	W31-24	t:Pugh,Butler,Ostler,Dandy,Campbell g:Kaighan(5) fg:Kaighan	7th(P2)	1,366
26/2/12	Swinton (h) (NRC)	W32-16	t:Ballard,Toal(2),Nixon,Gordon,Larkin g:Holt(4)	5th(P2)	1,083
4/3/12	Whitehaven (a) (NRC)	W10-18	t:Toal(2),Harrison,Haney g:Kaighan	4th(P2)	902
11/3/12	North Wales (a)	W24-26	t:Dixon,Larkin(2),Toal,L Finch g:Holt(3)	4th	1,513
18/3/12	Doncaster (h)	W25-8	t:Campbell,Larkin,Low,Holt g:Holt(4) fg:Holt	2nd	1,365
25/3/12	Lezignan (h) (CCR3)	W32-22	t:Campbell(2),Harrison,J Finch,Haney g:Holt(6)	N/A	1,340
1/4/12	Oldham (a)	L32-26	t:Pugh,Pedley,Ostler,Nixon,J Finch g:Kaighan(3)	3rd	1,114
6/4/12	Gateshead (h)	W40-12	t:Toal(3),Campbell(3),Low g:Kaighan(6)	2nd	1,371
15/4/12	Oldham (a) (CCR4)	L26-14	t:Nixon,Harrison g:Holt(3)	N/A	773
22/4/12	Rochdale (h)	W44-18	t:Low,Ballard(2),Larkin,Nixon(2),Campbell(2) g:Holt(6)	2nd	1,332
6/5/12	South Wales (a)	W24-42	t:Gordon,Campbell,Nixon(2),Ballard(2),Ostler g:Holt(7)	3rd	337
13/5/12	Workington (h)	W20-12	t:Toal(2),Larkin g:Holt(4)	2nd	1,808
20/5/12	London Skolars (a)	W42-12	t:Campbell(2),Harrison,J Finch,Ballard,Toal,McGoff g:Shaw(7)	1st	1,159
27/5/12	Whitehaven (a)	W28-42	t:Bracek,Campbell(3),Dandy,J Finch,Shaw g:Shaw(7)	1st	1,124
10/6/12	Gateshead (a) ●	W18-40	t:Haney,Butler,Kaighan(3),Shaw,Nixon g:Shaw(6)	1st	398
17/6/12	Halifax (a) (NRCQF)	L54-24	t:Toal(2),Duffy,Backhouse g:Shaw(4)	N/A	1,448
24/6/12	North Wales (h)	W40-24	t:Harrison(3),Ballard,Campbell,Toal,Kaighan g:Shaw(6)	1st	1,438
1/7/12	London Skolars (a)	W17-30	t:Harrison,Dandy,Ballard(2),Ostler g:Shaw(5)	1st	472
15/7/12	Doncaster (a)	L28-24	t:Nixon,Campbell,Shaw,Backhouse g:Shaw(4)	2nd	997
19/7/12	Whitehaven (h)	W48-16	t:Bracek,Campbell,Haney,Nixon,Ballard,Harrison,Butler,L Finch g:Shaw(8)	1st	1,710
5/8/12	Oldham (h)	W42-16	t:Campbell,Harrison(2),Shaw(4),Haney g:Shaw(5)	1st	1,337
12/8/12	Workington (a)	L48-34	t:L Finch,Dandy,Ballard(2),Toal,Kaighan g:Shaw(5)	1st	1,710
19/8/12	Rochdale (a)	L24-18	t:Ballard,Larkin(2),Shaw g:Shaw	2nd	446
2/9/12	South Wales (h)	W34-22	t:Campbell,Ballard,Larkin,Harrison(2),McGoff g:Ballard(5)	2nd	1,245
16/9/12	Doncaster (h) (QSF)	W20-22	t:Low(2),Larkin,Dandy g:Ballard(3)	N/A	744
30/9/12	Doncaster (GF) ●●	L13-16	t:Larkin,Low g:Ballard(2) fg:Kaighan	N/A	N/A

● Played at Filtrona Park, South Shields
●● Played at Halliwell Jones Stadium, Warrington

		APP		TRIES		GOALS		FG		PTS	
	D.O.B.	ALL	Ch1	ALL	Ch1	ALL	Ch1	ALL	Ch1	ALL	Ch1
Mike Backhouse	14/6/82	15	12	2	1	0	0	0	0	8	4
Andy Ballard	10/5/86	24	19	14	13	10	10	0	0	76	72
Andy Bracek	21/3/84	18(3)	14(2)	2	2	0	0	0	0	8	8
Bradley Brennan	18/1/93	9	8	0	0	0	0	0	0	0	0
Jamie Butler	29/8/80	11(7)	8(6)	3	2	0	0	0	0	12	8
Liam Campbell	5/6/86	26	19	21	17	0	0	0	0	84	68
James Dandy	23/5/90	15(5)	10(5)	5	4	0	0	0	0	20	16
Andrew Dawson	12/3/89	5(19)	2(17)	0	0	0	0	0	0	0	0
Marc Dixon	6/3/85	3	1	1	1	0	0	0	0	4	4
Ryan Duffy	13/5/92	3(7)	3(6)	1	0	0	0	0	0	4	0
Lee Dutton	3/11/80	1(3)	1(1)	0	0	0	0	0	0	0	0
James Finch	9/7/83	6(3)	3(1)	4	3	0	0	0	0	16	12
Liam Finch	19/3/85	12(12)	10(8)	3	3	0	0	0	0	12	12
James Gordon	26/6/86	14(5)	11(3)	2	1	0	0	0	0	8	4
Lee Haney	11/6/88	15	10	5	3	0	0	0	0	20	12
Liam Harrison	3/12/82	26	19	13	10	0	0	0	0	52	40
Darren Holt	21/9/76	9(1)	5(1)	1	1	39	24	1	1	83	53
Scott Kaighan	11/11/88	18	15	5	5	15	9	2	1	52	39
Chris Larkin	20/6/86	23	17	11	10	0	0	0	0	44	40
Andy Litherland	15/4/90	1	0	0	0	0	0	0	0	0	0
Aaron Low	5/5/88	13	10	6	6	0	0	0	0	24	24
Brad Marwood	4/11/93	1(3)	1	0	0	0	0	0	0	0	0
Ruairi McGoff	5/1/85	12(5)	8(4)	2	2	0	0	0	0	8	8
James Nixon	10/8/85	23	17	11	8	0	0	0	0	44	32
Martin Ostler	21/6/80	4(15)	4(12)	4	3	0	0	0	0	16	12
Jack Pedley	9/11/89	(8)	(7)	1	1	0	0	0	0	4	4
Barry Pugh	17/10/84	5(5)	2(4)	2	1	0	0	0	0	8	4
Ryan Shaw	27/2/92	12	11	8	8	58	54	0	0	148	140
Daniel Toal	22/9/89	25	18	16	9	0	0	0	0	64	36
Andries Venter	4/10/86	2(6)	2(2)	0	0	0	0	0	0	0	0

Liam Campbell

LEAGUE RECORD
P18-W14-D0-L4-BP3
(2nd, Championship 1/
Grand Final Runners-Up)
F617, A383, Diff+234
45 points.

CHALLENGE CUP
Round Four

NORTHERN RAIL CUP
Quarter Finalists/4th, Pool 2

ATTENDANCES
Best - v Workington (Ch1 - 1,808)
Worst - v Swinton (NRC - 1,083)
Total (excluding Challenge Cup) - 15,214
Average (excluding
Challenge Cup) - 1,383
(Down by 144 on 2011, Championship)

CLUB RECORDS
MATCH RECORDS
Highest score: 138-0 v Nottingham City, 27/11/94 **Highest score against:** 0-90 v Leeds, 11/2/90 **Record attendance:** 21,651 v Salford, 15/4/38
Tries: 6 Val Cumberbatch v Batley, 21/11/36; Jim Thornburrow v Maryport, 19/2/38; Steve Rowan v Nottingham City, 15/11/92
Goals: 17 Darren Carter v Nottingham City, 27/11/94 **Points:** 42 Darren Carter v Nottingham City, 27/11/94
SEASON RECORDS
CAREER RECORDS
Tries: 50 Jim Lewthwaite 1956-57 **Goals:** 135 Joe Ball 1956-57 **Points:** 323 Jamie Rooney 2010
Tries: 352 Jim Lewthwaite 1943-57 **Goals:** 1,099 *(inc 63fg)* Darren Holt 1998-2002; 2004-2009; 2012
Points: 2,403 Darren Holt 1998-2002; 2004-2009; 2012 **Appearances:** 500 Jim Lewthwaite 1943-57

DONCASTER

DATE	FIXTURE	RESULT	SCORERS	LGE	ATT
15/2/12	Gateshead (a) (NRC)	W10-48	t:Waterman(4),Sanderson,Hodson(2),Cunningham,Butterfield,Kesik g:Waterman,Hodson(3)	N/A	243
19/2/12	York (h) (NRC)	L18-29	t:Cunningham(2),Butterfield g:Cooke(3)	4th(P2)	702
26/2/12	Sheffield (h) (NRC)	L12-56	t:Edwards,Colton g:Waterman(2)	7th(P2)	731
4/3/12	Hunslet (a) (NRC)	L20-10	t:Hughes(2) g:Cooke	7th(P2)	310
11/3/12	Whitehaven (h)	W48-16	t:Cooke(2),Waterman(2),Hyde,Kesik,Hodson,Cunningham g:Cooke(8)	2nd	781
18/3/12	Barrow (a)	L25-8	t:Hodson,Waterman	5th	1,365
24/3/12	Sharlston (h) (CCR3)	W57-10	t:Waterman(6),Hodson(2),Hyde(2),Sanderson g:Waterman(4),Hyde(2) fg:Hyde	N/A	496
1/4/12	South Wales (h)	W46-12	t:Robinson,Ely,Hodson(3),Cunningham,Bibb,Waterman,Hyde g:Cooke(4),Waterman	4th	606
6/4/12	London Skolars (h)	W58-16	t:Waterman(3),Hodson(5),Hyde,Bibb,Edwards g:Cooke(7)	4th	541
15/4/12	Bradford (a) (CCR4)	L72-6	t:Spiers g:Hyde	N/A	3,210
22/4/12	Gateshead (a)	W22-40	t:Fawcett,Spurr,Hodson(2),Butterfield(2),Kesik g:Hodson(6)	3rd	326
29/4/12	Rochdale (a)	W6-38	t:Kelly(2),Cooke,Waterman(2),Kesik,Fawcett g:Hodson(5)	1st	301
6/5/12	Rochdale (h)	W48-26	t:Colton(2),Spiers,Kesik,Fawcett(2),Spurr,Butterfield,Hodson g:Hodson(6)	1st	720
13/5/12	Oldham (h)	W40-18	t:Fawcett,Hodson,Welsh,Kelly,Cowling,Kesik,Ely g:Hodson(6)	1st	653
20/5/12	Workington (a)	L45-18	t:Cowling,Butterfield,Waterman g:Hodson(3)	2nd	804
27/5/12	North Wales (a)	W28-41	t:Spiers(2),Spurr,Cooke,Fawcett(2),Butterfield g:Hodson(6) fg:Fawcett	2nd	705
24/6/12	Gateshead (h)	W78-6	t:Ely(2),Powley,Emmett,Waterman(4),Fawcett(2),Kelly,Butterfield,Rowe,Sanderson g:Hodson(11)	3rd	656
1/7/12	South Wales (a)	W30-44	t:Waterman(2),Sanderson,Butterfield(2),Fawcett(2),Hughes g:Hodson(6)	3rd	360
15/7/12	Barrow (h)	W28-24	t:Waterman(2),Castle,Emmett,Kelly,Fawcett g:Waterman(2)	3rd	997
26/7/12	Workington (h)	W22-6	t:Robinson,Cooke,Waterman g:Cooke(5)	2nd	891
5/8/12	Whitehaven (a)	L25-18	t:Sanderson,Hughes(2) g:Cooke(3)	2nd	833
12/8/12	Oldham (a)	W22-46	t:Waterman(2),Spurr,Kelly,Colton,Fawcett(2),Castle g:Cooke(7)	2nd	500
19/8/12	North Wales (h)	W48-12	t:Cowling(2),Spurr,Hughes,Waterman(2),Fawcett,Edwards,Powley g:Cooke(5),Waterman	1st	891
2/9/12	London Skolars (a)	W8-48	t:Hughes,Fawcett,Walshaw(2),Cowling,Colton,Waterman(2),Spurr g:Cooke(6)	1st	578
16/9/12	Barrow (h) (QSF)	L20-22	t:Kesik,Hughes,Walshaw,Sanderson g:Waterman(2)	N/A	744
23/9/12	Workington (h) (FE)	W20-0	t:Spurr,Sanderson,Fawcett,Powley g:Hodson(2)	N/A	576
30/9/12	Barrow (GF) ●	W13-16	t:Sanderson,Waterman,Fawcett g:Hodson(2)	N/A	N/A

● Played at Halliwell Jones Stadium, Warrington

	D.O.B.	APP		TRIES		GOALS		FG		PTS	
		ALL	Ch1	ALL	Ch1	ALL	Ch1	ALL	Ch1	ALL	Ch1
Kyle Bibb	25/1/88	2(7)	(4)	2	2	0	0	0	0	8	8
Mike Burnett	6/10/88	(2)	0	0	0	0	0	0	0	0	0
Mick Butterfield	5/12/84	17	13	10	8	0	0	0	0	40	32
Mark Castle	19/2/86	26	21	2	2	0	0	0	0	8	8
Dean Colton	18/2/83	16(1)	12(1)	5	4	0	0	0	0	20	16
Paul Cooke	17/4/81	21	18	5	5	49	45	0	0	118	110
Danny Cowling	20/12/92	11	11	5	5	0	0	0	0	20	20
Jamie Crowther	28/10/92	(1)	0	0	0	0	0	0	0	0	0
Liam Cunningham	28/10/89	9(3)	4(3)	5	2	0	0	0	0	20	8
Grant Edwards	22/3/87	12(4)	8(4)	3	2	0	0	0	0	12	8
Jack Ely	3/12/89	5(2)	3(2)	4	4	0	0	0	0	16	16
Mike Emmett	13/5/87	18(5)	15(4)	2	2	0	0	0	0	8	8
Craig Fawcett	8/11/85	21	17	18	18	0	0	1	1	73	73
Tom Hodson	27/9/90	19	14	18	14	56	53	0	0	184	162
Carl Hughes	30/11/82	7(8)	6(6)	8	6	0	0	0	0	32	24
Kieran Hyde	10/10/89	7(1)	4(1)	5	3	3	0	1	0	27	12
Michael Kelly	23/5/89	19(1)	15(1)	6	6	0	0	0	0	24	24
Kyle Kesik	3/6/89	18(7)	15(5)	7	6	0	0	0	0	28	24
Craig Lawton	17/2/81	12(6)	9(5)	0	0	0	0	0	0	0	0
Dean O'Loughlin	25/9/82	16	12	0	0	0	0	0	0	0	0
Nathan Powley	15/8/91	(20)	(16)	3	3	0	0	0	0	12	12
Craig Robinson	30/7/85	15(8)	9(8)	2	2	0	0	0	0	8	8
Alex Rowe	11/3/85	(4)	(4)	1	1	0	0	0	0	4	4
Kyle Sampson	13/9/89	(2)	0	0	0	0	0	0	0	0	0
Stewart Sanderson	10/4/85	21(2)	16(1)	8	6	0	0	0	0	32	24
Russ Spiers	28/4/91	10(9)	9(9)	4	3	0	0	0	0	16	12
Chris Spurr	7/7/80	16	15	7	7	0	0	0	0	28	28
Andy Townend	18/12/82	(1)	0	0	0	0	0	0	0	0	0
Lucas Walshaw	4/8/92	6	6	3	3	0	0	0	0	12	12
Lee Waterman	13/4/87	27	21	36	26	13	6	0	0	170	116
Francis Welsh	9/11/92	(14)	(10)	1	1	0	0	0	0	4	4

Lee Waterman

LEAGUE RECORD
P18-W15-D0-L3-BP1
(1st, Championship 1/
Grand Final Winners, Champions)
F717, A347, Diff+370
46 points.

CHALLENGE CUP
Round Four

NORTHERN RAIL CUP
7th, Pool 2

ATTENDANCES
Best - v Barrow (Ch1 - 997)
Worst - v Sharlston (CC - 496)
Total (excluding Challenge Cup) - 9,489
Average (excluding Challenge Cup) - 730
(Up by 155 on 2011)

CLUB RECORDS

MATCH RECORDS

Highest score: 96-0 v Highfield, 20/3/94 **Highest score against:** 4-90 v Widnes, 10/6/2007
Record attendance: 10,000 v Bradford, 16/2/52 *(York Road)*; 6,528 v Castleford, 12/4/2007 *(Keepmoat Stadium)*
Tries: 6 Kane Epati v Oldham, 30/7/2006; Lee Waterman v Sharlston, 24/3/2012
Goals: 12 Tony Zelei v Nottingham City, 1/9/91; Robert Turner v Highfield, 20/3/94
Points: 32 Tony Zelei v Nottingham City, 1/9/91; Lee Waterman v Sharlston, 24/3/2012

SEASON RECORDS
CAREER RECORDS
Tries: 36 Lee Waterman 2012 **Goals:** 129 Jonny Woodcock 2002 **Points:** 306 Jonny Woodcock 2002
Tries: 112 Mark Roache 1985-97 **Goals:** 850 David Noble 1976-77; 1980-89; 1992 **Points:** 1,751 David Noble 1976-77; 1980-89; 1992
Appearances: 327 Audley Pennant 1980-83; 1985-97

GATESHEAD THUNDER

DATE	FIXTURE	RESULT	SCORERS	LGE	ATT
15/2/12	Doncaster (h) (NRC)	L10-48	t:Payne,Waller g:Clarke	N/A	243
19/2/12	Whitehaven (a) (NRC)	L44-18	t:Waller,Williams,Welton g:Clarke(3)	10th(P2)	649
26/2/12	York (a) (NRC)	L26-22	t:Mitchell(2),Hodgson,Neilson g:Clarke,Welton,Hodgson	10th(P2)	635
4/3/12	Leigh (h) (NRC) ●	L0-42		10th(P2)	276
11/3/12	South Wales (h)	L30-32	t:Williams,Brown,Mitchell,Waller,Neilson(2) g:Stamp(3)	6th	233
18/3/12	Oldham (a)	L40-14	t:Steen,Neilson,Mitchell g:Stamp	9th	539
24/3/12	York Acorn (h) (CCR3)	W28-20	t:Waller,Thackeray(2),Mitchell,Brown g:Stamp(4)	N/A	179
1/4/12	Whitehaven (h)	L18-30	t:Peers,Mitchell,Clarke g:Clarke,Stamp(2)	9th	347
6/4/12	Barrow (a)	L40-12	t:Barron,Hodgson g:Clarke,Stamp	9th	1,371
14/4/12	Swinton (a) (CCR4)	L70-10	t:McBride,Welton g:Clarke	N/A	415
22/4/12	Doncaster (h)	L22-40	t:Thackeray(3),Stamp,Condron g:Beasley	10th	326
6/5/12	Workington (a)	L58-6	t:O'Sullivan g:Beasley	10th	467
13/5/12	Rochdale (a)	L46-24	t:Beasley,Thackeray,Payne,Neilson,Waller g:Parker Jnr(2)	10th	350
27/5/12	London Skolars (a)	L48-22	t:Hodgson,Brown,Waller,Stamp g:Beasley,Parker Jnr(2)	10th	353
10/6/12	Barrow (h) ●●	L18-40	t:Parker Jnr,Stamp,Barron g:Parker Jnr(3)	10th	398
24/6/12	Doncaster (a)	L78-6	t:Waller g:Parker Jnr	10th	656
1/7/12	Rochdale (h) ●●	L0-32		10th	231
8/7/12	North Wales (a)	L46-18	t:Waller(2),Thackeray g:Stamp,Barker(2)	10th	719
15/7/12	North Wales (h) ●●	L10-60	t:Barron,Stoker g:Stamp	10th	336
22/7/12	London Skolars (h) ●●	L16-64	t:Stamp,O'Mara,Brown g:Beasley,Stamp	10th	186
12/8/12	Whitehaven (a)	L60-12	t:O'Mara,Waller g:Beasley(2)	10th	733
19/8/12	South Wales (a)	L32-10	t:Payne(2) g:Beasley	10th	219
29/8/12	Workington (h)	W24-22	t:Payne(2),Capper,Waller g:Beasley(4)	10th	256
2/9/12	Oldham (h)	L12-56	t:Brown,Waller g:Beasley,Stamp	10th	273

● Played at Kingston Park, Newcastle
●● Played at Filtrona Park, South Shields

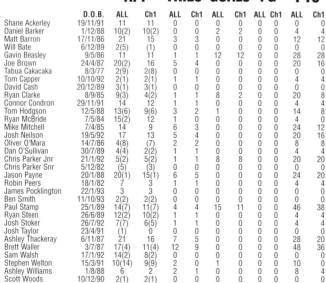

		APP		TRIES		GOALS		FG		PTS	
	D.O.B.	ALL	Ch1	ALL	Ch1	ALL	Ch1	ALL	Ch1	ALL	Ch1
Shane Ackerley	19/11/91	11	11	0	0	0	0	0	0	0	0
Daniel Barker	1/12/88	10(2)	10(2)	0	0	2	2	0	0	4	4
Matt Barron	17/11/86	21	15	3	3	0	0	0	0	12	12
Will Bate	6/12/89	2(5)	(1)	0	0	0	0	0	0	0	0
Gavin Beasley	9/5/86	11	11	1	1	12	12	0	0	28	28
Joe Brown	24/4/87	20(2)	16	5	4	0	0	0	0	20	16
Tabua Cakacaka	8/3/77	2(9)	2(8)	0	0	0	0	0	0	0	0
Tom Capper	10/10/92	2(1)	2(1)	1	1	0	0	0	0	4	4
David Cash	20/12/89	3(1)	3(1)	0	0	0	0	0	0	0	0
Ryan Clarke	8/9/85	9(3)	4(2)	1	1	8	2	0	0	20	8
Connor Condron	29/11/91	14	12	1	1	0	0	0	0	4	4
Tom Hodgson	12/5/88	13(6)	9(6)	3	2	1	0	0	0	14	8
Ryan McBride	7/5/84	15(2)	12	1	0	0	0	0	0	4	0
Mike Mitchell	7/4/85	14	9	6	3	0	0	0	0	24	12
Josh Neilson	19/5/92	17	13	5	4	0	0	0	0	20	16
Oliver O'Mara	14/7/86	4(8)	(7)	2	2	0	0	0	0	8	8
Dan O'Sullivan	30/7/89	4(4)	2(2)	1	1	0	0	0	0	4	4
Chris Parker Jnr	21/1/92	5(2)	5(2)	1	1	8	8	0	0	20	20
Chris Parker Snr	5/12/82	(5)	(3)	0	0	0	0	0	0	0	0
Jason Payne	20/1/88	20(1)	15(1)	6	5	0	0	0	0	24	20
Robin Peers	18/1/82	7	3	1	1	0	0	0	0	4	4
James Pocklington	22/1/93	3	3	0	0	0	0	0	0	0	0
Ben Smith	11/10/93	2(2)	2(2)	0	0	0	0	0	0	0	0
Paul Stamp	25/1/89	14(7)	11(7)	4	4	15	11	0	0	46	38
Ryan Steen	26/6/89	12(2)	10(2)	1	1	0	0	0	0	4	4
Josh Stoker	26/7/92	7(7)	6(5)	1	1	0	0	0	0	4	4
Josh Taylor	23/4/91	(1)	0	0	0	0	0	0	0	0	0
Ashley Thackeray	6/11/87	21	16	7	5	0	0	0	0	28	20
Brett Waller	3/7/87	17(4)	11(4)	12	9	0	0	0	0	48	36
Sam Walsh	17/1/92	14(2)	8(2)	0	0	0	0	0	0	0	0
Stephen Welton	15/3/91	10(14)	9(9)	2	0	1	0	0	0	10	0
Ashley Williams	1/8/88	6	2	2	1	0	0	0	0	8	4
Scott Woods	10/12/90	2(1)	2(1)	0	0	0	0	0	0	0	0

Brett Waller

LEAGUE RECORD
P18-W1-D0-L17-BP2
(10th, Championship 1)
F274, A824, Diff-550
5 points.

CHALLENGE CUP
Round Four

NORTHERN RAIL CUP
10th, Pool 2

ATTENDANCES
Best - v Barrow (Ch1 - 398)
Worst - v York Acorn (CC - 179)
Total (excluding Challenge Cup) - 3,105
Average (excluding Challenge Cup) - 282
(Down by 29 on 2011)

CLUB RECORDS	**Highest score:** 66-6 v Wakefield, 5/9/99 **Highest score against:** 0-132 v Blackpool Panthers, 16/5/2010 **Record attendance:** 6,631 v Bradford, 16/5/99
MATCH RECORDS	**Tries:** 5 Andy Walker v London Skolars, 22/6/2003 **Goals:** 11 Ian Herron v Wakefield, 5/9/99 **Points:** 26 Ian Herron v Wakefield, 5/9/99
SEASON RECORDS	**Tries:** 25 Matt Daylight 1999 **Goals:** 129 *(inc 1fg)* Dan Russell 2008 **Points:** 293 Dan Russell 2008
CAREER RECORDS	**Tries:** 74 Kevin Neighbour 2001-2006; 2008-2010 **Goals:** 151 Paul Thorman 2001-2004 **Points:** 387 Paul Thorman 2001-2004 **Appearances:** 218 Robin Peers 2002-2012

LONDON SKOLARS

DATE	FIXTURE	RESULT	SCORERS	LGE	ATT
19/2/12	Batley (a) (NRC)	L50-16	t:Adebisi,B Bolger,Smith g:McLean,Skee	9th(P1)	601
26/2/12	South Wales (a) (NRC)	W30-38	t:Robinson,Bryan,Price,Adebisi,R Thomas,Skee,McLean g:Skee(5)	6th(P1)	205
4/3/12	Halifax (h) (NRC)	L12-16	t:Aggrey,Adebisi g:Skee(2)	7th(P1)	613
11/3/12	Rochdale (a)	L36-4	t:Price	10th	359
18/3/12	North Wales (h)	W66-16	t:Skee(2),Bryan,Paxton,Price,Thorman,Bate,Hopkins(2),McNamara,M Thomas, R Thomas g:Skee(9)	4th	535
24/3/12	Leigh (h) (CCR3)	L26-43	t:Junor,Hopkins,Purslow,Adebisi,Skee g:Skee(3)	N/A	376
1/4/12	Workington (a)	L27-20	t:McNamara,Adebisi(3) g:Skee(2)	7th	439
6/4/12	Doncaster (a)	L58-16	t:Anthony(2),Hopkins g:Thorman(2)	7th	541
9/4/12	Toulouse (h) (NRC)	L16-32	t:Junor,Bloom,Fletcher g:McLean(2)	7th(P1)	242
22/4/12	Oldham (h)	D20-20	t:Anthony,Smith,Skee g:Skee(4)	7th	492
6/5/12	Whitehaven (a)	L36-28	t:Adebisi(2),Hopkins,Williams,Worrincy g:Skee(4)	7th	627
20/5/12	Barrow (a)	L42-12	t:Worrincy,R Thomas g:Skee(2)	8th	1,159
27/5/12	Gateshead (h)	W48-22	t:Adebisi(3),Hopkins(2),Bryan,Worrincy,Anthony,Smith g:Skee(6)	7th	353
10/6/12	Workington (h)	L12-44	t:Anthony,Worrincy g:Skee(2)	8th	623
24/6/12	South Wales (a)	W32-36	t:McLean(2),Colleran,Skee(2),Price g:Skee(6)	7th	307
1/7/12	Barrow (h)	L17-30	t:Anthony,McLean,Hopkins g:Skee(2) fg:McLean	7th	472
15/7/12	Oldham (a)	L25-24	t:Colleran,Price(2),Bryan,M Thomas g:Skee(2)	8th	487
22/7/12	Gateshead (a) ●	W16-64	t:Price(3),Junor(3),Thorman,Hopkins(2),McLean,M Thomas,Skee g:Skee(8)	8th	186
29/7/12	South Wales (h)	W64-6	t:M Thomas,Skee(2),Bryan,Paxton,Hopkins(2),B Bolger,Williams,Junor,Thorman g:Skee(10)	7th	290
5/8/12	Rochdale (h)	W56-36	t:Bryan,Hopkins,Skee,Anthony,Adebisi,McLean(3),M Thomas g:Skee(10)	5th	407
12/8/12	North Wales (a)	L40-22	t:Price,Anthony(2),Bryan g:Skee(3)	7th	800
24/8/12	Whitehaven (h)	W41-26	t:Thorman,Bryan,Skee,Hopkins,R Thomas,McLean g:Skee(8) fg:Thorman	6th	1,174
2/9/12	Doncaster (h)	L8-48	t:Paxton(2)	7th	578

● Played at Filtrona Park, South Shields

		APP		TRIES		GOALS		FG		PTS	
	D.O.B.	ALL	Ch1	ALL	Ch1	ALL	Ch1	ALL	Ch1	ALL	Ch1
Ade Adebisi	7/1/86	16	12	13	9	0	0	0	0	52	36
Austen Aggrey	12/5/79	2(11)	1(9)	1	0	0	0	0	0	4	0
James Anthony	18/2/86	21	18	9	9	0	0	0	0	36	36
Dave Arnot	27/6/88	10(1)	9	0	0	0	0	0	0	0	0
Alex Bate	25/4/91	9(5)	6(4)	1	1	0	0	0	0	4	4
Oliver Bloom	16/4/86	1(4)	(4)	1	0	0	0	0	0	4	0
Ben Bolger	13/9/89	3	2	2	1	0	0	0	0	8	4
Sam Bolger	1/11/91	(1)	(1)	0	0	0	0	0	0	0	0
Lamont Bryan	12/4/88	18	15	8	7	0	0	0	0	32	28
Danny Burke	26/7/86	1(1)	0	0	0	0	0	0	0	0	0
Dion Chapman	16/2/92	(1)	0	0	0	0	0	0	0	0	0
Will Colleran	24/5/91	4	3	2	2	0	0	0	0	8	8
James Fletcher	25/2/87	(1)	0	1	0	0	0	0	0	4	0
Brad Hopkins	22/10/89	17(1)	16(1)	14	13	0	0	0	0	56	52
Lameck Juma	6/12/90	3	0	0	0	0	0	0	0	0	0
Smokie Junor	15/4/90	8	6	6	4	0	0	0	0	24	16
Olsi Krasniqi	26/6/92	1	1	0	0	0	0	0	0	0	0
Joe Mbu	6/11/83	1(4)	1(4)	0	0	0	0	0	0	0	0
Connor McDonald	27/8/88	(1)	0	0	0	0	0	0	0	0	0
Andy McLean	28/7/82	18	13	9	8	3	0	1	1	43	33
Chris McNamara	13/7/88	7	4	2	2	0	0	0	0	8	8
Jaroslaw Obuchowski	20/9/90	1	0	0	0	0	0	0	0	0	0
John Paxton	20/4/85	21	18	4	4	0	0	0	0	16	16
Joe Price	7/10/85	20	17	10	9	0	0	0	0	40	36
Oliver Purslow	17/9/87	5(11)	5(7)	1	0	0	0	0	0	4	0
Joe Ridley	14/4/91	3(2)	2(1)	0	0	0	0	0	0	0	0
Louis Robinson	9/1/91	2(5)	(3)	1	0	0	0	0	0	4	0
James Roche	14/7/85	5(4)	4(4)	0	0	0	0	0	0	0	0
Dylan Skee	13/1/86	22	18	12	10	89	78	0	0	226	196
Aaron Small	28/10/91	1	0	0	0	0	0	0	0	0	0
Martyn Smith	27/2/92	4(17)	4(14)	3	2	0	0	0	0	12	8
Michael Sykes	10/12/86	1(8)	1(8)	0	0	0	0	0	0	0	0
Matt Thomas	8/1/80	13(5)	10(5)	5	5	0	0	0	0	20	20
Rob Thomas	9/10/90	9(9)	6(8)	4	3	0	0	0	0	16	12
Neil Thorman	4/6/84	22	18	4	4	2	2	1	1	21	21
Andre Vine	9/11/91	(1)	0	0	0	0	0	0	0	0	0
Dave Williams	29/1/87	21	17	2	2	0	0	0	0	8	8
Michael Worrincy	16/2/86	8	7	4	4	0	0	0	0	16	16

Dylan Skee

LEAGUE RECORD
P18-W7-D1-L10-BP3
(7th, Championship 1)
F558, A560, Diff-2
26 points.

CHALLENGE CUP
Round Three

NORTHERN RAIL CUP
7th, Pool 1

ATTENDANCES
Best - v Whitehaven (Ch1 - 1,174)
Worst - v Toulouse (NRC - 242)
Total (excluding Challenge Cup) - 5,779
Average (excluding Challenge Cup) - 525
(Up by 16 on 2011)

CLUB RECORDS MATCH RECORDS	**Highest score:** 70-28 v St Albans, 19/3/2006 **Highest score against:** 4-98 v Sheffield, 3/8/2003 **Record attendance:** 1,427 v Keighley, 29/8/2008
	Tries: 5 Mark Cantoni v Gateshead, 27/6/2004
	Goals: 10 Jake Johnstone v Gateshead, 24/8/2003; Dylan Skee v South Wales, 29/7/2012; Dylan Skee v Rochdale, 5/8/2012
	Points: 28 Dylan Skee v South Wales, 29/7/2012
SEASON RECORDS CAREER RECORDS	**Tries:** 20 Mark Cantoni 2004 **Goals:** 89 Dylan Skee 2012 **Points:** 226 Dylan Skee 2012
	Tries: 57 Austen Aggrey 2004-2012 **Goals:** 223 *(inc 2fg)* Paul Thorman 2007-2010 **Points:** 488 Paul Thorman 2007-2010
	Appearances: 198 Gareth Honor 2003-2011

NORTH WALES CRUSADERS

DATE	FIXTURE	RESULT	SCORERS	LGE	ATT
11/3/12	Barrow (h)	L24-26	t:Moulsdale,Durbin,Massam(2),Brennan g:Brennan(2)	7th	1,513
18/3/12	London Skolars (a)	L66-16	t:D Hulme(2),Hudson g:Johnson,Brennan	10th	535
24/3/12	Toulouse (h) (CCR3)	W28-10	t:Morrison,D Hulme(3),Massam,Moulsdale,Johnson	N/A	567
1/4/12	Rochdale (h)	L18-54	t:Wilkes(2),Massam,D Hulme g:Smith	10th	1,047
9/4/12	South Wales (h)	W34-22	t:Moulsdale,Johnson(2),Brennan(2),Smith,I Brown g:Cross,Smith(2)	9th	1,204
15/4/12	Wigan (a) (CCR4)	L98-4	t:O Brown	N/A	4,198
22/4/12	Workington (a)	L58-0		9th	776
6/5/12	Oldham (a)	W32-36	t:Clay,Moulsdale,Broadbent,Clarke,Morrison,Cross,Massam g:Cross(4)	8th	580
13/5/12	Whitehaven (h)	L10-17	t:Sheen(2) g:Broadbent	7th	804
27/5/12	Doncaster (h)	L28-41	t:Stephens,Sheen,Moulsdale,Massam,Clay g:Broadbent(4)	9th	705
10/6/12	Oldham (h)	W30-28	t:Brennan(3),Sheen,Clay,Smith g:Broadbent,Johnson(2)	7th	822
24/6/12	Barrow (a)	L40-24	t:Gorski(2),Smith,Brennan g:Johnson(4)	9th	1,438
1/7/12	Workington (h)	L20-30	t:Wilkes,Massam,D Hulme,McConnell g:Johnson(2)	8th	733
8/7/12	Gateshead (h)	W46-18	t:D Hulme(2),Gorski,Clarke,Durbin,L Hulme,Smith,McConnell g:Johnson(7)	7th	719
15/7/12	Gateshead (a) ●	W10-60	t:Moulsdale(3),Sheen(3),Adamson,Brennan,J Walker,L Hulme g:Johnson(10)	7th	336
22/7/12	Rochdale (a)	L34-6	t:Sheen g:Johnson	7th	648
5/8/12	South Wales (a)	W24-36	t:Gorski,Durbin,Massam,Clay(2),L Hulme,Smith g:Johnson(4)	8th	687
12/8/12	London Skolars (h)	W40-22	t:Brennan,J Walker,Massam,Weaver,Moulsdale,Smith,Clay g:Johnson(6)	6th	800
19/8/12	Doncaster (a)	L48-12	t:Brennan,Moulsdale g:Johnson(2)	7th	891
2/9/12	Whitehaven (a)	L58-20	t:Gorski,Massam(2),Stephens g:Johnson(2)	8th	701

● Played at Filtrona Park, South Shields

		APP		TRIES		GOALS		FG		PTS	
	D.O.B.	ALL	Ch1	ALL	Ch1	ALL	Ch1	ALL	Ch1	ALL	Ch1
Toby Adamson	28/5/90	7(1)	7(1)	1	1	0	0	0	0	4	4
Leon Brennan	11/2/87	17	15	10	10	3	3	0	0	46	46
Sam Broadbent	28/10/88	4(1)	3(1)	1	1	6	6	0	0	16	16
Iwan Brown	3/3/86	7(4)	5(4)	1	1	0	0	0	0	4	4
Owain Brown	30/7/84	4(11)	2(11)	1	0	0	0	0	0	4	0
Jamie Clarke	15/11/84	4(7)	3(7)	2	2	0	0	0	0	8	8
Adam Clay	7/10/90	10	10	6	6	0	0	0	0	24	24
Ian Cross	15/9/89	6(1)	5(1)	1	1	5	5	0	0	14	14
Jamie Durbin	7/9/84	13	12	3	3	0	0	0	0	12	12
Gareth Frodsham	18/12/89	1(1)	1(1)	0	0	0	0	0	0	0	0
Andy Gorski	31/3/81	10	10	5	5	0	0	0	0	20	20
Owain Griffiths	18/7/91	(8)	(7)	0	0	0	0	0	0	0	0
Kurt Haggerty	8/1/89	1	1	0	0	0	0	0	0	0	0
Mark Hamon	24/11/90	1(1)	1	0	0	0	0	0	0	0	0
Lee Hudson	28/9/90	15(3)	13(3)	1	1	0	0	0	0	4	4
Danny Hulme	15/2/91	6(3)	5(3)	9	6	0	0	0	0	36	24
Liam Hulme	28/10/91	5(1)	5(1)	3	3	0	0	0	0	12	12
Tommy Johnson	19/4/91	16(4)	15(3)	3	2	41	41	0	0	94	90
Craig Lawton	5/11/90	(1)	0	0	0	0	0	0	0	0	0
Chris Lunt	18/12/90	(2)	(2)	0	0	0	0	0	0	0	0
Rob Massam	29/11/87	19	17	11	10	0	0	0	0	44	40
Aaron McCloskey	20/7/88	(1)	(1)	0	0	0	0	0	0	0	0
Dave McConnell	25/3/81	4(1)	4(1)	2	2	0	0	0	0	8	8
Anthony Morrison	12/4/91	9(6)	8(6)	2	1	0	0	0	0	8	4
Andrew Moulsdale	22/1/87	19(1)	17(1)	10	9	0	0	0	0	40	36
David Orwell	31/1/91	(2)	(2)	0	0	0	0	0	0	0	0
Christiaan Roets	5/9/80	11	10	0	0	0	0	0	0	0	0
Billy Sheen	8/12/89	7(7)	7(5)	8	8	0	0	0	0	32	32
Jono Smith	12/11/88	15(1)	13(1)	6	6	3	3	0	0	30	30
Simon Stephens	11/10/83	14	14	2	2	0	0	0	0	8	8
Alex Trumper	5/4/91	(3)	(3)	0	0	0	0	0	0	0	0
Chris Tyrer	10/10/85	2(7)	2(5)	0	0	0	0	0	0	0	0
Chris Walker	25/5/87	1	1	0	0	0	0	0	0	0	0
Jonny Walker	26/9/86	20	18	2	2	0	0	0	0	8	8
Adam Walsh	27/6/87	3	2	0	0	0	0	0	0	0	0
Lewys Weaver	14/9/93	(2)	(2)	1	1	0	0	0	0	4	4
Kriss Wilkes	22/11/90	9	8	3	3	0	0	0	0	12	12

Danny Hulme

LEAGUE RECORD
P18-W7-D0-L11-BP3
(8th, Championship 1)
F460, A628, Diff-168
24 points.

CHALLENGE CUP
Round Four

NORTHERN RAIL CUP
Not entered

ATTENDANCES
Best - v Barrow (Ch1 - 1,513)
Worst - v Toulouse (CC - 567)
Total (excluding Challenge Cup) - 8,347
Average (excluding Challenge Cup) - 927

CLUB RECORDS MATCH RECORDS	**Highest score:** 60-10 v Gateshead, 15/7/2012 **Highest score against:** 4-98 v Wigan, 15/4/2012 **Record attendance:** 1,513 v Barrow, 11/3/2012 **Tries:** 3 Danny Hulme v Toulouse, 24/3/2012; Leon Brennan v Oldham, 10/6/2012; Andrew Moulsdale v Gateshead, 15/7/2012; Billy Sheen v Gateshead, 15/7/2012 **Goals:** 10 Tommy Johnson v Gateshead, 15/7/2012 **Points:** 20 Tommy Johnson v Gateshead, 15/7/2012
SEASON RECORDS CAREER RECORDS	**Tries:** 11 Rob Massam 2012 **Goals:** 41 Tommy Johnson 2012 **Points:** 94 Tommy Johnson 2012 **Tries:** 11 Rob Massam 2012 **Goals:** 41 Tommy Johnson 2012 **Points:** 94 Tommy Johnson 2012 **Appearances:** 20 Tommy Johnson 2012; Andrew Moulsdale 2012; Jonny Walker 2012

OLDHAM

DATE	FIXTURE	RESULT	SCORERS	LGE	ATT
15/2/12	Featherstone (h) (NRC)	L0-68		N/A	672
19/2/12	South Wales (a) (NRC)	D36-36	t:Clough(2),Dallimore(2),Johnson,Fogarty g:Dallimore(6)	7th(P1)	849
26/2/12	Dewsbury (h) (NRC)	L28-30	t:Gillam(3),N Roden,Clough g:Dallimore(4)	8th(P1)	573
4/3/12	Keighley (a) (NRC)	L26-12	t:Robinson,Greenwood g:Dallimore(2)	9th(P1)	827
11/3/12	Workington (a)	W14-24	t:Gillam,Greenwood,McCully,Clarke g:Dallimore(4)	3rd	760
18/3/12	Gateshead (h)	W40-14	t:P Smith,Ballard(2),N Roden,Greenwood(2),Noone g:Dallimore(6)	1st	539
23/3/12	Egremont (a) (CCR3)	W14-22	t:Clough,Clarke,Whitmore,Thompson g:Dallimore(3)	N/A	468
1/4/12	Barrow (h)	W32-26	t:Onyango,Ellison,Whitmore,Dallimore,Cookson,Greenwood g:Dallimore(4)	1st	1,114
6/4/12	Rochdale (a)	L18-10	t:Onyango,Thompson g:Dallimore	3rd	1,020
15/4/12	Barrow (h) (CCR4)	W26-14	t:Thompson,Noone,Fogarty,Greenwood g:Dallimore(5)	N/A	773
22/4/12	London Skolars (a)	D20-20	t:Greenwood(2),Thompson(2) g:Dallimore(2)	4th	492
27/4/12	St Helens (h) (CCR5) ●	L0-76		N/A	5,746
6/5/12	North Wales (h)	L32-36	t:Robinson,Clough,Fogarty(2),Ellison,Greenwood g:Dallimore(4)	4th	580
13/5/12	Doncaster (h)	L40-18	t:Robinson,Ward,Cookson,Greenwood g:Dallimore	5th	653
20/5/12	Whitehaven (h)	L16-26	t:Cookson(2),Brocklehurst g:Dallimore,Holroyd	5th	624
26/5/12	South Wales (h)	L30-35	t:Reed,Clough,Ward,Greenwood,Tootill g:Holroyd(5)	5th	471
10/6/12	North Wales (a)	L30-28	t:Ward(2),Ellison,Whitmore,Greenwood g:Holroyde(4)	5th	822
24/6/12	Rochdale (h)	L4-30	t:Greenwood	6th	599
1/7/12	Whitehaven (a)	L42-20	t:McCully,Thompson,Dallimore,Ward g:Dallimore(2)	6th	701
15/7/12	London Skolars (h)	W25-24	t:Murphy,Dallimore,Greenwood(2) g:Dallimore(4) fg:N Roden	6th	487
22/7/12	South Wales (a)	W12-44	t:Cookson,P Smith,Thompson(2),Dallimore,Gillam,Murphy,McCully g:Dallimore(6)	6th	196
5/8/12	Barrow (a)	L42-16	t:Dallimore,Gilchrist,P Smith g:Dallimore(2)	7th	1,337
12/8/12	Doncaster (h)	L22-46	t:Greenwood(3),Clough g:Dallimore(3)	8th	500
19/8/12	Workington (h)	W28-18	t:Greenwood,N Roden,Ward,Onyango g:Dallimore(6)	6th	538
2/9/12	Gateshead (a)	W12-56	t:Thompson(3),Brocklehurst(2),Clough,Greenwood,Dallimore,Joy,Onyango g:Dallimore(8)	6th	273
9/9/12	Workington (a) (EPO)	L34-29	t:N Roden,Thompson,P Smith(3) g:Dallimore(4) fg:N Roden	N/A	563

● Played at Langtree Park

		APP		TRIES		GOALS		FG		PTS	
	D.O.B.	ALL	Ch1	ALL	Ch1	ALL	Ch1	ALL	Ch1	ALL	Ch1
Jamie Acton	4/4/92	3(3)	3(2)	0	0	0	0	0	0	0	0
Paul Ballard	4/9/84	5	3	2	2	0	0	0	0	8	8
Valu Bentley	9/10/82	13(4)	9(4)	0	0	0	0	0	0	0	0
Jason Boults	7/9/83	26	19	0	0	0	0	0	0	0	0
Mark Brocklehurst	27/9/86	13	10	3	3	0	0	0	0	12	12
Chris Clarke	29/3/89	15(3)	9(3)	2	1	0	0	0	0	8	4
John Clough	13/9/84	17(7)	13(5)	8	4	0	0	0	0	32	16
David Cookson	1/10/88	18	12	5	5	0	0	0	0	20	20
Sam Cunningham	4/4/90	1(1)	1(1)	0	0	0	0	0	0	0	0
Jamie Dallimore	20/8/88	23	16	8	6	78	58	0	0	188	140
Dave Ellison	2/4/82	(18)	(11)	3	3	0	0	0	0	12	12
Matthew Fogarty	16/3/92	9	3	4	2	0	0	0	0	16	8
Rob Foxen	12/12/87	4	4	0	0	0	0	0	0	0	0
Liam Gilchrist	28/3/89	10(6)	6(6)	1	1	0	0	0	0	4	4
John Gillam	15/10/84	9	7	5	2	0	0	0	0	20	8
Miles Greenwood	30/7/87	25	18	20	18	0	0	0	0	80	72
Graham Holroyd	25/10/75	5	5	0	0	6	6	0	0	12	12
Chris Holroyde	6/12/89	2	2	0	0	4	4	0	0	8	8
Bruce Johnson	26/1/84	2(6)	1(2)	1	0	0	0	0	0	4	0
Phil Joy	4/9/91	1(1)	1(1)	1	1	0	0	0	0	4	4
Danny Langtree	18/2/91	(2)	(2)	0	0	0	0	0	0	0	0
Mark McCully	24/10/79	17(1)	15(1)	3	3	0	0	0	0	12	12
Chris Murphy	19/9/89	4	3	2	2	0	0	0	0	8	8
Paul Noone	22/4/81	17(2)	14(1)	2	1	0	0	0	0	8	4
Lucas Onyango	12/4/81	11	9	4	4	0	0	0	0	16	16
Lewis Reed	24/3/91	3(1)	3(1)	1	1	0	0	0	0	4	4
Jack Reid	24/3/91	1	0	0	0	0	0	0	0	0	0
Tom Rigby	6/12/90	1	0	0	0	0	0	0	0	0	0
Shaun Robinson	13/7/89	8	4	3	2	0	0	0	0	12	8
Colton Roche	23/6/93	1(1)	1(1)	0	0	0	0	0	0	0	0
Martin Roden	26/12/79	13(3)	10(1)	0	0	0	0	0	0	0	0
Neil Roden	9/4/80	17	13	4	3	0	0	2	2	18	14
Daniel Smith	20/3/93	(4)	(4)	0	0	0	0	0	0	0	0
Paul Smith	17/5/77	16(1)	14	6	6	0	0	0	0	24	24
Luke Stenchion	15/2/86	(4)	(4)	0	0	0	0	0	0	0	0
Matty Syron	24/2/91	(7)	(4)	0	0	0	0	0	0	0	0
Alex Thompson	11/2/90	8(11)	4(9)	12	10	0	0	0	0	48	40
David Tootill	22/5/86	3	3	1	1	0	0	0	0	4	4
Michael Ward	10/2/91	11(7)	8(6)	6	6	0	0	0	0	24	24
Danny Whitmore	22/12/88	6(11)	4(7)	3	2	0	0	0	0	12	8

Miles Greenwood

LEAGUE RECORD
P18-W7-D1-L10-BP5
(6th, Championship 1/
Elimination Play-Off)
F465, A485, Diff-20
28 points.

CHALLENGE CUP
Round Five

NORTHERN RAIL CUP
10th, Pool 1

ATTENDANCES
Best - v Barrow (Ch1 - 1,114)
Worst - v South Wales (Ch1 - 471)
Total (excluding Challenge Cup) - 6,697
Average (excluding Challenge Cup) - 609
(Down by 18 on 2011)

CLUB RECORDS	**Highest score:** 80-6 v Blackwood, 7/3/2010 **Highest score against:** 0-84 v Widnes, 25/7/99
MATCH RECORDS	**Record attendance:** 28,000 v Huddersfield, 24/2/1912 *(Watersheddings)*; 1,275 v York, 12/9/2010 *(Whitebank Stadium)*
	Tries: 7 James Miller v Barry, 31/10/1908
	Goals: 14 Bernard Ganley v Liverpool City, 4/4/59 **Points:** 34 Andy Ballard v London Skolars, 2/5/2009; Chris Baines v Hunslet, 20/9/2009
SEASON RECORDS	**Tries:** 49 Reg Farrar 1921-22 **Goals:** 200 Bernard Ganley 1957-58 **Points:** 412 Bernard Ganley 1957-58
CAREER RECORDS	**Tries:** 174 Alan Davies 1950-61 **Goals:** 1,358 Bernard Ganley 1951-61 **Points:** 2,761 Bernard Ganley 1951-61 **Appearances:** 627 Joe Ferguson 1899-1923

ROCHDALE HORNETS

DATE	FIXTURE	RESULT	SCORERS	LGE	ATT
19/2/12	Halifax (a) (NRC)	L38-6	t:McDermott g:Crook	8th(P1)	1,881
26/2/12	Keighley (h) (NRC)	L16-40	t:Pyke(2),Bowman g:Crook,Hough	10th(P1)	604
4/3/12	Dewsbury (a) (NRC)	L32-10	t:Leather,McDermott g:Crook	10th(P1)	701
11/3/12	London Skolars (h)	W36-4	t:Middlehurst(3),English,O'Connor,McDermott,Bannister g:Crook(4)	1st	359
18/3/12	Whitehaven (a)	L30-10	t:Newton,Bloomfield g:Baines	6th	714
25/3/12	East Hull (a) (CCR3) ●	W20-48	t:Middlehurst(3),Baines,Cookson,Wood,O'Connor,Leather g:Baines(8)	N/A	303
1/4/12	North Wales (a)	W18-54	t:O'Connor,Hobson,Braddish,Roper,Leather(2),Hough,Cookson,Bowman g:Baines(9)	5th	1,047
6/4/12	Oldham (h)	W18-10	t:English,Davies,Baines,McDermott g:Hough	5th	1,020
15/4/12	Leigh (a) (CCR4)	L68-18	t:Bannister,Lucas,O'Connor g:Baines(2),Hough	N/A	1,229
22/4/12	Barrow (a)	L44-18	t:Davies,Crook,McDermott g:Crook(3)	5th	1,332
29/4/12	Doncaster (h)	L6-38	t:Baines g:Crook	6th	301
6/5/12	Doncaster (a)	L48-26	t:Bloomfield(2),Gorton,O'Connor,Braddish g:Crook(3)	6th	720
9/5/12	South Wales (h) (NRC)	W46-24	t:Wood,Crook,Clarke(2),Middlehurst,Leather(2),Chadwick g:Crook(7)	9th(P1)	238
13/5/12	Gateshead (h)	W46-24	t:Bloomfield,Leather,Crook(2),Middlehurst,Davies,English(2) g:Crook(7)	6th	350
20/5/12	South Wales (a)	L32-30	t:Gorton(2),English,Davies,Cookson,McDermott g:Crook(3)	6th	557
3/6/12	Workington (h)	L24-37	t:Clarke,English,Bloomfield,Cookson,Davies g:Crook(2)	6th	512
24/6/12	Oldham (a)	W4-30	t:Leather(3),English,Braddish g:Crook(5)	5th	599
1/7/12	Gateshead (a) ●●	W0-32	t:Crook(2),Middlehurst(2),Leather,Hough g:Crook(4)	5th	231
22/7/12	North Wales (h)	W34-6	t:Bloomfield(2),Roper,English(2),Leather g:Crook(5)	5th	648
29/7/12	Whitehaven (h)	L12-31	t:Crook,Leather g:Crook(2)	5th	581
5/8/12	London Skolars (a)	L56-36	t:Bannister,Donoghue,Bloomfield,McDermott(2),Ekis g:Crook(6)	6th	407
12/8/12	South Wales (h)	W42-12	t:Bloomfield(3),Roper,Leather(2),Bannister,Taylor g:Crook(5)	5th	311
19/8/12	Barrow (h)	W24-18	t:Donoghue(2),Crook,English,Leather g:Crook(2)	5th	446
2/9/12	Workington (a)	L48-18	t:Bowman,Roper,Unsworth g:Crook(3)	5th	514
9/9/12	Whitehaven (a) (EPO)	L40-12	t:Roper,Stewart g:Crook(2)	N/A	601

● Played at Spotland
●● Played at Filtrona Park, South Shields

		APP		TRIES		GOALS		FG		PTS	
	D.O.B.	ALL	Ch1	ALL	Ch1	ALL	Ch1	ALL	Ch1	ALL	Ch1
Chris Baines	25/9/84	18(3)	14(2)	3	2	20	10	0	0	52	28
Steve Bannister	10/10/87	9(3)	7(2)	4	3	0	0	0	0	16	12
Dale Bloomfield	24/10/87	20	18	11	11	0	0	0	0	44	44
Adam Bowman	12/11/87	8(13)	6(10)	3	2	0	0	0	0	12	8
Phil Braddish	30/7/82	3(12)	2(12)	3	3	0	0	0	0	12	12
Paul Brearley	5/2/92	(1)	0	0	0	0	0	0	0	0	0
Ryan Brown	17/2/92	4(2)	4(1)	0	0	0	0	0	0	0	0
Will Chadwick	24/9/92	3(3)	1(3)	1	0	0	0	0	0	4	0
Barry Clarke	11/7/92	4	3	3	1	0	0	0	0	12	4
Chris Clough	20/1/87	1	1	0	0	0	0	0	0	0	0
John Cookson	12/12/84	20(2)	17(1)	4	3	0	0	0	0	16	12
Paul Crook	28/8/86	21	17	8	7	67	57	0	0	166	142
Daniel Davies	14/7/87	10	9	5	5	0	0	0	0	20	20
Dayne Donoghue	22/9/88	21	17	3	3	0	0	0	0	12	12
Danny Ekis	17/1/82	(7)	(6)	1	1	0	0	0	0	4	4
Wayne English	8/3/80	20	16	10	10	0	0	0	0	40	40
Joe Fitzpatrick	22/10/85	2(3)	1(3)	0	0	0	0	0	0	0	0
Dean Gorton	16/1/84	7(1)	5(1)	3	3	0	0	0	0	12	12
Stephen Hickey	9/10/91	(1)	(1)	0	0	0	0	0	0	0	0
Mark Hobson	14/1/87	16(3)	12(3)	1	1	0	0	0	0	4	4
Chris Hough	30/8/81	12(6)	10(4)	2	2	3	1	0	0	14	10
Craig Johnson	17/4/87	2	0	0	0	0	0	0	0	0	0
Fraser Jones-Lake	30/11/92	3(1)	2(1)	0	0	0	0	0	0	0	0
Mark Kellett	14/2/88	1	0	0	0	0	0	0	0	0	0
Jonny Leather	29/7/89	13(3)	10(2)	16	12	0	0	0	0	64	48
Stephen Lucas	22/11/89	(7)	(2)	1	0	0	0	0	0	4	0
Ben Marsden	11/5/90	1	0	0	0	0	0	0	0	0	0
Steve McDermott	27/12/85	9(9)	7(6)	8	6	0	0	0	0	32	24
Gary Middlehurst	24/10/83	18	13	10	6	0	0	0	0	40	24
Henry Mitchell	18/11/89	(1)	(1)	0	0	0	0	0	0	0	0
Charles Moore	10/10/92	(1)	0	0	0	0	0	0	0	0	0
Dave Newton	22/12/81	15(4)	11(4)	1	1	0	0	0	0	4	4
Paul O'Connor	3/6/84	11(1)	7(1)	5	3	0	0	0	0	20	12
Danny Price	5/10/92	2(1)	2(1)	0	0	0	0	0	0	0	0
Danny Pyke	1/10/86	3	0	2	0	0	0	0	0	8	0
Steve Roper	10/11/86	16	12	5	5	0	0	0	0	20	20
Danny Samuel	8/8/85	4(1)	4(1)	0	0	0	0	0	0	0	0
Anthony Stewart	5/3/79	12	9	1	0	0	0	0	0	4	0
Andy Taylor	29/6/90	5	4	1	1	0	0	0	0	4	4
Damien Turner	29/10/86	(1)	0	0	0	0	0	0	0	0	0
Andy Unsworth	14/9/92	2(2)	2(1)	1	1	0	0	0	0	4	4
Alex West	22/8/90	3	2	0	0	0	0	0	0	0	0
Phil Wood	25/10/83	6(8)	2(7)	2	0	0	0	0	0	8	0

Dale Bloomfield

LEAGUE RECORD
P18-W9-D0-L9-BP1
(5th, Championship 1/
Elimination Play-Off)
F496, A460, Diff+36
28 points.

CHALLENGE CUP
Round Four

NORTHERN RAIL CUP
9th, Pool 1

ATTENDANCES
Best - v Oldham (Ch1 - 1,020)
Worst - v South Wales (NRC - 238)
Total (excluding Challenge Cup) - 5,370
Average (excluding Challenge Cup) - 488
(Down by 117 on 2011)

CLUB RECORDS
Highest score: 120-4 v Illingworth, 13/3/2005 Highest score against: 0-106 v Castleford, 9/9/2007
Record attendance: 26,664 v Oldham, 25/3/22 *(Athletic Grounds)*; 8,061 v Oldham, 26/12/89 *(Spotland)*

MATCH RECORDS
Tries: 5 Jack Corsi v Barrow, 31/12/21; Jack Corsi v Broughton Moor, 25/2/22; Jack Williams v St Helens, 4/4/33; Norman Brelsford v Whitehaven, 3/9/73; Marlon Billy v York, 8/4/2001 Goals: 18 Lee Birdseye v Illingworth, 13/3/2005 Points: 44 Lee Birdseye v Illingworth, 13/3/2005

SEASON RECORDS
Tries: 31 Marlon Billy 2001 Goals: 150 Martin Strett 1994-95 Points: 350 Mick Nanyn 2003

CAREER RECORDS
Tries: 103 Jack Williams 1931-37 Goals: 741 Walter Gowers 1922-36 Points: 1,497 Walter Gowers 1922-36 Appearances: 456 Walter Gowers 1922-36

SOUTH WALES SCORPIONS

DATE	FIXTURE	RESULT	SCORERS	LGE	ATT
19/2/12	Oldham (h) (NRC)	D36-36	t:J Burke,Acton,Mossop,Greenwood,Reece,C Cunningham g:Rooney(6)	5th(P1)	849
26/2/12	London Skolars (h) (NRC)	L30-38	t:Fox,Mossop(2),Pope,D James g:Rooney(5)	5th(P1)	205
3/3/12	Toulouse (a) (NRC)	L44-30	t:Prescott,J Burke,Reece,Leatherbarrow,Mossop g:Reece(5)	8th(P1)	685
11/3/12	Gateshead (a)	W30-32	t:D James(2),Mossop,Peake,Reece,Bateman g:Rooney(4)	5th	233
18/3/12	Workington (h)	L10-40	t:Rooney(2) g:Rooney	8th	374
24/3/12	Wath Brow (a) (CCR3)	W22-24	t:D James,Parry,Peake(2),Callow g:Rooney(2)	N/A	350
1/4/12	Doncaster (a)	L46-12	t:Grant,Reece g:Rooney(2)	8th	606
9/4/12	North Wales (a)	L34-22	t:Spencer,Greenwood(2),Mossop g:Rooney(3)	8th	1,204
14/4/12	Halifax (h) (CCR4) ●	L28-84	t:D James(2),Peake,Parry,Jack Murphy g:Leatherbarrow(4)	N/A	879
22/4/12	Whitehaven (h)	L0-34		8th	231
6/5/12	Barrow (h)	L24-42	t:Parry(2),Jamie Murphy,T Morgan(2) g:Reece,Jamie Murphy	9th	337
9/5/12	Rochdale (a) (NRC)	L46-24	t:Crow(2),K James,J Morgan g:Wildbore(4)	8th(P1)	238
20/5/12	Rochdale (h)	W32-30	t:Mossop,Parry(2),K James g:Jamie Murphy(4)	9th	557
26/5/12	Oldham (a)	W30-35	t:King,Greenwood,Parry(2),Jamie Murphy,K James g:Jamie Murphy(5) fg:Wildbore	8th	471
10/6/12	Whitehaven (a)	L34-18	t:Greenwood,T Morgan,Bateman g:Jamie Murphy(3)	9th	648
24/6/12	London Skolars (h)	L32-36	t:K James,T Morgan,Parry(2),G Burke,Mossop g:Wildbore(4)	8th	307
1/7/12	Doncaster (h)	L30-44	t:Mossop,Owens,Grant,D James,C Davies g:Owens(3),C Davies(2)	9th	360
15/7/12	Workington (a)	L50-10	t:Mossop,Grant g:C Davies	9th	653
22/7/12	Oldham (h)	L12-44	t:Pope,C Davies g:Owens(2)	9th	196
29/7/12	London Skolars (a)	L64-6	t:Lloyd g:Owens	9th	290
5/8/12	North Wales (h)	L24-36	t:Owens,Mossop,T G Morgan,Parry g:Owens(4)	9th	687
12/8/12	Rochdale (h)	L42-12	t:Gilbert,D James g:C Davies,Hawkes	9th	311
19/8/12	Gateshead (h)	W32-10	t:T G Morgan(2),Mossop(2),Pope,Owens g:Owens(3),Mossop	9th	219
2/9/12	Barrow (a)	L34-22	t:Lloyd,Pope,Grant,Hawkes g:C Davies(3)	9th	1,245

● Played at The Shay

	D.O.B.	APP ALL	Ch1	TRIES ALL	Ch1	GOALS ALL	Ch1	FG ALL	Ch1	PTS ALL	Ch1
Jamie Acton	4/4/92	2(1)	0	1	0	0	0	0	0	4	0
Ashley Bateman	11/2/90	13(7)	11(4)	2	2	0	0	0	0	8	8
Joe Bullock	27/11/92	5	4	0	0	0	0	0	0	0	0
Greg Burke	12/2/93	7(1)	5	1	1	0	0	0	0	4	4
Joe Burke	18/5/90	23	18	2	0	0	0	0	0	8	0
Greg Callow	1/10/86	3(1)	3	1	0	0	0	0	0	4	0
Liam Carberry	24/2/93	(1)	0	0	0	0	0	0	0	0	0
Phil Carleton	2/5/83	5(4)	(4)	0	0	0	0	0	0	0	0
TJ Collin	6/4/94	1	0	0	0	0	0	0	0	0	0
Mike Connor	27/3/94	(2)	(2)	0	0	0	0	0	0	0	0
Dominic Crosby	11/12/90	2	2	0	0	0	0	0	0	0	0
Matthew Crow	8/5/93	2(1)	1(1)	2	0	0	0	0	0	8	0
Andrew Cunningham	23/6/93	1	0	0	0	0	0	0	0	0	0
Curtis Cunningham	16/12/86	3	0	1	0	0	0	0	0	4	0
Ryan Curtis	19/3/92	(1)	0	0	0	0	0	0	0	0	0
Neil Dallimore	24/2/81	3(3)	2(2)	0	0	0	0	0	0	0	0
Alun-Wyn Davies	14/9/84	2(7)	2(7)	0	0	0	0	0	0	0	0
Courtney Davies	1/7/94	2(4)	2(4)	2	2	7	7	0	0	22	22
Geraint Davies	7/3/86	6(1)	5(1)	0	0	0	0	0	0	0	0
Rhys Davies	9/6/96	(3)	(3)	0	0	0	0	0	0	0	0
Gil Dudson	16/6/90	5	4	0	0	0	0	0	0	0	0
Dale Evans	26/6/93	(1)	(1)	0	0	0	0	0	0	0	0
Connor Farrer	6/6/95	(1)	(1)	0	0	0	0	0	0	0	0
Rhys Fitzgerald	16/8/95	(1)	(1)	0	0	0	0	0	0	0	0
Lewis Fox	30/6/87	1	0	1	0	0	0	0	0	4	0
James Gahan	10/3/95	2	0	0	0	0	0	0	0	0	0
Ben Gilbert	10/12/89	9	9	1	1	0	0	0	0	4	4
Rhys Godwin	10/12/84	(1)	0	0	0	0	0	0	0	0	0
Dalton Grant	21/4/90	16	12	4	4	0	0	0	0	16	16
James Greenwood	17/6/91	8(1)	6	5	4	0	0	0	0	20	16
Kieran Harrison	2/10/91	2(1)	1(1)	0	0	0	0	0	0	0	0
Kristian Hawkes	11/12/90	2(1)	2(1)	1	1	1	1	0	0	6	6
Jason Howells	27/5/87	3(1)	3(1)	0	0	0	0	0	0	0	0
David James	1/9/85	23	18	8	4	0	0	0	0	32	16
Kevin James	13/10/80	10	9	4	3	0	0	0	0	16	12
Alex Jones	28/9/93	2	2	0	0	0	0	0	0	0	0
Karl Jones	20/9/88	(1)	0	0	0	0	0	0	0	0	0
Luke Kell	23/12/93	3(2)	3(2)	0	0	0	0	0	0	0	0
Ryan King	23/1/92	2	2	1	1	0	0	0	0	4	4
Scott Leatherbarrow	3/9/90	4	1	1	0	4	0	0	0	12	0
Chris Leyshon	24/12/94	1(1)	1(1)	0	0	0	0	0	0	0	0

	D.O.B.	APP ALL	Ch1	TRIES ALL	Ch1	GOALS ALL	Ch1	FG ALL	Ch1	PTS ALL	Ch1
Rhodri Lloyd	22/7/93	3	3	2	2	0	0	0	0	8	8
Shae Lyon-Fraser	6/2/93	1	1	0	0	0	0	0	0	0	0
Alistair McDonald	18/1/84	2(3)	1(1)	0	0	0	0	0	0	0	0
Joe McKenna	21/8/87	5(1)	3(1)	0	0	0	0	0	0	0	0
Tom McKeown	28/4/86	(1)	(1)	0	0	0	0	0	0	0	0
Jacob Morgan	3/12/93	1	0	1	0	0	0	0	0	4	0
Thomas Gwyn Morgan	3/1/90	3(1)	3(1)	3	3	0	0	0	0	12	12
Tom Morgan	18/10/89	6	6	4	4	0	0	0	0	16	16
Nathan Mossop	21/2/88	18(2)	15(1)	15	11	1	1	0	0	62	46
Jack Murphy	18/3/92	1	1	1	0	0	0	0	0	4	0
Jamie Murphy	29/12/89	4	4	2	2	13	13	0	0	34	34
Shaun Owens	29/11/88	14(2)	11(2)	3	3	13	13	0	0	38	38
Yannic Parker	29/12/90	4(4)	2(4)	0	0	0	0	0	0	0	0
Steve Parry	19/10/88	15(8)	13(5)	11	9	0	0	0	0	44	36
Rodney Peake	29/4/86	9	4	4	1	0	0	0	0	16	4
Osian Phillips	2/5/94	2(4)	2(4)	0	0	0	0	0	0	0	0
Rory Pitman	6/10/89	(1)	(1)	0	0	0	0	0	0	0	0
Alan Pope	1/4/85	10(3)	9(3)	4	3	0	0	0	0	16	12
Paul Prescott	1/1/86	2	1	1	0	0	0	0	0	4	0
Lewis Reece	17/6/91	9(2)	6(1)	4	2	6	1	0	0	28	10
Jamie Rooney	17/3/80	7	4	2	2	23	10	0	0	54	28
Lewis Singleton	29/9/91	1	0	0	0	0	0	0	0	0	0
Tom Spencer	2/1/91	2	2	1	1	0	0	0	0	4	4
Chris Vitalini	5/5/87	13(2)	10(1)	0	0	0	0	0	0	0	0
Liam Watton	7/12/90	(1)	0	0	0	0	0	0	0	0	0
Sam Wellings	13/12/89	2	2	0	0	0	0	0	0	0	0
Loz Wildbore	23/9/84	5	4	0	0	8	4	1	1	17	9
Callum Wilkinson	17/2/91	(7)	(5)	0	0	0	0	0	0	0	0

LEAGUE RECORD
P18-W4-D0-L14-BP4
(9th, Championship 1)
F365, A680, Diff-315
16 points.

CHALLENGE CUP
Round Four

NORTHERN RAIL CUP
8th, Pool 1

ATTENDANCES
Best - v Oldham (NRC - 849)
Worst - v Oldham (Ch1 - 196)
Total (excluding
Challenge Cup) - 4,322
Average (excluding
Challenge Cup) - 393
(Up by 59 on 2011)

CLUB RECORDS   Highest score: 70-22 v London Skolars, 23/5/2010; 70-16 v Gateshead, 11/7/2010   **Highest score against:** 28-84 v Halifax, 14/4/2012
  Record attendance: 890 v Swinton, 13/6/2010
MATCH RECORDS   **Tries:** 4 Dalton Grant v Gateshead, 22/5/2011   **Goals:** 11 Lewis Reece v Gateshead, 11/7/2010   **Points:** 30 Lewis Reece v Gateshead, 11/7/2010
SEASON RECORDS   **Tries:** 19 Steve Parry 2010   **Goals:** 55 Lewis Reece 2011   **Points:** 130 Lewis Reece 2011
CAREER RECORDS   **Tries:** 43 Steve Parry 2010-2012   **Goals:** 72 Lewis Reece 2010-2012   **Points:** 188 Lewis Reece 2010-2012   **Appearances:** 64 Steve Parry 2010-2012

WHITEHAVEN

DATE	FIXTURE	RESULT	SCORERS	LGE	ATT
15/2/12	Hunslet (a) (NRC)	L34-18	t:Fleming,Houghton,Calvert g:Rudd(3)	N/A	305
19/2/12	Gateshead (h) (NRC)	W44-18	t:Calvert(3),McAvoy,Smith,Fleming,Varkulis,Bauer g:Rudd(6)	6th(P2)	649
26/2/12	Workington (a) (NRC)	L44-16	t:Fleming,Bauer,Sice g:Rudd(2)	8th(P2)	1,147
4/3/12	Barrow (h) (NRC)	L10-18	t:Hamzat,Gee g:Rudd	9th(P2)	902
11/3/12	Doncaster (a)	L48-16	t:Crellin,Bauer,Rudd g:Rudd(2)	9th	781
18/3/12	Rochdale (h)	W30-10	t:Bauer,Calvert(2),McAvoy(2) g:Rudd(5)	7th	714
25/3/12	Hunslet Warriors (h) (CCR3)	W52-6	t:Fox(3),Calvert,Rudd,Bauer,McAvoy,Isakka,Varkulis g:Rudd(8)	N/A	534
1/4/12	Gateshead (a)	W18-30	t:Karalius,Wiper,Varkulis,Calvert(2),Bauer g:Rudd(3)	6th	347
6/4/12	Workington (h)	L12-30	t:Calvert,Wilson g:Rudd(2)	6th	1,529
15/4/12	Salford (h) (CCR4)	L18-58	t:Gee,Varkulis,Houghton g:Rudd(3)	N/A	751
22/4/12	South Wales (a)	W0-34	t:McAvoy,Sice(3),Gee(2) g:Karalius(5)	6th	231
6/5/12	London Skolars (h)	W36-28	t:Cullnean,Doran,Bauer,Rooney(2),Hamzat g:Rudd(6)	5th	627
13/5/12	North Wales (a)	W10-17	t:Sice,Calvert,Doran g:Rudd,Rooney fg:Rooney	4th	804
20/5/12	Oldham (a)	W16-26	t:Gee,Wiper,Calvert,Houghton g:Rudd(3),Rooney(2)	4th	624
27/5/12	Barrow (h)	L28-42	t:Rudd,Varkulis,Houghton,Sice,Parker g:Rudd(4)	4th	1,124
10/6/12	South Wales (h)	W34-18	t:Calvert(4),Wiper(2) g:Rudd(2),Rooney(3)	4th	648
24/6/12	Workington (a)	L30-28	t:Rooney,Doran(2),Beattie,Mullally g:Rudd(3),Rooney	4th	1,954
1/7/12	Oldham (h)	W42-20	t:Calvert(3),Wiper,Parker,Houghton,Beattie g:Rudd(4),Rooney(3)	4th	701
19/7/12	Barrow (a)	L48-16	t:Hemingway,Calvert,Rooney g:Rudd,Rooney	4th	1,710
29/7/12	Rochdale (a)	W12-31	t:Rooney,Palfrey,Calvert,Parker,Hamzat g:Rudd,Rooney(3),Sice fg:Rooney	4th	581
5/8/12	Doncaster (h)	W25-18	t:Sice(2),Parker,Varkulis g:Rudd(2),Rooney(2) fg:Rooney	4th	833
12/8/12	Gateshead (h)	W60-12	t:Calvert(3),Varkulis(2),Rudd,Parker(2),Hemingway,Cullnean,Doran g:Rudd(8)	4th	733
24/8/12	London Skolars (a)	L41-26	t:Rooney(2),Calvert(2),Hamzat g:Rudd(2),Rooney	4th	1,174
2/9/12	North Wales (h)	W58-20	t:Hemingway,Calvert,Rooney(2),Beattie(3),Parker,Crellin,Hamzat g:Rudd(9)	4th	701
9/9/12	Rochdale (h) (EPO)	W40-12	t:Parker(2),Rudd,Doran,Wiper,Palfrey,Cullnean,Rooney g:Rudd(2),Rooney,Beattie	N/A	601
16/9/12	Workington (a) (ESF)	L26-2	g:Rudd	N/A	1,273

		APP		TRIES		GOALS		FG		PTS	
	D.O.B.	ALL	Ch1	ALL	Ch1	ALL	Ch1	ALL	Ch1	ALL	Ch1
Shane Ackerley	19/11/91	3	1	0	0	0	0	0	0	0	0
Daniel Barker	1/12/88	1(2)	(1)	0	0	0	0	0	0	0	0
Andreas Bauer	26/9/82	15(3)	12(1)	7	4	0	0	0	0	28	16
Andrew Beattie	12/1/81	14(6)	11(5)	5	5	1	1	0	0	22	22
Peter Bewsher	16/7/89	(3)	(1)	0	0	0	0	0	0	0	0
Craig Calvert	10/2/84	24	18	27	22	0	0	0	0	108	88
Brad Crellin	2/7/89	11(2)	7(2)	2	2	0	0	0	0	8	8
Paul Cullnean	8/1/77	15(11)	15(5)	3	3	0	0	0	0	12	12
Sam Cunningham	4/4/90	1	0	0	0	0	0	0	0	0	0
Lee Doran	23/3/81	24	19	6	6	0	0	0	0	24	24
Chris Fleming	11/1/91	3	0	3	0	0	0	0	0	12	0
Steve Fox	13/2/90	8(3)	7(2)	3	0	0	0	0	0	12	0
Sam Gee	28/2/87	9(4)	6(4)	5	3	0	0	0	0	20	12
Scott George	21/11/90	(2)	0	0	0	0	0	0	0	0	0
Matthew Haggerty	8/1/91	2(16)	1(16)	0	0	0	0	0	0	0	0
Loz Hamzat	26/10/90	14	12	5	4	0	0	0	0	20	16
Tom Hemingway	6/12/86	7	7	3	3	0	0	0	0	12	12
Howard Hill	16/1/75	4(4)	3(3)	0	0	0	0	0	0	0	0
David Houghton	2/11/89	25	20	5	3	0	0	0	0	20	12
Luke Isakka	1/11/80	8(12)	3(12)	1	0	0	0	0	0	4	0
Ben Karalius	6/12/91	13(1)	9(1)	1	1	5	5	0	0	14	14
Scott McAvoy	9/4/86	8(1)	4(1)	5	3	0	0	0	0	20	12
Anthony Mullally	28/6/91	2(1)	2(1)	1	1	0	0	0	0	4	4
Martin O'Neill	4/2/94	(1)	0	0	0	0	0	0	0	0	0
Lewis Palfrey	25/2/90	7	7	2	2	0	0	0	0	8	8
Jessie Joe Parker	22/8/85	17(1)	16(1)	9	9	0	0	0	0	36	36
Jamie Rooney	17/3/80	15	15	10	10	18	18	3	3	79	79
Carl Rudd	10/10/82	25	19	5	4	84	61	0	0	188	138
Carl Sice	13/4/80	9(12)	7(10)	8	7	1	1	0	0	34	30
Chris Smith	21/1/90	4(4)	2(2)	1	0	0	0	0	0	4	0
Richard Varkulis	21/5/82	14(11)	10(9)	8	5	0	0	0	0	32	20
Martyn Wilson	22/10/82	7(3)	6(3)	1	1	0	0	0	0	4	4
Max Wiper	18/9/90	25(1)	20	6	6	0	0	0	0	24	24
Jonathan Youds	12/10/90	4	1	0	0	0	0	0	0	0	0

Craig Calvert

LEAGUE RECORD
P18-W12-D0-L6-BP1
(4th, Championship 1/
Elimination Semi-Final)
F549, A421, Diff+128
37 points.

CHALLENGE CUP
Round Four

NORTHERN RAIL CUP
9th, Pool 2

ATTENDANCES
Best - v Workington (Ch1 - 1,529)
Worst - v Hunslet Warriors (CC - 534)
Total (excluding Challenge Cup) - 9,762
Average (excluding Challenge Cup) - 814
(Down by 52 on 2011)

CLUB RECORDS	**Highest score:** 86-6 v Highfield, 25/1/95 **Highest score against:** 8-106 v Wigan, 12/5/2008 **Record attendance:** 18,500 v Wakefield, 19/3/60
MATCH RECORDS	**Tries:** 6 Vince Gribbin v Doncaster, 18/11/84 **Goals:** 13 Lee Anderson v Highfield, 25/1/95 **Points:** 32 Mick Nanyn v Batley, 22/8/2004
SEASON RECORDS	**Tries:** 34 Mike Pechey 1994-95 **Goals:** 141 John McKeown 1956-57 **Points:** 398 Mick Nanyn 2004
CAREER RECORDS	**Tries:** 248 David Seeds 1993-2007 **Goals:** 1,050 John McKeown 1948-61 **Points:** 2,133 John McKeown 1948-61
	Appearances: 417 John McKeown 1948-61

WORKINGTON TOWN

DATE	FIXTURE	RESULT	SCORERS	LGE	ATT
12/2/12	Sheffield (h) (NRC)	L14-28	t:Mossop,Carter g:Forber(3)	N/A	532
19/2/12	Barrow (a) (NRC)	L31-24	t:Coward,Petersen,Thackray,Forber g:Forber(4)	9th(P2)	1,366
26/2/12	Whitehaven (h) (NRC)	W44-16	t:Forber,Rooney,Miller,Carter,Thackray(2),Phillips,Shackley g:Forber(6)	6th(P2)	1,147
4/3/12	Swinton (a) (NRC)	L30-12	t:Miller,Shackley g:Forber(2)	8th(P2)	503
11/3/12	Oldham (h)	L14-24	t:Rooney,Mossop,Olstrum g:Forber	8th	760
18/3/12	South Wales (a)	W10-40	t:Phillips,Whitehead,Miller,Thackray,Patrick(2),S Dawes,Mossop g:Forber(4)	3rd	374
25/3/12	Batley (h) (CCR3)	L6-22	t:Shackley g:Forber	N/A	601
1/4/12	London Skolars (h)	W27-20	t:Petersen(2),Miller(2),Thackray g:Forber(3) fg:Forber	2nd	439
6/4/12	Whitehaven (a)	W12-30	t:Mossop,Miller,Stack,Phillips g:Forber(6),McDonald	1st	1,529
22/4/12	North Wales (h)	W58-0	t:Stack,Bainbridge,Carter(2),Miller(2),Petersen(2),Shackley,S Dawes,Mossop g:Forber(3),Bainbridge(4)	1st	776
6/5/12	Gateshead (h)	W58-6	t:Mattinson,Coward(2),McDonald,Patrick,Stack,Phillips,Miller(2),Rooney,Olstrum g:Bainbridge(7)	2nd	467
13/5/12	Barrow (a)	L20-12	t:Mattinson,Miller,S Dawes	3rd	1,808
20/5/12	Doncaster (h)	W45-18	t:Miller(3),Stack(2),Rooney,Carter,Thackray,Calderwood g:Bainbridge(2),Forber(2) fg:Lupton	3rd	804
3/6/12	Rochdale (a)	W24-37	t:Lupton(2),Carter(2),Thackray,Miller g:Bainbridge(6) fg:Bainbridge	3rd	512
10/6/12	London Skolars (a)	W12-44	t:Coward,Mattinson,Stack,Olstrum(2),Calderwood(2),Miller g:Bainbridge(6)	2nd	623
24/6/12	Whitehaven (h)	W30-28	t:Miller,Stack,Mattinson,Lupton,Petersen,Phillips g:Bainbridge(3)	2nd	1,954
1/7/12	North Wales (a)	W20-30	t:Coward,Thackray,Newton,Carter,Petersen g:Forber(5)	2nd	733
15/7/12	South Wales (h)	W50-10	t:Miller(5),Stack,Calderwood(2),Thackray,Mattinson g:Forber(5)	1st	653
26/7/12	Doncaster (a)	L22-6	t:Lupton g:Forber	3rd	891
12/8/12	Barrow (h)	W48-34	t:Stack(2),Thackray(2),Walne,Miller(2),Whitehead g:Forber(8)	3rd	1,710
19/8/12	Oldham (a)	L28-18	t:Miller,Lupton,Morris g:Forber(3)	3rd	538
29/8/12	Gateshead (a)	L24-22	t:Coward,Stack,Patrick,Shackley g:Forber(3)	3rd	256
2/9/12	Rochdale (h)	W48-18	t:Petersen,Phillips(2),Patrick,Annakin,Forber,McAvoy,Mossop,Frazer g:Forber(6)	3rd	514
9/9/12	Oldham (h) (EPO)	W34-29	t:Coward,Mattinson,Miller,Carter,Frazer,Mossop g:Forber(5)	N/A	563
16/9/12	Whitehaven (h) (ESF)	W26-2	t:Patrick,Calderwood,Shackley g:Forber(7)	N/A	1,273
23/9/12	Doncaster (a) (FE)	L20-0		N/A	576

		APP		TRIES		GOALS		FG		PTS	
	D.O.B.	ALL	Ch1	ALL	Ch1	ALL	Ch1	ALL	Ch1	ALL	Ch1
Chris Annakin	30/1/91	7	7	1	1	0	0	0	0	4	4
Marc Bainbridge	22/12/87	11(4)	11(3)	1	1	28	28	1	1	61	61
Mark Calderwood	25/10/81	14	14	6	6	0	0	0	0	24	24
Brett Carter	9/7/88	19	14	9	7	0	0	0	0	36	28
Kris Coward	1/10/89	22(1)	19	7	6	0	0	0	0	28	24
Jonathan Dawes	5/12/84	4	1	0	0	0	0	0	0	0	0
Stephen Dawes	14/1/85	8	7	3	3	0	0	0	0	12	12
Peter Dobson	23/11/85	(1)	0	0	0	0	0	0	0	0	0
Richard Farrer	25/11/85	2(4)	(3)	0	0	0	0	0	0	0	0
Carl Forber	17/3/85	21(1)	16(1)	3	1	78	62	1	1	169	129
Neil Frazer	7/3/76	6	5	2	2	0	0	0	0	8	8
Jack Gaskell	21/1/95	1(2)	1	0	0	0	0	0	0	0	0
James Green	29/11/92	2(1)	(1)	0	0	0	0	0	0	0	0
Nick Johnson	18/12/90	3	1	0	0	0	0	0	0	0	0
Darren King	9/3/82	3(1)	0	0	0	0	0	0	0	0	0
Peter Lupton	7/3/82	10(2)	10(2)	5	5	0	0	1	1	21	21
Graeme Mattinson	24/4/85	17(2)	15(1)	6	6	0	0	0	0	24	24
Kieran McAvoy	4/9/92	1(1)	1(1)	1	1	0	0	0	0	4	4
Ryan McDonald	24/2/78	15(5)	12(5)	1	1	1	1	0	0	6	6
Elliott Miller	14/9/90	22	17	26	24	0	0	0	0	104	96
Andy Morris	15/5/93	3	3	1	1	0	0	0	0	4	4
Jason Mossop	12/9/85	25	21	7	6	0	0	0	0	28	24
James Newton	20/12/91	(3)	(3)	1	1	0	0	0	0	4	4
Karl Olstrum	21/9/91	13(6)	10(6)	4	4	0	0	0	0	16	16
John Patrick	29/11/82	11	8	6	6	0	0	0	0	24	24
Dave Petersen	6/3/92	14	12	8	7	0	0	0	0	32	28
Brett Phillips	25/10/88	22(1)	19	7	6	0	0	0	0	28	24
James Robinson	4/3/79	4(11)	1(10)	0	0	0	0	0	0	0	0
Daniel Rooney	6/1/90	14(2)	11(1)	4	3	0	0	0	0	16	12
Marc Shackley	14/1/89	7(15)	4(14)	6	3	0	0	0	0	24	12
Jarrad Stack	13/2/88	18(2)	17(2)	11	11	0	0	0	0	44	44
Jamie Thackray	30/9/79	6(20)	6(15)	11	8	0	0	0	0	44	32
Matthew Tunstall	7/9/77	3(2)	3	0	0	0	0	0	0	0	0
Adam Walne	3/10/90	(2)	(2)	1	1	0	0	0	0	4	4
Mike Whitehead	25/8/78	10(13)	7(12)	2	2	0	0	0	0	8	8

Jamie Thackray

LEAGUE RECORD
P18-W13-D0-L5-BP4
(3rd, Championship 1/
Final Eliminator)
F617, A330, Diff+287
43 points.

CHALLENGE CUP
Round Three

NORTHERN RAIL CUP
8th, Pool 2

ATTENDANCES
Best - v Whitehaven (Ch1 - 1,954)
Worst - v London Skolars (Ch1 - 439)
Total (excluding Challenge Cup) - 11,592
Average (excluding Challenge Cup) - 892
(Up by 309 on 2011)

CLUB RECORDS **MATCH RECORDS**	**Highest score:** 94-4 v Leigh, 26/2/95 **Highest score against:** 0-92 v Bradford, 14/2/99 **Record attendance:** 17,741 v Wigan, 3/3/65 **Tries:** 7 Ike Southward v Blackpool, 17/9/55 **Goals:** 14 Darren Holt v Gateshead, 12/6/2011 **Points:** 42 Dean Marwood v Highfield, 1/11/92; Dean Marwood v Leigh, 26/2/95
SEASON RECORDS **CAREER RECORDS**	**Tries:** 49 Johnny Lawrenson 1951-52 **Goals:** 186 Lyn Hopkins 1981-82 **Points:** 438 Lyn Hopkins 1981-82 **Tries:** 274 Ike Southward 1952-68 **Goals:** 809 Iain MacCorquodale 1972-80 **Points:** 1,800 Iain MacCorquodale 1972-80 **Appearances:** 419 Paul Charlton 1961-69; 1975-80

CHAMPIONSHIP ONE 2012
Round by Round

ROUND 1

Sunday 11th March 2012

NORTH WALES CRUSADERS 24 BARROW RAIDERS 26

CRUSADERS: 1 Danny Hulme; 2 Chris Walker; 3 Christiaan Roets; 4 Rob Massam; 5 Adam Walsh; 6 Andrew Moulsdale; 7 Jamie Durbin; 8 Chris Tyrer; 9 Lee Hudson; 10 Jonny Walker; 11 Leon Brennan; 12 Mark Hamon; 13 Jono Smith. Subs (all used): 14 Billy Sheen; 15 Tommy Johnson; 16 Owain Brown; 17 Iwan Brown.
Tries: Moulsdale (14), Durbin (20), Massam (36, 38), Brennan (61); **Goals:** Brennan 2/5.
RAIDERS: 1 Andy Ballard; 2 Marc Dixon; 3 Chris Larkin; 4 Aaron Low; 5 James Nixon; 6 Darren Holt; 7 Liam Campbell; 8 Andy Bracek; 9 Liam Finch; 10 Andrew Dawson; 11 Liam Harrison; 12 James Gordon; 13 Daniel Toal. Subs (all used): 14 Jack Pedley; 15 Martin Ostler; 16 Barry Pugh; 17 Ruairi McGoff.
Tries: Dixon (7), Larkin (45, 63), Toal (61), L Finch (72); **Goals:** Holt 3/5.
Rugby Leaguer & League Express Men of the Match: *Crusaders:* Jamie Durbin; *Raiders:* Liam Harrison.
Penalty count: 6-5; **Half-time:** 20-4;
Referee: Matthew Kidd; **Attendance:** 1,513.

DONCASTER 48 WHITEHAVEN 16

DONCASTER: 1 Mick Butterfield; 2 Dean Colton; 3 Liam Cunningham; 4 Lee Waterman; 5 Tom Hodson; 6 Paul Cooke; 7 Kieran Hyde; 8 Mark Castle; 9 Mike Emmett; 10 Craig Robinson; 11 Dean O'Loughlin; 12 Craig Lawton; 13 Grant Edwards. Subs (all used): 14 Kyle Kesik; 15 Kyle Bibb; 16 Carl Hughes; 17 Francis Welsh.
Tries: Cooke (7, 72), Waterman (20, 79), Hyde (25), Kesik (30), Hodson (39), Cunningham (52);
Goals: Cooke 8/8.
WHITEHAVEN: 1 Shane Ackerley; 2 Andreas Bauer; 3 Max Wiper; 4 Steve Fox; 5 Martyn Wilson; 6 Carl Rudd; 7 Ben Karalius; 8 David Houghton; 9 Chris Smith; 10 Richard Varkulis; 11 Luke Isakka; 12 Andrew Beattie; 13 Brad Crellin. Subs (all used): 14 Carl Sice; 15 Peter Bewsher; 16 Paul Cullnean; 17 Matthew Haggerty.
Tries: Crellin (16), Bauer (44), Rudd (63);
Goals: Rudd 2/3.
Rugby Leaguer & League Express Men of the Match: *Doncaster:* Paul Cooke; *Whitehaven:* Steve Fox.
Penalty count: 6-5; **Half-time:** 30-6;
Referee: Chris Leatherbarrow; **Attendance:** 781.

GATESHEAD THUNDER 30 SOUTH WALES SCORPIONS 32

THUNDER: 1 Robin Peers; 2 Ashley Thackeray; 3 Mike Mitchell; 4 Josh Neilson; 5 Ashley Williams; 6 Sam Walsh; 7 Ryan Clarke; 8 Stephen Welton; 9 Tom Hodgson; 10 Brett Waller; 11 Matt Barron; 12 Joe Brown; 13 Ryan Steen. Subs: 14 Paul Stamp; 15 Chris Parker Snr; 16 Dan O'Sullivan (not used); 17 Josh Stoker.
Tries: Williams (2), Brown (24), Mitchell (46), Waller (59), Neilson (65, 75); **Goals:** Clarke 0/1, Stamp 3/5.
SCORPIONS: 1 Rodney Peake; 2 Dalton Grant; 3 Lewis Reece; 4 Ashley Bateman; 5 David James; 6 Jamie Rooney; 7 Shaun Owens; 8 Gil Dudson; 9 Nathan Mossop; 10 Paul Prescott; 11 Joe Burke; 12 Chris Vitalini; 13 Joe McKenna. Subs: 14 Steve Parry; 15 Phil Carleton (not used); 16 Callum Wilkinson; 17 Dale Evans.
Tries: D James (6, 70), Mossop (18), Peake (33), Reece (55), Bateman (79); **Goals:** Rooney 4/6.
Rugby Leaguer & League Express Men of the Match: *Thunder:* Brett Waller; *Scorpions:* Jamie Rooney.
Penalty count: 6-8; **Half-time:** 10-18;
Referee: Dave Merrick; **Attendance:** 233.

ROCHDALE HORNETS 36 LONDON SKOLARS 4

HORNETS: 1 Paul O'Connor; 2 Dale Bloomfield; 3 Daniel Davies; 4 Steve Bannister; 5 Wayne English; 6 Paul Crook; 7 Steve Roper; 8 Mark Hobson; 9 Steve McDermott; 10 John Cookson; 11 Gary Middlehurst; 12 Chris Baines; 13 Dayne Donoghue. Subs (all used): 14 Phil Wood; 15 Chris Hough; 16 Adam Bowman; 17 Stephen Lucas.
Tries: Middlehurst (12, 59, 79), English (16), O'Connor (25), McDermott (69), Bannister (75); **Goals:** Crook 4/7.
SKOLARS: 1 James Anthony; 2 John Paxton; 3 Joe Price; 4 Chris McNamara; 5 Ade Adebisi; 6 Andy McLean; 7 Dylan Skee; 8 Rob Thomas; 9 Neil Thorman; 10 Dave Williams; 11 Alex Bate; 12 Matt Thomas; 13 Lamont Bryan. Subs (all used): 14 Oliver Purslow; 15 Austen Aggrey; 16 Martyn Smith; 17 Joe Ridley.
Try: Price (21); **Goals:** Skee 0/1.
Dismissal: Anthony (59) - use of the elbow on Wood.
Rugby Leaguer & League Express Men of the Match: *Hornets:* Paul O'Connor; *Skolars:* Lamont Bryan.
Penalty count: 7-5; **Half-time:** 14-4;
Referee: Clint Sharrad; **Attendance:** 359.

WORKINGTON TOWN 14 OLDHAM 24

TOWN: 1 Jonathan Dawes; 2 Karl Olstrum; 3 Jason Mossop; 4 Daniel Rooney; 5 Nick Johnson; 6 Marc Bainbridge; 7 Carl Forber; 8 Ryan McDonald; 9 Graeme Mattinson; 10 Kris Coward; 11 Brett Phillips; 12 Jarrad Stack; 13 Dave Petersen. Subs (all used): 14 James Green; 15 Mike Whitehead; 16 Marc Shackley; 17 Jamie Thackray.
Tries: Rooney (6), Mossop (40), Olstrum (71);
Goals: Forber 1/3.
OLDHAM: 1 Miles Greenwood; 2 Shaun Robinson; 3 Matthew Fogarty; 4 Mark Brocklehurst; 5 John Gillam; 6 Neil Roden; 7 Jamie Dallimore; 8 Jason Boults; 9 John Clough; 10 Chris Clarke; 11 Paul Noone; 12 Paul Smith; 13 Martin Roden. Subs (all used): 14 Mark McCully; 15 Danny Whitmore; 16 Dave Ellison; 17 Matty Syron.
Tries: Gillam (25), Greenwood (53), McCully (61), Clarke (77); **Goals:** Dallimore 4/4.
Rugby Leaguer & League Express Men of the Match: *Town:* Jamie Thackray; *Oldham:* Chris Clarke.
Penalty count: 8-12; **Half-time:** 10-6;
Referee: Warren Turley; **Attendance:** 760.

ROUND 2

Sunday 18th March 2012

SOUTH WALES SCORPIONS 10 WORKINGTON TOWN 40

SCORPIONS: 1 Rodney Peake; 2 Ashley Bateman; 3 Lewis Reece; 4 Shae Lyon-Fraser; 5 David James; 6 Jamie Rooney; 7 Scott Leatherbarrow; 8 Gil Dudson; 9 Steve Parry; 10 James Greenwood; 11 Joe Burke; 12 Chris Vitalini; 13 Joe McKenna. Subs (all used): 14 Shaun Owens; 15 Alan Pope; 16 Callum Wilkinson; 17 Phil Carleton.
Tries: Rooney (47, 76); **Goals:** Rooney 1/2.
TOWN: 1 Elliott Miller; 2 Stephen Dawes; 3 Jason Mossop; 4 Daniel Rooney; 5 John Patrick; 6 Carl Forber; 7 Marc Bainbridge; 8 Ryan McDonald; 9 Graeme Mattinson; 10 Kris Coward; 11 Mike Whitehead; 12 Brett Phillips; 13 James Robinson. Subs (all used): 14 Karl Olstrum; 15 Richard Farrer; 16 Marc Shackley; 17 Jamie Thackray.
Tries: Phillips (12), Whitehead (16), Miller (22), Thackray (26), Patrick (31, 54), S Dawes (36), Mossop (64); **Goals:** Forber 4/9.
Rugby Leaguer & League Express Men of the Match: *Scorpions:* Jamie Rooney; *Town:* Jamie Thackray.
Penalty count: 6-12; **Half-time:** 0-28;
Referee: Warren Turley; **Attendance:** 374.

BARROW RAIDERS 25 DONCASTER 8

RAIDERS: 1 Andy Ballard; 2 Lee Haney; 3 Chris Larkin; 4 Aaron Low; 5 James Nixon; 6 Darren Holt; 7 Liam Campbell; 8 Andy Bracek; 9 Liam Finch; 10 Jamie Butler; 11 Liam Harrison; 12 Barry Pugh; 13 Daniel Toal. Subs (all used): 14 Jack Pedley; 15 Andrew Dawson; 16 James Gordon; 17 Lee Dutton.
Tries: Campbell (14), Larkin (40), Low (43), Holt (73);
Goals: Holt 4/4; **Field goal:** Holt (73).
DONCASTER: 1 Mick Butterfield; 2 Dean Colton; 3 Liam Cunningham; 4 Lee Waterman; 5 Tom Hodson; 6 Paul Cooke; 7 Kieran Hyde; 8 Mark Castle; 9 Mike Emmett; 10 Dean O'Loughlin; 11 Craig Robinson; 12 Craig Lawton; 13 Grant Edwards. Subs (all used): 14 Kyle Kesik; 15 Kyle Bibb; 16 Francis Welsh; 17 Michael Kelly.
Tries: Hodson (18), Waterman (48); **Goals:** Cooke 0/2.
Rugby Leaguer & League Express Men of the Match: *Raiders:* Darren Holt; *Doncaster:* Kyle Kesik.
Penalty count: 11-12; **Half-time:** 12-4;
Referee: Jamie Leahy; **Attendance:** 1,365.

LONDON SKOLARS 66 NORTH WALES CRUSADERS 16

SKOLARS: 1 James Anthony; 2 John Paxton; 3 Joe Price; 4 Chris McNamara; 5 Ade Adebisi; 6 Andy McLean; 7 Dylan Skee; 8 Rob Thomas; 9 Neil Thorman; 10 Dave Williams; 11 Alex Bate; 12 Matt Thomas; 13 Lamont Bryan. Subs (all used): 14 Oliver Purslow; 15 Austen Aggrey; 16 Martyn Smith; 17 Brad Hopkins.
Tries: Skee (2, 72), Bryan (4), Paxton (12), Price (15), Thorman (26), Bate (36), Hopkins (39, 79), McNamara (57), M Thomas (60), R Thomas (62); **Goals:** Skee 9/12.
CRUSADERS: 1 Danny Hulme; 2 Adam Walsh; 3 Tommy Johnson; 4 Rob Massam; 5 Kriss Wilkes; 6 Andrew Moulsdale; 7 Jamie Durbin; 8 Jonny Walker; 9 Lee Hudson; 10 Chris Tyrer; 11 Anthony Morrison; 12 Leon Brennan; 13 Jono Smith. Subs (all used): 14 Billy Sheen; 15 Iwan Brown; 16 Aaron McCloskey; 17 Ian Cross.
Tries: D Hulme (46, 76), Hudson (50);
Goals: Johnson 1/2, Brennan 1/1.
Sin bin: J Walker (56) - high tackle.
Rugby Leaguer & League Express Men of the Match: *Skolars:* Dylan Skee; *Crusaders:* Danny Hulme.
Penalty count: 7-11; **Half-time:** 40-0;
Referee: Tom Crashley; **Attendance:** 535.

OLDHAM 40 GATESHEAD THUNDER 14

OLDHAM: 1 Miles Greenwood; 2 Mark Brocklehurst; 3 David Cookson; 4 Mark McCully; 5 Paul Ballard; 6 Neil Roden; 7 Jamie Dallimore; 8 Jason Boults; 9 John Clough; 10 Chris Clarke; 11 Paul Noone; 12 Paul Smith; 13 Martin Roden. Subs (all used): 14 Matty Syron; 15 Danny Whitmore; 16 Dave Ellison; 17 Alex Thompson.
Tries: P Smith (19), Ballard (29, 32), N Roden (39), Greenwood (42, 67), Noone (56); **Goals:** Dallimore 6/7.
THUNDER: 1 Robin Peers; 2 Ashley Thackeray; 3 Mike Mitchell; 4 Josh Neilson; 5 Ashley Williams; 6 Sam Walsh; 7 Paul Stamp; 8 Brett Waller; 9 Tom Hodgson; 10 Stephen Welton; 11 Matt Barron; 12 Joe Brown; 13 Ryan Steen. Subs (all used): 14 Ryan Clarke; 15 Chris Parker Snr; 16 Dan O'Sullivan; 17 Josh Stoker.
Tries: Steen (51), Neilson (59), Mitchell (64);
Goals: Stamp 1/3.
Rugby Leaguer & League Express Men of the Match: *Oldham:* Neil Roden; *Thunder:* Paul Stamp.
Penalty count: 6-7; **Half-time:** 22-0;
Referee: George Stokes; **Attendance:** 539.

WHITEHAVEN 30 ROCHDALE HORNETS 10

WHITEHAVEN: 1 Andreas Bauer; 2 Craig Calvert; 3 Steve Fox; 4 Scott McAvoy; 5 Max Wiper; 6 Carl Rudd; 7 Ben Karalius; 8 David Houghton; 9 Carl Sice; 10 Howard Hill; 11 Luke Isakka; 12 Lee Doran; 13 Andrew Beattie. Subs (all used): 14 Chris Smith; 15 Richard Varkulis; 16 Daniel Barker; 17 Paul Cullnean.
Tries: Bauer (19), Calvert (34, 57), McAvoy (72, 76);
Goals: Rudd 5/7.
Sin bin: Bauer (44) - dissent.
On report: Beattie (16) - alleged late challenge.
HORNETS: 1 Paul O'Connor; 2 Dale Bloomfield; 3 Daniel Davies; 4 Steve Bannister; 5 Wayne English; 6 Paul Crook; 7 Steve Roper; 8 Mark Hobson; 9 Steve McDermott; 10 John Cookson; 11 Gary Middlehurst; 12 Chris Baines; 13 Dayne Donoghue. Subs (all used): 14 Phil Wood; 15 Adam Bowman; 16 Stephen Lucas; 17 Dave Newton.
Tries: Newton (29), Bloomfield (66);
Goals: Baines 1/2.
Rugby Leaguer & League Express Men of the Match: *Whitehaven:* Andreas Bauer; *Hornets:* Paul O'Connor.
Penalty count: 13-6; **Half-time:** 12-6;
Referee: Dave Merrick; **Attendance:** 714.

ROUND 3

Sunday 1st April 2012

WORKINGTON TOWN 27 LONDON SKOLARS 20

TOWN: 1 Brett Carter; 2 Elliott Miller; 3 Jason Mossop; 4 Daniel Rooney; 5 John Patrick; 6 Marc Bainbridge; 7 Carl Forber; 8 Ryan McDonald; 9 Graeme Mattinson; 10 Kris Coward; 11 Brett Phillips; 12 Marc Shackley; 13 Dave Petersen. Subs (all used): 14 Karl Olstrum; 15 Richard Farrer; 16 Jarrad Stack; 17 Jamie Thackray.
Tries: Petersen (13, 55), Miller (28, 43), Thackray (33);
Goals: Forber 3/5; **Field goal:** Forber (75).
Sin bin: Thackray (50) - dissent.
SKOLARS: 1 James Anthony; 2 John Paxton; 3 Joe Price; 4 Chris McNamara; 5 Ade Adebisi; 6 Andy McLean; 7 Dylan Skee; 8 Dave Williams; 9 Neil Thorman; 10 Rob Thomas; 11 Alex Bate; 12 Brad Hopkins; 13 Lamont Bryan. Subs (all used): 14 Oliver Purslow; 15 Martyn Smith; 16 Austen Aggrey; 17 Matt Thomas.
Tries: McNamara (8), Adebisi (20, 36, 57);
Goals: Skee 2/4.
Rugby Leaguer & League Express Men of the Match: *Town:* Dave Petersen; *Skolars:* Ade Adebisi.
Penalty count: 6-6; **Half-time:** 16-16;
Referee: Chris Leatherbarrow; **Attendance:** 439.

NORTH WALES CRUSADERS 18 ROCHDALE HORNETS 54

CRUSADERS: 1 Danny Hulme; 2 Kriss Wilkes; 3 Ian Cross; 4 Leon Brennan; 5 Rob Massam; 6 Andrew Moulsdale; 7 Jamie Durbin; 8 Owain Brown; 9 Lee Hudson; 10 Jonny Walker; 11 Anthony Morrison; 12 Kurt Haggerty; 13 Jono Smith. Subs (all used): 14 Chris Lunt; 15 Gareth Frodsham; 16 Chris Tyrer; 17 Tommy Johnson.
Tries: Wilkes (6, 59), Massam (71), D Hulme (73);
Goals: Cross 0/3, Smith 1/1.
Dismissal: Morrison (57) - fighting.
On report: Haggerty (46) - alleged dangerous tackle.
HORNETS: 1 Paul O'Connor; 2 Dale Bloomfield; 3 Chris Baines; 4 Steve Bannister; 5 Wayne English; 6 Chris Hough; 7 Steve Roper; 8 Dave Newton; 9 Steve McDermott; 10 John Cookson; 11 Gary Middlehurst; 12 Mark Hobson; 13 Dayne Donoghue. Subs (all used): 14 Phil Wood; 15 Jonny Leather; 16 Adam Bowman; 17 Phil Braddish.
Tries: O'Connor (16), Hobson (26), Braddish (32), Roper (34), Leather (37, 63), Hough (52), Cookson (65), Bowman (78); **Goals:** Baines 9/10.
Dismissal: Middlehurst (57) - fighting.
Rugby Leaguer & League Express Men of the Match: *Crusaders:* Jono Smith; *Hornets:* Steve Roper.
Penalty count: 7-12; **Half-time:** 4-28;
Referee: Warren Turley; **Attendance:** 1,047.

DONCASTER 46 SOUTH WALES SCORPIONS 12

DONCASTER: 1 Mick Butterfield; 2 Stewart Sanderson; 3 Liam Cunningham; 4 Lee Waterman; 5 Tom Hodson; 6 Paul Cooke; 7 Kieran Hyde; 8 Mark Castle; 9 Jack Ely; 10 Craig Robinson; 11 Dean O'Loughlin; 12 Craig Lawton; 13 Grant Edwards. Subs (all used): 14 Kyle Kesik; 15 Mike Emmett; 16 Russ Spiers; 17 Kyle Bibb.
Tries: Robinson (3), Ely (6), Hodson (17, 34, 43), Cunningham (25), Bibb (50), Waterman (60), Hyde (77);
Goals: Cooke 4/8, Waterman 1/1.
SCORPIONS: 1 Lewis Reece; 2 Dalton Grant; 3 David James; 4 Alan Pope; 5 Greg Callow; 6 Shaun Owens; 7 Jamie Rooney; 8 Gil Dudson; 9 Steve Parry; 10 Alistair McDonald; 11 Joe Burke; 12 Chris Vitalini; 13 Joe McKenna. Subs (all used): 14 Nathan Mossop; 15 Phil Carleton; 16 Callum Wilkinson; 17 Ashley Bateman.
Tries: Grant (14), Reece (73); **Goals:** Rooney 2/2.
Rugby Leaguer & League Express Men of the Match: *Doncaster:* Kieran Hyde; *Scorpions:* Dalton Grant.
Penalty count: 4-7; **Half-time:** 26-6;
Referee: Dave Merrick; **Attendance:** 606.

GATESHEAD THUNDER 18 WHITEHAVEN 30

THUNDER: 1 Robin Peers; 2 Ashley Thackeray; 3 Mike Mitchell; 4 Josh Neilson; 5 Joe Brown; 6 Sam Walsh; 7 Paul Stamp; 8 Stephen Welton; 9 Tom Hodgson; 10 Brett Waller; 11 Matt Barron; 12 Jason Payne; 13 Ryan Steen. Subs (all used): 14 Ryan Clarke; 15 Josh Stoker; 16 Tabua Cakacaka; 17 Chris Parker Snr.
Tries: Peers (3), Mitchell (26), Clarke (56);
Goals: Clarke 1/1, Stamp 2/4.
WHITEHAVEN: 1 Andreas Bauer; 2 Craig Calvert; 3 Steve Fox; 4 Scott McAvoy; 5 Max Wiper; 6 Carl Rudd; 7 Ben Karalius; 8 David Houghton; 9 Carl Sice; 10 Howard Hill; 11 Matthew Haggerty; 12 Lee Doran; 13 Andrew Beattie. Subs (all used): 14 Chris Smith; 15 Luke Isakka; 16 Paul Cullnean; 17 Richard Varkulis.
Tries: Karalius (17), Wiper (22), Varkulis (32), Calvert (48, 72), Bauer (64); **Goals:** Rudd 3/6.

Rugby Leaguer & League Express Men of the Match: *Thunder:* Ryan Clarke; *Whitehaven:* Craig Calvert.
Penalty count: 9-6; **Half-time:** 10-16;
Referee: Joe Cobb; **Attendance:** 347.

OLDHAM 32 BARROW RAIDERS 26

OLDHAM: 1 Miles Greenwood; 2 Lucas Onyango; 3 David Cookson; 4 Mark McCully; 5 Paul Ballard; 6 Danny Whitmore; 7 Jamie Dallimore; 8 Jason Boults; 9 Martin Roden; 10 Bruce Johnson; 11 Paul Noone; 12 Paul Smith; 13 Chris Clarke. Subs (all used): 14 Alex Thompson; 15 John Clough; 16 Dave Ellison; 17 Matty Syron.
Tries: Onyango (16), Ellison (23), Whitmore (38), Dallimore (43), Cookson (49), Greenwood (75);
Goals: Dallimore 4/6.
RAIDERS: 1 Andy Ballard; 2 Lee Haney; 3 Chris Larkin; 4 James Finch; 5 James Nixon; 6 Scott Kaighan; 7 Liam Campbell; 8 Andy Bracek; 9 Liam Finch; 10 Lee Dutton; 11 Liam Harrison; 12 Barry Pugh; 13 Daniel Toal. Subs (all used): 14 Jack Pedley; 15 Martin Ostler; 16 James Gordon; 17 Andrew Dawson.
Tries: Pugh (11), Pedley (32), Ostler (35), Nixon (70), J Finch (78); **Goals:** Kaighan 3/5.
Rugby Leaguer & League Express Men of the Match: *Oldham:* Dave Ellison; *Raiders:* Liam Harrison.
Penalty count: 6-7; **Half-time:** 18-18;
Referee: Clint Sharrad; **Attendance:** 1,114.

ROUND 4

Friday 6th April 2012

ROCHDALE HORNETS 18 OLDHAM 10

HORNETS: 1 Paul O'Connor; 2 Dale Bloomfield; 3 Daniel Davies; 4 Chris Baines; 5 Wayne English; 6 Jonny Leather; 7 Chris Hough; 8 Phil Braddish; 9 Steve McDermott; 10 Dave Newton; 11 Gary Middlehurst; 12 Mark Hobson; 13 Dayne Donoghue. Subs (all used): 14 Phil Wood; 15 Adam Bowman; 16 Steve Bannister; 17 John Cookson.
Tries: English (6), Davies (26), Baines (45), McDermott (56); **Goals:** Baines 0/4, Hough 1/1.
OLDHAM: 1 Miles Greenwood; 2 Lucas Onyango; 3 David Cookson; 4 Mark McCully; 5 Paul Ballard; 6 Neil Roden; 7 Jamie Dallimore; 8 Jason Boults; 9 John Clough; 10 Chris Clarke; 11 Paul Noone; 12 Paul Smith; 13 Martin Roden. Subs (all used): 14 Alex Thompson; 15 Danny Whitmore; 16 Dave Ellison; 17 Bruce Johnson.
Tries: Onyango (13), Thompson (39);
Goals: Dallimore 1/2.
Sin bin: Thompson (67) - punching.
On report: Clough (80) - alleged pushing of Bowman into advertising hoardings.
Rugby Leaguer & League Express Men of the Match: *Hornets:* Gary Middlehurst; *Oldham:* Alex Thompson.
Penalty count: 9-10; **Half-time:** 8-10;
Referee: Gareth Hewer; **Attendance:** 1,020.

BARROW RAIDERS 40 GATESHEAD THUNDER 12

RAIDERS: 1 Andy Ballard; 2 Mike Backhouse; 3 Chris Larkin; 4 Aaron Low; 5 James Nixon; 6 Scott Kaighan; 7 Liam Campbell; 8 Jamie Butler; 9 James Dandy; 10 Andrew Dawson; 11 Liam Harrison; 12 James Gordon; 13 Daniel Toal. Subs (all used): 14 Jack Pedley; 15 Barry Pugh; 16 Andy Bracek; 17 Andries Venter.
Tries: Toal (8, 52, 60), Campbell (40, 45, 71), Low (76);
Goals: Kaighan 6/7.
THUNDER: 1 Connor Condron; 2 Ashley Thackeray; 3 Dan O'Sullivan; 4 Josh Neilson; 5 Joe Brown; 6 Sam Walsh; 7 Paul Stamp; 8 Brett Waller; 9 Ryan Clarke; 10 Jason Payne; 11 Matt Barron; 12 Josh Stoker; 13 Ryan Steen. Subs (all used): 14 Tom Hodgson; 15 Tabua Cakacaka; 16 Stephen Welton; 17 Will Bate.
Tries: Barron (4), Hodgson (29);
Goals: Clarke 1/1, Stamp 1/1.
Rugby Leaguer & League Express Men of the Match: *Raiders:* Daniel Toal; *Thunder:* Sam Walsh.
Penalty count: 8-2; **Half-time:** 12-12;
Referee: Peter Brooke; **Attendance:** 1,371.

DONCASTER 58 LONDON SKOLARS 16

DONCASTER: 1 Mick Butterfield; 2 Stewart Sanderson; 3 Liam Cunningham; 4 Lee Waterman; 5 Tom Hodson; 6 Paul Cooke; 7 Kieran Hyde; 8 Mark Castle; 9 Craig Lawton; 10 Jack Ely; 11 Craig Robinson; 12 Grant Edwards; 13 Russ Spiers. Subs (all used): 14 Francis Welsh; 15 Mike Emmett; 16 Kyle Bibb; 17 Kyle Kesik.
Tries: Waterman (6, 38, 46), Hodson (11, 24, 31, 38, 74), Hyde (15), Bibb (54), Edwards (60); **Goals:** Cooke 7/11.
SKOLARS: 1 James Anthony; 2 John Paxton; 3 Joe Price; 4 Chris McNamara; 5 Ade Adebisi; 6 Neil Thorman; 7 Dylan Skee; 8 Lamont Bryan; 9 Martyn Smith; 10 Dave Williams; 11 Michael Worrincy; 12 Brad Hopkins; 13 Austen Aggrey. Subs (all used): 14 James Roche; 15 Oliver Purslow; 16 Louis Robinson; 17 Alex Bate.
Tries: Anthony (21, 27), Hopkins (71);
Goals: Thorman 2/3.
Rugby Leaguer & League Express Men of the Match: *Doncaster:* Tom Hodson; *Skolars:* James Anthony.
Penalty count: 7-3; **Half-time:** 34-10;
Referee: George Stokes; **Attendance:** 541.

WHITEHAVEN 12 WORKINGTON TOWN 30

WHITEHAVEN: 1 Jonathan Youds; 2 Craig Calvert; 3 Martyn Wilson; 4 Scott McAvoy; 5 Max Wiper; 6 Carl Rudd; 7 Ben Karalius; 8 David Houghton; 9 Chris Smith; 10 Howard Hill; 11 Luke Isakka; 12 Lee Doran; 13 Andrew Beattie. Subs (all used): 14 Jessie Joe Parker; 15 Richard Varkulis; 16 Paul Cullnean; 17 Matthew Haggerty.
Tries: Calvert (59), Wilson (71); **Goals:** Rudd 2/3.
TOWN: 1 Brett Carter; 2 Elliott Miller; 3 Jason Mossop; 4 Daniel Rooney; 5 Stephen Dawes; 6 Marc Bainbridge; 7 Carl Forber; 8 Ryan McDonald; 9 Graeme Mattinson; 10 Kris Coward; 11 Brett Phillips; 12 Marc Shackley; 13 Karl Olstrum. Subs (all used): 14 Jarrad Stack; 15 Mike Whitehead; 16 Jamie Thackray; 17 James Robinson.
Tries: Mossop (10), Miller (40), Stack (50), Phillips (63);
Goals: Forber 6/7, McDonald 1/1.
Rugby Leaguer & League Express Men of the Match: *Whitehaven:* Carl Rudd; *Town:* Brett Carter.
Penalty count: 11-14; **Half-time:** 2-16;
Referee: Matthew Thomason; **Attendance:** 1,529.

Monday 9th April 2012

NORTH WALES CRUSADERS 34
SOUTH WALES SCORPIONS 22

CRUSADERS: 1 Danny Hulme; 2 Kriss Wilkes; 3 Ian Cross; 4 Leon Brennan; 5 Rob Massam; 6 Andrew Moulsdale; 7 Jamie Durbin; 8 Jonny Walker; 9 Lee Hudson; 10 Owain Brown; 11 Iwan Brown; 12 Anthony Morrison; 13 Jono Smith. Subs (all used): 14 Billy Sheen; 15 Chris Tyrer; 16 Jamie Clarke; 17 Tommy Johnson.
Tries: Moulsdale (9), Johnson (34, 54), Brennan (48, 73), Smith (63), I Brown (69);
Goals: Cross 1/4, Smith 2/3.
SCORPIONS: 1 David James; 2 Greg Callow; 3 Lewis Reece; 4 Rodney Peake; 5 Dalton Grant; 6 Jamie Rooney; 7 Shaun Owens; 8 Tom Spencer; 9 Nathan Mossop; 10 James Greenwood; 11 Joe Burke; 12 Chris Vitalini; 13 Geraint Davies. Subs (all used): 14 Steve Parry; 15 Joe McKenna; 16 Ashley Bateman; 17 Alistair McDonald.
Tries: Spencer (25), Greenwood (27, 64), Mossop (57);
Goals: Rooney 3/4.
Rugby Leaguer & League Express Men of the Match: *Crusaders:* Jamie Durbin; *Scorpions:* James Greenwood.
Penalty count: 9-4; **Half-time:** 10-10;
Referee: Chris Leatherbarrow; **Attendance:** 1,204.

ROUND 5

Sunday 22nd April 2012

BARROW RAIDERS 44 ROCHDALE HORNETS 18

RAIDERS: 1 Andy Ballard; 2 Mike Backhouse; 3 Chris Larkin; 4 Aaron Low; 5 James Nixon; 6 Darren Holt; 7 Liam Campbell; 8 Andy Bracek; 9 James Dandy; 10 Ruairi McGoff; 11 Liam Harrison; 12 Martin Ostler; 13 Daniel Toal. Subs (all used): 14 Liam Finch; 15 Jamie Butler; 16 Barry Pugh; 17 Andrew Dawson.
Tries: Low (8), Ballard (50, 80), Larkin (53), Nixon (56, 67), Campbell (58, 63); **Goals:** Holt 6/8.
HORNETS: 1 Paul O'Connor; 2 Dale Bloomfield; 3 Daniel Davies; 4 Anthony Stewart; 5 Wayne English; 6 Paul Crook; 7 Chris Hough; 8 Phil Braddish; 9 Steve McDermott; 10 John Cookson; 11 Chris Baines; 12 Mark Hobson; 13 Dave Newton. Subs (all used): 14 Phil Wood; 15 Dean Gorton; 16 Jonny Leather; 17 Danny Ekis.
Tries: Davies (25), Crook (42), McDermott (77);
Goals: Crook 3/4.
Rugby Leaguer & League Express Men of the Match: *Raiders:* Liam Finch; *Hornets:* Steve McDermott.
Penalty count: 9-3; **Half-time:** 6-6;
Referee: Dave Merrick; **Attendance:** 1,332.

GATESHEAD THUNDER 22 DONCASTER 40

THUNDER: 1 Connor Condron; 2 Ashley Thackeray; 3 Mike Mitchell; 4 Josh Stoker; 5 Joe Brown; 6 Sam Walsh; 7 Gavin Beasley; 8 Brett Waller; 9 Ryan Clarke; 10 Ryan McBride; 11 Daniel Barker; 12 Ryan Steen; 13 Jason Payne. Subs (all used): 14 Paul Stamp; 15 Dan O'Sullivan; 16 Stephen Welton; 17 Tabua Cakacaka.
Tries: Thackeray (8, 40, 43), Stamp (48), Condron (68);
Goals: Beasley 1/5.
DONCASTER: 1 Mick Butterfield; 2 Dean Colton; 3 Chris Spurr; 4 Lee Waterman; 5 Tom Hodson; 6 Paul Cooke; 7 Craig Fawcett; 8 Mark Castle; 9 Kyle Kesik; 10 Dean O'Loughlin; 11 Michael Kelly; 12 Craig Lawton; 13 Grant Edwards. Subs (all used): 14 Nathan Powley; 15 Francis Welsh; 16 Russ Spiers; 17 Kieran Hyde.
Tries: Fawcett (4), Spurr (17), Hodson (21, 62), Butterfield (33, 36), Kesik (56); **Goals:** Hodson 6/7.
Rugby Leaguer & League Express Men of the Match: *Thunder:* Ashley Thackeray; *Doncaster:* Mick Butterfield.
Penalty count: 6-3; **Half-time:** 8-30;
Referee: Ronnie Laughton; **Attendance:** 326.

LONDON SKOLARS 20 OLDHAM 20

SKOLARS: 1 James Anthony; 2 John Paxton; 3 Joe Price; 4 Joe Ridley; 5 Ade Adebisi; 6 Andy McLean; 7 Dylan Skee; 8 Rob Thomas; 9 Neil Thorman; 10 Dave Williams; 11 Brad Hopkins; 12 Michael Worrincy; 13 Alex Bate. Subs (all used): 14 Austen Aggrey; 15 Oliver Purslow; 16 Martyn Smith; 17 James Roche.
Tries: Anthony (4), Smith (47), Skee (75);
Goals: Skee 4/5.
OLDHAM: 1 Miles Greenwood; 2 Lucas Onyango; 3 Matthew Fogarty; 4 Mark McCully; 5 Shaun Robinson; 6 Graham Holroyd; 7 Jamie Dallimore; 8 Jason Boults; 9 Martin Roden; 10 Chris Clarke; 11 Paul Noone; 12 Paul Smith; 13 Valu Bentley. Subs (all used): 14 Matty Syron; 15 Alex Thompson; 16 Dave Ellison; 17 Michael Ward.
Tries: Greenwood (23, 77), Thompson (30, 37);
Goals: Dallimore 2/4.
Rugby Leaguer & League Express Men of the Match: *Skolars:* James Anthony; *Oldham:* Graham Holroyd.
Penalty count: 10-4; **Half-time:** 8-16;
Referee: Joe Cobb; **Attendance:** 492.

SOUTH WALES SCORPIONS 0 WHITEHAVEN 34

SCORPIONS: 1 David James; 2 Dalton Grant; 3 Yannic Parker; 4 Lewis Reece; 5 Greg Callow; 6 Rodney Peake; 7 Shaun Owens; 8 Tom Spencer; 9 Nathan Mossop; 10 James Greenwood; 11 Ashley Bateman; 12 Joe Burke; 13 Geraint Davies. Subs (all used): 14 Steve Parry; 15 Callum Wilkinson; 16 Chris Vitalini; 17 Rory Pitman.
WHITEHAVEN: 1 Jessie Joe Parker; 2 Craig Calvert; 3 Max Wiper; 4 Scott McAvoy; 5 Loz Hamzat; 6 Carl Sice; 7 Ben Karalius; 8 David Houghton; 9 Sam Gee; 10 Richard Varkulis; 11 Andrew Beattie; 12 Lee Doran; 13 Brad Crellin. Subs (all used): 14 Martyn Wilson; 15 Luke Isakka; 16 Paul Cullnean; 17 Matthew Haggerty.
Tries: McAvoy (20), Sice (32, 70, 79), Gee (45, 77);
Goals: Karalius 5/6.
Rugby Leaguer & League Express Men of the Match: *Scorpions:* Geraint Davies; *Whitehaven:* Carl Sice.
Penalty count: 6-6; **Half-time:** 0-12;
Referee: Chris Leatherbarrow; **Attendance:** 231.

WORKINGTON TOWN 58 NORTH WALES CRUSADERS 0

TOWN: 1 Brett Carter; 2 Elliott Miller; 3 Jason Mossop; 4 Karl Olstrum; 5 Stephen Dawes; 6 Marc Bainbridge; 7 Carl Forber; 8 Matthew Tunstall; 9 Graeme Mattinson; 10 Kris Coward; 11 Marc Shackley; 12 Jarrad Stack; 13 Dave Petersen. Subs (all used): 14 Mike Whitehead; 15 Peter Lupton; 16 Daniel Rooney; 17 Jamie Thackray.
Tries: Stack (7), Bainbridge (12), Carter (16, 29), Miller (32, 39), Petersen (37, 46), Shackley (43), S Dawes (64), Mossop (66); **Goals:** Forber 3/6, Bainbridge 4/5.
CRUSADERS: 1 Tommy Johnson; 2 Adam Clay; 3 Rob Massam; 4 Leon Brennan; 5 Kriss Wilkes; 6 Andrew Moulsdale; 7 Jamie Durbin; 8 Jonny Walker; 9 Lee Hudson; 10 Iwan Brown; 11 Jamie Clarke; 12 Anthony Morrison; 13 Simon Stephens. Subs (all used): 14 Chris Tyrer; 15 Owain Brown; 16 Owain Griffiths; 17 Billy Sheen.
Rugby Leaguer & League Express Men of the Match: *Town:* Jamie Thackray; *Crusaders:* Jamie Durbin.
Penalty count: 12-4; **Half-time:** 36-0;
Referee: Tom Crashley; **Attendance:** 776.

ROUND 10

Sunday 29th April 2012

ROCHDALE HORNETS 6 DONCASTER 38

HORNETS: 1 Paul O'Connor; 2 Anthony Stewart; 3 Dean Gorton; 4 Daniel Davies; 5 Dale Bloomfield; 6 Paul Crook; 7 Chris Hough; 8 Dave Newton; 9 Phil Wood; 10 John Cookson; 11 Mark Hobson; 12 Steve Bannister; 13 Dayne Donoghue. Subs (all used): 14 Steve McDermott; 15 Chris Baines; 16 Adam Bowman; 17 Phil Braddish.
Try: Baines (47); **Goals:** Crook 1/1.
DONCASTER: 1 Mick Butterfield; 2 Dean Colton; 3 Danny Cowling; 4 Lee Waterman; 5 Tom Hodson; 6 Paul Cooke; 7 Craig Fawcett; 8 Mark Castle; 9 Kyle Kesik; 10 Dean O'Loughlin; 11 Craig Lawton; 12 Michael Kelly; 13 Grant Edwards. Subs (all used): 14 Nathan Powley; 15 Stewart Sanderson; 16 Francis Welsh; 17 Jack Ely.
Tries: Kelly (12, 35), Cooke (32), Waterman (59, 63), Kesik (69), Fawcett (75); **Goals:** Hodson 5/7.
Rugby Leaguer & League Express Men of the Match: *Hornets:* John Cookson; *Doncaster:* Paul Cooke.
Penalty count: 6-5; **Half-time:** 0-16;
Referee: Gareth Hewer; **Attendance:** 301.

ROUND 6

Sunday 6th May 2012

WHITEHAVEN 36 LONDON SKOLARS 28

WHITEHAVEN: 1 Andreas Bauer; 2 Craig Calvert; 3 Max Wiper; 4 Jessie Joe Parker; 5 Loz Hamzat; 6 Jamie Rooney; 7 Ben Karalius; 8 David Houghton; 9 Sam Gee; 10 Paul Cullnean; 11 Andrew Beattie; 12 Lee Doran; 13 Carl Rudd. Subs (all used): 14 Carl Sice; 15 Luke Isakka; 16 Howard Hill; 17 Matthew Haggerty.
Tries: Cullnean (6), Doran (11), Bauer (26), Rooney (41, 67), Hamzat (54); **Goals:** Rudd 6/7.
Sin bin: Sice (51) - fighting.
SKOLARS: 1 James Anthony; 2 John Paxton; 3 Joe Price; 4 Dave Arnot; 5 Ade Adebisi; 6 Joe Ridley; 7 Dylan Skee; 8 Oliver Purslow; 9 Neil Thorman; 10 Dave Williams; 11 Brad Hopkins; 12 Michael Worrincy; 13 Alex Bate. Subs (all used): 14 Martyn Smith; 15 Oliver Bloom; 16 Joe Mbu; 17 Matt Thomas.
Tries: Adebisi (13, 76), Hopkins (58), Williams (64), Worrincy (78); **Goals:** Skee 4/5.
Sin bin: Worrincy (19) - interference;
Arnot (51) - fighting.
Rugby Leaguer & League Express Men of the Match: *Whitehaven:* Jamie Rooney; *Skolars:* James Anthony.
Penalty count: 12-11; **Half-time:** 18-6;
Referee: Matthew Thomason; **Attendance:** 627.

DONCASTER 48 ROCHDALE HORNETS 26

DONCASTER: 1 Mick Butterfield; 2 Dean Colton; 3 Danny Cowling; 4 Lee Waterman; 5 Tom Hodson; 6 Paul Cooke; 7 Craig Fawcett; 8 Mark Castle; 9 Kyle Kesik; 10 Dean O'Loughlin; 11 Chris Spurr; 12 Craig Lawton; 13 Grant Edwards. Subs (all used): 14 Mike Emmett; 15 Russ Spiers; 16 Nathan Powley; 17 Francis Welsh.
Tries: Colton (8, 22), Spiers (19), Kesik (29), Fawcett (32, 69), Spurr (52), Butterfield (66), Hodson (79); **Goals:** Hodson 6/9.

North Wales' Rob Massam makes a break against Oldham

HORNETS: 1 Paul O'Connor; 2 Andy Taylor; 3 Daniel Davies; 4 Dean Gorton; 5 Dale Bloomfield; 6 Paul Crook; 7 Chris Hough; 8 Dave Newton; 9 Steve McDermott; 10 John Cookson; 11 Chris Baines; 12 Mark Hobson; 13 Dayne Donoghue. Subs (all used): 14 Phil Wood; 15 Will Chadwick; 16 Danny Ekis; 17 Phil Braddish.
Tries: Bloomfield (15, 43), Gorton (46), O'Connor (49), Braddish (77); **Goals:** Crook 3/5.
Dismissal: McDermott (36) - punching.
Rugby Leaguer & League Express Men of the Match: *Doncaster:* Craig Lawton; *Hornets:* Paul Crook.
Penalty count: 7-3; **Half-time:** 26-4;
Referee: Peter Brooke; **Attendance:** 720.

OLDHAM 32 NORTH WALES CRUSADERS 36

OLDHAM: 1 Miles Greenwood; 2 Mark Brocklehurst; 3 Matthew Fogarty; 4 Mark McCully; 5 Shaun Robinson; 6 Jamie Dallimore; 7 Graham Holroyd; 8 Jason Boults; 9 John Clough; 10 Chris Clarke; 11 Paul Smith; 12 Jamie Acton; 13 Martin Roden. Subs (all used): 14 Valu Bentley; 15 Danny Whitmore; 16 Dave Ellison; 17 Luke Stenchion.
Tries: Robinson (3), Clough (16), Fogarty (36, 48), Ellison (76), Greenwood (78); **Goals:** Dallimore 4/6.
CRUSADERS: 1 Tommy Johnson; 2 Adam Clay; 3 Ian Cross; 4 Christiaan Roets; 5 Rob Massam; 6 Andrew Moulsdale; 7 Jamie Durbin; 8 Jonny Walker; 9 Lee Hudson; 10 Gareth Frodsham; 11 Jamie Clarke; 12 Anthony Morrison; 13 Simon Stephens. Subs (all used): 14 Owain Griffiths; 15 Sam Broadbent; 16 Chris Tyrer; 17 Iwan Brown.
Tries: Clay (11), Moulsdale (19), Broadbent (22), Clarke (31), Morrison (42), Cross (58), Massam (64); **Goals:** Cross 4/7.
Sin bin: Clarke (75) - professional foul.
Rugby Leaguer & League Express Men of the Match: *Oldham:* Shaun Robinson; *Crusaders:* Jamie Durbin.
Penalty count: 10-4; **Half-time:** 16-20;
Referee: Chris Leatherbarrow; **Attendance:** 580.

SOUTH WALES SCORPIONS 24 BARROW RAIDERS 42

SCORPIONS: 1 Jamie Murphy; 2 Dalton Grant; 3 Tom Morgan; 4 Lewis Reece; 5 David James; 6 Shaun Owens; 7 Steve Parry; 8 Kieran Harrison; 9 Nathan Mossop; 10 Greg Burke; 11 Ashley Bateman; 12 Chris Vitalini; 13 Joe Burke. Subs (all used): 14 Geraint Davies; 15 Alan Pope; 16 Alun-Wyn Davies; 17 Phil Carleton.
Tries: Parry (5, 57), Jamie Murphy (10), T Morgan (66, 75); **Goals:** Reece 1/2, Jamie Murphy 1/3.
RAIDERS: 1 Andy Ballard; 2 Mike Backhouse; 3 Chris Larkin; 4 Aaron Low; 5 James Nixon; 6 Darren Holt; 7 Liam Campbell; 8 Andy Bracek; 9 James Dandy; 10 Ruairi McGoff; 11 Liam Harrison; 12 Martin Ostler; 13 James Gordon. Subs (all used): 14 Liam Finch; 15 Jack Pedley; 16 Jamie Butler; 17 Andrew Dawson.
Tries: Gordon (18), Campbell (31), Nixon (47, 50), Ballard (55, 69), Ostler (60); **Goals:** Holt 7/7.
Rugby Leaguer & League Express Men of the Match: *Scorpions:* Steve Parry; *Raiders:* Andy Ballard.
Penalty count: 8-9; **Half-time:** 10-12;
Referee: Matthew Kidd; **Attendance:** 337.

WORKINGTON TOWN 58 GATESHEAD THUNDER 6

TOWN: 1 Elliott Miller; 2 John Patrick; 3 Jason Mossop; 4 Daniel Rooney; 5 Stephen Dawes; 6 Peter Lupton; 7 Marc Bainbridge; 8 Ryan McDonald; 9 Graeme Mattinson; 10 Kris Coward; 11 Brett Phillips; 12 Jarrad Stack; 13 Dave Petersen. Subs (all used): 14 Karl Olstrum; 15 Richard Farrer; 16 James Robinson; 17 Jamie Thackray.
Tries: Mattinson (1), Coward (7, 77), McDonald (18), Patrick (27), Stack (34), Phillips (45), Miller (47, 52), Rooney (70), Olstrum (72); **Goals:** Bainbridge 7/11.
THUNDER: 1 Shane Ackerley; 2 Ashley Thackeray; 3 Mike Mitchell; 4 Dan O'Sullivan; 5 Joe Brown; 6 Paul Stamp; 7 Gavin Beasley; 8 Brett Waller; 9 Ryan Clarke; 10 Ryan McBride; 11 Daniel Barker; 12 Ryan Steen; 13 Matt Barron. Subs (all used): 14 Tom Hodgson; 15 Tabua Cakacaka; 16 Stephen Welton; 17 Jason Payne.
Try: O'Sullivan (55); **Goals:** Beasley 1/1.
Rugby Leaguer & League Express Men of the Match: *Town:* Brett Phillips; *Thunder:* Ryan Steen.
Penalty count: 10-12; **Half-time:** 28-0;
Referee: Jamie Bloem; **Attendance:** 467.

ROUND 7

Sunday 13th May 2012

NORTH WALES CRUSADERS 10 WHITEHAVEN 17

CRUSADERS: 1 Tommy Johnson; 2 Adam Clay; 3 Ian Cross; 4 Sam Broadbent; 5 Rob Massam; 6 Andrew Moulsdale; 7 Jamie Durbin; 8 Jonny Walker; 9 Lee Hudson; 10 Iwan Brown; 11 Jamie Clarke; 12 Anthony Morrison; 13 Simon Stephens. Subs (all used): 14 Billy Sheen; 15 Chris Lunt; 16 Owain Brown; 17 Chris Tyrer.
Tries: Sheen (23, 46); **Goals:** Cross 0/1, Broadbent 1/1.
WHITEHAVEN: 1 Andreas Bauer; 2 Loz Hamzat; 3 Max Wiper; 4 Jessie Joe Parker; 5 Craig Calvert; 6 Jamie Rooney; 7 Ben Karalius; 8 David Houghton; 9 Sam Gee; 10 Paul Cullnean; 11 Brad Crellin; 12 Lee Doran; 13 Carl Rudd. Subs (all used): 14 Carl Sice, 15 Richard Varkulis; 16 Howard Hill; 17 Matthew Haggerty.
Tries: Sice (28), Calvert (51), Doran (60);
Goals: Rudd 1/3, Rooney 1/1; **Field goal:** Rooney (74).
Rugby Leaguer & League Express Men of the Match: *Crusaders:* Billy Sheen; *Whitehaven:* Max Wiper.
Penalty count: 11-6; **Half-time:** 4-6;
Referee: Matthew Kidd; **Attendance:** 804.

BARROW RAIDERS 20 WORKINGTON TOWN 12

RAIDERS: 1 Andy Ballard; 2 Mike Backhouse; 3 Chris Larkin; 4 Ryan Shaw; 5 James Nixon; 6 Darren Holt; 7 Liam Campbell; 8 Andy Bracek; 9 Liam Finch; 10 Ruairi McGoff; 11 Liam Harrison; 12 Martin Ostler; 13 David Toal. Subs (all used): 14 Jack Pedley; 15 Barry Pugh; 16 Jamie Butler; 17 Andrew Dawson.
Tries: Toal (24, 32), Larkin (52); **Goals:** Holt 4/4.
TOWN: 1 Brett Carter; 2 Elliott Miller; 3 Jason Mossop; 4 Daniel Rooney; 5 Stephen Dawes; 6 Peter Lupton; 7 Carl Forber; 8 Ryan McDonald; 9 Graeme Mattinson; 10 Kris Coward; 11 Brett Phillips; 12 Jarrad Stack; 13 Dave Petersen. Subs (all used): 14 Marc Bainbridge; 15 Marc Shackley; 16 Mike Whitehead; 17 Jamie Thackray.
Tries: Mattinson (3), Miller (48), S Dawes (57);
Goals: Forber 0/1, Bainbridge 0/2.
Rugby Leaguer & League Express Men of the Match: *Raiders:* Daniel Toal; *Town:* Graeme Mattinson.
Penalty count: 8-10; **Half-time:** 12-4;
Referee: Chris Leatherbarrow; **Attendance:** 1,808.

DONCASTER 40 OLDHAM 18

DONCASTER: 1 Mick Butterfield; 2 Stewart Sanderson; 3 Danny Cowling; 4 Lee Waterman; 5 Tom Hodson; 6 Paul Cooke; 7 Craig Fawcett; 8 Mark Castle; 9 Kyle Kesik; 10 Dean O'Loughlin; 11 Michael Kelly; 12 Craig Lawton; 13 Mike Emmett. Subs (all used): 14 Francis Welsh; 15 Jack Ely; 16 Russ Spiers; 17 Nathan Powley.
Tries: Fawcett (16), Welsh (45), Kelly (49), Cowling (60), Kesik (67), Ely (73); **Goals:** Hodson 6/7.
OLDHAM: 1 Miles Greenwood; 2 Lucas Onyango; 3 David Cookson; 4 Mark Brocklehurst; 5 Shaun Robinson; 6 Graham Holroyd; 7 Jamie Dallimore; 8 Jason Boults; 9 John Clough; 10 Liam Gilchrist; 11 Michael Ward; 12 Valu Bentley; 13 Martin Roden. Subs (all used): 14 Jamie Acton; 15 Sam Cunningham; 16 Dave Ellison; 17 Bruce Johnson.
Tries: Robinson (12), Ward (63), Cookson (70), Greenwood (80); **Goals:** Dallimore 1/4.
Sin bin: Clough (39) - delaying restart.
On report: Bentley (66) - alleged kicking.
Rugby Leaguer & League Express Men of the Match: *Doncaster:* Lee Waterman; *Oldham:* Michael Ward.
Penalty count: 9-6; **Half-time:** 10-4;
Referee: Dave Merrick; **Attendance:** 653.

ROCHDALE HORNETS 46 GATESHEAD THUNDER 24

HORNETS: 1 Wayne English; 2 Dale Bloomfield; 3 Daniel Davies; 4 Dean Gorton; 5 Jonny Leather; 6 Paul Crook; 7 Will Chadwick; 8 Mark Hobson; 9 Steve McDermott; 10 Adam Bowman; 11 Gary Middlehurst; 12 Andy Unsworth; 13 Dayne Donoghue. Subs (all used): 14 Phil Wood; 15 Paul O'Connor; 16 Joe Fitzpatrick; 17 Phil Braddish.

South Wales' Kevin James crashes over for a try against Rochdale

Tries: Bloomfield (21), Leather (28), Crook (32, 71), Middlehurst (47), Davies (53), English (57, 65); **Goals:** Crook 7/8.
THUNDER: 1 Shane Ackerley; 2 Ashley Thackeray; 3 Josh Neilson; 4 Ryan Steen; 5 Joe Brown; 6 Chris Parker Jnr; 7 Gavin Beasley; 8 Ryan McBride; 9 Tom Hodgson; 10 Tabua Cakacaka; 11 Matt Barron; 12 Daniel Barker; 13 Jason Payne. Subs (all used): 14 Paul Stamp; 15 Brett Waller; 16 Stephen Welton; 17 Scott Woods.
Tries: Beasley (5), Thackeray (10), Payne (39), Neilson (44), Waller (49); **Goals:** Parker Jnr 2/5.
Rugby Leaguer & League Express Men of the Match:
Hornets: Paul Crook; *Thunder:* Jason Payne.
Penalty count: 8-9; **Half-time:** 18-14;
Referee: Greg Dolan; **Attendance:** 350.

ROUND 8

Sunday 20th May 2012

BARROW RAIDERS 42 LONDON SKOLARS 12

RAIDERS: 1 Andy Ballard; 2 Mike Backhouse; 3 Ryan Shaw; 4 Chris Larkin; 5 Lee Haney; 6 Scott Kaighan; 7 Liam Campbell; 8 Andy Bracek; 9 Liam Finch; 10 Ruairi McGoff; 11 Liam Harrison; 12 James Gordon; 13 David Toal. Subs (all used): 14 James Dandy; 15 James Finch; 16 Jamie Butler; 17 Andrew Dawson.
Tries: Campbell (25, 72), Harrison (44), J Finch (67), Ballard (74), Toal (77), McGoff (80); **Goals:** Shaw 7/7.
SKOLARS: 1 James Anthony; 2 John Paxton; 3 Joe Price; 4 Dave Arnot; 5 Ade Adebisi; 6 Neil Thorman; 7 Dylan Skee; 8 Oliver Purslow; 9 Martyn Smith; 10 Dave Williams; 11 Brad Hopkins; 12 Michael Worrincy; 13 Lamont Bryan. Subs (all used): 14 Rob Thomas; 15 Oliver Bloom; 16 Alex Bate; 17 Joe Mbu.
Tries: Worrincy (7), R Thomas (49); **Goals:** Skee 2/2.
Rugby Leaguer & League Express Men of the Match:
Raiders: James Gordon; *Skolars:* Brad Hopkins.
Penalty count: 7-10; **Half-time:** 6-6;
Referee: Joe Cobb; **Attendance:** 1,159.

OLDHAM 16 WHITEHAVEN 26

OLDHAM: 1 Miles Greenwood; 2 Lucas Onyango; 3 David Cookson; 4 Mark McCully; 5 Mark Brocklehurst; 6 Graham Holroyd; 7 Jamie Dallimore; 8 Jason Boults; 9 John Clough; 10 David Tootill; 11 Michael Ward; 12 Valu Bentley; 13 Martin Roden. Subs (all used): 14 Alex Thompson; 15 Danny Whitmore; 16 Lewis Reed; 17 Liam Gilchrist.
Tries: Cookson (21, 62), Brocklehurst (75);
Goals: Dallimore 2/3, Holroyd 1/1.
WHITEHAVEN: 1 Andreas Bauer; 2 Loz Hamzat; 3 Jessie Joe Parker; 4 Max Wiper; 5 Craig Calvert; 6 Jamie Rooney; 7 Ben Karalius; 8 David Houghton; 9 Sam Gee;
10 Paul Cullnean; 11 Richard Varkulis; 12 Lee Doran; 13 Carl Rudd. Subs (all used): 14 Carl Sice; 15 Luke Isakka; 16 Howard Hill; 17 Matthew Haggerty.
Tries: Gee (6), Wiper (27), Calvert (35), Houghton (73);
Goals: Rudd 3/3, Rooney 2/2.
Rugby Leaguer & League Express Men of the Match:
Oldham: Lewis Reed; *Whitehaven:* Lee Doran.
Penalty count: 11-6; **Half-time:** 4-18;
Referee: Chris Leatherbarrow; **Attendance:** 624.

SOUTH WALES SCORPIONS 32 ROCHDALE HORNETS 30

SCORPIONS: 1 Jamie Murphy; 2 David James; 3 Tom Morgan; 4 Kevin James; 5 Dalton Grant; 6 Loz Wildbore; 7 Steve Parry; 8 Greg Burke; 9 Nathan Mossop; 10 Joe Burke; 11 Chris Vitalini; 12 Geraint Davies; 13 Ashley Bateman. Subs: 14 Shaun Owens (not used); 15 Phil Carleton; 16 Alun-Wyn Davies; 17 Callum Wilkinson.
Tries: Mossop (15, 24, 73), Parry (30, 67), K James (50); **Goals:** Jamie Murphy 4/6.
HORNETS: 1 Wayne English; 2 Dale Bloomfield; 3 Daniel Davies; 4 Chris Baines; 5 Dean Gorton; 6 Paul Crook; 7 Jonny Leather; 8 Joe Fitzpatrick; 9 Chris Hough; 10 John Cookson; 11 Gary Middlehurst; 12 Adam Bowman; 13 Dayne Donoghue. Subs (all used): 14 Steve McDermott; 15 Mark Hobson; 16 Dave Newton; 17 Phil Braddish.
Tries: Gorton (8, 64), English (21), Davies (40), Cookson (54), McDermott (80); **Goals:** Crook 3/6.
Rugby Leaguer & League Express Men of the Match:
Scorpions: Nathan Mossop; *Hornets:* Daniel Davies.
Penalty count: 5-6; **Half-time:** 16-12;
Referee: Warren Turley; **Attendance:** 557.

WORKINGTON TOWN 45 DONCASTER 18

TOWN: 1 Brett Carter; 2 Elliott Miller; 3 Jason Mossop; 4 Daniel Rooney; 5 Mark Calderwood; 6 Peter Lupton; 7 Marc Bainbridge; 8 Ryan McDonald; 9 Graeme Mattinson; 10 Matthew Tunstall; 11 Brett Phillips; 12 Jarrad Stack; 13 Dave Petersen. Subs (all used): 14 Karl Olstrum; 15 Carl Forber; 16 Mike Whitehead; 17 Jamie Thackray.
Tries: Miller (21, 33, 79), Stack (29, 77), Rooney (55), Carter (62), Thackray (66), Calderwood (69);
Goals: Bainbridge 2/5, Forber 2/4; **Field goal:** Lupton (73).
DONCASTER: 1 Mick Butterfield; 2 Stewart Sanderson; 3 Danny Cowling; 4 Lee Waterman; 5 Tom Hodson; 6 Paul Cooke; 7 Craig Fawcett; 8 Mark Castle; 9 Kyle Kesik; 10 Dean O'Loughlin; 11 Michael Kelly; 12 Chris Spurr; 13 Mike Emmett. Subs (all used): 14 Nathan Powley; 15 Francis Welsh; 16 Craig Robinson; 17 Russ Spiers.
Tries: Cowling (3), Butterfield (7), Waterman (19);
Goals: Hodson 3/3.
Rugby Leaguer & League Express Men of the Match:
Town: Jamie Thackray; *Doncaster:* Tom Hodson.
Penalty count: 3-4; **Half-time:** 14-18;
Referee: Gareth Hewer; **Attendance:** 804.

ROUND 9

Saturday 26th May 2012

OLDHAM 30 SOUTH WALES SCORPIONS 35

OLDHAM: 1 Miles Greenwood; 2 Chris Holroyde; 3 David Cookson; 4 Mark Brocklehurst; 5 John Gillam; 6 Graham Holroyd; 7 Danny Whitmore; 8 Jason Boults; 9 Martin Roden; 10 David Tootill; 11 Paul Noone; 12 Michael Ward; 13 Lewis Reed. Subs (all used): 14 Valu Bentley; 15 John Clough; 16 Dave Ellison; 17 Liam Gilchrist.
Tries: Reed (15), Clough (25), Ward (39), Greenwood (50), Tootill (78); **Goals:** Holroyd 5/5.
SCORPIONS: 1 Jamie Murphy; 2 David James; 3 David James; 4 Tom Morgan; 5 Ryan King; 6 Loz Wildbore; 7 Steve Parry; 8 James Greenwood; 9 Nathan Mossop; 10 Greg Burke; 11 Chris Vitalini; 12 Geraint Davies; 13 Joe Burke. Subs (all used): 14 Alun-Wyn Davies; 15 Ashley Bateman; 16 Lewis Reece; 17 Shaun Owens.
Tries: King (11), Greenwood (18), Parry (33, 68), Jamie Murphy (44), K James (56);
Goals: Jamie Murphy 5/6; **Field goal:** Wildbore (70).
Rugby Leaguer & League Express Men of the Match:
Oldham: Michael Ward; *Scorpions:* Steve Parry.
Penalty count: 8-6; **Half-time:** 18-18;
Referee: Greg Dolan; **Attendance:** 471.

Sunday 27th May 2012

LONDON SKOLARS 48 GATESHEAD THUNDER 22

SKOLARS: 1 James Anthony; 2 John Paxton; 3 Joe Price; 4 Dave Arnot; 5 Ade Adebisi; 6 Neil Thorman; 7 Dylan Skee; 8 Oliver Purslow; 9 Martyn Smith; 10 Dave Williams; 11 Brad Hopkins; 12 Michael Worrincy; 13 Lamont Bryan. Subs (all used): 14 Rob Thomas; 15 Oliver Bloom; 16 Alex Bate; 17 Joe Mbu.
Tries: Adebisi (3, 46, 77), Hopkins (6, 73), Bryan (11), Worrincy (19), Anthony (61), Smith (79);
Goals: Skee 6/9.
THUNDER: 1 Shane Ackerley; 2 Ashley Thackeray; 3 Mike Mitchell; 4 Josh Neilson; 5 Joe Brown; 6 Chris Parker Jnr; 7 Gavin Beasley; 8 Brett Waller; 9 Tom Hodgson; 10 Tabua Cakacaka; 11 Matt Barron; 12 Daniel Barker; 13 Jason Payne. Subs (all used): 14 Paul Stamp; 15 Josh Stoker; 16 Stephen Welton; 17 Oliver O'Mara.
Tries: Hodgson (8), Brown (23), Waller (37), Stamp (65); **Goals:** Beasley 1/2, Parker Jnr 2/2.
Rugby Leaguer & League Express Men of the Match:
Skolars: Ade Adebisi; *Thunder:* Brett Waller.
Penalty count: 9-9; **Half-time:** 20-16;
Referee: Dave Sharpe; **Attendance:** 353.

NORTH WALES CRUSADERS 28 DONCASTER 41

CRUSADERS: 1 Tommy Johnson; 2 Adam Clay; 3 Ian

Cross; 4 Sam Broadbent; 5 Rob Massam; 6 Andrew Moulsdale; 7 Billy Sheen; 8 Jonny Walker; 9 Lee Hudson; 10 Iwan Brown; 11 Andy Gorski; 12 Anthony Morrison; 13 Simon Stephens. Subs (all used): 14 Owain Brown; 15 Jamie Clarke; 16 Alex Trumper; 17 Owain Griffiths.
Tries: Stephens (8), Sheen (25), Moulsdale (29), Massam (57), Clay (72); **Goals:** Broadbent 4/5.
DONCASTER: 1 Mick Butterfield; 2 Stewart Sanderson; 3 Chris Spurr; 4 Lee Waterman; 5 Tom Hodson; 6 Paul Cooke; 7 Craig Fawcett; 8 Mark Castle; 9 Kyle Kesik; 10 Russ Spiers; 11 Michael Kelly; 12 Craig Lawton; 13 Mike Emmett. Subs (all used): 14 Nathan Powley; 15 Francis Welsh; 16 Craig Robinson; 17 Dean Colton.
Tries: Spiers (3, 36), Spurr (20), Cooke (47), Fawcett (51, 66), Butterfield (61); **Goals:** Hodson 6/7; **Field goal:** Fawcett (76).
Rugby Leaguer & League Express Men of the Match: *Crusaders:* Iwan Brown; *Doncaster:* Craig Fawcett.
Penalty count: 7-8; **Half-time:** 18-18;
Referee: Jamie Bloem; **Attendance:** 705.

WHITEHAVEN 28 BARROW RAIDERS 42

WHITEHAVEN: 1 Andreas Bauer; 2 Craig Calvert; 3 Max Wiper; 4 Jessie Joe Parker; 5 Loz Hamzat; 6 Jamie Rooney; 7 Ben Karalius; 8 David Houghton; 9 Sam Gee; 10 Paul Cullnean; 11 Richard Varkulis; 12 Lee Doran; 13 Carl Rudd. Subs (all used): 14 Carl Sice; 15 Luke Isakka; 16 Brad Crellin; 17 Matthew Haggerty.
Tries: Rudd (4), Varkulis (21), Houghton (27), Sice (40), Parker (47); **Goals:** Rudd 4/5.
Sin bin: Haggerty (32) - late challenge.
RAIDERS: 1 Andy Ballard; 2 Mike Backhouse; 3 James Finch; 4 Ryan Shaw; 5 James Nixon; 6 Scott Kaighan; 7 Liam Campbell; 8 Jamie Butler; 9 James Dandy; 10 Ruairi McGoff; 11 Andy Bracek; 12 James Gordon; 13 Daniel Toal. Subs (all used): 14 Liam Finch; 15 Martin Ostler; 16 Andrew Dawson; 17 Andries Venter.
Tries: Bracek (8), Campbell (18, 72, 74), Dandy (23), J Finch (32), Shaw (51); **Goals:** Shaw 7/7.
Rugby Leaguer & League Express Men of the Match: *Whitehaven:* David Houghton; *Raiders:* Liam Campbell.
Penalty count: 9-11; **Half-time:** 24-24;
Referee: Tom Crashley; **Attendance:** 1,124.

Sunday 3rd June 2012

ROCHDALE HORNETS 24 WORKINGTON TOWN 37

HORNETS: 1 Wayne English; 2 Dale Bloomfield; 3 Daniel Davies; 4 Anthony Stewart; 5 Barry Clarke; 6 Paul Crook; 7 Danny Price; 8 Chris Clough; 9 Phil Wood; 10 John Cookson; 11 Steve Bannister; 12 Gary Middlehurst; 13 Dayne Donoghue. Subs (all used): 14 Ryan Brown; 15 Chris Hough; 16 Danny Samuel; 17 Adam Bowman.
Tries: Clarke (36), English (41), Bloomfield (46), Cookson (53), Davies (67); **Goals:** Crook 2/5.
TOWN: 1 Brett Carter; 2 Elliott Miller; 3 Jason Mossop; 4 Daniel Rooney; 5 Mark Calderwood; 6 Peter Lupton; 7 Marc Bainbridge; 8 Mike Whitehead; 9 Graeme Mattinson; 10 Matthew Tunstall; 11 Brett Phillips; 12 Jarrad Stack; 13 Dave Petersen. Subs (all used): 14 Karl Olstrum; 15 Marc Shackley; 16 James Newton; 17 Jamie Thackray.
Tries: Lupton (7, 25), Carter (22, 76), Thackray (29), Miller (72); **Goals:** Bainbridge 6/6;
Field goal: Bainbridge (75).
Rugby Leaguer & League Express Men of the Match: *Hornets:* Paul Crook; *Town:* Brett Carter.
Penalty count: 8-5; **Half-time:** 4-24;
Referee: Ronnie Laughton; **Attendance:** 512.

ROUND 10

Sunday 10th June 2012

LONDON SKOLARS 12 WORKINGTON TOWN 44

SKOLARS: 1 James Anthony; 2 John Paxton; 3 Alex Bate; 4 Dave Arnot; 5 Smokie Junor; 6 Neil Thorman; 7 Dylan Skee; 8 Lamont Bryan; 9 Martyn Smith; 10 Dave Williams; 11 Brad Hopkins; 12 Michael Worrincy; 13 Joe Mbu. Subs (all used): 14 Oliver Bloom; 15 Oliver Purslow; 16 Sam Bolger; 17 Matt Thomas.
Tries: Anthony (23), Worrincy (33); **Goals:** Skee 2/2.
TOWN: 1 Brett Carter; 2 Elliott Miller; 3 Jason Mossop; 4 Daniel Rooney; 5 Mark Calderwood; 6 Dave Petersen; 7 Marc Bainbridge; 8 Ryan McDonald; 9 Graeme Mattinson; 10 Kris Coward; 11 Brett Phillips; 12 Jarrad Stack; 13 Karl Olstrum. Subs (all used): 14 Peter Lupton; 15 Marc Shackley; 16 Mike Whitehead; 17 Jamie Thackray.
Tries: Coward (9), Mattinson (20), Stack (27), Olstrum (29, 45), Calderwood (72, 76), Miller (79);
Goals: Bainbridge 6/8.
Rugby Leaguer & League Express Men of the Match: *Skolars:* James Anthony; *Town:* Graeme Mattinson.
Penalty count: 7-9; **Half-time:** 12-20;
Referee: Greg Dolan; **Attendance:** 623.

NORTH WALES CRUSADERS 30 OLDHAM 28

CRUSADERS: 1 Tommy Johnson; 2 Adam Clay; 3 Sam Broadbent; 4 Leon Brennan; 5 Rob Massam; 6 Andrew Moulsdale; 7 Billy Sheen; 8 Jonny Walker; 9 Lee Hudson; 10 Iwan Brown; 11 Andy Gorski; 12 Anthony Morrison; 13 Simon Stephens. Subs (all used): 14 Jono Smith; 15 Alex Trumper; 16 Toby Adamson; 17 Owain Brown.
Tries: Brennan (2, 66, 73), Sheen (11), Clay (49), Smith (51); **Goals:** Broadbent 1/3, Johnson 2/3.
OLDHAM: 1 Miles Greenwood; 2 Chris Holroyde; 3 Mark Brocklehurst; 4 Mark McCully; 5 John Gillam; 6 Neil Roden; 7 Danny Whitmore; 8 Jason Boults; 9 Martin Roden; 10 David Tootill; 11 Michael Ward; 12 Valu Bentley; 13 Lewis Reed. Subs (all used): 14 Colton Roche; 15 John Clough; 16 Dave Ellison; 17 Liam Gilchrist.
Tries: Ward (21, 27), Ellison (31), Whitmore (39), Greenwood (62); **Goals:** Holroyde 4/5.
Rugby Leaguer & League Express Men of the Match: *Crusaders:* Leon Brennan; *Oldham:* Michael Ward.
Penalty count: 14-5; **Half-time:** 10-22;
Referee: Matthew Thomason; **Attendance:** 822.

GATESHEAD THUNDER 18 BARROW RAIDERS 40

THUNDER: 1 Connor Condron; 2 Ashley Thackeray; 3 Josh Neilson; 4 Joe Brown; 5 Shane Ackerley; 6 Chris Parker Jnr; 7 Gavin Beasley; 8 Brett Waller; 9 Tom Hodgson; 10 Ryan McBride; 11 Matt Barron; 12 Daniel Barker; 13 Jason Payne. Subs: 14 Paul Stamp; 15 Ryan Steen; 16 Stephen Welton; 17 Oliver O'Mara (not used).
Tries: Parker Jnr (35), Stamp (50), Barron (69);
Goals: Parker Jnr 3/3.
RAIDERS: 1 Lee Haney; 2 Mike Backhouse; 3 Ryan Shaw; 4 James Finch; 5 James Nixon; 6 Scott Kaighan; 7 Liam Campbell; 8 Jamie Butler; 9 James Dandy; 10 Andries Venter; 11 Liam Harrison; 12 Andy Bracek; 13 Daniel Toal. Subs: 14 Liam Finch; 15 Darren Holt (not used); 16 Martin Ostler; 17 Andrew Dawson.
Tries: Haney (5), Butler (15), Kaighan (20, 76, 79), Shaw (45), Nixon (58); **Goals:** Shaw 6/7.
Rugby Leaguer & League Express Men of the Match: *Thunder:* Chris Parker Jnr; *Raiders:* Lee Haney.
Penalty count: 13-9; **Half-time:** 6-16;
Referee: Dave Sharpe; **Attendance:** 398
(at Filtrona Park, South Shields).

WHITEHAVEN 34 SOUTH WALES SCORPIONS 18

WHITEHAVEN: 1 Andreas Bauer; 2 Craig Calvert; 3 Jessie Joe Parker; 4 Steve Fox; 5 Max Wiper; 6 Jamie Rooney; 7 Carl Rudd; 8 David Houghton; 9 Carl Sice; 10 Paul Cullnean; 11 Lee Doran; 12 Richard Varkulis; 13 Brad Crellin. Subs (all used): 14 Ben Karalius; 15 Matthew Haggerty; 16 Luke Isakka; 17 Anthony Mullally.
Tries: Calvert (5, 15, 40, 64), Wiper (50, 61);
Goals: Rudd 2/5, Rooney 3/3.
SCORPIONS: 1 Jamie Murphy; 2 Ryan King; 3 Tom Morgan; 4 David James; 5 Kevin James; 6 Loz Wildbore; 7 Steve Parry; 8 James Greenwood; 9 Nathan Mossop; 10 Greg Burke; 11 Chris Vitalini; 12 Geraint Davies; 13 Joe Burke. Subs (all used): 14 Connor Farrer; 15 Alun-Wyn Davies; 16 Ashley Bateman; 17 Neil Dallimore.
Tries: Greenwood (18), T Morgan (23), Bateman (32);
Goals: Jamie Murphy 3/3.
Sin bin: T Morgan (78) - punching.
Rugby Leaguer & League Express Men of the Match: *Whitehaven:* Craig Calvert; *Scorpions:* Jamie Murphy.
Penalty count: 5-8; **Half-time:** 16-18;
Referee: Dave Merrick; **Attendance:** 648.

ROUND 11

Sunday 24th June 2012

BARROW RAIDERS 40 NORTH WALES CRUSADERS 24

RAIDERS: 1 Andy Ballard; 2 Mike Backhouse; 3 Chris Larkin; 4 Ryan Shaw; 5 James Nixon; 6 Scott Kaighan; 7 Liam Campbell; 8 Bradley Brennan; 9 Liam Finch; 10 Ruairi McGoff; 11 Liam Harrison; 12 Andy Bracek; 13 Daniel Toal. Subs (all used): 14 Jack Pedley; 15 James Gordon; 16 Ryan Duffy; 17 Andrew Dawson.
Tries: Harrison (10, 64, 68), Ballard (20), Campbell (33), Toal (43), Kaighan (77); **Goals:** Shaw 6/7.
CRUSADERS: 1 Tommy Johnson; 2 Adam Clay; 3 Leon Brennan; 4 Christiaan Roets; 5 Rob Massam; 6 Andrew Moulsdale; 7 Jamie Durbin; 8 Jonny Walker; 9 Lee Hudson; 10 Simon Stephens; 11 Andy Gorski; 12 Toby Adamson; 13 Jono Smith. Subs (all used): 14 Jamie Clarke; 15 Danny Hulme; 16 Iwan Brown; 17 Alex Trumper.
Tries: Gorski (16, 48), Smith (37), Brennan (58);
Goals: Johnson 4/4.
Rugby Leaguer & League Express Men of the Match: *Raiders:* Liam Harrison; *Crusaders:* Jono Smith.
Penalty count: 5-6; **Half-time:** 18-12;
Referee: Peter Brooke; **Attendance:** 1,438.

DONCASTER 78 GATESHEAD THUNDER 6

DONCASTER: 1 Mick Butterfield; 2 Stewart Sanderson; 3 Chris Spurr; 4 Lee Waterman; 5 Tom Hodson; 6 Kyle Kesik; 7 Craig Fawcett; 8 Mark Castle; 9 Jack Ely; 10 Dean O'Loughlin; 11 Michael Kelly; 12 Craig Robinson; 13 Mike Emmett. Subs (all used): 14 Alex Rowe; 15 Russ Spiers; 16 Carl Hughes; 17 Nathan Powley.
Tries: Ely (14, 71), Powley (22), Emmett (25), Waterman (28, 45, 56, 67), Fawcett (34, 37), Kelly (40), Butterfield (51), Rowe (72), Sanderson (76); **Goals:** Hodson 11/14.
THUNDER: 1 Connor Condron; 2 Ashley Thackeray; 3 Josh Neilson; 4 Joe Brown; 5 Shane Ackerley; 6 Chris Parker Jnr; 7 Gavin Beasley; 8 Brett Waller; 9 Tom Hodgson; 10 Ryan McBride; 11 Matt Barron; 12 Ryan Steen; 13 Jason Payne. Subs (all used): 14 Paul Stamp; 15 Daniel Barker; 16 Oliver O'Mara; 17 Stephen Welton.
Try: Waller (60); **Goals:** Parker Jnr 1/1.
Rugby Leaguer & League Express Men of the Match: *Doncaster:* Lee Waterman; *Thunder:* Brett Waller.
Penalty count: 8-7; **Half-time:** 38-0;
Referee: Matthew Kidd; **Attendance:** 656.

OLDHAM 4 ROCHDALE HORNETS 30

OLDHAM: 1 Miles Greenwood; 2 Lucas Onyango; 3 Colton Roche; 4 Mark McCully; 5 John Gillam; 6 Neil Roden; 7 Danny Whitmore; 8 Jason Boults; 9 John Clough; 10 Lewis Reed; 11 Paul Noone; 12 Paul Smith; 13 Valu Bentley. Subs (all used): 14 Michael Ward; 15 Alex Thompson; 16 Dave Ellison; 17 Daniel Smith.
Try: Greenwood (37); **Goals:** D Smith 0/1.
Sin bin: N Roden (79) - professional foul.
HORNETS: 1 Wayne English; 2 Dale Bloomfield; 3 Dean Gorton; 4 Anthony Stewart; 5 Jonny Leather; 6 Paul Crook; 7 Steve Roper; 8 Dave Newton; 9 Chris Hough; 10 John Cookson; 11 Danny Samuel; 12 Gary Middlehurst; 13 Dayne Donoghue. Subs (all used): 14 Chris Baines; 15 Phil Braddish; 16 Joe Fitzpatrick; 17 Adam Bowman.
Tries: Leather (26, 54, 74), English (65), Braddish (77);
Goals: Crook 5/5.
Rugby Leaguer & League Express Men of the Match: *Oldham:* Miles Greenwood; *Hornets:* Wayne English.
Penalty count: 9-14; **Half-time:** 4-6;
Referee: Joe Cobb; **Attendance:** 599.

SOUTH WALES SCORPIONS 32 LONDON SKOLARS 36

SCORPIONS: 1 David James; 2 Kevin James; 3 Ben Gilbert; 4 Tom Morgan; 5 Dalton Grant; 6 Loz Wildbore; 7 Steve Parry; 8 James Greenwood; 9 Nathan Mossop; 10 Greg Burke; 11 Chris Vitalini; 12 Ashley Bateman; 13 Joe Burke. Subs: 14 Shaun Owens (not used); 15 Neil Dallimore; 16 Alan Pope; 17 Keiran Harrison.
Tries: K James (6), T Morgan (18), Parry (21, 28), G Burke (50), Mossop (53); **Goals:** Wildbore 4/6.
SKOLARS: 1 James Anthony; 2 John Paxton; 3 Joe Price; 4 Will Colleran; 5 Ade Adebisi; 6 Andy McLean; 7 Dylan Skee; 8 Olsi Krasniqi; 9 Neil Thorman; 10 Dave Williams; 11 Brad Hopkins; 12 Michael Worrincy; 13 Lamont Bryan. Subs (all used): 14 Michael Sykes; 15 Martyn Smith; 16 Matt Thomas; 17 Louis Robinson.
Tries: McLean (2, 63), Colleran (10), Skee (39, 56), Price (42); **Goals:** Skee 6/6.
Rugby Leaguer & League Express Men of the Match: *Scorpions:* Steve Parry; *Skolars:* Andy McLean.
Penalty count: 8-8; **Half-time:** 22-18;
Referee: Warren Turley; **Attendance:** 307.

WORKINGTON TOWN 30 WHITEHAVEN 28

TOWN: 1 Brett Carter; 2 Elliott Miller; 3 Daniel Rooney; 4 Jason Mossop; 5 Mark Calderwood; 6 Peter Lupton; 7 Marc Bainbridge; 8 Ryan McDonald; 9 Graeme Mattinson; 10 Kris Coward; 11 Brett Phillips; 12 Jarrad Stack; 13 Dave Petersen. Subs (all used): 14 Karl Olstrum; 15 Marc Shackley; 16 Mike Whitehead; 17 Jamie Thackray.
Tries: Miller (13), Stack (38), Mattinson (44), Lupton (56), Petersen (59), Phillips (66); **Goals:** Bainbridge 3/8.
WHITEHAVEN: 1 Andreas Bauer; 2 Craig Calvert; 3 Jessie Joe Parker; 4 Steve Fox; 5 Max Wiper; 6 Jamie Rooney; 7 Carl Rudd; 8 David Houghton; 9 Carl Sice; 10 Paul Cullnean; 11 Richard Varkulis; 12 Anthony Mullally; 13 Lee Doran. Subs (all used): 14 Sam Gee; 15 Luke Isakka; 16 Andrew Beattie; 17 Matthew Haggerty.
Tries: Rooney (20), Doran (31, 78), Beattie (51), Mullally (72); **Goals:** Rudd 3/4, Rooney 1/1.
Rugby Leaguer & League Express Men of the Match: *Town:* Graeme Mattinson; *Whitehaven:* Jamie Rooney.
Penalty count: 10-7; **Half-time:** 10-12;
Referee: Matthew Thomason; **Attendance:** 1,954.

ROUND 12

Sunday 1st July 2012

LONDON SKOLARS 17 BARROW RAIDERS 30

SKOLARS: 1 James Anthony; 2 John Paxton; 3 Joe Price; 4 Dave Arnot; 5 Ade Adebisi; 6 Andy McLean; 7 Dylan Skee; 8 Michael Sykes; 9 Neil Thorman; 10 Dave Williams; 11 Brad Hopkins; 12 Matt Thomas; 13 Lamont Bryan. Subs (all used): 14 Rob Thomas; 15 Martyn Smith; 16 Louis Robinson; 17 Joe Mbu.
Tries: Anthony (13), McLean (39), Hopkins (61);
Goals: Skee 2/3; **Field goal:** McLean (40).
Sin bin: Thorman (10) - obstruction;
Mbu (33) - late challenge on Kaighan.
RAIDERS: 1 Andy Ballard; 2 Mike Backhouse; 3 Chris Larkin; 4 Ryan Shaw; 5 Lee Haney; 6 Scott Kaighan; 7 Liam Campbell; 8 Jamie Butler; 9 Liam Finch; 10 Bradley Brennan; 11 Liam Harrison; 12 James Gordon; 13 Daniel Toal. Subs (all used): 14 James Dandy; 15 Martin Ostler; 16 Ryan Duffy; 17 Ruairi McGoff.
Tries: Harrison (43), Dandy (47), Ballard (49, 69), Ostler (67); **Goals:** Shaw 5/5.
Rugby Leaguer & League Express Men of the Match: *Skolars:* Andy McLean; *Raiders:* Liam Harrison.
Penalty count: 8-5; **Half-time:** 11-0;
Referee: Tom Crashley; **Attendance:** 472.

SOUTH WALES SCORPIONS 30 DONCASTER 44

SCORPIONS: 1 David James; 2 Kevin James; 3 Ben Gilbert; 4 Tom Morgan; 5 Dalton Grant; 6 Shaun Owens; 7 Steve Parry; 8 Neil Dallimore; 9 Nathan Mossop; 10 Joe Burke; 11 Alan Pope; 12 Chris Vitalini; 13 Ashley Bateman. Subs (all used): 14 Yannic Parker; 15 Courtney Davies; 16 Alun-Wyn Davies; 17 Rhys Davies.
Tries: Mossop (16), Owens (41), Grant (43), D James (67), C Davies (76); **Goals:** Owens 3/3, C Davies 2/2.
DONCASTER: 1 Mick Butterfield; 2 Stewart Sanderson; 3 Chris Spurr; 4 Lee Waterman; 5 Tom Hodson; 6 Paul Cooke; 7 Craig Fawcett; 8 Mark Castle; 9 Kyle Kesik; 10 Dean O'Loughlin; 11 Craig Robinson; 12 Michael Kelly; 13 Mike Emmett. Subs (all used): 14 Nathan Powley; 15 Carl Hughes; 16 Russ Spiers; 17 Alex Rowe.
Tries: Waterman (3, 26), Sanderson (9), Butterfield (40, 55), Fawcett (47, 72), Hughes (61); **Goals:** Hodson 6/8.
Rugby Leaguer & League Express Men of the Match: *Scorpions:* Dalton Grant; *Doncaster:* Dean O'Loughlin.
Penalty count: 3-8; **Half-time:** 6-20;
Referee: Peter Brooke; **Attendance:** 360.

NORTH WALES CRUSADERS 20
WORKINGTON TOWN 30

CRUSADERS: 1 Tommy Johnson; 2 Kriss Wilkes; 3 Leon Brennan; 4 Christiaan Roets; 5 Rob Massam; 6 Andrew Moulsdale; 7 Jamie Durbin; 8 Jonny Walker; 9 Lee Hudson; 10 Simon Stephens; 11 Andy Gorski; 12 Toby Adamson; 13 Jono Smith. Subs (all used): 14 Owain Brown; 15 Jamie Clarke; 16 Danny Hulme; 17 Dave McConnell.
Tries: Wilkes (17), Massam (28), D Hulme (73), McConnell (78); **Goals:** Johnson 2/4.
TOWN: 1 Brett Carter; 2 Elliott Miller; 3 Jason Mossop; 4 Stephen Dawes; 5 Mark Calderwood; 6 Peter Lupton; 7 Carl Forber; 8 Ryan McDonald; 9 Graeme Mattinson; 10 Kris Coward; 11 Brett Phillips; 12 Mike Whitehead; 13 Dave Petersen. Subs (all used): 14 James Newton; 15 Marc Shackley; 16 James Robinson; 17 Jamie Thackray.
Tries: Coward (8), Thackray (32), Newton (37), Carter (55), Petersen (70); **Goals:** Forber 5/6.
Rugby Leaguer & League Express Men of the Match: *Crusaders:* Andy Gorski; *Town:* Jamie Thackray.
Penalty count: 6-6; **Half-time:** 10-16;
Referee: Ronnie Laughton; **Attendance:** 733.

GATESHEAD THUNDER 0 ROCHDALE HORNETS 32

THUNDER: 1 Connor Condron; 2 Ashley Thackeray; 3 Josh Neilson; 4 Mike Mitchell; 5 Shane Ackerley; 6 Chris Parker Jnr; 7 Sam Walsh; 8 Ryan McBride; 9 Tom Hodgson; 10 Brett Waller; 11 Matt Barron; 12 Jason Payne; 13 Ryan Steen. Subs (all used): 14 Paul Stamp; 15 Stephen Welton; 16 Tabua Cakacaka; 17 Daniel Barker.
Dismissal: Waller (67) - head-butt on Donoghue.
Sin bin: Walsh (67) - fighting.
HORNETS: 1 Wayne English; 2 Dale Bloomfield; 3 Chris Baines; 4 Anthony Stewart; 5 Jonny Leather; 6 Paul Crook; 7 Steve Roper; 8 Dave Newton; 9 Chris Hough; 10 John Cookson; 11 Danny Samuel; 12 Gary Middlehurst; 13 Dayne Donoghue. Subs (all used): 14 Joe Fitzpatrick; 15 Adam Bowman; 16 Phil Braddish; 17 Mark Hobson.
Tries: Crook (5, 80), Middlehurst (13, 72), Leather (52), Hough (61); **Goals:** Crook 4/6.
Sin bin: Newton (67) - fighting.
Rugby Leaguer & League Express Men of the Match: *Thunder:* Ryan McBride; *Hornets:* Paul Crook.
Penalty count: 5-2; **Half-time:** 0-8;
Referee: Dave Merrick; **Attendance:** 231
(at Filtrona Park, South Shields).

WHITEHAVEN 42 OLDHAM 20

WHITEHAVEN: 1 Andreas Bauer; 2 Craig Calvert; 3 Jessie Joe Parker; 4 Steve Fox; 5 Max Wiper; 6 Jamie Rooney; 7 Carl Rudd; 8 David Houghton; 9 Carl Sice; 10 Paul Cullnean; 11 Andrew Beattie; 12 Anthony Mullally; 13 Lee Doran. Subs (all used): 14 Sam Gee; 15 Luke Isakka; 16 Richard Varkulis; 17 Martyn Wilson.
Tries: Calvert (11, 33, 80), Wiper (18), Parker (31), Houghton (53), Beattie (67);
Goals: Rudd 4/4, Rooney 3/3.
OLDHAM: 1 Miles Greenwood; 2 Rob Foxen; 3 David Cookson; 4 Mark McCully; 5 John Gillam; 6 Neil Roden; 7 Jamie Dallimore; 8 Jason Boults; 9 John Clough; 10 Liam Gilchrist; 11 Paul Noone; 12 Paul Smith; 13 Valu Bentley. Subs (all used): 14 Michael Ward; 15 Alex Thompson; 16 Dave Ellison; 17 Daniel Smith.
Tries: McCully (4), Thompson (37), Dallimore (47), Ward (72); **Goals:** Dallimore 2/4.
Rugby Leaguer & League Express Men of the Match: *Whitehaven:* David Houghton; *Oldham:* Jamie Dallimore.
Penalty count: 5-5; **Half-time:** 24-10;
Referee: Clint Sharrad; **Attendance:** 701.

ROUND 8

Sunday 8th July 2012

NORTH WALES CRUSADERS 46
GATESHEAD THUNDER 18

CRUSADERS: 1 Danny Hulme; 2 Christiaan Roets; 3 Tommy Johnson; 4 Leon Brennan; 5 Kriss Wilkes; 6 Andrew Moulsdale; 7 Jamie Durbin; 8 Jonny Walker; 9 Dave McConnell; 10 Simon Stephens; 11 Andy Gorski; 12 Toby Adamson; 13 Jono Smith. Subs (all used): 14 Owain Brown; 15 Jamie Clarke; 16 Liam Hulme; 17 Lee Hudson.
Tries: D Hulme (15, 71), Gorski (21), Clarke (25), Durbin (27), L Hulme (31), Smith (57), McConnell (77);
Goals: Johnson 7/8.
THUNDER: 1 Connor Condron; 2 Ashley Thackeray; 3 Mike Mitchell; 4 Josh Neilson; 5 Shane Ackerley; 6 Sam Walsh; 7 Scott Woods; 8 Brett Waller; 9 Paul Stamp; 10 Ryan McBride; 11 Matt Barron; 12 Daniel Barker; 13 Jason Payne. Subs (all used): 14 Tom Hodgson; 15 David Cash; 16 Stephen Welton; 17 Tabua Cakacaka.
Tries: Waller (18, 53), Thackeray (35);
Goals: Stamp 1/1, Barker 2/2.
Rugby Leaguer & League Express Men of the Match: *Crusaders:* Dave McConnell; *Thunder:* Brett Waller.
Penalty count: 6-10; **Half-time:** 28-12;
Referee: Greg Dolan; **Attendance:** 719.

ROUND 13

Sunday 15th July 2012

WORKINGTON TOWN 50
SOUTH WALES SCORPIONS 10

TOWN: 1 Brett Carter; 2 Elliott Miller; 3 Jason Mossop; 4 Daniel Rooney; 5 Mark Calderwood; 6 Peter Lupton; 7 Carl Forber; 8 Ryan McDonald; 9 Graeme Mattinson; 10 Kris Coward; 11 Brett Phillips; 12 Jarrad Stack; 13 Dave Petersen. Subs (all used): 14 James Newton; 15 James Robinson; 16 Mike Whitehead; 17 Jamie Thackray.
Tries: Miller (8, 10, 73, 76, 78), Stack (27), Calderwood (38, 73), Thackray (44), Mattinson (46);
Goals: Forber 5/10.
SCORPIONS: 1 David James; 2 Kevin James; 3 Ben Gilbert; 4 Yannic Parker; 5 Dalton Grant; 6 Shaun Owens; 7 Steve Parry; 8 Dominic Crosby; 9 Nathan Mossop; 10 Neil Dallimore; 11 Joe Burke; 12 Alan Pope; 13 Ashley Bateman. Subs (all used): 14 Rhys Davies; 15 Courtney Davies; 16 Jason Howells; 17 Alun-Wyn Davies.
Tries: Mossop (52), Grant (69); **Goals:** C Davies 1/2.
Rugby Leaguer & League Express Men of the Match: *Town:* Elliott Miller; *Scorpions:* Nathan Mossop.
Penalty count: 9-9; **Half-time:** 22-0;
Referee: Joe Cobb; **Attendance:** 653.

DONCASTER 28 BARROW RAIDERS 24

DONCASTER: 1 Mick Butterfield; 2 Dean Colton; 3 Chris Spurr; 4 Lee Waterman; 5 Stewart Sanderson; 6 Paul Cooke; 7 Craig Fawcett; 8 Mark Castle; 9 Kyle Kesik; 10 Russ Spiers; 11 Craig Robinson; 12 Michael Kelly; 13 Mike Emmett. Subs (all used): 14 Francis Welsh; 15 Alex Rowe; 16 Carl Hughes; 17 Nathan Powley.
Tries: Waterman (6, 41), Castle (16), Emmett (36), Kelly (55), Fawcett (62); **Goals:** Waterman 2/5, Cooke 0/1.
Sin bin: Rowe (69) - fighting.
RAIDERS: 1 Andy Ballard; 2 Mike Backhouse; 3 Chris Larkin; 4 Ryan Shaw; 5 James Nixon; 6 Scott Kaighan; 7 Liam Campbell; 8 Andy Bracek; 9 James Dandy; 10 Bradley Brennan; 11 Liam Harrison; 12 James Gordon; 13 Daniel Toal. Subs (all used): 14 Liam Finch; 15 Martin Ostler; 16 Ryan Duffy; 17 Andrew Dawson.
Tries: Nixon (26), Campbell (31), Shaw (48), Backhouse (67); **Goals:** Shaw 4/5.
Sin bin: Bracek (69) - fighting.
Rugby Leaguer & League Express Men of the Match: *Doncaster:* Paul Cooke; *Raiders:* Liam Campbell.
Penalty count: 9-6; **Half-time:** 16-12;
Referee: Jamie Leahy; **Attendance:** 997.

GATESHEAD THUNDER 10
NORTH WALES CRUSADERS 60

THUNDER: 1 Connor Condron; 2 Ashley Thackeray; 3 Mike Mitchell; 4 Joe Brown; 5 Shane Ackerley; 6 Sam Walsh; 7 Scott Woods; 8 Matt Barron; 9 Paul Stamp; 10 Stephen Welton; 11 David Cash; 12 Daniel Barker; 13 Jason Payne. Subs (all used): 14 Tom Hodgson; 15 Ryan Steen; 16 Josh Stoker; 17 Tabua Cakacaka.
Tries: Barron (21), Stoker (32); **Goals:** Stamp 1/2.
CRUSADERS: 1 Tommy Johnson; 2 Kriss Wilkes; 3 Christiaan Roets; 4 Leon Brennan; 5 Rob Massam; 6 Andrew Moulsdale; 7 Billy Sheen; 8 Jonny Walker; 9 Dave McConnell; 10 Simon Stephens; 11 Liam Hulme; 12 Toby Adamson; 13 Jono Smith. Subs (all used): 14 Anthony Morrison; 15 Jamie Clarke; 16 Owain Griffiths; 17 David Orwell.
Tries: Moulsdale (4, 17, 46), Sheen (9, 25, 75), Adamson (12), Brennan (42), J Walker (58), L Hulme (65); **Goals:** Johnson 10/10.
Rugby Leaguer & League Express Men of the Match: *Thunder:* Tabua Cakacaka; *Crusaders:* Andrew Moulsdale.
Penalty count: 7-6; **Half-time:** 10-30; **Referee:** Matthew Kidd; **Attendance:** 336 *(at Filtrona Park, South Shields).*

OLDHAM 25 LONDON SKOLARS 24

OLDHAM: 1 Miles Greenwood; 2 Rob Foxen; 3 David Cookson; 4 Mark McCully; 5 Chris Murphy; 6 Neil Roden; 7 Jamie Dallimore; 8 Jason Boults; 9 John Clough; 10 Liam Gilchrist; 11 Paul Noone; 12 Paul Smith; 13 Valu Bentley. Subs (all used): 14 Martin Roden; 15 Chris Clarke; 16 Michael Ward; 17 Daniel Smith.
Tries: Murphy (14), Dallimore (24), Greenwood (51, 77);
Goals: Dallimore 4/4; **Field goal:** N Roden (80).
SKOLARS: 1 James Anthony; 2 John Paxton; 3 Joe Price; 4 Will Colleran; 5 Ade Adebisi; 6 Andy McLean; 7 Dylan Skee; 8 Lamont Bryan; 9 Neil Thorman; 10 Dave Williams; 11 Brad Hopkins; 12 Matt Thomas; 13 Ben Bolger. Subs (all used): 14 Rob Thomas; 15 Michael Sykes; 16 Martyn Smith; 17 Austen Aggrey.
Tries: Colleran (5), Price (19, 44), Bryan (69), M Thomas (72); **Goals:** Skee 2/5.
Rugby Leaguer & League Express Men of the Match: *Oldham:* Miles Greenwood; *Skolars:* Lamont Bryan.
Penalty count: 5-9; **Half-time:** 12-10;
Referee: Chris Leatherbarrow; **Attendance:** 487.

ROUND 14

Thursday 19th July 2012

BARROW RAIDERS 48 WHITEHAVEN 16

RAIDERS: 1 Andy Ballard; 2 Lee Haney; 3 Chris Larkin; 4 Ryan Shaw; 5 James Nixon; 6 Scott Kaighan; 7 Liam Campbell; 8 Bradley Brennan; 9 James Dandy; 10 Jamie Butler; 11 Liam Harrison; 12 Andy Bracek; 13 Daniel Toal. Subs (all used): 14 Liam Finch; 15 Martin Ostler; 16 Ryan Duffy; 17 Andrew Dawson.
Tries: Bracek (4), Campbell (26), Haney (36), Nixon (43), Ballard (47), Harrison (54), Butler (61), L Finch (80); **Goals:** Shaw 8/9.
WHITEHAVEN: 1 Andreas Bauer; 2 Craig Calvert; 3 Jessie Joe Parker; 4 Steve Fox; 5 Max Wiper; 6 Jamie Rooney; 7 Carl Rudd; 8 David Houghton; 9 Carl Sice; 10 Paul Cullnean; 11 Andrew Beattie; 12 Lee Doran; 13 Tom Hemingway. Subs (all used): 14 Sam Gee; 15 Luke Isakka; 16 Richard Varkulis; 17 Martyn Wilson.
Tries: Hemingway (18), Calvert (70), Rooney (71);
Goals: Rudd 1/1, Rooney 1/2.
Rugby Leaguer & League Express Men of the Match: *Raiders:* Liam Campbell; *Whitehaven:* Tom Hemingway.
Penalty count: 4-5; **Half-time:** 18-6;
Referee: Chris Leatherbarrow; **Attendance:** 1,710.

Sunday 22nd July 2012

GATESHEAD THUNDER 16 LONDON SKOLARS 64

THUNDER: 1 Connor Condron; 2 Ashley Thackeray; 3 Josh Neilson; 4 Joe Brown; 5 Shane Ackerley; 6 Ryan Steen; 7 Gavin Beasley; 8 Stephen Welton; 9 Paul Stamp; 10 Ryan McBride; 11 Jason Payne; 12 David Cash; 13 Matt Barron. Subs (all used): 14 Tom Hodgson; 15 Sam Walsh; 16 Oliver O'Mara; 17 Tabua Cakacaka.
Tries: Stamp (24), O'Mara (62), Brown (79);
Goals: Beasley 1/1, Stamp 1/2.
SKOLARS: 1 James Anthony; 2 John Paxton; 3 Joe Price; 4 Will Colleran; 5 Smokie Junor; 6 Andy McLean; 7 Dylan Skee; 8 Rob Thomas; 9 Neil Thorman; 10 Dave Williams; 11 Brad Hopkins; 12 Matt Thomas; 13 Lamont Bryan. Subs (all used): 14 Michael Sykes; 15 Oliver Purslow; 16 Martyn Smith; 17 James Roche.
Tries: Price (2, 5, 45), Junor (10, 19, 33), Thorman (29), Hopkins (36, 70), McLean (58), M Thomas (65), Skee (76); **Goals:** Skee 8/12.
Rugby Leaguer & League Express Men of the Match: *Thunder:* Paul Stamp; *Skolars:* Dylan Skee.
Penalty count: 5-8; **Half-time:** 6-38;
Referee: Tom Crashley; **Attendance:** 186
(at Filtrona Park, South Shields).

ROCHDALE HORNETS 34
NORTH WALES CRUSADERS 6

HORNETS: 1 Wayne English; 2 Dale Bloomfield; 3 Chris Baines; 4 Anthony Stewart; 5 Jonny Leather; 6 Paul Crook; 7 Steve Roper; 8 Dave Newton; 9 Chris Hough; 10 John Cookson; 11 Danny Samuel; 12 Gary Middlehurst; 13 Dayne Donoghue. Subs (all used): 14 Steve McDermott; 15 Mark Hobson; 16 Danny Ekis; 17 Phil Braddish.
Tries: Bloomfield (14, 19), Roper (33), English (51, 70), Leather (77); **Goals:** Crook 5/6.
CRUSADERS: 1 Tommy Johnson; 2 Rob Massam; 3 Leon Brennan; 4 Christiaan Roets; 5 Kriss Wilkes; 6 Andrew Moulsdale; 7 Billy Sheen; 8 Jonny Walker; 9 Dave McConnell; 10 Simon Stephens; 11 Andy Gorski; 12 Liam Hulme; 13 Jono Smith. Subs (all used): 14 Anthony Morrison; 15 Jamie Clarke; 16 David Orwell; 17 Lee Hudson.
Try: Sheen (25); **Goals:** Johnson 1/1.
Rugby Leaguer & League Express Men of the Match: *Hornets:* Gary Middlehurst; *Crusaders:* Billy Sheen.
Penalty count: 10-8; **Half-time:** 16-6;
Referee: Clint Sharrad; **Attendance:** 648.

SOUTH WALES SCORPIONS 12 OLDHAM 44

SCORPIONS: 1 David James; 2 Jason Howells; 3 Ben Gilbert; 4 Kevin James; 5 Dalton Grant; 6 Shaun Owens; 7 Steve Parry; 8 Joe Burke; 9 Nathan Mossop; 10 Alun-Wyn Davies; 11 Alan Pope; 12 Luke Kell; 13 Ashley Bateman. Subs (all used): 14 Yannic Parker; 15 Courtney Davies; 16 Osian Phillips; 17 Rhys Fitzgerald.
Tries: Pope (25), C Davies (64); **Goals:** Owens 2/2.
OLDHAM: 1 Chris Murphy; 2 Rob Foxen; 3 David Cookson; 4 Mark McCully; 5 John Gillam; 6 Neil Roden; 7 Jamie Dallimore; 8 Jason Boults; 9 John Clough; 10 Liam Gilchrist; 11 Paul Noone; 12 Paul Smith; 13 Valu Bentley. Subs (all used): 14 Michael Ward; 15 Alex Thompson; 16 Chris Clarke; 17 Daniel Smith.
Tries: Cookson (3), P Smith (10), Thompson (30, 34), Dallimore (41), Gillam (49), Murphy (68), McCully (73);
Goals: Dallimore 6/8.
Rugby Leaguer & League Express Men of the Match: *Scorpions:* Ashley Bateman; *Oldham:* David Cookson.
Penalty count: 8-9; **Half-time:** 6-22;
Referee: Peter Brooke; **Attendance:** 196.

Thursday 26th July 2012

DONCASTER 22 WORKINGTON TOWN 6

DONCASTER: 1 Lee Waterman; 2 Dean Colton; 3 Chris Spurr; 4 Danny Cowling; 5 Stewart Sanderson; 6 Paul Cooke; 7 Craig Fawcett; 8 Mark Castle; 9 Kyle Kesik; 10 Dean O'Loughlin; 11 Craig Robinson; 12 Michael Kelly; 13 Mike Emmett. Subs (all used): 14 Alex Rowe; 15 Carl Hughes; 16 Russ Spiers; 17 Nathan Powley.
Tries: Robinson (3), Cooke (23), Waterman (44);
Goals: Cooke 5/5.
TOWN: 1 Brett Carter; 2 Mark Calderwood; 3 Karl Olstrum; 4 Jason Mossop; 5 Elliott Miller; 6 Peter Lupton; 7 Carl Forber; 8 Ryan McDonald; 9 Graeme Mattinson; 10 Kris Coward; 11 Brett Phillips; 12 Mike Whitehead; 13 Jarrad Stack. Subs (all used): 14 Marc Bainbridge; 15 Marc Shackley; 16 Jamie Thackray; 17 James Robinson.
Try: Lupton (74); **Goals:** Forber 1/1.
On report: Thackray (60) - alleged trip on Powley.
Rugby Leaguer & League Express Men of the Match: *Doncaster:* Lee Waterman; *Town:* Brett Phillips.
Penalty count: 10-12; **Half-time:** 16-0;
Referee: Matthew Thomason; **Attendance:** 891.

ROUND 7

Sunday 29th July 2012

LONDON SKOLARS 64 SOUTH WALES SCORPIONS 6

SKOLARS: 1 James Anthony; 2 John Paxton; 3 Joe

Whitehaven's Jessie Joe Parker finds his path blocked against Doncaster

Price; 4 Dave Arnot; 5 Smokie Junor; 6 Andy McLean; 7 Dylan Skee; 8 Lamont Bryan; 9 Neil Thorman; 10 Dave Williams; 11 Brad Hopkins; 12 Matt Thomas; 13 Ben Bolger. Subs (all used): 14 Rob Thomas; 15 Michael Sykes; 16 Martyn Smith; 17 James Roche.
Tries: M Thomas (6), Skee (9, 43), Bryan (30), Paxton (51), Hopkins (54, 66), B Bolger (57), Williams (74), Junor (76), Thorman (79); **Goals:** Skee 10/11.
SCORPIONS: 1 David James; 2 Jason Howells; 3 Alan Pope; 4 Kevin James; 5 Dalton Grant; 6 Ben Gilbert; 7 Shaun Owens; 8 Joe Burke; 9 Nathan Mossop; 10 Alun-Wyn Davies; 11 Matthew Crow; 12 Rhodri Lloyd; 13 Ashley Bateman. Subs (all used): 14 Steve Parry; 15 Osian Phillips; 16 Luke Kell; 17 Yannic Parker.
Try: Lloyd (3); **Goals:** Owens 1/1.
Rugby Leaguer & League Express Men of the Match:
Skolars: Dylan Skee; *Scorpions:* Shaun Owens.
Penalty count: 11-5; **Half-time:** 18-6;
Referee: Greg Dolan; **Attendance:** 290.

ROUND 13

Sunday 29th July 2012

ROCHDALE HORNETS 12 WHITEHAVEN 31

HORNETS: 1 Wayne English; 2 Dale Bloomfield; 3 Chris Baines; 4 Anthony Stewart; 5 Jonny Leather; 6 Paul Crook; 7 Steve Roper; 8 Dave Newton; 9 Chris Hough; 10 John Cookson; 11 Mark Hobson; 12 Danny Samuel; 13 Dayne Donoghue. Subs (all used): 14 Steve McDermott; 15 Adam Bowman; 16 Danny Ekis; 17 Phil Braddish.
Tries: Crook (16), Leather (30); **Goals:** Crook 2/2.
WHITEHAVEN: 1 Lewis Palfrey; 2 Craig Calvert; 3 Max Wiper; 4 Jessie Joe Parker; 5 Loz Hamzat; 6 Jamie Rooney; 7 Carl Rudd; 8 David Houghton; 9 Tom Hemingway; 10 Paul Cullnean; 11 Richard Varkulis; 12 Martyn Wilson; 13 Lee Doran. Subs (all used): 14 Carl Sice; 15 Steve Fox; 16 Andrew Beattie; 17 Matthew Haggerty.
Tries: Rooney (8), Palfrey (38), Calvert (57), Parker (64), Hamzat (74); **Goals:** Rudd 1/1, Rooney 3/4, Sice 1/1; **Field goal:** Rooney (67).
Rugby Leaguer & League Express Men of the Match:
Hornets: Wayne English; *Whitehaven:* Jamie Rooney.
Penalty count: 6-11; **Half-time:** 12-12;
Referee: Warren Turley; **Attendance:** 581.

ROUND 15

Sunday 5th August 2012

BARROW RAIDERS 42 OLDHAM 16

RAIDERS: 1 Andy Ballard; 2 Lee Haney; 3 Ryan Shaw; 4

Aaron Low; 5 James Nixon; 6 Scott Kaighan; 7 Liam Campbell; 8 Bradley Brennan; 9 James Dandy; 10 Andries Venter; 11 Liam Harrison; 12 Andy Bracek; 13 James Gordon. Subs (all used): 14 Liam Finch; 15 Martin Ostler; 16 Ryan Duffy; 17 Andrew Dawson.
Tries: Campbell (6), Harrison (13, 38), Shaw (21, 29, 41, 61), Haney (79); **Goals:** Shaw 5/8.
OLDHAM: 1 Miles Greenwood; 2 Rob Foxen; 3 David Cookson; 4 Mark McCully; 5 John Gillam; 6 Neil Roden; 7 Jamie Dallimore; 8 Jason Boults; 9 John Clough; 10 Liam Gilchrist; 11 Paul Noone; 12 Paul Smith; 13 Valu Bentley. Subs (all used): 14 Michael Ward; 15 Alex Thompson; 16 Chris Clarke; 17 Luke Stenchion.
Tries: Dallimore (32), Gilchrist (66), P Smith (71); **Goals:** Dallimore 2/3.
Sin bin: N Roden (58) - late challenge.
Rugby Leaguer & League Express Men of the Match:
Raiders: Ryan Shaw; *Oldham:* Miles Greenwood.
Penalty count: 9-7; **Half-time:** 26-6;
Referee: Peter Brooke; **Attendance:** 1,337.

LONDON SKOLARS 56 ROCHDALE HORNETS 36

SKOLARS: 1 James Anthony; 2 Smokie Junor; 3 Joe Price; 4 John Paxton; 5 Ade Adebisi; 6 Andy McLean; 7 Dylan Skee; 8 Lamont Bryan; 9 Neil Thorman; 10 Dave Williams; 11 Brad Hopkins; 12 Matt Thomas; 13 James Roche. Subs (all used): 14 Rob Thomas; 15 Michael Sykes; 16 Martyn Smith; 17 Austen Aggrey.
Tries: Bryan (1), Hopkins (18), Skee (40), Anthony (42), Adebisi (50), McLean (53, 65, 66), M Thomas (80); **Goals:** Skee 10/11.
HORNETS: 1 Dale Bloomfield; 2 Andy Taylor; 3 Chris Baines; 4 Steve Bannister; 5 Barry Clarke; 6 Paul Crook; 7 Steve Roper; 8 Dave Newton; 9 Danny Price; 10 John Cookson; 11 Dayne Donoghue; 12 Mark Hobson; 13 Gary Middlehurst. Subs (all used): 14 Steve McDermott; 15 Adam Bowman; 16 Danny Ekis; 17 Phil Braddish.
Tries: Bannister (7), Donoghue (14), Bloomfield (27), McDermott (35, 61), Ekis (44); **Goals:** Crook 6/6.
Sin bin: Roper (56) - dissent;
McDermott (78) - interference; Price (80) - dissent.
Rugby Leaguer & League Express Men of the Match:
Skolars: Andy McLean; *Hornets:* Dale Bloomfield.
Penalty count: 16-8; **Half-time:** 18-24;
Referee: Joe Cobb; **Attendance:** 407.

SOUTH WALES SCORPIONS 24 NORTH WALES CRUSADERS 36

SCORPIONS: 1 David James; 2 Alex Jones; 3 Ben Gilbert; 4 Kevin James; 5 Joe Bullock; 6 Shaun Owens; 7 Steve Parry; 8 Joe Burke; 9 Nathan Mossop; 10 Osian Phillips; 11 Alan Pope; 12 Luke Kell; 13 Ashley Bateman. Subs (all used): 14 Thomas Gwyn Morgan; 15 Yannic Parker; 16 Courtney Davies; 17 Tom McKeown.
Tries: Owens (14), Mossop (29), T G Morgan (32), Parry (61); **Goals:** Owens 4/4.

CRUSADERS: 1 Tommy Johnson; 2 Adam Clay; 3 Christiaan Roets; 4 Leon Brennan; 5 Rob Massam; 6 Andrew Moulsdale; 7 Jamie Durbin; 8 Jonny Walker; 9 Liam Hulme; 10 Simon Stephens; 11 Andy Gorski; 12 Toby Adamson; 13 Jono Smith. Subs (all used): 14 Owain Griffiths; 15 Owain Brown; 16 Danny Hulme; 17 Anthony Morrison.
Tries: Gorski (4), Durbin (8), Massam (19), Clay (23, 72), L Hulme (64), Smith (68); **Goals:** Johnson 4/7.
Sin bin: Adamson (13) - late challenge on Parry.
Rugby Leaguer & League Express Men of the Match:
Scorpions: Shaun Owens; *Crusaders:* Liam Hulme.
Penalty count: 6-7; **Half-time:** 18-22;
Referee: Clint Sharrad; **Attendance:** 687.

WHITEHAVEN 25 DONCASTER 18

WHITEHAVEN: 1 Lewis Palfrey; 2 Craig Calvert; 3 Max Wiper; 4 Jessie Joe Parker; 5 Loz Hamzat; 6 Jamie Rooney; 7 Carl Rudd; 8 David Houghton; 9 Tom Hemingway; 10 Paul Cullnean; 11 Richard Varkulis; 12 Martyn Wilson; 13 Lee Doran. Subs (all used): 14 Carl Sice; 15 Steve Fox; 16 Andrew Beattie; 17 Matthew Haggerty.
Tries: Sice (32, 45), Parker (65), Varkulis (72);
Goals: Rudd 2/2, Rooney 2/3; **Field goal:** Rooney (61).
DONCASTER: 1 Lee Waterman; 2 Dean Colton; 3 Chris Spurr; 4 Danny Cowling; 5 Stewart Sanderson; 6 Paul Cooke; 7 Craig Fawcett; 8 Mark Castle; 9 Kyle Kesik; 10 Dean O'Loughlin; 11 Craig Robinson; 12 Michael Kelly; 13 Mike Emmett. Subs (all used): 14 Nathan Powley; 15 Carl Hughes; 16 Craig Lawton; 17 Russ Spiers.
Tries: Sanderson (9), Hughes (70, 75); **Goals:** Cooke 3/3.
Rugby Leaguer & League Express Men of the Match:
Whitehaven: Jamie Rooney; *Doncaster:* Paul Cooke.
Penalty count: 10-12; **Half-time:** 6-6;
Referee: Warren Turley; **Attendance:** 833.

ROUND 16

Sunday 12th August 2012

NORTH WALES CRUSADERS 40 LONDON SKOLARS 22

CRUSADERS: 1 Tommy Johnson; 2 Adam Clay; 3 Christiaan Roets; 4 Leon Brennan; 5 Rob Massam; 6 Andrew Moulsdale; 7 Billy Sheen; 8 Jonny Walker; 9 Dave McConnell; 10 Simon Stephens; 11 Andy Gorski; 12 Liam Hulme; 13 Jono Smith. Subs (all used): 14 Owain Brown; 15 Anthony Morrison; 16 Lewys Weaver; 17 Lee Hudson.
Tries: Brennan (2), J Walker (22), Massam (31), Weaver (54), Moulsdale (65), Smith (73), Clay (79); **Goals:** Johnson 6/7.

SKOLARS: 1 James Anthony; 2 John Paxton; 3 Matt Thomas; 4 Joe Price; 5 Dave Arnot; 6 Andy McLean; 7 Dylan Skee; 8 Rob Thomas; 9 Neil Thorman; 10 Oliver Purslow; 11 Brad Hopkins; 12 James Roche; 13 Lamont Bryan. Subs (all used): 14 Austen Aggrey; 15 Michael Sykes; 16 Alex Bate; 17 Martyn Smith.
Tries: Price (5), Anthony (12, 50), Bryan (47);
Goals: Skee 3/4.
Rugby Leaguer & League Express Men of the Match:
Crusaders: Rob Massam; *Skolars:* Dylan Skee.
Penalty count: 8-3; **Half-time:** 18-10;
Referee: Gareth Hewer; **Attendance:** 800.

OLDHAM 22 DONCASTER 46

OLDHAM: 1 Miles Greenwood; 2 Lucas Onyango; 3 David Cookson; 4 Mark McCully; 5 Chris Murphy; 6 Neil Roden; 7 Jamie Dallimore; 8 Jason Boults; 9 Alex Thompson; 10 Liam Gilchrist; 11 Paul Noone; 12 Michael Ward; 13 Chris Clarke. Subs (all used): 14 Valu Bentley; 15 John Clough; 16 Luke Stenchion; 17 Jamie Acton.
Tries: Greenwood (15, 38, 42), Clough (79);
Goals: Dallimore 3/4.
DONCASTER: 1 Lee Waterman; 2 Dean Colton; 3 Chris Spurr; 4 Lucas Walshaw; 5 Stewart Sanderson; 6 Paul Cooke; 7 Craig Fawcett; 8 Mark Castle; 9 Kyle Kesik; 10 Russ Spiers; 11 Mike Emmett; 12 Michael Kelly; 13 Carl Hughes. Subs (all used): 14 Craig Lawton; 15 Grant Edwards; 16 Nathan Powley; 17 Craig Robinson.
Tries: Waterman (2, 27), Spurr (6), Kelly (12), Colton (25), Fawcett (54, 65), Castle (69); **Goals:** Cooke 7/8.
Rugby Leaguer & League Express Men of the Match:
Oldham: Miles Greenwood; *Doncaster:* Craig Fawcett.
Penalty count: 5-7; **Half-time:** 10-28;
Referee: Matthew Kidd; **Attendance:** 500.

ROCHDALE HORNETS 42
SOUTH WALES SCORPIONS 12

HORNETS: 1 Wayne English; 2 Andy Taylor; 3 Dale Bloomfield; 4 Steve Bannister; 5 Jonny Leather; 6 Paul Crook; 7 Steve Roper; 8 Adam Bowman; 9 Ryan Brown; 10 John Cookson; 11 Mark Hobson; 12 Gary Middlehurst; 13 Dayne Donoghue. Subs (all used): 14 Fraser Jones-Lake; 15 Chris Hough; 16 Danny Ekis; 17 Phil Braddish.
Tries: Bloomfield (15, 42, 68), Roper (29), Leather (57, 78), Bannister (65), Taylor (72), **Goals:** Crook 5/8.
Dismissals: Middlehurst (40) - fighting; Braddish (40) - fighting.
SCORPIONS: 1 David James; 2 Alex Jones; 3 Ben Gilbert; 4 Chris Leyshon; 5 Joe Bullock; 6 Courtney Davies; 7 Kristian Hawkes; 8 Thomas Gwyn Morgan; 9 Nathan Mossop; 10 Dominic Crosby; 11 Alan Pope; 12 Luke Kell; 13 Joe Burke. Subs: 14 Steve Parry; 15 Osian Phillips; 16 Jason Howells (not used - dismissed); 17 Mike Connor.
Tries: Gilbert (21), D James (34);
Goals: C Davies 1/1, Hawkes 1/1.
Dismissals: Mossop (40) - fighting;
Howells (40) - fighting; Crosby (63) - punching.
Rugby Leaguer & League Express Men of the Match:
Hornets: Dale Bloomfield; *Scorpions:* Joe Burke.
Penalty count: 13-5; **Half-time:** 12-12;
Referee: Dave Merrick; **Attendance:** 311.

WHITEHAVEN 60 GATESHEAD THUNDER 12

WHITEHAVEN: 1 Lewis Palfrey; 2 Craig Calvert; 3 Max Wiper; 4 Jessie Joe Parker; 5 Loz Hamzat; 6 Jamie Rooney; 7 Carl Rudd; 8 David Houghton; 9 Tom Hemingway; 10 Paul Cullnean; 11 Richard Varkulis; 12 Martyn Wilson; 13 Lee Doran. Subs (all used): 14 Carl Sice; 15 Brad Crellin; 16 Andrew Beattie; 17 Matthew Haggerty.
Tries: Calvert (4, 52, 63), Varkulis (9, 21), Rudd (16), Parker (23, 70), Hemingway (29), Cullnean (37), Doran (78); **Goals:** Rudd 8/11.
Sin bin: Cullnean (46) - late challenge.
THUNDER: 1 Connor Condron; 2 Ashley Thackeray; 3 Josh Neilson; 4 Joe Brown; 5 Josh Stoker; 6 Gavin Beasley; 7 Paul Stamp; 8 Ryan McBride; 9 Tom Hodgson; 10 Stephen Welton; 11 David Cash; 12 Jason Payne; 13 Matt Barron. Subs (all used): 14 Brett Waller; 15 Sam Walsh; 16 Oliver O'Mara; 17 Ben Smith.
Tries: O'Mara (42), Waller (47); **Goals:** Beasley 2/2.
Rugby Leaguer & League Express Men of the Match:
Whitehaven: Jessie Joe Parker; *Thunder:* Jason Payne.
Penalty count: 5-3; **Half-time:** 40-0;
Referee: Tom Crashley; **Attendance:** 733.

WORKINGTON TOWN 48 BARROW RAIDERS 34

TOWN: 1 Elliott Miller; 2 Stephen Dawes; 3 Jason Mossop; 4 Andy Morris; 5 Mark Calderwood; 6 Peter Lupton; 7 Carl Forber; 8 Jamie Thackray; 9 Graeme Mattinson; 10 Kris Coward; 11 Brett Phillips; 12 Jarrad Stack; 13 Chris Annakin. Subs (all used): 14 Marc Shackley; 15 Adam Walne; 16 Marc Bainbridge; 17 Mike Whitehead.
Tries: Stack (3, 23), Thackray (9, 63), Walne (36), Miller (45, 56), Whitehead (74); **Goals:** Forber 8/8.
RAIDERS: 1 Andy Ballard; 2 Mike Backhouse; 3 Chris Larkin; 4 Ryan Shaw; 5 Lee Haney; 6 Scott Kaighan; 7 Liam Campbell; 8 Bradley Brennan; 9 Liam Finch; 10 Jamie Butler; 11 Liam Harrison; 12 Andy Bracek; 13 Daniel Toal. Subs (all used): 14 James Dandy; 15 Martin Ostler; 16 Ryan Duffy; 17 Andrew Dawson.
Tries: L Finch (6), Dandy (29), Ballard (40, 68), Toal (42), Kaighan (50); **Goals:** Shaw 5/6.
Rugby Leaguer & League Express Men of the Match:
Town: Jamie Thackray; *Raiders:* Scott Kaighan.
Penalty count: 13-7; **Half-time:** 24-18;
Referee: Dave Leatherbarrow; **Attendance:** 1,710.

Workington's Peter Lupton brings down Barrow's Andy Bracek

ROUND 17

Sunday 19th August 2012

DONCASTER 48 NORTH WALES CRUSADERS 12

DONCASTER: 1 Lee Waterman; 2 Dean Colton; 3 Chris Spurr; 4 Danny Cowling; 5 Stewart Sanderson; 6 Paul Cooke; 7 Craig Fawcett; 8 Mark Castle; 9 Mike Emmett; 10 Russ Spiers; 11 Lucas Walshaw; 12 Grant Edwards; 13 Carl Hughes. Subs (all used): 14 Craig Lawton; 15 Liam Cunningham; 16 Nathan Powley; 17 Craig Robinson.
Tries: Cowling (4, 34), Spurr (15), Hughes (24), Waterman (48, 54), Fawcett (56), Edwards (73), Powley (79); **Goals:** Cooke 5/8, Waterman 1/1.
On report: Walshaw (27) - alleged dangerous tackle.
CRUSADERS: 1 Tommy Johnson; 2 Adam Clay; 3 Toby Adamson; 4 Leon Brennan; 5 Rob Massam; 6 Jamie Durbin; 7 Billy Sheen; 8 Jonny Walker; 9 Lee Hudson; 10 Simon Stephens; 11 Andy Gorski; 12 Liam Hulme; 13 Jono Smith. Subs (all used): 14 Owain Brown; 15 Anthony Morrison; 16 Andrew Moulsdale; 17 Owain Griffiths.
Tries: Brennan (21), Moulsdale (69); **Goals:** Johnson 2/2.
Rugby Leaguer & League Express Men of the Match:
Doncaster: Danny Cowling; *Crusaders:* Leon Brennan.
Penalty count: 2-10; **Half-time:** 22-6;
Referee: Dave Merrick; **Attendance:** 891.

OLDHAM 28 WORKINGTON TOWN 18

OLDHAM: 1 Miles Greenwood; 2 Lucas Onyango; 3 David Cookson; 4 Michael Ward; 5 Andy Morris; 6 Neil Roden; 7 Jamie Dallimore; 8 Jason Boults; 9 Alex Thompson; 10 Jamie Acton; 11 Paul Noone; 12 Paul Smith; 13 Chris Clarke. Subs (all used): 14 Danny Langtree; 15 John Clough; 16 Luke Stenchion; 17 Liam Gilchrist.
Tries: Greenwood (5), N Roden (19), Ward (29), Onyango (34); **Goals:** Dallimore 6/7.
Dismissal: Acton (79) - fighting.
Sin bin: Stenchion (79) - fighting.
TOWN: 1 Elliott Miller; 2 Neil Frazer; 3 Andy Morris; 4 Jason Mossop; 5 Mark Calderwood; 6 Peter Lupton; 7 Carl Forber; 8 Jamie Thackray; 9 Marc Bainbridge; 10 Kris Coward; 11 Brett Phillips; 12 Jarrad Stack; 13 Chris Annakin. Subs (all used): 14 Marc Shackley; 15 Mike Whitehead; 16 Ryan McDonald; 17 James Robinson.
Tries: Miller (52), Lupton (62), Morris (68);
Goals: Forber 3/3.
Dismissal: Miller (79) - fighting.
Sin bin: Phillips (79) - fighting.
Rugby Leaguer & League Express Men of the Match:
Oldham: Neil Roden; *Town:* Elliott Miller.
Penalty count: 11-20; **Half-time:** 24-0;
Referee: Joe Cobb; **Attendance:** 538.

ROCHDALE HORNETS 24 BARROW RAIDERS 18

HORNETS: 1 Wayne English; 2 Dale Bloomfield; 3 Dayne Donoghue; 4 Anthony Stewart; 5 Jonny Leather; 6 Paul Crook; 7 Steve Roper; 8 Adam Bowman; 9 Ryan Brown; 10 John Cookson; 11 Mark Hobson; 12 Gary Middlehurst; 13 Chris Baines. Subs (all used): 14 Steve McDermott; 15 Chris Hough; 16 Dave Newton; 17 Phil Braddish.
Tries: Donoghue (7, 75), Crook (13), English (33), Leather (48); **Goals:** Crook 2/5.
RAIDERS: 1 Andy Ballard; 2 Ryan Shaw; 3 Chris Larkin; 4 Aaron Low; 5 James Nixon; 6 Scott Kaighan; 7 Brad Marwood; 8 Bradley Brennan; 9 Liam Finch; 10 Ryan Duffy; 11 Liam Harrison; 12 Martin Ostler; 13 Daniel Toal. Subs (all used): 14 James Dandy; 15 Andy Bracek; 16 Ruairi McGoff; 17 Andrew Dawson.
Tries: Ballard (25), Larkin (29, 67), Shaw (55);
Goals: Shaw 1/4.
Rugby Leaguer & League Express Men of the Match:
Hornets: Steve Roper; *Raiders:* Scott Kaighan.
Penalty count: 6-2; **Half-time:** 14-10;
Referee: Peter Brooke; **Attendance:** 446.

SOUTH WALES SCORPIONS 32
GATESHEAD THUNDER 10

SCORPIONS: 1 David James; 2 Jason Howells; 3 Ben Gilbert; 4 Alan Pope; 5 Joe Bullock; 6 Shaun Owens; 7 Steve Parry; 8 Thomas Gwyn Morgan; 9 Nathan Mossop; 10 Osian Phillips; 11 Sam Wellings; 12 Rhodri Lloyd; 13 Joe Burke. Subs (all used): 14 Mike Connor; 15 Kristian Hawkes; 16 Luke Kell; 17 Chris Leyshon.
Tries: T G Morgan (16, 22), Mossop (30, 52), Pope (38), Owens (77); **Goals:** Owens 3/5, Mossop 1/1.
THUNDER: 1 James Pocklington; 2 Shane Ackerley; 3 Josh Neilson; 4 Joe Brown; 5 Josh Stoker; 6 Gavin Beasley; 7 Paul Stamp; 8 Ryan McBride; 9 Connor Condron; 10 Stephen Welton; 11 Daniel Barker; 12 Jason Payne; 13 Matt Barron. Subs (all used): 14 Oliver O'Mara; 15 Chris Parker Jnr; 16 Tom Capper; 17 Ben Smith.
Tries: Payne (47, 57); **Goals:** Beasley 1/2.
Sin bin: Ackerley (34) - high tackle.
Rugby Leaguer & League Express Men of the Match:
Scorpions: Thomas Gwyn Morgan; *Thunder:* Jason Payne.
Penalty count: 7-6; **Half-time:** 22-0;
Referee: Greg Dolan; **Attendance:** 219.

Friday 24th August 2012

LONDON SKOLARS 41 WHITEHAVEN 26

SKOLARS: 1 James Anthony; 2 John Paxton; 3 Joe Price; 4 Dave Arnot; 5 Smokie Junor; 6 Andy McLean; 7 Dylan Skee; 8 Lamont Bryan; 9 Neil Thorman; 10 Dave Williams; 11 Brad Hopkins; 12 Matt Thomas; 13 James Roche. Subs (all used): 14 Rob Thomas; 15 Michael Sykes; 16 Martyn Smith; 17 Austen Aggrey.
Tries: Thorman (2), Bryan (29), Skee (32), Hopkins (49), R Thomas (51), McLean (78); **Goals:** Skee 8/8;
Field goal: Thorman (67).
WHITEHAVEN: 1 Lewis Palfrey; 2 Craig Calvert; 3 Max Wiper; 4 Jessie Joe Parker; 5 Loz Hamzat; 6 Jamie Rooney; 7 Carl Rudd; 8 David Houghton; 9 Tom Hemingway; 10 Paul Cullnean; 11 Richard Varkulis; 12 Martyn Wilson; 13 Lee Doran. Subs (all used): 14 Andreas Bauer; 15 Luke Isakka; 16 Andrew Beattie; 17 Matthew Haggerty.
Tries: Rooney (7, 73), Calvert (36, 71), Hamzat (69);
Goals: Rudd 2/4, Rooney 1/1.
Rugby Leaguer & League Express Men of the Match:
Skolars: Dylan Skee; *Whitehaven:* Craig Calvert.
Penalty count: 9-8; **Half-time:** 18-12;
Referee: Warren Turley; **Attendance:** 1,174.

Doncaster's Lee Waterman takes on London Skolars' Matt Thomas and Michael Sykes

ROUND 15

Wednesday 29th August 2012

GATESHEAD THUNDER 24 WORKINGTON TOWN 22

THUNDER: 1 James Pocklington; 2 Shane Ackerley; 3 Tom Capper; 4 Joe Brown; 5 Josh Stoker; 6 Gavin Beasley; 7 Paul Stamp; 8 Ryan McBride; 9 Connor Condron; 10 Stephen Welton; 11 Daniel Barker; 12 Jason Payne; 13 Ben Smith. Subs: 14 Brett Waller; 15 Oliver O'Mara; 16 Tom Hodgson; 17 Chris Parker Jnr (not used).
Tries: Payne (25, 76), Capper (37), Waller (51);
Goals: Beasley 4/6.
TOWN: 1 Mark Calderwood; 2 Neil Frazer; 3 John Patrick; 4 Jason Mossop; 5 Jack Gaskell; 6 Jarrad Stack; 7 Carl Forber; 8 Jamie Thackray; 9 Karl Olstrum; 10 Kris Coward; 11 Mike Whitehead; 12 Marc Shackley; 13 Chris Annakin. Subs: 14 Kieran McAvoy; 15 Stephen Dawes (not used); 16 James Robinson; 17 Daniel Rooney (not used).
Tries: Coward (13), Stack (62), Patrick (66), Shackley (70); **Goals:** Forber 3/4.
Rugby Leaguer & League Express Men of the Match:
Thunder: Jason Payne; *Town:* Jarrad Stack.
Penalty count: 8-15; **Half-time:** 12-6;
Referee: Dave Sharpe; **Attendance:** 256.

ROUND 18

Sunday 2nd September 2012

BARROW RAIDERS 34 SOUTH WALES SCORPIONS 22

RAIDERS: 1 Andy Ballard; 2 Lee Haney; 3 Chris Larkin; 4 Aaron Low; 5 James Nixon; 6 Scott Kaighan; 7 Liam Campbell; 8 Bradley Brennan; 9 James Dandy; 10 Ruairi McGoff; 11 Liam Harrison; 12 James Gordon; 13 Daniel Toal. Subs (all used): 14 Darren Holt; 15 Martin Ostler; 16 Jamie Butler; 17 Andrew Dawson.
Tries: Campbell (5), Ballard (9), Larkin (13), Harrison (40, 80), McGoff (65); **Goals:** Ballard 5/5, Holt 0/1.
SCORPIONS: 1 David James; 2 Joe Bullock; 3 Alan Pope; 4 Ben Gilbert; 5 Dalton Grant; 6 Courtney Davies; 7 Kristian Hawkes; 8 Thomas Gwyn Morgan; 9 Steve Parry; 10 Gil Dudson; 11 Sam Wellings; 12 Rhodri Lloyd; 13 Joe Burke. Subs (all used): 14 Rhys Davies; 15 Alun-Wyn Davies; 16 Osian Phillips; 17 Matthew Crow.
Tries: Lloyd (3), Pope (18), Grant (32), Hawkes (51);
Goals: C Davies 3/4.

Rugby Leaguer & League Express Men of the Match:
Raiders: Jamie Butler; *Scorpions:* Courtney Davies.
Penalty count: 8-6; **Half-time:** 24-16;
Referee: Matthew Kidd; **Attendance:** 1,245.

GATESHEAD THUNDER 12 OLDHAM 56

THUNDER: 1 James Pocklington; 2 Ashley Thackeray; 3 Tom Capper; 4 Joe Brown; 5 Josh Stoker; 6 Gavin Beasley; 7 Paul Stamp; 8 Ryan McBride; 9 Connor Condron; 10 Stephen Welton; 11 Daniel Barker; 12 Jason Payne; 13 Ben Smith. Subs: 14 Oliver O'Mara; 15 Brett Waller; 16 Tom Hodgson (not used); 17 Chris Parker Jnr.
Tries: Brown (30), Waller (77);
Goals: Beasley 1/1, Stamp 1/1.
OLDHAM: 1 Miles Greenwood; 2 Lucas Onyango; 3 Michael Ward; 4 Mark McCully; 5 Mark Brocklehurst; 6 Neil Roden; 7 Jamie Dallimore; 8 Jason Boults; 9 John Clough; 10 Chris Clarke; 11 Paul Smith; 12 Sam Cunningham; 13 Alex Thompson. Subs (all used): 14 Paul Noone; 15 Danny Whitmore; 16 Phil Joy; 17 Liam Gilchrist.
Tries: Thompson (18, 62, 66), Brocklehurst (24, 37), Clough (40), Greenwood (45), Dallimore (59), Joy (74), Onyango (80); **Goals:** Dallimore 8/10.
Rugby Leaguer & League Express Men of the Match:
Thunder: Joe Brown; *Oldham:* Jamie Dallimore.
Penalty count: 5-6; **Half-time:** 6-24;
Referee: Greg Dolan; **Attendance:** 273.

LONDON SKOLARS 8 DONCASTER 48

SKOLARS: 1 James Anthony; 2 John Paxton; 3 Joe Price; 4 Dave Arnot; 5 Smokie Junor; 6 Andy McLean; 7 Dylan Skee; 8 Oliver Purslow; 9 Neil Thorman; 10 Dave Williams; 11 Brad Hopkins; 12 Matt Thomas; 13 James Roche. Subs (all used): 14 Rob Thomas; 15 Michael Sykes; 16 Martyn Smith; 17 Austen Aggrey.
Tries: Paxton (28, 40); **Goals:** Skee 0/2.
DONCASTER: 1 Lee Waterman; 2 Dean Colton; 3 Chris Spurr; 4 Danny Cowling; 5 Stewart Sanderson; 6 Paul Cooke; 7 Craig Fawcett; 8 Russ Spiers; 9 Mike Emmett; 10 Mark Castle; 11 Lucas Walshaw; 12 Michael Kelly; 13 Carl Hughes. Subs (all used): 14 Kyle Kesik; 15 Grant Edwards; 16 Craig Lawton; 17 Craig Robinson.
Tries: Hughes (7), Fawcett (11), Walshaw (15, 35), Cowling (38), Colton (45), Waterman (57, 74), Spurr (67); **Goals:** Cooke 6/9.
Rugby Leaguer & League Express Men of the Match:
Skolars: John Paxton; *Doncaster:* Lee Waterman.
Penalty count: 7-6; **Half-time:** 8-26;
Referee: Peter Brooke; **Attendance:** 578.

WHITEHAVEN 58 NORTH WALES CRUSADERS 20

WHITEHAVEN: 1 Lewis Palfrey; 2 Craig Calvert; 3 Max Wiper; 4 Jessie Joe Parker; 5 Loz Hamzat; 6 Jamie Rooney; 7 Carl Rudd; 8 David Houghton; 9 Tom Hemingway; 10 Paul Cullinean; 11 Brad Crellin; 12 Andrew Beattie; 13 Lee Doran. Subs (all used): 14 Sam Gee; 15 Luke Isakka; 16 Richard Varkulis; 17 Matthew Haggerty.
Tries: Hemingway (16), Calvert (26), Rooney (33, 66), Beattie (37, 52, 57), Parker (39), Crellin (51), Hamzat (79); **Goals:** Rudd 9/10.
On report: Doran (46) - alleged stamping.
CRUSADERS: 1 Tommy Johnson; 2 Adam Clay; 3 Christiaan Roets; 4 Leon Brennan; 5 Rob Massam; 6 Andrew Moulsdale; 7 Billy Sheen; 8 Jonny Walker; 9 Lee Hudson; 10 Simon Stephens; 11 Andy Gorski; 12 Toby Adamson; 13 Jono Smith. Subs (all used): 14 Owain Brown; 15 Anthony Morrison; 16 Lewys Weaver; 17 Owain Griffiths.
Tries: Gorski (4), Massam (28, 44), Stephens (63);
Goals: Johnson 2/4.
Rugby Leaguer & League Express Men of the Match:
Whitehaven: Andrew Beattie; *Crusaders:* Leon Brennan.
Penalty count: 5-7; **Half-time:** 30-10;
Referee: Chris Leatherbarrow; **Attendance:** 701.

WORKINGTON TOWN 48 ROCHDALE HORNETS 18

TOWN: 1 Mark Calderwood; 2 Kieran McAvoy; 3 John Patrick; 4 Jason Mossop; 5 Neil Frazer; 6 Dave Petersen; 7 Carl Forber; 8 Jamie Thackray; 9 Karl Olstrum; 10 Kris Coward; 11 Brett Phillips; 12 Jarrad Stack; 13 Chris Annakin. Subs (all used): 14 Mike Whitehead; 15 Marc Shackley; 16 Ryan McDonald; 17 James Robinson.
Tries: Petersen (10), Phillips (14, 23), Patrick (20), Annakin (28), Forber (31), McAvoy (57), Mossop (64), Frazer (75); **Goals:** Forber 6/9.
HORNETS: 1 Wayne English; 2 Dale Bloomfield; 3 Jonny Leather; 4 Alex West; 5 Barry Clarke; 6 Paul Crook; 7 Steve Roper; 8 Andy Unsworth; 9 Ryan Brown; 10 John Cookson; 11 Chris Baines; 12 Fraser Jones-Lake; 13 Adam Bowman. Subs (all used): 14 Will Chadwick; 15 Stephen Hickey; 16 Dave Newton; 17 Henry Mitchell.
Tries: Bowman (4), Roper (39), Unsworth (71);
Goals: Crook 3/3.
Rugby Leaguer & League Express Men of the Match:
Town: Karl Olstrum; *Hornets:* John Cookson.
Penalty count: 6-8; **Half-time:** 36-12;
Referee: Ronnie Laughton; **Attendance:** 514.

Whitehaven's Lee Doran swamped by the Rochdale defence

PLAY-OFFS

ELIMINATION PLAY-OFFS

Sunday 9th September 2012

WORKINGTON TOWN 34 OLDHAM 29

TOWN: 1 Elliott Miller; 2 Neil Frazer; 3 Jason Mossop; 4 John Patrick; 5 Mark Calderwood; 6 Brett Carter; 7 Carl Forber; 8 Mike Whitehead; 9 Karl Olstrum; 10 Kris Coward; 11 Brett Phillips; 12 Jarrad Stack; 13 Chris Annakin. Subs (all used): 14 Graeme Mattinson; 15 Marc Shackley; 16 Ryan McDonald; 17 Jamie Thackray.
Tries: Coward (5), Mattinson (35), Miller (57), Carter (62), Frazer (74), Mossop (76); **Goals:** Forber 5/7.
OLDHAM: 1 Miles Greenwood; 2 Mark McCully; 3 Michael Ward; 4 Paul Noone; 5 Mark Brocklehurst; 6 Neil Roden; 7 Jamie Dallimore; 8 Jason Boults; 9 John Clough; 10 Jamie Acton; 11 Phil Joy; 12 Paul Smith; 13 Alex Thompson. Subs (all used): 14 Valu Bentley; 15 Danny Whitmore; 16 Danny Langtree; 17 Liam Gilchrist.
Tries: N Roden (12), Thompson (25), P Smith (28, 48, 70); **Goals:** Dallimore 4/5;
Field goal: N Roden (30).
Sin bin: Acton (4) - late challenge.
On report: Acton (37) - alleged biting.
Rugby Leaguer & League Express Men of the Match: *Town:* Brett Carter; *Oldham:* Neil Roden.
Penalty count: 15-7; **Half-time:** 10-19;
Referee: Gareth Hewer; **Attendance:** 563.

WHITEHAVEN 40 ROCHDALE HORNETS 12

WHITEHAVEN: 1 Lewis Palfrey; 2 Craig Calvert; 3 Max Wiper; 4 Jessie Joe Parker; 5 Loz Hamzat; 6 Jamie Rooney; 7 Carl Rudd; 8 David Houghton; 9 Tom Hemingway; 10 Paul Cullnean; 11 Brad Crellin; 12 Andrew Beattie; 13 Lee Doran. Subs (all used): 14 Carl Sice; 15 Luke Isakka; 16 Richard Varkulis; 17 Matthew Haggerty.
Tries: Parker (23, 34), Rudd (25), Doran (37), Wiper (52), Palfrey (62), Cullnean (64), Rooney (79); **Goals:** Rudd 2/5, Rooney 1/2, Beattie 1/1.
HORNETS: 1 Wayne English; 2 Alex West; 3 Anthony Stewart; 4 Dayne Donoghue; 5 Andy Taylor; 6 Paul Crook; 7 Steve Roper; 8 Dave Newton; 9 Ryan Brown; 10 John Cookson; 11 Chris Baines; 12 Fraser Jones-Lake; 13 Adam Bowman. Subs (all used): 14 Danny Price; 15 Steve Bannister; 16 Will Chadwick; 17 Andy Unsworth.
Tries: Roper (42), Stewart (75); **Goals:** Crook 2/2.
Rugby Leaguer & League Express Men of the Match: *Whitehaven:* Paul Cullnean; *Hornets:* Wayne English.
Penalty count: 13-7; **Half-time:** 20-0;
Referee: Matthew Thomason; **Attendance:** 601.

QUALIFYING SEMI-FINAL

Sunday 16th September 2012

DONCASTER 20 BARROW RAIDERS 22

DONCASTER: 1 Lee Waterman; 2 Dean Colton; 3 Chris Spurr; 4 Danny Cowling; 5 Stewart Sanderson; 6 Paul Cooke; 7 Craig Fawcett; 8 Mark Castle; 9 Kyle Kesik; 10 Russ Spiers; 11 Michael Kelly; 12 Lucas Walshaw; 13 Carl Hughes. Subs (all used): 14 Mike Emmett; 15 Liam Cunningham; 16 Nathan Powley; 17 Craig Robinson.
Tries: Kesik (2), Hughes (28), Walshaw (48), Sanderson (58); **Goals:** Waterman 2/4.
Sin bin: Kesik (20) - late challenge.
RAIDERS: 1 Andy Ballard; 2 Mike Backhouse; 3 Chris Larkin; 4 Aaron Low; 5 James Nixon; 6 Scott Kaighan; 7 Liam Campbell; 8 Ryan Duffy; 9 Liam Finch; 10 Ruairi McGoff; 11 Liam Harrison; 12 James Gordon; 13 Daniel Toal. Subs (all used): 14 James Dandy; 15 Martin Ostler; 16 Jamie Butler; 17 Andrew Dawson.
Tries: Low (22, 32), Larkin (37), Dandy (46); **Goals:** Ballard 3/4.
Rugby Leaguer & League Express Men of the Match: *Doncaster:* Carl Hughes; *Raiders:* Scott Kaighan.
Penalty count: 13-8; **Half-time:** 12-16;
Referee: Matthew Thomason; **Attendance:** 744.

ELIMINATION SEMI-FINAL

Sunday 16th September 2012

WORKINGTON TOWN 26 WHITEHAVEN 2

TOWN: 1 Elliott Miller; 2 John Patrick; 3 Jason Mossop; 4 Andy Morris; 5 Mark Calderwood; 6 Brett Carter; 7 Carl Forber; 8 Jamie Thackray; 9 Karl Olstrum; 10 Kris Coward; 11 Brett Phillips; 12 Jarrad Stack; 13 Chris Annakin. Subs (all used): 14 James Robinson; 15 Marc Shackley; 16 Ryan McDonald; 17 Mike Whitehead.
Tries: Patrick (33), Calderwood (45), Shackley (70); **Goals:** Forber 7/7.
WHITEHAVEN: 1 Lewis Palfrey; 2 Andreas Bauer; 3 Max Wiper; 4 Jessie Joe Parker; 5 Loz Hamzat; 6 Jamie Rooney; 7 Carl Rudd; 8 David Houghton; 9 Sam Gee; 10 Paul Cullnean; 11 Brad Crellin; 12 Andrew Beattie; 13 Lee Doran. Subs (all used): 14 Carl Sice; 15 Scott McAvoy; 16 Richard Varkulis; 17 Matthew Haggerty.
Goals: Rudd 1/2.
Sin bin: Rooney (59) - dissent.
On report: Beattie (34) - challenge on Miller.
Rugby Leaguer & League Express Men of the Match: *Town:* Karl Olstrum; *Whitehaven:* Lee Doran.
Penalty count: 14-13; **Half-time:** 10-2;
Referee: Robert Hicks; **Attendance:** 1,273.

FINAL ELIMINATOR

Sunday 23rd September 2012

DONCASTER 20 WORKINGTON TOWN 0

DONCASTER: 1 Lee Waterman; 2 Tom Hodson; 3 Chris Spurr; 4 Danny Cowling; 5 Stewart Sanderson; 6 Kyle Kesik; 7 Craig Fawcett; 8 Mark Castle; 9 Mike Emmett; 10 Russ Spiers; 11 Michael Kelly; 12 Lucas Walshaw; 13 Carl Hughes. Subs (all used): 14 Grant Edwards; 15 Craig Robinson; 16 Nathan Powley; 17 Craig Lawton.
Tries: Spurr (2), Sanderson (22), Fawcett (49), Powley (79); **Goals:** Hodson 2/4.
TOWN: 1 Mark Calderwood; 2 Neil Frazer; 3 Jason Mossop; 4 Jarrad Stack; 5 John Patrick; 6 Brett Carter; 7 Carl Forber; 8 Jamie Thackray; 9 Karl Olstrum; 10 Kris Coward; 11 Brett Phillips; 12 Mike Whitehead; 13 Chris Annakin. Subs (all used): 14 Adam Walne; 15 Marc Shackley; 16 James Robinson; 17 Ryan McDonald.
Dismissal: Annakin (43) - dangerous tackle.
Rugby Leaguer & League Express Men of the Match: *Doncaster:* Lee Waterman; *Town:* Brett Carter.
Penalty count: 10-11; **Half-time:** 10-0;
Referee: Jamie Leahy; **Attendance:** 576.

GRAND FINAL

Sunday 30th September 2012

BARROW RAIDERS 13 DONCASTER 16

RAIDERS: 1 Andy Ballard; 2 Lee Haney; 3 Chris Larkin; 4 Aaron Low; 5 James Nixon; 6 Scott Kaighan; 7 Liam Campbell; 8 Jamie Butler; 9 James Dandy; 10 Ryan Duffy; 11 Liam Harrison; 12 Daniel Toal. Subs (all used): 14 Liam Finch; 15 Martin Ostler; 16 Ruairi McGoff; 17 Andrew Dawson.
Tries: Larkin (4), Low (77); **Goals:** Ballard 2/3;
Field goal: Kaighan (39).
DONCASTER: 1 Lee Waterman; 2 Tom Hodson; 3 Chris Spurr; 4 Danny Cowling; 5 Stewart Sanderson; 6 Kyle Kesik; 7 Craig Fawcett; 8 Mark Castle; 9 Mike Emmett; 10 Russ Spiers; 11 Michael Kelly; 12 Lucas Walshaw; 13 Carl Hughes. Subs (all used): 14 Nathan Powley; 15 Craig Robinson; 16 Grant Edwards; 17 Liam Cunningham.
Tries: Sanderson (11), Waterman (46), Fawcett (57); **Goals:** Hodson 2/3.
Rugby Leaguer & League Express Men of the Match: *Raiders:* Liam Harrison; *Doncaster:* Craig Fawcett.
Penalty count: 4-5; **Half-time:** 7-4;
Referee: Jamie Leahy.
(at Halliwell Jones Stadium, Warrington).

Doncaster's Craig Fawcett looks for a gap against Barrow during the Championship One Grand Final

NORTHERN RAIL CUP 2012
Round by Round

ROUND 1

Sunday 12th February 2012

POOL 1

KEIGHLEY COUGARS 16 BATLEY BULLDOGS 22

COUGARS: 1 Craig Moss; 2 Richie Barnett; 3 Matt Parata; 4 Semi Tadulala; 5 Gavin Duffy; 6 Danny Jones; 7 Sam Obst; 8 Andy Shickell; 9 James Feather; 10 Michael Korkidas; 11 Richard Jones; 12 Jason Demetriou; 13 Jy-Mel Coleman. Subs (all used): 14 Jamaine Wray; 15 Paul March; 16 Brendan Rawlins; 17 Neil Cherryholme.
Tries: Demetriou (14), Barnett (29), Feather (47);
Goals: D Jones 2/3.
BULLDOGS: 1 Johnny Campbell; 2 Gareth Potts; 3 Jason Walton; 4 Danny Maun; 5 Danny Mills; 6 Ben Black; 7 Tom Henderson; 8 Byron Smith; 9 Paul Mennell; 10 Craig Potter; 11 Alex Bretherton; 12 Jonny Walker; 13 Kris Lythe. Subs (all used): 14 Gareth Moore; 15 Alex Walmsley; 16 Ashley Lindsay; 17 Mark Applegarth.
Tries: Mennell (12), Walker (55), Maun (71), Applegarth (74), Potts (78);
Goals: Henderson 0/1, Moore 1/4.
Rugby Leaguer & League Express Men of the Match: *Cougars:* Danny Jones; *Bulldogs:* Ben Black.
Penalty count: 7-3; **Half-time:** 10-4;
Referee: Gareth Hewer; **Attendance:** 1,095.

DEWSBURY RAMS 6 HALIFAX 36

RAMS: 1 James Craven; 2 Michael Wainwright; 3 Ryan Esders; 4 Ayden Faal; 5 Austin Buchanan; 6 Craig Cook; 7 Pat Walker; 8 Nick Fozzard; 9 Luke Blake; 10 Steve Crossley; 11 Rob Spicer; 12 Josh Tonks; 13 Dwayne Barker. Subs (all used): 14 Mark Barlow; 15 Andy Smith; 16 Ben Jones; 17 Danny Samuel.
Try: Crossley (67); **Goals:** Walker 1/1.
Sin bin: Smith (74) - late challenge.
On report: Fozzard (79) - alleged punching.
HALIFAX: 1 Ryan Fieldhouse; 2 Paul White; 3 Steve Tyrer; 4 Ben Heaton; 5 Wayne Reittie; 6 Paul Handforth; 7 Anthony Bowman; 8 Adam Robinson; 9 Sean Penkywicz; 10 Sean Hesketh; 11 Dane Manning; 12 Iain Morrison; 13 Craig Ashall. Subs (all used): 14 Anthony Thackeray; 15 Matt James; 16 Jim Gannon; 17 Josh Barlow.
Tries: Ashall (9), Reittie (13), Penkywicz (39), Bowman (45), Robinson (60), Thackeray (71), Handforth (75); **Goals:** Tyrer 4/7.
Sin bin: Penkywicz (67) - dissent.
On report: Penkywicz (79) - alleged punching.
Rugby Leaguer & League Express Men of the Match: *Rams:* Steve Crossley; *Halifax:* Paul Handforth.
Penalty count: 9-9; **Half-time:** 0-14;
Referee: Tim Roby; **Attendance:** 1,347.

POOL 2

LEIGH CENTURIONS 48 BARROW RAIDERS 16

CENTURIONS: 1 Gregg McNally; 2 Steve Maden; 3 Stuart Littler; 4 Matt Gardner; 5 Dean McGilvray; 6 Martyn Ridyard; 7 John Duffy; 8 Ricky Bibey; 9 Bob Beswick; 10 Rob Parker; 11 Craig Briscoe; 12 Tommy Goulden; 13 Sam Hopkins. Subs (all used): 14 Ryan Brierley; 15 Michael Worrincy; 16 Anthony Nicholson; 17 Tommy Gallagher.
Tries: Goulden (25), Littler (33, 54), Worrincy (36), McGilvray (51), Brierley (56, 72), Parker (60);
Goals: Ridyard 5/5, Brierley 3/3.
RAIDERS: 1 Andy Ballard; 2 Lee Haney; 3 Chris Larkin; 4 Aaron Low; 5 James Nixon; 6 Darren Holt; 7 Liam Campbell; 8 Jamie Butler; 9 James Dandy; 10 Andrew Dawson; 11 Liam Harrison; 12 James Gordon; 13 Daniel Toal. Subs (all used): 14 Liam Finch; 15 Martin Ostler; 16 Ruairi McGoff; 17 Andries Venter.
Tries: Toal (4), Nixon (39), Campbell (79);
Goals: Holt 2/3.
Rugby Leaguer & League Express Men of the Match: *Centurions:* Anthony Nicholson; *Raiders:* Daniel Toal.
Penalty count: 11-7; **Half-time:** 18-10;
Referee: George Stokes; **Attendance:** 1,860.

WORKINGTON TOWN 14 SHEFFIELD EAGLES 28

TOWN: 1 Elliott Miller; 2 John Patrick; 3 Daniel Rooney; 4 Jason Mossop; 5 Neil Frazer; 6 Brett Carter; 7 Carl Forber; 8 Ryan McDonald; 9 Darren King; 10 Richard Farrer; 11 Mike Whitehead; 12 Brett Phillips; 13 James Robinson. Subs (all used): 14 Jack Gaskell; 15 Jamie Thackray; 16 Matthew Tunstall; 17 Peter Dobson.
Tries: Mossop (11), Carter (23); **Goals:** Forber 3/3.
EAGLES: 1 Misi Taulapapa; 2 Vinny Finigan; 3 Menzie Yere; 4 Nev Morrison; 5 Tim Bergin; 6 Simon Brown; 7 Dominic Brambani; 8 Jack Howieson; 9 Andrew Henderson; 10 Ryan Hepworth; 11 Alex Szostak; 12 Peter Green; 13 Michael Knowles. Subs (all used): 14 Joe Hirst; 15 Sam Scott; 16 Quentin Laulu-Togagae; 17 Liam Higgins.
Tries: Scott (29), Taulapapa (47), Henderson (60), Morrison (74), Szostak (76);
Goals: Brown 2/3, Brambani 2/2.
Rugby Leaguer & League Express Men of the Match: *Town:* Brett Carter; *Eagles:* Andrew Henderson.
Penalty count: 9-9; **Half-time:** 14-6;
Referee: Chris Leatherbarrow; **Attendance:** 532.

Wednesday 15th February 2012

POOL 1

OLDHAM 0 FEATHERSTONE ROVERS 68

OLDHAM: 1 Miles Greenwood; 2 Paul Ballard; 3 David Cookson; 4 Matthew Fogarty; 5 Chris Murphy; 6 Jamie Dallimore; 7 Neil Roden; 8 Jason Boults; 9 John Clough; 10 Liam Gilchrist; 11 Chris Clarke; 12 Paul Smith; 13 Valu Bentley. Subs (all used): 14 Michael Ward; 15 Danny Whitmore; 16 Dave Ellison; 17 Bruce Johnson.
ROVERS: 1 Ian Hardman; 2 Tangi Ropati; 3 Sam Smeaton; 4 Greg Worthington; 5 Tom Saxton; 6 Andy Kain; 7 Liam Finn; 8 James Lockwood; 9 Ben Kaye; 10 Stuart Dickens; 11 Jon Grayshon; 12 Tim Spears; 13 Matty Dale. Subs (all used): 14 Kyle Briggs; 15 Nathan Freer; 16 Michael Haley; 17 Andrew Bostock.
Tries: Ropati (3), Finn (17, 71, 79), Grayshon (28, 50), Kain (42, 63, 73), Hardman (53, 65), Worthington (58);
Goals: Finn 10/12.
Rugby Leaguer & League Express Men of the Match: *Oldham:* Jamie Dallimore; *Rovers:* Liam Finn.
Penalty count: 6-6; **Half-time:** 0-14;
Referee: Jamie Leahy; **Attendance:** 672.

POOL 2

GATESHEAD THUNDER 10 DONCASTER 48

THUNDER: 1 Josh Neilson; 2 Robin Peers; 3 Mike Mitchell; 4 Joe Brown; 5 Ashley Williams; 6 Sam Walsh; 7 Paul Stamp; 8 Brett Waller; 9 Ryan Clarke; 10 Jason Payne; 11 Matt Barron; 12 Oliver O'Mara; 13 Will Bate. Subs (all used): 14 Josh Stoker; 15 Stephen Welton; 16 Ryan McBride; 17 Dan O'Sullivan.
Tries: Payne (39), Waller (54); **Goals:** Clarke 1/2.
DONCASTER: 1 Mick Butterfield; 2 Stewart Sanderson; 3 Liam Cunningham; 4 Lee Waterman; 5 Tom Hodson; 6 Paul Cooke; 7 Craig Fawcett; 8 Craig Robinson; 9 Kyle Kesik; 10 Mark Castle; 11 Dean O'Loughlin; 12 Michael Kelly; 13 Grant Edwards. Subs (all used): 14 Nathan Powley; 15 Carl Hughes; 16 Kyle Bibb; 17 Kyle Sampson.
Tries: Waterman (6, 25, 50, 71), Sanderson (16), Hodson (20, 42), Cunningham (33), Butterfield (48), Kesik (59); **Goals:** Waterman 1/6, Hodson 3/4.
Rugby Leaguer & League Express Men of the Match: *Thunder:* Oliver O'Mara; *Doncaster:* Dean O'Loughlin.
Penalty count: 6-7; **Half-time:** 4-22;
Referee: Joe Cobb; **Attendance:** 243.

HUNSLET HAWKS 34 WHITEHAVEN 18

HAWKS: 1 Danny Ratcliffe; 2 Stuart Kain; 3 Lee Brickwood; 4 Josh Nathaniel; 5 Dennis Tuffour; 6 Luke Helliwell; 7 Danny Allan; 8 Andrew Yates; 9 Luke Haigh; 10 Steve Lewis; 11 Richard Blakeway; 12 John Oakes; 13 David March. Subs (all used): 14 Joe McLocklan; 15 Steve Dooler; 16 Ryan Benjafield; 17 David Tootill.
Tries: Nathaniel (10), March (27), Ratcliffe (30, 43), Lewis (67), Oakes (79); **Goals:** Ratcliffe 5/6.
WHITEHAVEN: 1 Jonathan Youds; 2 Craig Calvert; 3 Max Wiper; 4 Scott McAvoy; 5 Chris Fleming; 6 Carl Rudd; 7 Ben Karalius; 8 David Houghton; 9 Sam Gee; 10 Richard Varkulis; 11 Luke Isakka; 12 Lee Doran; 13 Brad Crellin. Subs (all used): 14 Andreas Bauer; 15 Paul Cullnean; 16 Andrew Beattie; 17 Chris Smith.
Tries: Fleming (24), Houghton (50), Calvert (73);
Goals: Rudd 3/3.
Rugby Leaguer & League Express Men of the Match: *Hawks:* Danny Ratcliffe; *Whitehaven:* Ben Karalius.
Penalty count: 5-6; **Half-time:** 18-6;
Referee: Dave Merrick; **Attendance:** 305.

ROUND 2

Saturday 18th February 2012

POOL 1

TOULOUSE OLYMPIQUE 24 KEIGHLEY COUGARS 24

OLYMPIQUE: 1 Nathan Ross; 2 Greg White; 3 Damien Couturier; 4 Antoine Reveillon; 5 Adam Innes; 6 Johnathan Ford; 7 Mourad Kriouache; 8 Eloni Vunakece; 9 Luke Fahy; 10 Jerome Gout; 11 Kevin Larroyer; 12 Guy Williams; 13 Sylvain Houles. Subs (all used): 14 Yohann Gigord; 15 Sebastien Planas; 16 Theo Gonzalez-Trique; 17 Jean-Christophe Borlin.
Tries: Ross (14), Kriouache (25), Innes (64, 77);
Goals: Couturier 4/4.
COUGARS: 1 James Haythornthwaite; 2 Danny Lawton; 3 Matt Parata; 4 Jake Normington; 5 Richie Barnett; 6 Paul March; 7 Sam Obst; 8 Neil Cherryholme; 9 James Feather; 10 Michael Korkidas; 11 Oliver Pursglove; 12 Jamie Shepherd; 13 Jason Demetriou. Subs (all used): 14 Jamaine Wray; 15 Chris Clough; 16 Brendan Rawlins; 17 Andy Shickell.
Tries: Feather (18), Demetriou (44), March (54), Lawton (60); **Goals:** Lawton 4/5.
Rugby Leaguer & League Express Men of the Match: *Olympique:* Luke Fahy; *Cougars:* Matt Parata.
Penalty count: 5-10; **Half-time:** 12-6;
Referee: Jamie Bloem; **Attendance:** 650.

Sunday 19th February 2012

POOL 1

BATLEY BULLDOGS 50 LONDON SKOLARS 16

BULLDOGS: 1 Ian Preece; 2 Gareth Potts; 3 Jason Walton; 4 Danny Maun; 5 Danny Mills; 6 Ben Black; 7 Gareth Moore; 8 Byron Smith; 9 Paul Mennell; 10 Luke Menzies; 11 Adam Scott; 12 Jonny Walker; 13 Kris Lythe. Subs (all used): 14 Chris Buttery; 15 Keegan Hirst; 16 Mark Applegarth; 17 Ashley Lindsay.
Tries: Potts (7), Mennell (13), Maun (19, 23), Preece (27), Lythe (29), Black (40), Moore (51), Mills (70); **Goals:** Moore 6/8, Mennell 1/1.
SKOLARS: 1 James Anthony; 2 Ade Adebisi; 3 John Paxton; 4 Joe Price; 5 Lameck Juma; 6 Dylan Skee; 7 Andy McLean; 8 Rob Thomas; 9 Neil Thorman; 10 Dave Williams; 11 Matt Thomas; 12 Ben Bolger; 13 Lamont Bryan. Subs (all used): 14 Oliver Purslow; 15 Louis Robinson; 16 Martyn Smith; 17 Alex Bate.
Tries: Adebisi (58), B Bolger (64), Smith (80);
Goals: McLean 1/2, Skee 1/1.
Rugby Leaguer & League Express Men of the Match: *Bulldogs:* Ben Black; *Skolars:* Martyn Smith.
Penalty count: 6-8; **Half-time:** 40-0;
Referee: Warren Turley; **Attendance:** 601.

FEATHERSTONE ROVERS 38 DEWSBURY RAMS 6

ROVERS: 1 Ian Hardman; 2 Gareth Raynor; 3 Sam Smeaton; 4 Greg Worthington; 5 Tangi Ropati; 6 Andy Kain; 7 Liam Finn; 8 James Lockwood; 9 Ben Kaye; 10 Stuart Dickens; 11 Jon Grayshon; 12 Tim Spears; 13 Matty Dale. Subs (all used): 14 Kyle Briggs; 15 Anthony England; 16 Michael Haley; 17 Andrew Bostock.
Tries: Smeaton (32), Kain (37), Briggs (59, 72), Ropati (67), Kaye (76), Hardman (78); **Goals:** Finn 5/7.
RAMS: 1 Derrell Olpherts; 2 Michael Wainwright; 3 Ryan Esders; 4 Rob Spicer; 5 Austin Buchanan; 6 Ed Barber; 7 Scott Spaven; 8 Ben Jones; 9 Craig Cook; 10 Steve Crossley; 11 John Davies; 12 Josh Tonks; 13 Dwayne Barker. Subs (all used): 14 Matt Nicholson; 15 Billy Harris; 16 Nick Fozzard; 17 George Flanagan.
Try: Esders (3); **Goals:** Spaven 1/1.
Rugby Leaguer & League Express Men of the Match: *Rovers:* Kyle Briggs; *Rams:* Derrell Olpherts.
Penalty count: 7-6; **Half-time:** 10-6;
Referee: Clint Sharrad; **Attendance:** 1,943.

HALIFAX 38 ROCHDALE HORNETS 6

HALIFAX: 1 Ryan Fieldhouse; 2 Rob Worrincy; 3 Steve Tyrer; 4 Ben Heaton; 5 Paul White; 6 Paul Handforth; 7 Anthony Thackeray; 8 Adam Robinson; 9 Sean Penkywicz; 10 Sean Hesketh; 11 Dane Manning; 12 Iain Morrison; 13 Craig Ashall. Subs (all used): 14 Anthony Bowman; 15 Joe Chandler; 16 Jim Gannon; 17 Josh Barlow.
Tries: Fieldhouse (7), Thackeray (18), Gannon (28), Worrincy (35), White (39), Ashall (50), Tyrer (72);
Goals: Tyrer 5/7.
HORNETS: 1 Paul O'Connor; 2 Dean Gorton; 3 Dayne Donoghue; 4 Anthony Stewart; 5 Wayne English; 6 Paul Crook; 7 Steve Roper; 8 John Cookson; 9 Phil Wood; 10 Dave Newton; 11 Chris Baines; 12 Mark Hobson; 13 Gary Middlehurst. Subs (all used): 14 Steve McDermott; 15 Chris Hough; 16 Adam Bowman; 17 Stephen Lucas.
Try: McDermott (43); **Goals:** Crook 1/1.
Rugby Leaguer & League Express Men of the Match: *Halifax:* Ryan Fieldhouse; *Hornets:* Gary Middlehurst.
Penalty count: 11-11; **Half-time:** 26-0;
Referee: Matthew Thomason; **Attendance:** 1,881.

SOUTH WALES SCORPIONS 36 OLDHAM 36

SCORPIONS: 1 Rodney Peake; 2 Dalton Grant; 3 Lewis Reece; 4 David James; 5 Curtis Cunningham; 6 Jamie Rooney; 7 Shaun Owens; 8 Joe Burke; 9 Steve Parry; 10 Neil Dallimore; 11 Joe McKenna; 12 Jamie Acton; 13 Phil Carleton. Subs (all used): 14 Nathan Mossop; 15 James Greenwood; 16 Chris Vitalini; 17 Ashley Bateman.
Tries: J Burke (21), Acton (29), Mossop (37), Greenwood (42), Reece (46), C Cunningham (67);
Goals: Rooney 6/6.
OLDHAM: 1 Miles Greenwood; 2 Paul Ballard; 3 David Cookson; 4 Matthew Fogarty; 5 Tom Rigby; 6 Neil Roden; 7 Jamie Dallimore; 8 Jason Boults; 9 John Clough; 10 Liam Gilchrist; 11 Alex Thompson; 12 Michael Ward; 13 Valu Bentley. Subs (all used): 14 Martin Roden; 15 Danny Whitmore; 16 Dave Ellison; 17 Bruce Johnson.
Tries: Clough (9, 77), Dallimore (25, 63), Johnson (58), Fogarty (71); **Goals:** Dallimore 6/6.
Rugby Leaguer & League Express Men of the Match: *Scorpions:* Nathan Mossop; *Oldham:* Jamie Dallimore.
Penalty count: 7-6; **Half-time:** 18-12;
Referee: Peter Brooke; **Attendance:** 849.

POOL 2

BARROW RAIDERS 31 WORKINGTON TOWN 24

RAIDERS: 1 Lee Haney; 2 Marc Dixon; 3 Chris Larkin; 4 Andy Litherland; 5 James Nixon; 6 Scott Kaighan; 7 Liam Campbell; 8 Andrew Dawson; 9 James Dandy; 10 Jamie Butler; 11 Liam Harrison; 12 Barry Pugh; 13 Daniel Toal. Subs (all used): 14 Brad Marwood; 15 James Finch; 16 Martin Ostler; 17 Andries Venter.
Tries: Pugh (12), Butler (15), Ostler (36), Dandy (42), Campbell (62); **Goals:** Kaighan 5/6;
Field goal: Kaighan (80).
TOWN: 1 Elliott Miller; 2 Nick Johnson; 3 Jason Mossop; 4 Jonathan Dawes; 5 John Patrick; 6 Brett Carter; 7 Carl Forber; 8 James Green; 9 Graeme Mattinson; 10 Kris Coward; 11 Marc Shackley; 12 Jarrad Stack; 13 Dave Petersen. Subs (all used): 14 Brett Phillips; 15 Daniel Rooney; 16 Mike Whitehead; 17 Jamie Thackray.
Tries: Coward (6), Petersen (67), Thackray (72), Forber (77); **Goals:** Forber 4/4.
Rugby Leaguer & League Express Men of the Match: *Raiders:* Andrew Dawson; *Town:* Dave Petersen.
Penalty count: 7-7; **Half-time:** 16-6;
Referee: Jamie Leahy; **Attendance:** 1,366.

SWINTON LIONS 18 HUNSLET HAWKS 24

LIONS: 1 Ian Mort; 2 Gavin Dodd; 3 Adam Higson; 4 Tom Armstrong; 5 Kevin Penny; 6 Martin Ainscough; 7 Ian Watson; 8 Danny Meekin; 9 Mark Smith; 10 Neil

Holland; 11 Lee Wingfield; 12 Darren Hawkyard; 13 Dale Cunniffe. Subs (all used): 14 Mike Morrison; 15 David Mills; 16 Karl Ashall; 17 Chaz I'Anson.
Tries: Armstrong (22), Ainscough (45), Dodd (58);
Goals: Mort 3/3.
HAWKS: 1 Danny Ratcliffe; 2 Stuart Kain; 3 David Clayton; 4 Josh Nathaniel; 5 Lee Brickwood; 6 Luke Helliwell; 7 Danny Allan; 8 Andrew Yates; 9 Luke Haigh; 10 Steve Lewis; 11 Richard Blakeway; 12 John Oakes; 13 David March. Subs (all used): 14 Joe McLocklan; 15 Steve Dooler; 16 David Tootill; 17 Ryan Benjafield.
Tries: Brickwood (10), Clayton (32, 69), Nathaniel (51), Helliwell (80); **Goals:** Ratcliffe 1/3, Allan 1/2.
Rugby Leaguer & League Express Men of the Match: *Lions:* Darren Hawkyard; *Hawks:* Danny Ratcliffe.
Penalty count: 7-12; **Half-time:** 6-10;
Referee: Thierry Alibert; **Attendance:** 475.

DONCASTER 18 YORK CITY KNIGHTS 29

DONCASTER: 1 Mick Butterfield; 2 Dean Colton; 3 Liam Cunningham; 4 Lee Waterman; 5 Stewart Sanderson; 6 Paul Cooke; 7 Craig Fawcett; 8 Kyle Bibb; 9 Mike Emmett; 10 Mark Castle; 11 Craig Robinson; 12 Craig Lawton; 13 Carl Hughes. Subs (all used): 14 Kyle Kesik; 15 Francis Welsh; 16 Mike Burnett; 17 Jamie Crowther.
Tries: Cunningham (31, 65), Butterfield (69);
Goals: Cooke 3/3.
CITY KNIGHTS: 1 Ben Hellewell; 2 Waine Pryce; 3 James Ford; 4 Matt Garside; 5 Dave Sutton; 6 Chris Thorman; 7 Jordan Tansey; 8 Adam Sullivan; 9 Jack Lee; 10 James Houston; 11 Rhys Clarke; 12 Ed Smith; 13 Jack Aldous. Subs (all used): 14 Tom Bush; 15 Alex Benson; 16 Tom Haughey; 17 Brooke Broughton.
Tries: Ford (9, 21), Lee (17), Clarke (37), Pryce (53);
Goals: Thorman 4/5; **Field goal:** Thorman (40).
Rugby Leaguer & League Express Men of the Match: *Doncaster:* Mark Castle; *City Knights:* James Ford.
Penalty count: 5-5; **Half-time:** 6-25;
Referee: Ronnie Laughton; **Attendance:** 702.

SHEFFIELD EAGLES 23 LEIGH CENTURIONS 22

EAGLES: 1 Quentin Laulu-Togagae; 2 Vinny Finigan; 3 Menzie Yere; 4 Misi Taulapapa; 5 Nev Morrison; 6 Simon Brown; 7 Dominic Brambani; 8 Jack Howieson; 9 Andrew Henderson; 10 Liam Higgins; 11 Sam Scott; 12 Michael Knowles; 13 Joe Hirst. Subs (all used): 14 Duane Straugheir; 15 Peter Green; 16 Alex Szostak; 17 Ryan Hepworth.
Tries: Szostak (59), Hirst (62), Scott (73), Finigan (79);
Goals: Brown 3/4; **Field goal:** Brambani (80).
On report:
Yere (30) - alleged dangerous tackle on Worrincy.
CENTURIONS: 1 Gregg McNally; 2 Steve Maden; 3 Stuart Littler; 4 Matt Gardner; 5 Dean McGilvray; 6 Martyn Ridyard; 7 Bob Beswick; 8 Tom Spencer; 9 Anthony Nicholson; 10 Rob Parker; 11 Michael Worrincy; 12 Tommy Goulden; 13 Sam Hopkins. Subs (all used): 14 Ryan Brierley; 15 Craig Briscoe; 16 James Taylor; 17 Tommy Gallagher.
Tries: Hopkins (6, 38), McNally (27), Brierley (53);
Goals: Ridyard 3/4.
Rugby Leaguer & League Express Men of the Match: *Eagles:* Dominic Brambani; *Centurions:* Martyn Ridyard.
Penalty count: 6-7; **Half-time:** 0-18; **Referee:** Robert Hicks; **Attendance:** 1,045 *(at Don Valley Stadium).*

WHITEHAVEN 44 GATESHEAD THUNDER 18

WHITEHAVEN: 1 Jonathan Youds; 2 Craig Calvert; 3 Andreas Bauer; 4 Scott McAvoy; 5 Chris Fleming; 6 Carl Rudd; 7 Ben Karalius; 8 David Houghton; 9 Chris Smith; 10 Richard Varkulis; 11 Luke Isakka; 12 Lee Doran; 13 Brad Crellin. Subs (all used): 14 Scott George; 15 Paul Cullnean; 16 Max Wiper; 17 Peter Bewsher.
Tries: Calvert (7, 10, 28), McAvoy (14), Smith (31), Fleming (55), Varkulis (72), Bauer (79); **Goals:** Rudd 6/8.
THUNDER: 1 Robin Peers; 2 Ashley Thackeray; 3 Mike Mitchell; 4 Josh Neilson; 5 Ashley Williams; 6 Sam Walsh; 7 Ryan Clarke; 8 Brett Waller; 9 Tom Hodgson; 10 Jason Payne; 11 Matt Barron; 12 Oliver O'Mara; 13 Will Bate. Subs (all used): 14 Joe Brown; 15 Ryan McBride; 16 Stephen Welton; 17 Josh Taylor.
Tries: Waller (21), Williams (49), Welton (59);
Goals: Clarke 3/3.
On report: Walsh (47) - alleged biting on Calvert.
Rugby Leaguer & League Express Men of the Match: *Whitehaven:* Lee Doran; *Thunder:* Brett Waller.
Penalty count: 10-5; **Half-time:** 26-6;
Referee: Greg Dolan; **Attendance:** 649.

ROUND 1

Thursday 23rd February 2012

POOL 2

YORK CITY KNIGHTS 30 SWINTON LIONS 22

CITY KNIGHTS: 1 Ben Hellewell; 2 Waine Pryce; 3 James Ford; 4 Matt Garside; 5 Tom Bush; 6 Chris Thorman; 7 Jordan Tansey; 8 Adam Sullivan; 9 Jack Lee; 10 Paul King; 11 Tom Haughey; 12 Ed Smith; 13 Jack Aldous. Subs (all used): 14 George Elliott; 15 James Houston; 16 Rhys Clarke; 17 Brooke Broughton.
Tries: Pryce (12), Elliott (45), Bush (55), Lee (64, 67);
Goals: Thorman 5/5.
LIONS: 1 Richie Hawkyard; 2 Alex Hurst; 3 Sam Reay; 4 Tom Armstrong; 5 Ian Mort; 6 Martin Ainscough; 7 Ian Watson; 8 David Mills; 9 Mark Smith; 10 Mike Morrison; 11 Dale Cunniffe; 12 Darren Hawkyard; 13 Chaz I'Anson. Subs (all used): 14 Neil Holland; 15 Danny Meekin; 16 Karl Ashall; 17 Rob Foxen.
Tries: R Hawkyard (26), Mort (36), Morrison (49), Cunniffe (70); **Goals:** Mort 3/5.
On report: D Hawkyard (9) - alleged incident with King; Morrison (66) - alleged use of the elbow.
Rugby Leaguer & League Express Men of the Match: *City Knights:* Chris Thorman; *Lions:* Ian Watson;
Penalty count: 7-4; **Half-time:** 6-10;
Referee: Matthew Thomason; **Attendance:** 504.

ROUND 3

Saturday 25th February 2012

POOL 1

BATLEY BULLDOGS 34 TOULOUSE OLYMPIQUE 12

BULLDOGS: 1 Ian Preece; 2 Johnny Campbell; 3 Jason Walton; 4 Danny Maun; 5 Alex Brown; 6 Ben Black; 7 Gareth Moore; 8 Byron Smith; 9 Paul Mennell; 10 Craig Potter; 11 Alex Bretherton; 12 Jonny Walker; 13 Kris Lythe. Subs (all used): 14 Ashley Lindsay; 15 Alex Walmsley; 16 Mark Applegarth; 17 Mark Toohey.
Tries: Moore (18), Lythe (23), Walton (27), A Walmsley (40), Preece (54), Campbell (62); **Goals:** Moore 5/6.
OLYMPIQUE: 1 Nathan Ross; 2 Ryan Houston; 3 Damien Couturier; 4 Antoine Reveillon; 5 Jean-Baptiste Meurin; 6 Johnathan Ford; 7 Nicolas Delgal; 8 Theo Gonzalez-Trique; 9 Yohann Gigord; 10 David Delpoux; 11 Olivier Saintignan; 12 Guy Williams; 13 Sebastien Planas. Subs (all used): 14 Karim Djemi; 15 Joris Canton; 16 Cyril Moliner; 17 Yohan Barthau.
Tries: Ross (51), Houston (57); **Goals:** Couturier 2/2.
Rugby Leaguer & League Express Men of the Match: *Bulldogs:* Johnny Campbell; *Olympique:* Nathan Ross.
Penalty count: 11-5; **Half-time:** 24-0;
Referee: Greg Dolan; **Attendance:** 620.

Sunday 26th February 2012

POOL 1

HALIFAX 32 FEATHERSTONE ROVERS 34

HALIFAX: 1 Ryan Fieldhouse; 2 Wayne Reittie; 3 Steve Tyrer; 4 Ben Heaton; 5 Paul White; 6 Paul Handforth; 7 Anthony Thackeray; 8 Jim Gannon; 9 Sean Penkywicz; 10 Sean Hesketh; 11 Dane Manning; 12 Adam Robinson; 13 Craig Ashall. Subs (all used): 14 Anthony Bowman; 15 Joe Chandler; 16 Luke Ambler; 17 Josh Barlow.
Tries: Tyrer (8), Heaton (13, 78), Ashall (49), Hesketh (56), White (68); **Goals:** Tyrer 4/6.
Dismissal: Ashall (55) - fighting.
ROVERS: 1 Ian Hardman; 2 Tom Saxton; 3 Sam Smeaton; 4 Greg Worthington; 5 Tangi Ropati; 6 Kyle Briggs; 7 Liam Finn; 8 James Lockwood; 9 Ben Kaye; 10 Stuart Dickens; 11 Jon Grayshon; 12 Tim Spears; 13 Matty Dale. Subs (all used): 14 Andy Kain; 15 Andrew Bostock; 16 Michael Haley; 17 Anthony England.
Tries: Hardman (39, 65, 71), Ropati (61), Bostock (76), Worthington (79); **Goals:** Finn 5/6.
Dismissal: Haley (55) - fighting.
Rugby Leaguer & League Express Men of the Match: *Halifax:* Dane Manning; *Rovers:* Ian Hardman.
Penalty count: 8-6; **Half-time:** 10-6;
Referee: Robert Hicks; **Attendance:** 2,530.

OLDHAM 28 DEWSBURY RAMS 30

OLDHAM: 1 Miles Greenwood; 2 Shaun Robinson; 3 David Cookson; 4 Matthew Fogarty; 5 John Gillam; 6 Neil Roden; 7 Jamie Dallimore; 8 Jason Boults; 9 John Clough; 10 Liam Gilchrist; 11 Chris Clarke; 12 Michael Ward; 13 Alex Thompson. Subs (all used): 14 Paul Noone; 15 Danny Whitmore; 16 Dave Ellison; 17 Bruce Johnson.
Tries: Gillam (35, 65, 72), N Roden (58), Clough (78);
Goals: Dallimore 4/5.
On report: Thompson (46) - alleged punching.
RAMS: 1 Derrell Olpherts; 2 Michael Wainwright; 3 Andy Smith; 4 Ayden Faal; 5 Austin Buchanan; 6 Ed Barber; 7 Scott Spaven; 8 Ben Jones; 9 Craig Cook; 10 Steve Crossley; 11 Dwayne Barker; 12 Ryan Esders; 13 Josh Tonks. Subs (all used): 14 Luke Blake; 15 Matt Nicholson; 16 John Davies; 17 Danny Samuel.
Tries: Faal (3), Jones (8), Barber (24), Barker (39), Olpherts (48), Nicholson (53); **Goals:** Spaven 3/6.
On report: Barker (46) - alleged punching.
Rugby Leaguer & League Express Men of the Match: *Oldham:* John Gillam; *Rams:* Dwayne Barker.
Penalty count: 10-10; **Half-time:** 4-20;
Referee: Jamie Bloem; **Attendance:** 573.

ROCHDALE HORNETS 16 KEIGHLEY COUGARS 40

HORNETS: 1 Wayne English; 2 Paul O'Connor; 3 Dayne Donoghue; 4 Danny Pyke; 5 Craig Johnson; 6 Paul Crook; 7 Steve Roper; 8 Dave Newton; 9 Steve McDermott; 10 John Cookson; 11 Chris Baines; 12 Mark Hobson; 13 Gary Middlehurst. Subs (all used): 14 Phil Wood; 15 Chris Hough; 16 Adam Bowman; 17 Steve Bannister.
Tries: Pyke (12, 68), Bowman (72);
Goals: Crook 1/2, Hough 1/1.
Sin bin: Newton (58) - persistent offending.
COUGARS: 1 Craig Moss; 2 James Haythornthwaite; 3 Matt Parata; 4 Danny Lawton; 5 Semi Tadulala; 6 Danny Jones; 7 Sam Obst; 8 Andy Shickell; 9 James Feather; 10 Jode Sheriffe; 11 Richard Jones; 12 Oliver Pursglove; 13 Jamie Shepherd. Subs (all used): 14 Jamaine Wray; 15 Jy-Mel Coleman; 16 Michael Korkidas; 17 Neil Cherryholme.
Tries: Parata (4, 44, 64, 70), Feather (26), Obst (36), Coleman (39), Lawton (62); **Goals:** D Jones 4/8.
Rugby Leaguer & League Express Men of the Match: *Hornets:* Paul Crook; *Cougars:* Matt Parata.
Penalty count: 10-9; **Half-time:** 6-22;
Referee: George Stokes; **Attendance:** 604.

SOUTH WALES SCORPIONS 30 LONDON SKOLARS 38

SCORPIONS: 1 Rodney Peake; 2 David James; 3 Lewis Fox; 4 Alan Pope; 5 Ashley Bateman; 6 Jamie Rooney; 7 Scott Leatherbarrow; 8 Joe Burke; 9 Nathan Mossop; 10 Alistair McDonald; 11 Chris Vitalini; 12 Jamie Acton; 13 Phil Carleton. Subs (all used): 14 Steve Parry; 15 Neil Dallimore; 16 Callum Wilkinson; 17 Lewis Reece.
Tries: Fox (8), Mossop (59, 64), Pope (67), D James (78); **Goals:** Rooney 5/5.
SKOLARS: 1 James Anthony; 2 Ade Adebisi; 3 Chris McNamara; 4 Joe Price; 5 Lameck Juma; 6 Andy McLean; 7 Dylan Skee; 8 Louis Robinson; 9 Neil Thorman; 10 Dave Williams; 11 Alex Bate; 12 Matt Thomas; 13 Lamont Bryan. Subs (all used): 14 Rob Thomas; 15 Austen Aggrey; 16 Martyn Smith; 17 Oliver Purslow.
Tries: Robinson (11), Bryan (16), Price (24), Adebisi (35), R Thomas (43), Skee (55), McLean (62);
Goals: Skee 5/7.
Rugby Leaguer & League Express Men of the Match: *Scorpions:* Nathan Mossop; *Skolars:* Lamont Bryan.
Penalty count: 3-10; **Half-time:** 6-22;
Referee: Tom Crashley; **Attendance:** 205.

POOL 2

BARROW RAIDERS 32 SWINTON LIONS 16

RAIDERS: 1 Andy Ballard; 2 James Nixon; 3 Chris Larkin; 4 Aaron Low; 5 Marc Dixon; 6 Darren Holt; 7 Liam Campbell; 8 Andy Bracek; 9 James Dandy; 10 Andrew Dawson; 11 Liam Harrison; 12 James Gordon; 13 Daniel Toal. Subs (all used): 14 Liam Finch; 15 James Finch; 16 Jamie Butler; 17 Martin Ostler.
Tries: Ballard (3), Toal (18, 52), Nixon (24), Gordon (28), Larkin (80); **Goals:** Holt 4/6.
LIONS: 1 Richie Hawkyard; 2 Gavin Dodd; 3 Alex Hurst; 4 Tom Armstrong; 5 Kevin Penny; 6 Martin Ainscough; 7 Ian Watson; 8 David Mills; 9 Mark Smith; 10 Mike Morrison; 11 Dale Cunniffe; 12 Andy Gorski; 13 Chaz I'Anson. Subs (all used): 14 Neil Holland; 15 Danny Meekin; 16 Rob Foxen; 17 Lee Wingfield.
Tries: Dodd (34), Watson (58), I'Anson (70);
Goals: Dodd 2/3.
Rugby Leaguer & League Express Men of the Match: *Raiders:* Daniel Toal; *Lions:* Lee Wingfield.
Penalty count: 7-7; **Half-time:** 20-4;
Referee: Dave Merrick; **Attendance:** 1,083.

DONCASTER 12 SHEFFIELD EAGLES 56

DONCASTER: 1 Tom Hodson; 2 Dean Colton; 3 Liam Cunningham; 4 Lee Waterman; 5 Stewart Sanderson; 6 Grant Edwards; 7 Craig Fawcett; 8 Kyle Bibb; 9 Kyle Kesik; 10 Craig Robinson; 11 Dean O'Loughlin; 12 Michael Kelly; 13 Mike Emmett. Subs (all used): 14 Nathan Powley; 15 Mike Burnett; 16 Andy Townend; 17 Kyle Sampson.
Tries: Edwards (69), Colton (73); **Goals:** Waterman 2/2.
EAGLES: 1 Quentin Laulu-Togagae; 2 Vinny Finigan; 3 Menzie Yere; 4 Misi Taulapapa; 5 Nev Morrison; 6 Simon Brown; 7 Dominic Brambani; 8 Jack Howieson; 9 Andrew Henderson; 10 Liam Higgins; 11 Alex Szostak; 12 Peter Green; 13 Joe Hirst. Subs (all used): 14 Duane Straugheir; 15 Sam Scott; 16 Pat Smith; 17 Mitchell Stringer.
Tries: Morrison (8), Hirst (19, 22), Szostak (24), Taulapapa (30), Laulu-Togagae (32, 55), Stringer (37), Brambani (44, 53); **Goals:** Brown 8/10.
Rugby Leaguer & League Express Men of the Match: *Doncaster:* Grant Edwards; *Eagles:* Mitchell Stringer.
Penalty count: 8-8; **Half-time:** 0-40;
Referee: Warren Turley; **Attendance:** 731.

LEIGH CENTURIONS 30 HUNSLET HAWKS 12

CENTURIONS: 1 Gregg McNally; 2 Steve Maden; 3 Stuart Littler; 4 Matt Gardner; 5 Dean McGilvray; 6 Martyn Ridyard; 7 John Duffy; 8 Sam Hopkins; 9 Anthony Nicholson; 10 Rob Parker; 11 Michael Worrincy; 12 Tommy Goulden; 13 James Taylor. Subs (all used): 14 Ryan Brierley; 15 Craig Briscoe; 16 Michael Ostick; 17 Tommy Gallagher.
Tries: Taylor (15), Hopkins (22), Littler (25), Nicholson (31), McNally (62), Worrincy (79); **Goals:** Ridyard 3/6.
HAWKS: 1 Danny Ratcliffe; 2 Stuart Kain; 3 David Clayton; 4 Josh Nathaniel; 5 Lee Brickwood; 6 Luke Helliwell; 7 Danny Allan; 8 Andrew Yates; 9 Luke Haigh; 10 Steve Lewis; 11 Steve Dooler; 12 John Oakes; 13 David March. Subs (all used): 14 Joe McLocklan; 15 David Tootill; 16 Joe Pickets; 17 Ryan Benjafield.
Tries: Ratcliffe (36, 43); **Goals:** Ratcliffe 2/2.
Rugby Leaguer & League Express Men of the Match: *Centurions:* Anthony Nicholson; *Hawks:* Danny Ratcliffe.
Penalty count: 9-8; **Half-time:** 22-6;
Referee: Chris Leatherbarrow; **Attendance:** 1,374.

WORKINGTON TOWN 44 WHITEHAVEN 16

TOWN: 1 Elliott Miller; 2 Jonathan Dawes; 3 Daniel Rooney; 4 Jason Mossop; 5 Karl Olstrum; 6 Brett Carter; 7 Carl Forber; 8 Ryan McDonald; 9 Graeme Mattinson; 10 Kris Coward; 11 Mike Whitehead; 12 Brett Phillips; 13 James Robinson. Subs (all used): 14 Darren King; 15 Marc Shackley; 16 Matthew Tunstall; 17 Jamie Thackray.
Tries: Forber (3), Rooney (19), Miller (28), Carter (33), Thackray (43, 55), Phillips (54), Shackley (67);
Goals: Forber 6/8.
Sin bin: Carter (46) - fighting.
On report: Brawl (46).

WHITEHAVEN: 1 Jonathan Youds; 2 Craig Calvert; 3 Andreas Bauer; 4 Max Wiper; 5 Chris Fleming; 6 Carl Rudd; 7 Ben Karalius; 8 David Houghton; 9 Chris Smith; 10 Richard Varkulis; 11 Luke Isakka; 12 Lee Doran; 13 Brad Crellin. Subs (all used): 14 Carl Sice; 15 Scott George; 16 Peter Bewsher; 17 Paul Cullnean.
Tries: Fleming (8), Bauer (47), Sice (79);
Goals: Rudd 2/2, George 0/1.
Sin bin: Calvert (46) - fighting.
On report: Brawl (46).
Rugby Leaguer & League Express Men of the Match: *Town:* Brett Phillips; *Whitehaven:* Luke Isakka.
Penalty count: 12-10; **Half-time:** 20-6;
Referee: Matthew Kidd; **Attendance:** 1,147.

YORK CITY KNIGHTS 26 GATESHEAD THUNDER 22

CITY KNIGHTS: 1 Tom Bush; 2 Ben Dent; 3 Tom Haughey; 4 George Elliott; 5 Dave Sutton; 6 Brett Turner; 7 Jordan Tansey; 8 Brooke Broughton; 9 Kris Brining; 10 Alex Benson; 11 Rhys Clarke; 12 Joe Hemmings; 13 Paul King. Subs (all used): 14 Jack Lee; 15 Chris Green; 16 Adam Howard; 17 Davey Burns.
Tries: Turner (20), Hemmings (25, 29), Green (60, 67);
Goals: Tansey 0/1, Bush 3/4.
Dismissal: Howard (72) - kicking.
THUNDER: 1 Robin Peers; 2 Ashley Thackeray; 3 Mike Mitchell; 4 Josh Neilson; 5 Ashley Williams; 6 Sam Walsh; 7 Ryan Clarke; 8 Brett Waller; 9 Tom Hodgson; 10 Ryan McBride; 11 Matt Barron; 12 Oliver O'Mara; 13 Jason Payne. Subs: 14 Will Bate; 15 Joe Brown; 16 Chris Parker Snr (not used); 17 Stephen Welton.
Tries: Mitchell (3, 53), Hodgson (7), Neilson (45);
Goals: Clarke 1/2, Welton 1/1, Hodgson 1/1.
Rugby Leaguer & League Express Men of the Match: *City Knights:* Paul King; *Thunder:* Ryan Clarke.
Penalty count: 9-7; **Half-time:** 14-10;
Referee: Dave Sharpe; **Attendance:** 635.

ROUND 4

Friday 2nd March 2012

POOL 2

SHEFFIELD EAGLES 36 YORK CITY KNIGHTS 4

EAGLES: 1 Quentin Laulu-Togagae; 2 Vinny Finigan; 3 Menzie Yere; 4 Misi Taulapapa; 5 Nev Morrison; 6 Simon Brown; 7 Dominic Brambani; 8 Jack Howieson; 9 Andrew Henderson; 10 Mitchell Stringer; 11 Alex Szostak; 12 Peter Green; 13 Joe Hirst. Subs (all used): 14 Pat Smith; 15 Ryan Hepworth; 16 Duane Straugheir; 17 Alex Rowe.
Tries: Morrison (14), Brambani (22, 61), Yere (47), Straugheir (67), Taulapapa (73); **Goals:** Brown 6/6.
CITY KNIGHTS: 1 Ben Hellewell; 2 George Elliott; 3 James Ford; 4 Matt Garside; 5 Tom Bush; 6 Brett Turner; 7 Jordan Tansey; 8 Adam Sullivan; 9 Jack Lee; 10 James Houston; 11 Rhys Clarke; 12 Ed Smith; 13 Jack Aldous. Subs (all used): 14 Kris Brining; 15 Chris Green; 16 Tom Haughey; 17 Alex Benson.
Try: Clarke (34); **Goals:** Bush 0/1.
Rugby Leaguer & League Express Men of the Match: *Eagles:* Peter Green; *City Knights:* Jack Lee.
Penalty count: 5-3; **Half-time:** 12-4; **Referee:** Robert Hicks; **Attendance:** 725 *(at Don Valley Stadium).*

Saturday 3rd March 2012

POOL 1

TOULOUSE OLYMPIQUE 44 SOUTH WALES SCORPIONS 30

OLYMPIQUE: 1 Nathan Ross; 2 Gregory White; 3 Bruno Ormeno; 4 Damien Couturier; 5 Adam Innes; 6 Johnathan Ford; 7 Nicolas Delgal; 8 David Delpoux; 9 Mourad Kriouache; 10 Jerome Gout; 11 Kevin Larroyer; 12 Guy Williams; 13 Sebastien Planas. Subs (all used): 14 Karim Djemi; 15 Yohan Barthau; 16 Cyril Moliner; 17 Jean-Christophe Borlin.
Tries: Ross (1, 55), Couturier (6), White (26), Williams (34), Innes (37), Ormeno (44), Larroyer (70);
Goals: Couturier 6/8.
SCORPIONS: 1 Rodney Peake; 2 Dalton Grant; 3 Lewis Reece; 4 David James; 5 Curtis Cunningham; 6 Scott Leatherbarrow; 7 Shaun Owens; 8 Gil Dudson; 9 Nathan Mossop; 10 Paul Prescott; 11 Joe Burke; 12 Chris Vitalini; 13 Phil Carleton. Subs (all used): 14 Steve Parry; 15 Greg Burke; 16 Jamie Acton; 17 Ashley Bateman.
Tries: Prescott (12), J Burke (42), Reece (57), Leatherbarrow (63), Mossop (75); **Goals:** Reece 5/5.
Rugby Leaguer & League Express Men of the Match: *Olympique:* Guy Williams; *Scorpions:* Gil Dudson.
Penalty count: 7-6; **Half-time:** 28-6;
Referee: Matthew Thomason; **Attendance:** 685.

Sunday 4th March 2012

POOL 1

KEIGHLEY COUGARS 26 OLDHAM 12

COUGARS: 1 James Haythornthwaite; 2 Gavin Duffy; 3 Matt Parata; 4 Jake Normington; 5 Richie Barnett; 6 Danny Jones; 7 Paul March; 8 Michael Korkidas; 9 Sam Obst; 10 Brendan Rawlins; 11 Oliver Pursglove; 12 Chris Clough; 13 Richard Jones. Subs (all used): 14 Jason Demetriou; 15 Jy-Mel Coleman; 16 Jode Sheriffe; 17 Andy Shickell.
Tries: Obst (12, 39), R Jones (33), Barnett (63), Duffy (66); **Goals:** D Jones 3/5.
Sin bin: Duffy (75) - dissent.
OLDHAM: 1 Miles Greenwood; 2 Shaun Robinson; 3 David Cookson; 4 Mark Brocklehurst; 5 John Gillam; 6 Jamie Dallimore; 7 Jack Reid; 8 Jason Boults; 9 Martin Roden; 10 Liam Gilchrist; 11 Chris Clarke; 12 Paul Noone; 13 Alex Thompson. Subs (all used): 14 Paul Smith; 15 John Clough; 16 Dave Ellison; 17 Bruce Johnson.
Tries: Robinson (26), Greenwood (79);
Goals: Dallimore 2/2.
Rugby Leaguer & League Express Men of the Match: *Cougars:* Paul March; *Oldham:* Jamie Dallimore.
Penalty count: 10-10; **Half-time:** 18-6;
Referee: Ronnie Laughton; **Attendance:** 827.

DEWSBURY RAMS 32 ROCHDALE HORNETS 10

RAMS: 1 James Craven; 2 Jermaine Akaidere; 3 Ryan Esders; 4 Ayden Faal; 5 Austin Buchanan; 6 Pat Walker; 7 Scott Spaven; 8 Ben Jones; 9 Luke Blake; 10 Steve Crossley; 11 Josh Tonks; 12 Dwayne Barker; 13 Ed Barber. Subs (all used): 14 Billy Harris; 15 Derrell Olpherts; 16 Matthew Tebb; 17 Matt Nicholson.
Tries: Faal (1), Crossley (5), Esders (24), Akaidere (37, 49), Craven (43); **Goals:** Walker 4/6.
HORNETS: 1 Jonny Leather; 2 Wayne English; 3 Danny Pyke; 4 Steve Bannister; 5 Mark Kellett; 6 Paul Crook; 7 Steve Roper; 8 Dave Newton; 9 Steve McDermott; 10 Mark Hobson; 11 Chris Baines; 12 Gary Middlehurst; 13 Dayne Donoghue. Subs (all used): 14 Stephen Lucas; 15 Paul Brearley; 16 Damien Turner; 17 John Cookson.
Tries: Leather (62), McDermott (76); **Goals:** Crook 1/2.
Sin bin: Brearley (70) - dangerous tackle.
Rugby Leaguer & League Express Men of the Match: *Rams:* Steve Crossley; *Hornets:* Paul Crook.
Penalty count: 5-5; **Half-time:** 22-0;
Referee: Matthew Kidd; **Attendance:** 701.

FEATHERSTONE ROVERS 22 BATLEY BULLDOGS 34

ROVERS: 1 Tom Carr; 2 Tom Saxton; 3 Sam Smeaton; 4 Greg Worthington; 5 Tangi Ropati; 6 Kyle Briggs; 7 Liam Finn; 8 Anthony England; 9 Ben Kaye; 10 Stuart Dickens; 11 Matty Dale; 12 Tim Spears; 13 Jon Hepworth. Subs (all used): 14 Andy Kain; 15 Mufaro Mvududu; 16 Dominic Maloney; 17 Nathan Freer.
Tries: Worthington (2), Spears (15), Dickens (51), Dale (70), Ropati (78); **Goals:** Finn 1/5.
Dismissal: Spears (77) - punching.
Sin bin: Smeaton (74) - fighting.
BULLDOGS: 1 Ian Preece; 2 Johnny Campbell; 3 Chris Buttery; 4 Daley Williams; 5 Danny Mills; 6 Lewis Palfrey; 7 Tom Henderson; 8 Craig Potter; 9 Kris Lythe; 10 Luke Menzies; 11 Mark Toohey; 12 Adam Scott; 13 Mark Applegarth. Subs (all used): 14 Paul Mennell; 15 Keegan Hirst; 16 Alex Bretherton; 17 Gareth Frodsham.
Tries: Potter (18), Frodsham (23), Campbell (26), Daley Williams (31), Buttery (54, 66); **Goals:** Palfrey 5/7.
Sin bin: Bretherton (74) - fighting.
Rugby Leaguer & League Express Men of the Match: *Rovers:* Stuart Dickens; *Bulldogs:* Lewis Palfrey.
Penalty count: 8-6; **Half-time:** 8-24;
Referee: Jamie Leahy; **Attendance:** 1,652.

LONDON SKOLARS 12 HALIFAX 16

SKOLARS: 1 James Anthony; 2 John Paxton; 3 Joe Price; 4 Chris McNamara; 5 Ade Adebisi; 6 Andy McLean; 7 Dylan Skee; 8 Rob Thomas; 9 Neil Thorman; 10 Dave Williams; 11 Alex Bate; 12 Matt Thomas; 13 Lamont Bryan. Subs (all used): 14 Oliver Purslow; 15 Austen Aggrey; 16 Danny Burke; 17 Joe Ridley.
Tries: Aggrey (30), Adebisi (55); **Goals:** Skee 2/3.
HALIFAX: 1 Ryan Fieldhouse; 2 Wayne Reittie; 3 Steve Tyrer; 4 Ben Heaton; 5 Rob Worrincy; 6 Paul Handforth; 7 Anthony Thackeray; 8 Jim Gannon; 9 Sean Penkywicz; 10 Sean Hesketh; 11 Dane Manning; 12 Adam Robinson; 13 Craig Ashall. Subs (all used): 14 Anthony Bowman; 15 Callum Casey; 16 Luke Ambler; 17 Lee Paterson.
Tries: Fieldhouse (48), Tyrer (71), Reittie (80);
Goals: Tyrer 2/3.
Sin bin: Heaton (51) - late challenge.
Rugby Leaguer & League Express Men of the Match: *Skolars:* Ade Adebisi; *Halifax:* Ryan Fieldhouse.
Penalty count: 10-9; **Half-time:** 6-0;
Referee: Joe Cobb; **Attendance:** 613.

POOL 2

SWINTON LIONS 30 WORKINGTON TOWN 12

LIONS: 1 Richie Hawkyard; 2 Gavin Dodd; 3 Adam Higson; 4 Tom Armstrong; 5 Rob Foxen; 6 Martin Ainscough; 7 Ian Watson; 8 Neil Holland; 9 Mark Smith; 10 Lee Wingfield; 11 Andy Gorski; 12 Darren Hawkyard; 13 Chaz I'Anson. Subs (all used): 14 David Mills; 15 Danny Meekin; 16 Dale Cunniffe; 17 Karl Ashall.
Tries: Armstrong (2, 46), Ainscough (19), D Hawkyard (27, 36), Dodd (54); **Goals:** Dodd 2/5, Ashall 1/1.
TOWN: 1 Brett Carter; 2 Elliott Miller; 3 Karl Olstrum; 4 Jonathan Dawes; 5 Nick Johnson; 6 Dave Petersen; 7 Carl Forber; 8 James Green; 9 Darren King; 10 Richard Farrer; 11 Mike Whitehead; 12 Marc Shackley; 13 James Robinson. Subs (all used): 14 Jack Gaskell; 15 Graeme Mattinson; 16 Kris Coward; 17 Jamie Thackray.
Tries: Miller (33), Shackley (65); **Goals:** Forber 2/2.
Rugby Leaguer & League Express Men of the Match: *Lions:* Ian Watson; *Town:* Graeme Mattinson.
Penalty count: 6-10; **Half-time:** 20-6;
Referee: Clint Sharrad; **Attendance:** 503.

GATESHEAD THUNDER 0 LEIGH CENTURIONS 42

THUNDER: 1 Robin Peers; 2 Ashley Thackeray; 3 Joe Brown; 4 Josh Neilson; 5 Ashley Williams; 6 Sam Walsh; 7 Ryan Clarke; 8 Brett Waller; 9 Tom Hodgson; 10 Ryan McBride; 11 Matt Barron; 12 Oliver O'Mara; 13 Jason Payne. Subs (all used): 14 Will Bate; 15 Chris Parker Snr; 16 Stephen Welton; 17 Dan O'Sullivan.
CENTURIONS: 1 Matthew Russell; 2 Adam Clay; 3 Stuart Littler; 4 Matt Gardner; 5 Ryan Shaw; 6 Martyn Ridyard; 7 John Duffy; 8 Ricky Bibey; 9 Anthony Nicholson; 10 Tom Spencer; 11 Craig Briscoe; 12 Michael Worrincy; 13 James Taylor. Subs (all used): 14 Bob Beswick; 15 Steve Maden; 16 Michael Ostick; 17 Tommy Gallagher.
Tries: Russell (1, 20), Shaw (27), Gallagher (38), Taylor (45), Gardner (51), Spencer (54), Clay (68);
Goals: Ridyard 5/8.
Rugby Leaguer & League Express Men of the Match: *Thunder:* Brett Waller; *Centurions:* Matthew Russell.
Penalty count: 5-5; **Half-time:** 0-22; **Referee:** Tom Crashley; **Attendance:** 276 *(at Kingston Park, Newcastle).*

HUNSLET HAWKS 20 DONCASTER 10

HAWKS: 1 Danny Ratcliffe; 2 Lee Brickwood; 3 David Clayton; 4 Josh Nathaniel; 5 Dennis Tuffour; 6 Danny Grimshaw; 7 Luke Helliwell; 8 Steve Lewis; 9 Luke Haigh; 10 Andrew Yates; 11 Richard Blakeway; 12 John Oakes; 13 David March. Subs (all used): 14 Joe McLocklan; 15 Steve Dooler; 16 David Tootill; 17 Ryan Benjafield.
Tries: Lewis (12), Haigh (21), Oakes (50), Brickwood (78); **Goals:** Ratcliffe 2/4.
DONCASTER: 1 Stewart Sanderson; 2 Tom Hodson; 3 Liam Cunningham; 4 Lee Waterman; 5 Dean Colton; 6 Paul Cooke; 7 Keiran Hyde; 8 Dean O'Loughlin; 9 Jack Ely; 10 Mark Castle; 11 Craig Robinson; 12 Craig Lawton; 13 Mike Emmett. Subs (all used): 14 Nathan Powley; 15 Kyle Bibb; 16 Francis Welsh; 17 Carl Hughes.
Tries: Hughes (45, 55); **Goals:** Cooke 1/2.
Rugby Leaguer & League Express Men of the Match: *Hawks:* Luke Haigh; *Doncaster:* Carl Hughes.
Penalty count: 6-4; **Half-time:** 10-0;
Referee: Peter Brooke; **Attendance:** 310.

WHITEHAVEN 10 BARROW RAIDERS 18

WHITEHAVEN: 1 Shane Ackerley; 2 Craig Calvert; 3 Martyn Wilson; 4 Max Wiper; 5 Loz Hamzat; 6 Carl Rudd; 7 Sam Gee; 8 Matthew Haggerty; 9 Carl Sice; 10 Richard Varkulis; 11 Sam Cunningham; 12 Daniel Barker; 13 Andrew Beattie. Subs (all used): 14 Steve Fox; 15 Martin O'Neill; 16 Andreas Bauer; 17 Paul Cullnean.
Tries: Hamzat (43), Gee (59); **Goals:** Rudd 1/2.
RAIDERS: 1 Andy Ballard; 2 Lee Haney; 3 James Finch; 4 Chris Larkin; 5 Mike Backhouse; 6 Scott Kaighan; 7 Liam Campbell; 8 Andy Bracek; 9 Liam Finch; 10 Ruairi McGoff; 11 Liam Harrison; 12 Barry Pugh; 13 Daniel Toal. Subs (all used): 14 Brad Marwood; 15 Andries Venter; 16 Lee Dutton; 17 James Gordon.
Tries: Toal (12, 23), Harrison (18), Haney (78);
Goals: Kaighan 1/4.
Sin bin: Larkin (52) - high tackle.
On report: McGoff (74) - alleged dangerous tackle.
Rugby Leaguer & League Express Men of the Match: *Whitehaven:* Richard Varkulis; *Raiders:* Daniel Toal.
Penalty count: 14-7; **Half-time:** 0-14;
Referee: Gareth Hewer; **Attendance:** 902.

ROUND 1

Monday 9th April 2012

POOL 1

LONDON SKOLARS 16 TOULOUSE OLYMPIQUE 32

SKOLARS: 1 Will Colleran; 2 Aaron Small; 3 Lameck Juma; 4 Dave Arnot; 5 Smokie Junor; 6 Andy McLean; 7 Joe Ridley; 8 Louis Robinson; 9 Danny Burke; 10 Oliver Bloom; 11 Jaroslaw Obuchowski; 12 James Roche; 13 Michael Worrincy. Subs (all used): 14 Connor McDonald; 15 James Fletcher; 16 Andre Vine; 17 Dion Chapman.
Tries: Junor (62), Bloom (72), Fletcher (75);
Goals: McLean 2/3.
OLYMPIQUE: 1 Nathan Ross; 2 Ryan Houston; 3 Guy Williams; 4 Antoine Reveillon; 5 Jean-Baptiste Meurin; 6 Johnathan Ford; 7 Mourad Kriouache; 8 Theo Gonzalez-Trique; 9 Yohann Gigord; 10 Jean-Christophe Borlin; 11 Cyril Moliner; 12 Olivier Saintignan; 13 Kevin Larroyer. Subs (all used): 14 Adrien Viala; 15 Luke Fahy; 16 Yohan Barthau; 17 David Delpoux.
Tries: Ross (25, 33, 50, 70), Meurin (30), Houston (79);
Goals: Kriouache 4/6.
Dismissal: Borlin (15) - use of the elbow.
Rugby Leaguer & League Express Men of the Match: *Skolars:* James Fletcher; *Olympique:* Nathan Ross.
Penalty count: 6-6; **Half-time:** 0-16;
Referee: Dave Sharpe; **Attendance:** 242.

Wednesday 9th May 2012

POOL 1

ROCHDALE HORNETS 46 SOUTH WALES SCORPIONS 24

HORNETS: 1 Jonny Leather; 2 Barry Clarke; 3 Alex West; 4 Dean Gorton; 5 Andy Taylor; 6 Paul Crook; 7 Will Chadwick; 8 Joe Fitzpatrick; 9 Phil Wood; 10 Adam Bowman; 11 Gary Middlehurst; 12 Fraser Jones-Lake; 13 Ben Marsden. Subs (all used): 14 Ryan Brown; 15 Stephen Lucas; 16 Andy Unsworth; 17 Charles Moore.
Tries: Wood (1), Crook (4), Clarke (8, 34), Middlehurst (14), Leather (37, 46), Chadwick (43); **Goals:** Crook 7/8.
SCORPIONS: 1 Jacob Morgan; 2 Joe Bullock; 3 Kevin James; 4 Yannic Parker; 5 James Gahan; 6 Loz Wildbore; 7 Andrew Cunningham; 8 Greg Burke; 9 Lewis Singleton; 10 Kieran Harrison; 11 TJ Collin; 12 Matthew Crow; 13 Phil Carleton. Subs (all used): 14 Rhys Godwin; 15 Ryan Curtis; 16 Karl Jones; 17 Liam Watton.
Tries: Crow (23, 61), K James (53), J Morgan (70);
Goals: Wildbore 4/4.
Rugby Leaguer & League Express Men of the Match: *Hornets:* Will Chadwick; *Scorpions:* Matthew Crow.
Penalty count: 5-3; **Half-time:** 34-6;
Referee: Dave Sharpe; **Attendance:** 238.

FINAL TABLES

POOL 1

	P	W	D	L	BP	F	A	Diff	Pts
Batley Bulldogs	4	4	0	0	0	140	66	74	12
Featherstone Rovers	4	3	0	1	1	162	72	90	10
Halifax	4	3	0	1	1	122	58	64	10
Keighley Cougars	4	2	1	1	1	106	74	32	9
Toulouse Olympique	4	2	1	1	0	112	104	8	8
Dewsbury Rams	4	2	0	2	0	74	112	-38	6
London Skolars	4	1	0	3	1	82	128	-46	4
Sth Wales Scorpions	4	1	0	3	1	120	164	-44	3
Rochdale Hornets	4	1	0	3	0	78	134	-56	3
Oldham	4	0	1	3	1	76	160	-84	3

POOL 2

	P	W	D	L	BP	F	A	Diff	Pts
Sheffield Eagles	4	4	0	0	0	143	52	91	12
Leigh Centurions	4	3	0	1	1	142	51	91	10
Hunslet Hawks	4	3	0	1	0	90	76	14	9
Barrow Raiders	4	3	0	1	0	97	98	-1	9
York City Knights	4	3	0	1	0	89	98	-9	9
Swinton Lions	4	1	0	3	2	86	98	-12	5
Doncaster	4	1	0	3	2	88	115	-27	5
Workington Town	4	1	0	3	1	94	105	-11	4
Whitehaven	4	1	0	3	1	88	114	-26	4
Gateshead Thunder	4	0	0	4	1	50	160	-110	1

Top four teams from each Pool progressed to Quarter Finals.

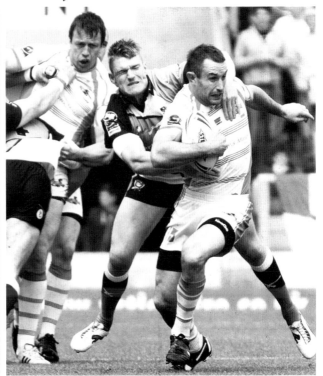

Leigh's Bob Beswick on the attack against Batley

QUARTER FINALS

Thursday 14th June 2012

KEIGHLEY COUGARS 12 FEATHERSTONE ROVERS 60

COUGARS: 1 Craig Moss; 2 Richie Barnett; 3 James Haythornthwaite; 4 Danny Lawton; 5 Jesse Sheriffe; 6 Jy-Mel Coleman; 7 Sam Obst; 8 Andy Shickell; 9 James Feather; 10 Neil Cherryholme; 11 Oliver Pursglove; 12 Jamie Shepherd; 13 Jason Demetriou. Subs (all used): 14 Ryan Smith; 15 Brendan Rawlins; 16 Jode Sheriffe; 17 Michael Korkidas.
Tries: Coleman (43), Obst (79); **Goals:** Lawton 2/2.
ROVERS: 1 Ian Hardman; 2 Jack Briscoe; 3 Sam Smeaton; 4 Greg Worthington; 5 Tom Saxton; 6 Andy Kain; 7 Liam Finn; 8 Anthony England; 9 Ben Kaye; 10 Stuart Dickens; 11 Matty Dale; 12 Tim Spears; 13 Jon Hepworth. Subs (all used): 14 James Lockwood; 15 Michael Haley; 16 Dominic Maloney; 17 Andrew Bostock.
Tries: England (7), Briscoe (11), Finn (16), Spears (26), Bostock (31), Kain (33, 69), Hardman (38), Lockwood (60), Saxton (73); **Goals:** Finn 10/10.
Rugby Leaguer & League Express Men of the Match: *Cougars:* Jy-Mel Coleman; *Rovers:* Liam Finn.
Penalty count: 3-4; **Half-time:** 0-42;
Referee: Jamie Leahy; **Attendance:** 828.

Friday 15th June 2012

SHEFFIELD EAGLES 48 HUNSLET HAWKS 0

EAGLES: 1 Quentin Laulu-Togagae; 2 Vinny Finigan; 3 Menzie Yere; 4 Misi Taulapapa; 5 Nev Morrison; 6 Simon Brown; 7 Dominic Brambani; 8 Jack Howieson; 9 Andrew Henderson; 10 Mitchell Stringer; 11 Michael Knowles; 12 Joe Hirst; 13 Dane McDonald. Subs (all used): 14 Alex Szostak; 15 Peter Green; 16 Liam Higgins; 17 Sam Scott.
Tries: Laulu-Togagae (5, 34, 37, 69), McDonald (22), Morrison (27), Yere (42), Henderson (66), Szostak (77); **Goals:** Brown 3/6, Brambani 1/1.
HAWKS: 1 Elliot Hodgson; 2 Stuart Kain; 3 Lee Brickwood; 4 John Oakes; 5 Dennis Tuffour; 6 Luke Helliwell; 7 Aaron Dobek; 8 Andrew Yates; 9 Luke Haigh; 10 Ryan Benjafield; 11 Tom Haughey; 12 Richard Blakeway; 13 David March. Subs (all used): 14 Joe McLocklan; 15 Josh Nathaniel; 16 Steve Lewis; 17 Tom Henderson.
On report: March (20) - alleged contact with referee.
Rugby Leaguer & League Express Men of the Match: *Eagles:* Quentin Laulu-Togagae; *Hawks:* Luke Helliwell.
Penalty count: 11-5; **Half-time:** 24-0; **Referee:** Ronnie Laughton; **Attendance:** 286 *(at Don Valley Stadium)*.

Sunday 17th June 2012

HALIFAX 54 BARROW RAIDERS 24

HALIFAX: 1 Ryan Fieldhouse; 2 Rob Worrincy; 3 Lee Paterson; 4 James Haley; 5 Paul White; 6 Paul Handforth; 7 Anthony Thackeray; 8 Sam Barlow; 9 Sean Penkywicz; 10 Luke Ambler; 11 Dane Manning; 12 Adam Robinson; 13 Craig Ashall. Subs (all used): 14 Anthony Bowman; 15 Josh Barlow; 16 Sean Hesketh; 17 Jim Gannon.
Tries: S Barlow (9), Thackeray (15, 44), Paterson (31), Robinson (34, 49), Penkywicz (64), Fieldhouse (72), Bowman (76), Worrincy (80); **Goals:** Paterson 7/10.
RAIDERS: 1 Lee Haney; 2 Mike Backhouse; 3 Ryan Shaw; 4 James Finch; 5 James Nixon; 6 Scott Kaighan; 7 Liam Campbell; 8 Andy Bracek; 9 James Dandy; 10 Ruairi McGoff; 11 Liam Harrison; 12 Bradley Brennan; 13 Daniel Toal. Subs (all used): 14 Brad Marwood; 15 Liam Finch; 16 Ryan Duffy; 17 Andrew Dawson.
Tries: Toal (18, 57), Duffy (28), Backhouse (60); **Goals:** Shaw 4/4.
Rugby Leaguer & League Express Men of the Match: *Halifax:* Adam Robinson; *Raiders:* Liam Harrison.
Penalty count: 9-10; **Half-time:** 22-12;
Referee: George Stokes; **Attendance:** 1,448.

LEIGH CENTURIONS 32 BATLEY BULLDOGS 12

CENTURIONS: 1 Gregg McNally; 2 Steve Maden; 3 Stuart Littler; 4 Matt Gardner; 5 Jonathan Pownall; 6 Martyn Ridyard; 7 Ryan Brierley; 8 Michael Ostick; 9 Bob Beswick; 10 Rob Parker; 11 James Laithwaite; 12 Tommy Goulden; 13 Sam Hopkins. Subs (all used): 14 Kevin Henderson; 15 Craig Briscoe; 16 Tom Spencer; 17 Tommy Gallagher.
Tries: Gardner (11), Maden (25, 80), Littler (54), McNally (65), Beswick (77); **Goals:** Ridyard 4/7.
BULLDOGS: 1 Ian Preece; 2 Gareth Potts; 3 Jason Walton; 4 Danny Maun; 5 Alex Brown; 6 Ben Black; 7 Gareth Moore; 8 Byron Smith; 9 Paul Mennell; 10 Craig Potter; 11 Alex Bretherton; 12 Jonny Walker; 13 Mark Applegarth. Subs (all used): 14 Matthew Wildie; 15 Keegan Hirst; 16 Lewis Palfrey; 17 Kris Lythe.
Tries: Potts (18), Wildie (32); **Goals:** Moore 2/3.
Sin bin: Black (55) - holding down.
On report: Hirst (76) - alleged high tackle on Parker.
Rugby Leaguer & League Express Men of the Match: *Centurions:* Matt Gardner; *Bulldogs:* Mark Applegarth.
Penalty count: 9-3; **Half-time:** 10-12;
Referee: Clint Sharrad; **Attendance:** 2,002.

SEMI-FINALS

Thursday 5th July 2012

FEATHERSTONE ROVERS 54 LEIGH CENTURIONS 16

ROVERS: 1 Ian Hardman; 2 Jack Briscoe; 3 Sam Smeaton; 4 Greg Worthington; 5 Tom Saxton; 6 Andy Kain; 7 Liam Finn; 8 Anthony England; 9 Ben Kaye; 10 Stuart Dickens; 11 James Lockwood; 12 Tim Spears; 13 Matty Dale. Subs (all used): 14 Andy Ellis; 15 Dominic Maloney; 16 Michael Haley; 17 Andrew Bostock.
Tries: Briscoe (13, 76), Smeaton (15, 19, 38, 50), Saxton (29, 55), Dickens (64), Finn (69); **Goals:** Finn 7/10.
CENTURIONS: 1 Gregg McNally; 2 Steve Maden; 3 Stuart Littler; 4 Matt Gardner; 5 Adam Clay; 6 Martyn Ridyard; 7 Ryan Brierley; 8 Stephen Nash; 9 Anthony Nicholson; 10 Tom Spencer; 11 Sam Hopkins; 12 Andy Thornley; 13 Craig Briscoe. Subs (all used): 14 Kevin Henderson; 15 John Duffy; 16 Michael Ostick; 17 Rob Parker.
Tries: Henderson (38), Hopkins (43), Littler (58); **Goals:** Ridyard 2/3.
Rugby Leaguer & League Express Men of the Match: *Rovers:* Sam Smeaton; *Centurions:* Rob Parker.
Penalty count: 9-3; **Half-time:** 24-4;
Referee: Jamie Leahy; **Attendance:** 1,721.

Friday 6th July 2012

SHEFFIELD EAGLES 22 HALIFAX 24

EAGLES: 1 Quentin Laulu-Togagae; 2 Scott Turner; 3 Menzie Yere; 4 Misi Taulapapa; 5 Nev Morrison; 6 Simon Brown; 7 Dominic Brambani; 8 Jack Howieson; 9 Andrew Henderson; 10 Mitchell Stringer; 11 Michael Knowles; 12 Sam Scott; 13 Joe Hirst. Subs (all used): 14 Pat Smith; 15 Duane Straugheir; 16 Peter Green; 17 Liam Higgins.
Tries: Knowles (10, 74), Henderson (15), Turner (25); **Goals:** Brown 3/5.
HALIFAX: 1 Ryan Fieldhouse; 2 Rob Worrincy; 3 Steve Tyrer; 4 Lee Paterson; 5 Wayne Reittie; 6 Paul Handforth; 7 Anthony Thackeray; 8 Jim Gannon; 9 Sean Penkywicz; 10 Luke Ambler; 11 Dane Manning; 12 Adam Robinson; 13 Craig Ashall. Subs (all used): 14 Anthony Bowman; 15 Callum Casey; 16 Sam Barlow; 17 Makali Aizue.
Tries: Fieldhouse (28), Worrincy (49), Thackeray (58), Reittie (66); **Goals:** Paterson 0/1, Tyrer 4/4.
Rugby Leaguer & League Express Men of the Match: *Eagles:* Andrew Henderson; *Halifax:* Anthony Thackeray.
Penalty count: 7-9; **Half-time:** 18-4; **Referee:** Ronnie Laughton; **Attendance:** 671 *(at Don Valley Stadium)*.

FINAL

Sunday 29th July 2012

FEATHERSTONE ROVERS 12 HALIFAX 21

ROVERS: 1 Ian Hardman; 2 Jack Briscoe; 3 Sam Smeaton; 4 Greg Worthington; 5 Tom Saxton; 6 Andy Kain; 7 Liam Finn; 8 Anthony England; 9 Ben Kaye; 10 Stuart Dickens; 11 Jon Grayshon; 12 Tim Spears; 13 Matty Dale. Subs (all used): 14 James Lockwood; 15 Dominic Maloney; 16 Michael Haley; 17 Andrew Bostock.
Tries: Finn (26), Smeaton (43); **Goals:** Finn 2/3.
HALIFAX: 1 Ryan Fieldhouse; 2 Rob Worrincy; 3 Lee Paterson; 4 Steve Tyrer; 5 Wayne Reittie; 6 Paul Handforth; 7 Anthony Thackeray; 8 Jim Gannon; 9 Craig Ashall; 10 Sean Hesketh; 11 Dane Manning; 12 Luke Ambler; 13 Adam Robinson. Subs (all used): 14 Anthony Bowman; 15 Makali Aizue; 16 Sam Barlow; 17 Sean Penkywicz.
Tries: Thackeray (4), S Barlow (36), Tyrer (78); **Goals:** Tyrer 4/5; **Field goal:** Ashall (72).
Rugby Leaguer & League Express Men of the Match: *Rovers:* Anthony England; *Halifax:* Sean Penkywicz.
Penalty count: 5-10; **Half-time:** 6-12;
Referee: Jamie Leahy;
Attendance: 6,691 *(at Bloomfield Road, Blackpool)*.

Featherstone's Sam Smeaton and Andrew Bostock pursue Halifax's Ryan Fieldhouse during the
Northern Rail Cup Final

CHALLENGE CUP 2012
Round by Round

ROUND 3

Friday 23rd March 2012

EGREMONT RANGERS 14 OLDHAM 22

RANGERS: 1 Rhys Davies; 2 Ryan Barnes; 3 Ben Walker; 4 Clayton Sutton; 5 Leon Crellin; 6 John-Paul Brocklebank; 7 Paul Corkhill; 8 Tom Whalley; 9 Daniel Telford; 10 Chris Murphy; 11 Matt Bewsher; 12 Kieran Glenn; 13 Matty Palmer. Subs (all used): 14 Paul Telford; 15 Jack Stainton; 16 Kevin Brown; 17 Malcolm Caton.
Tries: Davies (3), Sutton (57); **Goals:** Brocklebank 3/4.
OLDHAM: 1 Miles Greenwood; 2 Lucas Onyango; 3 David Cookson; 4 Matthew Fogarty; 5 Mark Brocklehurst; 6 Neil Roden; 7 Jamie Dallimore; 8 Jason Boults; 9 John Clough; 10 Bruce Johnson; 11 Paul Noone; 12 Chris Clarke; 13 Alex Thompson. Subs (all used): 14 Martin Roden; 15 Danny Whitmore; 16 Dave Ellison; 17 Matty Syron.
Tries: Clough (17), Clarke (30), Whitmore (54), Thompson (72); **Goals:** Dallimore 3/4.
Rugby Leaguer & League Express Men of the Match: *Rangers:* Daniel Telford; *Oldham:* John Clough.
Penalty count: 8-10; **Half-time:** 10-10;
Referee: Joe Cobb; **Attendance:** 468
(at Recreation Ground, Whitehaven).

Saturday 24th March 2012

DONCASTER 57 SHARLSTON ROVERS 10

DONCASTER: 1 Mick Butterfield; 2 Stewart Sanderson; 3 Liam Cunningham; 4 Lee Waterman; 5 Tom Hodson; 6 Kieran Hyde; 7 Craig Fawcett; 8 Mark Castle; 9 Kyle Kesik; 10 Craig Robinson; 11 Dean O'Loughlin; 12 Michael Kelly; 13 Grant Edwards. Subs (all used): 14 Nathan Powley; 15 Mike Emmett; 16 Francis Welsh; 17 Craig Lawton.
Tries: Waterman (5, 22, 34, 56, 60, 79), Hodson (8, 14), Hyde (12, 65), Sanderson (48); **Goals:** Waterman 4/8, Kesik 0/1, Hyde 2/2; **Field goal:** Hyde (40).
Dismissal: O'Loughlin (80) - fighting.
Sin bin: Fawcett (46) - dissent.
ROVERS: 1 Ian Jackson; 2 Geoff Hick; 3 Danny Glassell; 4 Greg Wilby; 5 Tom Malyan; 6 Matt Johnson; 7 Lee Bettinson; 8 Craig Miles; 9 Scott Glassell; 10 Sean Emblem; 11 Carl Saville; 12 Brian Sutton; 13 Jon Waddle. Subs (all used): 14 Chris Bingham; 15 Lee Holmes; 16 Adam Saynor; 17 Lee Maskill.
Tries: D Glassell (25), Hick (30); **Goals:** Jackson 1/2.
Dismissal: Emblem (80) - fighting.
Sin bin: Miles (7) - dissent.
Rugby Leaguer & League Express Men of the Match: *Doncaster:* Lee Waterman; *Rovers:* Danny Glassell.
Penalty count: 11-3; **Half-time:** 33-10;
Referee: Chris Leatherbarrow; **Attendance:** 496.

GATESHEAD THUNDER 28 YORK ACORN 20

THUNDER: 1 Connor Condron; 2 Ashley Thackeray; 3 Mike Mitchell; 4 Dan O'Sullivan; 5 Joe Brown; 6 Sam Walsh; 7 Paul Stamp; 8 Stephen Welton; 9 Tom Hodgson; 10 Brett Waller; 11 Matt Barron; 12 Josh Stoker; 13 Ryan Steen. Subs (all used): 14 Ryan Clarke; 15 Chris Parker Snr; 16 Oliver O'Mara; 17 Will Bate.
Tries: Waller (8), Thackeray (34, 51), Mitchell (44), Brown (70); **Goals:** Stamp 4/7.
ACORN: 1 Joe Budd; 2 Matt Woods; 3 Jordan Hyde; 4 Adam Sellers; 5 Damien Hilton; 6 Anthony Chilton; 7 Tim Elliott; 8 Nick Caldwell; 9 Kevin Brayshaw; 10 Adam Endersby; 11 Tom Hill; 12 Mike Embleton; 13 Leigh Rientoul. Subs (all used): 14 Fran Starkey; 15 Steve Mackley; 16 Matt Withers; 17 Danny Caldwell.
Tries: Rientoul (36), Woods (39), Endersby (66);
Goals: Chilton 4/4.
Dismissal: Chilton (73) - high tackle on Condron.
Rugby Leaguer & League Express Men of the Match: *Thunder:* Ashley Thackeray; *Acorn:* Adam Endersby.
Penalty count: 7-4; **Half-time:** 12-14;
Referee: Peter Brooke; **Attendance:** 179.

LONDON SKOLARS 26 LEIGH CENTURIONS 43

SKOLARS: 1 John Paxton; 2 Smokie Junor; 3 Joe Price; 4 Chris McNamara; 5 Ade Adebisi; 6 Andy McLean; 7 Dylan Skee; 8 Rob Thomas; 9 Neil Thorman; 10 Dave Williams; 11 Brad Hopkins; 12 Alex Bate; 13 Austen Aggrey. Subs (all used): 14 Oliver Purslow; 15 Louis Robinson; 16 Martyn Smith; 17 Dave Arnot.
Tries: Junor (6), Hopkins (38), Purslow (40), Adebisi (54), Skee (80); **Goals:** Skee 3/5.
CENTURIONS: 1 Gregg McNally; 2 Steve Maden; 3 Stuart Littler; 4 Matt Gardner; 5 Jonathan Pownall; 6 Martyn Ridyard; 7 John Duffy; 8 Ricky Bibey; 9 Anthony Nicholson; 10 Rob Parker; 11 Craig Briscoe; 12 Michael Worrincy; 13 James Taylor. Subs (all used): 14 Bob Beswick; 15 Sam Hopkins; 16 Michael Ostick; 17 Tommy Gallagher.
Tries: Pownall (15), Littler (18, 40, 70), Maden (21), Gardner (30), Worrincy (44), McNally (47);
Goals: Ridyard 5/8; **Field goal:** Beswick (76).
Rugby Leaguer & League Express Men of the Match: *Skolars:* Oliver Purslow; *Centurions:* Stuart Littler.
Penalty count: 16-8; **Half-time:** 14-26;
Referee: Matthew Kidd; **Attendance:** 376.

OULTON RAIDERS 8 SHEFFIELD EAGLES 58

RAIDERS: 1 Tommy Griffiths; 2 Dane Charles; 3 Andy Eastland; 4 Danny Hardy; 5 Adrian Holdsworth; 6 Matt Stogden; 7 Matt Bullough; 8 Dave Jessey; 9 Andy Kay; 10 Josh Lancaster; 11 Kyle Wharton; 12 Dave Stogden; 13 Danny Stanley. Subs (all used): 14 Luke Richardson; 15 Hayden Mann; 16 Alan White; 17 Craig Jones.
Tries: Hardy (15), Richardson (62); **Goals:** Stanley 0/2.
EAGLES: 1 Quentin Laulu-Togagae; 2 Scott Turner; 3 Menzie Yere; 4 Nev Morrison; 5 Vinny Finigan; 6 Simon Brown; 7 Dominic Brambani; 8 Ryan Hepworth; 9 Pat Smith; 10 Liam Higgins; 11 Sam Scott; 12 Duane Straugheir; 13 Michael Knowles. Subs (all used): 14 Aaron Smith; 15 Alex Rowe; 16 Dane McDonald; 17 Mitchell Stringer.
Tries: Laulu-Togagae (4, 22, 24, 35), McDonald (37, 47), Morrison (42), Hepworth (69), Scott (73), P Smith (78), Straugheir (80); **Goals:** Brown 3/7, Knowles 4/4.
Rugby Leaguer & League Express Men of the Match: *Raiders:* Danny Stanley; *Eagles:* Quentin Laulu-Togagae.
Penalty count: 4-9; **Half-time:** 4-26;
Referee: Warren Turley; **Attendance:** 360
(at Rapid Solicitors Stadium, Wakefield).

WATH BROW HORNETS 22
SOUTH WALES SCORPIONS 24

HORNETS: 1 Peter Caddy; 2 Jamie Martin; 3 Francis King; 4 Ryan Amor; 5 Scott Pink; 6 Karl Dixon; 7 Charlie Tomlinson; 8 David Pettit; 9 Ryan Doran; 10 Paul Murphy; 11 Matt Huby; 12 James Toman; 13 Richard Huby. Subs (all used): 14 Ian Curnow; 15 Ryan Campbell; 16 Liam Martin; 17 James Dixon.
Tries: King (16, 21, 49), R Huby (28), K Dixon (37);
Goals: Caddy 1/5.
SCORPIONS: 1 Rodney Peake; 2 Dalton Grant; 3 Lewis Reece; 4 David James; 5 Curtis Cunningham; 6 Shaun Owens; 7 Jamie Rooney; 8 Joe Burke; 9 Steve Parry; 10 James Greenwood; 11 Joe McKenna; 12 Ashley Bateman; 13 Phil Carleton. Subs: 14 Dale Evans (not used); 15 Callum Wilkinson; 16 Alistair McDonald; 17 Greg Callow.
Tries: D James (4), Parry (31), Peake (34, 42), Callow (67); **Goals:** Rooney 2/5.
Rugby Leaguer & League Express Men of the Match: *Hornets:* Francis King; *Scorpions:* Steve Parry.
Penalty count: 9-5; **Half-time:** 18-16;
Referee: Jamie Bloem; **Attendance:** 350
(at Recreation Ground, Whitehaven).

NORTH WALES CRUSADERS 28
TOULOUSE OLYMPIQUE 10

CRUSADERS: 1 Danny Hulme; 2 Kriss Wilkes; 3 Ian Cross; 4 Christiaan Roets; 5 Rob Massam; 6 Andrew Moulsdale; 7 Leon Brennan; 8 Jonny Walker; 9 Lee Hudson; 10 Owain Brown; 11 Iwan Brown; 12 Anthony Morrison; 13 Jono Smith. Subs (all used): 14 Billy Sheen; 15 Tommy Johnson; 16 Craig Lawton; 17 Chris Tyrer.
Tries: Morrison (19), D Hulme (31, 40, 79), Massam (63), Moulsdale (64), Johnson (74);
Goals: Brennan 0/3, Cross 0/3, Moulsdale 0/1.
OLYMPIQUE: 1 Adam Innes; 2 Sebastien Ader; 3 Kevin Larroyer; 4 Yoanne Didone; 5 Antoine Reveillon; 6 Johnathan Ford; 7 Nicolas Delgal; 8 David Delpoux; 9 Luke Fahy; 10 Shane Brackett; 11 Yohan Barthau; 12 Guy Williams; 13 Sebastien Planas. Subs (all used): 14 Sylvain Houles; 15 Jean-Christophe Borlin; 16 Theo Gonzalez-Trique; 17 Mourad Kriouache.
Tries: Houles (37, 39); **Goals:** Didone 1/2.
Sin bin: Larroyer (43) - late challenge on Moulsdale.
On report:
Fahy (61) - alleged dangerous tackle on Moulsdale.
Rugby Leaguer & League Express Men of the Match: *Crusaders:* Andrew Moulsdale; *Olympique:* Luke Fahy.
Penalty count: 9-7; **Half-time:** 12-10;
Referee: George Stokes; **Attendance:** 567.

Sunday 25th March 2012

BRADFORD DUDLEY HILL 6 KEIGHLEY COUGARS 58

DUDLEY HILL: 1 Aiden Batey; 2 Martin Southwell; 3 Craig Tyman; 4 Alex Dickinson; 5 Neil Wall; 6 Daniel Softley; 7 Mick Hill; 8 Kyle Bateman; 9 Nathan Kitson; 10 Adam Jefferson; 11 Steve Lamond; 12 Lewis Evans; 13 Anthony Huby. Subs (all used): 14 Anthony Lawton; 15 Lee O'Connor; 16 Simon Kenefick; 17 Sam Broadley.
Try: Huby (66); **Goals:** Kitson 1/1.
COUGARS: 1 Craig Moss; 2 Gavin Duffy; 3 James Haythornthwaite; 4 Danny Lawton; 5 Jesse Sheriffe; 6 Danny Jones; 7 Paul March; 8 Jode Sheriffe; 9 James Feather; 10 Neil Cherryholme; 11 Oliver Pursglove; 12 Richard Jones; 13 Jamie Shepherd. Subs (all used): 14 Jy-Mel Coleman; 15 Chris Clough; 16 Michael Korkidas; 17 Andy Shickell.
Tries: Duffy (4), Jesse Sheriffe (8), Lawton (11, 17, 63, 77), Shepherd (15), R Jones (24, 34), Shickell (31), D Jones (73); **Goals:** D Jones 7/11.
Rugby Leaguer & League Express Men of the Match: *Dudley Hill:* Anthony Huby; *Cougars:* Paul March.
Penalty count: 6-9; **Half-time:** 0-44; **Referee:** Brandon Robinson; **Attendance:** 814 *(at Cougar Park).*

HUNSLET HAWKS 34 ROYAL NAVY 14

HAWKS: 1 Danny Ratcliffe; 2 Lee Brickwood; 3 David Clayton; 4 Josh Nathaniel; 5 Dennis Tuffour; 6 Luke Helliwell; 7 Danny Allan; 8 Andrew Yates; 9 Luke Haigh; 10 David Tootill; 11 Neil Lowe; 12 Scott Watson; 13 David March. Subs (all used): 14 Jack Bradbury; 15 Anthony Henderson; 16 Ryan Benjafield; 17 Gareth Davies.
Tries: Clayton (1), Watson (39), March (60), Ratcliffe (69), Tuffour (72), Nathaniel (76), Benjafield (80); **Goals:** Ratcliffe 2/5, Allan 1/2.
ROYAL NAVY: 1 Darren Bamford; 2 Silivenuisi Buinimasi; 3 Tommy Wilkinson; 4 James Wagstaffe; 5 Mick Haldenby; 6 Kevin Botwood; 7 Steve Lockton; 8 Richie Metcalfe; 9 Kyle Larvin; 10 Lewis Taylor; 11 Craig Sutton; 12 Ben Taylor; 13 Mark Robinson. Subs (all used): 14 Jack Savage; 15 Ash Hedges; 16 Dave Gee; 17 Matt Corrigan.
Tries: Wilkinson (8), Lockton (11); **Goals:** Botwood 3/4.
Rugby Leaguer & League Express Men of the Match: *Hawks:* Danny Ratcliffe; *Royal Navy:* Steve Lockton.
Penalty count: 7-6; **Half-time:** 10-14;
Referee: Ronnie Laughton; **Attendance:** 302.

HUNSLET OLD BOYS 12 FEATHERSTONE ROVERS 86

OLD BOYS: 1 Wayne Rawson; 2 Chris Thompson; 3 Kieron Murphy; 4 Mark Stubley; 5 Jerome Malcolm; 6 Luke O'Malley; 7 Ben Dean; 8 Tom Saunders; 9 Jamie Bradley; 10 Jamie Fields; 11 Carl Briggs; 12 Ricky Hazelwood; 13 Ryan Campbell. Subs (all used): 14 Wayne Foster; 15 Johnny Bradley; 16 Jack Raby; 17 Kyle McDermott.
Tries: Jamie Bradley (17), Fields (53); **Goals:** Fields 2/2.
ROVERS: 1 Ian Hardman; 2 Tom Saxton; 3 Sam Smeaton; 4 Andrew Bostock; 5 Tangi Ropati; 6 Kyle Briggs; 7 Liam Finn; 8 Anthony England; 9 Ben Kaye; 10 Stuart Dickens; 11 Mufaro Mvududu; 12 James Lockwood; 13 Jon Hepworth. Subs (all used): 14 Jack Bussey; 15 Dave Nurse; 16 Liam Mackay; 17 Lewis Jones.
Tries: Dickens (9, 35), Briggs (13, 57, 64), Hardman (15, 26, 32, 61), Mvududu (29, 39), Finn (49, 66), Saxton (73), Hepworth (80); **Goals:** Finn 13/15.
Rugby Leaguer & League Express Men of the Match: *Old Boys:* Jamie Fields; *Rovers:* Ian Hardman.
Penalty count: 7-12; **Half-time:** 6-46; **Referee:** Tom Crashley; **Attendance:** 785 *(at Big Fellas Stadium).*

SWINTON LIONS 66 SIDDAL 0

LIONS: 1 Richie Hawkyard; 2 Alex Hurst; 3 Adam Higson; 4 Tom Armstrong; 5 Ian Mort; 6 Martin Ainscough; 7 Ian Watson; 8 Mike Morrison; 9 Karl Ashall; 10 Neil Holland; 11 Dale Cunniffe; 12 Darren Hawkyard; 13 Chaz I'Anson. Subs (all used): 14 David Mills; 15 Dave McConnell; 16 Rob Foxen; 17 Andy Gorski.
Tries: Higson (2, 60), I'Anson (7), Ashall (13, 67), Holland (18), Ainscough (25, 36), Mort (27, 56), Armstrong (75), D Hawkyard (80); **Goals:** Mort 9/12.
SIDDAL: 1 Scott Caley; 2 Gareth Blackburn; 3 Matthew Batley; 4 Ross Coates; 5 Emerson Newburn; 6 Chris Brooke; 7 Stephen Illingworth; 8 Gareth Blackburn; 9 Simeon Hoyle; 10 Scott Law; 11 Chris Geoghegan; 12 Nick Smith; 13 Luke Simeunovich. Subs (all used): 14 Craig Sanderson; 15 Shaun Blackburn; 16 Liam Green; 17 Gary Lewis.
Rugby Leaguer & League Express Men of the Match: *Lions:* Adam Higson; *Siddal:* Simeon Hoyle.
Penalty count: 4-5; **Half-time:** 36-0;
Referee: Dave Sharpe; **Attendance:** 404.

BARROW RAIDERS 32 LEZIGNAN 22

RAIDERS: 1 Andy Ballard; 2 Lee Haney; 3 Chris Larkin; 4 James Finch; 5 James Nixon; 6 Darren Holt; 7 Liam Campbell; 8 Andy Bracek; 9 Liam Finch; 10 Ruairi McGoff; 11 Liam Harrison; 12 Barry Pugh; 13 Daniel Toal. Subs (all used): 14 Jack Pedley; 15 Andrew Dawson; 16 James Gordon; 17 Lee Dutton.
Tries: Campbell (35, 72), Harrison (38), J Finch (47), Haney (78); **Goals:** Holt 6/7.
Sin bin: Bracek (65) - fighting.
LEZIGNAN: 1 Rhys Lenarduzzi; 2 Nicolas Piquemal; 3 Vincent Michau; 4 Christophe Calegari; 5 Fabien Poggi; 6 Nicolas Munoz; 7 Nathan Wynn; 8 Franck Rovira; 9 Kane Bentley; 10 Charly Clottes; 11 Florian Quintilla; 12 Yoan Tisseyre; 13 Jordi Lingeres. Subs (all used): 14 Mathieu Alberola; 15 Arnaud Astruc; 16 Pierre Negre; 17 Aurebien Bourrel.
Tries: Lenarduzzi (6), Tisseyre (13), Michau (23), Bentley (74); **Goals:** Wynn 3/4.
Sin bin: Rovira (65) - fighting.
Rugby Leaguer & League Express Men of the Match: *Raiders:* Liam Harrison; *Lezignan:* Yoan Tisseyre.
Penalty count: 14-6; **Half-time:** 12-16;
Referee: Greg Dolan; **Attendance:** 1,340.

DEWSBURY RAMS 84 THATTO HEATH CRUSADERS 12

RAMS: 1 James Craven; 2 Michael Wainwright; 3 Ryan Esders; 4 Rob Spicer; 5 Austin Buchanan; 6 Pat Walker; 7 Scott Spaven; 8 Ben Jones; 9 Craig Cook; 10 Steve Crossley; 11 Josh Tonks; 12 Dwayne Barker; 13 Ed Barber. Subs (all used): 14 George Flanagan; 15 Matt Nicholson; 16 Greg Scott; 17 Billy Harris.
Tries: Barber (6), Buchanan (19, 24, 29, 50, 75), Flanagan (25, 39), Spicer (32), Craven (34, 65, 69), Esders (40), Harris (47), Wainwright (59);
Goals: Walker 12/15.
CRUSADERS: 1 Shaun Quinn; 2 Jordan Houghton; 3 Dave Hill; 4 Darren Woods; 5 Phil Morrison; 6 Andrew Stott; 7 Chris Frodsham; 8 Mark Beech; 9 Keiron Maddocks; 10 Glenn Holland; 11 Luke Bradshaw; 12 Anthony Bate; 13 Jack Jones. Subs (all used): 14 Dave Bates; 15 Andy Lea; 16 Nathan Ashurst; 17 Greg Mannion.
Tries: Bradshaw (50), Lea (56); **Goals:** Quinn 2/2.
Rugby Leaguer & League Express Men of the Match: *Rams:* Austin Buchanan; *Crusaders:* Andrew Stott.
Penalty count: 6-7; **Half-time:** 50-0;
Referee: Chris Kendall; **Attendance:** 606.

EAST HULL 20 ROCHDALE HORNETS 48

EAST HULL: 1 Matt Spenceley; 2 Jamie Edwards; 3 Tommy Brett; 4 Stuart Coates; 5 Andy Moody; 6 Carl Puckering; 7 Scott Partis; 8 Lee Brown; 9 Matty Brookes; 10 Chris Lyth; 11 Liam Reid; 12 Gary Noble; 13 Jordan Precious. Subs (all used): 14 Craig Murray; 15 Lee Roberts; 16 James Morris; 17 Chris Spenceley.
Tries: Coates (2), Edwards (10, 47), Moody (79);
Goals: Precious 1/3, Puckering 1/1.

HORNETS: 1 Paul O'Connor; 2 Dale Bloomfield; 3 Danny Pyke; 4 Anthony Stewart; 5 Craig Johnson; 6 Chris Hough; 7 Steve Roper; 8 Dave Newton; 9 Phil Wood; 10 John Cookson; 11 Gary Middlehurst; 12 Chris Baines; 13 Dayne Donoghue. Subs (all used): 14 Steve McDermott; 15 Adam Bowman; 16 Jonny Leather; 17 Stephen Lucas.
Tries: Middlehurst (6, 20, 70), Baines (13), Cookson (26), Wood (60), O'Connor (63), Leather (67); **Goals:** Baines 8/8.
Rugby Leaguer & League Express Men of the Match: *East Hull:* Scott Partis; *Hornets:* John Cookson.
Penalty count: 4-13; **Half-time:** 10-24;
Referee: Dave Merrick; **Attendance:** 303 *(at Spotland)*.

MYTON WARRIORS 4 HALIFAX 94

WARRIORS: 1 Chris Wainman; 2 Nick Halstead; 3 Gavin Drewery; 4 Carl Booth; 5 Lee James; 6 Dave Richmond; 7 Kris Walker; 8 Allan Dunham; 9 Nathan Slater; 10 Lee Fewlass; 11 Richard Dunham; 12 Steve Atkinson; 13 Ricky Hough. Subs (all used): 14 Alec Hobman; 15 Bradley Krebs; 16 James Johnson; 17 Adam Humphrey.
Try: James (63); **Goals:** Walker 0/1.
HALIFAX: 1 Paul White; 2 Lee Paterson; 3 Steve Tyrer; 4 Wayne Reittie; 5 Rob Worrincy; 6 Anthony Bowman; 7 Anthony Thackeray; 8 Sean Hesketh; 9 Craig Ashall; 10 Sam Barlow; 11 Dane Manning; 12 Ross Divorty; 13 Callum Casey. Subs (all used): 14 Mark Goodman; 15 Joe Chandler; 16 Makali Aizue; 17 Josh Barlow.
Tries: White (4, 42), Manning (9), S Barlow (12, 40), Worrincy (20), Bowman (25), Chandler (28), Thackeray (32), Tyrer (35), Ashall (38, 55), Casey (46), Paterson (67), Reittie (59, 70), J Barlow (77);
Goals: Paterson 13/17.
Rugby Leaguer & League Express Men of the Match: *Warriors:* Kris Walker; *Halifax:* Anthony Thackeray.
Penalty count: 1-10; **Half-time:** 0-56; **Referee:** Jamie Callaghan; **Attendance:** 1,011 *(at The Shay)*.

WHITEHAVEN 52 HUNSLET WARRIORS 6

WHITEHAVEN: 1 Andreas Bauer; 2 Craig Calvert; 3 Steve Fox; 4 Scott McAvoy; 5 Max Wiper; 6 Carl Rudd; 7 Ben Karalius; 8 David Houghton; 9 Carl Sice; 10 Howard Hill; 11 Luke Isakka; 12 Lee Doran; 13 Andrew Beattie. Subs (all used): 14 Paul Cullnean; 15 Chris Smith; 16 Richard Varkulis; 17 Daniel Barker.
Tries: Fox (3, 10, 54), Calvert (16), Rudd (23), Bauer (29), McAvoy (70), Isakka (75), Varkulis (78);
Goals: Rudd 8/10.
WARRIORS: 1 Gary McClelland; 2 Luke Rayner; 3 Mark Cunningham; 4 Mickey Lyons; 5 Gareth Brain; 6 Richard Wheelhouse; 7 James Baker; 8 Amir Benatmane; 9 Arron Pratt; 10 Johnny Dawson; 11 Mark Holmes; 12 Omar Mehdi; 13 Caldon Bravo. Subs (all used): 14 Nathan Sheard; 15 Karl Featherstone; 16 Matty Scott; 17 Liam Gale.
Try: Cunningham (57); **Goals:** McClelland 1/1.
Rugby Leaguer & League Express Men of the Match: *Whitehaven:* Andreas Bauer; *Warriors:* Mark Cunningham.
Penalty count: 12-6; **Half-time:** 28-0;
Referee: Scott Mikalauskas; **Attendance:** 534.

WORKINGTON TOWN 6 BATLEY BULLDOGS 22

TOWN: 1 Elliott Miller; 2 Stephen Dawes; 3 Jason Mossop; 4 Daniel Rooney; 5 John Patrick; 6 Brett Carter; 7 Carl Forber; 8 Ryan McDonald; 9 Darren King; 10 Kris Coward; 11 Marc Shackley; 12 Brett Phillips; 13 Karl Olstrum. Subs (all used): 14 Marc Bainbridge; 15 Richard Farrer; 16 James Robinson; 17 Jamie Thackray.
Try: Shackley (58); **Goals:** Forber 1/1.
BULLDOGS: 1 Johnny Campbell; 2 Darren Williams; 3 Jason Walton; 4 Daley Williams; 5 Danny Mills; 6 Ben Black; 7 Lewis Palfrey; 8 Luke Menzies; 9 Tom Henderson; 10 Keegan Hirst; 11 Alex Bretherton; 12 Mark Applegarth; 13 Ashley Lindsay. Subs (all used): 14 Paul Mennell; 15 Alex Walmsley; 16 Alex Brown; 17 Byron Smith.
Tries: Lindsay (8), Bretherton (32), Brown (41), Black (55); **Goals:** Palfrey 3/4.
Rugby Leaguer & League Express Men of the Match: *Town:* Marc Shackley; *Bulldogs:* Johnny Campbell.
Penalty count: 15-4; **Half-time:** 0-10;
Referee: Jamie Leahy; **Attendance:** 601.

YORK CITY KNIGHTS 40 HULL DOCKERS 14

CITY KNIGHTS: 1 Jordan Tansey; 2 Tom Bush; 3 George Elliott; 4 Matt Garside; 5 Dave Sutton; 6 James Ford; 7 Brett Turner; 8 Adam Sullivan; 9 Jack Lee; 10 James Houston; 11 Tom Haughey; 12 Ed Smith; 13 Jack Aldous. Subs (all used): 14 John Gay; 15 Alex Benson; 16 Joe Hemmings; 17 Adam Howard.
Tries: Lee (11), Haughey (20), Elliott (37), Garside (40), Ford (62, 69, 72), Turner (76);
Goals: Bush 2/4, Tansey 0/1, Turner 2/3.
DOCKERS: 1 Danny Ulyatt; 2 Kris Birch; 3 Martin Johnson; 4 Craig Skelton; 5 Anthony Tognola; 6 Andy Kay; 7 Karl Smirk; 8 Aaron Bradley; 9 Steve Sellers; 10 Darren Bumby; 11 Jason Bowsley; 12 Jon Eccles; 13 Nick Powley. Subs (all used): 14 Dominic Proctor; 15 Alex Everitt; 16 Paul Fletcher; 17 Callum Birch.
Tries: Powley (7), Johnson (29); **Goals:** Skelton 3/3.
Rugby Leaguer & League Express Men of the Match: *City Knights:* James Ford; *Dockers:* Karl Smirk.
Penalty count: 13-10; **Half-time:** 20-14;
Referee: Gareth Hewer; **Attendance:** 346.

ROUND 4

Friday 13th April 2012

LEEDS RHINOS 38 WAKEFIELD TRINITY WILDCATS 18

RHINOS: 1 Brent Webb; 2 Ben Jones-Bishop; 12 Carl Ablett; 4 Zak Hardaker; 5 Ryan Hall; 13 Kevin Sinfield (C); 6 Danny McGuire; 8 Kylie Leuluai; 7 Rob Burrow; 10 Jamie Peacock; 18 Chris Clarkson; 15 Brett Delaney; 16 Ryan Bailey. Subs (all used): 9 Paul McShane; 17 Ian Kirke; 14 Lee Smith; 20 Darrell Griffin.
Tries: Bailey (23), McGuire (45), Hardaker (47, 57), Ablett (67), McShane (70), Jones-Bishop (75);
Goals: Sinfield 5/7.
On report: Sinfield (35) - alleged kicking on Kirmond.
WILDCATS: 1 Richard Mathers; 2 Peter Fox; 34 Paul Sykes; 3 Dean Collis; 5 Ben Cockayne; 13 Danny Washbrook; 20 Tim Smith; 10 Andy Raleigh; 7 Kyle Wood; 15 Kyle Amor; 17 Danny Kirmond (C); 33 Lucas Walshaw; 14 Paul Aiton. Subs (all used): 4 Vince Mellars; 6 Isaac John; 8 Oliver Wilkes; 25 Matt James (D).
Tries: Amor (17), Kirmond (31), John (77);
Goals: Sykes 3/3.
On report:
Aiton (3) - alleged dangerous tackle on Burrow.
Rugby Leaguer & League Express Men of the Match: *Rhinos:* Brett Delaney; *Wildcats:* Danny Kirmond.
Penalty count: 8-8; **Half-time:** 6-12;
Referee: Richard Silverwood; **Attendance:** 7,140.

Saturday 14th April 2012

SWINTON LIONS 70 GATESHEAD THUNDER 10

LIONS: 1 Richie Hawkyard; 2 Ian Mort; 3 Adam Higson; 4 Tom Armstrong; 5 Kevin Penny; 6 Martin Ainscough; 7 Ian Watson; 8 David Mills; 9 Mark Smith; 10 Danny Meekin; 11 Dale Cunniffe; 12 Darren Hawkyard; 13 Chaz I'Anson. Subs (all used): 14 Lee Wingfield; 15 Dave McConnell; 16 Sam Reay; 17 Andy Gorski.
Tries: Mills (7), Meekin (12), Watson (16), Penny (21, 51), Higson (26), Cunniffe (36), Ainscough (55, 64), D Hawkyard (60), Gorski (75), I'Anson (78); **Goals:** Mort 11/12.
THUNDER: 1 Connor Condron; 2 Ashley Thackeray; 3 Mike Mitchell; 4 Dan O'Sullivan; 5 Joe Brown; 6 Sam Walsh; 7 Paul Stamp; 8 Brett Waller; 9 Ryan Clarke; 10 Ryan McBride; 11 Matt Barron; 12 Jason Payne; 13 Ryan Steen. Subs (all used): 14 Will Bate; 15 Tabua Cakacaka; 16 Stephen Welton; 17 Josh Stoker.
Tries: McBride (29), Welton (72); **Goals:** Clarke 1/2.
Rugby Leaguer & League Express Men of the Match: *Lions:* Chaz I'Anson; *Thunder:* Stephen Welton.
Penalty count: 6-6; **Half-time:** 34-4;
Referee: Warren Turley; **Attendance:** 415.

FEATHERSTONE ROVERS 23 CASTLEFORD TIGERS 16

ROVERS: 1 Ian Hardman; 2 Tom Saxton; 3 Sam Smeaton; 4 Greg Worthington; 5 Tangi Ropati; 6 Kyle Briggs; 7 Liam Finn; 8 James Lockwood; 9 Ben Kaye; 10 Stuart Dickens; 11 Matty Dale; 12 Tim Spears; 13 Jon Hepworth. Subs (all used): 14 Andy Kain; 15 Michael Haley; 16 Jon Grayshon; 17 Dominic Maloney.
Tries: Ropati (11), Briggs (14), Hardman (18), Worthington (31); **Goals:** Finn 3/5; **Field goal:** Finn (73).
TIGERS: 1 Richard Owen; 2 Nick Youngquest; 11 Brett Ferres; 4 Kirk Dixon; 5 Josh Griffin; 6 Rangi Chase; 7 Danny Orr (C); 22 Nathan Massey; 9 Daryl Clark; 12 Jonathan Walker; 13 Steve Snitch; 21 Oliver Holmes; 8 Jake Emmitt. Subs (all used): 10 Craig Huby; 14 Stuart Jones; 20 Grant Millington; 23 Ryan McGoldrick.
Tries: Clark (4), Griffin (36), Youngquest (68);
Goals: Dixon 1/2, Orr 1/1.
Sin bin: Clark (13) - professional foul.
Rugby Leaguer & League Express Men of the Match: *Rovers:* Jon Hepworth; *Tigers:* Nick Youngquest.
Penalty count: 8-6; **Half-time:** 20-10;
Referee: Ben Thaler; **Attendance:** 4,165.

SOUTH WALES SCORPIONS 28 HALIFAX 84

SCORPIONS: 1 David James; 2 James Gahan; 3 Jack Murphy; 4 Yannic Parker; 5 Dalton Grant; 6 Scott Leatherbarrow; 7 Rodney Peake; 8 Joe Burke; 9 Nathan Mossop; 10 James Greenwood; 11 Greg Burke; 12 Chris Vitalini; 13 Geraint Davies. Subs (all used): 14 Steve Parry; 15 Liam Carberry; 16 Ashley Bateman; 17 Alistair McDonald.
Tries: D James (3, 59), Peake (34), Parry (49), Jack Murphy (57); **Goals:** Leatherbarrow 4/5.
HALIFAX: 1 Paul White; 2 Rob Worrincy; 3 Steve Tyrer; 4 Ben Heaton; 5 Lee Paterson; 6 Paul Handforth; 7 Anthony Bowman; 8 Sean Hesketh; 9 Callum Casey; 10 Makali Aizue; 11 Dane Manning; 12 Ross Divorty; 13 Craig Ashall. Subs (all used): 14 Sean Penkywicz; 15 Josh Barlow; 16 Sam Barlow; 17 Joe Chandler.
Tries: Casey (13), Ashall (18), Bowman (24, 44), Paterson (26), White (37, 80), Chandler (40), Handforth (42), Tyrer (51, 64), Hesketh (67), Manning (69), Aizue (71), Penkywicz (73); **Goals:** Paterson 12/15.
Rugby Leaguer & League Express Men of the Match: *Scorpions:* Scott Leatherbarrow; *Halifax:* Craig Ashall.
Penalty count: 1-6; **Half-time:** 12-36;
Referee: Robert Hicks; **Attendance:** 879 *(at The Shay)*.

WIDNES VIKINGS 38 ST HELENS 40

VIKINGS: 29 Jack Owens; 2 Paddy Flynn; 3 Chris Dean; 4 Willie Isa; 5 Patrick Ah Van; 25 Danny Craven; 7 Rhys Hanbury; 8 Ben Cross; 13 Jon Clarke (C); 17 Steve Pickersgill; 11 Frank Winterstein; 24 Kurt Haggerty; 12 Hep Cahill. Subs (all used): 6 Lloyd White; 18 Sione Kite; 22 Macgraff Leuluai; 26 Anthony Mullally.
Tries: Ah Van (3, 75), Hanbury (21), White (45, 78), Haggerty (58), Cahill (73); **Goals:** Ah Van 5/7.
SAINTS: 1 Paul Wellens (C); 34 Adam Swift (D); 3 Michael Shenton; 26 Josh Jones; 5 Francis Meli; 6 Lance Hohaia; 7 Jonny Lomax; 8 Josh Perry; 9 James Roby; 14 Anthony Laffranchi; 13 Chris Flannery; 4 Iosia Soliola; 15 Mark Flanagan. Subs (all used): 10 Louie McCarthy-Scarsbrook; 16 Paul Clough; 18 Shaun Magennis; 19 Andrew Dixon.
Tries: Jones (7, 49), Wellens (14, 55), Flannery (28), Hohaia (31), McCarthy-Scarsbrook (38);
Goals: Lomax 6/7.
Sin bin: Roby (71) - professional foul.
Rugby Leaguer & League Express Men of the Match: *Vikings:* Patrick Ah Van; *Saints:* James Roby.
Penalty count: 4-4; **Half-time:** 10-28;
Referee: James Child; **Attendance:** 3,069.

Sunday 15th April 2012

LONDON BRONCOS 72 DEWSBURY RAMS 4

BRONCOS: 1 Luke Dorn; 23 Omari Caro; 3 Jamie O'Callaghan; 19 Dan Sarginson; 21 Kieran Dixon; 6 Michael Witt; 7 Craig Gower (C); 8 Antonio Kaufusi; 9 Chad Randall; 13 Tony Clubb; 20 Matt Cook; 11 Shane Rodney; 12 Chris Bailey. Subs (all used): 10 Mark Bryant; 15 Karl Temata; 27 Sam Bolger (D); 16 Chris Melling.
Tries: Kaufusi (6, 55), Dixon (10, 29), Randall (22), Sarginson (24), Dorn (37), O'Callaghan (42, 77), Witt (46, 68), Bailey (49), Cook (72);
Goals: Witt 7/10, Gower 3/3.
RAMS: 1 Derrell Olpherts; 2 Jermaine Akaidere; 3 Greg Scott; 4 Andy Smith; 5 Michael Wainwright; 6 Ed Barber; 7 Cain Southernwood; 8 Matt Nicholson; 9 Craig Cook; 10 Steve Crossley; 11 Rob Spicer; 12 Billy Harris; 13 Josh Tonks. Subs (all used): 14 Mark Barlow; 15 Jonathan Schofield; 16 Danny Samuel; 17 Matthew Tebb.
Try: Akaidere (62); **Goals:** Barber 0/1.
Rugby Leaguer & League Express Men of the Match: *Broncos:* Michael Witt; *Rams:* Matt Nicholson.
Penalty count: 7-7; **Half-time:** 32-0;
Referee: Matthew Thomason; **Attendance:** 652.

KEIGHLEY COUGARS 18 WARRINGTON WOLVES 44

COUGARS: 1 Craig Moss; 2 Richie Barnett; 3 James Haythornthwaite; 4 Danny Lawton; 5 Semi Tadulala; 6 Danny Jones; 7 Sam Obst; 8 Andy Shickell; 9 James Feather; 10 Michael Korkidas; 11 Oliver Pursglove; 12 Richard Jones; 13 Paul March. Subs (all used): 14 James Davey; 15 Jamie Shepherd; 16 Jode Sheriffe; 17 Neil Cherryholme.
Tries: Barnett (39), Obst (76, 79); **Goals:** D Jones 3/3.
WOLVES: 31 Jordan Burke (D); 2 Chris Riley; 18 Matty Blythe; 5 Joel Monaghan; 22 Rhys Williams; 6 Lee Briers (C); 24 Gareth O'Brien; 20 Chris Hill; 14 Mick Higham; 16 Paul Wood; 11 Trent Waterhouse; 12 Ben Westwood; 21 Tyrone McCarthy. Subs (all used): 33 Brad Dwyer; 17 Michael Cooper; 32 Ben Currie; 13 Ben Harrison.
Tries: J Monaghan (7), Westwood (14), Hill (18), Williams (25), Dwyer (48), Riley (54), Harrison (57), Wood (71); **Goals:** Briers 6/8.
Rugby Leaguer & League Express Men of the Match: *Cougars:* Paul March; *Wolves:* Ben Westwood.
Penalty count: 8-13; **Half-time:** 6-22;
Referee: Tim Roby; **Attendance:** 2,196.

BRADFORD BULLS 72 DONCASTER 6

BULLS: 2 Adrian Purtell; 29 Michael Platt; 12 Elliott Whitehead; 3 Keith Lulia; 18 Shaun Ainscough; 23 Danny Addy; 6 Ben Jeffries; 16 Manase Manuokafoa; 14 Matt Diskin (C); 15 Bryn Hargreaves; 11 Olivier Elima; 19 Tom Olbison; 13 Jamie Langley. Subs (all used): 37 Callum Windley (D); 21 Tom Burgess; 10 Craig Kopczak; 26 John Bateman.
Tries: Whitehead (3, 59, 76), Jeffries (8), Diskin (14, 27), Ainscough (24, 29, 70), Bateman (35), Kopczak (48), Lulia (51, 65); **Goals:** Addy 10/13.
DONCASTER: 1 Mick Butterfield; 2 Dean Colton; 3 Chris Spurr; 4 Lee Waterman; 5 Tom Hodson; 6 Grant Edwards; 7 Kieran Hyde; 8 Mark Castle; 9 Jack Ely; 10 Russ Spiers; 11 Craig Lawton; 12 Michael Kelly; 13 Craig Robinson. Subs (all used): 14 Francis Welsh; 15 Kyle Bibb; 16 Kyle Kesik; 17 Stewart Sanderson.
Try: Spiers (1); **Goals:** Hyde 1/1.
Rugby Leaguer & League Express Men of the Match: *Bulls:* John Bateman; *Doncaster:* Mick Butterfield.
Penalty count: 11-4; **Half-time:** 38-6;
Referee: Jamie Leahy; **Attendance:** 3,210.

HULL FC 16 HUDDERSFIELD GIANTS 42

HULL: 21 Reece Lyne; 2 Will Sharp; 3 Tony Martin; 19 Jordan Turner; 5 Tom Briscoe; 20 Jamie Ellis; 7 Brett Seymour; 17 Sam Moa; 9 Danny Houghton; 10 Andy Lynch (C); 11 Willie Manu; 12 Danny Tickle; 34 Jay Pitts. Subs (all used): 27 Chris Green; 15 Richard Whiting; 24 Liam Kent; 23 Ben Crooks (D).
Tries: Briscoe (11, 24); **Goals:** Tickle 4/4.
GIANTS: 29 Greg Eden; 5 Jermaine McGillvary; 3 Leroy Cudjoe; 17 Joe Wardle; 20 Luke George; 7 Danny Brough; 1 Scott Grix; 8 Eorl Crabtree; 9 Luke Robinson; 4 Lee Gilmour; 2 Michael Lawrence; 18 Jason Chan; 6 Kevin Brown (C). Subs (all used): 13 David Faiumu; 12 David Fa'alogo; 15 Larne Patrick; 11 Luke O'Donnell.
Tries: George (40, 42), Eden (49), Cudjoe (55, 61), Wardle (57), Robinson (66), Chan (70);
Goals: Brough 5/8.
Rugby Leaguer & League Express Men of the Match: *Hull:* Sam Moa; *Giants:* Scott Grix.
Penalty count: 7-1; **Half-time:** 14-6;
Referee: Thierry Alibert; **Attendance:** 8,327.

HULL KINGSTON ROVERS 18 CATALAN DRAGONS 20

ROVERS: 1 Shannon McDonnell; 2 Craig Hall; 3 Kris Welham; 29 Liam Salter; 21 Sam Latus; 6 Blake Green; 7 Michael Dobson; 15 Liam Watts; 14 Lincoln Withers; 23 Mickey Paea; 11 Constantine Mika; 18 Graeme Horne; 12 Ben Galea (C). Subs (all used): 19 Scott Murrell; 10 Scott Taylor; 13 Rhys Lovegrove; 9 Josh Hodgson.
Tries: Taylor (48), B Green (53), J Hodgson (65), Latus (72); **Goals:** Dobson 1/4.
DRAGONS: 18 Daryl Millard; 5 Cyril Stacul; 4 Setaimata Sa; 25 Vincent Duport; 28 Damien Cardace; 3 Leon Pryce; 7 Scott Dureau; 20 Michael Simon; 9 Ian Henderson; 10 Remi Casty (C); 23 Lopini Paea; 12 Louis Anderson; 24 Jason Baitieri. Subs (all used): 8 David Ferriol; 11 Steve Menzies; 16 Eloi Pelissier; 22 Jamal Fakir.
Tries: Pryce (7, 36), Henderson (39); **Goals:** Dureau 4/4.
Rugby Leaguer & League Express Men of the Match: *Rovers:* Blake Green; *Dragons:* Leon Pryce.
Penalty count: 5-6; **Half-time:** 0-20;
Referee: Phil Bentham; **Attendance:** 4,425.

HUNSLET HAWKS 18 BATLEY BULLDOGS 21

HAWKS: 1 Elliot Hodgson; 2 Lee Brickwood; 3 Gareth Davies; 4 David Clayton; 5 Stuart Kain; 6 Luke Helliwell; 7 Ryan Smith; 8 Andrew Yates; 9 Luke Haigh; 10 Anthony Henderson; 11 Scott Watson; 12 John Oakes; 13 David March. Subs (all used): 14 Joe McLocklan; 15 Steve Lewis; 16 Ryan Benjafield; 17 David Tootill.
Tries: Yates (10, 74), March (49, 79);
Goals: Helliwell 1/2, McLocklan 0/1, Hodgson 0/1.
Sin bin: Tootill (79) - fighting.
BULLDOGS: 1 Ian Preece; 2 Gareth Potts; 3 Jason Walton; 4 Daley Williams; 5 Alex Brown; 6 Ben Black; 7 Gareth Moore; 8 Byron Smith; 9 Paul Mennell; 10 Craig Potter; 11 Alex Bretherton; 12 Jonny Walker; 13 Kris Lythe. Subs (all used): 14 Lewis Palfrey; 15 Alex Walmsley; 16 Mark Applegarth; 17 Ashley Lindsay.
Tries: Preece (30), Moore (34), A Walmsley (40), Potts (44); **Goals:** Moore 2/4; **Field goal:** Moore (77).
Sin bin: Brown (79) - fighting.
Rugby Leaguer & League Express Men of the Match: *Hawks:* David March; *Bulldogs:* Gareth Moore.
Penalty count: 5-4; **Half-time:** 6-14;
Referee: Gareth Hewer; **Attendance:** 664.

LEIGH CENTURIONS 68 ROCHDALE HORNETS 18

CENTURIONS: 1 Gregg McNally; 2 Steve Maden; 3 Stuart Littler; 4 Matt Gardner; 5 Jonathan Pownall; 6 Martyn Ridyard; 7 Ryan Brierley; 8 Michael Ostick; 9 Bob Beswick; 10 Rob Parker; 11 Craig Briscoe; 12 Tommy Goulden; 13 James Taylor. Subs (all used): 14 Anthony Nicholson; 15 Sam Hopkins; 16 Ricky Bibey; 17 Tommy Gallagher.
Tries: Briscoe (4), Ridyard (9), Brierley (15, 45, 69, 71), Littler (23, 49), Maden (28), Hopkins (42, 66), Gardner (77); **Goals:** Ridyard 10/12.
On report: Littler (35) - alleged dangerous contact.
HORNETS: 1 Paul O'Connor; 2 Dale Bloomfield; 3 Daniel Davies; 4 Anthony Stewart; 5 Wayne English; 6 Jonny Leather; 7 Will Chadwick; 8 Adam Bowman; 9 Phil Wood; 10 Phil Braddish; 11 Mark Hobson; 12 Steve Bannister; 13 Chris Hough. Subs (all used): 14 Steve McDermott; 15 Chris Baines; 16 Stephen Lucas; 17 Danny Ekis.
Tries: Bannister (18), Lucas (34), O'Connor (59);
Goals: Baines 2/2, Hough 1/1.
On report: Leather (41) - alleged dangerous tackle.
Rugby Leaguer & League Express Men of the Match: *Centurions:* Ryan Brierley; *Hornets:* Steve McDermott.
Penalty count: 10-5; **Half-time:** 26-12;
Referee: Chris Leatherbarrow; **Attendance:** 1,229.

OLDHAM 26 BARROW RAIDERS 14

OLDHAM: 1 Miles Greenwood; 2 Lucas Onyango; 3 Matthew Fogarty; 4 Mark McCully; 5 Shaun Robinson; 6 Jamie Dallimore; 7 Danny Whitmore; 8 Jason Boults; 9 Martin Roden; 10 Chris Clarke; 11 Paul Noone; 12 Paul Smith; 13 Valu Bentley. Subs (all used): 14 Alex Thompson; 15 John Clough; 16 Dave Ellison; 17 Matty Syron.
Tries: Thompson (40), Noone (48), Fogarty (59), Greenwood (68); **Goals:** Dallimore 5/6.
RAIDERS: 1 Andy Ballard; 2 Mike Backhouse; 3 Aaron Low; 4 Chris Larkin; 5 James Nixon; 6 Darren Holt; 7 Liam Campbell; 8 Jamie Butler; 9 James Dandy; 10 Ruairi McGoff; 11 Liam Harrison; 12 James Gordon; 13 Daniel Toal. Subs (all used): 14 Liam Finch; 15 Barry Pugh; 16 Andy Bracek; 17 Andries Venter.
Tries: Nixon (15), Harrison (20); **Goals:** Holt 3/3.
Rugby Leaguer & League Express Men of the Match: *Oldham:* Jamie Dallimore; *Raiders:* Liam Harrison.
Penalty count: 15-4; **Half-time:** 6-14;
Referee: Dave Merrick; **Attendance:** 773.

WHITEHAVEN 18 SALFORD CITY REDS 58

WHITEHAVEN: 1 Shane Ackerley; 2 Craig Calvert; 3 Jessie Joe Parker; 4 Scott McAvoy; 5 Loz Hamzat; 6 Max Wiper; 7 Carl Rudd; 8 David Houghton; 9 Sam Gee; 10 Luke Isakka; 11 Andrew Beattie; 12 Lee Doran; 13 Brad Crellin. Subs (all used): 14 Carl Sice; 15 Paul Cullnean; 16 Howard Hill; 17 Richard Varkulis.
Tries: Gee (18), Varkulis (44), Houghton (62);
Goals: Rudd 3/3.
CITY REDS: 25 Josh Veivers; 18 Ashley Gibson; 3 Sean Gleeson; 4 Joel Moon; 5 Danny Williams; 22 Marc Sneyd; 7 Matty Smith (C); 17 Iafeta Palea'aesina; 9 Wayne Godwin; 15 Adam Sidlow; 14 Chris Nero; 19 Adam Neal; 16 Luke Adamson. Subs (all used): 8 Lee Jewitt; 21 Jordan James; 24 Stuart Howarth; 11 Matty Ashurst.
Tries: Nero (6), Sneyd (13, 28), Moon (21, 65), Adamson (31), Gleeson (33), Veivers (48), Smith (50), Ashurst (73); **Goals:** Sneyd 9/10.
Rugby Leaguer & League Express Men of the Match: *Whitehaven:* Lee Doran; *City Reds:* Matty Smith.
Penalty count: 8-4; **Half-time:** 6-34;
Referee: Steve Ganson; **Attendance:** 751.

WIGAN WARRIORS 98 NORTH WALES CRUSADERS 4

WARRIORS: 1 Sam Tomkins; 2 Josh Charnley; 3 Darrell Goulding; 4 George Carmont; 30 Ryan King (D); 25 Joe Mellor; 7 Thomas Leuluai (C); 8 Paul Prescott; 28 Logan Tomkins; 21 Epalahame Lauaki; 26 Jack Hughes; 12 Gareth Hock; 16 Liam Farrell. Subs (all used): 17 Chris Tuson; 22 Gil Dudson; 33 Dominic Crosby (D); 9 Michael McIlorum.
Tries: King (4, 24), S Tomkins (8, 16, 32, 37, 56, 69), Charnley (21, 41), Farrell (29, 46, 60), Mellor (36), Tuson (43), Prescott (52), L Tomkins (66), Crosby (72);
Goals: Charnley 13/18.
CRUSADERS: 1 Tommy Johnson; 2 Adam Walsh; 3 Sam Broadbent; 4 Leon Brennan; 5 Rob Massam; 6 Andrew Moulsdale; 7 Jamie Durbin; 8 Jonny Walker; 9 Lee Hudson; 10 Owain Brown; 11 Iwan Brown; 12 Jamie Clarke; 13 Jono Smith. Subs (all used): 14 Billy Sheen; 15 Owain Griffiths; 16 Chris Tyrer; 17 Mark Hamon.
Try: O Brown (78); **Goals:** Brennan 0/1.
Rugby Leaguer & League Express Men of the Match: *Warriors:* Sam Tomkins; *Crusaders:* Andrew Moulsdale.
Penalty count: 5-0; **Half-time:** 48-0;
Referee: George Stokes; **Attendance:** 4,198.

YORK CITY KNIGHTS 12 SHEFFIELD EAGLES 50

CITY KNIGHTS: 1 Jordan Tansey; 2 Tom Bush; 3 George Elliott; 4 Matt Garside; 5 Ben Dent; 6 James Ford; 7 Chris Thorman; 8 Adam Sullivan; 9 Kris Brining; 10 Nathan Freer; 11 Joe Hemmings; 12 James Houston; 13 Rhys Clarke. Subs (all used): 14 Jack Lee; 15 Alex Benson; 16 Dave Sutton; 17 Jack Aldous.
Tries: Elliott (59), Sutton (78); **Goals:** Thorman 2/2.
EAGLES: 1 Quentin Laulu-Togagae; 2 Scott Turner; 3 Menzie Yere; 4 Misi Taulapapa; 5 Nev Morrison; 6 Dane McDonald; 7 Dominic Brambani; 8 Jack Howieson; 9 Andrew Henderson; 10 Liam Higgins; 11 Alex Szostak; 12 Peter Green; 13 Joe Hirst. Subs (all used): 14 Michael Knowles; 15 Ryan Hepworth; 16 Alex Rowe; 17 Mitchell Stringer.
Tries: Brambani (13), Morrison (24, 43), Henderson (28), Yere (50), Turner (56), Szostak (66), Laulu-Togagae (69, 75); **Goals:** Brambani 7/9.
Rugby Leaguer & League Express Men of the Match: *City Knights:* Nathan Freer; *Eagles:* Dominic Brambani.
Penalty count: 5-4; **Half-time:** 0-18;
Referee: Ronnie Laughton; **Attendance:** 551.

ROUND 5

Friday 27th April 2012

FEATHERSTONE ROVERS 16 WIGAN WARRIORS 32

ROVERS: 1 Ian Hardman; 2 Gareth Raynor; 3 Sam Smeaton; 4 Greg Worthington; 5 Tom Saxton; 6 Kyle Briggs; 7 Liam Finn; 8 Michael Haley; 9 Ben Kaye; 10 Stuart Dickens; 11 James Lockwood; 12 Tim Spears; 13 Jon Hepworth. Subs (all used): 14 Andy Kain; 15 Dominic Maloney; 16 Jon Grayshon; 17 Anthony England.
Tries: Saxton (19), Hardman (21), Raynor (60);
Goals: Finn 2/4.
WARRIORS: 1 Sam Tomkins; 2 Josh Charnley; 3 Darrell Goulding; 26 Jack Hughes; 24 Anthony Gelling; 6 Brett Finch; 7 Thomas Leuluai; 8 Paul Prescott; 9 Michael McIlorum; 14 Jeff Lima; 11 Harrison Hansen; 12 Gareth Hock; 13 Sean O'Loughlin (C). Subs (all used): 10 Lee Mossop; 16 Liam Farrell; 17 Chris Tuson; 21 Epalahame Lauaki.
Tries: O'Loughlin (4), Goulding (24), Hock (39, 79), Leuluai (53), Charnley (65);
Goals: Charnley 3/4, S Tomkins 1/2.
Rugby Leaguer & League Express Men of the Match: *Rovers:* Liam Finn; *Warriors:* Josh Charnley.
Penalty count: 7-10; **Half-time:** 12-16;
Referee: Richard Silverwood; **Attendance:** 4,082.

OLDHAM 0 ST HELENS 76

OLDHAM: 1 Miles Greenwood; 2 Mark Brocklehurst; 3 David Cookson; 4 Matthew Fogarty; 5 Shaun Robinson; 6 Danny Whitmore; 7 Jamie Dallimore; 8 Jason Boults; 9 Martin Roden; 10 Chris Clarke; 11 Mark McCully; 12 Michael Ward; 13 Valu Bentley. Subs (all used): 14 Jamie Acton; 15 Alex Thompson; 16 Dave Ellison; 17 Matty Syron.
Sin bin: Dallimore (44) - dangerous tackle.
SAINTS: 1 Paul Wellens (C); 21 Tom Makinson; 3 Michael Shenton; 26 Josh Jones; 5 Francis Meli; 6 Lance Hohaia; 7 Jonny Lomax; 10 Louie McCarthy-Scarsbrook; 9 James Roby; 16 Paul Clough; 19 Andrew Dixon; 4 Iosia Soliola; 15 Mark Flanagan. Subs (all used): 13 Chris Flannery; 18 Shaun Magennis; 25 Carl Forster; 28 Joe Greenwood (D).
Tries: Lomax (5, 71), Clough (9), McCarthy-Scarsbrook (21), Jones (23, 77), Soliola (32), Makinson (35), Wellens (40), Meli (44, 66, 80), Shenton (47), Magennis (55); **Goals:** Lomax 10/14.
Rugby Leaguer & League Express Men of the Match: *Oldham:* Jamie Dallimore; *Saints:* Jonny Lomax.
Penalty count: 5-10; **Half-time:** 0-38;
Referee: George Stokes; **Attendance:** 5,746 *(at Langtree Park).*

Saturday 28th April 2012

WARRINGTON WOLVES 32 BRADFORD BULLS 16

WOLVES: 1 Brett Hodgson (C); 2 Chris Riley; 4 Ryan Atkins; 3 Chris Bridge; 5 Joel Monaghan; 6 Lee Briers; 24 Gareth O'Brien; 20 Chris Hill; 14 Mick Higham; 16 Paul Wood; 11 Trent Waterhouse; 12 Ben Westwood; 21 Tyrone McCarthy. Subs (all used): 10 Garreth Carvell; 13 Ben Harrison; 15 Simon Grix; 17 Michael Cooper.
Tries: J Monaghan (22, 44, 79), Hodgson (37), Riley (40), Atkins (48); **Goals:** Hodgson 4/7.
Sin bin: Hill (65) - interference.
BULLS: 33 Karl Pryce; 2 Adrian Purtell; 12 Elliott Whitehead; 3 Keith Lulia; 18 Shaun Ainscough; 6 Ben Jeffries; 7 Luke Gale; 15 Bryn Hargreaves; 14 Matt Diskin (C); 10 Craig Kopczak; 11 Olivier Elima; 26 John Bateman; 13 Jamie Langley. Subs (all used): 9 Heath L'Estrange (C); 16 Manase Manuokafoa; 21 Tom Burgess; 23 Danny Addy.
Tries: Purtell (12), Lulia (54), Elima (76); **Goals:** Gale 2/3.
On report:
Bateman (36) - alleged dangerous contact on Hodgson.
Rugby Leaguer & League Express Men of the Match: *Wolves:* Brett Hodgson; *Bulls:* John Bateman.
Penalty count: 8-11; **Half-time:** 16-6;
Referee: James Child; **Attendance:** 5,505.

CATALAN DRAGONS 68 SHEFFIELD EAGLES 6

DRAGONS: 6 Thomas Bosc; 5 Cyril Stacul; 25 Vincent Duport; 18 Daryl Millard; 28 Damien Cardace; 3 Leon Pryce; 7 Scott Dureau; 8 David Ferriol; 9 Ian Henderson; 20 Michael Simon; 11 Steve Menzies; 4 Setaimata Sa; 24 Jason Baitieri. Subs (all used): 10 Remi Casty (C); 14 Sebastien Raguin; 16 Eloi Pelissier; 22 Jamal Fakir.
Tries: Cardace (12, 26, 65), Duport (18), Pryce (24, 47), Bosc (32, 50), Menzies (44), Pelissier (60, 68), Stacul (72); **Goals:** Dureau 10/12.
EAGLES: 1 Scott Turner; 2 Vinny Finigan; 3 Menzie Yere; 4 Misi Taulapapa; 5 Nev Morrison; 6 Simon Brown; 7 Dominic Brambani; 8 Jack Howieson; 9 Andrew Henderson; 10 Mitchell Stringer; 11 Alex Szostak; 12 Michael Knowles; 13 Joe Hirst. Subs (all used): 14 Peter Green; 15 Liam Higgins; 16 Sam Scott; 17 Alex Rowe.
Try: Finigan (55); **Goals:** Brown 1/1.
Rugby Leaguer & League Express Men of the Match: *Dragons:* Scott Dureau; *Eagles:* Michael Knowles.
Penalty count: 12-5; **Half-time:** 26-0;
Referee: Robert Hicks; **Attendance:** 3,102.

Sunday 29th April 2012

BATLEY BULLDOGS 16 LONDON BRONCOS 22

BULLDOGS: 1 Ian Preece; 2 Gareth Potts; 3 Jason Walton; 4 Danny Maun; 5 Alex Brown; 6 Ben Black; 7 Gareth Moore; 8 Byron Smith; 9 Paul Mennell; 10 Craig Potter; 11 Alex Bretherton; 12 Mark Applegarth; 13 Kris Lythe. Subs (all used): 14 James Grehan; 15 Keegan Hirst; 16 Alex Walmsley; 17 Lewis Palfrey.
Tries: Maun (17), Applegarth (20), Preece (73);
Goals: Moore 2/3.
BRONCOS: 5 Michael Robertson; 3 Jamie O'Callaghan; 28 Michael Channing; 19 Dan Sarginson; 21 Kieran Dixon; 6 Michael Witt; 7 Craig Gower (C); 8 Antonio Kaufusi; 9 Chad Randall; 10 Mark Bryant; 20 Matt Cook; 11 Shane Rodney; 12 Chris Bailey. Subs (all used): 15 Karl Temata; 18 Olsi Krasniqi; 16 Chris Melling; 1 Luke Dorn.
Tries: O'Callaghan (9), Cook (13), Kaufusi (15), Randall (70); **Goals:** Rodney 3/4.
Rugby Leaguer & League Express Men of the Match: *Bulldogs:* Jason Walton; *Broncos:* Michael Witt.
Penalty count: 7-6; **Half-time:** 12-16;
Referee: Thierry Alibert; **Attendance:** 1,025.

LEIGH CENTURIONS 19 HALIFAX 18
(after golden point extra time)

CENTURIONS: 1 Gregg McNally; 2 Steve Maden; 3 Stuart Littler; 4 Matt Gardner; 5 Jonathan Pownall; 6 Martyn Ridyard; 7 John Duffy; 8 Michael Ostick; 9 Bob Beswick; 10 Rob Parker; 11 James Laithwaite; 12 Tommy Goulden; 13 Craig Briscoe. Subs (all used): 14 Ryan Brierley; 15 Sam Hopkins; 16 Stephen Nash; 17 Tommy Gallagher.
Tries: Duffy (30), Goulden (55), Laithwaite (62);
Goals: Ridyard 3/3; **Field goal:** Ridyard (87).
On report: Hopkins (72) - alleged biting on S Barlow.
HALIFAX: 1 Ryan Fieldhouse; 2 Rob Worrincy; 3 Lee Paterson; 4 Ben Heaton; 5 Wayne Reittie; 6 Paul Handforth; 7 Anthony Thackeray; 8 Adam Robinson; 9 Sean Penkywicz; 10 Luke Ambler; 11 Dane Manning; 12 Ross Divorty; 13 Craig Ashall. Subs (all used): 14 Callum Casey; 15 Jim Gannon; 16 Sam Barlow; 17 Iain Morrison.
Tries: Thackeray (25), Worrincy (36), Paterson (39);
Goals: Paterson 2/3, Handforth 1/1.
Rugby Leaguer & League Express Men of the Match: *Centurions:* Sam Hopkins; *Halifax:* Dane Manning.
Penalty count: 12-11; **Half-time:** 6-16;
Referee: Phil Bentham; **Attendance:** 2,182.

HUDDERSFIELD GIANTS 52 SWINTON LIONS 0

GIANTS: 29 Greg Eden; 21 Aaron Murphy; 3 Leroy Cudjoe; 17 Joe Wardle; 20 Luke George; 1 Scott Grix; 7 Danny Brough; 11 Luke O'Donnell; 13 David Faiumu; 16 Dale Ferguson; 4 Lee Gilmour; 18 Jason Chan; 9 Luke Robinson (C). Subs (all used): 10 Keith Mason; 35 Scott Moore (D2); 26 Jamie Cording; 25 Jon Molloy.
Tries: Brough (7), Faiumu (11), Gilmour (15), Eden (29, 43), Chan (33), Grix (36), Cording (68, 76);
Goals: Brough 8/9.

LIONS: 1 Richie Hawkyard; 2 Ian Mort; 3 Sam Reay; 4 Tom Armstrong; 5 Kevin Penny; 6 Martin Ainscough; 7 Ian Watson; 8 David Mills; 8 Mark Smith; 10 Danny Meekin; 11 Dale Cunniffe; 12 Darren Hawkyard; 13 Chaz l'Anson. Subs (all used): 14 Mike Morrison; 15 Glenn Riley; 16 Chris Clarke; 17 Karl Ashall.
Rugby Leaguer & League Express Men of the Match: *Giants:* Danny Brough; *Lions:* Darren Hawkyard.
Penalty count: 3-2; **Half-time:** 34-0;
Referee: Tim Roby; **Attendance:** 2,617.

SALFORD CITY REDS 10 LEEDS RHINOS 16

CITY REDS: 1 Luke Patten; 2 Jodie Broughton; 3 Sean Gleeson; 4 Joel Moon; 18 Ashley Gibson; 6 Daniel Holdsworth; 7 Matty Smith; 15 Adam Sidlow; 9 Wayne Godwin; 8 Lee Jewitt; 11 Matty Ashurst; 16 Luke Adamson; 13 Stephen Wild (C). Subs (all used): 24 Stuart Howarth; 17 Iafeta Palea'aesina; 21 Jordan James; 14 Chris Nero.
Tries: Jewitt (6), Broughton (51); **Goals:** Holdsworth 1/2.
RHINOS: 1 Brent Webb; 2 Ben Jones-Bishop; 12 Carl Ablett; 4 Zak Hardaker; 5 Ryan Hall; 13 Kevin Sinfield (C); 6 Danny McGuire; 8 Kylie Leuluai; 31 Shaun Lunt; 10 Jamie Peacock; 18 Chris Clarkson; 15 Brett Delaney; 16 Ryan Bailey. Subs: 14 Lee Smith; 20 Darrell Griffin; 21 Richard Moore; 17 Ian Kirke (not used).
Tries: Webb (38), Jones-Bishop (64), Lunt (72);
Goals: Sinfield 2/3.
Rugby Leaguer & League Express Men of the Match: *City Reds:* Jodie Broughton; *Rhinos:* Danny McGuire.
Penalty count: 6-11; **Half-time:** 6-6;
Referee: Steve Ganson; **Attendance:** 4,500.

QUARTER FINALS

Friday 11th May 2012

LEIGH CENTURIONS 12 LEEDS RHINOS 60

CENTURIONS: 1 Gregg McNally; 2 Steve Maden; 3 Stuart Littler; 4 Matt Gardner; 5 Jonathan Pownall; 6 Martyn Ridyard; 7 Bob Beswick; 8 Michael Ostick; 9 Anthony Nicholson; 10 Rob Parker; 11 James Laithwaite; 12 Tommy Goulden; 13 Stephen Nash. Subs (all used): 14 Ryan Brierley; 15 Craig Briscoe; 16 Sam Hopkins; 17 Tommy Gallagher.
Tries: Goulden (12), McNally (62); **Goals:** Ridyard 2/2.
RHINOS: 1 Brent Webb; 2 Ben Jones-Bishop; 14 Lee Smith; 4 Zak Hardaker; 5 Ryan Hall; 13 Kevin Sinfield (C); 6 Danny McGuire; 8 Kylie Leuluai; 7 Rob Burrow; 17 Ian Kirke; 11 Jamie Jones-Buchanan; 19 Weller Hauraki; 18 Chris Clarkson. Subs (all used): 9 Paul McShane; 16 Ryan Bailey; 21 Richard Moore; 31 Shaun Lunt.
Tries: McGuire (6), Webb (21), Jones-Bishop (31), Hall (34, 79), Burrow (49), Lunt (55), Sinfield (58, 74), Smith (71); **Goals:** Sinfield 10/10.
Rugby Leaguer & League Express Men of the Match: *Centurions:* Tommy Goulden; *Rhinos:* Kevin Sinfield.
Penalty count: 6-6; **Half-time:** 6-24;
Referee: Ben Thaler; **Attendance:** 5,290.

Saturday 12th May 2012

WIGAN WARRIORS 18 ST HELENS 4

WARRIORS: 1 Sam Tomkins; 2 Josh Charnley; 26 Jack Hughes; 4 George Carmont; 24 Anthony Gelling; 6 Brett Finch; 7 Thomas Leuluai; 8 Paul Prescott; 9 Michael McIlorum; 10 Lee Mossop; 11 Harrison Hansen; 12 Gareth Hock; 13 Sean O'Loughlin (C). Subs (all used): 14 Jeff Lima; 16 Liam Farrell; 17 Chris Tuson; 21 Epalahame Lauaki.
Tries: S Tomkins (12), O'Loughlin (21), Finch (50);
Goals: Charnley 3/4.
SAINTS: 1 Paul Wellens (C); 21 Tom Makinson; 3 Michael Shenton; 17 Gary Wheeler; 5 Francis Meli; 6 Lance Hohaia; 7 Jonny Lomax; 14 Anthony Laffranchi; 9 James Roby; 8 Josh Perry; 13 Chris Flannery; 4 Iosia Soliola; 12 Jon Wilkin. Subs (all used): 10 Louie McCarthy-Scarsbrook; 15 Mark Flanagan; 16 Paul Clough; 18 Shaun Magennis.
Try: Wellens (6); **Goals:** Lomax 0/1.
Rugby Leaguer & League Express Men of the Match: *Warriors:* Brett Finch; *Saints:* Paul Wellens.
Penalty count: 11-6; **Half-time:** 12-4;
Referee: Richard Silverwood; **Attendance:** 12,864.

Sunday 13th May 2012

CATALAN DRAGONS 22 WARRINGTON WOLVES 32

DRAGONS: 1 Clint Greenshields; 6 Thomas Bosc; 25 Vincent Duport; 18 Daryl Millard; 28 Damien Cardace; 3 Leon Pryce; 7 Scott Dureau; 23 Lopini Paea; 9 Ian Henderson; 10 Remi Casty (C); 14 Sebastien Raguin; 20 Michael Simon; 22 Jamal Fakir; 26 Ben Fisher.
Tries: Paea (20), Simon (43), Fisher (49), Duport (71); **Goals:** Dureau 3/4.
WOLVES: 1 Brett Hodgson (C); 5 Joel Monaghan; 3 Chris Bridge; 4 Ryan Atkins; 2 Chris Riley; 6 Lee Briers; 24 Gareth O'Brien; 10 Garreth Carvell; 14 Mick Higham; 20 Chris Hill; 11 Trent Waterhouse; 12 Ben Westwood; 13 Ben Harrison. Subs (all used): 15 Simon Grix; 16 Paul Wood; 17 Michael Cooper; 21 Tyrone McCarthy.
Tries: J Monaghan (9), Hodgson (31), Riley (35), Wood (52), Bridge (74); **Goals:** Hodgson 6/6.
Rugby Leaguer & League Express Men of the Match: *Dragons:* Clint Greenshields; *Wolves:* Lee Briers.
Penalty count: 19-9; **Half-time:** 6-20;
Referee: Steve Ganson; **Attendance:** 7,476.

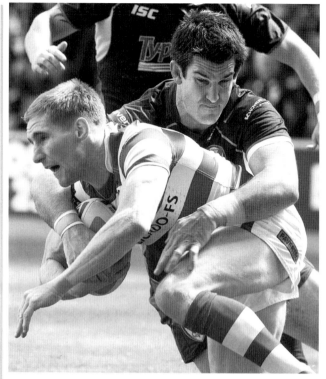

Wigan's Sam Tomkins brought down by St Helens' Chris Flannery

HUDDERSFIELD GIANTS 50 LONDON BRONCOS 14

GIANTS: 29 Greg Eden; 5 Jermaine McGillvary; 3 Leroy Cudjoe; 17 Joe Wardle; 21 Aaron Murphy; 1 Scott Grix; 7 Danny Brough; 8 Eorl Crabtree; 13 David Faiumu; 4 Lee Gilmour; 2 Michael Lawrence; 18 Jason Chan; 6 Kevin Brown (C). Subs (all used): 9 Luke Robinson; 10 Keith Mason; 15 Larne Patrick; 16 Dale Ferguson.
Tries: Murphy (9, 59), Eden (13, 39), Patrick (33), Robinson (48, 50), McGillvary (65), Ferguson (72);
Goals: Brough 5/6, Grix 2/3.
BRONCOS: 5 Michael Robertson; 21 Kieran Dixon; 28 Michael Channing; 4 David Howell; 3 Jamie O'Callaghan; 6 Michael Witt; 7 Craig Gower (C); 8 Antonio Kaufusi; 9 Chad Randall; 10 Mark Bryant; 20 Matt Cook; 11 Shane Rodney; 12 Chris Bailey. Subs (all used): 30 Scott Wheeldon; 13 Tony Clubb; 16 Chris Melling; 15 Karl Temata.
Tries: Dixon (7, 26), Wheeldon (52); **Goals:** Witt 1/3.
Rugby Leaguer & League Express Men of the Match: *Giants:* Luke Robinson; *Broncos:* Kieran Dixon.
Penalty count: 7-4; **Half-time:** 22-8;
Referee: James Child; **Attendance:** 2,574.

SEMI-FINALS

Saturday 14th July 2012

LEEDS RHINOS 39 WIGAN WARRIORS 28

RHINOS: 4 Zak Hardaker; 2 Ben Jones-Bishop; 3 Kallum Watkins; 12 Carl Ablett; 5 Ryan Hall; 13 Kevin Sinfield (C); 6 Danny McGuire; 8 Kylie Leuluai; 7 Rob Burrow; 10 Jamie Peacock; 11 Jamie Jones-Buchanan; 15 Brett Delaney; 16 Ryan Bailey. Subs (all used): 17 Ian Kirke; 20 Darrell Griffin; 25 Stevie Ward; 31 Shaun Lunt.
Tries: Hall (4, 26), Jones-Bishop (7, 34), Hardaker (11, 49), Bailey (31); **Goals:** Sinfield 5/8;
Field goal: Sinfield (64).
WARRIORS: 1 Sam Tomkins; 2 Josh Charnley; 3 Darrell Goulding; 4 George Carmont; 24 Anthony Gelling; 13 Sean O'Loughlin (C); 6 Brett Finch; 14 Jeff Lima; 9 Michael McIlorum; 10 Lee Mossop; 11 Harrison Hansen; 12 Gareth Hock; 17 Chris Tuson. Subs (all used): 16 Liam Farrell; 21 Epalahame Lauaki; 23 Ben Flower; 26 Jack Hughes.
Tries: Carmont (21), Hock (23), Flower (38), O'Loughlin (58), Charnley (74); **Goals:** S Tomkins 4/6.
Rugby Leaguer & League Express Men of the Match: *Rhinos:* Kevin Sinfield; *Warriors:* Gareth Hock.
Penalty count: 4-4; **Half-time:** 30-20;
Referee: Ben Thaler; **Attendance:** 12,860.
(at Galpharm Stadium, Huddersfield).

Sunday 15th July 2012

HUDDERSFIELD GIANTS 6 WARRINGTON WOLVES 33

GIANTS: 1 Scott Grix; 5 Jermaine McGillvary; 3 Leroy Cudjoe; 4 Lee Gilmour; 21 Aaron Murphy; 6 Kevin Brown (C); 7 Danny Brough; 8 Eorl Crabtree; 35 Scott Moore; 10 Keith Mason; 12 David Fa'alogo; 16 Dale Ferguson; 2 Michael Lawrence. Subs (all used): 9 Luke Robinson; 13 David Faiumu; 15 Larne Patrick; 23 Jacob Fairbank.
Try: Moore (9); **Goals:** Brough 1/1.
WOLVES: 1 Brett Hodgson; 5 Joel Monaghan; 3 Chris Bridge; 4 Ryan Atkins; 2 Chris Riley; 6 Lee Briers; 19 Stefan Ratchford; 10 Garreth Carvell; 14 Mick Higham; 20 Chris Hill; 11 Trent Waterhouse; 12 Ben Westwood; 13 Ben Harrison. Subs (all used): 16 Paul Wood; 8 Adrian Morley (C); 9 Michael Monaghan; 21 Tyrone McCarthy.
Tries: Carvell (15), Atkins (24), J Monaghan (28), Hodgson (56), Ratchford (77); **Goals:** Hodgson 6/6;
Field goal: Hodgson (66).
Rugby Leaguer & League Express Men of the Match: *Giants:* Leroy Cudjoe; *Wolves:* Lee Briers.
Penalty count: 5-5; **Half-time:** 6-18;
Referee: Richard Silverwood; **Attendance:** 9,473.
(at City of Salford Community Stadium).

FINAL

Saturday 25th August 2012

LEEDS RHINOS 18 WARRINGTON WOLVES 35

RHINOS: 4 Zak Hardaker; 2 Ben Jones-Bishop; 3 Kallum Watkins; 12 Carl Ablett; 5 Ryan Hall; 13 Kevin Sinfield (C); 25 Stevie Ward; 8 Kylie Leuluai; 7 Rob Burrow; 10 Jamie Peacock; 11 Jamie Jones-Buchanan; 15 Brett Delaney; 16 Ryan Bailey. Subs (all used): 20 Darrell Griffin; 31 Shaun Lunt; 17 Ian Kirke; 32 Jimmy Keinhorst.
Tries: Kirke (19), Watkins (70, 79); **Goals:** Sinfield 3/5.
WOLVES: 1 Brett Hodgson; 5 Joel Monaghan; 19 Stefan Ratchford; 4 Ryan Atkins; 2 Chris Riley; 6 Lee Briers; 7 Richard Myler; 10 Garreth Carvell; 14 Mick Higham; 20 Chris Hill; 11 Trent Waterhouse; 12 Ben Westwood; 13 Ben Harrison. Subs (all used): 16 Paul Wood; 8 Adrian Morley (C); 16 Paul Wood; 9 Michael Monaghan; 21 Tyrone McCarthy.
Tries: J Monaghan (7), Waterhouse (29), Riley (49), Atkins (54), McCarthy (59), Hodgson (74);
Goals: Hodgson 5/6; **Field goal:** Briers (63).
Rugby Leaguer & League Express Men of the Match: *Rhinos:* Jamie Peacock; *Wolves:* Brett Hodgson.
Penalty count: 8-9; **Half-time:** 10-12;
Referee: Richard Silverwood; **Attendance:** 79,180.
(at Wembley Stadium).

Leeds' Darrell Griffin and Kylie Leuluai combine to halt Warrington's Paul Wood during the Challenge Cup Final

AMATEUR, RESERVES & ACADEMY 2012

THE CO-OPERATIVE RUGBY LEAGUE CONFERENCE NATIONAL THREE

FINAL TABLE

	P	W	D	L	F	A	D	BP	Pts
Hudds-Underbank	18	16	0	2	702	160	542	2	50
Hemel Stags	18	15	0	3	612	229	383	2	47
Coventry Bears	18	13	0	5	512	320	192	1	40
Warrington Wizards	18	12	0	6	543	402	141	1	37
Bramley Buffaloes	18	8	0	10	378	402	-24	5	29
Nottingham Outlaws	18	6	0	12	366	620	-254	3	21
St Albans Centurions	18	5	0	13	362	626	-264	5	20
Kippax Knights *	18	5	1	12	302	454	-152	4	19
Bristol Sonics *	18	5	1	12	333	583	-250	3	18
South Wales Hornets	18	4	0	14	297	611	-314	2	14

Denotes points deducted

ELIMINATION PLAY-OFFS

Sunday 9th September 2012
Coventry Bears 40 ....Nottingham Outlaws 16
Warrington Wizards 64 ....Bramley Buffaloes 22

QUALIFYING SEMI-FINAL

Sunday 16th September 2012
Huddersfield Underbank Rangers 14 ....Hemel Stags 24

ELIMINATION SEMI-FINAL

Sunday 16th September 2012
Coventry Bears 44 ....Warrington Wizards 34

FINAL ELIMINATOR

Saturday 22nd September 2012
Huddersfield Underbank Rangers 36..Coventry Bears 18

GRAND FINAL

Saturday 29th September 2012
Hemel Stags..17
Huddersfield Underbank Rangers 10
Stags: T - Kelly (5), Henderson (29), Butcher (38);
G - Butcher 2; FG - Butcher
Rangers: T - Lang (10), Chatterton (25); G - Barrett
(at Big Fellas Stadium, Featherstone)

NATIONAL CONFERENCE - INTERIM SEASON

GROUP A

	P	W	D	L	F	A	D	Pts
Leigh East	12	8	0	4	302	266	36	16
Wath Brow Hornets	12	7	0	5	211	83	128	14
Egremont Rangers	12	6	1	5	251	226	25	13
Leigh Miners	12	6	1	5	260	236	24	13
Thatto Heath	12	6	0	6	328	286	42	12

GROUP B

	P	W	D	L	F	A	D	Pts
St Patricks	12	11	0	1	404	152	252	22
Ince Rose Bridge	12	6	0	6	300	326	-26	12
Millom	12	4	0	8	182	260	-78	8
St Judes	12	3	0	9	232	320	-88	6
Askam	12	2	0	10	116	404	-288	4

GROUP C

	P	W	D	L	F	A	D	Pts
Siddal	12	11	0	1	541	136	405	22
Ovenden	12	4	0	8	242	266	-24	8
Rochdale Mayfield	12	4	0	8	259	318	-59	8
Saddleworth	12	4	0	8	228	388	-160	8
Elland	12	4	0	8	194	393	-199	8

GROUP D

	P	W	D	L	F	A	D	Pts
Hunslet Warriors	12	8	1	3	363	192	171	17
East Leeds	12	8	1	3	261	185	76	17
Milford Marlins	12	8	1	3	257	190	67	17
Oulton Raiders	12	4	0	8	230	303	-73	8
Stanningley	12	3	1	8	194	398	-204	7

GROUP E

	P	W	D	L	F	A	D	Pts
Widnes West Bank	12	12	0	0	383	189	194	24
Waterhead	12	9	0	3	396	202	194	18
Oldham St Annes	12	7	1	4	380	272	108	15
Eccles	12	4	0	8	296	374	-78	8
Crosfields	12	2	0	10	198	457	-259	4

GROUP F

	P	W	D	L	F	A	D	Pts
Lock Lane	12	9	1	2	386	202	184	19
Eastmoor Dragons	12	7	0	5	312	342	-30	14
Stanley Rangers	12	3	1	8	341	334	7	7
Normanton Knights	12	3	1	8	228	446	-218	7
Castleford Panthers	12	1	2	9	253	465	-212	4

GROUP G

	P	W	D	L	F	A	D	Pts
Bradford Dudley Hill	10	7	0	3	372	232	140	14
York Acorn	10	6	0	4	290	187	103	12
Shaw Cross Sharks	10	3	0	7	176	385	-209	6
Heworth	10	0	0	10	131	452	-321	0

GROUP H

	P	W	D	L	F	A	D	Pts
Skirlaugh	12	11	0	1	428	159	269	22
Myton Warriors	10	7	0	3	279	190	89	14
East Hull	12	6	0	6	298	272	26	12
West Hull	10	4	0	6	236	283	-47	8
Hull Dockers	12	4	0	8	312	362	-50	8

QUARTER-FINALS

Saturday 12th November 2011
Bradford Dudley Hill 26 ....Skirlaugh 14
Castleford Lock Lane 4 ....Hunslet Warriors 22
Leigh East 22................................Wigan St Patricks 44
Siddal 30 ....Widnes West Bank 12

SEMI-FINALS

Saturday 19th November 2011
Hunslet Warriors 24....................Bradford Dudley Hill 18
Siddal 22 ....Wigan St Patricks 23

GRAND FINAL

Saturday 26th November 2011
Hunslet Warriors 18
Wigan St Patricks 14
(after extra time)
Warriors: T - Medhi (31), Cunningham (84), Rayner (90);
G - McClelland 3
St Patricks: T - Higham (75), Birkett (98); G - Schofield 3
(at the Arthur Miller Stadium, Stanningley)

ACE INSURANCE BARLA NATIONAL CUP

QUARTER FINALS

Saturday 24th March 2012
Bank Quay Bulls 24 ....Blackbrook 10
Queensbury 26...Queens 44
Saturday 31st March 2012
Hunslet Old Boys 0 ....Siddal 26
Sharlston Rovers 38 ....Fryston Warriors 22
(Abandoned after 72 mins - result stood)

SEMI-FINALS

Saturday 21st April 2012
Sharlston Rovers 36 ....Bank Quay Bulls 32
Saturday 28th April 2012
Siddal 4 ....Queens 18

FINAL

Saturday 2nd June 2012
Queens 33
Sharlston Rovers 10
Queens: T - Brown (19, 24, 54), Henry (50), Alrawi (58);
G - Milner 6; FG - Milner
Rovers: T - D Glassell (35), Malyan (62); G - Jackson
(at Woodlands Memorial Ground, Fylde)

TIER 4

WALES PREMIER

	P	W	D	L	F	A	D	Pts
Bonymaen Broncos	8	7	1	0	348	96	252	15
Bridgend Blue Bulls	8	5	1	2	340	210	130	11
Valley Cougars	8	5	0	3	238	210	28	10
Titans	7	2	0	5	164	270	-106	4
Cardiff Demons	7	2	0	5	134	292	-158	4
Dyffryn Devils	6	0	0	6	78	224	-146	0

SOUTHERN PREMIER

	P	W	D	L	F	A	D	Pts
London Skolars	11	10	0	1	492	150	342	20
Hammersmith HH	11	10	0	1	355	164	191	20
Eastern Rhinos	11	4	0	7	276	324	-48	8
Sth London Storm	11	4	0	7	234	443	-209	8
Elmbridge Eagles	10	3	0	7	254	368	-114	6
W London Sharks	10	1	0	9	80	242	-162	2

LONDON & SOUTH EAST

	P	W	D	L	F	A	D	Pts
Portsmouth NS	10	8	1	1	390	153	237	17
Southampton S	10	5	0	5	228	284	-56	10
Medway Dragons	10	4	1	5	315	332	-17	9
Guildford Giants	10	4	1	5	202	228	-26	9
Sussex Merlins	10	4	0	6	218	278	-60	8
Greenwich Admirals	10	2	3	5	182	260	-78	7

NORTH EAST PREMIER

	P	W	D	L	F	A	D	Pts
Jarrow Vikings	12	11	1	0	520	118	402	23
Gateshead Storm	12	10	0	2	526	204	322	20
Wallsend Eagles	11	4	1	6	246	314	-68	9
Peterlee Pumas	12	4	0	8	358	459	-101	8
Sunderland	12	4	0	8	313	568	-255	8
Gateshead Spartans	11	3	1	7	230	348	-118	7
East Cumbria C	12	2	3	7	196	378	-182	7

MIDLANDS PREMIER

	P	W	D	L	F	A	D	Pts
Northampton D	12	10	1	1	362	94	268	21
Leicester Storm	11	7	2	2	394	215	179	16
Birmingham B	11	4	1	6	238	266	-28	9
Gloucestershire W	12	4	1	7	319	422	-103	9
Coventry Bears A	12	1	1	10	154	470	-316	3

SCOTTISH CONFERENCE LEAGUE CENTRAL

	P	W	D	L	F	A	D	Pts
Edinburgh Eagles	9	7	0	2	412	179	233	14
Ayrshire Storm	8	6	0	2	308	224	84	12
Easterhouse P	8	5	0	3	257	154	103	10
Aberdeen Warriors	11	4	1	6	262	296	-34	9
Fife Lions	8	2	1	5	88	290	-202	5
Victoria Knights	8	1	0	7	54	238	-184	2

HARRY JEPSON TROPHY SEMI-FINALS

Sunday 9th September 2012
Gloucestershire Warriors 22 ....London Skolars A 46
Northampton Demons 24...........Edinburgh Eagles 12

HARRY JEPSON TROPHY GRAND FINAL

Sunday 16th September 2012
London Skolars 'A' 56
Northampton Demons 12
Skolars A: T - Roche (12), Burke (19, 56), Bloom (36),
McLean (41), Chapman (46), Ronayne (64), Powell (70),
Aggrey (72), Clover (74); G - McLean 8
Demons: T - Hulme (32, 51); G - Young 2
(at Pennine Way, Hemel Hempstead)

Warrington Wolves - Valvoline Cup Winners

THE CO-OPERATIVE RUGBY LEAGUE CONFERENCE REGIONAL

NORTH WALES CHAMPIONSHIP

	P	W	D	L	F	A	D	Pts
Prestatyn & Rhyl	8	7	1	0	292	104	188	15
Conwy Celts	8	6	0	2	305	190	115	12
Dee Valley Dragons	9	5	0	4	384	215	169	10
Flintshire Falcons	9	1	1	7	214	350	-136	3
Wrexham Bradley R	8	1	0	7	114	450	-336	2

NORTH EAST REGIONAL

	P	W	D	L	F	A	D	Pts
Cramlington Rockets	18	17	1	0	876	344	532	35
Teesside Bulls	17	13	0	4	842	380	462	26
Peterlee Pumas	18	11	0	7	740	582	158	22
Miner RL	18	10	1	7	875	512	363	21
Durham Demons	17	10	0	7	708	436	272	18
Consett Steelers	17	7	2	8	508	788	-288	16
Whitley Bay B	18	7	1	10	368	689	-321	15
Durham Tigers	17	5	2	10	272	716	-444	12
Hartlepool	18	3	0	15	380	660	-280	6
Warriors	18	1	1	16	320	774	-454	3

SCOTTISH CONFERENCE LEAGUE NORTH

	P	W	D	L	F	A	D	Pts
Edinburgh Eagles	6	4	1	1	188	100	88	9
Aberdeen Warriors	5	3	2	0	290	146	144	8
Moray Eels	5	2	1	2	174	148	26	5
Moray Titans RFC	6	0	0	6	118	376	-258	0

WEST OF ENGLAND

	P	W	D	L	F	A	D	Pts
Oxford Cavaliers	8	5	0	3	348	224	124	10
Somerset Vikings	8	5	0	3	270	210	60	10
Bristol Sonics A	8	4	0	4	242	220	22	8
Swindon St George	8	3	0	5	212	314	-102	6
Gloucestershire	8	3	0	5	200	304	-104	6

EAST

	P	W	D	L	F	A	D	Pts
North Herts C	12	10	0	2	495	286	209	20
St Ives Roosters	12	9	0	3	496	322	174	18
Bedford Tigers	11	7	0	4	351	274	77	14
Bury Titans	11	3	0	8	160	356	-196	6
Kings Lynn BK	10	2	1	7	252	362	-110	5
Milton Keynes W	10	1	1	8	156	310	-154	3

YORKSHIRE PREMIER

	P	W	D	L	F	A	D	Pts
Fryston Warriors	10	10	0	0	470	112	358	20
West Hull Lions	10	6	0	4	246	188	58	12
Skirlaugh Bulls	10	6	0	4	234	200	34	12
Oulton Raiders	10	5	0	5	186	250	-64	10
Cutsyke Raiders	10	2	1	7	149	280	-131	5
Bradford DH 'A'	10	0	1	9	96	351	-255	1

COMMUNITY CHALLENGE SHIELD

QUARTER-FINALS

Saturday 1st September 2012
Distington 16 ....Kells 39
Elmbridge Eagles 24 ....Hammersmith Hill Hoists 34
Leigh East 38 ....Walton Warriors 30
Skirlaugh Bulls 6 ....Fryston Warriors 28

SEMI-FINALS

Saturday 22nd September 2012
Fryston Warriors 48 ....Hammersmith Hill Hoists 0
Kells 42 ....Leigh East 10

FINAL

Sunday 7th October 2012
Fryston Warriors **35**
Kells **18**
Warriors: T - Land 3, Dickinson, Scott, McHugh;
G - Cogan 3, McHugh 2; FG - Speake
Kells; T - Boyd, McCourt, Schofield; G - Gainford 3
(at Ince Rose Bridge)

VALVOLINE CUP *(Under-20s)*

FINAL TABLE

	P	W	D	L	F	A	D	Pts
Warrington Wolves	20	17	0	3	871	335	536	34
Salford City Reds	20	15	1	4	741	537	204	31
Leeds Rhinos	20	14	2	4	696	412	284	30
St Helens	20	14	0	6	704	405	299	28
Wakefield T Wildcats	20	13	0	7	622	444	178	26
Wigan Warriors	20	12	1	7	754	382	372	25
Hull FC	20	11	1	8	522	548	-26	23
Castleford Tigers	19	7	0	12	504	668	-164	14
Widnes Vikings	20	6	1	13	548	740	-192	13
Hull Kingston Rovers	20	6	0	14	430	644	-214	12
London Broncos	19	4	0	15	399	710	-311	8
Bradford Bulls *	17	4	0	13	308	683	-375	8
Huddersfield Giants	19	1	0	18	296	887	-591	2

* Bradford Bulls only completed 17 fixtures

QUALIFYING PLAY-OFFS

Friday 7th September 2012
Warrington Wolves 42 ....St Helens 4
Salford City Reds 30 ....Leeds Rhinos 50

ELIMINATION PLAY-OFFS

Saturday 8th September 2012
Wakefield Trinity Wildcats 48 ....Castleford Tigers 28
Wigan Warriors 50 ....Hull FC 0

PRELIMINARY SEMI-FINALS

Saturday 15th September 2012
St Helens 60 ....Wakefield Trinity Wildcats 0

Sunday 16th September 2012
Salford City Reds 16 ....Wigan Warriors 52

QUALIFYING SEMI-FINALS

Saturday 22nd September 2012
Warrington Wolves 42 ....St Helens 26
Sunday 23rd September 2012
Leeds Rhinos 18 ....Wigan Warriors 14

GRAND FINAL

Saturday 29th September 2012
Warrington Wolves **36**
Leeds Rhinos **20**
Wolves: T - R Evans (10), Broughton (26), Bennion (40),
Currie (49), Hulme (52), Blythe (58); G - Goulding 6
Rhinos: T - Foster (21, 46), Hauraki (37), Agoro (42);
G - White 2
(at The Halliwell Jones Stadium)

RESERVES CHAMPIONSHIP *(Under-23s)*

FINAL TABLE

	P	W	D	L	F	A	D	Pts
Featherstone Rovers	15	14	1	0	754	224	530	29
Halifax	16	10	0	6	424	327	97	20
Oldham	15	7	2	6	396	386	10	16
Keighley Cougars	16	7	1	8	437	472	-35	15
Sheffield Eagles	15	5	0	10	344	582	-238	10
York City Knights	13	0	0	13	216	580	-364	0

PLAY-OFF

Friday 10th August 2012
Halifax 12 ....Oldham 18
(Featherstone Rovers advanced directly to Grand Final)

GRAND FINAL

Saturday 18th August 2012
Featherstone Rovers **72**
Oldham **6**
Rovers: T - Bussey (3, 18), Kitchen (23, 77), Johnson
(25, 74), Lyons (29), Jones (40), Iley (48), Mackay (51),
Mvududu (57), Humphries (70); G - Carr 12
Oldham: T - Lloyd (15); G - Nield
(at Big Fellas Stadium, Featherstone)

Featherstone Rovers - Reserves Championship Winners

GRAND FINALS
1998-2011

1998

DIVISION ONE GRAND FINAL

Saturday 26th September 1998

FEATHERSTONE ROVERS 22 WAKEFIELD TRINITY 24

ROVERS: 1 Steve Collins; 2 Carl Hall; 3 Shaun Irwin; 4 Danny Baker; 5 Karl Pratt; 6 Jamie Coventry; 7 Ty Fallins; 8 Chico Jackson; 9 Richard Chapman; 10 Stuart Dickens; 11 Gary Price; 12 Neil Lowe; 13 Richard Slater. Subs: 14 Paddy Handley for Coventry (70); 15 Asa Amone for Lowe (50); 16 Micky Clarkson for Jackson (50); 17 Steve Dooler (not used). **Tries:** Baker (15), Jackson (45), Collins (49), Hall (69); **Goals:** Chapman 3.
TRINITY: 1 Martyn Holland; 2 Josh Bostock; 3 Adam Hughes; 4 Martin Law; 5 Kevin Gray; 6 Garen Casey; 7 Roger Kenworthy; 8 Francis Stephenson; 9 Roy Southernwood; 10 Gary Lord; 11 Ian Hughes; 12 Sonny Whakarau; 13 Matt Fuller. Subs: 14 Sean Richardson for I Hughes (32); 15 Andy Fisher for Lord (26); 16 David Mycoe (not used); 17 Wayne McDonald for Whakarau (70); Lord for Stephenson (40); Stephenson for Lord (70). **Tries:** Southernwood (2), Bostock (7, 25), Casey (58), Stephenson (76); **Goals:** Casey 2.
League Express Men of the Match:
Rovers: Richard Chapman; *Trinity:* Garen Casey.
Penalty count: 8-3; **Half time:** 6-12; **Referee:** Nick Oddy (Halifax); **Attendance:** 8,224 *(at McAlpine Stadium, Huddersfield).*

SUPER LEAGUE GRAND FINAL

Saturday 24th October 1998

LEEDS RHINOS 4 WIGAN WARRIORS 10

RHINOS: 1 Iestyn Harris (C); 22 Leroy Rivett; 3 Richie Blackmore; 4 Brad Godden; 5 Francis Cummins; 13 Daryl Powell; 7 Ryan Sheridan; 8 Martin Masella; 21 Terry Newton; 25 Darren Fleary; 11 Adrian Morley; 17 Anthony Farrell; 12 Marc Glanville. Subs: 20 Jamie Mathiou for Masella (25); 24 Marcus St Hilaire for Powell (40); 14 Graham Holroyd for Newton (49); 27 Andy Hay for Fleary (54); Powell for Godden (58); Masella for Mathiou (71).
Try: Blackmore (20).
WARRIORS: 1 Kris Radlinski; 2 Jason Robinson; 3 Danny Moore; 4 Gary Connolly; 5 Mark Bell; 6 Henry Paul; 7 Tony Smith; 16 Terry O'Connor; 9 Robbie McCormack; 10 Tony Mestrov; 20 Lee Gilmour; 17 Stephen Holgate; 13 Andy Farrell (C). Subs: 8 Neil Cowie for O'Connor (18BB, rev 48); 14 Mick Cassidy for McCormack (19BB, rev 27); 25 Paul Johnson for Moore (37); 12 Simon Haughton for Gilmour (27BB, rev 33); Haughton for Holgate (33); Cowie for Mestrov (54); Cassidy for Haughton (64); Holgate for Cowie (68); Haughton for Gilmour (71BB, rev 75); Mestrov for O'Connor (75BB).
Try: Robinson (37); **Goals:** Farrell 3.
League Express Men of the Match:
Rhinos: Iestyn Harris; *Warriors:* Jason Robinson.
Penalty count: 7-13; **Half-time:** 4-6; **Referee:** Russell Smith (Castleford); **Attendance:** 43,553 *(at Old Trafford, Manchester).*

1999

NORTHERN FORD PREMIERSHIP GRAND FINAL

Saturday 25th September 1999

DEWSBURY RAMS 11 HUNSLET HAWKS 12

RAMS: 1 Nathan Graham; 2 Alex Godfrey; 3 Paul Evans; 4 Brendan O'Meara; 5 Adrian Flynn; 6 Richard Agar; 7 Barry Eaton; 8 Alan Boothroyd; 9 Paul Delaney; 10 Matthew Long; 11 Andy Spink; 12 Mark Haigh; 13 Damian Ball. Subs: 14 Brendan Williams for Eaton (5BB, rev 15); 15 Sean Richardson for Haigh (50); 16 Simon Hicks for Long (25); 17 Paul Medley for Spink (50); Williams for Evans (61); Long for Boothroyd (71); Spink for Long (78).
Tries: Flynn (27), Ball (54); **Goal:** Eaton; **Field goal:** Agar.
HAWKS: 1 Abraham Fatnowna; 2 Chris Ross; 3 Shaun Irwin; 4 Paul Cook; 5 Iain Higgins; 6 Marcus Vassilakopoulos; 7 Latham Tawhai; 8 Richard Hayes; 9 Richard Pachniuk; 10 Steve Pryce; 11 Rob Wilson; 12 Jamie Leighton; 13 Lee St Hilaire. Subs: 14 Mick Coyle for Wilson (57); 15 Phil Kennedy for Pryce (35); 16 Jamie Thackray for St Hilaire (25); 17 Richard Baker for Higgins (55); Higgins for Fatnowna (62); Pryce for Kennedy (65).
Tries: Cook (31), Higgins (46);
Goal: Ross; **Field goals:** Tawhai, Leighton.
League Express Men of the Match:
Rams: Barry Eaton; *Hawks:* Latham Tawhai.
Penalty count: 8-5; **Half-time:** 7-7; **Referee:** Steve Ganson (St Helens); **Attendance:** 5,783 *(at Headingley Stadium, Leeds).*

SUPER LEAGUE GRAND FINAL

Saturday 9th October 1999

BRADFORD BULLS 6 ST HELENS 8

BULLS: 28 Stuart Spruce; 2 Tevita Vaikona; 20 Scott Naylor; 5 Michael Withers; 17 Leon Pryce; 6 Henry Paul; 1 Robbie Paul (C); 10 Paul Anderson; 9 James Lowes; 29 Stuart Fielden; 15 David Boyle; 23 Bernard Dwyer; 13 Steve McNamara. Subs: 14 Paul Deacon for R Paul (53); 4 Nathan McAvoy (not used); 12 Mike Forshaw for McNamara (18); 22 Brian McDermott for Anderson (18); Anderson for Fielden (61); Fielden for Dwyer (65); R Paul for Deacon (72).
Try: H Paul (18); **Goal:** H Paul.
SAINTS: 1 Paul Atcheson; 14 Chris Smith; 3 Kevin Iro; 4 Paul Newlove; 5 Anthony Sullivan; 13 Paul Sculthorpe; 20 Tommy Martyn; 8 Apollo Perelini; 9 Keiron Cunningham; 10 Julian O'Neill; 2 Fereti Tuilagi; 21 Sonny Nickle; 11 Chris Joynt (C). Subs: 26 Paul Wellens for Martyn (52); 6 Sean Hoppe for Newlove (43); 16 Vila Matautia for O'Neill (20); 7 Sean Long for Perelini (24); Perelini for Matautia (46); O'Neill for Perelini (69).
Tries: Iro (65); **Goals:** Long 2.
League Express Men of the Match:
Bulls: Henry Paul; *Saints:* Kevin Iro.
Penalty count: 4-7; **Half-time:** 6-2; **Referee:** Stuart Cummings (Widnes); **Attendance:** 50,717 *(at Old Trafford, Manchester).*

1998...Jason Robinson shows off the Harry Sunderland Trophy

1999...Apollo Perelini offloads under pressure from Mike Forshaw and David Boyle

2000

NORTHERN FORD PREMIERSHIP GRAND FINAL

Saturday 29th July 2000

DEWSBURY RAMS 13 LEIGH CENTURIONS 12

RAMS: 1 Nathan Graham; 2 Richard Baker; 4 Dan Potter; 3 Brendan O'Meara; 5 Adrian Flynn; 6 Richard Agar; 7 Barry Eaton; 8 Shayne Williams; 9 David Mycoe; 10 Mark Haigh; 11 Sean Richardson; 12 Daniel Frame; 13 Damian Ball. Subs: 14 Gavin Wood (not used); 15 Paul Delaney for Mycoe (53); 16 Ryan McDonald for Haigh (30); 17 Matthew Long for Williams (23); Haigh for McDonald (64).
Tries: Eaton (2), Long (23); **Goals:** Eaton 2; **Field goal:** Agar.
Sin bin: Williams (66) - use of the elbow.
On report: Richardson (20) - high tackle on Donlan.
CENTURIONS: 1 Stuart Donlan; 5 David Ingram; 3 Paul Anderson; 4 Andy Fairclough; 2 Alan Cross; 6 Liam Bretherton; 7 Kieron Purtill; 8 Tim Street; 9 Mick Higham; 10 Andy Leathem; 11 Simon Baldwin; 12 Heath Cruckshank; 13 Adam Bristow. Subs: 14 James Arkwright for Cross (68); 15 Paul Norman for Street (36); 16 Radney Bowker (not used); 17 David Whittle for Leathem (24); Street for Norman (62).
Tries: Higham (29, 69); **Goals:** Bretherton 2.
Sin bin: Whittle (66) - retaliation.
League Express Men of the Match:
Rams: Richard Agar; *Centurions:* Mick Higham.
Penalty count: 4-4; **Half-time:** 10-6; **Referee:** Robert Connolly (Wigan); **Attendance:** 8,487 *(at Gigg Lane, Bury).*

SUPER LEAGUE GRAND FINAL

Saturday 14th October 2000

ST HELENS 29 WIGAN WARRIORS 16

SAINTS: 17 Paul Wellens; 24 Steve Hall; 3 Kevin Iro; 15 Sean Hoppe; 5 Anthony Sullivan; 20 Tommy Martyn; 7 Sean Long; 8 Apollo Perelini; 9 Keiron Cunningham; 10 Julian O'Neill; 11 Chris Joynt (C); 22 Tim Jonkers; 13 Paul Sculthorpe. Subs: 14 Fereti Tuilagi for O'Neill (20); 12 Sonny Nickle for Perelini (28); 26 John Stankevitch for Jonkers (50); 23 Scott Barrow (not used); Perelini for Nickle (52); Jonkers for Stankevitch (66); Stankevitch for Perelini (67BB); O'Neill for Hall (74).
Tries: Hoppe (7), Joynt (28, 50), Tuilagi (69), Jonkers (80); **Goals:** Long 4; **Field goal:** Sculthorpe.
WARRIORS: 5 Jason Robinson; 2 Brett Dallas; 1 Kris Radlinski; 3 Steve Renouf; 26 David Hodgson; 6 Tony Smith; 7 Willie Peters; 8 Terry O'Connor; 9 Terry Newton; 10 Neil Cowie; 11 Mick Cassidy; 12 Denis Betts; 13 Andy Farrell (C). Subs: 23 Brady Malam for Cowie (30); 17 Tony Mestrov for O'Connor (43); 19 Chris Chester for Cassidy (47BB, rev 69); 14 Lee Gilmour for Betts (51); O'Connor for Mestrov (61); Cowie for Malam (67); Chester for Newton (75).
Tries: Farrell (13), Hodgson (61), Smith (61); **Goals:** Farrell 2.
League Express Men of the Match:
Saints: Chris Joynt; *Warriors:* Andy Farrell.
Penalty count: 10-6; **Half-time:** 11-4; **Referee:** Russell Smith (Castleford); **Attendance:** 58,132 *(at Old Trafford, Manchester).*

2001

NORTHERN FORD PREMIERSHIP GRAND FINAL

Saturday 28th July 2001

OLDHAM 14 WIDNES VIKINGS 24

OLDHAM: 1 Mark Sibson; 2 Joey Hayes; 3 Anthony Gibbons; 4 Pat Rich; 5 Joe McNicholas; 6 David Gibbons; 7 Neil Roden; 8 Leo Casey; 9 Keith Brennan; 10 Paul Norton; 11 Phil Farrell; 12 Bryan Henare; 13 Kevin Mannion. Subs: 14 Mike Ford for Mannion (27); 15 Jason Clegg for Casey (18); 16 John Hough for Brennan (44); 17 Danny Guest for Norton (40BB, rev 54); Mannion for Henare (66); Guest for Clegg (73).
Tries: Brennan (9), Ford (74), Mannion (80); **Goal:** Rich.
VIKINGS: 1 Paul Atcheson; 2 Damian Munro; 3 Craig Weston; 4 Jason Demetriou; 5 Chris Percival; 6 Richard Agar; 7 Martin Crompton; 8 Simon Knox; 9 Phil Cantillon; 10 Stephen Holgate; 11 Steve Gee; 12 Sean Richardson; 13 Tommy Hodgkinson. Subs: 14 Andy Craig for Gee (41); 16 Joe Faimalo for Knox (32); 17 Matthew Long for Holgate (23); Knox for Long (49BB, rev 61); Holgate for Long (74).
Tries: Gee (17), Demetriou (38, 60), Cantillon (50), Munro (69); **Goals:** Weston 2.
League Express Men of the Match:
Oldham: Jason Clegg; *Vikings:* Phil Cantillon.
Penalty count: 8-5; **Half-time:** 4-10; **Referee:** Steve Ganson (St Helens); **Attendance:** 8,974 *(at Spotland, Rochdale).*

SUPER LEAGUE GRAND FINAL

Saturday 13th October 2001

BRADFORD BULLS 37 WIGAN WARRIORS 6

BULLS: 5 Michael Withers; 2 Tevita Vaikona; 20 Scott Naylor; 23 Graham Mackay; 3 Leon Pryce; 6 Henry Paul; 1 Robbie Paul (C); 8 Joe Vagana; 9 James Lowes; 22 Brian McDermott; 11 Daniel Gartner; 19 Jamie Peacock; 12 Mike Forshaw. Subs: 29 Stuart Fielden for McDermott (21BB, rev 65); 10 Paul Anderson for Vagana (22); 15 Shane Rigon for Pryce (40); 7 Paul Deacon for R Paul (69); Vagana for Anderson (53); Fielden for Gartner (72); Anderson for Vagana (74).
Tries: Lowes (9), Withers (11, 27, 31), Fielden (65), Mackay (72); **Goals:** H Paul 5, Mackay; **Field goal:** H Paul.
WARRIORS: 1 Kris Radlinski; 2 Brett Dallas; 4 Gary Connolly; 3 Steve Renouf; 5 Brian Carney; 6 Matthew Johns; 7 Adrian Lam; 8 Terry O'Connor; 9 Terry Newton; 20 Harvey Howard; 11 Mick Cassidy; 14 David Furner; 13 Andy Farrell (C). Subs: 15 Paul Johnson for Carney (12BB); 10 Neil Cowie for Howard (17); 12 Denis Betts for O'Connor (32); 19 Chris Chester for Farrell (59); O'Connor for Cowie (55); Howard for Newton (64); Cowie for Cassidy (72).
Try: Lam (63); **Goal:** Furner.
League Express Men of the Match:
Bulls: Michael Withers; *Warriors:* Adrian Lam.
Penalty count: 6-7; **Half-time:** 26-0; **Referee:** Stuart Cummings (Widnes); **Attendance:** 60,164 *(at Old Trafford, Manchester).*

2000...Dewsbury Rams get the party started

2001...Henry Paul races away from Adrian Lam and Kris Radlinski

2002

NORTHERN FORD PREMIERSHIP GRAND FINAL

Saturday 12th October 2002

HUDDERSFIELD GIANTS 38 LEIGH CENTURIONS 16

GIANTS: 1 Ben Cooper; 2 Hefin O'Hare; 3 Eorl Crabtree; 4 Graeme Hallas; 5 Marcus St Hilaire; 6 Stanley Gene; 7 Chris Thorman; 8 Michael Slicker; 9 Paul March; 10 Jeff Wittenberg; 11 David Atkins; 12 Robert Roberts; 13 Steve McNamara. Subs: 14 Heath Cruckshank for Roberts (24BB); 15 Chris Molyneux for Slicker (53); 16 Darren Turner for March (21); 17 Andy Rice for Cruckshank (57); Roberts for Wittenberg (34); Wittenberg for Roberts (74).
Tries: O'Hare (12, 78), St Hilaire (34, 53), Thorman (46), Gene (57); **Goals:** McNamara 7.
Sin bin: Roberts (47) - fighting.
CENTURIONS: 1 Neil Turley; 2 Leon Felton; 4 Jon Roper; 3 Dale Cardoza; 5 Oliver Marns; 6 Willie Swann; 7 Bobbie Goulding; 8 Vila Matautia; 9 Paul Rowley; 10 David Bradbury; 11 Simon Baldwin; 12 Andrew Isherwood; 13 Adam Bristow. Subs: 14 Gareth Price for Bradbury (24BB, rev 35); 15 John Duffy for Swann (32); 16 John Hamilton for Bristow (46BB, rev 57); 17 David Whittle for Matautia (22); Matautia for Bradbury (53BB); Swann for Goulding (58); Hamilton for Whittle (67); Bradbury for Turley (72); Goulding for Swann (75).
Tries: Cardoza (9), Marns (18), Hamilton (70); **Goals:** Turley 2.
Sin bin: Whittle (47) - fighting; Bristow (47) - interference.
On report: Isherwood (66) - high tackle on Roberts.
Rugby Leaguer & League Express Men of the Match:
Giants: Chris Thorman; *Centurions:* Adam Bristow.
Penalty count: 11-11; **Half-time:** 14-10;
Referee: Karl Kirkpatrick (Warrington);
Attendance: 9,051 *(at Halton Stadium, Widnes).*

SUPER LEAGUE GRAND FINAL

Saturday 19th October 2002

BRADFORD BULLS 18 ST HELENS 19

BULLS: 6 Michael Withers; 2 Tevita Vaikona; 20 Scott Naylor; 15 Brandon Costin; 5 Lesley Vainikolo; 1 Robbie Paul (C); 7 Paul Deacon; 8 Joe Vagana; 9 James Lowes; 29 Stuart Fielden; 11 Daniel Gartner; 12 Jamie Peacock; 13 Mike Forshaw. Subs: 14 Lee Gilmour for Gartner (21); 10 Paul Anderson for Vagana (25); 22 Brian McDermott for Fielden (34); 3 Leon Pryce for Vainikolo (53); Fielden for Anderson (55); Vainikolo for Paul (77).
Tries: Naylor (3), Paul (44), Withers (47); **Goals:** Deacon 3.
SAINTS: 1 Paul Wellens; 5 Darren Albert; 3 Martin Gleeson; 4 Paul Newlove; 19 Anthony Stewart; 13 Paul Sculthorpe; 7 Sean Long; 8 Darren Britt; 9 Keiron Cunningham; 10 Barry Ward; 23 Mike Bennett; 15 Tim Jonkers; 11 Chris Joynt (C). Subs: 2 Sean Hoppe for Wellens (3); 12 Peter Shiels for Ward (27); 14 John Stankevitch for Britt (31BB, rev 58); 17 Mick Higham for Joynt (54); Stankevitch for Shiels (58); Joynt for Britt (75); Shiels for Jonkers (77).
Tries: Bennett (24), Long (32), Gleeson (56);
Goals: Long 3; **Field goal:** Long.
Rugby Leaguer & League Express Men of the Match:
Bulls: Paul Deacon; *Saints:* Mike Bennett.
Penalty count: 5-4; **Half-time:** 12-8; **Referee:** Russell Smith (Castleford); **Attendance:** 61,138 *(at Old Trafford, Manchester).*

2002...Huddersfield celebrate promotion

2003

NATIONAL LEAGUE TWO GRAND FINAL

Sunday 5th October 2003

KEIGHLEY COUGARS 13 SHEFFIELD EAGLES 11

COUGARS: 1 Matt Foster; 2 Max Tomlinson; 3 David Foster; 4 James Rushforth; 5 Andy Robinson; 6 Paul Ashton; 7 Matt Firth; 8 Phil Stephenson; 9 Simeon Hoyle; 10 Danny Ekis; 11 Oliver Wilkes; 12 Ian Sinfield; 13 Lee Patterson. Subs (all used): 14 Chris Wainwright; 15 Richard Mervill; 16 Mick Durham; 17 Jason Ramshaw.
Tries: M Foster (7), Robinson (74); **Goals:** Ashton 2;
Field goal: Firth.
EAGLES: 1 Andy Poynter; 2 Tony Weller; 3 Richard Goddard; 4 Tom O'Reilly; 5 Greg Hurst; 6 Gavin Brown; 7 Mark Aston; 8 Jack Howieson; 9 Gareth Stanley; 10 Dale Laughton; 11 Andy Raleigh; 12 Craig Brown; 13 Wayne Flynn. Subs (all used): 14 Peter Reilly; 15 Simon Tillyer; 16 Nick Turnbull; 17 Mitchell Stringer.
Try: O'Reilly (51); **Goals:** G Brown 3; **Field goal:** Reilly.
Rugby Leaguer & League Express Men of the Match:
Cougars: Simeon Hoyle; *Eagles:* Andy Raleigh.
Penalty count: 6-8; **Half-time:** 9-4; **Referee:** Peter Taberner (Wigan). *(at Halton Stadium, Widnes).*

NATIONAL LEAGUE ONE GRAND FINAL

Sunday 5th October 2003

LEIGH CENTURIONS 14 SALFORD CITY REDS 31

CENTURIONS: 1 Neil Turley; 2 Damian Munro; 3 Alan Hadcroft; 4 Danny Halliwell; 5 Leroy Rivett; 6 John Duffy; 7 Tommy Martyn; 8 Sonny Nickle; 9 Patrick Weisner; 10 Paul Norman; 11 Sean Richardson; 12 Willie Swann; 13 Adam Bristow. Subs (all used): 14 David Bradbury; 15 Lee Sanderson; 16 Bryan Henare; 17 Ricky Bibey.
Tries: Richardson (33), Halliwell (38), Swann (65);
Goal: Turley.
On report: Nickle (60) - late tackle on Clinch.
CITY REDS: 1 Jason Flowers; 2 Danny Arnold; 3 Stuart Littler; 4 Alan Hunte; 5 Andy Kirk; 6 Cliff Beverley; 7 Gavin Clinch; 8 Neil Baynes; 9 Malcolm Alker; 10 Andy Coley; 11 Simon Baldwin; 12 Paul Highton; 13 Chris Charles. Subs (all used): 14 Steve Blakeley; 15 David Highton; 16 Martin Moana; 17 Gareth Haggerty.
Tries: Hunte (3, 52), Beverley (23), Littler (73);
Goals: Charles 6, Blakeley; **Field goal:** Blakeley.
Rugby Leaguer & League Express Men of the Match:
Centurions: Willie Swann; *City Reds:* Gavin Clinch.
Penalty count: 10-10; **Half-time:** 10-16;
Referee: Richard Silverwood (Dewsbury);
Attendance: 9,186 *(at Halton Stadium, Widnes).*

SUPER LEAGUE GRAND FINAL

Saturday 18th October 2003

BRADFORD BULLS 25 WIGAN WARRIORS 12

BULLS: 17 Stuart Reardon; 2 Tevita Vaikona; 6 Michael Withers; 4 Shontayne Hape; 5 Lesley Vainikolo; 15 Karl Pratt; 7 Paul Deacon; 8 Joe Vagana; 9 James Lowes; 29 Stuart Fielden; 11 Daniel Gartner; 12 Jamie Peacock; 13 Mike Forshaw. Subs (all used): 10 Paul Anderson; 18 Lee Radford; 3 Leon Pryce; 1 Robbie Paul (C).
Tries: Reardon (51), Hape (59), Lowes (75);
Goals: Deacon 6/6; **Field goal:** Deacon.
WARRIORS: 1 Kris Radlinski; 5 Brian Carney; 18 Martin Aspinwall; 14 David Hodgson; 2 Brett Dallas; 15 Sean O'Loughlin; 20 Luke Robinson; 30 Quentin Pongia; 9 Terry Newton; 10 Craig Smith; 11 Mick Cassidy; 12 Danny Tickle; 13 Andy Farrell (C). Subs (all used): 4 Paul Johnson; 8 Terry O'Connor; 23 Gareth Hock; 17 Mark Smith.
Tries: Tickle (17), Radlinski (72); **Goals:** Farrell 2/3.
Rugby Leaguer & League Express Men of the Match:
Bulls: Stuart Reardon; *Warriors:* Kris Radlinski.
Penalty count: 7-6; **Half-time:** 4-6; **Referee:** Karl Kirkpatrick (Warrington); **Attendance:** 65,537 *(at Old Trafford, Manchester).*

2004

NATIONAL LEAGUE ONE GRAND FINAL

Sunday 10th October 2004

LEIGH CENTURIONS 32 WHITEHAVEN 16
(after extra time)

CENTURIONS: 1 Neil Turley; 2 Rob Smyth; 3 Danny Halliwell; 4 Ben Cooper; 5 David Alstead; 6 John Duffy; 7 Tommy Martyn; 8 Simon Knox; 9 Paul Rowley; 10 Matt Sturm; 11 David Larder; 12 Oliver Wilkes; 13 Ian Knott. Subs (all used): 14 Dave McConnell; 15 Heath Cruckshank; 16 Richard Marshall; 17 Willie Swann.
Tries: Cooper (27, 83), Martyn (61), Turley (87);
Goals: Turley 6/8; **Field goals:** Turley 2, Rowley, Martyn.
WHITEHAVEN: 1 Gary Broadbent; 2 Craig Calvert; 3 David Seeds; 4 Mick Nanyn; 5 Wesley Wilson; 6 Leroy Joe; 7 Sam Obst; 8 Marc Jackson; 9 Aaron Lester; 10 David Fatialofa; 11 Paul Davidson; 12 Howard Hill; 13 Craig Walsh. Subs (all used): 14 Spencer Miller; 15 Carl Sice; 16 Chris McKinney; 17 Ryan Tandy.
Tries: Wilson (2, 71), Calvert (45); **Goals:** Nanyn 2/6.
Rugby Leaguer & League Express Men of the Match:
Centurions: Neil Turley; *Whitehaven:* Aaron Lester.
Penalty count: 5-9; **Half-time:** 7-6; **Full-time:** 16-16;
Referee: Ronnie Laughton (Barnsley);
Attendance: 11,005 *(at Halton Stadium, Widnes).*

SUPER LEAGUE GRAND FINAL

Saturday 16th October 2004

BRADFORD BULLS 8 LEEDS RHINOS 16

BULLS: 6 Michael Withers; 17 Stuart Reardon; 16 Paul Johnson; 4 Shontayne Hape; 5 Lesley Vainikolo; 18 Iestyn Harris; 7 Paul Deacon; 8 Joe Vagana; 1 Robbie Paul (C); 29 Stuart Fielden; 12 Jamie Peacock; 13 Logan Swann; 11 Lee Radford. Subs: 10 Paul Anderson for Vagana (14); 15 Karl Pratt for Paul (23); 27 Rob Parker for Anderson (24); 19 Jamie Langley for Peacock (32); Paul for Withers (ht); Peacock for Radford (48); Radford for Swann (54); Vagana for Parker (56); Parker for Fielden (63); Fielden for Vagana (67); Swann for Langley (68).
Tries: Vainikolo (7), Hape (43); **Goals:** Deacon 0/2.
RHINOS: 21 Richard Mathers; 18 Mark Calderwood; 5 Chev Walker; 4 Keith Senior; 22 Marcus Bai; 13 Kevin Sinfield (C); 6 Danny McGuire; 19 Danny Ward; 9 Matt Diskin; 8 Ryan Bailey; 3 Chris McKenna; 29 Ali Lauitiiti; 11 David Furner. Subs: 16 Willie Poching for Furner (19); 10 Barrie McDermott for Ward (22); Ward for Bailey (29); 7 Rob Burrow for Lauitiiti (30); Bailey for McDermott (41); 20 Jamie Jones-Buchanan for McKenna (48); Lauitiiti for Ward (50); Furner for Sinfield (60); McKenna for Poching (63); Sinfield for Diskin (67); Poching for McKenna (72); Ward for Bailey (73).
Tries: Diskin (15), McGuire (75); **Goals:** Sinfield 4/4.
Rugby Leaguer & League Express Men of the Match:
Bulls: Lesley Vainikolo; *Rhinos:* Richard Mathers.
Penalty count: 5-5; **Half-time:** 4-10; **Referee:** Steve Ganson (St Helens); **Attendance:** 65,547 *(at Old Trafford, Manchester).*

2005

NATIONAL LEAGUE ONE GRAND FINAL

Sunday 9th October 2005

CASTLEFORD TIGERS 36 WHITEHAVEN 8

TIGERS: 1 Michael Platt; 2 Waine Pryce; 3 Michael Shenton; 4 Jon Hepworth; 5 Damien Blanch; 6 Brad Davis; 7 Andrew Henderson; 8 Adam Watene; 9 Aaron Smith; 10 Richard Fletcher; 11 Tom Haughey; 12 Steve Crouch; 13 Deon Bird. Subs (all used): 14 Paul Handforth; 15 Craig Huby; 16 Adrian Vowles; 17 Frank Watene.
Tries: Huby (22), Crouch (24), Blanch (26), Davis (33, 45), Haughey (52); **Goals:** Fletcher 2/3, Huby 3/4, Hepworth 1/1.
WHITEHAVEN: 1 Gary Broadbent; 2 Craig Calvert; 3 David Seeds; 4 Mick Nanyn; 5 Wesley Wilson; 6 Leroy Joe; 7 Joel Penny; 8 Ryan Tandy; 9 Carl Sice; 10 David Fatialofa; 11 Spencer Miller; 12 Howard Hill; 13 Aaron Lester. Subs (all used): 14 Carl Rudd; 15 Aaron Summers; 16 Craig Chambers; 17 Marc Jackson.
Tries: Seeds (56), Calvert (78); **Goals:** Nanyn 0/2.
Sin bin: Joe (16) - late tackle on Davis.
On report: Joe (16) - late tackle on Davis;
Sice (40) - alleged biting.
Rugby Leaguer & League Express Men of the Match:
Tigers: Brad Davis; *Whitehaven:* Wesley Wilson.
Penalty count: 4-9; **Half-time:** 26-0;
Referee: Steve Ganson (St Helens);
Attendance: 13,300 *(at Halton Stadium, Widnes).*

SUPER LEAGUE GRAND FINAL

Saturday 15th October 2005

BRADFORD BULLS 15 LEEDS RHINOS 6

BULLS: 6 Michael Withers; 3 Leon Pryce; 13 Ben Harris; 4 Shontayne Hape; 5 Lesley Vainikolo; 18 Iestyn Harris; 7 Paul Deacon; 12 Jamie Peacock (C); 9 Ian Henderson; 29 Stuart Fielden; 16 Paul Johnson; 10 Brad Meyers; 11 Lee Radford. Subs (all used): 24 Adrian Morley for Johnson (5); 19 Jamie Langley for Peacock (24); 8 Joe Vagana for Fielden (24); Johnson for Radford (24); 1 Robbie Paul for Henderson (31); Peacock for Vagana (45); Fielden for Morley (49); Henderson for Paul (54); Radford for Meyers (60); Morley for Peacock (62); Meyers for Langley (73); Peacock for Johnson (74).
Tries: L Pryce (29), Vainikolo (53); **Goals:** Deacon 3/5;
Field goal: I Harris.
RHINOS: 1 Richard Mathers; 2 Mark Calderwood; 3 Chev Walker; 12 Chris McKenna; 5 Marcus Bai; 6 Danny McGuire; 7 Rob Burrow; 8 Ryan Bailey; 14 Andrew Dunemann; 15 Danny Ward; 20 Gareth Ellis; 16 Willie Poching; 13 Kevin Sinfield (C). Subs (all used): 10 Barrie McDermott for Ward (17); 11 Ali Lauitiiti for Poching (21); 18 Jamie Jones-Buchanan for Bailey (31); Ward for McDermott (34); 9 Matt Diskin for Ellis (48); Poching for Lauitiiti (48); McDermott for Ward (54); Ellis for Poching (54); Lauitiiti for McDermott (61); Poching for Dunemann (65); Ward for Jones-Buchanan (68); Dunemann for Ellis (71).
Try: McGuire (22); **Goals:** Sinfield 1/2.
Rugby Leaguer & League Express Men of the Match:
Bulls: Leon Pryce; *Rhinos:* Danny McGuire.
Penalty count: 6-8; **Half-time:** 8-6; **Referee:** Ashley Klein (Keighley); **Attendance:** 65,537 *(at Old Trafford, Manchester).*

2004...Kevin Sinfield leads the Rhinos' celebrations

2005...Craig Huby shows his delight at scoring

2006

NATIONAL LEAGUE TWO GRAND FINAL

Sunday 8th October 2006

SHEFFIELD EAGLES 35 SWINTON LIONS 10

EAGLES: 1 Johnny Woodcock; 5 Greg Hurst; 4 Jimmy Walker; 3 James Ford; 2 Rob Worrincy; 6 Brendon Lindsay; 7 Gavin Brown; 8 Jack Howieson; 9 Paul Pickering; 10 Mitchell Stringer; 11 Andy Hay; 12 Dale Holdstock; 13 Andy Smith. Subs (all used): 14 Craig Poucher; 15 Martin Ostler; 16 Sean Dickinson; 17 Waisale Sovatabua.
Tries: Worrincy (21, 43), Lindsay (38), Woodcock (39), Walker (51), Hay (60); **Goals:** Woodcock 5/6;
Field goal: G Brown.
LIONS: 1 Wayne English; 2 Andy Saywell; 3 Darren Woods; 4 David Alstead; 5 Marlon Billy; 6 Martin Moana; 7 Chris Hough; 8 Bruce Johnson; 9 Phil Wood; 10 Dave Newton; 11 Kris Smith; 12 Ian Sinfield; 13 Lee Marsh. Subs (all used): 14 Liam McGovern; 15 Chris Morley; 16 Danny Aboushakra; 17 Ian Parry.
Tries: Saywell (35), Alstead (74); **Goals:** McGovern 1/2.
Rugby Leaguer & League Express Men of the Match:
Eagles: Johnny Woodcock; *Lions:* Wayne English.
Penalty count: 3-4; **Half-time:** 16-4;
Referee: Peter Taberner (Wigan).
(at Halliwell Jones Stadium, Warrington).

Dewsbury Rams were National League Two Champions in 2006. This game was to determine who took the second promotion place.

NATIONAL LEAGUE ONE GRAND FINAL

Sunday 8th October 2006

HULL KINGSTON ROVERS 29 WIDNES VIKINGS 16

ROVERS: 1 Ben Cockayne; 2 Leroy Rivett; 3 Gareth Morton; 4 Jon Goddard; 5 Byron Ford; 6 Scott Murrell; 7 James Webster; 8 Makali Aizue; 9 Ben Fisher; 10 David Tangata-Toa; 11 Iain Morrison; 12 Michael Smith; 13 Tommy Gallagher. Subs (all used): 14 Pat Weisner; 15 Dwayne Barker; 16 Jason Netherton; 17 Dave Wilson.
Tries: Ford (6), Goddard (18, 36), Murrell (24), Weisner (43); **Goals:** Morton 4/6; **Field goal:** Murrell.
VIKINGS: 1 Gavin Dodd; 2 Damien Blanch; 3 Sean Gleeson; 4 Daryl Cardiss; 5 John Kirkpatrick; 6 Dennis Moran; 7 Ian Watson; 8 Terry O'Connor; 9 Mark Smith; 10 Barrie McDermott; 11 Mick Cassidy; 12 David Allen; 13 Bob Beswick. Subs (all used): 14 Aaron Summers; 15 Oliver Wilkes; 16 Jordan James; 17 Ryan Tandy.
Tries: Dodd (32), Tandy (57), Blanch (70); **Goals:** Dodd 2/3.
Rugby Leaguer & League Express Men of the Match:
Rovers: James Webster; *Vikings:* Mark Smith.
Penalty count: 8-5; **Half-time:** 22-4;
Referee: Phil Bentham (Warrington);
Attendance: 13,024 *(at Halliwell Jones Stadium, Warrington).*

2006...The departing Jamie Lyon carried from the Old Trafford pitch by his teammates

SUPER LEAGUE GRAND FINAL

Saturday 14th October 2006

HULL FC 4 ST HELENS 26

HULL: 1 Shaun Briscoe; 14 Motu Tony; 4 Sid Domic; 3 Kirk Yeaman; 5 Gareth Raynor; 13 Paul Cooke; 7 Richard Horne; 8 Ewan Dowes; 9 Richard Swain (C); 10 Garreth Carvell; 11 Lee Radford; 12 Shayne McMenemy; 24 Danny Washbrook. Subs: 15 Paul King for Carvell (17); 19 Graeme Horne for Radford (23); 26 Scott Wheeldon for Dowes (27); 6 Richard Whiting for McMenemy (29); Dowes for Wheeldon (49); Carvell for King (49); Radford for G Horne (51); McMenemy for Whiting (54); King for Carvell (68); Wheeldon for Dowes (73); Whiting for Tony (76); G Horne for Radford (77).
Try: Domic (24); **Goals:** Cooke 0/1.
SAINTS: 1 Paul Wellens; 2 Ade Gardner; 3 Jamie Lyon; 4 Willie Talau; 5 Francis Meli; 6 Leon Pryce; 7 Sean Long (C); 17 Paul Anderson; 9 Keiron Cunningham; 10 Jason Cayless; 11 Lee Gilmour; 12 Jon Wilkin; 16 Jason Hooper. Subs: 23 Maurie Fa'asavalu for P Anderson (12); 19 James Graham for Cayless (25); 15 Mike Bennett for Fa'asavalu (28); 14 James Roby for Cunningham (31); P Anderson for Wilkin (33); Cunningham for Gilmour (49); Cayless for P Anderson (52); Wilkin for Hooper (56); Fa'asavalu for Cayless (58); Gilmour for Graham (66); Cayless for Fa'asavalu (72); P Anderson for Wilkin (75).
Tries: Meli (17), Pryce (29), Talau (49), Gardner (52), Cunningham (62); **Goals:** Lyon 3/5.
Rugby Leaguer & League Express Men of the Match:
Hull: Shaun Briscoe; *Saints:* Paul Wellens.
Penalty count: 4-2; **Half-time:** 4-10;
Referee: Karl Kirkpatrick (Warrington);
Attendance: 72,582 *(at Old Trafford, Manchester).*

2007

NATIONAL LEAGUE TWO GRAND FINAL

Sunday 7th October 2007

FEATHERSTONE ROVERS 24 OLDHAM 6

ROVERS: 1 Loz Wildbore; 2 Danny Kirmond; 3 Jon Whittle; 4 Wayne McHugh; 5 Ade Adebisi; 6 Andy Kain; 7 Paul Handforth; 8 Gareth Handford; 9 Joe McLocklan; 10 Stuart Dickens; 11 Jamie Field; 12 Richard Blakeway; 13 Tom Haughey. Subs (all used): 14 Jamie Benn; 15 Ian Tonks; 16 James Houston; 17 Gavin Swinson.
Tries: McHugh (39, 49), Handforth (46); **Goals:** Dickens 5/6;
Field goals: Wildbore (66, 70).
Dismissal: Blakeway (64) – head butt on Roberts.
OLDHAM: 1 Gareth Langley; 2 Byron Ford; 3 Craig Littler; 4 Adam Hughes; 5 Lucas Onyango; 6 Neil Roden; 7 James Coyle; 8 Anthony Tonks; 9 Simeon Hoyle; 10 Richard Mervill; 11 Ian Sinfield; 12 Robert Roberts; 13 Geno Costin. Subs (all used): 14 Ian Hodson; 15 Alex Wilkinson; 16 Said Tamghart; 17 Matty Brooks.
Try: Hughes (31); **Goals:** Langley 1/2.
Rugby Leaguer & League Express Men of the Match:
Rovers: Paul Handforth; *Oldham:* Robert Roberts.
Penalty count: 9-5; **Half-time:** 10-6; **Referee:** Gareth Hewer.
(at Headingley Carnegie, Leeds).

Celtic Crusaders were National League Two Champions in 2007. This game was to determine who took the second promotion place.

NATIONAL LEAGUE ONE GRAND FINAL

Sunday 7th October 2007

CASTLEFORD TIGERS 42 WIDNES VIKINGS 10

TIGERS: 1 Stuart Donlan; 2 Danny Williams; 3 Michael Shenton; 4 Ryan McGoldrick; 5 Kirk Dixon; 6 Anthony Thackeray; 7 Danny Brough; 8 Liam Higgins; 9 Andrew Henderson; 10 Awen Guttenbeil; 11 Joe Westerman; 12 Ryan Clayton; 13 Peter Lupton. Subs (all used): 14 Mark Leafa; 15 Chris Charles; 16 Michael Wainwright; 17 Ryan Boyle.
Tries: Wainwright (20), McGoldrick (29), Guttenbeil (44, 76), M Shenton (52), Westerman (62), Clayton (66);
Goals: Brough 6/9; **Field goals:** Brough (25, 55).
VIKINGS: 1 Scott Grix; 2 Damien Blanch; 3 Toa Kohe-Love; 4 Mick Nanyn; 5 Gavin Dodd; 6 Dennis Moran; 7 Joel Penny; 8 Mick Cassidy; 9 Mark Smith; 10 Oliver Wilkes; 11 Joel Tomkins; 12 Paul Noone; 13 Bob Beswick. Subs (all used): 14 Aaron Summers; 15 Jordan James; 16 Ian Webster; 17 Lee Doran.
Tries: Nanyn (35), Wilkes (69); **Goals:** Nanyn 1/2.
Rugby Leaguer & League Express Men of the Match:
Tigers: Danny Brough; *Vikings:* Scott Grix.
Penalty count: 7-2; **Half-time:** 13-4; **Referee:** Phil Bentham;
Attendance: 20,814 *(at Headingley Carnegie, Leeds)*.

SUPER LEAGUE GRAND FINAL

Saturday 13th October 2007

LEEDS RHINOS 33 ST HELENS 6

RHINOS: 1 Brent Webb; 5 Lee Smith; 3 Clinton Toopi; 4 Keith Senior; 2 Scott Donald; 6 Danny McGuire; 7 Rob Burrow; 8 Kylie Leuluai; 9 Matt Diskin; 10 Jamie Peacock; 11 Jamie Jones-Buchanan; 12 Gareth Ellis; 13 Kevin Sinfield (C). Subs (all used): 14 Ali Lauitiiti for Diskin (23); 16 Ryan Bailey for Leuluai (18); 18 Ian Kirke for Jones-Buchanan (33); 22 Carl Ablett for Kirke (57); Leuluai for Bailey (55); Jones-Buchanan for Lauitiiti (60); Diskin for Ablett (63); Kirke for Leuluai (65); Bailey for Kirke (76).
Tries: Webb (19), Lauitiiti (50), Donald (52), Smith (69), Jones-Buchanan (80); **Goals:** Sinfield 6/7;
Field goal: Burrow (55).
SAINTS: 1 Paul Wellens; 2 Ade Gardner; 3 Matt Gidley; 4 Willie Talau; 5 Francis Meli; 6 Leon Pryce; 7 Sean Long; 8 Nick Fozzard; 9 Keiron Cunningham (C); 10 Jason Cayless; 11 Lee Gilmour; 30 Chris Flannery; 12 Jon Wilkin. Subs (all used): 17 James Graham for Cayless (15); 14 James Roby for Cunningham (23); 23 Maurie Fa'asavalu for Fozzard (23); 15 Mike Bennett for Wilkin (31); Cayless for Fa'asavalu (34); Cunningham for Flannery (51); Wilkin for Bennett (55); Fa'asavalu for Cayless (55); Fozzard for Graham (57); Cayless for Fozzard (68); Graham for Fa'asavalu (68); Bennett for Gilmour (72).
Try: Roby (27); **Goals:** Long 1/2.
Rugby Leaguer & League Express Men of the Match:
Rhinos: Rob Burrow; *Saints:* Sean Long.
Penalty count: 4-5; **Half-time:** 8-6; **Referee:** Ashley Klein;
Attendance: 71,352 *(at Old Trafford, Manchester)*.

2007...Jon Whittle brought down by Ian Sinfield

2008

NATIONAL LEAGUE TWO GRAND FINAL

Sunday 28th September 2008

DONCASTER 18 OLDHAM 10

DONCASTER: 1 Zebastian Luisi; 2 Dean Colton; 3 Andreas Bauer; 4 Shaun Leaf; 5 Wayne Reittie; 6 Kyle Wood; 7 Luke Gale; 8 Nathan Freer; 9 Corey Lawrie; 10 Alex Benson; 11 Peter Green; 12 Craig Lawton; 13 Josh Weeden. Subs (all used): 14 Kyle Briggs; 15 Chris Buttery; 16 Michael Haley; 17 Mark Castle.
Tries: Buttery (44), Gale (49), Briggs (73); **Goals:** Gale 3/4.
OLDHAM: 1 Paul O'Connor; 2 Gareth Langley; 3 Marcus St Hilaire; 4 Mick Nanyn; 5 Daryl Cardiss; 6 Phil Joseph; 7 James Coyle; 8 Adam Robinson; 9 Matty Brooks; 10 Richard Mervill; 11 Tommy Goulden; 12 Danny Halliwell; 13 Robert Roberts. Subs (all used): 14 Ian Hodson; 15 Luke Menzies; 16 Chris Baines; 17 Said Tamghart.
Tries: Hodson (34), Nanyn (62); **Goals:** Nanyn 1/4.
Rugby Leaguer & League Express Men of the Match:
Doncaster: Luke Gale; *Oldham:* Adam Robinson.
Penalty count: 7-8; **Half-time:** 2-6; **Referee:** Ronnie Laughton. *(at Halliwell Jones Stadium, Warrington)*.

Gateshead Thunder were National League Two Champions in 2008. This game was to determine who took the second promotion place.

NATIONAL LEAGUE ONE GRAND FINAL

Sunday 28th September 2008

CELTIC CRUSADERS 18 SALFORD CITY REDS 36
(after extra time)

CRUSADERS: 1 Tony Duggan; 2 Luke Dyer; 3 Josh Hannay; 4 Mark Dalle Cort; 5 Anthony Blackwood; 6 Damien Quinn; 7 Jace Van Dijk; 8 Jordan James; 9 Neil Budworth; 10 David Tangata-Toa; 11 Chris Beasley; 12 Darren Mapp; 13 Terry Martin. Subs (all used): 14 Aaron Summers; 15 Ian Webster; 16 Mark Lennon; 17 Neale Wyatt.
Tries: Blackwood (38), Dyer (50), J James (54), Tangata-Toa (66); **Goals:** Hannay 0/1, Lennon 1/3.
CITY REDS: 1 Karl Fitzpatrick; 2 Matt Gardner; 3 Stuart Littler; 4 John Wilshere; 5 Paul White; 6 Robbie Paul; 7 Richard Myler; 8 Paul Highton; 9 Malcolm Alker; 10 Craig Stapleton; 11 Ian Sibbit; 12 Luke Adamson; 13 Jordan Turner. Subs (all used): 14 Stefan Ratchford; 15 Steve Bannister; 16 Lee Jewitt; 17 Phil Leuluai.
Tries: White (5, 86), Gardner (26), Fitzpatrick (63), Sibbit (83), Myler (99); **Goals:** Wilshere 6/7.
Rugby Leaguer & League Express Men of the Match:
Crusaders: Tony Duggan; *City Reds:* John Wilshere.
Penalty count: 5-5; **Half-time:** 4-10; **Full-time:** 18-18;
Referee: Ben Thaler; **Attendance:** 7,104
(at Halliwell Jones Stadium, Warrington).

SUPER LEAGUE GRAND FINAL

Saturday 4th October 2008

LEEDS RHINOS 24 ST HELENS 16

RHINOS: 5 Lee Smith; 22 Ryan Hall; 19 Carl Ablett; 4 Keith Senior; 2 Scott Donald; 6 Danny McGuire; 7 Rob Burrow; 8 Kylie Leuluai; 9 Matt Diskin; 10 Jamie Peacock; 11 Jamie Jones-Buchanan; 12 Gareth Ellis; 13 Kevin Sinfield (C). Subs (all used): 17 Nick Scruton; 14 Ali Lauitiiti; 18 Ian Kirke; 16 Ryan Bailey.
Tries: Smith (23), Hall (37), McGuire (49, 63);
Goals: Sinfield 4/4.
SAINTS: 1 Paul Wellens; 2 Ade Gardner; 3 Matt Gidley; 4 Willie Talau; 5 Francis Meli; 6 Leon Pryce; 7 Sean Long; 18 Bryn Hargreaves; 9 Keiron Cunningham (C); 17 James Graham; 11 Lee Gilmour; 12 Jon Wilkin; 16 Chris Flannery. Subs (all used): 8 Nick Fozzard; 21 Paul Clough; 14 James Roby; 23 Maurie Fa'asavalu.
Tries: Graham (6), Gidley (43), Gardner (59); **Goals:** Long 2/3.
Rugby Leaguer & League Express Men of the Match:
Rhinos: Jamie Peacock; *Saints:* Sean Long.
Penalty count: 6-8; **Half-time:** 12-6; **Referee:** Ashley Klein;
Attendance: 68,810 *(at Old Trafford, Manchester)*.

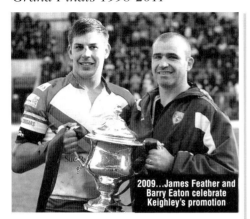

2009...James Feather and Barry Eaton celebrate Keighley's promotion

2009...Zebastian Luisi gets a pass away under pressure from Shad Royston

2009

CHAMPIONSHIP ONE GRAND FINAL

Sunday 4th October 2009

KEIGHLEY COUGARS 28 OLDHAM 26

COUGARS: 1 George Rayner; 2 Sam Gardner; 3 Dan Potter; 4 Oliver Pursglove; 5 Gavin Duffy; 6 Jon Presley; 7 Danny Jones; 17 Scott Law; 14 Jamaine Wray; 8 Andy Shickell; 11 Will Cartledge; 18 Greg Nicholson; 13 Carl Hughes. Subs (all used): 21 Ryan Smith; 28 Ryan Benjafield; 9 James Feather; 16 Brendan Rawlins.
Tries: Gardner (24), Jones (42, 50), Presley (63), Pursglove (67); **Goals:** Jones 4/5.
OLDHAM: 4 Paul Reilly; 21 Lucas Onyango; 24 Marcus St Hilaire; 22 Phil Joseph; 1 Paul O'Connor; 18 Neil Roden; 7 Thomas Coyle; 15 Jason Boults; 30 Martin Roden; 16 Wayne Kerr; 23 Chris Baines; 12 Tommy Goulden; 28 Craig Lawton. Subs (all used): 10 Jamie l'Anson; 25 Luke Menzies; 27 Matt Ashe; 29 Ben Heaton.
Tries: Menzies (35, 76), N Roden (54), St Hilaire (70), Kerr (78); **Goals:** Baines 3/4, Ashe 0/1.
Rugby Leaguer & League Express Men of the Match:
Cougars: Danny Jones; *Oldham:* Luke Menzies.
Penalty count: 9-2; **Half-time:** 4-6; **Referee:** Ronnie Laughton. *(at Halliwell Jones Stadium, Warrington).*

Dewsbury Rams were Championship One Champions in 2009. This game was to determine who took the second promotion place.

CHAMPIONSHIP GRAND FINAL

Sunday 4th October 2009

BARROW RAIDERS 26 HALIFAX 18

RAIDERS: 1 Gary Broadbent; 36 Andy Ballard; 32 Andreas Bauer; 4 Liam Harrison; 5 James Nixon; 24 Jamie Rooney; 31 James Coyle; 34 Rob Roberts; 9 Andy Ellis; 8 Brett McDermott; 33 Dave Allen; 22 Ned Catic; 26 Zebastian Luisi. Subs (all used): 15 Chris Young; 13 Andy Bracek; 35 Danny Halliwell; 14 Paul Noone.
Tries: Harrison (33), Ballard (37), Allen (61), Bauer (66, 78); **Goals:** Rooney 3/5.
HALIFAX: 4 Shad Royston; 5 James Haley; 15 Mark Roberts; 2 Lee Paterson; 23 Rob Worrincy; 19 Mick Govin; 7 Ben Black; 21 Neil Cherryholme; 9 Sean Penkywicz; 22 David Wrench; 11 David Larder; 27 Steve Bannister; 12 Paul Smith. Subs (all used): 13 Bob Beswick; 14 Mark Gleeson; 16 Said Tamghart; 26 Dominic Maloney.
Tries: Haley (12), Royston (31), Black (45), Govin (70); **Goals:** Paterson 1/5.
Rugby Leaguer & League Express Men of the Match:
Raiders: Gary Broadbent; *Halifax:* Mick Govin.
Penalty count: 8-5; **Half-time:** 10-10; **Referee:** Phil Bentham; **Attendance:** 11,398 *(at Halliwell Jones Stadium, Warrington).*

SUPER LEAGUE GRAND FINAL

Saturday 10th October 2009

LEEDS RHINOS 18 ST HELENS 10

RHINOS: 1 Brent Webb; 2 Scott Donald; 3 Lee Smith; 4 Keith Senior; 5 Ryan Hall; 6 Danny McGuire; 7 Rob Burrow; 8 Kylie Leuluai; 14 Matt Diskin; 10 Jamie Peacock; 11 Jamie Jones-Buchanan; 18 Carl Ablett; 13 Kevin Sinfield (C). Subs (all used): 16 Ryan Bailey for Leuluai (19); 19 Luke Burgess for Peacock (29); 17 Ian Kirke for Jones-Buchanan (29); 12 Ali Lauitiiti for Ablett (29); Jones-Buchanan for Lauitiiti (36); Peacock for Burgess (46); Leuluai for Bailey (53); Ablett for Kirke (57); Burgess for Diskin (62); Bailey for Leuluai (67); Diskin for Burgess (69); Kirke for Jones-Buchanan (76).
Tries: Diskin (30), Smith (37, 72); **Goals:** Sinfield 2/4.
Field goals: Sinfield (42), Burrow (78).
SAINTS: 1 Paul Wellens; 2 Ade Gardner; 3 Matt Gidley; 18 Kyle Eastmond; 5 Francis Meli; 6 Leon Pryce; 7 Sean Long; 10 James Graham; 9 Keiron Cunningham (C); 16 Tony Puletua; 12 Jon Wilkin; 11 Lee Gilmour; 13 Chris Flannery. Subs (all used): 14 James Roby for Cunningham (25); 15 Bryn Hargreaves for Puletua (24); 17 Paul Clough for Gilmour (31); 23 Maurie Fa'asavalu for Graham (31); Graham for Fa'asavalu (48); Puletua for Hargreaves (50); Gilmour for Wilkin (55); Cunningham for Clough (61); Wilkin for Roby (65); Roby for Flannery (73).
Try: Eastmond (13); **Goals:** Eastmond 3/3.
Rugby Leaguer & League Express Men of the Match:
Rhinos: Kevin Sinfield; *Saints:* James Graham.
Penalty count: 8-7; **Half-time:** 8-8; **Referee:** Steve Ganson; **Attendance:** 63,259 *(at Old Trafford, Manchester).*

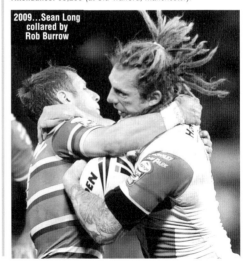

2009...Sean Long collared by Rob Burrow

2010...York celebrate defeating Oldham

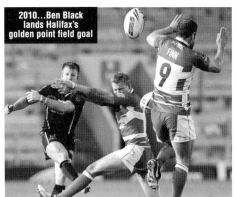
2010...Ben Black lands Halifax's golden point field goal

2010

CHAMPIONSHIP ONE GRAND FINAL

Sunday 26th September 2010

OLDHAM 4 YORK CITY KNIGHTS 25

OLDHAM: 1 Paul O'Connor; 2 Lucas Onyango; 24 Marcus St Hilaire; 4 Mick Fogerty; 5 Jon Gillam; 6 Neil Roden; 28 Gregg McNally; 8 Jason Boults; 9 Martin Roden; 16 Wayne Kerr; 18 Chris Clarke; 13 Joe Chandler; 21 Valu Bentley. Subs (all used): 10 Dave Ellison; 19 Ben Heaton; 17 Danny Whitmore; 7 Matt Ashe.
Try: Fogerty (20); **Goals:** McNally 0/1.
CITY KNIGHTS: 31 James Haynes; 2 Wayne Reittie; 3 Mike Mitchell; 4 Lee Waterman; 28 Danny Wilson; 6 Chris Thorman; 1 Danny Ratcliffe; 17 Nathan Freer; 33 Jack Lee; 10 Alex Benson; 11 Jordan Ross; 29 Ryan Esders; 15 Luke Hardbottle. Subs (all used): 32 Paul Stamp; 36 Callum Dinsdale; 26 Steve Lewis; 30 Jack Stearman.
Tries: Reittie (7), Haynes (26), Thorman (64), Lewis (74); **Goals:** Waterman 2/3, Thorman 2/2; **Field goal:** Thorman (69).
Rugby Leaguer & League Express Men of the Match: *Oldham:* Neil Roden; *City Knights:* Chris Thorman.
Penalty count: 2-7; **Half-time:** 4-10; **Referee:** Gareth Hewer.
(at Halliwell Jones Stadium, Warrington).

Hunslet Hawks were Championship One Champions in 2010. This game was to determine who took the second promotion place.

CHAMPIONSHIP GRAND FINAL

Sunday 26th September 2010

FEATHERSTONE ROVERS 22 HALIFAX 23
(after golden point extra time)

ROVERS: 1 Ian Hardman; 26 Zak Hardaker; 3 Sam Smeaton; 4 Liam Welham; 2 Tom Saxton; 6 Kyle Briggs; 9 Liam Finn; 17 Tony Tonks; 31 Ben Kaye; 10 Stuart Dickens; 18 Tim Spears; 13 Jamie Field; 11 Matty Dale. Subs (all used): 19 Ross Divorty; 16 Dane Manning; 12 Jon Grayshon; 7 Andy Kain.
Tries: Briggs (28), Hardaker (30, 52), Dale (45);
Goals: Briggs 3/4.
HALIFAX: 4 Shad Royston; 2 Lee Paterson; 6 Luke Branighan; 18 Dylan Nash; 23 Rob Worrincy; 26 Graham Holroyd; 7 Ben Black; 10 Neil Cherryholme; 13 Bob Beswick; 8 Makali Aizue; 11 David Larder; 22 David Wrench; 27 Sam Barlow. Subs (all used): 9 Sean Penkywicz; 17 Frank Watene; 19 Dominic Maloney; 24 Steve Bannister.
Tries: Worrincy (20), Black (58), Branighan (60), Bannister (75); **Goals:** Paterson 3/4; **Field goal:** Black (82).
On report: Barlow (35) - alleged high tackle on Divorty.
Rugby Leaguer & League Express Men of the Match: *Rovers:* Tom Saxton; *Halifax:* Ben Black.
Penalty count: 6-3; **Half-time:** 12-4; **Full-time:** 22-22;
Referee: Robert Hicks; **Attendance:** 9,443
(at Halliwell Jones Stadium, Warrington).

SUPER LEAGUE GRAND FINAL

Saturday 2nd October 2010

ST HELENS 10 WIGAN WARRIORS 22

SAINTS: 1 Paul Wellens; 30 Jamie Foster; 3 Matt Gidley; 5 Francis Meli; 24 Jonny Lomax; 12 Jon Wilkin; 34 Matty Smith; 10 James Graham; 9 Keiron Cunningham (C); 15 Bryn Hargreaves; 4 Iosia Soliola; 13 Chris Flannery; 11 Tony Puletua. Subs (all used): 17 Paul Clough; 14 James Roby; 22 Andrew Dixon; 25 Jacob Emmitt.
Tries: Dixon (28), Meli (74); **Goals:** Foster 1/2.
WARRIORS: 6 Sam Tomkins; 24 Darrell Goulding; 3 Martin Gleeson; 4 George Carmont; 5 Pat Richards; 19 Paul Deacon; 7 Thomas Leuluai; 8 Stuart Fielden; 15 Michael McIlorum; 10 Andy Coley; 11 Harrison Hansen; 12 Joel Tomkins; 13 Sean O'Loughlin (C). Subs (all used): 9 Mark Riddell; 17 Iafeta Palea'aesina; 25 Liam Farrell; 14 Paul Prescott.
Tries: Gleeson (4, 16), Goulding (20), S Tomkins (53);
Goals: Richards 2/3, Riddell 1/3, S Tomkins 0/1.
Rugby Leaguer & League Express Men of the Match: *Saints:* Tony Puletua; *Warriors:* Thomas Leuluai.
Penalty count: 6-11; **Half-time:** 6-16;
Referee: Richard Silverwood;
Attendance: 71,526 *(at Old Trafford, Manchester).*

2010...Sam and Joel Tomkins show off the Super League Trophy

2011...Player-coach Jason Demetriou shows his delight as Keighley win promotion

2011

CHAMPIONSHIP ONE GRAND FINAL

Sunday 2nd October 2011

KEIGHLEY COUGARS 32 WORKINGTON TOWN 12

COUGARS: 18 James Haythornthwaite; 4 Danny Lawton; 22 Ben Sagar; 33 Jake Normington; 5 Gavin Duffy; 6 Jason Demetriou; 36 Jy-Mel Coleman; 17 Ryan Benjafield; 9 James Feather; 10 Scott Law; 11 Will Cartledge; 12 Oliver Pursglove; 21 Richard Jones. Subs (all used): 14 Jamaine Wray; 8 Andy Shickell; 16 Brendan Rawlins; 7 Ryan Smith.
Tries: Lawton (5), Feather (20), Rawlins (25), Pursglove (32), Normington (69, 77); **Goals:** Lawton 4/6.
TOWN: 1 Brett Carter; 2 Elliott Miller; 3 Jason Mossop; 4 Aaron Low; 5 Neil Frazer; 24 Darren Holt; 7 Scott Kaighan; 10 Kris Coward; 13 Karl Olstrum; 29 Dave Armitstead; 11 Mike Whitehead; 18 Joe McKenna; 12 Jarrad Stack. Subs (all used): 23 Marc Bainbridge; 15 Ruairi McGoff; 32 Chris Clough; 17 James Robinson.
Tries: Kaighan (65), Frazer (74); **Goals:** Holt 2/2.
Rugby Leaguer & League Express Men of the Match:
Cougars: Jason Demetriou; *Town:* Jarrad Stack.
Penalty count: 7-5; **Half-time:** 22-0; **Referee:** Tim Roby.
(at Halliwell Jones Stadium, Warrington).

Swinton Lions were Championship One Champions in 2011. This game was to determine who took the second promotion place.

CHAMPIONSHIP GRAND FINAL

Sunday 2nd October 2011

FEATHERSTONE ROVERS 40 SHEFFIELD EAGLES 4

ROVERS: 1 Ian Hardman; 33 Ben Cockayne; 3 Sam Smeaton; 17 Greg Worthington; 5 Tom Saxton; 6 Andy Kain; 7 Liam Finn; 8 Tony Tonks; 9 Ben Kaye; 10 Stuart Dickens; 11 Jon Grayshon; 12 Tim Spears; 28 Jon Hepworth. Subs (all used): 18 Ross Divorty; 13 Matty Dale; 4 Andrew Bostock; 30 Kirk Netherton.
Tries: Spears (4), Finn (7, 39), Hardman (42), Cockayne (56), Hepworth (59), Saxton (79); **Goals:** Finn 6/7.
Sin bin: Netherton (54) - fighting.
EAGLES: 6 Quentin Laulu-Togagae; 5 Tim Bergin; 26 Corey Hanson; 1 Misi Taulapapa; 3 Vinny Finigan; 13 Dane McDonald; 7 Simon Brown; 8 Jack Howieson; 9 Andrew Henderson; 10 Mitchell Stringer; 11 Alex Szostak; 12 Peter Green; 19 Joe Hirst. Subs (all used): 22 Ryan Hepworth; 30 Sam Scott; 20 Pat Smith; 14 Jonny Woodcock.
Try: McDonald (12); **Goals:** Brown 0/1.
Sin bin: Hirst (54) - fighting.
Rugby Leaguer & League Express Men of the Match:
Rovers: Liam Finn; *Eagles:* Joe Hirst.
Penalty count: 7-11; **Half-time:** 18-4;
Referee: Matthew Thomason; **Attendance:** 7,263
(at Halliwell Jones Stadium, Warrington).

2011...No way through the Sheffield defence for Stuart Dickens

SUPER LEAGUE GRAND FINAL

Saturday 8th October 2011

LEEDS RHINOS 32 ST HELENS 16

RHINOS: 1 Brent Webb; 23 Ben Jones-Bishop; 27 Zak Hardaker; 12 Carl Ablett; 5 Ryan Hall; 13 Kevin Sinfield (C); 6 Danny McGuire; 8 Kylie Leuluai; 9 Danny Buderus; 10 Jamie Peacock; 11 Jamie Jones-Buchanan; 3 Brett Delaney; 21 Chris Clarkson. Subs (all used): 7 Rob Burrow; 16 Ryan Bailey; 17 Ian Kirke; 14 Ali Lauitiiti.
Tries: Burrow (34), Webb (65), Hall (70), Ablett (74), Hardaker (80); **Goals:** Sinfield 6/7.
SAINTS: 1 Paul Wellens (C); 28 Tom Makinson; 3 Michael Shenton; 5 Francis Meli; 22 Jamie Foster; 25 Lee Gaskell; 20 Jonny Lomax; 10 James Graham (C); 9 James Roby; 11 Tony Puletua; 12 Jon Wilkin; 4 Iosia Soliola; 16 Paul Clough. Subs (all used): 19 Andrew Dixon; 14 Scott Moore; 15 Louie McCarthy-Scarsbrook; 17 Gary Wheeler.
Tries: Makinson (50), Shenton (55); **Goals:** Foster 4/5.
Rugby Leaguer & League Express Men of the Match:
Rhinos: Rob Burrow; *Saints:* Lee Gaskell.
Penalty count: 5-7; **Half-time:** 8-2; **Referee:** Phil Bentham;
Attendance: 69,107 *(at Old Trafford, Manchester).*

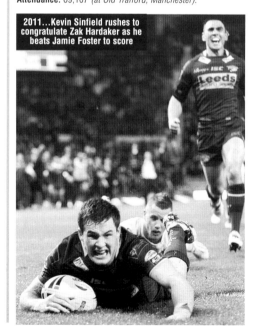

2011...Kevin Sinfield rushes to congratulate Zak Hardaker as he beats Jamie Foster to score

LONGEST SERVING PLAYERS 2012

SUPER LEAGUE

PLAYER	CLUB	DEBUT vs	COMP	DATE	APPS
Jamie Langley	Bradford Bulls	Wakefield Trinity Wildcats (a)	SL	1/4/02	238
Craig Huby	Castleford Tigers	Leeds Rhinos (a)	SL	7/6/03	184
Jamal Fakir	Catalan Dragons	Wigan Warriors (h)	SL	11/2/06	142
Gregory Mounis	Catalan Dragons	Wigan Warriors (h)	SL	11/2/06	186
Eorl Crabtree	Huddersfield Giants	London Broncos (a)	SL	13/4/01	312
Richard Horne	Hull FC	Leeds Rhinos (a)	SL	16/4/99	347
Jason Netherton	Hull Kingston Rovers	Keighley Cougars (a)	NRC	13/2/05	157
Kevin Sinfield	Leeds Rhinos	Sheffield Eagles (h)	SL	22/8/97	436
Karl Temata	London Broncos	Salford City Reds (a)	SL	9/9/05	137
Luke Adamson	Salford City Reds	Wakefield Trinity Wildcats (a)	SL	11/6/06	145
Paul Wellens	St Helens	Halifax Blue Sox (h)	SL	30/8/98	435
Matthew Wildie	Wakefield Trinity Wildcats	Huddersfield Giants (a)	SL	1/8/10	22
Lee Briers	Warrington Wolves	St Helens (a)	SL	20/4/97	406
Ben Kavanagh	Widnes Vikings	Blackpool Panthers (a)	NRC	3/2/08	116
Sean O'Loughlin	Wigan Warriors	Hull FC (h)	SL	5/4/02	299

Lee Briers

CHAMPIONSHIP

PLAYER	CLUB	DEBUT vs	COMP	DATE	APPS
Mark Toohey	Batley Bulldogs	Widnes Vikings (h)	NFP	6/6/01	206
Pat Walker	Dewsbury Rams	Oldham (a)	NRC	18/3/07	126
Stuart Dickens	Featherstone Rovers	Halifax (a) (D2)	NL1	14/8/05	209
	Featherstone Rovers	Widnes Vikings (h) (D)	D1	15/3/98	212
James Haley	Halifax	Batley Bulldogs (h)	NL1	9/5/04	177
Steve Dooler	Hunslet Hawks	Oldham (h)	NRC	1/3/09	62
James Feather	Keighley Cougars	Oldham (a)	NRC	26/2/06	191
James Taylor	Leigh Centurions	London Broncos (h)	SL	28/3/05	173
Jack Howieson	Sheffield Eagles	Doncaster Dragons (h)	NFP	13/4/01	265
Richie Hawkyard	Swinton Lions	Oldham (a)	NRC	1/2/08	98
Jack Stearman	York City Knights	London Skolars (h)	NRC	1/3/09	35

Jack Howieson

CHAMPIONSHIP ONE

PLAYER	CLUB	DEBUT vs	COMP	DATE	APPS
James Nixon	Barrow Raiders	Gateshead Thunder (a)	NL2	4/7/04	175
Dean Colton	Doncaster	London Skolars (h) (D2)	NRC	1/2/08	93
	Doncaster	Sheffield Eagles (a) (D)	NFP	13/4/01	122
Robin Peers	Gateshead Thunder	Oldham (a)	NFP	17/2/02	218
Austen Aggrey	London Skolars	Dewsbury Rams (h)	NL2	1/5/04	178
Jason Boults	Oldham	Rochdale Hornets (h)	NRC	11/2/07	155
Neil Roden	Oldham	Rochdale Hornets (h) (D2)	NRC	11/2/07	151
	Oldham	Sheffield Eagles (a) (D)	NFP	2/4/00	131
Chris Hough	Rochdale Hornets	Swinton Lions (a) (D2)	NRC	10/2/08	66
	Rochdale Hornets	Wigan St Judes (h) (D)	CC	31/1/99	6
Ashley Bateman	South Wales Scorpions	Workington Town (h)	Ch1	28/2/10	61
Neil Dallimore	South Wales Scorpions	Workington Town (h)	Ch1	28/2/10	43
Steve Parry	South Wales Scorpions	Workington Town (h)	Ch1	28/2/10	64
Craig Calvert	Whitehaven	Rochdale Hornets (h)	NL1	11/7/04	221
James Robinson	Workington Town	Chorley Lynx (a)	ATC	9/3/03	166

Robin Peers

- Player's continuous service, beginning with first team debut, and finishing the season as a registered player with that club.

- All information correct up to the end of the 2012 domestic season.

- If player has had two spells with club, both debuts and separate appearance totals are included.

2012 SEASON
Stats round-up

Josh
Charnley

Kevin
Sinfield

TRIES *(play-offs in brackets, included in total)*

1	Josh Charnley	Wigan Warriors	32 (1)
2	Sam Tomkins	Wigan Warriors	29 (1)
3	Ryan Hall	Leeds Rhinos	27 (1)
4	Chris Riley	Warrington Wolves	25 (2)
5	Ryan Atkins	Warrington Wolves	24 (1)
6	Joel Monaghan	Warrington Wolves	22 (2)
7	Tom Briscoe	Hull FC	20 (3)
	Danny McGuire	Leeds Rhinos	20 (2)
	Paul Wellens	St Helens	20 (1)
	George Carmont	Wigan Warriors	20 (3)

GOALS *(play-offs in brackets, included in total)*

1	Kevin Sinfield	Leeds Rhinos	140 (21)
2	Scott Dureau	Catalan Dragons	117 (3)
3	Michael Dobson	Hull Kingston Rovers	103 (-)
4	Danny Brough	Huddersfield Giants	101 (0)
5	Brett Hodgson	Warrington Wolves	82 (14)
6	Danny Tickle	Hull FC	76 (0)
7	Paul Sykes *	Wakefield Trinity Wildcats	72 (2)
8	Daniel Holdsworth	Salford City Reds	69 (-)
9	Luke Gale	Bradford Bulls	65 (-)
10	Jamie Foster **	Hull FC	63 (9)
	Pat Richards	Wigan Warriors	63 (9)

* includes 2 for Bradford Bulls   ** includes 18 for St Helens

GOALS PERCENTAGE *(play-offs included)*

			G	Att	%
1	Gareth O'Brien	Warrington Wolves/ Widnes Vikings	43	49	87.75
2	Danny Tickle	Hull FC	76	89	85.39
3	Pat Richards	Wigan Warriors	63	76	82.89
4	Kevin Sinfield	Leeds Rhinos	140	169	82.84
5	Brett Hodgson	Warrington Wolves	82	100	82.00
6	Craig Hall	Hull Kingston Rovers	9	11	81.81
7	Luke Gale	Bradford Bulls	65	80	81.25
8	Patrick Ah Van	Widnes Vikings	29	36	80.55
9	Craig Gower	London Broncos	24	30	80.00
	Danny Orr	Castleford Tigers	16	20	80.00
	Shane Rodney	London Broncos	12	15	80.00

(10 minimum attempts to qualify)

POINTS *(play-offs in brackets, included in total)*

			T	G	FG	Pts
1	Kevin Sinfield	Leeds Rhinos	5	140	4	304 (47)
2	Scott Dureau	Catalan Dragons	12	117	3	285 (6)
3	Michael Dobson	Hull Kingston Rovers	9	103	1	243 (-)
4	Josh Charnley	Wigan Warriors	32	56	0	240 (4)
5	Danny Brough	Huddersfield Giants	6	101	1	227 (0)
6	Brett Hodgson	Warrington Wolves	8	82	0	196 (36)
7	Danny Tickle	Hull FC	9	76	0	188 (0)
8	Pat Richards	Wigan Warriors	15	63	0	186 (22)
9	Daniel Holdsworth	Salford City Reds	6	69	0	162 (-)
10	Paul Sykes *	Wakefield Trinity Wildcats	3	72	3	159 (4)

* includes 4 for Bradford Bulls

CONSECUTIVE APPEARANCES
(Super League, including play-offs, Challenge Cup and World Club Challenge)

1	Kevin Sinfield	Leeds Rhinos	78
2	Tom Briscoe	Hull FC	72
3	Andy Lynch	Hull FC/Bradford Bulls	68
4	Ryan Hall	Leeds Rhinos	51
	Willie Manu	Hull FC	51
6	Remi Casty	Catalan Dragons	43
	Zak Hardaker	Leeds Rhinos	43
8	Scott Dureau	Catalan Dragons	38
9	Chad Randall	London Broncos/Harlequins	36
10	Danny Washbrook	Wakefield Trinity Wildcats/Hull FC	35

FINAL TABLE

	P	W	D	L	F	A	D	Pts
Wigan Warriors	27	21	0	6	994	449	545	42
Warrington Wolves	27	20	1	6	909	539	370	41
St Helens	27	17	2	8	795	480	315	36
Catalan Dragons	27	18	0	9	812	611	201	36
Leeds Rhinos	27	16	0	11	823	662	161	32
Hull FC	27	15	2	10	696	621	75	32
Huddersfield Giants	27	14	0	13	699	664	35	28
Wakefield Trinity Wildcats	27	13	0	14	633	764	-131	26
Bradford Bulls *	27	14	1	12	633	756	-123	23
Hull Kingston Rovers	27	10	1	16	753	729	24	21
Salford City Reds	27	8	1	18	618	844	-226	17
London Broncos	27	7	0	20	588	890	-302	14
Castleford Tigers	27	6	0	21	554	948	-394	12
Widnes Vikings	27	6	0	21	532	1082	-550	12

* 6 points deducted for entering administration

AVERAGE ATTENDANCES

	2012 Avg	*2011 Avg*	*Diff*
Wigan Warriors	15,208	15,287	-79
Leeds Rhinos	14,526	14,669	-143
St Helens	14,113	7,975	+6,138
			(Stobart Stadium)
Bradford Bulls	11,755	13,967	-2,212
Hull FC	11,654	12,431	-777
Warrington Wolves	11,070	11,149	-79
Catalan Dragons	9,280	8,387	+893
Wakefield Trinity Wildcats	8,172	6,552	+1,620
Hull Kingston Rovers	7,786	8,320	-534
Huddersfield Giants	7,709	7,147	+562
Castleford Tigers	6,709	7,156	-447
Widnes Vikings	6,046	3,744	+2,302
			(Championship)
Salford City Reds	5,192	4,754	+438
			(The Willows)
London Broncos	2,808	3,132	-324
			(Harlequins)

2012 Average	9,431	
2011 Average	8,879	
Difference	+552	

BEST ATTENDANCES

		Round	*Date*
70,676	Leeds v Warrington	GF	6/10/12
	(at Old Trafford, Manchester)		
21,522	Wigan v St Helens	27	7/9/12
21,267	Wigan v Warrington	8	23/3/12
20,851	Bradford v Leeds	10	6/4/12
19,628	Wigan v Bradford	19	29/6/12
18,979	Hull FC v Hull KR	10	6/4/12
18,520	Leeds v Bradford	21	20/7/12
17,980	St Helens v Wigan	10	6/4/12
17,736	Wigan v Hull FC	23	3/8/12
17,120	Leeds v Warrington	6	9/3/12

WORST ATTENDANCES

		Round	*Date*
1,517	London Broncos v Salford	23	4/8/12
1,829	London Broncos v Catalan Dragons	10	5/4/12
1,970	London Broncos v Huddersfield	4	26/2/12
2,117	London Broncos v Widnes	17	9/6/12
2,261	London Broncos v Warrington	25	17/8/12
2,268	London Broncos v Wakefield	9	31/3/12
2,380	Salford v Wakefield	27	8/9/12
	(at Leigh Sports Village)		
2,381	London Broncos v Castleford	6	10/3/12
2,525	London Broncos v Hull KR	27	8/9/12
2,844	London Broncos v Bradford	13	6/5/12
	(at Brisbane Road, Leyton)		

* Super League attendance figures include play-offs.

CHALLENGE CUP

TRIES

1	Joel Monaghan	Warrington Wolves	7
	Sam Tomkins	Wigan Warriors	7
3	Lee Waterman	Doncaster	6
	Ian Hardman	Featherstone Rovers	6
	Quentin Laulu-Togagae		
		Sheffield Eagles	6

GOALS

1	Lee Paterson	Halifax	27
2	Kevin Sinfield	Leeds Rhinos	25
3	Brett Hodgson	Warrington Wolves	21
4	Ian Mort	Swinton Lions	20
	Martyn Ridyard	Leigh Centurions	20

POINTS

			T	*G*	*FG*	*Pts*
1	Lee Paterson	Halifax	3	27	0	66
2	Brett Hodgson	Warrington Wolves	4	21	1	59
	Kevin Sinfield	Leeds Rhinos	2	25	1	59
4	Josh Charnley	Wigan Warriors	4	19	0	54
5	Ian Mort	Swinton Lions	2	20	0	48

BEST ATTENDANCES

		Round	*Date*
79,180	Leeds v Warrington	F	25/8/12
	(at Wembley Stadium)		
12,864	Wigan v St Helens	QF	12/5/12
12,860	Leeds v Wigan	SF	14/7/12
	(at Galpharm Stadium, Huddersfield)		
9,473	Huddersfield v Warrington	SF	15/7/12
	(at City of Salford Community Stadium)		
8,327	Hull FC v Huddersfield	4	15/4/12

WORST ATTENDANCES

		Round	*Date*
179	Gateshead v York Acorn	3	24/3/12
302	Hunslet v Royal Navy	3	25/3/12
303	East Hull v Rochdale	3	25/3/12
	(at Spotland)		
346	York v Hull Dockers	3	25/3/12
350	Wath Brow v South Wales	3	24/3/12

NORTHERN RAIL CUP

TRIES

1	Nathan Ross	Toulouse Olympique	8
2	Daniel Toal	Barrow Raiders	7
	Ian Hardman	Featherstone Rovers	7
4	Liam Finn	Featherstone Rovers	6
	Andy Kain	Featherstone Rovers	6
	Sam Smeaton	Featherstone Rovers	6
	Anthony Thackeray	Halifax	6
	Quentin Laulu-Togagae		
		Sheffield Eagles	6

GOALS

1	Liam Finn	Featherstone Rovers	40
2	Simon Brown	Sheffield Eagles	25
3	Steve Tyrer	Halifax	23
4	Martyn Ridyard	Leigh Centurions	22
5	Carl Forber	Workington Town	15

POINTS

			T	*G*	*FG*	*Pts*
1	Liam Finn	Featherstone Rovers	6	40	0	104
2	Steve Tyrer	Halifax	4	23	0	62
3	Simon Brown	Sheffield Eagles	0	25	0	50
4	Martyn Ridyard	Leigh Centurions	0	22	0	44
5	Carl Forber	Workington Town	2	15	0	38

BEST ATTENDANCES

		Round	*Date*
6,691	Featherstone v Halifax	F	29/7/12
	(at Bloomfield Road, Blackpool)		
2,530	Halifax v Featherstone	3	26/2/12
2,002	Leigh v Batley	QF	17/6/12
1,943	Featherstone v Dewsbury	2	19/2/12
1,881	Halifax v Rochdale	2	19/2/12

WORST ATTENDANCES

		Round	*Date*
205	South Wales v London Skolars	3	26/2/12
238	Rochdale v South Wales	1	9/5/12
242	London Skolars v Toulouse	1	9/4/12
243	Gateshead v Doncaster	1	15/2/12
276	Gateshead v Leigh	4	4/3/12
	(at Kingston Park, Newcastle)		

CHAMPIONSHIP

Liam Finn

TRIES *(play-offs in brackets, included in total)*

1	Andy Kain	Featherstone Rovers	22 (0)
2	Quentin Laulu-Togagae		
		Sheffield Eagles	21 (3)
3	Gareth Potts	Batley Bulldogs	15 (0)
	Ryan Brierley	Leigh Centurions	15 (1)
	Menzie Yere	Sheffield Eagles	15 (3)
6	Misi Taulapapa	Sheffield Eagles	13 (4)
7	Nathan Chappell	Featherstone Rovers	12 (0)
	Gregg McNally	Leigh Centurions	12 (0)
	Michael Knowles	Sheffield Eagles	12 (2)

(5 players tied on 11)

GOALS *(play-offs in brackets, included in total)*

1	Liam Finn	Featherstone Rovers	115 (12)
2	Gareth Moore	Batley Bulldogs	88 (2)
3	Martyn Ridyard	Leigh Centurions	86 (4)
4	Simon Brown	Sheffield Eagles	79 (22)
5	Pat Walker	Dewsbury Rams	57 (-)
6	Lee Paterson	Halifax	49 (0)
7	Danny Lawton	Keighley Cougars	37 (4)
8	Chris Thorman	York City Knights	36 (-)
	Steve Tyrer	Halifax	36 (4)
10	Ian Mort	Swinton Lions	30 (-)

POINTS *(play-offs in brackets, included in total)*

			T	G	FG	Pts
1	Liam Finn	Featherstone Rovers	10	115	1	271 (24)
2	Gareth Moore	Batley Bulldogs	9	88	1	213 (4)
3	Martyn Ridyard	Leigh Centurions	10	86	0	212 (8)
4	Simon Brown	Sheffield Eagles	1	79	1	163 (44)
5	Pat Walker	Dewsbury Rams	2	57	1	123 (-)
6	Lee Paterson	Halifax	6	49	0	122 (4)
7	Danny Lawton	Keighley Cougars	7	37	0	102 (8)
8	Andy Kain	Featherstone Rovers	22	0	1	89 (0)
9	Steve Tyrer	Halifax	4	36	0	88 (12)
10	Quentin Laulu-Togagae					
		Sheffield Eagles	21	0	0	84 (12)

FINAL TABLE

	P	W	D	L	BP	F	A	D	Pts
Featherstone Rovers	18	15	1	2	0	684	354	330	47
Leigh Centurions	18	14	0	4	2	612	310	302	44
Halifax	18	14	0	4	2	597	377	220	44
Sheffield Eagles	18	12	1	5	3	565	437	128	41
Batley Bulldogs	18	11	0	7	7	551	326	225	40
Keighley Cougars	18	8	1	9	5	395	368	27	31
Dewsbury Rams	18	7	0	11	4	371	528	-157	25
Swinton Lions	18	4	1	13	5	366	632	-266	19
Hunslet Hawks	18	2	0	16	4	248	684	-436	10
York City Knights	18	1	0	17	4	272	645	-373	7

AVERAGE ATTENDANCES

	2012 Avg	2011 Avg	Diff
Featherstone Rovers	2,060	1,675	+385
Halifax	2,041	2,061	-20
Leigh Centurions	1,692	2,248	-556
Dewsbury Rams	1,114	1,048	+66
Keighley Cougars	1,027	830	+197
(Championship One)			
Sheffield Eagles	1,003	1,118	-115
Batley Bulldogs	939	1,065	-126
York City Knights	768	1,149	-381
Swinton Lions	711	709	+2
(Championship One, The Willows)			
Hunslet Hawks	494	749	-255
2012 Average	1,185		
2011 Average	1,590		
Difference	-405		

BEST ATTENDANCES

		Round	Date
6,409	Featherstone v Sheffield	GF	30/9/12
	(at Halliwell Jones Stadium, Warrington)		
2,816	Featherstone v Keighley	18	2/9/12
2,806	Featherstone v Halifax	6	6/5/12
2,792	Halifax v Featherstone	12	28/6/12
2,382	Featherstone v Leigh	2	15/3/12
2,378	Halifax v Keighley	4	6/4/12
2,377	Halifax v Dewsbury	7	13/5/12
2,344	Halifax v Batley	18	2/9/12
2,304	Featherstone v Batley	14	22/7/12
2,293	Featherstone v Sheffield	4	7/4/12

WORST ATTENDANCES

		Round	Date
410	Swinton v York	6	6/5/12
419	Hunslet v Sheffield	2	18/3/12
426	Hunslet v Swinton	7	13/5/12
462	York v Sheffield	7	10/5/12
463	Hunslet v Dewsbury	17	19/8/12
505	Hunslet v York	4	8/4/12
505	Hunslet v Keighley	12	1/7/12
506	Hunslet v Batley	6	6/5/12
506	Swinton v Sheffield	12	1/7/12
515	Swinton v Keighley	17	19/8/12

* Championship attendance figures include play-offs and Northern Rail Cup. Challenge Cup not included.

CHAMPIONSHIP ONE

TRIES *(play-offs in brackets, included in total)*

1	Lee Waterman	Doncaster	26 (1)
2	Elliott Miller	Workington Town	24 (1)
3	Craig Calvert	Whitehaven	22 (0)
4	Craig Fawcett	Doncaster	18 (2)
	Miles Greenwood	Oldham	18 (0)
6	Liam Campbell	Barrow Raiders	17 (0)
7	Tom Hodson	Doncaster	14 (0)
8	Andy Ballard	Barrow Raiders	13 (0)
	Brad Hopkins	London Skolars	13 (-)
10	Jonny Leather	Rochdale Hornets	12 (0)
	Jamie Rooney *	Whitehaven	12 (1)

* includes 2 for South Wales Scorpions

GOALS *(play-offs in brackets, included in total)*

1	Dylan Skee	London Skolars	78 (-)
2	Carl Forber	Workington Town	62 (12)
3	Carl Rudd	Whitehaven	61 (3)
4	Jamie Dallimore	Oldham	58 (4)
5	Paul Crook	Rochdale Hornets	57 (2)
6	Ryan Shaw	Barrow Raiders	54 (0)
7	Tom Hodson	Doncaster	53 (4)
8	Paul Cooke	Doncaster	45 (0)
9	Tommy Johnson	North Wales Crusaders	41 (-)
10	Marc Bainbridge	Workington Town	28 (0)
	Jamie Rooney *	Whitehaven	28 (1)

* includes 10 for South Wales Scorpions

POINTS *(play-offs in brackets, included in total)*

			T	G	FG	Pts
1	Dylan Skee	London Skolars	10	78	0	196 (-)
2	Tom Hodson	Doncaster	14	53	0	162 (8)
3	Paul Crook	Rochdale Hornets	7	57	0	142 (4)
4	Jamie Dallimore	Oldham	6	58	0	140 (8)
	Ryan Shaw	Barrow Raiders	8	54	0	140 (0)
6	Carl Rudd	Whitehaven	4	61	0	138 (10)
7	Carl Forber	Workington Town	1	62	1	129 (24)
8	Lee Waterman	Doncaster	26	6	0	116 (8)
9	Paul Cooke	Doncaster	5	45	0	110 (0)
10	Jamie Rooney *	Whitehaven	12	28	3	107 (6)

* includes 28 for South Wales Scorpions

FINAL TABLE

	P	W	D	L	BP	F	A	D	Pts
Doncaster	18	15	0	3	1	717	347	370	46
Barrow Raiders	18	14	0	4	3	617	383	234	45
Workington Town	18	13	0	5	4	617	330	287	43
Whitehaven	18	12	0	6	1	549	421	128	37
Rochdale Hornets	18	9	0	9	1	496	460	36	28
Oldham	18	7	1	10	5	465	485	-20	28
London Skolars	18	7	1	10	3	558	560	-2	26
North Wales Crusaders	18	7	0	11	3	460	628	-168	24
South Wales Scorpions	18	4	0	14	4	365	680	-315	16
Gateshead Thunder	18	1	0	17	2	274	824	-550	5

Top four teams promoted to Championship
- top six play-off to decide Champions

AVERAGE ATTENDANCES

	2012 Avg	2011 Avg	Diff
Barrow Raiders	1,383	1,527	-144
			(Championship)
North Wales Crusaders	927	N/A	N/A
Workington Town	892	583	+309
Whitehaven	814	866	-52
Doncaster	730	575	+155
Oldham	609	627	-18
London Skolars	525	509	+16
Rochdale Hornets	488	605	-117
South Wales Scorpions	393	334	+59
Gateshead Thunder	282	311	-29
2012 Average	704		
2011 Average	595		
Difference	+109		

BEST ATTENDANCES *(figure unavailable for Grand Final)*

		Round	Date
1,954	Workington v Whitehaven	11	24/6/12
1,808	Barrow v Workington	7	13/5/12
1,710	Barrow v Whitehaven	14	19/7/12
1,710	Workington v Barrow	16	12/8/12
1,529	Whitehaven v Workington	4	6/4/12
1,513	North Wales v Barrow	1	11/3/12
1,438	Barrow v North Wales	11	24/6/12
1,371	Barrow v Gateshead	4	6/4/12
1,365	Barrow v Doncaster	2	18/3/12
1,337	Barrow v Oldham	15	5/8/12

WORST ATTENDANCES

		Round	Date
186	Gateshead v London Skolars	14	22/7/12
	(at Filtrona Park, South Shields)		
196	South Wales v Oldham	14	22/7/12
219	South Wales v Gateshead	17	19/8/12
231	South Wales v Whitehaven	5	22/4/12
231	Gateshead v Rochdale	12	1/7/12
	(at Filtrona Park, South Shields)		
233	Gateshead v South Wales	1	11/3/12
256	Gateshead v Workington	15	29/8/12
273	Gateshead v Oldham	18	2/9/12
290	London Skolars v South Wales	7	29/7/12
301	Rochdale v Doncaster	10	29/4/12

* Championship One attendance figures include play-offs and
Northern Rail Cup. Challenge Cup not included.

2012 TOP SCORERS - ALL COMPETITIONS

Lee Waterman

TRIES

1	Lee Waterman	Doncaster	36
	Josh Charnley	Wigan Warriors	36
	Sam Tomkins	Wigan Warriors	36
4	Quentin Laulu-Togagae	Sheffield Eagles	35
5	Ryan Hall	Leeds Rhinos	33
6	Andy Kain	Featherstone Rovers	30
7	Joel Monaghan	Warrington Wolves	29
	Chris Riley	Warrington Wolves	29
9	Ryan Atkins	Warrington Wolves	27
	Craig Calvert	Whitehaven	27

GOALS

1	Liam Finn	Featherstone Rovers	181
2	Kevin Sinfield	Leeds Rhinos	168
3	Scott Dureau	Catalan Dragons	134
4	Martyn Ridyard	Leigh Centurions	132
5	Danny Brough	Huddersfield Giants	120
6	Simon Brown	Sheffield Eagles	112
7	Gareth Moore	Batley Bulldogs	106
8	Michael Dobson	Hull Kingston Rovers	104
9	Brett Hodgson	Warrington Wolves	103
10	Lee Paterson	Halifax	92

POINTS

			T	G	FG	Pts
1	Liam Finn	Featherstone Rovers	18	181	2	436
2	Kevin Sinfield	Leeds Rhinos	7	168	5	369
3	Martyn Ridyard	Leigh Centurions	14	132	1	321
4	Scott Dureau	Catalan Dragons	12	134	3	319
5	Josh Charnley	Wigan Warriors	36	75	0	294
6	Danny Brough	Huddersfield Giants	7	120	1	269
7	Gareth Moore	Batley Bulldogs	12	106	2	262
8	Brett Hodgson	Warrington Wolves	12	103	1	255
9	Michael Dobson	Hull Kingston Rovers	9	104	1	245
10	Simon Brown	Sheffield Eagles	1	112	1	229

FIELD GOALS

1	Kevin Sinfield	Leeds Rhinos	5
2	Scott Dureau	Catalan Dragons	3
	Paul Sykes	Wakefield Trinity Wildcats	3
	Lee Briers	Warrington Wolves	3
	Jamie Rooney	Whitehaven	3

319